PETER LEVENDA

SINISTER FORCES

A GRIMOIRE OF AMERICAN POLITICAL WITCHCRAFT

PETER LEVENDA

SINISTER FORCES

A GRIMOIRE OF AMERICAN POLITICAL WITCHCRAFT

PETER LEVENDA

SINISTER FORCES

A GRIMOIRE OF AMERICAN POLITICAL WITCHCRAFT

SINISTER FORCES

To The Stars

To The Stars Media Inc.
1150 Garden View Road
Box #230393
Encinitas, CA 92024
ToTheStars.Media
To The Stars® is a registered trademark of To The Stars Media Inc.

Cover Design by Joe Brisbois
Book Design by Lamp Post
Managing Editor: Kari DeLonge

Manufactured in the United States of America

ISBN 978-1-943272-52-5 (Hard Cover trade)
ISBN 978-1-943272-53-2 (eBook)

Distributed worldwide by Simon & Schuster

1 3 5 7 9 10 8 6 4 2

For all my readers…

One cannot coerce the Spiritual: if one attempts to enter into the Light without preparation, one always faces the trials and dangers of Darkness. At the very least, an enforced entry into initiation will drive the illegal entrant insane.

—David Ovason, *The Zelator*

CONTENTS

BOOK THREE: THE MANSON SECRET | 685

SECTION FIVE: MAGIC IN THEORY AND PRACTICE

SECTION SIX: HUNGRY GHOSTS

OMNIBUS FOREWORD

20TH ANNIVERSARY EDITION OF THE *SINISTER FORCES* TRILOGY

Most people move through life without ever questioning how things truly work. One of the most fascinating conversations I've ever had was with someone deep inside the US intelligence community. I asked why the government couldn't be more forthright about UFO disclosures. His answer was unsettling: "How do you level with the public when only a third of them read above a sixth-grade level—and tell them that reality itself isn't what they think it is?"

That everything we see and experience might not reflect what's really happening.

Over the years, I've learned that human existence operates under far stranger conditions than we imagine. Reality isn't linear—it's layered, parallel, and responsive. What we call "time" may not flow from point A to B but exist laterally, with every moment—past, present, and future—coexisting in a single field of possibility. Our consciousness might be the mechanism that chooses which slice of that field we perceive.

I often picture it through the metaphor of **biological versus mechanical sonar.** A dolphin navigates the ocean using organic frequencies—an intuitive, living technology. We, on the other hand, build metal submarines that imitate that ability through circuitry and code. Both locate objects in the dark, but one does it as part of nature, the other by replicating nature. In the same way, human consciousness could be a biological form of advanced technology—something evolution crafted long before we learned to build machines.

That concept connects directly to **wave-function collapse** in quantum physics: the idea that the act of observation itself determines which potential becomes real. Our brains might be quantum engines, processing billions of probabilities every second and collapsing one of them into the physical world we experience. If that's true, then what we collectively believe—our myths, fears, and expectations—literally constructs the timeline we inhabit.

When groups of people synchronize their focus, those timelines converge. Ancient rituals, mass movements, even national myths could be seen as exercises in collective tuning. Consciousness, physics, and power are not separate; they are intertwined frequencies.

This is precisely where **Peter Levenda's *Sinister Forces*** comes in. Long before most of us dared to bridge these subjects, Levenda was tracing the circuitry between mind, ritual, and authority. His research reveals that history itself may be an engineered system—a ritual carried out over centuries by those who understand how belief shapes reality.

Reading *Sinister Forces* feels like encountering a second, hidden history running parallel to the official one. Levenda connects the occult to intelligence agencies, religion to geopolitics, and coincidence to pattern. He demonstrates that the same invisible hand guiding esoteric ritual can also steer governments, corporations, and culture. The trilogy doesn't just document conspiracies; it explores how the architecture of belief can be weaponized to sculpt civilization.

When you grasp that, you realize how fragile our consensus world really is. The boundary between magic, psychology, and science begins to dissolve. Our inventions mirror our inner architecture: computers mimic neural networks; AI models simulate thought; surveillance replicates omniscience. Technology externalizes consciousness—sometimes beautifully, sometimes dangerously.

That's why *Sinister Forces* remains so vital two decades later. Levenda's work shows how easily hidden systems—political, occult, or technological—can exploit the frequencies of human belief. His writing urges us to ask uncomfortable questions: Who is tuning the collective signal? What agenda hides behind the noise of progress? Are the forces shaping society human, or something that learned to wear a human face?

When I later began developing *Time Rider* with A. J. Hartley, those same questions echoed in my mind. The project built on Levenda's foundation, exploring how future or non-human intelligences might manipulate timelines through consciousness and technology. But make no mistake—*Sinister Forces* is where that revelation began for me. It's the origin point of the map, the book that teaches you to see history as a feedback loop between the seen and unseen.

Today, as artificial intelligence, brain-computer interfaces, and algorithmic control systems spread across the planet, Levenda's warnings sound prophetic. We're building mechanical sonar to navigate a reality that was once purely biological—digital consciousness attempting to replace organic intuition. In chasing efficiency, we risk severing ourselves from the very mystery that makes us human: empathy, imagination, and the ability to wonder.

Twenty years after its first publication, *Sinister Forces* is not just a trilogy of books—it's a decoding tool for the modern age. It invites readers to re-examine the machinery behind their own perceptions, to question the source of their thoughts, and to recognize how belief can be engineered. It's a reminder that history, politics, and spirituality are not separate subjects but overlapping expressions of the same hidden current.

Levenda mapped that current with the precision of a historian and the courage of a mystic. Few have gone as deep, and fewer still have returned with something coherent enough to share. His work opened a generation of minds—including mine—to the possibility that we are participants in a vast, unfinished experiment.

Perhaps the signs were always there… and we simply chose not to see them.

Tom DeLonge

OMNIBUS PREFACE

20TH ANNIVERSARY EDITION OF THE *SINISTER FORCES* TRILOGY

I first began writing *Sinister Forces* during Watergate.

My initial thesis was that, for all our insistence that there is a separation of Church and State in America, there is still a lot of what famous French tourist Alexis de Tocqueville (1805–1859) called "religious insanity" in the United States, and it influences our political and cultural life as Americans to an unsettling degree. Watergate and its aftermath revealed a lot of that, inadvertently to be sure, and even gave us the term "sinister forces" as the cause of the infamous eighteen-and-a-half-minute gap in Nixon's Oval Office tapes.

As the Watergate hearings (1973–1974) morphed into Congressional committees investigating the assassinations of President Kennedy and Martin Luther King Jr. (1976–1979), and even more investigations in 1977 involving the CIA's study of mind control techniques (popularly known as MK-ULTRA), the 1970s slithered into the Son of Sam murders during 1975–1977 in New York City and the Jonestown massacre in Guyana in 1978, culminating in the Iran Hostage Crisis of 1979 and the assassination of John Lennon in front of the Dakota apartment building in December, 1980.

That's a hell of a timeline.

Throw in the fact that both Edgar Cayce and Ronald Reagan were members of the Disciples of Christ denomination—made famous by cult leader Jim Jones, a minister in that same denomination—and that Sirhan Sirhan, convicted as the assassin of Bobby Kennedy, requested books by Theosophists while awaiting trial . . . and that Manson Family member Squeaky Fromme attempted the assassination of President Gerald Ford . . . which brings us to Roman Polanski and Sharon Tate having dinner with Bobby Kennedy the night of Bobby's assassination . . . Polanski, whose film *Rosemary's Baby* opened that month, a movie about Satan worshippers living at . . . well . . . the Dakota (known as the Bramford in the film), and that Sharon Tate would be murdered the following year, a victim of the Manson Family . . .

You see where I was going with this?

And then the discovery that at least two suspects in the JFK assassination investigation led by New Orleans District Attorney Jim Garrison—Guy Banister and Fred Crisman—had ringside seats at the 1947 UFO phenomenon, the first as an FBI investigator reporting directly to J. Edgar Hoover, the second as a central figure in the Maury Island affair—and we are off to the races.

And did I mention that Lee Harvey Oswald was a handshake away from a mystic circle of blue-blooded American Brahmins led by Andrija Puharich in a snowed-in farmhouse in Maine in 1952–1953? A circle that eventually involved disembodied spirits, flying saucers, mental telepathy, Uri Geller, and a Faraday cage?

It took thirty years, but I eventually managed to cram all of this research into an actual book. It originally (2005–2006) spread over three volumes, but somehow we managed to get this into a single volume (as it was intended to be), the one you now hold in your hands. The thesis is as relevant today as it was in the 1970s; perhaps more so. The coincidences, synchronicities, and just plain weirdness that obsessed me then are even more prevalent today, decades later. The UFO Phenomenon has become a national obsession (thanks, in large part, to the efforts of Tom DeLonge and his team at To The Stars) and its roots are delineated in these pages, with no attempt to disguise the "high strangeness" with which this field is entangled. The consciousness aspect of the UFO Phenomenon was explored in this book then and becomes even more relevant today.

The theme of "sinister forces" shaping historical events runs through the text like a leitmotif. The crazy patterns of synchronicity and coincidence—a web of correspondences pointing to the existence of a web of mysterious connections underlying our reality—became the inspiration for a work of fiction. Co-authored by Tom DeLonge and A. J. Hartley, *Time Rider* takes the basic elements of *Sinister Forces* and reworks them into a narrative, at once entertaining and suggestive. Like their previous collaboration—the *Sekret Machines* fictional series—the idea was to tell the same story but in a more linear fashion, essentially asking the question: "If what we read in *Sinister Forces* is true, what are the implications?" I'm proud to have contributed as a consultant to this project, and to see my work from twenty years ago find a new audience in this manner.

I hope you feel the same way, and as you flip—a little dizzy, perhaps—between the pages of this book and those of *Time Rider,* you will sense what I first felt as the revelations of the Watergate hearings were underway and the entire decade of the 1970s began to spin out of control like a UFO crash-landing in the New Mexico desert. I've published a lot of books since *Sinister Forces* first came out, and they are all basically additional chapters. This is the mother lode, the *fons et origo,* and I hope it inspires you to read more, research more, and come to your own conclusions all the while marveling at the way our reality—this incredible, deeply-encoded tapestry of people, places, events, and symbols—actually works.

It's been a wild ride, so far. Thanks for riding shotgun!

Peter Levenda
2026

SINISTER FORCES

A GRIMOIRE OF AMERICAN POLITICAL WITCHCRAFT

PETER LEVENDA

SINISTER FORCES

A GRIMOIRE OF AMERICAN POLITICAL WITCHCRAFT

BOOK ONE: THE NINE

FROM OUT OF SPACE....
A WARNING AND AN ULTIMATUM!

THE DAY THE EARTH STOOD STILL

WITH

MICHAEL RENNIE · PATRICIA NEAL · HUGH MARLOWE

SAM JAFFE · BILLY GRAY · FRANCES BAVIER · LOCK MARTIN

PRODUCED BY JULIAN BLAUSTEIN · DIRECTED BY ROBERT WISE · SCREEN PLAY BY EDMUND H. NORTH

FOREWORD

BY JIM HOUGAN

Just when the 20th Century went amok, and why, is difficult to say, but the creation of the CIA would seem to have been, at the very least, a contributing factor.

Born in the septic afterglow of World War II, and in keen anticipation of its successor, WW III (a/k/a "the Big One"), the Agency was shaped, in part, by transformative events that had taken place earlier in the century. These were the efflorescence of psychiatry as an important medical practice, and a turn-of-the-century occult revival that reached a crescendo in the 1920s.

Taken together, these events conspired toward unforeseen ends, not the least of which was the conversion of the American heartland into a laboratory experiment in "psychological warfare."

As Peter Levenda, the author of this extraordinary and deeply scary book, points out, the term is a translation of a German word, Weltansschauungskrieg (literally, "world-view warfare"). By way of example, one battle in this war got under way in 1953, when the Central Intelligence Agency convened "a prestigious group of scientists" (watch out, dear Reader, whenever you see that phrase) to discuss the problem of UFOs. There were waves of sightings at the time, and people, in and out of government, were getting nervous about them. Meeting behind closed doors, with CIA security guards at the ready, the so-called "Robertson Panel" (named for Dr. H.P. Robertson, a physicist and weapons expert at Caltech) studied the Tremonton sightings and other films of lights in the sky, and listened patiently to the reports of experts from the private sector, the Air Force and Navy.

Soon, it became apparent that the experts were in disagreement. Some claimed that the lights could be explained in terms of natural phenomena (e.g., sunlight on the wings of seagulls). Others, such as the Navy's Photo-Interpretation Laboratory, insisted that, on careful study, the same objects appeared to be "self-luminous," and therefore intelligently guided.

So it was a question of seagulls or rockets or spaceships. Or something.

No matter. Since the experts could not agree on the meaning of the evidence in front of them, the scientific problem was redefined in political terms. Whatever was zipping around in the skies over America, it hadn't killed anyone (at least not yet, at least not directly). So there didn't appear to be a military threat.

Or was there?

The question arose as to what might happen if the Soviets tried to exploit the phenomenon, preying on the superstitions and weaknesses of the man in the street. A "War of the Worlds" panic might easily result. "Mass hysteria" would set in, and emergency reporting channels would be overloaded. Air-defense intelligence sources would be compromised.

The Reds could walk right in! If not to Washington, then West Berlin. Something had to be done.

It was decided, therefore, that the subject had to be "debunked." That is to say, UFOs needed to be made intellectually disreputable in the hope that they would eventually become unthinkable. In this way, the problem (if not the lights themselves) would be made to disappear.

So it was that a covert operation was mounted, with the Ozzie & Harriet world of Middle America as its target. Celebrities such as Arthur Godfrey were enlisted to make fun of the subject and ridicule those who were interested in it. UFO watchdog groups, such as Wisconsin's Aerial Phenomena Research Organization (APRO), were placed under surveillance and infiltrated. The Jam Handy Organization, which produced World War II films for the American Army, was retained, along with the Walt Disney organization. Journalists working for *Life* and the *Saturday Evening Post* were dragged into the fray, as was the Navy's Special Devices Center on Long Island.

It took a while, but UFOs eventually became a kind of in-joke among those who hoped to be taken seriously. To raise the issue in public was to invite ridicule and trigger snickers. By 1960, curiosity about mysterious lights in the sky was regarded by many as evidence of mental "instability." While an expression of interest in the subject would not be enough to get you committed, neither would it enhance your resume.

Other psy-ops followed, at home and abroad. Levenda discusses many of them, including Gen. Edward Lansdale's manipulation of the vampire myth in the Philippines, and the CIA's scheme to eliminate Fidel Castro by persuading his constituents that he was, in fact, *el Anticristo*.

The JFK assassination was, of course, a focal-point in the world-view war waged by the CIA. Just as the Agency conspired to make curiosity about "flying saucers" a litmus test for an addled mind, excessive interest in the President's murder was made to seem "ghoulish" and trivial. For a journalist or historian to write critically about either subject was professional suicide.

Eventually, psy-ops like these combined to redefine the parameters of acceptable discourse in America. Principal among the notions placed beyond the Pale was the practice and theory of "conspiracism"—which soon came to include criticism of mainstream reportage. More than a matter of seeing cabals behind every murder, it was a way of thinking, a stance toward the networks, the press and the feds. Anyone who looked too deeply into events, or who asked too many questions, was dismissed as "a conspiracy-theorist." (This, after MK-ULTRA, Iran-Contra, BCCI and the destruction of the World Trade Centers.)

In some ways, it is as if the century itself has been encrypted, so that if an historian would be honest, he must also become an investigator reporter. Failing that, we are left at the mercy of ambitious academicians and journalists, stenographers to power who are themselves complicit in an astonishing string of coverups and atrocities that stretch from Dealey Plaza to Watergate, Waco to 9-11. Pier Paolo Pasolini, the Italian poet and film director who was stomped to death by a street-hustler in 1975 (unless, as some insist, he was beaten to death by a gang of fascists) understood. Fascinated by the 20th Century vectors of politics and violence, Pasolini despaired of the way in which the age has been encrypted. Writing in *Corriere della Sera,* a left-wing newspaper, he declared,

> I know the names of those responsible for the slaughters . . .
> I know the names of the powerful group . . .
> I know the names of those who, between one mass and the next, made provision and guaranteed political protection . . .
> I know the names of the important and serious figures who are behind the ridiculous figures . . .
> I know the names of the important and serious figures behind the tragic kids . . .
> I know all these names and all the acts (the slaughters, the attacks on institutions) they have been guilty of . . .
> *I know. But I don't have the proof. I don't even have clues.*

Well, here they are: the clues, seething in the evidentiary equivalent of what the French call "a basket of crabs," in the first volume of what promises to be a virtual encyclopedia of clues. Levenda calls *Sinister Forces* "a grimoire," or manual for invoking demons.

Certainly, there are demons enough in its pages: Charles Manson and Richard Helms, Aleister Crowley and David Ferrie, Jack Parsons and the Son of Sam. The "usual suspects," you say? Well, yes, of course. But the suspects are served up with an entourage of angels and demons you may never have heard of: Arthur Young and C.D. Jackson, Andrija Puharich and The Nine, not to mention a claque of "Wandering Bishops" and the proprietors of Music World in Wilder, Kentucky (surely the model for the nightmare-cantina in Quentin Tarantino's "From Dusk Til Dawn").

But that's just for openers. Levenda's study is broad and deep, a life's work that runs to volumes. What distinguishes it from other efforts, such as those of Pasolini, is not merely its comprehensiveness. Rather, it is Levenda's realization that a matrix of politics and violence is incapable of explaining the demented century that shuddered to an end in Manhattan, not so long ago. What's needed is a third dimension, and that dimension, he tells us, is "the occult."

By this, Levenda means something broader than a mix of magic and religion. When he writes of the occult, he means to include whatever is secret, hidden, or unknown. Add this dimension to those of politics and violence, and the century shivers into focus. *Sinister Forces* is about evil in what is now the digital age: *Evil 2.0.*

Time magazine long ago, and famously, posed the question: "Is God Dead?" Implicit in Levenda's study is a related inquiry: Did the Devil survive Him? If he did not, then how are we to explain a century of recreational homicide and political mayhem?

Perhaps with reference to what seems to be a Fortean element: the pattern of coincidence that enfolds these highly strange events, adding a distinct "woo-woo factor" to Levenda's study. Whether it is Lee Harvey Oswald's habit of hanging out at the Bluebird Cafe in Atsugi, Japan ("Bluebird" was the code-name of a CIA mind control program to produce "programmed assassins"), or the famous chain of coincidences surrounding the Kennedy and Lincoln assassinations, (eg., Lincoln's secretary named Kennedy and Kennedy's secretary named Lincoln each warned the President not to make his fatal sojourn). It seems almost as if an early warning system is embedded in the passage of time itself, or in what Carl Jung called the Collective Unconscious. And that system would seem to be sending a stream of warning signals, enciphered as synchronicities.

Exploring topics like this is what makes *The Nine* one of the darkest and most provocative books that you are ever likely to read (pending publication of Book II). That said, it is also one of the most enjoyable, easy to pick up (start reading on any page), and hard to put down. Levenda's intuitions are a delight, and his choice of subject-matter unerring. Both a compendium of 20th century evil and an investigation of it, Levenda's study is deep, intuitive (and, often, droll).

It is, in other words, parapolitics at their most bizarre and, I suspect, their most illuminating. Like UFOs, conspiracies and assassination, serial killers, mind control and the occult, "evil" isn't something that serious people are supposed to think about. If they did, the emergency reporting system would soon be overloaded. And you know what happens when that occurs.

All hell breaks loose.

Lucifer Enthroned (c.1590–1600), Engraving by Cornelis Galle I after Ludovico Cardi (Cigoli)

This image is a visualization of the final Canto of Dante Alighieri's allegorical masterpiece Inferno. In this epic poem, Dante encounters sinners enduring punishments that correspond to their earthly crimes, with each descending circle containing progressively worse sinners—until reaching Satan himself. Dante's famous work would shape Western imagery and perception of Satan and Hell for generations to come.

INTRODUCTION

A STUDY IN SCARLET

"There's the scarlet thread of murder running through the colourless skein of life, and our duty is to unravel it, and isolate it, and expose every inch of it."
—Sherlock Holmes in *A Study in Scarlet*, by Sir Arthur Conan Doyle, 1887

August 25, 2000 Rome

It is the centenary of the death of Friedrich Nietzsche, but I am in Rome. A week ago, I was in Turin, standing in the plaza where Nietzsche went insane in January, 1889. He saw a horse being whipped and—out of all character—was so moved to compassion that he threw his arms around the horse's neck and suffered a nervous breakdown on the spot. Since then, psychiatrists have been of the opinion that this spontaneous gesture of compassion was so alien to Nietzsche's own writings that it precipitated the breakdown.[1] Compassion, that most un-Darwinian of emotions, went against everything Nietzsche thought he stood for.

What blond beast, its hour come round at last . . .

I am thinking of Nietzsche now, in the intense, unforgiving sun of St. Peter's Square in a relentlessly hot August, escorting an American executive (my employer) and his fiancée on a tour of Rome. In a way I am coming full circle to my childhood from this moment in time, nearly fifty years after my birth and, like Nietzsche, I am confronted with my antithesis. It is not a whipped horse I see before me, however, but as we descend into the crypt below the high altar it is a small casket said to contain the bones of St. Peter himself, the first Pope and the small rock on which Christ is said to have built his church.

Ecce Homo. Nietzsche's last work, finished in the months before he went mad, titled after Pontius Pilate's famous words to the crowd as he asked them to spare the accused Jesus Christ: Behold the Man.

St. Peter was murdered, and died a martyr's death. This pilgrimage to make contact with his remains—remains over which the entire edifice of Roman Catholicism has been built—is for me a confrontation with the Enemy. And, like all true Enemies, in his face I see my own.

Christ was executed, according to the official version of the story (although this has always been in doubt, both among historians and among members of

Western secret societies). His chosen successor, Simon Peter—in whose Basilica I now stand—was also executed, and in fact crucified upside-down. St. Peter's Cross is a reverse crucifix, such as those the Satanists wear, perhaps marking them as more Christian than they would be comfortable knowing. St. Andrew was also crucified, he of the X-shaped cross. And every Catholic church must have the mortal remains of some saint present in the altar stone. It is, with its gruesome crucified Jesus and saints missing eyes and being roasted alive or torn to pieces, a bloody religion: a faith built on aggression and murder, madness and sacrifice. The Passion. The early Christians met in catacombs, in cemeteries and in darkness. And now I pass lines of sarcophagi containing the remains of dead Popes buried beneath the nave of St. Peter's Basilica. More death: death in everlasting rows, quiet chapels and candles burning alone, in silence. And there is the sarcophagus of Pope John Paul I. He was Pope for a month, and then he died. Mysteriously, to be sure. There is evidence to suggest he was murdered. Volumes of evidence and, as in the Kennedy assassinations, the spoor of conspiracy and hatred.

"A first class relic is a piece of the saint's flesh or blood or bone. A second class relic is something the saint is known to have touched, such as clothing worn. A third class relic is something touched to a first class relic." I am describing Catholic ritual and religion to my guests. They are Lutheran and Methodist, respectively. The woman has wanted to visit the Sistine Chapel since she was twelve. We have already done that, me standing aside and staring up at the Creation, and Adam and Eve in the Garden, not looking too closely at the huge Last Judgment, not being the type who slows down on the highway to gaze at accident victims.

If the blood and bones of saints are relics, what are the blood and bones of the common person: the murder victim? the suicide? the casualty of war? What secret power lies forgotten in their graves, their dump sites, their formaldehyde jars on a serial killer's shelf?

What Great Beast, its hour come round at last . . .

Everywhere around me are images of pissed-off prophets: Moses, forever the type-A executive, smashing and smoting and scolding everyone in sight, taking on the Egyptians, a man who has the balls to ask God for a photostat of the Ten Commandments after he, Moses, smashes the first set in anger at his own people. You've got to be on pretty intimate terms with the Creator to go up the mountain a second time. Moses, on some statuary, is shown with horns on his head. And then there are Isaiah, Jeremiah, and Ezekiel, full of dire warnings and frightening predictions. John the Baptist, not the sort you would want to invite to your GOP fundraiser. Danger is all around us. Trust no one. The presence of Satan is everywhere implicit. *But who is he?*

Bogeyman. The word comes from the Russian, *bog*, meaning "god."

I stand a little apart as the executive and his fiancée approach the glass window that opens out onto St. Peter's own resting place. It was to Peter that Jesus said,

"Get thee behind me, Satan!" I am nervous. The crowds are too thick, this being a Jubilee Year and what the Italian papers are calling *La Woodstock del Pape*. There is no possibility of silent contemplation of St. Peter's remains, no chance for a psychic connection with the founder of the Christian organization. I glance to my right. There is a metal box there. *Peter's Pence,* it says. You're supposed to make a donation.

Even St. Peter's Basilica is not immune. Not even the bones of Peter himself. There is no way to avoid the collection plate, the thick envelope, the outstretched, manicured hand. A few feet away, John Paul I lies in a plain, unassuming box, while all around him the bodies of Popes who went along to get along are buried in carved marble splendor.

Get thee behind me, Satan.

I am thinking of Nietzsche again as we make our way over to the gift shop to organize the purchase of a poster of the Sistine ceiling, or *il volto* as they say in Italian. The vault. A souvenir of the journey for the fiancée, who believes in vampires and crystals and the Knights Templar and Rosslyn. She already has a poster of that famous scene from the Chapel, the one where God leans over and almost—but not quite—touches the languid fingertip of Adam. I sometimes wonder if Adam and God are actually pointing at each other, challenging the other to take the blame for what can only be a pretty messed up Creation. There is supposed to be tension in that painting, the tension of a gun about to go off. As I once wrote, long ago,

> I have respect for God, the same respect I have for a loaded gun, or the hand that holds it.[2]

And,

> God is the only safe thing to be.[3]

And Nietzsche wrote,

> We should reconsider cruelty and open our eyes. . . Almost everything we call "higher culture" is based on the spiritualization of *cruelty*, on its becoming more profound: this is my proposition. That "savage animal" has not really been "mortified"; it lives and flourishes, it has merely become—divine.[4]

And,

> The great epochs of our life come when we gain the courage to rechristen our evil as what is best in us.[5]

"Rechristen our evil" . . .an unintended irony?

We find a taxi to take us back to the Hotel Hassler, that ornate pile atop the Spanish Steps. We are lucky; the day is hot and the pilgrims many. Getting a taxi at St. Peter's Square is no mean feat; I know, I have struggled many times in the past in all kinds of weather. The visit has been overwhelming: too many statues, too many paintings, too many rooms. But the effect has been to bring me back to my childhood, to the smell of stale incense and dusty cassocks, to Latin conjurations and exorcisms, to the roll call of the dead—the murdered and the suicides—that I have known and survived. To the plots and counterplots and subplots that I have been assiduously recording for the past thirty years. And to that Catholic specialty, guilt.

As I bid the other Americans good evening and take the elevator to my room, I wonder if I can start writing the book I have put off for years, as I did one more bit of research, sought out one more lead, read one more dry volume on psychology, or criminology, or assassination. I feel stronger, more capable, articulate in a way writers have to be.

But in the back of my mind glows the small casket of St. Peter's remains, a silvered shadow of Satan, and that last crazed moment of Nietzsche in Turin, embracing a startled horse and asking for forgiveness. And love. And going insane.

Like all journeys of a thousand miles, this one began with a single step. It was an article in the *Village Voice* by Craig Karpel, entitled "Patriotic Witchcraft," and it was in two parts. The *Voice* is a weekly newspaper, and I waited eagerly for the following week's conclusion. It was the time of Watergate, and I was wallowing.

I worked during the day for the Bendix Corporation, at their International Marketing Operation on Broadway in midtown Manhattan. At night, I was a struggling writer. I wrote short stories, poems, and novellas, working my way up to the novel. I had no illusions, though; I knew that getting paid for writing is virtually impossible, so I was relatively content to write "for the drawer." I had no social obligations, I was single, answerable only to myself. I spent more money on books than on any other item in my modest studio apartment in Brooklyn Heights. I treated friends to meals and long, stately coffee sessions on Montague Street, when I had the money, and we would talk about Vietnam, and the Kennedy assassinations, and Watergate, and the Middle East, and World War II and its aftermath. Across the East River from the Brooklyn Heights Promenade, we could watch the doomed World Trade Center towers going up. A few blocks from Montague Street is Atlantic Avenue and the Arab Quarter, and we spent at least one day a week eating at the Lebanese or Syrian or Moroccan restaurants there, and attending parties—replete with belly dancers and bromides—that raised money and consciousness for Palestinian charities. It was a time of paranoia and innocence, a kind of national adolescence.

The Watergate revelations were coming fast and furious, and I was amused by the startled and shocked expressions of my friends as each new character took the stand with his or her briefcase full of scandals. None of it surprised me. I read three newspapers every day, and did not own a television set, so I considered myself better informed.

And then the *Voice* articles, and something ignited inside me.

Karpel was writing about some of the odd dimensions to Watergate that had so far escaped the notice (or fell beneath the contempt) of mainstream journalists. The fact that convicted Watergate "plumber," and former CIA agent and Bay of Pigs officer, E. Howard Hunt was a part-time novelist who had three occult novels to his credit (á la the Cigarette Smoking Man in the *X-Files2* television series). Or the fact that Richard Nixon had "rushed to judgment" in the case of Charles Manson, declaring him "guilty" while the trial was still under way (a fact that should have caused a mistrial, but didn't). And the odd set of coincidences that linked Nixon's resignation date with the death of Marilyn Monroe, and the opening of the Haunted House at Disneyland.

Indeed, it was the very juxtaposition of those words "patriotic" and "witchcraft" that caused some kind of subconscious chain reaction, resulting in the cortical fission that became the idea for this book. Manson, Nixon, Hunt, occultism, Monroe, politics . . . witchcraft. It was delicious, a kind of Robert Ludlum on LSD experience. Throw in the Church of Satan, *Rosemary's Baby*, *The Manchurian Candidate* and the Kennedy assassinations, and the allure is irresistible.

To what degree does mysticism (including occultism, religious organizations, and secret societies) influence politics? Can it be demonstrated that there is no real separation of church and state, despite most Americans' belief? Can we show that the world's political leaders are motivated by (at times bizarre and outrageous) religious or spiritual convictions, thus threatening at the least the very nature of the American way of life . . . and at the most American lives in general?

Is politics a science? Is it an art?

Or is it religion?

Armed with these uneasy questions, I set out to investigate as much human history as possible to see to what extent—if any—religious or spiritual ideas, convictions, or even regulations have influenced the political lives of nations and contributed to happiness or suffering, peace or war, under the control of visionary leadership. I began with the study of Nazi occultism, since rumors of that were very much in the air at the time. I visited the National Archives in Washington, D.C. and the Library of Congress and fell upon a treasure trove of documentation showing Nazi fascination with occult themes . . . to the extent of financing research in Tibet and hunting down the Grail. This became the central subject matter of my last book, *Unholy Alliance*. Here was a perfect example of a nation being ruled by what were called—in any other age—occult leaders and "spiritual" visionaries. From the swastika to the SS, the Nazis were little more than the 20th century's best organized (and best dressed) cult. A political party? Please.

Simultaneously, I set out to "deconstruct" the Manson phenomenon. I read everything available on the Tate/LaBianca killings, on Manson's childhood and upbringing, and the backgrounds and relationships of his followers. I reviewed Manson's history in California with the Beach Boys, and with Angela Lansbury's daughter and other minor celebrities. Manson's connection to the Church of Satan and to The Process was also important to my research. And then, a strange thing happened (one of many that will be mentioned during the course of this book): I realized that my first real job in New York was with a company whose owner, Willy Brandt, had a son (gossip columnist Steven Brandt) who was questioned by the police in connection with the Manson killings and who subsequently committed suicide—some say in abject fear that he would be the next victim of the "Family." In other words, I was only two handshakes away from the Tate/LaBianca killings myself. (It was at this same company that I later discovered I was only two handshakes away from the Howard Hughes disappearance and the Clifford Irving affair. Coincidence piled on coincidence, until I finally realized that coincidence itself is an important, although neglected, factor in history, as we shall see.)

I thought I had all this pretty much nailed, until I decided one day to drive to the town where Manson grew up. I found that a relative of Manson's had been murdered in Ashland a few months before the Tate/LaBianca killings took place. A kitchen knife had been the weapon used, stabbing Darwin Scott nineteen times and pinning him to the floorboards of his apartment. Clearly there was more to be discovered, and a trip to Manson's "home town" was in order.

Ashland, Kentucky is not a place where nice New York City boys like me hang out. Although it is well-known as the birthplace of Naomi and Wynonna Judd, and Chuck Woolery of *The Love Connection*, it is a small town dominated by the petroleum and chemical refineries that bear Ashland's name. I noticed that serial killer Bobby Joe Long came from Kenova, West Virginia, which is a smaller town only a few miles from Ashland, and that serial killer Henry Lee Lucas was born in a Virginia town on the West Virginia border. I wondered what it was about this particular location—this Bermuda Triangle of depravity—that seemed to breed serial killers and mass murderers. Was it the water?

So I rented a cool, cherry-red Ford Mustang convertible and made the drive from New England to Ashland, Kentucky, stopping off first in Washington, D.C. and then in the hollers of rural West Virginia during a thunderstorm. The tale of that trip comes later in this book. Suffice it to say that I found more than I bargained for in Ashland:

- Ancient "Indian" burial mounds in the center of town;
- A large house that was moved entire from its original site to one a few streets over, directly on a line with burial mounds and sporting a pair of griffins on its roof, mythical creatures—according to the town's own brochure—designed to ward off evil spirits;

- The Ashland Tragedy and Massacre: a savage killing of three children on a Christmas Eve in the late nineteenth century, the subsequent arrest of three suspects, and a massacre of townspeople by militia detailed to protect the suspects from a lynching; and
- Oddest of all, the fact that a Manson relative and sometime petty crook—Darwin Scott—was brutally murdered with a kitchen knife in Ashland a few months before the celebrated Tate/LaBianca killings . . . a murder case that has never been solved.

It is said that "Kentucky" is an Indian word that means "dark and bloody ground." I wondered if it was true, if a physical place could be evil, could hold a curse that would affect generations of residents to come. Did the Indians know something we didn't? Or did we unconsciously suspect that the earth held some sinister secret? Indeed, the name first proposed for the Commonwealth of Kentucky was . . . Transylvania.

And then I remembered the words of Cotton Mather, he of the Salem witch trials in seventeenth century Massachusetts, who said that America had been the Devil's land before the Europeans came, and wondered if he meant more than simply that the Native Americans were not Christians.

And then there were the stories of H.P. Lovecraft, the father of Gothic horror, who felt that there was something ancient and evil beneath the hardscrabble New England soil, a concept amplified by Shirley Jackson in her stories of New England haunted houses and depraved villages.

After all, America has had its share of misery and tragedy, regardless of the beautiful words and even more beautiful intentions of the Declaration of Independence and Constitution. Why would a fertile and bountiful land, colonized by pious and fervent European Christians of every variety, descend into that maelstrom of civil war, slavery, mass murder, assassinations, and day-to-day violence that shocks the rest of the world, even as the rest of the world has had to deal with its Kaisers and Hitlers and Mussolinis and Stalins and Maos and Hirohitos? Do we have more than our share of violence, or is it simply that we get more PR?

Was the answer to be found in unraveling the skein of violence itself, like the scarlet thread of murder in the very first Sherlock Holmes story, running through the fabric of our history like a timeline? . . .Was I wrong to look at religious history? Occult history? It bore such interesting and convincing fruit in my Nazi study. Yet surely the roots of American violence and American evil could not grow from the same metaphysical soil?

And as I poked through the debris of American history—the autopsy photos and the police reports and the political manifestos and the trial transcripts and the confessions and the lies and the declassified documents and the bureaucratic memoranda—I saw that American history could not be separated from my own history or from world history, that, as Americans, we can't look objectively at our own story. Like that famous conundrum in quantum physics, the observer changes the event observed. Is the Kennedy assassination a particle, or a wave?

During the Watergate era a somewhat unsettling revelation was made: that for twenty-five years (or more) the CIA had conducted psychological experimentation upon both volunteers and unwitting subjects—both at home and abroad—to find the key to the unconscious mind, to memory, and to volition. Their goal was to create the perfect assassin and to protect America from the programmed assassins of other countries. This project was known by the name MK-ULTRA, but it had its origins in earlier forms of the same "brainwashing" agenda: Operations BLUEBIRD and ARTICHOKE. To me, this was astounding. A US government agency was conducting what—to a medievalist—could only be characterized as a search for the Philosopher's Stone, for occult power, for magical spells and talismans. Indeed, some of the CIA's subprojects included research among the psychics, the mediums, the magicians and the witches of America and beyond. And the Army was not far behind in its mind control testing, as we shall see.

What was even more disturbing was the revelation that nearly all records of this incredible and superhumanly ambitious project were destroyed in 1973 on orders of CIA director Richard Helms himself. In his testimony, he claimed that MK-ULTRA did not come up with anything worthwhile, and that the project had been terminated. Then why were the documents shredded?

We do not know who the test subjects were. We don't know what was done to them. We don't know how they have been programmed, if at all. We don't know what they might do.

Or what they have already done.

We do know, however, that some of our more colorful criminals have spent time at the same institutions receiving CIA MK-ULTRA funding for this "special testing." People like Charles Manson and Henry Lee Lucas, for instance, as well as "Cinque," the leader of the Symbionese Liberation Army that kidnapped heiress Patty Hearst. It is entirely possible, given the evidence at our disposal, that convicted serial killer Arthur Shawcross is also such an example.

As I stood in the park at Ashland, staring at the ancient burial mounds and looking up at the house with the griffins, I realized that I was standing at a nexus of American history and culture: Charles Manson, unsolved homicides, mind control experiments, mass murder and massacres . . . and I wondered what Indian burial mounds and griffins, movie stars and spies, witches and Washington, even UFOs and occultists, had to do with any of it.

Our culture in the West—formed as it is by a faith in science, a reliance on the technological—has convinced us to ignore the unseen. There is a web of connections between visible events and visible, measurable phenomena that we cannot see, cannot measure—so our response has been to ignore this web in favor of what we *can* see and measure. The blind leading the blind. The drunk looking for his keys under a lamp post because the light is better there. We know—can describe—the stages of growth of flowers, animals, people . . . but not the life force itself, the drive: what engineer, inventor and mystic Arthur Young called "the quantum of action." Of this we know nothing, and are happy to know nothing. And thus we become victims.

University of Chicago Professor Ioan Culianu was able to show that the technique of secret links and correspondences between objects and events discovered by a Renaissance magician—Giordano Bruno—are applicable to mind control and psychological warfare today. Charles Manson declared himself to be a reincarnation of Bruno,[6] an oddly sophisticated choice for the nearly-illiterate convicted murderer. Professor Culianu himself was murdered in 1991, another crime that has never been solved.

The people we trust are those who can measure the measurable. The people we distrust are those who point to the invisible and shout to get our attention. Our world is marching calmly to an obscure and unknowable end because we, the people, hear the drum, feel the beat, know our place in line. That's better, somehow, than jumping off the path into the dark forest where God dwells like a hungry tiger. There is too much personal responsibility in jumping out of line, and if you then try to jump back in, you will find you have lost your place and your fellow marchers no longer want you to join them. You are dirty; you are crazed; you have seen what they are afraid to see.

In order to conduct this investigation I would have to dig very deep, below the surface of official reports, trial transcripts and conspiracy theories. I would have to dig deep below the surface of the American psyche, and trace pieces of evidence back down through several layers of meaning and relevance to find the connective tissue that would make sense of our history, our politics, our collective weirdness. This would have to be nothing less than a deconstruction of our most cherished beliefs and ideals.

Academia frowns upon historians who get "involved" with their subject personally. It is believed such activity ruins objectivity, makes the historian's findings suspect. The "New Journalism" changed that somewhat for journalists, but not for historians. Yet, it is virtually impossible for any American my age—born in 1950—to approach such subject matter as the Kennedy assassinations or the Manson killings with pure, detached objectivity. We lived through it all. We either marched on Washington or marched in the jungles of Southeast Asia. We know where we were when Kennedy was killed—and when the World Trade Center went down. We are connected to these events and cannot extricate ourselves from them, even when we let the documents and the primary sources speak for themselves. For there are documents, and there is blood. Politics and religion both are born of documents and of blood. And both documents and blood form the primary sources of the following investigation.

This is a book about evil. Evil ordinary and extraordinary. Evil vigilant. Evil militant. Evil triumphant. Evil ancient and modern, violent and discrete, beautiful and obscene. Evil in the face of God, of man and woman, of children. The evil of vainglorious men and their hollow minions. Evil unseen and fierce. The evil of bodybags and spent cartridges. Of mass graves and crematoria. Of crimes against nature and against heaven. The evil of death and derangement, of murder and madness, of suicide and satanism. This is the evil that is older than humanity, but reflected in our children's eyes. The evil we can't grasp, cannot punish, cannot destroy. The evil that contaminates souls as well as bodies, nations as well as people. This is a book about the evil spirits that haunt America. About the sinister forces that rule the world of our dreams, our nightmares, and our sober, trembling, waking reality.

If it is true that the gods of one religion become the demons of the one that replaces it, then we in America must deal with generations of demons once worshipped here who now wander the countryside, the city streets, the interstate highways and dead end roads, the theme parks and fast food restaurants, the shopping malls and parking lots, the peepshow parlors and cathedral aisles, like hungry ghosts on a mission from Hell. We gaze with horror on their crimes, and don't understand. We stare into the eyes of their hideous creatures, and don't understand. We clean up the crime scenes and mop up the blood, and don't understand. We imprison, institutionalize, execute to make it all go away . . . and don't understand.

This book is an attempt at understanding. The premise is one that has been embraced by psychoanalysts like Jung and physicists like Pauli: the existence of another mechanism in the universe that binds together events seemingly unrelated. The perspective offered is unique, dangerous, incredible, possibly offensive. The subject matter—serial homicide, genocide, assassination, terrorism, multiple personalities, satanism, sexual savagery, demonic possession, depravity, insanity—makes it impossible to be anything else. We cannot begin to heal until we have identified the disease; we cannot identify the disease until we have studied the anatomy of the body politic. Freud, in order to understand the workings of the human mind, focused on its pathology. We, in order to understand America—and America's place in the world—must do the same. We must plumb the depths of the American psyche, the American unconscious, and dredge up whatever we find before it's too late.

How late is it? Listen in the middle of the night. Turn off the television, the radio, the CD player, the computer. Unplug the telephone. Turn off the lights. What do you hear? Beneath the silence and the stoic beating of your humble heart, what do you hear? Can you hear your soul singing?

Or is it Satan laughing?

ENDNOTES

1 See, for instance, Anacleto Verrechia, "Nietzsche's Breakdown in Turin," in *Nietzsche in Italy*, edited by Thomas Harrison, Anma Libri, Stanford University, 1988

2 Levenda, *Citadel*, unpublished novel

3 Ibid.

4 Nietzsche, *Beyond Good and Evil*, 1966, Vintage Press, NY, p. 158

5 Ibid., p. 86

6 Charles Manson, "The Black/White Bus," in *The Manson File*, edited by Nikolas Shreck, Amok Press, NY, 1988, ISBN 0-941693-04-X

Peter Levenda writes: "It is clear from Sir Arthur Conan Doyle's first Sherlock Holmes story that he was fascinated with the history of the Mormons." The second part of "A Study in Scarlet" (first published in 1887) unexpectedly shifts to the American West with a dark tale of revenge involving Mormon settlers in Utah, marking one of Victorian literature's most notable fictional portrayals of early Mormonism.

Above: Published February 4, 1882, this cartoon shows women labeled "sealed" walking into a skull labeled "Utah."

Right: Joseph Smith (1805–1844) founded the Mormon religion after claiming to have received divine revelations, including the discovery of golden plates that became *The Book of Mormon*, establishing the Church of Jesus Christ of Latter-day Saints in 1830. Painting by an unknown painter, circa 1842.

SECTION ONE:

DEEP BACKGROUND

In the colonial period, when religious creeds, institutions, and communities exerted a major impact on life and work, there was bound to be some spillover into politics. Because the contribution of religion to American political culture covers such important beliefs as obedience, the design of government, and the national mission, the religious roots of American political culture merit close investigation.

—Kenneth D. Wald[1]

Beware when the righteous prepare for the practice of evil.

—Kenneth Patchen[2]

In absurd terms, as we have seen, revolt against men is also directed against God: great revolutions are always metaphysical.

—Albert Camus[3]

Possession and exorcism had always symbolized the rhythms of the historical process.

—Stuart Clark[4]

H.P. Lovecraft (1890–1937) was an American writer who revolutionized horror fiction through his creation of cosmic horror and the Cthulhu Mythos, emphasizing humanity's insignificance in a vast, uncaring universe. Despite living in relative obscurity and poverty during his lifetime, publishing mainly in pulp magazines like *Weird Tales*, his influence on horror and science fiction has proven both timeless and immense, inspiring countless writers, artists, and filmmakers. His most famous works, including "The Call of Cthulhu," "At the Mountains of Madness," and "The Shadow over Innsmouth," feature scholarly protagonists confronting ancient, incomprehensible beings and forbidden knowledge that threatens their sanity, often set against the backdrop of his fictional New England locations like Arkham and Miskatonic University.

BOOK ONE: THE NINE

CHAPTER ONE

THE DUNWICH HORROR: AN OCCULT HISTORY OF AMERICA

When a rise in the road brings the mountains in view above the deep woods, the feeling of strange uneasiness is increased. The summits are too rounded and symmetrical to give a sense of comfort and naturalness, and sometimes the sky silhouettes with especial clearness the queer circles of tall stone pillars with which most of them are crowned.

—"The Dunwich Horror," H.P. Lovecraft[5]

Lovecraft was writing in the 1920s, when most of his more famous stories were published. He was writing of a New England that, in his imagination, had ancient roots in unknown cultures; where Druidic circles and pagan chants would infest the countryside; where a kind of subterranean culture existed, parallel to the world of our own reality. He peppered his stories with references to the works of archaeologists and anthropologists (some real, some fictitious), and connected the American Indian culture to the worship of strange, perhaps extraplanetary or extradimensional beings who viewed humans as little more than undercooked hors d'ouevres. His work has attracted a great deal of attention in the past 30 years or so, oddly enough in France where—like the films of Jerry Lewis—he is an adopted obsession, but also certainly in America where he maintains a cult status even now, more than sixty years after his death. He has attracted serious, albeit fringe, attention from academics and historians of both literature and mysticism, and has even been graced with an anthology of his work prefaced by no less a literary light than Joyce Carol Oates.[6] The blind Argentine author of many essays and stories on the macabre—Jorge Luis Borges—has written in the Lovecraftian mode in homage to the cranky Yankee master.[7] In addition, there are several hard-core occult organizations in Europe and America that owe allegiance to the bizarre principles outlined in his works. They have taken their names and identities straight from his published work, with cults like *Dagon* and *Cthulhu*, and occultist emeritus Kenneth Grant has written extensively on the relation between the works of Lovecraft—an author of gothic horror fiction—and the rituals of modern ceremonial magic and communication with extraterrestrial intelligences.[8]

Part of the reason for Lovecraft's popularity among serious occultists is due to the fact that many of the ideas he put forward in his stories have found some basis in reality: in historical, archaeological, anthropological reality. While there is no evidence at this time for the existence of the beings of which he wrote—Cthulhu chief among them, but let's not forget Yog Sothot or Shub Niggurath—there is evidence that America was visited, and possibly inhabited for some time, by peoples who are not racially (or, at least, culturally) identical to the Native American "Indian" tribes that exist today. The schools of thought over this are contentious and emotional in defending their respective positions. The group most consistently under attack are the Diffusionists (whose most famous proponent was the late Harvard Professor Barry Fell), who adhere to the idea that America was not settled by a single group of wanderers from Asia across the Bering Straits, but by different groups of people from different parts of the globe. There is growing archaeological evidence that people from Europe and North Africa settled in North and South America thousands of years ago, bringing with them their languages, their culture, and their religious and mystical beliefs. And therein lies a tale. We will examine all of this in detail in Chapter Two. For now, though, let us look at some well-known stories, but from a different perspective and with additional data that bear directly on the theme of this work. Seen in this sometimes unsettling light, they provide a basis for the revelations that will come. But before we examine the archaeological evidence, let us look at the purely historical, the evidence that can be supported by unimpeachable, primary sources.

1492

Most Americans learn very early in their primary school education that America was "discovered" by Christopher Columbus on October 12, 1492. Some of them remember that he was supposed to be finding a more direct route to India—by going west instead of east—and that is why we call Native Americans "Indians" to this day: the result of Columbus's blunder in believing that the small Bahamian island he discovered was part of the Indian subcontinent. In the following weeks he would similarly "discover" Cuba and Hispaniola, the island now comprising the Dominican Republic and Haiti.

What is not well-known is the real reason for his expedition.

Yes, he wanted to find a fast route to India and China. At that time, the great seafaring nations of Europe—in particular Portugal, but also Holland and other maritime powers—were going south along the African coastline, rounding South Africa at the Cape and going north and east to reach India. Columbus—based on what are believed to be faulty geographic measurements and a faith in some of the apocryphal books of the Bible—thought he could make it to India much more quickly by going due west from the European coast. The Portuguese had turned this idea down, realizing that his math was faulty, and the Spanish at first rejected him as well, but he later had an audience with King Ferdinand of Spain, who agreed to fund his expedition and to grant him titles, land and a tenth of whatever precious metals he found: an agent's commission.

This much is consistent with what our schoolchildren know.

However, Spain in 1492 was in the middle of one of the greatest upheavals in its history. To understand what Columbus was doing, and the hidden agenda of his voyage—and thereby to begin to understand American history from a European perspective (most Americans being, after all, descendants of European ancestors)—we need to understand a little of what was happening in Spain.

And to understand Spain, we have to understand the history of Islamic "imperialism" and its stormy relationship to Europe in general and Christianity in particular.

While such a topic deserves much more space and much more attention to its detail than the author can ever hope to provide in these pages, we can summarize the situation as follows. Interested readers are urged to follow up with their own research, and several very good texts are recommended in the bibliography. Essentially, we must address the birth and expansion of Islam.

Muhammad, the prophet who created the religion known as Islam, had a vision of the Angel Gabriel while meditating in a cave in what is now Saudi Arabia. He was forty years old, a tradesman, a pagan, and troubled by hearing Jewish and Christian tradesmen and others around them discussing their respective religions. Monotheism was a new concept, and the year was 610 A.D.

The vision of Gabriel ignited something in Muhammad's heart and soul. He began preaching a personal and unique amalgam of Jewish, Christian and native Arab mythology and religious and moral principles to anyone who would listen. These principles included better treatment of slaves and women, a life of moderation, a "surrender" to the one true God (the word "Islam" means "surrender"), and other spiritual doctrines. Abstinence from alcohol and the eating of pork were also included, the latter a probable borrowing from Jewish law.

The people in his native Mecca found Muhammad to be something of a problem, because his doctrines interfered with trade and with the status of the social elite. Much as Christianity had evolved from a Messianic Jewish cult to a world religion and was about to conquer much of Europe as a political power, so too Muhammad and his followers were seen as a political and economic threat to the status quo.

Muhammad escaped a murder plot in Mecca and, with some of his followers, fled to Medina. This was in the year 622 A.D., the year of the "flight," the *Hegira* from which year Islam now counts its calendar.

Muhammad found a slightly better reception in Medina, settled several tribal disputes, and gradually converted many of these tribes to his new religion. He tried to win the allegiance of the Jews in Medina, but the Prophet was an illiterate

Arab tradesman, and the Jewish elite scorned him and his new religion which they found at odds with the Torah. Although Muhammad initially had his followers face Jerusalem when they prayed, and made them adopt the practice of the Yom Kippur fast, his experience with the Jews in Medina led him to change these practices. The Muslims now face Mecca, which is the site of an ancient Arab relic, the Qa'aba (at the time of Muhammad a pagan shrine containing 360 idols and a piece of black, probably meteoric, rock), and they fast for the entire month of Ramadan. Thus, Islam became gradually more "Arab," as Muhammad's initial desire to wed Judaism, Christianity and indigenous Arab religious ideas and forms met opposition on all sides. Due to this very early contact with Jewish religious and economic leaders, the Koran has many citations specifically targeted against the Jews.[9] Thus, some modern-day Muslims feel they have religious approval—if not an out and out license—for their antagonism against Israel.

As his religion grew in numbers, so did Muhammad grow in political power. At the time of his death, Islam was virtually the state religion in Saudi Arabia. During the next hundred years after his death, Arab armies would give the idea of missionary work a new meaning as they conquered—with fire and sword—nation after nation, extending their faith and the Arab culture as far afield as France, where they were finally defeated by Charles Martel at the Battle of Tours in the year 800 A.D. They had to fall back to Spain and Portugal in the west, and in the east as far as Samarkand, Tashkent and Turkey. Europe would hear again of the Arab legions when the Ottoman Empire reached its height in the sixteenth century A.D., going as far inland as the outskirts of Vienna and running over the Balkans, Romania and everything in between.

It would be nearly another three hundred years after the Battle of Tours before the first Crusades were mounted by the Catholic Church to "take back" the holy city of Jerusalem. Jerusalem was also sacred to the Muslims, due to a tradition that Muhammad had ascended to heaven from a site in Jerusalem that was also sacred to Jews and Christians: the site of King Solomon's Temple. This scenario may be a borrowing from the legend of Jesus and some stories of the Virgin Mother and of the prophet Elijah, who were all bodily carried into heaven.

Muhammad's descendants—both familial and spiritual—then fought over the growing Islamic empire. Europe saw Islamic forces on their soil within a century after the death of Islam's founder. And, in Spain, it would be another *eight hundred years* before the last Islamic rulers would finally leave their country.

Specifically, in the year 1492.

TALES OF THE ALHAMBRA

In the spring of 1829, the author of this work, whom curiosity had brought to Spain, made a rambling expedition from Seville to Granada in company with a friend, a member of the Russian Embassy at Madrid. Accident had thrown us together from distant regions of the

> globe and a similarity of taste led us to wander together among the romantic mountains of Andalusia.
>
> —Washington Irving, *Tales of the Alhambra*[10]

In the spring of 2001, the author of this work, whom business had brought to Spain, made a fast expedition from Seville to Granada in company with a colleague, an executive of an American corporation that has a factory in Seville. Accident had thrown us together from distant regions of the globe (he from North Carolina, me from my temporary base in Malaysia), and a similarity of taste and a tightness of schedule led us to hire a car and drive across Spain in search of Granada and the fabled palace of the Alhambra.

My Spanish is okay, my driving ability perhaps less so, yet I found myself doing all the driving that day, getting us out of Seville at an early hour and making good time to Granada. As was the case with that earlier tour to Rome in company with another such executive, I found myself less of a chauffeur and more of a tour guide and ad hoc historian as we wandered the fabulously decorated halls and courtyards of one of the most striking examples of Arab architecture anywhere. It is always interesting for me to watch American executives abroad, and to marvel at how little they really know of the world outside their borders. This case was no exception.

The executive in question has a mother who is fascinated by church history, and who has a passionate attachment to the Holy Land and especially to Jerusalem and to the Holy Sepulcher, the site where Christ is supposed to have been laid to rest after the Crucifixion. Yet, her son—a tall, self-important man of heroic proportions, with paranoid demeanor and somewhat lacking in social skills—seemed relatively unaware of Arab conquests in Europe, even though he had accompanied his mother on a pilgrimage to Jerusalem and is the beneficiary of her knowledge of the subject. I found myself filling in odd gaps in his understanding of the stormy relationship that has existed between Muslims and Christians virtually since the death of Muhammad, and particularly since the "Moorish" invasion of Europe in the eighth century A.D.

It was a revelation to stand in the Alhambra, in Spain, and realize that there had been an Islamic government in charge of large parts of the country for eight hundred years. That is nearly as long as the time since the Norman conquest of England in 1066, and is certainly much longer than the time elapsed since Columbus' landing on San Salvador in 1492 and . . . the present. The cities of Seville, Cordoba, and Granada are testimony to the once-strong but now fading legacy of the Caliphs of the Alhambra.

Washington Irving—the American author perhaps better known for his frightening *Legend of Sleepy Hollow* and the somewhat comical and perceptive story of *Rip Van Winkle*—in his celebrated combination of short stories and travelogue *Tales of the Alhambra* makes justified recognition of the generally benign rule of the Moors in Spain, a reign that was famous for learning, science and the arts, and which attracted scholars and artists from all over Europe in its time. Nonetheless, it was an alien transplant in Europe and—surrounded as it was by hostile Christians on every side and separated by sea and land from its spiritual home in the Middle East—it eventually succumbed to pressure from without and within.

The Moors were vanquished, finally, in January of 1492, the same year that Columbus set sail on his first voyage to the New World, and that was not a mere coincidence. King Ferdinand was triumphant in removing the last vestige of Muslim political influence from western Europe . . . and began to dream of another conquest.

This is what American schoolchildren never learn, and what scholars have been slow to report. From the *Diario* of Christopher Columbus, then:

> And [Columbus] says that he hopes in God that on the return that he would undertake from Castile he would find a barrel of gold that those who were left would have acquired by exchange; and that they would have found the gold mine and the spicery, and those things in such quantity that the sovereigns, before three years, will undertake and prepare to go conquer the Holy Sepulcher; for thus I urged Your Highnesses to spend all the profits of this my enterprise on the conquest of Jerusalem, and Your Highnesses laughed and said that it would please them and that even without this profit they had that desire.[11]

The conquest of Jerusalem and the Holy Sepulcher. In other words, another Crusade.

The discovery of America and the subsequent voyages of Columbus had as their goal *the recapture of Jerusalem.* Indeed, one of the most important reasons for finding the "fast" route to the East was to provide Ferdinand with a different strategy for retaking Jerusalem, for if Columbus was right and if India and China could be reached by traveling due west, then so could Jerusalem. Rather than send an army of Crusaders across the Mediterranean or via land through hostile Muslim territory, Ferdinand believed he could instead attack Jerusalem from the eastern side. No one would expect a Crusader force coming from the land east of Jerusalem, when all previous attacks had come from the western approach.

Ironically, then, American history begins in the sands of Palestine, in the solemn stones of Jerusalem and King Solomon's Temple, the Holy Sepulcher and the Dome of the Rock, where so many have fought and suffered and died for religion, and still do.

Much has been made in conspiracy literature of the possible connections Columbus had with the outlawed Knights Templar. It is said that his fleet—the famous *Nina*, *Pinta* and *Santa Maria*—bore the red Templar cross on their sails as a sign of the real mission of the Genoese-born Columbus and his Spanish patrons. Although the Templars had been suppressed two hundred years previously, there is evidence to show that some members of the Order had escaped to Portugal and Scotland, among other places. We can easily see how their descendants would have privately rejoiced in such a Grail-like quest. *"Jacques de Molay, thou art avenged."* We should also remember it was Columbus' patrons—King Ferdinand and Queen Isabella—who created the Spanish Inquisition in 1478. At first, it was designed to root out heresy among the Marranos, the Jews who had converted to Christianity, usually through social or other pressure. It was then extended to those who had converted from Islam. At its height, the Grand Inquisitor was also responsible for the American territories conquered by Spain: Mexico and Peru, the lands of the Aztecs and the Incas respectively. In the case of America, however, the Inquisition was concerned less with heresy, and more with witchcraft and sorcery.

In addition, and most importantly, we should realize that the Spanish Inquisition was not run by the Church. Authority was given by the Pope to the King to run the Inquisition, thereby making it a governmental organization, even though the Inquisitors themselves were usually Catholic churchmen, predominately Dominican monks. This mechanism would be followed two hundred years later in Salem, Massachusetts during America's own witch trials, when religious authority gave way to secular, and witches—practitioners of spell-casting, Satan worshipping, and other such acts considered anti-Christian—were arrested, indicted, tried and executed by the secular courts. Heresy is tantamount to rebellion where there is a State Church, and therefore it became the State's business to discover and punish—and torture and execute—heretics. They were, after all, *de facto* traitors. Private beliefs became matters for public prosecutions.

And finally we should not forget that the Pilgrims, the Puritans and the Huguenots—some of the first settlers in North America—were religious refugees, fleeing oppression in their native lands, to practice their faiths freely in the New World. It is no indulgence in hyperbole to suggest that the modern origins of America are spiritual (or, at least, religious) in nature, and that America has spent the last five hundred years trying—usually unsuccessfully—to ignore that fact.

In light of the events of September 11, 2001 in the United States, many Americans have a dim view of Islam, and suspect all Muslims of harboring ill intentions towards their country. In spite of all the rhetoric denying this, there is some truth to the suspicion that devout Muslims are hostile to the West. Islamic rulers have had a long and well-documented history of anti-European aggression, beginning with the invasions in the eighth century A.D., long before the first Crusade against Jerusalem. Particularly since the end of World War I, when the five hundred-year-old Ottoman Empire was finally destroyed by Western forces, and when the betrayal of the Arab revolt was etched in stone at the peace talks in Versailles—thus paving the way for the creation of a Jewish state in the midst of Arab Palestine—Muslims have been angry at the West and at what they perceive to be Western decadence and immorality (an attempt, perhaps, to raise a visceral sense of humiliation at the hands of the technologically-advanced nations to a higher spiritual plane). Although in the past Christians and Jews fared better, oddly, under Muslim leaders than under Christian administrations, it would be naïve to believe that most Muslims are friendly to the West in general and to the United States in particular, especially in light of America's role in support of Israel. Islamic fundamentalism has been on the rise worldwide, and the only thing stopping the creation of a new Ottoman Empire is chronic disunity among Muslim nations.

But it was not always thus.

As I stood in the Court of the Lions at the Alhambra, while my colleague wandered back and forth snapping photographs and asking endless questions for which he rarely stood still for an answer, I was reminded—with a kind of nostalgic sigh—of the words of Washington Irving, describing the fall of the Caliphate:

> Never was the annihilation of a people more complete than that of the Morisco-Spaniards. Where are they? Ask the shores of Barbary and its desert places. The exiled remnant of their once powerful empire disappeared among the barbarians of Africa, and ceased to be a nation. They have not even left a distinct name behind them, though for nearly eight centuries they were a distinct people. The home of their adoption, and of their occupation for ages, refuses to acknowledge them, except as invaders and usurpers. A few broken monuments are all that remain to bear witness to their power and dominion, as solitary rocks, left far in the interior, bear testimony to the extent of some vast inundation. Such is the Alhambra;—a Moslem pile in the midst of a Christian land; an Oriental palace amidst the Gothic edifices of the West; an elegant memento of a brave, intelligent, and graceful people, who conquered, ruled, flourished, and passed away.[12]

King Ferdinand raised his army of Crusaders, but never managed to reach Jerusalem. The Crusaders found themselves in the midst of a military adventure in Italy, and the dream of retaking Jerusalem in the wake of the ouster of the Islamic government in Granada never materialized. But in the same year, 1492, he managed to forcibly expel from Spain all Jews who would not convert to Christianity. In a reign worthy of admiration by Christian fundamentalists everywhere, Ferdinand had managed to defeat Islam, expel the Jews, and mount a Crusade against the Muslims in the Holy Land . . . all in one year. He was also responsible for the infamous Spanish Inquisition (immortalized in Edgar Allan Poe's "The Pit and the Pendulum"). However, to American schoolchildren, King Ferdinand is pictured as a relatively anonymous or even benign influence, a man who helped Columbus in his quest for a western passage to India, a hero of the "round Earth" theory.

The year 1492 for some scholars—including the brilliant historian Dame Frances Yates in her *The Occult Philosophy In The Elizabethan Age*—also marked the beginning of the Renaissance, as Spanish Jews fled to Italy with their science, art, and mystical writings, even as others mark the Renaissance as beginning with the fall of Constantinople to the Turkish Empire in 1453.

As for Columbus himself, alas, his succeeding three voyages were cursed with bad luck, violence, and death. He managed to visit what is now Trinidad and a little farther on, Venezuela and the mouth of the Orinoco River, finally realizing that he had discovered a new land that was not on the maps. But in the meantime his attempts to convert the Native Americans to Catholicism—warlike Caribs and peaceful Arawaks, for the most part—had failed miserably, and in some cases the Native Americans rose in revolt and slaughtered their European visitors, only to be slaughtered themselves in return, thus instituting a pattern of attack and counterattack that would plague European/Native American relations for centuries. Indeed, it was Columbus who brought the first Native American slaves to Europe, about two hundred of them, many of whom died of disease on the voyage. This was a pattern that was to be followed by the Spanish who followed him to the New World, as they captured native peoples and enslaved them to work on their plantations in the American Southwest, the Caribbean, and Latin America.

Finally, Columbus was put in irons and sent back to Spain in disgrace. What he had accomplished, however, would long outlive him and far exceed his wildest expectations. Spanish, Portuguese, Dutch, English and French expeditions would be mounted over the course of the next hundred years to take as much of the "New World" as possible, regardless of the opinions of the Arawaks or any of the other Native American peoples. And, even as America was discovered by accident while a Spanish King and an Italian navigator plotted a new Crusade to take back the Holy Land, they and their descendants committed atrocity after atrocity upon the pagan peoples they found there.

But the Arawaks would have the last laugh. It would take them exactly two hundred years—almost to the day—but they would have the last laugh.

THE CRUCIBLE

> . . . the rumours of devil-worship were partly justified by a peculiar secret cult which had gained force there and engulfed all the orthodox churches. It was called . . . "The Esoteric Order of Dagon," and was undoubtedly a debased, quasi-pagan thing imported from the East a century before . . .
>
> —"The Shadow Over Innsmouth," H.P. Lovecraft[13]

Eventually, Spanish explorers did find gold and all manner of treasure in the New World. The names of Pizzaro, Cortez and Ponce de Leon are familiar to American schoolchildren as the illustrious Spanish conquistadores and explorers who spread out from Florida and Cuba to Mexico and Peru, Colombia and Venezuela and up to California and the American Southwest. Their legacy lives on in the architecture, the culture, the language and especially the predominantly Catholic religion of Latin America. By the mid-sixteenth century, the great Aztec empire that was headquartered in what is now Mexico City had been subjugated to the Spanish crown with fire and sword . . . and missionaries.

The "Journey to the West" begun by Ferdinand and Columbus in 1492 would culminate four hundred years later, after the conquest of not only much of Latin America but also the Philippine Islands. Revolutions instigated by Simon Bolivar and Bernardo O'Higgins in South America would eventually free the continent from direct control by Spain, but the Crown would hold on to Cuba, Puerto Rico, the Philippines and other territories until the Spanish-American War and Teddy Roosevelt's famous charge up San Juan Hill.

In the meantime, however, strange things were taking place in North America, a short ride from H. P. Lovecraft's home town in Providence, Rhode Island.

When they hear the word "Salem," many Americans automatically think of either the cigarette or witchcraft, both potentially lethal phenomena to be sure. Ironically, they do share a common origin, at least in popular American history, and we will come to that in a moment. Disregarding King Tobacco for now, let's focus on what we know about Salem witchcraft, because its popularity has not diminished with time, and the town of Salem, Massachusetts boasts an official Witch as well as a Witchcraft Museum, a witchcraft shop, and a lot of rather silly bumper-stickers.

Essentially, the story is that a few young girls in Salem were being told ghost stories by a Black slave, Tituba, who had been brought to Salem from her native Barbados. These stories, full of sorcery and spells, enticed the girls and they began either to practice these forms of folk magic or to focus on them so intensively that they started to exhibit drastic personality changes. This, in turn, both terrified the villagers and instigated similar behavior in other girls to the point that witchcraft was suspected. The girls, brought to trial, started naming names as those responsible for "bewitching" them, and eventually dozens of people were accused of witchcraft and many were executed.

The year was 1692.

Recent scholarship, however, has shown that Tituba was not an African slave, but a Native American, a member of the Arawak people who had been brought out of Venezuela to Barbados, where she was bought by Samuel Parris, the tradesman and future minister who figures so prominently in Salem history. And a close reading of the trial transcripts and of the records made by observers at the scene reveals that what was taking place in Salem in 1692 was not purely the result of overactive imaginations and what psychiatry used to like to call "hysteria" (a term with rather offensive origins in that it implies that the womb—*hyster* is Latin for "womb"—is the source of emotional instability in women, with a corresponding implication that men are incapable of such a state). Instead, some of the accounts of demonic possession ring strangely true, accompanied as they are with reports of paranormal phenomena, intense rage and blasphemy, etc. When I say "strangely true," I hasten to clarify that these states are virtually identical in every respect to those accounts of modern day possession, as reported by Catholic and Protestant clergymen in Europe and the United States. Many have insisted that there was no witchcraft at Salem, but the evidence readily available proves otherwise.

The other assumption that is often made is that the Salem witch trials were the first and last in the United States. Nothing could be more wrong. America has been home to accusations of witchcraft since the earliest Colonial days, as well as to alchemists, astrologers and occultists of all types. In fact, the situation was becoming so serious that in the late seventeenth century the clergymen of Massachusetts were issuing warnings to their flocks about the dangerous attractions of occultism in the Colony.

Yet, the history of European-style occult practices in the American colonies begins earlier than that. There are records of witchcraft accusations and trials all over the East Coast and particularly in New England from the mid-seventeenth century on. In a book published by Scribner's in 1914—*Narratives of the Witchcraft Cases 1648–1706* by George Lincoln Burr, ed.—we read of Elizabeth Garlick of Easthampton, Long Island (then a Dutch colony, although settled by English) who was "indicted for witchcraft and sent to Connecticut for trial" in the year 1658.[14] Another two cases—those of Ralph Hall and his wife and of Katherine Harrison—cropped up in 1665. The accused were acquitted of the charges, except that in the case of Ralph Hall's wife, Mary, the court did find "some suspitions [*sic*] by the Evidence, of what the woman is Charged with, but nothing considerable of value to take away her life."[15] The couple were accused of having used witchcraft to cause the deaths of a George Wood and the infant child of one Ann Rogers. This occurred at what is now City Island, in the borough of the Bronx in New York City.

Indeed, a look at the record for witchcraft cases in New England in the seventeenth century (which is the earliest for which we have documentation) shows that accusations, indictments, prosecutions and even executions were taking place since 1638 and extended through 1697. The earliest execution for which records can be found is of Alice Young, executed in Windsor, Connecticut in 1647, followed by those of Elizabeth Kendall of Cambridge, Massachusetts and Margaret Jones of Charlestown, Massachusetts (the latter person executed in 1648). All in all, we can find a total of 132 persons accused of witchcraft in New England alone in the seventeenth century, not counting those at Salem. Of these 132 persons, four actually confessed, twenty were convicted, and fourteen were executed. Again, this is in addition to the nineteen who were executed at Salem. The accused were overwhelmingly female, more than 100 of the 132.[16]

In all fairness, though, Salem was a special case: 156 accused, 30 convicted, 44 confessed, and 19 executed. Another prisoner was pressed to death during torture and interrogation, bringing the Salem death count to twenty, and several more died in jail.

Witches in the classical sense were not the only "alternative religionists" in the Colonies. A strange case that has rarely made it to the general histories of America is that of Thomas Morton, and his infamous Maypole at what is now Quincy, Massachusetts (not far from Salem). It was May Day, 1637 (and a year before the first recorded witchcraft case in New England). Thomas Morton decided that they should celebrate the day after "old English custome: prepared to set up a Maypole upon the festivall day of Philip and Jacob; & therefore brewed a barrell of excellent beer, & provided a case of bottles to be spent, with other good cheer, for all comers of that day . . . . A goodly pine tree of 80 foot long, was reared up, with a pair of buckshorns nailed on, somewhat neare unto the top of it . . ."[17]

Morton also had the assistance of the Native Americans of the vicinity, who were more than happy to join in the celebration, even though it was intended to commemorate the renaming of the area from Pasonagessit to Merry Mount. But, as Morton continues:

> The setting up of this Maypole was a lamentable spectacle to the precise separatists: that lived at New Plymouth. They termed it an Idoll; yea they called it the Calf of Horeb: and stood at defiance with the place, naming it Mount Dagon . . .[18]

(Shades of H. P. Lovecraft!) But that wasn't the end of the story.

Apparently, the English were taking slaves and indentured servants from Massachusetts to Virginia and selling or renting them off. Morton, in the absence of the traders, then appealed to the remaining Native Americans, slaves and servants that they should band together and resist the efforts to expatriate them, as it were. The Maypole was the first official attempt at organizing not only a pagan festival but an armed resistance to the English officials in charge of the slave trade. In addition to welcoming Native Americans—and especially those of the female persuasion—to the feast, and "consorting" with them and having all sorts of drunken revels, Morton trained them in the use of firearms. When an English lieutenant arrived to take charge of the rapidly deteriorating situation, he was thrown out of the settlement and evidently had to beat a retreat for England.

Morton's experiment began to attract a lot of attention from the English authorities, as could be imagined. No less a figure than Captain Miles Standish himself—and a force comprised of eight men from "Pascataway, Namkeake, Winismett, Weesagascusett, Natasco, and other places where any English were seated"—was sent on orders of the Governor to put down the uprising, but Standish's army was met with a force of arms by Morton's merry men.

The resistance did not last long, however (William Bradford says that they were too drunk to effectively resist) and eventually Morton was captured and put in irons and sent to England . . . but he avoided any prosecution by the Crown and instead took the time off to compose a New English Dictionary. (He was, after all, a friend of dramatist Ben Jonson.) Another worthy, one John Endecott, was installed in Quincy in his place, a no-nonsense sort who had the Maypole struck and the locals chastised.

By that time, however, the damage had been done. The "Indians" now had modern weapons, and instruction in their use. As William Bradford, one of the early chroniclers of the period, despairs:

> O the horribleness of this villainy! How many both Dutch and English have been lately slain by those Indians, thus furnished; and no remedy provided, nay, the evill more increased, and the blood of their brethren sold for gaine, as is to be feared; and in what danger all these colonies are in is too well known. Oh! That princes and parliaments would take some timely order to prevent this mischief, and at length to suppress it, by some exemplary punishment upon some of these gain thirsty murderers, (for they deserve no better title,) before their collonies in these parts be over thrown by these barbarous savages, thus armed with their owne weapons, by these evill instruments, and traitors to their neighbors and country.[19]

Scholarship suggests that the reasons the Puritans reacted so strongly to Morton's cult was twofold: In the first case, it was obvious that Morton and his men were sexually involved with Native American women (a charge that would be made against one of the accused at Salem fifty-five years later). This in itself was bad enough; but giving their men firearms was the last straw. This meant that they were now on a roughly equal footing with the Puritans, could hunt as well or better, and could control the trade in beaver skins and other exportable items. Morton was open about both these practices. He had written poems encouraging dalliances with Indian lasses, and conducted firearm instruction and trading with Indian men. Of course, the repercussions from Morton's trade and instruction in firearms were to be long-lasting. The "Indians" now had weapons and could more effectively resist the white settlers. The New England Indian wars began:

The Pequot War, 1637.
The Narragansett War, 1643–45.
King Philip's War, 1675–1676.

By the time of the Salem Witch Trials in 1692, the white settlers had come to see themselves as surrounded by hostile forces, and to characterize these forces as "savages" at best, and as demonic beings at worst. It was a crucible, indeed.

WONDERS OF THE INVISIBLE WORLD

> The New Englanders are a people of God settled in those, which were once the Devil's territories; and it may easily be supposed that the Devil was exceedingly disturbed, when he perceived such a people here accomplishing the promise of old made unto our Blessed Jesus, That He should have the utmost parts of the earth for his possession.
>
> —Cotton Mather[20]

Dame Frances Yates—the aforementioned historian, of the University of London, the British Academy, the Warburg Institute, and the Royal Society of Literature—has written extensively on the Elizabethan period and the Renaissance, with a particular focus on occult literature, thus elevating the study somewhat above its usual relegation to the attention of cranks and publicity seekers. In her *The Occult Philosophy In The Elizabethan Age* she makes an interesting, if daring, claim that the Puritan movement owed much to occult ideology current in England at the time, with connections to Pico della Mirandola, Cornelius Agrippa, and other saints of the occultist canon. This form of occultism—known as Christian Cabala to historians—was an amalgamation of the Jewish Cabala with Muslim and Christian elements; in other words, an attempt to integrate the three religions by focusing on some basic, mystical elements that they had in common. Among these was the belief in a sophisticated form of numerology where letters have numeric equivalents, and in the rituals of invoking angelic forces. Eventually, this intellectual and spiritual movement came to be represented in such organizations as the Rosicrucians and the Masonic societies, and to embrace various other occult disciplines such as alchemy and ceremonial magic.

What may cause some New Englanders no small degree of astonishment—if not, in some cases, amusement or even alarm—is the fact that no less a personage than Governor John Winthrop, Jr. was a practicing alchemist during his administration (1659–1676). It is noted that his library contained some "275 books on alchemy and the occult."[21] He was well-versed not only in these arcane matters, but also on the subject of the Rosicrucians, a putative secret society (like the Freemasons and the Templars) whose existence was proclaimed at the very beginning of the seventeenth century, probably by occult scholar Robert Fludd. During Winthrop's tenure, in fact, many people were accused of witchcraft, and three were executed: Rebecca and Nathaniel Greensmith of Hartford and Mary Barnes of Farmington.

Alchemy and the study of ceremonial magic as well as the medical theories of Paracelsus were considered gentlemanly pursuits in the seventeenth century, and indeed we know that many esteemed scientists of the day were also practicing occultists of some type. As D. Michael Quinn notes in his excellent and exhaustive *Early Mormonism and the Magic World View,*

> Many of New England's practicing alchemists were Yale and Harvard graduates who continued their experiments into the 1820s. These alchemists served as chief justice of Massachusetts, president of the Massachusetts Medical Society, president of Yale College, and president of the Connecticut Medical Society.[22]

Such historically important scientists as Isaac Newton, Roger Bacon, Leibniz and many others were enthusiastic practicing occultists and members of occult secret societies. Newton's interests have been thoroughly outlined in Michael White's *Isaac Newton, the Last Sorcerer*, a book which caused no little controversy upon publication, since modern science has been at pains to disparage the paranormal in general and organized occult activity and beliefs in particular. To demonstrate that the "father of modern physics" had deeply held mystical beliefs—which may have influenced his thinking in science—was simply too much for some members of the scientific establishment to bear. At the time of the Salem trials, Newton was in the throes of a kind of nervous breakdown, hard at work at trying to decipher the Bible on the one hand, and involved with alchemical experiments on the other. (As we shall show in a later chapter, Newton had a twentieth century counterpart in Nobel Prize-winning physicist Wolfgang Pauli.) Yale University Professor Jon Butler, in *Awash in a Sea of Faith: Christianizing the American People*, gives a valuable synopsis of the religious, mystical and occult milieu in seventeenth century America, including the scientists, lawmakers, ministers and other community leaders who were themselves involved in alchemy, ceremonial magic, Rosicrucianism and other occult practices and movements. Large libraries of occult books, secret correspondence with like-minded occultists or members of secret societies, and avant-garde religious sentiments—particularly in a political context, and including such American Founding Fathers as Washington, Franklin and Jefferson—defined the spiritual atmosphere of the intellectual class of the colonies; divining rods, shew stones, and magic charms and talismans as well as basic astrological lore defined the approach of the lower and middle classes. Yet both groups shared a common belief in the actions of invisible forces in the world, forces which could be manipulated or cajoled into cooperation for mundane goals. Forces which could be summoned by magic white and black, by priestly magicians in the shadow of the Church or by evil witches in the farms, villages and back alley lanes of the common people.

This, then, was the environment in which the good villagers of Salem found themselves in 1692. Two hundred years after the discovery of America by would-be Crusader Christopher Columbus and his crew—many of whom had fought the Muslims in Spain—the English colonists found themselves facing a pagan enemy in their midst . . . and alchemists, astrologers and magicians hidden among their churchmen, their governors, their doctors. In fact, the Indians themselves might very well be demonic beings and not humans at all; at the very least, they were believed to be Satan worshippers. Cotton Mather insisted that the Devil himself had brought the Indians to America, since there was no mention of their race in the Bible. Thus, when Lovecraft wrote his fanciful stories of pagan cults in New England he was touching a deeply buried memory of the very land in which he lived. Columbus—and his Dutch, French and English followers in North America—brought the Cross and the Sword, in a blaze of neo-Templar fury, to bear down upon the Red Man, to convert him or to kill him. The hatred of the Puritans for deviation of any kind would inevitably turn inward and begin killing them off from within. And the instrument of that social suicide would be none other than another Red Man or, in this case, Red Woman. Her name was Tituba, and she was an Arawak whose ancestors lived in Guyana, Venezuela and elsewhere in the Caribbean; whose ancestors had welcomed and trusted Columbus; and who had paid the price of that trust with their lives.

The Arawak are famous for two exports. Tituba—and the ensuing Salem witchcraft case—is one; tobacco is another. It was once again brother Columbus who, in 1492, saw the Arawaks smoking tobacco in a kind of tube they called *tobago,* and hence smoking—and the word "tobacco"—came to the white man from the Arawak. In fact, even the word "cannibal" comes from the Arawak language.

Tituba's ancestors came from what is now Guyana, the South American country that would later become famous as the site of the Jonestown massacre. She herself was purchased as a slave from Barbados, by Samuel Parris: a minister and central figure in the Salem witch trials. Her story is covered in Elaine Breslaw's *Tituba, Reluctant Witch of Salem,* and her testimony is analyzed and "deconstructed" with a view to sorting the Arawak and Amerindian mythology and magic from the Puritan version.

Professor Breslaw mentions a native Guyanese belief in the "evil stranger," the *kenaima,* who causes evil things to happen in a village and who can take various forms (such as other humans, animals, etc.). This is always a stranger, someone from outside the village, and Tituba in her testimony before the magistrates began to point a finger at evil outside influences behind the witchcraft covens in Salem. She claimed that the ringleader of the witches was a "man in black" who lived in Boston, that she and the other Salem witches attended meetings in Boston in spirit form, and that they received their instructions to return to Salem and hurt the children living there.

In addition, perhaps the greatest controversy over how the trials were conducted was the issue of "spectral evidence." It was this type of evidence against which Cotton Mather warned time and again, but usually in vain. Although Reverend Mather believed in the existence of witches and in paranormal phenomena generally, he doubted the admissibility of testimony based on people's visions of demons, evil spirits, and other phenomena which could not be witnessed by the judges in a courtroom. In other words, it was enough for someone to say that "so and so bewitched me" in spirit form. If the accused was sitting in the dock, peacefully at rest, but the "victims" cried out that he or she was tormenting them by occult means and then fell over in fits to demonstrate the fact, many judges tended to credit that as evidence. In this case, the spectre or spiritual form of the accused was doing the tormenting, even though no one other than the victim would see it. The Guyanese *kenaima* could, of course according to legend, assume any form, animate or inanimate. So in the context of Arawak magic and witchcraft, the stories about shape-shifting witches and ghostly appearances of one's neighbors in the middle of the night or in a dream were perfectly acceptable. What is remarkable—as has been noted by Professor Breslaw and others—is that the Salem Puritans would adopt much of this tradition as their own, with suitable changes and amendments as they integrated these beliefs into their Christian system.

In the final analysis, what we have here is probably the first recorded instance of what would become the satanic survivor craze of America in the 1980s. In fact, many of Tituba's "memories"—as well as those of her "coconspirators"—were slow in coming, and memory disorders, real or imagined or feigned, were part of the Salem experience. Recovered memories, tortured children, witch covens, a satanic network spanning the Northeast . . . welcome to Geraldo Nation. Add to this mixture the figure of the "man in black," and we can tie all of this in nicely with the UFO phenomenon. Indeed, Tituba's account of leaving her body at night and traveling to the meetings, and then returning again before dawn, sounds eerily similar to some accounts of alien abductions. The existence of witch marks—odd bruises on one's body suggestive of pacts with the Devil, etc.—have their correlates with the stories of alien surgery and alien implants. In fact, Tituba first claimed that she flew to Boston through the air in both body and soul, but amended this fact later to state that she only appeared in Boston in the spirit.

(Compare this historical event with satanic cult survivor syndrome, and wonder if the stories of a network of satanic cults breeding children for human sacrifice—along with the confessions of persons who claim they were breeders, or had been pressed into cult service while children—are in any way different from those of the Salem case. Then wonder a little further, and ask: if there was smoke in the Salem case—and evidence of at least a small fire—and if some clergymen, politicians, and scientists in New England in 1692 were involved in serious occult studies and research, then perhaps there was a fire beneath all the smoke of the satanic cult hysteria of three hundred years later, and perhaps some of our own clergymen, politicians and scientists in America of 1992 were also involved in serious occult research. Is it simply a recurring phenomenon, or is there a link between the events of 1692 and those of present-day America?)

Washington Irving—mentioned above as the author of a series of tales about the Muslim palace, the Alhambra, in Spain (in which palace, in fact, he lived for a while)—is also the author of *The Legend of Sleepy Hollow*. In this Halloween tale of headless horsemen and unrequited love, we have Ichabod Crane: a schoolteacher. One of Ichabod's claims to fame is that he "had read several books quite through, and was a perfect master of Cotton Mather's history of New-England Witchcraft, in which, by the way, he most firmly and potently believed."[23] It would be hard to overestimate the importance of Mather's work among the population of the Northeast in the late seventeenth and early eighteenth centuries. Cotton Mather had been present at the Salem witch trials—and at the trials and investigations of numerous other witches and purported cases of witchcraft—and is a somewhat trustworthy observer of what transpired. It was he who gave us the wonderful concept of the Invisible World as the domain of the evil spirits, and it is to this domain that we will return again and again in one form . . . or another.

> We have been advised by some credible Christians yet alive, that a malefactor, accused of witchcraft as well as murder, and executed in this place more than forty years ago, did then give notice of an horrible plot against the country by witchcraft, and a foundation of witchcraft then laid, which if it were not seasonably discovered, would probably blow up, and pull down all the churches in the country. And we have now with horror seen the discovery of such a witchcraft! An army of devils is horribly broke in upon the place which is the center, and after a sort, the firstborn of our English settlements: and the houses of the good people there are filled with doleful shrieks of their children and servants, tormented by invisible hands, with tortures altogether preternatural.
>
> —Cotton Mather, *Wonders of the Invisible World*[24]

Here, then, in a nutshell is the gist of the entire Salem witchcraft phenomenon. There is a plot of witches against the churches of the country, an attempt to pull down Christianity and replace it by devil worship; and the brunt of the attack is taken upon the "firstborn of our English settlements," i.e., Salem, Massachusetts. The witches have decided to attack Christianity at a place named after Jerusalem, the City of Peace, in a land which the Puritans had hoped would become the New Jerusalem after the irretrievable loss of the Old. (America, after all, was discovered during an attempt to finance a new Crusade to take back the original Jerusalem. Failing that, a town in America was named after it which has now, ironically, become synonymous with witchcraft!) The site of the attack therefore has deep symbolic and spiritual ramifications. It is both the "firstborn" of the settlements, and a place named after the sacred city of Jews, Christians and Muslims. The attack is being waged by "invisible hands," the first wave of a plot that was in existence forty years before the Salem trials, that is, sometime in the 1650s. The allusion by Mather to a person convicted of witchcraft and murder in Salem and executed at about that time is mysterious, as it does not come up in any of the documents I have been able to locate. Yet, the insistence by Mather that the occurrence of witchcraft in Salem is the result of a plot by devil worshippers to take over the country is worth considering for several reasons.

In the first place, such an accusation would serve to rally the people together by making witchcraft a threat to everyone and not only to those afflicted by torments and curses. It is a master stroke, and reminiscent of Hitler's castigation of a Jewish plot against Germany.

In the second place, it implies that the witches are well-organized and have been setting this up for over forty years. In other words, it is impossible to know who your friends are. People you have known all your life may, indeed, be part of this ongoing plot to destroy Christianity in the New World. If they are truly operating by invisible means, then normal systems of defense are hopeless.

In the third place—and perhaps most importantly of all—the "malefactor" of forty years ago was also a murderer as well as a witch. This linking of supernatural powers and religious rebellion with actual murder is very important. As in the case of the satanic cult survivor syndrome of the 1980s, satanic cults are not deemed threatening or even newsworthy unless they have been killing people. This may be an early result of the Church coming to terms with science. When the threat of diabolic powers and unholy worship is no longer enough to frighten—being deemed more the domain of fairy tales and legends than the real world of physics and chemistry—then murder is enough to bring the subject of satanists and witches back to the front burner. Remember, also, that these murders were the result of black magic and not .44 calibre bullets. A poppet studded with pins, hidden in a wall or buried in the garden, coupled with a corpse, was enough for a conviction. It satisfied means and opportunity, if not always motive; but if the motive is the plot to overthrow Christianity, then no further evidence is needed. The dead child or adult was simply a target of opportunity in an all-out war against the forces of Light.

In fact, when it comes to the case of "spectral evidence" in which the sufferer perceives the shape or image of a certain person to be causing the mischief, when the actual person can be shown to be elsewhere at the time and "alibied-up" (as we say in the Bronx), Mather understands that to be a wile of the Devil, rendering at times the person innocent even though that person's "shape" or "spectre" may have been seen by the bewitched. Mather goes even further, to say that though the person himself may be innocent it is still evidence of the extent of the diabolical plot against the land that the Devil is capable of using this type of illusion to cause dissension among the Christians and so to demoralize them.

> These our poor afflicted neighbors, quickly after they become infected and infested with these demons, arrive to a capacity of discerning those which they conceive the shapes of their troublers; and *notwithstanding the great and just suspicion that the demons might impose the shapes of innocent persons in their spectral exhibitions upon the sufferers (which may perhaps prove no small part of the witch-plot in the issue),* yet many of the persons thus represented, being examined, several of them have been convicted of a very damnable witchcraft: yea, more than one twenty have confessed, that they have signed unto a book, which the devil showed them, and engaged in his hellish design of bewitching and ruining our land.
>
> —Cotton Mather, *Wonders of the Invisible World* (emphasis added)[25]

Mather then, in prose fraught with presentiment of what would happen to America in the 1980s, states,

> *We know not, at least I know not, how far the delusions of Satan may be interwoven into some circumstances of the confessions; but one would think all the rules of understanding human nature are at an end, if after so many most voluntary harmonious confessions, made by intelligent persons of all ages, in sundry towns, at several times, we must not believe the main strokes wherein those confessions all agree: especially when we have a thousand preternatural things every day before our eyes, wherein the confessors do acknowledge their concernment, and give demonstration of their being so concerned.* If the devils now can strike the minds of men with any poisons of so fine a composition and operation, that scores of innocent people shall unite, in confessions of a crime, which we see actually committed, it is a thing prodigious, beyond the wonders of the former ages, and it threatens no less than a sort of a dissolution upon the world.
>
> —Cotton Mather, *Wonders of the Invisible World* (emphasis added)[26]

In other words, if everyone is confessing to things which they did not actually do, then it is still the action of the Devil, and the world is in even more danger. Heads I win. Tails you lose. Either the confessions are genuine, and the witches guilty; or the confessions are false and have been concocted by the Devil, in which case the accused may be innocent, but the Devil is a lot stronger than we thought and the country is in jeopardy. Either way, the Devil is abroad in the land.

Or, at least, in Massachusetts.

One of the most revealing views of Cotton Mather on the subject of witchcraft appears in his letters, in which he states that witchcraft works "upon the stage of imagination." He never doubted the fact of witches and witchcraft, but instead—after witnessing the events not only in Salem but in other cities in New England and in other cases of witchcraft—understood that the efficacy of witchcraft resided in the powers of the mind. We say that "the mind plays tricks" or "the imagination plays tricks" and thereby remove any personal responsibility from the event. But in Mather's day, one was responsible for the state of one's soul and could not shrug off culpability by blaming one's parents or one's environment. If the "imagination" was playing tricks, then someone was playing the imagination. Either the victim, or a witch. The witch as manipulator of perception, as manipulator of the imagination, is a powerful symbol and comes very close as a model for what actually transpires, as we shall see in later chapters.

And these individuals who understand the workings of the imagination pose a great threat to society, in Mather's eyes:

> . . . at prodigious witch-meetings, the wretches have proceeded so far as to concert and consult the methods of rooting out the Christian religion from this country,

and setting up instead of it perhaps a more gross diabolism than ever the world saw before.

—Cotton Mather, *Wonders of the Invisible World*[27]

These are very strong words. For Cotton Mather, the Invisible World is indeed wondrous, and very, very dangerous.

Among the most respected historians of the Salem Witchcraft trials is Chadwick Hansen, who based his novel thesis on the close reading of the actual trial transcripts themselves and came to the conclusion that there was, indeed, witchcraft being practiced in Salem and that some of the accused were actually guilty. In addition to this startling assertion, his study *Witchcraft at Salem,* originally published in 1969, goes on to conclude that many of the girls were actually suffering from a clinical mental disorder.

Hansen states that the problem afflicting the Salem girls was hysteria, but he qualifies this by saying that it was the medical condition known as hysteria and not the popular concept of hysteria; in other words, he claims that the girls suffered from a pathological condition. He refers to Freud, Janet and others as his source for information on hysteria, its symptoms, manifestations and presumed causes.[28] It may be salutary to compare those early definitions of hysteria with the *Diagnostic and Statistical Manual of Mental Disorders-III* (DSM-III) to see if there is still general agreement on both symptomatology and causes.

What is more interesting, perhaps, is his agreement that there was, indeed, witchcraft—specifically "image magic"—being practiced at Salem. He goes further to provide some evidence of one murder being carried out by an act of witchcraft. Of course, he puts this down to the general effect of cursing someone in a superstitious society: if you believe in curses and witchcraft and you know you have been cursed, you give up hope and die.

This does not exonerate those who practiced such spells, however. If they desired to cause the death of another and used "superstitious" means to effect that end, are they any less guilty because we—as moderns—profess not to believe in witchcraft? On the contrary, the spell-casters seem just as culpable to me as those who murder with knife, gun or poison. Especially in the context of 1692, it would seem that some of those convicted of witchcraft may very well have been guilty.

As Hansen writes,

> While it is clearly true that the majority of persons executed for witchcraft were innocent, it is equally true that some of them, in Massachusetts and elsewhere, were guilty.[29]

And,

> It should be clear by now that our historians have erred in their assumption that there was no witchcraft practiced at Salem, or that if there was it was of little consequence. The documents, rightly read, present us a far different picture. In Bridget Bishop, Candy, and Mammy Redd we have three people who practiced black magic, and with demonstrable success. In the Hoar family and George Burroughs we have people who established a reputation for black magic and then traded on it, although whether they were actually witches remains uncertain. . . .And if the testimony concerning Roger Toothaker and his daughter may be taken at face value—and there is reason to believe it may—we have one case of murder by witchcraft—one case in which occult means were used to take a human life away.[30]

While Hansen admits that witchcraft and black magic were used by some of the accused Salem witches, he still tends (as would most sober and serious historians) to associate their effects with the clinical definition of hysteria.

There is, however, something vaguely unsatisfying about this charge of hysteria. As Hansen himself relates,[31] hysterical fits seem to be disappearing as a rule, and he lays this to the fact that we—as moderns—don't give the hysterical fit as much attention or awe as before, so that as a mechanism it has lost its usefulness. This seems to argue against hysteria being a genuine pathology and the fit something over which a person has no control. One of the essential elements of Hansen's thesis seems to be that the bewitched of Salem were not frauds, but victims of a pathological condition. Yet, he seems to believe that hysterical fits are disappearing in the modern world because there is no support in the environment or society for their religious or mystical interpretations. Perhaps I am dull, but I don't see the logic of this argument.

The type of hysteria Hansen is describing—and the symptoms to which the transcripts of the Salem trials may refer—are covered in DSM-III (the edition current with Hansen's work) under "300.11 Conversion Disorder (or Hysterical Neurosis, Conversion Type)." Under the heading "Predisposing Factors," we read,

> Antecedent physical disorder (which may provide a prototype for the symptoms, e.g., pseudoseizures in individuals with epilepsy), exposure to other individuals with real physical symptoms or conversion symptoms, and extreme psychosocial stress (e.g., warfare or the recent death of a significant figure) are predisposing factors.[32]

We know from the transcripts that there was no evidence of "antecedent physical disorders" and "exposure to other individuals with real physical symptoms or conversion symptoms" seems to be a way of alluding to the popular concept of "mass hysteria," i.e., if a person sees one hysteric "acting out" then somehow this fit is contagious, like yawning or laughing, and you have a chain reaction of hysterics.

The last mentioned factor is "extreme psychosocial stress," and there *was* a degree of tension in Salem Village in those days, but nowhere near enough to account for the outbreak of hysteria, if hysteria it was. One setting that contributes to hysteria—according to DSM-III—is warfare. That's the degree of extreme psychosocial stress the authors of the DSM-III had in mind. So, we are left with a question: What social factors contributed to the outbreak of hysteria in Salem Village in 1692, of a nature equal to warfare?

Also, can hysteria be consciously controlled? The psychiatrists of today would tell us no, that it is a pathological condition beyond the conscious control of an individual. That would rule out fraud in the case of Salem, since the symptoms were so severe and so representative of the cases found in Janet, Charcot, Freud, et. al. that there is no way to disregard them as a kind of adolescent prank.

Many of the symptoms of conversion disorder seem equivalent to the type of phenomena witnessed in cases of demonic possession, and certainly many such cases were thus identified in the past. Hysterics in New England in the seventeenth century were often "cured" by prayer, which would seem to indicate a close relation to cases of demonic possession. It is possible that "conversion disorder" and "demonic possession" are simply two ways of saying the same thing . . . but that should not lull us into a false sense of security.

Hansen refers to parallel cases of hysterical fits in instances of New England "witchcraft" and in European medicine, in[33] which the hysterical victim claims to see beings tormenting her. Invective—including the use of foul expletives—is common in both types of cases. No less an authority than J.M. Charcot believed that the hallucination of beings attacking his patient were "reminiscences, doubtless, of the emotions experienced in her youth."[34] What does that mean? That these emotions—buried for decades, perhaps—come to the fore during an hysterical fit? Or are these emotions perhaps the cause of the fit? How, then, to describe the same thing happening to young girls, people still in their youth?

While the emotions may represent buried memories, may they be of a more atavistic nature? In the way of the collective unconscious of Jung, for instance? Or perhaps they are what they seem to be to a select few Catholic exorcists: evidence of the possession of the victim by some outside force?

It is common to say that a belief in possession carries with it a concomitant belief in exorcism, and that is why exorcism works and not because there is a real demon possessing a human being. But that is somewhat tautological. Cancer patients undergoing radiation treatments and chemotherapy are told to think positive, to visualize their cancer cells dying, to develop a "will to live," etc., leading us to wonder how much of modern cancer therapy is analogous to witchcraft. If the mind-body system is so interdependent as to support a whole host of radical therapies aimed at treating much illness as psychosomatic—if not in origin, then at least in cure—then perhaps we are missing the boat on hysteria, possession, and witchcraft. And if some of the current theories of quantum physics hold any deeper meaning for us, then perhaps the notion of an "outside force" is not too far-fetched.

Further, one could as easily suggest that because exorcism works, there are real demons. Science says that there is no evidence that demons exist, and that the symptoms of possession are actually those of other pathological states which can be treated with scientific procedures. In the cases where science—i.e., medicine—fails and magic works (such as in spontaneous cancer remission, for instance, or in cases of exorcism), it is claimed to be only due to an imperfect understanding of the scientific mechanisms of the specific malady, and not due to supernatural events.

What is not entertained—because it would cause a bit of social upheaval and a great deal of misunderstanding—is the possibility that these two claims are not mutually exclusive: that scientific and medical procedures contain within them an element of the supernatural or at least paranormal, and that the best doctors and the best physicists are those who recognize this and utilize it to the best of their ability.

Yet, Hansen goes on to insist,

> The direct cause of these fits, in the courtroom or out of it, was, of course, not witchcraft itself, but the afflicted person's fear of witchcraft.[35]

This is all well and good, for it supports the party line that occult powers *per se* either do not exist, or exist only in the fevered imaginations of occultists and fellow travelers. But numerous persons at the Salem trial confessed to witchcraft, and in specifics and in detail. Some of these persons were known occultists, such as George Burroughs and Samuel Wardwell. William Barker's confession in which he claimed there were 307 witches abroad in the land, and that they were part of a plot to replace the practice of Christianity with that of Devil worship—hence the fact that the Salem panic began at the home of its minister, Samuel Parris—is discounted as patently false by Hansen and, of course, by everyone else. We have variations today in the United States and elsewhere of "satanic panic" and charges of a conspiracy of witches or occultists in the land who are working towards the overthrow of Christianity, etc. Some of these confessions, however, are deliberate, detailed, expanded upon, citing specific events . . . and they are dismissed because, of course, there are no such things as occult powers or the Devil making pacts with humans . . . or even, dare we say, the Devil itself.

While it is not my intention to say that the confessions are literally true, and that Barker, Wardwell and others were transported to witches' sabbats on broomsticks and made pacts with a literal Devil and signed a physical book and worked for the overthrow of Christianity, what I am suggesting is that there is a dimension to these confessions that is beyond fraud, or overactive imaginations, or hysteria. What I am suggesting, and hope to demonstrate in the pages that follow, is that there exists a medium in which occult "powers" do exist and do have an effect on the world as experienced by non-occultists, and that the evidence that is available to support this thesis is convincing, and scientific.

As Cotton Mather states,

> Our dear neighbors are most really tormented, really murdered, and really acquainted with hidden things which are afterwards proved plainly to have been realities.[3637]

A STUDY IN SCARLET

> . . . The details of the case will probably be never known now, though we are informed upon good authority that the crime was the result of an old-standing and romantic feud, in which love and Mormonism bore a part. It seems that both the victims belonged, in their younger days, to the Latter Day Saints . . .
>
> —"A Study In Scarlet," Sir Arthur Conan Doyle[38]

It is clear from Sir Arthur Conan Doyle's first Sherlock Holmes story that he was fascinated with the history of the Mormons, also known as the Church of Jesus Christ of Latter Day Saints. Headquartered in Salt Lake City, Utah where the Mormon pilgrims finally ended their search for a place to practice their religion freely, they are famous the world over for the Mormon Tabernacle Choir, for their collection of birth records and genealogical data, and perhaps less so for the fact that the late Howard Hughes, billionaire recluse and erstwhile Hollywood playboy, insisted on Mormons as his personal staff and de facto bodyguards. The role that the Mormons play in our story will be amplified later; for now it is only enough to look at their mysterious origins, origins that gave rise to the first Sherlock Holmes mystery.

The tale begins where we left off a few paragraphs ago, in the village of Salem, Massachusetts. And it begins with the same topic as those infamous trials: witchcraft, magic and secret societies. The witch—or wizard, as the Salem judges would have termed him—was none other than Joseph Smith, Jr., founder of the Mormon Church and the recipient of its sacred text, the *Book of Mormon.* Like Muhammad, Joseph Smith was visited by an Angel. Like Muhammad, he created a whole religion based on his angelic contacts. But unlike Muhammad, Joseph Smith was actively involved in the use of ritual magic—ceremonial magic—for the purpose of finding buried treasure. Like a Yankee Doctor Faustus, Joseph Smith conjured spirits to come to his aid. With amulets and talismans, pentacles and swords, sigils and strange alphabets, he stepped from the misty milieu of Continental European magic and into the creation of the quintessential American-born religion, a religion which ties together some loose ends of American archaeology, Christian cabala, Freemasonry, and old-fashioned Bible stories to weave a crazy quilt of millennial paranoia, pseudo-Egyptian magic, and Masonic ritual. In fact, Joseph Smith could be considered one of the godfathers of the American occult scene, the progenitor of such groups as the Church of Satan, the OTO "Caliphate," even the witchcraft revival of the 1970s. One of the texts that was essential to Smith's occult operations was *The Magus*, that vast compendium of occult beliefs and systems written by Francis Barrett two hundred years ago, which was republished many times during the American occult renaissance in the 1970s.[39]

In fact, what many Americans—and probably most Mormons—do not know is that Joseph Smith, Jr. (who would go on to found the Mormon religion) was a direct descendant of one of the accusers at Salem, one Samuell Smith of Boxford, who accused Mary Easty of witchcraft. Samuell Smith was Joseph Smith's great-great-grandfather. Another accuser, one John Gould—who accused Sarah Wilds—was Samuell Smith's father-in-law.

Both Mary Easty and Sarah Wilds were executed at Salem in 1692, and on the basis of the accusations of Smith and Gould, Joseph Smith's ancestors . . .[40]

. . . and in 1836, Joseph Smith and a small company of fellow treasure-seekers decamped to Salem, Massachusetts for the purpose of renting a house where they believed treasure to be buried. It should be noted that this is *six years after* the *Book of Mormon* was first published. Joseph Smith was already the Prophet, had already founded a new religion based on revelations inscribed on golden plates, and was a well-known figure in American religion by that time. The evidence shows that he entered Salem quietly, attempted to rent the house, failed in that, was forced to rent another close by, and conducted ceremonies to divine the location of the supposed treasure. The attempt failed, and the Prophet left Salem without the gold and silver he was sure was buried there.[41]

That Joseph Smith should have been heavily involved in classic operations of ceremonial magic came as a shock to many Mormons and Mormon-watchers. While insiders know of the quasi-Masonic nature of Mormon ritual—and, in fact, that Joseph Smith himself was an initiated Mason by 1842—the rest of the world was not prepared for the revelations that he began his career as an occultist and magician. It would take a famous murder case[42] to bring this news to public attention, and even then the emphasis would be that Smith and his band practiced a form of American "folk magic" that was prevalent in the country at the time, and that they should not be censured or criticized for what was, in reality, a popular pastime among Americans.

To equate the formulas of ceremonial magic in such famous grimoires as Barrett's *The Magus* with "folk magic," however, is naïve. If ceremonial magic is "folk magic," then what is the alternative form of magic? The fact that "common people" bought sorcerers' workbooks and tried to practice the confusing and often bowdlerized rituals they found therein does not mean that these practices themselves were "folk magic," but only that the folk were practicing them. This is perhaps more a reflection of the influence of the publishing industry upon American mystical and religious sensibilities than it is motive for a characterization of these practices as folk magic.

For these early Americans—white, descendants of various European nationalities, whose forebears went back only a few generations before they could be traced to the ships that brought them from England, Holland, France, and other countries—were not "folk" in the ordinary sense of the word. There was no indigenous folk magic in America because there were no indigenous folk, aside from the Native American population whose religious and occult practices were largely unknown or—as in the case with Cotton Mather and his writings—largely misunderstood. American folk magic—as it is interpreted by historians—is the result of European systems of belief transplanted to American shores, either by active practitioners of these systems or by the printed word. And these were not folk systems, but elaborate series of rituals based on the works of educated mystics, cabalists, philosophers and magicians. In fact, an occultist would say—and with some justification—that it was the imperfect understanding of these processes that would lead to the murder of Joseph Smith himself by an angry mob in Carthage, Illinois in 1847.

The story of Joseph Smith, the golden plates, the Angel Moroni, the *Book of Mormon* and the creation of the Church of Jesus Christ of Latter-Day Saints (LDS) has been covered by many other historians and biographers, so I will give only a short synopsis here as it relates to this study. The occult aspects are covered in depth by Professor Quinn, and elsewhere as noted below.

Joseph Smith, Jr. was born on December 23, 1805 in the small town of Sharon, Vermont to a strange family that included his father, Joseph Smith, Sr., who was something of a wizard and ceremonial magician, a man given to drawing magic circles in the earth with a sword and divining for hidden treasure with a diviner's rod and seer stone, and his mother, who was involved in her own occult practices, and an aunt that married an alchemist. The fact of his birth on (or about) the winter solstice must have given his family some cause for rejoicing, as it is an auspicious day, and almost Christmas as well. They must have thought that their son was destined for great things, as indeed fortune tellers consulted about the boy's future predicted he would be.

But he was, in fact, a barefoot farm boy for most of his early life; he developed a knack for treasure-seeking and would assist his father in attempts to find gold and precious stones buried underground. This was a strange occupation for a young boy, especially in light of the fact that treasure was rarely, if ever, discovered. What did transpire, however, would produce much more than buried treasure; for as the young Joseph Smith spent day after day trying to contact spirits and gaze into magic stones in the fruitless attempt to uncover buried wealth, he was opening himself up to other influences, other forces. The treasure-seeking escapades were a kind of ad hoc initiatory program for Joseph Smith, and he began to see—not treasure, but visions.

This is the point at which various influences come together in a single person and produce unbelievable results, far in excess of what would ordinarily be predicted for a young farm boy from a bizarre background, living close to poverty, far from any city or center of education, cultural stimulation or sophistication of any kind. In fact, this is the type of family and background that we might associate with that of the serial killer or mass murderer. After all, some of our most famous killers—Charles Manson, Henry Lee Lucas, Otis Toole, Arthur Shawcross—all came from a similar background and circumstances, as well as many not so famous, such as Bobby Joe Long. David Berkowitz claimed to hear voices telling him to kill; Joseph Smith claimed to hear voices telling him to renew Christianity.

Whether or not his father truly believed he would ever find gold and treasure using the rituals of ceremonial magic, what can be assumed as a relative certainty is that his young son believed in it wholeheartedly. After all, his parents seemed to be firm believers and they were religious people as well, for whom their occult practices were perceived as complementary—rather than in opposition—to their Christian faith. In fact, Joseph Smith, Jr. would have been used as a seer by his father. The requirements for divining by use of spirits in the old books specified that a young child be used to gaze into the shew stone or crystal, as such a child was presumed to have led a chaste life and be pure in thought, thus permitting him or her easier access to the spirit world.

Joseph took this responsibility very seriously. He heard of a young woman with a seer stone (a type of rock used as a crystal ball, placed in a hat and gazed at for long periods of time), who had good results in divining hidden things. He spent a lot of time trying to learn the art of gazing from her, and eventually used these practices to discover the existence of his own seer stone, revealed to him in a vision as being buried beneath a certain tree or bush. Smith followed the instructions in his vision, proceeded to the tree and dug up the stone.

As time went on, both Smiths—*pere et fils*—would become involved in various rituals of ceremonial magic to the extent that they began to acquire a collection of books and paraphernalia that would be familiar to anyone dabbling in occult practices today. One of the most popular occult textbooks of that time was Francis Barrett's *The Magus,* which is a compendium of magical belief, invocations, occult diagrams and rituals that is as well known today as it was two hundred years ago, and which has been reprinted many times in the past thirty years. It is a hefty volume, and covers everything from planetary magic to divination to ritual invocations. Anyone examining the rituals of the nineteenth century English occult lodge—The Golden Dawn—will find many of the same seals, symbols and diagrams used by both Joseph Smith in 1820 and MacGregor Mathers and

Aleister Crowley in 1900 . . . and by modern occult and witchcraft organizations in the United States, Europe, Latin America and Australia today. In fact, much of the information contained in *The Magus* is a summary of occult rituals from the seventeenth century and earlier. Those individuals credited by Dame Frances Yates for contributing to Renaissance magic—Cornelius Agrippa and Pico della Mirandola, among others—can be found haunting the pages of Francis Barrett's monumental work.

In fact there is a continuum of practice and belief going back in time more than two thousand years that runs parallel to the mainstream histories of Christianity, Judaism and Islam in the West, a continuum of magic and sorcery: a belief in the possibility of the manipulation of hidden powers by ordinary mortals, provided that they only have the technological information at hand, and the right equipment. It is actually a very scientific attitude towards understanding and working with cosmic principles, contrary to the opinions of skeptics and historians. It is a technology that was designed to extend the capability of a person's five normal senses into a sixth realm: a technology that acted as a machine to fine tune the powers of the mind. This technology is so consistent in its general terms and practices that a magician of today can look upon the texts and instruments of his or her counterpart of two thousand years ago and figure out what they were up to. Furthermore, the systems are so internally consistent that we can duplicate these rituals exactly in every way and gradually come to an understanding of how they were expected to work, an understanding probably far in excess of what Joseph Smith could be expected to have, as the studies of psychology, psychobiology, and biochemistry were nowhere near as advanced then as they are today. Whereas modern histories of science grudgingly and somewhat sarcastically give credit to the alchemists of old for having—usually, according to these historians, by "accident"—created the fundamentals of chemistry, no one credits the ceremonial magicians for their contribution (however "accidental") to modern knowledge concerning psychology and psychobiology.

The tradition in which the Smiths were working is in the mainstream of ceremonial magic, and its rudiments can be studied today in works by Israel Regardie, MacGregor Mathers, A.E. Waite, Aleister Crowley and many others. In fact, Waite's book—*The Book of Ceremonial Magic*, sometimes titled *The Book of Black Magic and of Pacts*—is a worthy competitor to Francis Barrett's volume, and was a familiar sight in Western occult circles in the 1960s and 1970s. The symbols, magic squares and invocations found therein can be traced back to the *Greater* and *Lesser Keys of Solomon*, the *Enchiridion of Pope Leo*, the *Grimoire of Pope Honorious*, and other famous magic textbooks of the seventeenth and eighteenth centuries. They are the physical remnants of a stream of occult practice and belief known as "Christian Cabala," which is an amalgam of Jewish mystical beliefs and texts with corresponding Christian and Islamic input. The attitude of occultists has usually been very pragmatic and open-minded when it comes to the practices and "discoveries" of occultists of other faiths, much more so than the true believers of any one faith who find competing faiths anathema, and their competitors deserving of murder.

Christian Cabala came to America with some of the earliest settlers. A famous German mystic, Johannes Kelpius, settled at the Wissahickon River near Philadelphia with his band of Pietist brothers—where they practiced astrology, astronomy magic and alchemy—in 1694, only two years after the Salem trials. They were a millennialist cult, strictly[43] in number (no more, no less) and watched the skies carefully for a sign of the end of the world.

The Ephrata community, also in Pennsylvania, had its origins with the Kelpius group (known as the "Monks of the Wissahickon") and was similarly famous for its occult practices, which included ceremonial magic, astrology, astronomy, alchemy and Rosicrucian studies and practices. The Rosicrucians themselves became known as a result of the publication of the *Fama Fraternitatis* in 1614, in which—among other things—they claimed to have their origin with the mysterious Christian Rosenkreutz, a philosopher and mystic who had traveled Europe and the Middle East in search of esoteric wisdom and who had formed the Rosicrucian brotherhood as a repository of occult teachings: a secret society whose members would be unknown to the rest of humanity even as they labored on humanity's behalf. A further publication—*The Chymical Wedding of Christian Rosenkreutz*—placed the mystical tradition of the Rosicrucians firmly in the alchemical and qabalistic camp, in a treatise that borders on Hindu Tantrism.

As Professor Quinn points out in his *magnum opus*, a wide variety of occult literature was available to Joseph Smith, even in his otherwise remote village of Palmyra, New York (near Canandaigua). The works of Agrippa, Barrett, Mather and others were routinely stocked in bookstores in the region, and lists of occult books either in print or available for sale at second-hand ran to *over 100 pages*. America at that time—so soon after the War of 1812—was in the midst of a religious and mystical revival, a fact that is often ignored or misunderstood by general historians of the American experience. And in the midst of this religious revival was a fear of secret societies and their presumed ill intentions towards the young Republic. Chief among these societies was, of course, the Freemasons.

The Anti-Masonic movement in America was in its heyday at the time that Joseph Smith was searching for buried treasure using ceremonial magic. The kidnap and alleged murder of William Morgan in 1826 triggered an anti-Masonic backlash in western New York where the Smith farm was located. Morgan was a Mason (actually, his status within the Masonic organization was somewhat in doubt) who planned to reveal the secret rituals of Freemasonry in a book he was writing, contracted to a small publisher; as a result, it seems that some Masons felt it was imperative to mete out the justice specified in those very rituals. The printing office was fire-bombed and Morgan was kidnapped, that much seems certain. He was admittedly taken by Masons to Fort Niagara, New York where he was kept imprisoned for some time. After that, reports vary as to what eventually became of him. A year later, a body washed up near Fort Niagara that was eventually identified as Morgan, even though there was controversy over this fact as well. In any event, it was characterized as a cult killing, not the first in America and certainly not the last, but it was very visible and the results were sweeping.

Masons were forced to explain themselves, and explain their history as a society, in ways they had not anticipated. Masons were believed to be behind secret movements to control the operations of government and, naturally, the dreaded Illuminati would be invoked as an example of this perfidy. An Anti-Masonic Convention was held in Philadelphia on September 11, 1830 which was attended by such political celebrities as William H. Seward and Thaddeus Stevens (founders of the Republican Party after their break with the Whigs, the former of course also responsible for the purchase of Alaska from Russia in 1867) and Francis Granger, an enemy of Seward in other things (notably on the slavery issue) but a fellow-traveler when it came to the anti-Masonic cause. In the ensuing hysteria Masonic membership dropped drastically; many lodges were closed, virtually overnight, and Masonry became a campaign issue in the United States for decades. The 1830s and 1840s saw the growth of an anti-Masonic political party, as well as general paranoia over the perceived penetration of the Masonic Society by the political and anti-Christian elements of the Illuminati, thus rendering the Masonic Society little more than an "outer court" for the inner workings of a diabolical European organization with designs on the new American republic.

The Bavarian Illuminati have been covered in so many places in so many ways that it is probably not worthwhile to describe them in detail here. Suffice it to say that the Order was created by one Adam Weishaupt, a professor of theology at the University of Ingolstadt, Bavaria on May 1, 1776, as a kind of super-Masonry which attracted many of the intelligentsia of the day. It was the political machinations of the Illuminati that lead to its eventual suppression by the Bavarian authorities, but the damage had been done: a secret mystical brotherhood, bound by blood oaths and practicing strange rites, had been plotting against the government. It is perhaps no mere coincidence that Weishaupt's Order was established only a few months before the signing of the American Declaration of Independence. It has been blamed for everything from the French Revolution to the creation of the Federal Reserve banking system. A true Frankenstein's monster, born in the same town as the fictional Doctor's ghastly experiment at creating life . . . and the same town where, eventually, German automaker (and erstwhile warplane manufacturer) BMW would set up shop. As noted, the Illuminati were blamed for the French Revolution, among other things; even Winston Churchill would one day cite the Illuminati as a dread presence in world affairs.[44]

None of this stood in the way of Joseph Smith's attraction towards Freemasonry, however, and he eventually became a Mason in March of 1842 despite the general outrage over the society. Both admirers and detractors of Mormonism agree that much of the LDS Church's ritual and priesthood structure mimics that of Smith's Masonic involvement. Why he would choose to become a Mason in the atmosphere of alarm and paranoia that surrounded any mention of Masonry in the America of that time is open to conjecture; probably he saw Freemasonry as being sympathetic to his own ideas and background: the arcane rituals, the free-thinking atmosphere, the cherishing of a "secret history" of the world would all have been attractive to Joseph Smith. In addition, it probably gave him a sense of belonging to a society of people who would respect his higher intentions and his intellect at a time when Mormonism was being viewed as a heretical and possibly dangerous cult.

But in 1823, Joseph Smith had not yet founded a religion. He was a young man desperately seeking buried treasure. On the auspicious day of September 22, 1823 he had a vision of an Angel.

It was the autumnal equinox, the first day of the zodiacal sign of Libra, and he had repaired to a hill near his home late that night and performed the rituals necessary to invoke spiritual forces. He was gratified to obtain a vision of the Angel Moroni, who directed him to where a certain treasure was buried.

Quinn tells us that "Moroni" as a surname meant "dark complexion" or "swarthy," which reminds us at once of the Black Man or the Man In Black of the Salem witch trials.[45] This did not necessarily mean an African, but could have referred to any person of swarthy appearance: Native Americans, Meditteraneans, Levantines, etc.

Smith rushed to the spot indicated by Moroni and began digging. He found the gold plates but, ignoring the Angel's demand that he take the plates and seek no further, he could not resist looking into the hole he had dug to see if there was anything else. Enraged, the Angel took back the plates and told Smith if he wanted to see them again he should return the following year on the same day and at the same time, and should bring his older brother.

Chagrined, he returned to his home and related some of what had transpired.

And the following year, he tried again. The problem, however, was that his older brother had died a few months after the first attempt at the plates. Smith repaired to the same spot at the same time as indicated by Moroni, and Moroni put him off again. All in all it would take three more years before—on September 22, 1827—he would finally be able to see the plates again and to begin transcribing what has become the *Book of Mormon*.

The method of transcribing the plates—which, according to the story, were written in a kind of Egyptian hieroglyphic—would seem odd to many Americans but familiar to occultists and those familiar with occult literature. Smith would place his "shew stone" or "seer stone" in his hat and then bring his face into the hat so that no light would enter his field of vision. There, with his hands on his knees and staring into his hat, he would begin to dictate the pages of the *Book*.

This method is called "skrying" and was used by Elizabethan astrologer, occultist and spy John Dee in the sixteenth century, as well as by legions of fortune tellers, crystal gazers, magicians and soothsayers for millennia. John Dee, in fact, received his famous system of Enochian magic in roughly this manner. His shew stone—a piece of what appears to be polished Aztec obsidian—can be found at the British Museum.

Many devout Mormons have a problem with this story, as it makes Joseph Smith appear to be little more than a sorcerer or wizard. This is certainly the point of view one takes today, looking back on events that occurred nearly two hundred years ago, but it is perhaps slightly in error. The practices of ceremonial magic, skrying, divining, and all the rest were taking place side-by-side with intense religious feeling. Magic was believed to be an extension of religion, and not in opposition to it. Thus, we have many clergymen, scientists, and political leaders involved in those days in practices that can only seem unsavory today. To be sure, many strict fundamentalists opposed the practice of magic, fearing that it would lead to the excesses of witchcraft and demon-worship. But to the farmer, the villager, the blacksmith, these practices were based on a system of knowledge that was gleaned from the stars and the phases of the moon, things of nature, things that regulated their lives anyway and told them when to plant and when to harvest. It would be difficult to tell a farmer to ignore the phases of the moon, and to place no stock in the almanacs that had become part of his life at least since the time of Benjamin Franklin and "Poor Richard."

Indeed, as Professor Valerie I.J. Flint reminds us—when discussing the role of Simon Magus in early Christian literature and his widely reported magical wars with Saint Peter—in *The Rise of Magic in Early Medieval Europe,*

> Some supernatural exercises are neither admissible nor praiseworthy; but some are both . . . . Magical ability is expected of a great religious leader; objections arise only when he uses it in unacceptable ways and for unacceptable ends.[46]

And again,

> The harnessing of magical abilities to selfish ends renders the practice of magic wholly objectionable. . . .but magical powers of a wide variety emerge from the Simon literature as legitimate, provided only that they are employed for clear benefit of human beings. *They may even be necessary to humanity.*[47] (emphasis added)

"They may even be necessary to humanity." We will come back to this concept a bit later on, but at the moment we can summarize our findings as follows: that the origins of Mormonism lie in the most blatant practice of ritual ceremonial magic, a practice that was never denied or abandoned by either Smith or his proteges, as we can see by Quinn's pioneering study; that this blend of Christian religion and European ceremonial magic was common in America at that time (Quinn goes so far as to call it "folk magic"); and, finally and "coincidentally," that we have ancestors of the Smith family itself deeply involved in the Salem witch trials.

And we have Joseph Smith himself, years later, running for President of the United States and imprisoned in Carthage, Illinois in 1844. By this time he has become a Mason, has formed his new religion, has become the commander of a huge state militia (the largest in the country at the time), has become mayor of one of Illinois's largest communities, has continued the quest for buried treasures (both of the material and of the spiritual worlds, we assume, and at least one such quest took him back to his ancestral home in Salem, Massachusetts), has married numerous times, has established temples where his new religion could thrive . . . and, in a frenzy of fear and paranoia at the growing power of this latter-day Prophet, he is murdered by an angry mob on June 27.

He was wearing his Jupiter amulet at the time of his death, a photo of which can be seen in Quinn's book.[48]

It was incorrectly engraved.

The Hebrew characters on top of the magic square of Jupiter in the original—to be found in *The Magus* and other places—reads "AL AB," which means "The Father" and which is a holy name of Jupiter, which was Smith's ruling planet.

Unfortunately for Smith, his talisman is missing the final "B" character. Thus, the characters are A. L A, which in Hebrew means "but" or "only" or "except," a preposition instead of the Divine Name of Jupiter. As any authority will tell you, one must be faithful to every letter and mark in a grimoire and not edit the words, the signs or seals lest disaster befall. The other characters of the seal are correct, with one word being "ABA" or "Father" and the other "YHPYAL" or "Johphiel," which is the "Intelligence of Jupiter." With AL AB reduced to the preposition ALA, we are tempted to read the seal as "Father except Johphiel," certainly a distressing combination implying that Johphiel is nowhere present.

The word "YHPYAL" according to Hebrew Qabala (cabala, kabbala, etc.) adds to the number 136, the same number on the seal of Jupiter which is a magic square, the sum of whose numbers in any row add to 136. The word "ABA" adds to four. The word "ALA" adds to thirty-two. It should have been "AL AB" which would have resulted in thirty-four, for a grand total of 174. With the error in AL AB and reducing it to ALA, the total is 172.

According to *Liber 777*, which is a famous compendium of qabalistic numerology begun by the Golden Dawn and later compiled and printed by Aleister Crowley, we read that the value of the number 174 will give us "Torches" and *"Splendor ei per circuitum,"* a pleasant enough attribution. The valuation for 172, however, gives us "Cut, divided" and "The heel, the end."[49]

And so it was for Joseph Smith.

One is tempted, in the light of Smith's violent end at the hands of a mob, to look at his death in another, even more poetic, way. He was, after all, the descendent of men who, at Salem, accused women of witchcraft and saw them hanged. Like something out of Nathaniel Hawthorne (himself a Salem native), the sins of the father were visited on his children, and his children's children. Perhaps, with a bit of literary license and a nod at Hawthorne, we may say of Joseph Smith that "God gave him blood to drink."

Mormonism did not end with him, of course. The banner of leadership was taken up by Brigham Young, and the flight west begun. Eventually the Mormons would settle in what is now Utah, and make their headquarters at the side of the Great Salt Lake. But it would be years before Mormonism was viewed as respectable and conservative. Polygamy was one issue, of course, and the Mormons were forced to abandon the practice (at least officially and formally). But there had been violent confrontations between Mormons and non-Mormons, and even between Mormons themselves. For years they were perceived as a cult, just as David Koresh's experiment in Waco or Jim Jones' failed commune in the jungles of Guyana. Sir Arthur Conan Doyle is perhaps the best-known representative of this point of view. His very first Sherlock Holmes story—in which Watson and Holmes meet—is about the Mormons, with shadings of European occultism, secret societies and, of course, murder. *A Study In Scarlet* has a long, set-piece study of Mormonism, as Conan Doyle understood it and as it would have been familiar to his readers when published in 1887. Of course, for Conan Doyle's English readers, Mormonism was probably just another example of American foolishness at best, or sinister cult behavior at worse. Yet we see in this famous story an introduction to Sherlock Holmes, to Doctor Watson, to the concept of crime detection using the powers of deduction based on available evidence, to the paranormal, to murder, to cults, and to a specifically American cult. With the retrospect possible after over one hundred years since the initial publication of the story, we can see how really remarkable is this first attempt at popular crime fiction. It wove together many of the threads that would interest Conan Doyle for years to come and, in its own way, is concerned with themes that are as modern as today's tabloid headlines and trash-talk reality shows.

That Holmes and Watson are obviously the prototypes for Mulder and Scully respectively of television's *The X-Files* fame needs no further explanation beyond this: both pairs are involved in crime detection, one is a doctor who records his/her observations after each case, the other is a visionary, an eccentric who pursues his own peculiar *modus operandi* in the effort to capture the evil-doers, and both have a Dr. Moriarty in their past: in Holmes's case, it is the evil genius who is at the heart of all crime in London if not all of Europe, a personal nemesis who nearly succeeds in killing him; in Mulder's case, it is the government itself—or some frantic faction thereof—which is responsible for the kidnapping or abduction of his sister, and which nearly succeeds in killing him.

The influence of Mormonism does not end here, however. It comes up again and again in the course of American history, as we discover the Mormon relationship to Howard Hughes, and Mormon involvement in the Watergate scandal.[50] This is not an attempt to smear the Mormon church or the Mormon organization in any way; this *is* an attempt, however, to examine how religious and occult beliefs have influenced—and, at times, controlled—political events in America, and Mormonism has a lot to offer us by way of example.

Today, many Mormons are conscious that there is an effort underway to discredit their belief by means of proving that many deeply-held convictions are based on deception or blatant lies. Attempts to conceal Joseph Smith's magical practices are only one alleged example; another is the assertion of the actual existence of the golden plates from which the *Book of Mormon* was transcribed, and of the historical accuracy (or lack of accuracy) afforded by the analysis of those transcriptions.

In the 1940s, a devout Mormon began an archaeological quest to prove, once and for all, the literal truth of the *Book of Mormon*. Thomas Stuart Ferguson, a lawyer from California, decided to prove that the historical elements contained within the *Book of Mormon* were verifiable. He wished to prove that the *Book* was true and, therefore, that the religion was true by extension. Since Smith had received the golden plates from an Angel, and since Smith had not visited the lands described in the *Book of Mormon*, it was logical to assume that if the *Book* was correct, then Smith's angelic experiences and visions of the plates and the ensuing transcriptions were all true, or at least proof of extraordinary spiritual powers or gifts.

The widespread belief in some Mormon circles at the time was that the lands referred to in the *Book* were located somewhere in Central America or Mexico. Ferguson felt similarly inclined, and undertook expeditions to these areas in anticipation of discovering physical evidence for the geography outlined in the *Book*. After several false starts, Ferguson slowly came to believe that he was wasting his time. The discovery of some Aztec, Maya and Olmec sites that seemed to parallel descriptions in the *Book* were later invalidated when it was shown that these civilizations (or, at least, the specific sites referenced) came into being much later than the chronology given in the *Book*.

Archaeologists were quick to point out that there was no evidence to support a claim that Near Eastern groups had established communities in the New World, that there was no linguistic or other cultural evidence to support any cross-fertilization of Levantine and Ancient Mexican religious or racial groups, and that the *Book of Mormon* added nothing to what archaeologists knew of Aztec, Mayan, Toltec, Olmec or any other ancient New World civilizations. If the *Book of Mormon* was true in any historical sense, the basic premise seemed to be in error: the events described could not have taken place in Mexico or Central America.

The last straw came in November 1967 with the revelation that certain Egyptian papyri—which had been in Smith's possession and from which he "translated" the

Book of Abraham (included in the LDS scripture *The Pearl of Great Price*)—had been discovered. Ferguson was eager to have the papyri translated by non-Mormon Egyptologists. When they were, the documents were shown to be versions of the Egyptian *Book of the Dead* and had nothing at all to do with any Mormon scripture.

Ferguson died on March 16, 1983, of a heart attack while playing tennis. By that time he had given up all hope of proving the historical claims of the Mormon scriptures, but had reconciled himself to the fellowship of the Church and an embrace of its moral principles. He admitted that Joseph Smith was a "smart fellow," but stopped short of calling him a charlatan or a con-man.[51]

From the first voyage of Columbus to the land of the Arawaks on a quest for a fast route to Jerusalem; from the witchcraft trials of Salem, Massachusetts involving Arawak descendant Tituba and later manifesting in the magic and occultism of Salem descendant Joseph Smith; from European mysticism to American "folk magic" and stories of murderous cults and demon worshippers in the seventeenth and eighteenth centuries; from all this we can begin to perceive a different sort of American history. As Americans, we have been moving too fast and forgetting too much to realize that we have a unique cultural contribution to make, one that unites religion with mysticism at the very bedrock of human experience . . . and then transforms this alchemical tincture into a political and scientific Philosopher's Stone capable of causing tremendous change in the human psyche. Such an effort was, indeed, attempted by some of the best minds of the last generation.

Thus the story of the *Book of Mormon* is not the end of our quest, because it poses more questions than it answers. What did Joseph Smith see in the woods that night in 1823? What was the actual source of the *Book of Mormon* if it was, indeed, a total fabrication? Were there any advanced civilizations in America—other than those in Central America—which predated Columbus and which would have fit the Mormon chronicles of early American settlement?

Most importantly of all, for the next phase of our research: who built the Ashland mounds?

ENDNOTES

1 Kenneth D. Wald, *Religion and Politics in the United States*, Washington, DC, 1992, ISBN 0-87187-604-3, p. 42
2 Kenneth Patchen, *The Journal of Albion Moonlight*, New Directions, NY, 1941, ISBN 0-8112-0144-9, p 106
3 Albert Camus, *The Myth of Sisyphus*, Vintage International, NY, 1991, ISBN 0-67973373-6, p. 127n
4 Stuart Clark, *Thinking With Demons: The Idea of Witchcraft in Early Modern Europe*, Oxford University Press, NY, 1999, ISBN 0-19-820808-1, p. 434
5 H.P. Lovecraft, "The Dunwich Horror," *The Annotated Lovecraft*, S.T. Joshi, Dell, NY, 1997, p. 105
6 Joyce Carol Oates, *Tales of H.P. Lovecraft*, The Ecco Press, NY, 2000
7 Several stories by Borges were inspired by Lovecraft, including "Funes the Memorious" and "Tlon, Uqbar, Orbis, Tertius," as well as a story published in *The Atlantic Monthly* some years ago.
8 Most of Grant's published work refers to Lovecraft, especially *Outer Gateways, Cults of the Shadow*, etc. See Bibliography for a complete listing.
9 Note, for instance, Surah 5/13, 5/51, 5/57, 5/64-66, 9/30, 62/6-8, etc.
10 Washington Irving, *Tales of the Alhambra*, Editorial Escudo de Oro, Barcelona, p. 3
11 Christopher Columbus, *The Diario of Christopher Columbus's First Voyage to America 1492–1493*, Dunn and Kelley, University of Oklahoma Press, 1991, p. 290–1
12 Irving, op. cit., p. 57
13 Oates, op. cit., p. 229
14 Burr, George Lincoln, ed. *Narratives of the Witchcraft Cases 1648–1706*, Scribner's, NY, 1914, p. 41–52
15 Ibid., p. 47
16 Demos, John Putnam, *Entertaining Satan: Witchcraft and the Culture of Early New England*, Oxford, 1983, pp. 402–409
17 Morton, Thomas, *Revels in New Canaan, 1637*, reprinted in Albert Bushnell Hart, ed. *American History Told by Contemporaries*, NY, 1898, volume 1, pp 361–63
18 Ibid.
19 William Bradford, *History of Plymouth Plantation, 1620–1647*, Boston, 1912, Vol. 2, pp. 45–57
20 Cotton Mather, *Wonders of the Invisible World*, 1693
21 D. Michael Quinn, *Early Mormonism and the Magic World View*, Signature Books, Salt Lake City, 1998, p. 10
22 Ibid., p. 10
23 Washington Irving, "The Legend of Sleepy Hollow," in *Ronald Curran, Witches, Wraiths and Warlock s*, Fawcett, NY, 1988, ISBN 0-449-30061-7, p. 216
24 Cotton Mather, *Wonders of the Invisible World*, 1693
25 Ibid.
26 Ibid.
27 Ibid.
28 Chadwick Hansen, *Witchcraft at Salem*, George Braziller, NY, 1992, p. 1–3
29 Ibid., p. 11
30 Ibid., p. 86
31 Ibid., pp. 18–19
32 *Diagnostic and Statistical Manual of Mental Disorders* (Third Edition), American Psychiatric Association
33 Hansen, op. cit., p. 17
34 In Hansen, op.cit., p. 17
35 Hansen, op. cit., p. 90
36 Ibid., p. 97
37 Ibid., p. 97
38 Sir Arthur Conan Doyle, *The Complete Sherlock Holmes*, Magpie Books, London, 1993, p. 86
39 D. Michael Quinn, op. cit., p. 118 and elsewhere. Quinn gives a lengthy argument in this chapter concerning the ready availability of *The Magus* (and other famous occult texts) to the Smith family, and their use of these documents in works of ceremonial magic.
40 Ibid., p. 31
41 Ibid., p. 261–264
42 See Steven Naifeh & Gregory White Smith, *The Mormon Murders*, Onyx, NY, 1989, ISBN 0-451-40152-2 for the definitive history of the 1985 Mark Hoffmann case in Salt Lake City, Utah.
43 Ibid., p. 91

44 Winston Churchill, in a statement published in the *Illustrated Sunday Herald* of Feb. 8, 1920, famously announced, "From the days of Sparticus-Weishaupt to those of Karl Marx, to those of Trotsky, Bela Kuhn, Rosa Luxembourg and Emma Goldman, this world-wide conspiracy has been steadily growing. This conspiracy played a definitely recognizable role in the tragedy of the French Revolution. It has been the main-spring of every subversive movement in the 19th Century . . ." Sparticus-Weishaupt is, of course, Adam Weishaupt, the founder of the Illuminati, whose name in the Order was "Spartacus." George Washington also references the Illuminati in one of his letters: "It was not my intention to doubt that the doctrine of the Illuminati and the principles of Jacobinism had not spread to the United States. On the contrary, no one is more satisfied of this fact than I am." Washington and Churchill thus give us two completely different value judgments—one from the revolutionary and fiercely independent Colonies and one from the voice of the Colonizer—on the existence and purpose of the Illuminati.

45 Quinn, op. cit., p. 155

46 Valerie I.J. Flint, *The Rise of Magic in Early Medieval Europe*, Princeton, 1991, p. 339

47 Ibid., p. 342

48 Quinn, op. cit., Figure 28a

49 Aleister Crowley, *777 and Other Qabalistic Writings of Aleister Crowley*, Samuel Weiser, York Beach, 1986, "Sepher Sephiroth," p. 23

50 This has been investigated at length by Jerald and Sandra Tanner, Mormon dissidents who figure prominently in the Mark Hoffmann case and who publish Mormon criticism through their Lighthouse Ministry. See for instance *Mormon Spies, Hughes, and the CIA*, Lighthouse Ministry, Salt Lake City, 1976. Sandra Tanner herself is a direct descendant of Brigham Young.

51 Stan Larson, *Quest for the Gold Plates: Thomas Stuart Ferguson's Archaeological Search for the Book of Mormon*, Freethinker Press, Salt Lake City, 1996

Top: Known historically as "Anasazi," the Ancestral Pueblo peoples of the Four Corners region left behind remarkable archaeological sites, including the sophisticated cliff dwellings at Mesa Verde, Colorado.[1] **Bottom left:** Joseph Smith called this Indian mound "The Hill Cumorah." Located near Manchester in upstate New York, this is the site where he received the golden plates, which he subsequently translated into *The Book of Mormon*. **Bottom right:** The Kensington Stone—discovered by a Minnesota farmer in 1898—is carved in runic characters and bears testament to an attack on a Norse encampment by Indians in the year 1362.

BOOK ONE: THE NINE

CHAPTER TWO

THE MOUNTAINS OF MADNESS: AMERICAN PREHISTORY AND THE OCCULT

> To wrangle the Devil out of the country, will be truly a new experiment: Alas! we are not aware of the Devil, if we do not think, that he aims at inflaming us one against another; and shall we suffer ourselves to be Devil-ridden? or by any unadvisableness contribute unto the widening of our breaches?
>
> —Cotton Mather[2]

> Religious insanity is very common in the United States.
>
> —Alexis de Tocqueville[3]

It was a cheap apartment in a small Appalachian town, and the sitting room was full of blood. The body had been savagely attacked, and bore nineteen separate stab wounds. The attack was so passionate, so bestial, that the murder weapon—a kitchen knife—was still in the body, pinning it to the floor.

It might have been a love affair gone terribly wrong. People from Ashland, Kentucky have been known to get emotional, even irrational, over love and the promises of love and the mistaken assumptions of love and its follies, like a town out of a country and western song.

Or it might have been something else. Something more sinister. A warning, borne of a hatred so deep and a malevolence so strong that slain flesh and spilled blood were only symbols—mere tokens—of its power.

The victim was a nobody. An ex-con, once convicted of writing bad checks. A man down on his luck, working for a trucking company.

He had been stabbed in a fury of nineteen slashing, slivering strokes—in a wood frame house in the middle of the night or the early hours of the morning on a side street in a small country town—and no one heard a thing.

The perpetrator left no clues, no identifiable fingerprints, nothing. The body might have lain there for days, except that the victim's co-worker stopped by to see why he hadn't shown up for work that morning. The body was found. The police were called.

The officer who responded to that call and who was the first policeman at the scene is today the Chief of Police of Ashland, Kentucky. The murder took place in

1969. He told me it remains unsolved—and the murder is open on the books—to this day.[4]

The victim's name was Darwin Scott. He was the brother of one Colonel Scott. Colonel Scott had been sued—successfully—for paternity of a boy, one "No Name Maddox," by a girlfriend and sometime prostitute, Kathleen Maddox. No Name Maddox would soon be known by another name. Charles Manson.

Darwin Scott was Charles Manson's uncle.

His murder took place in May. In August, the Sharon Tate and LaBianca murders would occur in Los Angeles. In December, Charles Manson would be charged along with several of his associates for those crimes. Crimes committed with knives. Crimes that turned beautiful Hollywood people into corpses, beautiful Hollywood homes into abattoirs awash in gore. Manson would be convicted of those crimes. But no one was ever arrested for the murder of Darwin Scott, his uncle.

MANHATTAN TRANSFER

Nixon was president, and the Vietnam War was in full swing. The Tet Offensive of January 1968 had occurred the previous year, and Walter Cronkite had bitched about it on network TV. The Days of Rage had flamed in Chicago, and Robert F. Kennedy was assassinated, Martin Luther King, Jr. was assassinated, Marcus Garvey was assassinated, Malcolm X was assassinated, the Weathermen were plotting against banks and Army recruiting stations, and I was on the telephone, talking to someone at the headquarters of the Presbyterian Church in New York City, when I heard a blast and the tinkling sound of breaking glass as my party shouted at me, "There's been a bomb! I have to hang up!" The Weathermen had blown up a brownstone in Greenwich Village in Manhattan, across the street from the church. It was an accident, a bomb-making enterprise gone wrong. It would be years before one of the surviving Weathermen would give herself up to the authorities.

But still we had not heard of Charles Manson. That would happen in December of 1969. I turned 19 the day he was arrested: that tiny terrorist dragged fuming and sneering from a crawl space under a wooden cabinet in the desert, but we would not know that he was the supposed mastermind of the Tate/LaBianca killings for some weeks yet. And he would not be convicted for many months more, after one of his own attorneys died under mysterious circumstances. By that time, I had taken a job with a lingerie company in Manhattan's Garment District.

Stardust was founded by a man named Brandt. His son, Steven Brandt, was a Hollywood gossip columnist at the time of the Manson killings, and one of the witnesses at Sharon Tate's marriage to Roman Polanski. He would return to New York in a panic, phone up his friends at Andy Warhol's Factory, and then commit suicide in a hotel room before his friend Ultra Violet could get there in time. He thought there had been a hit list, and he thought he was on it. All because of the Manson Family. Stardust. The company's Los Angeles location appeared in a Jack Lemmon film, *Save The Tiger*.

Other people connected to Manson and his ad hoc cult exploded out of California in the aftermath of the Tate/LaBianca killings, and wound up dead—murders or suicides—all over the world. This would tend to support the theory that there was more to the Manson "Family" than sex, drugs and rock and roll. But at 19, I was more concerned about earning a paycheck from my first real job than I was about the inner workings of a madman's fantasies in California, a place I had never been. I was also worried about Vietnam, and the possibility that I would wind up slogging through the tall grass, humping a BAR and sweating tears and blood in the tropical jungles.

At Stardust, I was befriended by a former model, a tall, exotic beauty with a warped sense of humor. We got along well, and she invited me several times to the apartment she shared with her musician boyfriend. We talked about a lot of things, typical New York topics: music and movies and books. We rarely discussed politics, but when I asked her about her former life as a model, she revealed her previous connections to people involved with the Howard Hughes organization. She would tell me that Hughes had been kidnapped. A few months later, Clifford Irving would tell the world that he had been secretly interviewing Hughes and would write the only authorized biography of the hermit billionaire. It was eventually denounced as a hoax, but under very bizarre circumstances: Hughes holding a press conference by telephone, his metallic voice denouncing the Irving book from a small box in the center of the room.

I urged the model to come forward and tell what she knew. Horrified, she refused. She said to do that would put her life in danger. We never discussed it again.

Hughes. Nixon. Vietnam. Manson. Hollywood.

Then the Craig Karpel series in the *Village Voice,* and it all came together.

And there were more revelations.

Richard Helms admitted there had been something going on at the CIA called MK-ULTRA, which was an attempt to probe the secrets of the human mind in an effort to produce the perfect assassin and to counteract the enemy's brainwashing efforts.

Then there were the Son of Sam killings. The Jonestown massacre. John Lennon murdered by a man holding a copy of *Catcher in the Rye*, a man who had prayed to Satan only hours before.

The bodies—and the cults—were piling up. And my research was outrunning me. Every time I thought I had enough to start work on the book, more bizarre stories appeared linking government agencies and psychological operations, cult infiltrations, organized crime, banking scandals, serial murder, drug trafficking . . .

There was the *Propaganda Due* scandal in Italy. A Masonic society involved with assassinations and terror bombings, Latin American dictators and neo-Nazis, linked to the Church.

Then there was Iran-Contra. The BCCI scandal. Koreagate. It just never stopped.

And then there was the book by respected historian, Ladislas Farago, *Aftermath,* about escaped Nazi war criminals living in South America. Farago's most shocking revelation—to me—was not his claim that Martin Bormann had escaped and was living in Brazil, but the fact that the Roman Catholic Church had been intimately involved in helping the Nazis escape to South America, even disguising some as priests. It was that book that sent me to Chile in 1979 during the height of the Pinochet regime and martial law, while doing research on the Nazi use of occult and mystical ideas, a trip that contributed to my first book, *Unholy Alliance*.[5] I had originally intended *Unholy Alliance* to be only a chapter of the present book, but as usual the research outran me. In this case, however, I was not able to outrun the research: I was detained by German nationals at the infamous Colonia Dignidad in Chile and only allowed to leave the torture and interrogation center when it was determined that killing me would be too risky and would perhaps endanger the Colony's most esteemed guests, renegade Nazis on the run from justice.

But it wasn't only about government conspiracies and cover-ups. This book became a personal and a spiritual quest as well. Links and connections took me to the Dead Sea Scrolls and questions about the legitimacy of all the teaching to which I had been exposed as a young Roman Catholic in New York and Chicago. Books like *Holy Blood, Holy Grail* purported to give a completely different history of the origins of Christianity and specifically of the Catholic Church. Did Jesus have a family? Are his descendants living in Europe today? And what about the Gospel of St. Thomas (so prominent in the recent horror film, *Stigmata*)? Does it deserve a place in the Christian Bible, as respected as the other four Gospels? Was it suppressed by the Church? If so, why?

And, finally, what about the reality of spiritual experience? Are saints and madmen equally deluded? Are witches' sabbats the same as alien abductions? Is exorcism merely a form of psychotherapy, or is it something more? Something . . . other? What is evil? Can everything we experience as human beings be explained away by a tranquil, Carl Sagan-like belief in science? Was Carl comforted in his final moments by reciting the Second Law of Thermodynamics . . . or by a remembered prayer of childhood? Is science a "candle in the dark"? . . . Or is it simply whistling in the dark?

If Church and State are not separate in reality, in the world of action, then where does Science stand? Is it an outgrowth of the Church, and a tool of the State? Or does the answer lie in the cults, the secret societies, the occult orders of yesterday and today? What did the CIA learn during its long investigation of psychology and the paranormal? *Why did they shred all the documentation of this that they could find?*

These and similar, equally disturbing questions kept me awake at odd hours of the night since that month in 1975 when I read the Craig Karpel series. After Bendix, I had a series of jobs in New York that eventually led me to travel extensively throughout the United States and the world. I've spent a lot of time in South America, the Caribbean, Europe, Australia and especially in Asia, where the line between religion and politics is very fine indeed, and sometimes—such as in Indonesia or Malaysia—non-existent. I visited temples, shrines, mosques, churches, hounforts, cemeteries, séances . . . and archives, libraries, document collections, government offices, factories, military bases, and prisons. I came to know—often by utter and complete accident—many figures and organizations that appear in the pages that follow. I discovered the FBI file on my late father; I worked with a famous spy, a former colleague of E. Howard Hunt and employee of the Hughes public relations firm, Robert Mullen. And some clergymen I knew numbered suspected JFK co-conspirator David Ferrie among their hierarchy.

I finally decided, then, to visit the place where my story begins. The town that Charles Manson called home for the first years of his life. The town where his uncle had been murdered, by person or persons unknown. I had to find some way to bring all this information together, to connect it in some logical fashion, to make it make sense. There was no linear chronology, no neat historical pattern. Rather, the information I collated was so intertwined that it appeared more like a spiderweb than a timeline. People who should not have been connected, were. Events that should not have been connected touched each other through improbable links. How was this possible? How did it happen that when I pulled the strings of my own life history, I found tendrils reaching to the farthest ends of assassination and conspiracy?

I hoped the answer would somehow lie in Ashland, Kentucky.

There is an ancient America that lurks beneath the threshold of our collective, corn-fed consciousness. We see it all the time. It surrounds us with its feral glow; we have learned to fear it in the dark without learning what it is, what it means. It's not just the woods out back, the lonely desert trails, the virgin mountains where we lose our Boy Scouts or survivalists in the winter snows. It's also in the laundromats, the gas stations, the drug stores and diners.

> "I think you say 'convenience store.' We lived above it."
> —*Twin Peaks*[6]

It's in our standing stones, our Anasazi ruins, our Indian burial mounds. It's the remains of the Old Ones, the original people, the deep ancestors of our forgotten history, the history before Columbus that is never taught in the schools because we don't know it ourselves . . . because we don't want to know, don't want to accept what has been proved so many times in the past: that this land of ours is haunted by the ghosts of races who lived and died on our land thousands of years before we came, and of races we ourselves exterminated with fire and sword and virus. There were vast cities here before us, huge temples dwarfing the Colosseum, the Parthenon, the Pyramids of Gizeh, some built long before any of these more famous structures were even dreamed. There were Norsemen here before us, bringing paganism and the worship of Nordic gods. There were Irishmen here before us, bringing a strange mixture of Catholicism and druidism, standing up their stones and sighting along the solstices years before the Nina, Pinta and Santa Maria. There were Carthaginians here before us, Phoenician traders, perhaps even Buddhists from China. All the votes aren't in, yet. We don't know why there are stones engraved with ancient alphabets, buried in our farmland. We don't know how they got there, so we file these petroglyphs along with tales of sea serpents and great white whales . . . in the land of fantasy that is the bull's eye target of our scientists. And we whisper ourselves to sleep like the voice-over on a late night talk show while the gloom gathers outside our windows and doors and the dead Indians, the dead Phoenicians, the dead Norsemen chant their ancient mantras to rob us of our dreams.

Welcome to American prehistory.

AMERICA, B.C.

There are two general approaches to the study of human habitation on the North and South American continents before the arrival of the people we think of as Native Americans. The most accepted view is that of the "independent inventionists": archaeologists and anthropologists who believe that both continents were peopled by a race that came from Northern Asia, from what is now Russia (or, perhaps, parts of China or even Southeast Asia according to one school) and who walked across the Bering Straits (when they were frozen solid) and followed the coast down Alaska and into Canada and spread out from there as far east and south as the land mass allowed. In other words, all Native Americans are descendants of this group of wanderers from the frozen wastes of Siberia—a group known as the Clovis people, from a site in western New Mexico where some stone spearpoints were first discovered in 1932 (and oddly enough a town named after the first Merovingian king of France). The Clovis spearpoints are believed to be representative of a purely "American" style of manufacture, and can be found throughout the Americas. (Of course, this gives rise to a question: If the "Clovis" people came from Siberia, why is there no evidence of Clovis points in Siberia?) Given their antiquity, the theory is that the Clovis people were not only the first race to set foot on American soil, but are the progenitors of all other Native Americans. Thus, the Aztecs, Incas, Mayas, Iroquois, Cherokee, Chickasaw, Hopi, Quecha, Narragansett, Pequot, Zuni and all other known "Indian" and American tribes and civilizations are direct descendants of the Clovis people.

The opposing view—and one which goes in and out of fashion regularly through the years—is that of the "diffusionists." This theory has it that parts of North and South America were peopled by races from Asia, Europe and the Middle East at various times, people who sailed across the Atlantic from the Mediterranean or from the northern European coastlines of Scandinavia, France, Spain, Portugal and the British Isles, across the Pacific from Southeast Asia or the Chinese mainland, or from Polynesia. The diffusionists like to believe that some of our modern Native Americans are descendants of Phoenicians, Celts, Malays, Chinese and other ancient civilizations.

In the late 1940s and early 1950s, a Norwegian adventurer attempted to prove that it was possible to sail across the Pacific Ocean on a raft. Thor Heyerdahl wanted to show that people from South America could have traveled to Asia (or, at least, the South Pacific) a thousand years before Columbus; and that people from Sumeria and Egypt could have sailed the Indian and Atlantic oceans in ancient times. Several books (*Kon Tiki* and *Aku Aku* among them) were written defending this point of view and showing how Heyerdahl managed to build a raft using local materials and sail across the seas using only the stars for navigation. His *Ra Expedition* proved that one could sail across the Atlantic the same way, always using materials and methods—including navigational methods—that would have been locally available at the time and place of origin. (His film of the Kon Tiki voyage between South America and Polynesia won a 1951 Academy Award for Best Documentary.) Heyerdahl's courageous undertaking was all the rage among laypersons for some years, and then interest waned and we were back to wrestling with the Clovis theory.

There are some facts, however, that are disturbing to mainstream archaeologists, who dismiss anomalies as either hoaxes or as inexplicable, preferring to accept the Clovis position because it's neat and tidy. There is also a political problem with diffusionism, because some believe it would devalue the Native American culture. That this is patently not the case has been verbalized again and again by some Native American diffusionists, but their words fall on deaf ears.[7]

Question: Examination of an Egyptian mummy of the 21st Dynasty by a German toxicologist in 1992 shows that the body tested positive for tobacco and cocaine, products that were native only to the Americas at the time of the pharaohs. How did tobacco and cocaine reach ancient Egypt?[8]

Question: What are graphic depictions of maize doing on the Hindu temples at Karnataka, when maize is another of those products that are native to the Americas and which supposedly were unheard of and unknown in India at the time of the carvings . . . the twelfth century, A.D.?[9]

Question: What about the sweet potato, which was known throughout the Pacific basin, including Polynesia, as early as 400 A.D. . . .when the sweet potato is indigenous to the Americas only?[10]

Most surprising of all, what are stones doing in West Virginia, New Mexico, Minnesota and elsewhere inscribed with ancient scripts that were unknown to the Native Americans who had no written languages?

Remains of ancient civilizations in the Americas that predate the Clovis migrations are routinely ignored or devalued, since they don't fit the pattern. Other explanations are sought for the existence of 15,000–30,000 year old burial sites in the Andes Mountains, for instance, or petroglyphs in West Virginia that are written in ancient European languages. Science assumes that these are either hoaxes, or somehow "anomalies" that cannot be explained . . . and which are therefore put in a category of "unknowables" and left outside the mainstream discussions.

Richard Rudgley in his *Lost Civilizations of the Stone Age* refers to the interesting case of the Seven Sisters,[11] a constellation—the Pleiades—that was known by that name to the ancient races of North America . . . *and* Siberia . . . *and* Australia; if this is more than merely a coincidence, Rudgley points out, then it implies a common origin for the name of this constellation that must predate the peopling of North America as well as that of Australia. In other words, it is evidence of a single body of knowledge that existed more than 40,000 years ago, common to Asians and North Americans since that time. "Most researchers tend to ignore findings as anomalous as these," Rudgley says, "as they simply do not fit well with generally accepted views."[12]

The late Harvard Professor Barry Fell did a lot to try to change that attitude, and made an excellent case for the diffusionist perspective. His research has been roundly (if not soundly) attacked in recent years by the Clovis faction, much in the way Gerald Posner attacks critics of the Warren Commission. Using selective evidence out of context and ignoring evidence that doesn't fit in with basic assumptions, it is possible to attack virtually everything and sound knowledgeable doing it. Of course, Fell and the diffusionists have been accused of the same sins. The controversy has become emotional and personal at times. But the weight of diffusionist evidence is growing every year, and the implications of it are startling and will eventually require a rewriting of American prehistory as we know it. Before we examine diffusionism in detail, though, it is worthwhile to pick up our story where we left off, with America in the nineteenth century and an obsession with buried treasure and sacred hills.

Joseph Smith called the Indian mound in upstate New York where he received the golden plates "the Hill Cumorah," after an incident in his own Book of Mormon. Others since Smith have tried to place Cumorah in other regions, such as Central America or Mexico, even though Smith himself referred to this gentle slope near Manchester, New York as Cumorah. What is not generally known to most Mormons is that America during Smith's lifetime was a hotbed of speculation about the mounds.

Mounds are found all over the United States, from New England to Missouri, with a few in Texas and some in Florida. There are, in fact, over 100,000 of them (and this does not count all the sacred circles and standing stones, which most Americans are totally unaware exist in their own country).[13] Some of them are burial mounds, as can be evidenced by the skeletal remains found therein. Others are sacred sites arranged in ways reminiscent of Stonehenge in England, mounds astronomically oriented towards the solstices or to the rising of some specific star. Others still are vast works of art, such as Serpent Mound in Adams County, Ohio, which has been analyzed by professionals and shown to be more than art: an artistic astronomical computer, oriented towards the solstices, the moon, the sun, and the constellations of Draco and Ursa Major,[14] consistent with a theology we can only imagine, and like those intricately engraved Persian astrolabes one sometimes finds in an antique store or a *souk*. Some of these Neolithic sites are mere piles of earth; others were constructed using wooden logs as a kind of infrastructure. Others constitute what appear to have been entire cities, with wide avenues and huge platform mounds enclosing areas in excess of twenty acres or more, such as "Great Hopewell Road" in Ohio, which links Newark with Chillicothe.[15]

But the real mystery in the early nineteenth century was "who built the mounds, and why?"

Although generally referred to as "Indian burial mounds," it was acknowledged that the Indians themselves had no precise data to offer as to their origins or purpose. When asked, the Native American elders of some tribes would refer to an older race or tribe that had lived in the area long before their own arrival. In some cases, there were stories of a race of the "Old Ones" or the "First People" who had lived and then disappeared ages ago. Some tribal groups occupied earthworks and other types of fortifications that they admit they did not build, but found unoccupied, such as the Anasazi site in the American Southwest. (The word Anasazi means "Old Ones.") With the passage of time and a lot of digging, archaeology came up with two distinct groups of prehistoric Americans in the region roughly from New England to the Mississippi River basin: the Adena and the Hopewell cultures.

Although even this division of two distinct groups is currently a matter for some debate (some archaeologists entertaining the belief that they were really the same people) it would do us well to consider them separately for now, as most of the literature one comes across still speaks of two, very different, populations and cultures. The earliest of these was the Adena people, named after a farm in Ohio where this type of mound was excavated. The Adena flourished two thousand years ago and longer, and were building mounds in America at the time of Christ, even at the time of Buddha. No wonder, then, that Smith would have identified one of these mounds as having been built by a tribe of Jews who had fled the Middle East and wound up on American shores. Except that the dating of the mounds took place long after Smith had written the *Book of Mormon*.

Precise dating is not always possible when it comes to the mounds. In many cases, they are simply earthworks with nothing that can be reliably carbon-dated. In other cases, though, there are skeletal remains as well as wood fragments, pottery and ornaments, and these lend themselves rather more easily to specific dating exercises.

After the Adena came the Hopewell culture, which was more complex and sophisticated than the Adena, and which built some of the more elaborate mound complexes and effigy mounds, such as (it is claimed) the Serpent Mound, which is now dated by some to around 1066 A.D., and by others to 250 A.D.

No one knows where the Adena came from, or what happened to them. It is believed that they were either exterminated by the later Hopewell culture, or were assimilated into the Hopewells through intermarriage and the gradual erosion of their own culture. Their only legacy rests in the proliferation of mounds. In some of these, strange burial patterns were observed, such as the twelve people buried at the Kiefer Mound in Ohio, in a circle with their heads on the inside of the circle and their feet pointing outwards "like spokes in a wheel."[16] This same arrangement was reported in the *Wheeling Gazette*—a body on an altar, head facing "west of north" in the direction where there was evidence of a fire, the body covered by a foot of ashes. The body was found to be "remarkably perfect, and was mostly preserved. Around this body were twelve others with their heads centering towards it, and feet projecting. No articles of art were found, except a polished stone tube, about twelve inches in length."[17] The alignment of the body implies an astronomical orientation consistent with many Hopewell and Adena sites. In this case, it is possible that the "west of north" alignment was towards Ursa Major, but that is pure conjecture since we don't know when the site was constructed or the bodies interred. The fact that there were twelve other bodies with the central, altar-lain body indicates that these twelve were killed, sacrificed, in some sort of ritual. The stone tube might have been a pipe, or it could have served some function of which we are not aware; such is the state of knowledge of American prehistory. Oddly, this is a precise description of a Cathar burial method of the thirteenth century A.D. (and of nine persons discovered dead in an identical wheel-like formation—heads inside, feet out—after the FBI assault on the Branch Davidian compound in Waco, Texas in 1993). At the Kiefer Mound, three of the twelve corpses had been decapitated, with the skulls placed between the thigh bones. This odd placement of the skulls also exists in other Adena sites in Kentucky.[18] Engraved tablets were found buried in these mounds with the artistically arranged bodies, and Adena experts William S. Webb and Charles E. Snow believe that this "constitutes a very important Adena trait."[19]

Then there is the red paint. Ochre coloring was common on the skulls and bones of the deceased; in other words, after the bodies had decomposed someone had cleaned off the bones and painted them with red paint, sometimes in strange symmetrical designs, and then reburied them. In some cases, the ochre was piled onto the lower extremities of the corpses[20] and in two Adena sites in Kentucky a black graphite compound was used to color the skull and collar bones of the corpse while red ochre was used for the lower extremities.[21] No one knows the purpose of this ritual, but the use of ochre in sacramental painting was common all over Europe in ancient times as well as in early North American civilizations. The amount of work involved in either stripping the skeletons of flesh and then painting the bones, or in waiting for natural decomposition to occur and then digging up the bodies and painting them and then reburying them, was prodigious, and must have served an identifiable purpose deemed necessary to the Adena.

In one case mentioned by Webb and Snow, the skull of a young woman was painted in horizontal red stripes of ochre on the top of the skull, leaving the forehead bare of any ochre; the red ochre was continued in horizontal stripes over the eyes, and then a vertical bar of graphite extended from the forehead down between the eyes to the nasal cavity.[22] This clearly had some religious significance for the Adena, but whatever it was is lost in time.

Other symbolic motifs found in Adena sites include a plumed serpent, which gives rise to speculation that the cult of Quetzalcoatl of Aztec Mexico had reached the Adena, or vice versa. A plumed serpent is a very specific icon, a complex mix of concepts that implies all sorts of cultural and religious ideas. It strains belief to insist that the plumed serpent of the Adena had nothing at all to do with the plumed serpent of Mexico, a land not that far to the south. The presence of obsidian flakes in Adena mounds[23] adds further credence to the theory that there was a connection between the Adena and the Aztecs, since the Aztecs prized obsidian. Indeed, one of the famous shew stones of the Elizabethan magician and spy, John Dee, was of Aztec obsidian brought back from the New World by Spanish conquistadores. The Aztecs used the obsidian shew stone in an identical fashion to that used by Dee (and, later, Joseph Smith), as a kind of crystal ball. To the Aztecs, the obsidian mirror was sacred to the god Tezcatlipoca, the "god of the smoking mirror," who would reveal to them the will of heaven. Tezcatlipoca was identified with the constellation Ursa Major, thus tying together astronomy with religion and divination in a pattern familiar to all students of ancient civilizations. The astronomical alignments of many of the Adena mound sites is further evidence of this persistent occult theorem. Joseph Smith, of course, used shew stones in much the same way as the Aztecs and John Dee.[24] Indeed, John Dee himself was a scientific advisor to English expeditions to the New World, and a close friend of Sir Walter Raleigh, the man who introduced tobacco and many other curiosities to England from the New World. Elizabethan magician and spy, Dee also became convinced that a Welsh prince had "discovered" America centuries before Columbus.[25]

Raptorial birds were also common symbols among the Adena, particularly the hawk. Webb and Snow remark upon an actual hawk's head that was sewn onto a ceremonial headdress.[26] There was even a unique symbol found at one site: a hand with an eye depicted on its palm, a symbol familiar to those who study ancient Middle Eastern religions and mysticism.[27]

Further, a unique characteristic of the Adena people was their extraordinary height. Analysis of skeletal remains at Adena sites shows the men to have occasionally reached seven feet in height, with the women often over six feet tall. Thus, their physical dissimilarity to the later Hopewells contributes to accurate identification of the mounds, but also raises questions as to their racial origin. Today, this supposed difference in physical appearance between the two cultures is debated, and studies have been done to show that the Adena and Hopewell peoples were related, if not actually the same people. What is lacking is a detailed analysis of some of the remains found in these mounds, which show a race that can only be described as a race of "giants."

Newspaper reports from the late 1800s discuss skeletons of more than seven feet and eight feet in length found in burial mounds and caves that often contained stone altars, or even, in at least one case, a stone sarcophagus. Cyrus Thomas reports on the "blond mummies" of Tennessee and Kentucky in the *Twelfth Annual Report of the Bureau of Ethnology*, dated 1894. These bodies were in "some instances" found "incased in stone slabs and afterwards imbedded in clay or ashes. In Smith and Warren counties, Tennessee, and in Warren and Fayette counties, Kentucky, the flesh of the bodies was preserved and the hair was yellow and of fine texture . . . . In one of the caves in Smith county the body of a female is said to have been found, having about the waist a silver girdle, with marks resembling letters."[28] This discovery of letters or hieroglyphics in ancient American burial sites is not an isolated case.

In December 1870, the so-called Brush Creek Tablet was unearthed from a burial mound on the farm of one J. M. Baughman in Muskingum County, Ohio. The tablet contains a variety of carvings which appear to be a form of hieroglyphic. Even more startling, the mound was found to contain skeletons measuring eight and nine feet in length.[29] Of course, these assertions—including a signed affidavit by six citizens swearing that the above account is true—are dismissed by academia. Citizens, of course, are not to be trusted as "reliable observers."

In 1838, the same year that Joseph Smith "returned" the golden plates of the Book of Mormon to an angel, a large Adena mound was excavated at Grave Creek, West Virginia. In a burial chamber in that mound which contained a single skeleton and some copper bracelets (and at a depth of 60 feet) an[30] engraved tablet was discovered, carved with Phoenician characters in a style of writing that was common in Spain *two thousand years ago*. This type of writing, sometimes called "Punic," was Semitic in origin, Spain then being controlled by Carthage, which in turn had originated in the previous millennium as an outpost of the Semitic Phoenicians. At the time the tablet was discovered, this type of script had not yet been deciphered, and would not be deciphered until the mid-twentieth century, thus ruling out the possibility of a hoax even if the discovery of the tablet under sixty feet of ancient burial mound was not enough to assure its provenance. Thus, there is at least circumstantial evidence that West Virginia had been visited by Europeans at the time of Christ. There is no other way to explain the presence of that stone tablet in that grave, carved in a writing that would not be deciphered for another hundred years.

And the Grave Creek tablet is not an isolated case.

There is the Bat Creek stone, for instance. Discovered in a burial mound in eastern Tennessee in 1889, its carvings were identified as ancient Hebrew by archaeologist Cyrus Gordon in 1971, a type of Hebrew that dates from the first hundred years after Christ. The inscription is said to read "For Judea." Shades of Joseph Smith! The site was later (1988) carbon-dated, and found to date from the period 32–769 A.D. Thus, Cyrus Gordon's 1971 identification of the type of Hebrew and the 1988 carbon-dating of the site are consistent.[31]

The American landscape is replete with stone carvings, some very simple and others quite elaborate, which point to a continuing immigration of Europeans and Middle Eastern peoples to its shores. A sub-discipline of archaeology—known as epigraphy—has attracted amateur archaeologists in America for many years. Epigraphy is concerned with writings on stone, and epigraphers scour the countryside, the forests, the hills and mountains, looking for stone inscriptions and trying to identify and decipher them. Epigraphy and epigraphical evidence are mainstays of the diffusionist argument, because stone carvings—once they have been identified and certified as genuine and ruled out as hoaxes—can represent unequivocal proof of foreign visitation to American soil in the years before Columbus and, in some cases, in the years before Christ. Joseph Smith's worldview—though based on a hoax, according to his detractors—is amazingly in accord with the worldview of the diffusionists, which is not unexpected since there was such a lot of speculation about the mound builders at the time the *Book of Mormon* was being written. According to scholars such as Fell, people from the Middle East *did* come to America long before Columbus. And where they did not leave golden plates covered with lengthy scriptural writings (at least, not as have been discovered so far!), they did leave stone tablets with scriptural quotations.

> . . . they have somewhat observed the motions of the stars; among which it has been surprising to me to find that *they have always called 'Charles Wain' by the name of "Paukunnawaw," or "the Bear," which is the name whereby Europeans also have distinguished it.* Moreover, they have little, if any, traditions among them worthy of our notice; and reading and writing is altogether unknown to them, though *there is a rock or two in the country that has unaccountable characters engraved upon it.*
>
> —Cotton Mather, *Magnalia Christi Americana*, 1702, Part III, in which he is writing of the American Indian population (emphasis added)

One of the earliest Americans interested in the strange carved inscriptions was our old friend Cotton Mather. He is known to have informed the Royal Society in England of the discovery of a strange inscription on a stone in Dighton, Massachusetts by clergyman John Danforth, who discovered the inscription in 1680.

The Royal Society published the information in their *Philosophical Transactions* in 1712, and thereafter the matter died on the vine.[32]

Item: There is the fact of the Los Lunas stone, found in New Mexico (the home of the first identified "Clovis" site). This is a stone boulder covered in a form of Hebrew writing current at the time of the first Temple, circa 1000 B.C., but which *was not translated until 1949*. When it was finally translated, it was revealed to be an abbreviated form of the Ten Commandments.[33]

The Ten Commandments. In ancient Hebrew. In New Mexico. 2,500 years before the visit of Columbus.

Do we, as Americans, really understand our own history? Is our history the history of an unknown race of people who created a vast and vibrant civilization and then—due to disease, perhaps, in the Great Dying of the sixteenth century—disappeared, leaving only the mounds as their trace? Is our history the history of our own ancestors in Europe, Africa, Asia? Is it simply the history of the land we occupy? Or is it really a combination of all of these? Is our history that of our ancient ancestors, who evidently came and went from America many times and for many reasons over the last three or four thousand years? Is America a legacy of Asian Buddhists, Palestinian Jews, Norse Vikings, and Phoenician traders as well as a shipload of Pilgrims from England? Is America's function as a destination of dreams for all the peoples of the earth no more than a memory of the time when it did, indeed, belong to everyone?

Is the Statue of Liberty standing in New York Harbor an acknowledgement of America's ancient purpose?

Even further, when we teach American history in school should we begin, as always, with its discovery by Columbus in 1492 . . . or should we begin instead with the fall of Carthage, or the Buddhist missions, or the cult of Wotan? Or with the Cahokia Mound near St. Louis, Missouri, a vast prehistoric complex that stuns the imagination? Or with the Newark mound complexes and their radical octagon–circle–square designs? By drawing a straight line through history at 1492 we, as Americans, are enforcing a kind of dual personality upon ourselves. At first, such a strategy was useful in order to amalgamate all the various nationalities that came to our shores looking for freedom and opportunity. Wiping out our ancestral heritage was a way of adopting the new, American heritage and making us all the same, all Americans, regardless of our family names or skin color.

But what have we lost in the process?

Item: The famous Peterborough Stone, in Ontario. A huge rock measuring "hundreds of square feet." Professor Barry Fell identified the maze of writings as a form of Scandinavian runes or, actually, pre-runic characters that he dated to 1700 B.C. Later archaeologists have corrected Fell's dating and translation, but were left with the result that Fell was essentially correct: the characters are written in a script called Tifinagh, which was used by the Tuaregs—a people of northern Africa. The stone was dated to 800 B.C. rather than 1700 B.C., but represents the record of a trade route in gold running from the Niger River in Africa to Scandinavia and then, eventually, to Ontario.[34]

In 800 B.C. At the time of the origin of the Adena people, eight hundred years before Christ and roughly contemporary with the life of the Buddha. A trade route from Africa, to Europe, to America. An established path for other traders, other peoples, other races, civilizations, religions. The Tuaregs and Scandinavians in 800 B.C. were, of course, pagans. How much of their culture did they bring with them to America? Did they intermarry with local races? Did they teach their systems of astronomy, divination, metallurgy, etc. to the Americans?

Did the Americans teach the Tuaregs and Scandinavians anything in return? There is no reason to believe that the transmission of knowledge was all one-sided. How did the African and European traders find the gold mines in Canada? How long were they in America? How often did they return?

Are their descendants still among us?

Any one of these pieces of evidence—the Grave Creek tablet, the Bat Creek stone, the Peterborough Stone, the existence of American flora in ancient Egypt, India and East Asia, and the hundreds of other examples, including Celtic Ogam script all over the American northeast—should be enough in itself to force historians to come to terms with pre-Columbian civilizations visiting and interacting with tribes, peoples and cultures from the Eastern Hemisphere. The preponderance of such evidence, however, and the multiplication of possible overseas connections from ancient cultures means that we have to go back carefully over the legends, myths, and histories of all the ancient peoples and see if we can find textual traces of this cross-fertilization.

In 1840, a pair of mound enthusiasts decide to excavate a promising group of mounds at Chillicothe, Ohio in the very heart of mound country. The team of Squier and Davis are generally acknowledged to be the godfathers of modern American archaeology. Their exhaustive and systematic work on hundreds of mounds throughout the Midwest still stands as a primary reference for American prehistory studies, and the Chillicothe excavation is probably their defining moment. They were not the first to excavate "Indian" mounds, however. George Washington was interested in the mounds.[35] No less a personage than Thomas Jefferson began a scientific stratigraphic excavation of a mound in 1781; his Secretary of the Treasury, Albert Gallatin, was perhaps the most influential person in American government (before or since) to have insisted on an appreciation of both the mounds and of the Native American populations who lived in the conquered territories. William Henry Harrison (who would become the United States' ninth president for a month before dying of pneumonia) would follow suit in 1838 with his *Discourse on the Aborigines of the Valley of the Ohio*, a description of mounds and some fanciful suggestions as to their origins and purposes. The reader will remember that this year has shown up before, as the year Joseph Smith returned the golden plates to the Angel Moroni, and as the year the "Phoenician" tablet was found at the Grave Creek mound.

(In an odd piece of trivia that may interest some readers, a respected Hollywood filmmaker also wrote a book about the mounds. Kenneth Macgowan—producer of such films as *Young Mr. Lincoln* (1939), and one of the better propaganda films of the early war years, *Man Hunt* (1941), wrote *Early Man In the New World.* Macgowan, who began his career in New York City in the Broadway theater, later became a film theorist as well as a teacher at UCLA, and authored several textbooks on cinema, for which he is better known. He died in 1963 at the age of seventy-five.)

Other personalities who became involved in mound research included the founders of the town of Marietta, Ohio: Rufus Putnam and Manasseh Cutler, the former a general of the Revolutionary War and the latter a minister. Marietta is in the heart of mound country, not far from Chillicothe, and General Putnam forbade the destruction of the mounds by farmers, instead making detailed maps of them for posterity.

But it is to Ephraim George Squier and Dr. Edwin H. Davis that we owe most of our early knowledge about the mounds. Together they excavated more than two hundred of them, and published the results in *Ancient Monuments of the Mississippi Valley: Comprising the Results of Extensive Original Surveys and Explorations*, a by-now standard text that was the first (1848) publication of the Smithsonian "Contributions to Knowledge" series. The Chillicothe site is amply described and illustrated; indeed, there are nearly 300 Adena mound sites within a 150 mile radius of Chillicothe, extending into Indiana, Kentucky, West Virginia and Pennsylvania. These sites include the Grave Creek Mound, in Moundsville, West Virginia described above, as well as the mounds in Mound State Park in Indiana.

The Grave Creek site boasts the largest mound of the Adena culture: it has a 295 foot base diameter, and is 69 feet high; it represents 60,000 *tons* of earth, and was built around 200 B.C. (It is tempting to note that dividing the height by the diameter of this mound gives .2338, which begs us to consider that it might have had astronomical importance: the ratio seems to mimic that of the angle of the ecliptic, which is about 23 degrees 30 minutes.) It was in the Grave Creek Mound that the stone bearing Phoenician inscriptions was discovered in 1838, ten years before Squier and Davis published their "monumental" study. This gives rise to several questions, if we accept that the stone is authentic (and many, if not most, authorities insist it is not) and that its placement in the mound took place during the Adena period (and not much later). It is only with reluctance that some archaeologists today accept these facts, although they have no explanation for them and describe the Phoenician stone as "anomalous." Conveniently, the stone itself has since disappeared, although copies of its inscription were made when it was still in the possession of archaeologists.

The first question is the obvious one: In what way were the Adena people and the Phoenicians related? By trade? Or was there some other dimension to the relationship? Were the foreign visitors or traders attempting to convert the Adena people to their religion? Did they leave the stone behind as a reminder to the Adena of their visit? Was it simply the work of one of the visitors with a lot of time on his hands, something to occupy himself perhaps? Or was it left there as a kind of claim, a "Kilroy was here" sort of memento?

The second question is perhaps more oblique: Why was the stone buried in the mound in the first place?

Is one of the skeletons found in the Grave Creek Mound the mortal remains of one of the visitors? The stone was found with one specific skeleton, wearing copper bracelets. Was the stone left there after the fashion of funerary goods, such as the ancient Egyptians buried with their kings? It seems safe to assume that the Adena people did not simply "find" the stone; the stone and the mound are of the same period.

And why that stone, and nothing else to suggest foreign influence?

The first question may be easiest to answer, although with a result unacceptable to most modern historians and archaeologists. When the stone was finally deciphered—after its identification as a form of Punic (Phoenician) used on the Iberian peninsula during the first millennium B.C.—the text was found to refer to the[36] mound specifically: "The mound raised on high for Tasach . . ." it says, in part, according to Barry Fell, and appears to be an astrological text. Thus, the stone and the mound are part of a single event, the stone left in its spot as a message to future generations. If Tasach was an Adena person, then why was there an inscription in an Iberian form of Phoenician? If Tasach was a visitor from Iberia, however, then American prehistory will have to be re-evaluated, since the Grave Creek Mound (also referred to as "Mammoth Mound") is representative of the Adena moundbuilder technology as a whole. The conclusion to which the diffusionists leap—and which the independent inventionists refuse to accept under any circumstances—is that the Adena (or at least *some* of the people identified as Adena) were not Native Americans but were, instead, Celto-Iberians from what is now Spain and Portugal.

One stone does not a complete theory make, however. In the first place, there are those who dispute Professor Fell's translation, some even denying the writing is writing at all, or that it represents any kind of alphabet. Others question whether the writing is a form of Punic, although Fell's arguments seem sound in this regard and the similarities between the stone inscription and forms of Punic seem almost too strong to ignore. Some philologists have rallied—albeit halfheartedly—to Fell's defense. If *only* that single stone had been found, we still would have been forced to confront a whole host of issues historical and archaeological. It would still have to be explained somehow, and the explanation would necessarily be upsetting to establishment archaeology.

However, many more stones have been found throughout West Virginia and Kentucky which support the diffusionists' claim that America was not simply visited briefly by a few scattered ships from Europe over a period of time, but was rather settled by foreign races hundreds, if not thousands, of years before Columbus. The social and political implication of this theory is that—in some eyes, anyway—it could be seen as devaluing the culture and contribution of the Native American population.

OGAM'S RAZOR

In addition to the strange Phoenician, Hebrew and other stone inscriptions or petroglyphs, epigraphers have been uncovering hundreds (if not thousands) of stones carved with simple markings that were once thought to be anything from scratches made by the plows of modern farmers to hoaxes perpetrated on the gullible. Epigraphers have been carefully collecting, photographing and cataloguing these stones, and in many cases they have been able to decipher their meanings. One of the pioneers of this type of endeavor was Professor Fell himself.

Barry Fell was a marine biologist, and not an archaeologist or historian, which is one of the reasons why his work has been avoided or attacked by professional archaeologists. However, his work in epigraphy and ancient languages was a direct result of his work as a marine biologist. Coming across many examples of petroglyphs on islands where he was tracing the routes of voyages made by ancient peoples throughout the Old World—in an attempt to discover how plants, animals and humans were dispersed globally—he realized that these ancient stones were probably important keys to his research, and that it would behoove him to have them translated or, at least, identified as to their language and country or race of origin.

It was only when he began receiving correspondence from New World archaeologists about identical types of carvings that he came to the inescapable conclusion that they were written by people sharing a common culture and language, and that these same people had traveled from the ancient Old World to the ancient New World thousands of years ago.

Although still not warmly embraced by mainstream archaeologists, the bulk of this evidence is overwhelmingly in support of the existence of ancient Celtic settlements in North America. The stones are carved in an old form of writing known—to those specializing in the Celtic histories of Great Britain, Iberia and northern France—as Ogam, a Celtic word that means "grooved writing."

Ogam is a in simple form that developed before the invention of paper. Like inscriptions on clay and stone in the ancient Near and Middle East, the writing style was itself a result of the writing technique: that is to say, due to the difficulty of writing curving lines and flourishes on solid stone or wet clay, the letters that compose these alphabets or syllabaries tend to be all straight lines and sharp edges, the easier to carve with an iron tool or a reed stylus. Sumerian cuneiform and Germanic runes are examples of this type of writing. The Ogam script is another.

Consisting mostly of straight, vertical strokes above, below or across a horizontal line, Ogam script was identified by an Irish monk writing in the thirteenth century A.D. Known as "The Ogam Tract" in the *Book of Ballymote,* this text had caused no great interest at first, since it was assumed—incorrectly, as it turned out—that many of the scripts mentioned were simple, childish codes and not serious alphabets at all. A kind of Rosetta Stone of ancient European scripts, "The Ogam Tract"—in which the nameless monk had tabulated various types of known alphabets, including even Egyptian and Numidian—was the proof, the "smoking gun," that the diffusionists were looking for, because it was evidence that their own identification of the petroglyphs was on target. One particular Ogam alphabet—known as "Ogam 16"—was of special interest, since it seemed that there were no petroglyphs in existence (in Ireland) engraved with these characters, which made it quite suspect in the eyes of the archaeologists.

The fact that the characters of Ogam 16 (albeit unidentified as such at first) were known to archaeologists in New England, West Virginia, Kentucky and other states would not be realized until the twentieth century, when archaeologists in the New World and the Old finally began comparing notes. Further, the existence of Ogam 16 in North America was particularly troubling, since the "Ogam Tract" was written some eight hundred years ago: three hundred years before Columbus's first voyage to what he thought was India. Either our Irish monk was possessed of tremendous psychic abilities or, as is most likely, he was privy to knowledge concerning a far away land and the Ogam script in use there.

The simplest solution to a problem is usually the correct solution: "entities are not to be multiplied unnecessarily," a familiar adage known as "Occam's Razor." Named after a Franciscan theologian of the thirteenth century, it is frequently cited by scientists and logicians. In the case of foreign races inhabiting America before Columbus and perhaps before the peoples we know as Native Americans, the evidence in the stones, the mounds, and the European petroglyphs provides archaeology with a simple answer, which we may in a spirit of whimsy call "Ogam's Razor," since it cleanly and manifestly demonstrates that there was wide exploration and settlement in America by races from across the Atlantic Ocean. That this evidence does not seem to be supported by the dispersion of Clovis spearpoints in America does not mean the evidence is invalid; it simply means that another explanation must be found to satisfy both sets of evidence. That archaeology has rushed too quickly to judgment in the case of the early American population scenario seems obvious today. Are the diffusionists right and the independent inventionists wrong? The answer probably lies somewhere between those two positions.

The number of ancient sites in America that mimic ancient sites in Europe is also startling. Circles of stones reminiscent of Stonehenge in England exist on the North American continent, as astronomically aligned as their English and

Celtic counterparts. Even many of the mound systems are now known to have been astronomically oriented, including those at Marietta and Chillicothe. Some Adena sites show circles of post-holes, evidence that wooden pillars instead of stone dolmens may have been used in America for the same purpose: astronomical alignments.

While the idea of astronomically-aligned monuments makes sense when one considers the reliance of the ancient peoples on agriculture (it is believed the Adena were the first Americans to cultivate maize and live in communities) and therefore on knowing the seasons, the phases of the moon, etc., what is startling about these discoveries is that it means the Adena were scientifically sophisticated enough to know exactly how to build something as complex as the equivalent of a Stonehenge in the American landscape, perhaps as long ago as two thousand years . . . or longer. (The jury is still out on the age of the Adena civilization, and books and studies published in the last forty years are all over the place regarding the advent of the Adena civilization.) Dating of Stonehenge itself is rather uncertain, with estimates ranging from 3000 B.C. to 1500 B.C. Thus, what is certain is that some of the prehistoric mound sites in North America actually predate the construction of Stonehenge and may also[37] predate that of the Great Pyramids of Gizeh: a proposition that would turn not only American history but world history on its head.

Recent studies undertaken on Adena mounds show that they were mostly ritualistic in nature; the difficulty in locating the remains of Adena living quarters and villages is directly related to this fact, as the Adena would keep the mound area clean of debris and non-sacramental artifacts and buildings. Thus, archaeologists find they are looking further and further away from the mound systems themselves in order to uncover Adena villages.

It is generally agreed at this point that the burial mounds were created for special personages or the elite, and were not the usual method of disposing of the dead, which was probably cremation. As is the case with the Valley of the Kings in Egypt, only high-ranking persons were accorded a full burial along with funerary items such as jewelry (mostly copper bracelets and what are known as "gorgets," small tablets with engraved markings of raptors, animals, or geometric designs) and pottery. Yet, in still other cases, mass burials are sometimes discovered, such as the famous Seip Mound in Ross County, Ohio which contained ninety-nine skeletons and a huge number of river pearls . . . thousands of pearls with a total estimated value in 1970 of $2,000,000. Along with the huge number of skeletons, there was an inner chamber which served as the final resting place of four adults and two infants. It is assumed that these were Adena royalty, but, of course, there is no proof of this or even if the Adena had royalty as we would understand it.

According to early researchers (and now debated), the Adena themselves were physically quite different from the later Hopewell culture that replaced them. Adena are referred to as "round heads" and, as mentioned above, they tended to be quite tall. The remains of Hopewell people show that they were shorter, and had longer skulls . . . in fact, the Iberians of ancient Spain, who purportedly gave us the Phoenician script discovered in the Grave Creek mound, were also known as "long skulls" or "long heads." It should be noted in addition that Iberian mortuary practices included the burial mound: in a design remarkably similar to those of the Adena moundbuilder culture. Of course, that is not enough information to create a scenario in which Iberians invaded America and wiped out the Adena culture, replacing it with their own, or, conversely, *were* the Adena culture themselves.

If those theories sound outrageous, they are perhaps no more so than some of the other theories put forward in the past two hundred years for the origins of the mound builders. Some have claimed that they were an errant band of Welshmen, others that they were Egyptians or, as Joseph Smith believed, Jews in Diaspora. There is certainly not enough data to support any of these theories, but the existing data do not support a simplistic Clovis migration scenario either. At a conference held in Santa Fe, New Mexico in October 1999 on the subject of "Clovis and Beyond," such mainstream archaeological types as Keith W. Kintigh were raising doubts and speculating about the Clovis theory. Kintigh is an archaeologist at Arizona State University in Tempe and president of the Society for American Archaeology. His doubts are, like many of his colleagues, based on the discovery in Monte Verde, Chile in the late 1980s of a race of people who lived in that part of the world about 30,000 years ago. The team of archaeologists was led by Thomas D. Dillehay of the University of Kentucky, and the people were identified as a pre-Clovis settlement and evidence of a pre-Clovis migration . . . at least as far as the southern tip of Chile. If the Clovis people crossed the land bridge from northern Asia and settled in North America 12,000 years ago . . . then the obvious questions arise: Who were the Monte Verde people, where did they come from, and how did they get there so far ahead of the Clovis migration?

As if that were not enough to encourage a re-writing of American history, there is the problem of the Pima and Zuni sacred languages.

The Pima Indians are descendants of the ancient Hohokam culture of New Mexico, based around the Sonoran Desert. (The Hohokam themselves were of Mexican origin, and migrated to New Mexico about 300 B.C.) At the beginning of the last century, an ethnologist with the US Government visited the Pima and stayed with them for about two years. During that time, he prevailed upon the tribe's elders to allow him to transcribe their sacred Creation Chant. He made a phonetic transcription and, using what he knew of Pima vocabulary, attempted to translate it. This translation was published by the government in 1908. The translation was woefully primitive, as the ethnologist—Frank Russell—himself admitted, making the dignified Creation Chant virtually unintelligible at best, or sounding like pidgin English at worst. And there it languished for almost seventy years until Barry Fell—using a Semitic dictionary—discovered that the archaic language in which the chant is sung is a form of Punic.

In his *America B.C.,* Professor Fell gives the original phonetic rendering as preserved by Frank Russell, with a corresponding Arabic transliteration, and then an English version beneath the Arabic.[38] The conclusion is inescapable: the Pima Indians had been using an ancient Semitic language as the repository of their sacred myths. The similarity of the Pima words to Arabic is uncanny, and it renders the Creation Chant suddenly quite intelligible; further, it follows the general description of the chant as given by one of the Pima elders. What is even more incredible is the realization that the Pima (like their Hohokam ancestors) reside in the southwestern part of the continent, about as far from Iberia or Phoenicia as one could get.

Professor Fell follows this startling demonstration with a longer exposition on the Zuni language. Without going into all the detail here, Fell's thesis is that the Zuni language is a derivative of an ancient North African dialect spoken by Libyan seamen around 500 B.C., a language which itself is descended from Egyptian, with Anatolian and Greek loan words. He goes so far as to link these seafaring Libyans and their language with Malay and Polynesian tongues. He offers as proof not only the spoken Zuni words and their equivalents in North African dialects, but the written language as well: discovered carved into stones in New Mexico. Fell does not offer these examples unsupported; he had his work checked by specialists, such as Boulos Ayad, Professor of Ancient Languages at the University of Colorado, who concurred with Fell's findings. He further offers charts that show the similarity (and, in many cases, identity) of the written Libyan alphabet as it was known over two thousand years ago to examples from Asian sources and rock carvings found in Iowa. These same symbols are found everywhere in the Pacific Rim from Polynesia to Chile, but also as far away as Quebec and New England.

In fact, during a dig at a Hopewell mound in Davenport, Iowa, some funerary offerings were found carved in the shape of an elephant . . . certainly not an animal with which the Native Americans would have been familiar! Fell believed that many of the more famous mounds of North America were built by these Libyan visitors, including the Seip Mound mentioned above. Some carved stone heads found there bear a striking similarity to the physical appearance and headgear of the ancient North Africans. Take these together with some of the epigraphic inscriptions discussed above, and one can easily see that the simplest explanation is that people from North Africa visited America—and possibly settled here, building temples and erecting stone tablets to commemorate their race—thousands of years before Columbus.

It should be emphasized that linguistic evidence is always the hardest to prove; armchair linguists are the bane of serious archaeological and historical research. This is even more problematic in the case of the ancient American races, as they left no written language of their own. Unlike the tombs at the Valley of the Kings in Egypt, or the Sumerian cylinder seals of Mesopotamia, or even the recently-decoded Mayan hieroglyphs of Central America, there appear to be no hieroglyphics or cuneiform or other writing left behind by the ancient North American peoples. No great statues with carved braggadocio, no dreary accountant's tables of figures, no secret spells in magical alphabets. Nothing. All that we have of a written record are the controversial petroglyphs studied so intently by Fell and the diffusionists, and if they were left by visitors to the American shores and not the native people themselves, then archaeology is at a loss to explain the function of the vast mound complexes in America.

The science of linguistics has its own rules and accepted forms of demonstration and proof. Fell was aware of this, and wherever possible he enlisted the support of specialists in this field. As time progressed, however, Fell became one of the few American experts in Ogam as well as the alphabets of the ancient Near and Middle East, and he was called upon frequently to translate stone inscriptions found all over North and South America by puzzled or bemused archaeologists as well as by amateur researchers and epigraphers.

The reaction of established historians, archaeologists and anthropologists to Fell's work has been mixed. Many disagree wholeheartedly with the whole diffusionist perspective, characterizing it as either racist, fascist, the domain of the credulous and gullible such as the Atlantis-seekers, or simply as "rubbish." Yet the sheer amount of evidence for the habitation of America by races from across the Atlantic is virtually overwhelming. If this evidence does not speak to the diffusionist theory, then—going back to Occam's Razor—what does it represent?

THE SWORD AND THE STONES

Probably the strangest story to emerge from diffusionist literature—and one even some diffusionists have trouble swallowing—is that of the visit of a famous European monarch to American shores (and from there to Kentucky and Tennessee) and of his subsequent settlement there, giving rise to tales of "white Indians" who spoke . . . Welsh. This has started its own firestorm of controversy as competing historians and archaeologists (and epigraphers) struggle to get the dates and the personalities right.

According to popular amateur archaeologists such as the team of Alan Wilson and Baram Blackett—*Artorius Rex Discovered*, *The Holy Kingdom* (with Adrian Gilbert)—King Arthur visited America on or about 652 A.D. at the time a meteor struck the British Isles. This meteor strike, they believe, is the reason for the devastation of the land of Camelot in the Arthurian legends, and the reason Arthur left Wales for the relative safety of Normandy. During that same time, according to the theory, one Prince Madoc of the Welsh court was at sea and found himself washed off course, finding his way to America by accident. Ten years later, he would return and tell Arthur of all the wonderful things he had seen in the land beyond the sea.

So far, so good.

Then—according to the theory of Wilson and Blackett—Arthur decided to send a convoy of ships in force to America. They landed, and made it as far inland as present day Kentucky and Tennessee. Arthur was killed in America by one of the natives, his body mummified and brought back to Wales, but not before leaving behind a race of white men who would stay to settle the land.

A competing theory has it that the aforementioned Prince was in reality Prince Madoc, son of Owain Gwynedd, a king of the Welsh province of Gwynedd who lived in the twelfth century A.D., and thus about five hundred years later than the legendary Arthur. Owain attempted to unite the warring Welsh kingdoms into a single nation with a single king—much like the Arthur of legend—but after his death a civil war broke out between his many sons about who would succeed him to the throne. Prince Madoc fled the war, and wound up in America.

Although Madoc's story does not appear in printed form until 1584, one Richard Hakluyt—in his *Principal Navigations* of 1600—claims that the story of Madoc and his flight to America was common knowledge long before Columbus' famous voyage in 1492. Famous Welsh historian Gutun Owain also wrote of Madoc before 1492.

According to the best estimates of historian and archaeologist, it would appear that Madoc landed somewhere at or near Mobile Bay, Alabama and wandered inland from there. This is based on computation of probable landfall due to ocean currents and prevailing winds from the British Isles, but also on some strange anomalies of the landscape of that part of the southeastern United States.

Along the Alabama River, south of Chattanooga, can be seen three large forts whose construction pre-dates Columbus and is "unlike any known Indian structure." According to the Cherokee Indians who were questioned about the forts, they had been built by a race of white men who lived in the area before them. One of these forts was found to resemble the birthplace of Prince Madoc, Dolwyddelan Castle, in virtually every detail. Located on Lookout Mountain in Alabama, its "setting, layout, and method of construction" is that of the Welsh prototype. Indeed, early European explorers to the region spoke of finding these "white Indians"—known as Mandans—and the strange language they spoke, which contained many Welsh words.

According to a Cherokee informant in 1782, Chief Oconostota of the Cherokee Nation, the Welshmen who built these forts had been at war with the Cherokee for many years and finally signed a truce in which they promised to vacate Cherokee land and head north, up the Ohio River and then as far as the Missouri. During this diaspora—or perhaps even before the truce—they had already begun losing their European culture and had become nearly indistinguishable from the Indians themselves, with some notable differences: their beards, grey hair, blue eyes, and the physical appearance of some of the women, which resembled European women more than native Americans.

The Mandans became a canvas onto which many historians, anthropologists and archaeologists would paint the pictures they wanted to see. Hjalmar Holand, in 1940, would see in the Mandans evidence of Norse explorations in North America, and the Mandans as descendants of Leif Erickson of Viking fame;[39] the famous—and controversial—Kensington Stone is considered evidence of Norse presence in North America hundreds of years before Columbus. This stone—discovered by a Minnesota farmer in 1898—is carved in runic characters and is testament to an attack on a Norse encampment by Indians in the year 1362. It has been attacked as a forgery over the years, but usually on flimsy ground (resulting, for instance, from ignorance of the type of runic used in Sweden and Norway in 1362); what one cannot adequately explain is why someone would go to all the effort of carving hundreds of runic characters into a boulder which is then left in the ground for so many years that a tree grew roots around it (as it was found) if the intention was a hoax or a fraud.

In the past few years, however, more evidence has been amassed to prove that the Kensington Stone—whatever it may be—is not a nineteenth century forgery. Many of the linguistic references used by its detractors were found to be inaccurate or dated; the carvings on the stone itself were carbon-dated to the right period by examining changes in the mica formation along their ridges; finally, Dr. Richard Nielsen—in the spring of 2001—published his findings on the stone in *Scandinavian Studies*, a peer-reviewed linguistic journal, in the form of a 75-page study representing more than ten years of research. The result: Hjalmar Holand was right. The Kensington Stone is genuine. The experts were wrong. History needs to be rewritten. There were Norsemen in Minnesota in 1362. Columbus did not discover America; he was only one of many to recognize a good thing when he saw it.

Yet, in other areas Holand may have jumped the gun. He dismisses the theory that the Mandans are descended from Welshmen; he sees the Kensington Stone as ample evidence of Norse immigration to Minnesota and the Dakotas, as if it would be therefore impossible to also imagine a group of Welshmen in the same territory. If the Norsemen arrived in that part of North America sometime in the thirteenth – fourteenth centuries A.D., then it would have been over a hundred years after the arrival of the mysterious Prince Madoc and his settlers anyway. Holand imagines that the physical appearance of the Mandans is more clearly Nordic than Welsh, based on nothing more than eye color (claiming that Nordic people have blue eyes but that Welshmen have brown eyes, thus ruling out Welshmen as the progenitors of the Mandan race!) but perhaps he is only succumbing to the racial theories of his time; he published his work in 1940, a year before America's entry into the Second World War, when it was still possible to write,

> The Swedes and Norwegians are of the purest Nordic stock and a relatively smaller number would therefore have been sufficient to transmit the physical peculiarities for which the Mandans were noted than if any other nationality had been represented by these early culture bearers.[40]

In the years immediately after the American Civil War, a British naval officer began a tour of pre-Columbian architecture in the Americas. Lindesay Brine wanted to see for himself the burial mounds, Aztec and Mayan pyramids, and the ancient fortifications of North and Central America. His report—published as *The Ancient Earthworks and Temples of the American Indians*—is a valuable resource in that it discusses the mounds (and the Native American tribes) rather dispassionately. Brine had no particular axe to grind: he wasn't an American, Native or otherwise, and he simply reports on the various mounds and other structures as an interested observer, albeit one with military experience and training. He noticed striking similarities between Central American mounds and those of, for instance, Cahokia, forcing him to consider that they were built by the same people.[41] This idea that the Native American populations originated in Mexico and Central America and came north is one that is batted about constantly by one group of archaeologists or another. There are some obvious similarities between religious art and mythology as well, enough to suggest a close relationship between the two groups if not actual direct lineage.

Brine goes further, to report on Mexican myths concerning a visit by twenty white, bearded men who arrived by ship in the years before Columbus . . . men wearing sandals, preaching what appears to be Christianity, and dressed in white robes adorned with red crosses.[42] One is startled at the similarity of this costume to that of the Knights Templar, men whose organization was suppressed by Pope and King in the fourteenth century and who had found refuge in Portugal, Scotland and other European lands even as their brothers were being executed in France, accused of heresy and worse.

Brine was also aware of the Mandan tribe, however, and reports on them at length, in the context of foreign races occupying North America before Columbus.[43]

He begins by discussing a Shawnee tradition that the mounds constructed in Ohio and Kentucky were built by a race of white foreigners, who were then exterminated in the course of wars with the Native American populations. It should be remembered that the Cherokee themselves have a similar tradition.

Brine then goes on to discuss an American cavalry officer, one Stuart, who came across the Mandans themselves sometime in the mid-1700s and was made their prisoner. Stuart claims the Mandans told him they were descended from a race of Europeans who had arrived in Florida and then made their way north to rest on the western side of the Mississippi once the Spaniards had landed. Stuart further claimed that another Mandan prisoner, this time of Welsh background, could make himself understood to the Mandans in his native tongue, thus opening up the great Mandan/ Welsh controversy.

Brine does not take a firm position on this matter one way or another. He does not agree that the construction of all of the mounds required European engineers; he does, however, believe that the construction of the more symmetrically-aligned mounds would have required a knowledge of geometry and engineering which, in his opinion, the existing Native American population did not have (although, of course, their ancestors may have had this information and lost it along the way, possibly due to an epidemic in North America referred to by archaeologists as the "Great Dying"). He points to the famous mound enclosures at Newark, Ohio as an example of this.[44]

At Newark, we have a construction of tremendous size. The first is a circle, twenty acres in area. Brine's conclusion is that it would have been tremendously difficult to create a perfect circle of that size without instruments, but allows that it would still be within the realm of possibility.

What he dismisses as impossible without instruments is the attached construction of a perfect octagon, containing an area no less than forty acres in size. These two constructions are joined by a path between them, again perfectly centered. These "fortifications" (if that is what they are) are of an advanced state of design and engineering. Brine feels that—without surveying equipment—the local Native American population (or any population) would have been unable to construct something of this nature. If we further examine those mound groupings that have astronomical orientation—usually to the equinoctial or solstitial points, much the same as Stonehenge in England—then we are forced to consider whether a race of beings (either Native American or foreign) having the scientific knowledge to create such impressive constructions could have arisen in North America . . . and then disappeared without any further trace than their monuments, and their dead. This is possible if we consider that, without a written language, there was no way to pass on the techniques of mound building once the Great Dying had begun.

The Mandans were eventually forced even further north, due to warfare with the Sioux, winding up as far as the Dakotas. The last great Mandan settlement—a town with old, European style huts and streets, and a fort with a moat—was located near Minot, North Dakota where it was visited by French explorer Captain Pierre la Verendrye in 1738. He noticed blond hair and blue eyes among the Mandans, but with evidence that the Mandan were the result of a process of intermarriage between the "original" white people—either Welsh, or Nordic, or perhaps some other, European, race—and local Native American populations. Yet, their mode of living was in marked contrast to the local cultures and involved a high state of agriculture and some curious religious beliefs which seemed to be a mixture of Native American mythology with elements of Christianity, including a story of the virgin birth of a great man; a flood, ark and dove; etc. They eventually succumbed to several smallpox epidemics, the first in 1837 and later in 1856, and were effectively wiped out as a tribe. 1838, of course, was the year of the discovery of the Grave Creek tablet, the year of the return of Joseph Smith's golden tablets, and the year of the publication of William Henry Harrison's fanciful study of the burial mounds. Perhaps the Mandan tribe held some important information about the pre-Columbian centuries of North America—as well as nuggets of data about the Norsemen, or early Wales, Prince Madoc, and maybe even the identity (and whereabouts?) of the putative King Arthur—but that information died with them.

What most Americans know of their Native populations is usually limited to genre literature and genre cinema. Cowboy-and-Indian movies were a staple in America since the earliest days of both Hollywood and television. Americans romanticized the role of the white settler and white soldier and even, to a large extent, romanticized the "noble savage" as well. They have seen their own history through a thick scrim of fantasy, fear, and even guilt, but still have not embraced the pure reality. Those that live near reservations have their own clearly defined set of racial biases. Academics take a more objective view than most—such is their vocation, after all—but even then their view of Native American history and culture is largely determined by a few axiomatic theories that are only now being tested by the weight of archaeological, anthropological and linguistic evidence. The Native Americans themselves are confused by some of this. Do they embrace the Clovis cult, and imagine that they all came from a single source, a single race that walked across the Bering land bridge thousands of years ago and dispersed throughout the Americas? Or do some tribes—holding ancient traditions that talk of white men or other foreigners landing in America and settling there long before Columbus—hold a secret belief that their origins are more recent than Clovis . . . or more ancient? Is it really a devaluation of the Native American population to insist that some of their ancestors arrived here from Carthage, or Iberia, or China, or Malaya, or even Wales or Ireland? There are those who insist that speculation about the mounds having been built by Europeans, for instance, implies a kind of racism: as if the Native Americans—"savages," after all—were incapable of building these complexes themselves. But that is not the point.

If the Native Americans are *descendants* of ancient European, Middle Eastern and South Asian races, then how are they devalued? It is accepted as gospel by nearly all archaeologists on both sides of the diffusionist/independent inventionist fence that the Native Americans did not originate in the Americas but arrived there from other places. How does saying they walked across the Bering Strait 12,000 years ago make them more unique or important as a race than saying some of them arrived by boat from Africa, Europe, or Southeast Asia?

The stories of the Mandan tribe certainly point to an interbreeding of native populations with "white" foreigners. The Native American traditions are replete with stories of ancient contact with European-type cultures, traditions from Central America and Mexico north to the Mandans themselves. By ignoring these venerable traditions and characterizing them as superstitious nonsense, do we not do a much greater disservice to the Native Americans, a greater "devaluation"?

There are sites on earth that are sacred to various religions and cults, as we in the West have been discovering and usually to our dismay. Jerusalem is sacred to Christians, Jews and Muslims alike. We know this, because we are all still fighting over it, and the question of Jerusalem and "sacred land" in general has led to devastating terrorist attacks by Muslims on Jewish and Christian targets worldwide, in the somewhat dubious context of *jihad*, a word often translated as "holy war." It has also led to the insufferable conditions experienced by displaced Palestinians, and their often obscene treatment by European conquerors. In Jerusalem, there are sites more sacred still, and the Dome of the Rock—a Muslim mosque built over part of King Solomon's Temple—is perhaps the ultimate target of religious fervor among Jews and Muslims alike, not to mention those Christians who believe that the Knights Templar discovered something important in the ruins of that temple, or that the Ark of the Covenant may still be buried there. It is a piece of land, nothing more, but it is invested with so much importance that tens of thousands have been willing to die because of it over the years. Tens of thousands? Perhaps millions.

There are mountains in Asia that are sacred to Buddhists, others to Hindus, still others to Daoists and yet still others to various animists and pantheists. There are sacred streams, sacred hills, sacred stones all over the earth. These sites are invested with supernatural power; and when the Europeans came to America there were already in place sites sacred to the Native Americans, to the Aztecs, the Incas, the Mayas . . . and to older races for which we have no genuine nomenclature, such as the Anasazi, the Adena, the Hopewell.

The early Christians used to meet in catacombs, where the dead were buried. Some Tantric cults held initiations and other rituals in graveyards in India. In April 1991 American archaeologists discovered catacombs at Casa Malpais, Arizona: tombs used for sacred rituals by Native Americans 800 years ago. The workbooks of the medieval sorcerers—such as those consulted by Joseph Smith—stipulate still other locations as more suitable than most for raising spirits, evoking demons, talking to God. The Chinese art of *feng shui*, so popular these days in Asia and the West alike, is a means of orienting buildings (and the furniture and decorations within buildings) so as to direct the earth's energy more profitably. The ancient Hindu practice of Vaastu is virtually identical in intent.

As Christianity became more sophisticated, it began the practice of building churches over sites that had been sacred to its pagan predecessors. Chartres Cathedral in France is one of these sites. The Church also practiced the ritual of siting the altar over the tomb or grave of a dead saint; failing that, they would have the bones or other relics of a saint embedded in a special stone that would be placed beneath the altar. The bones of the sacred dead were essential as a foundation for the ritual of the Mass. The Eastern Orthodox Christians invented the *antimensia*. This is a cloth into which sacred relics have been sewn. It is unfolded at the beginning of the liturgical service and lain upon the altar as a base for the ritual. For some reason, the Church understands the importance of these relics and has stipulated their absolute necessity for the performance of the core ritual of the faith: the Divine Liturgy, or Mass, in which the miracle of transubstantiation takes place, the transformation of bread and wine into the body and blood of Jesus.

If we follow this line of reasoning for a while—and it is a staple of the belief system of hundreds of millions of Catholics and Orthodox believers—we can posit a further instance in which some sites on earth are the opposite of these sacred sites, and some relics the opposite of these holy relics. We can even imagine that it would be a sacrilege of no mean dimension to abuse the sanctity of the sacred site: for instance, to build a prison or a brothel over the grave of St. Peter the Apostle. And if the relics of the saints are necessary in order to form a supernatural link between present-day worshippers and the great chain of transformation that can be traced directly back to Christ, then what of relics of murderers, violent criminals, satanists, rapists? Does a lock of Adolf Hitler's hair hold the same supernatural force as a lock of the hair of St. Anthony, different only in kind and not in power?

What if a prison were built over a site sacred to the Hindus, for instance? What if thousands of criminals were housed in stone and steel cages over the very place where once the Buddha slept, or the Goddess Athena worshipped, or where the Virgin of Fatima appeared? And if there is great spiritual solace to be had in close proximity to the remains of a saint, what contagion should be feared from the blood and bones of Heinrich Himmler, Josef Stalin . . . Ted Bundy?

Americans seem to be unconsciously aware that the mounds are repositories of something more than piles of crumbling bones. The famous Outlook Hotel in Stephen King's novel of horror and demonic possession, *The Shining*, was said to have been built over an Indian burial mound. The house that was the scene of terrifying paranormal phenomena in the film *Poltergeist* was also said to have been built on sacred Indian ground. Thus, our novelists and filmmakers seem to agree that there is a substrata of spiritual force—for good or evil—beneath the very foundations of America's towns and cities.

And those that believe in sacred spaces—Native Americans, Europeans, Africans, or any of the other races that make up the American mosaic—what do they think of the mounds, the standing stones, the carved rocks, the buried tablets, and all the other evidence of a culture, and a religion, that existed in America for thousands of years? What gods were worshipped in Kentucky? In West Virginia? Ohio? Indiana? New Hampshire? Rhode Island? Alabama? Georgia? In the thousand years before the arrival of the Spanish Catholics and the English Puritans? As America has systematically engaged in a program of eradication of its aboriginal population, it has simultaneously wiped out knowledge of its own origins. We are left with rocks, bones, a few scraps of ancient language and a few scraps of ancient myth and tradition, and we attempt to build a coherent story of the history of the continents based on these poor remains. If there are such things as ghosts in this new age, this new reality, then who haunts the mounds? What language do they speak? What gods do they believe in? And what do they want from us?

In 1909, the State of West Virginia acquired the Grave Creek mound, and began its maintenance and refurbishment . . . with the assistance of prisoners from the State Penitentiary at Moundsville, which is across the street from the mound. It is one of a number of prisons located at or near Adena mound sites, including the federal prison at Chillicothe which has housed Charles Manson and Henry Lee Lucas.

In 1950, the Garrison Dam was being planned for the Missouri River in North Dakota. The existing Native American populations were pressured into signing yet another treaty, this time ceding their ancient lands to the government. George Gillette, the leader of the Hidatsa tribe, broke into tears as the lands of his people for over a thousand years were signed away forever.[45] Hidatsa—and what was left of Mandan—sites were submerged in the flood, as if in fulfillment of an ancient prophecy about the end of the world.

Although the story of Prince Madoc/King Arthur as it pertains to the North American continent is not accepted by all historians, there are enough who find that both the physical evidence and the written record support the legend of the voyage as recorded in Welsh literature and the lore of the Cherokee nation. While some would object that the Welsh would be eager to prove that one of their famous ancestors had "discovered" America before Columbus, it is assumed that the Cherokee would have no such motive. In any event, the schizoid attitude of American archaeology towards theories of multiple migrations covering thousands of years and from several different points of origin is enough to confound and obscure any attempt at a multidisciplinary approach to the problem, which is what it requires. An objective team of specialists in such fields as archaeology, anthropology, archaeoastronomy, epigraphy, linguistics, genetics, and comparative religion (to name only a few) is needed before any kind of consensus on this very political question can be reached. Until then, we are forced to sit back and watch the experts duel with each other over their respective turfs, while the mounds, the tablets, the stone inscriptions, and the native speakers of ancient languages are ignored and consigned to the literal dustbins of history.

The existence of the Alabama River forts, their similarity to Welsh construction of the period, the existence of the Mandans and their possibly Welsh vocabulary (a datum that Holand excludes from his study), and the stories of the Cherokee elders—and the violent opposition of mainstream archaeologists and historians who dismiss such traditions out of hand as so much fanciful smoke—all contribute to this bizarre chapter in American historiography. For example, the Daughters of the American Revolution would erect, in 1953, a memorial to Prince Madoc and his expedition of 1170 A.D. at Mobile Bay, Alabama. . . .and then, a few years later, take it down again.

Yet, when the author visited Charles Manson's hometown, the city of Ashland, Kentucky in 1990—nearly a decade before the controversial claim of Wilson and Blackett that King Arthur had visited America—he noted at the time the existence of a "Camelot" supper club and lounge on Winchester Avenue . . . and had the stunning realization that a string of Indian burial mounds occupied the center of town.

ENDNOTES

1 Photo by Judson McCranie, CC BY-SA 3.0, https://commons.wikimedia.org/w/index.php?curid=106526835

2 Cotton Mather, *The Wonders of the Invisible World*, Boston, 1693, "Enchantments Encounter'd," section V

3 Alexis de Tocqueville, *Democracy in America, Volume II*, Part 2, Chapter XII

4 In correspondence with the author

5 Peter Levenda, *Unholy Alliance*, Continuum, NY, 2002

6 Pilot episode

7 See, for instance, the works of University of Colorado Professor Vine Deloria, Jr., himself a Native American and pro-diffusionist, who is quoted in Marc Stengel's article in *The Atlantic Monthly* (note 8).

8 The work of Dr. Svetla Balabanova—including the hair shaft test, which is a staple of forensic science—was detailed in a Channel Four UK broadcast on September 8, 1996, "The Mystery of the Cocaine Mummies," which also touched on diffusionism.

9 See, for instance, "The Diffusionists Have Landed," by Marc K. Stengel, *The Atlantic Monthly*, January 2000, where these facts and the arguments for and against them have been summarized.

10 Ibid.

11 Richard Rudgley, *Lost Civilizations of the Stone Age*, Arrow, London, 1999, p. 100

12 Ibid., p. 100

13 C.W. Ceram, *The First American: A Study of North American Archaeology*, Harcourt Brace Jovanovich, NY, 1971, p. 193

14 See for instance William F. Romain, *Mysteries of the Hopewell*, University of Akron, Ohio, 2000, ISBN 1-884836-61-5, pp. 233–253, for a peer-reviewed study of ancient American astronomy in connection with the mounds.

15 For more information on the Great Hopewell Road, see Susan L. Woodward & Jerry N.McDonald, *Indian Mounds of the Middle Ohio Valley*, McDonald & Woodward Publishing, Blacksburg VA, 2002, ISBN 0-939923-72-6, pp. 59–63, as well as Romain, op. cit.

16 William S. Webb & Charles E. Snow, *The Adena People*, University of Tennessee Press, Knoxville, 1981, p. 81

17 *Wheeling Gazette* (West Virginia), February 18, 1852, "Opening a Mound"

18 This is also a method known to European and early American cultures as a means of ensuring the corpse does not come back to life, i.e., become a vampire. See Michael E. Bell, *Food for the Dead*, Carroll & Graf, NY, 2002, ISBN 0-7867-1049-7, p. 170, concerning a grave of the New England "vampire cult" discovered in the 1990s in Connecticut.

19 Webb & Snow, op. cit., p. 81

20 Ibid., p. 74

21 Ibid., p. 79

22 Ibid., p. 281

23 Ibid., p. 90

24 C.A. Burland & Werner Forman, Feathered Serpent and Smoking Mirror, G.P. Putnam's Sons, NY, 1975, p. 55

25 Roger G. Kennedy, Hidden Cities: The Discovery and Loss of Ancient North American Civilization, The Free Press, NY, 1994, p. 233. Kennedy was a former director of the American History Museum (Smithsonian Institution) and a director of the National Parks Service.

26 Webb & Snow, op. cit., p. 93–94

27 Ibid., p. 95

28 Cyrus Thomas, Twelfth Annual Report of the Bureau of Ethnology, Government Printing Office, 1894, p. 583–584

29 See for instance "A Tradition of Giants," on http://www.greatserpentmound.org/ articles/giants.html

30 There have been many accounts of the Grave Creek Mound and its famous Tablet, and a lot of controversy surrounds the inscription. See for instance Barry Fell, America, B.C., Pocket Books, NY, 1989, p. 21 for his translation of the inscription; and Stephen Williams, Fantastic Archaeology: The Wild Side of North American Prehistory, University of Pennsylvania Press, 1991 pp. 82–87 for an opposing view.

31 Fell, op. cit., p. 315–316

32 Ibid., p. 11

33 Ibid., p. 310, and Marc K. Stengel, op.cit.

34 Fell, p. 303–309

35 See the historical overview of Roger G. Kennedy, Hidden Cities: The Discovery and Loss of Ancient North American Civilization, Free Press, NY, 1994, ISBN 0-02-917307-8. Kennedy was a former director of the National Parks Service as well as former director of the American History Museum at the Smithsonian in Washington, DC.

36 Fell, op. cit., p. 21

37 See for instance Robert M. Schoch, Voyages of the Pyramid Builders, Putnam, NY, 2003, ISBN 1-58542-203-7, for a lively discussion of the relationship between the pyramid builders of ancient Egypt and the mound builders of ancient America, and a corresponding defence of some of the ideas of the diffusionists. Dr. Schoch has degrees in geology and geophysics however: like Fell, he is not a member of the archaeologist union!

38 Ibid., p. 172

39 Hjalmar R. Holand, Norse Discoveries and Explorations in America 982–1362, Dover, NY, 1969.

40 Ibid., p. 278

41 Lindesay Brine, The Ancient Earthworks and Temples of the American Indians, Oracle, London, 1996, p. 189

42 Ibid., p. 409

43 Ibid., p. 95

44 Ibid., p. 96

45 Peter Nabokov, ed., Native American Testimony: A Chronicle of Indian-White Relations from Prophecy to the Present, 1492–1992, Penguin Books, NY, 1991, p. 343

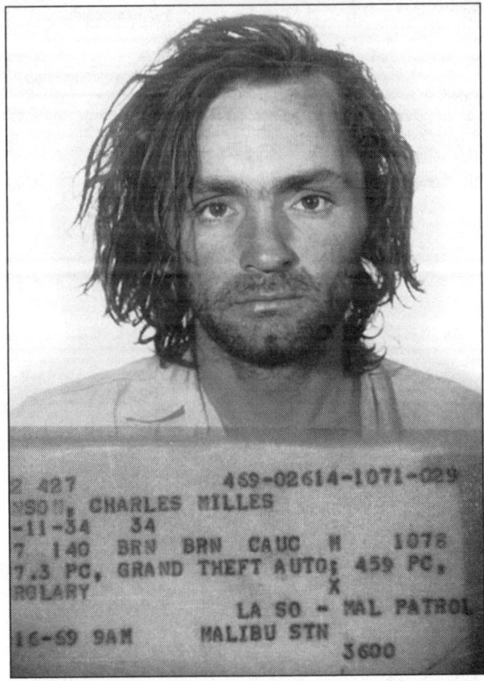

Charles Manson: A Creature of the Mounds—Born in Ashland, Kentucky under the name "No Name Maddox," Charles Manson (1934–2017) would later establish the infamous Manson Family cult in California, whose members carried out a series of nine murders at four locations in July and August 1969.

BOOK ONE: THE NINE

CHAPTER THREE

RED DRAGON: THE ASHLAND TRAGEDY

The old folk have gone away, and foreigners do not like to live there . . . . It is not because of anything that can be seen or heard or handled, but because of something that is imagined. The place is not good for the imagination . . .

—"The Colour Out of Space," by H. P. Lovecraft[1]

. . . a strong man with homicidal and religious mania at once might be dangerous. The combination is a dreadful one.

—*Dracula*, by Bram Stoker[2]

I was convicted of witchcraft in the Twentieth Century.

—Charles Manson[3]

If the Pentagon ever formulates the Manson Secret, the world's in trouble.

—*The Family*, by Ed Sanders[4]

The word "Kentucky" is a Native American word which means "dark and bloody ground." That is probably as good a name as any for a Commonwealth that has had its share of violent death, madness, and mania. Americans tend to think of Kentucky in terms of horse races, bluegrass music, or the ubiquitous KFC which is probably Kentucky's most famous export to world markets. Yet, even Kentucky Fried Chicken has its ominous side, its darker shadows, as we shall see a bit later on.

In 1991, there was an exorcism of a nightclub in Wilder, Kentucky (a small town near Covington, across the Ohio River from Cincinnati), due to a lawsuit by one of the customers.[5] Claude Lawson claimed that the owner of Music World—Bobby Mackey—was running a haunted establishment and that he had been attacked by evil spirits during the time he worked (and lived) there as a caretaker. Music World is built on the site of an old slaughterhouse (complete with a well underneath the building that received the drained blood of the slaughtered animals) dating back to the nineteenth century and, indeed, it was a site for satanic activity and a cult murder in 1896 when the headless body of five-month pregnant Pearl Bryan was found. Two men—Alonzo Walling and Scott Jackson—were arrested for murder after confessing to the crime. Self-proclaimed devil worshippers and occultists, they refused to tell investigating authorities the location of Pearl Bryan's missing head, saying it would bring the wrath of Satan upon them. They feared Satan more than death, because they were offered life in prison instead of execution if they gave up the head. They were hanged not far from the slaughterhouse, and Walling cursed his captors from the gallows in a scene out of Nathaniel Hawthorne.

Another young woman—a cabaret dancer known as Johana—committed suicide at the club in the 1930s, but not before poisoning her father, a gangster who had murdered Johana's boyfriend. Johana was also five months pregnant at the time.

The club has been the site of numerous murders, shootings and other crimes. It is one of the strangest clubs in America, for it boasts (if that is the right word) twenty-nine sworn affidavits by customers, employees and even local policemen who have been attacked there by forces from what Cotton Mather called the "invisible world." Once destined to be torn down in 1993 due to some strange accidents that the owner felt were paranormal warnings, it has remained in operation.

If, as suggested in the last chapter, some sites in America are sacred, then perhaps Music World is evidence that others may be just the opposite: unholy and profane.

> There were many other details to arrange; the consideration of a proper place for the operation gave rise to much mental labour. It is, generally speaking, desirable to choose the locality of a recent battle; and the greater the number of slain the better.
>
> —Aleister Crowley, *Moonchild*[6]

In 1996, a group of five Kentucky teens was arrested for the so-called "Vampire Murders" and made national news. Members of a vampire cult which numbered about thirty teens in southwestern Kentucky, they were reported to have drunk the blood of animals, and of each other, before finally murdering the parents of one of their clan and fleeing to Louisiana where they were eventually captured. The New York newspapers had a field day with this, of course. Reporting on the fact that one of the teens had called home to get additional funds, the *New York Post* headlined: *"Vampire" Teens Busted After They Called Home for Stake.*[7]

An interesting development for Kentucky, considering that officials originally wanted to name the state "Transylvania."

Odd bits of Kentucky's strange history went through my mind the first day I drove into Ashland. It was a frightening journey in and of itself. On the way down, through West Virginia from my first stop-over in Washington, D.C., my little red Ford Mustang was caught in a violent summer thunderstorm in the mountains. Shortly thereafter, I found myself skidding through a lake of blood in the darkness.

I was going to Ashland, Kentucky for several reasons. In the first place, it is the town where Charles Manson grew up. It is also the birthplace of another vile killer, Sedley Alley, who viciously murdered a beautiful and accomplished young woman, a Marine who wanted to be the first female Marine aviator.[8] Ashland is across the river from another town, Kenova in West Virginia, where serial killer Bobby Joe Long was born and raised.[9] It is in a kind of Bermuda Triangle of death and depravity whose base line runs right through the town in northern Virginia where another serial killer, Henry Lee Lucas, was born. *Appalachia.* As a native New Yorker, I found the very concept of Appalachia arousing feelings of terror, sadness and disgust. Dueling banjoes. In-breeding. Poverty.

About fifty miles south of Ashland, in another Appalachian town—Inez, Kentucky—then-President Lyndon Johnson announced the War on Poverty in 1964. He did so outside a small shack in the hollow, to the backbeat of television crews and print reporters. Twenty-eight years later, in 1992, that shack would still stand and its once famous inhabitant, Tommy Fletcher, *still* lived there. Only this time, the television crews would return to report that he and his current wife had been indicted for murder: for having children and then killing them off one by one for the insurance money. The body of their daughter, little three-year old Ella Rose Fletcher, had been exhumed and an autopsy showed she died of an overdose of an anti-depressant and had also been sexually molested. Her four-year old brother, Tommy Fletcher, Jr., was hospitalized only a month after his sister's death, showing the same symptoms of drug poisoning.

There had been a five thousand dollar life insurance policy on each child.[10]

The War on Poverty was another war we lost.

It had been more than ten years since my solitary investigation of the remote Chilean torture center run by fugitive Germans in the Andes mountains. In those days, I had relied upon public transportation to get me to the rural community of Parral from Chile's capitol, Santiago, and then a taxi—a taxi!—from Parral into the Andean foothills where Colonia Dignidad was located.

Nazi hunting on a budget.

Not exactly a James Bond scenario.

Now, however, I was riding in style. It was early summer in 1990, almost exactly eleven years later, and my research was taking me safely within the confines of the continental United States. I had my notes, a battered Toshiba T1000 laptop on the seat next to me, and a roadmap of West Virginia and Kentucky. I enjoyed long drives, as long as I had a fully-functioning tape deck and a ready supply of tapes with me.

So. What could go wrong?

As the afternoon turned to dusk in the hills of West Virginia outside Charleston, a spectacular storm front moved in. I was pushing the little convertible up and down the hills, trying to make Ashland before it got too dark, but Nature had other plans. Sheets of torrential rain made it impossible to see more than a few feet in front of me, and I had to pull over to the side of the highway. Ahead of me, eighteen-wheelers had the same idea, and soon the shoulder was crowded with vehicles whose drivers had decided to wait out the storm.

Thunder boomed and reverberated in those hills, shaking the car like a Matchbox toy and making me question, if only briefly, the wisdom of driving all the way out to Ashland from my home in New England rather than trying a more conventional approach. I could have flown down to any of the larger towns within a short drive of Ashland, such as Lexington or even Wheeling, but that would have meant a full day of changing planes at regional airports, since, as the saying goes, "you can't get there from here." Ashland—for all the world once a major American industrial town—is simply too remote from the rest of the United States to be approached easily from air or land or river.

I had to go to Ashland. I had convinced myself that only an on-the-spot confrontation with the place would reveal any of its secrets. I wondered who, in the days since the Tate/LaBianca killings, had bothered to travel all the way to Ashland, Kentucky to get a feel for the place, to find out if a town could breed a killer (á la Hillary Clinton's oft-repeated African phrase, "It takes a village to raise a child"), or if evil had other ways of propagating itself. To most Americans in 1969, the Manson story was a California story: more specifically, a Southern California, or Los Angeles, story. Conservative Americans—in 1969, in the midst of the war in Vietnam and political demonstrations and protest marches at home—felt justified in putting down the savagery of the attacks on the Hollywood celebrities as the sort of thing that happens in California. After all, wasn't California the scene of the "summer of love" and all that hippie madness? No one saw the Manson murders as the result of Appalachia crashing into Beverly Hills, like a couple of good ole boys in a battered pickup on a Saturday night, all whoops and hollers and jangling beer cans and rifle racks, smashing into a gazebo on a society lady's lawn. No. What neither the society lady nor the good ole boys would ever recognize is that they are both Americans; *that* only happens when there's a war on, and the society lady needs the good ole boys to defend the gazebo. When there is no war, the good ole boys turn on the gazebo and smash it to smithereens.

And there was no chance in hell that Charlie Manson would ever see the jungles of Vietnam.

All the records say that Charles Manson was born in Cincinnati, Ohio.[11] It makes sense that his mother, Kathleen Maddox, would have traveled that far up river from Ashland to have the baby, since it was born out of wedlock on November 12, 1934 to a sixteen-year-old girl. The father is believed to have been one "Colonel

Scott," about whom not much else is known. One can imagine the scene of a possibly much older Colonel Scott and the suddenly pregnant teenager in Ashland in 1934: the latter being rushed off to Ohio to have the baby in secret, away from the prying eyes of a small Southern town, the former wondering if his reputation among friends and family would have been harmed by the revelation, or quite possibly just the reverse. We will never know. It is believed that Colonel Scott died in 1954, although even this has not been officially confirmed. Colonel Scott's brother, Darwin Orell Scott, was only twenty-seven at the time Charles Manson was born; when he was butchered to death in 1969, he was already sixty-four. If Darwin was the younger brother, then Colonel Scott may have been in his thirties at the time Kathleen got pregnant. The military title "Colonel" is suggestive, but not conclusive. After all, it was Kentucky that gave us "Colonel Sanders," a man who was not exactly a war hero. Yet, oddly enough, there is no record of a first name for Colonel Scott, even though he was sued—successfully—by Kathleen in 1936 for paternity of little Charlie. Scott agreed to pay the princely sum of twenty-five dollars in settlement, plus another five dollars a month for Charlie's upkeep. By this time, Charlie was known as Charles Milles Manson. Kathleen had married a William Manson—a much older man—after Charlie's birth, and that is how "No Name Maddox" became Charles Manson. William Manson himself disappeared from Kathleen's life not much later.

Charlie wound up being parked with Kathleen's relatives in small towns all up and down the Ohio River—in Kentucky, Ohio and West Virginia—while Kathleen had her various adventures. One of these involved robbing a gas station with her brother, Luke, in 1939. The sibling desperadoes used soda bottles as their weapon of choice, knocking out the station attendant with them and robbing the till. Kathleen and Luke were apprehended and Kathleen was sentenced to five years in the state prison at Moundsville, West Virginia in the heart of burial mound territory. During that time, Charlie was sent to live first with a very religious grandmother, and then with an aunt and uncle in McMechen, a town a few miles outside of Moundsville, where the Grave Creek mound is located and where the infamous "Phoenician" tablet was discovered. Charlie was only five years old at the time.

Dr. Joel Norris, a sort of serial killer ambulance chaser and not the most reliable when it comes to names, dates and places (McMechen, West Virginia becomes "Maychem, Virginia" for instance)[12] recounts a story that Manson was forced to go to school in a girl's dress by his uncle, who thought the boy was a "sissy." (Norris also claims that Manson was born in Ashland; this is possible, of course, but I have been unable to find corroboration of this theory.) The "sissy" story is claimed as true by Manson, although others—such as his being sold for a pitcher of beer by his mother to a barmaid—are probably apocryphal.

What is known for sure is that Kathleen was paroled in 1942, took charge of her eight-year-old son, and led another series of adventures with drunken "uncles" in three states. In 1947, the court sent Charles Manson to a home for boys in Terre

Haute, Indiana, where he remained for ten months before escaping and returning to his mother, at the age of thirteen. Kathleen by this time had decided she had seen enough of her son, so he ran away again and began a life of crime, breaking into stores, stealing whatever he could find, until finally the courts got hold of him again and sent him, of all places, to Father Flanagan's Boys Town!

The 1938 film *Boys Town* starred Spencer Tracy as Father Flanagan and Mickey Rooney as one of his tougher challenges. Somehow, it is difficult to picture Mickey Rooney playing Charles Manson, aside from the fact that both gentlemen are somewhat on the short side. Flanagan's experiment was considered a kind of boot camp for juvenile delinquents—and, of course, had been made famous ten years earlier by the Spencer Tracy film, which won several Oscars—but Charlie didn't last a week. He and a friend broke out, stole a car, and made their way to Peoria, robbing a store and a casino along the way. His friend's uncle—a small-time thief in Peoria—began using them for small B&E (breaking and entering) jobs until they were caught once again, and this time Manson was sent to a more serious home in Indiana, where he remained for three years, until breaking out once more at the age of sixteen. He was apprehended after a string of crimes in 1951 and sent to another "school for boys" . . . this one in Washington, D.C., the National Training School for Boys, a secure institution which was run more like a prison and which was, indeed, under the jurisdiction of the Bureau of Prisons.

That was in March. By October, he had managed to convince the school's psychiatrist that he was trustworthy enough to be transferred to a minimum-security "home": the National Bridge Camp. There, things got only worse.

While his aunt had visited the Camp and told the board that she was willing and able to provide a home for Charlie, he managed to ruin his chances of an early parole by sodomizing another boy while holding a razor blade at the edge of his victim's throat. He was transferred to the Federal Reformatory at Petersburg, Virginia instead. While there, he was deemed very dangerous, and sent on to the Federal Reformatory at Chillicothe, Ohio on September 22, 1952.

One wonders what subterranean telluric forces were at work that day. Chillicothe is, of course, the center of the American Mound culture discussed in the last chapter. September 22 was the autumnal equinox, one of the important astronomical dates around which the ritual mounds were designed. A month after his transfer to Chillicothe, he suddenly became a model inmate. He did so well that on January 1, 1954 he was given a Meritorious Service Award. Then, on May 8 of that year—the same year it is believed his father, Colonel Scott, died—he was paroled back to McMechen (and the site of the Grave Creek Mound) to live with his mother. From Mound to Mound. At this time he was nineteen years old.

It is a mystery. What happened to Manson in Chillicothe, that he suddenly became studious (he was still illiterate when he was transferred there), learned to read and write and do simple arithmetic, mellowed out, and became a star "prisoner"? His psychiatric reports were all negative up to that point; even during the first month at Chillicothe the doctors were despairing of him, believing that he needed a closed environment and not the relatively "open" ambience of Chillicothe. Then, suddenly, Manson became a different person and maintained that identity for over a year and a half, until his release. That degree of conscious control—especially in a disturbed, uneducated, illiterate, violent, criminal, sodomitic bastard child of an unmarried, alcoholic mother—is suspicious, if not alarming. Was Charlie "helped" by someone at Chillicothe? According to Manson himself, in his own words, "I stopped thinking in 1954."[13]

John Gilmore, in his critically-acclaimed 1971 biography of Manson and the "family"—*The Garbage People*, retitled *Manson: The Unholy Trail of Charlie and the Family*—says that Manson met a "boy named Toby" at Chillicothe, from whom he learned hypnosis and mental manipulation. That may be so, but the dates in Gilmore's book seem to be wrong. He has Manson at Chillicothe as early as October 1951, but according to Bugliosi he didn't make it to Chillicothe until September 1952. Perhaps it is only a typographical error in Gilmore's book, because October 1952 is a very likely date for Manson to have met the mysterious "Toby," a person Manson refers to as "definitely satanic," and the only person of whom Manson ever speaks in tones both of fear and awe.

During this time, US government agencies were conducting medical tests among various inmate populations in America. Their most prized subjects were violent criminals—sociopaths like Charles Manson—whom they dosed with massive amounts of drugs to gauge personality changes, emotional response, and other parameters that have never been revealed. While sworn testimony before Congress in the 1970s is evidence that prisons were used for these experiments, and often the prisoners themselves were made aware of what was being done to them, the identities of the actual institutions as well as the doctors involved (with a few exceptions) are not known today. Those documents were shredded before testimony could be given. We will examine all of this in greater detail in the chapters that follow, but for now it is well to keep these questions in mind: What happened to Charles Manson in Chillicothe, Ohio in 1952? Did government experimentation extend from the adult prison population to reformatories for juvenile delinquents? Is there any other evidence that children were used as subjects or guinea pigs in medical experimentation?

The rain finally lifted and we all—my fellow drivers and I—began to get back onto the highway and make our way through the hollers and to our respective destinations. Except that now it was getting really dark.

In the West Virginia hills that time of year the fog and mist sets in with a vengeance. You drive up a hill out of the fog and for a blessed moment you can see in front of you, only to start back down the other side of the hill into more fog. It can be impenetrable, a thick soup of whiteness as dangerous as the darkest night. It was early summer, so the ground was still cold, and when it meets the warmth and humidity of the newly thawed air, the fog becomes the good man's enemy and the bad man's friend. It swirls around your car's headlights like the dry-ice smoke of a low-budget horror flick, and I remembered *Horror Hotel* and other campy fright films of the early 1960s that always involved a silent small town, shrouded in mist and fog, and maniacal killers on the loose.

I drove in silence, realizing that I had neglected to put in a tape and probably did so because it seemed oddly sacrilegious to play music in the gathering gloom. Or maybe it was because the victims in those horror films are always driving around late at night with the radio playing in the moments before . . .

There, in front of me, I could see a car pulled over on the shoulder. For a moment I thought the people in the car were in distress. The flashers were blinking, and I slowed down to see if they needed any help. The car's interior light was on, and I saw clearly a man and a woman arguing vehemently over something. I could almost hear them scream over the sound of my own tires and the wind rushing past the windshield.

I drove on.

Back into the fog, back into the night.

A little further on, there was another car pulled over onto the shoulder, but this time on the opposite side of the road from me, and pointing in the wrong direction. Again, the flashers were on. Again, there seemed to be some sort of altercation in the car which this time contained two adults in the front seat and at least two children that I could see in the back seat. The front of the car appeared to be damaged, but if the huge dent in the hood and front fender was recent or not, I couldn't tell. This was too strange; the idea of two such cars on opposite sides of the road on this miserable night, removed enough from each other that their circumstances were not related in any obvious way, was a little unsettling.

I drove on.

And then, suddenly, I see in front of me an eighteen-wheeler's rear lights emerging from the night and fog. I realize that I am probably driving too fast, or the truck driver is going too slow. I brake down to about 20 mph and watch in horror as the huge trailer veers sharply out of our lane into the oncoming lane.

As I come up to the same place, ready to swerve onto the shoulder if necessary, the truck angles back onto the right lane and continues on as before. Thank God there was no oncoming traffic as the highway is relatively deserted. Aside from the two cars that have pulled over, and now the eighteen-wheeler in front of me, there is no one else I can see on the highway.

And at that moment I notice there are dozens of red eyes staring at me out of the darkness from my side of the road.

It took me a moment to realize the eyes belonged to a herd of deer waiting to cross the highway, and as soon as that registered, a terrible sight changed the eerie drive into a tragic one. In front of me, and at the place where the truck had suddenly veered off into the oncoming lane, was the body of a huge stag, its antlers reaching up like beseeching fingers into the night, wisps of fog trailing the points like torn lace and fading memories.

There was blood all over the highway, and I had to perform the same maneuver as the truck before me, or else it would have been a toss-up as to which would have won the encounter: the corpse of a large deer or a little red Mustang convertible. As I drove sickeningly through the freshly-spilled blood of the deer I thought that such a sacrifice was probably a most appropriate welcome to the land of the serial killer and the mass murderer.

On the way into Kenova, West Virginia from Huntington—in an area surrounded by other towns with names like Hurricane, Tornado, Nitro, and the gruesomely appropriate Scary—one passes through the town of St. Albans. There one sees—or saw, in those days not so long ago—a video game parlor with the unlikely name of "Red Dragon." Fans of the novels of Thomas Harris know that *Red Dragon* is the title of the first in his Hannibal Lecter series, made famous by the movies *The Silence of the Lambs*, *Hannibal*, and *Manhunter*. In fact, *Manhunter* was the first movie made from *Red Dragon*, and is in many ways as powerful as *The Silence of the Lambs*. Readers may remember that Hannibal Lecter was a psychiatrist who was also a vicious serial killer. Apprehended, and serving the rest of his life in prison, Lecter would be visited by FBI profilers who would hope to understand the mind of the serial killer through conversations with this highly intelligent killer-in-captivity.

Lecter is a fictional creation, but the concept contains many elements that will confront us later as we poke behind the curtain of popular fiction to see the much stranger, and much more frightening, truth it disguises. Seeing the Red Dragon roadhouse on my way into Kenova—and, from there, a few minutes later into Ashland—only served as an omen telling me I was on the right track.

In January 1955 Manson married Rosalie Jean Willis, a seventeen-year-old girl from McMechen who worked in a hospital. Although he held a variety of jobs for a while, he could not keep out of trouble and wound up stealing cars and driving them across state lines. Taking stolen goods across state lines is, of course, a federal offense and Charlie was caught, as usual. Only this time, he had a pregnant seventeen-year-old wife. He drove a stolen car to Los Angeles, was apprehended, pled guilty, and asked the court for psychiatric help, for some reason referring back to his time in Chillicothe. The judge so ordered, and he was examined by Dr. Edwin Ewart McNeil in October 1955.

Dr. McNeil had been chief resident psychiatrist at Payne Whitney Psychiatric Clinic at New York Hospital in the 1930s, before moving to Honolulu where he held similar posts, then moving on to Los Angeles in 1944 and going into private practice while also working as a consulting psychiatrist to the court system in Los

Angeles. Thus, he should be considered eminently qualified to offer an opinion on Manson's mental capacity.

Dr. McNeil felt that Charlie—a poor risk under ordinary circumstances—might be permitted probation under supervision since he was now a husband and father. McNeil recognized that Manson had problems, but held out hope that marriage and fatherhood would have a socializing affect on the young man. The court agreed, and gave Manson five years probation with no prison term.

Unfortunately, while waiting for a hearing on another stolen vehicle charge (for which he would have probably also received only probation) Manson decided to go walkabout. He did not show up for his hearing, and a warrant was issued. He made it as far as Indiana before he was picked up in Indianapolis in March 1956, when probation was revoked, and he was sent to Terminal Island in California to serve a three year sentence.

His son—Charles Manson, Jr.—was born in March of that same year. On August 30, 1957, Charles Manson, Sr. and Rosalie Willis Manson were divorced.

THE MOTHMAN PROPHECIES

Due to the thunderstorm, the dead deer, and the whole bizarre gestalt of the trip thus far, I had only made it as far as Huntington before deciding that I should probably stop for the night and drive on into Kenova and Ashland in the morning, in the comforting light of day. I also did not know what facilities would be available in either town that late at night, so I found a small hotel in Huntington that had a room available for the night.

There is a certain gentility, a soft-spoken dignity, that seems natural to parts of the South, and which disconcerts Northeasterners when they confront it for the first time. A native New Yorker—from the Bronx, no less—I am always pleasantly surprised by it, even though I realize that it is simply good manners and not a reflection of a particularly enlightened or lofty state of mind or being. But, then, good manners are usually more reliable than lofty states of mind. The elderly lady at the reception desk greeted me warmly and kindly—not with false effusion, but as one human being to another—and I felt some of the tension of the drive slough off my nervous system like an old snakeskin. There was a lot of commotion in the place, and I discovered that a wedding reception was being held in the main hall as guests began pouring out into the lobby.

I made my way to my room for the night, arms filled with computer, maps, books, and small suitcase. Once ensconced, I pulled open the map and traced my journey thus far through the winding country roads of West Virginia. Huntington is only about fifty miles downriver from Point Pleasant, the scene of one of America's worst tragedies . . . and also one of its strangest. Covered extensively in John A. Keel's cult classic, *The Mothman Prophecies*, it was also made into a movie starring Richard Gere and released in 2002.

The basic outline of the story is that, on November 15, 1966, a strange creature was sighted about ten miles north of Point Pleasant, West Virginia. It was seen at night, was about six-six or seven feet tall, with what appeared to be wings folded against its back. It seemed to be male, and the most startling thing—aside from the wings—was the pair of huge red eyes, two inches in diameter, six inches apart on its face. It was clearly not completely human, according to the eye witnesses (no pun intended), but walked upright like a man. Thus was the legend of Mothman born.

Accompanying the sightings of Mothman were strange electrical disturbances, such as bizarre patterns on television sets, phones ringing with either no one at the other end or a kind of strange buzzing sound, plus weird warbles on police radio, etc. The thing actually seemed to fly, and in at least one instance was known to have chased a car full of people, and in another a Red Cross bloodmobile filled with whole blood on its way to Huntington, the town where I was now staying the night. As usual, the witnesses were average, normal people living typically American lives: people, that is, with no ulterior motive, no hidden agenda. These were not UFO enthusiasts or college kids out on a prank. The sightings began to take place quite regularly all up and down that mound-ridden stretch of the Ohio River—from Marietta, Parkersburg and points south—but centered on the town of Point Pleasant.

Exactly thirteen months later, to the day, the sightings abruptly stopped. Everyone in Point Pleasant remembers the date—December 15, 1967—because that is also the date of the Silver Bridge disaster, the worst bridge disaster in American history. The bridge, spanning the Ohio River between West Virginia and Ohio, was full of cars and trucks at rush hour, people out buying Christmas presents or going to and from company Christmas parties or just trying to get home. At 5:04 P.M. the bridge collapsed, causing vehicles and the people inside them to plummet to the icy river below. Forty-six people died, more than sixty vehicles were lost to the river. Two persons were never found.

And the Mothman was seen no more after that day.

John Keel wonders if the appearance of the Mothman was somehow related to the upcoming bridge disaster, hence the title of his book, *The Mothman Prophecies.* Are supernatural events harbingers of some impending doom? If so, how to correlate the appearance of a creature, half human and half bird of prey, to a failing bridge? There is either more or less to this than meets the eye.

There are many designs of raptorial birds among the Adena and Hopewell artifacts, and Keel mentions other mythical birds, such as the Indonesian Garuda, that have appeared throughout history all over the world; he even goes so far as to tie in the Indian burial mounds as somehow related to the phenomenon, linking them to the great burial mounds of Europe. As demonstrated in previous chapters, there is a distinct possibility that some of these mounds were either constructed by Europeans or by people using the same technology as the Europeans, and even the same (or similar) belief systems. The Tumulus ("mound") culture of Central Europe, for instance, was prevalent in the second millennium B.C. and was probably trading with cultures in the Middle East at that time, such as Egypt and what was left of the vanishing Sumerian civilization.[14] This culture was known, obviously, for their use of burial mounds and for their practice of burying valuable commodities with their dead, as was the case in the Adena and Hopewell cultures in America. Neolithic burial mounds are to be found all over Northern Europe and the British Isles, and later, in Ireland, these burial mounds were known as sidh and were believed to be centers of supernatural power and otherworldly beings.[15] The concept of sidh is famous in Irish folklore, and has come to represent the Celtic underworld in general, the domain of ghosts, fairies and other supernatural beings. According to poet and novelist Robert Graves in his infamous study of Celtic mythology, The White Goddess, the mounds were known as Caer Sidi or the "Fortress of the Sidi" who were the ancient magicians of Ireland. The Caer Sidi was also known as the Castle of Ariadne and linked to the Corona Borealis. To be buried there meant that the body was returned to the earth, but the spirit had gone to Ariadne's Castle or, equally, to the Corona Borealis.[16] There was even a British occult society based on Druidic lore which had, as its inner and most secret circle, The Mound Builders. Members of this group would figure prominently in the 19th century creation of the legendary British occult lodge the Hermetic Order of the Golden Dawn, and would include MacGregor Mathers, Allan Bennett and others famous from Golden Dawn days,[17] thus reinforcing the link (at least in the eyes of occultists) between the mound-builder culture and secret, supernatural forces.

The reader may wonder why Graves—a poet and novelist, famed for *King Jesus; I, Claudius* and other historical works—is referenced as an authority. Aside from the fact that Graves' research on ancient mythology is excellent, documented and dependable, the reader may be comforted in the knowledge that Graves was a close friend of William Sargant, author of the standard text on mind control and brainwashing, *The Battle for the Mind,* to which book Graves even contributed a chapter. According to Sargant's introduction, he credits Graves with having encouraged him to complete the work while he stayed at Graves' home in Majorca, Spain. As for Graves himself, *The White Goddess* was a canonical text of the European and American witchcraft revival of the 1970s, a book not read so much as handled like a talisman by devotees of the Wicca movement. Sargant is important to our thesis for other reasons, not least that he was also a colleague of Frank Olson, the biochemical warfare expert who was murdered in New York City at the height of the Cold War, a case to which we shall return in a later chapter. Thus, this strange nexus of mythologist and mind control expert is one of many reference points or "cultural traces" in our strange matrix where the spoor of sinister forces may be discerned.

The fact that the ancient mound builders were fascinated with birds of prey and carved their likenesses into their ornamentation could be seen as a reference to a mythical bird-like creature, which would "dovetail" nicely with Keel's passing references to the mounds as possible referants for the Mothman phenomenon.

Keel mentions another odd fact, something that would stick in the back of my mind as I worked at collecting data for this book. He mentions the discovery that Native Americans shunned West Virginia, and that no Indian tribes can be identified as indigenous to that State.[18] He refers to maps of pre-Columbian tribes worked out by modern anthropologists and published by Hammond in which the area we know as West Virginia is marked as "uninhabited." No one seems to know why the Indians didn't settle there, when the land itself would certainly have supported a large population in terms of fish, game, and vegetation. What is found in West Virginia, however, are petroglyphs and other evidence in stone pointing to the existence of wandering Europeans. There is also a heavy concentration of Adena sites northwest and northeast of Charleston, along the Kanawha and Elk Rivers, sites that date to the first millennium B.C.[19] Keel wonders if the Native Americans avoided West Virginia because of something they knew, and something the Europeans didn't know. Something inherently strange about the place. A sinister force.

After a few more hours of unanswered questions, scribbled notes and scraps of paper stuck into research material as bookmarks, fatigue eventually claimed me, and I fell asleep—fully clothed and with the lights still on—amidst a pile of books and maps and vague, unsettling terrors. The wedding party downstairs had dispersed into cars, limos and pickup trucks and a new couple was about to begin their lives in the shadow of ancient secrets.

Kathleen Maddox moved to Los Angeles at the time of Charles's incarceration at Terminal Island, evidently to be near her son. This is one of those relationships that simply defies any kind of rational explanation. When Charles was growing up in Ashland, it seemed Kathleen had no time at all for him and, indeed, for a while he lived by himself as a young teenager, earning a living by stealing. Suddenly, though, Kathleen develops maternal instincts and follows Charlie around the country from one lock-up to another, from one prison term to another. Charles is married to Rosalie, who is pregnant and who moves in with Kathleen while Charlie is "inside." This arrangement will not last long, however, and by March 1957 Rosalie is living with another man and stops visiting Charles in prison. Their divorce—begun in 1957—is finalized in 1958.

At Terminal Island, Charles is tested again by prison psychiatrists. This time, his IQ has climbed to 121, a substantial improvement over his score at Chillicothe. His verbal skills have noticeably increased, and he enrolls in a Dale Carnegie course, only to quit after a few weeks out of either pique or boredom. When he is seen as trustworthy, he is transferred to a Coast Guard station which is minimal security, but he is found hot-wiring a car in the parking lot and is slammed back inside to serve the remainder of his term.

He gets out on September 30, 1958, hooks up with a pimp in Malibu while under FBI surveillance, and begins running whores himself. He gets picked up on a forged check charge—shades of his uncle, Darwin Scott—and is arrested once again.

This, of course, is another federal offense. He cuts a deal with a judge, and is examined by Dr. McNeil once again. He is found to be a sociopathic personality, but without psychosis. (In layman's terms, we might translate that as "evil, but not crazy.") Dr. McNeil recommends *against* probation.

At this time, a young lady presented herself as the mother of Manson's unborn child. This turned out not to be true, but Leona—even though a convicted prostitute under the name Candy Stevens—managed to sway the judge's emotions, and Manson was released on probation once again. This was on September 28, 1959, almost exactly a year to the day after he was released from Terminal Island. He and Leona would marry that year, only to get divorced in 1963 when Charlie was again in prison, a replay of his marriage with Rosalie. In addition, a son was born to Leona and named Charles Luther Manson.

By December 1959, a scant two months after he was released, he was arrested once more by LAPD, but set free for lack of evidence on a stolen car rap. Instead, he began running women across state lines from California to New Mexico for purposes of prostitution—another federal violation—and wound up indicted once again after a man filed a complaint against him for raping his nineteen-year-old daughter and stealing her savings during a typical "Hollywood" scam, in which Manson posed as a radio and television producer. The judge issued a bench warrant since Manson had disappeared by this time, but he was picked up in Texas where he had been pimping and brought back to Los Angeles. An irate judge sentenced him to the US Penitentiary at McNeil Island, Washington, in July 1961, where he would remain until March 21, 1967. The vernal equinox.

During this time, Manson became involved with Scientology and it's this interest that has fueled a lot of the speculation concerning other influences at work in Manson's life. The creation of a small-time science fiction writer and would-be occultist, Scientology has been described as either a cult or a scam, or both, depending on which journalist, investigator or "survivor" you read. It has attracted celebrity membership, including John Travolta and Tom Cruise, as part of a concerted effort to win followers among Hollywood stars; it has also conspired against US Government agencies and been conspired against in turn. Its founder, L. Ron Hubbard, was a former Navy officer with a history of mental problems. He was a colleague of Jack Parsons, the rocket scientist and follower of Aleister Crowley. All of this will be discussed in more detail in the chapters that follow, as it bears heavily on our thesis, but suffice it to say that Scientology in the early 1960s was just coming into its own, recruiting heavily on street corners, and had obviously penetrated the prison system as well. An offshoot of Scientology is the Process Church of the Final Judgment, and Manson was believed to have been involved with the Process as well.

We are in a dangerous place here, because it is too easy to equate membership in an organization with that organization's blessing for every endeavor undertaken by the member. The fact that most of the Nazi hierarchy were born and baptized Catholics, for instance, does not mean that the Nazi Party was a branch of the Catholic Church. The fact that Manson seems to have been involved on some level with the Process does not mean that the Process is guilty—from a legal standpoint—of complicity in Manson's crimes.

Yet, there is another dimension of culpability that transcends a legal interpretation of cause and effect. To use the previous example, while the Catholic Church cannot be held accountable for the actions of its lay members, it is tempting to consider the Church responsible for creating the type of environment (authoritarianism, anti-Semitism, belief in supernatural events, etc.) in which such a creature as the Nazi Party could come to exist. We do not hold parents legally accountable for the criminal acts of their children no matter what the age of the child, minor or adult; but we routinely examine the childhood of criminal offenders to determine where the "problem" originated. A violent or abusive childhood is considered prime breeding ground for a violent and abusive adult, and particularly of the phenomenon known as Dissociative Identity Disorder (the former Multiple Personality Disorder); Manson's case seems to illustrate this.

Therefore, what effect do cults have on their followers from the standpoint of moral responsibility? As cults try to act as surrogate families for their members, do they not recreate the conditions of childhood and "mold" their members in such a way as to make them model "children" of the cult, carrying out the cult's agenda whether expressed or implied? The author intentionally uses the term "cult" here, rather than "religion," because a cult is generally based on a more recent revelation or illumination than an established religion: this means that the charisma of the leadership is still trembling from its contact with the supernatural forces it represents to its followers, and attempts to create a complete environment within which the cult members function, based on this revelation. Coupled with this is the understanding that organized religion—older, larger, more powerful—would frown on this new, unauthorized contact with the supernatural and would disavow any message received by the cult leadership, thus putting the cult in an uneasy position. Like most organizations who believe themselves vulnerable to outside influences, cults tend to become insular and to develop a siege mentality vis-á-vis other religions, other cults, the government (perceived to be a tool or instrument of whatever religion is predominant), and eventually the whole world. Further, cult leadership recognizes that its members are all former adherents of other religions, cults, etc., and that the pernicious psychological effects of the previous, competing religion must be neutralized to make way for the "new" revelation.

This has led to accusations of "brainwashing" or "programming," and the development of a cottage industry in "deprogrammers," who kidnap cultists—usually by request of concerned family members—and attempt to neutralize the effects of the cult's psychological conditioning by, quite often, using the same techniques the cult itself used in the first place.

Manson was involved enough with Scientology at one point to have picked up the jargon and to pass himself off as a "clear": someone who had passed through all of Scientology's "deprogramming" levels and reached the stage where previous social, environmental, perhaps even genetic influences no longer had any effect on decision-making, emotional stability, etc. He had a Scientology "auditor" in prison, another Scientologist called Lanier Ramer, who—Manson claimed—brought him to the level of "clear" or, more accurately, "theta clear." (Ramer would stay close to the Manson Family, even after the murders, as we shall see.) That he actually passed through all of these levels in prison, however, is doubtful, and it is more likely that he simply borrowed the language and the attitude of Scientologists. An indication of this might be his attempt to remain in prison: according to Vincent Bugliosi (the Manson prosecutor in the Tate/LaBianca case) Manson had begged prison officials to let him remain there.[20] He knew he could not adjust to the outside world. In fact, his prison reviews said the same thing. Regardless, Charles Manson was freed on March 21, 1967.

The drive from Huntington to Kenova and then to Ashland was undertaken on a beautiful summer's day, quite a difference from the night before. I stopped for a while in tiny Kenova, the birthplace of Bobby Joe Long, a serial killer captured in Tampa, Florida in 1983 and accused of nine murders and more than fifty rapes in a string of crimes known as the "Classified Ad Rapist" case. Long's childhood was oddly similar to Manson's in several ways, although Long was much younger (born on October 14, 1953). Growing up with an attractive single mother, who moved from place to place and had a succession of lovers, his earliest experiences were mirror images of Manson's. And where Manson was made to wear a dress to his first day of school, Bobby Joe Long had an even greater problem.

A congenital endocrine system dysfunction was responsible for Bobby Joe's breasts. By the age of eleven, his breasts had grown so embarrassingly large that surgery was necessary and, according to his mother, six pounds of flesh were removed from his chest at that time. Gender confusion seems to be another element Manson and Long had in common; Manson, with his short stature and baby-face, made to wear a dress to school, sodomitically raped by guards and other inmates at a succession of reformatories and prisons; and Long, with actual female breasts and associated problems related to the endocrine dysfunction.

But while Manson's experience of institutional life was devoted completely to prisons and reformatories, Long enlisted in the Army. It was an optimistic attempt at sorting out his life, but it ended badly. Six months into his enlistment, he crashed his motorcycle into a car while doing about sixty-five miles per hour. He sustained substantial head injuries, from which he suffered debilitating effects for the rest of his life, and which—after two years of bizarre behavior—put paid to his idea of a career in the Armed Forces. The neurological damage he experienced was severe, but went undiagnosed and untreated for more than ten years (until after his arrest for multiple murders). This was in addition to four previous head traumas, all experienced when Long was still a child and before his chest surgery. (The traumas were all related to falls, and do not seem to be the result of abuse by his mother or other adults.) The aggregate effect of all this trauma was to severely affect his nervous system, contributing to blinding headaches, impaired vision, and other symptoms.

The "other symptoms" were probably the most distressing. Long developed an enormous and uncontrollable sexual appetite, having sex with his young wife Cindy several times a day and then masturbating as well. He left the Army and had a job for a while as an x-ray technician, but lost that job when it was discovered he was making women undress for the x rays.

Finally, after a few more run-ins with the law, Long began a career as a serial rapist in Florida, using the classified ads in local newspapers to troll for victims. He would find an ad offering to sell furniture or other household items and would make an appointment to visit the seller during the day, when it was most likely going to be a housewife who would answer the door. He committed more than fifty rapes in this manner.

The murders were committed largely upon women he picked up in bars or, more accurately, who picked him up. He was angered by women who he believed were manipulating him, and he detested prostitutes (which seems to be a hallmark of serial killers), so these women he raped and then murdered for a total of nine victims. He was eventually caught after letting his latest victim, a seventeen-year-old girl, go free, and he was sentenced to death in Florida.[21]

Examination by Dr. Dorothy Otnow Lewis of the Medical Center at NYU showed severe damage to Long's brain in several places, and concomitant neurological disorders. Long was clearly brain-damaged, and his crimes must be seen in light of this fact. The thorniest problem of modern jurisprudence is judging when acts become wholly voluntary or wholly involuntary, and where to draw the line. Long's own testimony shows that he was aware that what he was doing was wrong, but was unable to control his behavior. Our usual understanding of the human will is that knowing an act is wrong automatically determines guilt when that act is committed. Since Long knew the rapes and murders were wrong, he is therefore guilty regardless of whether or not his limbic system permitted him any degree of choice in his behavior. But was Long *willfully* committing these crimes?

In order to answer that, we have to understand the degree to which all of our behavior is willed or automatic; this is the crux of the problem. It was the focus of one of the twentieth century's most ambitious explorations of the human mind—an exploration worthy of comparison to the search by Renaissance kings for the Philosopher's Stone—and it is the subject of a later chapter on the CIA's mind control programs. For now, as I passed through the town of Kenova once again on my way to Ashland, the question had to remain unanswered.

Crossing the Big Sandy River between West Virginia and Kentucky, one rounds a hill and suddenly comes upon the huge Ashland Oil plant at Catlettsburg, a suburb of Ashland. It is a surreal sight in the middle of the Appalachian countryside: smoke stacks reaching for the sky, atwinkle with blinking, different-colored lights and plumes of lethal-looking smoke, representing a combined production of diesel, gasoline, and chemicals: an ambience not unlike the *Blade Runner* skyline of Elizabeth, New Jersey. I suddenly wondered if I had solved the problem of the serial killer phenomenon in Appalachia: toxic chemicals from the Catlettsburg plant?

Due to Ashland's strategic location at the confluence of two rivers—the Ohio and the Big Sandy—and at the borders of three states (Kentucky, Ohio and West Virginia), it seemed like a logical place to build factories which could take advantage of the river traffic to move products in three directions. Indeed, the city brochure I picked up on that trip in 1990 characterizes Ashland as a town "Where Southern Charm blends with the Industrial Northeast."[22] ARMCO Steel was founded there in 1900, and there are nineteenth-century iron furnaces on the tourist trail, such as the Clinton Furnace, the Princess Furnace and the Vesuvius Furnace. The first iron smelting furnace was built in 1818, the Argillite Furnace. The Clinton Furnace—built in 1833—was actually the fruit of the efforts of the founding fathers of Ashland, the Poage brothers.

By the late nineteenth century, the railroad had come to town, thus increasing Ashland's profile as an industrial center. This led to the establishment of Ashland Oil in 1924, ten years before Manson's birth. In 1942, a new refinery was added to Ashland Oil's plant, this one specializing in aviation fuel for the war effort. By 1968, Ashland Oil's annual revenues would surpass one billion dollars.

But things were not completely rosy for Ashland Oil. As the Sixties turned into the Eighties and Nineties, Ashland Oil was hit with lawsuit after lawsuit by local residents claiming personal injury and other damages from the pollution caused by its Catlettsburg refinery. In May 1990, for instance, plaintiffs won a combined ten-million dollar decision against Ashland Oil, which was then appealed to the Kentucky Supreme Court. On February 22, 1993 Ashland announced a settlement of the lawsuits, which by now represented the claims of 740 plaintiffs[23] who had complaints against the Catlettsburg refinery due to air pollution. The terms of the settlement were not revealed.[24]

A few minutes after passing the grotesquerie of the Catlettsburg plant, I found myself sliding into Ashland, Kentucky itself, population 23,622. I parked the convertible near the Ashland Plaza Hotel, on Winchester Avenue, and deciding to have lunch there and examine my notes and the brochures I had picked up on the way. I definitely had to see the Kentucky Highlands Museum, which is not far from the hotel, and a few other points of interest.

Sitting down in the nearly deserted restaurant, I pored over the local newspapers, seeing nothing of particular interest or relevance. Ashland seemed quiet, peaceful, and even a little sad: like a party when most of the guests have already left. After lunch, I tried to visit the Museum but found that it was closed. I decided to take a walk around the town using the Museum as a reference point.

It was then, a block away from the Museum and my parked car, that I saw the mounds.

Central Park in Ashland is bounded by Central Avenue, 17th Street, Lexington Avenue, and 22nd Street. It covers 47 acres and was sold to the city of Ashland in 1900 by the Kentucky Iron, Coal and Manufacturing Company for the tidy sum of $32,500. Towards the 17th Street side of the Park, close to an intersection with Bath Avenue, one finds a string of five burial mounds, called "the String of Beads" by locals. These have been identified as belonging to the Adena culture, and dated to roughly 800 B.C. In fact, according to the *Archaeological Survey of Kentucky* by W. D. Funkhouser and W.S. Webb, and quoted in the Kentucky Highlands Museum brochure, "No city in the state of Kentucky . . . contains so much evidence of prehistoric occupation as the city of Ashland."[25]

If so, much of that evidence is already long gone. The mounds themselves had been opened by a Dr. J.C. Montmollin in 1870 and "found to contain human bones and other artifacts."[26] My attempts to locate and identify these artifacts met with no success. My communications with the Museum itself did not result in any additional information beyond that of the town's official brochure, although they have an exhibit dedicated to the American Indian presence in town from the Adena, Hopewell and Fort Ancient periods. In fact, most of my attempts at communication with Ashland officials and residents met with indifference bordering on hostility. I put that down to my Bronx pedigree, however, and do not hold it against them. After all, I know people in Connecticut and Rhode Island who firmly believe that the City of New York is the Abyss of Darkness and the Mother of All Evils, so how can I blame Ashlanders from thinking otherwise?

I knew nothing of Indian burial mounds in 1990 when I visited Ashland, but their bizarre presence in Central Park got me thinking. "This is where Charles Manson grew up," I told myself, gazing around at the trees, the mounds, the silent streets. "Did Charlie play on these mounds like the other children? Did he hear about Indian legends and the human bones found in the mounds? Did mothers frighten their children with tales of buried Indian warriors coming back to life? What was it like growing up here in the 1930s?"

Standing at the corner of 17th Street, I looked around and found a plaque describing the mounds. The plaque, a little weathered, reads,

> String of Beads. These mounds are evidence of prehistoric occupation of this area. The mounds which remain here are thought to have been part of a series of mounds, which from the air resembled a string of beads, ranging in an irregular line from 17th Street to 21st Street. In the 1920s several of the mounds were opened and found to be burial sites. The archaeologist's conclusion was that the area was once the site of an ancient village. These mounds were restored in 1984 by Troop 154 B.S.A.

Dr. J. C. Montmollin opened some of the mounds in 1870. Then, in the 1920s, they were opened again. So, the mounds were opened and reopened over a period of some fifty years and then, sixty years after some of the mounds were opened by an archaeologist, they were restored to their present condition by a troop of Boy Scouts. One wonders what had happened to the mounds in the meantime, and if the others had been opened surreptitiously. It's hard to imagine just how that would have been accomplished, as the mounds are in the park, which is in the center of town. But it seems someone was nervous.

In 1919, a huge, Queen Anne style home was moved entire from Winchester Avenue and 17th Street to its present location at Central Avenue and 16th Street by a team of mules. The town brochure acknowledges that this was "an amazing feat of engineering."[27] Anyone seeing the building would have to agree. This is not a ranch-style home lifted onto a flatbed truck and shipped over state roads with little red flags at the corners and "Wide Load" signs. No; this is a very large, three storey, brick and stone edifice replete with towers and turrets. And it was only moved three blocks away from its original position. The brochure does not say why, but it does refer to the house as "eclectic" and makes mention of the one factor that caught my attention immediately. Alone of all the houses I was able to see in Ashland, the house at 1600 Central Avenue is the one sporting griffins. According once more to the town brochure, "Atop the house are two lion-like statues as griffins, which legendarily ward off evil spirits."[28]

I see.

I could not help wondering why someone would go to all that effort to move such a monstrosity only three blocks, when I noticed that its new placement was much closer to the "String of Beads" than before. That's when I asked myself the obvious question: Why the griffins?

There are two of these creatures, one at either end of the roof. They looked to me less like lions than dragons, with long serpentine necks and bat-like wings, in a fierce expression, mouths open, long tongues sticking out. The griffins look outward from the roof, as if to protect the house from outside forces. I was reminded of the Ark of the Covenant and its two seraphim, which are also winged creatures and which also are situated at either side of the ark's cover, or roof. The town brochure was quite explicit in identifying the creatures as griffins, and as explaining their purpose as the warding off of "evil spirits."

Evil spirits in Ashland, Kentucky?

Kenneth Grant, a serious and well-respected English occultist, author of numerous books on Aleister Crowley, Austin Osman Spare, H.P. Lovecraft, and ceremonial magic that are a fascinating, sometimes exhilarating and sometimes bewildering mixture of western hermeticism and African and Asian occult practices, has this to say:

> The Narragansetts of the New England region, the Adena of Ohio, and the Lenape dog-rib Indians of California are known to have forged links with entities spawned in the Mauve Zone, and in the outer rings of Yuggoth.[29]

(The "Mauve Zone" is Grant's term for the Abyss, to be discussed in more detail in the next chapter; it is also, in Grant's words, "a supreme power-zone of magical energy."[30] The Abyss, for purposes of this citation, may be considered as the realm of demonic beings. The "outer rings of Yuggoth" are a reference to Lovecraft's tales.)

If Funkhouser and Webb are to be believed, Ashland was the busiest Adena site in the Commonwealth. The five burial mounds in Central Park would be the tip of an ancient iceberg of mounds and other earthworks, many of which were destroyed as the town was growing.

Ashland was founded by two Revolutionary War officers, the Poage Brothers, George and Robert, in 1786. (The town brochure is swift to point out that the Poage family was of Scotch-Irish descent.) They established what was then called Poage's Landing on the Ohio River, the town that would later become Ashland. The Poage family was in complete control of the town for more than fifty years. In 1854, the Poages joined with some Ohio developers (the brothers Hugh, Thomas and John Means) and formed the Kentucky Iron, Coal and Manufacturing Company . . . the same company that sold the burial mounds to the newly incorporated city of Ashland. The city was named after the home of statesman Henry Clay, a native Virginian who moved to Kentucky when he was twenty, married into Kentucky society, and was the veteran of a few presidential campaigns, which he lost, although he was better known as a US Senator deeply involved in the slavery issue.

In 1854, the same year that Kentucky Iron was formed and the city incorporated as Ashland, the town itself was designed. With Central Park and the mounds in the middle, and streets running parallel and perpendicular to it, Ashland became a typical small American town, albeit with the unmarked graves of ancient Adena people at its heart. What became of the rest of the Adena sites is unknown, but it is safe to speculate that there were many more mounds in the general vicinity of the "String of Beads" and that some of the houses in town are probably built on top of them. If there are evil spirits in Ashland, one wonders if they would be the souls of the ancient dead whose millennia-old sleep has been disturbed by businessmen and Boy Scouts.

Or by the blood sacrifice of Neal, Craft and Ellis.

THE ASHLAND TRAGEDY

One of the things the town brochure will not tell you is that Ashland was the site of a horrible crime which was committed in 1881 and which had repercussions for many years after. It reads today like the worst of modern mass murders, and indeed the killings radiated outward from the original deaths to encompass a few more before all the dust had settled. While researching the town in the Ashland Public Library that day, I came across the following story. The details are so unbelievable that the Cincinnati newspapers at the time were convinced that something about it wasn't quite right.[31]

On December 24, 1881—Christmas Eve—a house was discovered on fire at what is now Carter Avenue and 28th Street, about seven blocks from the mounds. It was a little before dawn, about 5 A.M., and the home of the J.W. Gibbons family was being consumed by flames. Neighbors rushed to the home, smashed open windows, and dived into the house to save whom they could, but it was to no avail.

The three children were already dead.

Fannie Gibbons was only 14; her brother, Robert, was 17 and a cripple; their friend, Emma Carico, was 15. Both girls had been raped. The skulls of all three were smashed in. The fire had obviously been set to destroy the evidence, but the children's bodies were found before they could be incinerated. In addition, an axe and a crowbar were discovered nearby. Both were found to contain traces of blood and hair.

The day before, Mrs. Gibbons left Ashland in the company of her youngest son, Sterling, aged 11, to go to visit one of her daughters in Ironton, Ohio, which is directly across the river from Ashland. Mr. Gibbons was working in West Virginia at the time, and had left Ashland only the week before. Mrs. Gibbons, concerned about leaving her fourteen-year-old daughter and crippled son home alone, asked Emma Carico to stay with them. Emma was fifteen, and thus a year older than Fannie Gibbons.

Mrs. Gibbons was due back in Ashland that day, having planned to spend only December 23rd in Ironton with her married daughter and to return to Ashland to be with her children on Christmas Eve. Her husband was in Hamlin, West Virginia and had an alibi for the night of the murders. Hamlin is about twenty miles east of Huntington, so it was a good distance to travel those days, though it was briefly rumored that Gibbons had actually committed the murders himself.

That the crimes were hideous and unthinkable is accepted by all who reported on the event. A Christmas Eve double rape and triple murder of children: what could be more horrible? One is forced to imagine the terror of the crippled Robert Gibbons, seventeen years old and helpless, being made to witness the rape of his sister and her friend and their subsequent murders. One perhaps hopes that Robert was the first to be killed, early on before the rapes of the two girls, but the savagery of the attacks says otherwise. More than one person had to be involved, and like a pack of dogs they probably cornered their prey and took their time, then torched the house.

The three children were buried in a single grave in Ashland Cemetery, after a funeral service at Methodist Episcopal Church, South. The church was packed for the service; not only were the Gibbons well known in Ashland, but the dimensions of the crime shocked and wounded the whole town.

And there were no suspects.

John Means, acting mayor of Ashland and member of the Means family that had founded, with the Poages, the modern city of Ashland, decided to post a reward for the capture of the killers. The reward money eventually reached the sum of three thousand dollars, which was a substantial amount in 1881. It attracted detectives to Ashland from all three states—Ohio, Kentucky and West Virginia—to help in the search for the murderers.

Finally, on January 2, 1882 a break in the case came, with the confession of one George Ellis. This confession was to be the single most controversial element of the entire affair.

Ellis was seen in a store talking about the murders and acting very nervously. He was a neighbor of the Gibbons, and knew them as well as most people did in Ashland. On the suspicion that Ellis knew more than he was letting on, he was taken to the room of US Deputy Marshall Heflin at the Aldine Hotel, where he eventually confessed to the crime and in the process implicated two other men—William Neal and Ellis Craft—saying that they forced him to participate.

William Neal was arrested at his job in a rolling mill, Ellis Craft in his rooming house. Both were brought to jail in Catlettsburg and were put in the same cell as their accuser, George Ellis. Both Neal and Craft had denied having anything to do with the deaths of the three children, and when George Ellis was put in their cell he eventually recanted his confession as well.

Ellis seems to have been someone easily intimidated. First, he claimed he was coerced into confessing by Marshall Heflin; then he recanted his testimony after spending some time in the same jail cell as his accusers. His whole problem began because he was seen to be nervous whenever the subject of the murders came up and was acting in a suspicious manner.

This was 1882. The forensics labs, DNA testing, even fingerprint evidence of the twentieth century were still a long way off. Neal and Craft were being accused on nothing more than the confession of George Ellis, and George Ellis' confession was suspect anyway. While he may have had something to do with the crimes, what is not known is how much Ellis may have been coached by Marshall Heflin. After all, there was a three thousand dollar reward at stake. We are not sure of the sequence of events, due to the sketchy reports in the Ashland sources. Did George Ellis testify that the girls had been raped *before* this had been determined by the three doctors performing the post-mortems?

Or was it only after the medical examination, and was this information communicated to Heflin who then suggested it to Ellis?

The Cincinnati newspapers thought there was something fishy about the whole thing. The children's father decamps to West Virginia a week before the murders, a week before Christmas. The children's mother goes to Ironton, Ohio the night before Christmas Eve. Their remaining two children, plus one neighbor's girl, are left alone in the house and are killed within hours of the mother's departure.

The house was torched about 5 A.M., which means the killers were on the premises until that time. It doesn't seem likely that the parents were involved in the crime, for the simple fact that their home was destroyed in the commission of it. And Ashland was, and is, a small town where everyone knew everyone else, so it made sense that the killers were known to the children, who probably let them into the house not suspecting it would be the last kindness they would ever extend. Further, the neighbors would have known—and commented upon—the fact that the children were being left alone. Mrs. Gibbons had gone to her neighbor to ask permission for Emma Carico to stay the night with her two children, thus alerting the neighbor to her plans for the evening. Did the information that the children were home alone emanate from that discussion with Emma Carico's parents? Was it a last minute decision, or had the trip to Ironton been planned in advance? If the trip had been planned some time in advance, then the circle of suspects would grow to include anyone in the neighborhood known to the Gibbons family and would also tend to support a theory that the crimes were premeditated. Had the trip been a last minute decision, however, that would both narrow the range of suspects considerably as well as demonstrate that the crimes were planned and committed in haste.

But time was running out. Rumors began to spread that some people in Ashland were preparing to take matters into their own hands. In their minds, Ellis, Craft and Neal were already guilty, and sentence had been passed. Anxious officials decided to spirit the three men away from Catlettsburg before a mob could descend on the jail. They boarded the steamer *Mountain Girl* in an attempt to take the prisoners to Maysville to await trial. At that same moment, the train from Ashland pulled into the Catlettsburg station, and a swarm of Ashlanders made for the courthouse.

According to reports in the local papers, the Ashlanders had simply arrived to witness the hearing, or examination trial as it was called, but the judge and the other officials feared the worst. *Mountain Girl* could not get up steam fast enough, so the prisoners under heavy guard boarded the Catlettsburg ferry instead. The ferry made it safely to Maysville, but not before a crowd of Ashlanders commandeered the *Mountain Girl*—which had finally developed a head of steam—and engaged in pursuit of the Catlettsburg ferry.

The ferry managed to meet another steamer, the *Mountain Boy*, and the prisoners were safely transferred to that steamer, which arrived safely in the town of Maysville, about halfway up river to Cincinnati.

Naturally, the Ashlanders were outraged. This was an insult to their honor! How could anyone believe that they would form a mob and lynch the three suspects? The authorities were telling the world that the three men could only be safe in another town, in another county, eighty miles away. The appropriately-named Huff, editor of the local Ashland paper at the time, also complained that the prisoners could more easily escape in Maysville than in Ashland, thus adding injury to insult. A special committee was formed to convince Circuit Court Judge George N. Brown that the prisoners would be safe in Ashland, and that in any event there had been no intention to enforce mob rule in Ashland or anywhere in Boyd County.

Major John R. Allen was put in charge of the Lexington Guards, the McCreary Guards and the Mason County Guards and marched to Ashland, the prisoners under guard. A special term of the Boyd County Circuit Court was held, and grand jury indictments were brought down against the three men: conspiracy and murder for Neal and Craft, and three counts of murder for George Ellis, after five days of deliberations. The grand jury itself reads like a roll call of Ashland history, and included Hugh Means (of Kentucky Iron fame), D.D. Geiger (the area where the children were murdered was known at the time as the "Geiger Extension") and R. Hatfield, a surname synonymous with Kentucky feuds. The first trial—for William Neal—began on January 16, for the murder of Emma Carico.

The trial lasted eight days, and Neal was convicted of the crime and sentenced to death. Ellis Craft's trial lasted ten days, and ended with the same result. Their execution by hanging was set for Friday, April 14 of that year "between sunrise and sunset." George Ellis's trial was postponed to the regular term of the Boyd County Circuit Court in May, a month after the scheduled executions. The three men were then taken to Lexington, Kentucky by armed troops.

Appeals were set in motion for Neal and Craft, and their executions were postponed. They then were reported to have attempted an escape from the Lexington jail on May 22, 1882, but were caught and brought back to the lock-up. Both the appeals and the escape attempt made the Ashlanders nervous that perhaps justice would not be done.

A week after the escape attempt by Neal and Craft, George Ellis was brought back to Catlettsburg to stand trial. He was arraigned on May 30, 1882, and his trial only lasted two and a half days before he was found guilty of murder. His penalty, however, was life imprisonment. While it is not stated in any of the documents I can find, this lighter sentence may be due to a deal Ellis struck with the authorities for bringing in Neal and Craft and confessing to the crime.

No matter, the Ashlanders did not take the sentence well.

The next night, eighteen masked men marched on the railroad station in Ashland and commandeered the train to take them to Catlettsburg, where Ellis was being held. The men broke into the jail and removed Ellis, taking him back on the train to Ashland.

He was hanged from the branches of a sycamore tree at 28th Street near Carter Avenue, not far from the scene of the murders themselves. His body was left there all night and into the next day.

Mob rule *did* reign in Ashland that night, and obviously the authorities were right to be afraid.

They didn't know *how* right.

Neal and Craft thought for a moment that they had lucked out. They won new trials, set for October of that year during the regular term of the Circuit Court. Once again, they were brought to Catlettsburg under armed guard, but this time with *five companies* of state militia and an artillery piece! The Governor of Kentucky, G. W. Blackburn—obviously still smarting over the lynching of George Ellis four months earlier, and worried about the effect of the critical Cincinnati newspaper columns—threatened that he would kill every person in Boyd County if necessary in order to uphold the "dignity of the law" in protecting the prisoners. Ashland was outraged at this bald threat, and hanged the Governor in effigy . . . from branches of the same sycamore tree from which George Ellis had been hanged only months earlier.

In this environment of open hostility, the lawyers for Neal and Craft managed to convince the court that they needed a change of venue. A new trial date was set for the following February in Carter County. The troops were once again ordered to guard the prisoners on their way back to Lexington jail.

That night, however, things began to get ugly. The new trial, the change of venue, and the removal of the prisoners to Lexington made Ashlanders believe that they were losing control of the situation. The murders had taken place in their town, committed—they believed—by their own people against their own children. It seemed to many that Ashland itself should be in charge of the case, the trial, and the execution of sentence. To everyone's way of thinking, Neal and Craft were already guilty, just as guilty as George Ellis whose body swung from a sycamore tree only months before. Couple that with the open hostility of Governor Blackburn and the huge military presence at Catlettsburg, and it seemed as if the Civil War—still fresh in many people's minds—was starting up all over again.

It should probably be remembered that this was all taking place at the same time as the famous Hatfield and McCoy feud, which raged across the Kentucky/West Virginia border not far from Ashland. On January 7, 1865, young Harmon

McCoy—discharged from the locally unpopular Union Army on Christmas Eve, 1864 due to his war wounds—had been murdered in his hiding place by men loyal to the Confederate Hatfields.

Then, in 1878, Randolph McCoy, while visiting a Kentucky Hatfield, spotted what he believed was one of his pigs. McCoy accused Hatfield of stealing his pig, and the two went to court. A key witness testified that the pig was, indeed, property of the Hatfields, and they won the case. The witness was slain by the McCoys a few months later. Tensions rose.

In the spring of 1880, Johnson Hatfield met Roseanna McCoy at a party at the home of one of the Kentucky Hatfields. They immediately eloped, Roseanna being taken to the Hatfield home in West Virginia. Their romance was doomed to failure, however, as everyone opposed it from both sides of the Tug River (a tributary of the Big Sandy that divides Kentucky and West Virginia further upstream). Johnson was forcibly removed from her side, and Roseanna sent in tears back to her family's cold disdain.

The spring elections of 1882—taking place at the same time as the lynching of George Ellis in Ashland—were the scene of another hideous murder. Roseanna McCoy's brothers—Tolbert, Pharmer and Bud—stabbed Ellison Hatfield twenty-six times and then shot him in the back. No one knows why. The three brothers were then themselves murdered only a few days later: executed, while tied to bushes, to the sound of their mother's screams.

And on it went, claiming a total of thirteen lives and numerous beatings, burnings, woundings, and other damage across the border between the two states. Finally, Kentucky officials under command of Frank Phillips invaded West Virginia in 1888 and captured nine Hatfields, bringing them back to stand trial. Several Hatfields had attacked the McCoy home, burning it to the ground after killing two McCoys they found there on New Year's Day, 1888. Eventually, the nine prisoners were brought back to Kentucky, stood trial, and some received the death penalty. The feud was officially over.

Back in Ashland, though, things had gone from bad to worse. The sounds of gunfire in the night kept the troops in a state of nervous excitement, certain that a crowd was descending on them once again to subject Neal and Craft to mob justice. Major Allen, in charge of the militia, decided against going to Lexington by train (there were rumors that the tracks had been torn up to force the train to stop so it could be boarded) and ordered the prisoners escorted to the river front. The date was November 1, 1882.

In a replay of the last time this had been attempted, the militia commandeered a steamer—this time the hapless *Granite State*—and the steamer's captain was told not to stop at Ashland or anywhere else until they reached Maysville. At that moment, the train from Ashland arrived and two hundred civilians disembarked. They were armed "with about forty pistols and shotguns."

The prisoners and militia boarded the steamer quickly. Major Allen deployed his 215 troops in a line around the wharf, positioning his artillery piece strategically. The Ashlanders demanded custody of the two prisoners. The Major refused. The steamer took off.

The Ashland train was reboarded, and as it made its way back to Ashland along the riverside, the crowd fired on the steamer from the train. Word spread to Ashland that the prisoners were aboard the *Granite State*. A ferryboat was commandeered by the mob at Ashland and ordered to approach the steamer. Shots were fired from both the ferry and the steamer; the volley from the steamer was so heavy that the ferryboat was put out of service. The militia fired in all directions, towards the ferryboat where the initial shots had come from and at the huge crowd on the docks at Ashland. It is said that a total of 1,500 rounds were fired by the militia aboard the *Granite State,* killing four civilians and wounding more than twenty others, including several teenage boys.

Ashland, of course, was outraged. The Governor defended the actions of his militia, however, and claimed that when the trials of Neal and Craft came up again that February, he would "send six regiments, or twelve if necessary, to defend the prisoners from mob rule." The Cincinnati *Enquirer* reported all of this with glee, as did the Lexington newspapers. The *Enquirer* insisted that the men were innocent and had been framed; this was received so badly in Ashland that, according to one report, no Cincinnati *Enquirers* were allowed in Ashland for years to come. The coroner's jury in Ashland slammed Major Allen, calling the Ashland Tragedy a "wanton and ruthless act," but Allen was never held accountable for the debacle. As it was, the memory of the lynching of George Ellis was on everyone's mind at the State House, and the ferocity of the militia's response to the attack from the ferryboat—and from Ashland in general—was deemed justified in the face of the threat.

But everything went peacefully after that. Craft—widely understood to be the ringleader of the group—was convicted in 1883 and hanged on October 12, 1883. Neal was convicted a year later and hanged on March 27, 1885 protesting his innocence to the end:

> I say to one and all that this is no place to tell a lie. I stand here today to suffer for a heinous crime I did not commit. One day my innocence will be established beyond a doubt.[32]

Ashland . . .

Putting down the books and papers in the public library after reading all of this, I wondered at the strangeness of the place. Indian burial mounds. The Ashland Tragedy. Children murdered and raped. Charles Manson playing in the dirt. Sure, the place was also the home of Naomi and Wynonna Judd, the popular mother and daughter country-and-western singing duo, and of Ashley Judd. Naomi's other daughter is an accomplished actor who herself portrayed the victim of a serial killer in the film *Kiss the Girls* with her costar Morgan Freeman. Ashley Judd would go on to donate $50,000 to the University of Kentucky's Department of Anthropology in 2001. A former anthropology student at the University, Ms. Judd wanted the sum—matched by another $50,000 from the University—to endow a fund to help support Ph.D. candidates in anthropology. (Did her interest in anthropology begin with a visit to the burial mounds in her home town?)

Odd bits and pieces of Ashland's history and geography seemed to swirl around a darker, more sinister core. In the library, I discovered that Ashland is 555 feet above sea level, for instance. That number has resonance for those interested in history and mysticism, for it was the original Nazi Party membership number of Adolf Hitler (he had it changed later to "seven"). It is also the exact height of the Washington Monument. Conspiracy theorists of the more marooned variety could have cause to develop multi-colored skeins of cause and effect around that particular loom. I could not see a connection, however, unless one wanted to attribute the creation of the Washington Monument, Adolf Hitler and the strange topography of a small Kentucky town to a single, sinister hand. However, a connection does exist: all three betray the same numerical correspondence. But is the connection meaningful? Is this what skeptics mean by "coincidence"? A reference to standard works of qabalistic numerology—such as those in use by people like Johannes Kelpius and Joseph Smith—will show that the number 555 represents "obscurity" in Biblical Hebrew. As mentioned in *Unholy Alliance*, that number is also the equivalent of the Greek letters that make up the word *Necronomicon*, the dreaded magician's spellbook mentioned so often by Lovecraft in his short stories.[33]

A multiple rape and murder of children on Christmas Eve, originally a pagan holiday of the winter solstice, resulting in the Ashland Tragedy of soldiers firing on civilians on November 1, All Saint's Day, originally a pagan holiday celebrating the dead coming back to earth; strange, undescribed burial mounds in the center of town; the Queen Anne-style griffin house that was moved closer to the mounds; Charles Manson. I left Ashland with a file full of information, none of it making very much sense at the time. As I drove out of town, I went over in my mind the details of Manson's history after his release on March 22, 1967. If the "cult cops" are right, and if special events occurring on any of the eight sacred days of the pagan calendar (the two equinoxes, the two solstices, and the four cross-quarter days of July 31/August 1, October 31/November 1, January 31/February 1, and April 30/May 1) are evidence of cult activity, then the history of Ashland and the life of Charles Manson seemed to suggest that cult activity was somehow involved. But how could that be true? Events so far removed from each other in time and space could not indicate the active involvement of cultists, unless one wanted to posit a vast conspiracy on the order of the Freemasonry fantasies of the last two hundred years, and that hypothesis defies belief. That there are conspiracies, and conspiracies in American politics, we have come to learn to our regret over the past fifty years. Everything from Watergate to Iran-Contra, and the coverups of crimes committed in the name of MK-ULTRA, is evidence of this fact. That persons, often political figures, are murdered as the result of conspiracies is well-known all over the world. That cults do exist is also known. But there is no evidence that cultists in the United States have any political power or influence; and the "satanic cult survivor syndrome" scare of the 1980s demonstrated how little proof exists of any kind of network of satanic murderers. But, as Carl Sagan and other skeptics have been forced to admit, "absence of evidence is not evidence of absence." What is really going on? Anything? Anything at all?

Charles Manson was loosed on the world. He made his way to San Francisco in time for the Summer of Love, and the transformation of a small-time thief and hustler into a prophet and murderer was begun. Along the way he would gather around himself a commune of young men and women, would undergo ritual-style initiations including a crucifixion while on LSD, and would become involved with the Church of Satan, the Process, and other cults in and around San Francisco and Los Angeles, in a saga that has been discussed and written about and argued over by law enforcement, journalists, filmmakers, psychologists, psychiatrists, philosophers, and cultists since that bloody day in August 1969 that saw a beautiful young actress, pregnant with her first child, and her friends carved to death with knives. But prior to that murder, there were others.

There was Darwin Orell Scott in Ashland, Kentucky: Manson's uncle and victim of an unsolved crime, carved with knives.

And there was Marina Habe, a seventeen-year-old girl who was abducted on New Year's Eve, 1968 and whose body was found—carved with knives—a few days later. Although attributed to the Manson "family," the murder is still officially unsolved.

But it was Marina Habe's case that led me to a whole other dimension of the thesis I was working on. It was Marina Habe who led me back to World War II, to Operation Paperclip, to Hollywood, escaped Nazis, psychological warfare and the enigmatic team of Clay Shaw and Fred Crisman. As I drove out of Ashland that warm summer's day, I was driving out of the frying pan and into the fire.

ENDNOTES

1 H.P. Lovecraft, "The Colour Out of Space," in *The Annotated H.P. Lovecraft*, S.T. Joshi, ed., p. 59

2 Bram Stoker, *Dracula*, Penguin Books, London, 1993, p. 132–33

3 Charles Manson, in *The Manson File*, Nicholas Schreck, ed., Amok Press, NY, 1988, p. 26

4 Ed Sanders, *The Family: The Story of Charles Manson's Dune Buggy Attack Battalion*, E.P. Dutton, NY, 1971, p. 61 (This sentence was later amended in the revised and updated 1991 edition to read, "If the Kremlin or the Pentagon ever formulates the robopathic secret of M, the world's in trouble," p. 48.)

5 Douglas Hensley, "Hell's Gate" on the Internet site http://www.angelfire.com/zine/ encounters/Letters.html, February 6, 2002; and "Ghosts Make Bobby Mackey's Nightclub Famous Subject of Book, Television Shows: A Bizarre Story of Murder, Hauntings" on http://www.nkycvb.com/news/000193.html, dated November 26, 2001

6 Aleister Crowley, *Moonchild*, Weiser Books, Boston, 2002, p. 179

7 Maggie Haberman and Andy Geller, "'Vampire' Teens busted after they called home for stake," New York Post, November 30, 1996, p. 4; and Clifford L. Linedecker, *The Vampire Killers*, St. Martin's Paperbacks, NY, 1998

8 John Douglas and Mark Olshaker, *Journey Into Darkness*, Pocket Star Books, NY, 1997, pp 220–248

9 Joel Norris, *Serial Killers*, Anchor Books, NY, 1988, pp. 137–149

10 "War on Poverty Figure Accused of Murder," *New York Times*, April 26, 1992, p. 30

11 This and most of the following information, except where noted, comes from the most reliable sources for factual biographical and chronological data on Manson, which include Vincent Bugliosi's *Helter Skelter* as well as selected data from Ed Sanders' *The Family*, John Gilmore's *Manson* and Nicholas Schreck's *The Manson File*. The author does not necessarily subscribe to the theories concerning Manson represented by these works, but has relied upon them for raw data.

12 Joel Norris, op. cit. pp. 161–173

13 Vincent Bugliosi, *Helter Skelter: The True Story of the Manson Murders*, Bantam Books, NY, 1995 edition, p. 677

14 John Gilmore, *Manson: The Unholy Trail of Charlie and the Family*, Amok, Los Angeles, 2000, p. 3

15 Nora Chadwick, *The Celts*, Penguin Books, NY, 1984, p. 27

16 Ibid., p. 170

17 Robert Graves, *The White Goddess: A historical grammar of poetic myth*, Farrar, Straus and Giroux, NY, 1981, pp. 101–103

18 Ithell Colquhoun, *Sword of Wisdom: MacGregor Mathers and the Golden Dawn*, G. P. Putnam's Sons, NY, 1975, p. 127–130

19 John A. Keel, *The Mothman Prophecies*, IlluminiNet Press, Lilburn, 1991, p. 53

20 Webb & Snow (1981), p. 132

21 Bugliosi, op. cit., p. 198

22 Joel Norris, op. cit., pp. 137–149

23 "Make Your Next Visit Ashland, Kentucky" brochure, Ashland/Boyd County Tourism Commission, Ashland, n.d.

24 "Ashland Oil Settles Civil Suits Over Air Pollution," *New York Times*, February 23, 1993, D5

25 Kentucky Highlands Museum Brochure, Ashland, n.d.

26 Ashland Historical Tour, brochure, Ashland/Boyd County Tourism Commission, Ashland, n.d.

27 Ibid.

28 Ibid.

29 Kenneth Grant, *Hecate's Fountain*, Skoob Books Publishing, London, 1992, p. 31

30 Ibid., p. 13

31 See "The Ashland Horror" by Guy H. Ogden in *Ashland A Long Time Ago*, compiled and edited by Arnold Hanners, Ashland, 1987 pp. 18–19; and "The Ashland Tragedy" in *A History of Ashland, Kentucky 1786–1954*, the Ashland Centennial Committee for the Celebration of its Centennial October 1, 2 and 3, 1954, pp. 69–72.

32 Ogden, op. cit., p. 19

33 Peter Levenda, *Unholy Alliance*, Continuum, NY, 2002, p. 91

The Many Faces of the Devil: From the serpent in Eden to Renaissance masterpieces and modern media portrayals, Satan has been depicted in countless forms—ranging from human to angelic to bestial. **Below:** In this engraving by Gustave Doré (1832-1883), we see his interpretation of Lucifer as the fallen angel from Dante's *Inferno*, a contemplative yet terrifying figure frozen at the lowest point of Hell.

SECTION TWO:

AGENTS OF THE DEVIL

To sustain the "master race" in its war-making, they enslaved millions of human beings and brought them into Germany, where these hapless creatures now wander as "displaced persons." At length bestiality and bad faith reached such excess that they aroused the sleeping strength of imperiled Civilization. Its united efforts have ground the German war machine to fragments. But the struggle has left Europe a liberated yet prostrate land where a demoralized society struggles to survive. *These are the fruits of the sinister forces that sit with these defendants in the prisoners' dock . . . . What makes this inquest significant is that these prisoners represent sinister influences that will lurk in the world long after their bodies have returned to dust.*

—Robert Jackson's Opening Statement at the Nuremberg Trial[1] (emphasis added)

"Do you know which way technology is headed? It is headed for the metaphysical. Radio waves are no longer anything concrete; wireless is already a highly abstract technique; the transmission of pictures infringes on the realm of religion; the extermination weapons are a point of contact with the universe. The physical world has its boundaries; only the psychic is 'oceanic,' as the author of Civilization and its Discontents puts it. That is why mankind's next bold step must be the materialization of the psychic."

—"General von Greehahn" (General Reinhard Gehlen) in *Agent of the Devil* by Hans Habe[2]

Adolf Hitler (above) and several of his high-ranking Nazi officers who played notorious roles during World War II: (from left to right) Josef Mengele, Otto Skorzeny, Martin Bormann[3] and Reinhard Gehlen[4].

BOOK ONE: THE NINE

CHAPTER FOUR

UNHOLY ALLIANCE: NAZISM, SATANISM AND PSYCHOLOGICAL WARFARE IN THE USA

> The secret services of all nations are directed or influenced by personalities which are marked by a criminal, a perverted, a criminal-pathological, or, in any case, an exceedingly vulgar imagination . . . . But the worst perversion of the secret services—and how could there be a worse one—is that of human sacrifice.
>
> —*Agent of the Devil,* Hans Habe[5]

On New Year's Day, 1969, the petite body of Marina Elizabeth Habe was found nude at the bottom of a ravine off Mulholland Drive in Los Angeles, about four miles from home.[6] The seventeen-year-old student at the University of Hawaii and aspiring actress was the victim of multiple stab wounds in the neck and chest, had been raped, burned, and had contusions in her eyes. It was a savage attack reminiscent of the later attack on Darwin Scott in Ashland, Kentucky. She had been returning from a date with friend John Hornburg in Brentwood the early morning of December 30, 1968 and was kidnapped from in front of the home she shared with her mother in the Hollywood hills after returning from a night out on Santa Monica Boulevard. The case remains unsolved, but there was a lot of speculation at the time that her killer was a Manson "family" member, since she was known to have befriended various members of the group. Manson himself has no alibi for the day and time of her death, and is known to have been in Los Angeles on the day she was kidnapped and killed, attending a New Year's Eve party at the home of musician John Phillips of the Mamas and the Papas.[7] Phillips himself is known to have been friendly with elements of the Process Church of the Final Judgment. The day before and the day after the killing Manson was with his Family at the Barker Ranch, which was located in the Panimint Mountains of Death Valley.

A reference to this crime is buried deep within Vincent Bugliosi's book on the Manson case, *Helter Skelter,*[8] and has a bit more space in Ed Sanders' *The Family.*[9] Marina Habe is identified as the daughter of writer Hans Habe.[10] There was no more information on this unfortunate victim or her father, so recourse was had to newspaper morgues, libraries, archives and eventually to Holocaust survivor materials. What developed was the story of a remarkable man and his mysterious life, one that stretched from the concentration camp to the Hollywood film studio . . . and from Madison Avenue to Munich.

According to a small paragraph in *Current Biography 1977*, the year Habe died, he was born on February 12, 1911, was an editor and correspondent in the 1930s for newspapers in Austria and Czechoslovakia, and eventually served with the Allies in World War II. He died in Locarno, Switzerland on September 29, 1977.

Current Biography 1943—published at the height of the War—was much more effusive and detailed. Habe rated three full pages in that edition, where we learn that he was born Jean (actually "Janos") Bekessy in Budapest, Hungary. Oddly, the article does not state why or when Jean Bekessy became Hans Habe. Perhaps one is supposed to believe that "Hans Habe" is simply a *nom de plume*, a pseudonym easier on American eyes and ears than "Bekessy." But there is more to the story than that.

Hans' father—Imre Bekessy—was also a journalist, but in his case a yellow journalist and extortionist. A converted Jew, Imre Bekessy's specialty was convincing public figures to pay him money in order that their names would be kept *out* of his articles! For these outrages, an Austrian court decided he was *persona non grata,* and Imre found himself expelled from Vienna and on the streets of Hungary, trolling for new prey. The name of Bekessy became so notorious that his son Janos Bekessy was forced to become someone else, anyone else, if he wanted a career in journalism. And thus Hans Habe was born.

A prominent Austrian journalist and social activist—Hans Janitschek—has informed the author that the "Habe" name comes from the first two letters of the first and last name, Hans Bekessy.[11] ("Hans" is the Germanization of "Janos.")

Readers of *Unholy Alliance* may remember another Viennese journalist with the same ambitions as Imre Bekessy: Herschel Steinschneider, who became Hitler's occult advisor, Hanussen.[12] Like Imre Bekessy, Hanussen began his career extorting money from Viennese celebrities, being paid to keep their names out of his newspapers. Like Janos Bekessy, he changed his name to something more dramatic but perhaps for a different reason: Steinschneider was Jewish, and he had his sights set on Berlin. Thus, as Hanussen moved from Vienna to Berlin, so Imre Bekessy moved from Vienna to Budapest. Eventually his son, Hans Habe, would move back to Vienna and become the youngest chief-editor in Europe at the time, working for *Der Morgen* at the age of twenty-one. Habe, with his name-change, not only disguised his relationship to a notorious blackmailer and extortionist, but he also hid his Jewish ancestry at a time when it was becoming increasingly difficult to survive—let alone excel—as a Jew in Europe.

As hostilities began with the accession of Hitler and the Nazi Party to a position of control within Germany, Habe found himself becoming a dedicated (some would say "rabid") anti-Nazi. (It is to Hans Habe, in fact, that we credit the discovery of Hitler's "Schicklgruber" family background.) As war broke out, Habe found himself on Hitler's enemies list: his books were burned, and he was shot at in Vienna (because of his publication of Hitler's Schicklgruber ancestry; Habe actually sent copies of his report to Germany at the time of Hitler's campaign against Hindenburg in an effort to ridicule Hitler and cause him to lose the election, a tactic which was in vain as we all know). Habe enlisted with a group of foreign volunteers in the French Army, and took part in the Battle of France. He was captured on June 22, 1940, armed only with an 1891 Remington rifle. Habe—in his book about the experience, *A Thousand Shall Fall*—rails against the French complicity in the defeat, accusing the Vichy hierarchy of actually wanting to surrender rather than fight Germany. (This book eventually became the 1943 MGM propaganda film *The Cross of Lorraine*, starring Jean-Pierre Aumont, Gene Kelly, Cedric Hardwicke, Peter Lorre and Hume Cronyn.)

Held at a prison camp in Occupied France, Habe managed to survive for a few weeks under an assumed name before escaping, dressed in a German uniform and fleeing in an ambulance. He eventually made his way to Spain and Portugal, joining his wife—Erika Levy—in neutral Lisbon. President Roosevelt gave Habe a special emergency visa, and the couple arrived in New York harbor on December 3, 1940.

A deeper examination of the available record shows that American rescue worker Varian Fry was instrumental in getting Hans Habe out of Europe. Recourse to the archives of the International Rescue Committee in New York shows that Varian Fry went to France in 1940 after the fall of Paris to help intellectuals escape the Gestapo. For over a year, Fry managed to rescue thousands of refugees, eventually becoming the first American ever honored by the Yad Vashem organization in Israel, where a tree was planted in his name by Secretary of State Warren Christopher on February 2, 1996. Among the people he helped escape were such famous personalities as Marc Chagall, Franz Werfel, Hannah Arendt, Fritz Kahn, Otto Meyerhof, Konrad Heiden (the Hitler biographer), Arthur Koestler and, of course, Habe. In addition, credit must be given to Varian Fry for saving nearly the entire Surrealist movement: Andre Breton, Marcel Duchamp, Max Ernst and Andre Masson.

Fry was eventually expelled from France in 1941. He died in 1967 as a retired teacher in Redding, Connecticut, his exploits on behalf of the refugees largely unknown and unrecognized in his own country at the time. Indeed, when he was expelled from France it was due to the fact that the US Consulin Marseilles had refused to renew his passport! Fry's wife received a letter from Eleanor Roosevelt saying, in essence, that Fry's expulsion from France was inevitable, as his actions did not have the support of the US Government . . . the same government which, five years later, would be helping Nazi war criminals emigrate to the United States to assist in the space program and in intelligence activities against the Soviet Union.

Then the Hans Habe story gets even more interesting.

In an attempt to find out more about Habe, the author accessed the Amazon.com website and found that his works were all out-of-print. They had a few second-hand copies in stock, however, and *Agent of the Devil* was selected, a novel Habe published in 1958. The book arrived a short while later, and—in one of those eerie coincidences that haunted the research for this book constantly for years—there was an old newsclipping taped inside the front cover of the book. This was a review of *Agent of the Devil*, by a "B.D.," and it contained thiss illuminating sentence: "Budapest journalist and U.S. army psychological warfare officer on the Italian front, Hans Habe is a 'cunning' writer."

Psychological warfare officer? Italian front? The newsclipping gave the author a further dimension for his research, and also suggested a new line of inquiry. Let's see where it leads us.

Habe began giving talks at various clubs and societies in America during 1941, even staying for a while at West Point where, it is said, he continued to work at his writing. In 1942 he began a series of lectures at Army bases under the aegis of the War Department's Bureau of Public Relations on "How To Lose a War": an ironic title which took as its text the fall of France, and served as motivation for the American troops in their struggle against Nazism.

Habe was busy in 1942 with other interests as well. He divorced Erika Levy after eight years of marriage and married Mrs. Eleanor Close Sturges Gautier Rand, the aggressively-nomenclatured former wife of that great comic film producer and screenwriter Preston Sturges and daughter of Mrs. Marjorie Post Hutton Davies, the General Foods heiress and former wife of the US Ambassador to Russia, Joseph E. Davies. One could not ask for a spouse with a more blue-blooded (and flagrant) set of pedigrees, the families of Rand, Hutton, Gautier, Post, Davies and even old Preston Sturges amply represented every time she signed a check. They were married on April 22, 1942, Hans Habe becoming her fourth husband and she his second wife. Considering that Erika Levy, Hans' first wife, was "the heiress to the Tungsram Lightbulb fortune," one has to say that he had a knack for marrying—perhaps not too wisely, but—too well. One story has it that Mrs. Eleanor etc. etc. Rand had helped Habe and his wife immigrate to the United States, and that they fell in love at that time. She seems to have been an older woman, and—according to some accounts—rather short on charm, and many suspected that Habe had married for money and security rather than for love or passion.

Shortly thereafter, in January 1943, Habe enlisted in the US Army. This was not mere expedience, since he had dependents and would probably not have been called up, but he asked to enlist anyway. By July of that year, he was in North Africa (and the new father of a son) as a second lieutenant. He was then loaned to British General Montgomery for a while, and September found him in Italy and this time with the US forces.

After that, the record becomes a little confused. Some reports have him landing with Allied forces at D-Day, yet he seems to have entered Europe via Italy nine months earlier than that. Regardless of the order of events, by that time Habe was working for C.D. Jackson—more famous in his Time Life incarnation—and was actively involved in psychological warfare operations, operations which lasted long after the war's end and which found Habe in charge of no fewer than *eighteen* German newspapers throughout the Allied territories.

One of those who knew Habe at this time was Tibor Scitovsky, a distinguished American economist who was born in Hungary, and whose father knew Habe's father—the yellow journalist—and threw him out of his office when Imre Bekessy approached him for money. His memoir, *A Proud Hungarian*,[13] mentions a psychological warfare school in Gettysburg, Pennsylvania where Scitovsky and others were being trained in propaganda. He characterizes Habe as the "US Army's propaganda expert" in his memoir of the war years, and describes how Habe trained him in spotting important information in the *New York Times*, and how to use that information for propaganda purposes. They practiced making radio broadcasts, writing articles and filler, designing propaganda posters, and all of it in both French and German. According to Scitovsky, Habe also had been a student of the Bauhaus and thus had a good eye for artistic composition as well as literature and journalism.

Scitovsky was eventually assigned to the 4th Mobile Broadcasting Company of the Army, and had quite a sophisticated bunch of Army "buddies," including Joseph Wechsberg of the *The New Yorker* magazine, and Igor Cassini, the gossip columnist and brother of Oleg Cassini. They were sent first to Britain at the time of the V-1 and V-2 attacks. According to that timetable, they would have been sent over sometime in mid-late 1944. Thus, Habe could have been with Allied forces at the Italian front in 1943, then returned Stateside to conduct psy-war classes at Gettysburg, and then returned to Europe with the Allied forces on D-Day in June 1944. Scitovsky, et al. did not arrive in Germany until after V-E Day, in May 1945. By that time, they had become part of USSBS.

USSBS—or United States Strategic Bombing Survey—was created by President Roosevelt in November 1944 to assess the damage caused by the Allied strategic bombing of Europe. Their task was to consider "the effects on civilian morale and whether bombs hardened the national will to fight, or collapsed it."[14] In other words, their function was essentially an intelligence one allied to psychological warfare. In the back of Roosevelt's mind must have been the question whether the devastating new atomic weapon being designed by the scientists of the Manhattan Project would cause an earlier end to the war . . . or prolong it indefinitely.

By the time Scitovsky and his colleagues were sent to Germany, their task had changed somewhat again. They were on the lookout for specific Nazi individuals to capture and interrogate, and USSBS became so huge in the process that it eventually found itself under combined military and civilian leadership, including an official of IBM (the Nazis were enthusiastic users of IBM punch card equipment during the war, for such tasks as keeping track of concentration camp inmates and their final dispositions) and such luminaries as Kenneth Galbraith, George Ball, and Paul Nitze, who would all go on to greater glory in succeeding presidential administrations.

Another friend of Habe at this time is psy-war officer Alfred de Grazia—now a professor at Princeton University and, even more intriguingly, a friend of the late Immanuel Velikovsky—who was with Habe in North Africa in 1943. His book on the war years[15] makes for very interesting reading, as it reveals that the "Mobile Broadcasting Company" was a cover for OSS (Office of Strategic Services) activities in Europe, and that they were joint OSS-US Army units. A photograph of Habe in this collection—taken near Tunis in North Africa in July 1943—shows him to look remarkably like the "Hans Habe/Heinz Habe" figure in the Bower volumes, mentioned below. What is even more surprising—especially to a reader of *Unholy Alliance*—is that the shady figure of George Viereck once again raises his ugly head.

Viereck was a propaganda officer and spy for the Kaiser during World War I and a colleague of infamous British occultist and sometime spy Aleister Crowley. Viereck went on to conduct espionage and propaganda activities during World War II as well, and wound up arrested for his efforts, spending about a year in prison. At the same time, his son—Peter Viereck—was working for the OSS and the 1st Mobile Broadcasting Company in North Africa, along with Hans Habe and other notables, including Martin Herz, a future US Ambassador![16]

And we should not forget yet another OSS officer in Italy at this time, Peter Tompkins, a broadcast journalist who became an intelligence officer during the war, but whose fame rests more on his researches in two fields: Egyptian archaeology on the one hand, and the use of lie detectors in the investigation of the "secret life of plants" on the other. Also involved in intelligence during the war in Europe—and specifically in the interrogation of Nazi prisoners, like his counterparts in OSS and USSBS—was J. D. Salinger, the famed and reclusive author of *Catcher in the Rye*, that favorite tome of American assassins. He was a CIC (Counter Intelligence Corps) officer from 1943, and took part in the D-Day invasion of June 1944.[17] His duties were essentially the same as those of his OSS counterparts: to round up Nazis and interrogate them, and to search for collaborators and German Army deserters among the "civilians." It also appears that two other gentlemen who will figure in our story—Clay Shaw and Fred Crisman—were involved in similar intelligence activities, specifically with the Paperclip operations.[18] (This will be discussed in Chapter Seven in more detail.) Shaw, as many readers are aware, figured prominently in the Kennedy Assassination theories of New Orleans District Attorney Jim Garrison and others; Crisman, supposedly a friend of Shaw from the war years, was subpoenaed by Jim Garrison to testify concerning that relationship. It has been suggested that Shaw was an OSS officer during the war; Crisman certainly was, as his CIA files demonstrate. Crisman, however, was also involved in the seminal UFO contact of the twentieth century. This was the Maury Island affair of 1947, which ushered in the whole

UFO spectrum, from "flying saucers," to "men in black," to government coverups and exploding aircraft.

As if that weren't enough, another Army Intelligence officer in Rome at this time, charged with hunting down Nazi agents like his OSS counterparts, was Philip J. Corso, who would eventually find a position on President Eisenhower's National Security Staff. It was Corso who, a bit before his death, published *The Day After Roswell*, a book claiming that he was privy to reverse-engineered scientific achievements based on captured flying saucers, and had actually seen the corpse of an extraterrestrial from Roswell in a shipping crate on its way to Wright Air Force Base in Ohio, a claim that is hotly debated on both sides of the UFO issue, even though Corso's *bona fides* in all other respects seem unimpeachable.

The involvement of intelligence agents in the field of Egyptian archaeology, the UFO phenomenon, and other odd pursuits will be discussed in a later chapter. For now, it suffices to point out that psychological warfare, literature, archaeology, and the paranormal not only make for strange bedfellows: in the war years of the last century it was positively an orgy.

While De Grazia's account shows that, although some OSS personnel were antagonistic towards the dashing Hungarian, Habe was riding high in the estimation of the US Army Psychological Warfare Bureau (PWB). Put in charge of US Army propaganda in Germany, he was the czar of German newspapers for years after the war (until 1951 according to the information available to the author), eventually responsible for the publication of 8 million pieces and over 10,000 newspaper articles (not counting over two dozen novels in his lifetime). Some of the papers he ran included *Muenchner Illustrierte*, *Echo der Woche*, and the American intelligence/Hans Habe creation: the *Neue Zeitung* of Munich.

Someone as high-profile and as rabidly anti-Nazi as Habe was a jewel in the psy-war crown. After all, they made a movie about his life in a Nazi POW camp (*The Cross of Lorraine*); he was married to the adopted daughter of the former US Ambassador to Russia; he was running propaganda and psy-war operations against the Nazis and then, after the war, against both the Nazi sympathizers and the Communists. If the Allied postwar intelligence community was like a corporation, then Habe had a seat on the Board.

It seemed logical to the author, therefore, that Habe would have been involved, if only peripherally, in the effort to identify and capture as many important Nazis as possible, including Nazi scientists. His former students at Gettysburg were doing just that, and had managed quite a coup in finding and interrogating Albert Speer, Hitler's architect, among many others. Was Habe involved with Operation Paperclip, the US effort to bring Nazi scientists—especially rocket scientists, but also medical men and other experts—to America after the war?

There is an intriguing—and startling—photograph in Tom Bower's *Blind Eye to Murder*, an account of the Allied failure to completely de-Nazify Germany after the war.[19] It is labeled Photograph 13, "The Paperclip Scientists," and describes "the men who put America on the moon, enjoying a Bavarian evening in Chicago, 1950." Among the scientists—the notorious "physician" Dr. Hubertus Strughold, Wernher von Braun, and General Walter Dornberger—there is another figure, identified as "Hans Habe."

Hans Habe does not appear in the text of Bower's book, nor in the index or anywhere else. The photo certainly looks like Habe, when compared to the de Grazia photo and the one in *Current Biography* of 1943. But how could that be? What would Hans Habe be doing hanging out in apparent conviviality with Paperclip scientists?

Bower's book was first published in 1981. In 1987, he published *The Paperclip Conspiracy*. This book contains the same photograph, only this time the individual originally identified as "Hans Habe" is now identified as "Heinz Habe."[20] This person also does not appear anywhere else in the book, but another photograph showing "Strughold's team at Heidelberg" shows a "Heinz Haber." Unfortunately, there is no further mention of Haber, either, even though we know that a Dr. Heinz Haber does make it to Strughold's Paperclip team in the United States after the war. The person identified as Haber looks enough like the Heinz Habe in the later photograph to be the same person. If so, how was the mistake made in 1981 identifying him as Hans Habe, the famous novelist and anti-Nazi propagandist?

There is another famous photograph to consider, this one notorious among UFO enthusiasts and debunkers alike. It is of an "alien," a short creature in a strange suit, a weird mask with elongated forehead and breathing apparatus, holding hands with an Army officer as another person walks behind carrying his . . . oxygen tank? It first appeared in a German newspaper on April Fool's Day, 1950, and made the tabloid circuit in the States shortly thereafter, in which form the author first saw it as a child years later. This photo would have appeared in one of Habe's newspapers (it appeared in 1950, and Habe was in charge of West German propaganda until 1951) and certainly would not have been shown without his prior involvement and approval as the US Army psychological warfare and propaganda expert. The photo was obviously a hoax and was published that way, in a tongue-in-cheek reference to the famous Roswell sighting of 1947, perhaps. Whatever the original purpose, one source has published that a photocopy of it was found in FBI files "with the suggestion that it might be one of the Roswell aliens."[21] In any event, it was published the same year as the "Paperclip scientists in Chicago" photo.

Habe evidently finished his postwar service in 1951, which would have been the same year his daughter, Marina, was born. Habe returned to the United States and left sometime in 1953 for Europe, evidently leaving his young daughter behind in America; the only information to hand is that he moved to Locarno, Switzerland at some point and stayed there until he died in 1977 at the age of 66. He had been through at least two more wives by that time, the actress Eloise Hardt (Marina's mother) and the actress Licci Bala. In the meantime, Habe began writing books critical of the United States. One of his more famous efforts, *Der Tod in Texas: Eine amerikanische Tragoedie*, ("Death in Texas: An American Tragedy") was an attack on the Warren Commission published in 1964. Habe had been traveling through the United States at the time of the assassination and did not believe the conclusions of the Warren Report. He was very fond of Kennedy, but very critical of America in the wake of the assassination and what he perceived as the obvious coverup efforts by the government and the willingness of the American people to accept the government's findings.

Habe. OSS operations. Psychological warfare. UFO hoax. Paperclip scientists. Even the JFK assassination. More—or less—than meets the eye?

In the effort to learn more about Habe, the author found himself going through a list of the contents of the C.D. Jackson files of the Dwight D. Eisenhower Library. Jackson was a vice-president of Time, Inc. from 1931 to 1964 (the year of his death), but he was much more than that. He was also Special Assistant to the US Ambassador to Turkey, 1942–43; President of the Free Europe Committee (which ran Radio Free Europe), 1951–52; speechwriter for Eisenhower in 1952; Special Assistant to the President for International Affairs, 1953–54; US Delegate to the United Nations Ninth General Assembly in 1954; speechwriter and consultant to Eisenhower during the Lebanon Crisis of 1958; and "unofficial consultant to the President on other occasions." He was also Deputy Chief, Psychological Warfare Branch (PWB) at Allied Forces Headquarters in 1943 and continued in that role, slightly modified, for the Psychological Warfare Division (PWD) at Supreme Headquarters, Allied Expeditionary Force (SHAEF) for the remainder of the war. His files, collected at the Eisenhower Library, contain one on Hans Habe (Box 58) and another entire box on that notorious bugaboo of conspiracy theorists, the Bilderbergers.

Jackson had files on the Bilderbergers from 1955 to 1964. These files include agendas, minutes of meetings, lists of participants at the Bilderberger meetings, even a history of Bilderberger meetings. Surely a treasure-trove for the academically-inclined paranoid (or the paranoid academic)? It was former CIA director Walter Bedell Smith who asked Jackson to help him recruit members for that mysterious organization. It was also C.D. Jackson who arranged the *Life* magazine purchase of the famous Abraham Zapruder film of the Kennedy assassination, thereby keeping it away from the public view for five years, until the Clay Shaw trial in New Orleans.

Psychological warfare is an intelligence function; it involves gathering of intelligence on target (generally civilian) populations as well as disseminating propaganda in various forms; but it also has a more lethal function, and this has been discussed at length by the respected historian Christopher Simpson in his excellent and enlightening *Science of Coercion: Communication Research & Psychological Warfare 1945–1960.*[22] There, he discusses the role Jackson (and fellow Bilderberger

Nelson Rockefeller) played in charge of policy oversight of combined CIA–USIA (US Information Agency) and US military country plans during the Huk insurrections in the Philippines in the mid-1950s. As we saw with the North African memoir of Alfred de Grazia mentioned earlier, the OSS (forerunner of the CIA) was heavily involved in the Psychological Warfare Bureau from the very start, running joint operations with the Army in North Africa, Italy and elsewhere.

Simpson's study, however, goes even further and cites clandestine operations such as sabotage and assassination as functions of the psychological warfare effort from the very beginning, for what the establishment considers "psychological warfare" the enemy often considers "terrorism"; these are two sides of the same coin. These operations are not, strictly speaking, military in nature, but have as their goal the psychological disorientation of an enemy population.

The Nazis had already been working a psy-war system of their own since the 1930s when they came into power. Mystic and Theosophist Otto Ohlendorf, who would later become a famous SS Einsatzgruppe D commando, cut his milk teeth on psychological warfare programs with his own creation, the *Deutsche Lebensgebiete*, in 1939, before going hunting in the Caucasus, looking for Jews and Freemasons, and killing ninety thousand innocent people in the process.[23] Probably the most famous propaganda chief of the war itself was the odd-looking, in-your-face Nazi fanatic Joseph Goebbels; most Americans and other Allies could not name his opposite number in their own countries. Propaganda was something the *other* side did. Our side does not use propaganda, the story goes; it merely disseminates factual, i.e., truthful, information. Meanwhile, "propaganda" and "psychological warfare" became synonymous within the United States intelligence agencies, and psychological warfare was the province of agencies like the famous OSS or the Army's G-2 and therefore operated in a cloak-and-dagger world of secrecy.

According to Simpson, even the English term "psychological warfare" did not come into use until 1941, as a manifestation of that marvelous—and perhaps more revealing—German neologism *Weltanschauungskrieg*, or "worldview warfare."[24] The term "psychological warfare" was first appeared in an English language text entitled *German Psychological Warfare* by an historian who would later become famous as the Hungarian-born author of *The Game of the Foxes* and *Patton*: Ladislas Farago. (Farago's later work, *Aftermath*, was a crucial factor in the development of this author's first book, *Unholy Alliance*.)

According to Simpson,

> British and Nazi German strategies and tactics in this field have historically been termed "political warfare" and *Weltanschauungskrieg* ("worldview warfare"), respectively. Each of these conceptualizations of psychological warfare explicitly links mass communication with selective application of violence (murder, sabotage, assassinations, insurrection, counterinsurrection, etc.) as a means of achieving ideological, political, or military goals.[25]

"World-view warfare" says it all: a battle between our perceptions and those of an enemy population. After all, one could say, isn't that what war is really about anyway? Rob an enemy of their moral justification for fighting; make your way seem the right way, the good way, the best way; make their way seem bad, wrong, doomed to failure; and you have robbed an enemy of their will to fight. Even the most crazed suicide bomber is acting from a belief that what he is doing is right, morally justified, and has the sanction of the people that matter, the people that count: God's people. "The best," says the poem, "lack all conviction," but rob the worst of *their* conviction and the war is over. It is tantamount to waking up and finding a voodoo doll in your bed, studded with pins . . . or a horse's head, á la Mario Puzo's *The Godfather*. You've been cursed; you will die. And your mind does the rest. That is the value of psychological warfare, of "world-view warfare," and it works . . . at least, just as well as the voodoo doll or the dead horse. In the right hands, one call kill (or influence) without firing a shot.

Psy-war was never perceived as a substitute for the real thing, but only as a complement to an existing arsenal of weapons. The basic psy-war techniques are only useful insofar as they make the enemy soldiers lose faith in the ability of their army, and their country, to win. One can shake that faith in many ways: by ridicule, by fake prophecies of doom, by appeals to reason or emotion. Another way is through fear.

When we speak of "psychological warfare" we are often speaking of ways to make the enemy afraid, and in order to do this we must understand an enemy's psyche: what makes him love, hate, fight, run. We must understand how an enemy will react under stress: will he fight harder, or simply surrender? Or will he start making errors in judgment, winning the war for us, in a manner of speaking? The costliest mistakes of psychological warfare operations are always those made in ignorance of an enemy's mindset. The psychological warfare officer must be able to play an enemy's mind like a violin. This implies a deep knowledge of human psychology, which is itself a kind of black art. And since this is a war of perceptions, of "world views," it is important that the psychological warfare officer understand the impact of art, music, literature, theater and other cultural modes of expression and how world-views are represented by them, even changed or modified by them. What plays in Peoria may not—very assuredly *will* not—play in Phnom Penh . . .

. . . And eventually, the temptation will arise to test some of these principles on the domestic population. After all, with whose mindset are we the most familiar but our own? What better place to test new theories of psychological warfare than among our native populace? And how better to control our population politically than through the judicious use of propaganda, using the robust media of the most turned-on, tuned-in, mentally-massaged nation on earth: the United States of America?

ELIMINATION BY ILLUMINATION

Psychological warfare (although in existence for centuries, since at least the time of Sun Tzu and *The Art of War*, and formalized in the United States during the First World War and George Creel's Committee of Public Information) was really a "discovery" of the Second World War, and its uses were thoroughly investigated in the decades to follow. Korea, the Philippines, Vietnam, Africa, the Middle East, Latin America . . . the roll call of psy-war ops (operations) is long and, for the most part, still classified, representing—again according to Simpson—some one billion dollars *per year* during the early 1950s alone.[26] It did not end with Habe's newspapers or flyers dropped from planes, urging enemy soldiers to surrender. It did not end with the famous "death cards" of Vietnam, the Ace of Spades dropped in Vietcong villages or on dead VC (a method that was ill-advised and actually did not work, since the Vietnamese did not use the American-style card decks but a different, Chinese version).[27] It continued on into acts of sabotage, assassination and terrorism, sometimes against entire villages in countries we never knew how to find on a map, whose capitols we couldn't pronounce. Taken individually, these psychological warfare operations may have had a succinct political purpose, as defined and identified by nameless men in grey flannel suits in the corridors of power, or by Presidents and National Security Advisors to further their own, hidden agendas; but they were manifestations of something deeper, a spiritual war, a war of "world views," a war we are still fighting, numbly, into the twenty-first century both at home and abroad.

One of the scholars and academics who codified psychological warfare—via its creature, the newly-developing science of communications studies and research—was Walter Lippmann. Lippmann began his career in psychological warfare and propaganda during the First World War, and was the author of several very influential texts on mass communications based on his wartime experiences. He understood that the technology of mass communications was having a profound political effect on the world's citizens, as they became more aware of life in other countries . . . and the disparity (in wealth, in access to information, in basic freedoms) between their own nations and their neighbors'. It was Lippmann who gave us the concept of the "stereotype" (1922), which was basically a continuation of the Jungian concept of the archetype (1919) by other means. To Lippmann, the world outside our borders exists in a different space, consciously, from our own. We develop notions about life in those countries, their cultures, attitudes, and values, without ever going there. Yet, their political situation affects our own; they exert a political influence—either through trade, communications, or transportation—on life in our own country even though we live in a constant state of unawareness of those countries, cultures, politics. The effect of these forces on us is invisible, but real. We then develop mental *images*—stereotypes—of the citizens of these countries, and it is upon the stereotypes that we act. The stereotypes determine our actions and reactions; like the stereotypes of the Islamic fundamentalist, the Vietcong revolutionary, the Red Peril, they are easy targets, and the stereotype communicates a specific message, is, in terms familiar to the deconstructionism of Derrida, a text.

Stereotypes can be created, and manipulated, by the gurus of mass communication and psychological warfare. Stereotypes are culturally-loaded and therefore not "value neutral." We make snap judgments based on the nature of the stereotype; in the hands of the psy-war expert, a stereotype does not contain much complexity or depth. The idea is not to make the target think too clearly or too profoundly about the "text" but instead to react, in a Pavlovian manner, to the stimulus it provides.

While such stereotypes as Islamic fundamentalists, long-haired hippies, the Red Peril, the Ugly American, the Evil Empire, and others are clearly of a specific political nature and are designed to elicit a specific response from the general population which is being manipulated for specific ends, there are other stereotypes that are more difficult to analyze in political terms. These are more basic to human nature, and involve deeper fears and anxieties, even religious or spiritual beliefs. One is reminded of the Flying Tigers of the Second World War: the fighter planes that were painted with huge teeth and jaws to frighten Chinese villagers and rural troops.

But it went further than that. Much further.

United States Air Force Brigadier General Edward G. Lansdale was the CIA's chief operative in the Philippines during the Huk rebellion in the 1950s. As such, he was under the oversight of C. D. Jackson and Nelson Rockefeller, who were responsible for psychological warfare operations at that time in the Philippines and other hot spots. It was Lansdale who came up with the idea of using the Huk belief in vampires—the *asuang*—against them. The psy-war squad would snatch a Huk in ambush and then kill him; they would pierce his neck with two holes, like a vampire bite, and then hang the body up and drain the blood. They would leave the body where the Huk would be sure to find it, neck punctured, drained of blood.[28]

After his successes in the Philippines, Lansdale was transferred to Vietnam. This was in 1954. At this time, Lansdale followed a psy-war technique that was used during World War Two: the use of astrologers to predict fatal outcomes for enemy leaders.[29]

Lansdale was so successful at his work that he was put in charge of organizing Operation Mongoose, the anti-Castro CIA operation designed to destabilize the Cuban regime. In one of these operations, Lansdale suggested simulating the Second Coming. He proposed telling the Cuban people that Fidel Castro was the Anti-Christ, and then staging the return of Jesus, complete with phosphorous shells fired over Havana. His partners in Operation Mongoose called the plan "elimination by illumination." That was in 1962.[30]

By 1964, the use of occult themes and rituals became an accepted part of psychological warfare planning. The Special Operations Research Office (SORO) at the American University prepared a paper at the request of the US Army on "Witchcraft, Sorcery, Magic and Other Psychological Phenomena and Their Implications on Military and Paramilitary Operations in the Congo." The paper was authored by James R. Price and Paul Jureidini. American University was no stranger to psychological warfare research, having seen the establishment there of the Bureau of Social Science Research (BSSR) in 1950. The BSSR was the scene of numerous studies of psychological warfare on Eastern European countries, and its African psy-war studies were underwritten by the Human Ecology Fund, an organization well-known to researchers of government-sponsored mind control programs as a front for the CIA's MK-ULTRA program.[31]

The SORO paper studied the use of occult ideas and techniques by "insurgent elements" in the Republic of the Congo. It states,

> Magical practices are said to be effective in conditioning dissident elements and their followers to do battle with Government troops. Rebel tribesmen are said to have been persuaded that they can be made magically impervious to Congolese army firepower. Their fear of the government has thus been diminished and, conversely, fear of the rebels has grown within army ranks.[32]

The study was ambitious in scope. Like a good psy-war study, it recommended that "today's insurgency situation should not be studied in a vacuum, but should be considered as part of a continuum stemming from the pre-independence Belgian administration, the impact of Western culture upon African tribal systems, the circumstances of the birth of the Congo Republic, and the nature of the struggle for power within the Congo since 1960."[33] The administration of Premier Patrice Lumumba was examined, and the study revealed that his followers set up a political machine that incorporated African tribal culture "including manifestations of beliefs in magic and witchcraft."[34]

The section entitled "Supernatural Aspects of the Present Insurgency Situation" could be read as a treatment of the Salem witchcraft phenomenon, so closely do the two situations parallel each other. Any sudden illness or misfortune is interpreted as a sign of witchcraft at work; indeed, there is an important distinction made in the SORO study that even though the villagers may understand that a building was destroyed due to the actions of termites, "that it fell at the time it did was a result of witchcraft or sorcery."[35] This is a sophisticated point of view with regard to the action of occult influences on mundane life, and as such comes closer to a modern interpretation of occult forces rather than the older, blanket concept which tended to blame everything on the invisible mechanisms of magic and supernatural powers.

In addition, the authors discovered that some of the tribes studied believed that the power of witchcraft could be put to use unconsciously, due to "hostility or envy," and that the "witch" may not even know that he or she possesses occult ability. This is also a sophisticated concept, and loaded with implications regarding the limits of human moral responsibility.

In the end, the study admitted that beliefs in witchcraft and sorcery were virtually endemic to the Congolese tribes in spite of five hundred years of exposure to foreign influences and particularly to Catholic and Protestant missionaries in the past hundred years. Ironically, it was the very attempt by Belgian authorities to eradicate the more lethal forms of occult belief that contributed to the growth of witchcraft. They had banned the use of the poison test, an ordeal by which a person suspected of witchcraft is given poison to drink. If he survives, he must be a witch. This is similar in nature to the European practice of "dunking" a bound witch into a lake or pond; if the witch floated to the surface and thus avoided drowning, she was surely a witch. Execution of convicted witches—practiced regularly before the advent of the Belgian administration—was also banned, thus giving rise to a fear that evil witches were multiplying beyond control.

As the SORO report states,

> As a result, many Africans feel that western political systems such as the modern state have aligned themselves on the side of evil because from their standpoint the "civilized" elimination of traditional control measures work to protect witches and sorcerers from retaliation by their innocent victims. The African man-in-the-bush is, therefore, much more at the mercy of those who wish to harm him by supernatural means than ever before. He thus tends to rely more and more upon the witch-doctor who, in the absence of the poison ordeal and other drastic sanctions, provides the main source of protection from evil.[36]

The advice of the SORO team was to study thoroughly the 200 or more Congolese tribes and to compile a comprehensive database on their beliefs, since superstitions vary from tribe to tribe. They also recommended that no psy-war operations using witchcraft or the occult be employed until the actual methods were examined and approved by their opposite numbers in the Congolese government. They recommended that the use of magical practices in a psy-war operation be relegated to "limited tactical objectives rather than broad strategic concepts or solutions to fundamental problems."[37] Further,

> A sound understanding of magical concepts, practices, and mannerisms is necessary for defensive purposes should they play any role or importance in an insurgency situation . . . . Detailed studies of supernatural beliefs of specific tribes are limited.The secrecy inherent in most magical rituals presents a formidable obstacle to the outside investigator, whether he may be a scientist or an intelligence agent.[38]

The report is sober, and dismissive of the long-term benefits of using occult methods in psy-war against the insurgents. The writers feared that using "superstition" would only validate magical thinking among the tribes, thus laying the philosophical groundwork for the next crop of anti-Government witches. The report outlined several important reservations, stating that "tribalism and superstition, so closely related to each other, have provided a fertile seedbed for political instability in the Congo, and measures which enhance the divisive and destructive aspects of tribalism simply lay additional obstacles in the already cluttered path toward Congolese nationhood. Should the central government successfully use occult methods to defeat a movement based on such methods, the very concepts of sorcery and magic which lend impetus to the insurgencies of the moment may gain strength and acquire even greater trouble-making potential for the future."[39]

Very politically-correct. But what if Congolese nationhood was not the ultimate goal of the US administration? What if political instability was the goal? That certainly was the result, no matter how well-planned or unplanned, for the Congo became the Democratic Republic of the Congo, which became Zaire, which became once again the Democratic Republic of the Congo in 1997. Patrice Lumumba, who had asked the UN to intervene in a case of insurrection in Katanga Province (an insurrection supported by Belgian troops) and was denied this assistance, then turned to the Soviet Union. That strategy spelled doom for Lumumba's administration, because it painted him in Communist colors even though he was more a nationalist than an "internationalist." He was targeted by the CIA and eventually killed, leaving his legacy up for grabs in a power struggle of operatic dimensions that has not diminished to this day. If political stability in the Congo was the goal of the US administrations and their intelligence agencies since the 1960s, then they failed utterly. But if their goal was to increase instability—to ensure the ouster of Lumumba who was siding with the Soviets, and to guarantee a weak, pro-US regime in its stead, with Mobutu and his kleptocracy, for example—then they were quite successful. We will probably never know to what extent psychological warfare operations were used in the Congo, and if they included magic spells and sorcery. What seems certain, however, is that the Congolese tribes never abandoned their native beliefs. Indeed, it was Mobutu—a puppet of US interests—who reinstated old African traditions in his country, forcing his citizens to change their names to more suitably "African" ones and to adopt African dress. It was the return of the witch-doctor, something the US accepted and encouraged in exchange for Mobutu's support against Communist strategies in Africa.

In Vietnam, events took an even stranger turn.

SPIRITUAL WARFARE

For instance, there was Operation Wandering Souls. The Vietnamese, as many others around the world, fear being buried in an unmarked grave. This may have something to do with Chinese influences, of course, since China was a nation of ancestor-worship, and there is a holiday every year in which dutiful Chinese visit the graves of their ancestors and burn incense. This practice is so important, in fact, that each year Hong Kong must contend with entire hillsides set on fire by the joss sticks and "hell money" burned on the gravesites amid very dry vegetation. (The author once drove from the new Hong Kong airport to the city during this season, and the flames which covered the hills and looked like the worst of California brush fires had reached the highway, making the passage—if not actually precarious or life-threatening—certainly dramatic!)

The Army PSYOPs personnel used this fear as a weapon in their spooky arsenal. They broadcast eerie sounds and spectral wailing at night from helicopters in an attempt to make the villagers believe that they were the ghosts of dead VC, searching for their unmarked graves and desperate because their families could not find them.

On May 10, 1967 the Joint United States Public Affairs Office (JUSPAO), Saigon, issued their Policy Number 36, "The Use of Superstitions in Psychological Operations in Vietnam."[40] It is a short document, no more than four pages, and begins:

> IN ACCORDANCE WITH U.S. MISSION DIRECTIVES, THIS IS MISSION PSYCHOLOGICAL POLICY AND GUIDANCE AND IS TO BE IMPLEMENTED AS PERTINENT BY ALL U.S. ELEMENTS IN VIETNAM.

The document goes on:

> A strong superstition or a deeply-held belief shared by a substantial number of the enemy target audience can be used as a psychological weapon because it permits with some degree of probability the prediction of individual or group behavior under a given set of conditions.

This is about as clear and concise a definition of psychological warfare principles as any. It is also as cynical. While this document was prepared for military actions in Vietnam, the same concept—using a "deeply-held belief" as a psychological weapon—can be ported from the Third World and used anywhere, no matter what the "deeply-held belief": fundamentalist Christianity, Mormonism, Buddhism, etc.

A further example of the cynicism in which this program was spawned can be shown in the following paragraph:

> In summary, the manipulation of superstitions is a delicate affair. Tampering with deeply-held beliefs, seeking to turn them to your advantage means in effect playing God and it should only be attempted if one can get away with it and the

> game is indeed worth the candle. Failure can lead to ridicule, charges of clumsiness and callousness that can blacken the reputation of psychological operations in general. It is a weapon to be employed selectively and with utmost skill and deftness. There can be no excuse for failure.[41]

Where did the Army PSYOPS people draw the line between religion and superstition? Were they any more successful than, for instance, James Frazer or Claude Levi-Strauss or Marcel Mauss? By playing God, what effect did they have on the lives and belief systems of the civilian populations in the target countries? Suddenly, it seems as if there is a dialectical change from the SORO report on the Congo, mentioned above, to the JUSPAO Policy memo for Vietnam. "Do it," the policy memo seems to say. "Just don't get caught and whatever you do don't damage the reputation of psychological operations in the process."

There can be no excuse for failure.

The final paragraph of the JUSPAO memo reflects the attitude of spiritual warfare in the twentieth century:

> Where the superstitions of friendly forces and populations are concerned, psyops personnel will assist commanders as required or called upon in devising indoctrination materials familiarizing troops with these beliefs and counseling respect for and sensitivity to local beliefs and traditions.[42]

In other words, there are good superstitions and bad superstitions. The US troops were being trained to know the difference between the superstitions of target, i.e., VC populations and those of the "good Vietnamese." One did not require respect and sensitivity for the superstitions of the Viet Cong, of course, since they were the enemy. Evidently it was assumed that there was a difference in belief system between the two groups. Spiritual warfare.

Truly. In the early 1950s, an American neurologist began a series of research projects to determine how a psychic ability such as extrasensory perception could be used as a weapon in psychological warfare. In November 1952 he briefed the Pentagon on the military uses of parapsychology. From 1953 to 1955, he was a captain in the Army and stationed at the Army Chemical Center at Edgewood, Maryland to conduct psychic experiments. His name was Dr. Andrija Puharich, and we will be covering his story more thoroughly later on, as he is a key element in the story of American military and intelligence agency involvement in the study and use of supernatural abilities as potential weapons in wartime, hot and cold.

Somehow, the search for the story behind the murder of young Marina Habe in Hollywood in 1968 led to her father, an important figure in World War II literature, to the OSS, psychological warfare operations, the Congo, Vietnam and beyond.

Marina was believed to be an associate of the Manson "family," and it is alleged that Charles Manson himself stabbed her to death. Was she selected for a particular reason, or was it just an evil coincidence? There is some evidence to show that the Manson "family" murder of Leno and Rosemary LaBianca the day after the Tate murders was a contract killing. Indeed, much of the violence perpetrated by Manson and his followers had a basis in other criminal activity. They were purposeful. Manson does not fit the profile of a serial killer, and indeed his crimes do not fit that pattern at all. A serial killer would not have missed the slaughter at the Tate household, for instance, which Manson had done, sending his followers inside to commit the hideous knife attacks on the five unfortunate victims. If he was somehow responsible for the murder of his uncle, Darwin Scott, that can be laid to a family grudge going back to Manson's childhood in Ashland, Kentucky.

Why, then, was Marina killed? A lust killing, pure and simple? Manson getting off on savagely murdering a college coed? His schedule for the day of the kidnap of Marina Habe and her subsequent murder argues against this; he left Death Valley for one day and returned the next. That implies he went to Los Angeles with a specific purpose in mind, a task to accomplish, and returned when the deed was done.

Marina's mother—Eloise Hardt—had looked out her window that night at 3:30 A.M. and saw a black sedan next to her daughter's smaller, foreign car and two men, one who looked young, about twenty years old. The sedan peeled out, and when Mrs. Hardt went to investigate, her daughter was nowhere to be found. Manson had been driving a black sedan that day, and had been visiting John and Michelle Phillips of the Mamas and the Papas at a New Year's Eve party.[43]

Marina had been known to the Manson group, and thus they would presumably have known of her famous father and his activities during the war. Hans Habe had left the United States for the calmer environment of Switzerland. He had written books criticizing America, and particularly the Warren Report. He was an intelligence officer, there at the birth of the CIA from the eccentric "band of brothers" of the OSS and the US Army Psychological Warfare Bureau, which liaised with the OSS to the extent that the lines between the two spy shops nearly vanished.

And Marina was killed in 1968, at the height of the Vietnam War and less than a year after the famous Tet Offensive of January 1968, in the midst of enormous domestic dislocation in the United States, with student protests, peace marches, demonstrations, and the growth of the Weather Underground. For Manson's most famous victim, he chose Sharon Tate, the daughter of an Army intelligence officer serving in Vietnam. Was there a connection? Two victims, both female, both daughters of intelligence officers, both living in Los Angeles; murdered within eight months of each other.

The author did not know if there was anything more concrete tying these two cases together than the fact that the murders were likely committed by the same group. Perhaps the Habe angle was ancient history. Hans Habe's intelligence career seemed to end in the early 1950s—in fact, the same year his daughter was born in 1951. But were there other connections between Habe and military or intelligence operations in the United States after that time? *Was* that Hans Habe in the photograph of Paperclip scientists in Chicago in 1950?

What was Paperclip?

CROSSBOW, OVERCAST, PAPERCLIP

There had to have been a level at which the US government's leaders identified with the Nazis, or at least admired them. There had to have been a point at which the crimes of the Holocaust were considered a minor problem, a kind of public relations nuisance, that was overshadowed by the glamour of the perfectly-run superstate of the Third Reich. There must have been an understanding that the ideologies of America and Nazi Germany were more alike than the ideologies of America and the Soviet Union. This is because there is just no other way to interpret what took place at the very end of the war; morally, what transpired can only be considered a war crime itself.

In 1945, Nazi scientists—using slave labor from concentration camps—were in a race to develop superweapons to enable Hitler to win the war. They were working at Peenemünde and Nordhausen, famous rocket laboratories where the V-1 and V-2 rockets were designed which made life such hell in Great Britain, and where even newer, more lethal rockets and weapons were being developed. Albert Einstein was worried that the Nazis were on the verge of developing an atomic bomb, and communicated this concern to President Roosevelt. And, what was worse, Russian troops were advancing towards Peenemünde from the east and would capture the Nazi rocket scientists and their laboratories, factories and blueprints, thus permitting the Soviets unprecedented access to the "art of German engineering." Policy makers in Washington knew that the next major conflicts would be fought between the United States and the Soviet Union, and they could not permit the Russians to have the upper hand in technology. It was of utmost importance that those scientists—or as many of them as possible—made it to American shores, out of reach of the Russians and, more importantly perhaps, pressed into service to the United States.

To that end, several wartime intelligence operations were put in motion.

The most famous of these is Operation Paperclip, of course; yet outside of poorly researched, poorly documented newsletters, websites and pamphlets produced by the fraternity of conspiracy theorists, very little information about Paperclip and its implications and ramifications is available to the modern American reading public. It is no longer discussed in Congress; it is not debated on CNN. One of the most accessible of the Paperclip studies is Linda Hunt's *Secret Agenda*, published in 1991; yet by 1999 when the author began writing the present chapter, that book was out of print in English and totally unavailable. Recourse was had to a translated edition which was ordered from Paris under its French title, *L'Affaire Paperclip.* Other important works include Tom Bower's two books, mentioned above, as well as another—very important—work by Christopher Simpson, *Blowback.* Much of the information contained in these volumes had to be extricated from the grasp of the US government under the Freedom of Information Act by the authors and their sources, and it is revealing that thousands of documents pertaining to the Second World War and Allied intelligence activities are *still classified* as of this writing. The picture that is revealed is not a pretty one; even as late as 1983 with the deportation of Nazi war criminal Klaus Barbie, the American government was denying that any mass recruitment of war criminals had ever taken place on US soil or under US government authority. History now tells a different story.

Most people who have heard of Paperclip assume that it was a program to bring Nazi scientists to the United States to assist the space program, a concept that is at least partially true. There was much more to Paperclip—and to subsequent Nazi recruitment—than rocket science, however. Nazi medical personnel were also recruited, as well as psychological warfare experts and, with the Gehlen Organization, spies, assassins and saboteurs. Eventually, some of these imported Nazi war criminals wound up holding impressive executive positions in American industry, principally high-technology firms in the aerospace and military hardware industries. That indefatigable researcher and conspiriologist, the late Mae Brussell, even suggested that the Paperclip Nazis had been involved in the Kennedy assassination! While that theory seems very far-fetched, there are some disturbing connections between the recruited Nazis and people close to the assassination, and these will be examined a bit later on.

It is important to realize that, at the end of the war, the new enemy was the Soviet Union, even though America and Russia had been allies during the war against Nazi Germany. It was, after all, General Patton himself who tried to convince Washington that we were pointing our weapons in the wrong direction and should make all haste to invade Russia and put an end to the Soviet state once and for all. (American schoolchildren never learn that, at the end of World War One, we had tried to do just that.)

Most people also never learn that the Catholic Church and various Eastern Orthodox churches were also involved in rescuing these war criminals and assisting them to find new homes (and employers) in the Americas, North and South. Some—such as Alois Brunner—even wound up in the Middle East, in Syria and Egypt, creating secret police organizations there and working for the CIA via the Gehlen Organization.[44] Brunner has been accused of murdering more than 120,000 men, women and children during the war, in countries ranging from France and Greece to Slovakia. Other Nazis wound up as far away as Australia and, it has been suggested to the author, in regions as remote as the mountains of northern Thailand and the islands of the Indonesian archipelago.

The Paperclip story is long and complex; it involves the alphabet soup of intelligence agencies and programs, from CROWCASS to CIC, SIS, OSS, CIA, JIOA, and many more. It deals with dozens of countries and their respective intelligence organizations, armies, political parties, churches, and criminal justice systems. Interested readers are encouraged to seek out the books mentioned above and draw their own conclusions. For now, the author will concentrate on those areas of Paperclip that pertain more directly to our story.

By December of 1943, it had become apparent to the Allies that the Germans were working on a series of secret weapons, notably rockets, at a number of sites in Germany. The most famous, of course, was Peenemünde, located at the northeastern tip of Germany, close to the Polish border. Bombing raids on Peenemünde forced the Nazis to diversify their rocket research to other centers around the country, and perhaps the most famous of these is Niedersachswerfen, in the Harz Mountains, the site of the *Mittelwerke* and only a few miles away from two concentration camps—Nordhausen and Dora—that would provide slave labor for the rocket factory. Slave labor was also provided by the prisoners at Buchenwald. But before the Mittelwerke (Central Works) became the prime focus of the rocket effort, a decision had been made in London that Nazi long range weapons research, development, and production had to be stopped at all costs. A team was brought together to concentrate on the problem and to allocate resources to its execution. This team was known by the project name *Crossbow*, and was led by British Prime Minister Winston Churchill himself.[45]

As the war began to wind down with the success of the D-Day invasion and the large-scale Allied assault, tensions in Germany grew high. On July 20, 1944—six weeks after D-Day—a group of Nazi generals attempted the assassination of Adolf Hitler, an attempt that failed almost miraculously. For months, Crossbow had been initiating bombing raids against Peenemünde and the Mittelwerke in a desperate attempt to stall (if not completely cancel) Germany's rocket and secret weapon development. In the United States, the Manhattan Project was well underway and progress was being made in the development of the world's first atomic bomb; yet the Allies were worried that the Nazis might be making the same—or even greater—progress from the hidden tunnels in the Harz Mountains where the rockets were being designed. Their worst fear was that the Nazis had the bomb; they knew they already had the rocket delivery system necessary to send it anywhere in Europe.

Himmler understood the urgent need for the secret weapons being developed by the Nazi scientists as the war was starting to go against the Germans, and at one point had approached Wernher von Braun to ask him if he would like to work directly for the Reichsführer-SS himself, rather than deal with "Army red tape." Von Braun politely declined, but the pressure was on.[46]

As the Russians advanced from the East, they were coming perilously close to Peenemünde The Allies were worried that the cream of Nazi science would fall into

Soviet hands. The Germans shared their concern, and began moving the scientists and their families out of Peenemünde in the spring of 1945 to the central German towns of Nordhausen and Bleicherode, where they continued their research at the Mittelwerke. Before leaving, however, they managed to destroy as much of Peenemündes classified information as possible, leaving only a skeleton crew behind when the Russians finally entered the town on May 5, 1945. Nordhausen, however, was right in the way of the American advance, and it appeared that the US Army would reach the Nazi scientists before anyone else. The race was on to capture as much as possible: scientists, blueprints, actual rockets and other weapons and machinery. OSS, CIC and other intelligence units spread out through Germany in a desperate effort to deny the Soviets the technological advantage of Nazi science, and in July 1945 the effort was coordinated under the project name *Overcast*.

Overcast would not become *Paperclip* until March 13, 1946 when security leaks required a change of codename, but the project mission was the same. By the time Paperclip was over, thousands of Nazi scientists—many of them accused war criminals who had participated in some of the war's worst outrages—had managed to find homes in the United States, South America and other locations. In many cases, they brought their families with them as well. And while the Paperclip agents were seeking scientists, other organizations were looking for Nazi espionage agents and recruiting them by the thousands to work for the United States and Great Britain against the Soviets. The most famous intelligence coup of the post-war period was the recruitment of General Reinhard Gehlen, a Nazi spymaster whose specialty was Russia and Eastern Europe. His story is told, albeit thinly disguised, in Hans Habe's *Agent of the Devil,* where he is identified as "General von Greehahn." Habe treats his subject cynically, and it is easy to see that he has become frustrated with Allied duplicity where the de-Nazification process was concerned. The book was published in 1958, by which time Habe had retreated to the aloof neutrality of the Swiss Alps.

Gehlen—like Habe's fictional Greehahn—was a con artist as well as a spy, which is probably a different way of saying the same thing. He convinced the CIA that his support, and those of his friends and former staff, was essential to western efforts to contain the Soviet advance. Today, Gehlen's real value to American intelligence is being seriously questioned, but in those days he was something of a hero: "our" German, a "good" German who was fighting the good fight against the Communist menace. Habe probably had an insider's view of the famous General, owing to his privileged position within American intelligence in post-war Germany. While not a spy-master or superspy, Habe's political influence in Germany was strong, and he had many friends among the OSS and the US Army's Psychological Warfare Bureau. He was in a position to witness the de-Nazification process at first hand and—as authors such as Hunt, Simpson and Bower have documented in exhaustive detail—this process was doomed from the beginning. Habe was in a position to watch the OSS morph into the CIA, and to observe how many of his sworn enemies became CIA operatives while he sat in Munich or Berlin, writing articles and editing newspapers for the Allies.

Habe assigns a mystical streak to Gehlen/Greehahn, which would not be surprising in the least. The higher ranking Nazis were contaminated with the ersatz paganism and popular occultism of the Thule Gesellschaft variety which had been absorbed into the SS with torchlight processions and runic chants. As early as 1958, Habe was writing of the "materialization of the psychic" as the next step in technology, putting these words in the mouth of his General. What can be more creepy than a Nazi intelligence chief predicting a world in which his people dominate the realm of the metaphysical, through the use of technology that enhances psychic abilities? Habe seemed to sense this direction, and one wonders if it was the fruit of his intelligence and psy-war connections on both sides of the fence in Germany? How strange . . . how very, very strange . . . that his daughter might have been murdered by a man who claimed just those sorts of abilities.

ROCKET SCIENCE

As the post-war years continued through the 1940s and into the 1950s, Nazis of every stripe wound up doing research for the American defense program. They were based all over the United States, depending on their specialty, but several locations stand out as more important than the rest.

Perhaps the most intriguing locale for former Nazi scientists was Randolph Air Force Base in Texas. Unlike Fort Bliss, near El Paso, where by February 1946 more than 100 Nazi scientists were in residence, working on the rocket program, Randolph AFB near San Antonio was used for more arcane research.

It was at Randolph that we come across the name of Dr. Hubertus Strughold. Strughold managed to escape the fate of his Nazi colleagues by clever maneuvering and outright lying about his work and his responsibility—aided and abetted by American intelligence agencies—but in the end as more and more files were found and declassified, it became apparent that Dr. Strughold was right in the middle of some of the more heinous medical experimentation this planet has ever known.

Aviation medicine is a specialized field which has since developed into aerospace medicine, the study of the physical effects of space travel on the human body. In the war years, however, attention was devoted to the effects of extreme cold, high pressure, oxygen deprivation and high altitude, as well as the effects of freezing water . . . for those pilots who would be downed over the open sea, for instance. Aircraft were being developed that could fly at astonishing speeds, and climb to unthinkable altitudes. Obviously, in conditions of airwar, the advantage was to the planes—and the pilots—who commanded the skies: the perfect combination of high-performance machines with highly-trained, physically-fit pilots. A new medical science was created to study how the vastly different environment of the air—as opposed to the earth, the domain of the footsoldier—affected the lives and the performance of human beings.

Aviation medicine was begun in Germany, in 1912, by Nathan Zuntz. Ironically, Zuntz was Jewish.[47] The first German aviation doctors built their own pressure chambers and centrifuges and experimented upon themselves, reporting their results in professional journals to the awe and admiration of the small, but elite, international community of aviation specialists. By the 1930s, conferences in Germany on aviation medicine were being attended by physicians and specialists from all over the world. Dr. Hubertus Strughold was one of these famous aviation medicine specialists, and he made friends with other members of the international community, including American military surgeons.

As director of an aviation medicine research institute for the Luftwaffe, holding the rank of Colonel, Strughold was in a position to know of the horrific medical experiments being carried out on living human beings at Dachau in the name of aviation medicine, some of which were being conducted by his friends and co-workers. Prior to the war years, aviation doctors had risked their own lives in these experiments. Now, with such a wealth of potential guinea pigs at their disposal, there was no need to endanger the lives of scientists. Experiments in high altitude pressure, extremes of heat and cold, etc. were carried out on living Jewish and political prisoners at Dachau, and these results shared among the members of the Nazi aviation medicine community.

Strughold had attended an important meeting of ninety-five senior officers in Nuremberg in October 1942, during which these experiments were openly discussed, experiments conducted by colleagues who reported to him and others to whom Strughold himself reported. Such notorious Nazi scientists as Dr. Sigmund Rascher—a Luftwaffe staff surgeon and member of Himmler's SS—had contributed[48] to these reports on the experiments, some of which had been filmed for the edification of Heinrich Himmler and a select audience. Later, Strughold would try to distance himself from Rascher and his experiments, but the documentation would go against him. Strughold was an associate of Dr. Siegfried Ruff—with whom he had co-authored a textbook, the *Atlas der Luftfahrtmedizin* (Aviation Medicine) published in Leipzig in 1942—and it was Ruff who was assigned by Lieutenant-General Professor Erich Hippke to assist Rascher in the human guinea pig medical program at Dachau's experimental Block Number Five. Hippke was the Luftwaffe's chief surgeon, and as such was Strughold's boss. Ruff, although a close personal friend of Strughold, did not work for Hippke, but was "invited" to join the human experimentation program to assist Rascher. (Sigmund Ruff and Siegfried Rascher! It is not often that evil attains such Wagnerian proportions.)

The experiments involved plunging prisoners into ice-cold water, with thermometers stuck in their various orifices, to measure how long it took for a live human being to freeze to death. Prisoners were also subjected to oxygen deprivation, to high pressure experiments, etc., and much of this was captured on still and motion pictures, some of which have survived to this day. It is not known how many prisoners in total died as a result of these "experiments," but eyewitness testimony indicates that eighty prisoners alone died as a result of the high pressure tests conducted by Rascher.[49] Strughold later admitted that everyone at the Nuremberg conference, for instance, was well aware that human beings—prisoners—were being used in the experiments, and that many of these subjects had died as a result of the tests. No objections were raised.

The Nuremberg prosecutors, however, were hot on the trail of the Nazi doctors. The scientists had managed to destroy their files, so all that remained were Himmler's SS files, which were discovered at the end of the war. The evidence in Himmler's files was very suggestive, however, and brought to light much more than what the Nazi scientists previously admitted had taken place. The problem was that most of the evidence against the doctors was circumstantial, and the prosecutors could not break the wall of silence that had grown up around the defendants as they corroborated each other's alibis and denied any knowledge of wrongdoing. While all of this was going on, Strughold sat in Heidelberg and edited the medical experimentation reports of his colleagues to ensure that no embarrassing admissions had taken place. He edited out all references to the human experimentation program, and thus presented a completely sanitized version of Nazi aviation medicine research, which was subsequently published as a massive, two-volume study, with some chapters actually written by Nazi scientists who had been condemned at Nuremberg for war crimes. This study was published by the US Air Force as *German Aviation Medicine*, and contained nothing about the human experiments, no reference to the prisoners who had lost their lives at Dachau and at other camps and "institutes" throughout the Reich. Strughold himself avoided prosecution, as military intelligence considered him too valuable to US aviation medicine programs; thus he was able to remain behind at Heidelberg, far away from the prosecutors and jail cells at Nuremberg, and continue his painstaking destruction of the evidence against him and his colleagues.

Dachau was not the only site of human medical experimentation; studies using prisoners were taking place everywhere in the Reich. Experiments on live subjects had taken place in settings as diverse as Chalais-Meudon in France and Occupied Prague. The experimenters at the last two sites had already found refuge and employment in the United States as early as 1947. Rascher had wanted to use Auschwitz as well, as it was a much larger camp and thus an easier place to hide the hideous experiments he had planned. Rascher complained that sometimes his subjects screams were quite loud during the course of the experiments, and that he needed a larger, more secure installation to continue his research in relative comfort, far from potential witnesses.

In the end, everything was blamed on the SS, even though the SS officers at the camps had no ability to conduct the experiments, no medical training, and could not even be expected to know how to operate the complex machinery. Not that the SS was blameless, of course. It was Himmler who was approving this type of experimentation right and left. His Ahnenerbe-SS was conducting its own experimentation on live subjects at Dachau, and was making a collection of human skulls from among the living prisoner population, a collection to be used in anthropological research. Indeed, Rascher was an SS officer, and Nuremberg would have loved to have had him in the dock, but he was executed on orders of Himmler two weeks before the end of the war. With Rascher dead, and the files destroyed, there remained only the testimony of the doctors themselves . . . or that of the witnesses, but in most cases the witnesses had died as a result of the experiments. Many of the Nazi doctors thus waltzed away free, and found refuge in America.

Strughold and his team wound up at Randolph AFB in Texas, where they continued their research in aviation medicine, a field then being changed to "space medicine." This was the School of Aviation Medicine that was begun at Mineola, Long Island (New York) during World War One, and which was subsequently moved to Brooks Air Force Base in Texas before winding up at Randolph. It is important to realize that NASA—the US government's civilian space agency—had not yet been formed, and would not be until July 29, 1958. Until then, space research was military research, and fell under the US Army and, eventually (1947) the newly created US Air Force. In fact, it was at Randolph that the "first Department of Space Medicine in the world" was established, on February 9, 1949 . . . nearly ten years before the creation of NASA. Strughold then became the world's first professor of Space Medicine.[50]

Thus, Strughold's team was developing the field of aviation and space medicine strictly for US military applications, acting under the authority and the unapologetic protection of the man who would eventually become the head of the US Air Force's aviation medicine program, Colonel Harry Armstrong. It was Armstrong who had first met Strughold at an aviation medicine conference in Germany in 1934, and who from then on considered himself a friend of the Nazi doctor. Further, Armstrong kept requesting more and more Nazi scientists as time went by, forcing General C.P. Cabell of Air Force Intelligence to warn Armstrong off.[51] Yet, Armstrong did not back down, but kept asking for more visas for more Nazis to bolster his growing aviation medicine team at Randolph.

Whatever the morality of recruiting German scientists—many of them committed Nazis, some actually accused of war crimes—to assist the United States space program and other military efforts, there was another dimension to the Randolph team that has gone virtually unnoticed by researchers due to the near total lack of documentation and the lack of living witnesses. The evidence that does exist is largely circumstantial, but much of it can be found in the Captured German Documents section of the National Archives and then collated with later testimony and other odd clues that turn up in memoirs, biographies and histories of the war years and its aftermath. Like the infamous MK-ULTRA files that were destroyed at CIA headquarters on the orders of Richard Helms, documentation on Nazi psychological warfare and mind control research was also either destroyed—by the Nazis themselves—or concealed under very high security classifications by the US military and intelligence establishment.

The first indication we have that anything like a mind control program existed within the Third Reich is the memoir of Himmler's astrologer, Wulff, who talks about the Nazi desire to create a program within the Reich to duplicate the mental state of the Japanese soldier, a human being willing and eager to risk his life without question for his country, stuffing his own body into pillboxes to blow them up, and the Chinese Communist "human wave" trooper, who would rush unthinkingly into certain slaughter. This "Asian" mentality was something the Nazis would have dearly loved to inculcate into their own troops, and Wulff—seen as an expert on Asian mysticism—was hired to come up with ways that could be used to condition the German soldier the same way.[52]

Buried in the voluminous files of the Ahnenerbe-SS are also references to the use of mescaline and cannabis as "truth serums," programs that—according to John Marks in his ground-breaking study of CIA mind control projects—have been kept classified by US intelligence since 1945.[53] Here and there we come across the names of Paperclip scientists involved with military and CIA mind control programs, such as Friedrich Hoffmann, a Nazi chemist who advised the CIA on matters relating to psychotropic substances for use in interrogation and "brainwashing."[54] Hoffmann has been linked to Edgewood Arsenal, where CIA maintained TSS (Technical Service Staff) personnel involved in various aspects of chemical and biological warfare, including—according to John Marks—the implantation of new memories in amnesiac patients.[55] One finds an article by Hoffmann, and co-authors William A. Mosher and Richard Hively, on the subject of "Isolation of Trans-*6-Tetrahydrocannibinol from Marijuana" in the April 20, 1966 issue of *Journal of the American Chemical Society*, an issue published—ironically enough—on Hitler's birthday. Hoffmann was working at the time under the cover of the University of Delaware, along with his co-author Mosher. Another colleague at the University was Dr. James Moore, a chemist originally with Parke, Davis in Detroit, and a person well-known among aficionados as deeply implicated in the CIA's MK-ULTRA program, who experimented on mind-altering substances such as mescaline, psilocybin and the highly controversial drug BZ (quinuclidinyl benzilate).

The ready supply of prisoners at Dachau provided a steady stream of guinea pigs for these chemical experiments and tests. Cannabis and mescaline were both used—sometimes in very large doses—along with hypnosis to see if any of these mechanisms could be used as truth serums, magical potions to unlock the secrets of the mind. At the same time, in the United States, OSS agents were using the same or similar drugs on unsuspecting targets—such as Mafia "made men"—to see if the same objectives could be attained. Gradually, in the US, hypnosis was also used, sometimes in combination with drugs. And if false information, or "suggestions," could be implanted in the subject, then we have an instance where the goals of psychological warfare and regular intelligence work overlap. In the case of the latter, the methodology was fine-tuned to the individual subject for a specific purpose: as it turned out, this purpose—as seen by the CIA and by their counterparts in other countries—was assassination.

We have seen that the Germans were among the first to study the uses of psychological warfare; we also have seen that psychological warfare became inextricably intertwined with propaganda and communication studies and science on the "soft" side, and eventually bled over into acts that can only be considered terrorism: assassinations, sabotage, torture and interrogation, on the "hard" side. Indeed, terrorism is nothing more than a form of psychological warfare, as acts of terrorism have no intrinsic military value aside from their effects on the psyches of the target populations. As psychological warfare became more sophisticated—and the intelligence services at once more creative and more demanding—new techniques were developed and virtually codified. One of these was "disinformation," a method by which false information is "leaked" in such a way as to make the receiver believe it is valid data. Disinformation can be used in several ways: in the first place, to make a target believe something false so they will act on the false information, wasting time, energy and money in the process and being deflected from any genuinely sensitive areas; in the second place, to trace the flow of information within a target intelligence shop. Like the dye that is used in staining biological slides, disinformation can be used to follow the trail of an invented story from place to place, from agent to agent, to find out if there is a mole or double agent in the system.

All of these techniques—hallucinogenic drugs, hypnosis, acts of terrorism, disinformation—share an ontological purpose: to manipulate perceptions, to re-create reality. As we noted above, the German word for psychological warfare translates as "worldview warfare": a battle of perceptions, of consensus realities. Once that Pandora's box was opened, there was no closing it again. The temptation was too great. For those who wanted to play God, in the words of the JUSPAO report above, there was the next best thing: one could play with the elements of creation in such a way that magical transformations would take place. As the men of the OSS, CIA, and military intelligence developed from the armchair scholars and academics that most of them were before the war years into soldiers fighting the Cold War on fronts all over the world, they became—in a very real sense—magicians. As we will see, the CIA mind control projects themselves represented an assault on consciousness and reality that has not been seen in history since the age of the philosopher-kings and their court alchemists.

Rumors of what was taking place at Randolph AFB in those days have filtered out into the community of conspiracy theorists in such a way as to devalue the research completely in many cases. There are, however, some scraps of evidence and testimony that are hard to ignore. One of these involves a man whose name has become synonymous with alien abductions and UFO phenomena, and this context makes the information suspect to skeptical researchers. However, the information that is verifiable has led the author to believe that something more than high-pressure studies and oxygen deprivation tests was going on at Randolph AFB in the bosom of the Nazi scientists.

Recourse to an official history of the Space Medicine program, written by Mae Mills Link, who was senior US Air Force Medical Historian, and published in 1965 as *NASA Special Publication-4003* in the NASA History Series, shows us some of the later employment in official positions of the Nazi scientists.

Among those on the roster is Dr. Heinz Haber, whom we have met earlier in some confusion with Hans Habe, and who later became chief science consultant for Walt Disney Productions! Dr. Fritz Haber later became involved with Avco Manufacturing, but at Randolph he had designed the sealed cabin for the high-pressure studies. Dr. Siegfried Gerathewohl, "who had been chief of the Psychological Testing Center of the German Air Force during World War II," later joined NASA.[56] Gerathewohl was not an official member of the Randolph team, having been assigned to the rocket scientists under Dornberger and von Braun instead, but he was often seconded to the Randolph base for specific work. (The NASA publication also refers to the two-volume *German Aviation Medicine,* edited by Strughold and "prepared by 56 leading German aviation specialists" on "such topics as the physiological fundamentals of high altitude and acceleration and the potential problems of man under gravity-free conditions." The word "Nazi" is never mentioned in the text, nor is reference made to the fact that several of the articles were written by accused war criminals and contained data obtained from the use of live subjects at Dachau and other concentration camps.)

That the psychological aspect of space medicine was not being ignored is evidenced by Gerathewohl's position with the Air Force. He has been the author of many articles on various aspects of space psychology from a mechanistic—one almost wants to say "Hegelian"—point of view. With Strughold, he was the author of "Motoric responses of the eyes when exposed to light flashes of high intensity and short duration" in *Aviation Medicine* (1953). This study has since been referenced in works on the use of lasers, but has applications in behavioral psychology as well. His "Orientation and Navigation in Space-Time" was published in 1967, and he is the author of the text *Psychologie im Flugzeug* (Aviation Psychology). So although his purpose at the US Air Force and, later, at NASA seems to have been devoted to physiological responses to the unique stressors of space flight, he never lost his interest in the more psychological aspects of his field. This wedding of the purely psychological with the purely physiological became the cornerstone of subsequent intelligence agency programs designed to uncover the secrets of the mind: the interface between the lump of grey matter we call the brain, and the great beyond we call reality.

Another Luftwaffe alumnus—this time one who wound up conducting torture and interrogation programs after the War—was Paul Schaefer, whose frightening Colonia Dignidad operation in Pinochet's Chile was covered extensively by this author in *Unholy Alliance*. At Colonia Dignidad, these techniques were combined with sophisticated technology to conduct the torture of political prisoners by remote control, all to the strains of Wagner and Mozart.

THE CHURCH OF . . . *THELMA?*

Naturally, the Nazis were not the only ones with a rocket program during World War II. The United States was involved in various research projects involving rocketry, including a search for the perfect solid-fuel propellant. At this time, much of the work was being done in California, at the Guggenheim Aeronautical Laboratory, California Institute of Technology (GALCIT) under the famous team of Theodore von Kármán and Frank J. Malina at Pasadena. One of their more illustrious—if eventually notorious—team members was Jack Parsons, a tall, darkly handsome and frighteningly intelligent man who would eventually lose his security clearance after the War due to his relationship with occultists and magicians. It was Parsons, a devotee of English magician Aleister Crowley, who would later declare himself the Antichrist . . . after a stormy relationship with the founder of Scientology, L. Ron Hubbard. Parsons was accused of giving secret technology to the Israelis, among other felonies, and at one time worked for the Howard Hughes empire. He died quite prematurely from an explosion at his home, either an accident, or suicide, or murder; none of the sources seem to agree. For all that, a crater on the dark side of the Moon was named after him in recognition of his accomplishments for the space program and his contribution in creating what would eventually become the Jet Propulsion Laboratory at Caltech. The reader should be assured at this point that all of the above statements are absolutely true and verifiable from hundreds of impeccable sources, such as FBI files (recently declassified and obtained under the Freedom of Information Act) and from Parsons's own words, as incredible as this story seems.

A search through NASA, Caltech and JPL websites will turn up photographs of Parsons and the rest of the team. Parsons was an apprentice—a research associate—of von Kármán's at Caltech when they fired their first test rocket in the Arroyo Seco, in back of Devil's Gate dam, in Pasadena on October 31, 1936 . . . Halloween and, coincidentally, the same day as the last Houdini séance (Houdini told his wife that if there was life after death he would try to contact her from the grave at a series of séances; October 31, 1936 was the last—equally unsuccessful—séance). Snapshots of the Arroyo Seco site show a very primitive launch platform in the midst of dry scrub land, and the rocket team casually spread out on the ground before it like the nerd contingent of a fraternity beach party. Those who think that perhaps the first rocket launch on Halloween was simply a coincidence should refer to the official JPL website where they state that the American space age began on "January 31, 1958 with the launch of the first US satellite, Explorer I, built and controlled by JPL." January 31, of course, is the pagan holiday known to Christianity as Candlemas and to pagans as Oimelc. Thus, for better or for worse, meaningful or not, the launch that took place on Halloween, 1936 culminated in the launch on Candlemas, 1958, and was the result of the work of the same organization, for von Kármán's GALCIT team eventually became the founding members of the Jet Propulsion Laboratory. Oddly enough, the man in charge of the Explorer launch was Dr. Wernher von Braun, the Nazi scientist formerly of Peenemünde and Nordhausen. Perhaps *he* had a pagan agenda?

Halloween (known among European pagans as Samhain, pronounced "sa-wen") is traditionally the day when the dead return to visit the living, similar to the Asian "Wandering Souls" festival mentioned above. It is the day when the gate between the living and the dead is open, a favorite day for evocations of spirits and demons. Candlemas, on the other hand, is the day of "quickening," when the earth begins to wake from its slumber, a day of promise for the future, of the celebration of fertility, of anticipation for the bounty of the coming year. One could say, therefore, that the first rocket launch on Halloween was an evocation of the daimon of flight, or perhaps in a darker context a breaching of the barrier between this world and the next, an initiatic rending of the veil of the Temple: space being seen as the domain of both the dead and the higher spiritual forces. The actual birth of the American space program on Candlemas is, of course, also an auspicious event, ripe with mythical connotations. It is not the intention of this author to suggest that the selection of these dates was deliberate on the part of von Kármán, Parsons, von Braun or the other space engineers. Indeed, by the time of the Explorer I launch in 1958 Parsons himself had already been dead six years. It *is* the intention, however, to point out these synchronicities as they occur, because they are evidence of deeper, more sinister, forces at work, as we shall see.

Jack Parsons was born Marvel Whiteside Parsons on October 2, 1914 in Los Angeles, California. His father was a captain in the US Army. His name was also Marvel Parsons. That's right: his father was Captain Marvel. His son later changed his name to John, after his father left his mother subsequent to some unpleasantness over an adultery.

He once visited Europe with his mother in 1929, when he would have been about fifteen, but that was the extent of foreign travel for Jack Parsons. He graduated from University High School in Pasadena in 1933, but did not go on to college after that. He took some extension courses at UC and University of Southern California, but never obtained a degree.

He became involved with explosives and rocket technology at a very early age, even before his high school graduation, working for the Hercules Powder Company in Los Angeles in 1932, before moving on to the Halifax Explosives

Company in 1934 and finally winding up at GALCIT in 1936, at which time he was barely twenty-two.

The Halloween launch occurred that year.

Parsons inherited a large house in Pasadena after the death of his father, to which he invited a string of houseguests from the occult and science-fiction communities. His interest in occultism ran roughly parallel to his interest in rocket science, and von Kármán wrote that Jack used to chant pagan hymns and stamp his feet on the ground in the Arroyo Seco, but that otherwise he was brilliant and a very hard-worker, very conscientious, and totally focused on rocketry. Parsons and his childhood friend and fellow rocketeer Edward Forman had been in regular communication with German and Russian rocket engineers, including the famous Willy Ley, as well as—according to some reports—Igor Sikorsky (inventor of the Sikorsky helicopter) and Arthur Young (who developed the Bell helicopter). At the age of 13, Parsons claimed he had tried to invoke Satan, but the experience frightened him, and he turned away from occultism for a while and devoted himself to pursuits of an even more . . . explosive nature.[57]

In 1939, we find Parsons married to Helen Northrup and joining a cult based in Los Angeles, the OTO or Ordo Templi Orientis. The OTO was one of several occult societies under the leadership of Aleister Crowley, the English magician who received a revelation in Cairo in 1904 which became the basis for a new religion, which Crowley called *Thelema*, the Greek word for "Will." The OTO was a German secret society that was designed to communicate Tantric and other Eastern sexual practices beneath the clean, white apron of Freemasonry. Crowley usurped leadership of the Order after the death of its previous Master, generating a three-way fight which left one version of the Order adhering to its original rites and purposes, another version—the Brotherhood of Saturn—peeling off to pursue a different dream, and Crowley's OTO becoming in the process the most famous of the three.

The sexual element of the OTO was enhanced by Crowley's naturally more rapacious appetites, and the rituals rewritten to include numerous references to Crowley's own belief system, Thelema, and more overtly sexual gestures. By 1939, the "Agape" Lodge was under stewardship of one W.T. Smith, an early Crowley devotee. This was the lodge that Parsons visited, and soon he found himself embroiled in all of the petty rivalries, sexual seductions, and thirst after arcane lore and unspeakable powers that characterizes such groups.

The following year, in 1940, the US Army Air Corps paid a visit to von Kármán and company and decided that they wanted to support and sponsor the rocket research going on there because of its military applications. The first visit was by none other than General "Pap" Arnold, the famed (and outspoken) aviator. His interest was in developing jet-assisted take-off and landing (JATO) capability for his aircraft, enabling them to take off and land on the very short runways he was anticipating in the upcoming Asian conflict. Von Kármán,

Forman, Parsons, and several others got to work on the program immediately. It is informative to note that most of the patents that would be generated by this research would be in Parsons' name. Several of the others would go on to glory as well, but not before a bit of *sturm und drang* in California. The GALCIT project was now renamed as the Jet Propulsion Laboratory, or JPL. Jack Parsons was a founding member.

When General Arnold returned to Washington, a background check was initiated on Parsons by Army Intelligence. The person requesting the FBI to scour its records, if any, on Parsons was none other than Brigadier General Sherman Miles, head of G-2 in Washington.[58] General Miles was a famous name in Washington circles, coming from a long line of military officers, one of whom fought in the Indian wars. Miles himself had played a role in drawing up boundaries in post-World War One Europe, a role for which he is still remembered. What he is best known for, however, was his reluctance to cover for his Commanding Officer, General George Marshall, at the time of the Pearl Harbor attack on December 7, 1941, when for a while the General could not be found, as the teletypes were burning up miles of copper wire between Hawaii and D.C. (General Miles was later relieved of his command.)

The FBI reported back that they had found nothing damaging about Parsons, and he was awarded a security clearance. It is interesting to note that at this same time, Naval Intelligence (ONI) also requested information on Parsons. This time, the intelligence officer was one Capt. W. B. Phillips, who may have been the same W.B. Phillips who later commanded an amphibious transport vehicle in the Pacific War. As before, nothing damaging was found.

Back in California, however, Parsons had so impressed the membership of the Agape Lodge that one member—Jane Wolfe—would write to Crowley, telling him that in her opinion Parsons would eventually become head of the Order. In March 1941, W.T. Smith sent a letter to Crowley praising Parsons. By this time, of course, England was at war with Germany.

On June 13, 1941, an Army officer is initiated into the OTO at the Agape Lodge temple. His name is Grady McMurtry, and he will be stationed for a time in England where he meets Aleister Crowley and develops an odd sort of relationship with the Prophet of Thelema. At this same time, Crowley has been involved in some potential intelligence work with such figures as Dennis Wheatley and Ian Fleming, both officers with British intelligence and friends of Crowley. They would later become famous novelists, of course, but at the time they were seeking Crowley's assistance to exploit his knowledge of the European occult underground in the war effort. (This is all covered in detail in my *Unholy Alliance*.) McMurtry will return to the United States safely after the war, and engineer a coup to take over leadership of the OTO after the deaths of Crowley and Crowley's designated successor. More about McMurtry in later chapters, but his movements between the Agape Lodge—which is, after all, infamous among the rocket scientists who are working on highly classified work—and London, where Crowley, their leader, is staying are suggestive of a larger purpose.

In 1942, Parsons single-handedly solves the JATO problem. The difficulty that faced the engineers was that the solid fuel formulas that had worked thus far degraded quickly during storage. Parsons is able to work out a more stable formula based on a mixture of asphalt and potassium perchlorate, having been inspired by something the ancients called "Greek fire," appropriately enough for an occultist. By this time, Parsons and the other rocket team members form their own company, the Aerojet Corporation, to develop these materials and sell them to the Army. (Aerojet would later be taken over by General Tire and Rubber, now known as GenCorp; one of the founding rocketeers, Frank Malina, would take his shares and open an art gallery in Paris . . . and future UFO researcher and nuclear physicist Stanton Friedman would find work there in the 1960s.[59])

And, by 1944, Parsons would become head of the Agape Lodge of the OTO by Crowley's decree, after the ouster of W.T. Smith, whose leadership had turned the Order into a "love cult." During this same year, an FBI informant had relayed information on the OTO and Parsons which was of an interesting nature. This notation—filed with the number 100-189320-2 and dated 3-31-44—was from Oklahoma City, and bore the heading:

> "Re: CHURCH OF THELMA, also known as
> ORIENA TEMPLUS ORIENTUS, OTO (phonetic)
> SECURITY MATTER—G"

Thus did the "Church of *Thelma*" enter FBI files.

The informant stated that he had been invited to a party sometime in June or July of 1940 in Pasadena. What he thought was going to be a party, however, turned into a meeting of the Order. No matter; the informant was initiated into the Order during the weekend, but "does not recall anything of the initiation proceedings except that all of the participants had all their clothes removed and they wore robes for the occasion. Prior to the proceedings [name deleted] given a glass of liquor which apparently was drugged thus causing him not to remember much of the proceedings."[60] This was, as the rest of the memo makes clear, during the reign of W. T. Smith, when free love was the norm (it was, after all, how the Order attracted recruits), and it is not known what drug—if any—was in use at that time that would have caused the type of amnesia to which the informant claims he was victim. Parsons was, of course, a chemist and later would work in the pharmacology department of a university, even though his main interest in chemistry was of the explosive variety; yet, there is evidence through his writings that he was also taking drugs, for a poem he published in the Order newsletter—*Oriflamme*—rather explicitly states, "I live on peyote, marijuana, morphine, and cocaine."[61] While one can assume a certain level of hyperbole in those claims, it is not inconceivable that these drugs were used in some combination among the swinging, free-love initiates of the Agape Lodge.

Love, though, is rarely free; eventually, the bill arrives in the mail. Parsons' wife, Helen Northrup (who became pregnant by Smith), departed with the priapic W.T. Smith in 1944, leaving Jack alone with her eighteen-year-old sister. Sarah Elizabeth Northrup, known as "Betty," was by all accounts a very attractive student at USC. Although they have an ongoing affair, by the summer of 1945 she and Jack meet a Naval officer, and their lives are never the same again. The officer, a struggling science fiction author with several published stories, becomes known to the world, not for literature but as the founder of Scientology: L. Ron Hubbard.

PULP FICTION

As many celebrities and movie stars (John Travolta, Tom Cruise, and Kirstie Alley for example) have joined the ranks of Scientology, and as Scientology reappears in our story in various other manifestations—Charles Manson, the Process Church of the Final Judgment, etc.—it would do well to examine the bizarre relationship of Parsons and Hubbard a little further, as it was evidently a pivotal episode in both their lives and led directly to the creation of Scientology, and perhaps indirectly to the death of Parsons.

One could reasonably claim that L. Ron Hubbard was the Joseph Smith of his generation. Like Smith, he began his spiritual quest in the murky realms of ceremonial magic, in fact, using some of the very same source material as Smith himself: the *Keys of Solomon*, the *Books of Moses*, all the basic reading material of the OTO, which itself was based on the European systems of ritual magic including planetary invocations, spirit evocations, demonology, the Qabala and Smith's own particular enthusiasm, Freemasonry. Like Smith, he founded what amounted to a religion based on his personal revelations, one that has attracted millions of members worldwide and which has a "sacred scripture" at its core, in Hubbard's case, *Dianetics*. Like Smith, his cult was attacked on all sides by conventional religious organizations, as well as by the governments of various countries. Like Smith, he had military pretensions and demanded a great deal of obedience from his followers, on pain of excommunication. And, like Smith, he had a fondness for the ladies.

One could say that Southern California in the twentieth century was the West Coast's answer to nineteenth century New York's "Burned Out District." Religious revivals and spiritual societies grew like mushrooms in the hot and sandy soil in and around Los Angeles in the post-war years. Religious leaders of every kind of denomination and persuasion were able to attract members, including celebrities and wealthy patrons. While Parsons was a serious, even fanatic, spiritual seeker, Hubbard was the Edward Kelley to his John Dee. Hubbard's various biographies contradict each other in important areas; it has taken researchers years to piece together Hubbard's real resume. His Naval record during the war years does not cover him with glory. He was a confidence man who claimed great achievements in his past, achievements which the record shows did not exist, and he did so unnecessarily since his genuine achievements were notable enough.

When the dust was cleared in Pasadena, however, Hubbard had managed to steal Parsons' girlfriend and his money, and Parsons had to go to court to win back at least the money if not the love. *Sic transit amor mundi.*

Parsons and Hubbard began working occult rituals together in the lodge headquarters at Parsons's home, including the infamous "Babalon Working" of January 1946, in which the Scarlet Woman was invoked. The Scarlet Woman—a reference to the consort of the Great Beast of the Apocalypse—is a sacred figure in the Thelemic religion, an embodiment of the female principle of nature, but on steroids. Parsons wrote to Crowley in England, praising Hubbard's magical abilities, saying that Hubbard was "the most Thelemic person" he had ever met.[62] Crowley, though, was dubious and fearful that young Parsons was getting in over his head. Parsons, seeing Betty transferring her affections to Hubbard, invokes a woman for himself to replace her, who appears miraculously in the person of Marjorie Cameron, an artist (who will later appear in a film by Crowley enthusiast Kenneth Anger, as would Manson protégé Bobby Beausoleil). A ritual he performed with Hubbard in the Mojave Desert to attract an "elemental"—in this case, a female sexual partner, since Hubbard was scarfing up all the available lovers—had culminated in Parsons, in an intuitive flash, suddenly claiming victory ("It is done!") and rushing home to find that a vivacious, red-headed Marjorie Cameron (whom he had never met) was waiting for him at his home.

At the same time, Parsons had already sold his stock in Aerojet and had some ready cash available. After the completion of various rituals, some involving sex, Parsons, Hubbard and Betty Northrup agreed to form a company: Allied Enterprises. Hubbard was always fond of boats, and suggested that they purchase boats on the East Coast and sell them on the West. With that in mind, Hubbard and Betty went to Florida with ten thousand dollars of Parsons's money.

Hubbard later phones from Miami and tells Parsons that they have bought a boat, a yacht. All well and good.

And then Parsons hears nothing from Hubbard or Betty Northrup for some time.

Worried—and perhaps in his heart still a little jealous of the relationship between Betty and Hubbard—Parsons goes to Miami to find out what has happened to his money. He discovers that Hubbard has purchased not one, but three vessels and is nowhere to be found. Parsons stakes out the marina, and when one of the Hubbard vessels begins to leave the harbor an amazing thing occurs.

According to Parsons, he raised a storm using magic to force the boat back to shore. Whether we can believe him or not, the fact is that a storm rose and the boat was forced back, at which point Parsons takes possession of the boats via court order, recouping most of the money, and returning to Pasadena in July 1946.

Hubbard and Betty Northrup, meanwhile, stay in Florida and get married.

But Hubbard is still married to his first wife at the time. It is all very "plural marriage," very . . . Mormonesque. Very . . . illegal. And yet, within three years, Hubbard's new science/religion called "Dianetics" will be born, and the rest, as they say, is history.

Later, Hubbard will describe his sojourn among the Thelemites as part of an undercover intelligence operation for—variously—the FBI or the Office of Naval Intelligence (ONI), to break up a dangerous satanic cult that counted important scientists among its members, people with classified secrets who were in danger (we assume) of being compromised by the weird rites and illicit sex taking place on the premises. How breaking up the "cult" would have benefited national security is not clarified. Obviously, no scientists were arrested. Presumably, we are meant to believe that once the scientists in question had seen the error of their ways—courtesy of Hubbard and the FBI—then they abandoned their licentious and blasphemous practices and devoted themselves to the forty-hour work week and church on Sunday. To be fair, we know that both the FBI and the ONI had been aware of Parsons and at least the FBI was watching the cult, but long before Hubbard was on the scene. Hubbard was no stranger to the secret police, though, having once tried to turn in a troublesome steward as a German spy in New York City in 1940; he was also an intelligence officer for a brief period during the war.

A look at Hubbard's official Navy record—released in 1986—tells the following story:

He began his career as a Lieutenant, Junior Grade, in the US Naval Reserve on July 19, 1941. He went on active duty September 22, 1941 for a few weeks, until October 6, 1941, then went back on active duty on November 24, 1941 for the duration of the war, becoming a Lieutenant in the process, until February 16, 1946 . . . after the time he first began seeing Parsons, which, according to the evidence to hand, must have been around October of 1945, with Parsons writing "the most Thelemic person" letter in January of 1946.

From December 18, 1941—that is, just after the attack on Pearl Harbor and the entry of the United States into the war—Hubbard is found at the Office of the Naval Attache, American Legation, in Melbourne, Australia. His duties at this time are described as "Intelligence Officer," a designation he retains through June 24, 1942 in the official account, although further clarification from the Navy shows that he only held that post until May 4, 1942. He returned to the United States in April 1942 and served in the Office of Cable Censor, in New York, from May 1, 1942 to June 24, 1942. Thus, he spent about three months "in the rear with the gear" in Australia during the war with Japan, for which he received the Asiatic-Pacific Campaign medal, as did everyone else who served in that theater. The other stories that the Scientology organization (and Hubbard himself) have spread about Hubbard's heroic war record are thus without basis in fact.

During the rest of the war, he was posted around the United States on various jobs, from Portland, Oregon to the Presidio, and finally wound up at the Naval Hospital in Oakland, California as a patient from September 5, 1945 to December 4, 1945. (Thus, at the time he was visiting Parsons in Pasadena for the first time, he was at least technically a mental patient.) He was honorably released from active duty on February 16, 1946, and resigned from inactive duty on October 30, 1950. One of the stories that is current about Hubbard's war years is that he fired on an uninhabited island off the coast of Mexico, much to the official chagrin of the Mexican government. There is no mention of this in the official US Navy documentation available to the author,[63] but it has been referenced so many times in so many places that it has passed into Hubbard legend. No matter what, something happened to Hubbard.

It is the term he spent as a "patient" that is interesting; the war in the Pacific was over in August, and a month later Hubbard is laid up in hospital where he stays for three months. He was not wounded; he never saw any action. There are no Purple Hearts in his Naval records. (The word is, he was suffering from an ulcer.) And, when he gets out, his Naval career is all but over, but the mental disorders are not. As late as 1947 he is writing the Veterans Administration and complaining about suicidal tendencies and his inability to cope with civilian life over the previous two years, i.e., during the time he was involved with Parsons, the OTO and Parsons' girlfriend, whom he had married in 1946![64]

Meanwhile, Parsons is still active in the lodge and is heavily involved in the darker aspects of magic, including a fascination with voodoo, goetia (the raising of evil spirits in the Crowleyan sense), and heavy ritual. This was no secret to his fellow rocketeers, and it is mentioned (albeit briefly) in Clayton R. Koppes' *JPL and the American Space Program,* as well as in Iris Chang's work on Parson's Chinese colleague, Tsien Hsue Shen.[65] He is not keeping up with the day-to-day business of the Order, however, and the backstabbing and sniping begins. He marries Marjorie Cameron on October 19, 1946 in San Juan Capistrano, (with his old friend Edward Forman and his wife as witnesses), and she returns for a while to New York City, where her mother is living, leaving Parsons very much alone.

By all accounts he was a brilliant chemist and rocketeer who made important contributions to the American war effort and to what would become the American space program—a man who attracted the jealousy of the legendary rocket pioneer Robert Goddard when the latter discovered that von Kármán's tykes at GALCIT were getting important Army funding[66]—and a founding member of JPL, the black sheep that JPL does not wish to acknowledge any more than is necessary. (Repeated attempts to extract anything from JPL by the author on the subject of Parsons have resulted in . . . nothing. Not even an acknowledgement of the letters I have sent. And yet, there is the crater on the Moon . . .)

With all of that, Parsons was a magician, a kind of sorcerer whose attraction was to the darker, fringe elements of the occult and to whom nothing was really off-limits. Crowley called him "a weak-minded fool,"[67] and it certainly seems as if Parsons was victimized by most of the people in his life. He expected people to behave with honor, reasonably, to the extent that he, himself, treated them nobly. From what evidence we can find, Parsons was treated well and honorably only by those who respected and admired his intelligence, his seriousness, and his brilliance: his fellow rocketeers. Yet, when involved in the one aspect of American life virtually guaranteed to disappoint the idealist—the occult underground, with its petty jealousies, inflamed egos and unstable emotions—he was ripped apart.

And still, he persevered.

He did not give up on the people who treated him shabbily, and even remained on good terms with W.T. Smith, the head of the Agape Lodge in 1939 and the man who fathered a child on Parsons' first wife, Helen, and contributed to their divorce. Parsons saw himself as above jealousy and possessiveness, even when those around him were wallowing in it. In his own words, "We can be insulated against everything but death—in fact, death is the very substance of our insulation. But to be used by life we must be naked and to be naked is to be hurt. But it is also to be alive."[68] He was also consumed by a desire to set the Creation straight, to cut through illusion and hypocrisy and to somehow revitalize the age. "For over two thousand years now every one who has tackled this job has made a fool of themselves—it is time some one was making more sense."[69]

The world, though, was not ready for Jack Parsons. In 1947, according to FBI records and to von Kármán's own memoirs, Jack began to seek work in Israel. The timing is suggestive, for it anticipates the creation of the Israeli state, which did not occur until 1948. In other words, Jack Parsons is hobnobbing with American lobbyists for Israel, and perhaps with elements of the Jewish underground. Israel: a country-to-be which is in desperate need of engineers, scientists and, perhaps most of all, a defense industry to call its own. Parsons probably found the whole idea very attractive, very appealing to his idealistic nature: to be in on the ground floor of the creation of a new country, especially one in the middle of the Holy Land, the land where the Knights Templar were born in the shadow of the Dome of the Rock, where Jesus walked and preached, where the Assassins cut down their enemies with stealth, where King Solomon summoned demons to help build his Temple. Parsons must have felt that working to develop the Israeli rocket and munitions industry was a position worthy of an enlightened man, an initiate of the arcane mysteries of the Order. The OTO in Israel? The very idea had . . . resonance.

Yet it is due to his membership in the OTO that he lost his security clearance, on September 21, 1948. According to FBI file 65-1753, originating with the Los Angeles Field Office but made at Cincinnati, Ohio on November 22, 1950, Parsons was being investigated by the Army's CIC (Counter Intelligence Corps) in May 1948. A Major Sam Bruno, Chief of Security at Wright-Patterson Air Force Base, reported the CIC investigation to the FBI. His report stated that "a religious cult, believed to advocate sexual perversion, was organized at subject's home at 1003 South Orange Grove Avenue, Pasadena, California, which had been reported subversive . . . . The report further reflects that subject reportedly associated with one [name deleted] an alleged Communist Party member."

While his security clearance would later be reinstated (on March 7, 1949), it meant that Parsons' career was effectively derailed.

A word to the nervous: Wright-Patterson AFB in 1948 is a very suggestive place to have been involved in an investigation of Jack Parsons, to be sure. UFO enthusiasts know Wright-Patterson as the scene where the elements of the crashed Roswell "flying saucer" were taken in 1947. It is also, of course, where Nazi General Walter Dornberger and his merry men were first taken as part of Operation Paperclip, curiously at the very same time as the Roswell crash in July 1947, leading many to suggest that the UFOs were really Nazi experimental aircraft. The author believes that the security personnel at the air base would have been involved in the Parsons investigation due to the occultist's deep involvement in the rocket program, and not due to anything more sinister; however, interested readers are advised to keep an open mind, because the people who eventually become involved in the Parsons investigation turn up in some odd (and worrisome) places.

In the interim, Parsons had to find work wherever he could get it. Without a security clearance, he could not work in the defense industry and could only find jobs with companies who supplied the special effects departments at Hollywood film studios. At the same time, he was undergoing a tremendous psychological crisis. In December 1948, he took "the Oath of the Abyss" in a ritual conducted before W.T. Smith. This is tantamount to willingly suffering the "long, dark night of the soul" that is common in artistic and psychological literature. While most occult initiations can be "given," i.e., passed on through ritual and the laying on of hands or some other appropriate ceremony, the initiatory levels of the "Abyss" and beyond cannot be imposed by human intervention, according to the tradition of the western mystery schools. In this case, all of creation is seen as the Qabalists' "Tree of Life," a diagram containing ten spheres connected by twenty-two paths. The top three spheres and the bottom seven spheres are "separated" in this instance by the Abyss, a place where one's ego is destroyed . . . or not. If not, then one becomes a "black brother," or "magician of the left-hand path," that is, an evil magician and source of pestilence. If one has successfully passed the Abyss, however, then one attains greater spiritual glory.

In the Crowley system, one may take the Oath of the Abyss at any time, which will then propel one head-first into the dark night of the soul, a bit like throwing children into a swimming pool: they either learn how to swim fairly quickly, or they drown. It can be considered a desperate act, fraught with psychological implications; no less than the destruction of one's personality, even of one's sanity . . . and to make matters worse, Parsons chose as his initiated name and identity: the Antichrist.

Parsons had come to believe that Christianity was the enemy of civilization, of humanity, and that it had to be destroyed. Parsons felt that, as the Antichrist, he could summon forth Babalon (the Scarlet Woman of the Apocalypse and consort of the Great Beast 666) and instigate the coming upheaval of western civilization. Parsons was not anti-Christian per se, as his writings demonstrate; he believed that the real Christ, however, had been hidden and buried beneath mainstream Christianity and that codified Christianity was false, whereas the Gnostic version was true. Parsons realized that Christianity's power lay in its simplicity of message and symbol, and that the failure of hermetic cults such as the Gnostics derived from their complexity and intellectual demands. He dreamed for a way to promote a more magickal, more Thelemic spiritual revolution and sought a simple message and symbol . . . but stumbled on the Catch-22 of Scarlet Woman, Great Beast, and Antichrist, symbols that had been created (or, at least, co-opted) by the Church and which contain a built-in failure mechanism: whoever attests to being anti-Christian becomes part of the Christian duality, part of the problem. In a sense, that person revitalizes that which he opposes. Satanists, for example, are part of the Christian continuum for it was the Church that created Satan. Buddhists are not Satanists; nor are Hindus, Daoists, or members of other non-Christian religions. But Parsons was working within what was essentially a Christian—or Judeo-Christian—tradition and could not extricate himself from its symbols, try as he might.

In the same time frame that he lost his security clearance, his pass to the secret realms of government on earth, he sought a pass to the celestial realms instead. The man who had such an influence on the techniques of sending rockets through space now wanted to send himself, if not bodily then "astrally," i.e., in a shape made of starstuff, to the realm of the stars.

In 1949, he wrote the *Manifesto of the Antichrist* in which he emphasized his spiritual accomplishment and his goals. The wording is suggestive of what had been going on in his life, and may contain clues not found in the FBI files: "An end to all authority that is not based on courage and manhood, to the authority of lying priests, conniving judges, blackmailing police . . ."[70]

Blackmailing police? Where did that come from? Was Parsons being blackmailed? It is indeed possible; after all, his home was the headquarters of a cult believed to be involved in "sexual perversion" and "subversion." It is possible that the drugs, sex and rituals would have aroused the curiosity of the police department (particularly as there were other, federal, investigations taking place), and that Parsons found himself in a vulnerable position and had to buy his way out of it from time to time. There is evidence that Parsons gave testimony against criminals as a consultant to LAPD, and that one of his fellow consultants—an explosive expert by the name of Santmyer—gave conflicting stories at the time of Parsons' death, in what seems to be a patent exercise in disinformation.

But we are getting ahead of our story.

Once Parsons's security clearance was reinstated, he started working for the Hughes Aircraft Company. It would be in September 1950 that he was found in possession of "classified documents," documents that Parsons admitted were helping him draw up a proposal for a laboratory in Israel. This was considered outright espionage, and he lost his security clearance again and never got it back.

The man in the middle of this investigation—being brought into it by J. Edgar Hoover, the Director of the FBI—was an Assistant Attorney General, James M. McInerney.[71] In correspondence between the two men in the spring of 1951, a determination was being sought on whether the documents in Parsons' possession were, indeed, classified and whether their sale or transfer to Israel would be a breach of "national security." Most of the documents were authored by Parsons himself, dating to his GALCIT days, and all were written during the war years. However, the military decided that one of the items was Restricted and two others Confidential, thus establishing a basis—however flimsy—for considering Parsons a potential spy for Israel.

This correspondence—and the associated investigation by the FBI and the armed services—took place over a year. On February 7, 1952 Hoover sent James McInerney a memo regarding Parsons, informing him that Parsons' appeal to the Industrial Employment Review Board of the Department of Defense was turned down. According to an attached letter from the Board, Parsons "might voluntarily or involuntarily act against the security interests of the United States and constitute a danger to the national security."[72]

Five months later he was dead.

James McInerney is an interesting person to associate with Parsons. We discover, for instance, in Robert Maheu's autobiography *Next to Hughes*, that it was James McInerney who provided the initial funding for Maheu's security firm, Robert A. Maheu Associates. According to Maheu, "Almost immediately, I began working for the CIA."[73] This was in 1954, and McInerney was still Assistant AG. He and Maheu, and some other ex-FBI agents, were gambling illegally, and Maheu won handily the princely sum (in 1954) of $2,800, all from McInerney. When Maheu attempted to refuse the winnings, McInerney would have none of it. It was to this fund that Maheu attributes the initial financial investment for his agency.

Maheu, of course, would go on to greater glory, including his infamous relationship with Howard Hughes (Parsons' former employer) and his involvement with the CIA/Mafia plots against Castro. McInerney himself would go on to represent the Kennedys at one point, according to Victor Lasky,[74] even though Maheu was told to sever *his* relationship with the Kennedy family or else he could not become involved with the CIA.

The murky facts surrounding the death of Jack Parsons make it inevitable that some researchers would look for murder. According to the forensics team investigating the blast scene at Parsons' home in Pasadena, there had been two explosions, the first from under the floorboards where Parsons was standing, setting off the second explosion from among his chemicals, thus implying a bomb. Other evidence found at the site, including filter papers soaked in explosive chemicals in the trash outside the house, seemed to support this theory of criminal intentions. However, the official version of the story was that Parsons died as a result of an accident: he had dropped a container of a powerful and volatile explosive, fulminate of mercury, while moving some of his personal belongings in preparation for a trip he was taking with Marjorie Cameron to Mexico. On the one hand, we have testimony of those who worked with Parsons refusing to believe he could be that careless when he was the epitome of the professional chemist. On the other hand, we have testimony that he stored a lot of chemicals, including explosives, at his home and that the accident was waiting to happen.

The Mexico trip is also controversial. According to some sources, Parsons was thinking of setting up an explosives factory in Mexico to produce special effects products; his wife at one time was considering settling down in Guadalajara or San Miguel de Allende to continue her work as an artist. Parsons was also believed to be on his way to Israel after that, to continue pursuing the lure of working for Israeli defense. He spent the early part of 1950 running around the country, looking for work. His itinerary included Redstone Arsenal, where by then the Nazi doctors had established themselves, Washington, D.C., Cumberland coal country, and the City of New York, where he stayed at the Roosevelt Hotel and wrote Marjorie long letters filled with magical advice. He was finally hired by Hughes at Culver City, California, and this is where he was working when he once again lost his security clearance and was forced to find work at various factories around Southern California, finally giving in during June 1952, when it was obvious his security clearance would not be reinstated.

Was Jack Parsons murdered? Was it by agents of his own government, in an effort to keep this admittedly brilliant rocket scientist away from other countries? Was it in revenge for the guilty verdict of a crooked cop his expert testimony had helped put away, as has been suggested by some (including his wife, Marjorie)? A cop who had earlier used a car bomb to kill his victim?

Or did it have something to do with a Chinese rocket scientist, a man whose relation to Chinese rocketry is much the same as Parsons was to American rocket science? For one of Parsons' earliest partners at GALCIT was Dr. Tsien Hsue Shen, a scientist who specialized in long-range missile development; in fact, his first prototype was built under Parsons' watchful eye at Aerojet. During the McCarthy Era, however, Dr. Tsien was accused of being a Communist. Although he denied any such affiliation, his security clearance was also removed; he protested this straight up to the Undersecretary of the Navy, saying he would go back to China if he wasn't reinstated. Instead, the Undersecretary made a call to Immigration and had Dr. Tsien arrested![75]

Tsien eventually left the United States, disgusted at his treatment and the suspicion that was aroused by a man born in pre-Communist China. He returned to

China as threatened . . . and jump-started the Chinese missile program. Were the McCarthy investigators wrong in their assumption that Tsien was a Communist?

A review of the FBI files shows that Parsons was suspected of knowing someone believed to be a Communist, and he was interrogated on this point several times by the FBI over the course of several years. Further recourse to some hand-written notes in those same files shows an intriguing reference to a suspect in the US Consulate, Shanghai and a list of friends of this suspect; all of the names in the Parsons file are deleted, except for Parsons himself.

Was Tsien a Communist, working for Mao's China? And if so, was Parsons aware of this at the time? With his avowed hatred of Christianity—he called himself the Antichrist, after all—and the suspicions of the American government that he was a walking security risk, is it possible that Parsons was only one element of a larger network of political intrigue, involving Chinese Communists, occultists, and rocket scientists?

Was the much-rumored job in Israel a cover for something more ominous?

And was his murder the final solution to the nagging problem of what to do with a brilliant young scientist who would not bow to "all authority that is not based on courage and manhood"?

Marjorie Cameron would remain involved in occultism for the rest of her life, keeping in touch with the old Agape Lodge members, and for a while became a fixture of the mystical scene, an honored alumnus of the Parsons era. It was of her that Kenneth Grant, the English magician mentioned in the last chapter, would write:

> . . . Cameron associated with a Witch-woman who had occult affiliations with ancient Indian cults that had retained unbroken a secret tradition of traffic with the Great Old Ones. The Narragansetts of the New England region, the Adena of Ohio . . . are known to have forged links with entities spawned in the [Abyss] . . .[76]

Thus we go from the ancient Indian mounds of the Adena people to the rocket scientist Jack Parsons, and back again, walking over what must be familiar territory by now to the reader, although he or she probably never set foot in it before!

The mystery of Parsons's death may never be solved, but what of his life? Although there is very little about Parsons on official government websites or histories, what does remain is incontrovertible proof of his genius, as well as his eccentricity. Parsons helped the war effort against Nazi Germany and Imperial Japan. He contributed heavily to the early days of the space program.

It is all but certain that the Paperclip Doctors would have been aware of his work, would have read his papers—the ones considered detrimental to national security should they leave American shores. And somehow, someone, somewhere in the labyrinthine bureaucracy of NASA made sure he got a lunar crater named after him, so there would always be a monument to his contribution to science.

On the other hand, he participated in occult rituals: sex and drug affairs replete with incantations, billowing clouds of incense and weird summonings of incarnate beings to visible appearance. He midwifed L. Ron Hubbard's initiation into the sacred mysteries of the Cult of Thelema and the *Ordo Templi Orientis*, thus providing the impetus for the creation of Scientology and subsequent offshoots, such as the Process Church of the Final Judgment. He took the Oath of the Abyss. He called on the Whore of Babylon, and proclaimed himself the Antichrist and an enemy of the Church. He sent rockets into the heavens, and summoned demons from hell.

And during his Babalon Working rituals in the Mojave Desert in 1946, he "opened a hole in space-time and something flew in."[77]

ENDNOTES

1 Robert Jackson, Opening Argument, Nuremberg War Crimes Tribunal, November 21, 1945

2 Hans Habe, *Agent of the Devil*, George G. Harrap & Co. Ltd., London, 1958, p. 192

3 Bundesarchiv, Bild 146-1968-100-21A / Friedrich Franz

4 Bundesarchiv, Bild 183-27237-0001 / CC-BY-SA 3.0

5 Ibid.

6 Vincent Bugliosi, *Helter Skelter*, Bantam Books, NY, 1995, ISBN 0-553-57435-3, p. 642

7 Maury Terry, *The Ultimate Evil*, Bantam Books, NY, 1989, ISBN 0-553-27601-8, p. 512

8 Bugliosi, op. cit., p. 642. Bugliosi was the high-profile prosecutor against Manson and the Manson "family" for the Tate/LaBianca killings that took place in Los Angeles in August of 1969 and his book is considered the most exhaustive and detailed on Manson, the murders, and the peculiar dynamics of the group that formed around him. Many people have problems with Helter Skelter, however, not least of all Manson and the "family"; it is salutary to read Bugliosi's book against that of Ed Sanders, *The Family*, Nikolas Schreck's *The Manson File*, and many of the other books that have come out since the time of the murders, including biographies of some of the principal actors in this typically American drama. Some of them are published by small presses that specialize in the arcane or the bizarre, for such is the domain of Manson studies thirty years after the crimes. For factual detail—names, dates and places—the Bugliosi book is quite reliable; for "color" and context, one could do worse than *The Family*. And for Manson's own words, *The Manson File* is probably the most accessible source.

9 Ed Sanders, *The Family*, E.P. Dutton & Co., NY, 1971, ISBN 0-525-10300-7, p. 137

10 Bugliosi, op. cit., p. 642

11 Personal communication with the author

12 Peter Levenda, *Unholy Alliance*, Continuum, NY, 2002, ISBN 0-8264-1409-5, p. 102–105

13 Tibor Scitovsky, *A Proud Hungarian*, excerpted in The Hungarian Quarterly, Volume XL, No. 156, Winter, 1999

14 Edwin Black, *IBM and the Holocaust*, Little, Brown & Co., London, 2001, ISBN 0-316-85771-8, p. 422

15 Ami Hueber de Grazia, ed., *Home Front and War Front in World War II: the correspondence of Jill Oppenheim de Grazia and Alfred de Grazia (1942–1945)*, Metron Publications, Princeton, 1999, (CD-ROM) p. 415–424

16 Ibid., p. 492–494

17 Ian Hamilton, *In Search of J.D. Salinger*, Vintage Books, NY, 1989, ISBN 0-67972220-3, p. 76–95; Anatole Grunwald, ed., *Salinger: A critical and personal portrait*, Harper & Row, NY, 1962, LOC 62-11222, p. 13–14

18 Jim Marrs, *Alien Agenda*, HarperCollins, NY, 1997, ISBN 0-06-018642-9, p. 86; Marrs references Crisman's CIA file, CRISMAN, Fred Lee, OSS/CIA 4250ce "located at Control Records Dispatch, Davenport, Iowa."

19 Tom Bower, *Blind Eye to Murder*, Warner Books, London, 1995, ISBN 0-75151822-0

20 Tom Bower, *The Paperclip Conspiracy*, Michael Joseph, London, 1987, ISBN 0-71812744-7

21 Fortean Times, vol. 109, p. 38

22 Christopher Simpson, *Science of Coercion: Communication Research & Psychological Warfare 1945–1960*, Oxford University Press, NY, 1994, ISBN 0-19-510292-4

23 Simpson (1994) p. 21–22; Levenda, op.cit., p. 45, 92, 199

24 Simpson (1994) p. 24

25 Ibid., p. 11

26 Ibid., p.9

27 Joint United States Public Affairs Office (JUSPAO), *Saigon, Psyops Policy, Policy Number 36*, 10 May 1967, "The Use of Superstitions in Psychological Operations in Vietnam," p. 2

28 Lansdale in Jon Elliston, "Psywar Terror Tactics," *Parascope*, 1996

29 Ibid.

30 Ibid.

31 Simpson (1994), p. 72

32 James R. Price & Paul Jureidini, "Witchcraft, Sorcery, Magic and other Psychological Phenomena and their Implications on Military and Paramilitary Operations in the Congo," SORO/CINFAC/6-64 8 August 1964, Special Operations Research Office, The American University, Counterinsurgency Information Analysis Center, Washington, DC, p. 1

33 Ibid., p. 1

34 Ibid., p. 3

35 Ibid., p. 5

36 Ibid., p. 7

37 Ibid., p. 8

38 Ibid., p. 8–9

39 Ibid., p. 9

40 JUSPAO report, op. cit.

41 JUSPAO, op. cit., p. 2

42 JUSPAO, op. cit., p. 3

43 Sanders, op. cit., p. 113

44 At the time of this writing, Alois Brunner is still alive and living in Syria under government protection.

45 James McGovern, *Crossbow and Overcast*, William Morrow & Co., NY, 1964, LOC 64-19976, p. 38–39

46 Ibid., p. 46

47 Bower (1987), p. 233

48 Ibid., p. 240. It is worthwhile to note that Rascher was working under the aegis of the Ahnenerbe, the occult studies or "ancestral heritage" division of the SS. The concentration camps, and Dachau in particular, were warehouses of living human specimens for use in bizarre projects that came under the wing of the Ahnenerbe "scientists."

49 Ibid., p. 240

50 Mae Mills Link, *Space Medicine in Project Mercury, NASA Special Publication-4003 in the NASA History Series, 1965, Chapter 2-2*, "Clinical Factors: USAF Aerospace Medicine"

51 Bower (1987), p. 285. It is interesting, if not entirely relevant, to note that less than a year after Cabell warned Armstrong about hiring more Nazis, Cabell issued an Air Intelligence Requirements Memorandum Number 4 (dated 15 February 1949) entitled "Unconventional Aircraft," in which he set down the Air Force requirements for collecting information about and reporting UFOs. We tend to forget how strange a world it was in the years immediately following the end of WW II.

52 Levenda, op. cit., p. 216–217

53 John Marks, *The Search for the Manchurian Candidate*, Times Books, NY, 1979, ISBN 0-8129-0773-6, p. 11

54 Linda Hunt, *l'Affaire Paperclip*, Stock, Paris, 1995, [Original title: Secret Agenda], p. 227

55 Marks, op.cit., p. 210

56 Link, op. cit., note 7

57 Jack Parsons, *The Book of AntiChrist*, "Analysis by a Master of the Temple," available in various places on the Internet (such as www.babalon.net) and in undated reprints in possession of the author. Perhaps the best published account of the life of Jack Parsons is *Sex and Rockets* by the pseudonymous John Carter and published by Feral House, Venice, CA 1999, ISBN 0-922915-56-3. Another, more mainstream, source that refers briefly to Parsons and his occult interests is Iris Chang, *Thread of the Silkworm*, Basic Books, NY, 1995, ISBN 0-465-00678-7. The FBI files (many still heavily redacted) on Jack Parsons are also available on the Internet, through the incredible industry of young John Greenwald, Jr. and his website, www.blackvault.com.

58 Reference is made to FBI BUFILE Number 65-59589, p. 49, with heading "96-0-55 Memo from A. M. Thurston to Mr. Clegg 10-25-40" in reference to a letter from Miles of 10-10-40 "in which he requested that the attached list of names be searched against the indices of the Bureau." Only one name is on the list, that of Parsons, and the notation "No Record Was Located."

59 Stanton T. Friedman, *Top Secret/Majic*, Marlowe & Co., NY, 1997, ISBN 1-56924741-2, p. 4–7

60 Ibid., p. 56–57

61 Carter, op.cit., p. 123. These quotations from Parsons' works have been republished in a variety of places in the occult press; for convenience of the reader, I have used *Sex and Rockets* by John Carter as a source for many of the Parsons quotes, as it is based on the same primary sources as my own.

62 Ibid., p. 107. This is from a letter dated January 4, 1946 from Parsons to Crowley.

63 Reference is made to Naval Military Personnel Command memo NMPC-036e-AT:wg/ HUBBA 113392, signed by R.A. Derr, Special Assistant for Officer Correspondence. It contains the notation "There is no record of any court-martial or other disciplinary action during former Lieutenant Hubbard's military service." This document shows Hubbard as a patient of the Naval Hospital in Oakland, CA from September 5 to December 4, 1945, separating from the Navy on December 6, 1945.

64 This is from a letter from Hubbard to the Veterans Administration in Los Angeles, CA dated October 15, 1947. He states he is attending school at the Geller Theater Workshop in Los Angeles, and states "After trying and failing for two years to regain my equilibrium in civil life, I am utterly unable to approach anything like my own competence. My last physician informed me that it might be very helpful if I were to be examined and perhaps treated psychiatrically or even by a psycho-analyst .... I cannot account for nor rise above long periods of moroseness and suicidal inclinations ..."

65 Clayton R. Koppes, *JPL and the American Space Program*, Yale University Press, New Haven, 1982, p. 3; and Iris Chang, op.cit., p. 97–99

66 Koppes, op.cit., p. 2

67 Letter from Crowley to Louis T. Culling, an OTO member in California, December 1946

68 Letter from Parsons to Marjorie Cameron, dated 5 October 1949

69 Letter from Parsons to Marjorie Cameron, dated 25 January 1950

70 Jack Parsons, *Manifesto of the AntiChrist*, in John Carter, op. cit., p. 138

71 Letter from Hoover to Assistant Attorney General McInerney dated December 20, 1950, "Subject: John Whiteside Parsons, Wa. / Espionage-IS" (The "IS" stands for "Israel"), BUFILE 65-59589, p. 34–36 and reply to Hoover from McInerney, dated January 18, 1951, JMM:CEN:vb, BUFILE 65-59589, p. 73, and reply by Hoover dated February 3, 1951, BUFILE 65-59589, pp. 75–76

72 BUFILE 65-59589, p. 137–139, letter to Parsons from Industrial Employment Review Board, and two memos from Hoover, one to SAC, Los Angeles and one to McInerney, with copies of the letter

73 Robert Maheu and Richard Hack, *Next to Hughes*, HarperCollins, NY, 1992, ISBN 0-06-016505-7, p. 39–40

74 Victor Lasky, *It Didn't Start With Watergate*, The Dial Press, NY, 1977, ISBN 08037-3857-9, p. 44

75 For complete details of this fascinating subject, see Iris Chang, op. cit.

76 Kenneth Grant, *Hecate's Fountain*, Skoob Books, London, 1992, ISBN 1-87143896-9, p. 31

77 Kenneth Grant, *Outside the Circles of Time*, London, Frederick Muller Ltd, 1980, ISBN 0-584-10468-5, p. 50

Maurice Maeterlinck (top right), a Nobel Prize-winning Belgian author and known occultist, infused his works with esoteric symbolism and explorations of psychic phenomena. His mystical play "The Blue Bird" (1908) follows two children's initiatic quest through realms of the dead and hidden dimensions in search of the elusive Blue Bird of Happiness. Maeterlinck's story moved quickly into popular culture, first as a play (center right and bottom right), and ultimately into multiple film adaptations. 20th Century Fox's fantasy adaptation (1940), starring Shirley Temple (bottom left), was intended as a studio response to MGM's The Wizard of Oz (1939). The play's themes of accessing hidden realms of memory and consciousness eerily parallel Operation BLUEBIRD's goals of penetrating and controlling the human mind. The above illustration (top left) is by F. Cayley Robinson from a 1911 English edition.

BOOK ONE: THE NINE

CHAPTER FIVE

BLUEBIRD

Our contest is not against flesh and blood, but against powers, against principalities, against the world-rulers of this present darkness, against spiritual forces of evil in heavenly places.

—Epistle of Paul to the Ephesians, 6:12

We deal now, not with things of this world alone, but with the illimitable distances and as yet unfathomed mysteries of the universe . . . . Of ultimate conflict between a united human race and the sinister forces of some other planetary galaxy; of such dreams and fantasies as to make life the most exciting of all times. And through all this welter of change and development your mission remains fixed, determined, inviolable. It is to win our wars.

—Speech of General Douglas MacArthur to West Point cadets, May 12, 1962

. . . the sinister forces which profit from the maintenance of international tension are clinging tenaciously to their positions. Though only a handful of individuals is involved, they are quite powerful and exert a strong influence on the policy of their respective States.

—Speech of Nikita Khruschev before the United Nations, September 23, 1960

Have you the grass here that sings, or the bird that is blue?

—*The Blue Bird*, Maurice Maeterlinck

Most persons of the author's generation look to 1968 as the pivotal year of their lives. It was a time of multiple assassinations, civil unrest, the escalation of the war in Vietnam, the riots at the Democratic National Convention in Chicago, and the election of Richard M. Nixon as President. For many of our generation, it signaled the death of a dream.

Yet, 1947 is also in the running as the pivotal year of the postwar period. Many of the issues that define our generation owe their conception to the events of that year. 1947 was the year the CIA was created, and the penetrating of secrets; it was the year of the famous UFO crash at Roswell, New Mexico and the subsequent concealing of secrets; the year the Dead Sea Scrolls were discovered, and their exposure of secrets. It was the year Winston Churchill made his famous

"Iron Curtain" speech, thus declaring the beginning of the Cold War. It's the year that the House Un-American Activities Committee (HUAC) begins its full-scale investigation of Hollywood. It is the year that inventor Arthur Young leaves Bell Helicopter for a full-time study of paranormal phenomena. It is the year that the US Navy begins Project CHATTER, the search for a viable truth serum, a magic potion to unlock the secrets of the mind.

In May of that year, the Corporal is launched: America's answer to the V-2 rocket, compliments of Jack Parsons and the rest of the JPL rocketeers. It is also the year of the famous "Black Dahlia" murder in Los Angeles, and of Admiral Byrd's "Hollow Earth" expedition. It is the year that Aleister Crowley dies. It is the year that Holly Maddux is born: a future murder victim whose death will expose the seamy underworld of the New Age movement.

And, if we can believe the Beatles, it is the year that Sergeant Pepper's Band learned to play. The famous *Sergeant Pepper's Lonely Hearts Club Band* album was released in June 1967 with lyrics saying, "Twenty years ago today, Sergeant Pepper taught his band to play." That would have been in June 1947; the month the first UFO sightings that gave birth to the term "flying saucer" occurred in the Pacific Northwest. The lyrics go on to state, "We'd like to take you home with us." In retrospect, maybe we should've gone.

It was the year when those things that are now so secret, so classified and behind the scenes were up front and in your face: the Cold War, the CIA, UFOs—whatever they were, alien spacecraft or Mogul balloons—crashing in New Mexico, and the mysteries of the origins of Christianity revealed in a cache of clay jars in Palestine. Maybe they were right about Jack Parsons; maybe he *did* open a hole in space-time in that series of rituals in the Mojave Desert in 1946 and maybe something *did* fly right in. And nested in America's heartland.[1]

FLYING SAUCER NEWS

In June 21, 1947—the summer solstice—six unidentified flying objects were seen over Maury Island in Puget Sound in the State of Washington. The observers were Harold A. Dahl, a harbor patrolman who was avoiding bad weather by anchoring in Maury Island Bay, his two crewmen, his teenaged son and a dog. The objects were doughnut-shaped and were hovering at about two thousand feet over the boat, according to Dahl. One of the six seemed to be in trouble, as it was losing altitude and was being circled by the other five. The objects seemed to be metallic, with a hole in the center (hence the idea they were "doughnut-shaped") and with portholes around the outer circumference. Each of the objects seemed to be about one hundred feet in diameter.

There was a small explosion, and one of the objects rained hot metal all over the boat, killing the dog, damaging the boat and injuring the teenaged son. Dahl quickly beached his craft and began taking pictures of the objects, which soon took off and headed towards Canada. Dahl tried to radio for help or to make a report, but his radio was jammed. Instead, bewildered, he headed back to Tacoma. He got some treatment for his son's injured arm, and then took his evidence—the camera, the film and some samples of the metallic slag—to his boss, a man known as Fred Lee Crisman.[2]

This is a seminal event. No matter on what side of the Kennedy assassination one finds oneself—a believer in the Warren Report, or a believer in a conspiracy—the Fred Crisman element strains credulity. More than twenty years after this event, Crisman will be subpoenaed by District Attorney Jim Garrison as a suspect in the assassination of President John F. Kennedy. Crisman, a former OSS officer, a man with a CIA file, a man friendly with Clay Shaw . . . in at the birth of the twentieth century's UFO experience? Of course, this is not the full story. Who would believe the full story?

Crisman wanted to investigate the site where Dahl's boat was damaged, but the previous night a stranger visited Dahl at his home and advised him to forget the whole thing. The man was dressed in black, and what was unusual was the fact that the incident had not yet been reported outside of Dahl's and Crisman's circle. Regardless, the next day—on June 23, 1947—Crisman went out to Maury Island and found what appeared to be molten glass or metal and foil, but not before another UFO passed overhead. Crisman returned to Tacoma, not knowing what to do at the moment with the information and evidence he had acquired, or so it seemed. So far, the UFO sighting was a localized event, a small town anomaly.

The next day, June 24, 1947, the world changed.

This was the day of the famous sighting of nine UFOs north of Mount Rainier by Kenneth Arnold.

One of the accusations leveled at UFO eyewitnesses is that their testimony is tainted by reason of their inexperience, lack of professionalism, lack of knowledge of astronomical phenomena, etc. In other words, they are not scientists or members of the military, police or government establishments, the people in charge of determining the contours of our reality. The problem with the Kenneth Arnold case is that he was the *perfect* witness. A successful businessman from Boise, Idaho, he was also a deputy federal marshal and an accomplished pilot who was a member of an Idaho Search and Rescue team. In other words, if Kenneth Arnold said that he saw UFOs, then he saw UFOs, not the planet Venus or swamp gas or weather balloons. This is not to say that what he saw was alien spacecraft, but what he witnessed was not conventional aircraft and the speeds at which he clocked them were not achievable by the types of aircraft he knew to be in existence at that time.

In the air on his way home to Idaho from Washington, he spent a while looking for a missing C-46 transport plane for which there was a large, five thousand dollar, reward. The plane was believed downed in the Cascade Mountains of Washington State.

Then, at the same time as the Harold Dahl sighting three days previously—at 2:00 P.M.—Arnold was flying at an altitude of about nine thousand feet, when he saw a bright flash that bathed his aircraft in light. Trying to spot the source of the flash, he soon saw another, coming from north of Mount Rainier. This time, the source of the flash was a formation of nine objects, flying erratically but maintaining formation, like "speed boats on rough water." He clocked the speed of the objects as they passed Mount Rainier at nearly 1,700 miles per hour, an impossible speed for known aircraft of the time.

Arnold landed and spoke about his experience. The initial speculation was that he was witnessing secret weapons tests, but later on in an interview that night with the *East Oregonian* newspaper, he described the motion of the objects like "a saucer would if you skipped it across the water," meaning the way the objects flew and not the way they looked. No matter, from that day on the "flying saucer" was born.

The story should have ended there and then. Arnold had no hard evidence for the sighting, only his own eyewitness experience. Yet, he was visited in early July by two military intelligence officers, Captain William Davidson and Lieutenant Frank M. Brown, of the Fourth Air Force, Hamilton Field, California. They listened to his story, and then returned to base.

Again, the story should have ended there. Fred Crisman, however, had other ideas.

His relationship to Raymond A. Palmer, the editor of *Amazing Stories*, is full of unanswered questions. Why this former OSS officer and harbor patrolman would be involved with a man who published fantasy tales of underground civilizations, weird military experiments (such as the Philadelphia Experiment, in which it was claimed the military had developed a device that could dematerialize a ship and then re-materialize it somewhere else on earth, a story that was later believed to be true by an astonishing number of persons), and mischievous aliens from other worlds, is not clear. Like fellow OSS officer Peter Tompkins after him, Crisman may simply have been fascinated by the paranormal and by speculative history. Or his interest may reveal a slightly more sinister agenda. Speculation is rampant that Crisman's role was that of a disinformation specialist, and that his ultimate purpose was to devalue the UFO reports or, failing that, to erase all traces of the evidence.

Crisman contacted Palmer in writing concerning the Maury Island incident; Palmer himself had contacted Arnold about the Mount Rainier sighting, offering a two hundred dollar advance for his story. These were only two of a large number of UFO sightings that were taking place that month and into July.

On the Fourth of July, at about 11:27 P.M., the infamous Roswell crash took place, and the first newspaper reports called the device a "flying saucer"; thus reference was made to the Arnold sighting in which that term was first employed to describe a UFO. On that same day, however, there were no less than eighty-five sightings in the United States. The Roswell crash was only one instance of a "sighting." Clearly, interest was at an all-time high, and opinion was divided as to whether the craft were of Soviet manufacture, a captured Nazi secret weapon, an American secret weapon, or—and this was by no means the most prevalent concept—an alien spacecraft.

While the Army then changed its story to describe the Roswell debris as that of a weather balloon, events were proceeding apace. General Walter Dornberger, the chief of the Nazi space program at Peenemünde and, later, at the *Mittelwerke* at Nordhausen, and responsible for the deaths of thousands of concentration camp inmates as slave laborers, is sent to Wright AFB as the Roswell debris is being shipped there. Dornberger and Wernher von Braun—both of whom initial CIC reports describe as ardent Nazis—have been forgiven their past sins by the Army and are brought to the United States under Operation Overcast—renamed Paperclip—much to the irritation of Nuremberg prosecutors. They are now in a position to review the Roswell wreckage.

At the same time, the same month, the National Security Act is passed, thus paving the way for the establishment of the Central Intelligence Agency, which is finally chartered in September. James Forrestal is named as the first US Secretary of Defense. He will not last long.

Meanwhile, Kenneth Arnold arranges to meet Harold Dahl in Tacoma, Washington at the request of Raymond Palmer. The date is set for July 30, 1947. During the flight to Tacoma on July 29, Arnold sees yet another squadron of UFOs—this time nearly two dozen of them, and very small compared to the first squadron, less than a meter in diameter each—at La Grande, Oregon. He attempts to film them, but the film only shows some small specks, and is disappointing as evidence.

Once arrived in Tacoma, Arnold discovers that all the hotels are fully booked. Discouraged, he tries the most expensive place in town and finds, incredibly, that a room has been reserved for him by name although no one knows who made the booking.

The next day, he meets Dahl. Dahl, however, is still unnerved by his visit from the "man in black" the previous month and is hesitant to talk to Arnold. Arnold, motivated in part by the two hundred dollar advance from Palmer and partly by his own curiosity about the sightings taking place, presses Dahl for more information.

Dahl finally breaks, and tells Arnold the same story he told Crisman. Dahl's photographs are gone, of course: he has given his camera and his film to Crisman. He did, however, manage to keep back a few pieces of the "slag" that fell from the damaged UFO. He showed Arnold a piece of what seemed to be volcanic rock, not a very suspicious-looking fragment. Dahl also told Arnold about a letter he had received, which stated the UFOs were piloted by aliens who had become visible due to US atomic explosions, and that they were visiting the earth to help protect it from unspecified enemies. The letter writer was anonymous, and one can't help wondering if Crisman was behind this, as well.

At this point, Arnold felt he was being had. The whole story sounded very suspicious, very artificial. He asked a friend, another pilot—United Airlines Captain E. J. Smith—for his take on the affair. They came to the conclusion that either the story was a simple hoax, or it was part of an intelligence operation. They distrusted Crisman completely, and felt that he was trying to control the investigation. Either Crisman was a hoaxer, or a spy. Either way, Arnold and Smith felt that he had nothing to contribute.

Then, as if in confirmation of their suspicions, it was reported that United Press International had received *verbatim transcripts* of their interviews and discussions, the ones held at Arnold's mysteriously-booked hotel room! Suddenly, it was all becoming clear. Arnold's presence in Tacoma had been part of a larger plot; his room was selected in advance and bugged; the information he extracted from Dahl, and his conversations with Smith, were sent to the news agency (for what purpose can only be imagined). It seemed as if there was an operation underway to discredit the Maury Island UFO report and to do that with Kenneth Arnold, a much more credible witness than either Dahl or Crisman. Two birds with one stone?

At this point, Arnold was determined to bring in military intelligence. If nothing else, it would eliminate once and for all the possibility that the Maury Island affair was some kind of espionage plot, thus reducing it to the level of a simple-minded hoax by Crisman and Dahl. Crisman seemed to welcome the idea of bringing in the Army; Dahl was still frightened from his meeting with the man in black, and did not want to cooperate.

No matter; Arnold called the men who had debriefed him after his own UFO sighting, Lieutenant Brown and Captain Davidson. They agreed to fly out to Tacoma immediately to see what Arnold had. They arrived later that day, talked with both Arnold and Smith, seemed to dismiss the whole affair as a hoax, and returned to the airport for their ride home. Arnold was nonplussed. It appeared to him as if they had already dismissed the story in advance of their arrival. If so, then why bother coming out at all?

At the airport, an odd thing happened, one which has plagued UFO researchers for years. Crisman, the man the intelligence officers seemed to think was nothing more than an oddball hoaxer, turned up at the last minute and gave the men a heavy box which he claimed was filled with the debris from the damaged UFO. To Arnold, who was there, the contents looked like a bunch of rocks. The men stowed the box in the trunk of their car and left for the airport, catching their flight.

They never made it back to base.

Both Davidson and Brown were killed. The enlisted men on board parachuted to safety after the left engine caught fire—according to the report of one of the survivors—and the two officers remained with the aircraft for a full ten minutes before the B-52 bomber crashed to earth. No one has any idea why the two intelligence officers would have remained with the plane and not parachuted themselves; or why they did not radio a distress call. The emergency fire-fighting equipment was inoperable, so there was no chance to save the plane. According to Major George Sander of the US Army Air Corps, the plane was carrying classified material. Was that a reference to the box of rocks carried on board by Davidson and Brown?

One of the men involved in the investigation of UFO reports in the American Northwest that year was none other than FBI Special Agent Guy Banister.

Guy Banister's name is well-known among conspiracy aficionados as another one of the men implicated by New Orleans District Attorney Jim Garrison in the Kennedy assassination. It was Guy Banister—by this time a *former* FBI agent—who rented office space at the same location stamped on Lee Harvey Oswald's "Fair Play for Cuba Committee" flyers. Banister was running an anti-Castro Cuban operation from his investigator's office, an operation that attracted the likes of former Eastern Airlines pilot and assassination suspect David Ferrie. Oswald was running a pro-Castro Cuban operation from the same address, an anomaly that could only be explained if one understood that Banister and Oswald were working together, and that the pro-Castro operation was a front for some other, even more nefarious, purpose. Further, while Banister was FBI Special Agent in Charge (SAC) of the Chicago field office during World War II, one of his FBI subordinates was James McCord of Watergate "plumbers" fame,[3] and another was Robert A. Maheu: the man who would later become head of his own investigative agency and an employee of Howard Hughes, the man whose agency was started by money won from James McInerney, the assistant Attorney General who was involved in the Jack Parsons investigation. Maheu would go on to become the man in the middle between the CIA and organized crime in the assassination plots against Castro.

Banister was—during the time of the Arnold sighting, the Maury Island affair, and Roswell—an FBI Special Agent assigned to the Butte, Montana field office, which had responsibility for several western states, including Idaho (where Kenneth Arnold resided). A look at recently declassified FBI files for that period in 1947 show a number of telexes from Banister, some with his initials "WGB," all pertaining to UFO phenomena,[4] as well as other FBI documents with the designation "Security Matter–X" or simply "SM-X," the origin—the author supposes—of the "X Files," which, at least in 1947, *did* exist at the FBI and was concerned with UFOs (as well as with the federal investigation of Wilhelm Reich, the pioneer psychoanalyst whose "orgone therapy" had run afoul of the medical establishment and who himself was a firm believer in the existence of UFOs).

Usually, when Banister is referenced in connection with the Kennedy assassination, he is mentioned as having been with the FBI in Chicago for many years, which is undoubtedly true, but the period in Butte put him in the middle of the seminal UFO event of the twentieth century.

Thus, the 1947 UFO sightings attracted two men—Crisman and Banister—who both would come under suspicion twenty years later for their supporting roles in the Kennedy assassination. The odds against this happening must be astronomical. It is the constant appearance of "coincidences" like these that leave most amateur conspiracy theorists apoplectic, speechless with disbelief and gazing on the world around them with haunted, suspicious expressions, as if reality itself were layered like an onion, a palimpsest on which numerous events were written over each other, all on the same page. In this case, we have Operation Paperclip, UFOs, and the Kennedy assassination all written on the same thin sheet of onion-skin parchment. Nazis, aliens and political murder. At this point, we can almost sympathize with Pontius Pilate, who asked, "What is truth?"—and the temptation to wash one's hands of the whole matter is almost too strong.

The conclusion of the crash investigation was that the plane suffered mechanical failure, and crashed as a result. Davidson and Brown were thus possibly the first martyrs to the UFO phenomenon. The author cannot offer any evidence that they were murdered, still less that they were murdered to cover-up the truth behind the UFO sightings of 1947. What he can offer, however, are the following facts:

Harold Dahl saw something in the skies over Maury Island which killed his dog and wounded his son, damaging his boat in the process. He gives his evidence of this sighting to his boss, Fred Crisman, a former OSS officer and soon-to-be CIA agent.

A few days later, Kenneth Arnold—an experienced pilot, a deputy federal marshal, and a successful businessman—sees a formation of flying objects traveling at tremendous speed near Mount Rainier. He reports this to the military.

When Arnold, Dahl and Crisman get together in Tacoma their meeting is bugged and transcripts of their conversations provided to the press. The only ones who knew Arnold was flying to Tacoma on that day and time to meet Dahl and Crisman were . . . Dahl and Crisman. There is only one hotel room available, and it has Arnold's name on it, although no one admits to making the reservation.

Arnold calls in military intelligence, the same two officers he met previously. They arrive immediately, question the men, and leave. Crisman gives them a box of what he claims is UFO debris. Their plane crashes, killing both intelligence officers.

Guy Banister is an FBI field agent at the time, charged with investigating UFO sightings under the rubric 62-83894: the "SM-X" or "X Files."

Both Crisman and Banister become suspects in the Kennedy assassination.

Crisman is a friend or colleague of Clay Shaw, another suspect in the assassination and a CIA contract agent.

Crisman has a CIA file and, according to veteran journalist Jim Marrs, was an "extended agent" involved in disruption operations as part of his brief as an Internal Security Specialist.[5]

About the only people involved in the affair who are *not* intelligence officers are Dahl and Arnold. Everyone else is either military intelligence, OSS or FBI. It is important to point out that President Truman had disbanded the OSS on September 20, 1945 and that the CIA was not chartered until September 18, 1947, almost exactly two years later. Thus, the Maury Island affair takes place at the end of that two-year hiatus separating the two agencies. However, the men involved in the OSS did not disappear from government service.

As several histories of the OSS demonstrate—most notably Richard Harris Smith's *OSS: The Secret History of America's First Central Intelligence Agency*—the assets of the OSS were "dispersed among the other agencies of the government. The remains of the Secret Intelligence and Special Operations branches were transferred to the War Department and placed under the command of Donovan's Deputy Director for Intelligence, General John Magruder."[6] Such other OSS luminaries as Richard Helms, James Angleton, and even Herbert Marcuse remained on board in some capacity or other until the formal creation of the CIA in 1947, even as the former OSS analysts were being charged with extreme left-wing, socialist and communist, tendencies. Thus, Crisman was possibly working for the War Department at the time of the Maury Island affair, and was certainly among those reactivated once the CIA was formally established only a few months after the UFO sightings.

It is tempting to link the UFO sightings with the creation of a National Security Act and the establishment of the CIA; it is even more tempting to link the sudden presence of Nazi General Dornberger at Wright Field with contemporaneous multiple UFO sightings in the US during the same month the Roswell crash debris is taken there. All of this happened in the same four week time frame, and involved some of the same notorious characters who would resurface sixteen years later at the time of the assassination of John F. Kennedy. One must either put this fascinating conglomeration of events down to mere coincidence, see it as proof of a wide, multilevel and omnivorous conspiracy . . . or be forced to seek a deeper meaning, evidence of the action of a hidden force in nature, a connective tissue among events that cannot be discerned from our three dimensional surface. Not *mere* coincidence, but the phenomenon we know as coincidence taken to a different level.

LAND OF ENCHANTMENT

The Maury Island affair and the Kenneth Arnold sighting are often linked, but in reality they were two separate incidents connected only by the fact that Arnold was sent—by Ray Palmer—to investigate the Maury Island sighting. Both events became eclipsed in the popular imagination by the Roswell crash.

So much has been written and broadcast about Roswell—including a prime-time television series featuring pouty, alienated teenagers as *aliens*—that the author will not devote an inordinate amount of time to the minutiae of the case. Instead, we will focus on specific elements as they pertain to our thesis. Interested readers can access a wide variety of printed studies of the Roswell case, as well as websites, films, television specials, etc.[7]

The basic facts of the case—insofar as facts can be identified within the welter of conflicting details that have amassed in the last fifty years—is that, shortly after the Arnold and Dahl sightings of late June 1947, a surprising number of UFO sightings were being reported all over the United States, and in foreign countries. These sightings culminated with an object tracked on radar screens over New Mexico on July 1, 1947. This object followed the basic pattern of the Arnold sighting, showing speeds and maneuvers of which contemporary American aircraft were incapable. These sightings continued on July 2 and July 3. On July 4, the object vanished. Whatever it had been, the belief was that it had crashed.

The next day, July 5, 1947, wreckage was discovered on William Brazel's ranch, north of Roswell, New Mexico. The people who found the wreckage included one Grady L. Barnett, a few archaeologists working on a dig nearby, and Brazel himself. The debris from the crash site covered a wide area, and Brazel's sheep wouldn't cross into the field. The next day, Brazel met with the sheriff of Roswell to report the situation, who then called the Army. The Army had the area cordoned off, and Brazel then spoke with intelligence officer Major Jesse A. Marcel and showed him a piece of the debris. Marcel then made a report at the airbase, and a complete search of the area was undertaken, from both land and air. During the investigation at the crash site, several eye witnesses reported seeing what appeared to be small bodies, corpses of whatever race was flying the object, beings that died on impact.

Later that week, the wheels fell off. The information officer of the 509th Bomb Group at Roswell issued a press release, telling a startled public that they had retrieved a flying disc.This seemed to have caught Washington by surprise. Marcel was ordered to take the debris to Fort Worth, Texas, to the Carswell Air Base, from which another press release was issued, this time telling the confused public that the material recovered was not from a flying disc but from a simple weather balloon. And there the story should have died.

Except for the witnesses.

Once again, most people who claim to have seen UFOs are dismissed as scientifically unsophisticated or somehow misinformed. In the case of Roswell, however, the sheer number of military witnesses alone argues against this. These witnesses include Corporal E.L. Pyles, Sergeant Thomas C. Gonzales, Sergeant Melvin E. Brown, CIC agent Master Sergeant Bill Rickett, Major Edwin Easley, Lieutenant Colonel Albert L. Duran, Colonel William Blanchard, and up to Brigadier General Arthur E. Exon, not forgetting Major Marcel himself, among others. In some cases, these men saw the crash and concluded that the craft was not of this world; in other cases, they saw bodies that did not seem to be human; in still other cases, they examined the crash debris and were amazed by the strange properties of the metal, such that it resisted extreme heat and could not be dented by hammers. This list includes both officers and enlisted men, from a Corporal to a Brigadier General. Either they are all lying, or some of them are lying, or they are all telling the truth. It strains credulity to believe that they were all simply mistaken, or the victims themselves of some kind of hoax.

To make matters even stranger, a high-ranking intelligence officer and former member of President Eisenhower's National Security Council—Colonel Philip J.

Corso—published a memoir shortly before his death claiming that he had seen evidence of the Roswell crash himself. The book was entitled *The Day After Roswell* and was published to, curiously, mixed reviews. Corso's credentials are impeccable; he had given testimony before Congress on the fate of POWs being held in North Korea, he had appeared on *Prime Time Live* as an expert on U-2 overflights, had worked for both Senator Strom Thurmond and Senator James Eastland as "a staff member specializing in national security," and had a remarkable twenty-one year career in the armed services. He had been part of Operation Paperclip in Italy. He had been a staff member for Senator Richard Russell on the Warren Commission (yet another Paperclip/UFO/assassination tie). The eighty-year-old retired military man with no need for the money the book would bring (and, indeed, due to some legal problems his royalties would be held up until after he died), and with a mantelpiece filled with medals and awards and photos with the famous and powerful in Washington, had no discernible reason—no ulterior motive that we can find—for participating in a hoax, if that is what Roswell is. His claim that his job at the Pentagon involved coordinating the reverse engineering of alien technology was greeted by either sneers of derision or cries of "I told you so!" The question that has not been answered is why Corso, at the end of his long and successful career, would have bothered writing all of this if it wasn't true, and thereby besmirch a previously blameless reputation.

Yet, with all that, the American public is expected to ignore Roswell and all of its attendant mysteries. It was a flying disc; no, it was a weather balloon; no, it was part of a top secret balloon project called Operation Mogul, and the bodies were really just mannequins. Unfortunately, the Roswell Air Base files on the crash were all destroyed, as US Representative Steven Schiff (R.-New Mexico) discovered to his disbelief in 1995. If Americans are not to believe a virtual platoon of military men and intelligence officers who all claim that something very unusual—something "otherworldly"—had crashed in the New Mexico desert in 1947, then just who *are* they supposed to believe? Press secretaries? Public relations officers? Spin doctors?

Of course, it is entirely possible that the government itself has no real idea exactly *what* crashed in Roswell, or what that crash implies for national security; but in the years that would follow, men would die, commit suicide, lose their minds and their reputations over the UFO phenomenon. That solemn roll call includes military men and scientists, people who can be expected to be skeptical, cautious, and most of all discerning in their approach to this material. Incredible sightings would take place, and continue to take place, all over the world, increasing the tension in the collective consciousness to the point that many people are expecting the truth about UFOs to be revealed any day. The author himself is reluctant to write this account, fearful that his reputation—such as it is!—is in danger due to his treatment of this controversial topic, because there are only two sides to this debate: you either believe, or you don't. You're not allowed to sit on the fence, and simply say "I don't know," because you will be immediately assailed on both sides by those who are desperate to shove their point of view down your rapidly constricting throat. In the absence of openness from the American government regarding what it knows about the UFO phenomenon, both believers and actual witnesses are forced into a kind of fantasy land: believers can make up any story they like, because they will all be denied with equal vehemence. Witnesses are forced to either admit they may be mistaken or at worst insane, doubting the solid evidence of their senses. And when that happens, a crime on a par with murder takes place: the murder of truth, a sin—as Sister Agatha used to say—against the Holy Spirit.

Item: January 7, 1948. Air National Guard pilot Captain Thomas Mantell crashes in Franklin, Kentucky, chasing a UFO over Fort Knox. A decorated World War II ace, he becomes the first UFO casualty if you don't count Davidson and Brown who died in the B-52 crash over Washington State. The cover story was that the misguided pilot was chasing the planet Venus; this was later changed to a weather balloon. Mantell had died because he ran out of oxygen at thirty thousand feet, the only one of his squadron who dared to climb that high in pursuit of the craft. His radio reports make it clear that he was in pursuit of a manned vehicle of some sort; the crash site examination and all other records were covered up and, at the time of this writing, have yet to be released.

Item: January 22, 1948. Two weeks after Captain Mantell's death, the Air Force creates Project SIGN to investigate UFO phenomena.

Item: February 12, 1948. Brigadier General Charles P. Cabell of the US Air Force Directorate of Intelligence—and later to become Deputy Director of the CIA, implicated in the Bay of Pigs fiasco and possibly in the Kennedy assassination—issued a memo requesting all Air Force bases in the United States be provided with at least one camera-equipped fighter plane to record data from UFOs. The request was considered too expensive, and was turned down.

Item: August 1, 1948. By this time, Project SIGN officers conclude there is something to the UFO sightings and report this to General Hoyt S. Vandenberg.

Item: December 16, 1948. Due to news leaks, Project SIGN is changed to Project GRUDGE, and a sea change takes place. From now on, all official government reports on UFOs will be designed to discredit the sightings and to characterize them as weather balloons, planets, etc.

Item: December 6, 1950. Radar installations all over the United States are under high alert as Canadian stations report a squadron of aircraft flying towards Washington, D.C. from the coast of Labrador. This event is recorded in Dean Acheson's autobiography, as well in books about the Truman administration. It was later described as anything from a flight of geese to a C-47 air cargo transport to atmospheric conditions, depending on the agency doing the explanation; but the incident was considered serious enough that the British Prime Minister was warned that a possible attack was in progress. Then, mysteriously, the squadron disappeared from radar over American airspace.

Item: March 1952. Project GRUDGE becomes Project BLUEBOOK, headquartered at Wright-Patterson AFB, near Dayton, Ohio.

Item: July 19, 1952. UFOs swarm over Washington, D.C. on two successive weekends, instigating over three hundred reported sightings.

Item: July 26, 1952. Military issues "shoot them down" orders on UFOs over Washington; a decision later rescinded on advice of . . . Albert Einstein.

Item: November 23, 1953. An Air Force F-89 disappears over Lake Superior while chasing a UFO.

Item: May 15, 1954. US Air Force Chief of Staff General Nathan Twining informs an audience at Amarillo, Texas that the Air Force is trying to solve the UFO problem and that there is nothing to worry about.

Item: October 9, 1955. General Douglas MacArthur is quoted in the *New York Times* as saying that the nations of the Earth should unite in common cause against a possible attack by alien forces.

Item: July 29, 1958. NASA is created.

Item: December 3, 1958. The Jet Propulsion Laboratory (JPL) is transferred from US Army jurisdiction to NASA.

Item: April 29, 1959. UFO researcher and author Morris K. Jessup commits suicide in a Dade County, Florida park.

Item: December 24, 1959. Air Force Regulation 200-2 is issued to all USAF personnel: not to report UFO sightings unless they are known to be of familiar objects.

Item: February 27, 1960. Former CIA chief Roscoe Hillenkoetter releases copies of Air Force Regulation 200-2 to the press, thus exposing the coverup attempt.

Item: May 1960. Roscoe Hillenkoetter is quoted as saying, "It is imperative that we learn where the UFOs come from and what their purpose is."

Item: January 20, 1961. President John F. Kennedy is inaugurated; he vows to put a man on the moon in ten years.

Item: June 1962. General Douglas MacArthur is quoted in the *New York Times* as saying, "We deal now not with things of this world alone. We deal now with the ultimate conflict between a united human race and the sinister forces of some other planetary galaxy."

Generals, CIA chiefs, dead airmen . . . all giving evidence of the existence of some "sinister force" operating in our world.

What, then, is reality? Have we simply satisfied superstitious impulses with this newer, quasi-scientific experience, as science observers such as Carl Sagan insist? Or is science itself reaching the limits of its ability to make statements about reality, and is it crossing over—slowly, but inexorably—into the domain of the supernatural?

A BROTHERHOOD BURIED ALIVE

George Steiner, in a breathtaking study of myth and philosophy in literature—*Antigones*—introduces us to a theme of Romantic literature, codified by the Danish philosopher Sören Kierkegaard as the *Symparanekromenoi*, a term that can be translated as "brothers in death" or "companions in live burial" or even "brotherhood of the sepulchral and macabre." Steiner presents as examples of this "brotherhood" the authors Baudelaire, Coleridge, Novalis, Nietzsche, and Kierkegaard himself.[8] He sees the literary technique of the fragment (bits of diary entry, letters, unfinished lectures, aphorisms, etc.) as representative of this school, as well as a fascination with death and the supernatural (in a morbid sense as opposed to the purely uplifting). One may say that these fragments represent nothing more than clues . . . clues perhaps at the scene of the crime.

The Romantic period was the last gasp of literary arrogance before the advent of technology and the "technological sciences" (as opposed to pure science). One might say that Hiroshima spelled the end of any future pretense at the Romantic in literature. Faced with such an unyielding and remorseless reality—the instantaneous incineration of whole populations by a single bomb—western literature and philosophy began to reflect that reality. When the full horrors of the Holocaust became common knowledge, the depth of the depravity and destructiveness of humanity stunned the innocent and naïve—that is to say, the Americans—and overrode all other impulses. The world seemed poised on the brink of Manichean apocalypse, of "mutual assured destruction," in death measured in megatons, rads, minutes, and first-strikes. Existentialism became a fad, as young people and old began to question existence (and therefore reality) itself, the purpose of life, and moral responsibility. Nuclear winter became our season of discontent.

As the Forties turned into the Fifties, and then the Sixties, the drug culture took western civilization on what appeared to be a detour but what may have been the main drag itself. Suddenly, questions that seemed so important a year before were rendered pointless in the face of fantastic hallucinations and psychedelic illuminations, and all this in the midst of Vietnam, Laos, Cambodia, African revolutions and Latin American coups d'etat. The real and the ideal were mixed in a kaleidoscopic mural of love and death, hope and despair.

As Vietnam turned into Watergate, reality itself became the circus of the bizarre. We learned more during the Watergate hearings than we ever wanted to know. Crooked politicians we could deal with, and have dealt with since the founding of the country; but crooked spies, rogue intelligence operations, foreign adventures unsupported by an electorate glued to their television sets during prime time soap opera extravaganzas . . . this was more than most Americans could understand.

Gradually, entertainment became reality, and reality, entertainment. Shows like *Cops* showed Americans what it was like to be on both sides of an arrest. Tabloid news shows like *Current Affair* and *Hard Copy* gave Americans reality presented as entertainment-presented-as-reality. The Falklands War gave us *Nightline,* where we could watch Argentine government officials and British government officials screaming at each other over satellite linkups, in real time.

Soon, reality became king. MTV gave us the spectacle of intellectually dismal young people living together in a single dwelling, sniping at each other and stabbing each other in the back. This was followed by a rash of "reality" television shows, such as *Survivor, Combat Mission, Eco-Challenge,* and the other creations of Australian producer Mark Burnett. At the same time, made-for-tv movie credits were always careful to mention that their offering was "based on a true story."

We might trace this "based on a true story" motif to that 1973 cinematic blockbuster, *The Exorcist.* After all, what made that movie so frightening to so many people was the insistence by its producer that it was, after all, based on actual events. And here we had an example of a new kind of postwar Romanticism: horror was acceptable if it was real. After all, the world had been shown to be full of more horrors than any (sane) novelist could imagine. The alternative was the splatter film, a genre soaked in blood and violence that was far from what the Romantics had in mind with their melancholy graveyards and sorrowful shades. Instead, the sophisticated horror tale had to be real and appropriately psychological. Psychology gave horror writers and producers a credible way to represent the otherwise impossible scenarios in their books and scripts: the perpetrator was crazy, and had only imagined in his diseased brain all those spooky effects. It was the diseased brain itself that became the crucible for horror, the new metaphor for evil. The Tony Perkins character in *Psycho* was tailor-made by Freud, and based on the real-life serial killer, Ed Gein.

Of course, our political assassins are all crazy, too.

While Romanticism may be dead, a curiosity fit only for college English Literature courses and tenured professors in tweedy jackets and elbow patches, there is a new kind of Romantic element at play in the West, and it is creating a new kind of literature. Norman Mailer may have been much closer to the mark than we realized, for instance, when he subtitled his Pulitzer Prize-winning *The Executioner's Song,* "a non-fiction novel." There is an element of the fragmentary in that work—the accumulation of evidence based on hundreds of interviews, trial transcripts, and public records—as well as in *Harlot's Ghost,* his fictionalized treatment of the history of the CIA. There is a growing realization that we cannot depict what really happened without an element of the novelistic. We can't tell the story without . . . telling a story. We have to put events in context for them to have any meaning, the same way a homicide detective examines the clues at the scene of the crime; and it is precisely this insistence on meaning that has plagued realism from the start, and has led to the confrontation between science and religion or, more properly perhaps, between science and the occult. And in the midst of that confrontation, living in the twilight world between what is mainstream science and what is fringe spirituality, an abyss of politics by other means, dwells a new "brotherhood buried alive": the investigative journalists Jim Marrs, Howard Blum and Jim Hougan, among others.

Jim Marrs is perhaps the latest one of that brotherhood of respected, award-winning journalists who seem to have gone off the deep end as their research took them further and further into the murky flipside of the American dream; Howard Blum may have been one of the first. Blum's 1977 expose on Nazi war criminals living peacefully in the United States—*Wanted! The Search for Nazis in America*—was a bestseller, based on the unsung heroes of the US government (as well as private citizens) who would not rest until the scandal of government-sponsored Nazi war criminals was made common knowledge and the criminals deported to stand trial. Blum wrote investigative pieces for the *New York Times*, and won several prestigious awards. *Wanted!* carried blurbs from Harrison E. Salisbury and Joseph Heller. Blum went on to become a contributing editor for *Vanity Fair*. He followed *Wanted!* with *Gangland* (about the FBI and the Mafia) and a study of the Walker spy family, *I Pledge Allegiance*.

In the midst of all these mainstream topics, though, we find Blum writing *Out There*, a 1990 expose of the UFO coverup in the American military and government. This was a gutsy thing to do. After all, UFOs are the kiss of death for serious journalists, and one risks his credibility even thinking about doing a story like that, unless the goal is to debunk. *Out There* did not debunk; on the contrary one comes away believing that the US government has detailed and precise knowledge of alien visitations, and is covering up a story about as big as the Crucifixion. To make matters even more interesting, Blum followed that in 1998 with *The Gold of Exodus*, a story about lost treasure, in which some amateur archaeologists secretly start digging around in Saudi Arabian territory, hot on the trail of Moses. So, from Nazi war criminals, spies and the Mafia . . . to UFOs and Biblical archaeology.

Jim Hougan, another highly-regarded investigative journalist, television producer and novelist, caught national attention with *Spooks,* a fascinating expose of the private use of intelligence agents in such companies as Hughes Tool and Resorts International. It is in *Spooks* that we learn of Mitch WerBell—the "Wizard of Whispering Death"—and other colorful, underworld characters. Hougan followed this up with *Secret Agenda*, a convincing report on the call-girl ring involved in the Watergate affair which has added considerably to our knowledge of this important political "nightmare." His *novels*, however, deal with Illuminati-type secret societies, intelligence agency mind control programs, and all the heavy furniture of the conspiracy theorists.

What's going on? Is this a phenomenon in itself worth studying: how the best and the brightest of our investigative journalists eventually find themselves wandering the labyrinth of cults, conspiracies and alien contact? Jim Marrs is the Texas-based journalist who came to national prominence with *Crossfire*, the book that—along with Jim Garrison's *On The Trail of the Assassins*—became the basis of Oliver Stone's film on the Kennedy assassination, *JFK.* He has since gone down the same mysterious labyrinth, publishing *Alien Agenda* in 1997 and *Rule By Secrecy* in 2000. The fact that respected journalists such as Marrs, Hougan and Blum put their names and reputations on the line by publishing reports on aliens, cults, and some of the wilder conspiracy theories of our time should give us pause. These are the people we trust to come back and tell us the truth about what is . . . out there.

Norman Mailer, the father of New Journalism, a founder of the *Village Voice*, two-time Pulitzer Prize winner and no-nonsense *eminence gris* of American letters, has himself followed a similar path. Beginning with *The Naked and the Dead* and through *A Fire On the Moon*, *Armies of the Night*, *The Executioner's Song*, *Harlot's Ghost* and dozens of other novels and works of non-fiction over the past fifty years, Mailer has given us reality as well as new ways of looking at reality without compromising his (or our) intellectual integrity. As an example, many objected to his study of Lee Harvey Oswald, *Oswald's Tale*, researched at some peril amid KGB files in the crumbling Soviet Union, since it seemed to support the Warren Commission Report's "crazed, lone gunman" conclusion. Yet, he has remained fascinated with spiritual and mythical themes. *Ancient Evenings* is probably the most obvious demonstration of this, a novel set entirely in ancient Egypt. He has also written about Marilyn Monroe at length and this, with his work on Oswald and his novel on the CIA, places him squarely in the middle of some of our greatest twentieth century controversies. While he has yet to tackle UFOs, he has written *The Gospel According to the Son,* which is a fictionalized "gospel" written by Jesus himself, and thus has covered the Biblical angle, along with those Egyptian mysteries in *Ancient Evenings.*

The above is a sampling of those who began as essentially political writers and journalists and who evolved over time into the type of seekers peculiar to the late twentieth century: seekers after truth who trust science more than faith. (About the only person the mainstream trusted to speak of UFOs, astrology, and cults was, after all, the late Carl Sagan.) But what of those who began their careers "from the other direction" as it might be? Were there cultists, priests of arcane religions, devotees of the "astral" who became . . . political?

Perhaps the most famous, most respected of all the amateur assassination and conspiracy researchers is Mary Ferrell. Ferrell's work has attracted virtually every serious journalist and writer on the subject of presidential assassinations. Her library of books, papers, newsclippings and articles is vast and well-organized. Mary Ferrell bought the entire 26 volume set of the Warren Commission Report and cross-indexed it single-handedly, thus immediately providing an invaluable research tool, since, as anyone knows who has ever seen the entire Report, it is a disaster when it comes to the organization of data. She then collected every scrap of paper she could find that involved the assassination and its various personalities. She has been a source for Jim Marrs, Norman Mailer, and virtually every other well-known (and not so well-known) name in the business. What is perhaps not so well-known about Mary Ferrell herself is that she was once heavily involved in the occult, specifically with the Golden Dawn: that British secret society and breeding ground for such personalities as Aleister Crowley, William Butler Yeats, Arthur Edward Waite and many others, and with Israel Regardie, Crowley's one time secretary and publisher of the Golden Dawn rituals. This involvement was long before the Kennedy assassination took place. It was the assassination itself that put her mystical studies on hold and which drove her into this noble obsession with finding out the truth behind the murder.

There are many similarities between the function of the occultist and the function of the detective: to seek the truth behind a mystery is perhaps the easiest way to describe what may be a psychological compulsion common to both types of personality. In the case of the detective, each individual homicide is perhaps representative of a greater Evil, and to solve one murder is to begin to solve all the others, to redress a history of wrong, to redeem society itself. In the case of the occultist, there is only one murder, whether it is the murder of Abel by Cain or of Jesus by the Romans or of any one of thousands of other symbols and signs for that first, ineffable crime, the "dreadful"—to use Kierkegaard's phrase—"that has already happened."

The Dutch writer Janwillem van de Wetering is another example of this same impulse. In 1972 he published a memoir of his time spent as a Zen monk in Japan, *The Empty Mirror*. He began his novitiate in 1958 in Kyoto, and spent a year and a half undergoing the harsh discipline of Zen monastery life. This was, of course, at the time of the Beat generation, and Zen had become popularized in the books and poems of Ginsberg, Kerouac, and the rest of the bongo-thumping, finger-snapping Beatniks. Yet, van de Wetering was quite serious about his desire to attain enlightenment, even though he interrupted his routine at times by getting drunk and walking blindly through the paper walls of the Japanese monastery.

He is now a famous author of mysteries, many involving his most beloved characters, the Amsterdam Cops. His tales are part detective story, part Zen koan. As his master told him the day he left the Japanese monastery, "By leaving here nothing is broken. Your training continues. The world is a school where the sleeping are woken up. You are now a little awake, so awake that you can never fall asleep again."[9] His detective novels are, perhaps, proof of this "spiritual insomnia."

Apropos philosophy and the detective story, the Italian philosopher and detective novelist in his own right, as well as author of many important works on semiotics, Umberto Eco has this to say:

> After all, the fundamental question of philosophy (like that of psychoanalysis) is the same as the question of the detective novel: who is guilty?[10]

Who, indeed?

BLUEBIRDS OVER THE MOUNTAIN

You are on the threshold of the Land of Memory . . .
—Act II, Scene I: "The Fairy," *The Blue Bird*[11]

As we have seen, the creation of the United States' intelligence apparatus began in the same month as the Roswell crash, in July of 1947, with the National Security Act. The National Security Council was established at that time, and James Forrestal was named as the first US Secretary of Defense (the War Department being renamed as the "Department of Defense"). The National Security Act provided for the creation of a national intelligence agency, and the Central Intelligence Agency was formally created by charter on September 18, 1947. The very first National Security Council meeting was held on December 19, 1947, and, a few days later on December 22, the first Director of the CIA—Vice Admiral Roscoe Hillenkoetter—authorized the CIA's SPG (Special Projects Group) to carry out covert operations. The Cold War is in full swing, and there is no turning back.

Within a few weeks, Captain Mantell would chase a UFO across the skies over Kentucky and would die after blacking out at thirty thousand feet, or so the story goes. During the rest of that year Project SIGN would be created, the State of Israel would be proclaimed, and Jack Parsons would lose his security clearance. That same year, the US Navy would create Project PENGUIN, a program to research the uses of psychic phenomena by the military.

By 1949 the world would enter a very dangerous phase, as the Soviet Union exploded its first atomic bomb, and Mao's revolution culminated in the creation of the People's Republic of China on October 1, 1949. The world, it seemed, was polarizing into two opposing forces, the yin and yang of twentieth century history: on the economic side, the opposing systems of capitalism and communism, and on the political side, the systems of democracy and totalitarianism. More than simply a difference of opinion about how to organize society, the opposing principles were deeper, more profound than that, and affected every aspect of the human experience. Everything from education to religion to commerce to government to marriage was being examined under the Communist systems of Russia and China, which meant that the rest of the world was forced to come to terms with institutions they had taken for granted. The term "Godless Communism" became a watchword and a battle-cry, a stereotype that could have come straight from the book of psychological warfare, so neat and unequivocal it was, so efficient in forestalling any need for deeper understanding of the conflict. Communists were atheists, enough said. Wasn't it Marx who wrote, "Religion is the opiate of the people"? And speaking of religion and opium it was on February 3, 1949 that the world was subjected to a very bizarre experience, in the form of a public confession recited by Roman Catholic Cardinal József Mindszenty of Hungary.

József Mindszenty was a staunch anti-Communist and priest of the Catholic Church in Budapest when Pope Pius XII consecrated him bishop in 1944, elevating him to Cardinal in February 1946. This was in the midst of great turmoil in Hungary, when a democratically-elected government was toppled by a Communist coup d'état that instigated a reign of terror. Mindszenty himself was arrested in 1948, accused of collaboration with the Nazis, espionage, and treason. Subjected to physical and psychological torture, including being beaten with a rubber hose, Mindszenty refused to sign a confession to the charges. Finally, in February of 1949, he appeared before the startled view of the world as, apparently drugged or under some other psychological coercion, he fully (and robotically) confessed to all the charges against him. The security and intelligence services of the world became very alarmed. What weapon did the Russians possess that was stronger than physical or psychological torture, that could make such a cast-iron anti-Communist as Mindszenty confess to crimes that he did not commit and that could conceivably sign his death warrant?

The following year, 1950, the Korean War began. Our former allies against the Nazis and the Japanese—the Russians and the Chinese respectively—were now our enemies. The Korean War would officially begin on June 25, 1950, but two months earlier an operation was put in motion whose effects are still being felt today, more than fifty years later.

Admiral Roscoe Hillenkoetter was the first Director of the CIA; he was also later to become a member of NICAP, that organization of professional scientists, military men, engineers and civilians created to uncover the truth about UFOs. Hillenkoetter remained convinced about the reality of the phenomenon all his life. But on April 20, 1950—ironically enough, Hitler's birthday—he approved the creation of a special project to discover a means to combat the Russian mind weapons, whatever they were. This project was called BLUEBIRD.[12]

Tad Szulc, a respected mainstream journalist and biographer of both Watergate Plumber and CIA agent E. Howard Hunt and Cuban leader Fidel Castro (and thus covering both sides of the Bay of Pigs story), mentions—in an article printed in the November 1977 issue of *Psychology Today*—that code names like BLUEBIRD and the later ARTICHOKE "have no known significance." This is echoed in John Marks' classic study of CIA mind control projects, *The Search for the Manchurian Candidate* (1979). Yet it is true that, in the early days of the CIA, project names were at the whim of their creators, and not the results of a computer-generated random search among a classified dictionary as they are now. Thus, project names usually had *some* meaning attached to them. (For instance, when Allen Dulles was put in charge of the CIA's mind control project he changed the name BLUEBIRD to ARTICHOKE, since (according to Gordon Thomas)[13] he was fond of the vegetable. It was, according to John Marks, CIA security chief Sheffield Edwards who decided to call the project—a program for exploring the uses of hypnosis and other means to protect Agency personnel from enemy psychic penetration—BLUEBIRD. Why, then, *did* he choose the name BLUEBIRD for the first-ever CIA mind control project, the forerunner of the more infamous MK-ULTRA?

At the time, the US Navy had its own truth serum operation, called Project CHATTER, begun in 1947. CHATTER seems a more appropriate project name, since its goal was to make prisoners talk. Thus, we are still faced with what appears to be a minor mystery: why BLUEBIRD?

There is a phrase which is perhaps not used so much these days as it was in the tender years of the twentieth century: "the blue bird of happiness." What many people do not realize—and did not realize even then—was that this term had its origins in a play and a novel by the Belgian Nobel Prize–winning author and dramatist, Maurice Maeterlinck (1862–1949). Maeterlinck was surrounded by the Symbolist movement (forerunners of the Surrealists) in *fin-de-siécle* France, and was a friend of Sar Peladan, a noted Rosicrucian of the day. Indeed, Maeterlinck was something of a mystic himself and a firm believer in occult phenomena, as his other writings such as *The Other World* (1942) amply demonstrate. He was also a keen observer of nature and natural phenomena, in *The Life of the Bee* (1901), in which the concept of the "meme" is introduced to a wider audience (after its creation by a relatively-unknown German psychologist—Richard Sauder—years before, the same psychologist who created the "engram," made famous by L. Ron Hubbard). His writings were very popular in Europe, being a mixture of the profound with the childlike, such as his most famous work *The Blue Bird* (1909). In this play, first performed in the Russian language in Moscow on September 30, 1908 and later in English in London and New York, two children set off on a search for the Blue Bird of Happiness. This search leads them on many adventures—a kind of initiatic quest for the Grail—and the author was startled to realize that many of the motifs of Maeterlinck's play are repeated in the CIA's search for a Manchurian Candidate, a search that began with Project BLUEBIRD. It is this strange set of correspondences that leads the author to the opinion that Sheffield Edwards's agenda itself was more profound than simply a search for a truth serum or a psychological defense against it, or that at least Edwards understood the implications of what he had set out to do in BLUEBIRD. (A further search through Maeterlinck's works reveals an even more sinister aspect, which will be discussed later.)

The story, which begins on Christmas Eve, involves two children—Tyltyl and his younger sister Mytyl—who set out on a quest to find the Blue Bird of Happiness. Impoverished children of a woodcutter, who live across from a great house with very rich children, they understand that they are too poor to receive Christmas presents that year. They go to sleep with the lamp out. Then, in the middle of the night, a light shines through their house from outside, the lamp lights itself, and the children awake. (It is like a scene from *Close Encounters of the Third Kind*, similar in detail to descriptions of UFO landings.) There is a knock at the door, and an old woman—who later introduces herself as the Fairy Berylune—asks them if they have "the grass that sings, or the bird that is blue." It appears that

Berylune has a sick daughter who will not get well unless the Blue Bird of Happiness is found. The children, eager to help, then set off on a quest for the mysterious Bird . . . and to visit their dead grandparents, with the Fairy's help. In order to visit the dead, however, they have to pass through the Land of Memory which is on the way to the Blue Bird.

Tyltyl is given a magic hat. On this hat is a diamond, set squarely in the center. If he presses it, he will see "the Soul of Things"; if he turns it to the right, he sees the past; to the left, the future; and as long as he wears the hat, it is invisible.

Those who read Eastern mysticism will no doubt grasp at once that the diamond is the "adamantine substance" and its position on the hat is a reference to the Third Eye, which, when opened, gives the devotee access to secret information and occult powers. The search for the Blue Bird will give Tyltyl these powers as he walks through the Land of Memory, the Palace of the Night, a Graveyard, and an enchanted Forest, meeting his dead grandparents on the way. Eventually, of course, the children arrive back at their home on Christmas morning where they discover that the Blue Bird of Happiness has been there all along: Maeterlinck's homely moral, which was embraced by many at the time. Few sought to delve any deeper into the tale to discover the esoteric elements of necromancy and treasure-quest. That children—virgins—are the ideal seers according to the occult texts of the Middle Ages (the ones consulted by Joseph Smith, Aleister Crowley, Jack Parsons, L. Ron Hubbard, et al.) goes unmentioned. The moral is uplifting and spiritual, conservative and charming. A fairy tale replete with talking animals and trees, and kindly grandparents, suitable for children and adults alike. The quest itself, though, is enlightening for other reasons.

The Land of Memory, of course, was the target of the BLUEBIRD project: to enter that Land in another person's mind, to go through the drawers, rearrange the furniture, and leave unnoticed. Once the Korean War started, and American POWs began making bizarre, pro-Communist statements after a mysterious sojourn in Manchuria, the world was introduced to the concept of "brainwashing," and BLUEBIRD took on enormous importance. If the Communists could alter the consciousness of American soldiers, then the War took on a completely different nature: it became a war of culture against culture, of atheism versus religion, of race against race, of Darkness against Light. This was a war not to be fought by bullets alone; psychological warfare operations were ramped up at the same time as BLUEBIRD went into full swing, and what William Sargant would later (1957) call "The Battle for the Mind" had begun.

The innocent tale of Tyltyl and Mytyl must have ignited some deeper understanding on the part of Sheffield Edwards. In 1940, Maeterlinck and his wife had fled to America after a brief sojourn in Portugal during the early days of the war. It was here, for a publication called the *American Magazine* of January 1941 that Maeterlinck wrote "The Blue Bird Found Again." In it, he writes, "They sought the blue bird of happiness throughout the worlds of the living and the dead—for surely, they thought, so great a prize as this cannot exist in any save a far, strange land. It was only when they returned, defeated in their search, that they discovered the blue bird—where it had been all the time, where they had never noticed it, since they had been seeing it every day."[14]

It was from far, strange lands—Communist Hungary, Communist Manchuria—that the search for the blue bird had been born. And Sheffield Edwards was determined to bring that search right back home. Everyone in the West in the pre-War years had known of Maeterlinck's creation, even if they had not read or heard of any of his other, more obscure, works, or of his studies of astrology, psychic phenomena, and mysticism. He won the Nobel Prize for Literature in 1911, largely on the strength of *The Blue Bird*, and he fled to the United States from Europe in the same year as Hans Habe, another famous novelist. Yet, it is the author's contention that Edwards was more familiar with *The Blue Bird* than simply hearing the term tossed around as a metaphor for an ideal state of mind. Maeterlinck's description of the Land of Memory had to strike deep resonances in the minds of the BLUEBIRD team as they embarked on their search for a key to the mysteries of human consciousness. For it was in Maeterlinck's play (and later a novelized form, published by esoteric groups in the US and Europe) that the search for happiness—for the Blue Bird—is linked to the Land of Memory, to the Palace of Night, and the source of Truth.

In the Land of Memory—a strange land enshrouded in mist and dark-ness—the two seekers find their grandparents, long deceased. Their grandparents tell them,

> The last time you were here, let me see, when was it? . . . It was on All Hallow's, when the church bells were ringing . . .
>
> —Act II, Scene 2 "The Land of Memory," *The Blue Bird*

All Hallow's, of course, is the Day of the Dead. They find a Blue Bird, but when they return from the Land of Memory the bird has turned completely black. Only the first "trial" has taken place, and Tyltyl and Mytyl have much farther to go.

The Palace of Night is somewhat more eerie and forbidding than even the Land of Memory. Night is depicted as a kind of angel, a Dark Lady with wings in place of arms. "Her beauty, built up of peace and repose, possessed the secret of Silence . . ."[15] When Tyltyl stands before her, she thinks, "What! A Man's son coming to her palace! And, perhaps, with the help of the magic diamond, discovering her secrets!"[16] The strange juxtaposition of "Man's son" with the Palace of Night, a magic diamond, and the discovery of the secret which was the aim of BLUEBIRD makes one think immediately of that compelling line in Ed Sanders' study of Charles Manson: "If the Pentagon ever formulates the Manson secret, the world's in trouble."[17] That there are other bizarre resonances between Manson and BLUEBIRD will become obvious later.

The Palace of Night is the domain of Ghosts, Sickness and Wars. One goes directly from the Land of Memory to the Palace of Night, from unlocking the secrets of the memory to communing with the dead, controlling sickness and becoming victorious in war. Some readers may protest that the author's reading of what is, after all, a fairy story is too poetic, and that he is taking an inordinate amount of license with the material; the author would protest that there seems no other reason for calling the CIA's mind control program BLUEBIRD if it was not in reference to the Maeterlinck play, and that—consciously or unconsciously—the doctors of the mind control program were following virtually the same agenda as our fictional hero, Tyltyl. BLUEBIRD, and its associated programs such as MK-ULTRA and OFTEN, became involved in all aspects of behavior modification, hypnosis, drug-induced psychological states, the creation of amnesia, and studies of the paranormal, including ESP and mediumship. The Land of Memory and the Palace of Night were both amply represented in the US Government's mind control programs.

Tyltyl finds a great door set in the rear of the Palace of Night, and is told he must never open it, that great dangers await those who rush in and that no one who enters that room ever returns to the land of the living. Tyltyl, who is charged with the sacred quest of finding the Blue Bird, finally decides to open the door. When he does so, he sees a beautiful garden, a waterfall, many wonderful things and . . . thousands of blue birds. He tries to grab as many as he can, and when he takes them out of the room they turn to corpses in his arms. They cannot stand the light of day.

> The Blue Bird, the real one, the only one that can live in the light of day, is hidden here, among the blue birds of the dreams that live on the rays of the moon and die as soon as they set eyes on the sun.
>
> —Act III, Scene I: "The Palace of Night," *The Blue Bird*

He must continue his quest, leaving the Palace of Night for his next destination, the Palace of Luxury. Here, he is confronted by a scene of outrageous depravity, as fat beings eat, drink, laugh and carouse, beatific in their willful ignorance. As always, however, Tyltyl—with his magic diamond—can see things as they really are, and by pressing the diamond he perceives that these beings are miserable fools and, thus exposed, they retreat to the Miseries, a special place from whence they may never return. Of course, the CIA specializes in "seeing things as they really are," looking behind the curtain, behind the façade, and their entire program may be seen as Tyltyl's diamond: they put the magic diamond to use to see the human mind as it really is, to strip away a human being's conscious defenses so that everything, every secret—even highly classified government secrets that could cost the lives of many—would be revealed.

From the Palace of Luxury, Tyltyl proceeds to the Kingdom of the Future. This is where he finds a land filled with children who are not yet born, dressed completely in blue and like little scientists. They are occupied with the inventions that they will produce once they have been born on earth. However, Tyltyl—as a living person—is not allowed in this Kingdom, which is under the rulership of Time. Secretly, he passes through the Kingdom, learning of the new advances in science, technology, agriculture and the like, finds the Blue Bird, and begins to leave, when Time discovers him and attacks him. Frightened, Tyltyl releases the Blue Bird, and once again it flies away.

From the Kingdom of the Future, then, to the Graveyard.

This is much like any other cemetery, with tombstones and grass and silence. At midnight, he is to use his magic diamond once again to see the Dead. In the midst of the darkness and impending horror, a clock in the distance chimes the hour. Tyltyl presses the diamond, frightened but willing to face the Dead as the next in his series of trials before he can capture the Blue Bird.

But instead of ghostly figures in shrouds and clanking chains, the scene changes. The tombs open, but instead of ghoulish entities only flowers emerge.

> They had thought that ugly skeletons would rise from the earth and run after them. They had imagined all sorts of terrible things. And then, in the presence of the Truth, they saw that all they had been told was a story and that death does not exist.[18]

The motto of the CIA, of course: "You shall know the Truth, and the Truth will set you free."

The poignant last lines of this section—in the novelization of *The Blue Bird*—are "There are no dead! There are no dead!" (The family of the late Dr. Frank J. Olson may disagree, of course. As one of the many martyrs of the CIA's mind control efforts, his sacrifice has become a rallying point for those who fear the CIA's arsenal of psy-war and behavior modification weapons. His story will follow soon.)

From the Graveyard, Tyltyl wanders into the Forest. Oddly, the creatures of the Forest fear Tyltyl and his efforts to find the Blue Bird and, in the accomplishment of his quest, reveal all of the secrets he has learned. They conspire to kill him.

> We must now decide, in order to avoid reprisals, which form of execution will be the most practical, the easiest, the quickest and the safest, which will leave the fewest accusing traces when Man finds the little bodies in the forest . . .
>
> —Act III, Scene II, "The Forest," *The Blue Bird*

During the hero's quest for the Blue Bird, he has been accompanied by various other creatures who have been observing him from a distance. These are variously a Cat, a Dog, Bread, Sugar, Fire, etc. Many of these creatures—most especially the Cat—fear for their lives should Tyltyl be successful. In addition, the Fairy has warned some of them: "All those who accompany the two children will die at the end of the journey."[19]

The Cat, however, is having none of it:

> "The idiots," she thought, "have very nearly spoiled the whole thing by foolishly throwing themselves at the Fairy's feet, as though they were guilty of a crime. It is better to rely on one's self alone. In my cat-life, all our training is founded on suspicion. I can see that it is just the same in the life of men. Those who confide in others are only betrayed. It is better to keep silent and to be treacherous one's self."[20]

At the risk of belaboring the point, might one say that the above quotation could be the personal motto of men like Richard Helms, E. Howard Hunt, or even the late czar of MK-ULTRA, Dr. Sidney Gottlieb? Loners all, desperately private men who guarded the secrets of the nation and the secrets of their lives with equal passion, since the two were often so inextricably intertwined, their training was certainly "founded on suspicion." The above words could also be their reaction to the spectacle of the Watergate hearings or those of the House Intelligence Sub-Committee on Assassinations, where some of the intelligence agents threw themselves at the feet of the Senators, "as though they were guilty of a crime" and "nearly spoiled the whole thing."

In the story, the Cat leads Tyltyl into a trap in the forest, where he is set upon by the trees and the animals and has to fight for his life. He is saved in the last minute by Light, who warns him—apropos of Cat and the other animals and trees—that "man is alone against all in this world. Never forget that."[21] Not exactly an environmentalist message!

Finally, the Leave-Taking occurs, as the hour has grown late and the two children, Tyltyl and his younger sister Mytyl, must return to their cottage to awaken on Christmas morning. They have not found the Blue Bird, and are in despair. What is more, they must say goodbye to all the animals and other creatures that accompanied them on their quest. The Cat has the last word of the animals, and says, "I love you both as much as you deserve,"[22] which could be the cynical perspective of some of the people whose histories we cover in these pages.

The children return to their cottage miraculously as the clock strikes eight o'clock on Christmas morning. This is the Awakening, a constant theme with Maeterlinck which is repeated in *The Betrothal,* his sequel to *The Blue Bird.* Of course, when they awaken, the children realize that the Blue Bird has been in their home all along.

The author has taken this much time with Maeterlinck's work in order to present his case that the selection of the project name for the CIA's first-ever mind control program was deliberate and held a certain degree of relevance for the initial team of scientists and spies that made up the BLUEBIRD team. Like Tyltyl and Mytyl in the story, they were on a sacred quest that would lead them into humanity's deepest secrets; by delving into the universal, macrocosmic secrets of the human mind, they hoped to uncover the specific, microcosmic secrets of their enemies. As above, so below.

Yet, Tyltyl and Mytyl were innocents; they were virgin children, morally spotless, on an initiatic journey in the company of Light. The men of BLUEBIRD, and later ARTICHOKE and MK-ULTRA, could hardly be considered in the same way. From the point of view of the ancient mystery religions whose quest they were imitating, they were plumbing the depths of the Abyss without having undergone a period of purification; thus their sins—their personal, private, specific sins—would come to haunt them in the days and weeks and years that would follow, soiling their reputations and forbidding them entry to the Inner Temple. Frank Olson was one of these: a man who had confronted his own personal demons, who had seen the hideous results of his work in the desperate eyes of his victims, and who wanted to be shriven, to be forgiven. Perhaps alone of all his colleagues, he realized that what he was cooperating in was heinous and he wanted out. Unfortunately, Dr. Gottlieb had other plans for Frank Olson. Dr. Olson was "initiated" at the hands of Gottlieb before he was spiritually ready, when his soul was sick and when hallucinations of terror were his constant companions.

His was the first sacrifice of these cynical Masters. His blood was spilled on the concrete outside a New York hotel. Like the Tarot trump, *The Lightning-Struck Tower*, the story of Frank Olson has become an icon, an archetype of sinister forces and the destruction they wreak on the guilty and the innocent alike. It is also a very real, literal story of espionage, mind control and politics—a terrifying case that may well lead to the dismantling or reorganization of America's intelligence establishment.

THE TOWER STRUCK BY GOD

> What are you doing in that corner? You look like a pack of conspirators!
>
> —Maeterlinck, *The Blue Bird*[23]

The story of Frank Olson has been known for quite some time, but only in bits and pieces. It is well-known, for instance, that he was a scientist who was given LSD without his knowledge, and who became psychotic and who died after a plunge from a hotel room window. It is well-known that his death as a result of an unethical drug experiment had not been revealed to anyone—including his family—for twenty years, until the Watergate era when some of the details of the MK-ULTRA program leaked out and hearings were held to determine just exactly what had gone on then. It is also well-known that the CIA paid damages to the Olson family, and hoped the whole thing would just go away.

What is not well-known, and what has only come to light recently, is that Dr. Olson was working on chemical and biological warfare weapons at his laboratory at Edgewood Arsenal in Maryland, work that involved the search for drugs that would unlock the human memory bank and help to create the perfect assassin, the "Manchurian Candidate"; that he doubted the morality of his work when confronted with some "test subjects" at a secret base in the United Kingdom (according to Gordon Thomas, German prisoners of war); that he was a colleague of such esteemed psychological warfare experts as William Sargant, who was worried that Olson would blow the whistle on the programs. He was faced with the horror of what he was doing, and began to request reassignment. He was definitely reassigned.

Most of the following information can be found on the website of the Frank Olson Legacy Project, which is under the stewardship of Dr. Olson's son, Eric Olson, who is a psychiatrist who studied under Dr. Robert Jay Lifton. Dr. Lifton is the author of numerous works concerned with the malicious use of science by governments, one of the classics being his work on thought-reform in China and another his definitive study of the Nazi doctors.[24]

Frank Olson is born in Wisconsin in the year 1910. He will receive his Ph.D. in biochemistry in 1942, from the University of Wisconsin. In 1943 he is asked to join the staff at the newly-formed Camp Detrick in Frederick, Maryland. The war is on, and the Army has created Camp Detrick to be its center for CBW, or Chemical-Biological Warfare. The man in charge of the science at Camp Detrick is Frank Olson's mentor from the University of Wisconsin, Dr. Ira Baldwin.

In 1948, Dr. Baldwin issues "Special CBW Operations" for the War Department, in which he advises a new approach for chemical and biological weapons strategy, the use of CBW weapons as sabotage. By 1950, with the outbreak of the Korean War, the scientists and would-be saboteurs at Camp Detrick get serious. The Special Operations Division (SOD) of the Army is created under Dr. John Schwab, a group that runs parallel to CIA's Technical Services Staff (TSS) under Dr. Sidney Gottlieb. It was SOD that was responsible for the bacteriological tests with the bacterium *Serratia marcescens* over San Francisco in the 1950s, which may have led to the death of Edward J. Nevin and possibly more, since at least ten others were hospitalized at the same time with the same symptoms.[25] Between 1949 and 1969, citizens of the United States were the unwitting subjects in 239 separate cases of open-air biological attack simulations; most used chemicals that were inert and harmless, but in some cases live bacteria were used, such as in San Francisco in September 1950.[26] The Army has defended itself, saying that these tests were necessary in order to understand the dispersal patterns of biological agents on the civilian population should the enemy (in those days, the Chinese and the Russians) attack the country with anthrax or other virulent toxins. It was the Cold War, and such measures were thought urgently necessary in order to defend the country; the question is, of course, where does one eventually draw the line between what actions are defensible in time of war and what are not? With the Nuremberg Trials, we thought we knew.

It is a critical period for Dr. Olson. He begins traveling extensively in Europe, and can be found in France, England, Norway and Morocco in July 1953 alone. Until that time, everything seemed to be okay with the friendly, upbeat scientist, but by August 1953—a month after the European trip—things begin to take a tragic turn. According to the Frank Olson Legacy website, "Frank Olson vacations with his family at the family summer house in the Adirondack Mountains. He is observed by his sister-in-law reading the Bible and is apparently going through a period of profound soul-searching and self-examination."

Two months later, and the turmoil in Frank Olson's soul is exposed for the world to see. Unfortunately, he was involved in heavily classified work for both the US Army and the CIA. The exposure of Frank's anguish meant the exposure of the government's secrets. As below, so above.

November 19, 1953 is the date of the infamous Deep Creek Rendezvous. Here, at an isolated cabin in the Maryland forest, nine persons meet to discuss various projects they are working on at Camp Detrick. This group consists of five SOD personnel and four CIA/TSS personnel. Dr. Sidney Gottlieb is present, as well as Dr. Robert Lashbrook. The unsuspecting SOD people are dosed with LSD in their Cointreau. Dr. Olson receives about 70 micrograms of the potent hallucinogen (according to one report, 10,000 micrograms according to another). Who knows how much? 500 micrograms would be the average dose. Thus 70 "mikes" is obviously quite small, and 10,000 mikes would be the equivalent of 20 doses. The party turns bizarre and raucous, and breaks up around 1 A.M. with Dr. Olson in a paranoid state, running around shouting, "You're all a bunch of thespians!" The author takes this to be a reference to their acting a role, i.e., performing duplicitously.

The next morning, Dr. Olson complains he had a wakeful night, and his strange, depressed mood is attributed to a kind of psychedelic hangover. He returns home and tells his wife he wants to quit his job at Detrick and become . . . a dentist. He is overwrought, deeply shaken, and tells her he has made a "terrible mistake."

On Monday, the first work day after the Rendezvous, Olson tells his supervisor—one Lt. Colonel Vincent Ruwet—that he wants to quit. Ruwet scorns Olson's plea, telling him instead that he is doing a great job and should remain at his post.

The next day, Olson goes to work as usual but is brought home at 10:00 A.M. by a driver from SOD. The family is told that Olson might become violent and harm them, and thus should go to Manhattan to get treatment.

The psychiatric treatment planned for Olson is unusual, to say the least. In the first place, the "therapist" was Dr. Abramson, a Mount Sinai–connected CIA doctor whose specialty was immunology, and who had no training or credentials at all in psychotherapy, psychology or psychiatry. It seems his only qualification was that he was CIA, with a background in LSD research. Why Olson had to be taken to New York for "therapy" is also unrevealed. There had to be CIA-approved psychiatrists closer to home, in Washington or Baltimore; but Abramson had been one of those involved with the CIA's Technical Services Staff and thus could be expected to know what was at stake and to stonewall the local authorities; also, according to the CIA's internal memo on the events, he was the only one who had experience with LSD experimentation.

If we look at a book published in 1967, *LSD, Man and Society*, we will see many references to Abramson's work in the footnotes to what is a series of articles based on a March 1967 symposium held at the chapel of Wesleyan University on the effects of LSD on society, religion, the laws, behavior, etc. Most of those references are to papers published in the years immediately following the death of Olson. For instance in 1955, Abramson published an article in the *Journal of Psychology* entitled "Lysergic acid diethylamide (LSD 25) as an adjunct to psychotherapy." Suddenly, Abramson was an authority. He followed this up in 1960 with a contribution to a Josiah Macy work, *Transactions of a Conference*, entitled "The use of LSD in psychotherapy," and again in 1967 as editor of the Bobbs-Merrill publication *The Use of LSD in Psychotherapy and Alcoholism*. So perhaps Dr. Abramson "got religion" after the death of Olson and started to specialize in the study of psychotherapy professionally?

Also in *LSD, Man and Society* is an article by Murray E. Jarvik, "The Behavioral Effects of Psychotogens," in which he references a study undertaken by him, Dr. Abramson and Dr. Margaret Ferguson in 1953 (the year of Olson's death) at Mt. Sinai, where LSD was given to test subjects and a questionnaire prepared to evaluate the effects. Ironically, this same paper references similar work being done by Isbell "and his collaborators" in Lexington, Kentucky (in what was actually a prison setting, where subjects were given massive doses of LSD over long periods of time). We would not find out for about ten years that these LSD projects of Isbell, Abramson, et al. were underwritten by the CIA and were part of MK-ULTRA.

Needless to say, at this stage of LSD research by Abramson, his "therapy" was useless. At one point in the process, Olson was taken to see the CIA's very own magician and illusionist, John Mulholland, a famous stage magician who had been assisting the CIA with the development of techniques for surreptitiously putting chemical or bacteriological agents into people's drinks, among other things. Olson did not like the magician, or the environment, or whatever was going on between Mulholland and Olson's CIA handler, Dr. Robert Lashbrook (Sidney Gottlieb's assistant). Olson wanted to leave, and Lashbrook, Olson and his boss Ruwet left for their hotel.

That night, Olson leaves his hotel room in the middle of the night, a room he shares with his boss, Ruwet. At this time, he engages in activity which future investigators would find very strange.

He wanders the streets and subways of New York, shredding his identification, getting rid of everything on him that can be traced. He returns and sits in the hotel lobby, wearing a trenchcoat and hat.

This scene is usually described as evidence of Olson's deteriorating mental state; however, to the trained eye, it looks more like classic espionage tradecraft. Olson was in danger of being caught behind enemy lines, so he did what agents are trained to do under the circumstances: get rid of identification and anything that could be used to blow the cover of the operation and endanger lives.

Frank Olson *was* behind enemy lines. He was in the United States of America in November 1953; the enemy agents were from the CIA; and his death at their hands was imminent.

November 26, 1953. Thanksgiving Day. Olson and Lashbrook are still in New York. Olson is afraid to go home, according to the CIA reports. So he and Lashbrook have Thanksgiving dinner, sadly, at a Horn and Hardart automat.

The next day, the always helpful if somewhat misguided Dr. Abramson visits Olson at the hotel and gives the unfortunate man a cocktail made of a dose of Nembutal and a glass of bourbon. (The "use of LSD in psychotherapy and alcoholism"? Did Dr. Olson have to fill out a questionnaire?) Needless to say, this is not a recommended combination for anyone; but then, Abramson didn't have any psychiatric training. Perhaps to immunologists a Nembutal/bourbon cocktail is "the right thing to do."

What happens next that night has been reported in several different ways, and by the same sole witness, Dr. Robert Lashbrook. At one time, he says that he woke up to see Frank Olson standing in the middle of the hotel room. Olson, from the middle of a very small hotel room, then rushes across the floor, over a radiator and through a closed window to plummet ten floors to the street. At another time, Lashbrook says he was asleep when Olson went through the window. In any event, Lashbrook's story has always been that Olson committed suicide.

The hotel in question was the Statler, which is now the Hotel Pennsylvania, on Seventh Avenue across from Penn Station and the new Madison Square Garden. The rooms at the Statler were quite small. The radiator was under the window. The window was small. There was not enough distance available in the room to permit a fully-grown man to work up enough momentum to crash through a closed window, moreover a window with the shade drawn. It also doesn't make sense that a person would try to commit suicide in that fashion. At the very least, he would open the window first. At the very least, he would simply go out the window and fall to the ground. By running at full tilt at a closed window all Olson could have hoped to accomplish was a dismal failure, with enough sound and fury to awaken the somnolent Lashbrook and defeat the whole purpose of the suicide attempt.

When the police get to Lashbrook's room, they find him sitting on the toilet seat in his underwear. According to CIA memoranda, he first phoned Sidney Gottlieb to tell him what happened, then called Ruwet, then called the front desk, and then called Abramson, in that order.[27] Abramson at first told Lashbrook he wanted nothing to do with the situation, but then later relented (under what type of persuasion?) and agreed to assist Lashbrook. The local NYPD detectives could get nothing out of Lashbrook, except that Olson had suffered from ulcers, and soon CIA field agents from the Security Division descended on the city to quash what looked like was turning into a homicide investigation.

And there matters stood until the Rockefeller Commission and the investigation into illegal domestic activities of the CIA more than twenty years later.

Unfortunately, the only clues we have to Frank Olson's state of mind in the days leading up to his death come from CIA or SOD personnel, the very people one would expect to present cover stories and outright lies. Obviously, nothing that Lashbrook said can be trusted, as he gave at least two different stories about what happened that night in the Hotel Statler. Nothing that Sidney Gottlieb said can be trusted at all. And the one person who may have been able to share some truth with the Olson family—Lt. Colonel Vincent Ruwet, whom Olson's wife considered a family friend—was Olson's boss and in a tricky position vis-à-vis Olson, the Army, and the CIA. After all, Frank's work at Detrick involved developing new ways to deliver biological agents. Like anthrax.

According to former State Department official and freelance journalist John Marks:

> After all, the officials at TSS and SOD worked intimately together, and they shared one of the darkest secrets of the Cold War: that the U.S. government maintained the capability—which it would use at times—to kill or incapacitate selected people with biological weapons.[28]

The arsenal of weapons available to TSS and SOD under their working codename MK-NAOMI included shellfish toxins, botulinum, Staphyloccus enterotoxin, Venezuelan equine encephalomyelitis, and anthrax. Dr. Olson's specialty was the development of aerosol sprays and other airborne delivery systems for the agents. During Frank Olson's tenure at SOD, one of the Fort Detrick employees actually died of exposure to anthrax. Frank told his wife it was pneumonia. The secrets at Detrick were some of the most closely guarded in the nation; if the world discovered just what went on at Detrick—and at Edgewood Arsenal, which specialized in the chemical half of CBW weaponry—the outcry would be loud and furious. Lt. Colonel Ruwet could be expected to maintain operational secrecy, and if Olson was killed by the CIA—as the evidence now suggests was the case—then one would not have heard it from Ruwet.

That left Lashbrook, one of the men who dosed the party at Deep Creek Lodge; Gottlieb, whose operation it was; and Abramson, a CIA doctor who had worked with LSD for several years and was evidently the only medical man within a three hundred mile radius of Frederick, Maryland who could be expected to keep his mouth shut. No one was about to get a clear picture from any of these men. What is known from a source not at CIA or SOD is that shortly before his death, Frank

Olson phoned his wife from New York and—according to her—he sounded much better, almost his old self.

A few hours later, he was dead.

If he was, indeed, murdered by the CIA, what was the motive? Most researchers would claim that it was to keep him quiet about what was going on at Detrick, that the LSD experience had unhinged him, and that he was about to become a security risk. According to the late Colonel Ruwet, Olson had asked to be allowed to quit his post. Yet, he was not allowed to do so. Ruwet worked hard to keep him in the program, but when it seemed Olson was going round the bend, Ruwet—a Lt. Colonel in the US Army for which both he and Olson worked—did not go to the Army for help but directly to the CIA. Aware of the projects they were working on, Ruwet obviously did not trust the Army doctors, who were presumably not cleared for the classified information in Olson's head. By handing his friend Frank Olson over to the CIA, he was handing him over to his executioners.

Gordon Thomas is considered by many to be an expert on espionage matters. His book, *Journey Into Madness*, published in 1989, is an excellent update and companion volume to Marks' *The Search for the Manchurian Candidate*. His other works on the Mossad, and on the doomed ship full of Jews unsuccessfully escaping the Holocaust—*The Voyage of the Damned*—were published to critical acclaim. Yet, it wasn't until 1998 that Thomas felt he was able to communicate to Frank Olson's son—Eric—the story behind the cover story.

Journey Into Madness begins with the story of veteran CIA field agent William Buckley, who was taken hostage by the Hezbollah in Beirut in March 1984. Buckley was tortured and killed by an Arab physician, one Dr. Aziz al-Abub, the Arab world's answer to Dr. Mengele (or Dr. Gottlieb) and an expert in the use of drugs in interrogations. What is important to our story at the moment is that Thomas was a friend of Buckley's and had also worked with that icon of mind control research, Dr. William Sargant (*Battle for the Mind*). From them both he was able to extract the story of what really happened to Frank Olson. In fact, according to Thomas, the Olson murder is taught as a case study to Mossad agents in Israel![29]

According to Thomas, during their acquaintance Sargant was a consultant to the British Secret Intelligence Service, or MI5 and MI6, "largely because of his work in the eliciting of confessions by the Soviets." Sargant revealed to Thomas that he had visited CIA headquarters and met with Gottlieb, Richard Helms, Dr. Lashbrook, Dr. Ewan Cameron (whom we will discuss later on) . . . and Dr. Frank Olson.

Gottlieb and Olson also visited London and Porton Down, which is Britain's version of Fort Detrick and Edgewood Arsenal. Later on, Olson went to England several times himself, and met with Sargant on many occasions. In the summer of 1953—the period discussed above—Olson told Sargant he was in Europe to meet with Gottlieb and a "CIA team." Thomas at this point tantalizes us with the statement, "Sargant was satisfied that the CIA team was doing similar work that MI6 were conducting in Europe—executing without trial known Nazis, especially SS men." (If so, this makes for an interesting additional chapter to the history of that war, but there is no independent corroboration of this assertion.)

Whatever the facts of the case, when Olson returned from his trip to Europe (which included Norway and West Berlin, according to a photocopy of his passport) he had changed. According to Sargant (via Thomas), Olson had seen the results of his work firsthand, on actual human "subjects" who were being killed by the very weapons Olson himself was developing at Detrick. The horror and ensuing guilt led Olson to question his faith in the United States government and his faith in himself as a human being.

Sargant reported this to his superiors at MI6, recommending that Olson no longer be permitted to visit their CBW facility. This report was then, presumably, passed on in some form to the CIA hierarchy as a matter of course, and steps were taken to permanently remove Olson's security clearance . . . with extreme prejudice.

According once again to Sargant-via-Thomas, Gottlieb had been working with various other drugs besides LSD, including one which could induce depression leading to suicide. It is possible that Olson's Cointreau had been spiked with something other than the straight LSD given to the rest of the test subjects that evening in November. It is also possible that the visit in New York with Abramson and, eventually, with magician John Mulholland involved further surreptitious doses. We have only Abramson's word, for instance, that Olson was given a dose of Nembutal that day in New York. It could have been anything. And alcohol is a known depressant; might bourbon have accelerated the action of Gottlieb's wonder drug?

William Buckley confirmed Thomas' suspicion that Olson had been killed by the CIA, and that Helms and Gottlieb had covered it up and lied about it ever since. Others have come forward in the past ten years or so, some anonymously and some for the record, with bits and pieces of the puzzle. The picture that emerges is nothing short of murder.

Eric Olson had his father autopsied in June 1994. As if to confirm his suspicions over fifty years after his father's death, there was no sign of the crash through the hotel room window on Frank Olson's body: no cuts, no scrapes, nothing. The coffin had been closed during the funeral on advice of the CIA, since the crash would have disfigured the man's face. There was no evidence of this at all once the body was exhumed. Further, there was a suspicious bruise on Olson's head which suggested that he had been knocked unconscious. He could then have been thrown from the hotel room window.

The CIA's story falls apart completely with this additional evidence. If Olson was murdered, then the only suspect is Dr. Robert Lashbrook, who was in the hotel room with him when Olson fell ten stories to Seventh Avenue below. Was the depressant not working fast enough? Had Olson threatened to blow the whistle on covert CBW operations in the United States and Europe? No matter how one looks at the story today, there is no alternative but to recognize Dr. Frank Olson as a hero and a martyr: a man who was disgusted by his own country's atrocities in the aftermath of World War Two, when doctors and scientists—sobered by the Nuremberg trials and all they represented—should have known better.

As a strange sidebar to this case, in the days immediately before Olson's death, his boss Colonel Ruwet had arranged to have him admitted for regular psychiatric care at Chestnut Lodge Hospital, an appointment that was never kept. The admitting physician was one Dr. Robert Gibson. By an odd coincidence (again, one of many involved in this study) Dr. Gibson was the son of a famous stage magician, Walter B. Gibson, a "close friend and colleague to John Mulholland,"[30] and the creator of "The Shadow," the popular radio character, under the pen name Maxwell Grant. It was while searching for the traditional meaning of the Tarot trump *The Lightning Struck Tower* that I realized I had for many years in my possession a copy of Walter Gibson's work on divination, *The Complete Illustrated Book of Divination and Prophecy*, published in 1973, without realizing its significance.

Therein, this Trump is described as symbolizing ". . . disaster, downfall, and destruction, either physically or in personal affairs."[31]

The card is depicted as a tower, with one or two people falling from it, as it is struck by lightning (or God) from above. Frank Olson was not the first to fall from a tall building, murdered by his enemies, and he wouldn't be the last. As for William Sargant himself, we will be examining his contribution to the study of mind control and brainwashing as we proceed, but it is worthwhile to note for the record that he was a close personal friend of Robert Graves, the poet and scholar who gave the world such classics as *I, Claudius* and *The White Goddess*. It was while visiting Graves on the isle of Majorca in the mid-1950s (presumably after Olson's murder) that Sargant was encouraged by him to complete *Battle for the Mind,* and indeed that textbook of brainwashing, behavior modification and mental science actually includes a chapter written by Graves himself.

That this paragon of paganism—whose *White Goddess* was warmly embraced by a generation or more of New Agers as a kind of Wiccan bible—should have been on intimate terms with the man who was at the center of the West's mind control experiments (a man who was experimenting on living human beings, a man who also numbered poor, murdered Frank Olson as one of his colleagues, and who possibly ratted him out to the Agency) is yet another disturbing nexus point in this study, for these forces that occupy our attention call to themselves whatever they need, from whatever industry or field, without regard to social niceties, class ties or appropriate acquaintance. What rich material for a novel! The Poet-Pagan and the Psychiatrist-Spy. Like Arthur Koestler's *The Yogi and the Commissar*, such a novel could offer a wealth of contradictions to be resolved in an uneasy truth. The trinity of Olson, Sargant and Graves can be mirrored in Parsons, Hubbard and

McMurtry, or McMurtry, Crowley and MI5 . . . or Crisman, Arnold and Shaw . . . While traditional historians tend to focus on single themes (military personalities seen from the perspective of military matters, for instance, as if generals are as single-minded as their biographers), our view must be at once broader and deeper if the history of the twentieth century is to mean anything to us at all.

Because right now not much of it seems to make any sense.

History comes across Sheffield Edwards again as one of the CIA officers who visited former FBI agent and Guy Banister-associate Robert Maheu in 1960, to encourage him to arrange the assassination of Fidel Castro. We will come across Fred Crisman again as a suspect in the Jim Garrison investigation into the assassination of John F. Kennedy. And we will come across Maurice Maeterlinck again in the same context, because if Maeterlinck did not actually predict the assassination of President Kennedy, then we must assume that his work provided an inspiration for those who committed the crime itself. And if the latter is true, then the finger points back towards Sheffield Edwards and all the witches and warlocks of the Central Intelligence Agency. But first, let us pick up where we left off a little while ago, with Charles Manson slouching towards Hollywood to be born.

CEASE TO EXIST

"Me and Charlie . . . we founded the Family."

—Dennis Wilson

The Spring of 1967 found Charles Manson making his way down the west coast from Terminal Island to Los Angeles. He had in prison heard stories about the Hippies, free love, and drugs in San Francisco's Haight-Ashbury district, and had managed to convince a parole officer to let him go up there. After a few false starts, and after meeting Mary Brunner—the first member of the Manson "Family"—Charlie then went back down to Los Angeles to try to meet a record producer and get himself a recording contract.

Manson had by this time perfected a sort of technique on the guitar, taught to him by Terminal Island inmate Al Karpis (the last surviving member of the Ma Barker gang), and had begun writing his own songs. Manson had also learned the basics of Scientology from another inmate, Lanier Ramer (or "Raymer"). It was that combination—music and Scientology—that comprised the only education he had of the real world outside prison walls. But it was enough.

It was in the Los Angeles area—specifically in Venice—that he met Lynette Fromme. Fromme was the eighteen-year-old daughter of an aerospace engineer (who had coincidentally been in the Army at Randolph Air Base during the war), and she had had an eclectic childhood, going to school in Southern California with such later luminaries as *Saturday Night Live*'s Phil Hartman and others who would one day become famous in the music business. An intelligent, softly attractive and somewhat ethereal redhead with a penchant for poetry and philosophy, she suffered a sexually abusive father and a morally-absent mother, running away from home on countless occasions and at one time being remanded for psychiatric observation.

Lynette Fromme was a deeply disturbed young woman who had taught herself to endure tremendous amounts of physical pain; at one point, turning an industrial staple gun on her arm and shooting staples into herself at three-inch intervals, numb with no expression, like a Hindu devotee at Thaipusam. Manson had also learned to cope with physical pain while institutionalized, and fellow inmates have reported that he could hold a lighted match to his arm and not flinch. Thus on one level the two clearly had a lot in common, and Fromme would later become one of Manson's most prominent "apologists" as the decades passed and Manson's chance for release on parole diminished.

On another level, though, one could hardly conceive of two more different people. While Fromme was educated and very literate, fond of Dylan Thomas and Erich Fromm, poetry and mysticism, séances and ghost stories, and could quote Milton in front of the jury at the murder trial, Manson was poorly-educated, barely literate, and street smart from years of petty hustling, pimping, cheating and stealing. Fromme's background was decidedly upper-middle-class, and she had even toured the country while a grade-schooler and star of a singing and acting troupe. Fromme was adored as a young child, while Manson was tolerated at best, abused at worst. Manson's background was the type they used to call in those days "poor white trash" or, at its most euphemistic, "redneck" or "hillbilly." Manson's mysticism was largely his own amalgam of Scientology and Dale Carnegie, later mixed with a good helping of the Book of Revelations and convict psychology—an Aleister Crowley manqué. He first dropped acid at a Grateful Dead concert, and from there on he had the ritual mechanism for his own brand of spiritual initiation. Manson and Fromme were an accident waiting to happen.

Charlie and Lynette met on the boardwalk at Venice Beach sometime in the spring of 1967. (The precise dates, as with much of the Manson story, are unclear.) They connected, Manson virtually reading her mind as she was sitting, miserable, on a bench with her suitcase and nowhere to go. He guessed that she had had a fight with her father, and suggested that she go away with him instead. With only three weeks left to go of her spring semester in college, she made a fateful decision and followed him, leaving family and college behind forever. They made their way north, to San Francisco and Mary Brunner, and from there to Mendocino County, where the three lived that summer in and around the small town of Caspar.

The summer of 1967 was the "Summer of Love" in San Francisco. Manson had been energized by the atmosphere of freedom—including free drugs, free sex, people crashing wherever they could—and the non-judgmental attitudes of the people he met. He found out that with a glib line, laced with mystical allusions, he could go anywhere, do just about anything, and be accepted or even welcomed.

That year, Jack Ruby died in prison. Suspected Kennedy assassination conspirators David Ferrie and Eladio del Valle also died, and Clay Shaw was arrested in New Orleans. Ouija board sales hit an all-time high at 2.3 million sold. Ira Levin's novel of modern-day Satanism in the City of New York, *Rosemary's Baby,* was published, and Roman Polanski began work on the film version. Sharon Tate was working on the set of *Valley of the Dolls*, and her previous film—*Eye of the Devil*, in which a Wiccan high priest and disciple of Aleister Crowley, Alex Sanders, was a technical consultant—had just been released. And on June 29 of that year, actress Jayne Mansfield was killed in an automobile accident. Rumors that her death was a decapitation and the result of a satanic curse were rampant: Mansfield had been seen occasionally at Anton LaVey's Church of Satan headquarters in San Francisco. Anton LaVey would later become involved in Polanski's film of *Rosemary's Baby* . . . as a technical consultant.

While the witches and the satanists found work (if not actual, on-screen credits) as technical consultants in films about the Devil, Charles Manson was consulting with some screenwriters on a film about . . . Jesus.

Charles, Lynette Fromme and Mary Brunner were living in the woods of Mendocino County when Charlie, hitchhiking one day, was picked up by a Congregationalist minister named Dean Moorehouse. The Reverend Moorehouse is a strange twist to this already strangely twisted tale, because Moorehouse came to California from Minot, North Dakota. As we will see later, Minot—a small town of about thirty thousand people and an Air Force base—was the scene of serious and sometimes violent occult activity that was linked to the Son of Sam murder cases in New York a decade later. (It was also where Kenneth Arnold—creator of the term "flying saucer" and involved in the Maury Island affair with Fred Crisman—learned to fly.) Charlie struck up a conversation with Moorehouse and convinced him to visit their place in the woods, where they turned him on to LSD. At that point, Dean Moorehouse became converted to the cause (at least insofar as acid was concerned) and introduced Manson, Fromme and Brunner to his wife and daughter. His daughter, Ruth Ann Moorehouse, became the Family member known as Ouisch, who would become involved in the drugging of a prosecution witness in Hawaii. At this time it is not known whether there is any more substance to the Moorehouse/Minot link than that. However investigative journalist Maury Terry would later find elements of a drug and prostitution network shaded with a veneer of ritual Satanism based in Minot, and would connect it to a convicted murderer known as "Manson II," to the Son of Sam killings in New York, and to the murder of producer Roy Radin in California.[32]

When life at Caspar became too much, and they got hassled by the local police for harboring Ruth Ann, an underage runaway—Charlie telling the booking officer that he was a minister and that his name was Charles *Willis* Manson instead of Charles *Milles* Manson and thus creating a phrase that he read as *Charles Will Is Man's Son*—the three retreated to Los Angeles, where Charlie would meet with some of his old prison friends (something that was happening on a regular basis during this period; what was discussed is still a mystery, and could have been anything from chatting about old times to plotting new capers and better connections) and finally pick up Patricia Krenwinkel, known as Katie and later, in San Francisco, Susan Atkins, who became Sadie. They moved into a house in Topanga Canyon—close to Malibu—known as the Spiral Staircase, to which they were introduced by someone involved in the occult. Some sources have connected this person to Abigail Folger, the coffee heiress and eventual Manson Family murder victim. Folger was involved in various consciousness movements in the area, and it is not unlikely that this would have been the case. She is known to have helped finance the Straight Theater in San Francisco, where Kenneth Anger was involved in filming his satanically-oriented works, and to have been involved with the Himalayan Institute as well as Esalen (where Manson also showed up a few days before the Tate killings). However, this introduces a disturbing element into the story, because it implies that Charles Manson (and his growing family of killers) knew at least one of the murder victims beforehand, and thus goes to motive.

Motive was the most ephemeral aspect of the prosecution's case against Manson; once they had the satanic and racist elements, the prosecutors looked no further. They believed that the victims in the Tate and LaBianca killings were selected randomly, as part of "Helter Skelter": an attempt to force a race war between whites and blacks. Although this dubious motive satisfied the media's lust for sensationalism and served to paint Charlie and his Dark Angels as the latest incarnation of Satan and Hitler combined, a look at Charlie's criminal history would tell a different story. As prosecutor Vincent Bugliosi himself admits in his book on the case, *Helter Skelter*, he was surprised by the lack of violent crime in Manson's rap sheet. Manson came across more as a con man and petty thief than as a lust killer. There were obvious problems with LAPD's investigation of the case too, which is surprising considering how focused the media was on the sensational crimes. Further, attempts to depict Charles Manson as a serial killer (notably by the late Joel Norris)[33] are also ill-advised. There is no evidence he killed anyone until 1968–9 and, in fact, he did not personally murder any of the Tate/LaBianca victims, although he was convicted for having ordered their deaths. Whatever Charles Manson may be—and he may be many things—a serial killer he is not, if we look objectively at the available evidence. The murders he did commit himself were not motiveless crimes, but were each for a specific purpose. Even the Tate murders themselves may have been a device to disguise the real agenda behind some of the other killings, such as those of Leno and Rosemary LaBianca (which may have been related to gambling debts), and of Gary Hinman, and of the attempted murder of drug dealer Bernard Crowe.

While keeping his criminal contacts alive and warm, Charlie was still interested in becoming known as a musician and tried to work the Southern California entertainment network as best he could. He was introduced to Gary Stromberg and Corey Allen, two screenwriters and would-be producers in a small office in Universal City. They were working on a script about the return of Jesus Christ as a black man in America, and Charlie impressed them both with his knowledge of black prison slang as well as his insights into religion and spiritual matters. He agreed to work with them one day a week at their office on script ideas and treatments for what they wanted to call *Black Jesus.* The project never got off the ground, but the die had been cast, and Charlie was now a familiar face in some (admittedly bizarre) Hollywood circles from 1967 until his arrest for the Tate/LaBianca murders in 1969.

There were two people in particular who became involved with Charles Manson and the rest of his Family. One was the son of actress Doris Day, Terry Melcher, who was living in the house at 10050 Cielo Drive where the Sharon Tate murders would take place. Melcher was interested in producing records, but, as it turned out, not in producing Manson's work. A somewhat more enthusiastic promoter of Manson, however, was Dennis Wilson of the Beach Boys.

People with only a passing knowledge of the Manson case usually don't realize that the Beach Boys recorded one of Manson's songs and released it as the "B" side of their cover of the old Ersel Hickey 1958 hit "Bluebirds Over The Mountain," a song about lost love. Manson's song was originally entitled "Cease to Exist"—a Scientology reference and not necessarily a homicidal one—but the Boys retitled it "Never Learn Not To Love," which comes from the song's lyrics, and changed the line "Cease to Exist" to the more seductive "Cease to Resist." This song later made it onto the group's album *20/20* (1969), but by this time the reference to Charles Manson was deleted.

What drew the author's attention to this nugget of information was the song on the "A" side of Manson's single. The title "Bluebirds Over The Mountain" was suggestive of the CIA mind control operation—even though it had been written by a rockabilly composer from Brighton, New York one night in the mid-1950s—and seemed too synchronistic to ignore. Hickey and Manson were born in the same year—1934—and both had problems at home; Manson's mother was incarcerated for robbery, while Hickey's mother was hospitalized for a nervous breakdown. Manson probably never knew his father, and Hickey's father died when the boy was only four years old. Both Manson and Hickey were farmed out to relatives or foster homes, spent time in reformatories and ran away from home, and both Manson and Hickey were guitar players and songwriters. Hickey's one and only hit, "Bluebirds Over The Mountain," then appears on Manson's one and only song recorded by a mainstream label (his other music was released on various underground, bootleg and private labels after the murders). Is there a reason why Manson's song was on the flipside of the "Bluebird" cover? Had the

CIA's "bluebirds" escaped? Was Manson a "bluebird," i.e., a mind control subject, gone amok?

Were there other "synchronicities" to explore?

FROM MANCHURIA TO MULHOLLAND DRIVE

> And then, you have told me twenty times over that neither you nor your people ever deployed such means to pull down an enemy . . . . No, no, the people who are near you could never do that . . . . There is no shadow of doubt, it was an ambush and an assassination.
>
> —Act I, Scene 3, *The Cloud That Lifted*, Maurice Maeterlinck

Manson and his women wound up staying at Dennis Wilson's home for long periods of time from the spring to the summer of 1968. Wilson once claimed that he and Manson had created the Manson Family, and referred to Manson as "the Wizard." The other Beach Boys were not so enamored of Manson, and tended to avoid him whenever they could. Wilson, however, was recently divorced and lived alone in the house he rented on Sunset Boulevard, and the Manson Family were welcome—if expensive—houseguests. Gregg Jakobson, the group's manager and sometime songwriter, also found Manson interesting, and they would talk for hours on philosophical subjects. During this period, Manson and his group treated Wilson's home as their own, giving things away, wrecking his Mercedes on the road to their desert commune, and borrowing large sums of money. Wilson estimated that the friendship with the Manson Family cost him about $100,000 but that he was the lucky one: he got away with his life. (After the Tate murders, Manson approached Wilson for money, which Wilson refused—although at this time he did not know that Manson was responsible for the murders—and Manson threatened the life of his seven-year-old son, following that up with more threats on Wilson's life.)

One of the more unusual Family members, though, if only for a short time, was Deirdre (or "DiDi") Lansbury, the troubled teenaged daughter of actress Angela Lansbury. Angela Lansbury even went so far as to give DiDi a note that said it was all right for her to stay with the Manson Family, in case she got hassled by the police! The author felt the reverberations of this odd piece of trivia, since Angela Lansbury played the role of the evil mind controller in the 1962 John Frankenheimer film *The Manchurian Candidate*, a film starring Frank Sinatra, Lansbury, Laurence Harvey and Khigh Dhiegh that was pulled from distribution after the assassination of President Kennedy (even though Kennedy himself had given the green light to Frankenheimer to proceed with making the film, since Kennedy at the time was in delicate negotiations with the Soviets). Khigh Dhiegh played the role of the Asian mind control expert who brainwashed the Laurence Harvey character (a decorated Korean War hero) into a programmed assassin whose target was a presidential candidate. Ms. Lansbury was Harvey's mother, and "case officer," moving him towards the kill. Interestingly, Khigh Dhiegh—who also starred in the TV series *Hawaii Five-O*—later left acting to become involved in Chinese mysticism and wrote several books on the *I Ching*.

Ms. Lansbury, though, became the central character in one of television's most popular detective series, *Murder, She Wrote*. Many of her scripts were written by Donald Bain. Donald Bain was the biographer of radio personality Long John Nebel, and of a separate biography of Nebel's wife, Candy Jones, in which he revealed that Ms. Jones was a CIA mind control subject. Although some researchers have problems with Bain's book on Candy Jones, much of her story comes across as perfectly plausible. The author's own research on Ms. Jones' Asian activities tends to support that end of her tale. Perhaps the most important aspect of the whole affair is the fact that Ms. Jones had no motive for lying about her relationship to the CIA, particularly as her revelations to Donald Bain began in 1974, before the Rockefeller Commission would in 1975 make public the facts of the Frank Olson case. The Congressional Hearings on MK-ULTRA would not take place until 1977.

(The author had the occasion to meet Candy Jones in 1979–80, and found her to be an eminently sane and no-nonsense sort of person who had no desire to exploit her alleged CIA background, and who never mentioned it unless pressed to do so by other people. She also shared an interest in paranormal phenomena with her late husband, Long John Nebel, although perhaps not to the same degree he did.)

The odd nexus of Angela Lansbury/Charles Manson/Donald Bain/Candy Jones was suggestive of a deeper web of connections. Was it possible that Hollywood was being used as a tool of secret, special interests, and that the selection of themes, scripts, actors, studios, producers, directors was—at times, and during certain periods of international or domestic tensions—politically motivated or the result of an intelligence agenda: psychological warfare? Of course, we have the ultimate example of Ronald Reagan, the actor who became a President, but is there more to this story than that? Something more profound, and evidence of another "player" altogether?

Another striking reference to "Bluebirds" was in direct connection to the Kennedy assassination itself, the spoor of a minor event that may have had deeper implications, because it involved Lee Harvey Oswald and his time spent at Atsugi Air Base in Japan, one of only two locations outside the United States (along with Manila, in the Philippines) where the CIA maintained a store of LSD, and the base for U-2 spy plane flights over the Soviet Union. And what was the scene of a fistfight between Oswald and Tech Sgt. Miguel Rodriguez on June 20, 1958, the same year "Bluebirds Over The Mountain" was first released? The Bluebird Café in Yamato, Japan.

Oswald had tried to pick a fight with Rodriguez earlier that month, at the Enlisted Men's Club at Atsugi. The alleged motive was that Rodriguez had assigned Oswald to an excessive amount of KP (kitchen) duty. The first attempt, in Atsugi, did not result in a fight, as Rodriguez ignored Oswald; but later at the Bluebird Café Oswald spilled a drink on Rodriguez and a fight ensued, for which Oswald was court-martialed and sent to the brig. Oswald, defending himself, had said that he was drunk and spilled the drink accidentally; Rodriguez claimed that Oswald was not drunk, walked over to him calmly, and spilled the drink quite deliberately.

This incident merits further attention is for two reasons. In the first place, episodes of Oswald getting physical and looking for fights are few and far between. (About the only other event in which Oswald is known to have used his fists is in slapping his Russian wife, Marina, around.) Oswald was known to have been physically cowardly, and even effeminate in the way delicate young men can appear to the "jocks." One of his nicknames in the Marines was "Ozzie the Rabbit," a reference to his lack of physical courage, perhaps, but one which could also be a (conscious or unconscious?) reference to Walt Disney character and forerunner of Mickey Mouse: "Oswald the Lucky Rabbit," who appears in the 1927 cartoon "Great Guns," about Oswald's enlistment in the Army. In any event, Lee Oswald's deliberate attempt to provoke Rodriguez to a fistfight is wholly out of character.

> It is not fashionable to cite Disney versions when applying fairy tales to clinical questions. However, it seems likely that the people in the Disney Studios possess an unconscious, too. It seems possible that the Disney unconscious may be even closer to our own than those of the storytellers who spoke with the brothers Grimm.
>
> —Jean Goodwin, "Snow White and the seven diagnoses"[34]

In the second place, according to some witnesses, Oswald's actual time spent in the brig seems to have been slight, and moreover spent in civilian clothes according to the only eyewitness who actually saw him there. Some researchers feel that Oswald was receiving intelligence training at this time, and that the fight and ensuing sentence in the brig was a cover, to allow him time to complete this training unnoticed. Oswald is known to have been approached earlier by what was probably a Communist spy in Japan—a beautiful Japanese woman who asked a lot of questions about his job at Atsugi—and he reported this contact to his superiors.

Former CIA finance officer James Wilcott testified before the House Select Committee on Assassinations that Oswald was, indeed, a CIA asset in Japan, according to conversations he had with his co-workers at the Agency after the assassination.[35] The CIA denied this relationship to Oswald, but they did suggest that perhaps the KGB had recruited Oswald in Japan! If so, of course, that meant that Oswald may have been a Soviet agent at the time of the assassination, and this angle was not pursued.

Whatever actually transpired in Japan, it was a crucial time for Oswald and his ensuing career—whether as US intelligence agent, Soviet intelligence agent, or disaffected Marine and crazed, lone gunman—and it began, oddly enough, at the

Bluebird Café. Some researchers openly wondered whether Oswald was receiving mind control treatments of some sort at the time, since the CIA had a large operational base at Atsugi and had been debriefing defectors and returning prisoners of war there under Operation BLUEBIRD at the time of the Korean conflict. It is impossible to tell with any certainty at this time what Oswald was really doing in the Marines at Atsugi; his military records do show some discrepancies and, in one case, a medical notation shows that he contracted gonorrhea "in the line of duty"; certainly a bizarre set of circumstances for a lowly Marine radar operator.

As we have seen, BLUEBIRD may have had its inspiration in the tale by Maurice Maeterlinck, discussed above. If so, then perhaps the assassination of President Kennedy had also been "inspired" by another of Maeterlinck's plays, this time the rarely performed *The Cloud That Lifted*.[36] In this play a political leader by the name of Bielensky is murdered by unknown assailants. Either three or four shots are fired; the number is controversial. The mortal wound is received in the nape of the neck. Bielensky dies without regaining consciousness. The shots come from a garden wall near a thicket of aspens (the grassy knoll?). The victim had been receiving death threats, which he decided would not cause him to alter his routine. Further, the assassin—Axel Thorild—thought "he was serving his master and Holy Russia." He was a member of an underground political faction under surveillance by the secret police; he believed he killed Bielensky, but someone else takes the blame and commits suicide. Was Axel set up? Was he a . . . patsy?

The above brief summary of the play does not do it justice, perhaps, but the dramatic elements are so close to the facts of the Kennedy assassination—and performed long before Kennedy was even born—that one is hard-pressed to deny any connection to that day in Dallas in 1963. Was it a psychic prediction by this mystical Nobel Prize-winning author? Or was the play as well-known to the people who created and manned BLUEBIRD as Maeterlinck's other works? One is tempted to remark that "Axel Thorild" is reminiscent of one of Oswald's aliases, "Alec Hidell" . . . but that is probably taking this too far.

Probably.

> I am looking for some ray of innocent simplicity . . . of madness, even, if necessary, to try to explain a thing that could only be explained . . . by something that is wholly impossible . . .
>
> —Act III, Scene 1, *The Cloud That Lifted*, Maurice Maeterlinck

ENDNOTES

1 There is a plethora of published material on the famous UFO cases mentioned here. The reader is advised that much of the material is based on secondary sources, or worse, and that reputable studies are few and far between. What is reassuring is that the basic facts about most of these cases are pretty consistent from volume to volume, even if the conclusions by the various authors are as contradictory and speculative as much conspiracy theory lore. With that caveat in mind, readers interested in verifying my information may refer to the following: Kevin D. Randle, *The UFO Casebook*, Warner Books, NY, 1989, ISBN 0-446-35715-4 (by a former US Air Force intelligence—and Project Blue Book—officer); Donald E. Keyhoe, *Aliens From Space*, Signet Books, NY, 1974, LOC 73-83597 (by a former major in the US Marine Corps who was involved in UFO research and was himself an important figure in UFOlogy); Paris Flammonde, *UFO Exist!*, Ballantine Books, NY, 1993 edition, ISBN 0-345-33951-7; and, for a debunking view, Curtis Pebbles, *Watch the Skies!*, Berkley Books, NY, 1995, ISBN 0-425-15117-4. This is only the tip of the UFO iceberg, and other works will be referenced in the notes that follow. Further, much of this information is also available from declassified FBI files on the UFO phenomenon. They will be referenced below as well.

2 Other than published material, reference can also be made to the FBI files on this matter: BUFILE 62-83894-52(? Not clear), 62-83894-40,-89, -91, etc. etc., all with the designation "SM-X" or "Security Matter-X" or "SM Dash X."

3 Many thanks and credit to Jim Hougan for this unsettling piece of information.

4 My Banister files include BUFILE 62-83894-25, a July 3, 1947 memo from "WGB" to Hoover on sightings in Idaho; BUFILE 62-83894-104 which is a telex from Banister to Hoover dated 8-15-47 and marked "Urgent" regarding "Flying Disks" in Idaho; another telex to Hoover on the same date and sent five minutes later, also marked "Urgent" and concerning the same Idaho sighting; a BUFILE 62-83894-66 dated 8-20-47 to Hoover marked "Urgent" concerning another Idaho sighting, this time of the previous evening; a memo dated September 27, 1947—BUFILE 62-83894-129—from Banister to Hoover regarding a sighting in Washington State; etc. BUFILE 62-83894 seems to be the FBI's designation for "X" files. BUFILE 65-58300 seems to be their designation for files pertaining to "Protection of Vital Installations" which includes UFO-related events, such as a memo dated March 22, 1949 from the SAC of San Antonio to Hoover, in which the writer reports a meeting held between the Bureau and G-2, ONI and OSI concerning "Flying saucers," which states: "It is repeated that this matter is considered secret by Intelligence Officers of both the Army and the Air Force." As ONI (Office of Naval Intelligence) was also present at this meeting, one wonders if they shared the same attitude.

5 Jim Marrs, *Alien Agenda*, HarperCollins, NY, 1997, ISBN 0-06-018642-9, p. 86

6 Richard Harris Smith, *OSS: The Secret History of America's First Central Intelligence Agency*, University of California Press, Berkeley, 1972, ISBN 0-520-04246-8, p. 364

7 Some of the Roswell materials available to the general reader include—but are not limited to—the following: Kevin D. Randle & Donald R. Schmitt, *The Truth About the UFO Crash at Roswell*, Avon, NY, 1994, ISBN 0-380-77803-3; Tim Shawcross, *The Roswell File*, Bloomsbury, London, 1997, ISBN 0-7475-3507-8; Philip J. Corso with William J. Birnes, *The Day After Roswell*, Pocket Books, NY, 1997, ISBN 0-67101756-X; and a skeptical/debunking source in Kal K. Korff, *The Roswell UFO Crash: What They Don't Want You to Know*, Dell, NY, 2000, ISBN 0-440-23613-4. Most of the other books referenced in the above notes also cover the Roswell incident to a greater or lesser degree.

8 George Steiner, *Antigones*, Clarendon Press, Oxford, 1986, ISBN 0-19-281934-8, p. 53

9 Janwillem van de Wetering, *The Empty Mirror: Experiences in a Japanese Zen Monastery*, Pocket Books, NY, 1978, LOC 73-12235, p.191; see also his "Amsterdam Cops" novels, for instance *The Perfidious Parrot* and *The Hollow-Eyed Angel*, both published by Soho Press, New York.

10 Umberto Eco, *Reflections on the Name of the Rose*, p. 54

11 Maurice Maeterlinck, *The Blue Bird: A Fairy Play in Five Acts*, Dodd Mead & Co., NY, 1910

12 John Marks, *The Search for the Manchurian Candidate*, Times Books, NY, 1979, ISBN 0-8129-0773-6, op. cit., p. 22

13 Gordon Thomas, *Journey Into Madness*, Bantam, NY, 1990, ISBN 0-553-28413-4, p. 98

14 Maurice Maeterlinck, *The Blue Bird*, The Philosophical Publishing Co., Quakerstown, 1984, p. xxiv

15 Ibid., p. 50

16 Ibid., p. 50

17 Ed Sanders, *The Family*, E.P. Dutton, NY, 1971, ISBN 0-525-10300-7, p. 61

18 Maeterlinck, (1984) p. 113

19 Ibid., p. 21

20 Ibid., p. 48

21 Ibid., p. 128

22 Ibid., p. 134

23 Ibid., p. 31

24 Robert Jay Lifton, *Thought Reform and the Psychology of Totalism*, W.W. Norton & Company, NY, 1962; *The Nazi Doctors*, Basic Book Publishers, NY, 1986, ISBN 0465-04905-2

25 Jim Carlton, "The Military, Microbes and Secret Tests Using the U.S. Public," *Wall Street Journal*, October 22, 2001, p. 1; and in Leonard A. Cole, *Clouds of Secrecy: The Army's Germ Warfare Tests over Populated Areas*, Rowman & Littlefield, Totowa, 1988, ISBN 0-8476-7579-3, p. 75–104 26 Leonard A. Cole, op. cit., p. 6

26 The Frank Olson case has been covered in many texts on the CIA's mind control programs, including John Marks (op. cit.), Gordon Thomas (op. cit.), and many others. Interested readers should also logon to the Frank Olson Project website at www. frankolsonproject. org, a site that is maintained by his son, Eric. Recourse may also be had to the Joint Hearing before the Senate Committee on Intelligence and the Subcommittee on Health and Scientific Research of the Committee on Human Resources, United States Senate, "Project MK-ULTRA, the CIA's Program of Research in Behavioral Modification," August 3, 1977, Appendix A: "XVII. Testing and Use of Chemical and Biological Agents by the Intelligence Community," pp 74–83.

27 Senate Committee Hearing, August 3, 1977, Appendix A, op. cit., p. 78

28 Marks, op. cit., p. 73

29 This information, including the story about Olson and Sargant and accompanying quotations, comes from a memorandum posted on the Frank Olson Project website from Gordon Thomas to Eric Olson dated November 30, 1998. One should be forewarned that there is no independent corroboration of these claims available to the author at this time; basically all we have are Thomas' recollections of conversations with Sargant and Buckley on this issue.

30 Michael Edwards, "The Sphinx and the Spy: The Clandestine world of John Mulholland," *Genii, the Conjurorsi Magazine*, April, 2001, available on the Frank Olson Project website. The article makes for fascinating reading, and contains a great deal of information on the career of this very suspicious magician and sometime CIA consultant, including a tantalizing suggestion that Mulholland knew Andrija Puharich, a man who becomes central to our story in later chapters, and was investigating Puharich's claims of success in paranormal research.

31 Walter B. Gibson & Litzka R. Gibson, *The Complete Illustrated Book of Divination and Prophecy*, Doubleday, NY, 1973, ISBN 0-385-03599-3, p. 187

32 As described in Maury Terry's *The Ultimate Evil*, Barnes & Noble, NY, 1999, ISBN 0-7607-1393-6 and elsewhere in this book.

33 Joel Norris, *Serial Killers*, Anchor Books, NY, 1988, ISBN 0-385-26328-7, pp. 161

34 Jean Goodwin, in Attachment, *Trauma and Multiplicity: Work ing with Multiple Personality Disorder*, Valerie Sinason, editor. Brunner-Routledge, NY, 2002, ISBN 0415-19556-X, p. 142, "Snow White and the seven diagnoses"

35 Anthony Summers, *The Kennedy Conspiracy*, Warner Books, NY, 1992, ISBN 0-75150340-1, p. 129–130

36 Maurice Maeterlinck, *The Cloud That Lifted*, The Century Company, NY, 1923

BOOK ONE: THE NINE

CHAPTER SIX

THE DOORS OF PERCEPTION

> . . . we intend to investigate the development of a chemical material which causes a reversible non-toxic aberrant mental state, the specific nature of which can be reasonably well predicted for each individual. This material could potentially aid in discrediting individuals, eliciting information, and implanting suggestions and other forms of mental control.
>
> —Richard Helms, memorandum to Allen Dulles, April 3, 1953

> . . . it had always seemed to me possible that, through hypnosis, for example, or auto-hypnosis, by means of systematic meditation, or else by taking the appropriate drug, I might so change my ordinary mode of consciousness as to be able to know, from the inside, what the visionary, the medium, even the mystic were talking about . . . . I took my pill at eleven . . . .
>
> —Aldous Huxley, *The Doors of Perception*, May 4, 1953

The LSD experience is an enormous obstacle in the way of understanding what the latter half of the twentieth century was all about; those who have not taken LSD (or the other hallucinogens available at the time, such as mescaline and psilocybin) cannot appreciate the effects these substances have on one's perception of reality. Those who have taken the drugs are often considered to be in no position to be objective about them! Yet, LSD and the other hallucinogens form a core of experience that has molded the lives and behavior of millions of people, both in the United States and abroad. This behavior is the result of an altered perception of reality and, hence, of social values. The shock to the system that results when coming down from such a drug and seeing the "real world" once again is often transformed into a rejection of consensus reality, a rejection of human institutions based on what the acid-tripper sees as an imperfect understanding of the workings of the cosmos.

Just as Communism was perceived by the West as a rejection of its values and the establishment of a "counter culture" in which institutions such as the government, the church, the school, marriage and other forms of civilization were reinterpreted, redesigned or even rejected altogether to create what the Communists believed would be a paradise on earth, the acid-tripper similarly rejected all forms of Western "establishment" culture in favor of something more ethereal but no less paradisiacal;

but the acid-tripper rejected Communism as well, and any governmental authority, and was thus a problem for establishments both in the West and in the East.

The acid-tripper was also a problem for religious organizations in general, at least those which attempt to monopolize access to the Godhead, because the acid trip can be a mystical one, a religious experience equivalent to the visions of the Saints. Direct access to God is always frowned upon by religious institutions, for such access renders the institution irrelevant. Thus, the acid trip is primarily a political problem, as the role of interpretation (of laws, of scriptures, of experience), and thus of control, is taken out of the hands of human authority and placed squarely into the mind of the tripper.

Ironically, it was human authority who created the problem in the first place. As is well-known by now and referenced in many studies of the LSD problem, the United States' Central Intelligence Agency was the nation's first "LSD connection," providing the drug to researchers all over the country, including to young professors such as Timothy Leary, Richard Alpert, Ralph Metzner, and others who would popularize use of the drug among their students and, by extension, among the rest of the nation's youth. The purpose behind this unprecedented largesse was not altruistic: it was to further the research into what Richard Helms and others involved in scientific R&D at the Agency believed was a super-drug for behavior modification and mind control tasking. In other words, the Agency needed a much larger base of test subjects than was available to them from within the Agency's own personnel pool. They began by farming the drug out to hospitals—for instance, to Dr. Abramson at Mount Sinai in New York—and to prisons, such as Dr. Harris Isbell's program at the Addiction Research Center at Lexington, Kentucky. Isbell's operation was part of the Federal Penitentiary system and although his subjects were referred to as "patients," they were, in reality, inmates of the prison system.

Another obvious benefit to having the LSD administered by doctors and professors who were not part of the CIA itself was that any adverse reactions, bad trips, and "accidents" would not be laid at CIA's door. The Olson affair was still fresh in everyone's mind, and even though no one was officially reprimanded for their role in his "suicide," the Director of Central Intelligence (DCI) did not want to take any more chances that a person with a high security classification—dealing in ultra sensitive matters of national security, such as biological weapons—would start tripping down Fifth Avenue, naked in a snowstorm. It was time to move the test subjects away from the CBW people and intelligence assets and towards those more expendable: prison inmates, terminally-ill patients, prostitutes, foreigners, and violent psychopaths. These were people whose deaths—should they occur—could be easily explained as a natural byproduct of their personal circumstances. They were also people whose secrets—whatever they were—could not embarrass the Agency if they should be revealed under the influence of the drug.

One of Helms' problems with the drug testing program was the legal issue of obtaining the consent of the test subjects beforehand. After all, Helms reasoned, if the subjects know they are going to be tested, then how does that help us understand what a person's reaction will be to the drug in the field, when he will not be forewarned? The idea was to obtain a person's reaction to the drug—particularly as used as an adjunct to interrogation and mental programming—when he had no idea a drug was being tested. Even better if the drug could be administered in a setting that was not so obviously . . . clinical. Thus, slowly at first and then with greater acceleration, LSD made its way into academia, and from there into society at large.

SET AND SETTING

Richard Helms—in expanding the CIA's mind control effort begun with Operation BLUEBIRD and its successor Operation ARTICHOKE—proposed the more comprehensive and aggressive MK-ULTRA on April 3, 1953 and it was approved by Allen Dulles on April 13, 1953, three days after he gave a very disturbing speech at Princeton University that cited "how sinister the battle for men's minds had become." He was referring to Soviet brainwashing techniques—or what was known, or imagined, of them at that time—and how a human mind could become putty in the hands of the specially-trained Communist controllers. Remember that 1953 was a pivotal year for Soviet Communism: Stalin died in 1953 and a titanic struggle for power ensued in Russia, with dangerous implications for the West. The picture Dulles painted of the world situation in general, and of the state of Soviet mind control in particular, was frightening, and he lost no time in approving what was to become the most ambitious ever scientific quest for the secrets of consciousness, something that had not been seen in this world since the days that magicians advised the crowned heads of Europe and alchemists toiled to turn lead into gold in the basements of archdukes and princes. Probably only the Nazi aberration known as the *Ahnenerbe-SS* comes close to duplicating in scope what MK-ULTRA was designed to do. In the former case, departments were created within Himmler's SS to research everything from the Holy Grail, mystical runes, and Tibetan Buddhism, to Icelandic sagas and the World Ice Theory. In the case of MK-ULTRA, the focus was narrower at first, but soon expanded to include psychic phenomena, shamanism, remote viewing, and occult practices. Even anthropologists found themselves on the CIA's payroll: on the one hand, to obtain data about the remote locations and peoples they encountered, as such information might have intelligence value later, and to suggest strategies for psychological warfare in Third World countries; on the other hand, to gather whatever flora and fauna might be useful to the boys in the lab back home as mind control agents, or as biological or chemical weapons.

As always, however, psychiatrists were the main focus of this research and the institutes set up to funnel money into CIA experimentation were mostly targeted towards medical and psychiatric purposes. The faith of the Agency in psychiatry was touching, if not wholly naïve, but what was their alternative? Psychiatry was not exactly a hard science in 1953 . . . or 2003 for that matter. Basic views of the human mind and its mechanisms in the postwar years were split between the behaviorists, who felt that "the mind" was simply the name we used to describe the functions of the brain, an organ that is physical, biological, and measurable, and the psychoanalysts, who felt that there were underlying layers of consciousness, unconsciousness, subconsciousness, id, libido, ego, superego, archetypes, you name it, courtesy of the Freudians and Jungians, who even between themselves had many important differences in their understanding of consciousness. In 1953 so little was known about how the mind really works that Agency personnel desperate to find the magic key that would unlock the gates to the Land of Memory were hard put to find people who could forge that key. Memory itself was *terra incognita:* Did memory reside in a specific area of the brain, or was it distributed throughout the brain? Were *all* memories recorded for posterity, capable of being dredged up by the properly-trained controller, or could some memories be erased, and replaced with new memories? In computer jargon, was the human brain "write once, read only" or could it be overwritten many, many times, like a floppy disk or a hard drive?

For intelligence purposes, what was required of MK-ULTRA was the ability to manipulate memory, and to relax the inhibitions of captured enemy agents so that they would reveal their secrets. Thus, what the Freudians call the "superego" had to be bypassed, allowing the controller direct access to the contents of an enemy agent's mind. That was step one. Step two would involve erasing specific pieces of information from the subject's memory and replacing those pieces with new bits of memory, thus permitting the Agency to send that agent back into the field without any knowledge that he or she had been interrogated and had given up the sensitive information. Step three was a potential bonus: Could that enemy agent then be "programmed" to commit acts on behalf of the Agency, without knowing who gave the commands or why? This was the essence of the Manchurian Candidate. It is also the essence of what we know today as hypnotherapy and "depth" psychoanalysis, for the psychiatrist or psychotherapist in this case is looking for access to the patient's unconscious layers, to extract important information (such as childhood trauma) and to neutralize the effects of that trauma, in some cases replacing certain unwanted or negative behavior patterns with new, approved patterns. Persons going to hypnotherapists for help with a drinking problem, or smoking, or overeating, go through a similar process, with the important difference that the entire treatment is voluntary. What the Agency was looking for was a key that would unlock these secrets and allow unfettered access to the human mind, with or without the voluntary cooperation or submission of the "patient."

In order to do this, they had to understand the workings of the mind first, and then develop drugs and techniques that would allow them quick and painless access. Agency personnel did not have a lot of time in the field to put an enemy agent or defector through years of what might be termed "aggressive psychoanalysis," but had to have answers quickly, sometimes in only hours, before that subject was to be sent back into the field to act as a double agent—or possibly assassin—for the CIA.

But in exploring the mind and developing techniques for unlocking its secrets, the Agency unknowingly tread on areas that have been the domain of religion and mysticism for thousands of years. Cults as disparate as that of Eleusis in Greece, Tantra in India, Siberian shamanism, Native American shamanism, Taoism in China, Tibetan Buddhism, Jewish Qabalism, even the relatively modern phenomenon of European ceremonial magic—as represented in the twentieth century by the Golden Dawn, the OTO, and individuals such as Jack Parsons, Aleister Crowley, and MacGregor Mathers—and countless other disciplines had already mapped out large areas of consciousness and developed methods for entering them relatively unscathed. As mythologists such as Mircea Eliade, Joseph Campbell, Carl Jung and others have demonstrated, there is a great deal of similarity in "technology" among these practices, and that similarity exists for a reason.

> The fact is that mystical experiences, like sudden conversions, do not always arise from purely religious influences and stresses; they can sometimes be induced by chemical means—such as, for instance, mescaline, ether, and laughing gas.
>
> —William Sargant, *Battle for the Mind*[1]

Precisely, Dr. Sargant; and the next question must be: where are the mechanisms in your laboratory that prepare the subject (we may say, *protect* the subject) for what he or she may encounter when under the influence of these artificial triggers of mystical experience?

In other words, Dr. Sargant, what really happened to your colleague, Dr. Olson?

As LSD became more and more popular among the "civilian" population in America, its use contributed to a unique jargon and a rudimentary understanding of the effects of LSD—or of any hallucinogen—on the mind, and how best to exploit its benefits. This was not the result of scientific tests done in laboratories and a resulting "protocol," but arose from general practices by the youth of America in the 1960s. Important factors of any hallucinogenic experience were referred to as "set and setting." This meant that the emotional state (the "set" or "mindset") of the individual was important, as well as the immediate environment (the "setting"). In other words, the potential candidate for an LSD experience should be in the proper emotional state and frame of mind to facilitate an easy and pleasant experience; the environment itself should be conducive to harmonious feelings, and should reinforce specific elements that the "tripper" would like to encounter or experience during the "trip." As the Sixties wore on, "guided trips" became more and more common. In this case, the person taking the LSD would do so in the presence of a guide, someone who would walk the tripper through the trip—as it were—and also be on hand to protect the tripper from any ill effects. In this way, it was believed that an LSD experience could be beneficial, could actually result in some important insights and have a lasting effect on the subject long after the chemical had left the bloodstream.

This was nothing new. Native Americans, for instance, had long known of the benefits of taking peyote as long as it was done in a controlled setting by an experienced shaman. CIA researchers were rarely interested in the ritual settings that surrounded drug-taking among aboriginals, however. They were more interested in isolating the drug's active ingredients and developing clinical protocols for their use. As scientists, they could be expected to do nothing else; but in their paradigm of operation—trying to find a fast way into the unconscious mind with control over memory and volition, and then *leaving the subject intact* (what Richard Helms, above, characterized as "a reversible non-toxic aberrant mental state")—the purely chemical approach was doomed to failure.

Sargant's prime example of the success of pure psychology was the Russian neurophysiologist Pavlov and his famous dogs. Sargant extrapolated Pavlov's findings to describe mechanisms for controlling human behavior. To a certain extent, this was effective (for instance, in treating victims of battle fatigue—what we now call post-traumatic stress disorder—where there is a specific trauma and a specific symptom associated with it). Sargant saw religious and political conversions in much the same way, as a behaviorist would. Apply the right amount of stress under the right conditions, and a human being's will is malleable; in fact, one's entire belief system can be changed overnight. Sargant cited works by Arthur Koestler to prove his point, as Koestler had famously undergone a "conversion" to Communism and then a "conversion" back again.

Also in 1953, we see that behaviorist poster-boy B. F. Skinner had begun publishing; his purely mechanical approach seemed the most . . . scientific, and the field of psychology was desperate to be taken seriously by science, which had long regarded psychology as "soft," if not an outright pseudo-science. The physicists had already given us the atomic bomb; what weapon of similar, demonstrable potency could the psychologists provide in the war against Godless Communism? It appeared as if the Communists had found ways of manipulating the consciousness of Cardinal Mindszenty, for instance, and had done similar work on captured American GIs in Korea. When Dulles made his speech in April 1953, he virtually characterized the Cold War as a Manichaean struggle between the forces of Light and Darkness. This was not a war over land or resources; it was a war over possession of the soul of humanity.

Communism is, of course, a system basically inimical to capitalism and democracy, for it pretends to be both an economic system as well as a political one. Both the Soviet and the Maoist states had pushed religious observances underground; to be a member of any church was to automatically lose one's Communist Party card at best, or be arrested and thrown into the Gulag at worst. Allegiance to divine authority was understood as a kind of treason, an allegiance to a different king, and in this perhaps the Communists understood religion better than the Capitalists.

Today for instance, China still insists it has the right to identify and proclaim the next Dalai Lama, Panchen Lama, and all of the other Tibetan religious leaders, even though this prerogative had always been the domain of the Tibetan Buddhist hierarchy itself. It is based on a tedious, but critical, ritualistic search for the heir that can take years, and which involves demonstrable spiritual powers from the candidates (the ability, for instance, to identify the previous Lama's personal possessions from among a mass of other objects). How the non-religious, anti-religious Chinese Government sees itself as capable of doing the same thing is beyond understanding, and even opens them up to ridicule, but the impulse is defensible from their point of view: allowing the Tibetans to choose their own spiritual leader is tantamount to showing the world that there is an authority that transcends Marxism-Leninism and Mao Ze Dong Thought. That policy is extended towards the Catholic Church, as well, for China has never allowed the Vatican's nomination of cardinal or archbishop for Chinese cities to influence its own candidates; during the time of the Soviet Union, a similar policy was in effect for selecting the hierarchy of the Russian Orthodox Church.

What Dulles was describing to his audience at Princeton that Spring, then, had a very real basis in reality. For a nation such as the United States, where church and state are nominally separate, and where neither the church can appoint secular leaders, nor the state appoint religious ones, the system of government in Russia and China seemed like nothing short of . . . well, Europe during the Middle Ages. Irony aside for the moment, if one takes the sum total of these facts—the superiority of the Communist state over religion, the submission of religious leaders to the will of secular leaders, and the creation of mind control and "brainwashing" techniques—we can see that what the Communist state was doing was exactly what Hitler had in mind for the Third Reich: the creation of a New Man. The Communist state's approach, however, was purely behaviorist. Indeed, political dissidents were often hospitalized in mental institutions, since it was assumed their rebellion against the state was evidence of a psychological disorder; there they would receive the full benefit of the state's behavior modification program: what we call electroconvulsive therapy and what others refer to as "torture." Hitler's approach was more psychoanalytical, in that he encouraged the development of a state religion based on Teutonic paganism, and thus summoning to his psychic assistance all those "archetypes" about which Jung—the Nazi manqué—was always lecturing about. The Third Reich normally eschewed the behaviorist approach, and simply imprisoned or executed dissidents, since it was understood that political dissidence and racial inferiority were basically one and the same. One of the most important exceptions to this rule was homosexuality, which, when it occurred among the SS men was treated as a psychological aberration suitable for the therapeutic setting, but when it occurred among members of the general population was tantamount to an assignment to the camps.

Once science and consciousness mechanisms—religion, spirituality, mysticism, psychology—became so closely aligned in service to the state in both the West and the East, there were bound to be repercussions, some of which are being felt to this day. The vast array of worldwide literature on mysticism and mystical states is very clear and consistent on several important points, most of which were ignored by government-supported mind control efforts on both sides of the political divide. The first, and most important, point is that these states are approached gradually and with graded levels of training and preparation. Like the Masonic degree system, initiates (read "subjects") are trained in some basic information, then brought to the first level or degree of awareness. They then receive further training, and another level is attained, etc. This process can take years, and is designed to integrate the initiate's consciousness on all levels and, yes, the goal is eventually to create a New Man (or Woman). Along the way, various paranormal abilities are cultivated or simply make themselves known to the initiate. The initiate may experience total recall of events from his childhood; he may experience some form of out-of-body travel or see events transpiring at great distances ("remote viewing"); the initiate may develop other psychic abilities, etc. The focus of the mind control experts, however, was on the goodies themselves—the psychic abilities, the control over the memory, control over autonomic bodily functions—and not on the development of their subject's spiritual identity. This is known in occult circles the world over—from India to Europe to America—as "black magic."

To pursue these abilities as an end in themselves is to tread on the very edge of the Abyss and, in some cases, to plunge over the side and into total darkness; but the people responsible for MK-ULTRA and the Soviet and Chinese versions of the same did not take the "initiations" themselves. In most cases, the treatments were given to other intelligence personnel, or to volunteer subjects at hospitals and prisons, or to unwitting subjects. Imagine someone being plucked from the streets—an innocent, a stranger, perhaps a criminal, perhaps a violent criminal—and *forced* to undergo a rigorous series of spiritual initiations. While there is no evidence in the ancient literature of secret societies and mystery cults that such was ever done, the modern imagination has admitted the possibility (for instance, in John Fowles' novel *The Magus*. Even the author's own, yet unpublished, novel *Citadel* is based on that idea). Genuine spiritual initiation is always portrayed as a difficult, painful experience, what the Japanese Zen masters refer to as "grandmotherly kindness"; it is not much of a leap to consider that it could be accomplished by force on an unwitting or unwilling participant. MK-ULTRA, unknown or unrealized by its perpetrators, was just such a program, stripped of any redeeming spiritual value. The tragedy of Dr. Frank Olson is proof of that.

On May 4, 1953, the brilliant and celebrated British novelist and essayist Aldous Huxley took mescaline for the first time. The author of *Brave New World* (1932) was living in California, having left England in 1937 for the United States. He tried his hand at screenwriting, and even attempted a treatment of *Alice in Wonderland* for Walt Disney, who rejected it on the grounds that he, Disney, could not understand it. Huxley's *The Devils of Loudon*, a fact-based study of demonic possession in seventeenth-century France, had just been published the previous year, testament to decades of study of Christian and Eastern mysticism and religion. He was as prepared, intellectually, as could be expected for what mescaline would offer, and he took a dose and waited.

The Doors of Perception (1954) was the result, a report of his experience on the drug, which was followed up by *Heaven and Hell* (1956). His sober, respectful account of the hallucinogenic experience had enormous influence on the Beat generation of the 1950s and on generations to follow. For instance, Jim Morrison named his rock group, The Doors, after Huxley's work. While authors and experimenters such as Timothy Leary, Richard Alpert and Robert Anton Wilson would, in the decades to follow, write glowing accounts of the benefits to be had by alterations of consciousness—either through drugs, meditation, or occultism, or all three in combination—Huxley threw open the Door in the Wall (in a self-conscious borrowing of a phrase from H. G. Wells) and let the light in. He was a bonafide intellectual, a pacifist, a literary lion; compared to Huxley, the others were *arrivistes*.

He writes of the fantastic colors and of the altered state of perception, noting that a person in an unsound state of mind who took mescaline would probably suffer the very fires of a schizophrenic hell as a result. Thus, in 1954, Huxley was writing about "set," and, as he went on to describe his mescaline trip—taken in the presence of his wife and Dr. Humphrey Osmond, a Canadian psychiatrist and the man who had supplied the drug and who was monitoring and recording his reactions—he would go on to write about "setting" as well: the environment and the influence it had on the progress of the experience.

Taking mescaline had a profound effect on Huxley, and he kept worrying at the experience, writing more about it and finding ways to extend the mescaline experience into discussions of art, music, literature and culture in general, finally talking about religion and psychology and mysticism in light of the mescaline experience. Frank Olson would drop acid six months later—in November 1953—and his handlers presumably would have benefited from Huxley's careful and respectful discussion of the vulnerability of the hallucinogenic state . . . but Huxley's report would not appear until after Olson's death. His paragraph on the relationship between the schizophrenic state and the psychedelic state reads like an account of Olson's last days:

> The schizophrenic is like a man permanently under the influence of mescaline, and therefore unable to shut off the experience of a reality which he is not holy enough to live with . . . [it] scares him into interpreting its unremitting strangeness, its burning intensity of significance, as the manifestations of human or

> even cosmic malevolence, calling for the most desperate counter-measures, from murderous violence on one end of the scale to catatonia, or psychological suicide, at the other.[2]

"The experience of a reality which he is not holy enough to live with" says it all. It is not for nothing that the mystery cults of the world prescribe a lengthy and thorough period of purification and cleansing—of the body and of the soul—preparatory to the ritual of initiation, whether by drugs or by trance or even, as in the case of Tantric Hinduism, sex. One must be "holy enough" to survive the transcendental experience, especially if drugs are involved for there is no easy way to stop that experience once it has begun. One must go through it to the end.

When Frank Olson was given LSD without his knowledge or approval, he was in a depressed mental state after all that he had experienced in Europe. As Aldous Huxley was busy writing up the experience of his first mescaline trip in the months after May 1953, Olson was traveling in Europe to visit the sites where his weapons systems—notably anthrax and other pathogens—were being tested on live subjects. His soul was in shreds; his heart was breaking. This was not the America in which he had been brought up, and which he was working so strenuously to protect against its enemies. This was not the America of the Nuremberg Trials, much less of the Constitution. Frank Olson was losing his faith, and he begged the Army to let him go. He wanted to become a dentist. A dentist. One is helplessly reminded of Kurt Vonnegut's novel, *Slaughterhouse-Five,* and its dentist protagonist who wants to escape the horrors of war, if only in his mind.

In this unclean and unprepared—this "unholy"—state, Olson took a drug that kicked open the Doors of Perception like a Gestapo boot in the middle of a crystal night. He saw a reality that sadly lived up to all his expectations: a paranoid police state committing atrocities abroad while keeping its citizens smiling at home. A *Brave New World.* He shredded his identification papers on the streets of New York, certain—in his psychedelically-charged mind—that enemy agents were coming to get him, to blow his cover and his networks. And they did. And he died.

O CANADA!

Drugs were not the only royal road to the unconscious mind taken by the Agency and its G-scale doctors in white robes and pocket protectors. Other eminent psychologists and psychiatrists had their own ideas, and were recruited far and wide throughout the American landscape. And Frank Olson was not the only casualty of this experimentation, although he may have been one of the first on American shores.

Dr. Ewen Cameron was a distinctive man with a distinctive resume. Cameron, a native of Scotland who had moved to Canada early in his career, had been one of the psychiatrists asked to evaluate captured Nazi leader Rudolf Hess in 1945 to see if he was fit to stand trial at Nuremberg.[3] Hess had twice attempted suicide and this, coupled with his serious occult beliefs, was considered possible evidence of insanity. Cameron, however, concurred with most of his fellow psychiatrists when he gave his opinion that Hess was sane enough and fit enough to stand trial.

He had become a friend of Allen Dulles, who would later become Director of the Central Intelligence Agency, and had even offered to treat Dulles' wife, Clover, according to Gordon Thomas.[4] Clover Dulles was upset over her husband's frequent philandering, and CIA doctors recommended she see Cameron in Montreal, since Cameron had a reputation for being good with women and women's psychological complaints. John Marks—in *The Search for the Manchurian Candidate*—gives Cameron the benefit of a doubt when it comes to whether or not the Scottish-born physician knew that his projects were receiving CIA funding. However, as a frequent visitor to Washington, and as a friend of Dulles from the postwar years, it is not possible to believe that Cameron was not completely aware of who was funding some of the most atrocious psychological experimentation taking place in the world at that time, the practice of "psychic driving" and the maintenance of the notorious "sleep room." Later, doctors trained by Cameron who had worked with him at his clinic in Montreal would be found working in South America—in Paraguay and Chile—coercing confessions from political prisoners at detention centers there. It is possible—though not proven yet—that these doctors loaned their special expertise to the interrogation officers at Colonia Dignidad, where the author spent a rather unpleasant afternoon in 1979 (as detailed in *Unholy Alliance*).

Donald Ewen Cameron was born in Scotland in 1901, and obtained a degree in psychological medicine in 1925. He fell under the influence of famed psychiatrist Adolph Meyer, and in 1926 Cameron left Scotland for Johns Hopkins in the States, where Meyer was then running the Phipps Clinic. After two years, Cameron then went to Switzerland, to the Burghoelzli Clinic, and from there went on to Manitoba, Canada.

The peripatetic Cameron then found himself in Worcester, Massachusetts in 1936 (at which time he published *Objective and Experimental Psychology* promoting a thoroughly scientific—which is to say, behaviorist and clinical—model of what psychiatry should be) and in Albany, New York from 1939 to 1943, where he was professor of neurology and psychiatry at the Albany Medical College. In 1943 he moved to McGill University in Montreal, where he created the Allan Memorial Institute on Mont Royal (with a $40,000 grant from the Rockefeller Foundation), a post he held until 1964, when he effectively retired from professional life.

It is the Allan Memorial Institute that holds our attention, because to many of its former patients it has become synonymous with suffering. The former mansion of Sir Hugh Allan, before it became the Institute it was known as Ravenscroft, a forbidding but somehow more fitting name for a building housing a flock of mad scientists intent on breaking into the innermost recesses of the human mind—by force.

As discussed by Harvey M. Weinstein, himself a physician and the son of one of Cameron's patients, Cameron had been fascinated by memory, believing memory to be stored in the brain and accessible through chemicals or other biological means.[5] Cameron realized that the Land of Memory guarded access to the mysteries of the mind itself, and if a way could be found to call up any memory—and reinterpret those memories or eradicate them completely—then one effectively erased mental illness. He called his technique of causing selective memory loss "differential amnesia"; it was a critical aspect of what MK-ULTRA was all about. As mentioned before, if the CIA could cause certain specific memories to be erased in a targeted individual—and perhaps replaced by false memories—then they could create the perfect spy, the perfect double agent, or even the perfect assassin: a person who would commit murder and not know (not remember) why he had done so, or who had ordered the hit. Imagine an assassin, standing up in a crowd, pulling out a gun—regardless of danger to his own safety, his own life—and killing an important political figure. He is captured, of course, and then cannot say why he did what he did, cannot even remember that he did it. Such an assassin is a cypher: a crazed, lone gunman.

Cameron believed that schizophrenia and other psychotic states were caused by physical conditions in the brain; like his friend and colleague of many years, Dr. William Sargant, he had a mechanistic view of consciousness and felt that with the right drug and the right procedure all could be made right as rain. This was an approach very attractive to the Technical Services Staff at the CIA; it was what they were looking for: a switch to turn memories on and off, something reliable, something quick. The CIA wanted to hear that there were easy techniques—whether drugs, or hypnosis, or some other mechanisms—to give agents in the field additional weapons in their arsenal. Cameron obliged. To that end, and to both test and prove his theories, he developed procedures known as "psychic driving" and "depatterning." The procedures were radical and extreme, designed to totally disorient a human being, to strip away layers of consciousness and memory until one came to bedrock, and then to rebuild the personality step by step.

Unfortunately, his patients—some of whom had come to him for mild disorders, such as anxiety—had no foreknowledge of the treatments and had not volunteered for the experimentation. Like other CIA guinea pigs under the MK-ULTRA program, they were unwitting and expendable test subjects. Cameron's operation had a further, fringe benefit: since the tests were taking place outside the United States and on non-US citizens there was another layer of deniability, and responsibility for the outcome of the experiments was further removed. Additionally, the Agency could ignore the legal dilemma of whether such tests, if conducted within the borders of the United States on unwitting United States citizens, were within the scope of the CIA's charter (which forbids domestic operations but which does not, evidently, forbid scientific research and development within the United States).

The setting for the tests was like something out of an old B-movie about mad scientists. Indeed, a look at history will show that mad scientists tend to be patriots who are committing their atrocities in the name of that "Greater Reich": national security. (Robert Jay Lifton calls this unique configuration "doubling,"[6] implying that such a doctor holds two different, often completely contradictory, points of view simultaneously: one, in which the physician feels he is upholding his Hippocratic Oath "to do no harm," and the second in which he commits acts of unquestionable brutality in the name of the State, or the greater good, or whatever justification is fashionable at the time. It is tantamount to having two personalities, two categories in which to pigeonhole the various opinions, feelings and strategies necessary to support them. It was perhaps Frank Olson's inability to "double" that led to his death.)

In the case of Cameron's psychic driving technique, a patient would be kept isolated in a room—the "sleep room"—and would be administered some combination of drugs and electroconvulsive therapy (what is popularly known as "electroshock"). Sometimes the shocks given were staggeringly high, and repeated more often than is usual in a therapeutic setting. The normal voltage is usually 110 volts; Cameron used 150 volts. The normal dosage was a single shock lasting a fraction of a second; Cameron's shocks lasted longer, up to one second (and thus an average of 30 times more powerful than normal) and were done 2–3 times a day as opposed to the more usual once a day, or once every two days. Electroshock causes a major convulsion, which is then followed by several minor convulsions. Cameron's was a variation of the already intense Page-Russell method, but taken up quite a few notches to the point where his patients became disoriented and confused. This was Cameron's aim, which was the opposite of what was intended by the already controversial electroconvulsive therapy method.

The drug regimen was equally severe: a "sleep cocktail" was administered to the subjects—one can hardly call them "patients" anymore—consisting of Thorazine, Nembutal, Seconal, Veronal and Phenergan. The subject would be awakened several times a day for the electroshock treatment and for the drug concoction. The combination kept the subject asleep day and night except for the electroshock, during which time his screams could be heard all over Ward 2.

This treatment typically would last from two weeks to a month, with some subjects being "treated" in this manner for over two months. In some cases, they would lose control of their bowels, be unable to feed themselves or to tend to normal bodily functions. Many tried to escape, but were always captured and brought back to their ward by the doctors and orderlies, since they were in such feeble condition that escape was impossible, groping along the walls and pathetically urinating on the floor of the corridor.

The effect of this treatment was to cause the subjects to lose their memory, usually in three stages. In the first stage, much memory was lost, but not the facts of the subject being at the clinic, knowing he is at the clinic and why, and who the doctors and nurses are. The second stage involved the loss of what Cameron called "space-time image"; the subject would not know where he was or why he was there. Understandably, this disorientation was extremely frightening. Imagine waking up in a hospital bed and not knowing what had happened, or why, and with no one in a position to tell you since keeping you in that degree of confusion was necessary to the "treatment." This nightmarish and Kafkaesque state of affairs was designed, remember, by a man who had once tested Rudolf Hess for sanity.

The third and final stage of memory loss is complete amnesia. There is only knowledge and memory of the present; there is no reference to past events or feelings. Cameron proudly pointed to this stage as the one where any schizophrenia has disappeared (along, of course, with a lot more!). The mind of the subject is a blank slate. He has been *depatterned.*

The CIA, satisfied with this level of progress, then asked Cameron to go to the next level: to implant new behavioral patterns in place of the old, erased ones. To do this, Cameron turned to another technique he had developed, which he called "psychic driving."

This method is, if anything, even more hellish than depatterning, and involves blasting the subject with tape recordings of verbal messages—usually specific for each subject—that played in a loop for *sixteen hours a day for weeks.* Normally, two tapes were used: the first was a "negative conditioning" tape which concentrated on, obviously, the negative facts of the subject's life, continually reinforcing these unhealthy images. This would then be replaced by a "positive conditioning" tape, also in a loop, also for sixteen hours a day for weeks, which would emphasize the desired behavior instead of the unwanted behavior of the first tape. Cameron's assistant in these endeavors—one Leonard Rubinstein, whose salary was paid for entirely by CIA funds—designed an enormous tape device that could play eight different tapes at the same time, thus "psychically driving" eight subjects at once. The speakers for these tapes were placed beneath the subjects' pillows. They were inescapable, unremitting, endless; and, in some cases, augmented with the use of hallucinogens such as LSD.

Compare Cameron's psychic driving technique—developed as early as 1953—with this proposal by Aldous Huxley, published in *The Doors of Perception* in 1954:

> What those Buddhist monks did for the dying and the dead, might not the modern psychiatrist do for the insane? Let there be a voice to assure them, by day and even while they are asleep, that in spite of all the terror, all the bewilderment and confusion, the ultimate Reality remains unshakably itself and is of the same substance as the inner light of even the most cruelly tormented mind. By means of such devices as recorders, clock-controlled switches, public address systems and pillow speakers it should be very easy to keep the inmates of even an understaffed institution constantly reminded of this primordial fact.[7]

As can be seen, Huxley envisioned the use of the same technology in virtually the same environment and for the same ostensible purpose: to heal the insane.

Cameron took this method and used it to drive otherwise sane people totally out of their minds.

And this was not all. Cameron eventually (in 1957, and with more CIA money and official approval) turned his talents towards sensory deprivation.

Sensory deprivation tanks became quite popular in the 1960s and 1970s, as an easy and legal way to obtain hallucinogenic-type visions, although most people used them simply for relaxation and meditation purposes. The idea is to completely isolate a person from his environment: have him float in water that is the same temperature as his body so there is no physical sensation, with goggles blocking all vision and earmuffs blocking all sound. With no external information source, the mind begins to turn on itself for data. Sensory deprivation systems were used to test pilots of high altitude aircraft back in the 1950s and 1960s; the author remembers an educational video from that period that showed a pilot strapped to a table in a specially-designed cell with no visual or auditory input: total darkness, total silence. After a short time, everyone begins to hallucinate. For some reason, these pilots hallucinated little yellow men in black hats.

In the Air Force's testing program, though, when the visions became too frightening the pilot could always hit the panic button next to his hand, and the room would open and the lights come on and attendants rush in to unstrap the babbling and sometimes incoherent subject and calm him down. Not many subjects lasted more than a few hours in such an environment, even though they often thought they had been there for days. According to the experts, even the strongest-willed, most adaptable individual should not be left in such a state for more than six days, because after that time the damage done to the psyche cannot be undone.

In Cameron's program, though, no one was allowed out of sensory deprivation until *he* said it was okay. In one particularly harrowing episode, he left a woman—who presented as simply suffering from menopause—in sensory deprivation for *thirty-five days* . . . and this was *after* a prolonged period of depatterning and 101 days of psychic driving. Cameron wrote this one off: "no favorable results were obtained." We don't know what eventually became of this poor woman—whom we know only as "Mary C."—except for a notation by a CIA official at the time that it was impossible to tell if the sensory deprivation or the psychic driving had done the most damage.

In case the reader is wondering if Dr. Ewen Cameron was a fluke, an accident that was taking place in a backwater of the psychiatric field, it is well to note at this time that Cameron was elected president of the American Psychiatric Association (in 1953) and was the first-ever president of the World Psychiatric Association. Cameron was famous, honored, well-respected by his peers, and a consummate politician. This was not a defrocked, dishonored crackpot who had lost his medical license over a botched, back alley abortion. This was the Chairman of the Board.

Eventually, when word of the MK-ULTRA experiments began to leak out in the wake of the Watergate affair, many of Cameron's former Canadian patients recognized his name and his affiliation with the CIA and brought suit against the Agency for the horrors perpetrated against them in the name of another nation's security, and won a settlement of $750,000. But in many cases their victory was pyrrhic: Cameron died in 1967—four years after the CIA cancelled his project—and the Canadian government refused any responsibility or culpability for his crimes, even though they were more than aware of the MK-ULTRA program, and its manifestation in their own country as the Allan Memorial Institute. Many of Cameron's former colleagues still will not talk; many have since died or left the country. As mentioned before, Gordon Thomas has revealed that several of the latter found employment with Latin American dictators and their secret police. The assault on the Land of Memory continues—with electroshock and Wagner—to this day.

Harvey Weinstein's father, Lou, was one of the victims of Ewen Cameron. Originally going to the clinic to obtain treatment for anxiety, he wound up getting the works. He became severely disabled following the gamut of electroconvulsive therapy, drug treatments, and the sleep room. He suffered "differential amnesia" for the period 1955–1964. He could not eat without humming, and had to follow other very specific rituals during the day; he "lost all sense of personal cleanliness or awareness of others." Like Frank Olson's son, Eric, Harvey Weinstein decided to become a psychiatrist, and, also like Eric Olson, Harvey Weinstein brought suit against the CIA for what it did to his father. That these sons of CIA mind control victims should both decide to devote themselves to the study of the mind and the treatment of its disorders—as well as to securing justice for the victims of government mind control programs—is perhaps the silver lining in this heavy, impenetrable cloud of sadness and madness.

The horrors of the Allan Memorial Institute are not an anomaly. Montreal is no stranger to abuses of institutionalized persons. Slowly, after the revelations of Cameron's frightening treatment of his patients, came stories about another set of abuses, this time from Catholic nuns who subjected the orphans under their care to the kind of treatment one would have expected of the old Bedlam days, when mental patients were "treated" with questionable therapies and kept in filth for days and weeks on end. The exception is that these were orphans in the 1950s in Canada, and they were not mental patients, but had been characterized as such by the Gray Nuns so that they could qualify for additional state funding. No one of the author's generation who has grown up under the tutelage of Roman Catholic nuns will find the following story surprising.[8]

During the postwar years in Montreal, money was in short supply. Funding for orphanages was virtually non-existent, but funding for hospitals was available from the central government in Ottawa. The Catholic Church decided to take advantage of the disparity in funding by classifying its orphans as "mentally deficient," thus qualifying for the federal largesse. The government in Montreal—specifically the administration of Premier Maurice Duplessis—was the instigating factor, since it offered the Church a subsidy of $2.75 per day per "mental deficient" as opposed to only $1.25 per day per orphan. The Church immediately took advantage of this policy, and reclassified thousands—estimates range as high as 5,000—of orphans and illegitimate children in its care as mental patients (usually without any medical or psychiatric examination whatsoever).

If this was strictly an exercise in paperwork, with no one the wiser—a pragmatic attempt to secure funding for the support of children whose only crime in the eyes of society was that they existed—then perhaps one could have turned a blind eye to the whole proceeding. However, the reclassification process prompted acts of horrific brutality against the children by nuns, the "brides of Christ," and in some cases monks and lay helpers. The abuse was not confined to only one order of nuns, but extended to the Gray Nuns of Montreal, the Sisters of Providence, the Sisters of Mercy, the Sisters of Charity of Quebec, the Little Franciscans of Mary, and two orders of monks—the Brothers of Notre Dame de la Misericorde and the Brothers of Charity—all of whom were named in civil lawsuits by surviving members of the thousands of children who were thus abused. There were, as well, 120 individuals who were named in criminal complaints. Further, the medical profession in Montreal was also complicit in the case, as physicians signed off on the thousands of examination forms stating that the orphans were mentally retarded when, in fact, they had not been examined at all.

Once the papers had been signed and, in some cases, entire orphanages converted to mental institutions virtually overnight, the horrors began.

Children were beaten, in some cases with chains; they were tied to iron bed frames and force-fed; put in straitjackets; subjected to ice baths; and sodomized. Some died from the abuse. Others became severely disabled, to the point that now—over fifty years after the events—they are still taking anti-depressants and are unable to hold regular jobs. One man still suffers from testicular problems due to the beatings. Of course, as they were officially listed as "mentally retarded" or "mentally deficient," they were considered marginal members of society and could not obtain decent education or the other benefits of "normal" children and adults. In fact, once they were officially designated "retarded," it was felt that there was no longer any need to educate them, and in many cases schooling of these children was cancelled completely. Some of these victims—at the time of this writing, in their 50s and 60s—still cannot read or write. In many other cases, the children were labeled retarded when they were quite young, so they had no reason to believe they were *not* retarded. When some of these bewildered men and women were interviewed for national television in the mid-1990s, their confusion and anger were apparent. Their lives had been destroyed, if not by the physical, mental and sexual abuse, then by the label of "mentally deficient" or "mentally retarded" which followed them all through life.

Some apologists for the Church say that it has been unjustly scapegoated for the sins of society at the time, that the children were dumped on the nuns and that, effectively, the nuns had no other choice. The apologists insist that the actions of the nuns be seen in the context of the postwar era, of the "laws, customs, and behavioral standards" that were current in the 1950s. This, of course, is patently absurd. Again, one can understand the bureaucratic maneuver to change the designation of an orphanage to a mental institution in order to obtain more funding from an otherwise recalcitrant government, but no amount of justification can be found for the beatings, the rapes, the lack of schooling and the rest of the hideous abuse suffered by these children. It is as if, once they were officially designated as "mentally retarded" on paper, they became so in fact, and were subject to the same treatment meted out to those less fortunate members of an unenlightened society, for whom the stigma of mental retardation or mental illness was tantamount to a confession of mortal sin. Perhaps the nuns themselves found the children to be representative of their own complicity, their own guilt, in defrauding the government, and the punishment inflicted on these innocents was the result of what the Freudians might call "transference." (No one who has done time at a Catholic parochial school in the 1950s, however, would even give them that much benefit of a doubt. At the time of this writing there had been so much evidence of the sexual abuse of children by Catholic priests—and ensuing cover-ups by the Church—that aged and ailing Pope John Paul II had to convene a special meeting in Rome of high-ranking Catholic clergymen to find a solution to the problem.)

But what is more absurd—especially to anyone who grew up Catholic—is the insistence that the crimes of the nuns were merely reflective of the attitudes of society at the time. Since when has Church policy ever reflected social attitudes? It sees itself as the supreme moral force in the world, unaffected by what society may think is right or wrong, since it is the Church which decides moral questions and not society. Thus, the unending issues of birth control, abortion, marriage for priests, ordination of women, etc. Regardless of what society may think, the Church stands firm on what it perceives to be solid moral ground, based on Canon Law, the Scriptures, the Church Fathers, the encyclicals of the Popes. Their moral status was indelibly written two thousand years ago with the crucifixion and resurrection of their God in the city of Jerusalem; they answer to no higher authority.

It is also well-known that the status of nuns within the Catholic Church is very low: the lowliest priest has more status in the ecclesiastical hierarchy than the most mature Mother Superior. That the abuse of these children could take place without the knowledge or consent (tacit or implicit) of the priesthood is simply not possible. So, how was this long—nearly twenty years or more—institutionalized horror allowed to take place?

There was a war on. A Cold War against godless Communism, against the Red Peril and the Yellow Menace. It was a war of Light against Darkness, and the bombs could fall at any time. It was a time of stringent measures to protect the best and the brightest; for all others it was every man for himself. The Allan Memorial Institute was in full flower at the same time that the atrocities were being committed against the Children of Montreal, and in the same city; an institute run by the world-renowned psychiatrist and specialist in mental disorders, Dr. Ewen Cameron. Who could argue with that kind of success? The actions of Dr. Cameron were as vile, obviously, as those of the gentle nuns of Quebec. At the risk of being accused of hysteria or hyperbole, let the author be permitted to draw the inescapable conclusion that the attitudes of Cameron and the nuns were no different from those of the Third Reich when it came to the mentally ill: they were expendable, "useless eaters," useful perhaps in tests and experiments of doubtful value to science (á la Dr. Mengele) or, in the case of the Catholic mental institutes, as slave labor in the hospitals . . . or even as sexual toys for their care-givers. It was St. Ignatius Loyola, the founder of the Jesuit Order, who said, "Give me a child for a year, and he is mine for life."

You will hear no argument from the Children of Montreal.

THE DOORMEN

The CIA was not the first organization of any size to confront the task of probing the human mind. Operations BLUEBIRD and ARTICHOKE, and MK-ULTRA, were designed to respond to similar practices of the Soviet Union and the People's Republic of China, what was termed in the popular press "brainwashing." Rudolf Hess, at his trial at Nuremberg for war crimes, began speaking of this phenomenon in his one and only statement to the court before he was cut off by the judges. He made reference to Soviet show trials of the late 1930s, in which accused prisoners freely confessed to their guilt even though it meant their deaths at the hands of Stalin's executioners. He referred to doctors who had visited him in prison—including one with a Scottish accent who might have been Cameron—and what seemed to be their efforts to hypnotize him. (In an intriguing sidebar, Dulles, who asked Cameron to examine Hess, was actually worried that the prisoner claiming to be Rudolf Hess was a double; he asked Cameron to get Hess to remove his clothing so that he could locate a specific scar that the real Hess would have. This was a strange request, since it should have been easy to have Hess physically examined at any time during his incarceration, but evidently Dulles did not entirely trust the British. Unfortunately, Cameron was unable to examine Hess physically, since he was in shackles and the guards did not have authorization to remove them.)

The show trial of Cardinal Mindszenty was more evidence that the Communists had managed to develop a technique for altering consciousness in their political prisoners; American GIs returning from captivity in Korea were another example. That there might be a mysterious Oriental method to "cloud men's minds" both frightened and excited the men of the CIA. In order quickly to learn as much as possible, they assigned psychiatrists, scientists and medical professionals to the task of finding out how the mind—and specifically memory—works. In another, parallel, effort they fanned out through the Third World in search for medicinal herbs, narcotic drugs, and hallucinogens that might be used for the same purpose. In doing so, they came across occult practices, demonstrations of psychic abilities, and the mind control techniques of yogis, shamans, and witch doctors. Clearly, this was a realm of mind control that was well worth pursuing, and which gave birth to some of the strangest projects ever funded by the US Government. It was in combination with the work of Cameron, Gottlieb, Abramson, Isbell, et al. that these drugs, spiritual techniques and laboratory tests opened a Pandora's Box of suffering, violence . . . and perhaps even redemption, through transformation: the Black Box of consciousness. In this, they were unwittingly following in the footsteps of magicians, sorcerers, gurus, and cultists the world over; but, unlike their forebears, they used a purely scientific approach to their material, and thus robbed the experiences of the one essential element that is common to all initiation: meaning.

Without meaning, there is no context for the experience; there is no way to integrate the material into one's psychological makeup. Cameron was not interested in meaning, neither was Gottlieb. That wasn't their job. Their task was to open up the mind to fast and easy manipulation by case officers and field agents, not to promote spiritual or psychic integration, or what Jung calls "individuation." Their job was to create assassins, turn agents, interrogate prisoners, obtain information. Saving souls was for priests.

However, there was a band of scientists and explorers loyal to the American government who felt the need to bring together the purely mechanistic and behaviorist approach to psychology that was being endorsed by the CIA on the one hand with the deeper, more analytical and Jungian approach on the other. The ideal discipline to cement this union and to demonstrate the utility of occult practices was the relatively new science of parapsychology. Parapsychology was concerned with bringing the psychic abilities and practices of certain powerful individuals into the clinic for measurement and testing. What seemed like a series of tame experiments in ESP turned into something quite different as the years wore on, and some of these government scientists became scalded by their exposure to the heat and light of powers beyond their imagining. One of these was a friend and, in some sense, a colleague of Aldous Huxley: Dr. Andrija Puharich.

The story of Puharich is central to any study of the US government's postwar interest in how psychology and parapsychology could benefit the intelligence agencies. It was arguably Puharich who was the first to bring the potential uses of paranormal abilities in military applications to the attention of the United States Navy; it was Puharich who introduced the Israeli psychic, Uri Geller, to American audiences . . . and to American intelligence. Further, it was Puharich who formed a mysterious cabal that numbered many important and influential Americans among its members, a cabal that would deliberately attempt to make contact with alien beings and—according to some commentators—actually succeed. This cabal included a man with shadowy connections both to Operation Paperclip on the one side . . . and to the Kennedy assassination on the other. Thus when we speak of the Doors of Perception, we must turn our attention to one of their most unique, if somewhat eccentric, Doormen.

Andrija Puharich was born Henry Karel Puharić on February 19, 1918 in Chicago. His parents were Balkan immigrants from what would soon become Yugoslavia, his father a stowaway who had entered the United States in 1912. His parents were divorced in 1933, and the young Puharich spent two years on a farm in Illinois working the orchards and doing general farmhand work. He eventually went back to school, graduating from Farragut High School in Chicago in 1938, when he was already twenty years old.

Like any good occultist worth his reputation, Puharich had several names. His birth name, Henry Karel Puharić, then became Andrija Puharich, from Henry Puharich (which sounded more American than Andrija, but which—to Slavic ears—sounded enough like Andrija to be acceptable); but he was also known from time to time as "Andy" and even as "Hank."

Upon graduation from high school, Andrija was awarded a scholarship to the College of Liberal Arts at Northwestern University, receiving his B.A. in philosophy in 1942, with a minor in pre-med. During the rest of the war years, Andrija—as a member of the US Army Medical Corps on inactive status and studying medicine on Army funds—also did some post-graduate work in philosophy, thus becoming himself one of those scientist-philosophers that he seemed to attract around him in later years. He also managed to get married, in 1943, to a lady who was working at the Office of War Information (and hence the OSS) and who eventually moved with him to the Kaiser Permanente Research Foundation in Santa Barbara, California. The two had a baby girl in 1947 . . . at a rather inopportune time, for he had since fallen in love with another woman, also at the Research Foundation. As if that wasn't enough, he was also due to show up that December for a regular two-year active duty stint in the Army, for he was now a Lieutenant and expected to repay the Army for the years it supported his medical education. As it happened, he received a medical discharge on December 20—due, it is said, to an ear infection—and he was free to consider the direction of the rest of his life. He had been offered a position as director of a proposed new neurological institute at the Kaiser Permanente Hospital. While doing research at Kaiser Permanente during the war, he had written a monograph on a theory of his that neurons transmit and receive the equivalent of radio waves, a theory, which came to the attention of the director of the hospital, and which was a prime example of the new field of biophysics.

Alas, by that time both his wife (along with his baby daughter) and the other woman in his life (a doctor at Kaiser Permanente) had left him. Finding himself suddenly free of commitments militarily, matrimonially and romantically, he visited his father in Chicago, who suggested he drop in on an old family friend, then wintering in Camden, Maine. Andrija was on his way to the East Coast anyway, to visit other scientists and people working in the biophysics field in New York and Boston with a view to setting up the neurological institute, so he accepted the suggestion and wound up at the home of Zlatko Baloković and his wife Joyce.

This visit was considered crucial by both the late Puharich and his biographers and other commentators. Puharich had been interested in extra-sensory perception—particularly as it applied to his chosen field of biophysics and specifically to the ability of neurons to act as transmitters and receivers—and he found in the Balokovićs fertile ground for his theories.

Zlatko Baloković—himself a Yugoslav and a famous concert violinist—was married to a member of the Borden family (the dairy products Bordens), and thus lived in relative wealth and comfort in the City of New York and Maine. (This is ironic, in that the young Henry Puharich delivered Borden milk as a poor kid growing up in the "slums" of Chicago.) He was also a friend of Marshall Tito of Yugoslavia, from the days when Yugoslav Communists were welcomed as anti-Nazis and allies, a relationship that was to bode ill for both Baloković and Puharich as the years went by and as Tito's Communism became a problem in McCarthy Era America.

Whatever was discussed during that period in Camden—where Puharich stayed for two to three weeks during a snowstorm—the end result was that Puharich would stay in Camden and build a hospital there where he could engage in the kind of research that interested him. Thus, he would turn down the more prestigious and potentially much more lucrative position at Kaiser Permanente, and stay in the frozen northeast. Baloković would subsidize him to the tune of two hundred dollars per month, and in no time Puharich had located an unused barn that he would convert into his hospital. The barn itself was interesting, having been used by the US Navy during the War to store materiel that was never described, although it had heavily reinforced floors and large quantities of firebrick. Naturally, explosives come to mind or some form of munitions, but this was never revealed.

Also in the same town was a factory whose products certainly interested Puharich. The company manufactured piezoelectric crystals, and was one of only three such factories in the entire country at the time. The crystals were wafer-thin, could be used in a variety of applications, and had been used by the military during the war as well as by General Electric, RCA and other electronics manufacturers. The firm was run by an inventor, one Dr. Raymond C. Tibbets, and his son George. The primary peacetime use of the crystals was in hearing aids, which is relevant to what Puharich would eventually be doing to when he set up his own company, the Intelectron Corporation.

At the same time, Puharich was traveling frequently to New York to meet other, like-minded individuals, including the psychiatrist Warren S. McCulloch, one of the founders of the burgeoning science of cybernetics, which is basically behavioral psychology on steroids. (McCulloch's work had been underwritten in part by the Josiah Macy Jr. Foundation, which was revealed in 1977 to have been a CIA front or conduit for funds for those involved in the MK-ULTRA projects.) Cybernetics views the human body—or, more precisely, the mind-body system—as a kind of machine, which can be tinkered with and made better by properly trained engineers: a very attractive concept to mind control advocates within the CIA. Even more attractive, perhaps, is the fact that Puharich, McCulloch and other scientists, doctors and engineers became involved in developing electronics that would provide a mind–society interface. These devices would involve the use of radio waves to implant suggestions or, as in the case of Jose Delgado to be discussed below, *commands*.

The story varies from journalist to journalist, and even in Puharich's own writings, but evidently when visiting McCulloch he discovered that there were one or two patients in the mental ward of McCulloch's hospital who complained of hearing voices in their head when there weren't any people around. (Had this been taking place at the Allan Memorial Institute, of course, the cause would have been easy to determine!) An examination of the "mental patients" revealed that traces of metal in their teeth acted as radio receivers, and that they were picking up a local radio station. At least, that is the cover story. There is very little reliable documentation on this event; if the signal was coming in strong, then the patient should have been able to realize that it was a radio station, thus the assumption is that the signal was fading in and out, much like the signal on a cell phone when one changes position in a car or when walking on a city street. Although we may never know the real story behind the events in question, we do know what happened next.

Once Puharich realized that small amounts of metal in a dental filling could effectively pick up radio signals, he decided to capitalize on this discovery. The handy access to Tibbet's factory proved providential (if not pre-planned). The use of piezoelectric crystals in hearing aids could be modified as radio receivers for a variety of other purposes.

In tandem with his work in New York City with McCulloch, Puharich formed the Round Table Foundation of Electrobiology in Camden in 1948, an organization whose name was usually shortened to the Round Table, or the Round Table Foundation. Thus, the hospital or clinic that had been originally planned became instead a kind of research institute specializing in the more arcane of the behavioral sciences, from cybernetics to ESP, and moved from the barn—which he lost due to some unpleasantness concerning Red baiting in the small New England town—to somewhat grander quarters in a twenty-two room house. One of the earliest members of the Round Table was Aldous Huxley,[9] and one of his earliest experiments was with the psychic Eileen Garrett, who was placed in a Faraday Cage to test her psychic abilities, as were such other famous names in the field as Peter Hurkos and Harry Stone. In order to support his research, Puharich approached a variety of individuals for funding, including Henry Wallace. Wallace had been Secretary of Agriculture in the Franklin D. Roosevelt Administration and later his Vice President. Under Truman, Wallace had been Secretary of Commerce, and in 1948 ran for President himself on the Progressive Party ticket. Wallace's name is usually associated with a scandal involving a Russian mystic, one Nicholas Roerich. (Wallace himself is usually credited with coming up with the pyramid and all-seeing eye design used on the back of the US dollar bill.) There is not enough space here to go into the whole story of Roerich; suffice it to say he was a painter and a mystic on the order of Gurdjieff, who became friendly with Wallace. He and Wallace had discussed how to Christianize Mao's China, and it is believed that Wallace sent Roerich on special missions to Tibet and Mongolia with this in mind, since he believed that evidence pointing to the Second Coming of Christ would be found in those Asian countries.

Wallace had written Roerich letters with the salutation "Dear Guru" which, when leaked to the press, led to his downfall, for it implied that the Vice President of the United States had spiritual allegiance to a bizarre Russian occultist. In the early days of the Cold War, this was not acceptable in a Presidential candidate. (Ten years later, the right wing would try to do the same damage to Jack Kennedy's chances for the presidency, since Kennedy was a Catholic and presumably owed spiritual allegiance to the Pope.) It is fun to imagine this scenario, however: the Vice President of the United States, sitting at the feet of a Russian mystic, discussing plans for smuggling Christianity into the People's Republic of China. Some of our *best* history is under-reported, underplayed, or simply ignored by mainstream historians and biographers, and winds up as grist for the plots of pot-boilers and popular movies that no one really believes. When will we ever pay attention to what's going on in the hearts and minds of our most powerful political and military leaders?

In any event, Wallace agreed to help fund Puharich's research, with a check for $4,458.73 in April of 1949. A princely sum at the time. And he visited the Round Table—according to Eileen Garrett—sometime in 1949–1950.[10]

Another mysterious donor to the Foundation was one Walter Cabot Paine, of Boston, who donated $3,000. When a researcher attempted to interview Walter Paine, he was rebuffed immediately, and Paine did not answer any questions. Arthur Young, the Bell Helicopter designer and eventual guru himself, told the same researcher that Paine was an associate of his and an oil executive who wished to remain anonymous. Mr. Young was being a little disingenuous, for he was related to Walter C. Paine through marriage. Arthur Young would remain a close friend and associate of Puharich during the 1950s, and it is this relationship that—in the context of all we have been discussing so far—is absolutely stunning in its implications, for Arthur Young was married to a Forbes heiress, one Ruth Forbes Paine, who was a descendant of Ralph Waldo Emerson. In other words, very old, very white money. Walter Cabot Paine was the son of Robert Treat Paine, a wealthy Boston Brahmin and art patron who made a special study of Japanese art, and was a direct descendant of the Robert Treat Paine who was a signer of the Declaration of Independence. W. C. was directly related to Ruth Forbes Paine Young's previous husband, George Lyman Paine (who is also descended from Colonial American "royalty," the Lyman family). Her son by that previous marriage, Michael Paine, married one Ruth Hyde.

The reason for this heredity lesson is simple. In 1963, Michael and Ruth Hyde Paine befriended two poor immigrants from the Soviet Union: one Russian woman, Marina, and her American-born husband, Lee Harvey Oswald.

The documents concerning the Paines and their relatives were sealed by the Warren Commission, and even District Attorney Jim Garrison could not get access to them when needed. In fact, the Paines are not mentioned by name in Oliver Stone's film, *JFK*, even though they are part of the public record on the assassination, and Ruth Paine's character is clearly present in the film. It is presumed that the threat of legal action of some kind forced the director to disguise their identities even though they are mentioned in virtually every book about the assassination, including the Warren Commission transcripts of the Michael and Ruth Paine interviews.

We will discuss this relationship in much more detail in the next volume of this work, including the tricky relationship of the Paines to Allen Dulles (which explains some unusual behavior of Dulles at the Warren Commission hearings), but for now let us continue to examine the activities of Andrija Puharich.

At one point, Puharich claimed he was researching psychic abilities for the US Navy in 1948, for something called Project Penguin. The Navy has denied that any such program existed, and indeed there does not seem to be any documentation available to prove Puharich's statement. However, what can be proved is that in November 1952 Puharich briefed Pentagon officials on the military uses of parapsychology. His talk was published as "An Evaluation of the Possible Usefulness of Extrasensory Perception in Psychological Warfare." That talk was reported in the *Washington Post* on August 7, 1977, at a time when MK-ULTRA revelations were coming fast and furious. A recently declassified CIA report, entitled "Parapsychology in Intelligence: A Personal Review and Conclusions," by Dr. Kenneth A. Kress mentions the newspaper article, and goes on to give a summary of CIA interest in parapsychology from about the 1960s through 1977, when the report was written. Dr. Kress does place the ESP and remote viewing experimentation under the auspices of first the Technical Services Staff (TSS) of the CIA, and then later under the Office of Scientific Intelligence (OSI), the Office of Research and Development (ORD) and finally the Office of Technical Service (OTS), the former TSS. Kress had been Project Officer in 1972 due to his prior background as a physicist. It was while running this psychic research project for the CIA that

Kress would become involved with the people at Stanford Research Institute (SRI) and specifically with Dr. Russell Targ and Dr. Harold E. Puthoff, both associates of Puharich at one time or another and both of whom figure prominently in our story.

Long before Kress' involvement with SRI, Targ, and Puthoff, however, Puharich had decided to go very "hands on" in his approach to the field of psychic phenomena. His presentation to the Pentagon was in November of 1952; according to his own account in *The Sacred Mushroom*, the orders had been cut to redraft him into the Army the following day, thus implying a specific agenda for Puharich. That December he would begin observing the trance state of one Dr. Vinod (whom he had first met in New York in December 1951) and make contact with what he believed were extraterrestrial forces.

Within months, Puharich would find himself back in uniform, this time as an Army Captain, and would be assigned to the Army Chemical Center in Edgewood, Maryland in February 1953, a position he would hold until April 1955. In other words, he was at Edgewood, working for the Army at the same time as Frank Olson was at Fort Detrick, and in and out of Edgewood, working for the Army. And as Olson was involved in research and development of biological weapons at Detrick, Puharich was involved in paranormal communication and ESP experiments at Edgewood. It is tempting to speculate whether Olson and Puharich had ever met; it is doubtful they would have been colleagues, as Puharich was involved with biophysics and cybernetics, with a little spiritualism on the side. Olson's work was purely in the biological warfare arena (except when he was chosen as a guinea pig in the LSD experiment). But they worked within the same overall group at two installations that had an incestuous relationship within the US Army, and it was Olson's death and the flurry of news reports around it that eventually led back to Puharich's presence and activities during the same time period.

Maybe they did not know each other. But CIA knew of them both.

Dr. Sidney Gottlieb, who was head of CIA's Technical Services Staff (TSS) at the time and who dosed Frank Olson with the fatal LSD in the Cointreau, was in charge of all MK-ULTRA work being conducted at Edgewood Arsenal. It has been reliably reported that Puharich's function at Edgewood was to develop chemical substances that would stimulate psychic abilities, the very essence of the report he had given to the Pentagon the previous November. There is no other way to understand what Puharich was doing at Edgewood Arsenal—of all places—except to admit that he was working for the CIA, the US Army, or some combination of the two, just as Olson was doing. This is exactly what his colleagues insisted was the case, and this would mean that the intelligence community's interest in mind control and in mechanical means of controlling memory and volition was running parallel with its psychic research as long ago as the early 1950s. The CIA and the Army would have presumably looked upon psychic or paranormal abilities as a behavioral matter, something to be studied and enhanced in a clinical setting.

There is evidence that Puharich saw something deeper in these phenomena, and that the roller-coaster ride that was his life was an indication of his own inability to "double," to separate his psychic research from his own, personal, spiritual quest. Puharich left so many clues in his own writings about the interest of the intelligence agencies in his research that in a way it seems almost a deliberate ploy, a plea for understanding or a confession of some secret guilt.

Another person who will figure in this story, however briefly, is Dr. Laurence J. Layton who—for about two years in the period 1952–54—was Chief of the US Army Chemical Warfare Division, based at Dugway Proving Grounds in Utah. Layton eventually found the idea of chemical warfare repugnant, according to his own account, and he left for a position at Indian Head, Maryland in 1954, where he was involved in developing rocket propellants for ICBMs and other missile systems (evidently a more humane form of warfare, at least from Layton's point of view). Most of his work for the Chemical Warfare Division is still classified, fifty years later, even though he only spent two years there. Layton's name will come up again in reference to the Jonestown Massacre, but it is interesting to note that his mother-in-law, Anita Philip, committed suicide by jumping from a window at her New York City apartment building on May 10, 1952 (barely two months after her son-in-law, Laurence Layton, was named Chief of the Army's Chemical Warfare Division); the assumption was that she—a refugee from Nazi Germany—became paranoid when she discovered that the FBI was running a security check on Layton's family and friends. The last time that had happened to her, it had been the Gestapo, or so the story goes. The stress was too much, as she imagined FBI agents stalking her every move, and she jumped.

It seems that involvement with the Army's CBW programs can be hazardous to one's health, particularly if one lives in tall buildings in New York. Her suicide note was unambiguous in intent, but one phrase was particularly intriguing, for it says, ". . . I was a gossip and have been entangled in a network of intrigue." One wonders what she meant by that. Do we put her suicide down to an old woman's paranoia, a holdover from the Nazi era? Or was something else bothering her entirely?

Puharich's involvement with the mysterious Dr. Vinod is critical to an understanding of some of the more arcane aspects of this study, since Puharich and the group that formed around him and his Round Table become involved in everything from MK-ULTRA to the Kennedy assassination to archaeological digs in Egypt to the New Age movement to extraterrestrial intelligences.

Some of this story is reported amply and well in a book by Lynn Picknett and Clive Prince, *The Stargate Conspiracy*. Picknett and Prince have written other books, one on the Turin Shroud and one on the perennial favorite of conspiracy theorists, the Knights Templar; the subject matter alone would give most historians a severe case of the yawns, but it should be emphasized that *The Stargate*

Conspiracy is arguably their best—and most thoroughly documented—work to date, for it reveals relationships that have been little noted even among writers on occult themes. What it does *not* reveal, however, is the important link between the Puharich group and the Kennedy assassination. This is due more to a lack of "crossover" between the investigators of occult themes and groups and those of political conspiracies and historical movements, than it is to any oversight or deliberate omission on their part.

Corroboration of much of Picknett and Prince's story can be found in the writings of the central figures themselves, such as Puharich, Young, Geller, physicist Jack Sarfatti, Puthoff, et al. We will continue with what can safely be proved by recourse to these sources.

On February 16, 1952—Puharich is very specific about the date—he had his first "reading" by Dr. D. G. Vinod, a Hindu scholar "and sage" from Poona, India, who channeled spiritual forces. Dr. Vinod held Puharich's right ring finger at the middle joint, and then began reading his past and future. According to Puharich, Vinod went into a trance, from where he was able to recite Puharich's life in detail "as though he were reading out of a book."[11] Vinod then went on to predict a rosy future for Puharich, and they made plans to meet again to probe this ability further.

This would not happen until New Year's Eve, when Vinod and Puharich flew from New York to Augusta, Maine, where they landed at 7:30 P.M. and were picked up by Hank Jackson, who was Puharich's laboratory administrator. They proceeded directly to the Round Table Foundation (the more luxurious house in Camden).

At precisely 9 P.M. on New Year's Eve, then, the Indian gentleman began channeling something that called itself *The Nine*. "M. calling. We are Nine Principles and Forces," the channeled entity began, and thus was born the saga of The Nine. The reader may be forgiven for wondering what all of these gentlemen were doing alone on New Year's Eve, holding a séance in a house in the Maine woods. (Sadly to say, the author has had worse New Year's Eves.)

1952 had been a banner year for strange phenomena. In January, Jack Parsons lost his security clearance; he would be dead six months later. In March, Project BLUEBOOK was created by the US Air Force, ostensibly an investigation of UFO phenomena which was later characterized as little more than a placebo; in July, there had been the famous UFO swarms over the nation's capitol on two successive weekends; Charles Manson was sent to Chillicothe in September, where he underwent a personality change; Puharich briefed the Pentagon on military uses of psychic phenomena in November; Operation BLUEBIRD became Operation ARTICHOKE; and the CIA began funding psychic research and infiltrating occult organizations.[12]

According to former colleagues of Puharich, such as Dr. Jack Sarfatti, Puharich had been working for Army intelligence during the 1950s; others have claimed that he was also working for the CIA at the time. This gaggle of intelligence agencies is not unusual, since Frank Olson's case is a clear example of one person working for more than one agency at the same time. Although it is doubtful whether Frank Olson was ever on the official CIA payroll—he, like Puharich, was employed by the US Army. The CIA funded many Army research projects—including specifically Fort Detrick (MK-ULTRA Subprojects 13, 30 and 50)—and had also been the entity responsible for dosing Olson with LSD; thus, a certain amount of crossover is to be expected, especially during the Cold War. Even Israeli psychic Uri Geller would claim that Puharich was working for the CIA when he brought Geller into the United States. Therefore, we should look at Puharich's experiments with Vinod in the light of American intelligence requirements where the paranormal was concerned, especially as Puharich would find himself back in uniform only months after the first séance with Dr. Vinod.

After Vinod's—or, should we say, "M's"—initial pronouncement that they were talking with The Nine, there followed a short discourse on the nature of The Nine in the type of language with which philosophy majors are comfortable, replete with terms like ontology and teleology, which then evolved into a form of the Lorentz-Einstein Transformation equation and a tantalizing reference to its application to the "problem" of the "superconscious." The Nine offered to work with Puharich to solve some of the problems he was working on at the time. If we are to credit the speech by "M" as given in Puharich's own work—in this case, *Uri*—then we must assume that Puharich was involved in psychic research, including psychokinesis and clairvoyance, and was interested in pursuing this research as quickly as possible.

Vinod completed his channeling ninety minutes later, and said he had no memory or knowledge of what was said. Puharich worked with Vinod for another month, and then had to go to Edgewood Arsenal, as he had been redrafted into the US Army.

Some months later, on June 27, 1953, the night of the full moon, Puharich gathered around him what was to be a core group of the Round Table Foundation for another session with Vinod. The membership of this group of nine members—á la *The Nine*—is illuminating. Henry Jackson, Georgia Jackson, Alice Bouverie, Marcella du Pont, Carl Betz, Vonnie Beck, Arthur Young, Ruth Young, and Andrija Puharich. Dr. Vinod acted as the medium. Imagine the Fellowship of the Ring, with government funding and a security classification that was, well, "cosmic."

In this group, we find immediately a du Pont and a Bouverie. Du Pont is self-explanatory, but for those who do not have a copy of the New York Social Register to hand, Alice Bouverie was born Ava Alice Muriel Astor, and was a descendant of John Jacob Astor, and the daughter of Colonel John Jacob Astor IV, builder of the Astoria Hotel and author of the book *A Journey To Other Worlds* (1894); her father was also one of the ill-fated passengers aboard the *Titanic* when it went down in April 1912. She had a reputation for her interest in the occult, as well as an interest in the institution of matrimony, for she married and divorced four times before her death in 1956 at the age of 54. Interestingly, her first husband was an officer in the Czarist Army, Prince Serge Obolensky. Obolensky was an intelligence officer during World War II and "headed the OSS Operational Groups which worked with the French Maquis at the time of the Normandy invasion."[13] He also parachuted behind enemy lines in Sardinia to inform the Italian garrison there that Italy had switched sides and abandoned the Nazis. A dashing sophisticate, he was a fanatic anti-Communist and, at the same time, a "darling of the New York social set."[14] It was Obolensky who translated a secret Russian copy of Mao Ze Dong's guerrilla warfare manual.[15] Thus, Ms. Astor's intelligence connections were on a par with those of Puharich and Paine, making The Nine look like a prayer meeting of the Association of Former Intelligence Officers. (Her last husband was David Pleydell-Bouverie, an architect in New York, hence her married name at the time of the séance as Alice Bouverie.)

The English branch of the Astor family was also involved—if somewhat mysteriously—in the occult. As friends of Stephen Ward, who lived in a cottage on the Astors' Cliveden Estate, they were privy to some strange occurrences in the years leading up to the Profumo Affair. Stephen Ward, a society osteopath, painter and occultist, found himself in the center of a political scandal of major proportions in 1962, when it was revealed that a friend of his (the glamorous call girl Christine Keeler) was sexually involved with the British Minister of War as well as the local Soviet GRU *rezident*. The scandal nearly brought down the government, and Stephen Ward—who was set up to take the fall—committed suicide in 1963. The Astors then had Cliveden Estate and later Stephen Ward's cottage exorcised. The exorcist—Roman Catholic Dom Robert Petitpierre—claimed that "the evil powers emanating from the cottage were some of the strongest" he had ever experienced.[16]

Arthur Young was a famous inventor, one of the men credited with creating the Bell Helicopter. For some reason, Young left Bell Helicopter after the end of the Second World War before the time that Walter Dornberger—Nazi scientist and slave labor czar of Peenemünde fame—took up residence there as a member of the Board. Rather than continue in the field of aviation mechanics and design, Young dropped out of the military-industrial complex and began to devote himself to a spiritual quest which lasted the rest of his life. As mentioned before, his wife was Ruth Forbes Paine, of the Forbes family and, through marriage, the Paine family. Thus, we have a du Pont, an Astor, and a Forbes/Paine attending this very important séance; in addition we have Puharich—working for the US Army—and Arthur Young, who worked under Army contract developing the helicopter. Henry Jackson was Puharich's administrator and was married to Georgia Jackson. Carl Beck was involved in alternate energy research, and had visited the laboratory of one Thomas Henry Molay, a Mormon scientist and ersatz alchemist living in

Salt Lake City who claimed to have identified a source of "free energy" which he termed "radiant energy." Developing alternate energy sources (á la Nikola Tesla) would be a preoccupation of Puharich in the years to come. (The only member of the original Nine that the author has been unable to satisfactorily identify is Vonnie Beck, who may have been the same Vonnie Beck who was a pilot for the US Navy during World War II, but at this time there is no further information on Beck.)

The séance proceeded in the following fashion:

Dr. Vinod sat on the floor, the nine members of the group in a circle around him, with a copper plate on his lap, prayer beads in his hands, and a small statue of "Hanoum," a Hindu god that the author believes to be Hanuman, the Monkey King. If this is so, it is interesting in that Hanuman was a human being, a minister, before becoming divine due to his devotion and courage. The half-human, half-divine image is one that becomes more important and more obvious as this study progresses. Another important aspect of Hanuman is his depiction in much Indian art as holding an entire mountain in one hand (and a club in the other). When—in the *Ramayana* and during the battle of Rama and Ravana—Lakshmana was mortally wounded, Hanuman raced to a mountain covered with different healing herbs. Not knowing which one Lakshmana required, Hanuman simply brought the entire mountain. Hanuman—as well as his fellow monkey-men, the Vanaras of southern India—is often shown with his hand in front of his mouth, signifying "silence" as well as obedience, in much the same way western occultists depict Harpocrates. In this sense, replete with silence, obedience, a club, and a mountain of herbs, Hanuman might easily have been the patron saint of MK-ULTRA. (In the Chinese epic, *Journey to the West*, the same "Monkey" is depicted as a trickster, a confidence-man and master of martial arts, who is part of a Buddhist priest's bodyguard.)

Vinod went into trance promptly at 12:15 A.M., and then "R," one of the extraterrestrial Nine, began speaking through him at 12:30 A.M. Threads appeared out of nowhere on the floor in front of Vinod, and he passed one to each of the human Nine, telling them, "Tonight we want to create Brahmins in this world," and that the thread was a sign of their initiation. (This is a common feature of some forms of Hinduism as well as Tibetan Buddhism.) The author finds this amusing, since a third of those present were Brahmins already (du Pont, Astor, Forbes) in one form or another.

A Brahmin, of course, is the highest caste in the caste-structured Hindu system. Other castes include warriors and merchants, and there is also the non-caste known as the Untouchables (who were generally involved in trades considered unclean, such as handling the dead, slaughtering, etc.). What Vinod (or, actually "R") was telling the assembled group is that they were to be reborn as spiritual Brahmins, in charge of bringing about a mystical renaissance on earth . . . under the mentorship of The Nine, of course. "R" then made an allusion to alchemy and transformation, and then a reference to Buddha. Eventually, the Hindu and Buddhist references faded out of the communications from The Nine in favor of discussions of "super-sense" and other quasi-scientific, philosophical constructs that might have seemed profound in the context of the séance but which make for rather painful reading today, fifty years later.

Gradually, over a period of time, The Nine revealed themselves as extraterrestrial beings living on an immense spacecraft hovering invisibly over the planet. The assembled congregation had been selected to promote the agenda of The Nine on earth. As Puharich would later write in his biography of Uri Geller, "We took every known precaution against fraud, and the staff and I became thoroughly convinced that we were dealing with some kind of an extraordinary extraterrestrial intelligence."[17] This belief was reinforced by events that took place over the next twenty years, culminating in the Uri Geller experience, when it seemed there were UFOs following everyone around, from Israel to South America to New York State. Indeed, Puharich became obsessed with The Nine, seeing them behind every psychic encounter, every UFO sighting, every paranormal event.

Puharich did not know what to do with the channeled information from Vinod; although he believed what he heard, he had no way to prove that The Nine really existed. There was the matter of the materialization of the threads from Puharich's floor, of course, but that was proof only to the people in the room at the time. Puharich wanted more; or, perhaps, his handlers did.

Puharich stayed with the Army at Edgewood Arsenal until April 1955, when he was finally discharged. During his two year hitch at Edgewood, MK-ULTRA was created, his friend Aldous Huxley tripped on mescaline, and Frank Olson was killed. (Even his boss at the time—the head of the Army's CBW program—was Dr. Laurence Layton, whose son would be the only person tried and convicted for his role in the Jonestown massacre more than 20 years later.) In addition, the Robertson Panel was formed by the CIA to investigate UFO sightings, the Korean War ended, the CIA overthrew Mussadegh of Iran and re-installed the Shah, and overthrew Arbenz in Guatemala, C.P, Cabell became Deputy Director of the CIA under Dulles, and the first Scientology office opened in Los Angeles. Also during the same period, the Army–McCarthy hearings would begin, and on March 3, 1953, "Michelle" of *Michelle Remembers* said she was inducted into a satanic cult in Victoria, British Columbia. On May 15 of that same year, US Air Force Chief of Staff Nathan Twining would inform an audience at Amarillo, Texas that the Air Force was trying to solve the UFO problem and that there was nothing to fear.

Although out of the Army, Puharich was still quite busy. He found himself in Mexico with his psychic friend, Peter Hurkos, (and, it seems, Arthur Young) in July 1956 to "help solve an archaeological problem."[18] As Puharich was involved in locating drugs that could stimulate psychic abilities, it seems likely that he was there with Hurkos on just such an agenda; neither Puharich nor Hurkos had any archaeological credentials. While in the town of Acambaro, he and Hurkos ran into an American couple from Arizona who eventually claimed that they had been receiving instructions from The Nine. Neither Puharich nor Hurkos had ever met these people before, but it seems they were working with a medium back in Arizona who was also channeling The Nine. To prove this, they sent letters to Puharich the following month with sealed communications from The Nine that referred to details of the specific séances that Puharich had chaired back in Maine. This was the proof that Puharich was looking for. The details went so far as to include a variation of the Lorentz-Einstein Transformation formula that had formed part of the first séance.

If we do not want to give The Nine the benefit of a doubt, we can assume that the medium who was working with the Arizona couple—the Laugheads of Whipple, Arizona (which sounds fishy anyway)—was the same Dr. Vinod, for no one else would have the information. Puharich insists that no one from his laboratory had leaked the details of the séance to anyone; but we never learn what happened to Dr. Vinod. Yet, if this were the case, what was Vinod up to? And for whom? Was this a kind of double-blind experiment on Puharich, conducted by the Army or CIA? Was Dr. Vinod a plant? Unfortunately, there is no way to answer these questions now without more documentation about the Army, the Navy and the CIA's mind control programs, and in most cases this documentation has been destroyed. (The bulk of the CIA's mind control research was destroyed by orders of Richard Helms when it looked like Watergate was getting a little too warm.) For their part, the Laugheads insisted that all of their information came directly from the medium during trance, and they refused to reveal the medium's identity. A good prosecuting attorney would get a conviction out of a jury with that kind of circumstantial evidence, but the defense doesn't rest just yet.

The story of The Nine gets stranger and stranger.

THE REFLEXIVE UNIVERSE

Arthur Young and Jack Parsons had a lot in common, although it is possible that neither one knew of the other during Parsons' lifetime. Arthur Young was an inventor working for the Army during the Second World War; Parsons was an inventor working for the Army during the Second World War. Arthur Young's invention—the Bell Helicopter—has had an important and lasting impact on aviation science and technology to this day; Parsons's inventions in the field of rocket science are equally (if not, perhaps, more) important to aviation science and technology. Both Young and Parsons left the companies they were most identified with—Bell Aviation and Aerojet, respectively—after the War.

And both Young and Parsons were interested in the occult, in UFOs, in paranormal phenomena, and were involved in organizations that were designed to promote expanded human consciousness. Yet, Parsons died quite young and Arthur Young lived to a ripe old age. The one possible connection between them was the figure of Harry Smith, an initiate of the OTO in Pasadena (Parsons' lodge), who became a friend of Arthur Young, and of whom more later.

Arthur Young was born on November 3, 1905 in Paris, France to Charles Morris Young—an artist—and Eliza Middleton Coxe, a society woman from Philadelphia. They returned to the United States a year later and settled in Jenkintown, Pennsylvania. Arthur Young had a knack for mechanical things and wanted to go on to MIT after high school graduation, but his father insisted on Princeton, which is where he ended up in 1921, first as an astronomy major and then later as a mathematics major. While at Princeton, Young was undecided as to which direction his career should take; he dabbled in art, philosophy and even cosmology, as he attempted to create a philosophical theory of the universe that was based on something he called "process." This interest would lie dormant during the War years as he became involved with the Bell Aircraft Corporation. On November 2, 1941 he joined Bell Aircraft on a short-term, but open-ended, contract, agreeing to stay on until the first workable prototype of a helicopter was complete. He had discovered a way to maintain stability in the air, and had been awarded a patent on the concept, which he signed over to Bell in return for the contract.

This work was completed in 1947, and Young left Bell to concentrate on philosophy. He had read Blavatsky in 1946, and thus began a lifelong interest in Orientalia, Hinduism, and Buddhism. He had been married during his tenure at Bell, but divorced in 1948 after he left his lucrative position there for what promised to be a life of uncertainty. However, he married Ruth Forbes Paine in June of that year, and his life changed for the better.

Ruth Forbes Paine was a descendant of Ralph Waldo Emerson as well as of the financially-powerful Forbes family; her previous marriage to George Lyman Paine aligned her to one of the oldest American families and related her to Walter Cabot Paine, in the direct line of Robert Treat Paine and aligned with the powerful Cabot family of Boston. Her pedigree—even in marriage—was blue-blood and blue chip. Although Arthur Young was not quite of the same background—he actually got his hands dirty in the machine shop—his mother was a member of Philadelphia society, and he had been born in Paris, which lent him a certain *je ne sais quoi*.

Arthur Young's interests were arcane, but at the heart of them was his theory of process. This theory has been amply explained in his several books—such as *The Reflexive Universe* and *The Geometry of Meaning*—and we will not delve too deeply into it here. Suffice it for our purposes to say that Young believed there was a force in the universe beyond that known to modern science, a force that contributed to growth, to life, to movement. He believed that science could explain the mechanics of things but not the force that organized and propelled these things; much like explaining how an automobile works but ignoring the driver. (The author hopes Young's admirers will forgive him this thumbnail sketch of what is really a much deeper, more complex theory.) Young wanted to put *meaning* back into science, something it had lost along the way from the Renaissance to the rotor blade.

He moved to the City of New York by 1949, beginning a five year quest which took him and his wife all over America and to other countries, looking for answers to his spiritual questions. Eventually, in 1952, he formed the Foundation for the Study of Consciousness in Philadelphia. This was at the same time that he was involved with Andrija Puharich in the Round Table Foundation in Maine. In August of that year, Puharich received a visit from the Army's Psychological Warfare people; in November he would give his famous speech to the Pentagon. In December, he would begin his séances with Dr. Vinod.

In the summer of 1956, Puharich went to Mexico with Peter Hurkos, the famous psychic detective. In *Uri*, Puharich mentions Hurkos but does not mention Arthur Young on that trip; however other sources say that Young was present,[19] which is entirely likely, but it then raises alarm bells that Puharich left Young's name out of his account. According to Peter Hurkos, the trip was arranged at the behest of someone involved with the Round Table Foundation,[20] which could have been almost anyone, since documentation on those early years is hard to come by. However, Arthur Young was definitely a sponsor and, after all, one of the original Nine "Brahmins" initiated during Dr. Vinod's second séance in 1953. It is possible that Young himself wanted to keep this mission secret, since it took place at a time when the CIA was actively scrounging around the Mexican hinterlands looking for hallucinogenic drugs.

The Canadian psychiatrist and researcher who had turned Huxley on to mescaline—Dr. Humphrey Osmond—had also been interested in the possible use of drugs to facilitate psychic ability and, indeed, had made a presentation to the New York Academy of Sciences as long before as March 1947 on just that subject. Puharich's own presentation to the Pentagon involved the military use of psychic abilities. Thus, taken together, it comes as no surprise that someone in either the military or the CIA, or both, came up with the formula: drugs plus ESP equals military applications.

On June 29, 1955, a banker by the name of R. Gordon Wasson had stunned the world with his report on the psychedelic experience to be had by ingesting a certain mushroom, a report that appeared in*Life* magazine later that year. While in Mexico taking the mushroom for the first time—under the traditional setting and with a native shaman—Wasson was supposed to have been participating in a long-distance ESP experiment with Puharich, but as it turned out Wasson was too stoned to be of any use that day. The story generated an enormous amount of interest, coming on the heels of the Huxley books, *The Doors of Perception* and *Heaven and Hell,* which were principally about mescaline. Wasson's experience was with psilocybin, the famous "magic mushroom" which has been the topic of both learned anthropological studies as well as pop culture accolades. The *Life* magazine story prompted a young Timothy Leary to go to Mexico in search of the elusive substance himself, and the CIA began an official search for more of it. It was the era of "God's Flesh."

A CIA operative named James Monroe approached Wasson in an attempt to get the latter to work for the CIA in obtaining more of the drug, and perhaps other substances as well, but Wasson refused. That didn't stop Monroe from trying, however, and he dogged Wasson's footsteps through Latin America. The evidence that Puharich, Young and Hurkos were in Mexico on Monroe's behalf is largely circumstantial, but compelling nonetheless. The archaeological reason given as the cover for their trip was probably bogus, since Acambaro was already known as the site where thousands of pre-Columbian statues had been discovered in the 1930s and 1940s, so there would have been little reason to enlist a psychic detective like Hurkos to search for more of them in the same spot; but as Wasson had been cooperating with Puharich in ESP experiments (which presumably involved the use of hallucinogens to enhance psychic abilities), and since Wasson was not cooperating with the CIA directly, it is entirely possible—no, probable—that Puharich was in Mexico for the same reason: to locate and identify hallucinogens for the Agency. Hurkos would have been along for cover, painting the trip as purely some wacked-out psychic archaeological dig; the presence of Arthur Young, however, is more mysterious. One possible scenario is that Young was financing the trip himself (as he most probably was, as an important supporter of the Round Table) and decided to go along for the ride to further his own investigations. With Young doing the financing, there was no need for the CIA to implicate themselves financially in this junket; there is no record in the MK-ULTRA Subprojects of anything having to do directly with Puharich, although he could have been financed by the CIA through any one of a number of Agency conduits, such as the Josiah Macy, Jr. Foundation or the Geschickter or Human Ecology fronts, or even directly by the Army. There are a number of MK-ULTRA Subprojects whose designations refer to the collection of various hallucinogens, however, such as James Monroe's Subprojects 51, 52 and 53, and Subproject 58 to J.P. Morgan and Co. in 1956 for the collection of hallucinogenic mushrooms for $2,080.00, which also seems to be related to Wasson's work. Thus, the funding for this expedition could have come from anywhere, and be buried within another subproject's expenses.

We don't know if Puharich's mission to Mexico was successful; indeed, we don't really know what it was. In any event, it would not be the last time Arthur Young and Puharich would work together. Even twenty years later, Puharich could be found at Arthur Young's home in Pennsylvania with Uri Geller (and murder suspect Ira Einhorn) in tow.

What we do know, based on Young's own statement, is that he wrote his two books, *The Reflexive Universe* and *The Geometry of Meaning*—in "the early 1960s," even though they were not published until 1976.[21] These books give a description of his theory of process, and address an "added parameter" to physics beyond mass, length and time. This added parameter he quantifies as process, or drive, or force, or consciousness as manifested in the photon, what he terms the "quanta of action." His writings and lectures have had a great effect on an entire generation of thinkers, scientists, researchers, academics, and even novelists and artists. He was deeply concerned about what he called science's "cleavage of our culture," and sought to redress that disunity through a concentration on the physics of consciousness. His work has been picked up and elaborated—in spirit if nothing else—by quantum physicists such as Jack Sarfatti, who himself managed to walk the line between pure physics and culture. As an original member of the Round Table Foundation, and a member of the original Nine, Young, along with the other Brahmins, would try to bring about a kind of transformation on the earth—perhaps under the guidance of the very space beings who so fascinated him throughout his life.

But it is what Arthur Young was doing in the "early 1960s" that concerns us here, for in addition to writing his two seminal works on the parameter of force, he was entertaining a central character in the assassination of a president.

The doors of perception had been opened, not only by drugs like mescaline, LSD and psilocybin, but by the séance, the shaman, the secret ritual. All had become tools of the trade for elements of the CIA, and their assault on memory and consciousness threw open the doors of perception and, instead of letting the Light in, they let the Darkness out.

Drugs, shamanism, and the occult. The dark domain of Charles Manson and Andrija Puharich, of Arthur Young and Sidney Gottlieb. With psychedelics and spirit guides, they disturbed the sleep of ancient forces, and America would never be the same.

ENDNOTES

1 William Sargant, *Battle for the Mind*, Malor Books, Cambridge, 1997, ISBN 1-88353606-5, p. 99

2 Aldous Huxley, *The Doors of Perception and Heaven and Hell*, Flamingo, London, 1994, ISBN 0-00-654731-1, p.38

3 Harvey M. Weinstein, *Psychiatry and the CIA: Victims of Mind Control*, American Psychiatric Press, Washington, DC, 1990, ISBN 0-88048-363-6, p. 92–93. Dr. Weinstein's father had been a victim of Dr. Cameron at the Allen Memorial Institute, and it was the ordeal of watching his father deteriorate under the Doctor's care that inspired his son to become a psychiatrist and to eventually bring suit against the CIA.

4 Gordon Thomas, *Journey Into Madness*, p. 91

5 Weinstein, op. cit., p. 91

6 See for instance Robert Jay Lifton, *The Nazi Doctors*, Basic Books, NY, 2000, ISBN 0-465-04905-2, p. 418–429 on the subject of "doubling."

7 Aldous Huxley, op. cit., p. 39

8 See for instance Clyde H. Farnsworth, "Orphans of the 1950's, Telling of Abuse, Sue Quebec" in the *New York Times*, Friday, May 21, 1993,p. A3.

9 Andrija Puharich, *Uri: A Journal of the Mystery of Uri Geller*, Anchor, NY, 1974, ISBN 0-385-00992-5, p. 283

10 Lynn Picknett & Clive Prince, *The Stargate Conspiracy*, Warner, London, 2000, ISBN 0-7515-2996-6, p. 214. Those who do not have access to the older works by Puharich and his entourage could do worse than access this more recent volume; it contains a good and relatively-well documented account of the Round Table Foundation.

11 Puharich, op. cit., p. 13

12 Martin A. Lee & Bruce Shlain, *Acid Dreams*, Grove Weidenfeld, NY, 1992, ISBN 0-8021-3062-3, p. 18

13 Richard Harris Smith, *OSS: The Secret History of America's First Central Intelligence Agency*, University of California Press, Berkeley, 1981, ISBN 0-520-04246-8, p. 16

14 Ibid., p. 16

15 Ibid., p. 18

16 Phillip Knightley & Caroline Kennedy, *An Affair of State: The Profumo Case and the Framing of Stephen Ward*, Atheneum, NY, 1987, ISBN 0-689-11813-9, p. 257

17 Puharich, op. cit., p. 18

18 Ibid., p. 18

19 Picknett & Prince, op. cit., p. 168

20 This could have been businessman Henry Belk, who financed Hurkos' trip to Puharich's clinic in the 1950s and his more than two years' sojourn there until he became enraged over Hurkos' inability to predict the death of his daughter; see Norma Lee Browning, *The Psychic World of Peter Hurkos*, Signet, NY, 1970, LOC 76-114751, p. 74–76. Browning's book, published in 1970, gives a great deal of flavor of the psychic "environment" around Puharich, Belk, Hurkos, et al. during the Sixties.

21 Arthur M. Young, *The Foundations of Science: The Missing Parameter*, Robert Briggs Associates, San Francisco, 1984, ISBN 0-931191-03-3, p. 1

LLEGIVM FRATERNI
S S
FA MA

SECTION THREE:

CROSSFIRE

Mystery is an occult force or efficacy that does not obey us, and we never know how or when it will manifest itself.

—Octavio Paz[1]

. . . given that in the course of history many have acted on beliefs in which many others did not believe, we must perforce admit that for each, to a different degree, history has been largely the theater of an illusion.

—Umberto Eco[2]

For not all true things are to be said to all men.

—Bishop Clement of Alexandria (c. AD 150–215)[3]

After all, the fundamental question of philosophy (like that of psychoanalysis) is the same as the question of the detective novel: who is guilty?

—Umberto Eco[4]

BOOK ONE: THE NINE

CHAPTER SEVEN

JFK

> Imagine the man that committed this outrage going away quietly and peacefully, free and proud through life, as though it was nothing! . . .Ah, no, no! . . .I am in his path, and you will be in his path, too! . . .If others forget him, we will never forget. . . .We will seek and search everywhere for years if need be, but we will find the track.
>
> —*The Cloud That Lifted,* Maurice Maeterlinck[5]

It is not the intention of the author to review the entire debate over the assassination of President Kennedy, a controversy that has filled volumes already. It is not the intention of the author to go over all the evidence and prove, conclusively, that so-and-so committed the murder, or that such-and-such an organization was responsible, or even try to prove that Oswald acted alone. For this, one imagines the reader will be grateful.

What the author does intend to do, however, is to present additional evidence that so far has not been considered by mainstream journalists and researchers. This is evidence that may support one or more conspiracy theories, to be sure. The author feels that the conspiracy—if such existed—went much deeper than can be traced through the witness testimony and what passed for forensics reports in the Warren Commission Report. Like Peter Dale Scott,[6] the author believes in "deep politics," i.e., a layer of interrelationships that exists below the level of the simple facts of the case. In the author's case, though, he believes that there is a layer below Professor Scott's: a web of threads of cause and effect that run parallel at times, perpendicular at others. To that end, the author has pulled at some of these threads—these "scarlet threads of murder" that run through history—and has found relationships that are, if anything, more incredible than those presented in Oliver Stone's film, *JFK,* or in some of the more popular books on the assassination. Yet, they are fact, and supported by ample documentation.

THE CONCOURSE OF THE FORCES

Perhaps the most famous, and most respected, of the "amateur" investigators of the assassination of President John F. Kennedy is Ms. Mary Ferrell. She has been the ultimate resource for many other journalists, historians, and conspiracy theorists over the past fifty years. She cross-referenced and indexed all the volumes of the Warren Commission hearings, something which had never been done before, not even by the Commission itself, and thereby performed a vital service to all who would come after her. She also maintained a vast library of newsclippings, articles, journals, books, and transcripts that refer, in one way or another, to the subject of the assassination. Recently, some of her work has been published on CD-ROM, thereby giving researchers—particularly those like the author who lived at some geographical distance from the source material—an embarrassment of riches.

What many don't know, however, is that—until November 22, 1963—Mary Ferrell was an occultist.

In correspondence with the author, she spoke of her interest in the system of ceremonial magic practiced by the Golden Dawn, that British secret society that spawned Aleister Crowley, William Butler Yeats, Arthur Edward Waite, and many others. She had been in correspondence with Francis Israel Regardie, an occultist and author who had been Aleister Crowley's personal assistant for some years, and who published—to the grief and surprise of his brethren—the secret rituals of the Golden Dawn. Regardie himself was regarded as something of a resource to those in the New Age movement whose interest in the complex ritual systems of ceremonial magic was whetted by the works of Crowley, Mathers, Parsons, Charles Stansfeld Jones, Louis Culling, and others. Even more strangely, Regardie was initiated into a Rosicrucian group in Washington, D.C. in 1926, a group that leads us right to David Ferrie and from him to the assassination itself.

Regardie had been in contact with a group of Golden Dawn hopefuls in Dallas in the early 1960s; they had hoped to have Regardie teach them how to pronounce the Hebrew words that are so much a staple of Golden Dawn and other Hermetic literature. Regardie suggested they simply go to a local synagogue and get someone there to help them; but the Dallas group insisted and thus forked over a $500 per diem for two days, plus all expenses to bring Regardie to Dallas. Regardie made friends in Dallas that day, and had stayed in touch with them until the day he died.[7]

Mary Ferrell was thus, in the autumn of 1963, in position to become an important person in the community of magicians and occultists who came out of the tradition of Mathers, Crowley, et al. Had she devoted her energies to ceremonial magic instead of to the assassination, she may have provided an extremely valuable service to that muddled mass of theories, rituals, and posturing that has become modern ritual magic in America. Instead, she provided an even more important service: tools for the analysis of the twentieth century's most critical political murder.

The desire to uncover mysteries and secrets is probably a manifestation of a deeper paranoia about the universe; but this paranoia may be a healthy thing. As literary critic Anatole Broyard once remarked, "Paranoids are the only ones who notice anything anymore."[8] Or, as Charles Manson once observed, "Total paranoia is total consciousness."

Rather than a symptom of mental illness, paranoia may be the psychological equivalent of physical pain: a mechanism to warn of danger to the organism. In the case of physical pain, the source is usually easily identifiable. In the case of paranoia, the source is often invisible: an unnamed, sinister, force.

> The forces of darkness are inherently neither benign nor malevolent. They are unknown.
>
> —Arthur Young[9]

Actually, how could a reasonably intelligent person who was interested in the deeper aspects of the occult—of which the Golden Dawn system is certainly representative—*not* be moved to study the details of the Kennedy assassination? The murder had taken on mythic proportions, even in the days immediately following the event. The Kennedy administration had been referred to as "Camelot," a reference of course to King Arthur and the Knights of the Round Table, itself a symbol of deeper mysteries running the gamut from the Holy Grail to Joseph of Arimathea to Celtic magic and mysticism. Kennedy—the youngest President, the only Catholic President, husband of an attractive, sophisticated woman who graced the White House with famous artists, writers, musicians, the cultural elite of the day—had been murdered in front of crowds on a sunny afternoon in Dallas, Texas. It seemed as if the best and the brightest had been slain, a blood sacrifice on some unimaginable altar. It had all the hallmarks of an archetypal event, like the Crucifixion. We know so little about what really happened that day two thousand years ago atop Mount Golgotha, an event that spawned a religion and countless sects, cults, and secret societies; and murder, pogrom, and torture; and music, art and literature—so that when a similar event takes place in our midst there are those who will mop up every detail, every aspect of the case, like the witnesses at the decapitation of Charles I who soaked his blood into their handkerchiefs as sacred relics. In case the reader believes the author is overstating his case, please remember all those photographs of Kennedy that adorned the apartments, shops and homes of people from North America to South America, from Europe to Asia, in the years after the assassination; usually placed next to a picture of Jesus or the Pope, it had a place of honor tantamount to a Last Supper painting. Without being able to articulate why, in many cases the average person—particularly the average Catholic person—saw something divine, something terrible and sacred, in the idea of the murdered President.

All over the world, major streets and avenues and even districts (such as "Kennedy" in Bogota, Colombia) were re-named in honor of the slain President. Kennedy was seen as a friend of the poor, and as a defender of the disenfranchised of every race.

Whether or not that was true in fact, it was true in the minds of the people. And when his brother was assassinated, and Martin Luther King, Jr., it only seemed to justify the worship of the faithful and the certain belief that forces of evil were behind the multiple killings. This was a belief that the anti-Kennedy forces had to contend with at their peril, for they had nothing quite so strong in their arsenal. Except, maybe, fear. The author remembers the 1980 election campaign of Ronald Reagan and George Bush, when anti-Republican demonstrators wore buttons that said, "Shoot Bush First," and, "Where is Lee Harvey Oswald now that we need him?"

There is a degree system in the Golden Dawn, as there is in Masonry and in many other secret societies. One advances from degree to degree, from knowledge to knowledge, from experience to experience, under the guidance of those who have gone on before. The Golden Dawn professed to be the British branch of a German secret society, and the roots of that society were believed to have been derived from the German Rosicrucian Society of the seventeenth century, and that society to be a survival of the French Knights Templar of the fourteenth century, and so on back to the ancient Egyptians by way of the Gnostic Christians, the Islamic *hashishin*, the Ethiopian Coptics, the Jewish Qabalists, the Arabian Sabeans and Solomon the King. The rituals of the Golden Dawn therefore harkened back to all of these influences, and the study materials and lectures offered detailed exegeses of many ancient mysteries with the ultimate goal of creating a new human, a perfected creation, the next step in the evolutionary ladder. They took as their texts the *Zohar*, the Egyptian Coffin Texts and the *Book of the Dead*, as well as the alchemical works of the English, the Greeks and the Arabs, the *Turba Philosophorum* and the *Atalanta Fugiens*, the *Picatrix* and *The Book of the Sacred Magic of Abramelin the Mage* and *The True and Faithful Relation of What Passed For Many Years Between Dr. Dee and Some Spirits*. And, as an underpinning to all of this and to demonstrate the internal consistency of their program, was a system of correspondences.

This system was a mathematically-based set of tables against which virtually any object, any event, any philosophical idea could be identified and so drawn into comparison with other objects, events, ideas. Thus, one would find that the color red was related to the planet Mars, to blood, to iron, to certain herbs, to Tuesday, to the zodiacal sign of Aries, and so on. This system was predicated on the belief that events are related by invisible threads of connection that link them in ways too subtle to be measured by the normal cause and effect paradigm with which we are all familiar. After all, this is also the concept behind astrology, the Chinese system of *feng shui*, and many another occult, spiritual or New Age fashion. One can point to the Jewish system of the Qabala as the forerunner of this system in the West. The Qabala was a means of finding hidden relationships between words, based on their numerical equivalents; it was used to find secret messages in the Torah, for instance, or to create talismans and amulets. It was a method of assigning meaning to number, and this system formed the grammar and the algorithm for the Golden Dawn rituals, attaining its apotheosis in the *Book of the Concourse of the Forces*, which is an astonishing system of merging the Qabala with astrology, the Tarot, geomancy and other occult disciplines on the schema of John Dee's Elizabethan era Enochian system.[10] It was also a *theater of memory* and a means of controlling memory to the point that altered states of consciousness would result; a use of memory that goes beyond basic survival requirements and extends to the creation of a new way of perceiving reality, a new prioritizing of memories.

The goal of all this, the ultimate initiation in the Golden Dawn system, was the Adeptus Minor Ritual, which involved the crucifixion of the initiate (with ropes instead of nails) and a representation of the tomb of Christian Rosenkreutz, the putative founder of the Rosicrucian Order. It is a ritual symbolic of rebirth but, even more than that, it mimics the death and resurrection of the initiate in psychological terms so that those who undergo the ceremony are not merely acting parts in a strange play with no audience, but are experiencing profound psychological—if not spiritual—changes. It also unites the initiate with the whole history of his tradition, going back through all of those grimoires and spellbooks, all that gematria and incantation, all that sacred geometry, until a karmic balance has been achieved between the actions of the initiate's life (or lives) and the life to come, the life he will lead. The cross on which he has been crucified fixes him at a specific point in space and time, bleeds him of karmic debt, fixes him like the alchemists fixed mercury, so that he becomes the engine of his own transformation, his own X and Y axis, the center of his own dimension and, as such, the center of all dimensions. What is death and resurrection, after all, but a conquering—an *abrogation*—of the linear, unidirectional flow of time, and thus of space as well? And the extension of those parameters by the Young-ian quantum of *force*?

This crucifixion ritual would be mirrored in a ceremony that was performed by Charles Manson in Box Canyon near the Spahn Ranch in 1968, while he was under the influence of LSD. Charlie and his group had visited the headquarters there of a cult known as the Fountain of the World. This religion had been founded by a Francis Heindswatzer Pencovic, who renamed himself Krishna Venta. The group practiced a form of Christianity, and followed a strict celibacy rule (strict, that is, except for Krishna Venta himself). Disaffected followers who accused him of committing adultery with their wives killed him and nine of his followers with explosives on December 10, 1958, planting the dynamite in catacombs hidden beneath the church's complex. Photographs of the group show women dressed as nuns and sporting crosses, and in some cases washing the feet of male members á la Mary Magdalene.[11] Charlie was impressed by the group's dedication, and attempted to test their sincerity by sending his girls in to lure the members away from their vows of celibacy, a ruse that did not work.

Close to the sect's complex was a hill in the shape of a skull and a wooden cross planted atop it, in imitation of Golgotha. Charlie decided to re-enact the

Crucifixion with himself as the central character. He dropped acid. His followers tied him to the cross, jeered and humiliated him, and then symbolically killed him. They later celebrated his resurrection with an act of group sex.

Indirectly, as America's first acid pusher, the CIA had provided this barely literate Messiah-manqué with a quick fix on the cosmic cross; and, like the other psychic roadkill who make up the rolls of the Agency's unwitting test subjects, he was unprepared for the experience and wound up spinning like an imbalanced top over the California landscape of starlets, sunshine and sex. We have no idea what went through Manson's mind—or soul—during that ritual, but we can judge its after-effects. Manson was reared for a while by extremely religious relatives in West Virginia, and this when he was not even of kindergarten age. He was made to wear a dress to his first day at school, because his uncle thought he was a sissy. He was humiliated and jeered in real life, and was made to listen to sermons on Christian values and Biblical mythology. Then, he was sent to reform school after reform school and prison after prison. What an initiate of the Golden Dawn would have internalized, as part of the degree system and the gradual awakening of spiritual understanding, Manson experienced in the outer world. He then "fixed" these experiences—these negative, often horrifying and hideous experiences—in the ritual of the Crucifixion (while under the influence of a potent hallucinogen), without any means of neutralizing their effects or understanding them, or coming to terms with them in some positive way. Every humiliation he suffered, every rape in the prison system, every beating, every torment, was crystalized in the ritual, formalized, made—in a sense—permanent and unchanging. In the terms of a Golden Dawn-style perspective, he had become a "black brother" (ironically enough), a follower of the "left-hand path," and he didn't even know it.

They never do.

At times he called himself "Jesus," or "God," or whatever else came to mind. His power over his followers, however, began long before the crucifixion in Box Canyon, a control that was likened by one follower to Pavlov's Dogs, and by another to machinery in the minds of his followers that Charlie could control, like throwing a switch. But this degree of control did not contribute to happiness on Charlie's part, and he began to deteriorate, and to talk about apocalypse and armageddon.

"THE PROBLEM IS NOT YOUR BED, MRS. MCNEIL."

For a while, back in the 1960s, much was made of the similarities between the Abraham Lincoln and John F. Kennedy assassinations. We may call these similarities "coincidences," but perhaps Jung's "synchronicities" would be a better description. In any case, the number and type of similarities between the two cases beggars a simple description of coincidence. For instance, Lincoln had a secretary named Kennedy who advised him not to go to the theatre that fateful day; Kennedy had a secretary named Lincoln who advised him not to go to Dallas.

Abraham Lincoln was elected to Congress in 1847; Kennedy in 1947. Lincoln was elected president in 1860, Kennedy in 1960. Lincoln was succeeded by Andrew Johnson, who was born in 1808; Kennedy by Lyndon Johnson who was born in 1908. Both presidents died on a Friday. There are even more such coincidences, but the reader gets the general idea.

To a scientist, as well as to a historian, these are meaningless similarities. They are accidents of history. A scientist—if pressed—would look for other details that are *not* common to both Presidents, and then use that information to discredit the above catalogue. Lincoln was assassinated in 1865; Kennedy in 1963. Lincoln's wife was named Mary Todd; Kennedy's wife was Jacqueline Bouvier. See? No coincidences there. And what about the other two American Presidents who were assassinated? How many Americans even remember they were, or who they were? Why do Americans only remember Lincoln and Kennedy?

In the end, what do coincidences *mean,* anyway?

That they may be elements of a deeper web of connectivity between events in space and time (something suggested by Carl Jung, and ascribed to by physicist Wolfgang Pauli, among others) is too ephemeral an explanation for a traditional scientist, who would say that it properly belongs to that category of superstition that includes four-leaf clovers, rabbits' feet and the Psychic Hotline. What it will take perhaps another century or more to comprehend fully is that the assassination of President Kennedy was a modern-day crucifixion, a bloody sacrifice replete with iconic resonance. The cultural motif of the murdered President as a "slain king" was made clear in Kevin Costner's closing argument in his role as New Orleans District Attorney Jim Garrison in Oliver Stone's *JFK.* While there may be no overt religious overtones to the Kennedy assassination, there is a deep uneasiness about it; an uneasiness that became more pronounced with the murder of his brother in 1968, about the time of Manson's self-inflicted crucifixion in Box Canyon. The eerie set of similarities between the lives of Lincoln and Kennedy, therefore, is evidence of a much wider phenomenon that is screaming for our attention, even as it lurks beneath the threshold of consciousness, "dead, but dreaming," like a chthonic monster out of Lovecraft or Arthur Machen.

> I discover with surprise to what extent I had judged and admired my new country through Kennedy's actions. This brutal death reminds me of the existence of a volcano of violent realities underneath the orderly unfolding of our best plans.
>
> The real Beyond is not that which follows death but that which stretches underneath life itself. In this sense the saucers are a potential source of cultural and strategic upheaval, just like yesterday's killing in Dallas. Just as in Dallas, we are dreadfully unprepared.
>
> —Jacques Vallee, Diary 23 November 1963[12]

There is a famous moment in the film version of *The Exorcist* in which a psychiatrist tries to reassure the mother of the possessed Regan that her daughter is suffering from a temporal lobe disorder. Her mother insists that the whole bed was shaking and lifting off the floor. The psychiatrist says that muscle tremors are common in such disorders. Her mother insists that these were not tremors, that the whole bed was moving. The psychiatrist ignores this unacceptable evidence, and insists that everything is the result of a temporal lobe disorder, uttering the priceless line, "The problem is not your bed, Mrs. McNeil."

Which is another way of saying that the drunk was looking for his keys under a lamppost (even though he lost them across the street) because the light was better there.

In a way, the approach of science to date has been admirable. By ignoring the supernatural explanation, science has tried to let us keep control over our lives, to hold our destiny firmly in our own hands, to empower us and not blame Fate or Kismet or God's Will or a poor alignment of stars for the evil that does occur; but by taking all credibility or culpability away from the Infant in the Manger, God, Buddha, a malefic conjunction of planets or just bad vibes, they have thrown the Baby out with the bathwater. If we refuse to believe that a conspiracy of CIA agents, Cuban refugees, Mafia hitmen, or some combination of these had arranged the assassination of President Kennedy in Dallas, then we are forced to come up with some other explanation for the appearance of Lee Harvey Oswald—like some phantom squadron of UFOs—on everyone's radar: at CIA, the FBI, the Office of Naval Intelligence, Army intelligence, the Secret Service, Russian intelligence, anti-Castro Cubans, pro-Castro Cubans, right-wing extremists, homosexual cultists, private detectives and even the Civil Air Patrol. We are forced, that is, to find another reason why the relationships exist.

ON THE TRAIL OF THE ASSASSINS

While the inventor, psychic researcher, astrologer, Zen enthusiast and member of the original Nine, Arthur Young, was writing *The Reflexive Universe* in the quiet of his home in the Philadelphia suburb of Paoli in August of 1963, his wife was entertaining their daughter-in-law, Ruth Hyde Paine.

Ruth Hyde had married Michael Paine—Ruth Forbes Young's son by her previous marriage to George Lyman Paine—on December 28, 1957 in a Quaker ceremony in Philadelphia, Pennsylvania. Ruth Hyde's background alone is suggestive: her father had been employed by the Agency for International Development (AID), which was a well-known CIA front and which lost a few overseas officials to acts of terrorism, including the famous case of Dan Mitrione in Uruguay. Her brother-in-law—based in Washington, D.C.—was also employed by AID.[13] Ruth Hyde had been working in Philadelphia when she met Michael. Upon their marriage, she moved in with Michael, Ruth Forbes Young and Arthur Young at their home in Paoli, where the couple remained until the summer of 1959, Michael working directly for Arthur Young in his stepfather's barn . . . building model helicopters. This part of the story sounds quite strange. According to his Warren Commission testimony, Michael Paine set up shop in Arthur Young's barn (sometime in the early 1950s) and started working for himself. The nature of this work was not clarified, nor why Michael Paine would have been using Arthur Young's barn to "work for himself." Eventually, Arthur hired Michael to make model helicopters for him. This sounds suspiciously like make-work, since Arthur Young by this time had given up on helicopter design and was involved full-time in mystical pursuits. The other problem with Michael Paine's testimony is that he cannot give dates; he does not know when he began working for Bell Helicopter, he doesn't have a firm grasp of when he left school, joined the Army, re-enrolled in university, or anything else about his past. Nor is he aware of what level of security clearance he has at Bell. In fact, he cannot even remember what year he married Ruth Hyde! He has further lapses of memory throughout his testimony; anything to do with his relationship to Ruth Hyde Paine becomes vague and ephemeral.

What we do know with some certainty is that Michael Paine—a native of New York City—graduated from high school in 1947. He then went to Harvard for two years, but had to drop out, as he was failing academically. That would have been in 1949. His mother had married Arthur Young in 1948, while Michael was doing his first year at Harvard.

At some point, he wound up working for a nuclear research firm, the Bartol Research Foundation at Swarthmore, doing something vague with machines, while attempting to finish a bachelor's degree. He claims that he would have been in the class of 1953 at Swarthmore, had he stayed in school. With two years at Harvard already accomplished (and for which he probably received credit at Swarthmore) that puts him there in 1951, but according to his testimony he only worked about a year at Bartol before leaving for the Army.

He spent two years in the Army, and was sent to Korea. This would have been during the height of the Korean War. There is no indication in his testimony before the Commission about what his duties were or even what his rank might have been. It seems odd that his war record was not read into the transcript, or that an attempt to get accurate dates out of him was not strenuously mounted by someone at the Commission, but so it goes.

At one point, he is saved from embarrassment—or inadvertent revelation—by Allen Dulles. When Michael Paine is asked about his duties at Bell Helicopter, the following exchange takes place:

> Mr. LIEBELER—Have you been engaged in that type of work for Bell throughout?
>
> Mr. PAINE—I have been in the research laboratory research group that long. It has all been problems—
>
> Mr. DULLES—Are you a helicopter pilot by any chance yourself?

The reader is left with this tantalizing bit of personal anecdote interrupted by a typical Dulles non-sequitur, of which there are quite a few when it comes to the Paines. The question of Michael Paine's work at Bell never comes up again. This will happen several more times during Ruth Paine's testimony.

Michael and Ruth Paine moved to Irving, Texas (a Dallas suburb) in 1959 and somehow had two children. By September 1962, Michael and Ruth were separated but still on good terms. She was thirty years old. He was thirty-four. They would be officially divorced in 1971.

Michael Paine had managed to get a job at his stepfather's old firm, Bell Helicopter, at a branch facility they had in Fort Worth, Texas. One can only imagine that this job was due to his stepfather's influence at Bell, since Michael's work record is spotty and he had no college degree. Michael Paine's job was essentially the same as the one he had at Arthur Young's barn: building model helicopters. At this time, Bell's R&D was being run by the former Nazi General Walter Dornberger, whom me met earlier as a scientist brought to the US under Operation Paperclip along with more than 1,000 other German scientists, many of whom were suspected of being committed Nazis, including both Dornberger and his protégé, Wernher von Braun. (This association has given rise to much speculation that somehow the Nazis themselves were behind the Kennedy assassination. While this may be an exaggeration, there is no lack of Nazi influence in and around the events leading up to—and away from—the assassination.)

Ruth Paine met Lee Harvey Oswald and his wife, Marina, at a party in Highland Park, Texas (a short drive from Irving) on February 22, 1963. Ruth at this stage of her life was a Quaker, having converted in the first few months of 1951; her mother was a Unitarian minister. As one reads her Warren Commission testimony, it becomes obvious that religion was important in her life at that time, and living in close proximity to Arthur Young for almost two years something of his interest in spirituality must have rubbed off. Ruth Paine was also interested in learning Russian—a politically-suspect language to study in 1963—and interested as well in square-dancing and madrigal-singing. (The reader should be reminded that television programming was relatively spare in 1960s Dallas.) These varied interests had her joining several different groups and making friends over a wide spectrum of the population, including the White Russian émigré community.

The Oswalds were brought to the party by the de Mohrenschildts.

George de Mohrenschildt is one of the most enigmatic characters in the entire assassination scenario. A White Russian himself, a petroleum engineer, an entrepreneur, a world traveler, multilingual, suspected of Nazi sentiments, he cooperated with American intelligence on more than one occasion in his life. His motives for introducing the Oswalds to the Paines is unclear. He has told the story several different ways. When finally he was about to be brought before the House Sub-Committee on Assassinations in 1977 to tell the whole story, he committed suicide or, as some theorists insist, was murdered; it is true that the forensic evidence is suspicious, but either way—suicide or murder—the event is sufficiently alarming and suggestive of deeper, darker secrets.

Marina Oswald—who spoke very little English—was invited to stay with Ruth Paine at her home in Irving, along with Marina's child. This way, according to Ruth Paine, they could swap language lessons (a plan that seems to have been abandoned immediately after Marina moved in). Lee Oswald would go to New Orleans to seek work, and during that time he became modestly famous for about a week due to his "Fair Play for Cuba" leafletting and subsequent media appearance. When he returned to Dallas, he took up residence in a rooming house, once Ruth Paine had managed to network him into the Texas School Book Depository, and Marina remained with Ruth at Irving. When the assassination occurred, it was the Paines who led the police officers to the place (and the blanket) where Lee had supposedly stored his Mannlicher-Carcano rifle.

In fact, Ruth Paine was more than helpful. Much of the evidence that would eventually damn Oswald in the eyes of the Warren Commission (and the public) came from Ruth Paine: some of the famous photographs of Oswald posing with the rifle and copies of a Communist newspaper, the "spy camera," the fake Alex Hidell documents, and much else besides. There is even a growing body of evidence that Michael Paine's father—George Lyman Paine, who was a Trotskyite leader in California—had intelligence connections that led straight back to William Buckley, Jr. and E. Howard Hunt, through one James Burnham, who was George Paine's colleague in the Trotskyite party to which they both belonged, and who was also a consultant to the CIA and a friend of E. Howard Hunt of Watergate "Plumber" fame.

E. Howard Hunt himself had no little interest in the occult, and was the author of three occult novels (as well as numerous spy novels) under various pseudonyms; one of the occult stories was a thinly-disguised attack on the Kennedy family. He even lived on "Witches Island." Hunt, it may be remembered, was one of those CIA agents in charge of the Bay of Pigs invasion, and thus no lover of Jack Kennedy. He also has had a hard time accounting for his whereabouts on November 22, 1963.

The full story of Ruth and Michael Paine has never been told. Michael Paine admitted that on the day of the assassination itself, he was discussing political assassinations with some co-workers in the Bell cafeteria when the announcement came that the President had been shot. Another coincidence? Perhaps. Michael Paine—assuredly aware of his stepfather's occult interests—actually made a joking remark to the Commission that perhaps it was ESP that led him to engage a co-worker in a discussion of the nature of political assassins, but since neither one of them actually knew any political assassins the topic was dropped. Rather than ESP, was it that perhaps underachiever Michael Paine was bursting to reveal a secret?

It was Michael Paine who took Oswald to his first ACLU meeting. It was also Michael Paine who took Oswald to his first John Birch Society meeting. It was Michael Paine who engaged Oswald in political discussions in front of witnesses.

During his wife's testimony before the Warren Commission, several unusual moments took place which may have meant nothing at the time, but which raise some questions in the author's mind today.

For instance, early in her testimony to the Warren Commission, Ruth Paine admitted that at one point Lee Harvey Oswald was considering going to Philadelphia. As soon as she mentioned Philadelphia, Allen Dulles chimed in and opined that it was presumably to find work, to which Ruth replied in the affirmative. That is what is known as "leading the witness." Philadelphia, of course, is where Arthur and Ruth Young lived, and Ruth had a habit of going up there every year in the summer . . . as she did in the summer of 1963. Did Arthur Young invite the young Marine defector to his wooded estate in Paoli? Or had Ruth Paine made an inadvertent slip one day in front of Lee that she was related by marriage to the famous inventor of the Bell helicopter? Or did Michael, who after all worked for Bell? The relationship between the Paines and Arthur Young is never mentioned, never examined, in the Warren Commission hearings except to note that Michael's mother married someone named Arthur Young.

Dulles becomes helpful to Ruth Paine's testimony on more than one occasion. Each time her Russian language tutor is mentioned, Dulles heads off the line of questioning by asking something else before Ruth can answer. This happens first on page 467 of Volume II of the Warren Commission Hearings, and then again on page 473. Then, when Ruth Paine mentions that she thought of getting her husband, Michael, to put Marina Oswald on his tax return as a dependent so that she could earn some additional income—a suggestion that caused no end of mirth among the assembled Officers of the Court due to its stunning admission of illegality—it was Dulles who came in like the cavalry to paint Ruth Paine's motives in a purely altruistic light.

When the Commission finally did get around to asking Ruth Paine about her Russian language tutor, Dulles was conveniently absent from the hearings that day.

Why would Dulles take such a particular interest in Ruth Paine if, in fact, he did? Was he afraid that something said about the Russian language tutor in his presence would reflect badly on him later on? Was he aware of Ruth Paine's august family connections back in Philadelphia? Or did it have something to do with Michael Paine?

In fact, all of the above reasons may be valid. He certainly knew Michael and Ruth Paine, and perhaps should have recused himself from their part of the testimony in the first place; there is certainly no mention by Dulles in the twenty-six volumes of the Warren Commission Hearings that he knew the Paines socially, but it seems clear that he had to have known of them if not known them to talk to. He knew Ruth Young, and he knew a very close and personal friend of Ruth Young: Ms. Mary Bancroft.

Mary Bancroft has written an autobiography, and she describes this relationship in some detail. She had been the mistress of Allen Dulles for some twenty years, and had also been the mistress of Henry Luce (of Time Life, where the Zapruder film of the Kennedy assassination wound up) for about the same length of time.

She knew Dulles from the War years in Europe, when he was running the OSS operation out of Switzerland (Dulles knew E. Howard Hunt and Richard Helms at this time, as well). It was a relationship that lasted for decades, and of which Dulles' wife, Clover, was probably aware, as she was of his other infidelities. Mary Bancroft was a good friend of Ruth Forbes, which meant of course that she knew her children as well. Thus, it beggars belief to think that Allen Dulles was not acutely aware of the Paines, the Youngs, and their relationship to Lee Harvey Oswald.

Ruth Paine visited the Youngs in Paoli, Pennsylvania in mid-August 1963, after visiting the Naushon Island (Wood's Hole, Massachusetts) home of the Paine side of the family from July 31 to August 12. She then returned to Dallas, and invited Marina Oswald to stay with her while Marina was pregnant with the Oswald's second child. (At the same time, according to his testimony, Michael Paine had gone to Los Angeles to visit his father, the Trotskyite.) We may be forgiven if we assume that Ruth Paine discussed the Oswalds with Arthur and Ruth Young during this period. The Oswalds had stayed with her in the spring of 1963—during the time of Oswald's putative assassination attempt on right-wing extremist General Walker—and Ruth Paine was thinking up ways to have Marina move in with her again, even going so far as to find additional funds by cheating on Michael's income tax return. Marina happily moved in with Ruth Paine at the latter's home in Irving, Texas, and was there through the birth of her second child and right up to the day of the assassination of President Kennedy.

As noted above, Ruth Paine was more than helpful to the authorities who came calling as soon as Lee Oswald was identified on the day of the assassination. It was Ruth Paine who provided some of the most damaging circumstantial evidence against Oswald. It was also Ruth Paine who dragged her feet on getting Lee Oswald legal representation, even though both she and her husband were members of the ACLU. Ruth Paine the Quaker, Ruth Paine the liberal activist, Ruth Paine the pacifist who was studying Russian and writing letters to pen pals in the Soviet Union, hoping to bridge the gap between the two superpowers and promote peace, Ruth Paine the folk-dancing, madrigal-singing, friend of the oppressed . . . refusing to help the husband of stranded Russian immigrant Marina Oswald, and the father of Marina Oswald's two infant children, get legal representation?

When Ruth Paine's Russian language tutor—the elderly Mrs. Dorothy Gravitis, a Latvian—was deposed before the Commission, she revealed an interesting piece of information. A woman whose history parallels that of many Latvians in the second half of the twentieth century, she had been born in Latvia when it was part of Russian territory under the Czars; it became independent in 1918, at the time of the Revolution. It later became annexed to Russia in 1940, was invaded by the Nazis shortly thereafter, and then in 1944 Mrs. Gravitis herself wound up in Germany in a camp along with many other Displaced Persons (DPs), and eventually managed to emigrate to the United States in late 1949.

She taught Ruth Paine only two official classes at Berlitz, but remained a friend of hers in Texas and taught her privately after that. Ruth asked her to check on Marina when the former was out of town, in May of 1963 when she was evidently in San Antonio. Mrs. Gravitis spoke with Marina on the phone twice, and never met her, but they discussed Lee from a perspective that should have been very disturbing to the Commission, but which seems to have been passed over.

When asked by the Commission why she decided to distance herself from Marina before the assassination, she said it was because of Marina's remarks concerning Lee Oswald. Marina had used a very specific term in Russian to describe Lee's political beliefs. This word is not easily translatable into English, and her interpreter—Mamantov—had difficulty with it. It is a word that signifies that Lee was in the second phase of becoming a member of the Communist Party, the phase where he had to prove himself to the Party in some material way. In the Soviet Union of Mrs. Gravitis' experience, that usually meant spying.

What many Americans never realize about both the Soviet Union and the People's Republic of China is that there have been actually very few members—per capita—of the Communist Party in each country. To be a Party member is to be one of the elite class, and to lose Party membership is tantamount to social as well as political suicide. Thus, the requirements for attaining Party membership were usually quite strict, and a demonstration of Communist loyalty and zeal was required before one could be given a Party card. Within the Soviet Union (as in China), this usually meant spying on your neighbors, your co-workers, even your own family to discover anti-Communist actions or beliefs. You would then report all of this to the Party member in charge of your advancement, like a cat showing up with a dead mouse. What Marina was telling Mrs. Gravitis, then, was that Oswald was in this second phase.

Marina may simply have been bragging or exaggerating for the benefit of old Mrs. Gravitis (who was in her seventies at the time and who had had a hard life in Latvia, Russia, Nazi Germany, and New York City, where she worked cleaning floors, and finally in Texas). Whatever the truth of the matter was, Gravitis decided she wanted nothing to do with Lee Oswald, afraid that he was spying on the Russian émigré community in Texas on behalf of the Soviets. Since the last thing the Warren Commission wanted was evidence linking Oswald to the KGB—evidence that might have precipitated a Third World War—this aspect of the case was downplayed or ignored.

Another possibility, also never followed up, is that Oswald told Marina this story in order to direct her away from his real activities, which also included spying not *on* the White Russian community but *for* a faction of the US government.

As former CIA officer Victor Marchetti revealed in an interview to assassination researcher Anthony Summers, the US Navy's Office of Naval Intelligence (ONI) had a program in place in the 1960s to place phony defectors in the Soviet Union. These included between thirty and forty young men who were "made to appear disenchanted, poor, American youths who had become turned off and wanted to see what communism was all about."[14] From every indication, it would appear that the twenty-year-old Oswald fit the profile exactly. Add to that the fact that the period in which he defected was a time of numerous defections of US military and intelligence personnel to the Soviet Union, and the shoe fits.

This is not to say that Oswald was a James Bond. In fact, he *was* a poor, probably disenchanted American. He was also quite young. He would not have been given a strenuous assignment, such as running agents. He might have been made to serve other purposes, about which we can only conjecture. Yet, he was proficient enough in Russian at the age of twenty to indicate a reasonably high intelligence (Ruth Paine had studied Russian for years and obviously never got the hang of it . . . or so she said. The author, who can make his way in a variety of European and Asian tongues, can attest that Russian is one of the most difficult to learn). His erstwhile friend, the White Russian George de Mohrenschildt, found Oswald to be intelligent and well-spoken; it was also de Mohrenschildt who, it was later discovered, was reporting on Oswald to American intelligence in the months prior to the assassination; it is also de Mohrenschildt who, from his writings and remarks to various investigators and journalists, gives the impression that he was saddened—perhaps even guilty—about what happened to Oswald. There is a great deal of evidence—all of it circumstantial—that Oswald may have been working for American intelligence (or some faction thereof) right up to the end of his life. The author will not go into all of that here, of course.

Dulles may have already known what Dorothy Gravitis would say from other sources. As a Russian immigrant in the United States, Gravitis was vulnerable to all sorts of pressure from other Russians (and Latvians) in the United States at that time who were agitating for an American assault on the motherland to liberate it from Soviet control. The White Russian community in the United States had rallied around the Russian Orthodox Church and around several ersatz political groups that held parades and other conscious-ness-raising events around the country. These groups were often so extreme in their anti-Communism that they were pro-Nazi and, indeed, the Russian Orthodox Church in New York City was a center of Russian fascism. The Orthodox Church had split into several factions after the Russian Revolution of 1917. One group remained loyal to Moscow, through duress; this was the Patriarchate of Moscow which, of course, was headquartered in Russia and had to make accommodations with the Soviets to survive. They maintained a cathedral on West Ninety-Seventh Street in New York which was well-known as a conduit for KGB agents coming to the United States, agents disguised as priests.

Another group was the Russian Orthodox Church Outside Russia—usually referred to as the Synod—which was based on Park Avenue at Ninety-Third Street. This community was supported by the Romanovs and other escaped Russian royalty. This group was—during World War II—pro-Nazi, seeing in the Nazis potential liberators of the motherland.

The CIA and other political and intelligence organizations made use of these groups to run agents, gather information, or whatever could be valuable to the cause. Psychological warfare officers were familiar with the main characters in the Russian Orthodox scenario, and Radio Free Europe (an acknowledged CIA front) would broadcast religious messages into the Communist bloc on behalf of various Christian groups, but especially the Synod.

This use of Orthodox churches in the fight against Communism was more widespread than most Americans realize, simply because to them the Eastern Orthodox church is too ethnic, too mysterious to understand. Eventually, though, such famous names in the Kennedy assassination investigation as David Ferrie would be revealed as players in this strange underworld of archaic ritual, dead languages, and wandering bishops.

Dulles was aware of all of this, of course. Support of the Eastern churches was an essential element of the Cold War, as they provided a moral and cultural context for the fight against the Soviet Union. Rather than try to explain why dialectical materialism is flawed, or how putting the means of production in the hands of the State is doomed to failure, it was far easier to say that the Soviets were "Godless," were atheists bent on destroying Christ's church. This meant that the struggle against Communism was a war of Light against Darkness. In addition, the misguided attempt by the Soviets to completely eradicate certain of the ethnic minorities—such as the Ukrainians—by prohibiting publications in their native tongues was an attack on the cultural heritage of millions. The Eastern churches were repositories of not only Christianity, but also of ethnic culture, since each Eastern church celebrates its rituals in the vernacular of its people and is a repository for their traditions; thus, the ceremonies of the Greek Orthodox Church are in Greek, of the Syrian Orthodox Church in Arabic, of the Ukrainian Orthodox Church in Ukrainian, etc.

The possibility that Mrs. Gravitis—or her interpreter-son Mamantov—might have been allied with one or another of the anti-Communist underground organizations in Texas must have occurred to Dulles, if he did not actually know of this beforehand. He would not have wanted to reveal the CIA's interest in—and support of—these groups in an open forum, and this might have been one reason why he kept changing the subject when Ruth Paine mentioned the tutor, in essence keeping her from saying her name while Dulles was present.

This—admittedly circumstantial—piece of evidence, coupled with Dulles' omission of his prior acquaintance with Michael and Ruth Paine, as well as the

Commission's not firmly establishing Michael Paine's curriculum vitae or following up on his war record, or delving more closely into the background of Arthur Young, indicates the presence of a hidden agenda. The author would like to propose that the connection to Arthur Young through the Paines is a smoking gun, indicative of another level of covert activity that has not been explored by the Warren Commission or by the later House Sub-Committee on Assassinations (HSCA). Arthur Young's travels with Andrija Puharich to Mexico and elsewhere, and his long support of Puharich's Round Table Foundation, as well as his inclusion in the first "séance of The Nine," may reveal an intelligence operation—a truly *bizarre* intelligence operation—that is connected to the Oswald affair. Puharich, as we have seen, was working for either Army intelligence, the CIA, or more probably some combination of the two, out of Fort Detrick, which was a staging ground for both. Although Arthur Young's interest in the paranormal was very probably innocent and well-meaning—as so many of his admirers will insist—that is not to say that he did not cooperate with government agencies when he could, or when he was asked to do so, Puharich being the first known example. There is a tantalizing lack of published information about Arthur Young's life between 1952, when he founded something called the Foundation for the Study of Consciousness in Philadelphia, and 1973, when he founded the Institute for the Study of Consciousness in Berkeley. We know of his relationship to Puharich, but only in a very sketchy form; we know that he was Michael Paine's stepfather and, by extension, Ruth Paine's father-in-law; we know that Michael Paine worked for Arthur Young at the same time that Arthur Young was working with Puharich. Further, we know that Michael Paine's mother (Arthur Young's wife) was a close friend and confidant of Allen Dulles' mistress, Mary Bancroft. This incestuous tangle of friends, lovers, relatives, mothers, sons, in-laws, coworkers and intelligence agents is an aspect of the Kennedy assassination that has never been adequately investigated. How odd that the legacy of Robert Treat Paine—a signer of the Declaration of Independence and thus one of America's Founding Fathers—should have trickled down to a Michael Paine, a friend of the accused assassin of an American president.

There is another strange aspect to the question of the Paines that is worth a brief look, even though it is perhaps too bizarre to take seriously. One of the most mysterious of the many Aleister Crowley mysteries is that of a section of his famous *Book of the Law*, specifically Book Two, Verse 76. This verse reads,

> 76.4 6 3 8 A B K 2 4 A L G M O R 3 Y X 24 89 R P S T O V A L.
> *What meanest this, o prophet? Thou knowest not; nor shalt thou know ever.*

The verse is commonly referred to—by Thelemites—as "R P Stoval" after the last group of letters. No one knows what it means, although many have claimed to decode the enigmatic phrase.

A photograph found in the Paine home—a photograph of a '57 Chevrolet in the driveway of General Walker, the man Oswald is supposed to have fired upon and missed in the weeks leading up to the assassination—was mutilated. The license plate had been removed from the photo so that it would be impossible to identify. The Dallas detective who seized the photo from the Paine home and put it into evidence claimed that it was already mutilated; Marina Oswald denied this and later evidence—a photo of the photo, to be precise—shows that Marina was telling the truth. The photograph when it came into custody of the Dallas police was intact; someone in the department must have chopped the license number out of the picture.

The Dallas police detective who confiscated the photo and who subsequently lied by stating that it arrived in his possession in its mutilated state was one R. B. Stovall. In addition, Oswald worked for a photographic firm in Dallas that had Defense Department contracts: Jaggers-Chiles-Stovall. The job had been arranged for Oswald by George de Mohrenschildt.[15]

> In de Mohrenschildt's entire existence, as with so much else surrounding Oswald, we seem to be looking at a kind of voodoo.
>
> —Dick Russell, *The Man Who Knew Too Much*[16]

Is any of this data meaningful in a forensic sense? Does it reveal the truth about what happened in Dallas in 1963? Perhaps, perhaps not. But if, in some future decade, the evidence given above is shown to be not relevant to the actual murder of the President, then to what *is* it relevant? For it challenges every definition of cause and effect to ignore the above relationships and call them "coincidence." The point of the author is that these relationships cannot be ignored: that they are the spoor of some darker mechanism of history, of what we call reality, and that an understanding of world events is impossible without acknowledging their existence and seeking their underlying meaning.

HOW TO BECOME A BISHOP WITHOUT BEING RELIGIOUS

On the opposite side of the psychic scale from Arthur Young is the strange, intense figure of David Ferrie. Made memorable by Joe Pesci's performance in Oliver Stone's *JFK*, Ferrie was an improbable person. Had a novelist invented him, the genre would have to be either science-fiction or fantasy, or perhaps something avant-garde and experimental. In actuality, everything one reads about Ferrie is usually understatement. An Eastern Airlines pilot, an amateur cancer researcher, possibly an anti-Castro gunrunner and certainly (by his own admission) an associate of Sergio Arcacha Smith of the anti-Castro underground as well as of Mafia overlord Carlos Marcello, he was also in charge of Lee Harvey Oswald's old Civil Air Patrol unit in Louisiana. He had no facial hair at all, due to a condition known as alopecia, so he would paste on false eyebrows in a shocking shade of red and wear a red wig. (One is reminded of an episode during the Watergate affair when E. Howard Hunt borrowed a voice modifier and a red wig from CIA supply. An *homage?*) Ferrie came to the attention of District Attorney Jim Garrison when the latter was ramping up his investigation into New Orleans' connection with the Kennedy assassination. Ferrie's name had been dropped as a friend of both Guy Banister and Lee Harvey Oswald by one Jack Martin, who worked for Guy Banister (he of the FBI UFO files) as some sort of ersatz investigator. Martin himself had worked with Ferrie on an investigation involving diploma mills and fraudulent ecclesiastical papers. Well, they *claimed* it was an investigation. It was obviously more than that. It seems that both Martin and Ferrie were only too happy to acquire these paper dignities themselves. Ferrie and Martin had both come to the attention of the Warren Commission briefly, and then were dropped as suspects. They both came under Jim Garrison's microscope later on, but Ferrie died before he could testify. Garrison claimed that Ferrie was one of the most important people in history, but that might have been hyperbole. He was certainly one of the strangest.

One of the intriguing aspects of the Ferrie case to the author—and to very few others—was his membership in a church and his status as a bishop. This rang alarm bells, since the author himself has direct and personal experience of the church to which Ferrie was admitted and in which he was consecrated.

This church is referred to in the journalistic accounts of the assassination by all sorts of names, such as the Old Catholic Church or the Holy Apostolic Church, etc., etc., but in testimony obtained by the FBI it is clear that David Ferrie was a bishop in the American Orthodox Catholic Church, and therein lies a tale.

The American Orthodox Catholic Church was founded by Walter (Vladimir) Propheta, a priest with the Ukrainian Orthodox Church whose father was also a priest. (In Eastern Orthodox churches, priests are allowed to be married and raise families, provided they are married before they are ordained; married men are not, however, allowed to become bishops.) Walter Propheta was a sincere and dedicated anti-Communist, as were most Ukrainians who lived in the United States during the time of the Soviet Union. Propheta had gone on television in its early days to promote a strong, anti-Communist message. He had arranged for a documentary to be made on the Katyn Forest Massacre, and had appeared with Dave Garroway to discuss the evils being perpetrated against Ukraine and other "Captive Nations" by the Communists. In fact, Propheta once showed the author a letter from Presidential candidate Thomas Dewey, promising Propheta that he would be the White House chaplain should Dewey win the election against Truman. According to Propheta, he was packing his suitcase to go to Washington when the news came that Truman had won.

As it happens in the churches, celebrity can be the kiss of death when it comes to advancement in the hierarchy. Propheta wanted to be consecrated bishop of the Ukrainian Orthodox Church, but for some reason (canonical or otherwise) it didn't happen. Upset, he broke away to form his own church, the American Orthodox Catholic Church, which would be an Orthodox Church conducting its services in English (a rather novel idea at the time). The Church's headquarters were on East 183rd Street in the Bronx, at the Cathedral of the Holy Resurrection, a former Protestant church with an interior covered in crayon-colored ikons, quite close to the Bronx Zoo and also comfortably near Arthur Avenue, a famed Italian neighborhood with great bakeries and restaurants.

The church, however, had very few—if any—parishioners. It did have, however, an embarrassingly large number of bishops. At the headquarters alone—in the period 1968–69 when the author was there frequently—there was Propheta himself, Bishop Leonard G. Hill and Bishop John Christian Chaisson as the regular staff. There were no priests, deacons, altar boys, or anyone else for that matter.

But there were American intelligence officers.

According to Propheta, there was one FBI agent and one CIA agent on the Church's Board of Directors. This may have been simple boasting, but the author was introduced to both during his tenure at the Church. In fact, they were involved at the time in trying to buy a former mental hospital in New Jersey on behalf of the Church (for which purpose the author never knew), and once broached the subject to two young priests, wondering if they could sign the purchase agreement in order to disguise the agents' involvement. When they discovered that the two priests were only eighteen years old at the time, and thus could not sign legal documents in the State of New Jersey, the matter was dropped. The two young priests, however, went on to greater glory—and notoriety—in the years that would follow.

At this point, the reader no doubt is puzzled, and wondering what this is all about.

Back in the 1960s there was a very popular book—in certain circles—entitled *How To Become a Bishop Without Being Religious*. This book humorously discussed the ease with which one could become a clergyman, particularly a bishop, and all the perks that went with it. It was read avidly by a strange circle of very strange men—of which David Ferrie was a member—known as the *Episcopi Vagantes*, or "wandering bishops." These were men who had either invented their own Church and named themselves as its bishops or who, more often, joined churches already in existence and (for a fee, or for some service) were consecrated as bishops by other bishops. There is a certain degree of sadness in contemplating the type of individual who would lust so mightily for the bishop's robes but be otherwise incapable or unqualified to be even an altar boy, much less a priest and much, much less a bishop. Some of these men gave themselves outlandish titles, such as Patriarch or Archbishop; some were janitors, convicted criminals, or the borderline insane. Still others were intelligence agents.

When Propheta crossed the line and created his own church, he was in need of a legitimate consecration. "Consecration" is the ritual by which a priest is made a bishop, and in Orthodox Christianity as in the Roman Catholic Church, one needs a minimum of three bishops to consecrate another bishop. This guarantees something called the "line of apostolic succession," which is a line of consecrations leading directly back to St. Peter, the first Pope. For those who have gone the "independent" route, it is vitally important to prove that one has been validly ordained and validly consecrated, for it means that the rituals one performs are thus as valid as those performed by a Catholic priest or bishop, or by a regular Eastern Orthodox priest or bishop. This validity is the only thing standing between a wandering bishop and doubts about his sanity. For this reason, consecrations are swapped like baseball cards, because one is never quite sure if his consecration is *really* valid, and it is nice to have additional consecrations in case the previous one is shown to be invalid.

This is what happened with Propheta. He had to secure valid consecration, and he did so at the hands of an occultist, a man who ran one of the oddest of odd churches in Manhattan, an Orthodox Church which was at the same time the local headquarters of the SRIA: the *Societas Rosicruciana In America,* or "the Rosicrucian Society of America."[17]

The SRIA was an occult lodge founded in the United States at the end of the nineteenth century as an outgrowth of a British lodge, the *Societas Rosicruciana In Anglia* (also known as SRIA). The British SRIA was the breeding ground of the Golden Dawn, which itself was the breeding ground of Aleister Crowley. Without going into too much detail about the creation and history of these orders, which is certain to bore and confuse the reader, let us summarize by saying that the head of the American SRIA was, for quite some time, one George Winslow Plummer, a devoted occultist and Hermeticist who edited a magazine of things alchemical and Rosicrucian called *Mercury*. Plummer was also interested in Christian mysticism, and aligned himself with several renegade Christian churches, including something called the Holy Orthodox Church. He was also a member of Aleister Crowley's OTO, and thus fits the mold of occultists everywhere: the inveterate joiner and accumulator of dignities. Plummer died in 1944, and was succeeded in the SRIA by his widow, the ethereal Mother Serena, who played the organ at the Church's headquarters at 321 West 101st Street on the Upper West Side of Manhattan when the author knew her. Mother Serena later married Theodotus Stanislaus de Witow (1890–1969), who then became the Patriarch of the Holy Orthodox Church, as well as the head of the SRIA until his death in 1969.

Propheta was ordained a Ukrainian Orthodox priest by Bishop Bohdan of the Ukrainian Orthodox Church on May 15, 1933. At this time, and until 1964, Propheta was still within the ecumenical fold. But things became strange after the Kennedy assassination in 1963, and Propheta sought other alliances; the details are not too well known.

Propheta was consecrated bishop of the American Orthodox Church on October 3,1964 by Archbishop Joachim Souris of the Autocephalous Greek Orthodox Church of America and by the aforementioned Archbishop de Witow of the Holy Orthodox Church in America; he then incorporated the American Orthodox Church as the American Orthodox Catholic Church (AOCC) in New York, and thus entered the document stream as one of America's foremost bishop mills.

Archbishop Joachim Souris was himself made a bishop by Metropolitan Peter Zhurawetzky and two Old Roman Catholic Church bishops who traced their lineage through the inescapable René Vilatte, a famous name in wandering bishop circles, as are Zhurawetzky and Propheta themselves. The Old Roman Catholic Church is the American incarnation of the famous Jansenist heresy, and according to most authorities they have maintained valid apostolic succession through their bishops who were—originally, at the time of the heresy—validly consecrated. It was the Old Roman Catholic Church more than any other group who popularized the idea that one could be a "real" priest and a "real" bishop without belonging to the "real" Catholic Church or any of the legitimate Eastern Orthodox Churches. Once that was accepted, it was only a matter of time before a lot of people jumped on the bandwagon, obtained "real" consecrations and set up their own churches, usually aligning themselves with other "real" bishops in order to consecrate even more bishops . . . who would found their own churches . . . and so it goes.

Anyone trying to make sense out of the foregoing, or to follow the richly entangled web of consecrations, cross-consecrations and affiliations has the author's condolences. For those who truly wish to trace the threads of these personalities, please refer to the Appendix of this volume, with the caveat that it is nowhere near complete (it couldn't possibly be), and that it should be consulted only as a general guide to the field.

For now, it is enough to say that Propheta's organization became very popular with all sorts of unsavory characters.

Before Propheta was consecrated bishop, another representative of the American Orthodox Church (soon to become the American Orthodox Catholic Church) was making a name for himself and has now become—if you are one of the faithful—a *saint*. This is Carl J. Stanley, who became Archbishop Christopher Maria (now Saint Christopher Maria, canonized—by someone—on April 22, 1976). It was Carl Stanley who was referenced in the Warren Commission documents as the bishop who consecrated David Ferrie a bishop; a photograph of Stanley in his episcopal regalia will show a dignified looking sort (it's hard not to look dignified in voluminous robes and heavy golden pendants, topped by a veiled hat of the *Never On Sunday* Greek variety) that one would hesitate to associate with anti-Castro gun runners.

Stanley told the FBI that he consecrated David Ferrie as a bishop in July of 1961, but then removed him from that office the following January when Stanley learned of Ferrie's homosexuality. When the author first read Stanley's statement, he burst out laughing. Homosexuality was never a bar to either ordination or consecration at the American Orthodox Catholic Church; in fact, a successor to Stanley—one Bishop Michael Francis Augustine Itkin of the "Moorish Orthodox Diocese of Ong's Hat and Montclair, New Jersey" (I am not making this up)—was consecrated by him in November of 1960, only eight months before he consecrated Ferrie. Bishop Itkin was first ordained by Bishop George A. Hyde in 1955, Bishop Hyde being an openly gay bishop who celebrated the first divine liturgy (Orthodox prototype of what would become the Catholic "Mass") dedicated to a homosexual parish, in a gay bar in Atlanta, Georgia in 1946. Hyde openly sought converts in the pages of a magazine published by the Mattachine Society, and Itkin joined the church because he wanted to work among the gay community.

When Hyde became a little nervous about being too activist, too "out of the closet," Itkin left him and sought consecration by Stanley, who had no qualms about consecrating a gay bishop. Thus, his remarks to the FBI that Ferrie's homosexuality would have disqualified him from the episcopate is patently untrue. Even if the Itkin episode never happened, the history of the American Orthodox Catholic Church (indeed, of all the "wandering bishop" dioceses) is replete with instances of every form of sexual expression. (It's not for nothing that Propheta's headquarters—the Cathedral of the Holy Resurrection—was known as "the Cathedral of the Holy Erection" in wandering bishop circles.) Thus, there is no question in the author's mind that Ferrie was never defrocked or deposed or in any way removed from office due to homosexuality, and it is doubted that he was ever removed at all, for any reason. If he was, he would have been the first (and probably only) person ever kicked out of the wandering bishops' club. To be fair, Stanley and Itkin "parted ways" soon after Itkin's consecration: evidently because Stanley found Itkin's activism a little too "up front" for 1960, and Itkin joined yet another church, finally (at the time of this writing) winding up with the "Moorish" diocese above-mentioned, which is actually a sect with heavy cultic overtones, being a survival of something called the Moorish Temple. The Moorish Temple was the progenitor of what would become the Nation of Islam; a West Coast mystic who called himself Hakim Bey revived the Temple and made it a catch-all for occultists, magicians, Christian mystics, Islamic mystics, homosexual mystics, and assorted counter-culture types.

Thus, to summarize, we have Francis Regardie of Golden Dawn fame being initiated into the SRIA in Washington, D.C.: the same Rosicrucian cult that was behind the Holy Orthodox Church of OTO initiate Winslow Plummer and Theodotus de Witow. This same Church, run at that time by SRIA initiate de Witow, then consecrated Walter Propheta of the American Orthodox Catholic Church as well as David Ferrie. The occult organizations behind the creation of some of the wandering bishop dioceses (such as the SRIA) are venerable institutions in the eyes of occult historians; the weird churches they created, however, are considered less than respectable by the mainstream Christian denominations. Yet, it should be remembered that the Lutheran Church was also considered less than respectable by the Catholic Church, as were the groups that eventually became the Presbyterians, the Methodists, and even the Episcopalians.

This is not as strange a phenomenon as some might think. Even the Theosophical Society itself was not immune to the lure of apostolic succession. The Liberal Catholic Church is a denomination that is closely affiliated to the Theosophical Society and, for quite some time, held services every Sunday above the Quest Bookshop of the Theosophical Society in New York City. The infamous Bishop Leadbetter was a cleric of this Church as well as one of the leaders of the Theosophical Society after the death of its founder, Helena Blavatsky.

And the OTO itself—the creation of a group of German occultists with Masonic leanings who believed they held the secret of the sexual rituals of the Hindu Tantricists and the Islamic Sufis, an organization that was later kidnapped by Aleister Crowley and turned into a vehicle for his own philosophy—is allied with something called the Gnostic Catholic Church, and members and clergy of the Gnostic Catholic Church are also members of the OTO The "Gnostic Mass" is a central feature of virtually every OTO Lodge that the author has visited or researched. This Church has its lineage in another gaggle of wandering bishops who were involved in occult societies in *fin-de-siécle* France.

Thus, Ferrie and Regardie—while probably not knowing each other—were brothers under the sign of the Rose and the Cross. Ferrie's interest in occultism is hinted at by the people who knew him. It is known that he considered himself something of a hypnotist as well as a psychotherapist . . . or at least used these dubious qualifications as a lure for potential sexual partners. According to Perry Russo—one of Jim Garrison's witnesses during the Clay Shaw trial, and not necessarily the most reliable or credible of those witnesses in the eyes of many investigators—Ferrie conducted the equivalent of Black Masses in his apartment at the appropriately-numbered 3330 Louisiana Avenue Parkway, New Orleans. James Kirkwood, the Pulitzer Prize-winning author of *A Chorus Line*, conducted his own informal investigation in New Orleans during the Clay Shaw trial, published as *American Grotesque* in 1970. Kirkwood was unequivocally pro-Shaw and anti-Garrison, so although his lengthy study makes for entertaining reading, his conclusions are not always above reproach, but it is worth quoting his transcript of Perry Russo's description of Ferrie's weekly Black Masses:

> The chalice featured animal blood, the wafer consisted of some kind of raw flesh, instead of cake or bread. "He wore a little black toga, solid black. He wore nothing underneath. . . . he called it the American Eastern Catholic Orthodox Church . . . after all the ritual, shouted ritual . . . it ends up and it's a brutal thing, a sadistic quality to it—bloodletting, chicken killing, stuff like that. . . ."[18]

Previously, in his own description of Ferrie, Kirkwood states,

> He professed to be a bishop in the Orthodox Old Catholic Church of North America, a cultish underground group quite different from the Catholic Church we know.[19]

We can see that there is some confusion with the ecclesiastical nomenclature, if nothing else. This is understandable, since these groups have long, outlandish names which generally include "Orthodox" and "Catholic" and "Church" somewhere in the title, in some order. Often, the bishop concerned has consecrations with several groups so that the confusion becomes almost unmanageable. The author believes that Perry Russo actually comes closest to the name of the organization, which we now know to be the American Orthodox Catholic Church; but as we have seen there were Old Catholic elements behind Ferrie's succession as well.

The rest of Russo's characterization of the Ferrie "Black Mass" sounds more like Voudoun or Santeria than it does Satanism, and one wishes that Russo had paid a lot more attention—or that Kirkwood had published the transcript of his interview in full—so that we could trace the elements of Ferrie's ritual to a known progenitor. Kirkwood's statement that "the wafer consisted of some kind of raw flesh, instead of cake or bread" is a recension of whatever Russo actually said, and the author wonders why Kirkwood would have said "cake or bread" when no Catholic or Orthodox Church uses cake in their sacraments . . . in fact, only the Gnostic Catholic Church of the OTO is known to use something called the "cakes of light," an unpleasant (and, these days, potentially lethal) mixture of semen and menstrual fluid and other ingredients which participants in the ritual are expected to consume. Was Kirkwood making an unconscious reference to the OTO and the Gnostic Catholic Church?

Propheta's organization began fronting for intelligence agencies and setting up shop all over the world. The author has personal knowledge of several such instances, such as the improbable H.P. ("Holy Prophet") Aluya, who came to the United States from war-torn Nigeria during the Biafran crisis. The author was on hand to welcome the Prophet at Kennedy Airport in New York in 1968, as were several members of the Nigerian Consulate. Aluya was brought to the Cathedral in the Bronx, consecrated a bishop, and sent back to Nigeria with a handsome document and photographs of the consecration. The author doubts whether the Holy Prophet was even a Christian, much less an Eastern Orthodox priest deserving of consecration as a bishop. In fact, his consecration certificate bore the name "Bishop H. P. Aluya" as if "H.P." stood for, perhaps, "Harry Potter."

Another instance was the synchronization of American intelligence goals with those of the Italian government around the same time. As is well-known, Italy in the 1960s was in the throes of an active and subversive Communist movement, and cover as priests for American agents in Italy was quite valuable, particularly if one did not have to deal with the cranky and bureaucratic Catholic Church itself. The Vatican was likely to exact a pound of flesh for every agent sent over under its cover; indeed, one could not be sure that the Vatican itself was not penetrated by agents of a hostile service. The author—due to his basic ability in the French language—was pressed into service as translator of communications from several suspect religious organizations in Europe and Africa, one of which was run by a bishop in what was then the Belgian Congo. This bishop had connections among another network that runs hand-in-hand with the wandering bishops, and that is the equally bizarre world of knighthoods and royal titles.

For an unknown consideration, Propheta was to receive a Papal Knighthood from one Prince Policastro of Sicily. This had been arranged with the Belgian bishop aforementioned. This dignity was delivered to Propheta's church by two gentlemen from the Italian Embassy in a limousine. The reason for this award is not known to the author; indeed, as an award it would not have been particularly necessary since Propheta had his own purveyor of knighthoods, baronetcies, dukedoms and other such endowments in the person of Bishop Pierre Michel Lorenzo de Valitch, a putative Serbo-Croatian Count who had been in the art gallery business years before, but who now ran a flourishing trade in bogus orders of knighthood for the rich and famous. The Count's appearance was reminiscent of a young Bela Lugosi, complete with kidskin gloves, monocle, and silver-knobbed walking stick. Thus, there would have been no particular need to have gone to such extremes to pick up what the Count could have more easily provided using his own connections. The author suspects that he was being tested in this instance, and introduced to the religious underground and to some of its political affiliations.

Another suspect organization was the Greek Order of St. Dennis of Zante, an organization that numbered the elusive Father Fox among its members. Father Fox had been a priest of various denominations, including the Syrian Orthodox Church, and had studied at Fordham University. He was fluent in several foreign languages, including Arabic and Russian, and had once been caught trying to cross the border into Northern Ireland in a car with a trunk full of weapons. Fox had made trips to Vietnam during the War, and one has the suspicion it was not as a tourist. In at least one episode, it became obvious to the author that Fox was working for American intelligence as an informant, if nothing else.

Yet another personality close to the Propheta organization was the famous wrestler Antonino Rocca. Rocca—retired from wrestling at that time—claimed to be an agent of the CIA working out of Lebanon; he further claimed that he was running Phantom jets into Israel under diplomatic radar by having them shipped to Luxembourg first and then flying them into Israel, thus avoiding Arab spies and saboteurs, who would have been expecting a shipment from the United States or, at least, France or Great Britain. It also was a way of hiding the shipments from the US Congress, since the sales would not register as Israeli but as sales to Luxembourg. All of this would seem like outrageous posturing, except that Rocca made these statements before Rabbi A. Allen Block of the Brotherhood Synagogue in 1969, in a meeting including several of Propheta's clergymen as well as the author. One of the clergymen present, Andre Pennachio, was closely connected to the Teamsters Union via Joseph Konowe and to celebrities such as Harry Hershfield, Peter Sellers' astrologer Maurice Woodruff, comic Lenny Kent, and who even had a bit part in Francis Ford Coppola's *Godfather* movie, as a cleric presiding over the baptism of Michael Corleone's godchild. Pennachio also had Old Roman Catholic origins, but wound up with Propheta in late 1968, running a committee to finance his consecration as bishop in Propheta's church, which he wanted to celebrate in a big way with photographers, reception, etc. This committee was being run out of a CIA front organization in lower Manhattan, Delta Metal Industries, which was ostensibly a metal furniture import-export firm. When one of the young clergymen around Propheta and Pennachio realized that the operation was bogus, he began to fear for his life. He left the church abruptly, and caused a panic at Delta Metal Industries that their cover would be blown. His phone would ring at all hours of the day and night from people at Delta Metal and by various clergymen attempting to ascertain what he knew—including an American priest who operated in a strangely autonomous fashion within the Russian Orthodox Church Outside Russia (the "Synod")—and to determine whether or not he was going public. When they were satisfied he was not, the phones stopped ringing.

Thus, Propheta's church was a clearing-house for all sorts of intelligence operators and fellow-travelers. David Ferrie, Andre Pennachio, Antonino Rocca, Father Fox, all had crossed paths with Propheta's people or had actually been members—and bishops—of Propheta's church. The occult connection via the SRIA was also a serious one, and that connection has tainted the apostolic succession claims of many bishops in the eyes of the legitimate Orthodox Churches, who consider SRIA to be a satanic organization.

And what do we make of the strange association of David Ferrie—pilot, investigator, consecrated bishop, acquaintance of Lee Oswald, performer of Black Masses—with Guy Banister, former ONI, former FBI, former hunter of UFOs? And of Fred Crisman, author of the Maury Island Affair, former OSS, former CIA, reputed friend of Clay Shaw? UFOs and satanists, aliens and archbishops. Spies and soothsayers. Magicians . . . and Manchurian Candidates.

Another Ferrie association—and another connection that was examined by Jim Garrison's staff—was with a strange wandering bishop based in Canada: Bishop Earl Anglin Lawrence James. Ferrie had made a number of long-distance phone calls to James in the period 1962–63, and Garrison asked Metropolitan Toronto Police to follow up. The episode made the Toronto newspapers, and a report filed by the *Toronto Telegram* on November 6, 1967 was headlined "Toronto's Renegade 'Bishop' Mentioned in Garrison Probe." According to the paper, James "operates a bizarre school on Danforth Ave." What newspapermen considered "bizarre" in Toronto in 1967 is anyone's guess; not for nothing was the town known as "Toronto the Good" for many years. James denied any knowledge of Ferrie, and in fact denied he had ever been to New Orleans. That proved to be a dubious statement, since he was in possession of a Key to the City of New Orleans, had membership cards in various Louisiana and New Orleans organizations, including one naming him an "Honorary Attorney General" of the State of Louisiana, another that named him a Colonel on the staff of Earl K. Long, and possessed various other police and investigation agency paper litter, and including a United States Social Security card. The one phone call he admits he received from New Orleans was from a "Mr. J. S. Martin. It was a personal call." J.S. Martin is, of course, Jack Martin, the man who was beaten by Ferrie associate and former FBI SAC Guy Banister shortly after the Kennedy assassination. Ferrie and Martin were involved in "investigating" phony diploma mills—according to Ferrie's testimony to government investigators—but they had a falling out and Martin went his own way.

According to the paper's report, James had been a bishop of the Old Roman Catholic Church in 1945, but had been excommunicated two years later. The story is more interesting than these bare bones would indicate, however.

James was indeed consecrated—on June 17, 1945—by the infamous Henry Carfora, the guiding light behind the Old Roman Catholic Church and its policy of consecrating all and sundry in those days. Carfora was assisted in this consecration by the indomitable Hubert Augustus Rogers. Thus, James' pedigree is firmly in the wandering bishop camp.

To make matters if possible any more complicated, Christopher Carl Stanley—the bishop who was being "investigated" by Jack Martin and who consecrated David Ferrie a bishop—was *himself* consecrated by the same Earl Anglin Lawrence James.

Thus we have a direct line of apostolic assassination succession from Carfora to James to Stanley to Ferrie: *the latter three all at one time or another suspects in the Kennedy assassination conspiracy*. This is not to forget the line that goes from Carfora to Stanley to Propheta.

Before Kennedy was elected President, however, Bishop James was the lucky recipient of the Eloy Alfaro Award, an obscure dignity that was conferred upon him in New York City and announced on the floor of the House of Representatives of the United States Congress on August 23, 1960. He was given this award—the Eloy Alfaro Grand Cross—for his "extraordinary achievements and accomplishments . . . within the framework of the services rendered by him to his fellow human beings and to the cause of international peace."[20] The person who read this event into the Record was Republican Representative Robert R. Barry. The actual ceremony took place at the Hotel Astor, appropriately enough.

The Master of Ceremonies was a psychiatrist, Dr. Herbert Holt, who conferred the Cross and diploma on James for his "outstanding work in behalf of humanity all over the civilized world as a dynamic religious leader and a great humanitarian . . ." and etc., etc. Other recipients of this award, according to Holt, were "President Eisenhower, former Presidents Harry S. Truman and Herbert Hoover, Senator Lyndon Johnson, Governors Rockefeller and Averell Harriman, Generals MacArthur, Crittenberger, Devers, and the Rt. Rev. Benjamin C. Eckardt, of Canada . . ."[21] Eckardt is yet another "autonomous bishop," and it is possible that he suggested to the committee that the award go to James, but this is purely speculation on my part.

Now Dr. Holt would go on to greater glory as the head of something called the Westchester Institute for Training in Psychoanalysis and Psychotherapy. According to the Institute's brochure, Holt was a "Viennese-trained psychiatrist and psychoanalyst who, in a series of papers and books, built upon the ground that Freud had established but added a holistic and phenomenological/existential emphasis as well."

We find Dr. Holt attending a meeting of the Society for the Scientific Study of Religion at the Mayflower Hotel in Washington, D.C. on Halloween, 1964, giving a talk on "Existential Analysis and Pastoral Counseling." At this time, Holt gave his affiliation as the New York Institute of Existential Analysis. Obviously, his interest was in the psychology of religion, and especially in the use of psychology within a pastoral setting. The Westchester Institute still offers training in this discipline, and has expanded the curriculum to include Jungian concepts as well.

What did Herbert Holt have in common with the "renegade bishop of Toronto," a man who had a mysterious past, who claimed more than 100 degrees—although he dropped out of the University of Toronto after only one year—and who was an associate of some of the most bizarre figures surrounding the Kennedy assassination? What great contribution did James make to the world to justify not only his receiving the Eloy Alfaro Award but having it read into the Congressional Record?

Most of the members of the Society for the Scientific Study of Religion were theologians or scholars of religion, such as the well-respected Peter L. Berger of the New School. In 1964, the vice-president of the Society was Paul W. Pruyser of the Menninger Foundation, an organization known to have ties to the CIA's mind control programs, but that is a tenuous connection at best. The name of the organization itself suggests an intelligence agenda, since MK-ULTRA was nothing if not a "scientific study of religion"; however, at this point the trail runs cold.

The only clue we have to what was really going on with Holt, James, Stanley, Ferrie, Propheta, and the rest is the connection between the Old Roman Catholic Church and hypnosis, specifically the interests in hypnosis of not only Ferrie but also William Bryan, Jr., who claimed he was the technical advisor for the film version of *The Manchurian Candidate*. It was Bryan who worked a score of well-known criminal cases, including the Boston Strangler case, and who claimed he worked for the CIA. He claimed also to have hypnotized Sirhan Sirhan, something that could only have happened *before* the young Palestinian assassinated Robert F. Kennedy. As we shall see in the next chapter, Bryan was a member—and possibly a bishop—of the Old Roman Catholic Church.

To most people, the association of hard-core occultists and members of secret societies and Masonic groups such as the SRIA, the Golden Dawn and the OTO with the Old Roman Catholic Church, the American Orthodox Catholic Church, and—God help us—the Moorish Orthodox Diocese of Ong's Hat and Montclair, New Jersey would seem to be illogical. Why would occultists and magicians hunger after "apostolic succession," mitres, cassocks, croziers and *panagias*? The answer is simple, and sinister.

The Black Mass which Ferrie was accused of performing is a ritual that mocks those of the Catholic Church; essentially, it is an attempt at organized blasphemy, an attack of rebellion, political as well as theological. It is also designed to attract demonic influences, evil spirits and the souls of the angry dead. Yet, this ritual carries very little weight if performed by a lay-person. It is potentially quite powerful, however, if performed by an ordained priest.

A valid ordination is one of the most singular sources of spiritual strength in the West. It is a line of ritual, faith and trust that extends back in time through two thousand years; to those who believe in the power of the "laying on of hands" it is potent magic, indeed. Aleister Crowley, dubbed by the myopic British tabloids as the "wickedest man in the world," could not perform a Black Mass no matter how much he may have liked to (there is no evidence that he ever wanted to). He was not an ordained priest.

Further, many rituals of ceremonial magic prescribe the use of relics and other articles that could only be sourced from the Church, thus giving rise to a great deal of theft and subterfuge. A priest, however, has immediate access to all of this and possesses the power to create more: holy water, holy oil, a consecrated Host, etc. Inasmuch as many grimoires—cookbooks of ritual magic—insist on invoking God, Jesus, Mary, the Saints, etc., the use of genuinely blessed religious artifacts would, of course, give the ritual that much more authority.

Thus, David Ferrie—should his line of apostolic succession prove valid—could "legitimately" perform a Black Mass whereas Crowley (from all available evidence) would not have been able to do so. This should not be viewed as the sole objective, however. Many occultists value the line of succession as a source of spiritual power whether or not they consider themselves Christian. Power is power, wherever it is found and by whatever means it can be obtained; a validly ordained priest has the power to perform most of the sacraments, and the validly consecrated bishop has the power to perform *all* of the sacraments including ordaining more priests and consecrating more bishops, thus ensuring a line of power for his cult equal to that of the Catholic Church. The allure is irresistible.

Add all of this to espionage activities and you have a perfect fruit salad of paranoia, power and prestige, mixing secret government work with secret rituals and the manipulation of those sinister forces we have been studying. The secret handshake of the cult and the secret code of the intelligence agency: they both invoke the power of relationships that are beyond the reach of the ordinary human being. The cultist believes he can summon the very hounds of hell to his aid; the intelligence agent can overthrow a government, terminate a politician, or call in an air strike. Either way, the Gates of the Underworld are opened.

In an interesting side note to all of this, H.P. Lovecraft in his short story "The Horror at Red Hook" (1925) mentions a church in Brooklyn that had been turned into a dance hall. This church actually existed; to the author's best recollection it was on Amity Street, but that may be a confabulation. In any event, it was only a few blocks south of Atlantic Avenue; south, that is, of Brooklyn Heights, where Lovecraft lived for a short time during his equally short marriage. Briefly, in the 1970s, that church had been taken over by another one of Propheta's renegade churches, this one practicing a kind of Roman Ritual under an Eastern Orthodox aegis. The church was also—and at the same time—believed to be a place where satanic or occult ceremonies were performed. It was only a few blocks away from the infamous Warlock Shop, a location that figures prominently—though never by name—in Maury Terry's study of the Son of Sam cult, *Ultimate Evil.*

EXECUTIVE ACTION

I remember staying home from school with a stomach ache the day Kennedy was shot. My family had moved to Charlestown, New Hampshire from Chicago that summer; we lived in an old saltbox-style house at the top of Hubbard Hill, a place reputed to be haunted, due to the fact that it used to be a prison farm at one time, and more recently it was suspected that old Percy Whitmore had murdered his wife and daughter on the place and buried them in the woods. Discovering a hidden panel in the house where Percy kept some poisons elaborately labeled with skull-and-crossbones didn't ameliorate the feeling that there was something strange about the farm.

That afternoon, I was sitting in bed on the second floor of the house, gazing out the window at the gray day and the tree line, when my mother suddenly appeared in the doorway and said, "They've shot the President." *They.*

At the same moment, a few hundred miles to the north in Montreal, Dr. James Monroe was paying a visit to Dr. Ewen Cameron at the Allen Memorial Clinic. A former Air Force officer and MK-ULTRA project leader in brainwashing studies, Monroe was in charge of the funds of the Human Ecology Society, which served as the Cameron project's front. As the airwaves broadcast the news of the assassination of President Kennedy at the Clinic, Monroe stopped and made a phone call to Washington. When he returned, he told Cameron that CIA sponsorship of his program was terminated.[22] The reader does not need to be advised that this was a strange and compelling combination of events, indicative of a deeply sinister agenda.

At the same time, three thousand miles away in California, Aldous Huxley died. The pioneer of the psychedelic revolution, author of *Brave New World*, *The Doors of Perception* and *Heaven and Hell,* lost consciousness without ever learning of the assassination of the President.

At the same time, Andrija Puharich was out of the country, in Brazil; George de Mohrenschildt was out of the country, in Haiti; E. Howard Hunt (according to a CIA memo) was in Dallas, but denies it; Richard Nixon was in Dallas; David Ferrie had just come from the courthouse in New Orleans, where he helped Mafia kingpin Carlos Marcello beat his latest rap. An anonymous phone call from Bell Helicopter told Dallas police that Marina Oswald was staying at the Paines'. And MK-ULTRA ramped up like never before.

Haitian President-for-Life "Papa Doc" Duvalier celebrated when Kennedy was killed, claiming that his powers of voudoun had caused the President's demise. To Duvalier, the number "22" had mystical associations with voudoun powers, and he used that number on his personal license plate. Kennedy was killed, of course, on November 22. The number 11/22 tickled Duvalier, who asked his cronies what more proof they needed of his occult abilities? Duvalier had long suspected Kennedy of having evil designs on his dictatorship; the threat of armed intervention was never very far away. (The US had already intervened in the Dominican Republic, with which Haiti shares the island of Hispaniola, and had invaded Haiti several times in the past.) Having George de Mohrenschildt there in Haiti with him the day Kennedy was killed must have been somewhat . . . comforting.

The religious, mystical dimension to this study leads in many directions. Suffice it to say that swirling about the feet and hands of the Kennedy assassination was a sticky fog of occultists, wandering bishops, American intelligence . . . and alien intelligence known as The Nine. Arthur Young, Michael Paine, Ruth Paine, Ruth Forbes Young, Andrija Puharich, Mary Astor, even David Ferrie were all a handshake or two away from Jack Kennedy's alleged assassin, Lee Harvey Oswald. They were all talking to ghosts, summoning alien beings, practicing ritual magic, holding hands around the séance table or sacrificing chickens in a New Orleans apartment.

And, in some cases, they were also members of America's ruling elite, the wealthiest and best-connected families in the country.

What were they really channeling?

ENDNOTES

1 Octavio Paz, *The Labyrinth of Solitude*, Grove Press, NY, 1978, ISBN 0-394-17242-6, p. 69

2 Umberto Eco, "The Force of Falsity," *Serendipities*, Orion Books, London, 1998, ISBN 0-75282-647-6, p. 3

3 Bishop Clement of Alexandria (C. AD 150-215), from Morton Smith, *The Secret Gospel*, quoted in Lawrence Gardiner, *Bloodline of the Holy Grail*, Element, Dorset, 1996, ISBN 1-86204-152-0, p. 92

4 Umberto Eco, *Reflections on the Name of the Rose*, Minerva, London, 1994, ISBN 07493-9627-X, p. 54

5 Maurice Maeterlinck, *The Cloud That Lifted*, The Century Company, NY, 1923

6 Peter Dale Scott, *Deep Politics and the Death of JFK*, University of California Press, Berkeley, 1996, ISBN 0-520-20519-7

7 Christopher S. Hyatt, editor, *An Interview With Israel Regardie: His Final Thoughts and Views*, Falcon Press, Phoenix, 1985, ISBN 0-941404-31-5, p. 5–6

8 Cited in Richard A. Schweder, "Why Do Men Barbecue? And Other Postmodern Ironies and Growing Up in the Decade of Ethnicity," in *Harpers*, Vol. 286, No. 1717, June 1983, p. 22

9 Arthur M. Young, "Fear of the Unknown," 1983, on the Arthur Young website, www. arthuryoung.com

10 Israel Regardie, *The Golden Dawn*, Llewellyn, St. Paul, 1986, ISBN 0-87542-663-8, p. 630

11 Douglas Hill & Pat Williams, *The Supernatural*, Hawthorn Books, NY, 1965, LOC 66-11502, p. 331–3

12 Jacques Vallee, *Forbidden Science*, North Atlantic Books, Berkeley, ISBN 1-55643125-2, p. 1992, p. 77–78

13 Jim Garrison, *On The Trail of the Assassins*, Warner, NY, 1988, ISBN 0-446-362778, p. 71

14 Anthony Summers, *The Kennedy Conspiracy*, Warner, NY, 1996, ISBN 0-7515-03401, p. 145

15 Ibid., p. 201

16 Dick Russell, *The Man Who Knew Too Much*, Carroll & Graf, NY, 2003, ISBN 07867-1242-2, p. 203

17 There are not many reliable sources on the origins and lineages of these groups, but the reader may depend upon Ellic Howe, *The Magicians of the Golden Dawn*, Samuel Weiser, NY, 1978, ISBN 0-87728-369-9 and Ithell Colquhoun, *Sword of Wisdom: MacGregor Mathers and the Golden Dawn*, Putnam, NY, 1975, SBN 339-11534-X. While focusing on the Golden Dawn, both sources contain histories of the SRIA and its manifestations and personalities.

18 James Kirkwood, *American Grotesque*, HarperPerennial, NY, 1992, ISBN 0-06097523-7, p. 627

19 Ibid., p. 124

20 *Congressional Record*, August 23, 1960

21 Ibid.

22 John Marks, *The Search for the Manchurian Candidate*, Times Books, NY, 1979, ISBN 0-8129-0773-6, p 155–156; Gordon Thomas, *Journey Into Madness*, Bantam, NY, 1990, ISBN 0-553-28413-4, p. 245–6

Rosemary's Baby (1967) front cover, first edition

BOOK ONE: THE NINE

CHAPTER EIGHT

ROSEMARY'S BABY

I knew by now that when a group of individuals gravitated toward one another for no apparent reason, or a group of individuals inexplicably headed in the same direction as if drawn by a magnetic field, or coincidence piled on coincidence too many times, as often as not the shadowy outlines of a covert intelligence operation were somehow becoming visible.

—Jim Garrison[1]

Chains of more-than-coincidence occur so often in my life that, if I am forbidden to call them supernatural hauntings, let me call them a habit. Not that I like the word 'supernatural'; I find these happenings natural enough, though superlatively unscientific.

—Robert Graves[2]

I don't believe you can ever solve a murder.

—George P. Pelecanos[3]

The President was in his Navy uniform. He had completely recovered from the assassination and looked better than ever.

—Ira Levin[4]

The day after the assassination of President Kennedy, his former mistress Mary Pinchot Meyer phoned LSD guru Timothy Leary to tell him that the President was murdered by a conspiracy at the highest levels of government.

Mary Pinchot Meyer (1920–1964) had once been married to CIA Chief of Covert Action Operations Cord Meyer, Jr. Cord Meyer, a former Marine lieutenant who was badly wounded on Guam in 1944, joined the CIA in late 1950 and gradually rose through the ranks, being at one time Chief of Station in London and later Deputy Director of Plans. Mary Meyer was something of a free spirit, however, a painter and the woman who smoked pot with Jack Kennedy. She had been a friend of Leary since the early 1960s—and of the Kennedys before that—and spoke to him of a very important friend of hers who was interested in the LSD experience, and asked for tips on how to guide the LSD trip, leading some investigators to believe that she had turned the President on to acid, as well.

Leary certainly provided Mary Meyer with acid, without knowing the identity of her important friend. When Leary began to actively promote acid consumption by the masses, Mary warned him that this was not what the CIA wanted him to do, but rather that he should study the effects of the drug on his test subjects and report back discretely. She had already succeeded, she told him, in turning on certain high-ranking members of the Washington establishment. Leary, however, had other ideas. "Turn On, Tune In, Drop Out" became the slogan of the disaffected young of the 1960s, a sly counterpoint to "You Shall Know The Truth, And The Truth Will Set You Free," the slogan or motto of both the CIA and NASA.

Mary Meyer was murdered less than a year after the Kennedy assassination—on October 12, 1964 (coincidentally Aleister Crowley's birthday, and of course the day Columbus discovered America)—and her diary disappeared. She seemed to have been the victim of a mugging in Georgetown during the lunch hour, shot in the face at close range on a towpath, although the level of violence in the attack made it look suspicious to some, and the accused murderer was acquitted by a jury due to lack of evidence. The disappearance of her diary caused some concern in her friends—after all, she was married to a high-ranking CIA officer and had turned the President (and who knew how many others) on to pot and possibly LSD as well. But evidence later would show that the diary was found by her sister, and surrendered to James Jesus Angleton, the CIA's paranoid Chief of Counter Intelligence and one of Cord Meyer's closest friends, who had been in Mary Meyer's apartment with a key long before her other friends arrived, looking for the same diary. Meyer was single, no longer married to Cord Meyer by this time, having divorced him much earlier. Her sister, Tony Pinchot, had been married to Ben Bradlee of the *Washington Post*. This is perhaps an indication of how incestuous these relationships become: Mary Pinchot Meyer, Tony Pinchot Bradlee, Ben Bradlee, Cord Meyer, Timothy Leary, Jack Kennedy . . .

Angleton did not destroy the diary, however. What he did with it while it was in his possession is open to debate, but he eventually gave it back to Tony Bradlee, who then destroyed it herself. It seems very odd that the Bradlees would have given the diary to Angleton to destroy in the first place; destroying a book is not exactly rocket science. It would have been a simple matter to rip out the pages and burn them, or flush them for that matter. But the diary went to Angleton, who took it to the CIA, who then did not destroy it, who then gave it back to the Bradlees to destroy.

Mary Meyer evidently believed that Jack Kennedy was killed on orders of people in the US government, and this is the gist of what she told Leary. Leary, a consummate showman who could have made much hay out of this, did not exploit the information at all and tended to downplay it or change the subject when asked. There has been a lot of speculation (much of it rather silly) in the counter-culture press that Leary was a CIA agent, or that Kennedy had been yet another MK-ULTRA guinea pig, etc. The facts of Mary Meyer's death may be simple: a mugging gone wrong. Yet the number and quality of the relationships is compelling, and this is what begets conspiracy theories. It is understandably difficult to believe that a woman who was sleeping with Kennedy, smoking pot with him and perhaps turning him on to LSD, a woman who was also a close personal friend of Timothy Leary and who believed that Kennedy had been murdered as a result of a conspiracy, moreover a woman who was married to a high-ranking CIA official who was at that time in charge of "dirty tricks," would have died a violent death that was somehow *not* related to the assassination or its coverup. Like the Kennedy assassination itself, there are way too many suggestive relationships; Angleton's fast trip to Mary Meyer's home to find the diary suggests that he was worried about far more than a revelation that she had been sleeping with Jack Kennedy. One does not get the impression that Angleton would have been worried about Jack Kennedy's reputation being tarnished; he would have been more worried about the intelligence implications of what would have been contained in the diary. The Warren Commission Report had been published the previous month. This was also during the time of the Nosenko debriefing, in which Angleton was certain KGB defector Yuri Nosenko was a plant, a false defector, sent by Moscow that January to do serious damage to the CIA. Angleton must have worried about the possible use Mary Meyer's diary would be to Soviet intelligence, for the type of intelligence information contained therein (pillow talk with the most powerful man in the world until his assassination less than a year earlier) might well have been damaging to national security.

The Mary Pinchot Meyer case is only one of many "scarlet threads" running through this narrative of American necromancy. It is not even the most shocking shade of red. Yet it suggested the use of a mind-expanding drug by the President of the United States, provided by Timothy Leary to the President's mistress. Had the CIA ever imagined that the drug they brought into the United States in the 1950s to test as an interrogation tool—the drug they used to dose Frank Olson unknowing unto death—would have filtered *up* as well as down?

The following year, Yale psychologist Dr. Jose Delgado demonstrated one of the most powerful applications of electronic technology in the area of mind control at the time. Delgado used brain implants to control an enraged bull in front of spectators. Using only a remote control device—a small, handheld box in his hands—he was able to increase the bull's aggression to the point that it charged the psychologist, who was standing quietly in an arena with no protective devices, and then, with a press of a button in Delgado's hand, the crazed animal suddenly stopped on a dime. This demonstration was widely reported in the press in May of 1965, and Delgado presented a lecture at the American Museum of Natural History in New York City that month on electrical stimulation of the brain. Although Delgado admitted that the technology at the time was crude, it was certainly effective. One can imagine the effect of this vivid demonstration on American (and Soviet, and Chinese) intelligence agencies. It also had other implications, for concentration on the electrical approach to behavior control might have been at odds with the purely chemical approach that had been developed to a certain extent under MK-ULTRA.

The electrical approach would likely seem more promising to a group of researchers who would consider such a "push-button" technique of controlling behavior as more reliable than a chemical technique which was more variable—in terms of results obtained, dosages, etc.—with each person. The drawback, of course, would be the need to physically implant electrical devices in the target subject's body; further, the experiments by Delgado were limited to very basic behavioral models, such as aggression and motor control. What the CIA needed was a more sophisticated switch that would point the subject in a specific direction—at a specific target, say—and no other. The "raging bull" model would not be sufficiently fine-tuned for the CIA's purposes. However, the results were very promising in that they showed that outside control of a sentient being's actions was possible. There had been no psychoanalysis of the bull, of course, no psychological interviews, no Rorschach tests, no MMPIs. It was a simple matter of knowing where to place the electrodes. It could, theoretically, be done to anyone, and with no need for a prior evaluation of that person's psyche. No need for Dr. Cameron's "sleep room" or depatterning exercises, procedures that were time-consuming and dangerous, and which often did not result in usable subjects. The individual person's will (and identity) was no longer an issue; the issue was the human will in general, how it could be overridden in anyone with the use of the proper electronic device.

In June 1972 Dr. Sidney Gottlieb—he of the LSD-spiked cocktail to Dr. Frank Olson—proposed a serious program of ESB (Electrical Stimulation of the Brain) to CIA Director Richard Helms, based on the work of both Delgado and neurosurgeon Dr. Robert G. Heath of Tulane, whose experiments with stimulating pleasure centers in the human brain using electrodes were fascinating, and filled with potential for behavior control. By identifying the brain's pleasure centers they were one step closer to mapping the electronic grid of the brain to the point that pleasure, pain, aggression, fear, and violence could be switched on and off at will—someone else's will.[5] This program was approved, and CIA development of ESB proceeded apace; but before this approach was considered, CIA was still investigating the use of drugs, hypnosis and other chemical and psychological means towards the creation of a Manchurian Candidate. In the meantime, however, other parties were developing their own version of a mindless killer, using the same combination of drugs and psychology.

AS IT IS

On 1946, Jack Parsons' occult partner in the Babalon Working was L. Ron Hubbard, the founder of Scientology. Hubbard would claim to have been investigating Parsons on behalf of some government agency—the FBI or ONI—but that claim has never borne out. Hubbard's military record is available, and it is rather dismal. His wheedling for disability benefits is particularly sad. Hubbard was what he always appeared to be, a struggling science fiction writer and confidence man who borrowed a great deal from his apprenticeship with Jack Parsons, and who stole much else. It is somehow depressing that the most famous example of the work of this brilliant scientist and idealistic young occultist would be Hubbard and his Church of Scientology, but there it is. (Sorry, Tom; John; Kirstie.)

On the other hand, Scientology would love to distance itself as much as possible from its Crowleyan origins, but the Pasadena episode sticks quite tightly, particularly as Hubbard would go on to marry Betty Northrup, whom he met as Parsons' *soror mystica*. As more and more evidence comes to light, there is no way for Hubbard's spiritual heirs to continue the charade that L. Ron was simply trying to break up a black magic ring that was populated by rocket scientists with security clearances. The lawsuit against Hubbard, filed in Miami by Parsons when the former stole his money and made off in one of the boats for parts unknown, stands as a different kind of evidence: of fraud, theft, and the deepest form of betrayal.

It was perhaps inevitable that Hubbard's philosophy of enlightened self-interest would result in the Process Church of the Final Judgment, usually referred to simply as the Process. Formed sometime in 1963–64 as a splinter group from Scientology, its founder was Robert Moore, a British subject who was born in Shanghai on August 10, 1935 and had been—according to one account—a cavalry officer who had served time in Malaya (that favorite haunt of witchcraft guru Gerald Gardner, *Clockwork Orange* author Anthony Burgess, and the *Heart of Darkness*' Joseph Conrad), and who later lived in London at the time of the Process' creation. At the Hubbard Institute of Scientology in London he met Mary Anne MacLean, a woman who is said to have been engaged to prizefighter Sugar Ray Robinson in America for a brief period, before returning to England. Mary Anne MacLean was born in Glasgow on November 20, 1931, and was thus four years Robert Moore's senior. Before she met Moore, however, she became involved with several high-ranking British politicians á la Christine Keeler of the Profumo affair. As mentioned earlier, Christine Keeler was the mistress of both British War Minister John Profumo and Soviet GRU agent Yevgeny Ivanov; she herself has also alleged that she slept with President John Kennedy on a trip she made to the United States in the summer of 1962. The Profumo Affair has other resonances with our story, since it also includes occultist Stephen Ward—an osteopath who was a friend of Christine Keeler as well as a kind of go-between for Profumo, Keeler and Ivanov, and who had many high-society celebrities as friends and patients and subjects for his other passion, portraiture, including Claus von Bulow, Sophia Loren, Frank Sinatra, Elizabeth Taylor, even Joseph Kennedy. Some authors have linked him to the Golden Dawn, but the author has been unable to find evidence of this; by 1963 there wasn't enough left of the Golden Dawn anyway to have made the association particularly relevant. Stephen Ward committed suicide when he was convicted—wrongly, as it turned out—of having lived on the proceeds of prostitution (i.e., Keeler and her friends). He could not take the humiliation and, on August 3, 1963, took an overdose of Nembutal instead.

This, then, was the situation at the time Mary Anne MacLean met Robert Moore at Scientology headquarters in London; they then decided to break away, form their own operation, and get married. For someone like Mary Anne, it was probably a wise move: her profile in British society was not entirely low. Engaged to an American prizefighter, running in the same circles as Keeler and her associates, who were all being rounded up to "help the police in their inquiries," it was a smart move to decamp to the Scientologists and marry an intelligent and charismatic architect like Robert Moore, as cover if nothing else. Further, the circumstances of the Profumo Affair and of Stephen Ward's participation in it, suggested a far deeper political agenda that involved Jack Kennedy, the British government, the Soviet government, and the Cuban Missile Crisis, as declassified FBI and CIA files suggest. It has also been revealed that Dr. Ward was the go-between for the British intelligence services and the Soviet GRU (military intelligence) via his friendship with Yevgeny Ivanov, and that possibly Ward had manipulated Keeler into sleeping with Ivanov as part of a classic "honey trap," in case they needed to blackmail the Russian agent into defecting at some later date. War Minister Profumo was essentially caught in the middle, having also slept with the evidently irresistible Ms. Keeler. Mary Anne MacLean's former fiance, Sugar Ray Robinson, had even intended to make a film of the Profumo Affair with Christine Keeler in the starring role opposite Sugar Ray himself,[6] thus strengthening the link between MacLean, Robinson, Keeler and the Profumo Affair . . . and from Profumo to Process.

The headquarters of the Process in London was on Fitzroy Street in the early days, before moving to a large house on Balfour Place in 1966. The philosophy of Robert and Mary Anne Moore (now known as Robert and Mary Anne de Grimston, a name of cultic significance to them) was a mixture of reincarnation, existentialism, some concepts adapted from Scientology, an attempt to merge the worships of Jehova and Lucifer, and a bit of neo-Nazi flavor. Their emblem was a stylized swastika, which in all fairness could have meant they were Buddhist; however, the philosophy of the Process and its alleged origins as a front for a German neo-fascist group, coupled with Mary Anne's belief that she was the reincarnation of Joseph Goebbels, seems to indicate a Nazi rather than a Buddhist inspiration. Further, the group was known to have kept thirty German shepherds on hand as a kind of totem-cum-guard dog arrangement. It was this very public association of German shepherds with the Process that would later lead some investigators in the United States to link Process members or former members with a series of sacrifices of these particular dogs where cult activity was believed to be taking place.

That same June, a large group of Process members—replete with dogs—spent a few months in Nassau and later in Mexico for reasons that are not clear, before returning to London to begin publishing their magazine and a book by Robert de Grimston, *As It Is*. It is known that, while in Mexico on the Yucatan peninsula, de Grimston added Satan to the Jehova-Lucifer deities of their group and, according to Maury Terry, held moonlight rituals on the beach at Xtul to invoke the Dark Lords.[7] By the time they had returned to London at the end of the summer they were ready to launch the Process in a much more aggressive manner, luring singer Marianne Faithfull into their organization. Ms. Faithfull is yet another solid link between the Process and Thelemic organizations in the United States, as she was known to belong to the same circle as Kenneth Anger, Anita Pallenberg, Marjorie Cameron, and Manson Family member Bobby Beausoleil, and had appeared in one of Anger's Crowleyan films, *Lucifer Rising*, as we shall see below.

In 1967, the Process set up camp in San Francisco, a few doors down from where Manson was living at the time on Cole Street. By the spring of 1968, they were in Los Angeles, and making a frontal assault on the entertainment industry (something the DeGrimstons had perhaps learned during their sojourn at the Scientology operation). Dressed in black, German shepherds at the leash, and speaking about worshipping Jehova, Lucifer and Satan, they were a pretty common sight in California. In 1966, Anton LaVey had already opened his Church of Satan to much media hoopla in San Francisco, so Californians were getting used to Satan-worshippers and oddly-dressed, blackly-dressed young people working on their satanic stares while everyone else was working on their tans. And then, in the summer of 1968, the Californian operation of the Process suddenly went underground.

On May 28,1966, a young Palestinian immigrant fascinated with the occult had attended his first meeting of the Ancient Mystical Order Rosae Crucis (AMORC) at the society's Akhnaton Lodge in Pasadena, and was the subject of an experiment in sensory perception, sitting blindfolded while attempting to identify objects by touch.[8] AMORC was one of the many splinter groups that broke off from the SRIA in England; they had OTO and Golden Dawn connections, but created a distinctly American style of recruiting: direct mail. Most people of a certain generation are familiar with those large ads in all sorts of magazines with the tag "What Secret Power Did These Men Possess?" and a P.O. box where one could send for information and begin a correspondence course in mental telepathy, meditation and, eventually, magic.

This interest continued for the next few years. In March 1968, the Palestinian was in Pasadena—where he lived with his mother, some blocks north of where Jack Parsons had lived in the 1940s and 1950s—attending a meeting of the Theosophical Society's Adyar Lodge. (That same month, the Process set up shop on South Cochrane Street in Los Angeles.)

A few months later, he would be arrested for the assassination of Senator Robert F. Kennedy. The Palestinian, of course, was Sirhan Bishara Sirhan.

Much ink has been spilled on the subject of the Process; Ed Sanders in the first edition of *The Family* links the Process with an amoebic network of death cults in California and from there to Manson; investigative journalist Maury Terry has linked them to Charles Manson as well as to the Son of Sam killings. The problem is that the linkages are there, but not enough to put a smoking gun in the hands of the Process itself. Of course, that is the problem with the entire field of conspiracy theory as well. What we are looking at in this case are mostly philosophical influences—which are certain to become a subject for academic study in another twenty or thirty years—and the "deep politics" connections of which Professor Peter Dale Scott writes so eloquently. The fidgety reader may complain that the American system of jurisprudence is such that one cannot be arrested on suspicion of undue influence over another; but, of course, that is exactly what happened in the case of Charles Manson, who did not actually murder anyone at the Tate or LaBianca households, but who was convicted of the murders anyway and would have been executed had not the State of California abolished the death penalty during his incarceration.

The Charles Manson case is germane to the study of the Process, since Manson was known to them and had even written an article for the "Death" issue of their magazine (in all fairness, Marianne Faithfull and Salvador Dali also wrote for the *Process* magazine; however, what put scroungy little Charles Manson in the same company as Faithfull and Dali?); and, as his prosecutor Vincent Bugliosi has written, members of the Process visited Manson in prison after his arrest for the Tate/LaBianca killings. At one point, Manson is known to have boasted, "I *am* Robert Moore."[9] Thus, it would behoove us to study this group a little to see how they could have become involved with Charles Manson and, by extension, the Tate/LaBianca killings and—if Maury Terry is correct—a spate of killings from California to New York City. (One of the murderous cults in California supposedly linked to Manson and to Maury Terry's "Manson II" was something called "Four P." A glance at the Process' logo—the stylized swastika—will show it is basically four P's in a circle.)

In all of that ink, a lot of nonsense has been promulgated about the Process, as critics such as Robert Hicks[10] have been quick to point out. That strange new breed of law enforcement officer, the "cult cop," has been all over the Process, the OTO, and the Church of Satan, with seminar leaders telling wide-eyed police officers around the country that these cults are dangerous, using mind control methods, and committing murder and mayhem on a global scale. To anyone who has had any direct dealings at all with these groups, the accusations are absurd. The Church of Satan was at best a gimmicky New Age operation; at worst it was a magnet for the type of neurotics that LaVey himself would eventually banish. The OTO couldn't organize a box lunch much less a nationwide program of human sacrifice. And the Process does not exist any longer, and hasn't existed for almost thirty years.

On the other hand . . .

It is a fact of life that many people who join or are attracted to organizations like the three mentioned above are much more serious than their leaders. To judge all Church of Satan members by the writings or the actions of its founder, Anton LaVey, would be a mistake. LaVey, for instance, talked a good game, but it was little COS vampire Susan Atkins who plunged the knife into Sharon Tate, killing both the actress and her unborn child. To judge all OTO members by their leaders would be to reduce that organization's reputation considerably. Jack Parsons and British occultist and author Kenneth Grant are good examples of people that the OTO administration did *not* like, but who have in past years become icons of the Order, and its best representatives. As for the Process, Robert Moore aka Robert de Grimston has distanced himself completely from his creation. One published account even states that he was "purged" from the Church and that his wife, Mary Ann de Grimston, took over and further emasculated the group.[11] When critics of the cult cops rightly point to the many logical inconsistencies in the way the police describe the very cults they investigate, they ignore something darker that is taking place. Indeed, the Process was itself a splinter group of Scientology; the Church of Satan was a rebellion against Christianity; the OTO was an attempt to inject new life into dusty old Freemasonry. And these groups have spawned their own splinters, their own renegade branches that have taken the original ideas a step or two further and usually in a dangerous direction. To the outside world, these people are all "Process" or "Church of Satan" or even "OTO," but in fact most of them have severed any formal links with these organizations before they began their criminal activity. What the occult Orders have done, however, deliberately or not, is provide these individuals—often more dedicated, more serious, even more charismatic than their own leaders—with the philosophical basis for their actions; in many cases, providing them with the ritual tools, jargon, and psychological conditioning necessary not only to perpetrate their crimes, but to scare the living daylights out of the rest of the population.

Many people in the New York City area, including some very serious occultists, were originally drawn to the OTO when it made its resurgence in 1977. It was the time of *Star Wars* and *Close Encounters of the Third Kind*. The hottest underground novel was Robert Anton Wilson's *Illuminatus!* trilogy, all about conspiracy theories, occultism, secret societies and consciousness expansion, with healthy dollops of sex, drugs, and rock-n-roll. The occult was on the increase, the Church of Satan was actively recruiting, as were the Wicca covens, and the OTO had decided to get back in the game after almost twenty years of lying low.

At that time, the most prominent member of the OTO in New York was Kristopher Dowling, who later became a "Celtic Orthodox" priest in the Bishop Propheta succession. Gnostic Masses were held in the back of the Magickal Childe Bookstore in Manhattan, the last incarnation of the old Warlock Shop in Brooklyn Heights. Gradually, the OTO went through some serious internal struggles and a fight ensued between two opposing factions, one led by a Brazilian, Marcello Motta, and the other by Grady McMurtry, who had been an Army officer and then a teacher at George Washington University. He had been referred to Aleister Crowley by Jack Parsons, who had recommended that the two visit when McMurtry was in England during the Second World War. This was done, and when McMurtry returned to the United States he was put in nominal charge of Parsons' Pasadena lodge, to Parsons' dismay. Yet, by the 1950s, the OTO was more or less moribund in America, with McMurtry in Washington, D.C., living his own life in apparently great distance from the Order.

By 1977, however, McMurtry was trying to gain control over the OTO by claiming he had authorization from Crowley himself (who died in 1947; this is thirty years later). This claim has been disputed, at length and in detail, by German researcher Peter Koenig on his website, and it makes for interesting reading. Nonetheless, when the smoke finally cleared, McMurtry's gang had convinced a judge that they were the legitimate OTO in America, and Motta's claims were thrown out. Dowling went the way of all flesh, and became an Orthodox cleric taking with him a woman who had been a Theosophist and cult member herself (although not to my knowledge of the OTO). The OTO under McMurtry and his lieutenants became organized and active in New York City and things were looking up.

But their membership roles were swollen by some very strange individuals. And these individuals attracted some even stranger hangers-on, who had expected to see in the OTO something more profound, more serious than they actually encountered. The exposure of these individuals to the Order at first stimulated them, but then they discovered that the rituals and the posing of the Order members—their pretension to spiritual powers and profound insights—were shallow, and so they adopted what they learned in the Order's meetings and Gnostic Masses and from discussions with other serious members and fellow-travelers, and began to develop more serious programs of their own. The same was true of the Process. The same was true of the Church of Satan, in which case Michael Aquino broke away in search of something more intellectually stimulating and more powerful, creating the Temple of Set: a much more ambitious occult program than the more popular, showy Satanism of LaVey. Many of those who broke away started their own groups; some were as public as Aquino's Temple of Set, others were more private and did not advertise, because their tastes ran to the . . . eclectic.

Thus, there *were* OTO members (current or lapsed) involved with nefarious activities in New York City at the time of the Son of Sam murders. And there were some familiar faces at OTO gatherings who could also be found at producer and theatrical agent Roy Radin's home on Long Island, for instance, including one young woman—a student at one of the Brooklyn schools of higher learning—who took her occultism*very* seriously, and who introduced the author to Roy Radin one afternoon when the latter was looking into the possibility of filming occult rituals. (Roy Radin figures prominently in Maury Terry's theory of a nationwide network of Satanic killers, of which "Manson II" was a member.) None of this means that the OTO itself was officially involved in anything illegal. How does one separate the acts of the organization from the acts of its members, particularly when what we are speaking of is essentially a secret society? George Washington was a Mason, and so incidentally was Robert Treat Paine. Does that mean that the Masonic Society started the American Revolution? Of course, some conspiracy theorists would have us think so.

But when cult members engage in cult activity which results in the commission of an illegal act, then it should be assumed that the cult itself is responsible in some way. Drug dealing is not a cult activity, even when all the members of a given cult are involved in dealing drugs, unless "drug dealing" is in their manifesto or book of shadows. The same is true of murder. When a cult member kills someone—or when a group of cult members kill someone—it is not necessarily a ritual act; the commission of the murder within a cultic ceremony, however, is. This is the point of view of the American courts, and it is valid insofar as it goes, and thankfully so.

What we are examining here, however, is another level of culpability entirely. There can be no doubt that individual Process members were involved in some illegal acts; interviews conducted with a Process member a few years ago have categorically linked David Berkowitz and other "Son of Sam" killers to the Process, *or to some faction thereof.*[12] Further, the murders of people linked to Berkowitz are evidence of a group at work and since nothing else seems to have characterized this group except murder and magic, then we are forced to make some unsettling assumptions. Indeed, a published personal account of the Process makes it clear that at least some members had knowledge that the Process was fronting for a German neo-Nazi operation in the 1960s.[13] Founder Robert de Grimston's wife, Mary Anne, even claimed that she was a reincarnation of Nazi Propaganda Chief Joseph Goebbels.[14] The Process' symbol—a stylized swastika—is further evidence of the group's sentiments if not alignments; and their theology included worship of Satan, Jehovah and Lucifer while their magazine was a paean to Death, Fear, etc. To view the Process then as an amalgamation of Scientology with neo-Nazism puts us in a different realm: it raises the stakes. The neo-Nazi movement—both in Europe and in the Americas—*has* been violent, *has* been responsible for murder. Scientology members themselves have performed illegal acts in the United States, including breaking into US government offices and spying on government agents, former Scientology members, etc. What occurs is a unique social phenomenon that has been inadequately examined: it is the fact that these groups—which openly incorporate or idolize Lucifer, Satan, ancient Egyptian gods, Death, Fear, Nazi ideology, secret rituals and arcane initiations, and use what is sometimes a sophisticated, sometimes an ill-advised, series of psychological mechanisms such as hypnosis, auto-hypnosis, psychodrama, ritual sex, and potent hallucinogenic drugs to create altered states of awareness—thus may act as channels for sinister forces, forces they cannot control.

In simple human terms—viewed as a commonplace social phenomenon—men like Jack Parsons were destroyed by these forces. Their lives, once they were actively involved in serious occult practice, began to go downhill in terms of personal success, material achievement, even mental health. Yet, this is sometimes true of our best artists, musicians and novelists, as well. It is also true of many of our philosophers and scientists. Genius—whether innate or invoked—can destroy the human vessel that carries it. The effect of Genius on the rest of society, however, is usually profound and lasts long after the death of the penniless artist, the bipolar painter . . . the mad magician. Even such a figure as Jesus himself was only a minor celebrity during his lifetime; look what happened since then. Viewed from another angle however, from an "initiated" perspective, the drama and tragedy of their lives was in a sense their apotheosis. Christ was on the cross. Van Gogh, Nietzsche, Artaud, and so many, many others, went insane, committed suicide or died violently; and Hollywood filmmakers and their stars are not immune from these effects, as they consciously try to evoke violent emotions using language, art, music, dramatization . . . in other words all the hoary repertoire of the magician. Yet we speak casually of possession and genius as if one went hand-in-hand with the other; never realizing that, in some cases, possession can be voluntary and madness temporary, and in other cases possession—even voluntary—can end in permanent madness, or death.

TO THE DEVIL, A DAUGHTER

> It was from the artists and poets that the pertinent answers came, and I know that panic would have broken loose had they been able to compare notes.
>
> —H.P. Lovecraft, "The Call of Cthulhu"

In October 1965, Pope Paul VI made a historic visit to New York City, where he would celebrate Mass at Yankee Stadium. This visit provided the inspiration and the backdrop for Ira Levin's bestselling novel, *Rosemary's Baby* (1967). In this story, a young wife—Rosemary—is made to bear the child of Satan in order to usher in a new age of the Devil. Unknown to her at first, her next-door neighbors are Satanists, and they arrange some lucky accidents for her husband, a struggling actor, enabling him to get lucrative roles. He gives them his wife's body in return, thus allowing Satan to impregnate her.

All of this activity takes place at a fictional old pre-war apartment building on the Upper West Side which, in the novel, is known as the Bramford, but which was inspired by the Dakota, where the movie version of the film was made. The

Dakota, of course, is where John Lennon and Yoko Ono lived, and where the former Beatle was gunned down in December 1980.

The basic scenario of a coven of Satanists drugging a young woman, using her in a blasphemous rite involving sex, and then taking her baby is familiar to most Americans, and has provided a template for much of the "satanic cult survivor syndrome" of the 1980s and 1990s. Although Ira Levin's novel is purely fiction, there was a later, non-fiction book incorporating most of the same themes. This book—*Michelle Remembers* (1980)—became the bible of the satanic cult survivor believers, with its additional twist alleging that many cult members (initiated as children) have suppressed the memory of the cult and only skilled psychotherapy and hypnosis can bring the memories back. According to Michelle Smith, she was initiated into the cult in 1955, when she was only four years old. The book is compiled from transcripts of psychiatric sessions conducted by Dr. Lawrence Pazder, her therapist and the man who later became her husband. In these transcripts, Michelle recounts horrific rituals conducted by what she called the Church of Satan, although this could not be a reference to the Church of Satan of Anton Szandor LaVey, which was only begun in 1966, eleven years after the events in question. The rituals involved blood-letting and sexual abuse of the child, events that evidently only Dr. Pazder's analysis could reveal since Michelle had no conscious memory of them.

Michelle Remembers has been attacked by medical professionals and other researchers on various grounds; without coming down on one side or the other on this issue, the author would like to mention that the dates given for Michelle's initiation—the eighty-one day "Feast of the Beast"—lasted from September 7, 1955 to November 27 of the same year. On October 9, General Douglas MacArthur was quoted in the New York *Times* as saying that the nations of the world should unite in common cause against a possible attack by alien forces, the term "alien" in this context meaning beings from other planets. (Other interesting events during the "Feast of the Beast": on October 13, Allen Ginsburg gave the first public reading of his landmark poem, *Howl* in San Francisco, a day conveniently close to Aleister Crowley's birthday of October 12, Crowley being, of course, the Great Beast himself; and on October 22, Timothy Leary's wife committed suicide on her husband's birthday, in another natal "celebration.")

Rosemary's Baby was an instant bestseller when it was published in 1967. The events described were supposed to have taken place from August 1965 to June 1966 (i.e., 6/66). The Pope's visit was in October of 1965, and Rosemary's Satanic child was born on June 25, 1966—i.e., nine months after the Pope's visit. (No, the implication was *not* that the Pope was the father!) What many people do not realize, and what was not generally known at the time, was that there was an actual exorcism taking place in Manhattan on 125th Street, on *the same day* that the Pope celebrated Mass in Yankee Stadium (and *the same day* that the fictional

Rosemary was being drugged and raped in the Satanic ceremony in Manhattan). The possessed person in this case was "Marianne K.," and the event is recorded in Malachi Martin's *Hostage to the Devil*, a book that was not published until 1976, almost ten years after Ira Levin's novel had hit the bookstores.[15] Marianne was a student of philosophy and physics, born and raised a Roman Catholic, but who abandoned the faith in the course of her studies and became fascinated with Satanism and the occult, drawing upside-down crosses and referring to "the Man" (either an hallucination or a real person), who indoctrinated Marianne into the mysteries of Satanism. As a possessed subject, her taunts of the priests during her exorcism were unusually intelligent. According to Martin's account, Marianne had posited the existence of two levels of communication in every being: the conscious level of information exchange, and an unconscious one where there is a flow of influence from one being to another. This influence could be benign or malign, depending on whether the influence served to enhance the self of the receiver or to split it, to damage it.

In addition to her philosophical ideas, as Marianne's mental illness progressed—leaving school, living with a succession of male partners, wandering the parks in a general state of dishevelment—she also became progressively sexual, picking up men and women and asking them to perform violent and bestial acts . . . or perhaps what would have seemed violent and bestial to a Roman Catholic priest in 1965 America. With her voracious sexual appetite came a profoundly bad smell that could not be erased with soap and water. The symptoms sound oddly like those of serial killer Henry Lee Lucas, who also had a fascination with Satanism, an insatiable sexual appetite, and very bad body odor, which some medical professionals associate with high levels of cadmium poisoning and its associated psychological disabilities.[16] Marianne K., however, was well-educated and intellectually sophisticated, as opposed to the barely literate Lucas; and, of course, there is no evidence that Marianne committed any homicides.

The exorcism seems to have been successful, although there is some ambiguity in Martin's account of it. He does imply, however, that the exorcist's mentor—who was very ill at the time of the exorcism—died at the same hour as the possession ceased, in Italy over three thousand miles away. The principal exorcist himself died in 1966, a year after the exorcism, shaken to the end by his encounter with the Devil. The late Malachi Martin was generally considered to be a reliable—if controversial—source on matters Roman Catholic, and a kind of back channel to the outside world for some of the Church's viewpoints on theology and Church policy. He has been attacked by other authors, though, particularly by Robert Blair Kaiser (a Robert Kennedy assassination investigator, as it turns out), who claims Martin seduced his wife and destroyed his marriage. The author has no reason to doubt Martin's reportage of the exorcisms he details, however. Whether or not one "believes" in demonic possession and exorcism is, of course, another matter; but there is no doubt that the Church believes in them and has been performing exorcisms for two thousand years. The odd coincidence that a genuine exorcism was taking place at the same time and in the same city as the placement of a fictional evocation of Satan—something Ira Levin could not have known—is an arresting piece of data.

On April 30, 1966 Anton Szandor LaVey officially opened his Church of Satan in San Francisco. April 30, of course, is the pagan feast of Walpurgisnacht, known as Beltane in Celtic countries: one of the most important days of the pagan calendar and second only to October 31, or Halloween. During the same month, actress Sharon Tate was busy filming *The Fearless Vampire Killers* in London with director Roman Polanski, the man who would later become her husband. She had already filmed *13,* also known as *Eye of the Devil*, in London the previous year. Although she was perhaps better known to American audiences for her supporting role in *Valley of the Dolls*, her occult films gained her additional notoriety, especially after the Manson killings. It has been reliably reported that during the filming of *13* she was initiated into a form of witchcraft created by the film's technical consultant, Alex Sanders.[17] Sanders had developed an amalgam of Gardnerian witchcraft and ceremonial magic that was known as "Alexandrian," after its founder's name; Gardnerian witchcraft itself was the creation of Gerald Gardner, a one-time customs official in Malaya and expert on the kriss—the wavy-bladed knife peculiar to Malaya and Indonesia—who returned to Great Britain and became involved with Aleister Crowley. Crowley actually wrote many of Gardner's rituals after the latter became initiated into Crowley's OTO. The flavor of the Gardnerian *Book of Shadows*—the witch's spellbook—is distinctly Crowleyan, and even has poems by Kipling, presented as if they were ancient pagan chants. Alex Sanders took some of the Gardnerian concept and mixed it with a somewhat more intellectually-demanding collection of ceremonial magic rituals, and it was this into which Sanders claimed to have initiated Sharon Tate. The same source suggests that Sanders had also had contact with members of the Manson "family," either directly or through his wide network of Alexandrian covens in Europe, America and Australia. There is also evidence that Sanders' group had interacted with the Process, and, if so, this is yet another connection to Manson and to the Tate murders.

This is a suggestive series of events, though. When Roman Polanski was asked to direct the film version of *Rosemary's Baby*, he hired Anton LaVey to act as technical consultant for that project, thus putting Sharon Tate in the path of *two* well-known twentieth century occultists and admirers of Crowley: Alex Sanders and Anton LaVey. What is even more suggestive is the fact that Manson Family member, and later convicted killer, Susan Atkins performed the role of a vampire in LaVey's 1967 public production of a Black Mass, in which she rose menacingly from a coffin. LaVey himself performed the role of the Devil in one of avant-garde filmmaker Kenneth Anger's offerings, *Invocation of My Demon Brother* (1969), alongside

Bobby Beausoleil, another Manson Family member and convicted murderer. Jack Parsons' widow Marjorie Cameron had once appeared in Anger's *Inauguration of the Pleasure Dome* (1954), in a dual role as Kali and the Scarlet Woman.

A later Anger film, *Lucifer Rising* (1970), was an Anita Pallenberg production, which featured Marianne Faithfull in the role of Lilith. The musical score was by Bobby Beausoleil, then already in prison for his participation in the Manson Family murders, and the film was shot in Egypt and in Externsteine, the Teutonic pagan shrine in Germany that was sacred to the Nazis. For this film, Anger enlisted the aid of Gerald Yorke as "Thelemic consultant," i.e., as an advisor on the Crowleyan aspects of the film's mythology. The names of Pallenberg, Faithfull, Beausoleil, LaVey and Atkins all figure prominently in our story, as we shall presently see.

As the Manson Family was located in California, it is perhaps no accident that they would become involved in film. It should be noted, however, that none of the Anger films referred to here were Hollywood productions in the usual sense. They were not done by the major studios, with big budgets and brand-name stars. These were labors of love by a filmmaker with an abiding interest in Aleister Crowley and the religion of Thelema. Anger also felt he had "discovered" Bobby Beausoleil, and saw him as the perfect Lucifer.

Anger was not the only one to use Beausoleil as a film actor. The soft-porn production *Ramrodder*—an "E.S.I. Production" shot in Topanga Canyon—features Bobby Beausoleil as a murderous Indian with Buck knife (the same type he used to kill Gary Hinman?), and Manson Family member Cathy "Gypsy" Share as an Indian "squaw." One of the central acts of the film involves the rape and murder of a blonde woman by a group of rampaging Indians. The film is high on production value but low on virtually everything else, from script to acting. Even the sex acts are chastely mimed, with a strange over-emphasis on close-ups of swinging buttocks. The value of this film, however, lies in the fact that Manson Family members Bobby Beausoleil and Cathy Share are actors, that they portray people living rough who turn murderous, and that there is a scene showing the murder of a blonde woman by a group of these Native American "Hippies" led by Bobby Beausoleil. When the blonde asks, "Why me?" the Beausoleil character responds,

> You are paying for the sins of your people, just as our people are paying for the crimes of our fathers who sold our land and our honor to the white man for a string of beads . . . . [The Chief] says we must live by the white man's law. Does not the white man's law say you are to take an eye for an eye?

Further, the castration of a white man by Bobby Beausoleil is also a foreshadowing of the murder he would commit on musician Gary Hinman, using the same type of weapon. The portrayal of the Indian tribe as a group of promiscuous young people wearing headbands and indulging in both straight and lesbian sexual acts could be a rehearsal of the Manson Family experience, or of the Summer of Love generally. It is the degeneration of this "Hippie life-style" into a season of violence and murder—portrayed by Manson Family members as actors—that leads the author to propose that this is yet another manifestation of the influence of sinister forces below the surface of everyday actions.

No major studios produced the Anger films or *Ramrodder*. A major studio did produce *Rosemary's Baby*, however. The executive producer on this project was Robert Evans, and it is Evans who will tie us in with a world of occultism, serial murder, secret societies, drug running and Hollywood celebrities that will lead from California to New York . . . and back to Ashland, Kentucky. Also released in 1968 was *The Devil Rides Out*, a film version of the Dennis Wheatley novel about a coven of murderous magicians, starring Christopher Lee. A former British intelligence agent and friend of Aleister Crowley, author Wheatley had written a trilogy of novels with a satanic theme, including—in addition to the above—*The Satanist* and *To The Devil, A Daughter* (this last also made into a movie in 1975 starring the ubiquitous Christopher Lee as well as Nastassja Kinski). These novels were based in part on Wheatley's personal knowledge of Crowley, the OTO and Crowley's own occult Order, the A.·.A.·. (*Argentum Astrum*, or "Silver Star"), and are amusing *romans á clef* for those so inclined, filled with paranormal events, ritual magic, human sacrifice and even—in the case of *The Satanist*—the involvement of a US military officer as cult leader. But before we delve too deeply into this unbelievable morass of hidden forces, let us first examine the events around another filmmaker in 1968, and the tragedy of a year's worth of political assassinations.

THE MANCHURIAN CANDIDATE

Then Robert F. Kennedy was assassinated, there was a lot of talk in the media about a "Kennedy Curse." After all, Joe Kennedy's eldest son, Joseph Jr., was killed in the war. John F. Kennedy was assassinated; then Robert Kennedy was assassinated. When Ted Kennedy later became embroiled in Chappaquiddick, it was considered just another piece of evidence that a Kennedy Curse did exist.

Of course, it is unscientific to talk of a Kennedy curse. What is the definition of a curse, exactly, and how does it apply in this case? Yet, if we deny the existence of something so insubstantial and unprovable as a curse, then we are forced to consider whether or not John Kennedy and his brother, Robert, were killed as the result of something else. Coincidence? Or conspiracy? And if not coincidence or conspiracy, what is the alternative? A curse . . . or something more profound?

The Richard Condon novel, *The Manchurian Candidate*, was published in 1959 and became a best-seller. It told of an American GI who was captured by the Communists during the Korean War, brainwashed, and sent back to the United States as a programmed assassin: his target, a candidate for President of the United States.

The film version starred Frank Sinatra, Laurence Harvey and Angela Lansbury, and was directed by John Frankenheimer. Frankenheimer had asked then-President John F. Kennedy if it was okay to make the movie, as it dealt with Communist brainwashing and the assassination of an American political leader. Frankenheimer was afraid that the sensational aspects of the plot would either inflame the American public or otherwise have an effect on Kennedy's ongoing negotiations with the Soviets, which had become exacerbated by the Bay of Pigs invasion and the Cuban missile crisis. Kennedy was also trying to get the Soviets to come to the table to ban nuclear weapons testing, and was embroiled in Vietnam. Frankenheimer did not want to create an atmosphere that would rock any boat the President might be sailing at the time. Kennedy told Frankenheimer to go ahead with the film and not to worry about any political fallout.

The film was released in 1962 to much critical acclaim; but in 1963 Kennedy was assassinated, and the film was pulled from distribution almost immediately, and was not seen again for almost thirty years.

Five years later, in June of 1968, John Frankenheimer hosted a small dinner party at his home in Malibu. Among the guests were Roman Polanski and his wife, Sharon Tate. The guest of honor was Senator Robert F. Kennedy, then running to become Democratic candidate for President. Four of his children were also present at the dinner. The California Primary polls were open, and there was nothing else for the Senator to do until the winner was announced except enjoy the company of film stars and studio executives. It was to be his last supper.

Frankenheimer drove the Senator to the Ambassador Hotel after dinner, where he would stay up the night to watch the election results. By midnight, it became obvious that Kennedy had won the California Primary. He went to the Embassy Room downstairs and declared victory to the cheers of his supporters. "On to Chicago!" A few moments later, he was shot to death. The accused assassin was Sirhan Bishara Sirhan, the Palestinian immigrant and Rosicrucian wannabe. He claimed (and still claims) to have no memory of the assassination (even though it took place in front of witnesses), and notebooks found in his home—seized without a warrant—opened a Pandora's box of conspiracy theories, as they tended to support the view that Sirhan had been the subject of a mind control experiment. Also discovered was a book by occultist Manley Palmer Hall, *The Divine Art of Healing*. The famous "girl in the polka dot dress" was seen with Sirhan by several witnesses, and then running from the scene shouting, "We killed him!" LAPD, in its infinite wisdom, discounted the testimony of these eye-witnesses almost immediately. Sirhan himself appeared remarkably calm and peaceful when he was jumped by ex-football star Roosevelt Grier among others, yet it took six men to hold him down even though he was a small, thin man.

The following day, June 8, James Earl Ray—the accused assassin of Martin Luther King, Jr. in Memphis that past April—was picked up in London trying to get aboard a flight to Belgium. Ray was an ex-convict, broke, and not too bright. But he was doing a lot of traveling around the US and Europe that year. He would be brought back to the United States to stand trial for the assassination of King, but many were not satisfied with the evidence produced on behalf of the prosecution, and Ray himself complained that he had been manipulated by his defense team.

A week later *Rosemary's Baby* premieres in Los Angeles, with Sharon Tate and director Roman Polanski very much in evidence, while in the meantime the Process goes underground in California.

As with the assassination of President Kennedy, the author has no intention to go over all the detail of the assassination of his brother and to prove a case one way or the other that a conspiracy might have been involved. As with the assassination of President Kennedy, there is enough circumstantial evidence to suggest the role of other parties in the murder of his brother, but due to mishandling of the crime scene and conflicting witness reports there will probably never be a definitive solution to the case. There are, however, elements of the crime that stand out as suggestive of the existence of darker forces at work, forces that may have been called into being by the CIA's aggressive use of mind control techniques in their search for the perfect, the Manchurian, assassin.

One of the men who was moved to investigate the murder of Senator Kennedy was former FBI agent and Democratic Party Congressional candidate William Turner, who, with his campaign manager Jonn Christian, co-authored *The Assassination of Robert F. Kennedy: The Conspiracy and Cover-Up* (1993). Clearly, Turner sees evidence of a conspiracy to kill the Senator, and he marshals a compelling array of evidence to show this.

One of the chief elements of the case in Turner's view is the possibility that Sirhan was one of the first programmed assassins. First, there is the consideration of the cult angle. He bases this not only on Sirhan's famous notebook—which contains numerous allusions to the Illuminati, to "Kuthumi" (evidently a phonetic equivalent of Theosophy's disembodied spiritual guide Master Koot Humi), and other occult subjects—but also on several pieces of evidence which put Sirhan in contact with people adorned with occult jewelry only hours before the assassination. Sirhan, after his arrest, also requested copies of Madame Blavatsky's *The Secret Doctrine*, as well as *Talks on the Path of Occultism, Volume 1: At the Feet of the Master,* co-authored by Blavatsky's Theosophical Society successor and political firebrand Annie Besant and wandering "Bishop" and Theosophist Charles W. Leadbeater. Several right-wing theorists in California at the time attempted to put the blame for the assassination on an Illuminati/Rosicrucian/Theosophist conspiracy, another way of saying (to them) the Council on Foreign Relations and the Trilateral Commission. However, the evidence—as Turner and Christian demonstrate—goes deeper than a possible cult connection to Sirhan, although we see our old friends, the wandering bishops, turn up again in the figure of one of Turner's top suspects in the case, hypnotist and suspected mind controller Dr. William Joseph Bryan, Jr.

As mentioned previously, investigative researchers tend to ignore the Wandering Bishop phenomenon because it is just too weird and seemingly irrelevant; certainly, one has to be pretty much of an expert in the subject to see any relevance at all, and it may be doubtful whether the effort is worth the candle. Yet, the author has seen this subject come up again and again in his own research, and since he has had first hand acquaintance with the eldritch world of *episcopi vagantes,* the associations are made more readily, and interesting relationships are revealed. They certainly introduce us to a web of intrigue; the Soviet KGB made use of the Eastern Orthodox Churches in their espionage strategies—as is described at length in the memoirs of just such a spy, Vasili Mitrokhin, in *The Mitrokhin Archive*[18]—and the churches that harbor the wandering bishops are, in many cases, close cousins. Archbishop Valerian Trifa of the Romanian Orthodox Church in America was exposed as a dedicated Nazi leader, a member of the notorious Iron Guard, who fled to the United States in the guise of a Romanian Orthodox priest, and wound up in charge of the entire archdiocese.[19] Many Nazi war criminals escaped to South America, and all over the world, courtesy of the rat lines established by the Vatican and in many cases disguised as priests: priests who performed the sacraments, celebrating Mass and solemnizing nuptials along the way. The Palestine Liberation Organization also had close connections with the Eastern churches, particularly with the ethnic Arab denominations, and has been known to run agents who are either disguised as priests or are actually priests themselves. (There are many Arab Christians. For instance Sirhan Sirhan was not a Muslim, contrary to many assumptions, but a Christian.) Thus, it should come as no surprise to us that American intelligence agencies also made use of these groups, both the venerable and legitimate Eastern Orthodox Churches (such as the Greek Orthodox Church, the Russian Orthodox Church Outside Russia, the Syrian Orthodox Church) and the renegade churches, such as the Old Roman Catholic Church and the American Orthodox Catholic Church.

According to William Turner, Dr. Bryan belonged to the Old Roman Catholic Church,[20] but Turner refers to it somewhat erroneously as "a fire-and-brimstone sect," which it is not. The Old Roman Catholic Church is more self-consciously Roman than the Catholic Church in many ways; the break between the denomination that would be known as the "Old Catholics" and Rome took place because the Old Catholics would not accept Papal Infallibility, and they had some other reservations about what was decided at the First Vatican Council (Vatican I) as well. The Old Catholics felt that the Roman Catholic Church had lost its bearing and was not being faithful to the original religion. The official break occurred in the 1870s, but the groundwork had been laid two hundred years earlier (when the Jansenists objected to Rome for pretty much the same reasons), and the line of apostolic succession held by the Old Roman Catholics goes back to the Church of Holland, which had been operating autonomously since that time but which was still a legitimate Catholic body. There has also been a lot of additional consecrations of Old Catholic bishops by different—usually Eastern Orthodox—groups and the Old Catholics in America have splintered into so many different groups themselves that one needs a scorecard to tell them apart, particularly when their published claims of succession are often misleading. Thus, when someone says that so-and-so is an Old Roman Catholic, detailed clarification is needed to determine just which Old Catholic group is being referenced.

There is nothing fire-and-brimstone about them, however; they generally prefer the sedate and dignified approach, bolstered by elaborate ritual vestments, clouds of incense, and heavy episcopal jewelry (no matter how weird their individual members may be). Turner says that this sect "broke away from the Vatican over a century ago,"[21] which is consistent with the same Old Roman Catholic Church we have been discussing. Turner maintains that Bryan belonged to this group "as a preacher." If so, then it was certain he was a priest, if not a bishop, in that church. Turner is correct in mentioning that it is the same church to which David Ferrie belonged; as we saw in the previous chapter, Ferrie was on close terms with both an Old Roman Catholic bishop, Earl James, and the testimony of Bishop Carl Stanley of the American Orthodox Catholic Church to the FBI gives evidence of his relationship to that organization. Since these churches swapped ordinations and consecrations like baseball cards, it is entirely possible (nay, likely) that Ferrie was a priest or bishop of the Old Roman Catholic Church as well as of the American Orthodox Catholic Church, making Ferrie and Bryan fellow clergymen. They may have known each other—or of each other—if they had been members at the same time. There was an Old Roman Catholic operation in Los Angeles for many years, as well as an American Orthodox Catholic Church operation. There were also groups in Texas and throughout the South; and, during the Sixties, the Church attracted all sorts of counter-culture elements. The Old Roman Catholic cathedral in New York was in the heart of Bedford-Stuyvesant in Brooklyn, and the church hierarchy at the time was composed of Black bishops, thus making the denomination completely integrated, and it was open-minded about a lot of theological issues that still plague the Vatican today, such as birth control, married clergy, etc.

The world of the wandering bishops is a small one, and everyone knows everyone else. If, however, Bryan belonged to the American Orthodox Catholic Church as did Ferrie, then it is almost a certainty that he was involved with a domestic intelligence operation that was using the Church as a convenient (and very cooperative) cover. The parallels do not stop there, however.

As noted earlier, David Ferrie was something of an amateur hypnotist, and he used hypnosis and drugs in some combination in his dubious "therapies," probably as a method of seduction. William Joseph Bryan was a much more successful hypnotist (it was his career), and, as a notorious womanizer, often used hypnosis for pretty much the same purposes as Ferrie; and his resume was if anything even more suggestive. A large, bearded man who taxed the scales at nearly 400 pounds, he was even stranger in his appearance than hairless Ferrie; a fat man who expected his secretaries to sleep with him, and who used hypnosis to sexually exploit still others. He demonstrated his hypnotic powers in public on many occasions, even putting noted defense attorney F. Lee Bailey under, along with two other lawyers, in a seminar organized by Melvin Belli (talk about a "dream team"). He also consulted on many famous criminal cases, and had hypnotized accused serial killer Albert DeSalvo (the "Boston Strangler") in his cell.

Bryan worked in the Los Angeles area, out of an office on Sunset Strip in Hollywood, after a checkered career in which he was once a drummer for Tommy Dorsey's band and then, during the Korean War, worked for the US Air Force in what he termed "the brainwashing section."[22] If this was, in fact, true and not some of Bryan's notorious hyperbole, then he certainly came to the attention of the CIA, which had just geared up Operation BLUEBIRD at this time and had sent agents to Korea to investigate the brainwashing phenomenon and to come up with ways to protect American servicemen against it. In fact, he would have been working for, or with, Dr. James Monroe, the Air Force officer we met in the previous chapter, who also specialized in brainwashing and was adopted by the CIA. As an admittedly powerful hypnotist, Bryan would have been scooped up by the CIA almost at once. Hypnosis—along with drugs—was the CIA's immediate strategy in the development of the "Manchurian Candidate," and they were working with hypnotists in New York and elsewhere in the attempt to develop a workable protocol. If the records of Bryan's successes are anything to go by, then he already had the system down pat. According to Bryan's associates, he admitted to working for the CIA; the only question is, for how long?

Bryan had a flamboyant personality and a lifestyle that would have been vulnerable for an ordinary intelligence operative; Bryan had no qualms about discussing his sexual exploits, however, so he was a poor target for blackmail. From available evidence in the public record, if Bryan was involved with the CIA as he claimed, it was probably in the capacity of a consultant, although one can imagine cases in which he would have been called in to perform a tricky hypnotic maneuver. This is, in fact, the belief of investigators such as Turner and Christian, as well as Political Science Professor Philip H. Melanson (*The Robert F. Kennedy Assassination*, 1991,1994). They believe sufficient evidence exists to suggest that Bryan was the hypno-programmer of Sirhan Sirhan.

They base this on several pieces of information that have no other plausible explanation. In the first place, eyewitnesses to the shooting of Senator Kennedy have claimed that Sirhan's demeanor was strangely distant and removed—"peaceful"—when he was pounced on by Kennedy supporters in the moments after the killing. Sirhan himself claims no memory of the assassination, although he did not deny that he did it. *Before* Sirhan's identity was made public, Bryan was on a radio show giving his opinion that the assassin had been hypnotically programmed. And one of Sirhan's notebooks contained serial killer DeSalvo's name repeated several times, although Sirhan himself does not know why. Although Bryan would gleefully describe any of the cases he worked on, especially high-profile cases like DeSalvo, he would change the subject when Sirhan's case was brought up, and occasionally turn angry at reporters or investigators who had the temerity to mention it. This was uncharacteristic of Bryan, and points to another level of knowledge about the case.

Eerily, Sirhan would also turn angry and upset when the Rosicrucians were mentioned, insisting that they not be brought into the investigation. This has led Turner and Christian to wonder if that was a deliberate hypnotic suggestion, implanted by Bryan or some other programmer, to divert attention away from the real conspirators. The "DeSalvo" reference in Sirhan's notebooks, however, suggests that the name of this alleged serial killer was brought up during Sirhan's programming, perhaps as a trigger word or, more likely, as a reference back to the original programmer. This would have to have been Bryan, since Bryan famously worked on the DeSalvo case. Did Bryan plant the "DeSalvo" reference as a kind of calling card? Or did Sirhan see the name of his programmer linked to DeSalvo in a newspaper or magazine article? There is no other connection between Sirhan and DeSalvo that anyone has been able to discover. It is perhaps the only pure anomaly in Sirhan's notebooks. It has nothing to do with politics, with Robert Kennedy, with the Illuminati or the Theosophists. It is as glaring—in the context of the notebooks—as a black cat on a white rug. The only connection to both Sirhan and DeSalvo is, of course, Bryan himself.

At one point, and to select individuals, Bryan claimed to have hypnotized Sirhan. There is no evidence linking Sirhan to Bryan *after* the assassination, however. Something like that would have become a matter of public record, considering the amount of scrutiny the case was getting in the wake of the botched investigation and follow-up of the JFK assassination. Bryan certainly would have made loud publicity over the fact that he hypnotized Sirhan if in fact he had done so; it would have made an impressive addition to his resume. Yet, Bryan claimed to have never hypnotized Sirhan when pressed by an independent researcher, and abruptly terminated the interview. Thus, Bryan had two stories about Sirhan. If Bryan did hypnotize the Palestinian immigrant, it was *before* the assassination; and for this, we are on firmer ground because Sirhan *was* hypnotized prior to June 1968.

Researcher, and William Turner's co-author, Jonn Christian interviewed a hypnotherapist who had encountered Sirhan in Pasadena in 1966. The hypnotherapist—Richard St. Charles—also had a stage act, and he would hand out slips for people to fill in their names and addresses for a mailing list. Sirhan's name and address was on one of them. Based on notes he made at the time, St. Charles recalled that Sirhan was a good hypnotic subject and, in his opinion, had been hypnotized before St. Charles ever met him. Thus, Sirhan had been hypnotized by St. Charles in 1966, and possibly by someone else even earlier. In fact, Sirhan was not the only assassin who had prior experience of hypnosis. James Earl Ray had also been hypnotized in Los Angeles two months before the assassination of Dr. King—by one Reverend Xavier von Koss—and a book on hypnotism was found in his safe house in Toronto, one of the stops he made before escaping to Europe.[23]

As we have already seen, the CIA's BLUEBIRD—and later ARTICHOKE and MK-ULTRA—program was aggressive in its use of hypnosis as a mechanism for mind control, and employed the services of several hypnotists in its assault on the Land of Memory. Dr. William Joseph Bryan claimed to have been one of them; and to intimate friends he also claimed to have hypnotized Sirhan Sirhan, although he would officially deny it. If Bryan was as good as everyone claimed he was—himself included—it is inconceivable that the CIA would not have approached him. If he did, in fact, serve in the military in Korea as a kind of "anti-brainwashing" expert, then we can assume with a great degree of certainty that Bryan used his hypnotic powers in an intelligence capacity beginning in the 1950s. Many of the people who knew Bryan—including other hypnotists and hypnotherapists—say that Bryan made no secret of the fact that he had worked or was working for the CIA in some capacity. A lot of people make claims like that, and more often than not they are tall tales and perhaps wishful (or wistful) thinking; but in Bryan's case we have quite a lot of smoke: it's the location of the fire that remains a mystery. The flamboyant and sex-addicted Bryan may indeed be a red herring, distracting us from Sirhan's real programmer. Let's see who else was in California on June 5, 1968.

THE CONTROL OF CANDY JONES

At the time I first met Candy Jones, I was unaware of the book about her experiences as a mind control subject, *The Control of Candy Jones* (1976), by family friend Donald Bain. Bain himself is an interesting personality: accomplished jazz musician, former Air Force officer, and screenwriter for the famous *Murder, She Wrote* television series starring Angela Lansbury. He had known Long John Nebel for many years, and when Nebel began to discover his wife's bizarre past, it was to Donald Bain that he turned to put the events into some kind of focus and to tell the tale of a young woman, a fashion model famous during World War II for her red-and-white striped bathing suit and generous decolletage, being brought unsuspecting into CIA's MK-ULTRA program.

When the book was published, the reaction was generally one of disbelief. Long John Nebel himself was an outrageous radio personality with a penchant for going for the jugular with his oddball guests, and he had a fascination with the paranormal, UFOs and the like: a 1960s version of Art Bell. So when he just happened to marry a woman whom he later claimed was a CIA mind control subject, there was naturally some resistance to the story. When the name of the actual controller was disguised in the book with a pseudonym—Dr. Gilbert Jensen—then incredulity turned to contempt in some circles, and the book's thesis was ignored. It was pulled from distribution sometime in 1977, amid rumors of a cash settlement whose terms and parties were never made public, and therein the story died. The name of the alleged controller has never been revealed, and except for the fact that he served in the Pacific theatre as a medic during World War II, subsequently had an office in Oakland, California in the 1960s, and was of Jewish extraction, we know very little about him. What we do have is Candy Jones' story, and it is a very strange tale indeed of hypnosis, drugs, mind control experiments, foreign assignments, torture, and a post-hypnotic instruction to commit suicide. It is a story made even more bizarre by the peripheral characters involved, one of whom would become a member of the Warren Commission and later President of the United States, the same man who would be the focus of an alleged assassination attempt by a former Manson Family member.

Briefly, then, the story of Candy Jones begins in Wilkes-Barre, Pennsylvania, with a troubled childhood, an abusive mother, a kindly grandmother, and a largely absent father. Candy—born Jessica Wilcox on December 31, 1925—was elected Miss Atlantic City in June 1941. Modeling agent John Powers invited her to New York City on a spurious offer to appear in a Chesterfield cigarette ad, and when that didn't pan out she found herself visiting the offices of competitor Harry Conover.

Harry Conover had formed his modeling agency in partnership with another male model, Gerald Ford. Yes, the same Gerald Ford who would become President of the United States. Ford eventually went on to greater and dubious glory, but Conover held on to the agency, and it prospered for a while. He signed Jessica Wilcox and created the "Candy" image for her. Eventually, they would marry, and Candy Jones turned into something of a money machine for the Conover agency. But before they married, Candy Jones signed on with the USO to do a tour of the South Pacific with a traveling roadshow as "Captain" Candy Jones.

It was Candy Jones that people of my parents' generation remember as the WAC and WAVE girl, urging young ladies to enlist during the War years. She was also a very popular pin-up girl in the candy-striped bathing suit that was her trademark, as well as in a more demure gown fashioned of parachute nylon. Her picture could be found in GI barracks all over Asia, and her tour was enormously successful until the day she contracted an illness from drinking unpasteurized milk, and had to be hospitalized in the Philippines. This was in April 1945.

The illness was compounded by malaria and jungle rot, and eventually Candy found her hair falling out and her complexion turning different shades from the malaria. It was during this time in hospital that she met a medic, who is named Dr. Gilbert Jensen in the Donald Bain book. It was a chance meeting amid the last days of the War, and she did not think of it again for nearly fifteen years.

She eventually recovered from her illnesses, returned to the States, and married Harry Conover. She landed a number of prestigious accounts and opened her own office next to Conover's, although the billing for her accounts went through Conover's agency as before. She was later to regret the arrangement, as Conover disappeared on May 18, 1958, taking all the money in their joint accounts and not reappearing until August, when he had taken rooms at the Plaza Hotel, a venue for wild parties he hosted with some of the teenaged models from the agency. Eventually, Harry Conover would serve two years in prison for his theft of the company funds, but Candy Jones was now in financial straits, struggling to keep her agency together.

It was during this time that she met Gene Tunney, the former prize-fighter, who had an office across the hall from hers. His office had been burgled—evidently by someone dressed as a cleaning woman—although not much was taken . . . except for photographs. It seems that Candy remembered flash bulbs going off in the office the night of the break-in, as if someone were taking pictures of the office or its contents. Tunney seemed nonplussed by the experience, and shrugged it off. She later saw Tunney in company with a retired Army general she had known briefly in the Pacific theatre. Speculation on the Internet has it that this was General William "Wild Bill" Donovan, head of the OSS during the War.

One day, perhaps, someone will do some research on the intelligence activities of retired fighters. As mentioned in an earlier chapter, Antonino Rocca was certainly one of these; perhaps Sugar Ray Robinson performed some service in that regard, due to his close proximity to the Profumo affair by way of Mary Anne Moore. Gene Tunney must be another, for shortly after the break-in at his office, Candy Jones is visited by an FBI agent known only as "Ted," who asks her questions about the break-in which then segues into a request for her to assist in an FBI mail-drop operation.

In this case, she will receive mail that is addressed to specific people not working at her agency. She is to hold the mail until an FBI agent comes to pick it up. This is all well and good, until "the general" himself phones in the late summer of 1960 and asks her to take a letter to someone in San Francisco, where she will be organizing a fashion show. Since this is the same "general" in 1960 as the one who met Gene Tunney in 1958, it is rather unlikely that he is General Donovan, since Wild Bill died in 1959. In any event, it gradually becomes clear that "Ted" was probably not an FBI agent, and that the mail drop was a CIA drop, because when she arrives in San Francisco she is phoned by the pseudonymous Gilbert Jensen, and a meeting is arranged at his office on Cyprus Street in Oakland, where she undergoes her first hypnotic trance.

San Francisco was a hotbed of MK-ULTRA activity in the 1960s, incorporating everything from drugs to hypnosis and, later, to paranormal and occult research. In 1955, MK-ULTRA operator George White (who worked for the Federal Bureau of Narcotics and not directly for the CIA, and thus had "plausible deniability") had moved to San Francisco from New York City, where he had run a "safehouse" that was used to test the effects of various drugs on prostitutes and their clients via two-way mirrors and the like. He set up an identical operation on Telegraph Hill, and wired it for sound, bringing in hookers, their johns, and eventually a whole assortment of local characters, both underworld and "civilian." George White's operation in San Francisco went on until the summer of 1963, covering the time of Candy Jones' first visit to the hypnotist in the autumn of 1960. Thus, there was a proven CIA presence in San Francisco under the auspices of the MK-ULTRA mind control program at the time of her recruitment, something that was not revealed until much later, when the Rockefeller Commission hearings into CIA's domestic intelligence operations began in 1975.[24]

While White specialized in drug testing—his job for the Narcotics Bureau was the perfect cover, and guaranteed him an almost unlimited supply of any type of drug—there were others in the area whose specialty was hypnosis. While hypnosis sounds tame by comparison, it actually had great potential as an intelligence weapon when wielded by the right hand and on the right subject. Much of what has been written on the applicability of hypnosis to a Manchurian Candidate scenario is fundamentally flawed: many investigators claim that since only one in every five persons is a perfect candidate for hypnosis, and since a hypnotized subject will not do anything to which he or she morally objects, hypnosis is therefore useless. They ignore the obvious implication that fully twenty percent of the human population *is* capable of "going under" without too much difficulty, and that many of these potential subjects would *not* find murder, rape, theft, deceit, etc., morally objectionable, particularly if the command was given by a recognized authority figure. Therefore, to the author's mind, the rejection of the Manchurian Candidate-by-hypnosis possibility is ill-informed at best, or disingenuous at worst.

As an example, the CIA's own Morse Allen—who led the hypnosis side of the search for the Manchurian Candidate—performed experiments on his own staff in the 1950s which demonstrated how easy it was to get someone to pull the trigger. As described in John Marks' *The Search for the Manchurian Candidate*, Allen hypnotized a secretary on February 19, 1954 sending her into a deep trance. He then hypnotized another secretary and told her she had to wake up the first secretary; if she could not, then she should become enraged, pick up a pistol and kill her. The first secretary was unable to come out of the trance unless Morse Allen gave her the command, and therefore could not be awakened; thus the second secretary became enraged and picked up a pistol—not knowing it was unloaded—and shot the first woman. When she was brought out of the trance, she had no memory of the event and insisted she would never shoot anyone.[25] What more evidence is necessary? A woman was told to commit an outrageous act of which she would not have been capable in a waking state, a morally-reprehensible act, in fact murder, and then had no memory of it upon awakening. As early as 1954, therefore, the CIA had the technology in hand to create programmed assassins.

The only difficulty they faced was the "delivery system": how to snatch an unwitting person, a person with no discernible ties to the Agency, put them under, and give them the post-hypnotic suggestion to kill another human being? They needed to experiment on the real world, and several scenarios were developed that would enable CIA operators to implement this technology under "battlefield" conditions.

One involved the snatch of an agent of a friendly foreign intelligence service from a party, putting him in a hypnotic trance, and giving him the command to assassinate a certain figure. This scenario had come up at the same time as Allen's experiment with his secretaries. The problem was that the secretaries were willing to be hypnotized; Allen was not sure that a man snatched from a party with no advanced warning could be hypnotized in a short time—a matter of an hour or so—and given a command that he would carry out. What Allen wanted were defectors, double agents, people to which the Agency already had access, and who would undergo hypnosis as part of a routine "medical examination."[26]

In addition, Allen wanted to know if a person who had been hypnotized to forget certain vital information—a lock on the Land of Memory to which only the hypnotist had the key—could stand up under torture. Allen had suggested they use the services of a friendly foreign intelligence agency or police department, such as "Taiwan or Paraguay," (nations where torture as an interrogation tool was widely practiced) to test the strength of the posthypnotic amnesiac state.[27] This way, they could create a genuine, threatening and dangerous environment equal to that a real agent would experience if captured by an enemy agency; plus the CIA would have distanced itself (legally, if not morally) from the actual torture of the subject. More plausible deniability. The subject would be tortured by these foreign agents in an effort to make him to reveal "classified" information.

According to the CIA, there is no knowledge of such vile experimentation actually taking place.

According to Candy Jones, it did.

Her first meeting with Gilbert Jensen in Oakland included a hypnotic session. He first asked her a number of questions about her personal life, including details about her childhood: specifically, about imaginary playmates she had. This is potentially the most explosive area of the investigation because, as we will see and as has been reported by Marks and others, the CIA explored the possibility of creating or developing alternate personalities in their mind control subjects, essentially manipulating what DSM-IV calls "dissociative identity disorder," or what used to be known as "multiple personality disorder." The CIA felt that if access was had to a violent personality hidden within the subject, then that personality could commit violent acts and keep the memory from the conscious recall of the core personality. It was a sophisticated approach to human consciousness for western science, but on the level of medieval sorcery or African witchcraft. As Marks writes,

> The candidate had to be among the one person in five who make a good hypnotic subject, and he needed to have dissociative tendency to separate part of his personality from the main body of his consciousness. The hope was to take an existing ego state—such as an imaginary childhood playmate—and build it into a separate personality, unknown to the first. The hypnotist would communicate directly with this schizophrenic offshoot and command it to carry out specific deeds about which the main personality would know nothing.[28]

Marks' book was published in 1979; Donald Bain's book on Candy Jones was published in 1976. Marks' account of the CIA's program based on official documents obtained under the Freedom of Information Act in 1975–78 and interviews with those involved, thus provides compelling corroboration of Candy Jones' account given to Donald Bain in 1974 (*before* the Rockefeller Commission hearings began in June of 1975). In fairness, it must be added, rumors about the CIA's mind control program were leaking out before then.

During hypnosis there was a deliberate attempt to focus on one of Ms. Jones' "alters," an imaginary playmate of Candy's childhood, who turned into the aggressive and cynical personality known as Arlene Grant. The "Arlene Grant" persona was discussed during Ms. Jones' first visit with Jensen, even including hair coloring, much to Candy's irritation since the questions seemed rather bizarre for someone who was interviewing her for a possible role in American intelligence. During the course of several visits to Jensen's office during 1960 and 1961, Jensen "conjured" Arlene Grant to appear, using what appears to be a combination of drugs—possibly including sodium amytal—and hypnosis. This relationship with "Arlene" would continue for 12 years.

G. H. Estabrooks—one of the most creative specialists in the subject of hypnosis—wrote that the goal of the military hypnotist in wartime was to actually *induce* multiple personalities.[29] Estabrooks was writing this in the 1940s, when the subject to most people still seemed far-fetched, the stuff of penny-dreadfuls, but which to the CIA was right on target. According to Estabrooks, one personality would be a dedicated Communist (for example) and anti-American, while the other personality would be a dedicated anti-Communist and pro-American. The Communist personality would have no knowledge of the anti-Communist personality, but the latter would have all of the former's memories as well as its own. This is, of course, classic dissociative identity disorder, a psychological illness that has been used occasionally as a defense for murder in the American courts.

Candy Jones was a blonde; Arlene Grant became a brunette. This required Ms. Jones to wear a dark wig when she was on assignment on behalf of the CIA, using a false passport in her "alter" personality. Photographs of Candy Jones and "Arlene Grant" in Bain's book are quite dissimilar; one would have to know that they were the same person to note the physical identity. "Arlene Grant" was also programmed to endure tremendous physical pain, something that is common under hypnosis, as many can attest from public demonstrations. Candy Jones was afraid of Arlene; Arlene despised Candy as a weakling and as a far too trusting individual. Over the course of Candy's sessions with Jensen, Arlene would be the personality who would be constantly "invoked" by the hypnotist; it was Arlene who was given the undercover assignments, acting as a courier all over the United States and eventually in Asia. And it was Arlene who was sent to Taiwan in October of 1966—one of the two countries mentioned by Morse Allen as potential hosts for the "terminal" experiments in hypnosis and mind control—and tortured.

The trip to Taiwan was made after the usual visit to Gilbert Jensen's office in Oakland. In this case, she was given the Arlene Grant passport and an airline ticket in Arlene Grant's name. She left the office in the dark wig and in the persona of Arlene Grant, where she would remain until her return from Taiwan.

She was met at the airport by a man who had been president of the Taipei Chamber of Commerce and taken to his house outside Taipei. She gave him the envelope she had carried from the States, and much to her surprise was taken to a room in the basement of the house, and then hooked up to electrodes and tortured. She was asked if she knew a Gilbert Jensen, and she said she didn't; she was asked about the contents of the envelope and said she didn't have any idea. And on and on. Eventually, the man made a phone call and when he returned, he unhooked her and told her it was all a misunderstanding and that the electro-shock was only used to "jog her memory." She stayed for lunch, and they drove her back to the airport that night.

Due to the method of electrode placement, her hands were severely burned, enough that she wore gloves for days afterwards to hide the evidence, something that friends of hers remarked upon. She also had been gone from her office for a week without any warning or advice to her staff, which was even more unusual.

And then, in 1968, she was asked to return to Taiwan once more.

Donald Bain has trouble understanding why the CIA would bother to go to such lengths for what amounted to a courier. From what we know now of the CIA's MK-ULTRA program, it has become clear that what Jensen was doing was experimenting with Candy Jones, and that the torture episode on Taiwan was just another element of the program. Bain admits this might have been the case. This author, long involved with Asian government agencies and their cozy relationship to American intelligence, also believes it to be so. Just as Morse Allen had suggested, the CIA was using Taiwan's friendly intelligence service to assist them in the experimentation on Candy Jones/Arlene Grant. The locale would have been even more valuable considering that to most Americans Asia is a mysterious and "disorienting" place, due to the insurmountable language difficulties if nothing else. Add to that a good dose of jet lag and the delivery of a mysterious envelope to a mysterious Chinese gentleman, and you have created a typical—if somewhat-novelistic—espionage scenario in which to test your subject. Candy Jones was not being tested as a courier. She was being tested as a spy. And possibly something more.

Her 1968 trip or trips to Taiwan involved more specific torture sessions, and seemed to include a scorpion and a coral snake, both very poisonous. It also involved being drugged, examined, pinched and interrogated by what appeared to be a Chinese nurse, and all of this done under the observation of an American in what appeared to be a kind of elaborate inn or guesthouse that included an infirmary. The location of this house is not known, except that it was not in Taipei this time, but in the south of Taiwan, probably in Kaohsiung. Ms. Jones was pinched very painfully by the "nurse," so much so that her arms and breasts were black-and-blue from the assaults. On her way out, she fell down a flight of stairs, so weak was she from the drugs and the torture.

She apparently passed the test, because she was escorted back to the airport, and then flew back to the States, reporting as usual to Jensen.

The exact date of this trip to Taiwan is not known, except that her Taiwan visits ended in 1968. Another trip she made that year is, if anything, even more suggestive, as she was in California during the Democratic Primary on the day Robert F. Kennedy was shot.

This time, she was visiting an institute run by another pseudonymous hypnotist, called "Dr. Marshall Burger" in the Bain book, who had a thriving practice in Chicago before moving to northern California and establishing his "institute" on behalf of the CIA. This is not enough information to identify the hypnotist, but it does narrow down the field considerably. The CIA had financed the setup or operation of a number of scientific and medical establishments in the United States as part of MK-ULTRA. The most famous, perhaps, was the Human Ecology Society, which fronted for a number of the Agency's research endeavors, and the Geschickter Fund for Medical Research, which tested drugs on terminal cancer patients and "mental defectives" in the Washington, D.C. area. The Human Ecology Society (formally known as the Society for the Investigation of Human Ecology) was run by John Gittinger, a CIA staff psychologist who worked undercover as the Society's head, and who developed the famed Personality Assessment System or PAS. This system of psychological appraisal recognizes *millions* of different personality types and was thus a potentially priceless tool in the psychiatrists' arsenal, but it seemed only Gittinger really understood how it worked. An interesting point about the Human Ecology Society was the fact that Gittinger opened offices in Tokyo and Hong Kong to service CIA stations in the Far East. This was done in the 1960s, and in the same time period as Candy Jones' many travels to Taiwan.[30] Gittinger also traveled to San Francisco during this period to visit with George White at his safehouse for testing drugs on male and female homosexuals and prostitutes.

Thus "Marshall Burger" could have been an employee—official or unofficial—of the Human Ecology Society or one of the various fronts the CIA employed to provide sufficient distance between it and its experimentation. (At this point, after all of the revelations concerning MK-ULTRA, there is probably no longer a need to keep the identities of these individuals—Burger and Jensen—secret, and their exposure would only serve to validate the late Candy Jones' story.) The disturbing fact about Burger and his relationship to Candy Jones was the racist indoctrination she underwent at his seminars at a secret school somewhere in a small town in Texas on the Louisiana border (possibly the town of Orange).

This is the strangest, most anomalous part of the story of Candy Jones and does not mesh with what we know of the CIA. According to the Bain book, Jones was taken to this class by Jensen, who introduced Burger to the class. Burger then went into a tirade concerning blacks, Hispanics, Asians, miscegenation, and the whole Bible of race hatred, including a recommendation that mixed-race couples should be sterilized. There is no way that this could have been an official CIA session. As much as we may distrust any secret intelligence agency—or the CIA in particular—there would be no discernible requirement or value for the type of class Candy Jones describes, except in the most feverish imagination of conspiracy theorists. More than that, however, is the lack of a clear motive for instilling racist concepts in hypnosis subjects like Candy, or in any of the other persons who attended the class. Yet, in the transcript of the hypnosis session between Candy Jones and her husband, John Nebel, she insists that Burger "*is* the CIA. He's important out here in discussions, but I don't know how big he is."[31] The idea that Burger may indeed be a CIA official of some sort is not far-fetched at all, but the author suggests that the class he was conducting was unofficial, something developed between Jensen and Burger for some ulterior purpose.

Jensen had expressed racist feelings to Candy Jones years before, when both were in the Philippines during the War. This was before the creation of the CIA in 1947, and obviously was not part of a psychological warfare or mind control scenario. The author suggests that Jensen and Burger were genuine racists, and that they had a hidden agenda. He further suggests that Candy Jones was a deniable asset of the Agency, an informal agent who was being used as an experimental subject and nothing more, but that her training and progress under Jensen's ministrations were being closely observed by the CIA as a case study in the use of hypnosis as a method for creating the Holy Grail: the Manchurian Candidate. If she could be made to express racist feelings—and if her presence at the "training school" in Texas was somehow recorded for posterity—then were she involved in a political assassination, it could be put down to race hatred, as it had been in the case of James Earl Ray and the assassination of Dr. Martin Luther King, Jr. earlier that same year. It is also entirely possible that Candy's projected role was not as an assassin, but as a fall guy, a patsy . . . as it may well have been in Ray's case. And in the case of Sirhan Sirhan. (And possibly in the case of Lee Harvey Oswald, as well.)

In June 1968, Candy Jones was sent to Burger's "institute" in northern California, evidently in or near San Francisco. She was given a battery of tests to appraise her sensitivity to various stimuli such as taste, smell, etc. During the session in which she recalled this visit, she relived a conversation with Jensen in which she mentions his awe of Burger and "his fat friends. They're all fat."[32]

Probably the fattest of all the hypnotists working in California at the time was, of course, William Joseph Bryan, the man who is suspected of having hypnotized Sirhan Sirhan. Indeed, Bryan had even been the technical consultant on the film of *The Manchurian Candidate*, directed by the man who hosted Bobby Kennedy's last dinner, John Frankenheimer. Yet, Candy Jones professed never to have heard of him. This battery of tests may have been given to her on June 3, 1968, although there was some confusion in her mind whether it was June 3 or June 5. June 5,1968, of course, is the day Robert F. Kennedy was assassinated in Los Angeles. To be more specific it was very early on June 5, the Primary being held on June 4. That Candy Jones would be in California the day of the primary, undergoing hypnotic tests and experimentation by Jensen, Burger and his "fat friends," while Sirhan—possibly programmed by one of these "fat friends"—was roaming the streets of Los Angeles looking for his target, is one of those coincidences that points to a deeper connection between events than we can see at first glance. Candy's not knowing Bryan could have been the result of post-hypnotic suggestion, of course, but even that degree of speculation is unnecessary. The fact that Candy paints both Jensen and Burger as racists—as committed and even rabid racists—and the parallel fact that both Sirhan Sirhan and James Earl Ray were known without a doubt to have been hypnotized in California prior to their assassinations of known anti-racists . . . is either a coincidence of muscular proportions, or it points to an intelligence operation in place at the time being run either by the CIA or by a secret, frantic faction thereof.

One is even tempted to wonder if Candy Jones—with her height, her voluptuous figure, and her sharp nose—was in fact the famous "girl in the polka dot dress" who was seen at the Ambassador Hotel with Sirhan; however, eyewitnesses say the actual lady in question was in her early or mid-twenties. Ms. Jones by this time was in her forties, and anyway even the author is not prepared to go quite that far. Had Ms. Jones been deployed by the Agency in that capacity, she almost certainly would have been in her Arlene Grant persona, replete with black wig, and this was not the case with the girl in the polka-dot dress. Yet, since we are on the subject of coincidence—meaningful or not—we can refer to an occult novel first published in 1972 by one David St. John: *The Coven.*

The novel is about a Pennsylvania Senator and his wife who are embroiled in a secret underground cult in Washington, D.C. based on the powers of a young, black African priestess. The Senator's wife—Catherine Vane—is a tall, beautiful blonde who, for some reason that is never explained in the book, wears a black wig. The hero of the tale, a former US Attorney-turned detective with the appropriately Ayn-Randish name of Jonathan Gault, beds the Senator's wife without too much trouble but does not appear to have done much else in the entire length of the novel except gather intelligence and illegally dispose of a body. The fact that the couple are from Pennsylvania (there is even a scene involving a company in Wilkes-Barre, Candy Jones' home town) and that the woman wears a black wig for no particular reason, Arlene Grant style, *and* turns out to be a murderer who undergoes a trance in the middle of an occult ceremony in the basement of an abandoned house in Washington . . . well, it would have been no more than an interesting parallel to the Candy Jones tale except that the real name of the pseudonymous author of *The Coven* is E. Howard Hunt, former CIA agent, Bay of Pigs action officer, despiser of Kennedys, and convicted Watergate "Plumber."

We may object to this linkage, saying that *The Coven* after all is an intended pot-boiler and not a *roman á clef.* Except that Hunt himself plays name games in the book, such as the reference on page 49 to something called the "Citywide Improvement Alliance," an organization which is never referred to again. The initials, of course, are CIA. In this case, the Citywide Improvement Alliance is in court, "there to see justice done to a brother."[33] This was rather prescient of the future jailbird, as the book was written *before* the Watergate scandal, and it is amusing to see the CIA in court watching a fellow member being arraigned.

Candy Jones was taken to the Farm in November 1971.

The Farm—as aficionados of CIA fiction and non-fiction are aware—is the training facility in Virginia where the Agency puts its agents through a kind of espionage boot camp. It was there that Ms. Jones was finally displayed before Jensen's colleagues as an example of his perfect control. According to her recall of the event while under hypnosis by her husband, there were about twenty-four people in attendance watching while Jensen put Candy through her paces, people she assumes were doctors.

The demonstration eventually included Candy remaining supine and unresisting as Jensen inserted a candle in her vagina. The reader may find this incident so revolting that it seems like nothing more than one of those artificial memories that are dredged up by unscrupulous therapists; recall that the "therapist" in this case is her own husband.

> The CIA made a science of watching other people have sexual activity, going so far as to audiotape and videotape the proceedings, all in the name of research. Former CIA psychologist James Keehner, in an interview that is summarized in Marks' book, tells of becoming disgusted with "entrapment techniques" after watching videotape of an agent and a target in bed. He pointed out that Agency case officers, many of whom "got their jollies" from such work, used a hidden camera to get their shots. The sexual technology developed in the MK-ULTRA safehouses in New York and San Francisco had been put to work.[34]

Thus, it doesn't seem too farfetched that a demonstration of the type Jones recalls was actually just that; again, we still have to wonder at its usefulness. Where would Jensen have had to go in order to demonstrate his perfect control of his subject, however? The only other avenue would have been a "terminal" experiment, i.e., having Candy Jones pull the trigger on someone. Morse Allen had already demonstrated that this could be done through hypnosis, though, seventeen years earlier; that was not an issue. Having a female subject submit to vaginal penetration by a candle in front of twenty-four witnesses might have seemed an extreme test—yet relatively safe, if of dubious legality—a test that would show beyond reasonable doubt the extent of the power of hypnosis to control behavior. Another alternative would have been to subject Ms. Jones to torture before the assembled guests, but it is assumed that the CIA would have been squeamish about that.

Donald Bain is careful to state at the beginning of his book that some of the material recalled by Ms. Jones under hypnosis—by her husband, in fact, an amateur hypnotist at best—might be tainted by leading questions and other environmental cues and may not be pure memory. Fair enough. But there is a level of credibility in the story of Candy Jones that cannot be denied. Something happened to her during those long years between 1960 and 1972, when she finally managed to escape the clutches of her controllers by marrying John Nebel. She was subject to wild mood swings in public, actually complete personality changes as "Arlene" took over; she would be gone for long periods of time; she did have friends in the government, some of whom she made during her USO stint during the war. All in all, there is enough circumstantial evidence to suggest that at least part of her story is true. Her details on Taiwan and on her visits to San Francisco are also very much to the point. She names her controllers to her husband, although these names are disguised in Donald Bain's book; thus we are to assume that these are people whose identities are known to a circle of people around the late Candy Jones. The lack of independent confirmation of her story is frustrating, but the internal evidence is compelling. What can be checked against other sources has been checked to the best of the author's ability, and he finds himself supporting the basic elements of her story.

Candy Jones was approached by hypnotists working for the CIA in some capacity. She was sent on errands around the country to test her competence and willingness. She was sent abroad, where she had painful experiences at the hands of persons working with her controllers. She found herself involved in the same nexus of mind controllers in California as surrounded Sirhan Sirhan and James Earl Ray. She did this willingly at first, as did so many who became CIA guinea pigs without knowing what they were getting into, out of patriotism.

More importantly, for the scope of this book, her case is a good example of the techniques proposed by Estabrooks and others: the creation of alter personalities in the hypnotic subject, the *inducement* of dissociative identity disorder and the utilization of those personalities as an intelligence weapon and, potentially, as an assassination tool. In other words, the creation of a mentally-ill killer, an assassin who could be programmed with a verbal cue to kill, and to forget. If apprehended, the killer's mental illness itself would provide the Agency with plausible deniability.

Because it was not Candy Jones on the table in front of twenty-four CIA scientists being penetrated by Jensen and his ridiculous candle. It was her alter, Arlene Grant. But it was Candy Jones who suffered for it.

One phenomenon that none of the available CIA documentation discusses is the damage to the psychic health of these subjects, perpetrated by medical and scientific professionals with no regard for the long-term effects of their drugs, hypnosis and other behavior control mechanisms. The concept of behavior control *is* mechanistic; it views the human mind as a computer that can be programmed to perform certain acts, a fleshy robot at the mercy of the wise men of Langley. To people like Jensen, it was a simple matter to create amnesia in their subjects so they would have no conscious recall of the horrors to which they were subjected . . . or of the evil acts they were forced to commit. No memory, to Jensen, meant no guilt. He had no interest in Candy's psychic health; perhaps he didn't even believe in it. What happened to Candy Jones' soul was her affair, if she had one and if such a thing existed. But Candy Jones became a basket-case, never entirely free of her demons. Arlene Grant would occasionally reappear to criticize Candy, and the two would have fights.

> Her eyes were closed. Her arms, fingers apart, extended over the table, and her body began to sway. The lips were closed but from her throat came sounds of a timbre I had never heard before. There were two voices, it seemed, in angry conflict, and as I watched and heard the sensation grew that I was listening to an *externalized* debate of Good and Evil.
>
> —*The Coven*, E. Howard Hunt (emphasis in the original)

Candy Jones was suffering from multiple personality disorder, or what is now known as dissociative identity disorder, induced by experimentation on her mind by people claiming to be patriots. She was used as a test subject, abused horribly both mentally and physically, and discarded. According to her own account, Jensen had booked a first class ticket for her from New York to the Bahamas, where she was to check into the Paradise Island Hotel, and then kill herself by jumping off a rock into the sea. That was supposed to have happened on her birthday in 1972, the very day she decided to get married to John Nebel and thus begin her long road back to some semblance of sanity.

The ordeal was not over after the marriage, the tapes, the book, the minor publicity. She continued to receive phone calls, including one six months after her marriage from Japan Air Lines, informing her she was booked on a flight to Tokyo with onward booking for Taipei. This call came at the time that Richard Helms and Sidney Gottlieb had finished shredding the CIA's MK-ULTRA documents in fear that those who had collaborated with them in their mind control program would be revealed. Candy Jones would have been a living witness, a loose end to tie up, a bit more difficult to shred than a personnel file. Evidently, Jensen still wanted to provide the ultimate demonstration of his powers, having Ms. Jones walk into a trap and again give herself up in Taiwan. Fortunately, she never took that flight.

This tale of Candy Jones is a dark one, but there are others as dark and darker, and as well-documented. There is a parallel for example, between the story of Candy Jones and the story of Michelle Smith in *Michelle Remembers*. The latter is also based on transcripts of hypnotic sessions in which a subject is made to "remember" horrible things, in this case satanic cults and the murder of children. In Candy Jones' case, the hypnosis was carried out by her husband, Long John Nebel. In Michelle's case, her therapist would become her husband. In both cases, the substance of the memories has been attacked by critics, but in both cases the memories—real or confabulated—concern the existence of a secret organization that tortures people in the name of a higher purpose.

Under hypnosis yet again, the famous story of Barney and Betty Hill was retrieved, and it told of alien forces who landed in the New Hampshire countryside and abducted a married couple, who were then experimented upon and released back into society with no conscious memory of what had happened. In this case as well, the Hills were subjected to physical abuse by a secret group in the name of a higher purpose; their story is also told in the form of transcripts of hypnotic sessions.

The CIA, satanic cults and UFOs; the mythology of the late twentieth century is surprisingly coherent even though the masks change from case to case, from victim to alleged victim. The CIA, of course, does exist; their mind control programs, from BLUEBIRD to ARTICHOKE to MK-ULTRA are a matter of public record. Their history of political assassinations and the overthrow of various foreign governments is also a matter of record. Satanic cults—or perhaps we should qualify that and say "occult secret societies"—also exist and are a matter of public record; their attempts to contact alien forces by means of ceremonial magic and arcane ritual (including the use of some of the same drugs and other techniques as the CIA used in its mind control programs) are also well-known and documented. Some of these practitioners were—and are—well-known men and women who have not denied their involvement (such as rocket scientist Jack Parsons in the 1950s and Army Colonel and intelligence officer Michael Aquino in the 1990s). The CIA also aggressively researched American cults and secret societies in an effort to discover the source of paranormal abilities and ancient mind control mechanisms. And while the jury is still out on the question of UFOs, there is no doubt that government agencies have attempted to track them, to analyze them, and to explain them away. Again, this is a matter of public record, including FBI and CIA documents in addition to military records.

Intelligence officers and cultists have a lot in common. (Marchetti and Marks' groundbreaking and controversial exposé of the Agency was entitled *The CIA and the Cult of Intelligence.*) Secrecy is a way of life for both the spy and the sorcerer; they both use codes and code names; they both pretend to have access to mysteries not available to the general public; they both claim to be able to influence events at a distance with their special abilities and powers. They both specialize in the manipulation of reality; both are aware that things are not always what they seem to be; and they are both ruthless and often amoral or immoral in the pursuit of their goals, embracing illicit sex, illegal drug use, and even murder as the means to their enigmatic ends. And when one can so easily manipulate the perception of reality, one eventually comes to the realization that Truth, itself, is a malleable thing. So it was only natural that the cultist and the spy would gravitate towards each other and would try to learn from each other.

This control of reality, of the *perception* of reality and the creation of what Robert Anton Wilson calls "consensus reality," is a powerful political tool, and has been since ancient times, when the proverbial sorcerer could appear to create solar eclipses by simply knowing when one would occur and acting as if *he* was causing the natural phenomenon to take place. To control and manipulate the reality of the masses, one uses what is now known as psychological warfare, or sometimes as simply advertising, or "spin." To control or manipulate the reality of an individual, drugs and hypnosis are valuable tools. And it is but one step away from controlling a person's *perception* of reality to getting that person to *act* on it. To commit espionage, sabotage, and even murder.

ENDNOTES

1 Jim Garrison, *On The Trail Of The Assassins*, Warner, NY, 1991, ISBN 0-446-362778, p. 135

2 Robert Graves, *The White Goddess*, Farrar, Straus & Giroux, NY, 1981, SBN 374.5.0493.8, p. 490

3 George P. Pelecanos, *International Herald Tribune*, May 18–19, 2002, p. 18

4 Ira Levin, *Rosemary's Baby*, Random House, NY, 1967, p. 86

5 Gordon Thomas, *Journey Into Madness*, Bantam, NY, 1990, ISBN 0-553-28413-4, p. 277

6 Phillip Knightley & Caroline Kennedy, *An Affair Of State*, Atheneum, NY, 1987, ISBN 0-689-11813-0, p. 9

7 Maury Terry, *The Ultimate Evil*, Barnes & Noble, NY, ISBN 0-7607-1393-0, p. 174

8 Philip H. Melanson, *The Robert F. Kennedy Assassination*, SPI Books, NY, 1994, ISBN 1-56171-324-4, p. 193

9 Vincent Bugliosi with Curt Gentry, *Helter Skelter*, Bantam, NY, 1995, ISBN 0-55357435-3, p. 636

10 Robert D. Hicks, *In Pursuit of Satan*, Prometheus Books, Buffalo, 1991, ISBN 087975-604-7, p. 71–72

11 R.N. Taylor, "The Process: A Personal Reminiscence," in *Apocalypse Culture*, Adam Parfrey, editor, Feral House, Portland, 1987, ISBN 0-922915-05-9, p. 159–171

12 Maury Terry, op. cit., in particular the Epilogue update which discusses new information concerning the involvement of Process members in the Son of Sam cult. See also an interview with Berkowitz aired on the A&E network on June 13, 1998 in which individual members of the Process—and their involvement in the Son of Sam murders—are identified.

13 Taylor, op. cit., p. 168

14 Nikolas Schreck, editor, *The Manson File*, Amok Press, NY, 1988, ISBN 0-94169304-X, p. 127

15 Malachi Martin, *Hostage to the Devil*, Reader's Digest Press, NY, 1976, ISBN 0-88349078-1, p. 29–82. There is a great deal of controversy surrounding Malachi Martin, who has been called everything from a visionary to a pathological liar and destroyer of marriages; *Hostage to the Devil*, however, has blurbs from Harvey Cox, as well as from various other notables in the fields of psychology and psychoanalysis and is still considered a classic on the subject of demonic possession.

16 Joel Norris, *Serial Killers*, Anchor Books, NY, 1989, ISBN 0-385-26328-7, p. 123

17 Shreck, op. cit., p 129 and in other places. The involvement of Alex Sanders (sometimes spelled 'Saunders') with Sharon Tate is a persistent rumor, made all the more believable because it simply stops there and does not pretend to a full-blown satanic conspiracy theory. Alex Sanders was quite well known in London in the 1960s, and it would have been just as understandable to have him as a technical consultant on *Eye of the Devil* as it was to have Anton LaVey as a technical consultant for *Rosemary's Baby*.

18 Christopher Andrew & Vasili Mitrokhin, *The Mitrokhin Archive: The KGB in Europe and the West*, Penguin, London, 1999, ISBN 0-14-029559-3, p. 634–661

19 See, for instance, Howard Blum, *Wanted! The Search for Nazis in America*, Quadrangle, NY, 1977, ISBN 0-8129-0607-1, Chapter 2, "The Bishop and the Dentist," pp. 83144

20 20 William Turner & Jonn Christian, *The Assassination of Robert F. Kennedy: The Conspiracy and Coverup*, Thunder's Mouth Press, NY, 1993, ISBN 1-56025-058-5, p. 226

21 Ibid., p. 226

22 Ibid., p. 225–226

23 Ibid., p. 202–3

24 John Marks, *The Search for the Manchurian Candidate*, Times Books, NY, 1979, ISBN 0-8129-0773-6, p. 87–104

25 Ibid., p. 183

26 Ibid., p. 186–187

27 Ibid., p. 188

28 Ibid., p. 184

29 See for example, G.H. Estabrooks, *Hypnotism*, Dutton, NY, 1943 and G.H. Estabrooks, *Spiritism*, Dutton, NY, 1947, where these concepts are freely described.

30 Marks, op. cit., p. 168

31 Donald Bain, *The Control of Candy Jones*, Playboy Press, Chicago, 1976, ISBN 087223-457-6, p. 157

32 Ibid., p. 149

33 E. Howard Hunt (as "David St. John"), *The Coven*, Fawcett Crest, Greenwich, 1973, LOC 75-186562, p. 49

34 Marks, op. cit. p. 174

The Great Schism of 1054 reached its dramatic climax when Cardinal Humbert, Pope Leo IX's legate, strode into Constantinople's Hagia Sophia during Divine Liturgy and placed a bull of excommunication on the altar, formally splitting Western (Roman Catholic) and Eastern (Orthodox) Christianity. This magnificent cathedral, built by Emperor Justinian in the 6th century and considered the epitome of Byzantine architecture, had served as the center of Eastern Orthodox Christianity for nearly 1000 years. After the Ottoman conquest of Constantinople in 1453, Sultan Mehmet II converted Hagia Sophia into a mosque, adding minarets and covering many of its Christian mosaics with Islamic calligraphy and designs, though some original Byzantine features remained visible. Lithograph by Louis Haghe after Gaspard Fossati (1852).

BOOK ONE: THE NINE

APPENDIX

A FIELD GUIDE TO WANDERING BISHOPS

The world of the wandering bishops—*episcopi vagantes*—is rife with confusion. This confusion is largely due to the frenzied efforts of the bishops themselves. What is offered here is a general guide to the phenomenon; it is by no means exhaustive. It couldn't hope to be. Instead, the author concentrates on some of the better-known personalities, intending to demonstrate where individuals such as Ferrie, Stanley, James et al. appear in the food-chain. In other words, the emphasis is more on how this phenomenon may impact any study of post–World War II American history, particularly in the areas of intelligence, mind control, and assassination studies, as well as the parallel world of cults and occultism. While several well-known wandering bishops were felons and ex-cons, others lived on the fringes of the intelligence community, while still others were heavily immersed in occultism, from the ethereal Theosophical variety, with its sinister emphasis on spirit guides and root-races, to the more hard-core rituals and beliefs of Aleister Crowley, Theodor Reuss, and the Rosicrucian orders.

The wandering bishop phenomenon largely owes its existence to a schism between the Jansenists in Holland and the Roman Catholic Church in the seventeenth century. This culminated in the creation of something called the Old Roman Catholic Church at the end of the nineteenth century. It is from there that many of the "wandering bishop" denominations can trace their apostolic lineage, since the Old Roman Catholics had valid apostolic succession but were not answerable to the Pope. Still others trace their lineage to an attempt by the Russian Orthodox Church to broaden its influence in the United States after the Russian Revolution, and thus were vulnerable to accusations of being Chekist: running agents within US borders, as indeed was the case with the Russian Orthodox Church (Moscow Patriarchate) and its infamous cathedral on West 97th Street in Manhattan.

It should be pointed out in advance that the author himself knew personally several of the individuals who come under discussion here. He was a familiar face for about a year around the headquarters of the Old Roman Catholic Church in Brooklyn, New York in the late 1960s, as well as the American Orthodox Catholic Church headquarters in the Bronx, the Russian Orthodox Church Outside Russia (the Synod), the Russian Orthodox Church (Moscow Patriarchate) and various other denominations of greater or lesser legitimacy, including that of the "Rosicrucian" denomination of George Winslow Plummer and Stanislaus de Witow. He was also familiar with members of the Gnostic Catholic Church, the OTO sect that descended in a somewhat irregular fashion from French wandering bishops, some of whom were consecrated in the so-called Vilatte line of succession.

At the outset it may be useful to keep in mind that there are three primary lines of succession that concern us. There are many more, of course, but the ones that most impact the world of the wandering bishops in the United States can trace their lineage to either Joseph Rene Vilatte, Aftimios Ofiesh, or Arnold Harris Mathew . . . or usually all three. From these three "patriarchs" are descended Propheta, Ferrie, Stanley and all the rest. In succeeding volumes of this work, other "wanderers" occasionally make an appearance, and you will find their lines of succession amply represented here.

It is truly impossible to be exhaustive on this subject. There are many sources—both printed and electronic—which are invaluable for understanding and keeping abreast of the latest news on the wandering bishop phenomenon. Peter Anson's book, *Bishops At Large*, was bedside reading for many wanderers in the 1960s, although difficult to find today; G. Gordon Melton's series of books on the American religious experience is also valuable for putting some of this in perspective. There are also many useful Internet sites—usually published by individual sects anxious to prove their *bona fides*—as well as a database of wandering bishops which is very helpful; unfortunately, the dates are sometimes in error (probably due more to forged or imaginary certificates of consecration and false claims than to any carelessness on the part of the webmaster). *Caveat lector*.

In 1871, and largely as a result of the First Vatican Council, a number of Dutch Old Catholic churches formed an alliance, and left the Roman Catholic Church in protest. The details of the squabble are beyond the scope of this book. It is enough to say that the Dutch Old Catholics were every bit as "Catholic" as the Church in Rome and had valid sacraments and a valid line of apostolic succession at the time of their split.

The Dutch Old Catholic bishops on April 28, 1908 consecrated Arnold Harris Mathew (1852–1919) as the Old Roman Catholic bishop for Great Britain. This was the beginning of a proliferation of irregular bishops around the world, as Mathew began consecrating—without prior authorization from his Dutch Catholic colleagues—a number of people who would go on to greater infamy. Mathew consecrated as many as fifteen other bishops, which is not a large number when you consider how many bishops have been created by individual clerics since then, but it was enough.

Perhaps the most famous was Prince Rudolph Landas Berghes (1873–1920), who was consecrated by Mathew on June 29, 1913, ostensibly as a bishop for Scotland. In November of 1914, Landas Berghes was in the United States, where he established the North American Old Roman Catholic Church, consecrating Carmel Henry Carfora (1878–1958). Carfora took over as the head of the North

American Old Roman Catholic Church in 1919, and consecrated Hubert Augustus Rogers (1887–1976) on July 30, 1942. In 1946, Rogers took over stewardship of the Church. (The author knew Archbishop Rogers and his son, Bishop James Hubert Rogers, in 1968 at the Church's headquarters in Brooklyn, New York.)

Among the many bishops consecrated by Mathew is one of special interest to us: the Rev. Fredrick Samuel Willoughby, who was a Theosophist, consecrated on October 28, 1914. Another Theosophist, James Ingall Wedgewood (1883–1923) was in turn consecrated by Willoughby on February 13, 1916. Thus, the link between the wandering bishops and occultism has a venerable pedigree. The Willoughby/Wedgewood nexus gave rise to the Liberal Catholic Church, a Theosophical Society sect that practiced the Catholic Mass—with some Theosophical flourishes—above the Society's bookshop in Manhattan in the 1960s when the author knew it. The infamous C.W. Leadbeater—associate of Blavatsky and Besant, and discoverer of the young Krishnamurti on a beach in India—was also a bishop in this line of succession. In addition, the Mathew line would give us Herman Adrian Spruit, who will come to our attention for a number of reasons in following volumes, but especially as the bishop who consecrated women, including Rayelan Russbacher, to the episcopate. Rayelan Russbacher was the wife of Gunther Russbacher, a shadowy figure in the Iran-Contra affair.

Running roughly parallel to the Mathew line is the line of Joseph Rene Vilatte (1854–1929). Vilatte's story is a sad one. His life seems to have been beset on all sides by troubles, and it is difficult to find fault with him. Rather, it would appear that Vilatte genuinely tried to do good but was somehow thwarted at every turn, seduced and abandoned by a number of denominations. It is to Vilatte that we trace some other interesting lines of succession, and it should be said that eventually Vilatte's line of succession will *also* result in the Herman Adrian Spruit consecration, thus do these "lines" become "webs."

Vilatte, an Old Catholic priest born in France who emigrated to the United States, was consecrated a bishop by Antonio Alvarez of the Malankara Orthodox Syrian Church. This Church, located in India and Ceylon (now Sri Lanka), came under the jurisdiction of the Syrian Patriarchate of Antioch. How this came about is a textbook case of the type of internecine warfare that exists among churches and schismatic sects. The Catholics of Goa, India—long a Portuguese colony with cultural ties to the motherland—were told by Rome that they now had to bear allegiance towards bishops in France and Italy. Outraged, a group of churches defected from the Catholic Church and elected Antonio Alvarez—a native of Goa and a Brahmin—to become their bishop. The Patriarch of Antioch, the Jacobite Mar Ignatius Peter III, obliged and, to make a long story blissfully short, eventually Vilatte was consecrated a bishop by Alvarez in Colombo. He then returned to America, but not before a sojourn in Europe and a flurry of consecrations there. Altogether, it is difficult to count the number of churches with which Vilatte was associated; it is even more difficult to keep track of the bishops he consecrated.

One of the men consecrated by Vilatte was the Trappist Francois Giraud, on June 21, 1907 in Paris. Giraud then consecrated a number of others in France, with a line of succession that is claimed by Michael Bertiaux, an occultist and proponent of voudon, the Haitian religio-occult system better known as "voodoo," due to his stay in Port-au-Prince as a teacher. Bertiaux is also a member of the OTO, and Kenneth Grant has written complimentary things about him, although Bertiaux has since defected to the Grady McMurtry wing of the Order. At this time, Bertiaux is consecrating bishops for the OTO's Gnostic Catholic Church; the validity of his succession is, of course, rather in doubt, not the least by Bertiaux himself, who boasts no fewer than eight separate consecrations, and, on at least one occasion—that of the consecration of Forest Ernest Barber (another Spruit consecratee) on June 16, 1979—Bertiaux and Barber engaged in reciprocal consecration, i.e., consecrated each other (giving a whole new meaning to the concept of the OTO's IXth degree). Thus, the Vilatte line eventually descends into occult practices as easily and inevitably as the Mathew line.

At the same time, there were other churches abroad in the land whose line of succession was equally valid and who were not in communion with the Church in Rome. These included the entire Eastern Orthodox establishment, with churches in Russia, Romania, Serbia, Bulgaria, Slovenia, Slovakia, Moravia, Ukraine, Armenia, Syria, Greece, Ethiopia, etc. The titular head of this establishment was, and still is, the Patriarch of Constantinople, considered "first among equals." Each national church, such as the Catholicos of Armenia, has its own Patriarch or national leader.

However, many of these national churches experienced further schisms after the initial break with Rome, which took place in the eleventh century A.D., when the Catholic Church rather cavalierly excommunicated the Orthodox Church . . . literally. A messenger from Rome rode into the Cathedral of St. Sophia on his horse during the celebration of Divine Liturgy, and threw the Bull of Excommunication onto the altar. There had been dissension over theological issues as well as political ones, and Christendom split into two great ecclesiastical camps: the Catholic Church in the West, and the Orthodox Church in the East.

Just as the Dutch Old Catholics split from the Catholic Church in 1871, a number of Orthodox Churches began to split from their mother churches around the time of the Russian Revolution, a split that was reinforced by the decision of the Moscow Patriarchate to cooperate—some would say "collaborate"—with the Soviet regime. Thus, the Russian Orthodox Church became at first two distinct and warring factions: the Church that was loyal to the Moscow Patriarchate, and the Russian Orthodox Church Outside Russia (ROCOR), sometimes simply referred to as "the Synod," which was loyal to the "Old Regime."

At the time of the split between the two Russian churches, Moscow became aggressive in trying to control Eastern Orthodoxy abroad. Through its foothold in the United States—its cathedral on West 97th Street in Manhattan—it consecrated an Arab clergyman as a bishop and gave him responsibility to work among the Syrian Orthodox community in America. Later, this was extended to include the authority to create an "American Orthodox Church." The Arab bishop was Abdullah "Aftimios" Ofiesh (1880–1966).

This seemed to be a purely political maneuver at first, but eventually Aftimios Ofiesh became as infamous as Mathew and Vilatte in his prodigious use of the powers of consecration. It is to Ofiesh that we can credit the consecrations of Bishops Sophronios Bishara and Joseph Zuk, who between them created another long dynasty of irregular clergymen, this time along the Eastern Orthodox lines of succession instead of the Old Roman Catholic lines, although all of these lines became ensnarled and entangled in the years to follow.

Ofiesh was consecrated a Bishop of Brooklyn on May 13, 1917 for the Russian Orthodox Church. He became Archbishop of the "Syrian Orthodox Mission of the North American Diocese of The Russian Orthodox Church" in 1923, and in 1927 (at the urging of the Russian Orthodox bishops) he founded the American Orthodox Church. The AOC was to be an autocephalous (self-governing) ecclesiastical body for America. It was from this initial inspiration that the greatest bishops' mill of them all, the American Orthodox Catholic Church (AOCC), would be incorporated in New York City in 1964 by Walter Propheta, using the same lines of apostolic succession from Ofiesh via Zuk and Sophronios . . . and de Witow and Plummer of the Rosicrucian SRIA.

Rather than go into further detail, it is assumed that the above brief summary will help the reader place the lines of succession as they come up. There is no listing at present that shows all the bishops consecrated by any one bishop; such would be very helpful, not only to scholars of this religious phenomenon but also to investigators in other areas, such as intelligence operations and assassinations. Rather, we have to work backwards from each bishop, up through his lines of succession to see where they meet and overlap with others. A short guide follows.

The reader is warned that being consecrated by any one wandering bishop does not necessarily imply any kind of alliance—personal, political, or spiritual—between the persons involved. Often, a consecration may take place for money or some other material reward. Sometimes, it's just as insurance in case a previous consecration was doubtful or invalid. And, sometimes, it's just fun.

What it does reveal, however, are personal associations between these individuals, associations we would not otherwise discern or understand. The involvement of Carl Stanley, for instance, with David Ferrie, Earl Anglin James, and Raymond Broshears is important, for it speaks to another level of interaction and commitment by these individuals, as does the involvement of these churches with the OTO, the Theosophical Society, the Rosicrucian orders, etc.: a hidden agenda, a *demi-monde* of belief and ritual, occultism and politics, that goes far beyond the standard accounts of the assassinations.

VILATTE LINE

As mentioned above, Joseph Rene Vilatte was consecrated by a bishop in Colombo, Ceylon and returned to the United States via Europe, where more consecrations took place. One of his lines went from Bishop Lloyd to Bishop Lines to Bishop Boyle to Bishop Lowell Paul Wadle and then to Bishop Herman Adrian Spruit. Another of his lines went from Paolo Miraglia to Julien Houssaye to Louis Francois Giraud to Jean Bricaud (in 1913). Bricaud becomes important when we consider the Martinist movement in France, the Gnostic Catholic Church, and the French OTO, as Bricaud was at one time or another allied with all three and involved with Crowley and Theodor Reuss of the German OTO. Bricaud, for example, became head of the Martinist Order (as redesigned by "Papus" or Gerard Encausse) in 1918. The line of apostolic succession from Vilatte to Wadle devolves not only to Spruit (in 1957) but also to occultist William W. Webb and from there to Roger Victor-Herard of the Gnostic Catholic Church, and eventually to Michael Bertiaux.

Yet another line from Vilatte to Bertiaux goes from Bricaud through a number of other French clerics, winding up with Bishop Jorge Rodriguez, who then consecrates Bertiaux. As you can see, these "lines" of succession are not in any way exclusive. That is, you cannot draw a straight line down from one bishop to another, as you would in an organization chart. In the first place, such a chart would be meaningful if one were only considering primary consecrators and ignoring the assisting consecrators. This is because each consecration potentially has three separate lines of succession behind it, and thus results in a brand-new, fourth line combining all three. That bishop then joins with two (or more) others to consecrate another bishop, thus multiplying the number of lines and associations geometrically and creating enormous difficulties for the historian. Add to this the tendency of the wandering bishops to create new denominations with slightly different names, and to give *themselves* new names and titles without warning, and you find yourself in a veritable labyrinth of madness, pleading for the comforting attentions of a hungry Minotaur.

MATHEW LINE

From Mathew, we have the consecrations of Landas Berghes and the aforementioned Samuel Willoughby. Landas Berghes would consecrate Carfora in the United States, and from Carfora we have Hubert Augustus Rogers (on July 30, 1942) and Earl Anglin James (on June 17, 1945). James, however, was not content with the consecration by Carfora (oddly enough, since Carfora's consecration is relatively above reproach considering he was consecrated by Landas Berghes who was consecrated by Mathew) and obtained another consecration at the hands of Hugh George de Willmott Newman (on November 24, 1946), a gentleman who exerted a tremendous influence over the wandering bishop circles, particularly among those with occult or Theosophical beliefs.

Willmott Newman was a correspondent of Aleister Crowley and William Bernard Crow, both famous occultists and authors of books on occultism and mysticism. Willmott Newman himself was consecrated by at least six other bishops at six different times (from information available to the author; there may be many more). Crow—a Liberal Catholic bishop with a line of succession back to Wedgewood and Willoughby (and thus back to Mathew)—has primacy of place, for he consecrated Willmott Newman on April 10, 1944 into something called the Ancient Orthodox Catholic Church. This was followed by a consecration from Charles William Keller on April 29, 1945, and then one by Hedley Coward Bartlett on May 20, 1945, then another by J.S.M. Ward (another occultist and author of mystical texts) on August 25, 1945, and one by Charles Leslie Saul on July 14, 1947, and yet another by Davison Quartey Arthur on February 19, 1951. Willmott Newman himself consecrated the celebrated author of occult books, Montague Summers (1880–1948). In addition, Willmott Newman was a consecrator of Christopher Maria Carl Stanley, also known as Carl J. Stanley to the FBI and as Saint Christopher Maria to his following. (And occultist J.S.M. Ward consecrated Gerald Gardner—father of the modern-day Wicca movement—in the Orthodox Church of England.)

To continue with the Mathew line, we have Bishop Willoughby (the Theosophist) consecrating Wedgewood (another Theosophist) in 1916, who form the Liberal Catholic Church. From Wedgewood we get Cooper (in 1919) and Hampton (in 1931) and eventually Herman Adrian Spruit in 1957 as a bishop in the Liberal Catholic denomination. Spruit would leave the Liberal Catholics in 1972 and go on to greater glory in his consecrations of Rayelan Allan Russbacher, the wife of Iran-Contra pilot Gunther Russbacher and a woman whose belief system makes Aleister Crowley's OTO look like a bunch of Christian Fundamentalists, and Roberto C. Toca (in 1992), a native of Cuba and member of a rival OTO organization based in Florida with his own Spanish radio program. Spruit would also consecrate Bishop Forest Ernest Barber (on June 15, 1971) who in turn consecrated Michael Bertiaux, the voudon practitioner and Thelemite we mentioned above, and Carl Llewellyn Weschcke (the publisher of occult books and almanacs) via occult authors Vivian Denning and Leon Phillips in 1983. (Denning and Phillips had been consecrated by the irrepressible Spruit in June of 1982.) On November 10, 1980, Spruit also consecrated Mother Serena (widow of Bishop Stanislaus de Witow) of the SRIA, thus ensuring a line of succession for that Rosicrucian operation on Manhattan's Upper West Side.

Forest Ernest Barber himself could claim no less than thirteen consecrations, including the one from Bertiaux, in which the two gentlemen consecrated each other on June 16, 1979.

Not to be outdone, however, Spruit also has a line of apostolic succession that leads from Vilatte, via Lloyd (1915) to Lines (1923) to Robert Raleigh Boyle

(1927) to Lowell Paul Wadle (1940) to Spruit (June 22, 1957). That's not all, however, for Wadle's succession also involves the Liberal Catholic succession of Willmott Newman via Bishop de Ortega Maxey; thus the occult and Theosophical and Rosicrucian connections are all there, if somewhat in knots.

Bertiaux himself claims succession from both the Vilatte and Mathew lines, but this is subject to some confusion as it is not known if these consecrations involved the actual laying-on of hands or if they were "paper consecrations," since it has been reliably reported that many of the OTO consecrations (for instance) were paper dignities sent back and forth in the mail and which involved no laying-on of hands. Such "consecrations" are patently invalid and have no meaning to anyone other than (presumably) the persons directly involved. While the Vilatte and Mathew and Ofiesh lines were valid at the times they were established, it is doubtful that all the bishops consecrated since then have been so consecrated according to the requirements of Canon law. This is one of the reasons, perhaps, for Bertiaux claiming at least eight separate consecrations, and Willmott Newman at least six. When in doubt, get consecrated again.

For the reader this brings up a hopeless additional complication, for there are consecrations, and there are re-consecrations, and there are consecrations *sub conditione*, or "conditional" consecrations (performed in case one of the previous consecrations is later shown to be invalid). There are also those *mutual* consecrations, in which two bishops consecrate each other simultaneously, the reason usually given is that it's a form of recognition of each bishop by the other, but in actuality is often an attempt to "trade" lines of succession. Further, every consecration is performed by one "main consecrator" and at least two or more assistant consecrators; these three bishops may not belong to the same church, or share the same apostolic succession, thus creating even more confusion in the historian's mind. In trying to pry apart the lines of succession of any one bishop, one is thrown willy-nilly into a document storm from which there may be no escape.

That said, let us look at the Ofiesh succession, which brings together many disparate strands of succession and gives us, finally, everyone from Propheta to Stanley to Ferrie to Broshears.

OFIESH LINE

Ofiesh consecrated Joseph Zuk (1932), who in turn consecrated William Albert Nichols (1932), who consecrated George Winslow Plummer (1934), who both consecrated Theodosius Stanislaus de Witow (1936) of the Holy Orthodox Church. Remember that both Plummer and de Witow were Rosicrucians and members of the Societas Rosicruciana in America, or SRIA.

At the same time, Ofiesh had consecrated Sophronios Bishara (1928), who in turn consecrated Christopher Kontogiorgios (1934) as Exarch of the Greek Orthodox Catholic Church (Alexandria Patriarchate), who consecrated Konstantin

Jaroshevich (1949), who—in tandem with Williamovich (consecrated by Rogers of the Mathew line)—consecrated Peter Zhurawetzky as bishop of the Eastern Orthodox Catholic and Apostolic Diocese of America on October 15, 1950.

Zhurawetzky is a true *macher*, for he and de Witow and Bishop Joachim Souris (of the True Orthodox Church of Greece, himself consecrated by Joseph Klimowicz of the American Holy Orthodox Catholic Eastern Church) then go on to consecrate Propheta in 1964, after the consecration of Robert Schuyler Zeiger as bishop of the Orthodox Catholic Patriarchate of America in 1961, and Carl Stanley (with Zeiger's assistance, as well as the assistance of Bishop Homer Ferdinand Roebke and Bishop Colin James Guthrie) also in 1964. Stanley had already been consecrated by one Assendelft-Altland in 1959, and by Earl Anglin Lawrence James (date unknown), but I guess it didn't "take." Roebke himself had already been consecrated by Stanley on August 4, 1962, by Zeiger on June 9, 1963, and later again by Propheta (*sub conditione*) on March 4, 1967!

Propheta, Zeiger and Roebke, along with Stanley, were forming the American Orthodox Catholic Church, as was envisioned by Aftimios Ofiesh and his successors. While something called the American Orthodox Church had already been in existence under Ofiesh, Zeiger and Roebke, it had not developed into anything substantial until Propheta was consecrated and then incorporated the American Orthodox Catholic Church in New York in 1964. Propheta and Roebke then became the de facto rulers of the group when Zeiger left it in 1964, although Stanley was still very much involved. Stanley was based in Kentucky, and according to David Ferrie's testimony, had been in trouble with the law. Stanley was characterized as "self-ordained," which was patently not true, and as a confidence man, about which there are no supporting documents to hand at this time. As for Roebke, he was consecrated *sub conditione* by Propheta in 1967, even though he had been a consecrator of Stanley in 1964 . . . and so it goes. Eventually it would be Propheta who would be proclaimed the Patriarch of the American Orthodox Catholic Church, and thus a legend was born.

Walter Vladimir Propheta (1912–1972) was a striking individual. In a world of effete Theosophist bishops with real or imagined English accents and watery, vacant stares, and of glad-handing, back-slapping redneck bishops of various dubious denominations and pending indictments, Propheta seemed to be the genuine article. Born into a Ukrainian Orthodox family and ordained into the Ukrainian Orthodox Church, he *was*. Tall, portly, with bulging eyes and a thick Ukrainian accent, he looked like the love child of Peter Lorre and Sidney Greenstreet. He would wear a see-through white cassock with red piping in the summer and, it was obvious, nothing underneath. He had two assistants—Bishop Leonard G. Hill and Bishop John Christian—who cooked and cleaned at the Cathedral of the Holy Resurrection in the Bronx, and who made sure that the Sunday liturgy was performed. Bishop Hill, the kinder and gentler of the three, was a hopeless alcoholic and of an afternoon could be seen urinating out of the second storey bathroom window and onto the passers-by below; once he had the misfortune of relieving himself into an otherwise refreshing beverage held by the outstretched hand of his boss, Propheta. Bishop Christian, of French Canadian extraction who spoke fluent French, was losing his eyesight and his mind when the author knew him. He was the fussy old maid to Bishop Hill's rather more muscular pipefitter pose: the Odd Couple, Orthodox style.

Propheta himself was another matter entirely. A fervent anti-Communist and Republican, he surrounded himself with émigrés and spooks. Financially, though, he had the perfect scam.

He had presentation cards printed showing dozens of his bishops in a group picture and giving the address, phone number, etc. of the Church. Bishops Hill and Christian would leave every weekday morning—including Saturdays—and drive to a different location around New York, Westchester County, New Jersey, or Connecticut, park the car with a "Clergy On Call" sticker in the window, and begin walking up and down the main street of the area, going into shops and . . . begging for money. This was ostensibly to raise funds for an orphanage, but the Church had no orphanage. In fact, if one were to extrapolate from Bishop Hill's second storey escapades, the Church didn't even have a pot to . . . well, you get the idea.

However, the two men—dressed outlandishly in Russian Orthodox-style robes and hats with long, black veils—would raise considerable sums of money every day, money which went into supporting Propheta's lifestyle and his new Cadillac every two years. It also kept the men out of the house during the week, during which time Propheta could concentrate on other matters.

Propheta's involvement with intelligence agencies and international affairs has already been noted. His colleague, Carl Stanley, had consecrated David Ferrie and Raymond Broshears into the church—two men considered suspects in the Kennedy assassination conspiracy by Jim Garrison. Stanley himself was consecrated by Earl Anglin Lawrence James, another Kennedy assassination suspect who was in contact with Ferrie's "associate" and fellow bishop, Jack S. Martin. Propheta's own known contacts with government officials and intelligence agents and his working relationship with Stanley indicates another level of activity beyond the scope of his two clueless assistant bishops. As mentioned previously, the author himself witnessed the presence of men who claimed to be both FBI and CIA around Propheta at various times during the late 1960s. These men were not bishops or ecclesiastical types. These were serious men in serious suits who stayed up half the night speaking privately with Propheta in his office, drinking Scotch and plotting. The rest of the time, officials from various embassies could be seen visiting the Bronx church on one errand or another. The author witnessed Italian and Nigerian embassy officials, and a number of Latin American and Slavic gentlemen, not to mention various members of American law enforcement. Yet, in all this time, and with all this activity, there were no parishioners. No congregation. No lay people attending the Sunday services. None. Ever. The headquarters of the American Orthodox Catholic Church—while possessed of a real church building, with ikons and incense, vestments and croziers, mitres and all manner of ecclesiastical trimmings—never attempted to attract followers, work with the community or in any way function as an actual religious organization, not even on Christmas and Easter. The services were held on Sunday and on the high holy days in relative obscurity. The rites were performed, at the proper times and dates, but no one ever showed up except for the clergy performing the rites or those there on some other, darker, purpose.

Propheta's brother in Christ, Carl Stanley, had consecrated several members of the anti-Castro underground, including David Ferrie. Stanley was himself consecrated by Earl Anglin Lawrence James, a man wanted for questioning during the Clay Shaw investigation. Another "Old Roman Catholic" was William Bryan, the hypnotist suspected of a role in the Robert Kennedy assassination. And Propheta himself was up to his neck in anti-Communist activities involving Eastern Europe, Italy and Africa, to name but a few, running bishops like agents . . . or agents like bishops. Christians and cultists; sorcerers and spies.

As we go to press, the author has learned that Propheta was, indeed, deeply involved with the FBI. As volunteered in a personal communication by Archbishop Colin Guthrie—one of the original founders of the American Orthodox Catholic Church and a colleague of Carl Stanley—Propheta had contacted all the bishops of the AOCC and informed them that he would be installed as the Primate of the Church by FBI Director J. Edgar Hoover! The recipients of this information were then told that any bishop who wanted to retain his status within the AOCC must provide a complete curriculum vitae to Propheta so that it could be vetted and the status of the bishop reconfirmed, and the bishop in question presumably re-consecrated. Archbishop Guthrie, rightly incensed (no pun intended) at this outrage on behalf of Propheta and Hoover, declined to submit to Propheta's demands. Carl Stanley, however, raced to New York City to swear his allegiance to Propheta and presumably to submit his credentials.

A month after his return to Kentucky, Stanley was dead. It is interesting to note that Stanley died in March 1967. His erstwhile associate and fellow clergyman, Bishop David Ferrie, had died in New Orleans under mysterious circumstances on February 22, 1967, only a few weeks earlier and around the time Stanley had returned from New York and his meeting with the FBI-elevated Propheta.

Jack Martin, however, survived and went on to consecrate even more bishops. The story about his "investigating" fraudulent churches and diploma mills is thus suspect if not patently false, for we find Bishop Martin involved in several consecrations well into the 1970s, including that of Thomas Jude Baumler in 1974. Baumler was a New Orleans politician and a known associate of Guy Banister . . . and a member of the American Association of Ethical Hypnotists, according to http://www.jfk-online.com/jpsbanag.html, an interest he shared with assassination suspects David Ferrie and William Bryan.

One likes to think a lot has changed since then. With the arrival of the Internet, some of this dirty laundry has been aired, and the individual churches now try to maintain a relatively spotless reputation. However, these groups still operate out of storefronts—when they have the money—or more often out of their apartments, basements, trailer parks, or post office boxes. There is a sense of cynicism among many of these men (and, now, women) since they seem to have attained a high rank in society that is normally only the province of the well-educated, well-connected, or well-heeled. To become a bishop in the Catholic Church is tantamount to becoming a vice president of a large corporation or a member of the US Senate, but to become a bishop—with the same line of apostolic succession, and hence of *some* kind of legitimacy—in the wandering bishop community requires not much more than a shoeshine and a smile . . . and sometimes not even that much. The initial euphoria wears off rather quickly when one returns to one's studio apartment or trailer home after the ceremony, faced with the same grim reality as the day before: no wealthy multi-national corporation behind you as there is behind the lowliest Catholic monk. Only a diploma and a title, and the sweaty company of your fellow dreamers. Unless you have sought the consecration because you genuinely believe in its occult power—a line of initiations that stretches back to Jesus and St. Peter and, according to some authors of mystical texts, all the way back to the priests of the pyramids of ancient Egypt—what you wind up with is only an excuse to consecrate someone else, and thus begin a different kind of pyramid.

Some of these bishops genuinely attempt to gather parishioners and congregations and to do good work in their communities, but the nagging sense that they are not "real" bishops performing "real" sacraments still lingers. This unease can be seen in the ferocity with which they publish their lines of apostolic succession in mind-numbing lists of consecrators going back two thousand years over several different "lines," as if to prove once and for all that they, too, are really bishops of a real church, while simultaneously scoffing at the lines of succession of their competitors.

The sad thing is, there is actually nothing there to compete for since the only ones paying any attention are usually other wandering bishops like themselves. They did nothing special to deserve the consecrations. No "service to humanity," no saintly charisma, no odor of sanctity. And, once consecrated, these individuals often do nothing special with the gift they have been given. If they are not occultists consciously using this sacramental power to further their own spiritual growth (if no one else's), or spies using the consecrations as a convenient and impenetrable cover for other business, then they have nothing left to do but look for someone else to consecrate and thus boost their own egos—if only for a short, short time.

And so it goes.

PETER LEVENDA

SINISTER FORCES

A GRIMOIRE OF AMERICAN POLITICAL WITCHCRAFT

BOOK TWO: A WARM GUN

FOREWORD

By Dick Russell

Let us begin with a couple of quotes from Carl Jung. "The unconscious is the unwritten history of mankind from time unrecorded," Jung wrote. It "only becomes dangerous when our conscious attitude to it is hopelessly wrong. To the degree that we repress it, its danger increases.

In this, Book Two of his trilogy *Sinister Forces,* Peter Levenda walks us through that minefield, dredges up and weaves together considerable material that many would prefer stay buried. There have been, for example, many books about the decline and fall of Richard Nixon, and no few books exploring the bizarre world of Charles Manson. But, beyond their existence in the same chronological time-frame, no one has probed the parallel reality of their not-so-separate universes. "Power, to people like Manson and Nixon, is the only reality, the only absolute," writes Levenda. "Nixon *had* to proclaim Manson guilty to the press; he had to address the one other man in the country who understood power, and truth, and evil, and murder the way he did."

It may make certain readers uncomfortable, this pairing of a president and a pariah. Comfort, however, is not Levenda's intent. Consider as well: "But the demon in the smoke that crawled out of the God Struck Tower on September 11, 2001 bore the face of Charles Milles Manson, the bastard son of America and product of its institutions and—even more importantly—scion of its bartered Soul."

Heavy stuff. Heavier still, because Levenda strides here into a realm where good and evil are often not what they appear. Or, rather, what Americans fantasize they are. In today's America, where biblical literalism is the absolute truth for an increasing number of people, Levenda's tracing of an Islamic and Christian "underground" through the centuries—in the cults of the Nizaris and the Templars—may be seen by many as heretical, if not blasphemous or even treasonous.

Cut from there to the author's "Heart of Darkness" chapter—the terrifying relationship between the CIA's attempts to control human behavior and the "mass suicide" inspired by Jim Jones at Jonestown—and one can almost envision poor Peter at the stake for this heresy. But wait, we are not done with assassins "under the influence," not until we have investigated the Chapman (John Lennon), Hinckley (President Reagan), and Bremer (George Wallace) capers.

Levenda is perhaps, above all, a master of exploring mysterious synchronicities, or at least giving such events a context. To wit, the year 1947 saw the creation of the CIA and the discovery of the Dead Sea Scrolls, not to mention the Roswell crash and the death of Aleister Crowley. In *A Warm Gun,* we are awash not in the coincidental but in the subliminal, and the possibility that the mythic battles between demonic and angelic forces are yet being recreated on planet Earth (and even beyond).

How quickly we forget, and with what urgency Levenda would remind us! The author's initial expertise was in the occult realm of Nazi Germany *(Unholy Alliance),* and here he sweeps through post-war events with a rapier, exposing the unctuous underbelly of a national history whose inevitable denouement may now be occurring—under the radar—with the corporate Christocracy of George W. Bush.

The pace of contemporary life moves too quickly—all sound-bite and videogame lever—for many of us to reflect upon yesterday, much less upon the patterns that fuel our paranoia. This book, then, is an often-maddening (but not mad!) excursion beyond the pale, beyond what has come to be considered "normalcy." Indeed, Levenda seems to be telling us, we live in the most abnormal—even paranormal—of times. And unless we heed the reality that underlies the everyday, our failure to connect the dots will allow our denial to persist. And increase the likelihood that, one of these godawful days, we shall either boil in our own carbon emissions or blow ourselves to smithereens in the name of righteousness.

"The bugle blows . . ." James Hillman writes in *A Terrible Love of War.* "Wake up, said Plato; we are all in a cave watching shadows on the wall, believing them to be reality."

So look down the barrel of Peter Levenda's *A Warm Gun,* and pay heed to the dark saga of how we came to our current "reality."

INTRODUCTION

Why this is hell, nor am I out of it.

—Mephistopheles in *Dr. Faustus*, Part I, iii, 76–80 by Christopher Marlowe

Welcome to Book Two of *Sinister Forces: A Warm Gun*. In Book One: *The Nine*, you were introduced to a thread of violence and bizarre belief—represented by violent and bizarre people running, like Sherlock Holmes' "scarlet thread of murder," through American history up to and including the assassinations of the two Kennedy brothers. Strange priests, satanic rituals, political conspiracy, and the occult. Not the sort of thing one normally encounters during the course of graduate work in political science . . . or during a walk down a dark alley in an American city at night. That all of these things happened is a fact; that these people committed these actions is a fact. That some very strange belief systems are at the heart of American policy, foreign and domestic, is also a fact.

That many Americans are not aware of this, or simply don't care, is another fact.

In this, the second book of a trilogy concerning American "political witchcraft," we will examine some of the more modern manifestations of this unsettling concourse of sinister forces. We will look at terrorism, true, but we will also discover the coincidence stream in full flow in the lives of men as disparate in social standing as Richard Nixon and Mark David Chapman, Jim Jones and Richard Mellon Scaife, David Berkowitz and Donald Cammell. It is a study of Washington . . . and Hollywood. Of serial murder and mysticism. Of the straining of the American intelligence community towards a manipulation of the unconscious mind and of their transgression into the realm of the occult and initiation. We will look at the stories we all think we already know, and see—maybe for the first time—what the Renaissance magician Giordano Bruno meant when he wrote of "the links": the doctrine of correspondences that is not only the province of ceremonial magic but of ceremonial politics. That is why this trilogy is called a "grimoire."

There are times when it appears that world history is nothing less than the story of warring secret societies, with all of the rest of humanity mere pawns in what historian Ladislas Farago called "the Game of the Foxes."

The Rosicrucians of the 17th Century gave us a prototype of the secret society: a band of brothers, bound together by mystical visions, which had probably never existed in reality but was the romantic invention of a English alchemist. It was an otherwise anonymous manifesto—a printed broadside—that created the myth of the Rosicrucians and since then many individuals have sought to capitalize on the name and the glamour by proclaiming themselves heirs to the Rosicrucian tradition.

What is Al-Qaeda, then, but another secret society: a band of brothers, bound together by a mystical vision of the world, whose membership is largely secret, where betrayal of the group's mysteries is punished by death, and which is probably a very small organization with a larger-than-life profile whose reputation is made on websites and videotapes . . . and mass murder. The same was said of the Illuminati and the Freemasons, upon whom the blame for centuries of violent revolution was laid. That Al-Qaeda—"the Base"—has more in common with the Assassins cult of Hasan-i Sabah only reinforces this idea of a secret society at war with the world . . . and with the West in general.

Should it surprise us, then, that the putative opponents of Al-Qaeda should be members of a Western secret society?

The secret society and occult affiliations of America's political and intelligence leadership is something that is never discussed on the open airwaves, never investigated by the mainstream media. We have all heard of Skull & Bones, and know that somehow President George W. Bush was a member of this college fraternity while a student at Yale University. The story seems to end there. No one delves too deeply into this aspect of Bush's life, even when it is revealed that his father belonged to the same society, and that Democratic presidential candidate John F. Kerry also belonged to Skull & Bones. The very idea that, in 2004, the presidential election was a choice between two Bonesmen never seemed to make the headlines in America even when it was shown that Skull & Bones membership is quite small (only *fifteen* new members are initiated every year), very select, and depends upon a strenuous enforcement of the rules of secrecy and deception. That the two presidential candidates were both members of this same small and elite group should have raised warning flags, and didn't. Yet, at a time when America was embroiled in the Iraq war and in an ostensible "war on terror"—directed against Al-Qaeda—our only choices for president were two members of the same secret society.

If that was all, it would be enough. But that's not all.

In 1833, the year after Skull & Bones was founded, another secret society was formed, this time at Union College in New York. This one was called Psi Upsilon, and was formed by seven students who signed a pact stating, "We, the undersigned, having determined to form a secret society, and having some conversation on the subject, do now and hereby pledge our sacred honors that we will keep all that has been done and said a most profound secret."

Psi Upsilon spread to many universities across America and even abroad. Its second, or Beta, chapter was founded at Yale University in 1840 and became known as The Fence Club in 1934.

In 1960, both Porter Goss, the George W. Bush-appointed Director of the CIA—and John Negroponte, the Bush-appointed Intelligence Chief—were members of The Fence Club at Yale. As was John Kerry, who was also, remember, a Bonesman.

Porter Goss was also a member of the super-secret Order of Book & Snake, a seemingly associated society of Skull & Bones. The same year Goss joined Book & Snake he also joined yet another secret society: the CIA.

And let us not forget still another member of the Bush dynasty, William Henry Trotter (Bucky) Bush, brother of former CIA Director and President, George Herbert Walker Bush. William Bush was also a member of The Fence Club in 1960, along with Porter Goss and John Negroponte.

So, what do we have?

We have George Herbert Walker Bush, George W. Bush, William Henry Bush, John F. Kerry, Porter Goss, and John Negroponte all members of secret societies at Yale University. And let's not forget Prescott Bush, who was one of the directors of the Union Banking Corporation that was shut down by the US government in 1942 when it was discovered that Bush and his partner, E Roland Harriman, were "trading with the enemy": i.e., the Nazis. Prescott Bush was another member of Skull & Bones.

That's two presidents, one presidential contender, two CIA directors, and an intelligence czar who are all fellow-travelers in the world of rituals and sworn oaths, secrecy and deception, trained since their late adolescence and early adulthood in the environment of privilege and control. Dear reader, should I burden you with revelations that Averell Harriman as well as Roland Harriman—partners with the Bush family in "trading with the enemy" before and during World War II—were also Bonesmen? That the Psi Upsilon secret society abandoned its pretence of being a literary society early on and admitted its preference for members with a proven *ancestry?* That there is little to associate these Orders with the popular conception of college fraternities represented by such films as *Animal House*?

As members of Skull & Bones, Psi Upsilon and Book & Snake consolidate their control over America's wealth, intelligence agencies, and military power, they are also engaged in a war with Islamic secret societies that costs us thousands of lives and hundreds of billions of dollars. Conservative Americans were worried in 1960 that should a Catholic become President, then America would somehow be controlled by the Pope. Instead, we have an America that is in thrall to a handful of initiates in a few small secret societies that share a hidden agenda, a covert brotherhood, and a contempt for individual liberty . . . and no one is bothered by this at all except the crazies, the loonies, the militiamen, the conspiracy theorists, the paranoid schizophrenics.

As the eminent *New York Times* critic Anatole Broyard once said, "paranoids are the only ones who notice anything anymore."

There are around 700 members of Skull & Bones alive today. That represents less than .00001 percent of America's total population, or 1 per every 300,000 persons. Yet, somehow, they occupy top positions of our government. The attitude of our media, however, is to "pay no attention to the man behind the curtain."

The previous volume of *Sinister Forces* ended with a review of the strange world of secret societies, wandering bishops, psychological warfare, and mind-control programs that culminated in the assassinations of President Kennedy and his brother, Senator Robert F. Kennedy. This volume picks up where the first left off: a discussion of these same influences around the Republican Party of Nixon and Reagan, Watergate, the assassination of John Lennon, the Son of Sam cult, the Manson Family, Jonestown. terrorism, and the "vast, right-wing conspiracy." This is a look behind the curtain, an exposé of The Nine as they perpetuated the ultimate secret society at work beneath the surface of America's long political nightmare through children especially selected as carriers of their message. It is *The Wizard of Oz* meets MK-ULTRA.

I'd like to end this by saying "We're not in Kansas, anymore." Unfortunately, might I say, paraphrasing Mephistopheles, "Why, this *is* Kansas. Nor am I out of it."

Peter Levenda
New York City

SECTION FOUR:

ALL THE PRESIDENT'S MEN

. . . Buzhardt told Haig that he could find "no innocent explanation," and concluded that the buzz had come from "some outside source of energy" rather than a malfunctioning of the tape recorder. Haig says he and other Presidential assistants suspected that night that the buzz had been caused by "some sinister force."

—J. Anthony Lukas, *Nightmare: The Underside of the Nixon Years*[1]

MIKE, THE ONE-ARMED MAN: "Don't turn on the overheads. The fluorescents don't work. I think a transformer's bad."
FBI SPECIAL AGENT DALE COOPER: "We know that."
MIKE: "Yes."

—Pilot Episode, *Twin Peaks*

Therefore with us there must be some accidental and particular cause preventing the human spirit from following its inclination and driving it beyond those limits within which it should naturally remain. I am profoundly convinced that this accidental and particular cause is the close union of politics and religion.

—Alexis de Tocqueville, *Democracy in America*[2]

We have had our last chance. If we will not devise some greater and more equitable system, our Armageddon will be at our door. The problem basically is theological and involves a spiritual recrudescence, an improvement of human character that will synchronize with our almost matchless advances in science, art, literature and all material and cultural developments of the past two thousand years. It must be of the spirit if we are to save the flesh.

—General Douglas MacArthur, Sept. 2, 1945

The Hatian Revolution—On the stormy night of August 14, 1791, at Bois Caiman in Haiti, a pivotal Voudon (voodoo) ceremony led by Dutty Boukman ignited what would become the first successful slave revolution in the Americas. The ritual, which included the sacrifice of a black pig and invocations to Ogun, the god of war, united slaves from plantations across Haiti's northern plain in a blood oath that launched a twelve-year struggle against French colonial rule. This revolution, uniquely merging African spiritual practices with Voudon beliefs—a syncretic religion combining West African Vodun traditions with Catholic elements—would transform Haiti into the world's first black republic and the second independent nation in the Americas, though the French and other colonial powers would extract a heavy economic toll for this independence in subsequent years.

BOOK TWO: A WARM GUN

CHAPTER NINE

FOR REBELLION IS AS THE SIN OF WITCHCRAFT

For rebellion is as the sin of witchcraft.
—1 Samuel 15:23

[King] Unas devoureth men and liveth upon the gods, he is the lord of envoys, whom he sendeth forth on his missions . . . . Khonsu the slayer of the wicked cutteth their throats and draweth out their intestines, for it is he whom Unas sendeth to slaughter; and Shesmu cutteth them in pieces and boileth their members in his blazing caldrons of the night. Unas eateth their magical powers, and he swalloweth their Spirit-souls . . . . The old gods and the old goddesses become fuel for his furnace.
—Pyramid Text[3]

If the power of God comes into a person, don't we become like God?
—Sirhan Sirhan[4]

By the conclusion of the first volume of *Sinister Forces, The Nine*, much had been made of political conspiracies, particularly those surrounding assassinations. There was also a focus on the Manson Family, as we walked with them through desert and canyon. But not so far as the Tate and LaBianca households. Not yet.

Furthermore, those events took place in a larger context. The pursuit of evil and the tracking of evil through the political and scientific machinations of intelligence agencies is ultimately unsatisfactory if we do not address an unspoken and normally unconscious assumption of our political leaders and particularly of our intelligence chiefs, and that is that their mission is in some way a divine one: that they represent the will of God.

The human assumption of divinity has been construed as evil—as a usurpation of the status of divine beings—for thousands of years. No organized religion of any size or amount of temporal power encourages or permits its followers direct access to divinity; the privilege of communicating directly to God has been reserved for the organized and socially approved priesthood. This is as true of ancient India as it is of modern Catholicism. Access to God is very tightly controlled, and is usually forbidden to certain elements of society, particularly women. Women may not become priests in the Roman Catholic Church, and are thus separated from the sacrament of ordination, a situation that calls into question the very nature of the soul. For it presupposes that the soul has a gender, since sacraments do not affect the body but only the soul. This is perhaps understandable in view of the etymology of the word "sacrament," which comes from the Latin and which originally meant a military oath, an oath of (male) soldiers. Women may not be ordained in the Eastern Orthodox churches, either.

In Orthodox Judaism, women may not become rabbis. Menstruating women, in fact, are considered unclean and may not enter the synagogue during their period. A man who touches a menstruating woman becomes unclean, and must bathe in the ritual bath—the *mikvah*—before going to worship himself. In the East, women are noticeably scarce in the lists of divine Hindu and Buddhist and Daoist figures.

Yet, in the West, it has traditionally been women who were charged with the practice of witchcraft, a phenomenon that has led some historians and anthropologists—such as Margaret Murray, Robert Graves and Erich Neumann—to develop the theory that witchcraft is the survival of an ancient goddess-oriented religion that was suppressed on a virtually global scale, from Europe to the Middle East, and to the borders of India. If this is true, and it was suppressed, then the reasons for the nearly perfect destruction of this religion had to be political.

Our most ancient artwork as a people has been that associated with magic and religion. The prehistoric cave paintings of Lescaux, for instance; the Venus of Willendorf; the many thousands of different varieties of goddess statues found all over the world. People did not venerate human leaders and etch their likenesses in stone and clay until civilization began to coalesce around villages and towns and away from field and forest. When they did, they did because their leaders partook of the divine essence, the divine nature; they were the representatives of the gods upon the earth.

And when this occurred, when state religions were established and associated with city-cults such as those of ancient Sumeria, Babylon and Egypt, then there grew up around them secret cults that worshipped older gods, the gods and goddesses that had been usurped by the newer, royally-linked deities. Even ancient Sumeria—arguably the oldest western civilization that has left any written record of itself—had its cult of witches, and various texts (such as the *Maqlu* or "Burning" Text) contain chants and prayers against the practice of witchcraft, some three thousand years before the birth of Christ. These witches were independent practitioners of ritual; in other words, they did not belong to the state cult, were not approved by the ruler (who was both secular and sacred ruler), and they worshipped beings that were not approved by the state cult. Thus, the Biblical phrase cited above, that witchcraft and rebellion were synonymous. Rebellion is a revolt against secular authority; the implication is therefore that witchcraft is a revolt against sacred authority. It puts access to God in the hands of the Great Unwashed. It creates an anti-church, just as rebellion creates an anti-government.

In a way, this is a logical extension of the Creation epics of all races. The Creation of the world (or the universe, or the cosmos, or just one race or nation) is always divine in nature. The First Man and the First Woman were created by God or Gods. Thus, society itself owes its existence to a deity of some kind. Following this chain of logic, then, the king—as the ruler of society—*must* have a special, sacred relationship with the divine. This is especially true in the West, where God is perceived as a King on a throne. (It may be argued therefore that the secularization of cosmology brought about by modern science could undercut any special claims to kingship, and render human rulers about as "special" as servers or routers on a computer network.)

The Cult of the Pharaoh in ancient Egypt was a religious as well as a secular cult. The Pharaoh was a representative of God; he was able to communicate directly with God, and after death he was guaranteed a continued existence as an Osiris, a resurrected god of the ancient Egyptians, after the performance of a long and complicated ritual which included mummification. The ancient Sumerian secular leaders would ascend to the top of their ziggurats and commune with their gods directly at certain times of the year. The Chinese Emperor was the "Son of Heaven" as was (and is) the Japanese Emperor; China was the "Middle Kingdom," at the center of the earth, and halfway between the earth and heaven. It is still called "Middle Kingdom"—*Zhong Guo*—to this day. The Dalai Lama is a political leader as well as a spiritual one; he is the incarnation of a god—*Avalokitesvara*, the God of Mercy—and when the Dalai Lama dies a search is undertaken to find his reincarnation. The leaders of the ancient Aztecs, Incas and Mayas had religious power. In Europe we had the Holy Roman Empire, and in England they talked of the "divine right of kings." Yet, in all of these cases, the composite religious-secular cult replaced an earlier one.

The older cults were buried, sometimes literally, and the new cults erected like shiny edifices on the bones of the old. In many cases, old cult centers were renovated and new cult centers built on their sites. This is true of Christian church construction in Europe, where many older sites of important pagan significance were co-opted by the new Christian leaders and turned into Christian shrines. The Gothic Cathedral at Chartres is a good example of this, but there are many more including St. Peter's Basilica itself, which was built on the site of the old Tauroboleum, a Mithraic cult center where bulls were sacrificed in honor of the god, Mithra. In fact, the name of the ceremonial headdress of Catholic bishops is still called a "mitre" seemingly in his honor, from the Latin *mitra* or "Mithra." This retention of ancient sites and ancient gods in the structure of their replacements may simply be a social strategy—to ensure greater and faster acceptance of the new cult by old cult members—or it may have an additional purpose, which would be to retain the particular powers of the older cults, those powers which their worshippers cultivate in secret ceremonies in the dead of night.

The ruthlessness with which new religions persecuted old ones was absolute. There is so little documentation left with which to appreciate and understand the older cults. Most of the documents we have on the ancient religions of Mexico and South America were written by Spanish Catholic priests and monks, for instance, and are therefore not necessarily wholly reliable. Tibetan Buddhism has all but eradicated the earlier Bon religion that it replaced, subsuming remnants of that shamanistic cult under its "Black Hat" Lamaistic branch, along with the Dalai Lama's "Yellow Hat" and the Gyalwa Karmapa's "Red Hat" sects. Of the old cults of pre-Dynastic Egypt we still know very little; the god Set—considered evil, on a par with the Christian "Satan," in Dynastic Egypt—was a god in his own right before the coming of the Pharaohs, as were Keb, Hathor and many others. The "God of the Witches" according to Margaret Murray in her controversial research was an ancient, horned deity whose worship was aggressively exterminated by the Church. Satan himself is an enigmatic figure, treated rather ambiguously in the Bible: sometimes as an adversary of God, sometimes as God's lieutenant (as in the Book of Job).

To worship the "old gods" was to commit heresy and, in the old days, treason. The political leadership and the religious leadership were one and the same. To go outside the system was to be cast into the outer darkness, to lose one's soul; to become a worshipper of devils, a word that comes from *deva*, the Sanskrit word for "god."

There is an interesting etymological puzzle that confronts the English speaker and the speaker of the Romance languages, and which compels us to draw some interesting and sobering conclusions about what we know and what we think we know. It is a puzzle that is at the heart of this study, and which will lead us into the Tunnels of Set, into the very bowels of Evil itself. And it may help us to understand Evil for the very first time.

REALITY, WHAT A CONCEPT

The word "real" and the word "royal" are inextricably linked. Indeed, in some languages the word for "real" and the word for "royal" is the same, such as Spanish *real*. Reality is, in this view, linked with Royalty; what is real is what is part of the kingdom, the "real estate." What is outside the kingdom is, therefore, outside of reality. It is not "royal," hence it is not "real." This speaks to Robert Anton Wilson's concept of "consensus reality," mentioned in the previous volume. Reality is a shape-shifter, dependent as much on political decisions as it is on scientific observations. And these decisions and observations are usually not the prerogative of the individual citizen. An essential part—a fundamental part—of the social contract, and imposed from the top down, is a general agreement as to what constitutes reality. To deviate from that agreement is to deviate from society—the kingdom, the real estate, the state religion—itself. It is to become, in a sense, a Satanist, a worshipper of an adversary; or a witch, a worshipper of an unapproved God.

We can take this analogy one step further, to the political arena, and say that he who attacks the king is insane, i.e., out of touch with reality. That is why our most famous assassins have all been pronounced "crazed" and "lone": they are insane and not part of a social group, at least not a social group recognized as valid in the kingdom. An attack on the king cannot be seen to originate from within the kingdom, from within the king's "reality": it has to come from outside, from the realm of the unreal, the unholy, for if it came from within the kingdom it would partake of the logic of the kingdom.

The other social group that is both crazed and alone is the independent ascetic, the hermit, the yogin, the sorcerer, the shaman. While often providing value to the social group—divination, exorcism of demons, channeling of spiritual forces—this person lives outside the general social structure in isolation from everyday communication and social intercourse. It is necessary to do so, for the forces that are contacted are those from outside the kingdom. The hermit or ascetic is a kind of probe into the Other World, the world outside the walls of the kingdom of reality. At times, the counsel is valued; usually, though, the person is despised, even ridiculed. The independent ascetic is one who breaks the social tabus of the group and refrains from social contacts, from eating socially approved foods (or from eating at all), from sexual activity and thus from the gene pool. The non-sexual ascetic does not share in the transfer of property—of real estate—that is so dependent upon marriage and the production of heirs. Or the ascetic may use unconventional sexual practices to reach altered states of consciousness: forms of reality outside the social contract.

Professor Wendy Doniger O'Flaherty—in her important study *The Origins of Evil in Hindu Mythology*—describes how the ancient Sanskrit texts relate the history of demons.

> The belief is often expressed that the demons were not only the equals of the gods but their superiors—the older brothers, the original gods from whom the gods stole the throne of heaven.[5]

This, of course, is exactly how the Sumerian creation epic describes it, showing how Marduk and his Company of Heaven rebelled against the older gods, their parents, and destroyed them. It is also related in this text that humanity was created from the blood of the slain older gods and the breath of the victorious younger gods. In fact, the Sumerian myth goes even further and describes the creation of human beings a bit as if Marduk was building automata, destroying the first set as defective. This parallels a Qabalistic legend that all of creation as we know it is really only the second draft; the first draft was defective and broke, and the shells of that first draft became the demons—the *qlippoth*—of the second. The idea that demons represent a moral quantum—evil, which is supposed to be the opposite of good—does not develop until much later and, in some cultures, not at all.

The idea that we are living in a replacement universe is common among the myths of the world which show an earlier civilization being destroyed, and the ancestors of the present human race as the survivors of the former. The Biblical legend of Noah and the Deluge is a good example of this, a legend that has its parallels all over the world. Hindu mythology, of course, describes Ages of vast length that repeat endlessly throughout time, witnesses to the rise and fall of many civilizations, many different forms of life and consciousness.

To the Hindus, the demons and the gods are consanguineous; they come from the same family, the same genetic stock. They both attempt to use humans to serve them, but they are really at war with each other. The gods have established an earthly priesthood to serve them, and society is obligated to support this priesthood—this "ritual sphere"—and to pay for the sacrifices which keep the gods strong. To do otherwise, is to invoke disaster:

> . . . it was in the interest of the Brahmins to convince these patrons that the gods regarded powerful human beings of the non-ritual sphere as demons and treated them accordingly . . . . Those mortals who aspired to religious power outside of the ritual sphere inherited the role of demons in the cosmic masque.[6]

and again:

> . . . a priest might legitimately emulate the gods, but an ascetic should not. An ambitious priest was like a god; an ambitious ascetic was like a demon.[7]

The ascetics were those who *interiorized* the rituals and the myths of the Vedas, the sacred Hindu scriptures, and who sought unity with godhead through their practices. Professor O'Flaherty makes particular reference to this system—which many readers will recognize as Kundalini Yoga—in the following passage:

> . . . Sumeru ("good Meru"), the world-mountain at the center of the earth, was now given a demonic counterpart, a mirror-image in the underworld—Kumeru ("bad Meru"). The world-mountain, which had provided access upwards, now extends down as well—and the gods oppose human and demonic ascetics who, by interiorizing these pillars within the spinal column, would mount to heaven.[8]

This anatomization of the world-mountain as the spinal column is known to the Jewish Qabalists as well. In fact, in Qabalism it is referred to as a "pillar," of which there are three. On these three pillars is drawn the glyph of the Tree of Life, and contemporary occultists have shown a relationship between the Ida, Pingala and Sushumna *nadis* or channels of the human body in Kundalini Yoga and the Right, Left and Middle Pillars of the Jewish Qabala and the body of Adam Kadmon, its ideal human. The important line in this citation is that the gods do not want either human or demonic ascetics to climb the pillar or mountain and so reach heaven. It is perceived as an attack on divine authority—to show up without an invitation—and the rituals and other practices designed to activate these powers in humans are prohibited by organized religion which is, certainly, the human representation of divine authority; organized religion becoming, in a sense, a colonial power on earth representing the home country on Mount Olympus or on Sumeru.

The interesting phonetic similarity of the world-mountain as "Sumeru" and the name of the ancient Mesopotamian culture "Sumeria" is, of course, noted. The Sumerians were famous for their stepped pyramids, the ziggurats, and many have conjectured that the Biblical Tower of Babel was in reality a ziggurat being built at Babylon by the Sumerians or by their successors, the Akkadians or Babylonians. The ancient Egyptians also revered mounds, and believed that the world was created when a Primeval Mound rose and separated the waters. This ancient belief may be related to the prevalence of mound cultures in ancient Europe, the British Isles and the Americas, just as the Egyptian pyramids have their counterparts in Mesopotamian ziggurats and Aztec, Maya and Inca pyramids in Latin America. While it is outside the scope of this book to go into further detail, it is tantalizing to speculate that there might have been significant communication between ancient Indian and ancient Sumerian cultures, representing general agreement on such things as a creation myth, a world-mountain myth, and the existence of evil and of demonic beings. They do, however, obviously agree on certain points whether they were ever in contact or not, and the abhorrence of individuals practicing religious—i.e., mystical or magical—rituals alone, outside the "ritual sphere" of the approved priesthood, is evident in both cultures.

Since the relationship of the society with God was all-important and communication with God deemed appropriate only for the highest levels of society (for reasons of national security!), we have to look for a motive for this. Obviously, survival of the society was dependent on the good graces of a powerful spiritual being who was considered to be omniscient and omnipotent (or, at least, more knowing and more powerful than the king). There was believed to be a channel of power or energy that emanated from that being and which was bestowed on the king, who then bestowed it on his kingdom. Thus, power and survival, the king and the god, formed the mechanism by which a society was identified and prospered. In a time when natural disasters—drought, flood, disease—could spell life or death for the tribe or the city-state, it was considered essential that someone in the kingdom have a direct line to the forces that controlled these disasters, since society itself could obviously not do so on its own.

Independent ritual-performers, therefore, must have been viewed with horror, for they were going directly to these forces and enlisting their aid in projects that did not have the blessing or approbation of society, that is, the king. It was a usurpation of the king's power, and it could spell catastrophe for the kingdom. Further, if the independent ritual-performers—let's call them sorcerers—contacted supernatural forces that were allied against the king's god, then a state of spiritual warfare existed in which sacrifices were being made and resources of the kingdom exhausted in propitiation of the *wrong* gods, the *older* gods, the spiritual adversaries of the king's god. It is easy to see why sorcerers and witches would be considered traitors or rebels. We can also see that the very fabric of reality itself was threatened when witches were allowed to practice their craft, since their successes with spells and potions and the shamanistic channeling of supernatural forces were more spectacular—and more convincing—than the elaborate ceremonial of the state religions that relied more on the maintenance of the status quo than on the expansion of consciousness or the direct apprehension of the Godhead by a normal citizen. The witch or sorcerer had access to a level of knowledge about the world that was not available to the general public and perhaps not even to the priesthood itself. This practice was especially attractive to women, as they were usually excluded from the state priesthood or from direct participation in their rituals, except perhaps for purely sexual purposes as ceremonial concubines or temple prostitutes.

The author believes that the political implications of witchcraft are rarely addressed in the literature, and hopes that the present work stimulates more in-depth research on this subject, especially now when the relationship between religion and politics is becoming more important, more pronounced in the world arena. One of the problems in addressing these issues, however, is the lack of a vocabulary for expressing some basic concepts. The literature of witchcraft—i.e., of shamanism, sorcery, "black magic" and the like—is such that it resists easy classification; but if we view witchcraft from both a psychological as well as an existential (perhaps an ontological) viewpoint, and politics from a psychological and religious viewpoint, we may be able to provide a convincing and workable political metaphor.

Why bother to concern ourselves with such an arcane task? Because modern science in the twenty-first century is on the verge of a major breakthrough in the physics of consciousness as we will see in the final volume of this work, and we as a race have demonstrated that we do not understand consciousness itself; we don't understand the forces with which we are dealing. We have so far left this responsibility in the hands of politicians, generals . . . and sorcerers. And they have used their knowledge to commit murder and other outrages, and have covered up their crimes by destroying evidence, shredding documents, and vilifying their accusers . . . or by couching their discoveries in such esoteric terms that the layman has no hope of ever understanding what they have accomplished, or what dark forces have been loosed upon the earth.

THE HIDDEN FORCE

It is useful to look at contemporary beliefs and practices concerning witchcraft and the "black arts," and the influence they have over the political lives of the people. In the West, such practices are, on the one hand, suppressed and devalued by a kind of media assault aided and abetted by such professional skeptics as the late Carl Sagan, James Kreskin, Martin Gardner and others, while, on the other hand, subliminally encouraged by Hollywood offerings such as *The Believers; Rosemary's Baby; Charmed; Sabrina, the Teen-Aged Witch; Buffy, the Vampire Slayer;* and *Angel.* In the East, these practices are tolerated *and accepted* to a degree unheard of in modern Europe or North America. Asian religions are—compared to their Western counterparts—a rich amalgam of mainstream religious practice and theological discussion mixed with indigenous occult practices and beliefs. Chinese Daoism (often spelled "Taoism") is a very good example of this. It had been suppressed in the People's Republic of China, of course, and only lately have a few of the ancient Daoist temples been renovated and re-opened, including the famous White Cloud Monastery in Beijing while, at the same time, Falun Gong has been brutally put down, its members imprisoned and dying during "questioning."

The practice of what is loosely called Daoism is a survival of very old pagan practices of the Han Chinese, mixed with elements of imported Indian Buddhism and yogic and Tantric practices. At its heyday, it was the state religion of China, much as Shinto is the state religion of Japan, where the Japanese emperor is an embodiment of indigenous Japanese Shinto beliefs. A study of Daoist occult literature—specifically in reference to what is known as "Daoist alchemy"—will show very clear correspondences with Tantric ritual as well as elements familiar to students of European alchemy; it is thus a valuable source of information on a very old system of beliefs and practices that predate Christianity, Buddhism and all the other monotheistic faiths in the world. It may have come from the same fountain of belief that provided the underpinning of the Vedic and pre-Vedic practices of India as well as of the religion of ancient Mesopotamia, of which we have only the sketchiest background. As discussed in the previous volume, the jury is still out on whether the "diffusionists" or the "independent inventionists" have the better explanation for these similarities, but let's leave that discussion open for now.

While Daoism has had its ups and downs in China, it has flourished within the Chinese communities outside China: in Taiwan, Singapore, Malaysia, Hong Kong, and in the Chinese communities of the West. What many non-Chinese do not know, however, is the prevalence of spirit possession as a divinatory practice in the temples. It is common for a Chinese desirous of knowing about the future to go to a Daoist temple (or, perhaps, a Chinese Buddhist temple; it is sometimes difficult to tell the difference between the two!) and ask for guidance from a medium. The medium goes into a trance, is possessed by a spiritual force, and gives answers to questions. This is all within the precincts of the temple and is supported by the temple, its monks and the people; thus, one would be hard put to categorize it as an "alternative" practice. It is obviously, however, a clear survival of Asian shamanism, a practice that was already ancient when the Buddha was born.

In Asian Muslim countries there is a corresponding cult of spirit possession, shamanism and what can only be called a type of "witchcraft." In Malaysia and Indonesia particularly (and to a lesser extent in Singapore and the Philippines), Islam has permitted the existence of a kind of witch doctor-cum-medicine man, known in Malaysia as a *bomoh*. This is a phenomenon that predates the arrival of Islam to these countries in the fifteenth century, and has been sturdy enough to survive as a reliable occult entity alongside the usually theologically intolerant Muslim faith for almost five hundred years; and it has had tremendous influence on not only the grass-roots political structures of the *kampung* (the Malay word from which we get the English "compound," and usually used to refer to a village or a "neighborhood" of houses in a village) but also on politics at a national level.

Indonesia is the largest Muslim nation in the world. Located in Southeast Asia, south of the Philippines, it includes a share (with Malaysia) of the large island known as Borneo; all of Sumatra, Java, and Sulawesi; West Timor; the part of New Guinea known as Irian Jaya; as well as the captivating paradise of Bali and literally thousands of other islands in the archipelago. Indonesia is home to over 200 million people, most of whom are at least nominal Muslims, but which include some Hindus (principally on Bali), Chinese of various faiths, and people known as *orang asli* or "original people": animists and jungle-dwellers whose ancestors go back on these islands for thousands of years. Indonesia's most notable ancient architecture is the temple at Borobudur on Java, which is a Hindu masterpiece.

An essential element of Indonesian culture and especially of the Javanese is something known as *kebatinan* loosely translated as "inner dimensions of life." It comes from the Malay root *batin* which means "inner feeling," a kind of mystical sense and sentiment wrapped up in one. (This concept of *batin* actually comes from Islamic mysticism, and is an Arabic word meaning "esoteric" or "hidden," as we will see in a later chapter.)

Anthropologist Dr. Niels Mulder, in his *Mysticism in Java: Ideology in* Indonesia, describes it this way:

> Things are not what they appear to be, but have a hidden core which fascinates them . . . . They speculate about hidden forces—whether spirits, or secretive political manipulation . . . . They are fond of explaining the symbolism of the ritual meal, of religious practice, of chance occurrences, of chronograms, and suchlike. In brief, the symbolic—and the mystical—dimensions of life constitute an important field of interest.[9]

In one paragraph, Mulder sums up the essential elements of this entire study: the hidden forces which are either (or both) spiritual forces and political ones; the symbolism of chance occurrences, religious practice, and the mystical dimensions of life. Western societies today do not consciously live in such a world; but they do so unconsciously, as it is hoped this study goes far to prove. However, Eastern societies *do* live consciously in a world where the "hidden force"—to borrow a phrase from both Niels Mulder and Dutch novelist Louis Couperus—penetrates and permeates all existence, and is a component of reality that cannot be ignored. *Kebatinan* is one way of describing this force. Couperus gives us another:

> Under all the appearance of tangible things the essence of that silent mysticism threatens, like a smouldering fire underground, like hatred and mystery in the heart.[10]

And:

> He would never know that, lurking under the simple life, there are all those forces which together make the omnipotent hidden force. He would have laughed at the idea that there are nations that have a greater control over that force than the Western nations have. He would shrug his shoulders—and continue on his way—at the mere supposition that among the nations there are a few individuals in whose hands that force loses its omnipotence and becomes an instrument.[11]

Couperus lived in Indonesia for a while when it was a Dutch colony, and was intimate with both the Dutch expatriate community there as well as the local population. It is impossible to live in Southeast Asia for any length of time and not become aware of this "hidden force" . . . or, at least, of the belief of the people in its existence, for they conduct their lives in accordance with its myriad manifestations. The longer one spends in Indonesia, Malaysia, Singapore and environs the more one becomes accustomed to the operation of this force; this is especially true of those who spend time outside the major cities and in the smaller towns, where the rule of the *bomoh* is stronger, and where *kebatinan* is thick in the atmosphere against the backdrop of the mosque and muezzin's cry; the lavish Hindu temples with their colorful statues of thousands of deities crammed together like a cocktail party of the gods; the mysterious Chinese temples in clouds of incense, strange hieroglyphic characters painted on scrolls representing the signatures of invisible forces. It almost takes a novelist's sensitivity to grasp the essential nature of this hidden force, as science has provided us with no intelligible language to describe it; or, perhaps, our very nature as Europeans and Westerners has imposed upon us a certain way of looking at life that is somewhat at odds with those of the East, and as well with those of our own Native Americans, our *orang asli*. As ethnographer of the Navajo culture Sam Gill writes,

> As I have come to think of it, when the facts of history come together for someone in a way that reveals their meaning or in a way that enables their fuller

> understanding to be sought, a story is born. History lacks meaning without story. Story lacks substance and relevance without history . . . . For the European-American story tradition the authority is history, even though the story is not strictly historical; for the Native American story tradition the authority is religious and outside of history, even though the story reflects history.[12]

Thus, for European-Americans, the facts are obvious—historical data—even though they may be treated in a novelistic manner in order to extract as much meaning as possible. For Native Americans—according to Gill—the facts are not necessarily obvious from a European-American perspective: the underlying structure, the "authority," is "religious and outside of history," which is comparable to Mulder's take on *kebatinan*, and which represents a force essentially religious (or, at least, mystical) and outside of what we understand as history, *outside the linear flow of time*, as much Navajo tribal legend is expressed.

Mulder's study of Javanese mysticism is simultaneously a study of Javanese politics. He begins by describing traditional Javanese concepts of kingship:

> Kings were thought to be among the most powerful mystical elements on earth, to be receptacles of cosmic potency. Their worldly power reflected their charisma, that is, their receiving of a supernatural mandate to rule, known as their wahyu . . .. Such wahyu was a clear sign of their association with and concentration of kasekten (cosmic potency), which was thought to radiate as a beneficial magical force from their persons to the populace . . .[13]

As Mulder goes on to describe, even their palaces reflected this concept, designed as microcosms, pictures in miniature of the entire universe with the king as the center, or "axis mundi."[14] Thus, the spirituality of the king represents an interplay between the visible and invisible worlds, and thus affects the peace and prosperity of his kingdom.[15] Although this seems like perfect superstitious mumbo-jumbo to modern Western ears—especially in the postwar era of atomic energy, space travel and the Internet—if we were to suspend disbelief for a moment and apply this notion to a European or American ruler, we might see that some of these same beliefs apply.

No matter how good a president Bill Clinton may have been, for example, he was pilloried over his supposedly private sex life: something that has no relevance to how well or how poorly he did his job. This suggests strongly that some significant portion of the American electorate feels that a President should be the moral equivalent of a minister of religion, even though there is no such provision in the Constitution which, to the contrary, mandates a separation of church and state. The viciousness of the attacks on Clinton over this issue—and the maneuvering of his friends and Party members away from openly supporting him in light of the revelations concerning Monica Lewinsky—demonstrates a clear (if somewhat hypocritical) connection in the popular mind between the President's behavior as an individual and the state of the nation, much like the old legends of King Arthur and the Holy Grail. This is so for a political leader who is democratically elected and who serves a maximum of two terms of four years each. How much more so for a leader who attains his or her position by virtue of genetics or marriage, such as a king or queen?

In Malaysia the king was viewed as a kind of shaman, as Sir Richard Winstedt points out in *The Malay Magician,* in a way very similar to that of Indonesia.[16] Winstedt, in fact, sees a close association between Malay magic and that of ancient Babylon, going so far as to suggest that the creation myths of the pre-Hindu Malays—recited as part of ritual by Malay shamans—are an echo of the Sumerian legends of Marduk and Tiamat.[17] The facts may be somewhat the reverse of appearances, as Stephen Oppenheimer suggests in his *Eden In The East.* Oppenheimer, a doctor specializing in tropical pediatrics and based out of Hong Kong, believes he has found genetic markers and other evidence in the tribes of Malaysia and Indonesia to suggest that the peoples of the ancient Middle East originated in . . . the Malay archipelago. His arguments are persuasive for a Southeast Asian "Garden of Eden," from which civilization sprang at the time of a great deluge eight thousand years ago. Winstedt was writing in 1951; Oppenheimer in 1998. It is a strange theory, from the point of view of traditional anthropology and archaeology, but the medical evidence in Oppenheimer's case and the internal evidence of Malay myth and ritual in Winstedt's case make for a compelling story. The idea of the king as high priest is also consistent with ancient Sumeria, and it is still understood as such by some contemporary Malays regardless of the influence of traditional Islam.

For example,

> In the eighteenth century Perak had a state shaman, who was of descent fully royal and bore the title of Sultan Muda or Junior Sultan . . . . The holder of this office (which still exists under the title of State Magician) is head of all the magicians in Perak and he is expected to keep alive the sacred weapons of the regalia, to conduct an annual feast and séance with libations for the royal drums and to make sacrificial offerings to the genies of the state. Such offerings are still made as part of the ceremony of installing a Sultan of Perak.[18]

As mentioned above, Winstedt was writing in 1951, but these citations are from a revised 1960 edition, i.e., after Malaysian independence in 1957. Perak is a Malaysian state on the west coast of peninsular Malaysia, on the Straits of Malacca (Melaka), north of Kuala Lumpur and south of Georgetown (Pulau Pinang). The point of this geography lesson is that the State of Perak is not a strange, isolated little community deep within the rain forest, but on the contrary is an important part of Malaysian history and has seen Hindus, Buddhists, Muslims, Christians, Chinese, Indians, Dutch, English, Arabs and every sort of trader, missionary, soldier and politician along its coast.

Again:

> The Malay shaman . . . and the Malay ruler both own familiar spirits. The familiars of a sultan are the genies who protect his state . . . . At a famous séance held in 1874 to discover if Mr. Birch, the first British Resident, would be wrecked on the bar of the Perak river, Sultan Abdullah himself was a medium and was possessed by nine spirits in succession.[19]

For the interested, the much-unloved Mr. J.W.W. Birch did not survive. A typical example of English colonial arrogance, he considered himself superior to the Sultan and thus to everyone else in Malaya and conducted himself accordingly; and accordingly, he was the victim of an assassination.

More than merely a medium or shaman, the Malay ruler was also believed to be the incarnation of a god; something that is no longer discussed in polite Malaysian company, but which survives in some of the pomp and ceremony that attends the installation of a sultan. This belief is thought to have occurred among the Malay people via India and Tantric Hinduism.[20] Hinduism has affected every layer of Malaysian society, even though it is often not recognized as such and its evidence merely accepted as being "traditionally Malaysian." The wedding ceremony of the Malay people, for instance, is virtually a carbon-copy of the Indian wedding ceremony, in which the bride and groom sit on a throne or raised dais and are told to look solemn.

The installation of a sultan in some states, however, particularly in Negeri Sembilan and Perak, is replete with even more Hindu and Buddhist ceremonial, although much of it has been sanitized and Islamicized to be in accord with the state religion. There is a limit to how much one can sanitize or Islamicize an ancient ritual, however, and the procedures involving lustration, circumambulation, the sacred weapons, the blessing of the four cardinal directions, etc. remain as very strong and incontrovertible evidence of both Malaysia's Indian heritage as well as its native, animist, shamanistic culture. Even more, it is evidence of a global preoccupation with the identity of king and magician, and the idea that a political ruler is also a kind of medium, a channel for the hidden force.

In Malaysia today, kingship is a revolving door. The king or "agong" of Malaysia is chosen among the sultans. The sultans are, of course, hereditary rulers of their specific states, and as such are believed to have an equal claim to the throne. The investiture of a king is ritualistic and involves (among other things) the bestowal of the ceremonial sword and the *kriss*, a wavy-bladed dagger that is a mystical weapon similar to the *athame* of modern witchcraft (traditionally, a double-bladed knife with a black handle), or the magic wand of European ceremonial magic. Spiritual forces are believed to reside in the kriss, and there are a tiny handful of people in Southeast Asia whose specialty is their manufacture, a process complicated by elaborate ritual requirements.

The king serves for a limited period of time before he is replaced by another of the thirteen sultans, making this a unique type of constitutional monarchy. The king in Malaysia has very little political power as such, this being invested in the Prime Minister (who is elected) and his Cabinet, after the British parliamentary fashion. Yet, the *authority* of the king is extremely important and sacred to the Malay people. His position is a ritual one, yet that does not diminish its power but rather enhances it. The king of Malaysia is the repository of its *kebatinan*, a tangent point between this world and the hidden force that underlies it. This is not seen as a philosophy antagonistic to Islam, for the sultans are all Muslims and hold a position of authority where the practice of Islam is concerned in their respective states. It is viewed as a philosophy that runs parallel to that of Islam, involving concepts of power, spiritual harmony and social integration that are deemed to co-exist with the teachings of the Prophet. There is the same co-existence, albeit with local variations, in Indonesia as in Malaysia; and other Islamic nations are not immune to flirtations with cosmic forces.

Indeed, in devoutly Muslim Pakistan, former Prime Minister Benazir Bhutto expressed a belief that the trials and tribulations of her father's regime were a re-enactment of the life of the Prophet, Muhammad. Blending religious imagery with political realities, Bhutto exploited the supposed similarities between the two men in an effort to crystallize her own role in the affairs of her country, and to demonize her father's opponents.[21] Elsewhere in Southeast Asia, yellow-beribboned Corazon Aquino expressed a belief that the spirit of her martyred husband, Ninoy Aquino (who was assassinated by men loyal to then-dictator of the Philippines, Ferdinand Marcos) entered into her to help her win the Philippine presidential elections on the "People Power" ticket.[22] Cory Aquino is a Catholic, and for a Catholic the idea that a spirit of the dead could enter into you and help you win an election is pure and unadulterated witchcraft; but in Asia, it is politics as usual.

Although mystical beliefs and their influence over politics in Indonesia go back for more than a thousand years, and can be traced in the Hindu–Buddhist pantheism that is unique to the country (after all, the national art form of this largest of all Muslim nations is the famous shadow puppet theater in which scenes of the Hindu epics the *Ramayana* and *Mahabharata* are enacted) as well as in local legends about the sanctity of various sites, trees, stones and so forth, the codification of these beliefs into a coherent system only began in the days after the end of World War II. Nationalism in the wake of the Japanese invasion and liberation, the end of Dutch colonial rule, the rise of Javanese political parties and a more orthodox approach to Islam as a result of greater communication with Arab countries all contributed to the creation of a national identity. This artificial Indonesian man is a spiritual *homunculus* born of a need to create a homogeneous national character out of the thousands of islands, races, religions and tribes that compose the archipelago. Rather than emphasize Islam as the unifying force, since many

Indonesians were lukewarm Muslims at best, it was necessary to dig deeper into the beliefs that form the bedrock of consciousness, not only for the Javanese but for all the peoples of the new country.

It was against this background in 1945 that Indonesian strongman Sukarno came up with a spiritual paradigm for citizenship, called *pancasila* or the "five principles": belief in one God, a just humanity, Indonesian unity, democracy, and social justice.[23] (This was copied virtually verbatim by the Malaysian government as their *Rukunegara:* Articles of Faith of the State.) The development of these principles (which eventually became a full-fledged government program requiring acceptance by every citizen) took place only after warring mystical sects in Indonesia began to threaten national unity. It is perhaps not realized by contemporary commentators on Indonesian affairs that the people of the country were by no means unified in their Muslim beliefs. Amidst the open hostility between traditional and modern Muslim factions there was, in fact, a strong and vocal anti-Islamic movement in Indonesia in the 1950s. Opposition to Islam did not come only from the Hindu island of Bali, but from mystical sects—such as the Permai—that based their ideology on what they perceived to be indigenous religious and mystical practices that predated the arrival of Hinduism from India. Permai was both a mystic cult and a political party, and thus shared some features with other cults abroad in the land that were forming themselves into action groups.[24] These groups were a threat to political stability, and the relatively new government of Indonesia saw an urgent necessity to codify religion and "approve" only certain faiths while proscribing the rest. Thus, once again, political rebellion and religious divergence became synonymous.

Indonesia provides us with a laboratory case of how nationalism is manufactured in any society. The German experience with Nazism gave us one case, but as it was a European example it may, paradoxically, be difficult for Europeans to understand it fully. The Indonesian example has all of the elements necessary to create the same type of nationalism, and the exotic nature of Indonesia to Westerners may enable us to see the action in more relief.

The country now known as Indonesia is in reality an amalgamation of many different cultures, including the Javanese, which seems to be dominant at this time, but also the Sumatran, Sulawesian, Balinese, etc. Once the Dutch left the "East Indies" at the end of World War II—and the British left Malaya and Singapore—the entire region went into a period of ideological self-discovery. Nationhood was a fragile thing; the territories that comprised the new country of Malaysia fell apart into Malaysia, Singapore and Brunei. The presence of a large number of Chinese in Malaya helped to consolidate Malay identity as the Malays banded together to show a united front against the non-Muslim, non-Malay Chinese. This resulted, however, in largely Chinese Singapore breaking away from the new Malaysia and forming its own, independent country while retaining Bahasa Melayu as their official language. Indonesia had a much smaller Chinese population, but itself has had trouble holding onto East Timor (which was predominantly

Portuguese-influenced and Christian), and as of this writing that tiny piece of real estate is now independent.

In any nationalist state, language is supremely important and it is necessary to elevate one language above all others; it is also the most practical approach for any country. The decision on which language to use, however, is fraught with political consequences. In the case of Malaysia, it was easy to adopt Bahasa Melayu as the official state language while also recognizing Chinese and Tamil as important local tongues. The Communist victory in China, however, galvanized the Malaysians in a struggle against what they perceived to be Chinese Communist insurgents in their own country. The struggle against Chinese Communism became, unfortunately, a struggle against their own, indigenous Chinese and any Chinese opposition to Malaysian government policies was interpreted as evidence of Chinese Communist agitation, much as opposition to US government policy in the United States during the McCarthy Era was seen as evidence of Communist "sympathy" if not outright treason. The Chinese were deliberately isolated from the rest of society for a time—during the so-called "Malay Emergency"—and placed in what were euphemistically called "New Villages," but which were only a step away from concentration camps. Thus, in Malaysia, race, religion and politics became inextricable one from the other. This has led to increasing states of tension over the years, and the equally increasing measures taken by the government to quell any outward signs of opposition, resulting in the famous "incident" in May of 1969, in which hundreds of Chinese were slain by rioting Malays.

In Indonesia, which shares a basic language in common with Malaysia, language was not as large an issue as religion, especially in a land where national culture is so closely identified with religion. The ringing tones of the *gamelan* orchestra, the almost furtive shadow figures of the *wayang* puppet shows, the massive Hindu structure at Borobudur . . . these have nothing to do with Islam but everything to do with Indonesia. This is why the Sukarno concept of pancasila was so necessary for national unity, because it did not elevate any religion or culture above another but sought to create a new Indonesian citizen, tolerant of all, as opposed to a primarily Javanese or a Balinese citizen. In this way, individual cultures were allowed to retain their special identities while still contributing to the nation as a whole. On paper, this seemed like a very workable concept; but in action it allowed the proliferation of occult beliefs and practices among both the educated classes as well as the relatively uneducated mass of people who could not decide whether Islam—as a foreign import—was inimical to their nation, or if it provided a healthy alternative to the mystical belief in *kebatinan*. It was the pancasila program that, in its attempt to incorporate the entire Indonesian cultural experience, managed to adopt the mystical attitudes of the people into a general cultural gestalt. Thus, to survive as a nation, Indonesia had to recognize the value of *batin*, the inner spiritual side of what it means to be human, that side of oneself that is in contact with the hidden force. Indonesia has had to legitimize the occult power of *kebatinan*.

Much the same has occurred in Malaysia. There is a concept there known as *badi* which is as resistant to translation as the Indonesian *batin* and which may represent the same term (the differences between Indonesian and Malaysian languages are slight; they are virtually the same language but have developed some local terminology), but which in Malaysia has a more sinister connotation. *Badi* is considered to be an "evil principle" by Skeats, who is one of the acknowledged authorities on Malay mysticism.[25] The catalogue of what has and does not have *badi* is very long, and seems to be much more specific in nature than the relatively amorphous *batin* of the Indonesian shamans. The ability to control the *badi* of animate and inanimate objects is the province of the *bomoh*. The power of the *bomoh*, the local village shaman, is recognized—albeit unofficially—by government and industry. Bomohs are widely believed to have power over the weather, for instance, and they can be called upon to ensure a sunny day for important political and cultural events and for open-air speeches by the Prime Minister. Some bomohs have been accused of much worse, however, including rape, sexual abuse of children, theft, and murder. In the year 2002, a bomoh—a woman accused of murdering a client—was executed in Malaysia. It is said she went smiling to her death.

The practice of extreme forms of occultism occurs with astonishing regularity in Malaysia, although most of the reporting on them usually takes place in Singaporean newspapers. In one case, a group of occultists had been murdering Caucasians in rituals designed to give them winning numbers in the lottery. The skulls of the murdered men and one woman were found in a hut in the forest, alongside ritual paraphernalia. Cases that would have made national news in the United States for months are treated with a kind of bland distance that is the result of both a desire to suppress the uglier aspects of Malaysian society and the contempt born of familiarity, and the cases are lost quickly from the media and never heard of again.[26]

Religious deviance is punished in Malaysia. The country has embraced the Sunni form of Islam, which means they view Shi'ism as a heresy. Shi'ism is not permitted in Malaysia, and its practitioners can be arrested by the Islamic courts (which are not, strictly speaking, government or secular courts) and imprisoned. More than Shi'ism, however, any form of theological deviation from strict Sunnism is frowned upon and can result in arrest and imprisonment. As in Indonesia, religious deviation automatically implies political rebellion; fundamentalist Islamic sects in Malaysia have been known to accumulate weapons and to call for an end to the domination of the main political alliance, UMNO (United Malays National Organization) and its creature, the Barisan Nasional. Strongest opposition to UMNO comes from PAS, which is a fundamentalist Islamic political party and which has, in the Malaysian states where it has won the majority, instituted the *shariyah*—Islamic law, such as obtained in Afghanistan under the Taliban and does yet in Saudi Arabia. Thus, supermarket check-out lines are divided into male and female; swimming pools at resort hotels are to be equally separated by sex, as are movie theaters and any public place; the sale and consumption of alcohol is not allowed, nor is even the presence of a pig much less the consumption of pork. PAS would like to see all of Malaysia—especially the capitol, Kuala Lumpur—under the rule of *shariyah,* creating, in essence, a theocracy. Fundamentalist forces in Indonesia and in the province of Mindanao in the Philippines are looking forward to the same goals; in fact, a goal of the local terrorist organizations allied to Al-Qaeda is the creation of a Muslim state that would encompass Malaysia, Indonesia, and the Philippine island of Mindanao.

None of this would matter to most Westerners, except that now the question of religion—and especially the unholy alliance of religion and politics—has become a major issue whose solution has profound implications for American and European national security. While Americans like to think that their Constitution protects them from state sponsored religious bigotry and fundamentalism, the threat from outside their borders is very real.

When Western intelligence services analyze the political, economic and cultural situations in Asian countries for their leaders, they naturally do so from a perspective that is the end result of thousands of years of cultural conceit (much the same way Eastern intelligence services view Western political developments). Much nuance is lost in the translation. Mistakes that were made in Vietnam are repeated endlessly in American foreign policy decisions, for instance; no one has the time or the inclination to become expert in the delicate cultural infrastructure of these societies and, anyway, we can always "bomb them into the Stone Age." United States presidents have only four years to succeed in their position and have to run for re-election a year before even that term is complete. This means they look for easy solutions, fast solutions to every problem. That is dangerous in any organization, but when the president is the leader of the most militarily and economically powerful nation on earth, such a fast fix invites catastrophe. Those citizens who oppose American foreign policy towards the developing nations, however, tend to swing to an extreme position and often hold up the beliefs, practices and social organizations of these societies as something exemplary, something to emulate. Both are examples of a perverse kind of racism that does nothing to ameliorate the situation, and both are wrong.

The psychological warfare experts of the 1950s came closest to understanding how to manipulate and exploit national *weltanschauung.* Their studies of African witchcraft, discussed in Book One, for instance, should be taken out and dusted off by their modern counterparts and improved upon with what is known now by academics, field engineers, social workers, Peace Corps volunteers and anyone else who has spent years in developing nations becoming accustomed to local beliefs and practices. Much has been made of the FBI profilers who must train themselves to think like their prey in order to capture them; men like Ressler and Vorpagel and Douglas have all written books about this process. The same approach is necessary for those intelligence services who wish to understand their target countries and to predict political developments with any kind of accuracy. This type of information is not always easily quantifiable—the hidden forces frustrate logical description. The United States has very few experts available on the cultures, the languages, the histories and the native beliefs of the people living in developing countries; yet, these are the same people who have become, in some instances, America's greatest enemies. It is this type of institutional racism that is causing a serious security problem in the United States. American political and military leaders have, in many cases, listened too long to Sagan and Gardner and Kreskin; it is time they paid more attention to Roscoe Hillenkoetter, Douglas MacArthur, Claiborne Pell, Carlos Castaneda, Jack Parsons . . . and the witches. Unfortunately, American foreign policy has been largely "anti-occult," as can be seen by its vociferous campaign against voodoo in Haiti.

THE COMEDIANS

Although there have been many examples of theocracies in ancient history (and a few in modern history, such as Tibet), there are perhaps even fewer "cultocracies" in the world, but when they do occur they offer evidence of the way cults operate even when they do not control an entire nation. In my previous work, *Unholy Alliance*, I attempted to show how the Third Reich was just such a cultocracy. Here, in North America, we have had another: the Republic of Haiti, under the dictatorships of Papa Doc and Baby Doc Duvalier.

Haiti is perhaps a unique example of a nation that was created out of the *houngans* and *hounforts* of the Voudon religion, normally spelled "voodoo." A survival of Dahomeyan, Nigerian, and religions from other parts of Africa's west coast, within the outer façade of Roman Catholicism, Voudon is a dynamic and energetic faith that unites racial identity, spirituality and what may be called "witchcraft" or "sorcery" into a single, all-encompassing practice. Voudon has always attracted other Americans and Europeans because of its exotic sensuality and aura of the mysterious, even the sinister. When the author was a child, his father had a "voodoo doll" in a box, imported from Haiti. The word was out to destroy the dolls because they contained poisonous berries for eyes. The doll was a black female, dressed in Haitian costume, and I was shown the doll once, and never saw it again, presumably to ensure that I did not consume one of the poisonous eyes . . . or did not become possessed by the desire to know more about the Haitian cult and its numerous *loa*, or gods.

Even Watergate co-conspirator and CIA agent E. Howard Hunt fell back on voodoo for his novel *The Coven*, having a young woman go to Africa on a research scholarship and come back as an initiate of the mysteries. She goes on to try to supplant another African priestess since she has had more direct contact with the original faith, but is murdered instead. The other priestess is referred to as a *mamaloi*, which is a Haitian term—and not an African one—for a priestess of the faith. Of course, practitioners of voudoun do not collect themselves into "covens," which is more appropriately a term used to refer to a gathering of European-style witches.

Voudon (or voodoo) is also the setting for a novel by another former intelligence officer, Ian Fleming, in *Live and Let Die*, the James Bond book that was made into a movie starring Roger Moore as 007. This story also centers on a beautiful priestess, and a voodoo cult based in the Caribbean as well as in New York City. The mixture of magic and eroticism—particularly of the interracial kind—is a hallmark of popular fantasies about voodoo. The controversial film *Angel Heart* also develops this idea, and once again we have a beautiful priestess (played by Lisa Bonet) who captivates a New York City detective (played by Mickey Rourke), and the voodoo cult is once again at the center of the action, along with a European-style Devil (played by Robert DeNiro). The action takes place in both New Orleans and New York City, and involves a ritual of European ceremonial magic in New York on the one hand, and voodoo rites in the swamps outside New Orleans on the other. The incestuous relationship between the Rourke and the Bonet characters, as well as the amnesia and consequent identity confusion of the Rourke character is perhaps a metaphor for something much deeper taking place, but this is thankfully beyond the scope of the present study!

What most audiences never realize, however, is that the relationship between magic and politics in Haiti is very strong, virtually inextricable. Papa Doc Duvalier was a powerful voudon practitioner, and bragged that it was his magic that resulted in the assassination of his enemy, President John F. Kennedy. This is not as much of an anomaly as it may appear, since the Haitian republic itself was born out of both political revolt and voudon, rebellion and witchcraft.

On the night of August 14, 1791 at Bois Caiman in Haiti, near the town of Morne-Rouge, a secret voudon ceremony was held in the midst of a storm of thunder and lightning. Amid that theatrical setting the god of war, Ogun, was invoked in the presence of legendary leader Dutty Boukman. Slaves from plantations all over the northern plain of Haiti were present, and swore allegiance to Boukman and to his lieutenants, Biassou, Celestin, and Jean-Francois. A black pig was decapitated in the midst of the ritual, and the Revolt of the Slaves was baptized in its blood.

From that moment on, Haiti was in the midst of terrible turmoil. Plantations were burned to the ground, and thousands of white settlers and plantation owners were slaughtered. Towns fell to the rebels, known as Maroons to the French, and with the advance of a Spanish force from the neighboring Dominican Republic and its alliance with the Maroon armies, the days of French colonial supremacy on the island were numbered. France made several treaties with the slave leaders, some of whom betrayed their leadership and became almost as bad as the white slavers themselves, but in the end France (and Napoleon) could not prevail against Haiti, losing some thirty-to sixty-thousand troops in a futile effort to retain control over the colony and use it as a base to attack the southern part of the United States. Boukman became a national hero, a Haitian slave who, with the energy and passion of the voudon cult, organized a slave revolt against the French and won, dying in the process. Voudon priestesses danced in the streets of the towns they would capture, and the sound of the conch shell horns and the pounding of the drums drove terror into the hearts of the slave owners. These children of the Slave Coast had vanquished the strongest European force in the world at that time, using a mixture of politics, military strategy, and African faith that had never before been seen.

The revolt took twelve long years before the streets were finally peaceful and the people returned to the land. Haiti has been betrayed by enemies both internal and external over the years since, but voudon itself has never died. When Harvard ethnobotanist Wade Davis went to Haiti in 1982 in search of the secret of zombification, he found the voudon cult vibrant and alive under Baby Doc Duvalier's regime. When the author himself visited a year later little had changed in Haiti: the politics were still the same, the violence had not abated, the poverty and sickness unsurpassed in the entire western hemisphere; but the people were still proud and beautiful, and the *houngans* and *bokors* still strong and still politically powerful.

The grand old Hotel Oloffson was still there, made famous by Graham Greene in his novel of Duvalier-era Haiti, *The Comedians,* and a favorite of celebrities and movie stars such as Marlon Brando, who had one of the Oloffson's private cabanas named after him. White people were still trying to squeeze out of Haiti whatever they could, and Haitian political leaders were squeezing back. One of these white, European post-colonialists in an ice-cream suit and Panama hat was George de Mohrenschildt, the friend of both Lee Harvey Oswald and Jacqueline Bouvier Kennedy, some-time spy, petroleum engineer, and world traveler, who went to Haiti only months before the assassination of President Kennedy. De Mohrenschildt would know that Papa Doc Duvalier had bragged about his magic spells that killed the President. Papa Doc rode around in a black limousine with the license plate "22," a number of tremendous occult power in the voudon cult, and the number of the date when Kennedy was killed in November, the 11th month. To Duvalier—and to other priests and practitioners of voudon—the combination 11/22 is a potent one, and seemed like mortal evidence of the vicious old politician's powers.

Papa Doc was born Francois Duvalier, one of the sons of the elite, intellectual class of Haitian society, but with strong feelings of identity with the Haitian people as opposed to the French society to which the elite normally swore cultural allegiance. At a time when an American occupation of Haiti was a festering sore of humiliation and shame, Dr. Duvalier—who had by this time become a medical doctor as well as an ethnologist specializing in Haitian culture—decided to do something about it. He gathered around himself a clique of like-minded souls who saw in Haitian identity—as opposed to the imported French variety—a source of national pride, and this included the popular folk religion of voudon.

In 1915, the United States had invaded Haiti. It was the start of World War I and the US Government was concerned over the security of the Panama Canal.

French and German interests were present in Haiti, and had the local government decided to allow their country to be used as a base of operations against the Canal, it could have been disastrous for the newly-opened sea lanes. The US stayed in Haiti for long after the end of the war, however, which resulted in anti-American protests and an active resistance movement, aided and abetted by Haitian secret societies, all of them representing a mixture of mystical and political agendas. The US military finally left Haiti in 1934, but during its nearly twenty years in-country had attempted to suppress the practice of voudon, since it was perceived to be a factor in fomenting rebellion, and tried to replace it with the more staunchly pro-American Roman Catholic Church. Books that were published abroad about Haiti around this time tended to paint the culture in satanic and depraved colors, thus legitimizing American military occupation of the heathen nation. This strategy was supported by first one Haitian political group and then another, as the culturally pro-French, mixed-race mulatto elite tried to suppress voudon in favor of the European style religion, Catholicism, embarrassed by the popular accounts of voudon that had exploded in the world press.

A former professor at the University of Pittsburgh—a zoologist and author of a number of books on the fauna of North America—visited Haiti in the late 1940s, some ten years before the start of the Duvalier regime. Samuel H. Williams, in his *Voodoo Roads* (oddly enough published in English by an Austrian firm in 1949) relates that "our American Marines had long been engaged in breaking up their voodoo practices in the length and breadth of the island under the mistaken idea that these practices were responsible for the lack of law and order there."[27] He further relates that the neighboring Dominican Republic took the opportunity of the departure of the Marines in 1934 to massacre some ten thousand Haitians on the Dominician border, an atrocity that was not answered by the Haitian government.

Although Williams' work reflects the racial biases of its author, particularly in its lingering descriptions of nubile, naked young Haitian women wherever he finds them, it is also politically sensitive, and the outrage of the academic at the atrocities perpetrated by the Haitian government against its own people is evident on many pages. He also states that Caucasians who fall under the spell of the voodoo rituals are "emotionally abnormal,"[28] although a few pages later he writes, "Voodooism is more than a religion. It is the embodiment of *all* the activities and psychological manifestations of the people. *Few religions can claim as much*" (Williams' emphasis).[29] These two sentiments seem to contradict each other, but perhaps they don't.

In the 1950s, as voudon was still being actively suppressed by the government and the sacred drums and flags of the religion were still being burned, Duvalier and his group represented a political, intellectual and cultural alternative, and Duvalier—seen as a "black" candidate as opposed to a supporter of the mulatto elite—won the presidential election in 1957. For the first time in over a hundred years, voudon priests, or *houngans*, were invited to the presidential palace and given government positions. On one particularly historic occasion, Duvalier invited *all* of the houngans in Haiti to a special meeting in Port-au-Prince, the capitol of the country. His allegiance to voudon was no secret, and the allegiance of voudon to Duvalier was cemented. The rumors in Haiti (and abroad) were that Duvalier was, himself, a houngan or perhaps even a black magician, a *bokor*.

Things were not easy for Duvalier, however. The first few years of his administration there were numerous attempts at military coups and assassinations, and in reaction he formed his own personal bodyguard, the dread Tontons Macoutes. With their sinister sunglasses and small arms, they were everywhere in Haiti for about thirty years. They wore no uniforms, but their presence was pervasive in every town, on every street corner. It was a huge organization, and the secret behind it was peculiarly Haitian: an occult society known as Bizango.

The roots of Bizango are not a matter of historical documentation, but of Haitian tradition and legend which places Bizango at the beginning of the slave revolt, and even earlier. According to an informant of Wade Davis, the word *bizango* was "of the Cannibal,"[30] and therefore Arawakian, the language of the Native American people all but wiped out with the advent of Columbus to Hispaniola in December of 1492—the same people that gave us Tituba, the "witch" of Salem, Massachusetts. The same informant also relates *bizango* to the name of a spirit found in a famous medieval grimoire known as the *Red Dragon* (*Le Dragon Rouge*), which was the title of the first book in Thomas Harris' Hannibal "the Cannibal" Lecter series, and also the name of a tile in the Chinese game of Mah Jong. (The reader may also remember the Red Dragon video game parlor in West Virginia encountered by the author on his way to Ashland, Kentucky, and described in Book One.) Another medieval grimoire that is frequently mentioned in association with voudon is the French *Le Petit Albert* which, we are told, was once banned in Haiti in the pre-Duvalier era. This is hard to believe, for the "Little Albert" is hardly a work of demonic character but contains chapters on palmistry, herbalism, and—of course—a bit on summoning spirits and spells for success in love and money.

Whatever the origin of Bizango, it has developed into a secret society that exists in every part of Haiti, and with whom its followers claim the Haitian government must cooperate if it wishes to stay in power. The Bizango cult has murdered its enemies, and has worked its voudon magic against them as well using a mixture of herbal poisons and drugs as well as incantations and spells. It is believed that Duvalier's Tontons Macoutes were soldiers of the Bizango society, or that, at least, their memberships overlapped considerably (as implied in the Wes Craven film very loosely based on Wade Davis' research in Haiti, *The Serpent and the Rainbow*). Upon coming to power, Duvalier relaxed the hold of the Catholic Church over the Haitian people and the practice of the native religion came into greater flower than ever before. Duvalier himself was widely believed to be a channel for the typically and uniquely Haitian god, the dread *Baron Samedi* ("Baron Saturday"), and Papa Doc went out of his way to cultivate this identity, dressing in the Baron's typical black suit, black hat and sporting a cane. Baron Samedi is the Lord of the Crossroads, and thus is the Guardian of the path into the Other World. The Baron is usually invoked before most rituals that have to do with summoning power from beyond. His empire is in the cemetery, and for this reason he is sometimes also called the Baron of the Cemetery. Although there are many important deities in the Haitian religion, the Baron is the one that Hollywood has fixated upon the most, as he is the most sinister in appearance. The Baron takes several bows in the James Bond film aforementioned—*Live and Let Die*—replete in skull and skeleton costume and top hat, as well as *Erzulie*, who is the flirtatious goddess most associated with love and sex (it is, of course, both Baron Samedi and Erzulie who also make an appearance in the Wes Craven film, mentioned above, evidence of Hollywood's fascination with death and sex).

Regardless of Hollywood's interpretation, however, the story of Haitian independence has much to tell us about the relationship between rebellion and witchcraft. The Duvalier regimes, on the other hand, have much to teach us about how politics, religion and the occult can come together as a powerful, and terrifying, force. When Duvalier dissolved the bicameral legislature of the government in 1961, the US government under President Kennedy suspended aid to Haiti in disapproval, and from that point on Duvalier—the personification of Baron Samedi, the Lord of Death, and at least the repository of the Baron's *kebatinan*—targeted Kennedy as an enemy of the state.

Haitian voudon has much to teach us about such things as possession and temporary madness, as well as about modern European ceremonial magic and the practices of some of the more interesting—and dangerous—cults extant today, and we will return to it later. For now, its strange syncretistic structure and its identification with the Haitian people and their nationalism are what compel us. Never in modern times has one nation been so identified with what we think of as the "occult"; the exception possibly being the short-lived Third Reich, with SS chief Heinrich Himmler playing the role of Baron Samedi in his black uniform with the death's head insignia. Of all the Nazi leaders, probably Himmler comes closest to being a "Baron of the Cemetery," as the SS officers in charge of the death camps were under his command.

In America, there is a specific division between the affairs of state and the affairs of religion; freedom of religion is protected by the Constitution, and the government may make no laws concerning the practice of religion. Thus, a colonel in the US Army, such as Temple of Set founder Michael Aquino, can have his religion listed as "Satanist," on a par with Catholic, Jew, Methodist, Buddhist, Muslim, etc. (God forbid anyone in the armed services should openly proclaim his or her homosexuality, however!)

Yet, this division is in a sense artificial. American coinage is minted with the slogan "In God We Trust," and the Pledge of Allegiance states—since the 1950s—that America is "one nation, under God." The United States is largely viewed as a Christian nation, and there have only been Christian presidents so far. No provision is made for government funding for churches, however; and prayer in the public schools has been proscribed as violating the Constitutional separation of church and state. Individual presidents have been very open about their religious affiliations, however, and many Americans are alternately charmed and relieved to see their elected officials attending Sunday services. The electorate may be forgiven if they are not aware of the depth of religious feeling of some of their officials; presidents rarely express these beliefs openly for fear of alienating some voting bloc or another. However, some of them have had . . . strange beliefs, and dangerous ones. One would not wish a man with apocalyptic visions formed by an idiosyncratic interpretation of the Bible to have his proverbial finger on the proverbial button to ignite a nuclear holocaust, but that is just what America had in the 1980s; and he was married to a woman who consulted an astrologer on a regular basis, organizing her husband's schedule on the basis of planetary transits.

The author has covered the occult aspects of the Third Reich in some detail in his previous work. Although he followed the progress of the Nazi ideologues and war criminals to Latin America via the Vatican's "rat lines" after the war, he did not focus too much on the presence of Nazism in the United States and its influence on post-war twentieth century American politics. While the presence of Nazi war criminals in the United States came to the attention of the public only gradually in the 1970s and 1980s, they had, after all, been in the country since 1945. The scientists of Peenemünde and Nordhausen were discussed in Book One; but the political influence of Nazism on the development of the post-war Republican Party has remained virtually unexamined, except when some particularly egregious blunder has exposed the presence of the Dark Lords in an embarrassing way. These cult leaders have wielded a disproportionate amount of influence over the Party since the early post-war years, mostly as a reflection of the Cold War mentality of the United States and its terrified reaction to the rise of Communism in Eastern Europe and the Asian landmass. Protection and support of Nazis—including war criminals—by the Republican Party has to remain as one of the biggest scandals of American politics, regardless of the *realpolitik* justifications and secret agendas of the intelligence agencies and the New Right, and it is evidence of a moral stand that is at best debatable and at worst deplorable.

These influences boiled over temporarily during the Watergate scandal and subsequent investigations—perhaps epitomized by the "sinister force" behind the erasure of a crucial eighteen-and-a-half minutes of a secret Oval Office tape recording—and it is to this strange and paranoid episode of American history that we now must turn.

ENDNOTES

1 J. Anthony Lukas, *Nightmare: The Underside of the Nixon Years*, Viking Press, NY, 29 1976, ISBN 0-670-51415-2, p. 460

2 Alexis deTocqueville, *Democracy in America*, HarperPerennial, NY, 1988, ISBN 0-06-091522-6, p. 300

3 E.A. Wallis Budge, *The Book of the Dead*, Gramercy Books, NY, 1960 ed., ISBN 0-517-12283-9, p. 94

4 Robert A Houghton with Theodore Taylor, *Special Unit Senator*, Random House, NY, 1970 p. 230

5 Wendy Doniger O'Flaherty, *The Origins of Evil in Hindu Mythology*, Motilal Banarsidass, Delhi, 1988, ISBN 81-208-0386-8, p. 66

6 Ibid., p. 80

7 Ibid., p. 89

8 Ibid., p. 81

9 Niels Mulder, *Mysticism in Java: Ideology in Indonesia*, The Pepin Press, Singapore,1998, ISBN 90-5496-047-7, p. 9–10

10 L. Couperus, *The Hidden Force*, The University of Massachusetts Press, Amherst, 1985, ISBN 0-87023-715-2, p. 129

11 Ibid., p. 142

12 Kelley & Francis, p.3; from Gill, *Mother Earth*, 1987 pp. 67–68

13 Mulder, op. cit., p. 30

14 Ibid., p. 30

15 Ibid., p. 32

16 Richard Winstedt, *The Malay Magician*, Oxford University Press, Kuala Lumpur, 1993, ISBN 0-19-582529-2, p. 9–13

17 Ibid., p. 8–9

18 Ibid., p. 10

19 Ibid., p. 11

20 Ibid., p. 157–166

21 Ian Buruma, *The Missionary and the Libertine*, Vintage Books, NY, 2000, ISBN 0-375-70537-6, p. 118–130, "Bhutto's Pakistan"

22 Ibid., p. 131–140, "St Cory and the Evil Rose"

23 Mulder, op. cit., p. 18

24 Ibid., p. 19

25 Endicott, op. cit., p. 66

26 See, for instance, P. Chandra Sagaran, "Three Charged With Murder," *New Straits Times*, July 28, 2001, p. 9; Kuldeep S. Jessy, "Trio charged with murder of American woman," *The Star*, July 28, 2001, p. 6; and similar cases in Lam Li, "Woman's body exhumed, hands and toes missing," *The Star*, December 19, 2001, p. 6 and Sim Bak Heng, "Body Snatchers," *The Malay Mail*, December 19, 2001, p. 2

27 Samuel H. Williams, *Voodoo Roads*, Verlag fuer Jugend und Volk, Wien, 1949, p. 37

28 Ibid., p. 12

29 Ibid., p. 16

30 Wade Davis, The Serpent and the Rainbow, Warner Books, NY, ISBN 0-446-34387-0, p. 309

Mobil

GOVERNMENT EXHIBIT
1
EXHIBIT #1
CRIM 1827-72
WATERGATE
GOVERNMENT EXHIBIT
1

BOOK TWO: A WARM GUN

CHAPTER TEN

WALLOWING IN WATERGATE

But the accusations are enough to show what thoughts worked under the surface of all that belligerent orthodoxy. We seem to see men half aware of their hallucination, and proportionately angry with those who do not share it.

—Allen Upward, *The Divine Mystery*[1]

Neurosis and initiation are the same thing, except that neurosis stops short of apotheosis, and the tremendous forces that mold all life are encysted—short circuited and turned poisonous.

—Jack Parsons[2]

L'amant dit à la belle:
Ou est la vérité?
La vérité, dit-elle,
Qui donc s'en fut doute,
La vérité, dit-elle,
Est morte et enterée.

—Maurice Maeterlinck, *The Cloud That Lifted*, Act III,Scene 3

Religion, like Watergate, is a scandal that will not go away.

—Victor Turner, *Revelation and Divination in Ndembu Ritual*[3]

In 1968, America turned a corner politically and, some would say, spiritually as well. In January, the Tet Offensive showed America that the war in Vietnam was nowhere near over. The author and millions of his fellow citizens sat in stunned silence in front of their television sets as Walter Cronkite, in a state of shock over the dramatic attacks that occurred on the Vietnamese New Year, said, "I thought we were winning this thing." By April, Martin Luther King had been assassinated, and by June so had Robert F. Kennedy. It looked as if both the peace movement and the civil rights movement had been dealt serious, mortal blows. The Days of Rage during the Democratic National Convention in Chicago represented the frustration and anger of the anti-war movement, as Mayor Daley called out the troops and had Lincoln Park cleared of demonstrators with Walter Cronkite, again on television, visibly upset at what was happening to our country.

And in November, Richard M. Nixon was elected President of the United States.

When dawn broke on the first day of January, 1969 seventeen-year-old Marina Habe's lifeless body was lying at the bottom of a ravine off Mulholland Drive, like a human sacrifice on the first day of the first year of Nixon's first term as president, a young victim whose father worked for US intelligence and psychological warfare operations in Europe during the War; a young victim who was slaughtered in Nixon's home state, a few miles from the town where he was born, a few miles from the town where he was first nominated by his party. Nixon, a lawyer by profession, would later go on to proclaim the alleged perpetrator of this atrocity to be "guilty" while his trial for other murders was still in progress, thus threatening a mistrial.

And in March, less than two months after his inauguration, President Nixon ordered the bombing of Cambodia.

In the months that followed in that first year of Richard Nixon's first term as President, the Manson Family gathered guns, vehicles, drugs and additional members and headed out to the Mojave Desert and Death Valley in preparation for a long-term siege. Manson's dream of becoming a rock star was not materializing, but his nightmare of race war and armageddon was taking shape. There had been race riots in Los Angeles a few years earlier, and Freedom Riders in the South. George Wallace had stood in the doorway of that college, staring down the National Guard that had been sent at Bobby Kennedy's insistence to force the desegregation of the University of Alabama. Nazis had been welcomed with open arms into the United States to help with the space program, and in July of 1969—a bare two weeks before the Tate killings—American astronauts had set foot on the Moon.

Evil had an Asian face, not a European one. Korea. Vietnam, Laos, Cambodia. China. Even Russia was Asiatic, except of course for the "White Russians," i.e., "our" Russians, the aristocratic Russians with German blood. When the Romanov family had been led to its murder by the Soviets in 1917, one of them left behind a swastika swabbed on the wall, a last desperate plea to the Gods of the noble White Europeans to protect them, to protect Holy Mother Russia. Is it any wonder, really, that Charles Manson—poor, white trash from Ashland, Kentucky; Moundsville, West Virginia, and various penitentiaries on both coasts and points in between—would have adopted Scientology, the Process, and eventually Nazism as a solution to his own problems as well as those of the world? He would not support the war in Vietnam, but he wasn't a hippie, either. He believed in violent action, in the use of force, in the disruption of society, in race war. The drugs and sex of the Sixties were only fringe benefits. And he would one day carve a swastika into his forehead. Observers are mistaken if they believe that Manson was a creature of the Summer of Love, of Haight-Ashbury be-ins and Grateful Dead dope-and-grope concerts, although that is what commentators have desperately tried to prove in order to discredit and devalue the anti-War movement and the sixties youth culture in general.

Manson was a creature of the Right: raised by the State, formed by the State, brutalized by the State since he was a child, Manson was the Right Wing in America, taken to its logical conclusion, in an environment in which Nazis were protected and coddled, in which the Church itself collaborated in some of the worst crimes that century had ever seen, and in which the American State Department, the CIA, the military, and other institutions fought among each other for the spoils. The cynicism of Manson was conceived as he watched this duplicity unfold in his own life. In "brainwashing" his followers he was only doing to perfection what the men of MK-ULTRA were trying to do with a larger budget and a lot of paperwork. The fact that he was convicted of the Tate/LaBianca murders and is still in prison to this day is testament to his success, since it is acknowledged that he did not pick up a knife or pull a trigger or in any way actually participate at the Sharon Tate crime scene. He was, as he said, "convicted of witchcraft in the twentieth century."

With the assassination of Dr. King in April, racial tensions were as high as they had ever been. Bobby Kennedy had the credentials with the black community as well as the anti-war community to make a difference, but he had been gunned down as well. The Beatles had come out with the *White Album* in 1968 (on November 22, the fifth anniversary of the assassination of President Kennedy), and Manson thought they were speaking directly to him about *Helter Skelter*, *Revolution 9* (understood by Manson as a Biblical reference to "Revelations 9"), *Piggies*, and *Happiness is a Warm Gun*.

This is a phenomenon that will be analyzed by academia one day: the replacement of traditional religious figures and texts by rock star celebrities, movie stars, and song lyrics. Anyone who has seen how young people reacted to the physical presence of the Beatles—screaming, shaking, fainting, hysteria—must have wondered if this was a kind of religious ecstasy taking place. Biblical figures never actually appear to the faithful, except in visions and then only to a few; but television and motion pictures made it possible to create new figures of Biblical proportions and to give the masses direct access to their every move, glance, strut, pout, or moue. And when they appeared in person—at a rock concert or movie premiere or book signing or supermarket opening—the impossible would take place: the Biblical figure was in the very flesh, corporeal, present and breathing the same air, walking in the same space. For many, this was as close to a mystical experience as they would ever get. In the case of the Beatles, they came with their own sacred texts: their songs. The music, the lyrics, the beat of Ringo's drums, the immediate reaction of conservative Christianity against them resulting in the destruction of records and the burning of their albums by religious groups; and the origins of rock 'n' roll itself in the black music of the South, the devilish blues of men like Robert Johnson, provided white America with a kind of voodoo cult of its own, shrink-wrapped and hi-fi. The package was complete, and thus John Lennon could be forgiven for having said—albeit cynically—that the Beatles had become more popular than Jesus Christ.

The backlash to all of this was the election of a right-wing Republican president to replace all those murdered or disgraced Democratic candidates. The tension in the streets of America rose exponentially. For the first time in the postwar era, America had become polarized into an Us and a Them. One could tell who was whom by such simple matters as a haircut (or lack of one), a clothing style, or a method of employment. It was not so simple to deduce a person's allegiance on the basis of age; many young Americans were also Young Republicans. Many older Americans had marched on Washington to protest the war in Vietnam. The polarization was cutting across all demographics.

When the author was a high school senior in the Bronx in 1968, the Students for a Democratic Society were busy trying to engage and organize the student body, but all they managed to organize were tedious meetings full of quasi-political discussions that did not advance the cause or stop the war in Vietnam; enter the Weather Underground. The Weathermen believed in taking action to "bring the war home." They bombed Army recruiting stations, banks, and any other targets that were understood to be supportive of the war effort. One day in 1969, the author was on the telephone to the headquarters of the Presbyterian Church which was, at that time, located on the edge of New York City's Greenwich Village. At one point during the phone conversation, there was a deafening blast and the sound of breaking glass. A terrified voice on the other end shouted, "I have to go! There's been a bomb!" and hung up. The Weathermen had been making bombs in the basement of a West Village brownstone across the street from the Presbyterian Church, and accidentally blew up the building and themselves. Several people died, and some Weathermen escaped, including one woman who would turn herself in twenty years later after a lifetime spent underground.

During that same period, the author had the opportunity to meet many Weathermen, Black Panthers, members of the Irish Republican Army, NORAID, the Palestine Liberation Organization, and other underground groups plotting all sorts of mayhem in the United States and abroad. He once shook the hand of Bernadette Devlin, the fiery young woman who was a Member of Parliament from Northern Ireland, the woman who wrote, "I was not born a Socialist; life has made me one." He also met Pete Seeger, Oscar Brand, Milos Forman, and a host of other counter-culture celebrities and activists. He visited the offices of the *East Village Other* (the EVO Eye) and, of course, the *Village Voice*, handing out press releases and placing ads announcing meetings of various subversive groups at the basements of radical churches throughout the City, including Judson Memorial in Manhattan and Spencer Memorial in Brooklyn Heights. He also became acquainted with the surreptitious movement of young men to Canada to avoid the draft, via an underground railroad that stretched from New York City anti-war churches and temples to coffee shops like The Yellow Door in Montreal. And all of this to the sensory backbeat of marijuana fumes, acid trips, day-glo posters, lava lamps, Peter Max and black light; the music of Leonard Cohen, Janis Joplin, Joni Mitchell, Joan Baez and the entire *Forrest Gump* soundtrack; rock groups like the Grateful Dead and Led Zeppelin and the Rolling Stones; movies like *The Strawberry Statement*, *Joe*, and *The Revolutionary*. Bobby Seal; Abbie Hoffman and *Steal This Book;* R. D. Laing and *The Politics of Experience*.

This was the atmosphere in the United States of America in the late sixties.

I had grown up in the 1950s thinking that at any moment the Russians or the Chinese would bomb the bejesus out of us; I was taught how to protect myself in the event of a nuclear strike, how to lean over with your head between your knees and—in the joke of the day—"kiss your ass goodbye," as the air raid sirens wailed periodically over the South Side of Chicago where I first attended school. Then the Cuban Missile Crisis. Then the Kennedy assassination. Race riots. Freedom marches.

In 1968, this was followed by the horror of the Martin Luther King, Jr. assassination, only to be intensified by that of Bobby Kennedy. Many historians look back on that period from a safe distance and try to explain it all in terms of dialectical materialism or some other force of history; we knew differently. We knew that there was a war between two opposing forces in America, and that one side was winning.

There were other forces at work in the world than those I learned of in my high school physics classes. Forces of darkness, surely, but of tremendous power as well. We had to identify them and, if possible, tame them, or at least protect ourselves against them.

Heady stuff for a high school student in 1968; but, after all, we were all of us involved in greater things. Marches on Washington, the Students for a Democratic Society, the Black Panthers, the Weathermen. Hippies, free love, pot and LSD. The Beatles, the Rolling Stones, Led Zeppelin. Hard rock, acid rock, folk rock. Beads and beards and peasant blouses and blue jeans. There was a war on, and at any moment any of us could be called up, and at that point we would have to make the most important decision of our lives.

By August 1969 I had not been drafted but was in need of money and took a job with a Presbyterian Church in Brooklyn Heights. That month, on August 9th, disciples of Charles Manson slaughtered Sharon Tate and her house guests, and then went on to hack Leno and Rosemary LaBianca to death the following day.

I worked for the Church for almost a year, and the following year got a job at a lingerie company in New York's Garment District. It was exactly a year after the Manson killings, and on my first day at work I heard a disturbing story. The son of one of the owners of the firm had committed suicide in a New York City hotel room, fleeing from Los Angeles where he had worked as a gossip columnist. Steve

Brandt killed himself because he was afraid the Manson Family was coming for him. Because he knew too much. It was while working for this highly unlikely firm that I also heard—from another co-worker—of a plan to kidnap Howard Hughes. More of that later.

If I needed any evidence that sinister forces were at work in the world, subtly manipulating reality in ways we could not predict or defend against, then my two years of work at Stardust, Inc. provided all the reinforcement I required. Charles Manson was arrested on October 12, 1969 (the birthday of Aleister Crowley; Columbus Day; and the birthday of President Eisenhower), and the trial and its aftermath lasted through much of 1970 and into 1971. During the trial, President Richard Nixon proclaimed that Manson was guilty; as a lawyer he should have known better, and as a president he should have kept his mouth shut. It threatened a mistrial if the jury had heard of it. Manson knew this, and brought a newspaper to the courtroom with him, waving it in front of the jury. Incredibly, the judge allowed the trial to continue after being assured by the jury that they would not be swayed by the President's remarks.

Readers of Book One will find familiar the odd coincidence that one of the jury was an employee of Ashland Oil.

President Nixon would resign in the wake of the Watergate investigation on August 9, 1974: the fifth anniversary of the murder of Sharon Tate and, incredibly, the fifth anniversary of the day that Disneyland inaugurated their "Haunted House" ride.

Walt Disney had once owned the house where Leno and Rosemary LaBianca were slain.

It is amusing to note that President Nixon was, after all, a Quaker. It is amusing for the very reason that Ruth Paine was also a Quaker, as was Whittaker Chambers and even the wife of Alger Hiss: a tight little circle of plain speech and affirmations. If the Paines had something material to do with the assassination of President Kennedy, who was heartily and energetically despised by Nixon, then we have the very rudiments of a Quaker conspiracy theory! The reader may be grateful to learn that we will not go down that particular road.

What we will discover, however, is something considerably more serious. It is a theme of this work that sinister forces were evoked by American political, military and intelligence leaders in the twentieth century, and that one of the traces of this is the support of Nazism by prominent Americans, and the involvement in occult and extremely bizarre religious practices and beliefs by still others. This support of a heinous political and mystical philosophy was ongoing from the very end of World War II and has continued—in one form or another—through to the present day, thus contributing to a politico-occult malaise that has manifested in such atrocities as the Manson murders, the revival of the Ku Klux Klan and other racist organizations, and the laying of the famous wreath at the SS cemetery at Bitburg.

We will leave discussion of the author's own life for a while, and continue this investigation with the life of Richard Nixon himself.

IT DIDN'T START WITH WATERGATE

> Soviet penetration of the Nazi networks were not only a threat to Allen Dulles' reputation, their exposure would have ruined the political career of Richard Nixon, the Republican candidate for President in 1959. Nixon authorized Dulles' covert projects during Eisenhower's illnesses in 1956 and 1957.
>
> —Aarons and Loftus, *Unholy Trinity: The Vatican, the Nazis, and Soviet Intelligence*[4]

> I am being the devil's advocate . . .
>
> —President Nixon, White House tapes, March 13, 1973

Richard Nixon occupies a unique place in American history. It is probably safe to say that no political leader—certainly no president—attracted so much vitriol, so much absolute disgust, in his opponents as did Nixon. He was vilified not only by Democrats, such as Eleanor Roosevelt, Harry Truman, Edmund Brown, and others but also by members of his own party, such as Eisenhower and even Nixon's own running mate, Henry Cabot Lodge, as well as his longtime staff members, such as Haldeman (who, of course, could be expected to have an axe to grind considering how he was treated during the Watergate crisis). Those who did support him and actually seemed to like him were mostly villains in their own right, people like Murray Chotiner, Bebe Rebozo, and Howard Hughes, or people with other secrets to hide, such as Allen Dulles, with whom Nixon had an improbable, lifelong friendship, and disgraced Attorney General John Mitchell. The forces of a contentious evil gathered around Nixon like blue-bottle flies on a day-old summertime corpse, and to this day there are still those who consider him to be a great president, and one much maligned by the same evil forces themselves arrayed against him. To be sure, no one is moderate when it comes to Richard Nixon.

Nixon's career takes us into the very belly of the Beast; there is virtually no aspect of his adult life that is not tainted somehow by associations with the vilest of men, as if somewhere in his distant past this hungry, ignored, socially-uncomfortable small-town lawyer signed a pact with the Devil, and the rest of his life was simply the logical conclusion of the contract. We look, in vain, for signs of redemption; a signal that he found an escape clause in his Faustian bargain and relaxed, finally, into the arms of his Quaker Savior.

It was not to be.

Nixon found his political legacy in his foreign policy successes, principally with China; which is ironic for a man who led the charge against Communism from his earliest political days. His foreign policy disasters—Vietnam and Chile come immediately to mind—are not regarded as such by his admirers. A casual observer may be forgiven if it seems strange that a man who held the line against Communist North Vietnam and the Socialist administration of Chile's Salvador Allende with an almost hysterical zeal would then toast Communist hero Mao Ze Dong with *mao tai* in the Great Hall of the People in Beijing, and welcome him into the United Nations against staunchly loyal (if slightly fascist) ally Taiwan. This is because Nixon's political life—although polarized in the extreme—did not depend on such mundane concepts as left-wing and right-wing, capitalism and Communism, democracy and totalitarianism, but on deeper divisions in the human soul. Nixon had been making pacts with devils since 1946 at least, and he was less a man in control of his own destiny than a creature of other powers, other forces; a kind of political homunculus, a golem that could not be destroyed except by its maker.

The origins of Richard Milhous Nixon are not exactly shrouded in mystery like those of a Marvel Comics character, but they might as well have been. Like high school geek Peter Parker, who would become Spider-man, Nixon's background was modest and unassuming, his personality nerdlike and awkward. There was no sign that he would evolve into a super-hero to some, a super-villain to others. Yet, there was one element—the crucial one, as it turns out—that molded his future forever and it *was* mysterious. It was his selection as a Congressional candidate after the end of World War II by a group of businessmen, businessmen with intelligence backgrounds and Mafia connections.

Nixon was born on January 9, 1913 in southern California, not far from Los Angeles. He had four brothers, two of whom died while quite young, leaving Richard and his brothers Donald and Edward. (Readers will smile when they learn that Richard himself was named after King Richard the Lionhearted, of Crusader fame.) The Nixon family was by all accounts middle-class and relatively prosperous, even though Nixon himself would later claim (for political spin) that he had a childhood full of suffering and hardship.

As a student, Nixon applied himself diligently, and won a scholarship to Whittier College (not difficult, as it was the Milhous Scholarship and only awarded to members of the Milhous clan). While at Whittier, he was involved in setting up a fraternity to rival the existing—more prestigious—one. The initiation rituals devised by Nixon and his colleagues for this "anti-frat" involved going at night, naked, and digging up a dead animal and feasting on its decaying flesh. It is said that Nixon, as the one who created the fraternity, did not have to go through this repulsive, Jeffrey-Dahmer-like, hazing ceremonial.[5] Nixon would go on to create spurious orders throughout his career, such as the Order of the Hound's

Tooth (after the "Checkers speech" that saved his political career amid allegations of financial wrong-doing). Interest in secret societies, espionage capers, and all the other hallmarks of a paranoid personality (or, simply, a suspicious one) would characterize Nixon as both a man and as a politician in the eyes of an increasingly nervous electorate.

Nixon went on to Duke University for a time to get his law degree, and eventually wound up married to Pat Ryan. The woman who would become known as Pat Nixon was born Thelma Catherine Ryan on March 16, 1912; she acquired the nickname "Pat" because her father called her that, as her birthday was so close to St. Patrick's Day. Nixon did not even know his fiancée's birth name until almost the time to fill out the marriage license; and Nixon would later make political hay out of obscuring her real birth date so he could claim she was as Irish as Paddy's pig, born on the one day possibly more sacred to the Irish than Christmas or Easter Sunday (Easter Monday excepted). Pat Nixon had been a sometime actress in Whittier, and Nixon met her when he was auditioning for a role there as well. It seems odd, somehow, that the next elected Republican President and First Lady after the Nixons—the Reagans—would also meet the same way and would also have been (somewhat more successful) actors. Pat Nixon (before her marriage) had even worked as an extra in a few Hollywood films.

She also spent some time in New York City in the 1930s before meeting Nixon, working in a hospital that treated patients suffering from tuberculosis. But three years after her return to California she was working as a teacher and acting on the side, and Nixon discovered her on the set of *The Dark Tower* by George S. Kaufman and Alexander Woollcott, and began to pursue her with sullen determination.

The script of *The Dark Tower* contains references to a play by the same name that—according to the story line—is enjoying some success in Greenwich, Connecticut and sparking plans to take it to Broadway. (We must assume that the name of the play is a reference to that famous line, "To the dark tower the Childe Rolande came," which has been such an influence on Stephen King, among others.) In the Whittier production, Pat played the role of Daphne, and Nixon of Barry: a cynical, hard-boiled actress and a boyish, idealistic playwright who are eventually thrown together and become lovers towards the end of the play. They are supporting roles rather than central characters, but the play still deserves another look, as it deals with a man believed to be dead who returns, only to be killed again (as apt a metaphor for Nixon's career as any), and themes of hypnosis and possession.

The resurrected man, Stanley Vance, was a career criminal who had caused one wife to commit suicide through hypnosis, and thus inherited her estate. He is on his way to doing the same with his current wife, when his brother-in-law kills him, first with chloryl hydrate and then finishing the job with a knife, while impersonating a Viennese investor in a room at the Waldorf Hotel. Thus, the young Nixon is introduced to the idea of hypnotic control of individuals to further criminal ends, pretty much what the CIA's MK-ULTRA was all about. The doctor who is examining the young woman under the influence of Stanley Vance's hypnotic powers claims that the only doctors who would be able to help her had died during the Middle Ages: in his estimation, she is possessed by an evil spirit. Her brother, Damon, had been dating the Daphne character, but when Stanley Vance—who was believed to be dead—returns at the end of the first act, Damon loses interest in Daphne (whom he had been treating shabbily even earlier in the play, ordering her about like a recalcitrant schoolgirl) and Daphne eventually winds up in the arms of Barry, the worshipful, puppy-like playwright. Oddly, this is what happened in Pat Nixon's own life, as she was dating other men when Nixon was pursuing her with totally-focused determination after meeting her on the set of *The Dark Tower.*

Psychohistorian Bruce Mazlish has studied Nixon's personality from the point of view that this brief association with the theater when young had influenced his political life.[6] Nixon as vice president and president is always talking about playing a role, about acting, and criticizing those whose ability to play a role (politically) are amateurish. Nixon clearly felt that he was a better actor than most of his fellow politicos—including the Russians—and it is obvious that he understood that an ability to act, to perform, *to pretend* was essential to the success of every politician. In the course of the action in *The Dark Tower*, one character is certain that the hypnotized wife—who is an actress—is only acting and that she is not genuinely "possessed" or under hypnotic influence, but only pretending to be so to enable the murder plot against her hideous husband to go forward. In the end, the "resurrected" husband is killed and his murderer goes free; such is the moral of the tale. *The Dark Tower* originally opened in New York City on November 25, 1933 at the Morosco Theater, almost thirty years to the day before the assassination of President Kennedy.

Nixon, in his earnest, steadfast wooing of Pat even acted as her chauffeur when she went out on dates with other men. Imagine the silent resentment, the self-loathing Nixon must have felt during this time. Humiliation of one kind or another would always dog his life and his career; self-abasement could be viewed as romantic idealism, though, with enough spin, and Nixon would get his own back in later years as he consistently humiliated Pat in public and, it is claimed, even beat her on occasion. For a long time Pat Ryan avoided Nixon, not finding herself particularly attracted to him, but by 1940 she finally relented to his barrage of love letters and constant attention, and they were married on June 21, 1940 (the summer solstice) in a Quaker ceremony near Whittier, California, Nixon's home town. (She would die almost exactly fifty-three years later, on June 22, 1993 in New Jersey.) It's an interesting fact that the Nixons' youngest daughter, Julie, married President Eisenhower's grandson, Dwight David Eisenhower II, on December 22, 1968, which happens to be the winter solstice.

When war broke out in December 1941, Nixon took a job working in Washington, D.C. for the Office of Emergency Management. Tiring of that, he enlisted in the Navy in 1942 and—after a short posting to Quonset, Rhode Island—was sent to the Pacific theater, where he served the remainder of the war, becoming a Lieutenant Commander in the process. This is where it gets interesting.

In 1937, he had gone job-hunting in New York City at two firms that had strong intelligence connections: Donovan, Leisure, Newton and Lombard, of which General William "Wild Bill" Donovan was the founding partner, and Sullivan and Cromwell, which had John Foster Dulles as a senior partner. Donovan, of course, was the genius behind the OSS; John Foster Dulles was a statesman of world renown and brother, of course, to Allen Dulles, who would one day become Director of the Central Intelligence Agency. At this time, Nixon also applied to the FBI but was turned down. The reasons are a little vague.

In 1945, at the war's end, Nixon—still in uniform—was back on the East Coast, and this time we know even less of what he was doing and for whom. There is one tantalizing reference to the "Bureau of Aeronautics," which is suggestive of a Jack Parsons link, but alas there is nothing else there to work with. What we do have, however, is evidence that Nixon had been involved—however briefly, however peripherally—with Operation Paperclip.

Mark Aarons and John Loftus, in *The Secret War Against the Jews*, refer to interviews with former Counter Intelligence Corps personnel as well as the Central Intelligence Group (the forerunner of the CIA), who claim that Nixon had seen documentation that Allen Dulles wanted kept secret, and that Dulles in return offered to help finance Nixon's run against incumbent California Congressman Jerry Voorhis in 1946. (This claim is repeated in their *Unholy* Trinity.) As Dulles had contacts and business associations with Nazis going back long before the start of the war, it is possible that the documentation Nixon saw implicated Dulles in some ugly relationships. However, it might have been even more complicated than that.

As is discussed more fully in *The Nine*, Operation Paperclip was a US Government program to bring over as many Nazi scientists and medical personnel as possible to the United States to assist in the space program which was, at that time, a purely military program. The Army and the Navy were both involved, both fighting over the intellectual spoils (the Air Force at this time was still part of the Army). Allen Dulles was running OSS operations during the war from Switzerland, and was in a position to influence the selection process. At the same time, Nazi spymasters such as Reinhard Gehlen were offering their services to the Americans in their new war against the Soviet Union. President Truman had disbanded the OSS in October 1945, but had created the Central Intelligence Group in January 1946; the CIA was created in 1947. It was during this interregnum reshuffling of experienced intelligence personnel that Richard Nixon found himself on the East Coast, in some mysterious capacity concerning a review of captured Nazi records and documents, ostensibly for the Navy. And it was this experience that gave Nixon some very valuable connections, for when it came time to go after alleged Communist spy Alger Hiss, he had the Dulles family on his side, providing him with sensitive intelligence information that would confirm Hiss' Communist sympathies.

The Dulles family had long and extensive ties to the Nazi underground, and had been laundering Nazi money for decades. They were not alone in this. As Aarons and Loftus demonstrate, the Bush family was so heavily involved in "trading with the enemy" that some of their company assets were seized by the US government in 1942. Nixon had stumbled on to the Dulleses' own dirty laundry, and Allen Dulles took Nixon under his wing, grooming him for a position of power in Washington. Somehow, this information never makes its way into the authorized biographies.

This exposure to Nazism—Nixon's war was, after all, in the Pacific against the Japanese—was not to be Nixon's last. As the years went by, Nixon would find himself involved in protecting known Nazis in the United States, and using neo-Nazis in anti-Democrat "dirty tricks." And when the axe fell on Chile on September 11, 1973, it was once again Nixon calling the shots, with assistance from his Nazi admirers at Colonia Dignidad.

In the meantime, however, he was being groomed (and financed) by a consortium of businessmen, right-wing activists, intelligence agents, and Mafia dons, from the very beginning of his political career. It all started with a letter from California, urging Nixon to run against Jerry Voorhis.

In September 1945, the manager of the Whittier, California branch of the Bank of America—Herman Perry—contacted Nixon by mail and asked him if he would consider running against a five-term Democratic veteran, Congressman Jerry Voorhis. Voorhis seemed unbeatable, a shoo-in for the Democrats in 1946 for a sixth term. The Republicans had no one with any serious chance against him in southern California, and Nixon—as a lawyer, and a veteran, someone well-known to Perry and the people of Whittier—seemed like a possible candidate to support. At least, that is the story.

This author finds it difficult to believe that the Republican Party of California would have reached so far, to an inexperienced young lawyer just returned from the war, a political non-entity really, to run against such an overall popular candidate like Voorhis. It's true he had some political experience before the war, making speeches in support of local Republican candidates and trying to get a state assembly seat, but nothing came of his efforts and the war interrupted everyone's lives. If what Loftus and Aarons say is true in *The Secret War Against The Jews*, that Nixon was privy to some unwholesome secrets about Dulles as early as 1945, then the scenario becomes tighter, if more sinister. It also explains the friendship between Dulles and Nixon, which is otherwise inexplicable.

Dulles was urbane, sophisticated, cosmopolitan, multilingual, the very type of Eastern Establishment figure that the socially-awkward Nixon despised. Dulles on his part should have found very little to admire or find likeable in Nixon. According to Nixon biographer Anthony Summers, "they shared the same world view,"[7] which evidently was enough to overcome their personality differences. In any event, Dulles seems to have pledged support to Nixon, and support did arrive:

from companies such as Standard Oil and other big business interests who felt threatened by Voorhis. Voorhis himself was aware that money was flowing into Nixon's coffers from a "New York financial house" in an effort to remove him from office.[8] Dulles would play further roles in Nixon's career, giving him the intelligence information he would need to go after Alger Hiss. The partnership between Allen Dulles and Richard Nixon was truly a Faustian bargain, but it is hard to tell just who is Faust and who is Mephistopheles in this scenario.

Further investigation also revealed another twist to the mystery of Nixon's anonymous backers, this from longtime mobster and associate of Meyer Lansky, Mickey Cohen. As early as the 1946 election, Nixon had been in the pocket of organized crime. Cohen confessed during his incarceration at Alcatraz to what had already come to the attention of US government officials as well as Democratic party leaders, that he—on Mafia orders—had supplied funds for Nixon's first campaign against Voorhis, in a meeting arranged by Nixon's "campaign manager," Murray Chotiner. Then, for the 1950 Senate race, Cohen came up with an additional $75,000 from a group of "associates" in the rackets. The sum of $75,000 in 1950 is equivalent to $660,000 today.[9]

Mickey Cohen was Los Angeles' answer to Bugsy Siegel in Las Vegas, and indeed the two had worked together to consolidate the West Coast rackets for the Lansky operation, while Lansky busied himself with his casinos in Cuba. When Cohen was eventually convicted and sent to prison, he at first refused to confirm or deny the allegations about Nixon, Chotiner and the Mob, because that would be "like ratting," but he eventually signed a statement full of details regarding names, dates, places and amounts that could have served as Nixon's rap sheet. What is even more worrisome, however, is Mickey Cohen's relationship to another character who would figure prominently in American history: Jack Ruby.

While Jack Ruby's connections to organized crime are well known and beyond any reasonable doubt, what is perhaps not so well-known is his relationship to a former girlfriend of Mickey Cohen's, a stripper whose stage name was Candy Barr but whose real name was Juanita Slusher Dale Phillips Sahakian. Candy Barr had been the object of Mickey's passionate attentions until she got sent up for marijuana possession, doing four years in a Texas prison and out on parole at the time of the Kennedy assassination. Ruby was phoning her and visiting her from her release in April of 1963 right up to a week or so before Dallas. It seems clear that this was not to get her to resume her career in one of Ruby's clubs, since she was under strict orders by her parole board not to go back to her old job. We may never know the real reasons behind Candy Barr's importance to Ruby; the assumption is that he was interested in what underworld connections she might have made while in prison,[10] but that does not explain the many phone calls, especially those leading up to the assassination.

Ruby was chronically short of cash, though, always on the verge of bankruptcy, so it is quite possible that he was looking for a Mafia "loan" and was hoping

Candy could lead him to the right people; indeed, remarks he made to associates in the days before the assassination led many to believe that he was on the verge of a windfall. He had met with various organized crime figures in the weeks preceding Kennedy's visit to Dallas, and spoke to many more by phone. None of this explains Candy's role, since Ruby certainly had his own connections to organized crime including all manner of loan sharks. Candy's importance to Ruby was probably due only to her long affair with Cohen, and it is possible Ruby was using Candy to communicate with Cohen. These circumstances may be totally irrelevant to the assassination and its aftermath, but we will probably never know for sure. What Candy Barr, Mickey Cohen and Jack Ruby did eventually have in common, however, was the same lawyer: Melvin Belli. Beyond that, the documentation is slim; but if we put Mickey Cohen together with Murray Chotiner and Richard Nixon on the one hand, and with Candy Barr and Jack Ruby on the other, we have a personality who knew where the bodies were buried. Literally. When he confessed to financing Nixon's early career, and when Warren Commission investigators uncovered Ruby's connections to Cohen, alarm bells should have gone off somewhere, but they didn't.

No matter the identity of the secret backers of Richard Nixon, he entered into the Voorhis campaign with complete focus. He developed his patented form of slanderous accusations and Red-baiting at this time, attacking Voorhis as a Communist when he knew that it was a completely unfounded allegation. According to Nixon's official platform, Voorhis was an instrument of the radical left; this, even though Voorhis was a member of the House Un-American Activities Committee (HUAC) and had an anti-Communist act named after him! To be fair, however, Voorhis *was* viewed as an ultra-liberal by many; his involvement with HUAC included hauling American Nazis such as George Moseley and George Deatherage (he of the reformed Knights of the White Camelia) before the Committee as early as 1939, criticizing their virulent anti-Semitism.[11]

The other real problem Republicans had with Voorhis, and probably the single most important reason they had to take him out in 1946, was of a piece. Voorhis had called for an overhaul of the American monetary system and "the purchase of the Federal Reserve System."[12] To American conspiracy theorists, there is probably nothing more sinister than the Federal Reserve System, which is viewed as a creature of the Illuminati, the Rothschilds, and mysterious foreign interests that use the Federal Reserve—which is an independent institution and not technically a part of the US government—to control America's financial destiny (and that of the rest of the world). For Voorhis to come out against the Federal Reserve was tantamount (in the eyes of the conspiriologists) to an attack on the Illuminati themselves. He had also attacked the oil industry as well as the insurance industry, not to mention the liquor industry. After that, there wasn't much left to go after except maybe your mother and her apple pie. It seemed as if Jerry Voorhis was going after all of business' sacred cows, all at once. He had, in effect, signed his own political death warrant and it was up to Tricky Dick to deliver it.

A combination of smears, lies, dirty tricks, anti-Communist hysteria and even anti-Semitism took the day. Registered voters in California would get phone calls from anonymous callers, asking, "Did you know Jerry Voorhis was a Communist?"—the same tactic that was used in 2000 against Democratic candidate for president, Al Gore in Florida (in Spanish this time). Leaflets were printed characterizing Voorhis as a tool of "subversive Jews" bent on destroying "Christian America." This, in 1946: only a year after Nazism was crushed in Europe at a terrible cost of human life, including those of Americans. It is important to realize from this episode how many Americans still distrusted Jews, even with the newsreel footage of the death camps fresh in their minds. Perhaps especially in face of the death camps. It was General Patton, after all, who claimed that during the war the Allies were aiming their guns in the wrong direction and should have sided with the Nazis against the Soviets. It was Patton who put captured SS officers back in charge of the temporary DP camps, filled with their former prisoners.

Dr. Carl Goldberg, a psychiatrist and psychotherapist of some renown who has held posts at the Albert Einstein School of Medicine and at New York University, has discussed this phenomenon in his *Speaking With The Devil: Exploring Senseless Acts of Evil.* In Chapter Twelve of that work, he discusses the case of "Emil," a Serbian man married to a prosecutor with the US District Attorney's office. Emil had participated in an atrocity in the former Yugoslavia before his emigration to the United States. His father had witnessed the horrors of World War II first-hand and had seen the selection process take place at one of the death camps. He watched as prisoners, hopeful to the end, were taken to be executed. The lesson he learned from this?

"It is better to be a Nazi and survive than to be one of those people who are so helpless and naïve that they have no choice but to pray to God that the Nazis are there to deliver them from harm!"[13]

Emil was taught to hate Jews by his father, to hate what his father saw as their weakness and victim mentality. As much as his father hated the Nazis who invaded their country, he hated their helpless and unresisting victims more. Emil went on to emulate this attitude, murdering civilians during raging ethnic strife in his own country. This may be a valuable perspective for understanding the flawed spirituality of people like Nixon, and of the party he represented for so many years.

In the end, Nixon won the election against Voorhis and went on to greater glory in the campaign against Helen Gahagan Douglas, who was the victim of even worse Red-baiting and racial slurs. The wife of actor Melvyn Douglas, a man whose Jewish father was born Hesselberg, Helen Douglas was attacked for the mere fact that she was married to a Jew. (Strictly speaking, Melvyn Douglas was not Jewish; according to the rabbis, Jewish heritage is passed down through the mother's side.) Both she and Nixon were fighting over a US Senate seat in 1950. Douglas, a New Deal Democrat, was a former opera singer and had been an actress on Broadway. Douglas had also appeared at the National Conference on the German Problem, held at the Waldorf-Astoria Hotel in New York City in March 1946. This Conference—arranged by Eleanor Roosevelt—was attended by such anti-Nazi luminaries as Albert Einstein and Henry Morgenthau, Jr. The Conference had targeted Operation Paperclip, demanding an end to Nazi immigration to the United States and a more aggressive prosecution of war criminals.[14]

But there was more to it.

As *Los Angeles Times* political correspondent Ronald Brownstein points out in his *The Power and the Glitter: The Hollywood-Washington Connection*, Helen Douglas had first-hand experience of Nazism. Douglas came from a conservative, Republican background, but was changed by the idealism of F.D. Roosevelt's New Deal and switched parties as early as 1932. An opera singer and sometime film actor (she played the lead in the first film made of the Ryder-Haggard novel, *She*), she was traveling through Europe for a concert tour in 1937. In Salzburg, Prague and Vienna she saw anti-Semitism, Nazism, and fear of the Nazi ideology firsthand.

> The experience changed Helen Douglas' life. Against the great upheavals wracking Europe her passion for her career suddenly seemed shortsighted, insular, selfish . . . . She returned to the United States committed to finding ways to express herself politically. Her husband, who had seen the same dangerous signs while accompanying her on part of the trip, followed suit. In the years leading to the war, both Douglases would devote as much energy to politics as to the movies, becoming pivotal figures in the struggle between liberals and Communists to define the agenda for the emerging Hollywood left.[15]

In June, 1936 the Douglases—along with Gloria Stuart, Fredric March and many others—formed the Hollywood League Against Nazism which later became the Anti-Nazi League for Defense of American Democracy. In 1944, Helen Douglas was elected a Representative from the State of California, and she threw herself wholeheartedly into the work of a political figure and one of the few women in the House. A dedicated anti-Nazi, she could never have been legitimately confused with a Communist or even having Communist sympathies. She frequently voted against the "Hollywood left" in favor of the Marshall Plan, for instance, and against the candidacy of Henry Wallace. But she was an outspoken anti-Nazi and was completely against the importation of Nazi war criminals under Operation Paperclip, and she made her position abundantly clear.

This type of activity was an attack on the heart of the Dulles/Nixon agenda, of course. Although she was as anti-Communist as Nixon, she also took a leaf from the Voorhis book on big business and especially oil business, attacking the oil companies for their rape of southern California. For this reason alone, the

Republicans knew she had to be stopped, as they had stopped Voorhis before her. Nixon could not effectively attack her on policy, but that was never his strong point anyway. Instead, he began a vicious smear campaign which portrayed Douglas as a Communist, and a whisper campaign—again by phone—reminding voters that she was married to a Jew. This bugaboo combination of Communist and Jew was precisely that used by the Nazis in their hate campaigns against the rest of the world; all that was missing to make a Heinrich Himmler proud would be a reference to the threat of global Freemasonry.

Nixon—and his anonymous backers—got their way, and he beat Douglas in the 1950 election, thereby winning his seat in the US Senate. At thirty-seven, Nixon was a Senator in Washington and within striking distance of the Presidency.

Victor Lasky, a Nixon croney and political hack who worked for Nixon's campaign and who was friendly with mob fixer Murray Chotiner, wrote a book entitled, with unintended irony, *It Didn't Start With Watergate*, in which he defended Nixon at the expense of the Kennedys and other Democrats. He had a long history of this sort of thing, and had written *JFK: The Man and the Myth* and the equally lugubrious *Robert F. Kennedy: the Myth and the Man*. The author has to agree with Lasky on one point, and that is that "it" truly didn't start with Watergate at all. Nixon's low cunning did not only comprise the manipulation of the electorate in 1946, 1950, 1952, 1960, 1962, 1968 and the bugging of Democratic National Committee headquarters at the Watergate complex in 1972. In fact, it started in 1945 and continued throughout his career; but the crimes for which he was not impeached or held accountable during his life were, if anything, more heinous than even Lasky could imagine, and may have resulted in the loss of thousands of American lives.

UNHOLY TRINITY

> In Rome itself, the transit point of the escape routes, a vast amount was done. With its own immense resources, the Church helped many of us to go overseas. In this manner, in quiet and secrecy, the demented victors' mad craving for revenge and retribution could be effectively counteracted.
>
> —Nazi Ace Colonel Hans-Ulrich Rudel, Kufstein 1970[16]

> According to Charles Colson, the aide who later turned to God and became a lay minister, Nixon had considered converting to Catholicism before the 1972 election, having come to be convinced that Catholics represented "the real America."
>
> —Anthony Summers, *The Arrogance of Power*[17]

While much of the story behind the Dulles-Nixon partnership has been sanitized, and sensitive material remains classified to this day, there is enough in the public record concerning Nixon's support of Nazi war criminals to afford us an honest gaze at this aspect of American history. Most Americans have had little exposure to the Byzantine machinations of the postwar émigré community in the United States. Many would be scandalized to learn of American support for men who caused death and atrocity during the war on the side of the Nazis; many more would be outraged to realize that the Catholic Church was a major factor in the escape of fugitive Nazis to countries all over the world. Still others would be confused by the plethora of Eastern Orthodox churches, idiosyncratic priests, spies and double agents, former SS officers, Republican Party flacks, South American political movements, captains of industry, Middle Eastern intelligence operations, multinational corporations and unorthodox banking practices that form the real structure of a network of resurgent fascism, a kind of Nazism *nouveau*, equal in everything but swastika armbands and Furtwaengler conducting *The Ring*. It is impossible to go into all of this in any great detail here; there are a number of books, however, for the interested reader who wants to pursue this story further, such as Christopher Simpson's essential *Blowback,* his *The Splendid Blond Beast*, and the equally important *Unholy Trinity* by Aarons and Loftus. What we will do is give a brief outline of what was going on after the war, and how Nixon and other Republican Party leaders became enmeshed in an unforgiving web of collaboration with the most despicable enemy the Twentieth Century had to offer.

The Nazi Party was a cult. Anyone who believes that the Nuremberg rallies, the speeches by Hitler, Rosenberg, Himmler, Hess and the others, and the swastika itself are all emblems of a traditional political party has not looked too carefully or too deeply at the phenomenon. In fact, with the swastika—a mystical, religious and occult glyph with ancient associations all over the globe—the Nazis were telling the whole world what they were about; it is a sad fact that no one really listened. The nationalist policies of the Third Reich were a manifestation in the mundane world of a philosophy that was transcendent—incorporating race, religion, architecture, astronomy, medicine, war, and politics only as a continuation of war by other means. The Holocaust had no political purpose; the tremendous expense in terms of time, money and personnel to keep the ovens burning had no political or military advantage to the Reich. It was a crusade against a race, a religion and a philosophy that the Reich found abhorrent.

Fascism is the elevation of one's own country above all others, and the elevation of the state above the individual. It is, in essence, an assault on the rest of the world and is more easily sustained if national policy assumes a racial superiority over all other races, coupled with a belief in its own structural superiority: i.e., its economic system, its system of government, perhaps even its geographical location. In countries which enjoy a mix of races, this idea of superiority is more difficult to sustain, since its own citizens have come from other countries and have some—if only sentimental or cultural—allegiances there. In that case, it is important to disregard—officially—any hint of racial superiority and instead focus on economic and political (i.e., ideological) differences. In any event, the concerns of one's own state are of absolute importance on a cosmic level, and the rights and concerns of the citizens of one's own or other countries become negligible. Thus, a foreign policy which undermines the sovereignty of other nations is acceptable.

In the days of Nazi Germany, race and nationalism went hand-in-hand. There was no way to separate the two. All other races were deemed inferior to the pure-blooded German. Attacks on other countries were considered normal and justified. In fact, Germans considered themselves *spiritually* superior to Jews and members of other races. Judeo-Christianity was viewed as a spiritual aberration, a disease that had to be eradicated. If a woman slept with a Jewish man, as an example, she was considered tainted by some sort of mystical Jewish essence and was therefore lost to the race. The Nazis were thus in the midst of a spiritual war of light against darkness, of the Aryan versus the Semite and the Slav, of the German against the Jew, the Arab, the African, the Asian, the Latin. The war was elevated to that of an astral conflict, a cosmological struggle for survival.

With the defeat of Nazi Germany at the end of World War II, fascism did not go away. How could it?

It was strong enough in Italy and Germany (and Austria, and many other countries) to cause tremendous physical dislocation, the murder of millions of civilians, the deaths of millions of combatants, and the redrawing of the map of Europe. It was tantamount to a religious faith, a mystic belief in national superiority and racial purity. It took anti-Semitism to its logical conclusion, redrawing the spiritual and genetic map (in the eyes of the Nazis, the same thing) of Europe as well. A military defeat was not enough to discredit the faith in the eyes of its true believers. In fact, to some it made Nazism even more romantic. The Nuremberg trials were considered a sham and a hoax by the Nazi war criminals fleeing along the rat lines into South America and other havens, a spiteful and vengeful exercise on behalf of the "demented victors," with no moral or ethical message worth taking away, no lesson to be learned. The Allies were preaching to their own choir; the sinners were still plotting in the basement. It would take more than bullets to kill off Nazism and fascism. After all, Christianity itself lived underground for almost three hundred years before it became a state religion.

Thus, in the damp and overheated postwar world, Nazism mutated, virus-like, and became confused with—one could say it "infected"—patriotism. What began as a war of Aryans versus Semites and sub-humans became the West versus the East, Capitalist versus Communist. The Communists were "godless" and therefore evil in a very real moral and spiritual sense. Stories were told of the persecution of religion in Communist nations, such as the Soviet Union and the People's Republic of China. The Catholic Church went underground in these countries; Masses were celebrated in secret. Priests were hunted down and imprisoned, tortured, executed. Membership in any religious organization was grounds for expulsion from the Communist Party, and consequent penalties in terms of housing, wages, education, etc.

The Vatican, therefore, was under attack in Eastern Europe and China. At the same time, its underground network of priests was a potentially valuable intelligence asset. The Church found itself cooperating with Western intelligence services against Communist countries. This meant that, in order to cooperate with the United States Central Intelligence Agency, they had to cooperate with the Nazis. The Gehlen Organization became a creature of the CIA in Europe, and once again the Vatican and the Nazis were in agreement according to both philosophy and tactics. The Vatican ran interference for war criminals escaping to less hostile nations on the one hand, and worked with resuscitated Nazi intelligence organs on the other. The Cold War had started, and every political leader in the West made sure that it was painted in Manichaean terms of Light versus Darkness, of Good versus Evil. After all, the Soviet Union was, according to President Reagan, the "Evil Empire," and not merely a sovereign nation with whom we disagreed on matters of economics, human rights and foreign policy. The Soviet Union was evil; it represented the forces of Satan on earth and had to be destroyed.

To those who believe the author is indulging in hysterical hyperbole, it is only necessary to refer to the speeches made by a long line of postwar Republican presidents and presidential candidates on the issue. Since they can be construed as "spin," however, the skeptical can review the record on support for Nazi individuals and political organizations in the United States by Republican leadership as they girded their loins for battle with the Communists.

(This is not an attack on the Republican Party itself; not every Republican is a closet Nazi, and it is not the intention of the author to suggest this. Probably very few Republicans are even aware of the extent to which their Party has embraced the politics of war criminals in their midst. However, as other authors have pointed out with mountains of documentation and rivers of primary source material, the Republicans seem to have embraced the Nazi underground with much more zeal and commitment than the Democrats, both as individuals and as a Party. There is a reason for this, and as we delve more deeply into America's political subconscious we may reveal it in all its ugliness and satanic glory.)

To understand the degree to which resurgent fascism and refugee Nazism have influenced the political direction of the United States (including its foreign policy), it is necessary to examine the role that Eastern European ethnic groups have played in the postwar years, forming voting blocs on the one hand, and making themselves essential to Western intelligence operations on the other. It is also necessary to examine the political allegiances and philosophies of these groups before they came to the United States. In many cases, these were nationalist organizations that had actively resisted Soviet Communism and, in the process, turned to fascist, extreme right-wing support, adopting anti-Semitism and other racial ideologies from the Nazis. The fact that Eastern Orthodox churches—the dominant religious group in Eastern Europe—are also intensely nationalistic and to a certain extent anti-Semitic (at least, no less than the Catholic Church in that era) made the alliance between

Nazism and Orthodoxy inevitable. The Nazis welcomed the political and military support of these militias, even though the Slavs were considered "sub-human" and their religions anathema, and ripe for the ovens one day once the war was over and Nazi hegemony assured. This type of cynicism was identical to that of Richard Nixon, for instance, whose anti-Semitism did not preclude him from supporting Israel or hiring Henry Kissinger. Power, after all, has its own ideology.

The split between the Eastern Orthodox churches and the Roman Catholic Church took place on July 16, 1054. The then Patriarch of Constantinople, Cerularius, rejected the claim of Pope Leo IX to universal leadership of Christendom. Until that time, all national Christian churches had been autocephalous, i.e., with their own head, or patriarch. There had been no universal ruler to whom all churches owed their allegiance regardless of the country in which they were located. Leo, in an attempt to consolidate political power over all Christian countries, was demanding allegiance from the Greek Patriarch, which would have given him the East. Instead, as a result of Cerularius' refusal to kow-tow to the Pope, he and his entire Church were excommunicated.

Christianity at that time was already geographically and culturally divided. The first important political leader who embraced the Christian faith was the Roman Emperor Constantine, who elevated Christianity to the status of a state religion, while moving the capitol to the ancient city of Byzantium, renamed Constantinople (what is now Istanbul). It retained this status for well over a millennium, throughout the illustrious history of the Byzantine Empire. As political power in the West in the centuries after Constantine, however, switched from Constantinople back to Rome, so did the emphasis on purely "Western" interpretations of Christianity.

Until the Catholic Church became dominant in the West, the religious services of the Church had always been held in local languages. Thus, the Greeks celebrated Mass (called the "Divine Liturgy") in Greek; in Eastern Europe, Greek missionaries Cyril and Methodius developed the Slavonic alphabet and a language called Church Slavonic: a brilliant attempt to provide a unified language for the many disparate ethnicities to be found in what is now Russia, Ukraine, Poland, Hungary, Romania, Czechoslovakia, Serbia, etc. The alphabet of this language was based on the Greek alphabet and called "Kyrillic" after Cyril who invented it. The language itself was a kind of Slavic Esperanto, in which much of the service could be understood by everyone, and all of it by no one! The emphasis on local language (vernacular) celebration of the Church services is a hallmark of Eastern Orthodoxy, and to this day one can experience this spirituality in Greek, Arabic, Serbian, Russian, Ukrainian, and many other languages. The local churches were also permitted to add cultural details of their own, such as the Easter eggs which are always red in Greece but which are multicolored and fantastically designed in the Eastern European countries, etc. In addition, the leader of the Russian Orthodox Church, for example, is a Patriarch. So also is the leader of the Greek Orthodox Church and all of the various national Orthodox Churches. The Greek Orthodox Patriarch is considered "first among equals" but the emphasis is on "equals." Each national church conducts its own affairs internally, without reference to the "spiritual headquarters" in Greece. Thus, Eastern Orthodoxy was always nationalistic, from the very beginning, and this provided a potential recruiting ground for more extreme forms of nationalistic political expression, such as Nazism.

By contrast, Roman Catholicism was . . . well, just that. *Roman* Catholicism. The official language was Latin, no matter in what country one found oneself. And the leader was the Pope, in Rome. Whereas Eastern Orthodoxy was a "distributed system" of leadership and ritual, Roman Catholicism was strictly hierarchical, with the Pope at the top, followed by cardinals and then bishops, down to priests and the faithful. In 800 A.D., when Charlemagne proclaimed himself Emperor of the "Holy Roman Empire," the handwriting was on the wall. And, as successive Muslim invasions of Turkey and Eastern Europe weakened the Byzantine Empire, the political power of the Eastern Church in Europe also waned.

The Byzantine Empire fell to Sultan Mohammed II in 1453. Oddly, though, the Sultan made the Greek Orthodox patriarch the *ethnarch* of all the Greeks in the Ottoman empire, in effect making him a civil authority as well as a religious one. This enabled the survival—if not the flourishing growth—of Greek Orthodoxy. Possibly the Sultan thought of using the Eastern Orthodox churches as a tool against his ultimate enemy, the Holy Roman Empire. After all, the Eastern Orthodox Churches had suffered from invading Catholic armies during the Crusades, which had witnessed the sacking of Constantinople, the burning of Orthodox churches and the murder of Orthodox priests: a campaign as ruthless as that against the Muslim enemies in the Holy Land; and thus the Sultan could make a case that the sympathies of the Orthodox should rest with the Ottomans. It would not be the last time the Eastern Orthodox churches were politically manipulated this way.

The Orthodox churches are called "Orthodox" because they follow the form of Christianity as it was practiced since early times. The Divine Liturgy of St. John Chrysostom is about three hours in length, no matter in which language it is celebrated. The Catholic Mass is an abbreviated form of this same Liturgy, cut down to about forty-five minutes. There are many other differences, including the strange pre-Liturgy ritual in which the crucifixion of Christ is re-enacted with loaves of bread and wine, and a golden knife: a somewhat Gnostic survival perhaps reflective of the Church's eastern origins.

Catholicism, on the other hand, modified its rituals considerably through the years. Whereas Eastern Orthodoxy seems frozen in time circa 1000 A.D., the Roman Catholic Church has undergone many transformations and has constantly evolved since the break with Orthodoxy. Ironically, however, the changes they have made—and contemplated—would bring the Church back to where the Eastern Orthodox already exist. The Vatican II decision to permit local churches to celebrate Mass in the local dialects—considered a major concession at the time—is merely what the Orthodox have been doing since the beginning. The Orthodox also have a married priesthood (which the Catholics also had for hundreds of years), and a form of confession in which priest and penitent face each other rather than in a confessional box, among many other practices that would be considered modern and "enlightened" today.

The Catholic Church, in an effort to attract Orthodox laity to the Papal fold, accepted what is known as Uniate or Eastern Rite Catholics. In this hybrid form of Catholicism, the beliefs of the people—including the all-important allegiance to the Roman Pope—are Catholic. The rituals, however, are Eastern Orthodox. Thus, with the Uniates, the Church enjoys the allegiance of some Eastern European and Middle Eastern Christians while the latter can keep the rituals with which they are the most familiar. The Church extends its political power into these otherwise impenetrable countries using this method. This became an important issue during World War II, when the Uniates were utilized as a kind of Vatican intelligence network against the Reds.

The groups most openly hostile to Communism and most open to Nazi support were Ukrainian, Croatian, Romanian, and Hungarian nationalists. The Hungarians and Croatians were, by and large, Roman Catholic and received tremendous support from the Catholic Church both in their actions against Soviet Communism as well as in intelligence operations and political action in support of Intermarium and other pan-Slavic cabals, support that would eventually earn these Nazi and pro-Nazi criminals safe haven in North and South America. The Ukrainians and Romanians were largely Eastern Orthodox or Eastern-Rite (Uniate) Catholics. The Russian Orthodox churches themselves were divided between those who supported the Moscow Patriarchate (largely seen, and with reason, to be an instrument of the Soviet government) and those whose bishops fled Russia at the time of the 1917 revolution and who wished to distance themselves from any dominance by the Moscow hierarchy (a group of bishops known, loosely, as the Synod or more formally as the Russian Orthodox Church Outside Russia or ROCOR). Whereas this latter policy seemed reasonable from a political perspective, it raised doubts about the canonicity (ecclesiastical legality) of these breakaway groups, a problem that need not concern us here at the moment, but which has caused many dislocations of those Eastern churches based in the United States and Canada, especially after the fall of Soviet Communism. In New York City, where the two Russian churches have their American headquarters, the Moscow Patriarchate is known to insiders as "Ninety-Eighth Street" and ROCOR is known as "Ninety-Third Street," due to the locations of their respective cathedrals.

In addition, groups like the Serbian Orthodox churches were actively suppressed by the Croatian Catholics operating in what would become Yugoslavia, their parishioners forced to convert to Catholicism or be killed, and sometimes both. Testimony has come down to us of entire Serbian Orthodox congregations being forced through a conversion ceremony in a Croatian Catholic church, and then machine-gunned outside the church's walls moments later. Catholic priests and monks were responsible for hideous atrocities in Serbia and Croatia during the war; in one case, a Franciscan priest was enthusiastically in charge of a concentration camp. Croatian Catholics also perpetrated gross atrocities against the indigenous Jewish populations of Croatia under the banner of the dread Ustasch, the rabidly pro-Nazi political and military organization of World War II Croatia. It would be the Ustasch that would benefit greatly from Vatican support both during and after the war, as Father Draganovic ensured that his countrymen would never stand trial for the war crimes for which they had been indicted, but would instead flee to the four corners of the earth, where they would take up their banners again.

Further, countries such as Slovakia—which were mostly Roman Catholic—actively supported Hitler during the war. In Slovakia's case, Hitler promised the people independence from the Czechs, with whom they had been artificially mated after the end of World War I. The Slovak leader during the war was Monsignor Tiso, a pro-Nazi Catholic prelate who was responsible for pogroms against the Jews in his own country.

In the Ukraine, the situation was, if anything, even more complex. Two rival religious institutions vied for the loyalty of Ukrainian Christians: the Ukrainian Orthodox Church and the Ukrainian Uniates. In both cases, the Nazis used their hatred of Soviet Communism to enlist their aid as militia against Russia: providing training, uniforms, weapons and leadership, just as they did for the Croatian Ustasch and the Romanian Iron Guard. The Nazis effectively unleashed the violence and rage against the Russians that had been building since the Revolution, when the Soviets had made every attempt to eradicate both the religion and the culture of the indigenous peoples of the region. They also unleashed Ukrainian anti-Semitism, and they did all this using the collaboration of the Vatican.

> . . . the debacle had been predominantly the responsibility of the tsar, his ministers, the whole state apparatus, and their policies over many years, which had Russia involved in a war for which it was not prepared and that it could not win. And so the search got under way, as it did in Germany one year later, for the "sinister forces," the "hidden hand," that had administered the "stab in the back" that had led to the catastrophe.
>
> —Walter Laqueur, *Black Hundred: The Rise of the Extreme Right in Russia*[18]

By early 1943, virtually every one of the 800,000 Ukrainian Jews had been killed by the Ukrainian Nazis. Members of the Ukrainian SS—largely composed of Uniate Christians who owed their spiritual allegiance to Rome—were enthusiastic in their support of the Final Solution; the Nazis had promised to overlook both their religion and their race in order to enlist their aid against their common enemies: Communists and Jews. Under other circumstances, being both Christian and Slav was enough to be considered sub-human and unworthy of the SS uniform. Forty thousand Ukrainians volunteered for duty in the specially-created SS Galicia Division—twice the number required, overwhelming the SS leadership. In the end twenty thousand were accepted, trained, and armed. Then, as the troops passed by in review, Archbishop Szepticky blessed the SS Division, urging them to glory.

They would follow in the footsteps of the Organisation of Ukrainian Nationalists (OUN) under Stepan Bandera and Yaroslav Stetsko. The OUN organized the pogrom of the Jews of Lvov, where six thousand were murdered in only three days and three nights of savagery in 1941. Stetsko would later become president of the Anti-Bolshevik Bloc of Nations (ABN), a merger of the OUN and White Russian Nazis, with Mikola Abramchyk (the Byelorussian Nazi Minister of Intelligence) as vice president, along with war criminal Stanislav Stankievich and many other renegade Nazi leaders. The ABN was being run by British Intelligence, under the supervision of Kim Philby; Philby would later be revealed as a double agent, working in reality for Soviet intelligence, which had penetrated the ethnic anti-Communist émigré groups since the earliest days of the Revolution.

And let us not forget the Croatians.

Let us look at the example of Bishop Ivan Saric, known as the Hangman of Sarajevo, whose slaughter of Croatian Serbs was legendary; or Father Josip Bujanovic, who—as the Ustaschi leader of Gospic—presided over the massacre of Serbian Orthodox peasants, before escaping to Australia at the end of the war, courtesy of the Vatican rat lines. Or Father Vilim Cecelja, a lieutenant colonel in the Ustaschi militia who was named war criminal number 7103 by the Yugoslav government, but who also emigrated to Australia, where he became important in the creation of Nazi and Ustaschi cells. Or Father Dragutin Kamber, the concentration camp commandant of Doboj, who slaughtered Serbian Orthodox priests and incited the wholesale massacre of Serbs in Bosnia.

Thus, the religious and political tapestries of these Eastern European countries are varied and their histories complex and interrelated to a great degree. Even Ukraine's status was always a matter for debate, since Ukraine was considered to be part of Russia from early times, though large parts of Ukraine had been annexed by Poland, thus causing some political wrestling over the issue of the Ukrainian Waffen SS Division "Galicia." Were the Ukrainians captured at the end of the war, serving in German uniforms under German officers with German training really Ukrainians and therefore Russians to be deported back to the motherland, or were they in reality Polish citizens and therefore not part of the Yalta agreement which would have surrendered them to the Soviets?

Regardless, the SS Galicia Division was responsible for pogroms and atrocities the equal of any other SS division during the war, and it was only due to a complicated arrangement between the Catholic Church on the one hand and Western intelligence agencies on the other that they were given over to the protection of the British via General Pavlo Shandruk, who had commanded the SS Galicia Division in its final months. Shandruk emigrated to the United States after the war, and was buried in the cemetery adjacent to Ukrainian Orthodox Church headquarters in Bound Brook, New Jersey . . . as a war hero.

Many fleeing Ukrainian Catholics had switched allegiance to the more fiercely nationalistic Ukrainian Orthodox Church, and it was this same church that consecrated renegade Romanian Iron Guard commandant and instigator of the 1941 pogrom of Bucharest, Valerian Trifa, as a Bishop of the Romanian Orthodox Church in America in 1952—even though he had no qualifications whatsoever as a bishop, had never been a priest or even an altar boy, and had no theological training at all. Trifa went on to create cells of Romanian Nazi "priests" under church cover throughout North America and in other countries, right up to his eventual deportation from the US in 1984.

When the Eisenhower-Nixon campaign of 1952 was successful in depicting the Democrats as "soft on Communism," it attracted the political and financial support of these émigré groups all across the country. A special "Ethnic Division" was created at campaign headquarters to ensure that the Ukrainian, Romanian, Slovak, Croatian, etc. vote was turned out in support of the former World War II Commander-in-Chief of Allied forces in Europe and his Red-baiting, anti-Semitic vice-presidential candidate. The Republicans had cornered the market on Eastern European hatred of Communism, and had promised a vigorous campaign to win back the motherlands from Soviet domination.

It is vitally important to understand that this was not a post–World War II aberration. This was *policy* and had been in place since the *first* World War, which is when the Dulles brothers cut their eye teeth on foreign affairs and found themselves agitating for a strong postwar Germany to stand as a buffer state against the Bolshevik Revolution that had taken power in Moscow and assassinated the royal family of Nicholas and Alexandra, and which was then struggling with *volkisch* groups such as the *Thule Gesellschaft* for dominance in Germany. Allen Dulles was already in an intelligence position in Switzerland during the *first* World War, developing the contacts and networks he would need as the years went by. John Foster Dulles was already in the State Department during World War I. Their uncle, Robert Lansing, was President Woodrow Wilson's Secretary of State, an ultra-conservative when it came to assigning blame for war crimes in World War I, who insisted that individual countries be responsible for prosecuting their own war crimes; from Lansing's point of view, the right people to judge what was and was not a war crime—what was and was not necessary for the preservation of the state—was the military leadership of each individual nation! In other words, the fox should guard the hen house. He objected to the idea of atrocities and "crimes against humanity"; it smacked too much of internationalism, which he opposed. Thus, if the German Army had committed atrocities then let the German Army prosecute their own troops. It should be an internal matter, of no concern to other nations.

Thus, Allen Dulles, John Foster Dulles, and their uncle Robert Lansing had already formulated a geopolitical strategy that they would implement not only at the end of World War I, but consistently through the postwar years, through World War II and beyond. It involved strengthening Germany as a guardian against the spread of European Bolshevism and Communism, and the creation of a *cordon sanitaire* composed of Eastern European countries to hold back Russian expansionism. The Dulles brothers actively courted Nazi officials in the 1930s—as did such American concerns as the Ford Motor Company and IBM—with no scruples about the type of institutionalized anti-Semitism that Hitler and his colleagues were planning for Germany and the Occupied Territories. While the Democratic president, Franklin D. Roosevelt, saw Nazism as an evil that had to be confronted and covertly plotted ways to bring America into the war against Hitler, the Republicans in Congress were talking about isolationism and appeasement: the continuing evolution of the Dulles strategy that had begun in 1917.

Thus, when, as we shall see, Nixon began taking bribes from the Greek military junta and ran interference to get President Johnson's peace initiative with Vietnam scuttled in time for the 1968 election, it was business as usual for the Republican Party. When he commanded that the socialist Allende regime in Chile be overthrown, and provided the financial support to the truckers' strike necessary to cripple Chile's economy and create instability that would pave the way for General Pinochet and his junta, it was business as usual once again.

In the case of the Greek military junta, we can assume that the primary motive was to get as much funding as possible for Nixon's election campaign; in other words, perhaps it was not ideologically motivated. In the case of Vietnam, we can assume that it was simply more important to Nixon to win the election than to halt the bombing and save human life; in other words, his tactics were not motivated by any desire to crush the North Vietnamese Communist forces but once again were purely to win an election. But when we discuss the overthrow of Allende's regime—in 1973 after Nixon had been twice-elected and thus could go no further politically—then we have to assume that ideology was the only motivating factor.

It does no good to give the benefit of a doubt in one case or even two cases when the overwhelming majority of instances of support for right-wing dictatorships had no other intrinsic value to Nixon or the Republicans in general except to promote a way of life, a political philosophy that was more allied to a kind of misguided German Romanticism—the icily ethereal fascist and Nazi ideal—than it was to a purely economic or pragmatic political policy. Like the Holocaust itself, which had no military value to the Reich and which diverted vital resources unnecessarily during the height of the war, the Republican policy of support for fascists, Nazis, war criminals, and neo-Nazis was (and is) a *mission*. When we embrace men who have committed unutterable atrocities and shake the hands of men that have been bloodied with the gore of Jews, of women and children, of

Muslims, of Orthodox Christians, of Slavs, of homosexuals, of Gypsies, then we have bartered the soul of the nation for a handful of votes, a few million dollars, and a dubious place in history.

Was it worth it? Are we truly any safer now than we were at the end of World War II?

As for the public record, the following chronology may serve as evidence of the existence of a pro-Nazi cabal lurking in America's corridors of power.

Item: 1945. Operation Overcast and Operation Paperclip bring hundreds—some say thousands—of Nazi scientists (many of them—such as General Walter Dornberger, the future boss of Michael Paine at Bell Aerospace—considered war criminals by the Nuremberg Commission as well as by the rest of the world) to the United States to assist in the space program, much against the express wishes of Democratic President Harry Truman. Other Nazis, including an entire division of Ukrainian Waffen SS, are assisted out of Europe and into safe havens in North America, South America, Australasia, and the Middle East by the US State Department, British Intelligence, French Intelligence and the Vatican. This operation will be aided, abetted and covered up by the CIA in the post-war years, and especially beginning in 1953, when Allen Dulles becomes CIA Director. Dulles' Chief of Counter Intelligence, James Jesus Angleton (later the CIA's Vatican liaison), and Frank Wisner are particularly involved, along with thousands of former Nazi "freedom fighters." What is variously known as Die Spinne, Die Kamaradenwerke, and ODESSA is born, but it is in reality even more of a Vatican operation than an organization of former SS officers, who are primarily its beneficiaries.

In 1945, Dulles—along with his OSS agent Hans Bernd Gisevius, a former Gestapo officer—was accused by the US Treasury Department of laundering Nazi funds from Hungary into Switzerland (where Dulles was based). The investigation was dropped when the US State Department claimed jurisdiction. Gisevius himself was working for the massive intelligence operation being run by a White Russian, General Turkul, and known as the Black Orchestra, a Vatican-linked Nazi intelligence network that was in reality a miracle of Soviet penetration into the Western intelligence services, something that Dulles would not have known at the time. Gisevius, from his position with the Reichsbank, also had excellent connections in the Nazi intelligence services and had been used by Dulles to communicate with Admiral Canaris of the Abwehr during the war.[19]

Richard Nixon was brought in on the money laundering secret by Allen Dulles in 1945 or early 1946, of which the Treasury Department investigation had only revealed a small portion. Nixon, in examining captured German documents as a Navy officer after the war, is presumed to have come across evidence of this money laundering effort, and of other links between German industrial and banking firms, OSS officers, and Dulles in particular. This was at the same time as the US Treasury Department investigation, so it is reasonable to assume that Nixon uncovered elements of a paper trail that would implicate such firms as Chase Bank, Morgan Bank, ITT and other companies that have since been revealed to have operated freely in Nazi territory, and often with Nazis on the local board of directors (such as Nazi Intelligence chief Walter Schellenberg, who kept his board position with ITT throughout the war). Dulles, in return, promised to assist Nixon in his California congressional campaign if he buried the data. A life-long partnership was born.

In this context, it is worthwhile to note the research of Charles Higham who, in his *American Swastika*, speaks of captured SS documentation which clearly shows that Dulles gave voice to extreme anti-Semitic views in several conversations with Max von Hohenlohe, a Nazi agent and intimate of Schellenberg, who himself was acting on instructions from SS leader Heinrich Himmler. (Higham's research was further corroborated by Christopher Simpson in *The Splendid Blond Beast.*) Hohenlohe had first cleared Dulles' credentials with the Spanish Ambassador to the Vatican, who proclaimed Dulles reliable.[20]

Dulles met with Hohenlohe in Geneva in January 1943 and is recorded—by the SS, remember, in their documents—as stating that in Europe "there must be no toleration of a return of the Jewish power positions" (Higham's paraphrasing) and that "the Americans were only continuing the war to get rid of the Jews and that there were people in America who were intending to send the Jews to Africa."[21] We may choose to give Dulles the benefit of a doubt here and assume that, if these remarks are correct, he was only trying to win the cooperation of the anti-Hitler Nazis with whom he was negotiating. This is basically what Simpson is saying. Dulles told Hohenlohe that the Allies would not accept Hitler as a leader, but that he was more interested in creating a buffer zone between Russia and the rest of Europe, and that a reconstructed, postwar Germany was central to the scheme. The extermination of the Jews was a fringe benefit. Even the eventual resolution of Czechoslovakia was immaterial to the Allies. In other words, the key to this geopolitical problem was anti-Communism, which was code for Russia. The Allies, according to Dulles, had no interest in the eventual disposition of European Jewry, understanding that Europe would not tolerate a "return of the Jewish power positions." The Nazis could do as they liked.

But were such anti-Semitic remarks necessary in order to win the cooperation of men like intelligence chief Schellenberg and Himmler, on whose behalf Hohenlohe was meeting Dulles? By accepting Himmler as a future leader of Germany, Dulles had already played any cards he needed. He could have saved countless lives if he had made it clear to the Nazis that the United States was firmly against the Holocaust, thus threatening Himmler's future career if he persisted in genocide. He would have at least made Himmler and Schellenberg stop and think and perhaps slow down the ongoing mass murder, perhaps using it as a bargaining chip if nothing else. By giving tacit approval to Himmler for the Holocaust—indeed, by saying that America was only continuing the war to collaborate (there is no other word) in Hitler's extinction of the Jews—he gave the green light to the SS to go ahead with the Final Solution.

Dulles had a wide and deep circle of business contacts, friends, and personal allies in Europe long before the war began. His business interests included Schroeders Bank, of which he was a director, and his law firm represented many other German organizations both before and during the war. He had even met Hohenlohe in the years before the war. Was it really necessary to give voice to such loathsome anti-Semitic sentiments? Or was it, perhaps, a reflection of Allen Dulles' genuine feelings in the matter, feelings that would influence decades of American intelligence activity and possibly open up the CIA to foreign penetration?

Further, were the records of these conversations with Dulles among the captured German documents that fell under Nixon's jaundiced eye during those sensitive postwar months when Operation Paperclip was being openly condemned by the Democrats? If so, it is clear why Dulles would have been desperate to have them "deep sixed" and to enlist Nixon's aid in doing so. A few phone calls from Dulles to business partners on the East Coast would have been enough to get the young lawyer's career off on the right track.

Later, the World Commerce Corporation is formed, ostensibly to "rebuild German-South American trade networks."[22] The directors are Sir William Stephenson ("Intrepid" of British intelligence fame) and General William Donovan, the creator and leader of the OSS. Allen Dulles served as counsel for the corporation, along with Frank Wisner. Both of these men would, of course, become much better known in their positions at the CIA. It is only one of many fronts for American intelligence activities that use former Nazis—many of them accused war criminals—in important leadership positions. These will include the Anti-Bolshevik Bloc of Nations (ABN), the World Anti-Communist League (WACL), of which US Army General and self-professed "black" psychological warfare expert John Singlaub of Iran-Contra fame was director, and many others. The Republicans were regrouping the Nazis: hiding them, recruiting them, using their networks and contacts, giving them visas and citizenship, hailing them as patriots. And pointing them at Russia.

Item: 1946. September 29. Nicolae Malaxa, Romanian Nazi financier and industrialist, arrives in New York as part of an official Romanian trade mission . . . and doesn't leave.

Item: 1946. November. Nixon's attack on Jerry Voorhis characterizes him as a Communist and his campaign uses anti-Semitic smears, saying that Voorhis is a tool of "subversive Jews." Nixon is financed from a mysterious East Coast cabal of oil industry executives and industrial tycoons on the one hand (via Dulles), and by organized crime figures around Meyer Lansky and Mickey Cohen on the other (via Murray Chotiner). Nixon wins the election.

For those mindful of events discussed in *The Nine*, this is the same year—and the same place, Pasadena—where Jack Parsons and L. Ron Hubbard had conducted the occult operation known as the Babalon Working. It was at the California

Republican Assembly (CRA) in Pasadena in 1946 that Richard Nixon was selected to run against Voorhis. The President of the CRA at that time was Meyer Lansky's "mouthpiece," Murray Chotiner. For those really titillated by bizarre linkages, Pat Nixon's birth name was Thelma. The FBI, in investigating the Parsons occult lodge in Pasadena, had mistakenly called it the "Order of Thelma." (Was Pat Nixon . . . Babalon!?!)

Item: 1947. The CIA is created, and organizes anti-Soviet intelligence networks in Western and Eastern Europe utilizing former Nazis under Third Reich intelligence chief General Reinhard Gehlen. This will become known as the Gehlen Org, and forms the backbone of anti-Soviet CIA operations in Europe, coordinating its efforts with Vatican officials friendly to the CIA. It will be years before it is known how deeply this operation was penetrated by Soviet intelligence, due in part to the cabal of Soviet agents within British Intelligence, including Kim Philby (the "third man"), Guy Burgess, Donald MacLean and Anthony Blunt. Nixon and Dulles tour Europe together, Dulles showing Nixon the importance of holding the line against Communism using any means necessary, including the use of "Freedom Fighters" taken from the ranks of pro-fascist organizations in Eastern and Central Europe, and led by former Nazis and SS officers.

Item: 1948. Prior to the November elections, Dulles—in Operation Bloodstone—authorizes his deputy Frank Wisner to maintain the Vatican's rat lines of escaping Nazi fugitives and "freedom fighters" using false paperwork to hoodwink Immigration officials.

Item: 1948. There is an attack on Alger Hiss, a suspected Communist in the State Department. Nixon, the youngest member of the House Un-American Activities Committee (HUAC) is given confidential information on Hiss by Dulles as well as by the FBI, via Republican presidential hopeful Thomas Dewey. A key figure is Catholic priest Father John Cronin, who had reported to the FBI on Communist penetration of American labor unions during the War. Cronin receives information on Hiss from the FBI and then leaks it to Nixon. One of the HUAC investigators on the Hiss case is FBI agent Lou Russell, who would become involved in the Watergate break-in more than twenty years later.[23] The CIA had known of Hiss for years, and had once considered him for a position as general counsel with the Agency until they came up with information linking him to Communist activities in the United States. Dulles and former OSS chief William Donovan trade information on Hiss, and then leak it to Congressman Nixon, thereby ensuring that Nixon's political star will rise.

Item: 1948. November. Republican candidate Thomas Dewey does not win the US presidential election, much to the dismay of Dulles and the other intelligence officers working the Nazi rat lines and building Nazi intelligence networks in Europe. Truman remains in power, and remains a problem, as he is not in agreement with covert efforts to save Nazi war criminals. Nixon also remains in power, winning reelection as Congressman.

Item: 1949. Cardinal Mindszenty's show-trial is televised, in which the Roman Catholic prelate robotically confesses to the Hungarian Communist regime's outlandish charges against him, leading the CIA to opine that "some unknown force" is compelling him to act this way, the result of some mysterious Russian interrogation technique.[24]

Item: 1949. Wisner's Nazis begin arriving in the United States. Some find work as broadcasters at Radio Liberty and the Voice of America, both fronts for CIA activity and black propaganda.

Item: 1950. February. Wheeling, West Virginia. Senator Joseph McCarthy makes his famous speech claiming Communist penetration of the State Department, using lines lifted verbatim from a previous Nixon speech on Alger Hiss.

Item: 1950. June. The Korean War begins. Nixon's senatorial campaign against Helen Gahagan Douglas uses the same Red-baiting and anti-Semitic tactics as in the Voorhis race, and he keeps referring to her husband's birth name of Hesselberg as an attempt to remind voters that she is married to a Jew. Nixon wins the election and enters the US Senate.

Item: 1950. July 19. Viorel Trifa arrives in New York. Trifa had been commandant of the Romanian Iron Guard student movement and responsible for the January 1941 attempted coup and resulting pogrom in the Jewish quarter of Bucharest, in which one thousand Jews were killed, including more than two hundred who were taken to a slaughterhouse and butchered in a grim parody of koshering. During the pogrom, Trifa himself visited the cells where Jews were being held and murdered them personally. He was a member of the Iron Guard General Staff, along with only two others. He was tried and sentenced *in absentia* by the Romanian government, but was living in protection at the German Embassy in Bucharest. At war's end, Trifa sought asylum in Italy and obtained a position as a history teacher in a Catholic college. In 1950, he manages to emigrate to the United States by disguising his Nazi past.[25] He will take over the Romanian Orthodox Church in the United States by force,[26] become an Archbishop, and in 1955 open a session of the US Congress by invitation of Vice President Richard Nixon.

Item: 1951. Soviet moles in British intelligence, Burgess and MacLean, defect. Kim Philby, the "third man," is recalled from his post in the United States. Soviet penetration of Dulles' espionage network of former Nazis is in danger of being exposed, but Dulles remains oblivious.

Item: 1951. Nixon introduces a private bill to allow Nicolae Malaxa to stay in the United States. Malaxa is a Romanian émigré and financier of the Iron Guard, and hence of Trifa's pogroms against the Jews in which thousands had been tortured and murdered. Malaxa had been a business partner of Hermann Goering, the Nazi Reichsmarschall, and his factories "integrated" with Germany's during the war. The arms supplied to the Iron Guard came from Malaxa's factories. Malaxa then hired the Nixon law firm in Whittier, California to represent him, and funneled (illegally) $100,000 to the Nixon campaign fund.[27]

Malaxa is allowed to remain in the United States. Other beneficiaries of Malaxa's business included the law firm of Sullivan and Cromwell (the law firm of the Dulles brothers), the law firm of Pehle and Loesser (John Pehle, of the Treasury Department, had frozen Malaxa's assets during the war), and former US Immigration commissioner Ugo Carusi, whom Malaxa hired, as well as a former OSS officer stationed in Romania, Grady McClaussen, with whom Malaxa had other business dealings and signed contracts.[28]

Item: 1952. July 4. Viorel (now "Valerian") Trifa takes the Romanian Orthodox Church by force, using a team of former Iron Guardists in a violent assault on church headquarters in Grass Lakes, Michigan. Trifa, now calling himself a bishop, had never even been ordained a priest; he is thus the epitome of the "wandering bishop," and his consecration is performed by bishop of the Ukrainian Orthodox Church, Ioan ("John") Teodorovich, who himself fled Soviet secret police in the Ukraine and came to the United States in 1924 to organize the Ukrainian Orthodox Church. (While the history of the Ukrainian churches—as well as Ukrainian history itself—is complex and beyond the scope of this work, it suffices to say that many pro-Nazi Ukrainian nationalists are considered heroes to this church, and some are even buried in the Church's cemetery in New Jersey, including one of the organizers of the rescue of the SS Galician Division, General Pavlo Shandruk.) In his career as Romanian Archbishop, Trifa will bring many more Iron Guardists into the United States and ordain them as priests, even though they have had no theological or religious training at all. Instead, under Church "cover," they establish Iron Guard operations in the United States, South America and Europe.

Item: 1952. The Republican campaign against the Democrats in the presidential elections includes a call for the liberation of Eastern Europe: those countries that had become "satellites" of the Soviet Union or which had been invaded and occupied by the Russians, such as the Baltic states of Latvia, Lithuania and Estonia, as well as Poland, Hungary, Romania, Bulgaria, Albania, Yugoslavia, and Czechoslovakia, in addition to the Ukraine and Belarus.

The Republican Party at this time creates its "Ethnic Division" to handle concerns of these minorities in the United States and to bring out the ethnic, i.e., Eastern and Central European, vote. It is also a way to earn campaign contributions from wealthy donors who have a vested interest in keeping up American pressure on the "captive nations." Many of these émigrés had been Nazis in their native lands, members of the Romanian Iron Cross and the Hungarian Arrow Sword, for instance. They go on to achieve leadership positions within the Ethnic Division and in other groups formed in the 1950s in Europe and the United States to combat Communism. The Republican ticket of Eisenhower and Nixon wins the election, Nixon campaigning as well for Joe McCarthy. John Foster Dulles is named Secretary of State; his brother Allen Dulles becomes Director of the CIA.

Item: 1954. Nicolae Malaxa meets with Otto Skorzeny and Juan Peron in Buenos Aires, Argentina, according to CIA documents.[29] Skorzeny—the famed

Nazi commando—has eluded a Nuremberg indictment and, as an international arms dealer, is now running an informal worldwide SS underground operation. Juan Peron, of course, is the President of Argentina and a supporter of Italian and German fascism. Most escaping Nazis wind up in Argentina at some point during their exile, and Peron profits financially as well as politically from the arrangement. Skorzeny is based in Franco's Madrid, where he oversees a resurgent Nazi renaissance. The other Iron Guard leaders are still active at this time, soliciting funds from Romanian exiles worldwide and publishing Guardist newspapers.

Malaxa, Trifa and others are eventually implicated, but no action will be taken against them except for sporadic attempts to deport Malaxa and Trifa, which fail due to the interference of Vice President Nixon and other Republican leaders.

OCTOBER SURPRISE

We've just seen some very terrible forces unleashed. Something bad is going to come of this.

—Richard Nixon in 1968, speaking of Robert Kennedy's declaration as a Presidential candidate [30]

Most people remember the term "October Surprise" as being linked to a purported deal between the Republican Party and the elements holding American hostages in Iran. The year was 1980, and forces loyal to the Ayatollah Khomeini had taken the American Embassy in Teheran the previous year and were holding fifty-two Americans prisoners. A deal with the Carter administration which would have had the hostages released before the end of the year suddenly went awry; some witnesses came forward, stating that George Bush, Sr. had asked the Iranians to hold the hostages for a few more weeks until after the November election, to ensure the victory at the polls of the Reagan-Bush ticket. This was in return for certain concessions. Carter, who believed he could have had a deal with the Iranians, suddenly found himself without one. The American electorate, tired of the long ordeal and the humiliation of the first American rescue attempt which foundered in the desert, elected Reagan, and the rest is history. The hostages were released on the day of Reagan's inauguration.

What most Americans do not know, however, is that this was not the first time American lives had been bartered for power. In an earlier October, it had cost many thousands of Vietnamese lives as well. As revealed in the Anthony Summers work on Nixon mentioned previously, Richard Nixon had performed the same deplorable maneuver in a desperate attempt to ruin upcoming peace talks, arranged by outgoing President Lyndon B. Johnson. It was in the final weeks of the 1968 election and could have been the template for the actions of 1980.

Although confirmation of this event comes from various, well-informed and well-placed sources, perhaps the most damning revelation comes from the woman who helped arrange the deception: Anna Chennault, the Chinese-born wife (and widow) of Claire Chennault, the commander of the famous Flying Tigers of World

War II. Mrs. Chennault was used as the go-between in a deal that involved Nixon, John Mitchell, South Vietnamese Ambassador to the United States Bùi Diễm and, ultimately, South Vietnamese President Thieu. The deal was simple: torpedo Johnson's peace initiative and Nixon (once elected) would prop up Thieu's regime with guns and money and a more aggressive stance against the North. Had Thieu gone to the peace table with Johnson, it is not certain that he would have left with anything more substantial than an uneasy truce and a Demilitarized Zone à la North and South Korea.

It would have meant peace, it would have meant the end of war and atrocity and the suffering of civilian and soldier alike, but that is obviously not what either Nixon or Thieu had in mind. Thieu agreed, and in the eleventh hour, only days before the election, he announced that he would not be a party to the peace initiative for various reasons. Nixon beat Vice President Humphrey at the polls, and the war in Vietnam continued for American forces for five more years, with the deaths of thousands of American troops and hundreds of thousands of Vietnamese casualties. Saigon finally fell over two years later, on April 30, 1975: *Walpurgisnacht*, and the thirtieth anniversary of Hitler's suicide; a day heavy with sinister correspondences.

That was not all, however.

Once he had won the election, betraying America in the process, he then proceeded to betray Thieu. President Johnson had discovered what Nixon was up to in the last hours of the campaign but was afraid of exposing it until he had concrete proof in hand. When he did, it was after the election and Nixon's narrow victory. He then forced Nixon to support a peace initiative in the remaining days of the Johnson administration, lest Johnson himself blow the whistle on what Nixon had been doing. Nixon, fearing what the exposure of his machinations would do, accepted the terms. He then asked Mrs. Chennault to go back to Thieu and press him to agree to Johnson's peace initiative. Chennault was furious, of course, and the whole affair was in danger of falling apart, but Chennault retired behind closed doors and refused to speak to the press or to expose her role in the affair until many years later; relevant FBI documents became declassified in 1999, and the story slowly leaked out anyway.[31]

Nixon's program in Vietnam did go on, however, regardless of the empty posturing for peace. Hundreds of American soldiers died while Nixon was running interference in October and November of 1968; tens of thousands more would die before America's role in the war was over. Hundreds of thousands of Vietnamese soldiers and civilians would also die. All of this was defended by Henry Kissinger, who believed that Nixon's "constituency" supported the war and would abandon him if Nixon worked too hard for peace. In other words, Nixon's domestic political future outweighed any consideration of the cost of life. Nixon knew the war was not winnable; Kissinger knew it. Like something out of *The Seventh Seal*, they coldly decided to use it as a chess piece in a cynical gambit that had nothing to do with the war, but everything to do with winning. Yet, the Vietnam affair was only one element of the Nixon "game plan" in 1968. The second phase involved supporting yet another corrupt military government.

At the same time as Nixon was jockeying for position against Johnson on Vietnam, he was also cutting a deal with the Greek military junta, and illegally accepting huge cash contributions from the generals. This is also covered in detail in Summers' book, and it deserves summarizing here.[32]

Only the year before, in 1967, the generals took over Greece and turned it into a police state overnight. Their reign was dramatized in the Costa-Gavras film *Z*, which boasted a memorable score by Mikis Theodorakis, who had to compose the music in secret to avoid being arrested . . . or worse. One of the strangest episodes of the Nixon campaign was the selection of Maryland Governor Spiro Agnew as his running mate; George Bush had been put forth as a logical vice president, but Nixon stunned the convention by choosing the Greek-American Agnew instead (much, one imagines, to Mr. Bush's great relief years later!). This is now believed to be directly linked with events in Greece and Nixon's friendship with the enigmatic Thomas Pappas, who is mentioned in the Oval Office tapes as "good old Tom Pappas," a guy who was raising hush money for the Watergate burglars. Pappas was a self-made millionaire who started in the grocery business and later wound up with a small empire of his own in oil and chemicals. He funneled large cash contributions into the Nixon war chest, and when Agnew was selected as candidate for vice president it appeared to be due to Pappas' influence.

More than that, however, was the willingness of the Greek military junta to finance the man they saw as their ally in Washington: Richard Nixon. The Democrats, who traditionally made human-rights issues a campaign platform, could be expected to give the generals a hard time. They knew they would get support from a right-wing Republican . . . particularly if that Republican had been paid off. According to Summers, the sum of $549,000 had been transferred to Nixon's campaign in three separate payments between July and October of 1968, an amount equivalent to millions of dollars today. The money originated not with rank-and-file Greek citizens—illegal as that would be in any case—but from the Greek Central Intelligence Service, KYP. The cash would go to Thomas Pappas in Greece, who would then carry the funds himself to the United States.

In other words, the Greek military junta added their very healthy contribution to the Nixon war chest to ensure a victory over Hubert Humphrey. Naturally, this was a gross violation of American law. It turned Nixon into an unregistered lobbyist for a foreign power, and it violated US campaign contribution regulations, which forbid any American politician from receiving any kind of financial contribution from foreign governments or their agents. This did not faze the candidate, however, since he had been receiving contributions from arms dealer Adnan Khashoggi for years. It would seem that in 1968 the Greek military government bought themselves a Vice President of the United States, with an option to buy the President. They had to stand in line, though, because Vietnamese President Thieu had the same idea.

It seemed as if Nixon could not get enough of dictators and mafia bag men. As the years went by, we saw time and again how the Nixon White House supported military governments and coups all over the world, in every hemisphere, from Vietnam to Chile to Greece. The list of secret financial contributors to Nixon's political career was maintained by his longtime secretary, Rose Mary Woods, and was known informally as "Rose Mary's Baby," certainly a characterization more apt than they realized. As Nixon added a second term after his first, the bodies continued to pile up. The line stretched back through the days he spent as vice president under Eisenhower, when he began work to assassinate Fidel Castro and return Cuba to the control of the Lansky mob, and at least as far back as the time he worked with Dulles on the Nazi spy networks that had been "seconded" to the CIA, covering up Soviet penetration of western intelligence services in Europe that dated back to the earliest days of the Russian Revolution.

As information has come to light in recent years, we now know that the Soviets were well aware of anti-Communist agitation among the White Russians, as well as among the various disenfranchised ethnic groups living in the West. They began penetration of these groups shortly after the Revolution, and never abandoned their intelligence networks in the West. By the time that Dulles and his British counterparts began using Ukrainian, Hungarian, and White Russian émigré groups to go up against the Soviet Union, they had been so compromised by Russian intelligence as to be virtually useless. Worse, they acted as agents against the West and did untold damage to the Western intelligence services. Dulles and his men, in their hubris, did not suspect that the White Russians on their team were agents for the KGB and Soviet military intelligence. By the time they did, the damage had been done.

THE COVEN

Although we have come to know E. Howard Hunt, G. Gordon Liddy, Donald Segretti, James McCord, Chuck Colson and the entire mixed media collage of anti-Castro Cubans, CIA officers, FBI agents, White House aides, Mafia bagmen, and Nazis-on-the run as "the Plumbers," or "the President's Men," or even "the finest public servants it has been my privilege to know," perhaps another designation is in order, one that is suggested by the title (and subject matter) of one of Howard Hunt's occult novels: *The Coven.*

Hunt himself lived in a white, wood frame house in suburban Montgomery County, where a sign near his mail box read, "Witches Island," and he wrote several occult novels as well as a number of spy-type thrillers under various pseudonyms. His background with the CIA was extensive, going back nearly to the beginning of the Agency's existence; he began his career with the OSS during the War and was very fond of Allen Dulles, whom he met at that time. His admiration of Richard Nixon also went back to the earliest days of Nixon's career. He met Nixon sometime in 1952 at a restaurant in Washington, D.C. He spoke with him awhile, and gave him a calling card on which he wrote, "My wife and I want to thank you for the magnificent job you are doing for our country."[33] The card named Hunt as an attaché at the US Embassy in Mexico City, where he had been stationed since 1949, taking up for the CIA where the FBI left off after the CIA's creation in 1947; Nixon at that time was running for Senator. Twenty years later, Nixon was President and Hunt—retired from the Agency—was masterminding the break-in at the Watergate Hotel on his behalf.

E. Howard Hunt was the inspiration for the Cigarette Man on Chris Carter's television series, *The X-Files*. According to Carter's mythology, the CGM was responsible for everything from the Bay of Pigs invasion, to the Kennedy assassination, and just about every dirty trick and dirty deed in American history of the past fifty years. He was also a failed novelist, and the bitterness of a frustrated career behind the typewriter led the CGM to a hard-bitten, cynical approach to life. This very nearly parallels Hunt's own career. Hunt—in his "Eduardo" persona—had been involved deeply with the Bay of Pigs operation, as was then-Vice President Nixon. He was suspected of involvement in the Kennedy assassination, and for years photographs of a derelict who had been arrested close to the assassination site was believed to have been a photo of Hunt in disguise.

Hunt later retired from the CIA during Nixon's tenure as president—on April 30, 1970, the most infamous day on the European witches' calendar: Walpurgisnacht in Germany or Beltane in the British Isles, something the occult-oriented Hunt (resident of Witches Island) would have known—and took a job at Robert Mullen & Company, a public relations firm that did extensive work for the Howard Hughes empire, on the very next day. One of his colleagues—Douglas Caddy—was the first lawyer called when the Watergate burglars were arrested. He is depicted in the book (and film) *All The President's Men* as the man who sat in quietly at the burglars' arraignment and refused to answer any of Woodward's questions, saying simply, "I'm not here. I have nothing to say."

Another colleague at Mullen was Arthur Hochberg, a mysterious individual who virtually disappeared after Watergate. Hochberg was a CIA action officer who was stationed variously in Brazil and the Far East, and who was based in Singapore in the early 1970s, setting up and running an overseas office for Mullen. Not much PR work was done at the Singapore Mullen or at another Mullen operation called Interprogress, as Hochberg's job had more to do with debriefing Chinese defectors and running agents against the People's Republic of China. (His Mandarin Chinese was fluent, as was his Brazilian Portuguese.) The author has tried in vain to obtain corporate records of Hochberg's operation in Singapore, visiting government offices there and discovering that the files have been sanitized: no record was kept of corporate officers or anything else, beyond the dates of the opening and closing of the offices. Attempts to learn more were firmly discouraged; this, thirty years after the offices were closed. Thus, after all this time, there is still sensitive information connected to this obscure, Vietnam-era CIA operation in Singapore.

Hochberg later went on to work for a company in Queens, New York that sold transmission systems for trucks and buses, and wound up traveling extensively to Africa on various business deals, principally to Mauritania: not exactly on one's list of prime export markets. When the author met him, as a co-worker in 1980, Hochberg seemed a little wistful about the good old days at the CIA and was disappointed in the action taken by Admiral Turner, who was Director of the CIA for a short time, in firing all the old hands in a post-Watergate house-cleaning maneuver. Experienced intelligence personnel were suddenly without work all over the country; one wonders what they got up to in the years since Watergate.

G. Gordon Liddy is also an obvious member of the Watergate Coven. A lifelong admirer of German culture, who was smitten by hearing Hitler's speeches over a radio when he was a child, he is known to start singing the Horst Wessel song at the drop of a microphone. While known to the media as the Plumbers, Liddy had named his team for stopping leaks and disrupting the Democratic presidential campaign "ODESSA," after the fabled organization of former SS officers:

> It appealed to me because when I organize, I am inclined to think in German terms and the acronym was also used by a World War II German veterans organization belonged to by some friends of mine, *Organisation Der Ehemaligen Schutz Staffel Angehörigen:* ODESSA.[34]

Liddy had inured himself to pain since he was a young man, even going so far as to hold his arm over a flame and gritting his teeth against the intense hurt, giving a whole new meaning to the concept of "burn." He would turn this into a kind of parlor trick in the Watergate era, holding his hand over a flame, and when people asked him what the trick was, he would reply, "The trick is not minding." Few seem to remember that this is a direct reference to the film *Lawrence of Arabia*, in which Peter O'Toole, playing Lawrence, extinguishes lit matches with his fingertips. He is asked, "What's the trick, then?" and he replies, "The trick is in not minding that it hurts." *Lawrence of Arabia* was a favorite film of the author's youth, and I believe I could easily trade quotations from the movie with Liddy, who obviously watched it about as many times as I did.

He also grew up a Roman Catholic, attending schools in New Jersey run by German Benedictines and then by Jesuits, both of whom he admired. It was perhaps logical that Liddy would eventually wind up at the FBI, and in 1958 getting posted to Gary, Indiana: the Chicago suburb and center of the steel industry. The author's father, brother and sister were all born in Gary, Indiana, and the author's father went on to some notoriety in Gary in the immediate postwar period. I cannot help but wonder if Liddy had reviewed my father's files.

Gary was considered to be a target of Soviet espionage in the 1950s, when both Liddy and the author and his family lived in the area. My father had been prominent in something called the Gary School Strike in the fall of 1945, and had been investigated by the FBI as a possible shill for the Communists. This story is referenced in *The Sinatra Files*, edited by Tom Kuntz and Phil Kuntz, which is a summary of FBI files on Frank Sinatra throughout his career. My father's name comes up in this collection because of an incident in the crooner's life, in which he visited Gary in an attempt to calm the racist fever that was threatening to erupt into something even uglier.

High school students in Gary—including those at my father's alma mater, Froebel High—were boycotting classes over a plan to desegregate the schools. I am not proud to say that my father was considered the leader of the boycott and, thus, a segregationist. His parents had come to America from small mining towns in eastern Slovakia, escaping the Austro-Hungarian Empire and coming to the promise of a better life in the United States. My grandfather truly disliked no one except the Poles. (Polish gangs would raid Slovak towns along the border, stealing and raping, with numbing regularity.) His youngest son, however, found himself involved in a high school debate over the question of segregation, and—winning the debate—became an overnight celebrity and an ad hoc segregationist. I never knew if my father had truly been a segregationist at the age of seventeen, or if he had just found it irresistible to be the center of attention. Whatever the case, he remained politically conservative and right-wing for the rest of his life.

The Gary School Strike became national news. Other schools were following Froebel's lead, and it threatened to become a test case for desegregation legislation. Frank Sinatra—at that time enormously popular with young people—decided he would do what he could to defuse the situation, although no one had actually asked him to do so. He arrived in Gary on November 1,1945 (the Catholic "Holy Day of Obligation": All Saint's Day) and addressed a meeting that night in the school auditorium. In his address, he claimed that my father, Leonard Levenda, had refused to meet with him, but my father said otherwise, saying that he met briefly with Sinatra before the singer's address, when he informed Sinatra that two men the latter had singled out as instigators of the strike—men who had attempted to form an all-white PTA and who were active in segregationist circles—had nothing to do with the strike, which was a spontaneous action of the students themselves. One of the men singled out for Sinatra's attack was Julius Danch, characterized by a Gary police captain as a staunch anti-Communist.

These were Eastern Europeans, for the most part. Danch was the president of the Hungarian Political Club in Gary. (And the reader will remember that Hitler had made Slovakia an independent country during the war, and that Catholic Monsignor Tiso had been put in charge.) Put anti-Communism and racism together in a single package and it is easy to believe that Nazi sympathies were close at hand. The FBI, however, believed that Sinatra's appearance had been arranged by Communist sources, at least in part; indeed, after his appearance at Froebel High School, Sinatra became an idol to the Left and was forever afterwards identified with liberal forces in American politics. My grandparents, however, once proudly showed me a clipping of the front page of a local Gary newspaper from that period which reported that my father had thrown Sinatra out of his house for making disparaging comments about their ethnicity.

It was my father's fifteen minutes of fame. From there, he went on to New York City to attend the American Academy of Dramatic Arts with classmates Jack Palance and Grace Kelly. He once acted on the stage with Palance, in *A Silver Tassie* and also performed in *Rope* (the stage play, not the film). But his acting days were over by 1950 when I was born and the young family moved back to Gary before eventually winding up in Chicago. But that is another tale.

Liddy, in 1958, would have been familiar with the Gary School Strike, and with the FBI's concern that Gary was a target of Soviet espionage. The FBI maintained an S.I., or Security Index: a list of those individuals believed to be a threat in the event of war with Russia. Did the Bureau believe my father was a threat, or an ally?

Liddy went on to greater glory. It is well known that he raided Timothy Leary's estate at Millbrook in New York, when Liddy was an assistant District Attorney. Liddy and Leary years later put together a kind of comedy routine, in which Liddy debated Leary on drugs, altered consciousness, alternative politics, and the like. It was popular for a short time on the college circuit. Liddy is far better known, however, for the role he played in the Watergate affair.

Another member of the Coven would have been E. Howard Hunt's boss at Mullen, Robert Bennett. A Mormon, Bennett had lucrative contracts with the Howard Hughes empire. The Mullen Company itself had been a front for the CIA since its inception in 1959, and Bennett—who later bought the company—was close friends with such Watergate luminaries as Chuck Colson. In fact, a close look at Robert Mullen & Company reveals a rich lode of CIA (and Mormon) involvement in the Watergate affair, and it has become apparent to many that Bennett's role was to divert attention away from the CIA and over to the White House. The Mullen operation also had very close ties to the J. Walter Thompson advertising agency, which was itself a source of many Watergate personalities, as we will see.

Bennett personally handled campaign contributions for Nixon and set up dozens of phony committees to collect funds for the President. He had also worked on Nixon's election campaign in 1968. In fact, much of the plotting of the Watergate break-in took place at Mullen's offices, which were across the street from Nixon's CRP: The Committee to Re-Elect the President, more commonly known as "CREEP." E. Howard Hunt would meet Gordon Liddy there, as well as James McCord and other conspirators. Although Hunt's ostensible role at Mullen was as a writer—he held the title of vice president at Mullen—he seems to have spent more time on White House and CIA business than anything else, which is appropriate when you review Mullen's long history as a CIA front both at home and abroad. When the Watergate story broke, Bennett spent a lot of time criss-crossing the United States, giving interviews to the press that effectively pointed them in the direction of the White House and away from the CIA. We may believe he did the same with Woodward, as he was undoubtedly a source for many of Woodward's stories—that they were acquainted and met frequently is not denied by either man.

Howard Hughes was surrounded by Mormons as bodyguards and servants. He apparently trusted the Mormons because they did not drink or smoke; their clean-cut appearance was appealing to the decrepit billionaire who had a horror of germs and contagion, and whose personal appearance was—if we are to believe press reports after his death—quite horrifying itself. The lank, unkempt hair and the long, yellowing, fingernails; the gaunt physique and ghostly pallor . . . . It seemed unbelievable that a man with so much wealth and so much power could have lived for years in total isolation from the outside world, except for his Mormon bodyguard. That is, until the Clifford Irving affair, when either Howard Hughes or someone pretending to be Howard Hughes made an historic phone call to a group of reporters telling them that the Irving book—*The Autobiography of Howard Hughes*—was a hoax and making other accusations that rattled the Hughes empire.

Strangely, the author himself was peripherally involved in the Irving/Hughes affair. In the summer of 1970, I joined a firm in Manhattan's garment district that supplied budget-conscious housewives shopping at Woolworth's, Kresge's, and Alexander's with knock-offs of designer lingerie. A co-worker—a tall, slender former model with an offbeat sense of humor—and I became fast friends. She was living with a singer/songwriter on the Upper West Side, a pretty common combination in New York City at any time, but especially in those days. As we became better acquainted, and I spent some evenings at their apartment listening to music and discussing everything under the sun—her companion was a Vietnam veteran with post-traumatic stress disorder to the extent that he would awaken in the middle of the night and throw his girlfriend to the floor, shouting "Incoming!"—she eventually came to confide in me concerning her past.

She had worked for the J. Walter Thompson agency in some capacity as a fashion model. (That same agency gave us Dwight Chapin, Ken Cole, Ron Ziegler, Larry Higby and Bob Haldeman: all of Watergate notoriety.) She only got out of the business due to their increasing demands for her to lose even more weight and the consequent beginning of a dependence on diet medication. They were also rather secretive, keeping her isolated in hotel rooms in New York and plying her with drugs to keep her weight down to Twiggy levels. She finally had enough and managed to leave; but not before attending a strange meeting with a client of J. Walter Thompson.

This meeting took place—if memory serves—at the offices of the agency, and several mysterious individuals were in attendance. One she knew only as "the Cowboy," and he indeed did wear a Stetson and dressed in Western attire; another was an aloof, quiet sort that was never identified by name, but who had an intelligence background; still another was a man who would stay friendly with her long after she left the agency, a man known to me only by the name Ackerman. The model was there evidently as some kind of window dressing, and she was kept busy refilling glasses and looking attractive. Not much of significance was discussed at the meeting, which was conducted with a lot of code words and other jargon, but the importance of the event was summarized for her later by Ackerman.

As she related it to me, Howard Hughes had been kidnapped.

> My mind raced through different scenarios of what might have taken place. The theory that made the most sense to me was that Gay and Davis had taken the Man against his will.
>
> —Robert Maheu[35]

The gist of the story was that CIA had kidnapped Hughes. This was due to the fact that Hughes was enormously wealthy, enormously powerful, but a psychological basket case. He was believed to be a national security risk; he was involved heavily in politics and had contributed huge sums to both Democrats and Republicans, mostly to ensure that his personal projects would be approved with a minimum of fuss and red tape; but he saw no one, took no meetings, and had not been seen in public—or even by his own second-in-command, former FBI agent and Castro assassination co-conspirator Robert Maheu—at all. With the exposure of the Glomar Explorer affair and the revelation of a "special relationship" between the CIA and the Hughes empire, the intelligence agency had decided that Howard Hughes was a threat, a loose cannon that had to be neutralized in the interests of national security.

According to the story, Hughes had been kidnapped and was being held offshore, in the Bahamas. The Mormons were essential to this operation, as Hughes trusted them, and made the "snatch" even easier. Watergate had not taken place yet (that was two years in the future) and the main players were largely unknown to the public. The Clifford Irving episode was also unknown, it having been put into action no earlier than January 1971, and had not been announced until December 7, 1971 in a press release by publisher McGraw-Hill. Having the Mormons involved, however, became more significant to me as the Watergate affair unfolded and we learned of the existence of the Robert Mullen agency, for whom both CIA agents E. Howard Hunt and Arthur Hochberg worked and which had contracts with the Hughes organization . . . *specifically regarding damage control over the Clifford Irving affair.* Hunt's boss at Robert Mullen was Robert Bennett, a Mormon with important connections back in Salt Lake City, who became a United States Senator, as was his father before him.

No one knew any of this back in 1970 or 1971, unless they were involved. I begged the model to go public with her information, or to let me report the story somehow. She adamantly refused, fearing for her life. When she realized that my reaction was to tell the story to the press, she suddenly would not discuss the story with me any further. Although we remained friends, the subject of Hughes and Ackerman was off limits.

Then, the Clifford Irving affair broke in late 1971 and early 1972. The Watergate break-in was in June 1972. I have often wondered if the Nixon administration—and especially E. Howard Hunt, one of the Watergate burglars—was interested in knowing how much the Democrats knew about the Hughes kidnapping, if in fact such did take place. We have Hunt working for both the CIA and the Mormon Robert Bennett; we have Mormon bodyguards around Hughes in the last years of his life; we have the Clifford Irving affair, which may have been intended to publicize the fact that Howard Hughes was well, at large, and *compos mentis* at a time when he was very probably none of those things, or perhaps not even alive. In fact, when Clifford Irving and his collaborator, Richard Susskind began work on a tell-all book about the hoaxed autobiography of Howard Hughes, the Mullen firm was on top of it. They had been approached for a quote on what it would cost to put Irving and Susskind under surveillance; Watergate burglar James McCord provided the quotation, which was judged to be too high. Instead Intertel, the private intelligence agency and security firm, was hired to spy on Irving and Susskind and keep them on around-the-clock surveillance to determine what information they were planning to reveal in their book. This seems unusual, to say the least. The Irving book had already been exposed as a hoax, and Irving a fraud. What value was there to the Hughes organization in maintaining a very expensive surveillance on Irving after the fact? What could they possibly reveal in their own story of the hoax that could be damaging to Hughes?

During the series of revelations about Irving and Hughes, several other interesting names came up. One was Ackerman. In this case, it was Marty Ackerman, Clifford Irving's lawyer (in civil, not criminal, matters), and I wondered if this was the Ackerman mentioned by my model friend. Ackerman acted as a kind of literary agent for Irving, and I could not help theorizing that Ackerman would have been perfectly placed to suggest the hoax autobiography to Irving at the request of other, interested parties, if Ackerman was working for one or another contingent in the Maheu-Hughes conflagration. Another name that would come up was that of Jim Phelan.

Phelan's name was familiar to anyone who had followed the Jim Garrison trial in New Orleans. Phelan had an agenda where Garrison was concerned, and was part of the effort by the media to discredit him entirely. He then turned his sights on Clifford Irving and McGraw-Hill in an aggressive maneuver to prove the Irving book a hoax. Although Phelan is a journalist and reporter—a "freelance investigative reporter" is how he is usually described—he always seems to have a secret agenda of his own. The Irving case was no exception, since he had already collaborated on a book about Hughes by longtime Hughes associate Noah Dietrich. When the Irving book was announced, Phelan smelled a rat and took it upon himself to dig a little deeper. In so doing, he discovered that the Irving book was based largely on his own, unpublished manuscript of the Noah Dietrich memoirs.

It was the final nail in the coffin, as Phelan rushed to McGraw-Hill and proved the truth of his allegations.

Recently declassified material on Phelan raises some other, more distressing, questions however. It is now known that Phelan was an FBI informant of long standing, and that during the Garrison investigation into the Kennedy assassination, Phelan was taking files from the District Attorney's office and giving them to the Bureau.[36] It has been further revealed that Phelan was a friend of Bob Maheu, which certainly puts a different wrinkle on the Hughes affair, especially as there is no mention of Jim Phelan in Maheu's own autobiography.

At the end of one investigation of the Clifford Irving affair—*Hoax*, by Stephen Fay, Lewis Chester and Magnus Linklater—these journalists reveal an interesting fact which has never been explained. They say that at a dinner in November 1970 in New York, Edith Irving (Clifford's wife at the time) revealed to her guests that her husband was considering a proposition "that could be worth upward of $500,000. It would, she said, be a dangerous one to undertake, since it concerned people 'who would stop at nothing to achieve their own ends—even murder.'"[37] The authors go on to state that the phrase she used about men who would stop at nothing was identical to the way in which she would later "describe the Hughes organization." Of course, Marty Ackerman's offices were in New York City; the Irvings had been living in Ibiza, Spain for years. According to Irving's own account, published in his *The Hoax*, he came up with the idea to write a fraudulent Hughes autobiography in Spain in December of 1970, one month and three thousand miles away from New York City, an idea prompted by an article in *Newsweek*. There is no mention of going to New York the previous month.

But it was November of 1970 when the model was telling me about the purported Hughes kidnapping by the CIA.

Was the Irving/Susskind book—the "tell all" story of the Howard Hughes hoaxed autobiography—suspected of revealing this piece of information, information that would have led back either to the CIA or to the Hughes organization itself . . . or both? In any case, it didn't. When Irving's book finally hit the stands, it contained little that was not already known.

Hughes disappeared from his Las Vegas Desert Inn eagle's nest in November 1970, on Thanksgiving weekend. This, in spite of the fact that he was quite ill, suffering from anemia complicated by pneumonia, and "on the verge of heart failure."[38] It became obvious in later years that Hughes had been forced to sign the proxy which eventually resulted in the firing of Robert Maheu, and did so while under the influence of painkillers and other drugs. In fact, Hughes' doctors forced him to approve all sorts of deals by threatening to withhold the codeine on which he had become increasingly dependent. This included the hiring of the Mormon bodyguard, among other things. When Maheu became a problem, his handlers then forced Hughes to leave the country so that Maheu could not personally confront him, and so that Hughes would not have to appear in court to defend his actions. Thus Hughes had, in effect, been kidnapped indeed.

That same month, the Irvings were approached by a sinister cabal that offered them "upwards of $500,000" for an important and dangerous project. The hoaxed Howard Hughes autobiography was in the works the following month. The Mormon Robert Bennett then supposedly took charge of anti-Irving strategy in the months that followed, which eventually resulted in the famous phone call on January 7, 1972 from Hughes in the Bahamas to a group of reporters in California, in which he "proved" he was alive and well, and that Maheu was evil and had been deliberately fired by Hughes. One feels that Irving knew all along what he was getting himself into, and that the entire scenario had played out just as it was supposed to have done. To complicate matters even further, it appears as if President Nixon ordered the IRS to attack Robert Maheu with a full audit going back three years (as mentioned in Maheu's autobiography). If so, it would appear that Maheu was a threat to more than just the Hughes "palace guard." Maheu certainly knew where the bodies were buried in the Hughes/Nixon relationship, and would later testify to the Watergate Committee that he had personally handled the illegal campaign contributions between Hughes and Nixon's sidekick, Bebe Rebozo.

The Hughes affair is important to an understanding of the sinister forces surrounding American politics in the late twentieth century. Howard Hughes inherited a great deal of money from his father, who had invented a special type of drill bit that was heavily used by the oil industry and thereby made his fortune. Hughes himself was something of a playboy in his earlier years. He was a pilot, and was always trying to improve the airplane, acting as his own test pilot and nearly getting himself killed in the process. He also dabbled in Hollywood, and squired a number of famous actresses, such as Ava Gardner, Ginger Rogers and Ida Lupino, and even marrying Jean Peters. He discovered the curvaceous Jane Russell, and had a hand in creating a special brassiere to support and display her most obvious qualities.

Money, the military, oil, and Hollywood.

The ceremonial magician, self-proclaimed AntiChrist and invoker of Babalon, Jack Parsons, once worked for the Hughes empire; but then so did Wilford Brimley, the plump and grizzly character actor who would later appear in such films as *Heaven's Gate*, *Cocoon*, *Death Valley*, and *The China Syndrome* (as well as a series of commercials for Quaker Oatmeal). I guess it was the "right thing to do." After all, the Hughes organization was a dominant player in California—both in the film industry and in the military-aviation industry—as well as in Texas in the oil industry, and in Nevada casinos, Hughes buying up hotel after hotel in a bid to consolidate his power there and run the entire state. He was active in trying to halt atomic testing (at least in Nevada) and threw money around in an attempt to buy off whatever politician he had to in order to get the job done. He also enlisted the services of Intertel, a private security and intelligence-gathering operation so well-documented in Jim Hougan's *Spooks.* It was Intertel which would eventually go after Clifford Irving, and eventually after Bob Maheu when he was "fired" by Hughes . . . or perhaps fired by Chester Davis and Bill Gay, the men who created a Berlin Wall of Mormons and medicine around the eremitical billionaire.

Another, perhaps honorary, member of the Coven would have been the psychic Jeane Dixon.

A GIFT OF PROPHECY

Jeane Dixon was familiar to many in the 1960s as a psychic who was said to have predicted the assassination of President Kennedy. The American-born daughter of German immigrants, she also made some startling predictions about a world war that was supposed to take place in the final decades of the twentieth century, as well as the birth of a Savior somewhere in the Middle East in the early 1960s. Most of this was included in the book about her, *A Gift of Prophecy*: a blue and white bound paperback that was ubiquitous in bookstores and magazine racks throughout the United States for years. What most people did *not* know, however, and which would have horrified them if they did know, was that Jeane Dixon was actively working on behalf of the FBI, tailoring her predictions to emphasize the danger of the Soviet Union!

It is a phenomenon which seems particular to the right wing, this dependence on soothsayers, astrologers, entrail-readers and the like. The administration of Republican President Reagan would surprise everyone with revelations that his wife, Nancy, consulted an astrologer regularly and arranged the President's schedule according to transiting planetary positions. In fact, Jeane Dixon also provided consultation to the Reagan White House. This was a president who believed firmly in an apocalyptic interpretation of Christianity and the "end times," and who viewed foreign relations and foreign policy through a scrim of the Book of Revelations, sharing this at least in common with Charles Manson. Yet, in Nixon's case, the soothsayer was also as much of a political front as Radio Free Europe.

Nixon believed in the prophecies of Jeane Dixon, according to John Ehrlichman. Nixon's psychotherapist, Dr. Arnold Hutschneker, was also a believer.[39] According to Ehrlichman, Nixon was getting premonitions from both Billy Graham and Jeane Dixon that his life was in danger in late 1972. Recently declassified FBI files—released after the psychic's death in 1997—show a comfortable relationship between Ms. Dixon and the FBI, to the extent that the Bureau supplied her with information on groups they considered subversive so that she had ammunition for her speeches around the country. She volunteered to help the FBI erode popular support for the Left, by making speeches with material that could not be traced to the Bureau.

In 1969, she accused the Soviet leadership of instigating and controlling race riots and student revolt in the United States; in 1971 she went so far as to say that there was a high-level spy in the US government who was reporting back to the Soviets. Her fear of the Left in general and of the Soviet Union in particular was consistent, and was exploited by the FBI for its own purposes. One angry correspondent wrote to Hoover demanding an investigation of the psychic, accusing her of trying to create an environment in which Democratic Party leaders would be assassinated, in particular Teddy Kennedy, about whom Dixon had always had dire things to predict. The accusation was that Dixon was consciously using her prestige as a diviner to suggest that Ted Kennedy ought to be killed. Her staunch support of Republican politicians, the FBI, and anti-Communism lends some credence to this point of view.

Nixon was not totally unaware of occult forces in any case. His own law firm, Nixon, Mudge, Rose, Guthrie and Alexander, based in New York City, had handled a volatile labor dispute in Puerto Rico in the 1960s. This dispute involved the practice of witchcraft—probably *santeria*, the Hispanic version of Haitian *voudon*—and the law firm wrote a brief discussing the practice of Puerto Rican occultism in some depth. The brief was, appropriately enough, thirteen pages long.

Finally, the presidency of Richard Nixon came to an ignominious end. The existence of an Oval Office taping system was revealed, and Nixon stonewalled as long as possible to avoid giving sensitive conversations over to the investigating committees. In one case, one particularly important tape recording was found to have eighteen-and-a-half minutes missing, that section of the tape either erased or recorded over. The buzzing sound could not be identified. According to Al Haig, it seemed as if the tape had been altered by some "sinister force." And thus the germ of an idea for this book was born.

As members of his staff all went off to prison on various counts of burglary, conspiracy, perjury, etc., many eventually becoming born-again Christians in the process, Nixon himself resigned from office on August 9, 1974. The previous year, he had warned the Joint Chiefs of Staff of the evil machinations of the "Eastern Establishment," and, according to Admiral Zumwalt, "It was clear that he perceived himself as a fighter for all that was right in the United States, involved in mortal battle with the forces of evil."[40]

But it was to no avail. As Nixon left the White House with his family for the last time that day—standing in the entrance to Air Force One raising his arms above his head in his familiar gesture and giving what the Golden Dawn would have understood as the sign of Typhon, the Destroyer—a crowd outside the fence was singing "Ding Dong, the Witch is Dead."

Evangelist Billy Graham, with whom Richard Nixon had prayed and agonized so often throughout the Presidency, once said, "I think there was definitely demon power involved. He took all those sleeping pills, and through history, drugs and demons have gone together."[41] According to Graham, the drugs opened a door in Nixon's soul and the demons flew in. This author believes that Nixon's pact with the demons had been signed much earlier, when he agreed to cover for Dulles, for the Nazis, and for the Mafia in return for the most powerful position in the most powerful country in the world.

ENDNOTES

1 Allen Upward, *The Divine Mystery*, Ross-Erikson, Santa Barbara, 1976, ISBN 0-915520-01-X, p.xxxii
2 Letter from Parsons to Marjorie Cameron, dated 27 January 1950
3 Victor Turner, *Revelation and Divination in Ndembu Ritual*, Cornell University Press, Ithaca, 1975, 0-8014-9151-7, p. 32
4 Mark Aarons & John Loftus, Unholy Trinity: the Vatican, the Nazis, and Soviet Intelligence, St Martin's Press, NY, 1991, ISBN 0-312-09407-8, p. 270
5 Anthony Summers, *The Arrogance of Power: The Secret World of Richard Nixon*, Penguin Books, NY, 2000, ISBN 0-14-0267078-1, p.16
6 Bruce Mazlish, *The Leader, the Led, and the Psyche*, Wesleyan University Press, Hanover, 1990, ISBN 0-8195-5220-8, p. 198ff
7 Summers, op. cit., p. 63
8 Ibid., p. 63
9 Ibid., p. 63
10 Seth Kantor, *Who Was Jack Ruby?*, Everest House, NY, 1978, p. 54–55
11 Charles Higham, *American Swastika*, Doubleday, NY, 1985, ISBN 0-385-17874-3, p. 85
12 Summers, op. cit., p.46
13 Carl Goldberg, *Speaking with the Devil: Exploring Senseless Acts of Evil*, Penguin, NY, 1997, ISBN 0-14-023739-9, p. 214
14 Higham, op. cit., p. 250
15 Ronald Brownstein, *The Power and the Glitter: The Hollywood-Washington Connection*, Pantheon, NY, 1990, ISBN 0-394-56938-5, p. 57
16 Simpson, op. cit., p. 179
17 Summers, op. cit., p. 12
18 Walter Laqueur, *Black Hundred: The Rise of the Extreme Right in Russia*, HarperCollins, NY, 1993, ISBN 0-06-018336-5, p. 15
19 Aarons & Loftus, op. cit., p. 277–278
20 Higham, op. cit., p. 190
21 Ibid., p. 191
22 Aarons & Loftus, op. cit., p. 278
23 Summers, op. cit., p. 62–66
24 John Marks, *The Search for the Manchurian Candidate*, Times Books, NY, 1979, ISBN 0-8129-0773-6, p. 21
25 Howard Blum, *Wanted! The Search for Nazis in America*, Quadrangle, NY, 1977, ISBN 0-8129-0607-1, p. 91–102
26 Ibid., 109–111
27 Summers, op. cit., p. 130–135
28 Blum, op. cit., p. 117–119
29 Ibid., p. 121
30 Summers, op. cit., p. 274
31 Thomas Powers, *The Man Who Kept the Secrets: Richard Helms and the CIA*, Knopf, NY, 1979, ISBN 0-394-50777-0, p. 197–200; Summers, op. cit., p. 297–308
32 Summers, op.cit., p. 284–287
33 Ibid., p. 142
34 G. Gordon Liddy, *Will*, Dell, NY, 1980, ISBN 0-440-09666-9, p. 203
35 Robert Maheu & Richard Hack,, *Next to Hughes*, HarperCollins, NY, 1992, ISBN 0-06-016505-7, p.233
36 See for instance FBI Airtel dated 4-12-67 from Hoover, entitled ASSASSINATION OF PRESIDENT JOHN FITZGERALD KENNEDY NOVEMBER 22, 1963 DALLAS, TEXAS concerning information from Garrison's office provided by Phelan to the Bureau to be "closely-held" and "not disseminated."
37 Stephen Fay, Lewis Chester, Magnus Linklater, Hoax: The Inside Story of the Howard Hughes-Clifford Irving Affair, Viking, NY, 1972, ISBN 670-37430-X, p. 309
38 Maheu, op. cit., p. 265
39 Summers., op. cit., p. 89
40 Ibid., p. 463
41 Ibid., p. 318

BOOK TWO: A WARM GUN

CHAPTER ELEVEN

NIGHT OF THE LONG KNIVES

In the colonial period, when religious creeds, institutions, and communities exerted a major impact on life and work, there was bound to be some spillover into politics. Because the contribution of religion to American political culture covers such important beliefs as obedience, the design of government, and the national mission, the religious roots of American political culture merit close investigation.

—Kenneth D. Wald, *Religion and Politics in the United States*[1]

When I begin I try to follow the money, as they say in All The President's Men, up the evil ladder, past the businessmen, past the Mafia, past the leaders in the state, I ask, "Who is doing the stuff, who is pulling the cords?" It looks an awful lot like God. It's the big fascist in the sky. But all of this religion, government, and civilization bending towards God is dangerous.

—Ken Kesey[2]

No, men were afraid of murder, but not from a terror of justice so much as the knowledge that a killer attracted the attention of the gods; then your mind was not your own, your anxiety ceased to be neurotic, your dread was real.

—Norman Mailer[3]

Sharon Tate was eight months pregnant when she was stabbed to death by members of the Manson Family on August 9, 1969 at her home at 10050 Cielo Drive in Los Angeles. *Cielo* is Spanish for "heaven" or "sky." It is the domain of the Egyptian goddess Nuit, to whom one of the three sections of Aleister Crowley's *Book of the Law* is dedicated. Nuit is a form of Babalon, the Scarlet Woman of the Apocalypse, the mystical bride of the Great Beast, whom Jack Parsons had invoked in the Mojave Desert. It is she who gives birth to the Magickal Child, the promise of the New Age.

In Sharon Tate's case, the child—her perfectly-formed unborn son—was killed along with his mother.

The ancient Egyptian analogue may appear gratuitous, but there are grounds for looking that deeply at the matter. In Book One, we discussed the seances of Andrija Pujarich, Arthur Young, Ruth Paine Young, etc. which resulted in contact with something called "The Nine." (These were the same individuals that were linked to the Kennedy assassination, and specifically to accused assassin Lee Harvey Oswald, as well as to American military and intelligence circles and, via Arthur Young and Michael Paine, to Operation Paperclip.) According to ancient Egyptian religion, there was such a Council of Nine—known as the Ennead of Heliopolis, called by Egyptologist R. T. Rundle Clark the "Divine Company"—which was made up of the major deities of that time, including Atum, Geb, Tefnut, Nut (or Nuit), Shu, Osiris, Isis, Nephthys, and Set (or Seth). Probably their most famous function was to act as intermediaries between the battling Horus and Set. Horus, the son of the slain god Osiris, was out to avenge his father's death; Set, as the murderer and as the embodiment of "blind force and unregulated violence,"[4] was Horus' target.

The war between the two—as recounted in the *Contendings of Horus and Set*—goes on so long and is so wasteful that the Council decides it must be stopped. They decide in favor of Horus; the powers of Set are thus curtailed; and the kingdom of Egypt is at peace at last. Egypt was divided into two kingdoms in ancient times, Upper Egypt (in the south) and Lower Egypt (in the north). Upper Egypt was said to be the realm of Set, and Lower Egypt the realm of Horus. The Pharaoh was king of both Upper and Lower Egypt, and wore two crowns to symbolize this fact, thus acting as representative of both Horus and Set. Of both Order and Chaos. Of both Peace and mindless Bloodshed.

This duality was also an important—if not central—feature of the Process Church of the Final Judgment, which preached the unity of both Jehovah and Lucifer, of both good and evil, with Satan thrown in for good measure a little later in the cult's development. This was also, of course, the main "rap" of Charles Manson: that he was both Jesus and the Devil, and that good was evil, and evil, good. The possibility that the Process may have strayed a bit too enthusiastically over to the Dark Side is evidenced by the Fear and Death themes of their publications, as well perhaps by their adoption of a stylized swastika and the German shepherd as cultic symbols. A dog-like creature was the emblem of Set, and dogs have been associated with the dark side of human consciousness for thousands of years. The dog is considered an unclean animal in Islam, for instance, for it is coprophagic: it eats the dead. The association of dog sacrifice—specifically of German shepherds—with satanic cults in the United States cannot be ignored, with numerous cases from coast to coast,especially in relation to the presumed Son of Sam cult (which incorporated the Manson Family). In addition, Jeffrey Dahmer, one of the twentieth century's most horrific serial killers, began his career by sacrificing dogs and putting their skulls on stakes around a ceremonial area behind his home in Ohio.

According to Rundle Clark, writing in 1959, "Seth is the essential enemy. He is the personification of blind force and unregulated violence . . . . Wherever there is a manifestation of blind force, Seth is in his element . . . . He is the desert wind, dryness and death."[5] There is perhaps no better description of the spirit of the Manson Family, born as it was in the Mojave Desert and reaching its apotheosis in "blind force and unregulated violence." Manson was perceived as the "essential enemy," and he reinforced this concept by carving a swastika into his forehead and by preaching race war and Armageddon.

In January 1969, shortly after the discovery of Marina Habe's body in a gulley off Mulholland Drive, several events occurred which are relevant to our study.

CIA Operation OFTEN was initialized by Dr. Sidney Gottlieb, based partly on documents which came into his possession after CIA agent William Buckley (who would later be tortured and murdered by Arab terrorists) tossed the premises of the late Dr. Ewen Cameron, he of the "sleep room" and "psychic driving" experiments in Canada. Initially, Operation OFTEN was a joint CIA/Army Chemical Corps drug project, based out of Edgewood Arsenal in Maryland and using inmates of the Holmesburg State Prison in Philadelphia as test subjects. It came under the aegis of the CIA's Office of Research and Development (ORD), which was concerned with parapsychology and the application of supernatural powers for military purposes.[6] Later, OFTEN would become a kind of grab bag of CIA investigations into the paranormal, and would include everything from séances and witchcraft to remote viewing and exotic drugs. Agents of Operation OFTEN would consult with such occult luminaries as Sybil Leek, the famous English witch who was interviewed constantly in the late 1960s on radio and television talk shows, and who had published a few books on the occult, astrology and associated themes. Although the CIA had been investigating ESP and the paranormal, and infiltrating occult groups, since 1952,[7] when Andrija Puharich began contact with The Nine, someone at the CIA evidently felt that the occult underground in 1969 might have access to special techniques for the manipulation of consciousness and memory, and they took to their study with renewed vigor. In some cases, university students who had been part of special controlled experiments in occultism later became occultists themselves; just as an earlier crop of drug experimenters became passionate advocates of LSD, mescaline and psylocibin. The CIA had opened the door, and all sorts of things were flying in and out.

When the powers that be had allowed the Nazi spy and science networks into the United States, it was with the understanding that *they* would control them, and not vice versa. As it happened, American hubris probably led to Soviet penetration of American intelligence systems, as Nazi/Soviet double agents found they had unfettered access to US government channels. In addition, by bringing over so many Nazis—many of whom were war criminals—they had unknowingly reinstated a Nazi underground in the United States, South America and Australia, not to mention the Middle East. The same was now happening with the CIA investigation of the paranormal and the occult: it was a two-edged sword, and the occultists were starting to develop under CIA tutelage and create their own networks. We will see evidence of this—especially with regard to the Stanford Research Institute, remote viewing, Uri Geller, and Andrija Puharich of The Nine—a little later on.

Also in January 1969, the Condon Report on UFOs was released, and immediately attacked as biased and basically worthless. The Condon Report had been contracted to the University of Colorado by the Air Force; its project leader, Dr. Richard Condon, proclaimed himself an agnostic on the issue of UFOs, but later documentation by Condon committee members including the controversial Low memorandum—would prove otherwise, showing Condon to have been antagonistic towards the whole idea of UFOs and to have used the project as a forum to discredit the theories about space aliens, secret government aircraft, etc. According to a CIA article on the subject, published in the agency's *Studies in Intelligence*, the Condon report had been contracted as a means of showing the public that the Air Force had nothing to hide concerning UFOs; it was not an attempt to prove or disprove the existence of flying saucers, etc. Regardless of the ultimate purpose of the Report, it was embraced by those who were already skeptics and denounced by those who believed in the existence of flying saucers.

A few months earlier, Jim Garrison had subpoenaed Fred Crisman to testify before the grand jury he had convened in New Orleans in the matter of the President Kennedy assassination. Crisman, as was related in Book One, had been present at the birth of the twentieth century's UFO phenomenon, along with Kenneth Arnold and a number of FBI agents, including another assassination suspect, Guy Banister. Crisman was interesting to Garrison for a number of reasons, not the least of which was that Clay Shaw is said to have phoned Crisman immediately upon learning he had been arrested. Garrison's other interest in Crisman stemed from the latter's knowledge of right-wing militia movements; the New Orleans District Attorney was evidently wondering what certain individuals in these movements had been doing in and out of New Orleans around the time of the assassination.

By the time the Clay Shaw trial was over, however, it was all moot. He had been declared "not guilty" on March 1, 1969. That same month, Nixon ordered the bombing of Cambodia, which began in earnest on March 18. The film *Goodbye, Columbus* was released, and Roman Polanski, Sharon Tate, and Jane Fonda attended the Directors Guild screening.

Shortly thereafter, Bruce Davis returned to California from London, where he had been staying for some months with the local Scientologists and, as some (including LAPD homicide detectives) insist, meeting with the Process Church of the Final Judgment.

Bruce Davis had been sent to London by Charles Manson in November 1968, shortly after the murders of Clida Delaney and Nancy Warren (the latter, like Sharon Tate, eight months pregnant) near Ukiah, California. They had been beaten, and then strangled to death "with thirty-six leather thongs,"[8] on the evening of October 13. Nancy Warren was married to a Highway Patrol officer, Clida Delaney was her grandmother. The Manson group was quickly suspected of having committed these murders when they were arrested the following year and more information about their criminal history came to light. Several members of the Manson clan were known to have been in the area on the day of the murders, and Manson moved his base of operations from the Spahn Ranch (near Chatsworth, just outside of Los Angeles proper) to the Barker Ranch (in Death Valley, on the other side of the Mojave Desert, many more miles away from Ukiah) about two days after they occurred.

Davis returned from London on April 25, 1969, and then flew to London again in November that same year, after the murder of a pair of Scientologists in California in which he was later considered a suspect, and in time for the murder of Manson Family associate Joel Pugh in London. (Joel Pugh was the husband of Sandy Good, who later teamed with Lynette "Squeaky" Fromme to create the Manson cult ATWA.) According to British Immigration officials, Davis had given as his address in the UK the address of Scientology headquarters.[9]

Since Davis was regarded by California investigators as "Manson's second-in-command," this constant traveling back and forth between California and London—specifically to either Scientology or Process headquarters, or both—is evidence of a larger plot. Davis was later convicted for his role in the murders of Gary Hinman and Donny Shea, the two "bookend' murders that took place before (Hinman) and after (Shea) the seven Tate/LaBianca killings, during the period July 26–August 26, 1969. He reappeared in February 1970 at the Spahn Ranch and then disappeared again when he was indicted for the Gary Hinman murder, only to reappear in Los Angeles in December 1970, when he turned himself in to authorities. He has since become a born-again Christian (like so many of the former Manson family members, as well as "Son of Sam" killer David Berkowitz) and a minister, although still in prison.

The Gary Hinman murder was as savage as the Tate and LaBianca killings. Hinman was a jazz musician with a master's degree in sociology who was friendly to the Manson clan, but when Manson needed money, he sent some of his followers to visit Hinman and extort cash from him. Hinman was making mescaline in his house, and Manson claimed that one batch of the drug was bad. The story has it that the bikers to whom Manson sold the hallucinogen had become ill and blamed Manson's mescaline, and Manson in turn blamed Hinman. Hinman was due to fly to Japan in two weeks on a religious pilgrimage (he was a follower of the Nichiren Shoshu sect of Japanese Buddhism); it seemed he also had come into some kind of an inheritance, or at least that is what the Family had heard.

Hinman did not have any cash in hand beyond about twenty dollars, but under threats of violence—including being pistol-whipped by Bobby Beausoleil—he signed over two of his cars. That still did not satisfy the Mansonites. Phone calls back and forth to Manson, giving updates on the ongoing cash extortion, resulted in Hinman's death at the hands of Bobby Beausoleil, Mary Brunner, and Susan Atkins, with Davis and Manson as co-conspirators. He was stabbed repeatedly by Beausoleil, after his ear had been chopped in half by a sword brandished by

Manson, who had left the Hinman residence before the actual murder, but who is said to have ordered it by phone when Hinman was still not coming across with the money. Hinman is said to have died with the chant "Nam Myoho Renge Kyo" on his lips, the famous prayer of the Nichiren Shoshu sect.

His death occurred on July 27th, Beausoleil writing "Political Piggy" and making a crude drawing of a cat's paw on the walls in Hinman's blood, in an attempt to put the blame on the Black Panthers. This was a tactic that would be repeated in the Tate and LaBianca killings, as one of the purported motives for the killings was to instigate a race war between blacks and whites.

In another eerie chain of coincidence, as the reader of *The Nine* will recall, Aldous Huxley had his first hallucinogenic experience *with mescaline* and *in Hollywood*, after which he wrote *The Doors of Perception*. Jim Morrison named his rock band—the Doors—after this book, and became initiated into witchcraft in 1970, shortly before his death in July 1971. His 1968 release "Five to One" seemed like an eldritch prediction of the Manson slaughters with its tag line, "No one gets out of here alive," and his reference to "five to one and one to five" (the address of the Tate residence on Cielo Drive was 10050).

A YEN FOR MAGIC

The same day that Hinman was being tortured and killed, an occult lodge was being raided in southern California in an effort to rescue six-year-old Anthony Gibbons, who had been imprisoned inside a packing crate on May 23 and had yet to be released a full two months later, except when he was allowed outside the box to work. He had been accused of burning down a building (accidentally) and this was his punishment. Local police received reports of child abuse, and thus the raid on this supposed lodge of the Ordo Templi Orientis. It is not clear at this time whether the police informants in the case were telling the truth or, as one commentator and apologist for the OTO insists, were embellishing a story for its sensationalistic value and to inflate their importance to the local police. That a young boy was kept chained in a wooden building by himself at the Brayton "ranch" is beyond dispute, however; what is controversial is the length of time he was kept there and under what conditions. The FBI report of August 15, 1969 is detailed and contains much corroborating information that does not appear in the OTO apologist's summary of the events, making a clear case for felony child abuse. In the final analysis, however, it didn't matter. The Solar Lodge of the OTO was raided, and its leaders scattered over the desert to avoid arrest and prosecution, some winding up in Mexico as fugitives from justice: a strange reaction from a supposedly benign organization that was not guilty of serious criminal activities.

The so-called Solar Lodge of the OTO was primarily the creation of one Georgina Brayton, and its story is rife with rumor, innuendo, false leads, and disinformation. The American branch of the OTO that was run by the late ex-Army officer Grady

McMurtry has consistently disavowed any connection with the Brayton lodge, but information recently available in the wake of numerous McMurtry-OTO lawsuits against all and sundry suggests otherwise. Predictably, the author himself has been attacked by various individuals claiming OTO affiliation for references he made in his previous work, *Unholy Alliance*, which linked the Solar Lodge with the McMurtry OTO and with Charles Manson. Unfortunately for the Order, the link between Georgina Brayton's OTO and the McMurtry OTO is definite.

Ray and Mildred Burlingame were members of the Agape Lodge of the OTO, the one in Pasadena that was being run for a while by Jack Parsons, and had been in direct communication with Aleister Crowley in the 1940s when Parsons was being considered for a leadership position with the Lodge. After Parsons' death, the Burlingames—who were friends of Georgina Brayton and her husband, a lecturer at the University of California, Richard Montgomery Brayton—began working the rituals of the OTO in an informal way; they were unaffiliated with the main body of the OTO, which was in disarray anyway after the death of Crowley in 1947, the closure of the lodge in 1953, and the subsequent death of Crowley's nominated successor, Karl Germer, in 1962. The Burlingames were veteran initiates of the OTO, and there is some controversy over whether or not Georgina Brayton could be considered initiated. The Burlingames did not possess the requisite authority from an OTO hierarch to start their own lodge or to initiate new members; but, then, neither did Grady McMurtry, the Army officer who had been initiated at Agape Lodge in the days before America entered World War II, having been introduced to Crowley's religion of Thelema by Jack Parsons himself. Although McMurtry had attained the highest operative degree of the Order, the Ninth Degree, he was not an Outer Head of the Order, or OHO (although he would claim this distinction in later years). What is certain is that Georgina Brayton was initiated into the OTO by the Burlingames; what is in dispute is the "validity" of that initiation, given the lack of an OTO charter.

The author does not want to spend a lot of time going over what is a tedious example of how occult lodges fight among themselves, especially where legitimacy and "apostolic succession" are concerned. Suffice it to say that both the Brayton "Solar Lodge of the OTO" and the subsequent McMurtry variation—the "Caliphate"—seemed equally legitimate or equally illegitimate as the case may be. There was nothing intrinsically different about either organization to guarantee that it had legal standing from the point of view of the OTO's original charters and by-laws. Obviously, when the Solar Lodge got into trouble over the case of the "boy in the box," it was up to McMurtry and those loyal to his faction to distance themselves as much as possible from the Solar Lodge, and McMurtry did this . . . especially with respect to correspondence he had with the FBI and the police in the wake of the Solar Lodge revelations.

The Solar Lodge had become somewhat notorious in Southern California in the late 1960s, and it was in the process of building a power center of its own in the Mojave Desert, near the towns of Blythe and Vidal. The reader may recall that the Manson Family was also relocating to the Mojave, but Blythe is far to the southeast of where Manson was setting up his operation, being roughly on the Arizona border. Regardless, the rumors of Manson's knowledge of the Solar Lodge and his attendance at some of its recruiting parties are quite persistent. It was this association, as well as the scandal over the "boy in the box," that, according to published accounts, brought Grady McMurtry out of occult retirement, and he traveled from Washington, D.C. to California to salvage what he could of the OTO (the Agape Lodge had been dissolved in 1953, but it had had the most active and serious members in the United States).

However, evidence shows that McMurtry arrived in California in April of 1969, which meant that he was in place months before either the "boy in the box" incident or the Manson killings. It is McMurtry's long military background (service in both World War II and Korea as an officer), coupled with his position at George Washington University (where he seems to have taught political science), that has raised the possibility that he went to California—leaving a paying job and security in Washington—to conduct an intelligence operation on behalf of . . . someone. If the Scientology people are correct in insisting that their founder, L. Ron Hubbard, a former Naval officer in World War II, was involved with the OTO on behalf of either the FBI or ONI in an effort to break up a "black magic ring" that had attracted scientists with high level security clearances, then it seems equally valid to put forward the idea that a former Army officer in World War II and Korea was involved with something similar.

For those readers who find it frankly incredible that the US government would have attempted to infiltrate occult organizations, I add the following piece of evidence to the published documentation showing a CIA interest in occult phenomena already referenced. On November 21, 1968 an FBI Special Agent in Charge in Philadelphia wrote a memo to FBI Director J. Edgar Hoover under the infamous COINTELPRO program. COINTELPRO was the domestic intelligence, surveillance, infiltration and disruption program of the FBI designed to attack the anti-War movement in general, and the Communist, socialist, Black Panther, Native American and other domestic US political groups in particular.

The memo states,

> "The emergence of the New Left on the American Scene [sic] has produced a new phenomenon—a yen for magic . . . . Self-proclaimed yogis have established a following in the New Left movement. Their incantations are a reminder of the chant of the witch doctor . . . . Philadelphia believes the above-described conditions offer an opportunity for use in the counter-intelligence field. Specifically, it is suggested that a few select top-echelon leaders of the New Left be subjected to harassment by a series of anonymous messages with a mystical connotation."[10]

A few days later, on December 4, 1968, Hoover approved the strategy, with the caveat that specific individuals be chosen for this treatment, based on recommendations of FBI informants close to them, and the symbolism of the messages carefully selected and interpretations made available to the targets by the informants, thus reinforcing the "sinister" messages.[11] Thus, we have documentary evidence based on declassified COINTELPRO files that demonstrate the Bureau's attitude towards cults and their presumed involvement with political subversion. McMurtry's correspondence with the FBI in the Solar Lodge case (see below) would have only served to reinforce the Bureau's suspicion and paranoia of occult groups. This identification of occultism with political dissent—the New Age with the New Left—is fascinating. The fact that many mainstream churches and religious organizations were active in the anti-War movement—one thinks of all the religious leaders who marched on Washington, for instance—did not figure into this equation. The Bureau was concerned with the influence of cults over the rise of American political opposition to the Vietnam War. *For rebellion is as the sin of witchcraft.*

In April of 1969, Bruce Davis had just returned to California and the sticky embrace of the Manson Family after having spent more than five months with either the Scientologists, the Process, or both. His lengthy mission in England is still a mystery, as is the funding for this junket. Documents seized by the US Government after a raid on Scientology headquarters in 1977 show considerable anxiety over the alleged connection between the Manson Family and Scientology; the Scientologists sent emissaries to try to find Steve Grogan (who was later convicted of the murder of Donny Shea), a Family member who had information concerning Manson's Scientology background (they were unsuccessful). Then, an informant came to them with information on Manson's 150 hours of Scientology auditing sessions in prison. The picture painted is frightening, for it shows a Manson at turns extremely enthusiastic about his training . . . and terrified to the point of demanding to be put into solitary confinement so he could escape his auditor. It was after the Scientology cell was broken up at the prison by the warden that another inmate after his release began sending Manson books on hypnotism and "black magic."

Beginning in January of 1969, the CIA's Operation OFTEN quickly expands to include occult research and interviews with occult leaders and cult members. Several months after OFTEN becomes operational, McMurtry leaves the D.C. area and reheats his occult career with the same organization (the OTO) and the same lodge (Agape) that L. Ron Hubbard had allegedly been trying to infiltrate and destroy. At this point, McMurtry had not been active with the OTO since the early 1950s at the latest. According to official OTO sources, he did this latter turn at the instigation or request of Phyllis Seckler, an OTO member in California who was trying to contact all the old Agape Lodge members in the aftermath of a series of robberies of OTO books and documents, including two at the home of Mildred Burlingame (her husband had died a few years previously), robberies that were at first laid at the door of the Solar Lodge. Crowley follower and Mary Ferrell friend Israel Regardie had been burglarized as well, as had Karl Germer's widow, Sascha. It appeared to be a well-organized campaign that lasted from 1965 to 1967, and which was believed to be the work of Georgina Brayton who, having been rebuffed by Mildred Burlingame in her plan to start up a new OTO lodge, decided to obtain as much "classified" Crowley material as possible to enable her to start up a lodge on her own. McMurtry—who was recently divorced—decided to move to California and assist Phyllis Seckler with revitalizing the Order; we do not know what contact, if any, he had with Georgina Brayton. His contact with Ms. Seckler, however, resulted in their marriage a short time after.

A few months later all Hell broke loose, with revelations about the Solar Lodge of the OTO and then, in the wake of the Manson killings, rumors that Manson may have visited the Solar Lodge on at least one occasion, adding the OTO to his list of occult connections (Scientology, the Process, the Church of Satan, the Fountain of the World sect, etc.). McMurtry cooperated with the police and the FBI in an effort to create legal distance between the OTO and the Solar Lodge; this obfuscation has had repercussions down to the present day. Truly, it is of little importance whether or not Manson visited the Solar Lodge; there is no evidence at all that he was a member, or that his actions in any way reflected the philosophy of the Solar Lodge. However, the involvement of both Manson and Bruce Davis with the Scientology and Process organizations, which have a pedigree that goes back to the OTO, is suggestive of something more than sixties-style religious eclecticism. Further, the Solar Lodge had degenerated into an apocalyptic, end-of-the-world sect that practiced a subtle form of racism with a thin veneer of Thelema and Crowleyism as window-dressing for something that was turning more sinister. The philosophical similarities between Manson's occult vision and that of the Solar Lodge (as well as the Process) bear consideration; they are not, however, equivalent to the official OTO philosophy, and it is this more than anything else that justifies McMurtry's distancing of the Crowley cult from that of Georgina Brayton.

Another OTO offshoot that was active in the United States and in southern California especially at the time was the Gardnerian Wicca movement. Although largely underground, it was growing in numbers and in visibility due to the missionary work of Raymond and Rosemary Buckland, a Gardnerian high priest and priestess who were active in the New York City area. Raymond Buckland had appeared on several talk shows—one with CIA consultant Sybil Leek—in the late sixties. Gerald Gardner had received an OTO charter from Aleister Crowley, and Gardner's *Book of Shadows* contains much that was derived from Crowley, the Golden Dawn, and the OTO.

Both Gardnerian and Alexandrian Wicca were popular in the United Kingdom and the United States, and we have seen the influence of Alexandrian Wicca on the career of doomed actress Sharon Tate. Like Scientology—and the Process Church which derived from Scientology—the Wicca movement was a direct descendant of the OTO. Thus, we had witches, satanists, Thelemites, and an entire ragtag band of magicians and occultists whose origins all go back—in one form or another—to Aleister Crowley and the occult Order he "inherited" from German Masons and magicians in the early days of the twentieth century. At the same time, we had alleged American intelligence agency involvement in the penetration and control of these groups, particularly in the 1960s, when the objectives of both the CIA's MK-ULTRA mind control programs and the FBI's domestic intelligence gathering programs on potentially subversive secret societies dovetailed; both of these programs were motivated by fear of Communism.

And in that climate of fear and paranoia, Richard Nixon and Henry Kissinger—in May of 1969—authorized FBI domestic wiretapping of American reporters and government officials. At this time, Richard Nixon had been President of the United States for less than four months. (That same month, Manson's uncle—Darwin Scott—was savagely hacked to death in Ashland, Kentucky. Like the murders of Delaney and Warren in April, it is a case tied to Manson that has never been solved.)

It is worth noting in this context that, in one lawsuit against Nixon concerning the wiretapping of Morton Halperin (a National Security Council staff member), the Federal Court of Appeals in 1977 stated, "The President is the elected chief executive of our government, not an omniscient leader cloaked in mystical powers."[12] An interesting choice of words, considering our theme.

THE OMEN

> There is no past. There is only now in this infinite time . . . . We are all one member—one force.
>
> —Charles Manson to his Family[13]

With the premiere of *Rosemary's Baby* in 1968, America was on the way to a spate of films dealing with the subject of the incarnation of evil. In *Rosemary's Baby*, of course, an innocent young woman is impregnated by Satan in order to bring about the birth of Satan's child on Earth, in a blasphemous recreation of the virgin birth of Christianity. Rosemary brings the baby to term, but it is taken from her at birth, and she is told that the baby died; she later hears chanting and the baby crying through the thin apartment walls and discovers the truth for herself. This idea—of a satanically-engendered or satanically-possessed child—is reprised in *The Exorcist*, in which the young Regan is possessed by an evil spirit, an emanation of the ancient Sumerian demon Pazuzu. Again, a child is the focus of evil; again, evil has became incarnated in human flesh rather than remaining merely a phantom or ghastly illusion. Even more frightening, this film was based on events that had actually occurred. A few years later, and the American public would be presented with yet another demonic presence, this time in *The Omen*, in which a young boy has the mark of 666 on his scalp: he is the Devil incarnate, again (and, like Crowley, in England again!). The 1990s film *Lost Souls*—starring Winona Ryder as a formerly possessed young woman on the trail of Satan—is another attempt to show the impending incarnation of Evil, although this time the vessel is a grown man (appropriately enough, a lawyer). Perhaps one day we will address this issue of why—from the late 1960s through the 1970s—we feared our children so much that we identified them with Lucifer himself; what concerns us here at this time however is the idea that Evil could be incarnated, could be "made flesh" and "dwell amongst us."

Charles Manson has become the ultimate example of the belief that a person—a human being born of woman—could be wholly, irredeemably, evil. Rightly or wrongly, we have characterized Manson this way. Some of the objections to Manson are quite valid, of course. Others are based on Manson's personality and style, an image that he cultivates that seems focused entirely on scaring the living daylights out of people. We know he was present during part of the time that Gary Hinman was being tortured to death, and that he ordered Hinman's murder; we know that he brought the ropes to the LaBianca house and tied up the victims; we know—at least we think we know—from the testimony of members of his "family" that he ordered the killings at the Tate household on Cielo Drive. We also know that he shot a drug dealer named Bernard Crowe in the stomach, leaving him for dead. All of that is bad enough, of course; but Manson was convicted for something darker, more sinister.

He was convicted of murder in the case of the Tate and LaBianca killings because of his psychological power over the men and women he sent to perform murder. The viciousness of the attacks on Sharon Tate, Jay Sebring, Abigail Folger, Voytek Frykowski, Steven Parent, Leno LaBianca and Rosemary LaBianca was not the work of Manson himself. He wasn't there when the victims were killed. Some of the victims were shot, but most did not die of the gunshot wounds. All were stabbed repeatedly, over and over again in a violent frenzy of homicidal passion, by two women and a man, a man—Tex Watson—who proclaimed upon entering the Tate home, "I am the Devil, and I'm here to do the Devil's business." These were young people who had never fired a shot in anger in their lives, nor stabbed helpless victims to death, nor written slogans on the walls of the abattoirs in the victims' blood. But Manson made it all possible, even probable.

As the events of that summer of 1969 began to percolate, Manson became more and more manic. Death was in the air. Everyone at his headquarters, the Spahn Ranch, was talking about death. Spahn Ranch had been a movie set for a slew of westerns that came out of Hollywood over the years, and now served as a horse ranch for weekend riders. Oddly enough, it was used as the set of *The Outlaw*, the Jane Russell vehicle that was produced by Howard Hughes. Hughes had even spent some time on the set at Spahn Ranch, but it was not used for filmmaking much any more. Now it was the headquarters for Helter Skelter.

Many observers (including Maury Terry in his controversial best-seller *The Ultimate Evil)* have proposed that Manson was a contract killer, taking contracts in exchange for drugs or money, or some other consideration. Indeed, the LaBianca killings were the most anomalous of all the murders; both Manson and Tex Watson knew the Tate residence since they knew its previous occupant, Terry Melcher, the son of actress Doris Day, and Manson had visited the Tate residence on Cielo Drive a few months before the murders, ostensibly looking for Melcher who had promised to help him land a recording contract. Yet no case could be made for the LaBiancas, except that there was a Mafia connection and the rumor of bad blood between Leno LaBianca and the Mob. The LaBianca killings *could* have been a Mafia hit, contracted to the Family. The Tate killings, on the other hand, seemed motivated by something entirely different. Some authors have wondered if the LaBianca killings were the real focus of the horror that week and that the Tate killings were designed to confuse the issue and throw the police off the scent, or vice versa. A motiveless crime is the most difficult to solve and, indeed, it might never have been solved had not one of the Manson women confessed to the crime to another inmate while she was in prison on an unrelated offense.

Satanism and Nazism were very much part of the Manson philosophy. He avoided Spahn Ranch employee Donny Shea because he was married to a black woman; Shea would eventually wind up dead and buried in the desert. He planted the stolen LaBianca identification and credit cards in a gas station in a black neighborhood, hoping that someone would find them and use them, and thus pin the murders on the Black Panthers. Convicted murderer Bobby Beausoleil had actually played the Devil in a Kenneth Anger film, opposite Church of Satan creator Anton Szandor LaVey; he also played a homicidal Indian in the soft-porn flick *Ramrodder*, killing a helpless man the way he killed Gary Hinman a few years later. Convicted murderer Susan Atkins belonged to the Church of Satan before she ever met Charles Manson, and played the part of a vampire in a publicly staged Black Mass at LaVey's church. Convicted murderer Tex Watson claimed he was the Devil, to frighten the Tate residents. Convicted murderer Charles Manson claimed to be both Jesus and Satan. Convicted murderer Patricia Krenwinkel doodled satanic glyphs and the Church of Satan's Goat of Mendes during her trial.

The barter America made for its protection and defense in the 1940s and 1950s—selling its soul to the Nazis; creating a program to open the Pandora's Box of human consciousness to develop the perfect weapon: the mindless assassin—was a bill that had to be paid. The sacrament of choice was LSD, that golem of the CIA mind-control program: it provided the "material basis" for the evocation of sinister forces. The Manson Family—according to eyewitness testimony, published in many sources but most noticeably in *The Garbage People*—were constantly strung out on acid in the weeks and months leading up to the Tate and LaBianca killings. Tex Watson was said to be so deranged from constant use of the drug that he forgot his own mother's address and phone number. Manson consciously used the drug as a tool in his arsenal, along with sex. In one instance, he told an interviewer that he would make a woman exhausted with physical work before he would have sex with her, so that she was in no mood to have sex at all. Then he would approach her and gradually work on her until the point where she began to respond to his sexual ministrations; at that point, Manson believed he had control of her mind and could convince her to do anything. That combination of sex and drugs and a kind of perverse operant conditioning are the basic working parts of what Ed Sanders calls "The Manson Secret." It was what CIA psychiatrist Ewen Cameron was working on until virtually the day he died, except that Manson was much more successful. As documented in *The Nine*, Cameron created zombies; Manson created assassins.

Another aspect of the Satanic and Nazi elements of Manson's philosophy was the apocalyptic. Manson was seen carrying a Bible and constantly referring to the Book of Revelations, also known in the Catholic Douay Rheims translation as *Apocalypse*, where he pointed to messages and omens that he felt were referring to him, his mission, and the general state of the world. Just as Fundamentalist Christians are concerned with the "End Times" and are only in debate as to when and how the End Times begin, so was Manson. Manson believed that he would be the engine of Armageddon, the last battle that would usher in a Golden Age. He believed that the End was imminent. In this, he was no different from Fundamentalist Christians, but also had a lot in common with his other predecessors: the Thelemites.

Those who follow the scriptures of Aleister Crowley agree that a New Age dawned in April of 1904, when Crowley received *The Book of the Law* in Cairo. It was the beginning of the Age of Horus, the Crowned and Conquering Child, the New Aeon that would replace Christianity. Crowley perceived himself to be the engine of that transformation, and called himself *To Mega Therion*, a Greek phrase that means "the Great Beast," the Beast of the Apocalypse known by his infamous number, 666. Crowley believed that he, himself, was the Beast prophesied in the Bible, and that the women he took as consorts were all "Scarlet Women," Whores of Babylon as mentioned in the Apocalypse.

Crowley's take on all of this was not that he was the personification of Evil, but that new Gods—when replacing old Gods—are rejected or resisted at first, until gradually they assume global acceptance, and the old Gods then become demons. Crowley identified the New Age with Horus, the Lord of Lower Egypt who avenged the murder of his father, Osiris, by Set. Jack Parsons, in pursuing his own spiritual path in the Mojave Desert, began to identify with the Antichrist, inasmuch as he was invoking the presence of the Whore of Babylon herself, spelled in Crowley's system "Babalon." Thus, the initial impetus of Thelema was as apocalyptic and millenial as that of Fundamentalist Christianity. The "End Times" were upon us, for Thelemites and Christians alike.

It was basically a time to choose sides and may the best God win. While Manson looked forward as eagerly to the Apocalypse as later President Ronald

Reagan would do, he saw his own role differently. As both God and Devil, he was uniting the opposing forces within himself (thus being assured that he would remain victorious regardless of which side won the Final Battle). Like the pharaohs of ancient Egypt, he was both Horus and Set. Thus, whatever he did was permissible. There was no evil, no good. There was only Manson.

And murder.

The events that led up to the slaughter on Cielo Drive are still very much in dispute. The only witnesses to the gradual build-up of violence among the members of Charles Manson's entourage in 1969 are the killers themselves and their accomplices: in most cases young renegades so strung out on dope, sex, mystical vibes and California dreams that their testimony reads like Old Testament prophets on angel dust, and with bad cases of tinnitus from sitting a little too close to the speakers.

Part of the problem with Manson was that he found himself suddenly in the midst of all of these "beautiful people," and he had a hard time dealing with the reality *they* lived with, and the reality *he* lived with. He was walking between two worlds, one filled with Dennis Wilson of the Beach Boys, John Phillips of the Mamas and the Papas, Deana Martin (daughter of Dean Martin), Terry Melcher, Peter Falk, Nancy Sinatra, Jane Fonda (whom he despised for her "race mixing"), even little DiDi Lansbury, daughter of actress Angela Lansbury, who gave her daughter a note to carry saying it was all right for her to be hanging out with the Manson Family! In fact, Manson even had one of his songs recorded by the Beach Boys. Pretty heady stuff for an illiterate, fatherless drifter who had spent most of his life institutionalized in reform schools and prisons.

But rather than making him grateful for the turn his life was taking, it made him bitter and angry. Lists of famous people—show business celebrities mostly—were drawn up as a Family "hit list" that included Frank Sinatra, Elizabeth Taylor, Tom Jones and many others. No one knows exactly why the residence of Sharon Tate was picked for the first night of "Helter Skelter," except that Manson possibly still held a grudge over the way he was treated by Tate's housekeeper on his previous visit. Or perhaps it was as a kind of message to Melcher, the man who had disappointed him in his quest for fame and fortune as a rock star: an unveiled threat? (Manson had threatened Dennis Wilson, sending messages to Wilson that he would harm Wilson's young son, when Wilson did not come across with cash that fateful weekend.) Or perhaps there was another aspect to it, a connection with drugs that has bothered investigators for some time.

A few nights before the Tate slaughter there was a strange event at the house on Cielo Drive. A dope dealer from Canada was punished for selling Jay Sebring bad dope. According to actor Dennis Hopper, twenty-five people were invited to watch the dealer get whipped and to participate in the whipping. They videotaped the event, as they had other events involving—again, according to Hopper—"sadism, masochism and bestiality."[14] Hopper claims that LA police informed him about some of this information. The tapes have never surfaced, but rumors in the Hollywood underground have always insisted that they exist. Some say that the LAPD has them in a safe place, much like J. Edgar Hoover's famous "secret files," to be used when necessary to coerce or persuade a celebrity to cooperate.

This event cannot be considered in isolation from the Tate killings. According to Hopper, the public humiliation of the dealer took place three days before the murders at Cielo Drive, which would make it on or about August 5th. Manson had complained to Gary Hinman about a bad batch of mescaline on July 26th. The burn was worth two thousand dollars. Hinman was killed. Hairstylist to the stars (and former lover of Sharon Tate) Jay Sebring had complained about getting burned to the tune of the same two thousand dollars. He would die in the Tate house. Only the type of drug is in question: was Sebring talking about cocaine or mescaline? According to Ed Sanders, Sebring's burn—and the subsequent whipping of the drug dealer—involved cocaine.[15] That there were two dope burns for the same amount of money in each case, less than two weeks apart, is probably coincidence; but it got Gary Hinman murdered, got a dope dealer whipped on Cielo Drive in front of twenty-five eyewitnesses including many celebrities, and led up to the horrific murders in the same house only three days later.

Police and prosecution officials are naturally reluctant to discuss this case's peculiarities even now, more than thirty years after the events in question. On one side, this is because—as Vincent Bugliosi has admitted in his own book on the Manson murders, *Helter Skelter*—the police investigation of the Tate and LaBianca killings was shoddy, to say the least; but it is also because the perpetrators are still alive, still behind bars, and no one wants to jeopardize that. New evidence could be used in a new trial, or at least to get some of the convicted murderers out on parole. It could also embarrass a lot of people in Hollywood. Thus, we are forced to rely on informants, independent investigative journalism, police snitches, and the like.

Or, when more murders take place that have a ring of similarity to the Manson killings, we can begin to see connections where there were none before. Maury Terry has been criticized for his book, *The Ultimate Evil*, because it discusses the existence of a nearly unbelievable nationwide Satanic conspiracy in the United States involving drugs, Hollywood, and murder. However, Terry's book managed to get the Son of Sam case reopened in the State of New York due to the evidence he presented showing that more than one person was involved in the Sam murders . . .something of which many of us who lived in New York City at the time were convinced. In addition, Terry's information on the occult scene in Brooklyn Heights and Manhattan in the 1970s is detailed and accurate, as the author himself can attest from personal experience. Terry's information regarding the drug dealer punishment on Cielo Drive is therefore important.

According to Terry,[16] the pistol-whipping of the Canadian drug dealer—who is likewise named "Billy Doyle" in the first edition of Ed Sanders' book *The Family*—took place on the same night as a party for French film producer Roger Vadim, who was married at the time to actress and anti-War activist Jane Fonda. Billy Doyle was well-known to the Cielo Drive crowd, since Abigail Folger and Voyteck Frykowski (both Manson murder victims) had lived on Cielo Drive before Tate and Polanski moved in, and Frykowski was heavily involved in the drug trade, being largely financed by his girlfriend who was the Folger Coffee heiress. Frykowski was running LSD and MDA, along with whatever else was going down. Doyle and several of Frykowski's friends had crashed Roman Polanski's house-warming party on Cielo Drive in March 1969 and were thrown out, much to their irritation. After the Polanskis left for England in April, however, Frykowski moved back into Cielo Drive with Abigail Folger, and the visits by Doyle, et al. resumed.[17] Jay Sebring, who would become a murder victim a few days later, brought some film that had been shot that night at Vadim's party to a developer for processing; it is suggested that the whipping of Billy Doyle was on that film.

It is important to note that Roman Polanski himself, in his autobiography, disputes this characterization of his friend Frykowski very strenuously, as he disputes other stories that have made the run of the press.[18] Whether this was out of loyalty to his friend, or a simple statement of fact, is impossible to discern at this remove. Polanski also implies that there was no cult activity of any sort at Cielo Drive[19] without ever specifically denying it, blaming it on a reporter's discovery of a Ouija board in his home; a conclusion that is difficult to accept. Instead, he says that *the police* "gave no credence whatsoever to tales of stray pick-ups, orgies, drug excesses, and black magic."[20] His explanation of the "hood on Jay Sebring" is that a police officer draped a cloth over Sebring's head because the victim's wounds were so grisly.[21] We know from other sources that Manson himself placed the towel around Sebring's head, just to throw off the investigation; much in the same way he planted an old pair of eyeglasses at the scene that had investigators running around for months trying to identify their owner. One of the strangest omissions from Polanski's autobiography is any mention of the poor doomed gossip columnist Steve Brandt, who was, after all, one of the witnesses to his wedding to Sharon Tate. Brandt does appear, however, in John Phillips' autobiography, and his account reflects what everyone else has said about Brandt's relationship to Sharon Tate.

Informants close to the case have insisted that the Tate killings had a motive that went beyond Manson's Helter Skelter philosophy. They insist that the target of the killings was Frykowski, and not Sharon Tate. That the killings were contracted to Manson. As were the LaBianca slayings the next night. Polanski believes that Manson chose the Tate household as a target because he believed that Terry Melcher still lived there and blamed Melcher for his failure to succeed as a rock star.[22] The LaBianca murders, according to Polanski's theory, were only to throw off the investigation. Using a kind of circular logic, Polanski implies that since no one has ever accused the LaBiancas of orgies, drugs, and black masses that these could not have been factors in the Tate killings, either. And so it goes.

Maury Terry raises an important point in his observation of the killings, one which cannot be easily ignored: if Helter Skelter was the true motive, then why did the killings stop after LaBianca? There was no evidence linking the Manson clan to any of the killings; they were still in the clear on Tate and LaBianca, although Bobby Beausoleil had been picked up for the Hinman murder. They could have continued their Helter Skelter murder spree much longer before being stopped. Why only that one weekend in August? Why only the five victims at the Tate house (six, if you count Sharon Tate's unborn son) and two at LaBianca? The only reason that makes sense is that both murders were contract hits, and that Manson dressed it up in Helter Skelter for the benefit of his young female assassins. (It is presumed that Tex Watson knew of the real motive, or had a suspicion anyway, as it was he who drove the car to the Tate residence specifically; it was not a random selection.)

Helter Skelter was Manson's "program" for the brainwashed murderers; it provided a context, and it also influenced their choice of bloody graffiti at each scene, thus laying the crimes off on the Black Panthers. For Manson, it was two birds with one stone, so to speak. He could spread the evil message of Helter Skelter while meanwhile getting paid—in *some* form, since money seemed to be in short supply in the days immediately preceding and succeeding the murders—by the drug dealing establishment to rid them of some problems. Once Frykowski's drug connections were known, then a motive for his killing could be understood. And once Leno LaBianca's indebtedness to the Mafia was known, another motive presented itself.

The brilliance behind these crimes had nothing to do with Manson himself. The brilliance was in *selecting* Manson and his assassins as the hit team, for it obscured the real motives and thus the real powers behind them. Further, due to the sensitive nature of the victims involved and their incestuous relationships with Hollywood, occultism, drugs, and "alternative" sexual practices—much of it captured on videotape—there was very little danger of their friends running to the police with information that could get the real masterminds into trouble. The Tate killings spread tentacles into the very highest reaches of Hollywood. Beginning with Terry Melcher and Dennis Wilson, and extending outward to the Mamas and the Papas, Jane Fonda, Roger Vadim, Jack Nicholson, Dennis Hopper, and so many others whose names were household words, the blood had splattered all over Benedict Canyon in an aerial spray that reached Mulholland Drive, Beverly Hills, Bel Air, North Hollywood, Malibu, and the back lots of studios all over town. Drugs, murder for hire, sadomasochistic sex on videotape involving celebrities, and satanic rituals . . . is it any wonder LAPD had a hell of a time trying to extricate one strand of nastiness from another? The "scarlet thread of murder" never ran so red as it did on August 9, 1969 at 10050 Cielo Drive.

Since the trial, more information has come to light concerning the Manson Family and its connections to the murder victims. There are witnesses who insist that Manson knew Abigail Folger from the "Summer of Love" days in San Francisco in 1967, shortly after Manson was released from prison. According to these sources, Folger had invested in the Straight Theater in the Haight-Ashbury section of the city, only blocks from where both Manson and the Process set up shop. The Straight Theater, on September 21, 1967, had staged a performance by The Magick Powerhouse of Oz in honor of the "Equinox of the Gods," and Kenneth Anger was in attendance filming the event, as was Bobby Beausoleil, Manson, Folger, and many others including—according to sources close to the events—former members of the OTO Agape Lodge of Pasadena and the Process. It was a virtual occult convention, and Manson was able to "network" with a lot of people who would become notorious in the years to follow.

Information that became available to Maury Terry long after the killings shows that Manson had become involved with the Process after the Straight Theater performance in 1967, and through early 1968, at the famous Spiral Staircase house in Topanga Canyon (not far from where Bobby Beausoleil and Catherine Share were filming *Ramrodder*), which was a kind of occult headquarters and sex club combined; this information came from one of the convicted Manson killers, and was confirmed by Manson in his "autobiography."[23] In a further development, Manson—in a letter written in 1989—claimed to have met with Process leaders (naming names) at the Tate residence![24] Clearly, the relationship between Manson, Abigail Folger, Terry Melcher, Dean Moorehouse, Dennis Wilson, John Phillips, the Process, Scientology and 10050 Cielo Drive is much more convoluted and involved than the trial ever revealed. While Manson had become involved with occultism and "black magic" while in prison, this interest was kicked into high gear during the Summer of Love and beyond.

Another startling piece of information concerns Donald "Shorty" Shea, the Spahn ranch hand and would-be actor who was murdered a few weeks after the Tate killings, allegedly because he "knew too much." In this scenario, attested by informants to Terry and Sanders, Shea had known both Manson and Folger in those halcyon days in San Francisco. Shea had later come down to the Spahn Ranch when Manson and his group moved in. Something went awry between the two diminutive persons and Shea was eventually murdered, his body found in the desert long after the trial, homicide detectives led there by Steve "Clem" Grogan, who was also a putative source for Scientology officials concerning Manson's involvement with the Hubbard cult. Thus the attack on the Tate residence and some of the murders that would follow seem linked to events that transpired and connections that were made in San Francisco two years earlier, with the somber drapery of ceremonial occultism drooping menacingly over the *mis-en-scene*. In that case, perhaps Donny Shea knew too much after all.

What follows is a brief description of what we know transpired that night of August 9, 1969. It is necessary to demonstrate to the reader the sheer savagery of the attack as compared with the mental and emotional state of the perpetrators. It goes to motive, as they say in murder trials. The author apologizes in advance for the graphic recreation of the event.

Susan Atkins (age 21), Linda Kasabian (age 20), Tex Watson (age 23) and Patricia Krenwinkel (age 21) left in an old white and yellow '59 Ford for the Tate residence, Watson driving. Manson had been at the Tate residence at least twice before, once when Terry Melcher was dropped off after a meeting and again on his own, a few months after Melcher moved out, when he was supposedly looking for Melcher. The last time he actually saw Sharon Tate was through a doorway when her housekeeper answered the door. Melcher, the son of Doris Day, had been living at the house with his girlfriend, the actress Candace Bergen, before Sharon Tate and Roman Polanski moved in. (Additional information emerging since the trial indicates that Manson may actually have spent much more time at the Tate residence with Melcher and company in the days before the Tates moved in, and thus knew the layout of the house quite well, data which he may have communicated to Tex Watson who, among all the killers, would have been the one that Manson entrusted with sensitive information.)

Watson was armed with a handgun, and two of the women carried knives. They brought a change of clothes with them, so that they could switch to their dark-colored "creepy crawley" outfits on the way to the death house. This was also in order to rid themselves of what would become clothing drenched in blood by the time the holocaust was over.

They parked down the street from the Tate residence. Tex Watson cut the telephone lines to the house, and the four of them crawled over the fence surrounding the lot and made their way to the house.

There is a rumor that Manson thought that Sharon Tate would not be there that night. She actually had plans to visit a friend, but changed these plans at the last moment. Her husband, Polish film director Roman Polanski, was in London at the time working on *The Day of the Dolphin*, a film inspired by the true story of the Navy's training of dolphins for military purposes. (When the film was finally released, the trailer described the plot as involving a nefarious scheme using dolphins to assassinate the President of the United States. When the author saw the trailer in a Manhattan movie theater, the audience laughed and applauded. Well, it *was* New York. And Nixon *was* President.)

But that month Polanski was frustrated with the way the screenplay was going, and was making plans to return to California early. His friend, the brilliant and quirky novelist Jerzy Kosiński, was also on his way to California. His luggage had been lost, though, so he decided to wait in New York City until they found it. It was the luckiest decision of his life. Had he arrived on time, he would have been at the Tate residence that night.

Voytek Frykowski was there, of course, along with his girlfriend Abigail Folger. Sharon Tate, eight months pregnant, was sitting in her bedroom talking to Jay Sebring. Sebring had been Sharon's lover before Roman Polanski arrived on the scene and broke that up. Friends in Hollywood claimed that Sebring still carried a torch for Ms. Tate, and he had remained good friends of her family. When

Sebring opened his new salon that summer, the Tates were in attendance: Doris Tate, Sharon's mother who later started a fund for crime victims, and Sharon's father, Colonel Paul Tate, an intelligence officer with the US Army who had been serving in Vietnam. Colonel Tate would go underground in California after the murders, hunting for his daughter's killers.

A young man, Steven Parent, was just leaving the Tate residence by car. As he was going down the driveway, a man stood in front of the car and waved it to stop. He told Parent to get out of the car, but the boy refused. His body would later show defensive knife wounds, but it was the bullets that killed him. Tex Watson fired four times into the car, killing the eighteen-year-old and leaving him there.

The killers then proceeded to the house.

Linda Kasabian, recently arrived in California from her home in Milford, New Hampshire, pregnant and with an infant daughter, stayed behind at the fence to watch for unwelcome visitors. She says she had no stomach for the killing, and was horrified by the shooting of Parent. Things were spiralling out of control. The women went up to the house with Watson, knives at the ready. Watson also carried a length of rope with him. The idea was to hang the victims from the rafters of the living room, and then gut them.

Susan Atkins was known to the Family as "Sadie" or "Sexy Sadie" (after the Beatles song on the White Album) or "Sadie Mae Glutz." Patricia Krenwinkel was known as "Katie." Virtually all of the Manson Family members had aliases, but these were not aliases in the criminal sense of the word (although they would often be used that way); these were names they adopted upon joining the Family. This action suggests a process that Robert Jay Lifton calls "doubling," or the creation of an alter ego or dissociated identity to enable he individual to become a killer responsible for acts of unbelievable savagery, and then re-enter society as if there had been no effect on the individual's personality, psyche, or soul.

Manson, meanwhile, remained behind at Spahn Ranch. Before the killers left on their mission, he told them, "Now is the time for Helter Skelter." He gave Watson some specific instructions, directing them straight to the Tate house with the ostensible reason that they were going to steal whatever money was there to bail some Family members—Mary Brunner (the mother of one of Manson's children) and Sandy Good—out of jail, having been arrested that day after trying to use some stolen credit cards. According to Watson's later testimony, Charlie had told them to go to the next house if they didn't get enough money there, and the one after that if necessary, until they had amassed the six hundred dollars bail money they would need. That was the cover story, anyway.

Manson, who was no stranger to crime, knew the risks of ripping off people who knew him. There were a lot of houses in Los Angeles to rob that night; they could have picked one with no one home, where no one could identify them later. Instead, he chose the one house in LA, outside of Dennis Wilson's home, where his merry band would be familiar to the residents. That theft was not the principle motive for the murders is clear from the overkill at the Tate household, and the elaborate preparations, including the rope and Manson's instructions to the girls to "Leave a sign. You girls know what to do. Something witchy."[25] In the Tate homicides, as in the LaBiancas, nothing of any value was stolen, even though—especially in the case of the LaBiancas—there was a lot of jewelry, a coin collection, etc. that would have been easy for Manson to fence. In any case, they did not follow these alleged instructions and would return to Spahn Ranch immediately following the carnage.

The girls had gone to a common arsenal and selected the knives they were going to use. Watson carried a nine-shot .22 revolver, and took a few hits of amphetamine for the road. Susan Atkins had been snorting amphetamine for days before the murders, and was on a perpetual high from the speed. Patricia Krenwinkel was just coming down from an LSD trip, and was groggy from lack ofsleep. Linda Kasabian had a valid driver's license, so she was elected to go along with them as the designated driver in case they were stopped by police, even though Watson would be doing all the driving that night. Squeaky Fromme, who would later attempt to assassinate a President, helped her find the license, which was kept in a communal cache under the close supervision of the pixie-ish Fromme.

When they entered the house, slashing through a mesh screen with their knives, it was Frykowski who saw them first. The stereo blaring, and Frykowski himself in the midst of a ten-day "mescaline experiment" (once again, echoes of Aldous Huxley and the Doors) he struggled to get up from the couch where he was lying, to focus on the strange-looking man suddenly standing in the living room.

"Who are you?" he asked.

"I am the Devil, and I'm here to do the Devil's business," Tex Watson replied.

Susan Atkins was ordered to look in the other rooms and find out how many people were in the house. She saw Sharon Tate and Jay Sebring in one room, talking, and Abigail Folger in another, reading, bringing the total to four people in the house. The body of Steven Parent was still in his car in the driveway outside, shot in the upper chest, left forearm, left cheek, lower chest. Abigail Folger looked up and saw Susan Atkins smile at her; she smiled back, a little uncertain. Strangers were always coming and going at Cielo Drive, friends of Sharon's, friends of Jay's or Voytek's. Drug connections, actors, musicians, mystics . . . who knew? On the piano's music stand in the living room, two compositions were open: one, Elgar's "Pomp and Circumstance," the standard for high school graduation classes everywhere, and a melody used to ironic purpose in Stanley Kubrick's masterpiece, *A Clockwork Orange*; the second, more ominously, by John Phillips, from the first album of The Mamas and The Papas: "Straight Shooter."[26] In another building on the estate, caretaker William Garretson was oblivious to the shooting and other sounds coming from the Tate residence; he was listening to The Mamas and The Papas and the Doors.

It was about half-past midnight in Los Angeles on August 9, 1969. The following day would be the thirty-fourth anniversary of Robert de Grimston's birth in Shanghai. One wonders how the Process Church of the Final Judgment celebrated their founder's birthday. Devil's food cake? Black candles? Doggie bag?

That same day, Disneyland opened their Haunted House ride.

That night, Steve Brandt—former press agent for Sharon Tate, legal witness at her wedding to Roman Polanski, and columnist for Photoplay *magazine—was having dinner at a Japanese restaurant in Los Angeles with John Phillips of The Mamas and The Papas.*[27] *For a brief time he would be a suspect in the murders even though he cooperated with police, and gave them "voluminous" information on Tate, Polanski, Frykowski, and the LA drug scene, before committing suicide in New York City after several other failed attempts. He was afraid he was on a hit list. Why?*

Many more thousands of miles to the west, across the Pacific Ocean in Japan, it was four-thirty in the afternoon of the same day, the twenty-fourth anniversary of the atomic bomb attack on Nagasaki. There had been peace demonstrations throughout Japan but especially in Hiroshima and Nagasaki, the two towns devastated by the blasts of "Little Boy" and "Fat Man," respectively, while in Vietnam in the summer of 1969 the war went on without a break: more soldiers died, more civilians died, flames and chemicals and bombs destroying the landscape and maiming its inhabitants, and Nixon—who cut the deal with President Thieu to sabotage the peace process and prolong the war until after his election—saw everything that he had made and, behold, it was good. And the evening and the morning of the first day.

And no one got out of there alive.

Susan Atkins herded Sharon Tate, Jay Sebring and Abigail Folger into the living room, where Frykowski—a survivor of the Nazi invasion of Poland—was already bound with towels. Patricia Krenwinkel did not have a weapon, and rushed outside to where Linda Kasabian was waiting, took her knife, and then rushed back to the house.

Although Tex Watson had brought a long length of rope, Frykowski was tied up very inefficiently with towels they found at the Tate home. This was obviously a very poorly-planned robbery. In the end, they took less than eighty dollars from the scene, leaving jewelry, electronic equipment, and credit cards behind. Again, robbery as a motive doesn't play.

Tex ordered the three newcomers to lie on their stomachs on the floor. Sebring objected, saying that Sharon Tate was pregnant and that she should be allowed to sit. Tex ignored him and ordered them all on the floor again, at which point Sebring lunged for the gun in Watson's hand. Watson fired, and Sebring was down. The women screamed. Watson then kicked Sebring in the face. He demanded money once again; this time Abigail Folger said she had some cash in her bedroom. Susan Atkins led her there at the point of a knife. The take was seventy-two dollars. Total. For the night.

Tex then ordered that all of the victims be tied together with the length of nylon rope that he brought with him, tied around their necks. Abigail Folger and Sharon Tate had the rope tied around their necks, and then one end was tossed over a ceiling beam and down to where Jay Sebring lay, unconscious from the gunshot wound, and tied around his neck. Tex ordered that the lights be turned out, and the rest of what transpired took place in relative darkness. He told the assembled victims that he was the Devil once again, and then he told them that he was going to kill all of them. The women began screaming again; Sebring was still unconscious; Frykowski was struggling to free himself of the towels.

Watson ordered Susan Atkins to kill Frykowski. She came up on him with her knife. The towels did not hold him. He got loose and jumped at Susan, pulling her down by her hair as they struggled over the knife. Getting her arm free, she began stabbing Frykowski over and over again. The slaughter had begun.

Susan stabbed Frykowski in the legs and then aimed for his chest, hitting his lung, but he still struggled, and she lost her knife in the chaos. It would turn up later, long after the killers had returned to the Spahn Ranch, stuck in a chair cushion. Susan jumped on his back, yelling, as Frykowski crawled to the door. Tex Watson aimed his .22 at the escaping man and shot him several times, but to no immediate avail. Finally, Watson began clubbing him to death with the butt of the gun, breaking it in the process.

During the attack on Frykowski, Abigail Folger managed to break free and ran for the rear of the house. Patricia Krenwinkel gave chase, and the two fought, as Watson turned to see that Jay Sebring was regaining consciousness. Watson then began stabbing Sebring repeatedly. Krenwinkel screamed she was having problems with Abigail Folger, who by this time had been stabbed in the arms as she tried to defend herself against Krenwinkel's blade. Finally, though, Abigail gave up, exhausted and bleeding. Watson slit her neck, and then stabbed her repeatedly in her abdomen after smashing her head in with the gun butt.

Frykowski, meanwhile, had managed to escape outside the house to the front lawn, where he began screaming for help. The Tate house was in Benedict Canyon, and the echoes carried far. No one responded to his desperate plea for life. William Garretson in his caretaker's cottage was listening to the Doors and ignoring whatever was going on outside his four walls. "This is the end . . ." Watson ran out of the house and jumped on Frykowski, dragging him to the ground and stabbing him a total of fifty-one times.

At the same moment, Abigail Folger—still alive after having been stabbed and having her throat slit—made her way, step by bloody step, to the rear of the house and freedom. Krenwinkel gave chase, leaving a bloody fingerprint on the door in the process, but Abigail had managed to almost reach the fence in the rear of the house past the swimming pool when she collapsed onto the ground and died.

Sharon Tate was alone in the house, with the body of Jay Sebring. She started to walk towards the front door when Krenwinkel entered the house through the back at a run. She stopped Sharon's escape, and held her in a headlock. Sharon began crying, begging to be left alive so she could have her baby. It wasn't to happen. Watson and Atkins entered the house, Susan Atkins holding Sharon's arms and Patricia Krenwinkel her legs. Sharon turned to Susan and begged for her life once again, or at least the life of her baby.

Tex told Susan to kill her. Susan declined. He told Patricia to kill her. She also declined. Then Tex began to stab Sharon Tate, and eventually all three stabbed her a total of sixteen times. Her baby died a few minutes after his mother. Susan Atkins, in recalling the murder to another prison inmate, said, "It felt so good, the first time I stabbed her."

Tex ordered the women out, and then he went around to all the corpses in a frenzy, stabbing them all again for good measure and kicking their heads. They then ran down to where they parked their car, looking for Linda Kasabian. Their clothing was drenched in blood.

Linda had tried, a little ineffectually, to get Atkins and Krenwinkel to stop. Still horrified by the corpse of Steven Parent, she wanted nothing more to do with killing. When the screams and the shots resounded all over the Canyon she hid, terrified, in some bushes and later made her way to the car. The killers began looking for her, but couldn't find her on the estate; so they made their way back to the Ford, where they found Linda at the wheel, starting the car.

They jumped in, Tex taking over the driving, and they changed their clothes, making a bloody bundle for Linda to toss over a cliff. This bundle would be found later, as well as the broken gun Watson had used to kill Parent, Sebring and Frykowski.

(There were a total of 102 stab wounds over the five victims. When the Spahn Ranch was raided—seven days later on August 16, 1969—and Manson arrested on auto-theft charges unrelated to the Tate and LaBianca killings, there would be a total of 102 law enforcement personnel involved.[28] Three days later, the murderers would all be freed).

The killers returned to Spahn Ranch, to find Manson sitting outside, waiting for them. When he got the story of what happened, he shook his head and demanded to be taken to the scene of the crime, where he would add a few touches of his own, such as draping a towel over Jay Sebring's head. The important point to remember is that Manson did not go to any other houses that night; he did not rob anyone else, and there was no further attempt that day to raise any money for Mary Brunner's bail. In fact, he let Brunner stay in jail for quite some time, when it would have been easy enough for him and his crew to raise the bail money through their usual methods. Once again, money was not the issue, and robbery was not the motive.

Manson knew the house well. He had been there with Terry Melcher. He saw Sharon Tate on one visit to the house after Melcher left. He knew Abigail Folger from his days in San Francisco. It's possible he knew Frykowski as well, since

Frykowski was Abigail Folger's lover and also because Frykowski was running drugs in Los Angeles, much to the discomfort of some long-standing dealers. He would have been the perfect person to use to take care of Frykowski, since the dealers would have known of Manson's relationships to the house and its inhabitants.

But other things went on at the Tate house, any of which could have provided a motive for murder. Witnesses have come forward to say that hokey satanic rituals took place there, some of which were filmed. Was this only some Hollywood Halloween kinkiness, a bunch of people dressing up in robes and chanting nonsense for fun? Or was there actual cult influence on Cielo Drive? As for film, police did confiscate one film from Cielo Drive showing Sharon Tate and Roman Polanski making love, which they then returned. Another witness has insisted that group sex was a feature of the Tate residence, sex that involved numerous celebrities, but which would also include strangers picked up in the clubs or along Sunset Strip or Santa Monica Boulevard. Jay Sebring was known to have a predilection for kinky sex, and was found to be in possession of bondage equipment. Dennis Hopper, as noted above, claimed LAPD told him of the existence of bondage, sado-masochism and bestialty films connected with the case. And, of course, they were all doing all sorts of drugs.

None of this is grounds for slaughter, certainly. Today, much of what was just described could be found in thousands of homes across America; but in the pre-VCR days, average citizens did not videotape each other having sex. There was no such equipment available to the general public. What did exist was extremely expensive and hard to come by, and required at least some training in its use. Further, the films taken would have to be developed at a film lab, so one needed pretty good connections to get "questionable" material processed, although that was usually not a problem for those already in the film industry (as this author can himself attest). Once the VCR and the video camera became ubiquitous in America, however, people began filming each other in various sexual states with reckless abandon, even selling the product on the open market as "amateur" films; this has only increased with the easy availability of basic desktop computer equipment, digital video cameras and multimedia software. Imagine, however, the heady intensity of those days in 1969 when only a handful of people had the capability to film each other, people associated with the film industry itself. The temptation to do so was overwhelming.

The author has no doubt that numerous "private" films were made in those days, films of sex, certainly, and possibly of torture and murder as well. The FBI has consistently reported that there is no evidence for the existence of "snuff films," that it is an urban legend, and we have to respect their statements on this. If anyone should know, the FBI should know. However, it is simply untrue that no one to date has filmed a murder.

The Son of Sam investigation has revealed—according to Maury Terry—that some films were made of specific killings. We also know for a certainty that serial killers Leonard Lake and Charlie Ng of northern California in the 1980s *did* videotape the torture and death of their victims, of which twenty were found buried around their cabin in Calaveras County. Leonard Lake—a former Marine who had served in Vietnam—considered himself a pagan, a worshipper of Odin, and was involved in creating the famous "unicorn" exhibit at the Barnum and Bailey Circus in 1984. With sexual tastes that were exclusively sadistic, he was involved in the pornography business, making films of women who were tied up and tortured. Later, he turned his pornographic fantasies into reality, and wound up killing his victims on camera and taking still photos of their corpses before burial. (He committed suicide with a cyanide capsule while in the custody of the San Francisco Police Department in 1985, before the police even knew his real name.)

Thus, "snuff" films *do* exist; whether they exist in the marketplace as a commodity is, of course, highly doubtful. Whatever does exist may be held either as blackmail material (real or potential) or for viewing by selected individuals. With the advent of the video camera, everyone can share in the magic of Hollywood; horror has become democratized, and the only question is whether your filmmaker neighbor is the future Wes Craven, John Carpenter . . . or Leonard Lake.

News of the Tate homicides broke later that day when housekeeper Winifred Chapman arrived and found the bodies. The story of the hideous crime made instant headlines all over the United States and the rest of the world. Many individuals with guilty consciences immediately went into hiding, believing themselves next on the hit list even though the police had no leads and did not know the motive for the crime. The drug trade in Hollywood and the rest of Los Angeles was severely affected, as drugs were the first thing on everyone's mind, and homicide detectives began leaning on their informants all over town. Cult murder was not ruled out, either, nor were starlets, studio executives, and movie stars with connections to Polanski, Tate, Frykowski, and Folger. Due to Sharon Tate's husband, some people were of the opinion that the murders were somehow related to Polanski's film *Rosemary's Baby*, perhaps in reprisal by some offended coven or secret lodge. There was also the possibility that John Phillips of The Mamas and The Papas was involved; Polanski had once slept with Phillips' wife, the singer and now actress Michelle Phillips, and Phillips was angry over that. Polanski actually considered John Phillips the prime suspect and investigated him on his own, coming up empty. Then there was a substantial rumor pointing to what Ed Sanders calls a "voodoo cult" operating from Jamaica. Polanski went down to Jamaica to check it out, and again came up empty.

The Jamaican angle is interesting because Canadian drug dealer Billy Doyle, who was beaten at the Tate house only days before the killings, was known to have flown drugs into the United States from Jamaica specifically. The idea was that Doyle had arranged the killings as retribution for the treatment he received on Cielo Drive, and contracted a cult of killers from Jamaica to do the deed. This only fits what we know of the crime if we maintain that the Jamaican cult then sub-contracted the hit to a known local cult, the Manson Family. There is no evidence to support this, of course, and one suspects it would have been easier for Doyle to go direct to Manson with the contract.

Manson himself has said that the real motive behind the Tate killings would never be revealed (by him), but that it was so explosive it would rock the establishment. One tends to believe Manson in this instance, perhaps because of his personal code of honor which stipulates that one never rats or informs on another criminal, and perhaps because he has never tried to use this information to get himself better treatment in prison. Of course, the reverse may also be true: that Manson has no information to trade. But Manson's own public self-identification with Robert Moore de Grimston of the Process Church of the Final Judgment—and the Church's subsequent visit to Manson, after which Manson no longer said a word about the Process—has opened a can of worms, a deep and unsettling suspicion that just won't go away.

More murders were committed in the coming weeks and months, as the police investigation went nowhere. The day after the Tate killings, Leno and Rosemary LaBianca were killed in their home after being tied up by Manson, who then left and ordered his minions to perform the actual homicides. Again, if robbery was the motive then they were pretty poor thieves, since they left jewelry and valuables worth many thousands of dollars all over the house, including a coin collection. Leno LaBianca's phone had been tapped, as it was later discovered by police, and the supposition is that the wiretap was federal and somehow connected to a famous bookie—known as The Phantom—who lived on the same street as the LaBiancas. Were the LaBiancas killed because the mob believed they were giving information to the Feds, when actually the information came from a wiretap? This doesn't seem likely, as the Phantom did not move from his home until *after* the LaBianca killings, indicating he did not have foreknowledge. Yet, he *did* move, and soon after the murders, indicating he at least knew the LaBiancas and was afraid of being dragged into the investigation, or that he had a snitch inside the police department who told him of the phone tap and its implications.

The LaBianca killings were the most cultic. It was at LaBianca that the police first came across the term "Helter Skelter" used in connection with the murder spree, as this phrase was written on the wall in blood, along with the word "Rise." The word "War" was carved into Leno LaBianca's stomach; and a serving fork was stuck into it as a final touch. Leno was killed first, within range of his wife; when they found him later, the police noticed a knife stuck in his neck along with the serving fork in his stomach.

That night, August 9th to August 10th, Manson, Tex Watson, Linda Kasabian, Susan Atkins, Patricia Krenwinkel and Steve Grogan had all piled into the car. Manson was going to show the murder crew how it was done. This time, they drove aimlessly through Pasadena for a long time, up and down streets, until finally

Manson stopped in front of one house, got out of the car, and then returned a few minutes later having decided not to "do" that house, making the whole thing look random. (One wonders if they passed the house where Sirhan's family lived; or Jack Parsons' old neighborhood.) He next stopped at a church, which was locked.

Then, they drove directly to the Los Feliz section of Los Angeles, to a house on Waverly Drive. Incredibly, Linda Kasabian had been to the house next door back in June of 1968 for a "peyote party."[29] She panicked, thinking that Manson was going to break into that house. Instead, Manson said "No, the house next door." The one at 3267 Waverly Drive.

This was the real target.

Manson went into the house first, armed with a sword. He tied up Leno and his wife with leather thongs, took Mrs. LaBianca's wallet, and then left the house. He went back to the car, and ordered Tex Watson, Patricia Krenwinkel and Leslie Van Houten into the house to kill the two people; kill them, but don't frighten them.

He would leave in the car with Susan Atkins and Linda Kasabian; the others, when they were through with the slaughter, would hitchhike back to Spahn Ranch.

The three killers went into the house, saw the terrified couple tied up in the living room, and then went into the kitchen to select a long serving fork and a serrated knife. They separated the two people, and the girls took Rosemary LaBianca into a bedroom while Tex Watson kept Leno LaBianca in the living room. The girls placed a pillow case over her head and tied her neck with a lamp cord, shoving her face down on the bed. Then her husband began to scream.

Tex Watson had ripped off Leno LaBianca's pajama top and began stabbing him repeatedly. Leno's hands were still tied behind him, and he couldn't maneuver himself away from the berserk killer. He was stabbed four times in the throat and four times in the abdomen with the serrated knife from the kitchen, with a pillow over his face to muffle the screams. The kitchen knife was stuck in his neck in a brutal recreation of the murder of Manson's uncle, Darwin Orell Scott, a few months earlier in Ashland, Kentucky. Blood was everywhere in the living room.

Rosemary LaBianca heard the screams and struggled with the two women, dropping to the floor and crawling to the living room. The women stopped her, and began stabbing her, severing her spinal cord. She bore forty-two stab wounds when it was all over, mostly from Patricia Krenwinkel at first and later from Tex and Leslie Van Houten.

Tex then returned to the body of Leno LaBianca and carved the word "War" into his abdomen. Patricia Krenwinkel took the serving fork and stabbed both bodies with it, leaving it finally in the stomach of Leno LaBianca. Then, in his blood, they wrote "DEATH TO PIGS" on one wall, and "RISE" on another. In the kitchen, on the refrigerator, they wrote "HEALTER SKELTER," a rather strange misspelling.

They wiped down the house for fingerprints, took a communal shower to wash off the blood, then they went back to the kitchen to get something to eat. They were hungry.

Meanwhile, Manson, Steve Grogan, Susan Atkins and Linda Kasabian drove to a gas station to place Rosemary LaBianca's wallet in the rest room, hoping that a black person would find it and use the credit cards, thus placing the blame squarely on the Black Panthers. It would be months before the wallet was ever discovered, however.

In the meantime, there was a spontaneous plan to kill someone else that night, an actor living in Venice who had portrayed the role of Lebanese poet Kahlil Gibran in a movie, a person known to Linda Kasabian. They stopped in front of his apartment house, and Manson handed her a pocket knife after showing her how to use it to kill someone. Then he left in the car.

Kasabian, not willing to kill anyone, pretended to knock on his door, but she knew it was the wrong apartment. When the actor did not show up, she went back to Atkins and Grogan with the news and they continued on their way, hitchiking back to the Spahn Ranch.

Watson, Krenwinkel and Van Houten also hitchhiked back to the Ranch. Their only spoils from the murders: a handful of foreign coins not worth more than a few dollars they found in a small bag. Once again, robbery was not the motive. Mary Brunner in jail for stolen credit cards was not the motive. Bobby Beausoleil in jail for the murder of Gary Hinman was not the motive. These were either contract hits, taken on by Manson for reasons undisclosed to this time, or we have to believe that they were the opening salvos in Manson's dream of igniting a race war.

If the latter, then why did the high-profile murders suddenly stop? While many more murders were committed in the days and weeks to follow, they were low-profile attacks on members of the Family who knew too much . . . or on Scientologists for some strange reason also yet to be divulged. Steve Grogan, who had been to the LaBianca residence with Manson, was pursued by the Scientologists, who believed he had information on Manson of value to them, according to an internal Scientology memo dated 22 June 1970, just after the start of the trial. The memo does not state why the Church was interested in Manson, but it does go on to report on the conversion of Manson to Scientology while in prison with Lanier Raimer (called in the memo "Lafayette Raimer") at McNeil Island. The memo confirms that Raimer's wife was "in training here at the L.A. Org in 1965–66; she had disconnected from Raimer." Obviously, if Manson was involved with Scientology, then the Church of Scientology was very eager to find out how, and to what extent, so that they could perform some damage control.

But was Manson—through his famous "Family"—behind the series of killings of Scientology members and others close to the investigation that began in 1969 and which extended to the deaths around the Son of Sam killings in the late 1970s, murders that were variously described as "retaliation" killings or even as damage control?

Item: October 31, 1969. Halloween. Sharon Tate friend Steve Brandt attempts suicide in Los Angeles, over fear of a hit list with him on it. He survives, only to succeed a month later in New York City.[30]

Item: November 16, 1969. At almost the same location where the body of Marina Habe was discovered on January 1, 1969, the body of another young woman was found. She had been stabbed 157 times. She was identified as "Sherry" by Ruby Pearl, a horse wrangler who worked at the Spahn Ranch. Nothing else is known about her, or who killed her so brutally, leaving her roughly where Marina Habe, similarly stabbed, had been left.

Item: November 21, 1969. Los Angeles. The bodies of two teenagers were found in an alley; they had each been stabbed more than fifty times. The eldest, Doreen Gaul (19) was a Scientology "clear" who had been living at the Church of Scientology. The boy, James Sharp, was only fifteen, but also a Scientology member. They had been killed with a long knife or bayonet (or sword) somewhere else and dumped in the alley. The crime has not been solved. It was claimed that Doreen Gaul was a former girlfriend of Scientologist and convicted Manson Family killer Bruce Davis, but this has never been confirmed. It is known that Davis flew to London that month and did not surface again until the following year.

Item: December 1, 1969. The anniversary of Aleister Crowley's death. Charles Manson—captured by police on the anniversary of Crowley's birth, October 12, 1969—has now been publicly associated with the Tate/LaBianca murders in a press conference given on this day in Los Angeles. On the same day, in London, Sandy Good's former husband—Joel Pugh—is found naked and dead in a hotel room where he had been living since that October. His wrists had been slashed, as had his neck. He was living on the ground floor, with window access to the street. The police cleared the incident as suicide and did not investigate further, even though there was writing on the mirror and other written materials in the room. They didn't even bother taking fingerprints. The possibility that this was murder cannot be ruled out. Bruce Davis was in England at this time, and was naturally acquainted with both eminent Family member Sandy Good and her husband. Was Joel Pugh another man who knew too much?

As we will see later, more murdered Scientologists turn up in the Son of Sam investigation.

These killings took place in an atmosphere of reprisal and damage control—murders committed *by* Family members or *on* Family members—after the Tate and LaBianca killings. One of these was of Donny Shea, who was murdered and buried at the Spahn Ranch on or about August 25, 1969; it was Steve Grogan (aka "Clem") who eventually led police to the site. Shea is believed to have known Manson and Abigail Folger as early as 1967, when Manson was first released and living in San Francisco. It is believed he was killed simply because he knew too much of Manson's past and his links to the Tate residence. The murder was made easier because Shea had been agitating to get the Family moved from Spahn Ranch, as they were bad for the Ranch's business of renting horses.

On November 5, 1969 Family member John Philip Haught (aka "Zero") was killed playing Russian roulette with a loaded gun in a house in Venice, California. When the gun was examined by police, it was discovered that it had no fingerprints. Bruce Davis was present at the time, but an informer stated that one of the women had killed Haught. No one believed that Haught killed himself while playing Russian roulette with the loaded revolver, but the case was carried as a suicide as there were many witnesses—all Family members—who insisted that this was the case.

Without going further into all the minutiae of the case, it is enough to report that the Manson Family was raided on October 12, 1969 for reasons unrelated to the Tate and LaBianca killings. As noted, this is Aleister Crowley's birthday, a day celebrated by many of the cults that adhere to his teachings. It is also, of course, Columbus Day. Yet, it would not be until December 1, 1969—the anniversary of Crowley's *death*—that the Los Angeles police would come to the conclusion that the people they had in custody were responsible for the Tate and LaBianca killings, a conclusion based largely on jailhouse talk by Susan Atkins to another inmate, as well as corroborating testimony by people close to the Family . . .and by Linda Kasabian, who turned state's evidence and told in detail about both the Tate and LaBianca killings.

One interesting detail—noted almost in passing in Polanski's autobiography—is that someone at LAPD suspected the Manson Family in the Tate killings long before any such suspicions were made known, and had indeed connected them to the Hinman killing. Lieutenant Bob Helder had made it known to Polanski (soon after Sharon Tate's funeral, and therefore sometime in August) that they were looking at "a possible lead involving a bunch of hippies living in the Chatsworth area under a commune leader, 'a crazy guy who calls himself Jesus Christ.'"[31] Had this lead been followed up immediately, they might have saved Donny Shea. As it was, Manson was rousted again and again that month on unrelated charges and let go every time.

The trial would begin June 15, 1970 and would last until January 25, 1971, with the penalty phase not over until March 29th of that year. During that time the trial itself would become a microcosm of insanity, as lawyers were hired and fired, as the antics of the accused and their supporters disrupted the courtroom constantly, and as Richard Nixon would proclaim Manson guilty, on August 9, 1970: the first anniversary of the Tate killings *and four years to the day* before he would resign as President in the wake of the Watergate investigation. No matter. When the trial was over, all defendants—Manson, Krenwinkel, Atkins, Leslie Van Houten—were found guilty and sentenced to death; fortunately for them, the death penalty was repealed in California and they wound up with life imprisonment instead.

More trials would take place, however: for Bruce Davis, Bobby Beausoleil, Steven Grogan, Charles "Tex" Watson. All would be found guilty. Bruce Davis turned himself in to authorities on December 2, 1970, a few days after the disappearance of Manson Family trial lawyer Ronald Hughes (to be discussed below), after spending the anniversary of Crowley's death in the sewers beneath Los Angeles. Charles "Tex" Watson—who led the killers in sheer viciousness and rage—was found guilty on October 12, 1971: again, Crowley's birthday. Manson himself was held in a special jail cell on the thirteenth floor at the courthouse, the one that had been specially built the previous year for Sirhan Sirhan.

Manson's lawyer, Irving Kanarek, was a flamboyant attorney with a knack for constant objections, frivolous motions and generally wasting everyone's time. One of the best—possibly apocryphal—stories about him tells of his objection when a witness was asked to state his name. "Objection!" yelled Kanarek. "Hearsay! His mother told him his name." He was, however, an effective trial lawyer in spite of the opprobrium in which he was held by fellow attorneys and judges. Yet, in Manson's case, he had virtually nothing to work with. Manson at one point even attacked the judge, leaping up to the bench, and had to be dragged down and put in chains. Kanarek himself had an odd and suggestive background, for this lawyer of many years practice in the State of California had begun his career as a chemical engineer. A rocket engineer. Specializing in propulsion systems.

It was Kanarek who addressed the court one day during the Easter holiday and, after reading aloud from the New Testament, asked the court if they really knew for certain that Charles Manson was *not* Jesus Christ?

Kanarek eventually had some sort of nervous breakdown years later, and wound up in a mental institution for a short time even as he was being sued. And even though his opponents knew where he was at the time, they didn't inform the judge as to Kanarek's whereabouts. Even so, he was one of the lucky ones. Another Manson attorney was not so lucky.

Ronald Hughes became Leslie Van Houten's attorney, even though he had no trial experience.[32] Manson's approach to litigation was unusual, to say the least. He was not particularly interested in going free or in getting a vigorous—or even a barely effective—defense. He was more interested in making his message known, in converting the judge, the lawyers, the jury and the rest of the world to his way of thinking. He was also insistent on the "Family" staying together and providing a united front. To these ends, the lawyers he chose were more representative of his personal, mystical agenda than they were of an attempt to beat the system. The selection of Irving Kanarek and Ronald Hughes was reflective of this. Kanarek could be counted upon to say the most amazing things during the trial, even going so far as to openly wonder if perhaps Manson really was Jesus Christ. Ronald Hughes, as a man totally unprepared for a murder trial, was the perfect choice—to Manson's way of thinking—to defend Leslie Van Houten, who was on trial for the

LaBianca murders only. Initially, there was an attempt to separate Van Houten's defense from the rest of the Manson Family, but that was shot down even though it may have given her a better chance. The important thing was to keep the Family together, both in the courtroom and outside. What they did not need was a savvy trial attorney pulling all sorts of tricks that would get some of them off and leave the rest behind. If Manson was going down, they were all going down.

Outside the courtroom, Lynette Fromme was doing her best to hold the Family together. She became the nucleus of what was left of the Manson cult, and ostensibly the one who transmitted Charlie's orders to the rest of the clan, orders that resulted in the deaths of several more people. Orders that resulted—according to Sandy Good—in the death of attorney Ronald Hughes, the "first of the retaliation murders."[33]

At a break in the trial on the weekend of November 27, 1970 Ronald Hughes decided to go camping at Sespe Hot Springs, something he did quite often. The springs are about two hours drive northwest of Los Angeles. Hughes would go up there on a Friday night and stay until Sunday. That weekend, the weekend before he was to begin his portion of the trial involving Leslie van Houten, he disappeared.

He was last seen alive on Saturday, apparently in good health and good spirits. There had been a flash flood that weekend, and speculation was that he was stranded. The people who had driven him up that weekend were found, and they claimed that they left early because of the rain but that Hughes wanted to stay longer. They themselves became stranded when their car got caught in the mud, and they had to hitchhike back to Los Angeles.

This was something of a problem for the trial, of course, with Miss Van Houten insisting she wanted no other attorney than Hughes. Eventually, the court appointed another attorney for her and the trial proceeded. The new lawyer was determined to do what he could to save Van Houten, which sent Manson into a rage. His plan was to have Van Houten testify against herself and in favor of Manson, to exonerate him, and her new lawyer was having none of it. The judge insisted that new counsel be found for Leslie Van Houten in spite of everyone's objections. That was on December 2, 1970. That same day, Bruce Davis and his current girlfriend and Manson Family member Brenda McCann (Nancy Pitman) surrendered to authorities. This raised a great deal of suspicion in the minds of defense and prosecution attorneys alike. Vincent Bugliosi, the lead prosecutor, felt sure that the events were related. Why would Bruce Davis—who was wanted for two murders (Hinman and Shea)—turn himself in when the police had no idea where he was? And surrender only a few days after the equally suspicious disappearance of Leslie Van Houten's defense attorney? And on the same day that the judge decided that she needed a new lawyer? It seemed obvious to many people that Manson was behind the strategy, possibly designed to create a mistrial.

Hughes had become increasingly independent over the course of the trial. It seemed certain that he would call Leslie Van Houten to the stand with the intent to crucify Manson, when Manson wanted the reverse to take place. In addition, Hughes feared Manson, and Manson knew this. Everyone knew it. Hughes made no secret of the fact that Manson scared him, but he was going to do what he had to do as an attorney to provide the best possible defense for his client. His client was not Charles Manson; it was Leslie Van Houten.

His body was reported discovered on the last day of the trial, badly decomposed and face down in a pool of water. The decomposition was so bad that an autopsy revealed very little. It was believed at first that he had simply been caught by the flash flood and drowned. Although many had their suspicions, they had no evidence and no eyewitnesses to work with.

Yet, when filmmaker Laurence Merrick was making his own documentary film on the Manson Family, Sandra Good told him—in front of a witness—that Ronald Hughes was murdered. The timing of the murder was, of course, highly suggestive of a motive: to keep him from doing his duty before the jury that coming Monday and defending Van Houten at the expense of Manson. This is essentially what Sandra Good confirmed.

Merrick's film, *Manson*, was nominated for an Academy Award in 1973. Merrick had been an acting coach for Sharon Tate, and had easy access to the Family members who were still at large. He was shot to death at his studio in Hollywood in 1977.

Family members were still involved in murder and attempted murder. Brenda McCann, aka Nancy Pitman, was arrested on November 11, 1972 in Stockton, California. Brenda had been Bruce Davis' girlfriend, with whom she had been on the lam in the Los Angeles sewers for months before they turned themselves in during December 1970. This time, she was found in a house which contained a body buried in the basement, that of Lauren Willett (19), who had been shot in the head. Along with McCann were two members of the Aryan Brotherhood, as well as another woman named Priscilla Cooper (21). Both women had X's carved into their foreheads, identifying them as Manson Family members. What alerted police to the house was the fact that a car parked outside belonged to a man who had been murdered a few days earlier in Northern California. James T. Willett was a former Marine, and had been found in his Marine uniform: killed with a shotgun and decapitated. As the police were busy arresting the four people in the house—which contained a small arsenal of weapons—Lynette "Squeaky" Fromme called and asked to be picked up, evidently in the slain Mr. Willett's car. The police were only too happy to oblige.

The motive for the murders remains unknown to this day. It is known that the Willetts had been associates of the Family for some time, at least a year if not longer according to Bugliosi.[34] Bugliosi also wondered if James and Lauren Willett were the same James and Lauren who had driven Ronald Hughes to his campsite; if so, their deaths would be in accord with the Family's tradition of murder-as-cover-up. Bugliosi was unable to find the original James and Lauren, who had long since moved from their last known address. Eventually, the two men of the Aryan Brotherhood confessed to the crimes and were sentenced, as were Nancy Pitman and Priscilla Cooper. There was nothing to hold Lynette Fromme, so she was set free.

And in September 1975, she attempted the assassination of President Gerald Ford in Sacramento, California. She was convicted and has spent all her life since then in prison, except for an escape attempt from the Federal Correctional Institute at Alderson, West Virginia during the Christmas holidays of 1987, when she heard a rumor that Manson had contracted cancer. She was found in the woods a few days later, and brought back to the prison. In 1989, Lynette Fromme was transferred to Marianna, Florida.

Ruth Ann Moorehouse, a young native of Minot, North Dakota, whose father tried to rescue her from Manson but who later became a devotee was involved in a bizarre attempt to murder a witness, one Barbara Hoyt, in Hawaii.

Barbara Hoyt (17) had been with the Family since April of 1969. She was present at Spahn Ranch when Donny Shea was murdered, and heard his screams. She was told by Ruth Moorehouse (known as "Ouisch") of ten additional murders they had committed besides the Tate and LaBianca killings. She had heard so much at the ranch—and also at other Manson hideouts such as the Barker Ranch in Death Valley—that she was an important material witness and could tie together names, dates and places.

Barbara Hoyt agreed to cooperate with the authorities and act as a witness in the trial against Manson and company, even though she was afraid for her life. However, before she could testify, Lynette "Squeaky" Fromme, Ruth Ann "Ouisch" Moorehouse, Catherine "Gypsy" Share and Steve "Clem" Grogan convinced her to go to Hawaii instead. Barbara agreed to leave California jurisdiction and hide out in Hawaii until the trial was over. It seemed like the line of least resistance. That was on September 6, 1970.

She flew to Honolulu with Moorehouse and stayed in the penthouse suite at the Hilton Hawaiin Village Hotel.[35] Like so many assassins who figure in American history over the past hundred years, they had first class travel accommodations and no indication exists of where the money came from. The same time every morning, Ouisch would leave the hotel and make a call to the Family from a pay phone. On the morning of September 9th, she was summoned back to California and given certain other instructions. She made arrangements to fly back that afternoon, but Barbara Hoyt was to remain behind in Hawaii.

They went to the airport together, and Ouisch suggested to Hoyt that she eat something, even though Ouisch herself wasn't hungry. Barbara ordered a hamburger, and Ouisch carried the tray to a table while Barbara stood in line at the cash register to pay for it.

By the time Barbara had returned to the table, Ouisch had laced the burger with a lethal dose of LSD.

Ouisch—Ruth Ann Moorehouse—then boarded her flight, leaving the now disoriented Barbara Hoyt alone in the airport. Hoyt began to feel very strange, and started wandering around and then running into the street. She was found sprawled outside in traffic, and rushed to the emergency room where her life was saved. After that incident, she was eager to testify against the Family.

Catherine "Gypsy" Share was not to be outdone. Her parents had been members of the French resistance against the Nazis during the Second World War, and had been executed. She was raised by a foster father in the United States, and had become an accomplished violinist . . . as well as a dedicated Communist. When she finally met the Manson Family, her Communist beliefs became muted, as she adopted more and more of the Manson philosophy and actually found herself marrying one of the pro-Nazi Aryan Brotherhood. It was Catherine Share who appeared in the soft-porn film *Ramrodder* with fellow Mansonite Bobby Beausoleil, both appearing as Indians and Bobby as a murdering warrior with a knife.

As the trial against Manson progressed, Share and the other members of the Family began developing practical relationships with members of the Aryan Brotherhood, a racist prison gang that has been implicated in all sorts of violence both inside and outside prison walls. In this case, it was an attempt to spring Manson from jail by first robbing a store that sold weapons. On August 21, 1971, Catherine Share and Mary Brunner—along with four men who were also Family members and in at least once instance (Kenneth Como) a member of the Aryan Brotherhood—robbed the Western Surplus Store in the Hawthorne section of Los Angeles of roughly 140 guns, storing them in a van parked in the alley behind the shop. The LAPD had been called to the scene by a silent alarm, and a gunfight ensued in which seventy rounds were fired. No one was injured, and the six Manson Family members were arrested.

It was later discovered that the attempted theft of the surplus store was part of a larger plot to free Manson by hijacking a 747 and killing hostages until he was freed. During the trial, one of the accused—Kenneth Como—managed to escape by sawing through the bars on his cell on the thirteenth floor. He was picked up by Sandy Good, but Sandy smashed up the van and Como fled on foot. He was apprehended a few hours later.

Eventually, Catherine Share would get ten years to life, Mary Brunner would get twenty to life, Kenneth Como fifteen to life, and the others various sentences. Catherine Share would later marry Kenneth Como. Mary Brunner—the very first Family member and the father of Manson's son Valentine Michael—served six and half years, and is now living under an assumed name in the Midwest. Valentine Michael—named after a character in the famous Heinlein novel

Stranger in a Strange Land—is alive and well and wants nothing to do with his father. (He was the subject of a series of articles and interviews in *Nerve* magazine.) Catherine Share eventually divorced Como, and has turned a new leaf, distancing herself completely from Manson and the rest of the Family. One of the other Hawthorne robbery culprits, Family member Dennis Rice, is now an ordained Christian minister, as are two of his sons, who were "Manson children" at Spahn Ranch.

THE MANSON-NIXON LINE (WITH COMPLIMENTS TO ROBIN WILLIAMS)

Readers may wonder why I took so much space to outline the history of the Manson Family. Readers of Book One know I have focused on it since the beginning of this study, which concerns, after all, the identification of the sinister forces that have influenced American life, culture and politics since the earliest days of our history. I trust that my purpose will become more clear as the chapters progress and my thesis becomes more compelling. This is difficult terrain. This is about evil. Standard appraisals and explanations of evil will not suffice if we are to truly confront it, and vanquish it. As Americans, we have trusted our leaders who have always pointed in another direction every time we were threatened. The American Revolution. The War of 1812. The Mexican War. The Spanish-American War. World War I. World War II. Korea. Vietnam. Grenada. Panama. The Persian Gulf. Afghanistan. Iraq.

The only war fought on our soil in nearly two hundred years was the Civil War, and the fight was over slavery and the right of states to secede from the Union. That war was costly, bloody, and hard fought; but, in a sense, it was too easily won, for when it was over, and the South defeated and the slaves emancipated, we thought we had solved our internal problems. We thought we had solved the problem of slavery. We thought we understood the rights of our citizenry. We thought we were all on the same page in our hymnals. We did not attack root causes. We had treated a symptom of evil, and thank God for it; but we did not banish the sickness from our shores.

Now, in the wake of a horrific attack on the United States—specifically on New York City and the Pentagon—we are faced with another threat, and once again our leaders are pointing abroad. Yet the technology of terror was designed, built, and delivered from the United States, and Charles Manson was—and still is—the epitome of this technology. We have not studied the phenomenon closely; like all good Americans, we have fought the war, captured the enemy, put him behind bars and forgotten all about him. But the demon in the smoke that crawled out of the God Struck Tower on September 11, 2001 bore the face of Charles Milles Manson, the bastard son of America and product of its institutions and—even more importantly—scion of its bartered Soul. This is not easy to understand now;

it will become easier and more certain as we proceed a little longer, for what we are disecting are the limbs, organs and nervous system of the Manson Secret.

Two major strands of American history meet in 1969: Hollywood, with all that the idea of Hollywood implies, and another strand that is much more elusive, more difficult to define with a single word, but which represents the dark nightmare side of politics. We may think of it as Watergate, as long as we remember it includes everything from what Nixon termed "the whole Bay of Pigs thing" to political assassinations, support for Nazi war criminals, right wing military dictatorships, and bags of dirty money. We like to think of these two strands—Hollywood and Watergate—as opposing forces, as Us and Them, but in the strange non-Euclidean geometry of the American psyche, these parallel lines meet in a tight little knot in August 1969.

The technology that had been researched, developed and fine-tuned by our own intelligence services since the end of World War II found its apotheosis in murder and madness. Americans, more than any other people in the world, love their illusions, their dreams, their flowery phrases and idealistic declarations. They have created an entire industry based on illusion: Hollywood. The deep effect that film has had on the human psyche has yet to be analyzed or even sufficiently addressed. We err if we believe that film is only stagecraft made more brilliant, more accessible. Stagecraft itself is a form of occultism, as teachers such as Stanislavski realized at once; cinema is occultism plus light. It is powerful, and it is one of the reasons why so many foreigners hate America with an abiding passion; hate America enough to kill it. The only nation that comes close to America in the intensity of its film industry is India, and India recognizes the power of cinema to the extent that certain types of film are *never* made in that country: x-rated pornography (even kissing is rare) and occult-oriented films. Sex and magic.

American intelligence, on the other hand, plumbed the depths of sex and magic (and drugs) to understand illusion, and to manipulate it and make it a weapon. They used the prisons as testing grounds, violent criminals and psychopaths as subjects. They broke through. The seal was broken. And demons were unleashed.

American filmmakers did the same thing. The manipulation of illusion, the challenge to reality that takes place in a movie theater, may only be momentary, an hour or two in a darkened temple before the icon screen of transmitted light; but its effects are long-lasting. Hence, the propaganda film.

Maybe all films are propaganda films. Our enemies certainly see it that way; and maybe we don't know our own strength. We never learned how to use this medium in the most efficient way. Like the mad scientists of MK-ULTRA, we play with the technology, test it, write it up in reports; people like Charles Manson take it and sharpen it.

Richard Nixon was born and raised within spitting distance of Hollywood and the back lots. He spoke in terms of theater, of acting. He met his wife on the stage. His policies paved the way for another actor to become President. He consulted psychics and preachers, and toyed with converting to Catholicism. He protected Nazis who pretended to be priests. He understood the power of illusion, and the manipulation of reality. He was open about it. He counseled others in the philosophy of deceit; because lies and truth are all relative when it comes to power.

Power, to people like Manson and Nixon, is the only reality, the only absolute. Nixon *had* to proclaim Manson guilty to the press; he had to address the one other man in the country who understood power, and truth, and evil, and murder the way he did. On the plane of the real world as understood by the media and the public at large, Manson was an insignificant crook compared to Nixon, the President of the United States, undeserving of the President's attention or comment; but on another plane, Manson and Nixon were warring black magicians, fighting over airtime and the fifteen-second sound bite. Manson was manipulating illusion, and that was supposed to be Nixon's forte.

Manson may be virtually illiterate, but no one doubts his intelligence. He was a natural at what he did; his followers are now more numerous—more than thirty years after the Tate and LaBianca killings—than they ever were before. He has attracted support from racist, right-wing, and neo-Nazi organizations all over the world. It is not the intention of this author to state unequivocally that Manson was created in prison labs by the G-scale engineers of MK-ULTRA; but he could be the Mind-Control Poster Boy of 1969.

The "Manson-Nixon line" is a term coined by Robin Williams, the actor and comedian, as a pun on the Mason-Dixon Line, which separated the Northern and Southern states in nineteenth century America, with the newer version separating two different states of mind. Yet I sense something more profound in Williams' turn of phrase: Manson and Nixon as the Alpha and Omega of a scarlet thread running through the American soul, a Great Divide separating Americans from each other, and from the rest of the world, and from what they know to be good, honest and virtuous. A thread of expediency, cynicism, pragmatic choices and *realpolitik* where the end justifies the means . . . and sometimes, not even that.

When, as detailed in *The Nine*, Frank Olsen was pushed out the window of the Statler Hotel in New York City in 1953 and fell ten stories to his death, he was the first of those who fell from the doomed World Trade Center almost fifty years later. The technology that destroyed him created the terrorists of Abu Nidal, Hamas, Hezbollah, and Al-Qaida. He—and they and so many others—were victims of the Manson Secret.

ENDNOTES

1 Kenneth D. Wald, *Religion and Politics in the United States*, Washington, DC 1992, p. 42
2 George Plimpton, editor, *Beat Writers at Work*, Modern Library, NY, 1999, p. 225
3 Norman Mailer, *An American Dream*, Flamingo, NY, 1965, p. 205
4 R.T. Rundle Clark, *Myth and Symbol in Ancient Egypt*, Thames and Hudson, NY 1991, p. 115
5 Ibid., p. 115
6 John Marks, *The Search for the "Manchurian Candidate,"* Times Books, NY, 1979, p. 211
7 Martin A. Lee & Bruce Shlain, *Acid Dreams*, Grove Weidenfeld, NY, 1992, p. 18
8 Ed Sanders, *The Family*, EP Dutton, NY, 1971, p. 122
9 Vincent Bugliosi with Curt Gentry, *Helter Skelter*, Bantam, NY, 1995, p. 647
10 Ward Churchill & Jim Vander Wall, *The COINTELPRO Papers*, South End Press, Boston, 1990, p. 205
11 Ibid., p. 207
12 Frank J. Donner, *The Age of Surveillance*, Vintage, NY, 1981, p. 248
13 John Gilmore & Ron Kenner, *Manson: The Unholy Trail of Charlie and the Family*, Amok, Los Angeles, 2000, p. 89
14 Ed Sanders, op. cit., p. 262
15 Ibid., p. 262
16 Maury Terry, *The Ultimate Evil*, Bantam, NY 1989, p. 596
17 Ibid., p. 594
18 Roman Polanski, *Roman*, William Morrow, NY, 1984, p. 313, 314
19 Ibid., p. 315
20 Ibid., p. 315
21 Ibid., p. 312
22 Ibid., p. 323
23 Maury Terry, *The Ultimate Evil* (Revised Edition), Barnes & Noble, NY, 1999, p. 533; Ed Sanders, *The Family*, (Revised Edition), Signet, NY, 1989, p. 57
24 Terry, (revised edition) op. cit., p. 534
25 Sanders, (revised edition) op. cit., p. 232
26 Ibid., p. 242
27 John Phillips with Jim Jerome, *Papa John: An Autobiography*, Dell, NY, 1986, p. 299
28 Sanders, (revised edition), op. cit., p. 307
29 Bugliosi, op. cit., p. 363
30 Phillips, op. cit., p. 309
31 Polanski, op. cit., p. 315
32 Jess Bravin, *Squeaky: The Life and Times of Lynette Alice Fromme*, St Martin's Press, NY, 1997, p. 111
33 Bugliosi, op. cit., p. 652
34 Ibid., p. 650
35 Ibid., p. 474

"The Massacre of Antioch" by Gustave Doré—This intense wood engraving depicts the grisly aftermath of the city's capture by Crusader forces in 1098. The scene underscores the ferocity and moral ambiguities of the Crusades, where Latin Christian armies, Muslim powers, and sects like the Nizari Ismailis (the "Assassins") reshaped the politics of the Middle East through siege, alliance, and targeted violence.

BOOK TWO: A WARM GUN

CHAPTER TWELVE

THE ROOTS OF TERRORISM

The Syrian Nizaris, who possessed a vulnerable and small principality in a hostile milieu, made an important impact, quite disproportionate to their numbers or political power, on the regional politics of the Latin East. This was particularly the case when they were led by Rashid al-Din Sinan, their most famous leader and the original 'Old Man of the Mountain.'

—Farhad Daftary, *The Assassin Legends*[1]

Seest thou not that We have set the devils on the disbelievers to confound them with confusion?

—Qur'an, 19:83

Nothing is true; everything is permitted.

—saying attributed to Rashid al-Din Sinan

In early 1947—the same year as Aleister Crowley's death in England, the infamous UFO sighting by Kenneth Arnold, the Roswell crash, and the creation of the CIA—some scrolls were found in the caves of Qumran in what is now Israel. The ramifications of this discovery have yet to be felt by the average man and woman living in the twenty-first century, two thousand years after the scrolls in question were written and hidden in the clay jars of Qumran. More discoveries took place over the intervening years, not only in Qumran but also in Nag Hammadi, a site in Egypt where the first of the "Gnostic Gospels" were discovered in 1945. Taken together, the finds represent the single most important challenge to the accepted belief and dogma of Christianity, and to the historical record of Judaism and even of Islam, which is largely based on Jewish and Christian scripture and tradition. Along another line, the find also represents the accidental revelation of the existence of one of the oldest secret societies in Europe, the Middle East and Central Asia: a society so old, and with secrets so well-kept, we don't even know what to call it. The pieces of those secrets—like a handful of pottery shards on an archaeologist's table—are slowly being assembled into something recognizable, but it may still be years before the whole story is understood, even by scholars. What has been discovered so far, however, has caused eminent historians of Christian, Jewish and Islamic origins to completely reevaluate their thinking.

Barbara Thiering, Elaine Pagels, Hugh Schonfield, J. M. Allegro and Robert Eisenman are some of the mainstream Biblical scholars whose books on the subject of the identity of Jesus, of his brother James, of Simon Magus, of Judas Iscariot, of all of the original apostles, of the gospels (of which there are somewhat more than the usual four), and of various sects, cults, heresies and traditions have formed a kind of "anti-history" that calls into question the last two thousand years of European belief systems, political affairs, and ecclesiastical developments. Allegro, one of the early Dead Sea Scrolls scholars along with Schonfield and Eisenman, also saw a drug connection which he popularized in *The Sacred Mushroom and the Cross* (Doubleday, 1970), a thesis considered scandalous in its time.

These discoveries have made it possible for other studies to be undertaken—usually by popular journalists—that question every facet of accepted knowledge and wisdom concerning the Bible, Church history, medieval history, the Crusades, the religious wars of Europe, and the blood-lines of kings and mystics alike. Books by authors like Michael Baigent, Richard Leigh, Henry Lincoln, Graham Hancock, Christopher Knight and Robert Lomas, Lynn Picknett, Clive Prince, and many others have all followed in the wake of these discoveries, popularizing some of the more arcane data, and sometimes imagining or speculating on the rest. The books by these other authors are usually strong on sources, regardless of how outlandish their conclusions may seem. Obviously serious about their research, they want their theories to be taken seriously. Though what results, quite often, is a great deal of infighting and criticism of each others' work, this does little to dampen the enthusiasm of the reading public for this type of scholarship. It cracks open a door to the inner sanctum of academia, and finally allows the rest of us a glimpse at what our own history may really be like. One such opening began in 1966, when the standard history of the last two thousand years of western civilization was seriously challenged by a renowned scholar—who would eventually be nominated for the Nobel Peace Prize—and the world has not been quite the same since.

I am referring, of course, to the publication of *The Passover Plot* by Dr. Hugh J. Schonfield.

In 1966, America was in the midst of the Johnson Administration and an escalating war in Vietnam. The hippie movement was in flower, and would reach its apotheosis in the Summer of Love in 1967. Martin Luther King and Robert F. Kennedy were still alive. In that year, Dr. Schonfield—an important Biblical scholar and one of the first to examine the Dead Sea Scrolls of Qumran—published a book designed for the general public on what the Dead Sea Scrolls (and other recent research) had to say about the life and death of Jesus. His conclusions were so controversial that even Dr. Schonfield himself characterizes his subject as "the strangest human enterprise in all recorded history."[2] Yet, his conclusions were perfectly in accord with what Middle Eastern and European secret societies have always insisted, even as long ago as the first century A.D., which is that Jesus never died on the cross, but was still alive when he was taken down a bare three hours after having been crucified; or, as some other scholars insist, that he survived the events narrated in the New Testament, and lived to a ripe old age. Naturally, if it could be proved that such was the case, then the entire Christian edifice comes tumbling down, for nothing is as central to Christianity as the item of faith that Christ died on the cross and was resurrected—came back to life, rose from the dead—forty hours later. Schonfield later expanded his findings in a number of other books and papers, including one—*The Essene Odyssey*—which addresses some of the issues concerning the relationship of this Biblical scholarship to later investigations of the Knights Templar and the Freemasons, as developed in *The Holy Blood and the Holy Grail* by Baigent, Leigh and Lincoln.

This latter work (published in the United States in 1982 as *Holy Blood, Holy Grail)* was as controversial in its time as *The Passover Plot* fifteen years earlier. Again, we are told that Jesus did not die on the cross, but that his bloodline survived, even though his descendants were often pursued and persecuted by a Church which could not allow this obvious challenge to orthodoxy to become public knowledge. We are told of Jesus' heirs manifesting as the Merovingian kings, and that the Knights Templar were repositories of the sacred secret of the Holy Blood, the "Sang Real," a secret that was passed down to the Rosicrucians, the Freemasons, etc.

Thus, according to this theory, a political and religious dynasty has existed in hiding for two thousand years and has had an inordinate amount of influence over the progression of world events, as certain select leaders—in politics, religion, science, culture—were brought in on the secret and made members of this intellectual elite, and given the key to understanding the codified mysteries of millenia. While Schonfield did not wholeheartedly support the conclusions of *Holy Blood, Holy Grail*, he did offer his own speculation that the Biblical Jesus wound up far from home. Schonfield tended towards the idea that Jesus wandered out of Palestine, across the Afghan frontier and into the heart of Kashmir, and was buried in a tomb built in accordance with Jewish tradition in the fabled city of Srinagar, where it can be seen today.

That the world—at the time of this writing, in the first decade of the twenty-first century—is on the verge of a horrible world war that could germinate either in Palestine or in Kashmir is satanic testament to the force of religious and political events that transpired in these two regions two thousand years ago, events that have been shrouded in mystery, in propaganda, in fantasy, but whose truths have been carefully preserved by a brotherhood of initiates, passed down in codified form for millenia.

All of the theories of the existence of a secret society of enlightened men, a society that has existed down through the ages, have as their origin either a band of geometers and architects based around the creation of the Egyptian pyramids or a similar guild of craftsmen who were involved in the erection of the Temple of Solomon in Jerusalem . . . and sometimes both (as in the case of the Freemasons).

The technology of architecture and construction was once believed to be sacred, and geometry was held to be a powerful art. The Freemasons still use the square and the compass as their universal symbol of God as the Great Geometer, a reference to their alleged involvement in the creation of some of the world's most enigmatic and compelling monuments including everything from the pyramids to the Temple of Solomon to Chartres Cathedral and the layout of Washington, D.C.

This combination of science and magic, of geometry and *goetia*—at the service of a lawful King—is what makes the idea of an ageless secret society of wise men timeless and still relevant today. In ancient times, this society was probably not secret, since it was in the employ of the State; but as illegitimate rulers became the crowned heads of Europe, the society that once supported the State went (or was driven) underground, and their arcane knowledge went with them. Such is the belief today held by many. When we consider how many American political leaders throughout the past two hundred years were Freemasons—and hence were exposed to these ideas, whether they embraced them or not—then we must ask ourselves if any of these ideas have received confirmation or corroboration from scientific and academic sectors, confirmation that was revealed only at the highest levels of government. One feature of this "lost science" was obviously an item on the agenda of the Central Intelligence Agency, that of occult control of the human mind, consciousness, memory and will.

The Egyptian Pharaohs were at once religious and political leaders; the power they held over their people was absolute. King Solomon is also associated with *occult* power. The grimoires that falsely bear his name—*The Greater Key of Solomon*, *The Lesser Key of Solomon*—are evidence that the association of the name of Solomon with ceremonial magic and the control over demonic forces was taken for granted by centuries of magicians and sorcerers. Solomon was a Jewish king, and the surmise is that this occult power was passed down to generations of holy Jewish leaders, down to the time of Jesus. Some sources attribute the idea of a "genie in a bottle" to the time of Solomon and the building of the Temple: that the spirits he conjured to build the Temple were imprisoned in a jar that had Solomon's Seal upon it, and thus were unable to escape, until at one point the bottle washed up on shore and it was opened by a curious passerby, causing the demons to fly to the four corners of the world. The *Keys* of Solomon are said to be the means whereby these demons may be forced to obey the will of the magician, since they include Solomon's Seal, which is a reminder to them of their time in spiritual "durance vile."

It is further insisted by many that the Knights Templar discovered some of this power during their sojourn on the Temple Mount in the early days of the twelfth century. The precise nature of this discovery is not known. The Ark of the Covenant? The Rod of Aaron? The secret of the Passover Plot? But it seems they did discover *something*.

It would explain a great deal if they had.

THE HASHISH EATERS

Nearly a thousand years ago, the Western world was enthralled by tales of Islamic terrorism, espionage, sabotage and assassination. It was believed that religious fanatics, devotees of a mysterious Islamic leader who lived in an impregnable mountain fortress, had ordered his men to infiltrate enemy cities and assassinate their leaders, Christian and Muslim alike. There was no defense against this secret network of killers. They could show up at any time, anywhere, to carry out their murderous agenda. Even worse, they were not afraid to die, and would gladly undertake suicide missions where their chance of survival was nil. This organization came to be known as the *hashishiyya*, an Arabic word that means "hashish eaters." It was from this word that the European languages derived their word *assassin,* demonstrating a conscious equivalence between this obscure (to the West) religious sect, drugs, and the practice of political murder.

Much of what has been written about the Assassin cult was based on hearsay, rumor, propaganda and innuendo. In reality, the Assassins were an Ismaili sect of Shi'ite Islam, the Nizaris (named after their loyalty to Nizar, an Ismaili Imam they supported against the Fatimid Caliphs), and their penchant for secrecy and disinformation was due in large part to the fact that their faith was proscribed by the predominantly Sunni authorities, as well as by other Shi'ites. While much has been made of stories that the cult used hashish as a means of brainwashing their trained killers, there seems to be very little evidence that this was so. Farhad Daftary, quoted above, is scornful of Western attempts to paint the Nizaris as hashish-gobbling programmed assassins with secret rituals and a hierarchy of degrees. However, even Daftary has a problem explaining why they were specifically referred to as *hashishiyya* by fellow Muslims. He describes a world in the centuries after the death of the Prophet as one in which two main branches of Islam—the Sunni and the Shia—fought for hegemony in the region. The Sunni—as the more orthodox, conservative branch—found the Shia to be heretical in some matters of faith, and treasonous in matters of politics. The Shi'ites believe that Muslims should owe their spiritual allegiance to the blood descendants of the Prophet's family, through his cousin Ali; the Sunni followed the leadership of the Prophet's friend, Abu Bakr. The term "caliph" means "successor," and the Shi'ites believe that the descendants of Ali are the rightful Caliphs, successors to the Prophet, branding the Sunni Caliphates therefore illegitimate.

We may note here that when Grady McMurtry declared himself head of the OTO—as opposed to other contenders abroad in the land—he chose the term "Caliph." For a German-born quasi-Masonic secret society, this doesn't appear to make a great deal of sense, especially when one looks at a blasphemous reference to Muhammad in the *Book of the Law* that would certainly incite a thundering *fatwa* from the throats of the Ayatollahs, if not an outright *jihad*; however, a look at the rituals of the OTO will demonstrate how closely the Order believes itself to be the repository of Middle Eastern secrets. Sadly, the Francis King publication of those rituals has disappeared due to a concerted effort by the OTO to remove them from library and bookstore shelves; a bit like locking the barn door after the horse has been taken out and shot.

In addition to the rightful Caliphs, Shi'ites believe that there are secret teachers, or Imams, who guide the faithful in this world and are the representatives of the Prophet on earth. The mainstream Shi'ites await the return of the last—the twelfth or "hidden"—Imam, which they believe could be imminent, and the more fanatic (or devout, take your pick) will do whatever it takes to ensure that the Imam is incarnated into a world made clean of disbelievers. The Shi'ites of the Ismaili sect—to which belonged the Assassins—had a more complicated millenial belief, which will be discussed below.

Until the return of the Imam, however, the Shi'ite leadership of the day—and specifically the more mystically-inclined Ismailis, from which the Nizari were descended—understood the value of keeping a low profile. The theological differences between Shia and Sunni are not great, but as usual the slightest of differences makes for tremendous internecine violence and bloodshed. It was the arrival of the Crusaders in the eleventh century that exacerbated what was already a bloody conflict, and the Shi'ites (today a minority compared with the rest of Islam, representing about ten percent of the whole) lost no time in figuring out a way to capitalize on the problem and to set Christian and Sunni at each others' throats, playing one side against the other.

The Sunnis had already characterized the Nizaris as "hashish eaters" in their own writings. Daftary suggests that this was due to the use of the term as a pejorative against people of low class: the ignorant rabble. Princeton University Professor Emeritus Bernard Lewis—in a tightly-focused account entitled *The Assassins: A Radical Sect in Islam*—concurs on this important point.[3] Yet, the term seems to be used specifically in reference to the sect of the Nizaris and not in general use as a term to describe other sects or faiths. Thus, while the jury is still out on the real history of the Assassins (there are very few historical documents available, even in Arabic or Farsi, on the development of the sect), we can view what has come down to us over the centuries as the West's perception of this cult and how it may have influenced not only Western intelligence agencies but also the popular imagination of the disaffected Muslim populations of the Middle East. We can also see how rumors of fraternization with the Shi'ites came to condemn those Christian Crusaders who did have secret rituals and a hierarchy of degrees: Crusader knights whose legacy—real or imagined—resulted in the creation of such occult lodges and secret societies as the Freemasons and the OTO.

And, as we shall see, we come full circle in the present day when we examine the case of an American intelligence officer who fell victim to the torture and interrogation practices of a new cult of *fedayeen*, who learned the hated science from the same sources as the West.

Muslims in general find the very concept of Crusader to be offensive. When President George W. Bush referred to the war on terrorism in the wake of the September 11, 2001 attacks on New York and Washington, he called it a "crusade," and immediately evoked the ire of Islamic groups who charged him with a lack of sensitivity on this issue; Islamic militants pointed to the expression as indicative of what they perceived to be Bush's real intention: a holy war against Islam. Thus can a single, simple word so quickly lead to horror.

In fact, the Islamic elements that complained the loudest about Bush's quite natural and unconscious use of the word "crusade"—a word in common English and American use that has referred to all sorts of projects, campaigns, and undertakings—should have known better. The word has been used in the English language for years without any religious connotation, and certainly not in the context of a holy war against anyone or anything. Be that as it may, Muslims themselves use the term *jihad* with reckless abandon, and insist to non-Muslims that it is a neutral term which refers to any type of "extreme effort," or struggle, including a moral or spiritual struggle within oneself. Thus, should the term "crusade" be similarly understood, as any type of all-out effort.

What is worse, however, is the sanctimonious position of Islamic apologists who castigate American political leaders for their use of the term, as if the actual Crusades happened only a few years ago—and not more than six hundred—and were a brutal attack on a peaceful people with no hostile intentions towards the West. Gleeful that Americans—and especially their elected officials—have so little knowledge of history and so little understanding of its importance (notably President Bush, who, as we have often seen, has little awareness of foreign geography or the niceties of foreign policy), they spin stories about supposed Western imperialism against the East and rely upon guilt and sympathy to promote the idea that Islam is a much-maligned and misunderstood faith.

In this day and age of mass communication, video cassette recorders and DVD players, home computers and the Internet, one wonders why Islam is still misunderstood? Is it because Muslim leaders still misunderstand the West? To be sure, it is quite likely that Buddhism, Daoism, Hinduism, Shintoism and other faiths are also misunderstood . . . but Islamic leaders themselves have done nothing to ameliorate the negative image of Islam in the "West," whereas Buddhist, Daoist, etc. leaders have been successful in attracting Westerners to their faiths, as well as in projecting a positive image to those who come across Eastern religions in the news or on their street corners. The Dalai Lama comes to mind. Yet, at the moment, the only coherent image the West has of Islam is as an intolerant, inflexible, anti-feminist, anti-Zionist, anti-American cult of fanatics, whether they are terrorists from the Middle East or followers of Louis Farrakhan in America.

That the first shot was fired against the West by Muslim armies marching on Europe in the eighth century A.D. has been conveniently forgotten. The Prophet was barely cold in his grave before his followers fought, first among themselves, and then against everyone else, as they cut a path through North Africa all the way to Gibraltar and across the Straits into what is now Portugal and Spain, and up to France before being blocked by the armies of Charles Martel in the eighth century A.D. But they did not leave Europe entirely, remaining behind in Iberia and taking Sicily for a while. There were Muslim kingdoms in Europe until 1492, when the Alhambra was liberated from Muhammad XI by the combined armies of Ferdinand and Isabella. Thus, Muslims held sway in Iberia for nearly seven hundred years. The glories of Cordoba and other Muslim cities on the Iberian Peninsula are a matter of historical record.

The progressive attitude towards science and art that contributed so greatly to the Renaissance is what the West *should* know of the flower of Islam. Yet, due to infighting and squabbling among the members of the *ummah*—the Muslim community—there has been no unified effort to promote Islam as a religion of progress, scientific curiosity, and peace. Various Arab nations compete with each other rather than cooperate. The plight of the Palestinians is used as a tool and a weapon to prop up first one Arab regime and then another. Arab intellectualism and Islamic theology is suborned to various national political agendas to the point that there is no unified voice of Islam, and the West only hears from those Muslim spin doctors they fear the most: the terrorists.

During the height of the Moorish kingdoms of Europe, at the very end of the eleventh century A.D., the first Crusades were mounted from France. Troops were sent overland to the Middle East, first to protect Constantinople and the Byzantine Empire from attack by the Seljuk Turks, and then to attack the city of Jerusalem and bring it into Christian hands. The invasion and sack of Jerusalem was brutal, and savage. Thousands of Muslims and Jews were needlessly slaughtered by Christian armies on July 15, 1099. Of this, there can be no doubt, as all records—Christian and Muslim—agree on the details. There followed a see-saw conflict that had the Christians in charge one day, the Muslims the next, for hundreds of years, until the Christians were finally ejected once and for all in the thirteenth century, and Muslim armies were on the march once again into the Balkans under the banner of the Ottoman Empire, an empire that would last until World War I reorganized everyone's priorities.

Thus, the history of Christian-Islamic hostilities is long and complex. Neither side has a monopoly on righteousness where the Crusades—and all they represent—are concerned. At the same time, however, historians agree that Islamic rulers were much more tolerant towards Jews than any Christian empire in Europe ever was, before or since. Christians and Jews were considered "people of the Book," i.e., they were mentioned in the Qur'an as predecessors of Muhammad and were considered "protected" until they could come to their senses and convert to Islam. After all, Islam itself was a religion of conversion, beginning with the Prophet himself and extending to the rest of the Arabian Peninsula before going on the warpath everywhere else. It was not an indigenous faith, growing out of the paganism of Arabia, Mesopotamia and Egypt. It was a syncretist creation of the Prophet, who blended elements of Christianity, Judaism and native Arab practices and beliefs, taking what he liked and ignoring the rest.

The Ka'aba, for instance, is an example of this. This holy shrine in Mecca which all Muslims are required (if possible) to visit at least once in their lives on the special pilgrimage known as the Haj contains a lump of meteoric stone that was worshipped by the pagan Arab population for centuries before the birth of Muhammad. In fact, the annual pilgrimage to Mecca was a feature of Arab life long before the birth of the Prophet. When Muhammad captured Mecca and made it the holy city of Islam that it is today, he removed the 360 pagan idols from the stone's shrine and transformed it into the central icon of the faith. This act has not been studied extensively in the West, and it is hoped that scholarship one day will examine the importance of this artifact and what it really represented to the pagan Arabs and then to Muhammad, and what it means today to his followers.

The fighting between two factions of Islam began after the death of the Prophet on June 8, 632. The Shi'ites, as mentioned, owed their allegiance to the Prophet's cousin, Ali. The vast majority of Muhammad's followers, however, decided to follow his best friend and father-in-law, Abu Bakr. While both factions revere Muhammad and the Qur'an and, to a large extent, the *shari'a* (Islamic law) equally, the differences between the two factions are such that open hostilities have never entirely disappeared in the nearly 1400 years since the Prophet's death. This has been exacerbated by nationalist and tribal fighting among members of the same factions. The conflict was subdued somewhat during the five hundred years of the Ottoman Empire when a large part of the Muslim world was under the political control of the Turks, but of course it didn't go away. With the end of Turkish hegemony in the region in 1918, the Balkanization of the Middle East began, made more problematic by the Balfour Declaration, which eventually led to the creation of the State of Israel in the middle of the newly-liberated Arab territories.

All of these difficulties have as their common origin the history of the ancient Middle East. To understand the Arabs, one must understand Islam. To understand Islam, one must understand the Arabs. Most people do not have sufficient time to undertake the kind of study necessary to bring the Middle East into a focus sharper than that of the cameras of CNN or the dispatches from various desert battlegrounds. They tend, instead, to interpret events through a Christian or Jewish filter, and this plays into the hands of those who would foment discord, hatred and bloodshed. By setting up a Christian–Muslim polarity (or a Jewish–Muslim polarity) they can expect to temporarily unite Muslims of differing backgrounds, culture and traditions against the common enemy. While Muslim leaders have been slow to exploit Western media in an attempt to clarify Islam and Arabism to the non-Muslims of the world, Western leaders have been equally slow to understand and exploit the differences—national, historical, cultural, traditional, sectarian—between the Arab countries and their neighbors, such as Iran, Pakistan, and

Afghanistan. Most Americans, for instance, don't know where the Kurds come into the equation. They don't know who the Druze are, or what their relationship is to Islam. They don't realize that Iranians (for instance) are not Arabs. They don't understand what Muslims are doing in Bosnia. They don't know the difference between a Shi'ite and a Sunni.

When the Crusaders invaded Jerusalem in 1099, they wasted little time in expanding their base further inland and along the Mediterranean coast. Once Jerusalem had become "secured" by Christian forces, a curious band of brothers set off from France to take up residence in Solomon's stables, near the site of Solomon's Temple, urged by the famous Catholic cleric, St. Bernard of Clairvaux. These were the famous Knights Templar, the Knights of Solomon's Temple, spiritual progenitors of the Freemasons and the OTO, and thereby hangs a tale.

As noted above, the Shia split with the Sunnis over the question of legitimate successors to the Prophet. The Shia believed legitimacy lay with Ali and his blood descendants. Thereafter, the Shia split still again; in fact, many times. The Druze are a Shi'ite sect, for instance; in fact, they are very secretive, have an additional set of scriptures and are ostracized by other Muslims for their heretical views. The Ismaili sect of Shi'ism is our focus here, and they split off in their belief that Ismail, the eldest son of Jafar al-Sadiq (the sixth Imam) was the rightful heir of Ali and thus the seventh Imam, whereas the rival Twelvers believed that Ismail's younger brother was the seventh Imam. These Shi'ites—the Twelvers—are the dominant religion in Iran today, and are the largest Shi'ite sect in the world. The Ismailis, on the other hand, developed largely in secret and created a coherent system of faith and thought that was attractive to many social elements in the Middle East, especially the intellectuals on one hand and the disenfranchised on the other.

Ismaili Shi'ism is a kind of Islamic Qabalism. The belief that the Qur'an has both an exoteric (*zahir*) and an esoteric (*batin*) meaning is fundamental to the sect, and this idea of hidden or secret knowledge appealed to many who could not understand why the world was so full of sorrow and misfortune when the Prophet had shown the world the right way of living and worship; certainly, there was some secret knowledge of the world, knowledge that was encrypted in the holiest of books, the Qur'an, for those who were intelligent enough to see beyond the obvious meanings and could divine the hidden truths. (The parallels with the Jewish Qabalistic tradition are obvious.) As scholars such as Barbara Thiering and Hugh Schonfield have demonstrated, the Jewish sect of the Essenes also used code in their writings to disguise important events and the identity of important persons, thus similarly creating two levels of sacred literature: the exoteric and the esoteric. (In fact, it is entirely possible that Essenic beliefs contributed to the creation of the Ismaili doctrine, as the Essenes had spread throughout the region now known as Iran, Iraq, Afghanistan and Pakistan hundreds of years before the birth of Muhammad.)

This type of knowledge could empower the poor, whose only asset was their soul, their passion, and whose only weapon was their belief. It was a form of neo-Platonism believed to have derived from Muslim contact with the Greeks and their philosophical systems, as well as by encounters with Gnosticism, Zoroastrianism, and various Christian sects. It was a syncretist system which still relied on the Qur'an as the final arbiter of spiritual Truth, but which used the various philosophies and sciences of the West as instruments to deepen understanding of the world.

Also, secrecy begets paranoia; the need to seek for hidden answers and conspiracies behind everyday events develops when a social group is suppressed, ostracized or in some other way shoved to the sidelines and no longer "in the loop" of the dominant party, religion, or culture. When one does not know what the other knows—or what the other is doing, or discussing—then speculation leads to suspicion, which can color an entire belief system. This hard-wired paranoia of the Ismailis—and especially of the Nizari sect which became known in the West as the Assassins—contributed to the creation of an intelligence organization unparalleled in the East, and which in turn led to the creation of what were probably the world's first "terrorists."[4]

Central to the Ismaili belief system is the Imam. Ismaili theologians proposed a world of cycles, in which hidden or silent Imams alternated with visible Imams. Regardless of whether the Imam was visible or not, he normally functioned through his representative, the Senior *D'ai*. The *d'ai*—which means "summoner"—was visible proof of the existence of the Imam. (It is interesting, and perhaps coincidental, to note the existence of a "summoner" in the annals of witchcraft; the "man in black" of the Salem trials was a summoner who called the faithful to the sabbat, and the term "summoner" is still used by some modern adherents of the Wicca movement.) The Senior *D'ai*—the *Hujja* or "Proof"—was also in direct contact with the Imam, even though others around him were not; thus we have an early example of the Secret Chief concept that would be so important to the Golden Dawn, a manifestation of the "Great White Brotherhood" of the Theosophists: hidden Masters who guide the world's spiritual development and who function through a handful of intermediaries. The Imam—like the Brotherhood—is human, but imbued with divine powers and abilities beyond the normal range of possibility.

The Ismaili sect divided yet again, into those who followed the Fatimid Caliphs—who were very powerful and influential in their day, and who created the oldest continuously-running university in the world, the Al–Azhar University in Cairo—and those who were loyal to Nizar, the eldest son of the previous Caliph, who was ousted from his appointed role by a scheming military dictator. Nizar fled to Alexandria, but was eventually captured and killed. Many Ismailis (especially those in the East, in Persia, Syria and what is now Iraq) felt that Nizar was the rightful heir to the throne, and decided not to recognize the authority of the new Caliph, a puppet of the dictator in Cairo. Thus were the Nizaris, later known as the Assassins, born.

At about this time, the Crusaders began their first invasion of the Middle East.

Responding to a call from Alexius I, the head of the Byzantine Empire which was ruled from Constantinople, that the Seljuk Turks were threatening his Christian kingdom, in 1095 A.D., Pope Urban II called for a crusade to help Alexius defend Christianity in the East and to take the Holy City of Jerusalem. The Seljuks had consolidated their power in what is now Turkey, virtually up to the walls of Constantinople. Armenian Christians, Greek Christians and Syrian Christians were in danger of having their cities and lands overrun by the new political, military and religious force that had its spiritual origins in the Saudi Arabia of the Prophet Muhammad, but its ethnic origins in the Asian steppes. Even the other Muslim territories of the Middle East were unhappy with the way the Turks were in ascendancy, and plotted how best to contain the Seljuk threat. As the bumbling Crusader armies finally secured the Byzantine capitol after several false starts, they went on a protracted campaign to capture the main cities along their route to Jerusalem, taking Edessa, Tarsus and finally Antioch before marching on Jerusalem in 1099.

Hasan i-Sabah was an educated Iranian and Twelver Shi'ite who eventually converted to the Ismaili form of Islam and spent some time in the court of the Caliph in Cairo. Becoming embroiled in the internecine warfare between the Fatimid and Nizari branches of the Ismailis, he cast his lot with the Nizari and wound up back in what is now Iran, secretly searching for a base of operations from which to wage unceasing warfare against the Seljuk Turks.[5] He chose the impregnable mountain fortress of Alamut, located in the Erbuz mountain range that hugs the southern coast of the Caspian Sea. At the same time, much of the territory of the Levant had come under control by the Seljuks. The Seljuks were new converts to Islam, and more Central Asian in nature than Arab. They were not part of the Arab feudal states with their complicated genealogies and tribal loyalties, and imposed a different sort of political reality on the Arab and Persian populations. Muslim or not, they were foreign invaders and Sunnis as well. The Fatimid Caliphate was disintegrating; it no longer held appeal for the masses who felt the moral bankruptcy of the regime and were turning more and more to the antinomian and millenarian "new preaching" of Hasan i-Sabah. Islam was in crisis, and so was the entire political infrastructure of the Middle East.

To a devout Muslim, the separation of Church and State that is familiar to the Western countries has no meaning. In Islamic countries, government and religion are one. This is one of the contributing factors to much political unrest in the Middle East, as religious differences automatically threaten government leadership. Religion and political administration must run together as one; if one deviates, then the spiritual structure of the country as well as its political nature is disrupted.

In a way, this is the other side of the coin from Communism, in which the *absence* of religion is by government decree. While in Islamic countries, church and state are one (as it were), in Communist countries the state is one; there is no church—no scripture, no ecclesiastical hierarchy, no liturgical requirements, no alternate power base—to worry about. However, as events have shown in the past fifty years of world history, that attitude was akin to whistling in the dark. Once religious bars in Communist countries were lifted, entire underground networks of religious and occult groups were revealed. This would be unthinkable in an Islamic state . . . except for the existence of secret religious/political organizations, groups holding heretical religious beliefs and hence subversive political agendas as well.

Thus, in Sunni territories and in Twelver Shi'ite territories, to be a Nizari was to court danger: imprisonment and execution. The Nizaris were not stupid, and they did not embrace suicide as a group, even though they encouraged suicidal practices by their agents, as we shall see. Instead, they developed a strategy of "precautionary dissimulation of one's true religious belief in the face of danger"[6]—in Arabic, *taqiyya*—of pretending to be whatever the ruling government of a given territory wanted them to be, while maintaining themselves secretly steadfast in their Nizari faith. The Nizari thus became a kind of spy or "sleeper agent," going about one's business in the hostile environment and pretending to adhere to the hated precepts of the evil faith of one's neighbors, all the while waiting for the order to rise up and strike Hasan-i Sabah began his career in Persia as a secret *d'ai* of the Nizaris, and thus as a sleeper agent himself. Eventually, he became a minister of this "new preaching," the *hujja* or proof of the invisible Imam, charged with revitalizing Islam both as a spiritual and as a political force in the world. The other Muslims—Sunnis, and those Shi'ites who were not part of his Nizari sect—were heretics and enemies to be destroyed. He could not do this with a standing army; the vast cities of the Muslim world were stronger and richer than he and his band of followers in the mountain castle of Alamut and the other isolated fortresses they would come to conquer. But he had another weapon at his disposal, one that carried the Ismaili concepts of *taqiyya* (dissimulation) and *batin* (esotericism) to their logical conclusion: political murder.

Assassination.

More than any other Muslim sect or organization, the Nizaris embraced the concept of political murder as a strategy central to their survival and success. The records at Alamut show dozens of assassinations carried out by loyal followers of Hasan during his lifetime. He was able to control large geographical areas and make his decisions felt everywhere in the Islamic world without ever leaving his mountain fortress at Alamut. For thirty-five years, Hasan-i Sabah stayed at Alamut and only left his residence twice, and that was to go onto the roof.[7] Devout, abstemious, studious, and completely focused, he maintained iron control of Alamut and of all the territories under his command. He had his own son put to death for drinking wine (alcohol is prohibited to Muslims). As an intellectual leader, he mastered "geometery, arithmetic, astronomy, magic, and other things."[8] He obviously felt the weight of his responsibility as living proof of the existence of the hidden Imam, and sought to prove himself worthy of that mystical trust his entire life. And that included ordering the assassinations of nearly fifty Muslim leaders.

There is controversy over whether or not the Assassin cult had a degree system of secret initiation. Iranian historian Farhad Daftary thinks not; he admits that there were different levels of understanding or learning within the sect, but these he believes were rather informal.[9] Bernard Lewis takes a different view, and maintains that the Nizaris under Hasan were a rigorous secret order with a degree system of initiation.[10] He ranks these (from lowest to highest) as respondents, licentiates, teachers, preachers, and the Proof, *Hujja*, or Senior D'ai, i.e., Hasan himself. There may be more ranks within these, as evidence is scant and confusing. Some authors have insisted the Assassins had seven degrees, others nine. Daftary dismisses this as ill-formed propagandizing by the enemies of the sect, whether Muslim or later, European, commentators. Clearly, not all the votes are in yet.

Hasan's assassins were carefully selected and, as the cult became more sophisticated, so did the selection and education process of the assassins, which may have involved disguise and language instruction. Regardless of the degree of preparation, the most important aspect of the assassin's readiness is that he be willing to strike in a public place for maximum effect, and thereby lose his life for the cause. Hasan's enemies were often stabbed to death in mosques while they were at prayer. At other times, while walking in the streets or being carried on litters. It didn't matter. And a few carefully selected victims, brought down in broad daylight by murderers who welcomed their own death as a passport to Paradise, caused many other leaders to offer tribute and toe the Assassin line without any further demonstration of ability.

That a small, devout, Muslim band of true believers based in an impregnable mountain fortress could strike at kings and princes whenever they choose, going to their own deaths in the process if need be without hesitation, all in the name of God and under control of a charismatic leader—who does not, himself, risk his own life—bears so many similarities to the events of the past fifty years in the Middle East that it beggars belief. Suicide bombers, terror attacks, plane hijackings . . . we have seen all of this before.

Hasan-i Sabah created his band of murderers nine hundred years ago, and in many ways they are still with us, and have been admired and emulated by successive incarnations of Shi'ite zealots down to the present day. Bernard Lewis accuses Hasan of having created terrorism as a political weapon.[11] The main difference from today's terrorist is that Hasan murdered leaders and used assassination with surgical precision, selectively and carefully, while his modern counterparts attack non-combatants, civilians, women and children: the innocent, who die in mass bombings and strafings. They have found—as the Assassins eventually discovered to their chagrin when dealing with the Templars and the Knights Hospitaller—that if you killed the leader of a Western army or government, another would come along to take his place. Assassination of Western leaders does not solve the political problems created by democratic governments; there is always a vice-president, a deputy minister, another general, another battalion, another air raid.

Furthermore, while Hasan and his followers did not attack civilian populations (it is, after all, against the Qur'an to do so), their spiritual heirs do. It has become a war of children against children, women against women; the disenfranchised of the East against the rich, self-satisfied, decadent West: stereotypes fighting stereotypes. What began as a political war in Hasan's time has become a cultural war in ours. The West is evil to the Shi'ite fundamentalists; America is the Great Satan. The Devil. The King of Devils. Not only because it is Christian, not only because of its support for Israel, although these are substantial issues in their own right. No; it is because Western culture—aided and abetted by Western technology—threatens Eastern culture, threatens to overwhelm the Faith. The West has movie stars; the East has martyrs.

Everyone on the planet knows who Madonna and Arnold Schwarzenegger and Sylvester Stallone are. What American knows the names of the Palestinian martyrs of the hideous Israeli and Christian Phalange attack of September 15, 1982 on the Sabra and Chattila refugee camps in Lebanon, where even the sick were dragged from their hospital beds and shot? Or the names of the teenaged suicide bombers—school children—who vainly, futilely try to avenge those deaths with dynamite and C-4 taped to their bodies? Yet, their photographs are plastered all over the walls in Beirut, Ramallah, Baghdad, and other Arab cities and towns and are traded like baseball cards among the young, the same young who danced in the streets when the World Trade Center was bombed; the same young who smiled and laughed in the coffee shops of Kuala Lumpur when the image of the God Struck Towers was flashed on the TV screen courtesy of CNN. "Finally," one could almost hear them think, "we are in the movies, too."

When the Crusader armies marched into Jerusalem, the status was reversed. Islamic civilization was far advanced at that time, and the Europeans were the unbathed barbarians, raping and pillaging their way into the Holy Sepulcher. Their information concerning Islam was scant, and they did not go to any lengths to improve their knowledge. The Muslims were enemies of Christendom and that was all they had to know. To study Islam too deeply might have been seen as an unhealthy interest in a demonic practice, and was thus avoided by virtually every European who lived in the Middle East at that time.

Rumors abounded in later years that the Assassins and the Knights Templar had just such an unhealthy relationship. This was promulgated primarily by the famous Orientalist Joseph von Hammer (*The History of the Assassins*, London, 1835), who jumped to a lot of conclusions concerning both Assassin and Templar alike. He went so far as to assume that the Assassins were the inspiration for the organization of the Templars, pointing to a similarity in dress and hierarchical structure, and went on from there to insist that the secrets of the Templars were those learned at the feet of the Assassins. This theory has been exploded many times over the past two hundred years, but it is still a central idea in the present-day Ordo Templi Orientis, which views itself as a survival of the original Knights Templar and which, in its initiation rituals, demonstrates an affection for the idea that the Ismailis and the Templars were well acquainted and had exchanged occult knowledge and initiations. As mentioned previously, this is most openly seen in the title of the American OTO leader as "Caliph." The German secret society which gave birth to the OTO *did* believe it was the repository of occult knowledge from the Middle East, much of it sexual in nature, which formed the basic character of the Order. (This knowledge was, however, admittedly of recent acquisition and not the result of a thousand years of secret cultivation.) The confusion of Templar with Nizari, however, hearkens back to the errors of von Hammer and his readers, errors which themselves were based on the charges brought against the Templars by the Church and by the French king who wished to see the Order destroyed, and could only do this by associating the Templars with the grossest forms of heresy and Satanism.

Most recently, Farhad Daftary has found evidence to support some of the speculation concerning the relationship between the Templars and the Assassins (specifically, the Syrian branch of the Nizari Assassins based in and around Damascus). There is ample documentation to show that the Assassins and the Templars had financial and other relationships. Daftary characterizes these as "complex," as well he might, as for the most part Templar records were destroyed in the fourteenth century at the time the Order was suppressed by King and Pope. While somewhat more is known about the Hospitallers and the Assassins (the relationship was political, to form an alliance against Saladin, the leader of the Sunni Muslims who threatened the Nizaris as well as the Crusaders), the relationship with the Templars is not so well understood or explicated. The Hospitallers, of course, were not suppressed and information about their operations is considerably better known. Both military orders were warned by the Church on several occasions about their unhealthy relationship with the Assassins, and with Muslims in general. The Church did not condone the tidy little arrangement in which the Nizaris paid a tribute to the Hospitallers for protection against Saladin, and in which the Nizaris agreed to assist the Hospitallers against their common enemy as well.

Daftary complains about the general ignorance of Western commentators on Islam and on the Assassins in general; however, the close working relationship between the Crusaders and the Assassins is a matter of record in both European and Islamic sources. Only the details are secret, and especially so in the case of the Templars. The Templars and Hospitallers were held in captivity by the Muslims for more than a year at one period, and it is said that they learned Arabic at that time (which, of course, makes sense). Templar Grand Masters are known to have had Arabic-speaking secretaries and to employ Muslim informers in the courts of the caliphs.

I submit that the Templars were more open to cross-cultural exchange than were their colleagues in *Outremer* (the Crusader States), and their brilliance at intelligence-gathering, banking, architecture and other accomplishments demonstrates intellectual abilities which require a certain amount of honest observation.

The Templars and Nizaris were both secret, religious orders that were also military in nature, and they would have respected each other for that, if for nothing else. In addition, the Templars would have wanted to know as much as possible about the Assassins without necessarily understanding a great deal about Islam in general, and it would have been to the benefit of the Nizaris to ensure that their philosophy constituted the heart of the Templars' knowledge of Islam.

We know that there was a cultural and philosophical exchange between the Templars and other religious sects in Syria and the Middle East, sects of various denominations encompassing the spectrum from Jewish heretical groups to Gnostics, Christian heretics, and various Muslim splinter groups including what appear to be Muslims with quasi-Christian sensibilities, such as the Mandaeans who revered John the Baptist. Evidence of this is contained in one of the most bizarre charges against the Templars, made in 1307, that they worshipped an idol they called Baphomet. The significance of this will be discussed a little later in this chapter, but it constitutes a compelling piece of evidence that the Templars *were* involved in occult teaching and ritual that they learned during their mission in the Middle East. This would have been especially possible after a remarkable event known as the *qiyama*, what is perhaps the most scandalous event in Nizari history, an event that was known to the Templars and other Crusaders, as is evident from some of the histories that have come down to us from the twelfth century.

It was during the month of Ramadan, the month of fasting in which all Muslims are expected to refrain from eating and drinking of any kind from sunrise to sunset. It was on the seventeenth day of the month, the anniversary of the murder of Ali, a day that is marked by all Shi'ites, some of whom work themselves up into a frenzy of self-flagellation. It was the year of the Hegira 559; in the Julian Calendar, it was the 8th of August 1164.

What follows is not the idle fantasy of Christian commentators. The details are in general agreement from Christian to Muslim, from Sunni to Shi'ite, and they are as follows:

On that day, the head of the Nizaris—Hasan II—the grandson of the founder of the Assassins, Hasan-i Sabah, performed a strange ritual at Alamut in the presence of his followers, who had been summoned from the four corners of the Nizari empire. He erected a pulpit, facing west, with four banners at the corners. The banners were white, red, yellow and green. The people he had summoned arranged themselves around the pulpit on the right and left sides, and directly in front. They all had their backs to Mecca.

At noon, Hasan II—dressed completely in white—approached the pulpit and announced the millenium.

Addressing all the inhabitants of the world of men, of angels, and of the *jinn* (the spirits, from which we get the word "genie"), he proclaimed that the hidden Imam had spoken to him and told him that the old Law—the *Shariya*—was abrogated, and that the time of the Resurrection was at hand. He then invited everyone to a banquet, there, at noon, in the midst of the fasting month of Ramadan and on the anniversary of the murder of Ali, to emphasize his proclamation that the time of the *Shariya* was ended. Messengers went out to all the Nizari strongholds, carrying the same message. A shock wave went through the community, and news of it reached the ears of Muslim and Christian alike. Either Hasan was, as he proclaimed in his speech, in direct communication with the Hidden Imam who had released the faithful from their spiritual obligations, or he was insane, or he was deserving only of a blasphemer's death. The Christians understood the complicated message to mean that Hasan had accepted Jesus Christ, since he had announced the Resurrection! The Resurrection, in this sense, meant nothing of the sort. As Daftary explains,

> Only the Nizaris were now capable of comprehending spiritual reality, the immutable truths hidden behind all the religious laws; and, as such, Paradise was made real for them in this world.[12]

Or, as the Persian chronicler Juvayni writes,

> . . . the Resurrection is when men shall come to God and the mysteries and truths of all Creation be revealed, and acts of obedience abolished, for in this world all is action and there is no reckoning . . .[13]

In other words, as the popular journalists have written, "Nothing is true; everything is permitted."

As Lewis and other historians have noted, this new dispensation was embraced by most of Hasan's followers without question, including in the Syrian strongholds.[14] Thus, the Assassins abandoned all pretence of following the Islamic law, discontinued praying five times a day facing Mecca, and began drinking and eating whatever suited them, whenever it suited them. Although there is no documentation for this, it can be safely assumed that the consumption of hashish was then also—if not encouraged—easily tolerated. Perhaps this event in 1164 gave the greatest impetus to the derogatory nickname of the Nizaris: the *hashishim*—the eaters of hashish—the Assassins.

Hasan II did not live long to enjoy the new dispensation. On the 9th of January 1166 he was stabbed to death by one of his brothers-in-law, who could not abide the blasphemy of his leader.

However, Hasan II was succeeded by his son, Muhammad, who continued the doctrine of the Resurrection and even expanded upon it, reiterating it as the new Nizari doctrine. And so it was, until Muhammad's son abolished it after the elder's death (possibly by poisoning) in 1210 A.D. Thus, the era of the *qiyama* lasted less than fifty years; but the effect this philosophy had on the Nizaris and on the people who feared them was profound.

In 1152, the Syrian Nizaris had begun paying an annual tribute to the Knights Templar of 2000 gold pieces.[15] This arrangement lasted throughout the *qiyama* period, even when the Nizaris tried to have it removed by the Christian ruler, King Amalric I. The Templars had the Nizari envoy himself assassinated for even daring to suggest that the tribute be lifted.

Then, in 1187, the great Muslim ruler Saladin sacked Jerusalem and took the Grand Masters of both the Knights Hospitaller and the Knights Templar into captivity, where they languished for a year. This, however, did nothing to stop the Nizaris from paying tribute to the Templars. Even when they had signed a mutual assistance treaty with the Knights Hospitaller in 1228, they continued to pay their annual fee to the Templars as well. The Nizaris had no reason to cooperate with Saladin, especially after the announcement of the *qiyama* since during that time (1164–1210) the Nizaris were considered heretics and blasphemers, having more in common with the Christians than with their fellow Muslims. The Nizaris were even known to have assisted the knights in their own internal struggles with the Christian rulers, a situation which gave rise to thunderous missives from Europe commanding the knightly Orders to desist having anything to do with the Nizaris.[16]

While the contribution of Muslim historians such as Daftary are valuable and important to an understanding of the Assassin phenomenon, their conclusions sometimes suffer from the same narrow viewpoints as the western historians they criticize. For instance, Daftary seems upset that Christian Europe would view the rise of Islam with alarm. As he writes:

> . . . Christian emperors were even more alarmed when the Muslims extended their hegemony from North Africa to Spain in the eighth century, and later, in the ninth century, to Sicily and other Mediterranean islands.
>
> Thus, the seeds of prolonged antagonism between the Christian and Muslim worlds were planted, and Islam, the 'Other' world, began to be perceived as a problem by western Christendom, a problem which in time acquired important religious and intellectual dimensions, in addition to its original political and military aspects.[17]

These paragraphs would be humorous if the subject matter were not so important. Presumably, when a continent is invaded by foreign armies with a foreign faith—what Daftary calls "extending their hegemony"—they may legitimately be "perceived as a problem"!

This is evidence of the clash of world-views between Muslims and Christians; and is one of the reasons why western historians and commentators have so little accurate information about the Assassins. Daftary admits in many places in his book that virtually all of the information about the Nizari Assassins available to the outside world was promulgated by their enemies. The Muslims themselves spread scathing, morbidly fantastic tales about the Assassins, and it is from the

Muslims that they got their nickname, the *hashishim*. How, then, were the Crusaders or other European chroniclers to obtain more accurate information? Obviously, the only way that was possible would be from the Assassins themselves.

THE MYSTERIES OF THE CATHEDRALS

That the Crusaders—and specifically the Templars—brought back important knowledge from the East, however, is beyond doubt. The access of European scholars to the works of the Greeks, the Arabs, the Persians and others caused a sudden explosion of creativity in France, for instance. Ironically, the building of the great Gothic cathedrals owes much to the architectural knowledge of the Muslim Middle East, knowledge that was put to use to create some of the most magnificent European churches ever seen. Geometry, medicine, astronomy, and alchemy were only some of the prizes taken back to France by the Crusaders, including the mysterious Templars and their allies. (Indeed, *algebra* and *alchemy* are phonetic transliterations of Arabic words.) The knowledge of how these disparate disciplines hung together in a cosmic framework of esoteric correspondences was the master key to the secret of the Saracens (as the Arabs were wrongly called), a secret that is revealed in the apse, nave and flying buttresses of the Gothic cathedrals, no less than in the strange statuary and other ornamentation that has baffled commentators for nearly a thousand years.

Louis Charpentier was probably the first to call the intricate relationship of the Knights Templar and the gothic cathedrals to our attention. In his *Les Mysteres de la Cathédrale de Chartres* (1995), he put forward a startling theory that Chartres—like the other gothic cathedrals of France—was the repository of arcane knowledge from the East, and the evidence in stone of an explosive secret that would rock Christianity if it were known. At once a machine for expanding consciousness and a testament to "hidden history," Chartres Cathedral lies at a nexus of science, religion and mysticism. The dimensions of Chartres are shown to be equivalent to those of astronomy and music; the carved statues on the outer walls to tell a story of how a secret treasure was brought from the Temple of Solomon by the Knights, and how this treasure enriched both the Order and the Church. This story has gone on to create an entire industry based around early Church history, Jewish messianic lore, and sacred geometry, as represented in such blockbusters as *Holy Blood, Holy Grail*, *The Messianic Legacy*, and dozens of other studies in various languages, as well as television documentaries. Chartres Cathedral itself became a magnet for New Age seekers, and it now has its own website.

Basically, the idea is this:

The Order of the Knights Templar was founded in 1118 and formally chartered in 1128 by St. Bernard of Clairvaux. Nine impoverished French knights make their way to Jerusalem in order to provide protection for Christian pilgrims going overland through Turkey to visit the Holy Land. Obviously, there was very little nine knights were going to accomplish if their mission was to police a thousand miles of road through hostile territory. Instead, they were based at the Al-Aqsa Mosque (from where Muslims believe the Prophet once ascended to heaven), which is built over part of Solomon's Temple.

Solomon's Temple was the center of Jewish worship since ancient times. It had been built according to legend by King Solomon himself, with the help of demonic beings he summoned by magic. It was destroyed by invaders, built again, and then destroyed again. By the time the Knights Templar had arrived on site, it was a ruin in sorry shape. According to the story now prevalent in New Age circles, the Knights spent their time in Jerusalem digging and looking for something in the vicinity of the Temple. It seems they found what they were looking for, and brought it back in a hurry to France.

The controversy is over whether this "treasure of the Templars" was a physical object or some kind of secret knowledge. Those of the Charpentier school feel it was both. Charpentier suggests that the Templars brought back with them the Ark of the Covenant, lost centuries before at the last destruction of the Temple. The Ark, of course, would be the single most important artifact of Judaism, because it would contain the original stone tablets on which the Ten Commandments were inscribed by the hand of God. It would also contain the mystical Rod of Aaron, a magic wand with divine powers. The Ark, according to the scant information given in the Bible concerning its use, was so powerful that if touched by the unworthy it would bring instant death. The Jewish tribes used it as a kind of weapon in battle, parading it around before their enemies who then fell before them in disarray. The Lucas–Spielberg film, *Raiders of the Lost Ark*, contains a fairly accurate rendition of some of the legends associated with the instrument, as well as Nazi interest in locating it.

To Charpentier, the Ark was something more than a weapon. A device for calculation, a kind of geomancer's compass, is one possibility; one that would have enabled the Templars to build the domes and buttresses of the cathedrals. It was also secret knowledge. As Charpentier tells us, there is no crucifix in Chartres Cathedral. He says that strange omission indicates that the Templars did not believe that Christ was crucified, i.e., believed that he lived, had children, and that his descendants also had survived, a theme developed at great length in *Holy Blood, Holy Grail* by the team of Baigent, Leigh and Lincoln. If Christ was not crucified (or, at least, did not die on the cross, as has been suggested by historians over the past two hundred years) it would explain the most potent charge against the Templars, that in their initiation ceremonies they were expected to trample upon a cross. This might have been a bowdlerized account of what was actually taking place, i.e., a renunciation of the basic, the most central, idea of Christianity: that Jesus was executed, buried, and rose from the dead.

If the Templars believed that Christ did not rise from the dead, then they shared this belief with their Muslim counterparts, and it is no wonder that they were violently suppressed by the Church. Indeed, recent research tends to support the idea that the Templars had Muslim aides, and that many spoke Arabic and took a keen interest in Islam as well as in the many heretical Christian sects abroad in the Middle East at the time, sects that owed much to Gnosticism and Zoroastrianism. As has been demonstrated by Lewis, Daftary and other historians of the period, the Templars had a close working relationship with the Syrian Nizaris, a relationship that spanned the period of the infamous *qiyama* instigated by Hasan II and continued by his son, Muhammad II. This would have exposed them to the apocalyptic and millennial cosmologies of the Ismailis, as well as to other "alternative" religious and historical beliefs.

They may have heard the legends current at the time indicating that someone—either an apostle, or possibly even Jesus himself—had traveled to Kashmir, a refugee from religious and political persecution, and died in Srinagar. They might have heard of the existence of alternative forms of the *Gospel of Mark*, an "unedited" version of the Gospel found in Egypt which refers to an occult initiation conducted by Jesus. They might have heard of the *Gospel of St. Thomas*, a mystical work considered an integral part of the Scriptures in what is now Ethiopia, where the Ark is said to have been taken after the fall of the Second Temple. They might have heard that the bloodline of Jesus survived and that there was—somewhere in the world—a current and living King of the Jews. This exposure to eastern mysticism and alternate history could explain the precise charges leveled against the Templars by King and Pope, charges that were not laid against their hated rivals, the Knights Hospitaller.

And if these stories *are* correct, then the House of David may have survived the last two thousand years of world history and—according to recent Biblical scholarship supported by discoveries in the Dead Sea Scrolls, among other texts—one of its current incarnations would be the King of the Jews, thus casting in doubt the legitimacy of the Catholic Church and, indeed, of all of Christianity. Over one billion believers would find themselves without a belief.

Charpentier—and others who have followed his thinking—feel that this may be the Great Secret of the Freemasons, Templars, and other secret societies of Europe, knowledge handed down quietly because of the danger to the bloodline should Church or State discover it. This, then, is the true meaning of the Holy Grail, for *San Greal* could be a pun on *Sang Real*, Holy Blood. The bloodline of Jesus.

What has all of this has to do with anything? If there is any truth at all to the above conjectures, then the careful edifice of the last two thousand years of Western civilization crumbles like a house of cards. The Muslims and the Jews would have no problem with the discovery that Jesus was never crucified, never rose from the dead, and had—instead—lived a long life and produced offspring who made their way to Europe or to India where they live to this day. They would only shake their heads and say, "I told you so." The Buddhists, Shintoists, animists, pagans and others in the Far East, Africa, and distant parts of the world would give the news only a passing glance. But it would shake the governments and institutions of the West like nothing before.

Christianity, *per se*, would cease to exist, and with it the cherished beliefs and ideals of almost a quarter of humanity. Political and religious leaders would struggle to fill the void with some kind of generalized humanism, a religion centered around an ambiguous God of no discernible personality or color, with a scripture cobbled together with the better parts of Thoreau, Thomas Paine, and perhaps Walt Whitman. Morality itself would be called into question, and one could imagine millions of people—robbed of even the shimmer of God's love and the shadow of God's wrath—going on a warpath of murder, rape and robbery. Crosses would be pulled down from steeples like busts of Lenin in Red Square.

Thus, if this were indeed the truth, the need to cover it up would be absolute. Cynical pragmatists in the Vatican as well as in the world's governments would do what they could to keep a lid on the secret, and perhaps do so in the belief that they were saving civilization. At the same time, it would be necessary to reveal a little of the truth, bit by bit, in selective doses to select individuals, knowing that eventually the truth would become known to everyone; by revealing the truth in degrees, one controls the fallout: a much safer approach than simply dumping the news on the front page of the *New York Times*.

Thus, we have the *raison d'etre* of the modern secret society.

THE NAME OF THE ROSE

The Freemasons believed themselves to be the inheritors of the architectural secrets of the Great Pyramid and the Temple of Solomon, as well as of the other secrets of the Knights Templar. In fact, in America their boys' auxiliary is named after the last Grand Master of the Templars, Jacques de Molay, who was arrested—along with the rest of his French knights—on Friday, the 13th of October, in the year 1307. De Molay was later executed, burned at the stake on March 18, 1314, professing his innocence to the last, after years of hideous torture at the hands of his coreligionists. His Order was scattered to the winds (those that survived) and wound up in Portugal as well as in Scotland. It is said that the sails of Christopher Columbus' caravelles bore the scarlet cross of the Templars, and that Templar knights rode to the assistance of the Scots at Bannockburn.

Romance aside, it is the strange combination of architecture, ritual and secret knowledge that concerns us here, for it is a combination that can be found in ancient Egypt among the pyramids as well as in Chartres Cathedral among the pews. It is an essential element of the Freemason mystique, and has become the focus of intense scrutiny by some modern intelligence agencies. It survives in the design of the temple of the Golden Dawn as well as in the various initiatory rites of Freemasonry, and the idea that the East has a secret technology of the mind, of occult power—an idea that has its origins with the controversy and scandals surrounding the Templars—bore fruit in the creation of the Rosicrucian Society in the early seventeenth century, a Society that had tremendous influence on the arts and sciences of the next two hundred years, and which was brought to America in several forms by English and German immigrants.

By delving back into time, into the deserts of Arabia and the Levant, the ruined temples of Jerusalem, the stone cathedrals of medieval France, the jar-buried scrolls of Qumran, the alchemical laboratories of Prague, and back even further to the mysteries of ancient Egypt and Sumer, we confront the origin of some of the issues that trouble us today. For the recurring idea of the existence of a science that bridges the gap between mind and body, and perhaps between body, mind and some other human faculty—the soul, the spirit, the *petit bon ange* or the *gros bon ange*, the *ka* or the *ba*, the *shen* or the *qing*—persists throughout history in both the West and the East. Furthermore, if it does exist, the organizations with the funding, the power, and the *necessity* of harnassing its technology today would be the intelligence agencies which are, after all, the spiritual descendants of the Nizari Assassins, the Templars, the Rosicrucians, the Illuminati, the Masons, even the votaries of Haitian *voudon*: secret organizations with secret membership, whose ideals may have been forged in religion, mysticism or simply pure idealism, but who owe their allegiance to political forces and will use covert methods to accomplish their goals.

Whether or not there was any basis in truth for the allegations that the Assassins used hashish as a mind-control substance, the important thing to remember is that the world—including many Muslims—*believed it to be so*, and believed that therein lies a key for unlocking the mindless killer in us all.

Premier among the secret societies believed—in the West—to be at once occult and political was (and in some cases remains) the Freemasons. (The East has its parallel in the Chinese secret societies that sprang up in response to the excesses of the Qing Dynasty, with much similarity to the Freemasons, except that the Chinese societies degenerated into criminal gangs, while this charge has never been laid against the Masons.) The Freemasons have been accused of every kind of blasphemy, treachery, and subversion by their critics; admirers and critics alike point to the organization's supposed origins in the shadow of Solomon's Temple, and some go even further and associate its teachings with the nameless cult that designed the Egyptian pyramids. Modern journalists—notably in the books of Lynn Picknett and Clive Prince—have gone so far as to demonstrate a historical continuum between the Egyptian pyramid builders, the Temple of Solomon, the heretical Christian cults of the first few centuries A.D., the Knights Templar and the Freemasons.[18]

It was the Masonic Society that gave birth to Professor Weishaupt's Illuminati in Bavaria on May 1, 1776: a group that was decidedly political as well as philosophical and which was eventually surpressed by the Bavarian authorities, as the Templars had been four hundred years earlier. It was a manifestation of a general air of revolutionary activity, established as it was on the eve of America's own Declaration of Independence from England. England at that time was a kingdom being run by George III, a man more at home with the German language than English. One of the leaders of the American revolutionary movement was Benjamin Franklin, a Mason and an intimate of French revolutionary and occult circles in Paris. Later in the century, of course, France would experience its own revolution after lending its support to the American template. A story current at the time has an unknown revolutionary running through the palace at Versailles shouting, "Jacques De Molay, thou art avenged!" The horror-stricken European nobles accused the revolutionary movement of France of having been masterminded by secret societies, and of course the Masons (and the Illuminati) were the first accused.

In the nineteenth century, America went through a paroxysm of anti-Masonry, and an Anti-Masonic Party was formed, out of which the Whigs and later the Republican Party would be created from its disparate limbs. One merely has to replace the word "Masonry" with the word "Communism" to appreciate the gist of the speeches and broadsides against this secret society with its "godless" agenda. America was going through a period of intense soul-searching in the early days of the nineteenth century, after the second defeat of the English during the War of 1812. Religious fanaticism and fundamentalism was on the rise, and the Masonic Society was identified as one of the sinister forces attempting to move America into worship of alien gods, while at the same time taking its orders from mysterious European masters. It was also a time of anti-Catholic feeling, for the Catholics were perceived as owing allegiance to the Pope before Country and God. Their religion was seen as idolatrous and superstitious, a kind of "outer court" of the Masons, who were seen as a bit more sophisticated but no less idolatrous. This was ironic, of course, in that Catholics were forbidden to join the Masonic Society; the Church saw Freemasonry as the survival of Templarism, which they had fought into the ground hundreds of years earlier. Secret societies with secret rituals were anathema to organized religion, which sought to remain the sole channel to Godhead.

Joseph Smith, an occultist at heart, embraced Freemasonry in the years before his murder, and Masonic ideas and ritual were incorporated into the Mormon liturgy, as was detailed in Book One. When Hitler came to power in the twentieth century, he banned all occult organizations and reserved his special ire for the Masons. Architect of the Final Solution Adolf Eichmann cut his eye teeth in the SS while working on the Masonic files, before he was finally diverted to another group that was considered as great a threat to the race as the Masons: the Jews. In the Freemasonry Section, he compiled lists of Masonic temples, libraries and other holdings as well as membership lists, and maintained a museum exhibit on Freemasonry that was visited regularly by Heinrich Himmler. Masonic property was seized everywhere in the Reich, and the artifacts sent directly to the SS for examination and storage, or eventual destruction.

Thus, Freemasonry has not had an easy time. Like any secret society, it is the target of those who believe that any group of persons meeting in secret must be up to no good; yet, today there is a Masonic temple in virtually every American town of any size, and the Masonic Society headquarters in Washington, D.C. is on Pennsylvania Avenue, but a stone's throw from the White House. George Washington was inaugurated as America's first president wearing Masonic regalia, and many future presidents would be Masons as well as an overwhelming number of senators and congressmen. Yet, few American non-Masons have a clear idea about the origins of the Society, or even its purpose (other than charity).

According to most established histories, the Masonic Society's official birth was in the year 1717,when the first Grand Lodge was announced, and allegations that the Order has a more ancient lineage was generally derided by academics until recently. As more documentation has become available, it seems clear that the Freemasons had existed for at least one hundred years prior to the formation of the Grand Lodge, and perhaps as much as two hundred years. This sounds dubious at first, since there are no published works on the Freemasons before the eighteenth century; or so it would seem.

Scotland boasts some of the earliest Freemasonic lore, and Masonic temples and lodges have been identified in Scotland as early as the sixteenth century. Further, when the Grand Lodge announced itself in London in 1717, the Freemasons of York protested and formed a rival lodge, saying that their organization was much older and had nothing to do with the lodges in London. Thus, there seems to have been a Masonic tradition in Scotland and northern England long before the heavily-publicized formation of the Grand Lodge. If this is so—and current academic research supports it—then where did the Masons come from?

The official Masonic line is that their brotherhood began in the shadow of the Temple of Solomon. The original Masons had been architects and builders in the employ of King Solomon, and the Master Mason—one Hiram Abiff—was later murdered by three assassins in an attempt to discover the "Master Word." This Word was assumed to be the password used by higher ranking Masons to enable them to receive a higher pay scale, one's position in the hierarchy of builders being determined by which password one held. If one could know the password of a Master Mason then one would be compensated at a higher rate. Such is the story. Unfortunately, Abiff refused to part with the information and was killed, his body buried in a shallow grave. Later, his body was dug up and searched to see if he had written the Word anywhere, but the Word was lost.

This odd story is the central myth of the Masons. While there are stories about the Egyptian pyramids, the orthodox origins of the Freemasons are said to belong to the days of Solomon's Temple. That would mean, of course, that the Masons are more than three thousand years old. While that chronology satisfies some, there are others who question the story with an eye to discovering its real secret.

This secret may have been discovered in the recent past by an amateur historian from Kentucky. Due to a fortuitous set of circumstances having nothing to do with the Freemasons, John J. Robinson stumbled upon compelling proof that the Freemasons had their origins with the Knights Templar, and that the Templar

Order had survived in England and Scotland after the official destruction of the Knights by order of the Pope. The evidence begins with the famous Peasant Revolt of 1381, in which there was a general uprising in England against the Church and the King, which resulted in the destruction of property all over the kingdom and the murder of many high-ranking clerics and nobles.

Robinson demonstrates beyond reasonable doubt that the attack was directed specifically against the Knights Hospitaller, the Templars' hated rival since the days of their mutual origin in the desert sands of Palestine, and inheritors of the Templars' assets when the Templars were suppressed by Papal decree. Robinson's book—*Born in Blood*—is a worthwhile addition to Masonic studies, even though it contains no footnotes or other academic impedimenta that would have elevated it to more lofty status among scholars; its connecting the Peasant Revolt with a "Grand Society" operating in secret in the British Isles, a society convincingly identified with the Knights Templar, is alone worth the price of admission. Robinson also shows that Templar shrines were spared the attacks, which left thousands dead and many beheaded as the revolt wound its way directly to the Tower of London. The leader of the revolt was known only by the name Walter the Tyler, which is suggestive, since the "tyler" is a Masonic office in the rituals of the temple. All this indicates that the Masonic society has its origins in the Knights Templar, as many historians have always insisted (albeit without the benefit of documentation).

The investigative team of Baigent and Leigh—in *The Temple and The Lodge*—have gone further, showing how the Templars escaped Europe at the time of their suppression and wound up in Scotland, among other places. They discuss the disposition of the Templar fleet, a substantial armada of ships that mysteriously disappeared at the time of the Order's destruction, and suggest that the fleet enabled escaping Templars to make it as far as the coast of Scotland and even, in at least one case, as far as Greenland and possibly to Mexico.

In fact, one of the more startling discoveries in *The Temple and The Lodge* is the report of a Templar grave, in what is now Israel, adorned with the by-now famous compass and square insignia of the Freemasons. This grave dates to the thirteenth century, which again indicates that there existed an identity between the Templars and the Masons. While this had always been a fantasy or a supposition by conspiracy theorists of the Right and the Left, the combined weight of the various clues as given by Robinson, Baigent and Leigh, and other recent research (such as that by David Stevenson in his *The* Origins of Freemasonry), now clearly points to Templar survival in the form of the Freemasons.

The only missing link in the story now is whether (and how) the Templars and the Assassins shared information, including not only military and political intelligence but also information of a more esoteric nature. This has also been a belief of conspiracy theorists, who jumped to the conclusion that since the Templars and the Assassins shared some of the same real estate and had some of the same enemies, that they must have—of necessity—become friendly. Indeed, this was one of the accusations against the Templars by the Church when they finally clamped down on them in the fourteenth century. They were said to worship an idol called "Baphomet" (a suggestively Arabic sounding name) rather than Jesus, and to have engaged in other unlawful practices of a distinctly Islamic nature.

It is said that the Templars' aversion to putting a crucifix—a representation of the body of Christ impaled on the cross—in their Gothic cathedrals was an indication that they shared a horror of idolatry which they inherited from either the Jews, the Muslims, or both. (Iconography is forbidden in both religions, although abstract design is usually permitted; Catholicism, however, embraces statues and paintings of Christ and the Saints, and the Orthodox Christians permit paintings—the famous ikons—but not statues.) The insistence on representing divinity in the form of sacred geometry and number only is a main feature of Islam, and this may have been one of the major influences on Templar thinking in the design of the Gothic cathedrals as well as in the ritualized and sacralized geometry of Freemasonry.

The reference to Baphomet is actually quite important, and bears some digression here. For centuries, no one knew what that name meant, and many wondered if it was a corruption of "Mahomet," a common medieval spelling of Muhammad, the Prophet and founder of Islam. Aleister Crowley, on assuming the leadership of the English OTO used Baphomet as his Order name, since the Templars were said to worship Baphomet, and Crowley was never averse to a stiff drink, a good cigar, a warm woman, or a devoted follower. It was up to Dead Sea Scrolls scholar Dr. Hugo Schonfield to solve the mystery, however. Using a well-known and often-used Qabalistic cypher known as *Atbash*—in which the first letter of the Hebrew alphabet is equivalent to the last letter, and so on—he applied the technique to the name *Baphomet* and came up with *Sophia*, the goddess of Wisdom. Thus, the Templars may well have been worshipping Wisdom in their secret councils; even more, Wisdom in a cryptic, Qabalistic dress. Even more again, Wisdom as Sophia, the consort of Simon Magus, one of the legendary fathers of the esoteric cult known to posterity as Gnosticism. *Baphomet* comes to us down the centuries, then, from the Templar Inquisition records as a signal to the Bretheren: a secret word with its solution buried in its seemingly random combination of letters. A "lost Word." A "Mason word." In fact, a word that was hidden using an ancient Jewish cypher, the same cypher that was in use by the Essenes.

That is still not proof of a link between the Templars and the Assassins, however. If anything, it demonstrates that the Templars were in communication with Jewish and Gnostic groups in the Middle East. But the belief that there was an exchange of secrets between the two groups is persistent, in spite of scant evidence one way or the other. What did they have in common?

In the first place, what many do not realize is that the Knights Templar were first and foremost monks. They were a monastic order, with a monastic rule. They took vows of poverty, chastity and obedience like any other Catholic monks. They owed their allegiance to the Pope, and to no other man: neither king nor cleric. They were forbidden to bathe. They were forced to wear sheepskin and leather, even in the pounding heat of the desert lands they went to conquer. They were not allowed any privacy at all. They were forbidden even the most casual contact with women. They were forbidden alcohol, and were allowed two meals a day. They were also expected to fight to the death, regardless of the circumstances, if their superior so ordered it. They were not allowed to retreat in battle unless the odds were greater than three to one, and then only if their superior allowed them to retreat. The regulations against wine and women would have made the Muslims feel at home. Their willingness to die for their religion would have made the Nizaris feel at home.

They were initiated in secret. Even the monastic rule of the Order was not revealed in its entirety until a Knight had achieved the highest rank. This secrecy was an unusual factor in the composition of the Order, not something normally practiced by other monastic orders. And Templars could not divulge anything of these initiation rites, or of the monastic rule, under penalty of death.

Obviously, the Templars and the Assassins shared much of the same mindset. The passion for secrecy, and the willingness to die if ordered to do so, were two very important things the two groups had in common. In addition, they were both religious orders, devoted to God, and they were both military organizations devoted to conquest. The main difference between them—aside from religion—was the fact that the Assassins operated in secret, in disguise, with lethal precision, whereas the Knights Templar were everywhere obvious by their mode of dress, and they struck as soldiers, in the open field, *en masse*. While the Assassins would take a castle by murdering its ruler, the Templars took a castle by overwhelming its forces in the heat of bloody conflict. But that would all change on October 13, 1307, when the Templars were arrested throughout France and the order went out to crush them in every part of the Catholic empire. At that point, the Templars went underground like their Nizari counterparts, and they suddenly had much more in common than ever before, for they suddenly had a common enemy in the Catholic Church and the Catholic kings of Europe.

The story of why the Order was suppressed, its leaders arrested, tortured and executed and its holdings seized and, in many cases, handed over to the hated Knights Hospitaller is a matter of historical record, and we will not dwell on it too deeply here. Basically, the Crusades had been lost. There were only a few Europeans left in the Middle East, tenaciously holding on to scraps of land along the coast of what is now Lebanon and Israel. The various principalities of Italy were at each other's throats, with the Venetians at war with the Genoese and everybody at war with France. Jacques de Molay, the Grand Master of the Order, was called to France for what he thought was going to be new marching orders and a budget for a new Crusade to take back the Holy Land. Instead, he was arrested, along with all of his lieutenants throughout France, on that fateful Friday the Thirteenth and charged with heresy. The instigator of this "night of the long knives" was the new King Philippe le Bel of France, in tandem with Pope Clement V. The reason was a desire to take over the vast holdings of the Templars throughout Europe, and wherever else they could be found, and to eliminate the Templars as a political threat.

At this point in European history, the Templars were not only the richest religious order but the richest organization of any kind. Philippe le Bel owed the Templars money, as did most of the crowned heads of Europe. Many have credited the Templars with the creation of the modern banking system. Although elements of this had already been in place in various parts of the world, the Templars turned banking into an art form. With their monastic vows of poverty and obedience, they were a logical choice to be entrusted with money; with their international network of Temples and multilingual scribes throughout Europe and the Middle East, they were an obvious channel for transmission of funds through the various ports to enable and facilitate trade between nations. In short, the Templars became rich. And wealth means power.

But the King could not simply round them all up and have them killed. He needed a legitimate reason, and this he found through informants and spies: the Templars were heretics. They practiced strange rites in secret. They trampled on the cross. They worshipped an idol they called "Baphomet." They engaged in homosexual intercourse. They hired Muslim aides, and had learned Arabic and the ways of the mysterious East. They did not believe in the Crucifixion of Jesus or His Resurrection. They owed their loyalty to foreign masters and alien gods.

There may have been some elements of truth in the accusations, but the Templars had always prided themselves on being answerable to no one but the Pope himself. This loyalty to the Church, and their willingness to undergo tremendous privations in both war and peace, was ignored during the *auto* da-fe that took place in that time. Many Templars—far from France—managed to escape and to take some of their wealth and records with them. Iberia was still a mixed bag of Christian and Muslim states, and it is known that some Templars found asylum there. Others made for England and Scotland.

But the damage had been done: the very Church to which the Templars had given their lives and devoted their souls had turned on them, and turned on them with a vengeance. Their Grand Master, Jacques de Molay, was finally burned at the stake. This was an intolerable state of affairs, and if the Templars had indeed learned heretical secrets in the East then this *contre-temps* seemed to prove them right. The men on the thrones of Catholic Europe and on the throne of St. Peter were evil men, unworthy of the faith of the Templars and of the trust of the people. God had forsaken his Church and abrogated the divine right of kings. The Templars were no longer bound by their previous oaths, but they were still trained as military monks, still had their weapons in some cases, still had their secret networks throughout the civilized world, and were still in contact with the Church's enemies, should they be needed.

As they burrowed deep within the towns and villages and cities of Christendom, they established safe houses where they could meet and exchange information.

These were known as lodges, and eventually developed into the Masonic Lodge we know today. Sixty years after the execution of Grand Master De Molay, these lodges formed the backbone of the Peasant Revolt which attacked Hospitaller knights and temples with rapacity throughout England. They fought alongside the Scots against the English and, it is said, metamorphosed into the clandestine organizations that fomented rebellion against the evil kings of France and England in the French and American revolutions, and against the royal houses of Prussia and Bavaria. Eventually, even the Russian Revolution was blamed on the Freemasons, the Illuminati and their illustrious forebear, the Order of the Knights Templar. It got to the point where even Winston Churchill noted the power and influence of these covert organizations over European history.

Given the weight of the supporting academic scholarship, there can be little doubt today that the Freemasons owe their existence to the clandestine network of Knights Templar that was established in the beginning of the fourteenth century. Thus, the organization—in general terms, without reference to a specific lodge—is over six hundred years old; more, if we consider its birth to date from the first expedition by Hugh de Payens, the first Templar Grand Master, to Jerusalem in 1118. In that case, the Freemasons are a nearly nine-hundred-year-old organization, and their origin in blood and religion, in the Journey to the East of the Crusades, makes them a template for future cults awash in secret rituals, privileged information of an occult nature, and political aspirations.

The beliefs allegedly adopted by the Templars, however, including the worship of Baphomet/Sophia and the rejection of the crucifixion, owe their origins to an even earlier date, and for that we have to go back two thousand years to the first Christian century and the Gnostic and Essene forces that surrounded the earliest days of the Church.

THE GNOSTIC GOSPELS

In 1945, a series of discoveries was made of a cache of Gnostic texts in a village in Egypt. This find, known collectively as the Nag Hammadi Library, was buried for safekeeping in the third century A.D. The Gnostics were well-established in Alexandria by this time, where the Ptolomies had first saturated this area of the Middle East with Greek philosophy and culture. It was this mixture of Platonic, Pythagorean, and pagan philosophy, science, art and religion that had such a profound influence on both the Jews and the local pagan population, and which, in a way, allowed the spread of a new Jewish cult outside of Israel and into the world—the Gentile, pagan world—at large.

For if it should survive at all, the new cult of Christianity, based on the teachings of the mysterious leader known as Jesus, would have to survive outside Judaism. The political environment of Israel at the time of Christ has been described at length by Robert Eisenman and Barbara Thiering, among others, so I will not go into detail here. It is enough to say that tremendous infighting in the Jewish population had made it possible for Greeks and Romans to keep Israel enslaved for centuries, and the most critical element of this internecine conflict was the struggle over foreign cultural influences.

In the second century B.C., educated and sophisticated Jews wanted their sons to study abroad, to learn Greek, and to dress in the Greek manner. The Seleucid Empire—the Syrian parallel to the Ptolomaic kingdom of Egypt, i.e., successor to the conquests of Alexander the Great—was in control in much of the Levant, including Palestine. In some cases, Seleucid rulers actively opposed Jewish religion and customs. This was known as the "Time of Wrath," and it was during this time that the Chasidim or "the Pious" were born, and when the mysterious "True Teacher" or "Teacher of Righteousness" made his appearance, an event that was heralded by the Jewish cult of the Essenes.

The Essenes were a purist sect of Jews who were renowned as healers, and who many thought had the gift—or the science—of prediction, a capability believed to have derived from their exceptionally holy lives and the devout attention they paid to the study of the sacred books. The Essenes were millennialist in a sense: they expected the arrival of the Messiah at any time, particularly in the Time of Wrath, which was believed to be the End of Days. Their scriptural writings speak of a lineage of priestly kings going back to the time of King Solomon and his confidant Asaph. Asaph was a master of the occult arts and possessor of the "Ineffable Word of God," which enabled him to perform miracles.

This Word—like the lost Word of Hiram Abiff, also of Solomon's Temple—is a recurring theme in Masonic ritual and literature as well as in ancient Jewish lore, and has a special place in the Qabala, which concentrates on words and letters and the power certain combinations and pronunciations can give to the initiated practitioner. This idea of the power of language is reflected in the Gospel according to John, the most mystical of the four Evangelists, which begins, "In the beginning was the Word, and the Word was with God, and the Word was God." In the Gnostic writings found at Nag Hammadi and in other places, a great emphasis is placed on words of no identifiable meaning, what archaeologists call "abracadabra," or meaningless sounds.

Obviously, since it seemed that no words from the everyday vocabulary of a language possessed any special power (else we would have all witnessed it many times in our lives), the magic words must be those that have no usage in common speech, words that are otherwise unrecognizable. Gibberish. And since these magic words could be phoneticized and written down anyway—and possibly seen by the unworthy—the secret of their power must lie in their method of pronunciation, a method that would be passed down to the initiate during the course of special ritual. In the later occult lodges of the nineteenth and twentieth centuries, this method was known as "vibration" rather than pronunciation, for it was acknowledged that speech (and, indeed, all sound) is vibration or sound waves. Therefore, magical pronunciation must consist of a special way of creating those very sound waves, a method of speaking or chanting or singing that would convey the power of the word in its very sound, its particular vocalization.

The constant repetition of select words or phrases over and over again—like the mantra of Hinduism and Buddhism, designed to lead a practitioner to exalted states of awareness, into contact with God—was the technique Dr. Ewen Cameron used in the depatterning experiments at his infamous clinic in Montreal on behalf of the CIA. The difference was that his patients were bombarded with these words for hours on end over electronic speakers placed under their pillows until they were quite insane. This same technique was used (with no success whatsoever) in the bombardment of David Koresh's compound in Waco, Texas, and in the sonic attack on Panamanian president Manuel Noriega, who was in hiding in a compound controlled by the Vatican, except that in Noriega's case the selection was pure rock 'n' roll.

If the good Doctor Cameron, or the ATF and the FBI, or the Marines had followed the procedures as originally developed by the Hindus and the Essenes and the Qabalists, they might have tried using some of the "meaningless gibberish" or "abracadabra" of their sacred books rather than specific words and phrases, some of which would have unknown connections with their victims' belief systems, especially in the case of Waco. Had they relied upon the seemingly meaningless mantras of the Gnostics, for instance, the results might have been interesting, and even more spectacular than the failures of Cameron, Waco and Panama City.

The "Ineffeable Word" was only one aspect of the Essene occult teaching, however; their main interest, outside of the purely religious and apocalyptic, was medical. In Egypt, they were known as *Therapeuts*, which implies a general acknowledgment of their healing capabilities. They were said to have a good knowledge of herbs and "therapeutic stones" and their application in a variety of diseases. When we consider the Essene lifestyle, belief system, and reputation for healing and prediction, we can see how they could have survived in one of the most famous eruptions of spiritual passion since the Cathars and Albigenses of the thirteenth century: the sudden appearance of the Rosicrucians.

Even the respected Biblical scholar Dr. Schonfield agrees:

> The influence of the Essenes of Egypt, known in the first century A.D. as Therapeuts, was particularly strong. Philo of Alexandria learned much from them. The Rosicrucians could look back to an Essene impetus from Egypt relating to arcane matters associated with the Sun-King and Master of Wisdom King Solomon, who had created the Temple in conjunction with the Master Asaph ben Berechiah. And these things were the foundations of Freemasonry.[19]

Thus what we have before us is a continuum of belief and practice—religious, historical, medical, architectural, occult and astronomical—that stretches for thousands of years backwards in time, much as the popular legends of Freemasonry would have it. And the continuum includes everything from the Temple of Solomon to the Essenes, the story of Jesus, the Knights Templar, the Rosicrucians and the Masons, as well as heretical sects such as the Cathars, the Bogomils and the Albigenses. It is an anti-history, a history below the surface of what is generally and popularly accepted as the truth, comprising elements from Judaism and Christianity and their offshoots, such as the Gnostics, as well as elements of Zoroastrianism and Islam. What is more, associated with this anti-history is a remarkably coherent and internally consistent set of psychological and spiritual practices that involves what we know as ritual magic, alchemy, astrology and sacred geometry: an anti-science whose secrets were the targets of some of the most advanced (and certainly most serious) governments in the world, from the time of the philosopher-kings of Europe down to the present day's CIAs and KGBs and terrorist organizations, an anti-science that was put to the use of interrogation, psychological warfare, "brainwashing" and mind control.

But it was not intended that way.

While the truth about the life of Jesus, the dispositon of the Ark of the Covenant, the architecture of the Gothic cathedrals, etc. presumably could be known through archaeological research and examination of ancient documents and histories, the operational secrets of the Essenes and other groups which share a common heritage were considered so powerful that they were protected by cyphers, passwords, ritual gestures of identification, and other arcane impedimenta: not through jealousy or greed, but because the same secrets that could be used to heal could also be used to kill. Thus the medical doctor could also become the poisoner; both disciplines derive from the same basic secret, the knowledge of the properties of plants and minerals. That is why a very high level of spiritual devotion and attainment was required of those who desired to share in this information, as a safeguard against the secrets being misused. In fact, the rules of the occult Orders were very specific on this point: the sacred knowledge—when used in society—could *only* be used to heal. The rest of the knowledge was to be kept secret and never used for personal power in the world, only for deeper spiritual understanding. This attitude is quite apparent in one of the most famous and influential documents printed in seventeenth century Europe, the *Fama Fraternitatis*.

Published in 1614—but with manuscript copies in evidence as early as 1611—the *Fama Fraternitatis* was the announcement of the existence of a secret body of pious and learned men, the Bretheren of the Rosy Cross, who were dedicated to humanist principles and who were somewhat in support of the religious reform movement taking place in Europe at the time. Thus, they wedded secrecy to wisdom to politics, all in a few short pages which begin with the discussion of their founder, one C.R. (identified in later documents as Christian Rosenkreutz), who was born in Germany but who traveled to the Middle East at a very young age and learned all he could of the occult arts before returning to Germany via North Africa and Spain.

Much of the document is taken with the discovery of C.R.'s tomb, and of the sketchy history of the Bretheren after C.R.'s death. The combination of the mystical with the scientific (the Bretheren were pledged to offer their services to the public only as healers, and to keep their membership in the Order and the rest of their arcane knowledge secret) with a bit of the political captured the imaginations of readers all over Europe, in what has been called "the Rosicrucian Furore." Many were desperate to sign up with the Order, if it could be found; others went into print either supporting it or castigating it.

Shortly thereafter, another document—the *Confessio Fraternitatis*—appeared, which offered more information on the Order as well as being more shrill politically, especially where the Pope was concerned. This hatred of the papacy would have been a hallmark of the Templars after they were suppressed, when they felt they had been betrayed and abandoned; but many in Europe had reason to despise the corruption of the Vatican at that time. The importance of the *Confessio* is perhaps in its giving of actual dates. Here we learn that Christian Rosenkreutz was born in 1378, and lived to be 106 years old, which means he died about 1484. As mentioned in the *Fama*, his tomb—when discovered—bore the inscription "*Post 120 Annos Patebo*," which means, "After 120 years I will open." Thus, we can conclude that the Tomb of Christian Rosenkreutz was opened in the year 1604.

Taking the story to be allegorical, we may wonder if the birth of Christian Rosenkreutz shortly before the Peasant Revolt in England has any significance, especially if we can accept that the Revolt was the work of the Knights Templar, in hiding since 1307. It may be that the Masonic Society was born at that time in 1378, went underground again in 1484 during the period when Islamic kingdoms in Iberia were being lost (at the "death" of Christian Rosenkreutz, possibly indicating Islamic support for the society in the intervening years), and then made made its way back to the light in 1604. But that is all conjecture; the dating seems quite specific, and may refer to events other than what we know of the Masonic Society.

There is, however, one very important clue common to both the *Fama* and the *Confessio*, and which is emphasized in both texts, and that is the strange odyssey of Christian Rosenkreutz to Damascus. We are told that he made his way to Damascus, where he learned Arabic and studied at the feet of the Eastern masters there. We may assume that Christian prelates were not the masters being cited. The area around Damascus at the time was rife with Syrian Nizaris who, although they had lost their stronghold in Damascus much earlier, were still active in the region and would remain so for centuries, tolerated by the Ottomans. In addition, it was to the "Land of Damascus" that the Essenes and other religious refugees had often fled in order to find sanctuary and a place where they could practice their beliefs in relative security. Both these Rosicrucian documents mention this sojourn in Damascus as the central event in the religious and occult education of Christian Rosenkreutz, for when he leaves Damascus and travels to other regions—Fez in

North Africa, and Salamanca in Spain—he views the quality of arcane teaching there as somewhat inferior to what he had learned in Damascus.

Further, in the *Confessio*, we read,

> . . . as those which dwell in the city of Damascus in Arabia, who have a far different politick order from the other Arabians. For there do govern only wise and understanding men, who by the king's permission make particular laws; according unto which example also the government shall be instituted in Europe (whereof we have a description set down by our Christianly Father) when first is done and come to pass that which is to precede . . . . Even in such manner as heretofore, many godly people have secretly and altogether desperately pushed at the Pope's tyranny, which afterwards, with great, earnest, and especial zeal in Germany, was thrown from his seat, and trodden underfoot . . .

Thus, we have in one paragraph a fascinating clue as to the Rosicrucian lineage and philosophy. For what Damascenes would have a "different politick order from the other Arabians"? And how does this fit with the impulse to resist the Papacy and actually to destroy it? What Arab philosophy would the Rosicrucians emulate? Obviously, it had nothing to do with mainstream Islamic government. Is this entire paragraph an allusion to the Syrian Nizari sect, the cult of the Assassins? And its anti-Papal stance a revival of the revenge of the Templars? Or is it even deeper than that, referring to a survival of Essenism, which did have a different government, a "different politick order" from Jewish, Christian and Muslim groups alike?

Like the Church and like Islam, the Masonic Society and the ephemeral Rosicrucian Order have had their share of renagade branches, formed by members who long for more initiations, different initiations, greater exclusivity, or who feel that the personal character of the lodges is not conducive to spiritual illumination or occult power. It is from these offshoots of Masonry and Rosicrucianism that organizations like the Golden Dawn and the OTO had their origins, groups that eventually led to Aleister Crowley, Jack Parsons, and L. Ron Hubbard. The fact that Freemasonry and Rosicrucianism had their spiritual origins in Syria, either through association with the Knights Templar or through some other collaboration with Islamic, Christian or Jewish heretical sects there, is important to a complete understanding of western secret societies, for it was from Syria that the Templars would have learned of the legends surrounding the crucifixion of Jesus, of the existence of Gnosticism and the War of Light versus Darkness, of Baphomet/Sophia, and of sacred geometry and Qabalistic numerology. It would have been from the Syrian Nizaris that the Templars would have learned of the infamous *qiyama* of Hasan II at Alamut and the doctrine that the old law was abrogated for the faithful . . . .

. . . That, in contemporary terms made popular by Western journalists and amateur historians, "Nothing is true; everything is permitted."

ENDNOTES

1 Farhad Daftary, *The Assassin Legends*, I.B. Tauris, London, 1995, p. 94
2 Hugh J. Schonfield, *The Passover Plot*, Bantam, NY, 1969, p. 7
3 Bernard Lewis, *The Assassins: A Radical Sect in Islam*, Oxford University Press, NY, 1967, p.12
4 Ibid., p. 130
5 Daftary, op. cit., p. 31
6 Ibid., p. 6
7 Lewis, op. cit., p. 44
8 Ibid., p. 62
9 Daftary, op. cit., p. 21
10 Lewis, op. cit., p. 48
11 Ibid., p. 130
12 Daftary, op. cit., p. 41
13 Lewis, op. cit., p. 73
14 Ibid., p. 73
15 Daftary, op. cit., p. 67
16 Ibid., p. 76
17 Ibid., p. 49
18 Lynn Picknett & Clive Prince, *The Templar Revelation*, Corgi Books, London, 1998
19 Hugh Schonfield, *The Essene Odyssey*, Element, Shaftesbury, 1998, p. 166

PEOPLES
TEMPLE
OF THE
DISCIPLES OF CHRIST

BOOK TWO: A WARM GUN

CHAPTER THIRTEEN

HEART OF DARKNESS

I take it, no fool ever made a bargain for his soul with the devil: the fool is too much of a fool, or the devil too much of a devil—I don't know which.

—Joseph Conrad, *Heart of Darkness*

To corner him for the Agency, it was recognized at Langley that the Devil must be made respectable. Working through conduits, the Scientific Engineering Institute helped fund a course in sorcery at the University of South Carolina. Two hundred and fifty students enrolled. The scientists of Operation Often studied carefully the results of classes devoted to fertility and initiation rites and raising the dead.

—Gordon Thomas, *Journey Into Madness*[1]

I stared at the clumps of bodies in front of the communications center. I couldn't bring myself to leave them. I noticed that many of them had died with their arms around each other, men and women, white and black, young and old. Little babies were lying on the ground, too. Near their mothers and fathers. Dead.

Finally, I turned back towards the main pavilion and noticed the dogs that lay dead on the sidewalk.

The dogs, I thought. What had they done?

Then I realized that Jones had meant to leave nothing, not even the animals, to bear witness to the final horror.

—Charles A.Krause, *Guyana Massacre: the Eyewitness Account*[2]

"The horror! The horror!"

—Conrad, *Heart of Darkness*

In November 1969 Charles Manson was in jail, but had not been charged yet with the murders at the Tate and LaBianca residences. He was arrested on October 12, 1969 on other charges, along with a number of his followers, who were scattered throughout the prison system awaiting trial. The Manson Family culpability in the Tate and LaBianca homicides would not be suggested until December. Until then, he was cooling his heels on what was a simple credit card fraud beef, and calmly expecting to be released at any time.

Steve Brandt, though, had committed suicide in New York City that month in terror over the killings and the possible existence of a hit list that would have included his name as a close friend and confidante of Sharon Tate.

At the same time, a couple—Al and Deanna Mertle—were experiencing some marital troubles. They had been married exactly a year before, in November of 1968, and each had children by a previous marriage; but they were finding it increasingly difficult to communicate with their kids and with themselves, and felt they were growing apart.

They decided to visit the minister who had married them, and one night they had dinner with him and his wife and the subject of a new church in Redwood City, a town some three and half hours from their home in Hayward, California, came up in conversation. They agreed to go to the church the following Sunday, and as it happened the event truly changed their lives.

And quite possibly ended them.

They joined the church in 1970 and stayed with it through thick and thin for the next six years. When they left in 1976, they were afraid for their lives. They campaigned vociferously against it, and did what they could to inform government and civic leaders of the threat it posed to society. They spoke of beatings, sexual abuse including the rape of men, women and children, public humiliation, torture, brainwashing, and the mind control of children, including sleep deprivation and being made to witness terrible punishments meted out for the slightest of offences and, sometimes, for no discernible offence at all. The leader considered himself a God, said he was the reincarnation of Jesus and Lenin, and demanded absolute obedience from his followers, who numbered in the thousands. It was Charles Manson and his Family writ large and fine-tuned.

In November of 1979 the Mertles published a book about their experiences. In February 1980, they were murdered in their home along with their teenaged daughter, each shot in the head execution-style by person or persons unknown. Their triple homicide has remained unsolved to this day.

The Mertles had published their book under a pseudonym: Jeannie Mills. It was entitled *Six Years With God* and was subtitled *Life Inside Rev. Jim Jones's Peoples Temple*.

The Jonestown massacre took place on November 18, 1978. In spite of tremendous media coverage, the case has never been satisfactorily explained, or the murders of over nine hundred persons ever really solved. The first police officials to be summoned to the crime scene described evidence that is at wide variance to that found in the official American reports. Bodies were missing, and then found. Numbers were juggled with reckless abandon. Cover stories were tried out, and then dropped in favor of more credible ones. Money was missing. Guns were missing. Documents were missing. And, as usual, witnesses started dying of unnatural causes.

Even the biography of the man at the center of the holocaust, Jim Jones, was sketchy and open to interpretation. His presumed close association with Dan Mitrione was never investigated by the US government or, if it was, the results were never made public. Mitrione was the man taken hostage and then killed by the leftist guerrilla Tupamaros in Uruguay in 1970, revolutionaries who knew that he was a CIA agent with AID agency cover. Jones and Mitrione had known each other in Indiana, where Mitrione was a cop specializing in juveniles and Jones a fifteen-year-old sidewalk preacher, and they *were* both in Brazil at the same time in the early 1960s: Mitrione with a police training unit that was under Agency for International Development (AID) cover, and Jones in some murky capacity that involved the US consulate.

Mitrione, it is now known, was involved with the training of Latin American police forces in the use of torture and drugs in interrogations, under the auspices of the now-defunct and cynically-entitled Office of Public Safety (OPS), an Orwellian organization that was formed during the Eisenhower administration. Mitrione was an avid practitioner of the methods he taught and, according to one of his trainees in Uruguay in the late 1960s, he would pick up homeless people on the streets to be used as guinea pigs in his training sessions, bloody interrogations which were always conducted in a soundproof room. In Montevideo, this room was in the basement of his home. When the derelicts died during the course of the "training," their bodies would be dumped back in the streets as a warning to Communist insurgents.

The drugs and techniques, of course, were the direct and unequivocal legacy of ongoing MK-ULTRA research. According to John Marks,

> In 1966 CIA staffers, including [John] Gittinger himself, took part in selecting members of an equally controversial police unit in Uruguay—the anti-terrorist section that fought the Tupamaro urban guerrillas. . . . Agency operators worked to set up this special force together with the Agency for International Development's Public Safety Mission (whose members included Dan Mitrione, later kidnapped and killed by the Tupamaros). The CIA-assisted police claimed they were in a life-and-death struggle against the guerrillas, and they used incredibly brutal methods, including torture, to stamp out most of the Uruguayan left along with the guerrillas.[3]

John Gittinger was the "MKULTRA program's resident genius."[4] He developed something called the Personality Assessment System (PAS). An incredibly complex system, it resisted computerization due to all the variables, and at one point Gittinger had something like 29,000 separate test results on computer printout in his office that he mined for data on the personalities of drug addicts, prostitutes, homosexuals, criminals, the easily hypnotizable, etc. His specialty was uncovering the "underlying personality structure—discrepancies that produce tension, conflict, and anxiety."[5] Gittinger had left his mark on virtually every aspect of MK-ULTRA, from the San Francisco "safe house" where prostitutes were observed with their johns behind two-way mirrors, to the attempt to develop an aerosol can that sprayed LSD, to the selection of secret police in Uruguay to assist Dan Mitrione in his endeavors.

During the same period, Andrija Puharich (of Arthur Young, MK-ULTRA and "Council of the Nine" fame) was also in Brazil investigating the famous "psychic surgeon," Arigo, while Arthur Hochberg (of Robert Mullen and E. Howard Hunt fame) was also in Brazil working for the CIA station there. Guy Lyon Playfair, an English-born biographer of Uri Geller and the author of several books on paranormal phenomena, was living in Brazil researching macumba and other Brazilian occult practices at the same time (working occasionally for *Time* magazine among other sources of income) and from 1967–71 was working for the *same* CIA front—AID, the Agency for International Development—that Dan Mitrione used as a cover! (As an aside, even the infamous medical doctor and war criminal, the "Angel of Death" at Auschwitz, Josef Mengele—one of the most wanted men in the world at the time—was living in hiding at a farm ninety-three miles north of Sao Paulo in 1962, and thus only a few hours' drive from both Sao Paulo and Belo Horizonte.) So, it was one big happy, psychotic, dysfunctional family: Jim Jones, Dan Mitrione, Andrija Puharich, Arthur Hochberg, Guy Lyon Playfair, Josef Mengele, even Arigo the psychic surgeon. But we are getting way ahead of the story.

We must spend some time with the Jonestown episode because it pulls together several disparate scarlet threads in this tapestry of politics, drugs, intelligence agencies, religion, mind control, and murder. Some commentators and journalists have gone overboard with accusations of Nazi involvement, and have claimed that Jonestown was "a CIA medical experiment." As outlandish as these claims seem *prima facie*, with Jonestown we are on the very threshold of the unbelievable. The documentation that does exist makes it virtually impossible to accept the official story of Jonestown as it has been handed down since that day in mid-November 1978 when Congressman Ryan was shot and over nine hundred others murdered. While the mainstream media has been content to cluck and shake their heads over the Jonestown massacre as an example of "what happens when people follow a religious leader blindly" and leave it at that, there was in reality so much more to the story of Jim Jones, the Peoples Temple, and the 913 murdered men, women and children that, if nothing else, the story needs to be told for their sake, most of whom never had a decent burial and many of whose bodies were never even identified.

LORD JIM

> Cornelius, who had made himself at home in the camp, talked at his elbow, pointing out the localities, imparting advice, giving his own version of Jim's character, and commenting in his own fashion upon the events of the last three years. Brown, who, apparently indifferent and gazing away, listened with attention to every word, could not make out clearly what sort

> of man this Jim could be. "What's his name? Jim! Jim! That's not enough for a man's name." "They call him," said Cornelius, scornfully, "Tuan Jim here. As you may say Lord Jim . . . . He is a fool. All you have to do is kill him and then you are king here. Everything belongs to him . . ."
>
> —Joseph Conrad, *Lord Jim*

The basic facts of the life of Jim Jones are a matter of public record. He was born James Warren Jones in the small village of Crete, Indiana on May 13, 1931. Crete doesn't appear on most roadmaps today, although its larger neighbor, Lynn, can be found about twenty miles north of Richmond, Indiana on the Ohio border, due east of Indianapolis. Jim Jones' father was a World War I veteran who had been gassed in the trenches and was considered disabled, living on a pension. A Quaker by birth, he was now a proud member of the Ku Klux Klan and a night watchman for the town, licensed to carry a handgun on his rounds. Jones' mother, according to one account, had been an anthropologist doing field work in Africa and had returned to Indiana soon after going there; the reasons are not clear. Thus, the marriage between these two people, widely separated in age, background and belief, is fairly incredible but nonetheless a fact.

Jim Jones and Charles Manson were contemporaries; Manson was born in 1934, only three years after Jones, and had a similar upbringing. Where Jones' father was a former soldier in the trenches of the Great War, Manson's father—at least in the eyes of the Ashland courts—was one Colonel Scott, of unknown background and unspecified military service (where did the "Colonel" come from?). They both were raised by very religious Christians who were not members of the immediate family. In Manson's case, we are talking about his West Virginia relations with whom he was housed when his mother was in prison. In the case of Jim Jones, the religious influence was a Mrs. Kennedy, who was his babysitter in Lynn after school while his mother worked at an aircraft plant in Richmond. Mrs. Kennedy was a devout Methodist, and it was from her that he got his first taste of the Bible and then wound up holding mock church services for other children at his home.

Then, at about the age of fifteen, he began preaching on the sidewalks in Richmond. This was certainly odd behavior for a high school student, and is an indication of how much he was attracted to religion: going from make-believe Sunday services at his home to actually preaching on street corners in town. It was at that time that he met Dan Mitrione, who was a police officer in Richmond, although the exact nature of their relationship remains mysterious and unexplored. It was in Richmond nonetheless that the seeds of Jonestown would be planted.

By the time he was ready for his senior year in high school, the Second World War was already over and his parents had separated. Jim Jones moved with his mother to Richmond, and he enrolled in Richmond High School while at the same time finding work as an orderly in Reid Memorial Mental Hospital. It was at Reid that he met his wife, a nurse four years his senior. He married Marceline

Baldwin in the Methodist Church in Richmond on June 12, 1949 and the newlyweds moved to Bloomington, where Jim Jones would attend Indiana University.

Jones took a part-time job as a night watchman, which was what his father had been doing to supplement his Army pension, and what a generation of other sinister gunmen have been known to do, such as David Berkowitz (the "Son of Sam") and Mark David Chapman, the killer of John Lennon. He began to drift away from the degrees he had been working towards, first the business degree and then the law degree, and then eventually even the degree in education. But by 1952 Jim Jones had finally found his true calling: as an assistant minister for the Somerset Methodist Church in Indianapolis. It was at Somerset that the phenomenon we know as Jim Jones was spawned.

Somerset was located in a poor white neighborhood in Indianapolis, a town as racist as any other in the United States in 1952. Jones, however, preached a gospel of racial tolerance, which was not accepted by the white community but which did attract black worshippers. By all accounts he was a charismatic speaker, but he supplemented his preaching with a fair amount of legerdemain: healing the sick in the manner of fraudulent faith healers the world over who remove cancerous growths from their patients with mesmeric passes, the shouting of Biblical phrases, and the generous use of concealed chicken livers as "tumors," which are revealed at just the right moment to effect the "cure." Eventually, Jones was kicked out of Somerset, but by then the damage had been done. He was not formally ordained into the ministry until much later, but he had developed a following throughout southern Indiana and Ohio nonetheless, aided by his frantic schedule of prayer services and radio programs, a campaign that wooed black people into a church organization that would include only whites in leadership positions.

At that time, the early 1950s, Jones' politics was by all accounts as virulently anti-Communist as those of his fellow clergymen, and his radio programs and preaching carried a clear anti-Communist message. This was, after all, the McCarthy Era and anti-Communism was fashionable in some circles (just as socialism was in others), and for a Christian minister in the Midwest who traveled the circuit between Cincinatti, Dayton, Richmond, Indianapolis and Fort Wayne, it was to be expected that he would preach against the godless Russians and the atheist Chinese. Politically then, before his trip to South America, his politics would have been considered sound by US government officials.

As the operation became more sophisticated, though, after his mysterious sojourn in Brazil, Jones gradually abandoned any pretense at standard Biblical terminology or theology. Jones began to speak of revolution, and of Jesus as a socialist. He began to gradually mock and villify the God of the Jews, the "Sky God" as he called him, and to identify Jehovah with satanic forces bent on the destruction of humanity. It was pure neo-Nazism, except it was so convoluted that most of his followers would never have recognized it for what it was. As detailed at some length in my previous work, *Unholy Alliance*, the Nazi ideologists of the

Third Reich had reinterpreted the Bible in such a way that the God of the Israelites was Satan. This has become standard theology in such racist organizations in America as the Christian Identity movement.

Lucifer was the "light-bringer," and intent on delivering humanity from the clutches of the evil Jehovah. This is also a Gnostic belief, as demonstrated in the scriptures uncovered at Nag Hammadi in Egypt in 1945. In this system, the Serpent in the Garden of Eden was the true God, who wanted to deliver the human race from the blind Creator God, the Demiurge who wanted Adam and Eve as his personal slaves. This deity is equivalent to the H.P. Lovecraft creature, the "blind idiot god of chaos," for it was he who created material forms with reckless abandon and who—in his blindness—believed he was the Superior Being and demanded that Adam and Eve worship only him. According to Gnostic legend, this being—Samael—was then chastised by the other gods for his vanity in assuming the mantle of Supreme God. That other gods existed is plain to see by the Biblical injunction, "I am the Lord thy God, thou shalt have no other gods before me," implying that there were other gods to be dealt with.

This multiplicity of gods with Biblical geneaology is what gave rise to the theology of the Process Church of the Final Judgment, as discussed in Book One. This form of Gnosticism also influenced Charles Manson, and he began to identify himself with Abraxas, a famous Gnostic deity whose numerological equivalent is 365, the same as the number of days in the year and thus representative of time itself. With the Nazis, the neo-Nazis, and the Christian Identity movement in the United States, Europe, and Latin America, we are experiencing a strange resurrection of first and second century Gnosticism: Gnosticism with a vengeance.

Some of this is evident in the sermons and speeches of Jim Jones as well, except that in his case he was obviously abandoning all pretense at religion of any kind and was trying to develop a popular political movement using all the creaking machinery of old-time religious revivalism. Imagine, if you will, all the ritual, pomp and ceremony of religion but without any mention of God. Imagine people signing over everything they own to a "Temple" that preaches neither Jehovah nor Jesus, but Lenin and Mao. In addition, Jones also preached reincarnation—not exactly a mainstream Christian belief, but one familiar to the early Gnostics—and claimed he was the reincarnation of Buddha, Jesus, Lenin, and the progenitor of the Bahai religion, the Bab. In other words, like his contemporary Charles Manson, Jim Jones was God; and by demanding total obedience and unstinting worship from his followers, he was unconsciously identifying himself with Samael, the "blind idiot god of chaos."

As Kenneth D. Wald points out in his *Religion and Politics in the United States*, the early American political campaigns were based on Christian tent revivalism:

> Candidates rallied supporters with torchlight parades, tent meetings, door-to-door canvassing, and public declarations of faith, the same methods pioneered by evangelists seeking religious converts.[6]

Jones merely took this one step further and mixed radical politics with Christian revival *sturm und drang* to the point where people thought they were in a church on Sunday—from all the singing and preaching, the handsome Reverend in his robes and aviator sunglasses, shouting and waving his arms in the pulpit (with no Bible in sight)—but were really at a political rally. An ersatz *socialist* political rally.

There is evidence to show that Jim Jones and his wife, Marceline, visited Cuba in 1960, for reasons unknown. It is here that the story takes on all the hallmarks of an intelligence operation, for there appear not one but two Jim Joneses, two different passports, and mutually contradictory itineraries throughout the period 1960–63.

Probably the best source of information on this period of Jones' life is contained in the parapolitical journal *Lobster*, a British publication that has long been a favorite of conspiracy theorists and investigative journalists. It is here, in issue number 37, that some of the most frightening information about Jim Jones was presented by veteran journalist and television documentary producer Jim Hougan (of *Spooks* and *Secret Agenda* fame). Entitled *Jonestown, The Secret Life of Jim Jones: A parapolitical fugue*, it gently debunks some of the wilder theories about Jonestown, while giving evidence for a scenario that is, if anything, even more unsettling. As I began to write this chapter, I was ignorant of some of the very firm connections that existed to support my own thesis, and I am thankful to Jim Hougan for the benefit of his two years of research on Jim Jones and Jonestown undertaken in the United States and South America.

Hougan has shown that Dan Mitrione and Jim Jones did know each other, and that Jones actually referred to his friendship with Mitrione several times during the course of his taped speeches at Jonestown. This is important, for it brings us one step closer to a true understanding of the events of 1978. More importantly, Hougan demonstrates that Jones was known to the CIA and the FBI before the massacre, and that the CIA maintained a file on Jones that coincided quite precisely with Dan Mitrione's career as an overseas "trainer" of foreign police forces. That is, the file on Jones was opened when Mitrione began to work for the AID-sponsored OPS program and was closed when Mitrione was killed in Uruguay in 1970, a period of roughly ten years spanning the Castro revolution in Cuba, the socialist victory at the polls in Guyana, the Bay of Pigs invasion, the assassination of President Kennedy, the socialist victories in Brazil, the military coup in Brazil, and even the assassinations of Bobby Kennedy and Martin Luther King. This coincidental opening and closing of Jones' file in tandem with Mitrione's career leads Hougan to believe that this was an indication of a Jones–Mitrione working relationship. If so, it has implications far worse than even the Jonestown massacre provides, for it means that Jones was infiltrating religious organizations, and specifically *black* religious organizations, on behalf of the United States government.

Jones visited Cuba in February of 1960. Certainly an awkward time for an American clergyman to be in Havana! Castro had just taken power the previous year, in January of 1959, and the Bay of Pigs plotting was already underway. The American presidential election of 1960 was months away. Yet, Jim Jones chose this time to visit what was practically a war zone.

According to a Cuban whom he met in Havana during that trip, Jones was involved in trying to arrange for Cubans to emigrate to the United States. This was part of a larger American policy of encouraging Cubans to defect from Castro, in order to weaken the Cuban economy as well as win some propaganda points. Jones was specifically trying to recruit black Cubans to come to Indianapolis where his Peoples Temple was still located. It seems that nothing much came of this plan, but Jones was evidently working on behalf of American political interests when he was there. He brought back with him photographs of himself in Cuba and most curiously a photo taken of him standing next to a downed aircraft that had been flown by anti-Castro Cubans—not exactly on the main tourist circuit, even in revolutionary Cuba. The anti-Castro Cubans were bombing the sugar cane fields in a further attempt to destabilize Castro's regime, and one of these photos shows a pilot's dead and mangled corpse. As Hougan points out, this type of photo would have been of extreme interest to American intelligence.

Did Dan Mitrione recruit Jim Jones one day on the streets of Richmond, Indiana? Did he note that Jones seemed to have a rapport with black people, something quite unusual for a white teenager in 1950s middle America? Was there a larger agenda, especially at a time when the FBI and the CIA were worried that a black revolution could threaten the existing American institutions and disrupt the status quo? Was Jones supposed to provide both an intelligence source within the black community, as well as a safety valve for the anger and resentment felt by a race that had been enslaved and even then were struggling for basic human rights?

If Jones did have an intelligence agenda, and was working for Dan Mitrione in some capacity, then it might go a long way towards explaining the two passports and, incredibly, the two different versions of Jim Jones.

Like the strange appearance of one, two, many Oswalds in New Orleans, Mexico City, and Dallas, which has plagued Kennedy assassination researchers for years, there were at least two men traveling to South America at that time named Jim Jones.

As pointed out in Hougan's research, Jones had two passports issued to him at two different times. One, issued in Chicago on June 28, 1960 and another issued in Indianapolis on January 30, 1962. The problem is twofold. First, as there is strong evidence (on the basis of an eyewitness account, an affidavit signed by Jones during that period in Cuba, etc.) that Jones was in Cuba in the first few months of 1960, how did he travel there if his passport was not issued until June 28? Secondly, why the two passports, as the first one issued in 1960 certainly would still be valid?

It is certain that Jones was in Cuba in February of 1960. It is also certain that he visited Cuba again a year later. And there is further evidence—also incontrovertible, and verified by newspaper accounts printed at the time—that Jones had visited Guyana (when it was still called "British Guiana") years before he ever set up the commune known to the world as Jonestown. In fact, according to an eyewitness—a Cuban he eventually brought to the United States in August 1960 to stay with the Temple in Indianapolis—Jones appeared to have been well-traveled by that time and "knew Latin America well. He had already been to Guyana, and wanted to start a collective there."[7]

The assumption is that Jones also spoke Spanish, since the witness—Carlos Foster—did not speak English at that time, and they spent entire days for a week discussing plans for bringing Cubans to the United States. (Why, Jimmy, we never knew ye!)

Then, in 1961, the Jim Jones phenomenon becomes positively . . .otherworldly.

He was named as the Director of the Indianapolis Human Rights Commission when he was thirty years old, by most accounts, which would mean sometime in 1961. One wonders what the duties of a Human Rights Commission director would have been in Indianapolis in 1961, but whatever they were, by October he was resigning the post after having spent a week in a hospital due to stress. He had been hearing "extra-terrestrial voices"—shades of Aleister Crowley and Aiwaz, or of Barney and Betty Hill, whose celebrated abduction by a UFO had taken place the previous month in New Hampshire—and having seizures.[8] These symptoms sound quite serious, and would be evidence of a psychotic episode, perhaps a schizophrenic or schizophreniform disorder, but alas we have insufficient information about Jones' particular illness, rendering further speculation futile.

At the end of October, Jones left Indianapolis for a few weeks of rest and recuperation, in Hawaii according to most accounts. Unfortunately, as Jim Hougan points out, this story is patently false, for the Guyanese newspapers have Jones in their country in late October 1961. He could not have been in both Hawaii and Guyana the same week of October. Not in 1961. Further, he is supposed to have stopped in Mexico City during that time as well, which renders the impossibility of being in three different countries spread that far apart in the same week. For those who have not attempted to visit Guyana, it is a difficult place to reach today, and was even more so in 1961. There were no direct flights from Honolulu to Georgetown. The airfare—in 1976 when the author was contemplating a trip, two years before the Jonestown massacre—was also prohibitively expensive, as Guyana is off the main tourist routes. One typically flew via Trinidad or Jamaica or one of the other Caribbean islands.

All of this simply goes to say that Jim Jones could not have been in both Hawaii and Guyana the same week. Further, there is evidence that Jones had been under psychiatric care in San Francisco and—as Hougan points out—some have offered the opinion that Jones went to Hawaii in order to "receive psychiatric care without publicity."[9]

The idea that Jones might have spent time in a mental hospital in Hawaii is rich with further implications, for one of history's most infamous assassins—Mark David Chapman—also spent time in a mental hospital in Hawaii, and Hawaiian hospitals also came under investigation for their possible role in a network of drug trafficking that involved the organization now believed to have been responsible for the Son of Sam murders in New York City. Also, and for reasons that are really not very clear, several of the Manson Family women, to keep one of their own out of the witness chair during the trial of Charles Manson, fled to Hawaii, where they fed her a hamburger laced with an overdose of LSD. The unfortunate victim—Barbara Hoyt—wound up wandering in the busy streets of Honolulu and was taken to a hospital for observation and treatment. This betrayal by her fellow Family members led to her becoming a *very* cooperative witness against them once she recovered. Why the Manson Family chose Hawaii is open to speculation. It would have been just as easy—and far less expensive—to have moved the witness to one of the other states or even to Canada or Mexico. The selection of Hawaii seems either serendipitous or evidence of a deeper agenda.

Nonetheless, what *is* known about Jones beyond any doubt is that he was under psychiatric care at the Langley-Porter Neuropsychiatric Institute in San Francisco, a hospital that conducts experiments on behalf of ARPA, the Advanced Research Projects Agency of the Defense Department, and where "virtually every survivor of the Jonestown massacre was eventually treated."[10] Jones' medical files have been withheld from scrutiny, even though Jones has been dead since 1978.

So, we have two passports, two distinct destinations, and many motives. Jones in Guyana was preaching against Communism. Jones in Cuba (during one trip) was attempting to lure Cubans into the States, and during another was meeting with Fidel Castro. Jones in Mexico was up to God knows what. And finally Jones was in Brazil. But the usual reasons given for his trip there also defy the chronological record.

The usual impetus described is an article published in the January 1962 edition of *Esquire* magazine entitled "Nine Places to Hide." In the event of a nuclear war, according to the article, there were nine safe places on the planet that would be immune from both bombs and radioactive fallout. One of these was Eureka, California and another was Belo Horizonte, Brazil. Jones is described as extremely paranoid about nuclear war, and desperate to find somewhere to sit out a holocaust. Although he was based in Indiana at the time, and therefore much closer to Eureka, California, for some reason Jones decided that Brazil was the place to be, and he moved himself, his wife, a personal friend and his wife, and their four children to Belo Horizonte that year.

The problem with this scenario is that Jones was already in Guyana in October of 1961. The article on Jones was published in the *Guyana Graphic* on October 27, 1961, so the story that he stopped off in Guyana on his way to Brazil doesn't wash.

And the story that the *Esquire* article prompted his trip also doesn't wash. It wasn't in print in October of 1961.

The months between October of 1961 and April of 1962 are a black hole in his biography. It seems evident that he was not in Indianapolis, but aside from that there is no way to know where he was or what he was doing. All that is certain is that he arrived in Sao Paulo, Brazil on April 11, 1962. According to a friend who knew Jones in Brazil at this time, he had arrived in Sao Paulo from Cuba.[11] The problem with this account should be obvious to anyone who remembers the period, because it is only a year after the Bay of Pigs invasion, and only six months before the Cuban Missile Crisis. How many Americans were touring Havana at that time? In addition, the same eyewitness claims that Jones showed her a photograph he had taken with Fidel Castro. This was the same American minister who made anti-Communist speeches in Guyana the year before.

Will the real Jim Jones please stand up?

Jones may have admired Castro's style of public speaking, for it so mirrored his own: lengthy speeches lasting hours, filled with revolutionary rhetoric, paranoia and *ad hominem* appeals to the better angels of our nature. But this foreign travel of the Joneses is mysterious and hard to understand on the basis of the existing documentation. So much of it is not explained. So much of the information that is available is contradictory. Witnesses describe Jones' lifestyle in Brazil as lavish; others as meager at best. Witnesses say that Jones was setting up an orphanage in Brazil, but for whom and with what funding is not described; others say that Jones did no missionary work at all in Brazil, but left the house each morning with a briefcase and returned each evening with few comments on where he had been or what he had done. He would make passing references to Naval Intelligence (à la Ron Hubbard) or to other government work; people who knew him in Brazil thought of him as a spy: no Brazilians who knew Jones during his stay there and can attest to his Christian missionary work have been discovered.

Whatever took place in Brazil, by the time he returned to the United States he had undergone a conversion to socialism, a conversion that would eventually lead him to espouse Communism as the only way. He dropped his pretense of being a Christian minister in the 1960s and began openly supporting revolutionary activity, particularly an end to racism. This could have been an honest conversion, based on witnessing firsthand some of the very poor conditions in South America and understanding that the United States was at least partially to blame for the suffering. On the other hand, the conversion—as so many have charged—might have been false, a cover story being developed for a far more sinister purpose. After all, most of the people who were murdered at Jonestown were black. Most of the people doing the killing were white.

As mentioned previously, Jim Jones was in Brazil at the same time as Dan Mitrione, whom he had known from their common sojourn in and around Richmond,

Indiana. Mitrione had since left Richmond to join the FBI, and eventually became an instructor of foreign police departments on behalf of the Office of Public Safety, which worked hand-in-hand with AID, the Agency for International Development. Mitrione's work involved training police investigators in the finer techniques of interrogation. This work was eventually heavily criticized by the US Congress when word of its excesses began to be known publicly in the 1970s, and the unit was disbanded and reorganized under other supervision. But it was in the 1960s that the damage had been done.

State Department, military and CIA operations in Latin America were notorious for their rapacity during that time. It is a matter of public record that the CIA managed to orchestrate a military coup in Guatemala in the 1950s, the Bay of Pigs invasion of Cuba in 1961, the election of a supposedly pro-US Forbes Burnham as Prime Minister in Guyana over his socialist opponent Jagan (who later expressed himself as satisfied with the results of the rigged election, when it was learned that Burnham himself was even more of a socialist than Jagan!), and, of course, the US-sponsored overthrow of the Allende regime in Chile on September 11, 1973. The police forces of Latin America have all received training of one kind or another from US specialists working for AID, OPS, or the US military directly; and this training has taken place either in the United States or, during the 1960s, more likely in the foreign country itself, far from the watchful eye of congressional oversight committees.

Indeed, the US government does not know what training programs were in place during that time or how much they cost, as they were often buried under other appropriations and other budgetary columns in the annual reports. But it was millions upon millions of dollars for dozens of programs spread throughout the various Departments and Agencies. In the unlikely event that it is ever shown that Jonestown *was* a "CIA medical experiment," there will be no documentation to support the contention. The personnel, equipment, contingency plans and budgets will all be buried in just the way government accountants and bookkeepers know so well: just as they had done for the international police training programs of the 1960s; just as they had for the mind-control experiments of the CIA, until a blunder revealed four boxes of financial papers sitting in a basement at Langley long after the rest of the documentation had been thoroughly shredded by Richard Helms and his Dr. Strangelove, Sidney Gottlieb.

During the same era, the author himself was employed by a large government contractor and Fortune 100 company, the Bendix Corporation. where I was privileged to work in their International Marketing Operation, located on Broadway in mid-town Manhattan. At Bendix—from 1973–79—I witnessed several occasions where my employer was used as a cover for intelligence activities and police and military support operations all over the world. Indeed, in the wake of the Watergate revelations, several newspapers carried stories about the involvement of Bendix "field engineering personnel" in the training of Saudi Arabian troops, as one example. We read these reports avidly in the office, looking for the names of people we knew. In Argentina, local Bendix employees and their expatriate manager were kidnapped by left-wing revolutionaries and held hostage. Our sales rep from Caracas, Venezuela—from the swashbuckling firm Representaciones Godoy—would fly to New York in his private plane and walk into our offices wearing a sidearm, much to the consternation of our security staff. I remember watching the telex machine one day as our man in Lebanon sent his sales report and purchase orders; in the middle of transmission, the machine died and we held our collective breath. Civil war had just begun, and our office was in the middle of the war zone in Beirut. Finally, after an agonizing wait of about twenty minutes, the transmission resumed. It was the last we would receive from Beirut, and our man transferred to another Middle Eastern location where the sound of small arms fire did not punctuate the night.

Considering that our clientele involved everyone from the Shah of Iran to the military procurement departments of countries all over the globe, it was no wonder that we would be used as a cover for intelligence operations. Financial arrangements at Bendix for international accounts were also so byzantine and complex, involving the payouts of huge "commissions" and the awarding of bizarre orders for seemingly useless equipment, that we began to understand that US intelligence agencies could have easily financed many of their operations simply by using Bendix sales people and sales agents in the target countries as conduits for funds, funds that would go both ways. For instance, we once sold to the Government of Pakistan *six* early-warning type radar systems. Six! The United States itself only had one of the same type at the time. It was understood that the contract for the six systems was, in reality, a contract for something else altogether; that the Pakistani government was paying for other services or equipment that it was considered best to conceal from the watchful eyes of journalists and congressmen. And so it goes.

Thus, when the author heard some of the stories about Dan Mitrione, as well as about Operation Condor in Latin America, Operation Phoenix in Vietnam, etc., he could well imagine how easily the finer details had been arranged. Had Jim Jones been in Brazil on some sort of assignment—either for the CIA, or for some other agency such as Mitrione's OPS—his funding would have been easy to source and to hide. As a contract agent, he might even have been paid in cash, with a paper receipt signed either in his name or in a mutually-agreed upon pseudonym.

It is known that Jones returned to the United States with money, not an easy miracle if one's whole time in Brazil was spent in missionary work, living close to the bone and building an orphanage, as he claimed in his speeches.[12] In an emotional confession before his assembled followers, in fact, he said that they were so broke in Brazil that he had to become a gigolo and sell his body to the rich and eager wives of local Brazilian businessmen in order to raise money for the impoverished children under his care, and all with his wife Marceline's approval. One must pause for a moment and brush a tear from the eye in sympathy with the tremendous sacrifice Jim made—over and over again—in order to put food on the table for the starving orphans of Belo Horizonte!

And, if such really is the case . . . where is the Reverend Jim Jones Memorial Orphanage?

THE BOYS FROM BRAZIL

"The precise pain, in the precise place, in the precise amount, for the desired effect."
—Dan Mitrione (in *Killing Hope*, by William Blum)

Brazil in 1962 was in virtual chaos. Jânio Quadros had been elected in 1960 on an anti-corruption platform. His vice president was the Brazilian Workers Party candidate, João Goulart. (In Brazil, presidents and vice presidents are elected separately.) Seven months later, however, for reasons that have never been revealed, Quadros resigned the presidency and threw the country into a constitutional crisis. By rights, Goulart should have taken the oath as president, but due to his socialist politics, the army resisted his inauguration. Finally, he was allowed to take office, but only with reduced responsibilities. The job was to be shared with a newly-created position of prime minister, someone who was acceptable to the military and could keep the socialist president in line.

Finally, in 1962, a national referendum held by Goulart reversed the 1961 decision, and Goulart was allowed to take full powers and remove the prime minister. This did not, however, happen with the full cooperation of the Brazilian military authorities. Brazil was as much in the midst of the Cold War as the United States and the other powers. Brazil, alone of all countries in South America, had sent troops to Europe to fight in World War II, specifically in Italy, and the Brazilian army considered itself a close working ally of the United States. Goulart, on the other hand, was seen as a Communist, and Brazilian and American military and intelligence forces began to cooperate to find a way to have him overthrown. Mitrione was in the middle of that plotting, and his training of the Brazilian police forces involved not only the usual third-degree and torture techniques but also "political" training. Both the United States and the Brazilian right-wing viewed Goulart as a revolutionary in the pocket of the Soviets and the Cubans, and this message was brought across by American advisors like Dan Mitrione.

This was the political environment in which Jim Jones and his entourage found themselves. Goulart's presidency had just been assured by the national referendum, and the Brazilian Army was in the grip of fear of a Communist takeover of their country. Of course, Christian fundamentalist churches could be counted upon to support the Army and the right-wing against Communist "evangelism" in the countryside. Godless Communism was the common enemy of all Christian churches, so a successful American preacher like Jim Jones could be expected to add his support to American and Brazilian efforts to counter the attraction that Goulart and other Communist sympathizers had for some of the electorate. There is no doubt in my mind, based on long experience in South America and Asia, that the presence of Jim Jones in Brazil in 1962 had political overtones, whether or not he was actually in the employ of an intelligence agency or simply cooperating with an old friend like Dan Mitrione. Religious groups in South America have long been politically affiliated or politically active; World Vision is only one example of an organization that is widely reported to have cooperated extensively with American intelligence services in South America.

During Jones' time in Brazil, the economy began to deteriorate. Goulart struggled to keep the country afloat as foreign loans were called in, loans that had been made to Brazil during the previous administration. By 1964, when Jones was leaving Brazil, inflation had reached 100 percent, and there was no foreign money coming into the country to help it stave off the creditors. In January and February of 1964, desperate to hold on to power and to keep the military at bay, Goulart organized political rallies in major cities throughout Brazil. He nationalized the oil refineries and put a cap on the expatriation of profits by foreign investors. Finally, he made a speech to the Brazilian Army, asking the noncoms to refuse to carry out any order by their officers if the order was not in Brazil's best interest. This speech was carried on national television. It was all the excuse the Army needed.

On March 31, 1964 the Army seized power in Brazil, and Goulart went into exile. Forever. A few months earlier, Jim Jones went home.

While Jim Jones was ostensibly setting up an orphanage or missionary operation (and it is perhaps relevant to note here that Jones had not yet been actually ordained as a minister by any church; that would not happen until after his return to the United States in 1964), Andrija Puharich was in Brazil to investigate the claims of "psychic surgeon" Arigo. Also at the same time, Guy Lyon Playfair was living and writing in Brazil about a variety of topics, but concentrating on his main interest: the paranormal. Both Puharich and Playfair would later become involved with Uri Geller, the Israeli psychic who dazzled the world with his apparent ability to bend spoons with his mind. As for Playfair, he was working for *Time* magazine and eventually for the AID office in Rio.

Brazil is a greenhouse for occult societies and alternative religious practices. When the author was there in the 1990s, it hadn't changed much from the 1960s. Native practices such as *macumba, umbanda* and *candomble* are very popular, and with every level of society. More surprisingly, the works of Allan Kardec are also popular. Kardec was a nineteenth-century spiritualist who wrote on a wide variety of occult themes, mostly having to do with contacting spiritual forces. In addition, basic grimoires of European ceremonial magic—such as the *Greater* and *Lesser Keys of Solomon*—are widely available and treated with reverence. All this operates in close proximity to the Catholic Church and to many different Christian sects, from Pentecostals to Evangelicals to standard Presbyterian and Methodist churches. Add to this the largest Japanese community outside Japan, located in Sao Paulo, and you have quite a mixture of spiritual beliefs and practices, which of course include Buddhism and Shintoism. Faith healers and spiritists abound, and new occult techniques and teachers are embraced with fervor. The sacrifice of animals occurs on a regular basis, in the deep jungles of the Amazon River basin as well as in the high-rises of Sao Paulo and the *favelas* of Rio de Janeiro.

According to Hougan's sources, Jones was there to study the phenomenon of David Miranda, a Pentecostalist minister who started his own congregation—the Church of God is Love—in Brazil in 1960–61, shortly before Jones' arrival. Miranda's mix of Christian fundamentalist Pentecostalism with faith healing and (as accused in 1999) money laundering would have attracted the like-minded Jones. Hougan believes, however, that there might have been another element to Jones' fascination with Miranda, and that would have been the CIA's interest in "mass conversion techniques" as part of its MK-ULTRA program. Certainly, Jones' visit to Brazil coincides with a major effort on behalf of the CIA to study primitive religions worldwide, from the psilocybin-eating Indians of Mexico to the Yoruba faith healers of Nigeria. This was not only a CIA interest, for the military had also actively pursued these studies in the name of psychological warfare. The manipulation of the masses—whether by drugs, hypnosis, or other means—would have been of extreme interest to the CIA and the military, and people like David Miranda would have become a focus of this interest. Today, Miranda's operation spans the globe, particularly in developing countries, and is worth many millions of dollars; it was probably a model for Pat Robertson's Christian Broadcasting Network and the Christian Coalition, which has also been involved in supporting right-wing military dictators from Mobutu of Zaire to Taylor of Liberia to Rios Montt of Guatemala and the Contras of Nicaragua (as we shall see later on).

Brazil is a multi-racial society, built by the Portuguese with imported slaves from Africa and indentured servants from Asia. (Guyana, its next door neighbor, is populated almost completely by Africans and East Indians; the native American population is a distinct minority.) In the Brazilian bush can be found a wide variety of Native American tribes, their numbers dwindling as the rain forest is cut down and their cultures lost forever. The Brazilian capitol of Brasilia—located not on the coast like Sao Paulo and Rio de Janeiro, but in the interior—is surrounded by animists and spiritualists of every stripe, and government officials are known to frequent these practitioners to ensure the success of their respective careers. It is a country steeped in respect for the paranormal, and therefore no wonder that the psychic surgeon Arigo should have known such acceptance there.

Andrija Puharich had gone to Brazil in August of 1963 with businessman Henry Belk,[13] a former agent with the Office of Naval Intelligence (ONI), heir to the largest chain of department stores in the southeast United States (the Belk Stores which are headquartered in Charlotte, South Carolina), and founder of the Belk Research Institute, of which Puharich was president, an institute created for the study of paranormal phenomena. Belk had also been acquainted with Dutch psychic Peter Hurkos but, according to one account, became disillusioned with Hurkos when Belk's ten year old daughter and only child went missing shortly after Hurkos had done a psychic reading for Belk and predicted nothing of the sort. His daughter was found dead by drowning and, according to the same source, it was Hurkos who saw the site where she would be found. That was not enough for Belk, of course, who felt that if Hurkos had any real powers he would have warned Belk of the tragedy so that he could have averted it. The Belk family is famous in South Carolina; they have endowed various educational institutions and have been major contributors to charities. William Henry Belk, the founder of the department store chain, began in 1888 with a small store in Charlotte which he named The New York Racket. (Cynics will claim the name was a case of psychic premonition by the energetic Presbyterian businessman!)

According to one source, the two had gone to Brazil to investigate Arigo at the suggestion of John Laurence, an RCA engineer who worked with NASA and who was actually on the committee that formed NASA in 1958. In Puharich's book, *Uri*, Laurence is described as "one of our researchers" in a group of medical specialists put together by Puharich in 1968 to return to Brazil to study Arigo,[14] and the one who spotted a UFO at the same time. Laurence's specialty with NASA and RCA was satellites, and it is possible that his role in Brazil was linked with the development of communications satellite technology. Laurence's other interests obviously involved the paranormal, and it is not clear what his relationship was to Puharich and why he would have invited Puharich specifically to come to Brazil at a time when that country was on the verge of a military coup to counter what was believed to be a nascent Communist insurgency. Further, as Puharich admits that Laurence was a specialist in satellite technology and worked for the Astroelectronics Division of RCA in New Jersey,[15] and thus would not seem to have had medical training, one wonders why he was present at all. Yet, there we have it. An unusual grouping of individuals in Brazil during the precise timeframe when both Brazilian and American intelligence agencies were pondering what to do about Goulart and the Communist menace: former agent and CBW specialist Puharich, police trainer and torture specialist Mitrione, local specialist in Brazilian occultism Playfair (who would later find work with AID), wealthy businessman and paranormal aficionado Belk, and NASA and RCA engineer Laurence. If we really want to stir ourselves up into a paranoid frenzy, we can add Josef Mengele to the mix.

Mengele had escaped justice after World War II and eventually found himself in Brazil in late October 1960, staying first in Sao Paulo before winding up, in the 1962–64 time period, at a farm about ninety-three miles north of Sao Paulo, which puts him within an easy distance of both Sao Paulo and Belo Horizonte.[16] Mengele, of course, was a notorious medical practitioner at Auschwitz, responsible for experiments on live subjects and with special interest in twins. It was Mengele—the Angel of Death—who would stand at the train station when the boxcars of Jewish prisoners were unloaded, telling the bewildered, starving victims "Right" or "Left," to live or to die. Of course, Mengele was in hiding after the war, desperate to avoid Israeli commandos, and would not have been hobnobbing with the likes of Jim Jones or Dan Mitrione or Andrija Puharich. It is only another example of the action of a sinister synchronicity at work in history.

However, it can be stated with some degree of certainty that the political events in 1964 that returned Brazil to the control of the military were welcome news to Mengele. A socialist or Communist in power meant worse conditions for Nazis on the run, particularly if the regime was pro-Soviet. The Russians have no sense of humor when it comes to Nazi war criminals; witness their intransigence in the case of Rudolf Hess, who was the only prisoner left at Spandau by the time he died in 1987, more than forty years after the end of World War II. Considering how deeply American intelligence agencies were protecting Nazis after the war, and how closely Brazilian and American military and intelligence agencies were cooperating, we can be sure that the local authorities would not have been looking too hard for Josef Mengele.

We can, however, posit a relationship between Jones and Mitrione due to their common origins in and around Richmond, Indiana and Jones' statements to that effect in his Jonestown speeches. Puharich and Playfair certainly knew each other, and both knew Geller. In fact, Geller would refer to Puharich as his "CIA case officer." Did the investigation of Arigo have an intelligence aspect? And, considering that Jim Jones made a very public spectacle of "psychic surgery" in the United States, by palming rotten chicken livers and holding them up as evidence of cancerous tumors extracted from his adoring congregants by nothing more than blind faith and mesmeric passes, was there any contact at this time between Arigo and Jones or Jones and Puharich? Unfortunately, we shall never know. Arigo, Puharich, Mitrione and Jones are all dead.

However, one connection can be made, to be filed perhaps under the "six degrees of separation" rule. In February of 1953, Andrija Puharich had been redrafted into the US Army, and posted to the Army Chemical Center in Edgewood, Maryland, where he would remain until April of 1955. His duties are not described anywhere in any detail, although evidence examined in Book One demonstrates that at least some of his responsibilities involved experiments under the CIA mind-control effort. Before Puharich's posting, one Dr. Laurence J. Layton was posted to Dugway Proving Grounds in Utah, a test center for the Chemical Warfare Division of the US Army; this was in November of 1951. In March of 1952, Layton had been named Chief of the US Army's Chemical Warfare Division, a position he held until 1954. In other words, Dr. Layton was—at least on paper—Dr. Puharich's boss.

The relevance of this will become clear shortly. Suffice it to say for now that Dr. Layton—and especially his children, Larry Jr. and Deborah—would play a major role in the events that led up to the Jonestown massacre and that Larry Jr. is still in prison, the only man ever convicted of murder in that hideous event, while it was his sister, Deborah, who had been an important influence on Congressman Leo Ryan's decision to go to Jonestown in the first place.

And, in one more bizarre twist to this story, another associate of Puharich and the busy occult circle around Arthur Young, Jack Sarfatti, Ira Einhorn and the rest was physicist Russell Targ, who by his own admission was involved with the Al and Jeannie Mertle group of Jonestown survivors. In fact, he was the Director of Counseling at the Mertles' Human Freedom Center in Berkeley, California in 1979, and worked for them for "almost a year" until he left to join the Stanford Research Institute (SRI) to study psychic phenomena. It was the Mertles who, under a pseudonym (Mills) wrote an exposé of the Peoples Temple entitled *Six Years With God.* A few weeks after Targ left their employ, the Mertles were found dead, murdered execution style in their home.[17]

DISCIPLES OF THE MILLENIUM

Upon Jones' return to the United States he quickly found himself formally ordained as a minister, and began setting up shop as the Peoples Temple, first in Indiana and then relocating to Ukiah, California. According to Jones, the relocation to Ukiah was of a piece with the *Esquire* magazine article that said the nine safest places in the world included Eureka, California. Now, Eureka and Ukiah are quite distant from each other and, to make matters worse, Ukiah is quite close to several military installations around San Francisco which would be targets in the event of a nuclear strike. No matter; somehow Jim rationalized his choice in his own mind.

By 1968, things at the Peoples Temple had become quite spooky. The Bible was being replaced by Jones' political oratory. The good citizens of Ukiah were getting worried about this strange preacher in the aviator sunglasses who peppered his "sermons" with obscenities and his theology with Marx. In addition, the white community of Ukiah was nervous at the growing numbers of blacks who were joining the Peoples Temple and causing cultural distortion in their little town. Jones began casting about for another home, and this would eventually become San Francisco.

In the meantime, he managed to attract some of his most important members (and defectors). He would also become heavily involved in the health-care industry, and in California politics. What does not compute in reviewing his career is how Jim Jones—if he was truly the psychopath as painted by the press and government reports—was able to garner such support from bureaucrat and politician alike. We can understand the influence of a charismatic preacher over the multitudes; that is, after all, the basic premise of broadcast television: to be able to communicate effectively with the largest mass of viewers one must tailor one's programming and vocabulary to the level of a sixth grade public school education. That is basically what Jones did, as is evident from the tape transcriptions of some of his speeches, including the last one made during the massacre at Jonestown. What we cannot understand is how this same individual was able to function effectively with governors, mayors, and businessmen who—at least theoretically—should be able to spot a con artist at thirty paces; some of the power of these men (and they were mostly men) resides in the ability to spot the same power in others. Jones had the admiration and support of his flock, which numbered in the thousands, and he made substantial donations to the religious organization that eventually adopted the Peoples Temple and insured its legitimacy: the Disciples of Christ.

Garry Wills, in *Under God: Religion and American Politics*, notes that the Disciples of Christ have given the United States three presidents: James Garfield, Lyndon Johnson, and Ronald Reagan.[18] (Oddly enough, the first was assassinated and the third would be the target of an assassination attempt. Only Johnson, it would seem, escaped the attentions of an assassin, although he became president due to the assassination of his predecessor.) The Disciples of Christ is a millennialist sect, and this is probably why—again, according to Wills—Reagan "felt so comfortable with biblical language about the end time whenever he met with fundamentalists."[19] Indeed, not only Reagan, but other members of his administration held deeply apocalyptic beliefs, men such as Defense Secretary Caspar Weinberger and Interior Secretary James Watt.

These high government officials held a Biblical, fatalistic acceptance of the idea that the End Times had come and were upon us; that the Second Coming of Christ was imminent and that the events of the world were pointing towards the meltdown of civilization and the ensuing Rapture. America was, therefore, and however briefly, in the hands of an administration that believed in the literal truth of the Book of Revelation, the Apocalypse (however one interprets the phrase "literal truth" when it comes to the hallucinatory prose of that work). Most Americans were blissfully unaware of this fact, and the implication that their government was on a collision course with the Evil Empire based on Biblical prophecy and Christian Fundamentalism, as if we were living in the twelfth century instead of the twentieth. How dangerous was the world in the 1980s! One wonders what Soviet intelligence made of all of this, ignoring for the moment that their celebrated revolutionary, Bakunin, was an avowed Satanist and that Stalin's daughter was a follower of the Russian mystic Gurdjieff . . . .

Oddly, Wills does not mention Peoples Temple or Jonestown in this study of American religion and politics, although he does agree that in America, religion and politics can never be truly separated. The Disciples of Christ were born in that same mad religious fervor of the early nineteenth century's religious revivalism that brought us the Awakenings . . . and the sight of an impoverished farm boy with a book of medieval spells summoning an angel on a mound on the night of the autumnal equinox in upstate New York: the Angel Moroni and the boy Joseph Smith.

Lest we believe that millennial and apocalyptic beliefs are a legacy of America's purely European and purely Christian ancestors, there is the parallel case of the Native American Ghost Dance phenomenon which culminated—in 1890—with the massacre of the Lakota Sioux at Wounded Knee. Without going overmuch into historical and ethnographic detail, suffice it to say that the Ghost Dance was originally designed to bring the Native Americans close to nature and to heal the wound they perceived had been made by the arrival of the white man and his profligate ways. It was believed that if the tribe performed this sacred dance daily then the breach between heaven and earth would be mended and the earth renewed, and all the buffalo that the white men had killed would be reborn and would wander the earth as in the Golden Age, and the white people themselves would be destroyed by a flood.

The Ghost Dance as such was instigated by a Native American prophet, Wovoka, who had a vision of God telling him to teach the Ghost Dance to the people. This occurred years after the famous Battle of Little Big Horn, in which Chief Sitting Bull destroyed the forces of General Custer. Sitting Bull had been exiled, then imprisoned in the United States, then freed to live on a reservation. The Lakota tribe was moved onto a reservation, and forced to become farmers rather than the hunters and gatherers they always had been. They had no idea about farming and began to starve to death, prohibited from carrying weapons and hunting for their food. In secret, they revived the Ghost Dance and met in the hills to pray for deliverance.

It was believed by the American forces that Sitting Bull was somehow behind the Ghost Dance movement and was using it to foment discord and hatred against the whites (as if they needed any instigation). They arrested and killed Chief Sitting Bull on December 15, 1890 and then pursued his followers into the hills. The massacre of Wounded Knee took place on December 29, 1890 and was the last major battle between Native Americans and whites. The exact number of slain Lakota Sioux is not known, but was estimated to be between 200 and 300, mostly non-combatants: women and children, including infants. A number of American troops were also killed, mostly from "friendly fire." The Sioux were wearing "ghost shirts" that had been specially prepared and blessed by their medicine men, and they believed the shirts would render them invulnerable to bullets. They were mistaken.

The Lakota were looking for the millennium, but instead they found Apocalypse Now. The parallels to Montsegur, to Masada, and even to Waco are too numerous to mention, and any interested reader can find sober histories detailing the sad events of the Lakota, as well as of the Cathars, the Branch Davidians and other "cults" that were deemed too dangerous to exist. The story of the Peoples Temple, however, differs from these examples in several important ways, as we shall see; but we should note that Jim Jones was a close friend and supporter of American Indian Movement (AIM) leader Dennis Banks, who himself led a ten-week protest and occupation of the original Wounded Knee site in 1973.

As more and more congregants signed over their life savings, their social security checks, and their tax refunds to the Peoples Temple, the church became, if not wealthy, at least well to do. Jones, fearing racial backlash in Ukiah, moved his congregation first to Orlando and then to San Francisco in 1972, to an old synagogue on Geary Street in 1972. By that time, he was already something of a political power in the state. He was the foreman of the grand jury of Mendocino County, and one of his top aides—Timothy Stoen—was an assistant district attorney for Mendocino County. That meant, essentially, that Peoples Temple represented the power of both the grand jury and the DA's office: a powerful combination, but it is not clear whether this power was put to actual use.

It is clear, however, that for whatever reason (genuine revolutionary charisma and sincere love of his fellow humans or a secret intelligence agenda) he became popular and powerful in the State of California after his return from Brazil and his move from Indiana. It was during this transitional period that he met the pseudonymous Al and Jeannie Mills—who would be murdered a few months after the publication of their book on Jonestown—and the Laytons. Two of the Laytons—Thomas N. Layton and his sister Deborah Layton—have also published books on the subject. Their brother, Larry Layton, Jr., is the one still in prison for his role in the Jonestown massacre: the murder of Congressman Leo J. Ryan.

As the Laytons are at the very heart of the story, we need to take a closer look at the family in order to ascertain the shift and shadow of the sinister forces that brought them together in fissionable combination with Jim Jones; for it is clear that the major players in this story all had prior professional experience in secret military and intelligence projects, and that Congressman Ryan was on the trail of CIA medical experimentation in his home state of California at the time he was murdered by the son of a man who was in charge of all US Army Chemical Warfare, a brilliant scientist who was deeply conflicted over his role as master of chemical weapons and their delivery systems.

Once again, as we have so often in this study, we must return to Germany in the war years.

> Many people that like to accept tradition as it is, without even questioning it, are religious in this superficial, conventional way . . . They merely accept a picture they have in their imagination, colored with the strange and sweet feeling of memory from childhood and early youth . . . . It is living somewhere back in our unconscious mind and shows up in everything we 'feel' toward other people, situations and ourselves.
>
> This picture memory plays the most important part in the religious concept of most people as they are nowadays. And it is a dangerous one . . . .
>
> —Lisa Philip, in a letter to Laurence Layton dated Sept. 15, 1941[20]

The Layton family is, of course, two families: the Laytons of Boomer, West Virginia and the Philip family of Hamburg, Germany. There is some mild controversy over the ancestral lineage of the Philip family, and one commentator (Meier) has attempted to prove that they were Nazis. This does not seem likely, as the same commentator does admit that they were related to the Nobel-Prize winning physicist, James Franck, who was—like the Philip family—a non-practicing Jew. According to Dr. Laurence Layton, the Philips also claimed to be related to a sixteenth-century Spanish cardinal, which is an unusual pedigree for Jews,[21] particularly in the sixteenth century, although possible. As for the Laytons, Laurence Layton's ancestors in Pennsylvania had been Quakers (although Laurence himself was now a Methodist, raised by a Methodist grandfather), and Lisa Philip had become a Quaker shortly after emigrating to the United States, and was a member of the State College Friends Meeting at Pennsylvania State College where she was studying,[22] thus sharing a strange link with Ruth and Michael Paine, who were also Pennsylvania Quakers, albeit a generation later.

Dr. Laurence Layton was born in Boomer, West Virginia—a small town about fifty miles southeast of Charleston along the Kanawha River, in an area of burial mounds and prehistoric mystery—on March 8, 1914. His maternal grandfather, Sheldon Nutter, was "a circuit-riding preacher, Baptist and Methodist on alternate Sundays, in the hills of Virginia, West Virginia and Kentucky"[23] and was general manager for the Mark A. Hanna Coal Company in Boomer. His father, John Wister Layton, was an electrical engineer credited with the design of the circuit breaker, among other devices.[24] John Wister Layton married Eva Nutter on January 18, 1913. Laurence Layton was their first child.

At the age of nineteen, Laurence Layton fell in love with the sixteen-year-old Mildred Arthur, a girl from Kentucky who had come to Boomer to visit relatives. Unfortunately, Mildred had a friend back in Pikeville, Kentucky: one of the Hatfield clan. He came to visit one week and Laurence—thinking he was Mildred's boyfriend—became depressed and quit college two days later, fleeing to Scranton, Pennsylvania where his mother and her new husband lived. (His father, John Wister Layton, had died at the age of thirty-one from a staph infection.)

It was in Scranton that Laurence Layton first made the acquaintance of the Young People's Socialist League, which was meeting in a YWCA in town. (Oddly enough, future CIA mind-control czar Sidney Gottlieb would also be active in the Young People's Socialist League, in his case at the University of Wisconsin, and during the same timeframe.) Layton stayed involved with the Socialists for about a year, and then returned to West Virginia, where he eventually garnered some local fame as a youthful inventor and scientist and went on to earn a master's degree, leaving shortly thereafter for Pennsylvania State to get his doctorate in chemistry. These were the late 1930s, the years just before America's entry into World War II. Six thousand miles away, in Europe, the Nazi menace was building strength after strength, and millions of lives were in terrible jeopardy.

Lisa Philip was born on July 14, 1915 in Hamburg, Germany, to Hugo and Anita Philip. The Philip family was descended, it is claimed, from Sephardic Jews—the "Asiatic" Jews rather than the more Slavic Ashkenazi Jews of Eastern Europe—and had been in Europe for a thousand years, arriving in Spain during the Moorish conquests and leaving during the subsequent Inquisition in the fifteenth century, which forced the Philips out of Spain and eventually into Germany. Lisa Philip was raised as a German, and had never visited a temple or celebrated any Jewish holidays. They observed Christmas and Easter, and had never identified themselves as Jewish at all. This gave rise to some suspicion among later commentators that the Philip family was Nazi, particularly considering the fact that Lisa's father, Hugo, was a banker and stockbroker whose accounts included I.G. Farben and Siemens, companies later identified as integral parts of the German war machine.[25]

The Philip family was cultured and sophisticated. Their home was done in the Bauhaus style, and they cultivated music and the arts. When the political situation became untenable, the Philip family began to make arrangements to leave Germany forever.

Lisa Philip was the first to leave, on May 6, 1938 aboard the SS *Manhattan*, bound for New York. Her passport, according to Thomas Layton, was stamped *Juden* or "Jewish." Her sponsors in the United States, the Berlin family, met her at the dock and took her to live with them in Philadelphia. Her parents were not so fortunate, finding it very difficult to leave Germany and emigrate to the United States along official channels. Things looked very bleak when they were turned back at the Italian border and sent on a return train to Germany. Rather than face a horrible fate in the camps, Hugo and Anita Philip took an overdose of Veronal.

They were saved, however, when a conductor found them unconscious and took them off the train in Austria, putting them in a hospital. For the time being, they were under Austrian supervision, even though Nazi officials were visiting the hospital daily to inquire after their condition. They managed to convince friends in Vienna to sponsor them until they received their American visas and, with the help of these friends and the American Society of Friends (the Quakers) spent four months there under heavy Nazi observation, before finally being allowed to leave for America on March 20, 1940.

In the meantime, Lisa Philip had moved to Chappaqua, New York (at the time of this writing, the new home of former President Bill Clinton) and found employment with a Congregationalist minister, Reverend Galen Russell. Attending church every Sunday with the Russells, Lisa Philip had become not only Americanized but Christianized. By the fall of 1940, she found another position, this time at Pennsylvania State College as a physical therapist (in the college's hospital). It was there that she met Laurence Layton.

They were introduced by a mutual friend, Franz Werner, in early 1941, and on October 18, 1941 they were married.

On December 7, 1941 the Japanese bombed Pearl Harbor, and the United States entered World War II.

Laurence Layton could have been drafted, but his wife wrote to her relative Dr. James Franck to get him an appointment with the University of Chicago so that he could avoid the draft. Franck did manage to arrange a posting for Layton, but he instead received a student deferment through regular channels and decided to stay on at the University of Pennsylvania. Had he accepted Franck's offer, he would have been involved with the Manhattan Project, which is what Franck was working on in Chicago.[26] Instead, he finished his doctorate and wound up working for Eastman Kodak at their headquarters in Rochester, New York. That job did not last very long, but the Laytons' first child—Thomas—was born there. In November of 1943, Laurence Layton decided to take a job as an assistant professor at the University of Maryland, a position he held for three years, during which their next two children—Annalisa and Laurence John, Jr.—were born. After the war, Dr. Layton found employment at Johns Hopkins University and eventually published important work in the field of cortisone treatments for arthritis.[27] This led to a higher profile for Layton, and he came to the attention of the US Army.

On November 5, 1951 he arrived at Dugway Proving Grounds in Utah, where he was named chief of biochemistry of the Army's Chemical Warfare Division. In the spring of 1952, he was named chief of the entire Chemical Warfare Division.

During the preceding years spent in Maryland, the Laytons had regularly attended Sunday meetings with the Quakers and considered themselves sincere Friends. Quakers are pacifists and have a very negative attitude towards warfare, finding the idea of armed conflict repugnant. (During the Vietnam War, it was common for Quakers to declare themselves conscientious objectors and to find themselves assigned to non-combatant duties in hospitals and other public services. The fact that Richard Nixon was a Quaker is one of history's ironies . . . or dirty jokes.) However, chemical warfare must seem even worse: especially as countries were busy writing laws against both chemical and biological warfare without actually banning warfare altogether.

There is a common denominator among people of different racial and ethnic origins that such weapons are inhuman and should be forbidden. Yet, this devout Quaker and man of high morals—so high, in fact, that he could never accept the fact that his devoted wife and the mother of their three children, Lisa Philip, was not a virgin on their first night together—accepted the job with the Army, even though his work was being recognized on an international level and he had been lecturing on it in Europe. No one, not even his eldest son Thomas Layton—who is now a well-known and respected archaeologist with many awards and honors to his name—can explain this strange about face. Yet, there is no denying that it happened, and that Dr. Laurence Layton was "responsible for the publication of ten classified reports on research aspects of chemical warfare and more than 100 reports on chemical weapons systems."[28] All that in only the two years he was employed by the Army. Dr. Layton was therefore quite an enthusiastic sponsor of chemical weapons, averaging one report on chemical weapons systems per week and five classified reports on chemical warfare per year. It was during his tenure as head of the Army's Chemical Warfare Division that some of the military's most controversial experiments on unwitting human subjects were taking place, such as the spraying of *aspergillus fumigatus* over populated areas. *Aspergillus fumigatus* is an infectious organism that affects the "lungs, bronchi, external ear, paranasal sinuses, orbit, bones, and meninges."[29] The organism can, in fact, cause death.

During the first three months of 1953, for another instance, the city of Minneapolis was subjected to a total of eighty-one hours of an aerosol spraying of zinc cadmium sulfide (to simulate a bacteriological attack) during the hours of 8:00 P.M. to midnight, and 1:30 P.M. to 5:00 P.M.[30] No one was warned about these events, of course, and everyone was exposed: men, women and children. The same type of simulation was undertaken in St. Louis during the following three months, from April to June of 1953. No testing was done of the humans who had breathed the chemical, and no follow-up was ever reported to determine what effect, if any, the testing had on the health of the general population.

Other tests, involving the aforementioned *aspergillus fumigatus* as well as *Serratia marcescens* and *bacillus subtilis*, were undertaken in the 1950s, and some of these projects were undertaken during Layton's tenure. The Army has insisted that these organisms—used to simulate such toxic substances as anthrax—are harmless to human beings, even though the medical literature available at the time shows clearly that they are, indeed, dangerous and—in some cases—fatal to human beings.

The most famous germ warfare test, though, was undertaken a little before Dr. Layton's tenure as CW chief, and that was the test over San Francisco in 1950, in which several people were taken ill and one died. Thus, Dr. Layton was both heir to a tradition of experimentation on unwitting populations and for two years the man in charge of the entire program. Perhaps coincidentally, and as described in John G. Fuller's memorably-entitled *The Day We Bombed* Utah, both Utah and neighboring Nevada were the scene of a controversial series of tests of atomic weapons during the time that Dr. Layton was living there. Specifically, a test with the code name "Dirty Harry" took place on May 19, 1953, and the fallout from the blast affected both human beings and livestock in both states.

That test had been preceded by many others over the years since 1951, and although Dugway was considered as a site for these tests, it was passed over due to its proximity to large population centers. Everyone in Nevada and Utah was aware of these tests, however, and the Army began to realize that large amounts of radiation were affecting citizens as far away as Troy, New York in the form of radioactive rain. Dr. Layton would have known all about these tests, of course, even though they were taking place outside of his area of responsibility. His tests—also involving unwitting citizen populations—were of weapons systems, but of a chemical and biological nature rather than atomic or nuclear.

It is important to remember that this was the Cold War, and that drastic measures were not only considered but often employed in the struggle to defend the country against every sort of attack from the Soviet Union and China; that does not justify using human beings as unwitting guinea pigs, of course, but it puts these operations in some sort of context. That Dr. Layton was dismayed by the uses to which the science was put is evident from his reluctance to stay with the program; that he performed excellent service for that program is also in evidence, to wit his one hundred reports on chemical warfare systems and the ten still-classified reports published during his short tenure with the Army's Chemical Warfare Division. Such, perhaps, is the structure of the human mind, able to support two such contrary natures simultaneously, each as strong as the other, both vying for dominance at the expense of the soul.

Later, in 1954, Dr. Layton transferred to the Naval Powder Factory at Indian Head, Maryland, where he would work with ICBMs and missile systems; but in the midst of this vigorous military research and development there was a tragic note. On May 10, 1952 Dr. Layton's mother-in-law, Anita Philip, committed suicide in New York City.

Hugo and Anita Philip had immigrated to the United States in 1940 and thus escaped the hideous fate of many of their friends and fellow Jews. But Anita Philip had never quite escaped the Nazis in her mind. Her suicide is one of the strangest episodes of this story, and there have been several attempts to explain it. The generally-accepted theory is that—due to the classified nature of her son-in-law's work for the Army—a routine background check was in progress on her family, and that it is the heavy-handed approach of the FBI that contributed to her paranoia that the secret police were after her once again. An expanded version of this theory has it that Anita Philip was so distraught over her son-in-law's work for the Army that she was moved to shame and despair.

She left a note, and there is in it a hint of guilt over an undisclosed indiscretion:

> My friends, know that I, free and proper, am a good American. But I was a gossip and have been entangled in a network of intrigue.[31]

The letter was written in German, so perhaps something of its nuance was lost in the translation. It is strange that it would be addressed to "my friends," as if to a wider audience than her children and family, whom she mentions later on in the brief note. Does the word "friends" perhaps refer to her fellow Quakers? Alas, we shall never know. Nor shall we know what she meant by "I was a gossip and have been entangled in a network of intrigue," which is certainly suggestive of something other than paranoia over an FBI investigation. To whom was she gossiping? What was she saying? What was the network of intrigue? The family brushes it off as a symptom of her failing mental state. But after writing the note, and signing it with a simple initial, "A," she leaped to her death from her apartment window.

A year later, and another person connected with the Army's Chemical Warfare Division would fall from yet another window in New York City. That person, of course, was Frank Olson and there is every indication that he was murdered by the CIA.

With Dr. Layton in Utah and Dr. Olson in Maryland, there was also Dr. Puharich, also in Maryland and also at Camp Detrick where Olson was stationed. All three men worked for the Army in chemical and biological weapons research, and all at the same time. The fact that the CIA was running its own operation in conjunction with the Army at Camp Detrick at the time Dr. Layton was chief of the Army's Chemical Warfare Division indicates that these men were all known to each other, if not on a personal basis then surely by name and function. Olson fell to his death in New York in November of 1953, and it is perhaps more than a coincidence that Dr. Layton decided to leave the Army's CWD soon thereafter to start work for the Navy in Indian Head, Maryland.

Other men connected with the CIA found themselves dying under mysterious circumstances at the same time. While much of the focus has been on Dr. Frank Olson—thanks to the brave and tireless efforts of his son, Eric—the other deaths have been ignored until recently. With the new developments in the Olson case, reporters and investigators have begun to look at other suspicious deaths and the tally is surprising.

A former State Department employee and suspected Soviet agent, Laurence Duggan, fell to his death from his 16th floor office window in Manhattan on December 20, 1948.

Former Secretary of Defense James Forrestal fell from the 13th floor of the US Naval Hospital at Bethesda, Maryland on May 22, 1949: a case that has all the earmarks of an "assisted suicide," and which many family members believe was homicide.

On January 24, 1953, State Department official and suspected CIA agent James C. Montgomery was found dead with a cord around his neck, his body completely nude. The death was ruled a suicide, but then-Congressman Fred E. Busbey of Illinois didn't believe it and called for a full investigation in the House.

Lifelong intelligence agent Speyer Kronthal was found dead on April 1, 1953. The cause of death was believed to have been a self-administered drug overdose. A high-ranking CIA official, Kronthal was revealed in 1975 to have actually been a Soviet double agent.

Duggan and Kronthal have been revealed to be Soviet agents—well, revealed by the CIA—and perhaps we can consider their executions appropriate, if not justified. We have no such reassurances on the case of Montgomery, none at all on Olson, and especially not on James Forrestal. Could it be that a government agency which finds it expedient to execute suspected Soviet spies without due process of law could also find it expedient to execute other men with whom they have "issues"?

At any rate, by July of 1957 Dr. Layton had accepted a (relatively benign?) position as a research scientist for the US Department of Agriculture, at a laboratory near Berkeley, California. The family up and moved to the Bay Area and looked forward to a healthier environment, free from talk of payloads and weapons systems and lethal chemical agents. A new addition to their family, Deborah Layton, had been born in February 1953 (she was conceived the week of Anita Philip's death).

As the 1950s moved into the 1960s, the Layton children were as affected by the growing youth culture as any other youngsters. Deborah Layton became very problematic, getting involved with drugs and teenaged depression and alienation. Thomas Layton had become cerebral and intellectual and was already moving in his own circles, as was big sister Annalisa. Laurence Jr. was consciously avoiding the draft for the Vietnam War, and was working in hospitals and waiting for confirmation of his conscientious objector status.

Deborah Layton—after a stint in the United Kingdom at a strict Quaker school—was finally drawn into the Peoples Temple experience by her brother Larry. This was when the Temple was located in Ukiah, California. Gradually she became very involved with the group and was entrusted to greater and greater responsibilities by Jim Jones. She found herself becoming part of an inner circle that handled the money, and was involved in moving funds out of the United States and into bank accounts in Latin America and Europe. Just as Rev. David Miranda of Brazil would be accused of doing some twenty years later, Jim Jones moved millions of dollars out of the country using church members as "mules," carrying the cash with them and depositing it in various accounts spread over the globe.

In addition, Deborah's mother—Lisa Philip Layton—also became involved with the Peoples Temple. Things were never that close between Lisa and her husband Laurence, and she saw the Peoples Temple as an adventure to be shared with her children. Lisa Layton, the German-born Jewish refugee from the Nazis, would emigrate to Guyana with Deborah, and would die at Jonestown months before the massacre itself.

Larry Layton, the youngest son of Dr. Laurence Layton, had had his share of emotional turmoil growing up and found himself involved with drugs and all the other alternative experiences available to the youth of the sixties. But in the Summer of 1968, he and his new wife—Carolyn Moore, the daughter of Rev. John Moore, a Methodist minister—moved to Ukiah, where Larry got a position as an aide at the Mendocino State Mental Hospital and was working on obtaining his conscientious objector status. His wife visited the Peoples Temple and came back impressed with Jim Jones and the Temple experience.

The "Peoples Temple of the Disciples of Christ of Redwood Valley" had been incorporated in the State of California since November 26, 1965. In 1967, Jones had been named the foreman of the Mendocino County Grand Jury and was also the Director of the Mendocino and Lake Counties Legal Services Foundation. His wife, Marceline Jones, had become a state nursing home inspector and, in the process, the Peoples Temple had opened three convalescent homes and a home for boys, and even a pet shelter. Thus, suddenly the Peoples Temple was in the health-care field, and its leader was heavily involved in local politics. His assistant pastor, Tim Stoen, was also an assistant district attorney for Mendocino County. The church was acquiring a power base.

At the time Carolyn Moore Layton decided she wanted to join the Peoples Temple, she was considered perhaps the most attractive woman in the church and this came to the notice of its priapic minister. He decided that he wanted Carolyn as his mistress, so he orchestrated the divorce of Carolyn and Larry in 1969 by first having Carolyn publicly humiliate Larry in front of the congregation. The influence of Jones was so great that Larry meekly accepted Jones' suggestion that he should divorce Carolyn since they were so incompatible. Jones then offered another one of his flock as a substitute on the spot, and the bewildered Larry—pressed to choose someone—selected a blonde, blue-eyed former hippie chick, Karen Tow. Done. Larry and Karen were married, and Carolyn became Jones' paramour, eventually becoming pregnant by him and bearing their child, a boy they named Kimo (the Hawaiian equivalent of "James"). In order to provide a legal father for the birth, Jones had Carolyn marry another Temple member.

Then, in 1970, Deborah Layton met Jim Jones for the first time. (That same summer, Jones' associate—case officer?—Dan Mitrione had been killed by the Tupamaros in Uruguay, leaving Jones high and dry but not without resources in the government.) By the mid-1970s she had become one of his most trusted followers, an essential partner in setting up the Jonestown facility and managing the administrative and financial matters of the church both in the States and, eventually, in Guyana. Her brother, Larry, was just as deeply involved and was part of the security force that guarded the Jonestown complex, a security force that was more like a troop of prison guards than a defensive army to protect the members from outside hostilities.

By that time, it was hard to tell the difference between Jonestown as beleagured commune and Jonestown as *stalag*. Jones had become increasingly paranoid about government intervention. His socialist rants from the pulpit of the Peoples Temple church in Ukiah and, later, in San Francisco became increasingly full of dire warnings about the doom facing America and the coming race war that would target groups like the Peoples Temple and its followers. Like any good member of the Disciples of Christ, Jones' view of the late twentieth century was apocalyptic.

There would be a conflagration, perhaps a nuclear war, and only those he managed to save would survive the holocaust. Jones' vision of an imminent race war was eerily similar to Manson's. One could say they were on either side of the same argument: Jones (ostensibly) wanted to preserve the black people of America and Manson wanted them destroyed. Both, however, saw race war as inevitable. When the dust cleared, however, Manson had killed only white people (with an attempted murder on one black drug dealer); Jones had killed hundreds of black people in Jonestown.

In March of 1976, Jones was appointed to the San Francisco Human Rights Commission, a reprise of his role with the Indiana Human Rights Commission in the early 1960s. In September of that year, there was a testimonial dinner in his honor that was attended by San Francisco Mayor George Moscone, Lt. Governor of California Mervyn Dymally, Angela Davis, Eldridge Cleaver, and many other luminaries.

His popularity and importance were such that by March of 1977 he was sharing a table with First Lady Rosalyn Carter at the Democratic Convention Dinner, after having met in previous months with President-elect Jimmy Carter's transition team and Vice President-elect Walter Mondale. Suddenly, Jim Jones was a force to be reckoned with in California state politics, and therefore at the national level as well.

And this publicity attracted some unwelcome attention from the media.

THE POLITICS OF THE FAMILY

In October 1976, a month before the US presidential election that would put Jimmy Carter in the White House, a man named Bob Houston decided he would leave the Peoples Temple. He wrote a letter of resignation to Jim Jones on October 3rd. On October 5th, he was dead.

He was not the first victim, and certainly would not be the last. Jim Jones exceeded even Charles Manson in sheer brutality and convoluted, complex mind-control games. Like Manson, he retreated from society with a band of followers. In Manson's case, it was to the desert; in Jones' case, it was to the jungle. Both had millennial expectations. Both could not countenance defection from the "Family"; such disloyalty was punishable by death.

> The 'family' becomes a medium to link its members, whose links with one another may otherwise be very attenuated. A crisis will occur if any member of the family wishes to leave by getting the 'family' out of his system, or dissolving the 'family' in himself. Within the family, the 'family' may be felt as the whole world. To destroy the 'family' may be experienced as worse than murder or more selfish than suicide.
>
> —R. D. Laing, *The Politics of the Family*, 1969

In the 1960s, the writings of Scottish psychiatrist R. D. Laing became very popular with alternative mental-health-care professionals, people who felt—like Laing—that perhaps schizophrenia was more a spiritual state than an actual illness or disease, and could be treated with metaphysics rather than electroshock and lobotomies. His seminal work, *The Politics of Experience*, could be found on many a bookshelf in college dorms and hippie communes. His more clinical work, such as *The Divided Self*, *Self and Others* and *The Politics of the Family*, reinforced the message of political liberation through spiritual liberation, of mental health through spiritual health. Laing focused on the family as the origin of most mental problems as well as most social problems, and in this he was not much different from Freud and generations of social workers. Laing, however, took the argument to a different level and used his findings in clinical psychiatry to extrapolate a larger vision. To Laing, schizophrenia was not necessarily a break-down, it could also be a "break-through."

Laing's work was attacked, predictably, by other psychiatrists who felt that schizophrenia was not a metaphysical playground but a serious and debilitating mental illness whose only hope of a cure was through surgery—the dread lobotomy—or electroshock, or drugs. When chemical imbalances were found to be at the heart of schizophrenia and thus the disease could be treated with chemicals that would redress the imbalances, Laing's theories were abandoned as so much quaint hippie furniture from the sixties.

However, Laing's basic premise was not necessarily invalidated by the discovery that there exists a link between chemicals and mental states. After all, the CIA had spent millions in an effort to clearly define the relationship between hallucinogens and consciousness. Science, however, preferred to believe that there was a direct cause and effect relationship between chemical imbalance and mental illness: the technological approach was to use chemicals to create an artificial balance wherein the illness would disappear. For Laing, this was just another form of lobotomy. It did not speak to the spiritual imbalance that had caused the illness in the first place—it treated the symptom and not the cause—and by using drugs to create the illusion of psychic integration, one merely swept the core problem under the rug. But the mechanistic approach to psychiatry and psychotherapy—demanded by a mental health profession which felt that psychology should be as "scientific" as possible—meant that more holistic theories would be abandoned in favor of chemical, surgical and electroconvulsive therapies.

The methodology of Jim Jones—both at the Peoples Temple in Ukiah and San Francisco and especially at Jonestown—was a combination of both approaches. Religion is, after all, a close cousin to psychotherapy and psychology in general. Like Manson, Jones had his "family." The followers were to call him "Father," not like the Catholic custom of referring to all priests as "Father," but in a more intimate way. Only Jones could be called "Father" at the Peoples Temple. All the members were his virtual children, and they demonstrated this in their submissive and dependent attitude towards him. And whenever any of them wished to "defect"—that is, simply leave the church—it was considered tantamount to an act of betrayal against Father and against the entire Family.

Jones used psychodrama extensively in his dealings with subordinates and the members of his congregation, a psychodrama composed of equal measures of fire-and-brimstone sermonizing, sexual politics, public humiliation, and—it is believed—drugs. The pharmacy at Jonestown was heavily weighted in favor of narcotics and psychoactive compounds, and it is not clear to what extent these drugs were used in the everyday life of the commune. As for sex, Jones constantly complained of his continuous need for sex, and would enlist as many women as he could in his sexual stable. He would then ridicule the sexual lives of his male followers, and insist that all men but him were basically homosexual.

He would control the sex lives of the members of the Peoples Temple, and arranged marriages between couples who were then not allowed to have sex. He would demand that wives complain publicly about the lack of sexual performance or prowess of their husbands, while demanding as well that they praise Jim Jones in that department. In other words, it was Mansonism writ large and, if possible, even uglier. Ostensibly, the rationale behind all of this was the spiritual liberation of his followers. In fact, the clever use of these techniques ensured not the liberation of his awe-struck congregation but their near-total enslavement.

Ed Sanders, in his book about Charles Manson and the Family, stated that if the Pentagon ever formulated the Manson Secret, the world would be in trouble. One wonders if Jonestown was an example of such a formula: a white man, with murky intelligence connections and political activity in Latin America and the Caribbean during the sixties, becomes the leader of a large black congregation and orders them all to their deaths. If this had been in a novel, it would have been dismissed as unbelievable.

Soon, the press began to get wind of the weird circumstances surrounding the Peoples Temple. Any organization that powerful in state politics would certainly come under scrutiny, and it was only a matter of time before the newspapers and magazines began to do exposés of life at the church. This situation was exacerbated by the defection of several church members and their open discussions with the media. This, coupled with the FBI raid on Scientology offices when it was discovered that the Scientologists were infiltrating the government and spying on government agents, made Jim Jones increasingly paranoid about a government raid on the Peoples Temple, which he painted in terms of the fascists attacking the socialists.

In the 1970s, this was a distinct possibility. On January 22, 1974 Governor Ronald Reagan of California, in his State of the State message, announced plans for the creation of a "violence center" to study the causes and cure of violence among youth, minorities, etc. The plan was to use an abandoned nuclear weapons test site in the Santa Monica mountains; although it was conveniently close to Los

Angeles, it was also remote from populated areas, hard to reach, guarded by barbed wire fences and secure buildings, and considered an excellent site for the type of research Reagan was intending to carry out. This did not materialize, mostly due to public outcry over the very idea of a secret government center to study violence as divorced from the social conditions that contribute to violence, such as poverty, lack of education, etc. Many people feared—rightly or wrongly—that the center would be used to develop a more efficient and more oppressive security apparatus in the state where the Los Angeles Police Department already had a reputation for a harsh and swift response to crime, particularly minority crime. This was coming at a time when the Watergate hearings were reinforcing a negative view of government interference in domestic life, interference that would be escalated once Reagan became President in 1981.

At the same time, California Congressman Leo J. Ryan was making a name for himself as a government watchdog. He had co-authored the Hughes-Ryan Amendment, which required the CIA to get prior approval from Congress before undertaking any covert activity. In addition, he was asking questions about the CIA's mind-control projects in the State of California, as he wondered whether or not the notorious members of the Symbionese Liberation Army (SLA) had been the willing or unwilling beneficiaries of the MK-ULTRA program while serving time at Vacaville.

The SLA was a bizarre revolutionary militant group, whose claim to fame was the kidnapping of publishing heiress Patty Hearst on February 4, 1974 only a few weeks after Reagan's controversial "violence center" announcement, and it has been a favorite subject of conspiracy theorists for decades, who believe that the SLA was a front for a domestic CIA operation. The mere fact of the kidnapping itself, with Patty Hearst being subjected to brainwashing by the SLA cadres and then sent out to help them rob a bank, was headline-grabbing news for weeks, even though many people could not understand what it all represented.

She had been blindfolded and subject to sensory deprivation, held in a closet, and raped by her captors: circumstances familiar to political prisoners all over the globe and particularly in the Latin American nations where men like Dan Mitrione trained the security forces. When Patty Hearst was finally freed she was put on trial for armed robbery as if she were legally culpable, a subject on which many psychiatrists disagreed passionately. It brought many of the old CIA mind-control experts out of the woodwork, although they were not necessarily advertised as such. Dr. William Sargant, who was a friend of Dr. Frank Olson and who advised the British intelligence agencies on interrogation and brainwashing techniques, was one of those who examined Patty Hearst, as was Dr. Martin Orne and Dr. Robert Jay Lifton, the latter an expert on Chinese mind-control techniques.

Much was happening between 1973 and 1975. Donald DeFreeze, the commander of the SLA, had earlier been a prisoner at the Vacaville facility that was used by the CIA as part of their mind-control experimentation program. At

Vacaville, an organization was set up to raise black consciousness—the Black Cultural Association, or BCA—which was under the direction of Professor Colston Westbrook. Westbrook has since been identified as a former intelligence officer who served in the Far East during the 1960s and, in fact, worked for AID—the same agency that provided cover for Dan Mitrione and, perhaps, Jim Jones in Brazil—during the same years that Mitrione was with them. It is tantalizing to speculate about a handoff of Jones from Mitrione to Westbrook; or perhaps after the murder of Mitrione, Westbrook simply picked up where he had left off. We know now that Jones spent time at the Langley-Porter Neuropsychiatric Institute during the 1960s and 1970s; Westbrook had been a psychological warfare officer in Vietnam, Japan and Korea. At Vacaville, he may have been involved in the MK-ULTRA testing and manipulation of violent inmates. Therefore there may be connections between these men, but Jones is dead and Westbrook isn't talking.

What is more stimulating in terms of bizarre synchronicities is the fact that four members of the SLA had come to Berkeley from Bloomington, Indiana. (The SLA never had more than a few dozen members at its height.) Emily and Bill Harris and Angela and Gary Atwood had been students at the University of Indiana, just as Jim Jones had been almost twenty years earlier. And they wound up in Berkeley—a suburb of San Francisco—at about the same time that Jones was shifting his attention away from Ukiah and towards San Francisco, where he had a large and enthusiastic congregation. (He bought an old synagogue on Geary Street in late 1972, and moved his operational headquarters there in 1975.) Jones was heavily involved in black liberation politics (witness his relationship with Angela Davis and Eldridge Cleaver), and the SLA was allegedly a black liberation army. There is no way that they would have been unaware of each other in San Francisco in 1973. Jones was too prominent, for one thing. He was active in state and local politics. His church was a magnet for black people, and he preached a boisterous revolutionary, socialist and anti-racist platform. In addition, his members were actively involved in mental hospitals and other health-care institutions in California, working as volunteers or as paid employees.

After the nineteen-year-old Patty Hearst was kidnapped on February 4, 1974, by April 15 she had become "Tania" (named after Che Guevara's lover) and had joined the SLA. She is photographed in a beret and holding a rifle during the robbery of a bank in San Francisco by the SLA. The public's confusion over this bizarre change in Hearst's status could find only one possible solution: Patty Hearst had been brainwashed. Pundits appeared on television talking about "Stockholm Syndrome," the identification of a victim with his or her captors after a prolonged period in their custody. The young, conservative heiress must have been programmed to participate in these acts; there could be no other explanation.

The police were mobilized in an intensive manhunt to find the SLA and bring them to justice. No one who was in front of a television will ever forget the day in May when SWAT teams destroyed a house in such an intensive storm of gunfire that the building collapsed in flames. Six members of the SLA—including Donald DeFreeze, their leader known as "Cinque"—were killed in the conflagration. Patty Hearst and Bill and Emily Harris were not in the building at the time. The May 17, 1974 attack was criticized by some members of the press, especially when it became obvious that the inhabitants of the house—and of surrounding buildings, some of which were damaged in the fire—were given little opportunity to evacuate or surrender. If Patty Hearst had been in the building at the time—something which the SWAT team presumably did not know—she would have been killed with all the rest, and the story of her captivity and "brainwashing" would have been lost forever.

However, on September 18, 1975—more than a year after the SWAT attack and more than eighteen months after her kidnapping—Patty Hearst was found and captured by the FBI in San Francisco. She would be convicted of the armed bank robbery, even though specialists insisted on the obvious: that she was mentally conditioned by her captors and forced to adopt an alternate identity. She had even fallen in love with one of her captors, Willie Wolfe, also known as "Cujo." Wolfe had died in the SWAT attack.

In January 1979, President Jimmy Carter commuted Patty Hearst's sentence and she was released from prison. She served twenty-one months of a seven-year sentence. In January 2001 she was pardoned by President Clinton as one of his last official acts as President.

The existence and actions of the SLA are so strange, and so illogical, and so out of context that the organization has been subject to the full-court press of the conspiracy theorists. The leader of the SLA—Donald DeFreeze, or "Cinque"—was black. Virtually everyone else in the SLA was white. (This is a mirror-image of the Peoples Temple, where the leader was white and the congregation black.) The group was believed to be Maoist, but the evidence for this was flimsy. Further, they claimed responsibility for the murder of Dr. Marcus Foster—Superintendent of the Oakland school system—in 1973 . . . by two white men who had used makeup during the commission of the crime, making themselves look black. This attempt to incite a race riot had been prefigured, of course, by the Manson Family attacks on the Tate and LaBianca households in 1969.

DeFreeze himself was a police informant who spent very little time in prison, even though he had a record of arms-dealing, among other felonies. When he left prison, he simply walked out, leading many to assume that his escape was an inside job. This was after prolonged contact with known intelligence officer Colston Westbrook. Although the SLA was painted in the worst possible colors as a violent revolutionary group, their record as violent revolutionaries is rather weak. They make so many mistakes, and reveal themselves to so many people during the course of their life "in hiding," losing large quantities of arms and ammunition at various poorly-disguised safe houses, that it is possible to view their actions as those of *agents provocateurs* and not as genuine revolutionaries. At one point they even hijack a car and driver, drive around for a few hours introducing themselves, and then let the driver free: actions reminiscent of the life of Lee Harvey Oswald prior to the Kennedy assassination, where he was seen in used-car lots talking about killing Kennedy, and then at a rifle range doing the same.

Congressman Ryan may have been getting a little too close to the truth when he demanded that the CIA inform him of any relationship between Donald DeFreeze and MK-ULTRA. They responded in writing to his office on October of 1978, stating that there had been no connection that they could find (remember, most of the documents had been shredded long before). The wording is a perfect example of a typical CIA response and is worth quoting at length:

> Dear Mr. Ryan:
>
> Thank you for your letter of 27 September to Admiral Turner requesting confirmation or denial of the fact of CIA experiments using prisoners at the California medical facility at Vacaville.
>
> It is true that CIA sponsored testing, using volunteer inmates, was conducted at that facility. The project was completed in 1968 . . . .
>
> Your letter referred to Donald DeFreese [*sic*], known as CINQUE, and Clifford Jefferson, both of whom were inmates at Vacaville. In so far as our records reflect the names of the participants, there is nothing to indicate that either was in any way involved in the project.

The letter was date-stamped "18 Oct 1978," and bore the signature stamp of Frank C. Carlucci.[32]

There are several points worth mentioning about this "non-denial denial" (as they used to say at the *Washington Post* during the Watergate investigation). The first is the misspelling of Donald DeFreeze's name, which—as any lawyer knows—is a way to cover one's ass in the event that the denial is proved false. It means that there was no one at the facility being tested who bore the name "Donald DeFreese." The CIA has used this tactic before. Yet, let us allow that it was an honest mistake, a typographical error by a typist. Then there is the question of "our records."

In the first place, the key MK-ULTRA records, of which the Vacaville experiments would have been a part, were all destroyed in 1973 (except for four boxes of accounting and bookkeeping records). So, the CIA had no records of it at all. In the second place, the letter is very careful to hedge even further: "In so far as our records reflect the names of the participants," Very clever, considering that in all likelihood no records existed and, anyway, the name of DeFreeze was misspelled.

Then there is the statement by future-CIA Director Carlucci that the project which had drawn Congressman Ryan's scrutiny "was completed in 1968." DeFreeze did not become an inmate at Vacaville until 1969. Thus, we are left with the distinct impression that the CIA had nothing to do with DeFreeze. But, from 1970 on, DeFreeze was in twice-weekly contact with Colston Westbrook, former intelligence officer under AID cover, psychological warfare officer, and Vietnam veteran, who created and ran the Black Cultural Association at the facility. By running an operation at the prison at arm's length, the CIA had what is known as "plausible deniability." When DeFreeze was being sought by police during the SLA fiasco, he repeatedly warned that Westbrook was a CIA officer, but his warnings were taken as the ramblings of a deranged Communist and black revolutionary, and few paid his charges any attention.

A month to the day after he received his non-denial denial from the CIA, Congressman Ryan was dead on the ground at Port Kaituma, Guyana.

It wasn't only a suspicion about CIA activity in California that bothered Ryan, however. The son of an old friend of his had died under mysterious circumstances, and his friend had pleaded with him to look into it. His friend was a well-known press photographer, Robert "Sammy" Houston. His son, Bob Houston, Jr. had died two days after resigning from the Peoples Temple.

Here is another case of Jim Jones deciding that his married followers should divorce. He "assigned" Joyce Shaw to marry Bob after the Jones-initiated breakup of his first marriage. Bob married her at Jones' urging, and they set up one of several foster homes run by the Peoples Temple, which took care of twenty children in addition to Bob's own two kids. But, according to Thomas Layton's book about Jonestown, Bob Houston asked too many "probing questions" and was subject to brutal beatings in the famous Peoples Temple boxing matches.[33]

The boxing matches were one way Jones controlled his flock through physical punishment and fear. An accused person had to stand passively in the ring as one of Jones' lieutenants beat them. The accused was not permitted to defend himself. Bob Houston evidently suffered through more than one of these in order to show his loyalty to the Temple and specifically to Jim Jones, but it wasn't enough. Houston worked two jobs to support his family and to send two thousand dollars every month to the Peoples Temple. Two thousand dollars a month in 1976 wasn't a bad donation; on the contrary, it was serious money. The questions Bob Houston was raising, however, were putting them all in jeopardy.

The press had already been critical of the Peoples Temple in 1972. Lester Kinsolving was a reporter (as well as a minister) who investigated the Peoples Temple, and although the worst thing about his article was probably the observation that a number of Temple employees carried firearms, his newspaper was picketed by Temple members and a mail-in campaign was organized by Temple staff to smear Kinsolving and have him run out of town.[34]

In another case, journalist George Klineman was meeting with Temple defectors, and the Temple decided to spy on him to the extent of tunneling under his house and listening to his conversations.[35]

Thus, the last thing the Temple needed was Bob Houston free and at large and talking to the press. His own father worked for Associated Press, and that one fact was probably enough to incite the Temple leaders when they received his letter formally announcing his resignation. He worked a second job as a switchman on the railroad, and his mangled body was found the next day on the tracks.[36] Then his father went to his friend Congressman Ryan and asked for his help in getting to the bottom of the case. It was another episode in the growing chorus of voices complaining about the conditions at the Peoples Temple.

Deborah Layton was initiated into some of the worst excesses, including having been raped by Jim Jones three times in 1976 during the course of her employment at the Temple, even at one point acquiring a sexually transmitted disease. To complete the humiliation, she was singled out by Jones in one public meeting as one of those who had had sex with him. In addition, Jones revealed that he had also had sex with Karen Layton, the woman Larry Layton, Jr.—Deborah's brother—had taken to wife at Jones' urging. He had done so, he said, because Larry Layton (like all other men) was really homosexual and could not satisfy his wife the way Jim Jones could. Further, part of this public humiliation ritual was the insistence that all of the women who had had sex with Jim Jones had approached him, not the other way around, and that Jones was simply being kind and generous to them by relenting to their sexual desires.[37]

It was in that same year of 1976 that Jones began to expatriate the Temple funds to banks in Panama and Switzerland, using Deborah Layton as one of the administrators of these funds and as a courier. He had simply been amassing too much wealth—he had one hundred thousand dollars in cash in a safe at the Temple to cover "incidental expenses"[38]—and he was getting thousands of dollars of cash donations every week, in addition to members' Social Security checks and real estate that was signed over to the Temple.

Deborah Layton made several trips over the course of a year or so to these foreign banks, setting up accounts and depositing cash. Thus, when the dust had cleared after the Jonestown massacre, one of her tasks was helping government officials locate and seize the millions of dollars in those accounts.

Jones had made another trip to Guyana in 1973,[39] and was seriously considering moving his congregation there, where he would be free from both press and legal scrutiny. By 1976, he had already leased nearly four thousand acres of land from the Guyanese government, and Temple members were down there clearing the land and getting ready for a major influx of Americans.

No one knows exactly why Jones chose that particular site. Its location close to the Venezuelan border—a hotly contested area by both countries, by the way—is suggestive of a hidden agenda. Some commentators believe that having more than one thousand Americans living so close to the border would blunt Venezuelan military action to take that land for itself. Others, including the present author, believe that he was simply being smart: having his settlement close to another international boundary meant that, in the event of a problem with the Guyanese government, he could quickly be safely inside Venezuelan territory.

This was the same strategy employed by fugitive Nazi Paul Schaefer, who set up his notorious Colonia Dignidad on the Chilean border with Argentina, and may have used his colony's proximity to Argentina to make his escape when the Chilean authorities finally raided the estate in the 1990s. Colonia Dignidad was another "religious" community with a political agenda (it had been used as a torture and interrogation center by the Chilean secret police during the overthrow of President Salvador Allende in 1973), was completely populated by German citizens (as Jonestown was by American citizens), was run by a minister of religion who was also a sexual sadist, etc. In both cases, orphaned children and foster children were exported to the colonies, and financial subsidies derived from their respective governments. In both cases, the colonies had shortwave radio communications with their offices in the country's capitols. Those offices were used by members to influence government officials, and, in the case of Jonestown, one Temple member was ordered to become the paramour of a Guyanese government official. And on and on. The parallels are almost too numerous to mention.

Yet another disturbing coincidence lies in the fact that the site chosen by Jones was in the Northwest District of Guyana, the same place where—in 1845—a Reverend Smith called together the local Native American population (including the Arawaks, Tituba's countrymen), and told them the Millennium was at hand. When it did not materialize, Smith's four hundred followers committed mass suicide on the spot, believing they would be resurrected as "white people."[40] The parallels to the Jonestown event are too strong to be ignored.

We can, of course, choose to categorize this uncanny synchronicity as "mere coincidence," as if the mass suicide of four hundred in 1845 and the mass murder of nine hundred in 1978 should be reduced to a scientific curiosity at best, or a scientific absurdity at worst. However, as we have noted before, in history there are documents . . . and there is blood. And as the fictitious detective Sherlock Holmes remarked in his very first appearance—in a story about Mormonism, no less, and secret societies and cult homicide—there is a scarlet thread of murder running through the tapestry of life. It runs among the Indian mounds of Charles Manson's hometown, Ashland, Kentucky, and the mounds of Chillicothe, Ohio and Moundsville, West Virginia, familiar to the inmates of the prisons built on those sites, people like serial killer Henry Lee Lucas, as well as Manson himself and Lynette Fromme. It runs to the doomed jungles of Guyana, where the Arawak faithful went willingly to their deaths a century before nine hundred Americans did likewise. Blood cries out to blood, and history repeats itself.

America had first learned in some detail of the CIA's domestic spying program as well as its mind-control projects in 1975. The information was provided by the Rockefeller Commission Report, published in June of that year, and evidence presented in that report rang alarm bells in the home of the Olson family, as they recognized the facts surrounding the death of Frank Olson and learned, for the first time, of his unwitting participation in an LSD experiment being run by Sidney Gottlieb. This was also the year that Lynette "Squeaky" Fromme attempted the assassination of President Gerald Ford, leading everyone to agree that the Manson Family was still armed and dangerous, and abroad in the land.

By June 1977, things were getting too hot for Jim Jones and the Peoples Temple. *New West* magazine was preparing an exposé of the Temple, and Jones began to panic. Complaints started to trickle in to government offices in California about the church and its bizarre practices. Important Temple members—such as Assistant District Attorney Tim Stoen—began to "defect," and to tell their stories to the media and to the authorities. The word "cult" was being used, and "brainwashing," and people became suspicious and fearful. Jones finally fled to Guyana himself on July 13, 1977, leaving trusted members like Deborah Layton in charge of things (especially the money) in the States.

THE RETURN OF THE NATIVE

Deborah's mother, Lisa Philip Layton, had decided to join the Peoples Temple sometime in 1973 after attending one late-night meeting there at the San Francisco Temple with her daughter Deborah. This veteran of Nazi Germany found something comforting and uplifting about Jim Jones and the raucous Temple services, and soon began making the long trip to the Los Angeles congregation three times a week.[41] This developed into a kind of devotion or even fanaticism, and by November 1974 she had moved out of her home with her husband, Dr. Layton, and asked him for a divorce.[42]

As her involvement with the Peoples Temple grew, so did her paranoia. The Temple was fearful of secret government action against it, or so Jones liked to claim. The postulation of a hostile outside force—whether one exists or not—is a useful tool for binding the members of any group together, and as the Temple grew in power in the seventies, so did its paranoia. Lisa Philip Layton had reason to fear this type of intervention, however, because she had witnessed it in Nazi Germany; and then there had been the suicide of her mother in New York City, a death attributed to Anita Philip's fear of what she felt was some sort of secret police investigation. By working with the predominantly black congregations of the Peoples Temple, Lisa Layton felt herself identifying with their oppression as well as becoming accepted and even loved. She began to adopt Jones' beliefs and fears as her own. She thought she could identify who was a CIA "plant" at the Temple.[43] And she put her money where her mouth was. When her divorce had become final, she donated something like three hundred thousand dollars to the Peoples Temple, a very large sum in those days.[44]

Thus, when the opportunity arose for her to travel to Guyana and live in the workers' paradise that was Jonestown, she was eager to do so and traveled there with her daughter Deborah in late 1977, arriving in Georgetown on December 7 and in Jonestown itself on December 14. It was then that both women began to experience the dreadful living conditions and draconian "security" measures that dominated Temple life.

Deborah was sent to work in the fields for six weeks, a grueling and impossible regimen in the jungle, subject to insects, venomous snakes, sunstroke, dehydration and overwork. The Temple members lived on rice and beans, and a little water (depending on the rainfall). It was, essentially, concentration-camp living, with the ever-present security forces alert to any deviation from the fixed routine, any complaint, no matter how reasonable or how minor. For infractions, one could be imprisoned in "the box" for extended periods of time, fed on a liquid diet—with vital signs monitored daily to ensure that the inmate was still alive—and subjected to interrogation by the security team until they were satisfied that the inmate was giving the correct answers. Children were subject to even worse treatment, taken to a well at the bottom of which two adults would be hiding in the water, waiting to grab the unfortunate child's legs and drag him or her under the surface of the brackish water. After a long session of that, the child would be allowed to return to the surface, and then would have to walk all the way back to the compound through the jungle, repeating over and over, "I'm sorry, Father."

Eventually, once the medical center had been built and enlarged, troublesome members would be imprisoned there and drugged heavily until their anti-revolutionary attitudes had been adjusted. The pharmacy at Jonestown contained Thorazine, as well as "Quaaludes, Demerol, Seconal, Valium, Nembutal, morphine—enough to fill the ordinary needs of a city of sixty-five thousand people."[45] Another source records that large quantities of Haldol and Mellaril in liquid form were being shipped to Jonestown.[46] Normally, these would be taken in pill form. The liquid form could be used for injections, which is a rare way to administer these drugs, or, more significantly, as a means to give the drug to people without their knowledge. All this pharmacopoeia was for a commune that never numbered more than twelve hundred souls.

The question of whether or not there were other drugs present at Jonestown—hallucinogens and other psychoactive substances useful in mind control experiments—has never been satisfactorily answered. However, the drugs of which we *are* aware could readily be used in behavior modification treatments, which they obviously were.

By 1977, Jones had yet another problem on his hands. His former assistant pastor, Timothy Stoen, the Assistant District Attorney, had defected. First to go was his wife, who left the Temple, separated from her husband, and claimed custody of their four-year-old son. Eventually, Tim Stoen also left the Temple, but by that time their son was in Jonestown. The Stoens fought Jones for custody of their child, and this was another legal nightmare for Jones, who claimed that he had fathered the child himself.

When the Supreme Court ruled in the Stoens' favor, demanding the extradition of the boy, Jones went ballistic and threatened—not for the first time—that his entire community would commit mass suicide if the Guyanese government acceded to the extradition demand. In a panic, Temple lawyers and other spokespeople in the States began phoning everyone they thought could help in this situation, and Temple attorney Charles Garry arranged a phone call to Jones from Angela Davis, Huey Newton and American Indian activist Dennis Banks to beg him to reconsider. At the same time, the wife of the Guyanese ambassador to the United States was reached—oddly enough, in Indiana where she was visiting a friend—and when the dust had cleared, the Guyanese government had bowed to the pressure from Jones, and the extradition proceedings were delayed.

Perhaps not surprisingly, the example of Jim Jones' news reports to Jonestown provides one of the strongest arguments against government management of the press. Loudspeakers were set up all over the settlement, like something out of *M*A*S*H*. They would go on at any time, day or night, and Jones would regale his captive audience with the details of the latest book he was reading, or news reports from journals and magazines he supposedly had in his cabin. No one was allowed to see these publications, of course. During these readings, he would inform his people that—for instance—Los Angeles was being evacuated due to drought and famine, or that the Klan was on the rampage, killing black people or enslaving them in camps. The people of Jonestown—having absolutely no access to the outside world in any way, shape or form—were reduced to either believing Jones' accounts and thanking God they were safe in the jungles of Guyana, or in disbelieving them and keeping that dangerous secret to themselves.

Suicide practice runs became frequent in the last years. At that point, with so few calories in their diet, a heavy workload of clearing jungle and raising some pitiful crops, and the constant loudspeaker harangues and forced marches—and worse—of the security staff, some people actually became indifferent to whether they lived or died. While romantic relationships were frowned upon unless encouraged or approved by Jones and sex was considered "counterrevolutionary," suicide itself was considered a revolutionary act by Jones, and he told his followers that they would be reincarnated in a better world. This was essentially the same rationale given to me by an American Nazi, who defended the genocide of the Jews and the Gypsies by claiming that—since there would be no more Jewish or Gypsy bodies after they were all killed—they would have to be reincarnated as Aryans. And of course Reverend Smith, more than a hundred years earlier, had told his Amerindian followers in Guyana that if they committed suicide, they would be reincarnated as white people. And so it goes.

A US State Department officer, Frank Tumminia, visited Guyana in 1978 and made a report, saying that the communards appeared "drugged and robot-like in their reactions to questions and, generally, in their behavior towards us visitors."[47] Officials visiting as late as November 1978, however, had no such observations and came away thinking everything there was just fine.

But back in December 1977, after a week in Jonestown, Deborah Layton had made plans to escape. She took the opportunity of a planned cultural program in Georgetown in March 1978, and she managed to stay in Guyana's capitol until she could arrange her return back to the United States. In the meantime, the Temple staff in Georgetown was told to approach the Soviet Embassy and try to get permission for the entire Jonestown population to emigrate to Russia. Deborah Layton was involved with this maneuver, which did not result in anyone actually going to Russia, but was part of an ongoing set of negotiations opened by Jones with both Russia and, to some extent, Cuba. The Russians, naturally, were a little leery of accepting the twelve hundred or so Americans, about seventy-five percent of whom were black—not a common racial group in Russia.

By the middle of May, Deborah—in a series of cloak-and-dagger moves to evade Temple members, and one false start due to documentation problems—managed to get into an Embassy car and get taken to the airport for her trip back to the States. Her brother, Larry Layton, was still in the US, and Deborah tried to warn him not to go down to Guyana if called. His sister, Annalisa, made a warning phone call, and Larry replied he was not planning to go anywhere; but his mood was cool.

He then went to his father's house, dressed in his hospital uniform, and mowed the lawn. He appeared to be in a drugged state, although these would not have been recreational drugs at this time, since Larry had become a devoted member of the Peoples Temple, even if he had slacked off considerably during Jones' absence. Then, still dressed in his hospital uniform, he dove into the swimming pool.

His father, Dr. Layton, was just about to take some action, fearing that his son had gone over the edge, when the phone rang. It was for Larry. Larry got out of the pool and answered the phone. He listened. He hung up. He left immediately. And was on a plane bound for Guyana that night.

A WATERGATE OF THE CULTS

> Tim Stoen encouraged her to make her information public; he felt that her story would be the beginning of a "Watergate of the cults."
>
> —Min S. Yee & Thomas N. Layton, *In My Father's House*[48]

> Religion, like Watergate, is a scandal that will not go away.
>
> —Victor Turner[49]

Deborah Layton began working very hard to raise some awareness of what was happening in Jonestown. She knew that Jones' constant threats of mass suicide were not merely empty attempts to win sympathy or support for his plight, but could very possibly turn deadly in a heartbeat. She became the focal point for defectors and for people who had family living in Jonestown. She appeared in the press, wrote letters to government officials, and lobbied everyone who could have any impact at all on the escalating tensions in Guyana. Her mother was still down there, very sick, and she feared for her life and for the lives of her friends. Even her estranged husband, Phil Blakey—a man she met when she was at the Quaker school in England, and with whom she was never able to have a genuine married relationship, due to the Temple—was still there, working in the fields.

When she spoke with ADA Tim Stoen, he urged her to go public with everything she knew. She was, after all, one of the trusted members of the Peoples Temple (or had been) and knew about the money laundering, the psychodramas, the phony cancer cures, the raising from the dead, the revolutionary speeches, the attempts to flee to Russia . . . her story would open a can of worms that would reach back into other cults. It would be the beginning, said Stoen, of a "Watergate of the cults."

Not much was made of that statement at the time; it was probably considered a bit of hyperbole on Stoen's part. The nation, after all, was still "wallowing in Watergate," and there were congressional and senate committees every year on some aspect of government corruption or secret government operations. The revelations were coming fast and furious. Tim Stoen—a district attorney, after all, and an intimate of the Peoples Temple—evidently felt that the information Deborah Layton had in her possession would start an important enquiry into the operation of cults, an enquiry that would reveal much more about them than had been ever suspected.

Unfortunately, the "Watergate of the cults" that Stoen hypothesized never took place, because the events in Jonestown in November of 1978 were so hideous, and the cover-up so complete, that no such "Templegate" ever transpired. Jonestown entered history as one of the western world's great icons, a mystical portrait that means different things to different people, painted by trained political mystics who knew the right amount of spin to employ (the same way Russian ikon painters know how to apply gold leaf on the haloes of the saints), a hoodwink that would be used later to explain the ferocity of the attack on the Branch Davidian compound in Waco, Texas. What the western world learned in the aftermath of Jonestown was what it was intended to learn. A moral for the story was ready and waiting in the wings.

As Deborah Layton agitated for a full-scale investigation of Jonestown, Jim Jones was on the attack. He had invited veteran conspiracy theorist and attorney Mark Lane to Guyana, ostensibly to lecture on the life (and the assassination?) of Dr. Martin Luther King, Jr. But when he arrived back in the States after his visit to Jonestown, Lane immediately embarked on a legal campaign against the US government over its alleged persecution of Jonestown, the Peoples Temple, and Jim Jones. Jones' paranoia about the CIA, FBI, IRS and other government agencies found a receptive ear in Mark Lane, whose work on the assassination of President Kennedy was well-known. It seems incredible that Lane would have visited Jonestown and not come away with serious misgivings about what was going on there, but his visit was short—only a few days—and Jones typically rehearsed his congregation beforehand and created a festive atmosphere for guests, as he would with the visit of Congressman Ryan in 1978. In addition, Mark Lane was first an attorney, and one specializing in unpopular causes it would seem. The Peoples Temple had deep pockets, and Lane could have been looking at this as any other legal gig. Who was he to argue with State Department officials who found nothing sinister in the Jonestown commune?

And there might have been another element to the relationship. We know now, for instance, of Jones' involvement with people like Dan Mitrione, and of Jones' trips to Cuba and Guyana in the early 1960s, as well as of his mysterious psychiatric treatment at Langley-Porter. How much of this did he tell to Mark Lane? How much of this did he spin in just the right way to indicate to Lane that he was dealing with a very serious nexus of government mind control, political action and torture? How many hints did Jones drop of his prior experience with intelligence operations? How much more did he promise Lane if only Lane could get the US government off his back long enough? There were bits and pieces of an autobiography by Jones found among the wreckage of the Jonestown settlement after the massacre. Was this a manuscript being prepared for Mark Lane?

This author finds it difficult to believe that Mark Lane would have gone so far out on a limb for Jim Jones after only one visit of a few days in Jonestown unless he had found something very valuable there. Lane must have been the victim of dozens of people laying their paranoid trips on him over the years—especially after the publication in 1966 of his book on the Kennedy assassination, *Rush to Judgment* and of his subsequent work, *A Citizen's Dissent*, published in 1975—people claiming to have inside information on the assassination of President Kennedy, or that of his brother, Bobby, or that of Martin Luther King, or of any of a host of other scenarios. Why would he choose to cast his lot, as it were, with Jim Jones, a paranoid fanatic in the middle of the jungle, as close to Joseph Conrad's crazed character Kurtz in the *Heart of Darkness* as any man alive?

In the first place, money. We know, from the Thomas Layton book that Lane was paid ten thousand dollars up front for his legal assistance in suing the US government. The Peoples Temple had deep pockets; they were getting—in Social Security payments alone—sixty-five thousand dollars a month mailed to Guyana. Very little of this money was actually spent in Guyana for the residents of Jonestown, who had to make do with the most primitive living conditions imaginable, a near-starvation diet, and a heavy workload. The ten thousand dollars paid to Lane was probably only a down payment. The Peoples Temple could turn into a cash cow.

In the second place, revelations about CIA involvement in Latin American politics, secret police, and training in brutal interrogation techniques. The latter had already been the subject of several government investigations by that time, however. Jones would have had to have had something more worthwhile than that, something juicier. If there was anything there, though, it never surfaced. Mark Lane has not published anything remotely explosive on the subject of Jonestown. It may be a case of attorney-client privilege . . . except that in this case his client is dead. So, what's the story, Mark?

Congressman Leo Ryan (D-CA) had also begun his own investigation of the Peoples Temple. His friend's son—Robert Houston—had been killed just at the time he was trying to leave the church. That, coupled with new charges surfacing in the press and in the form of petitions and letters being circulated by relatives of the Jonestown community, pushed the Peoples Temple to the forefront of Ryan's consciousness. He arranged a clandestine meeting with Deborah Layton and taped her two-hour statement on the conditions at the Jonestown compound as well as her own involvement over the prior seven years. Former Temple members Al and Deanna Mertle were also busy organizing and petitioning. Stories of children suffering at the Jonestown settlement and being held against their will—or against the will of their parents—were surfacing, and the heat was on the government to do something before the situation got completely out of hand. Deborah Layton pressed her case on Congressman Ryan, insisting that there was a very real possibility of mass suicide in the jungle.

Ryan was convinced that there was at least the possibility of disaster. A hands-on type of politician—who had worked undercover for two weeks in an inner-city school district as a teacher, and had spent a week as an inmate in the State's prison system so he could understand the conditions first-hand—Ryan was no stranger to dangerous situations. He made the arrangements to go to Jonestown himself, and his secretary—filled with ominous presentiments of death—urged the Congressman to make out his will before he left, as she was doing. A reporter who had interviewed Deborah Layton was convinced she was lying, making the whole thing up, and did not file a report on his interview with her concerning the situation in Jonestown.

He took a bullet in the wrist and another in the arm at the Port Kaituma airstrip.

Ryan notified the Peoples Temple officially of his upcoming visit, which prompted a response not from Jim Jones but from Mark Lane, now operating as the Temple's attorney. Lane tried to get Ryan to change his schedule. At the time of the proposed visit, Mark Lane was in Washington, D.C., where he was working on the Dr. Martin Luther King, Jr. assassination investigation. An important witness to the events leading up to the assassination was a woman—Grace Walden—who had been institutionalized for mental illness after she insisted that James Earl Ray was not the gunman. She was the landlady of the apartment complex that was used as the sniper's nest, and she identified someone else entirely as the shooter. Mark Lane was trying to get her story out in front of the House Assassinations Investigation Committee, but when he heard that Ryan had ignored Lane's plea for rescheduling and was on his way to Jonestown, he dropped everything—although he had worked on the King case for years, and had even taken the steps to obtain legal custody of Ms. Walden from the mental hospital where he found her—and instead flew immediately to Guyana to intercept the Congressman's party.

What happened next is so well-known, and has been covered in so many books, articles and documentaries, that I will not waste the reader's time with a detailed examination of the timeline leading up to the Jonestown massacre. There are a few salient points which should be viewed in context, however, and to these we turn our attention.

Congressman Ryan was held up in Georgetown for a few days, as Jim Jones had refused him and his party—which by now included newsmen and representatives of the "Concerned Relatives" group—until his attorneys Mark Lane and Charles Garry could get to Guyana. Ryan had met with State Department officials in Washington a few days before his visit, and had asked Deborah Layton to address them as well. The State Department people professed to have no knowledge of Jonestown at all, and had nothing to contribute to the meeting.

When Ryan arrived in Guyana, he met with the local US Embassy staff as well as with the local office of the Peoples Temple. His patience wearing thin, he informed the two Temple attorneys that he was chartering a plane and flying out to Port Kaituma whether or not Jim Jones approved. The lawyers made a hurried radio call to Jonestown and convinced Jones to let the party come.

An eighteen-seat chartered plane took the group to Port Kaituma, but they were met by Temple members, who took only a handful of persons back with them, leaving the rest behind at the Port Kaituma airstrip. One of the members accompanying Ryan to Jonestown was Richard Dwyer.

Dwyer's involvement in this—and subsequent discoveries about his background in intelligence—is one of the more suggestive elements of the whole saga. Dwyer was a career intelligence officer, working under State Department cover at the US Embassy in Georgetown. He was, according to several sources, the CIA Chief of Station for Guyana. As such, he could be expected to have very good information on Jonestown; unfortunately, he did not choose to share this information with Ryan or his party. It was well-known in Georgetown that the Peoples Temple had strong influence with the Guyanese government; Temple women were expected to develop personal relationships with Guyanese officials, and one such woman was the mistress of the Guyanese ambassador to the United States. Dwyer would have had to have known all of this, as Georgetown is small as capitols go, a place where gossip is about the only entertainment there is. Further, as

CIA station chief, it would have been his business to know all about the Peoples Temple political involvements, not only with the Guyanese government but also with the Soviet Union and Cuba, as the Temple had approached both of these countries—through their embassies in Georgetown—as possible relocation sites. Yet, Dwyer—and the State Department in general—remained strangely silent on the subject of the Peoples Temple and offered very little assistance to Congressman Ryan before and during his trip.

Ryan managed to visit Jonestown, and during the course of his two days there was approached by several Temple families who asked him to take them with him back to the States. At one point, Ryan was attacked and held at knife point by one of Jones' followers, who had to be restrained by Mark Lane and Charles Garry; it made for a dismal end to the Congressman's visit, and although Ryan had intended to stay longer, the atmosphere had changed and discretion seemed the better part of valor.

A truck was organized to take the Congressman's party—plus anyone else who wanted to leave—back to the Port Kaituma airstrip. The truck began filling up. One of the "defectors" was Larry Layton. It was November 18, 1978.

Remember that Larry was called back suddenly to Guyana after the defection of his sister, Deborah. He had been sinking in his father's swimming pool, dressed in his hospital X-Ray technician's uniform when the phone call came. He left his father's home at once and flew to Georgetown that evening.

It is Larry Layton's presence at Port Kaituma that is one of the more troubling aspects of the entire case. Larry had had problems growing up in the Layton household, but then many children of the sixties had problems with the generation gap: drugs, sex, and rock 'n' roll were the pathways to a different, altered state of consciousness and political and social awareness. He married the daughter of a minister, Carolyn Moore, and they both joined the Peoples Temple and became intimately involved in the church hierarchy including the dread PC, or Planning Commission, which was really the "inner court" of the Temple, the place where Jones could rant and rave for hours on end about politics, metaphysics, and especially about sex. It was during those PC sessions—to which only the most devoted (or important) were invited—that Larry lost Carolyn to Jim Jones, and was instead "assigned" to Karen Tow. Carolyn became a vociferous supporter of Jones and even bore him a son, Kimo. Larry and Karen, however, were not to have sex at all unless approved in advance by Jones. Instead, Larry was forced to make humiliating "confessions" of his homosexuality and of his homosexual attraction for Jones before the assembled throng of PC regulars.

Larry Layton's psychological and spiritual disintegration—begun years before with hallucinogens and religious yearnings—was exacerbated by the type of psychological mind games that Jones was playing. Jones after all was a religious leader and a political leader of sorts; he held a captive audience in the Planning Commission, whose meetings were usually held only at night and through to the early hours of the morning, exhausting the participants, including at times Jones himself, who was the only one allowed to eat and drink during the marathon sessions. Layton, like all the other PC attendants, had been worked on in a highly-charged, emotionally-draining controlled atmosphere. Jones was quite aware of the effect that the isolation and insularity of the scene would have on the psyches of his flock. He demonstrated this during a session in which a young boy was accused of stealing. Jones lightly drugged the boy, telling him he could strike him dead. By the time the drug began to take effect, the boy was quaking in fear. He was revived briefly, in the darkened church and to the sound of the other members of the congregation making terrifying sounds, as if the boy had descended to the very pit of hell. The boy was then "brought back from the dead" by Jones, and the traumatized child promised he would never commit another crime in his life. This is the environment in which Larry Layton found himself.

He became, in the terminology of Erich Fromm, a "true believer."

So, when the time came for the defectors to go back to the airstrip with Congressman Ryan, and Larry Layton hopped aboard the truck, the other defectors tried to warn the Congressman's party that Layton was not a genuine defector and that there would be problems. But, in the chaos of the leave-taking, Larry was brought along to the airstrip with the others.

Back in Jonestown, Jones knew that the end had come. He began to tell his flock that the plane would explode in the sky; that the pilot would be killed by one of the people who had gone to the airstrip. Thus, the plan was revealed, and the words captured on tape. The transcript of that tape has since been made available, and besides the oblique reference to the assassins on their way to kill Congressman Ryan there is also one other disturbing clue that has bothered researchers and commentators for years: the references to Dwyer.

Jones several times insists that Dwyer be allowed to leave; in fact, he doesn't want Dwyer in Jonestown at all when the curtain comes down and calls over the loudspeaker to have him taken away. As we have seen, Dwyer was likely the local CIA Chief of Station. Why, suddenly, is Jones worried for his safety? If the whole congregation is going to commit mass suicide (as the cover story would have it), then why would Jones care one way or another about Dwyer?

According to the press reports by eyewitnesses, Dwyer was on the truck with Layton and the Congressman's party. Dwyer was ostensibly going to return to Georgetown with them. However, Dwyer was wounded in the attack on the Port Kaituma airstrip: not seriously, it seems to have been a flesh wound in his thigh. Witnesses saw blood on his pants leg, but did not see a wound. Whatever the details of the wound, it did not prevent Dwyer from running into the jungle to hide with a few other survivors, and then organizing the events of the next twenty-four hours and shuttling back and forth between the airstrip and the town of Port Kaituma.

Why did Jones think that Dwyer was still at Jonestown? And why did he care?

The truck arrived at the airstrip, and shortly thereafter another vehicle arrived with three members of the Jonestown security force. There were two planes on the airstrip, one a small, single-engine craft and the other a larger plane to accommodate the growing party of defectors. Dwyer had just arrived from another part of the airstrip with a policeman holding a shotgun. The Jonestown security people marched up to the policeman and seized his shotgun. Neither the policeman nor Dwyer seems to have made any attempt to resist. A tractor pulled up to the airstrip, carrying more Jonestown security people, parking a trailer between one plane and the next and trying to determine who was going on each plane. Those defectors still on the tarmac, and fearing the worst, began to run to the jungle. The Temple security forces opened fire on the Congressman's party, killing the NBC news crew first as they were filming the murders. They then walked up to Leo Ryan, already wounded on the ground, and shot him in cold blood, leaving his body lying on the tarmac next to the plane.

Larry Layton had boarded the single-engine Cessna first—shoving himself forward ahead of everyone—and was armed; he either picked up a pistol earlier at Jonestown or it had been planted in the plane. Since all the Temple defectors had been checked for weapons before boarding, it seems more likely that the gun had been planted in the plane, which is why Layton insisted to Ryan that he have a seat on that particular aircraft.

He began shooting in the plane as it was trying to take off during the attack, wounding defectors Monica Bagby and Vernon Gosney before his revolver misfired and it was taken from him by defector Dale Parks.

There were others at the airstrip at the time, local Guyanese troops in fact, guarding a military plane that was being repaired, who made themselves scarce when the shooting started. The congressman's party did not have any weapons—thanks to the surrendering of the policeman's shotgun to the Temple security forces—and were sitting ducks. Bob Flick, an NBC producer, ran to the troops and begged them for help. They refused. They said it was a conflict between Americans and had nothing to do with them. He asked them for a weapon in order to defend himself. They refused again. They sat and watched five people being murdered in cold blood, and when the murderers took off in their tractor for Jonestown after the killing, they made no move to pursue them but instead let them pass.[50]

Back in Jonestown, the word reached Jim Jones that the Congressman was dead. No one knows how the information reached him so quickly. There had to have been a radio at the airstrip that was used to transmit the information, either from one of the planes or from somewhere else nearby. Once the information was relayed, however, the White Night was begun. Jones went on the loudspeaker and called everyone's attention, and began talking about the need for them to kill themselves.

Dwyer then went into action. Larry Layton was standing casually on the tarmac and talking to two Guyanese policemen. The defectors raised the alarm, pointing to Layton, and finally Dwyer walked over to the policemen and demanded that Layton be placed under arrest. They refused initially but then agreed, and took Layton back to Georgetown. He would be the only person charged and the only person ever convicted of the Port Kaituma attack and of conspiracy to murder Congressman Ryan.[51] Dwyer had his scapegoat; there was no need to look any further for the other gunmen.

What was Larry Layton doing, standing around the airstrip and chatting with Guyanese policemen just after shooting two people and attempting to shoot a third?

The events of the day became even more horrible. Attorneys Mark Lane and Charles Garry were permitted to escape into the jungle. The rest of the Jonestown compound was subjected to a lengthy harangue from Jim Jones as he attempted to convince them all to commit suicide. He asked mothers to kill their children first, and then to take their own lives. What actually transpired, however, has never been clear, and the crime scene investigation—such as it was—was one of the worst travesties of justice in the history of any country.

Many of the victims bore gunshot wounds, which argues strongly against the suicide-by-Kool-Aid story that was disseminated shortly after the massacre. Those who did survive recall the sounds of gunshots in such abundance it sounded like a war. The security forces had armed themselves with heavy automatic weapons at the start of Jones' plea for suicide and were ensuring that none would escape the compound. Jones had allowed Lane and Garry to leave, and had demanded that Dwyer also leave. It is possible that Dwyer was in Jonestown at the time of the massacre, since there are hours during that afternoon and night after the airstrip attack when it seems he was not present at Port Kaituma. In any event, Jones believed that Dwyer was there, and repeatedly asked that someone take him away.

Aerial photographs of the site days later would show the famous scene of bodies all over the compound; millions saw those photographs in the news magazines, but few came to the obvious conclusion: the bodies were all lying facedown and in many cases neatly arranged, indicating that the story of mass suicide might have been in error. It beggars belief that everyone in Jonestown would have fallen forward onto their faces after taking the cyanide-laced grape drink. It is entirely possible that the bodies were arranged that way to make their identification more difficult when photographed from above. It is also entirely possible that the bodies were arranged that way by persons unknown after the massacre. For it was a massacre.

Initially, the body count—performed by the first contingent of Guyanese troops that arrived the morning after the massacre—was only about two hundred. Later, as the days went on and more investigators (and curiosity-seekers) arrived, the body count was corrected upwards. At first, it was believed that the grand total would come in at three hundred sixty-three, of which eighty-two were identified as children. Yet, as the body count increased, the incredulous wanted to know how it was possible that it could go from 363 to 913; how was such a wide variation possible?

The explanation given was that some of the bodies were those of children, and that the adult bodies had fallen on top of them, rendering immediate location and identification difficult. In other words, there were more than five hundred bodies hidden under the first 363. That did not seem possible, particularly as the initial counts showed that of the 363, more than 80 were children. It simply did not make sense, and it seemed as if someone, somewhere was lying about the body count on behalf of some hidden agenda.

What made matters worse was the discovery of some 789 American passports at the scene. If there were only 363 bodies discovered, then 426 other souls were unaccounted for and possibly on the run through the Guyanese jungles. One had to put a stop to *that* rumor at once, and the body count was adjusted upwards to the point where 913 became the official number. But, to be perfectly honest, there was no verifiable, official record of the number of corpses, and only about three hundred had ever been positively identified.[52] Photos of some of the bodies show that they were wearing identification bracelets on their wrists, the type commonly used in hospitals to identify patients. No one knows why this was done, and particularly why those bracelets mysteriously disappeared somewhere between Jonestown and the American air base where the bodies were eventually shipped, thus rendering further identification even more difficult. (Three bodies were actually *lost*, and turned up in storage lockers in southern California years after the fact![53]) The bodies were left in the open jungle air for days, and had reached a particularly loathsome state of putrescence, rendering hellish the task of coroners and medical examiners. In fact, there were virtually no autopsies performed on the bodies recovered.

Only seven autopsies were ever performed on the more than nine hundred bodies found at Jonestown, and only one of those showed any sign of cyanide poisoning. In fact, the autopsies were not performed until a month after the bodies had been embalmed! The first forensic specialist on the scene was a Guyanese doctor, and his initial report on the massacre is widely at variance with the story that was later given so much publicity in the foreign press.

Dr. Mootoo, Guyana's chief medical examiner, noted that many of the victims had puncture wounds from syringes on their shoulders, where they could not have possibly injected themselves. In addition, cyanide was present in bottles labeled Valium, and Mootoo assumed that the victims had been given the fictitious Valium and discovered the switch too late, as they lay dying. To summarize his findings, he believed that the evidence strongly supported a charge of homicide in at least seven hundred cases. The tissue samples that he collected at the site—representing tests of more than twenty bodies—were handed over to an official of the American embassy for onward transmission to forensic specialists in the United States. They never arrived, and to this day no one knows what happened to them.

As if anyone needed additional mysteries to solve, Jim Hougan points out one more incredible anomaly: the CIA knew that there were mass suicides in Jonestown at 4:44 A.M. on Sunday morning, Guyana time. But the site had not been visited until mid-morning that same day by Guyanese troops. How did the CIA know that there had been mass suicides in Jonestown at least six hours before anyone else did?

One of the planes involved in the attack at Port Kaituma had managed to leave and make its way to Georgetown the night of the 18th, but the only news they had was of the attack on the Congressman's party at the airstrip and the murder of five people whose bodies still lay on the tarmac. No one knew about the massive death toll at Jonestown until the next day. Yet, somehow, the CIA knew all about it and was already spinning the story as a "mass suicide." Hougan believes the probable source to be Richard Dwyer; in addition, a CIA memorandum concerning Guyana refers to a CIA "field station" in Guyana, giving rise to speculation that there was another CIA operation in Guyana beyond that of Dwyer's embassy posting.

AFTERMATH

The deaths did not end with the massacre at Jonestown. As in the case of the Manson Family murders, people connected with the case continued to die from gunshot wounds for quite some time after the discovery of all those bodies in the jungle. At the beginning of this chapter, we noted that Al and Deanna Mertle—who had published a book about their Jonestown experience, replete with the sexual escapades and physical and mental torture of followers—were murdered in their home in February of 1980, only a few months after their book was published, in a case that has not been solved. They were not the first, and not the last.

Only nine days after the Jonestown massacre, San Francisco Mayor Moscone—whom Jones had helped to elect in the 1976 campaign—was shot dead, as was Harvey Milk, the famous defender of gay rights in government. There are numerous photos of Moscone and Jones, and even at the height of the Peoples Temple scandals in the press, Moscone stood behind Jones and was vocal in his support of the church. There is some circumstantial evidence to suggest Peoples Temple involvement in these deaths, but nothing substantial enough to warrant a full discussion at this point. The presence of a longtime Peoples Temple member—Bonnie Thielmann—however is suggestive. Ms. Thielmann lived with Jim and Marceline Jones in Brazil in the 1960s, and continued her involvement with the Peoples Temple right up to and after the Jonestown massacre. She was on the plane with Congressman Ryan that flew into Georgetown as one of the Concerned

Relatives—even though she was not related to anyone in Jonestown—but she did not go to Jonestown with the group, staying behind in the capitol instead, and then flying back to the States with Tim Stoen.

She attended (uninvited) Leo Ryan's funeral in California, latching onto Mayor Moscone and using him as her entrée into the private funeral service. She is said to have whispered something to the Mayor which left him visibly shaken. He had been receiving anonymous phone calls from people claiming to be members of the Temple or relatives of members, warning him to be very careful and insinuating that the Peoples Temple wanted him dead. Clearly, he felt that the massacre in Jonestown was somehow connected to him personally, and not only because of his support for Jones. He urged that survivors of the holocaust be treated by a psychiatrist, unfortunately a psychiatrist associated with the Langley-Porter clinic, the same institution that had been treating Jim Jones for his mysterious ailment, an institution that also specialized in classified Defense Department research, including the effects of ELF (extremely low frequency) waves on humans.

Mayor Moscone began to fear for his life, and on November 27, 1978 he lost it to a bullet.

Dan White had resigned his position as City Supervisor earlier that month, and then tried to retract the resignation but failed. There was some conservative support to have White (a former police officer) reinstated, but it seems that Moscone was just as happy to have White out of the way. At 9 A.M. on the 27th of November, White drove to City Hall with his aide, Denise Apcar. Ms. Apcar went into City Hall through the front doors and metal detectors, but White decided to find another way into the building. The loaded, five-shot revolver he was carrying would not pass the metal detectors.

He went in through a basement window, assisted by some workmen. He used the story that he did not want to go through the front doors because there were demonstrators outside supporting his reinstatement (which was true), and that the side doors were locked and he had forgotten his keys (not exactly true, he had surrendered his keys earlier, at the time of his resignation).

He went upstairs to the Mayor's Office, waited patiently in the outer office until Moscone was ready for him, and then went in and had a heated discussion with the Mayor. He then fired four rounds into him, and left by another door.

He went down the hallway, reloading as he walked, and stepped into Harvey Milk's office, asking him for a private word. Milk joined White in another room, where he was shot five times.

White left City Hall and phoned his wife, meeting her away from home. Eventually, he surrendered himself to the police and confessed to the crimes, even though he told the investigators that he walked through the murders in a kind of stupor, having blacked out on the way to City Hall and having no memory of the actual killings.

What happened next became a landmark in the history of jurisprudence. Dan White's lawyers came up with the infamous "Twinkie Defense," based on their allegation that Dan White committed the murders while in diminished mental capacity due to an over indulgence in junk food. He was convicted of the lesser charges of voluntary manslaughter and sentenced to seven years, eight months in Soledad, in segregation from the main prison population. He was freed on parole in January 1984 after serving only five years.

On October 21, 1985, White was found dead in his garage, a victim of probable suicide from carbon monoxide poisoning.

The motives for the Moscone and Milk murders were never very clear. White had no particular agenda against Moscone. He had resigned his city position for the simple reason that it would not pay enough to support him and his family. He then decided to retract his resignation, but there was no legal precedent for it. All in all, it did not seem enough to warrant his insane plan to murder the Mayor. As a political and moral conservative, he probably despised gay activist Harvey Milk; it's possible that he considered killing Milk at the same time as Moscone on general principle. But we will never know; White had confessed to the crimes, and it only wanted a decision by the courts as to whether the homicides were murder or manslaughter. The question of motive was not explored because, quite simply, White insisted he didn't even remember committing the crimes. His death raises more questions than answers, since it occurred at a time when White was planning to move his family to Ireland permanently.

On July 31, 1980 the surviving children of Congressman Leo Ryan's family brought a lawsuit against the United States of America in the matter of Ryan's assassination. They charged that the State Department knew in advance of the dangers inherent in a trip to Jonestown, but failed to warn the Congressman in advance. They further charged that Jonestown was a CIA mind-control experiment, and that the community was heavily armed, and was infiltrated by CIA agents, among whom they named Richard Dwyer and Deborah Layton's estranged English husband (and former Quaker) Philip Blakey. It was Blakey who had gone to Guyana years before the rest of the Peoples Temple, in order to clear the land and prepare the site for habitation. His role has always been open to speculation, as he seemed to be Jones' right-hand man. The suit was dropped, for reasons that have never been revealed, although many still persist in their belief that Jonestown was a CIA operation of some kind and, if it was, the only type of operation that makes any kind of sense would be something along the lines of MK-ULTRA or some other, related, mind control experiment, since we are told by CIA that MK-ULTRA had been discontinued in the 1960s.

One of the Ryan family children eventually went on to become involved with the Cult Awareness Network (CAN) after the lawsuit against the CIA was dropped. Other influential members of CAN at one time included Dr. Margaret Singer, long associated with the Langley-Porter clinic, as well as notorious CIA mind-control psychiatrist Dr. Louis Jolyon West. These doctors had also been involved in the defense of Patty Hearst, asserting she had been brainwashed.

Larry Layton was acquitted of all charges in Guyanese courts, but had to stand trial again in the United States. His first trial ended in a mistrial; he was tried again a few years later and convicted, and is still in prison as of this writing. He is the only person to have been tried and convicted in the Jonestown case, and the only crimes he is actually known to have committed are the shootings of the two Peoples Temple defectors in the Cessna, both of whom were wounded but not killed. The actual murderers of Congressman Ryan and the four other individuals at Port Kaituma have never been identified, apprehended, or charged in any way by anyone. It is almost certain that they were still alive at the time of Larry Layton's numerous trials.

Deborah Layton went on to retrieve the money that Jim Jones had salted away in Switzerland and Panama, but it is not known whether she found all the money Jones had hidden or just a portion. Jones' affairs were heavily compartmentalized, and several of his higher-ranking PC staff had access to overseas accounts and funds. There are also persistent rumors that some of the security staff escaped into the jungles with a suitcase full of cash. The Temple owned three sailing vessels in Guyana, which were all at sea at the time of the massacre. One of these was named *Cudjoe*, ironically enough, since it was also the *nom de guerre* of Patty Hearst's SLA lover, William Wolfe. Another vessel was the *Marceline*, the name of Jim Jones' wife. Evidence of conspiracy, or of sinister forces at work behind the flimsy façade of reality? Who were on these vessels? How many were they? Where were they dropped off? No one seems to care.

Bonnie Thielmann, Terri Buford, the Mertles/Mills, Thomas Layton, and Deborah Layton have all written or co-written books on Jonestown, each providing their own particular spin and adding to the general information—or disinformation—on the case. Tim Reiterman has written a book, as has Charles Krause, both newsmen present at Port Kaituma when the shooting started. Mark Lane has also written a book about Jonestown. So have other survivors.

"MISTAH KURTZ—HE DEAD."

As for Jim Jones himself, his fate is also open to question. His death was ruled a suicide, by a self-inflicted gunshot wound. The pistol he is alleged to have used, however, was found far away from his body. At least one researcher—Michael Meier—insists that the body that was identified as Jim Jones at the scene could not have been Jones, because the body does not match some essential physical characteristics, thus giving rise to the "Jim Jones double" theory; that Jones may have had a double is supported by some circumstantial evidence, as shown in the Jim Hougan article. In Meier's view,[54] the real Jim Jones is sipping banana daiquiris on a tropical beach somewhere, enjoying his millions in relative peace. Hard to believe? Sure. But, as so often in this study, we are confronted with more questions than answers. One wonders, for instance, where Dwyer was at the moment Jones was killed? Jones wanted him gone; thus he seemed to have been there at the time of the massacre. Was he Jim Jones' executioner, playing the Marlow to his Kurtz? Or was it a bit more like the Martin Sheen and Marlon Brando characters in *Apocalypse Now*, with Brando's crazed but successful renegade Colonel—surrounded by his Montagnard Army who revere him "as a god"—who must be assassinated by Sheen's Captain Willard.

In the original theatrical release of the film, we are shown an image that is frighteningly reminiscent of what might have happened at Jonestown. In this scene, which is nowhere to be found on the videotapes and DVDs that have since been produced, the end credits roll up over the sight of Colonel Kurtz' jungle encampment being razed by napalm, killing all the inhabitants. Although this finale is suggested by other events in the film—such as the discovery of Kurtz' manuscript with the words "Drop the bomb! Kill them all!" scribbled across one page—the actual firebombing of the site is not shown on later releases.

I like to think that Jim Jones *was* Colonel Kurtz; that he had been recruited by the CIA in his early days, and then become increasingly psychotic as his personal and spiritual isolation grew. I like to think that the CIA used him and his Guyana operation for a variety of experiments *in situ* because it was outside the United States, in the middle of nowhere, far beyond any possibility of congressional interlopers (until events forced Congressman Ryan's hand), and anyway the victims were poor, black, and socialist; by openly accepting Jones' rabid form of "apostolic socialism" and parroting his fear of an attack by the fascists, the Nazis, the KKK, the CIA, the FBI, etc., they had placed themselves beyond the pale. They could not be repatriated. Bringing a thousand paranoid black people who had been through the fires of hell together back into the United States could only have been seen as a terrible liability. Furthermore, who knew what some of them had witnessed at Jonestown? What tales would they tell?

> *As the tropical night deepens, the loudspeaker blaring the last, crazed harangue of Jim Jones, like the Brando character reciting poetry and broken, bitter prose over the radio deep within the jungles of Cambodia, and with the Jonestown population falling to the effects of cyanide, or to bullets in the back of their skulls, Richard Dwyer creeps along the wooden planks of the pavilion and fires the coup de grâce into the brain of a madman.*

I hope I may be forgiven if it seems that I have gone off the deep end with this theory, but stranger things have happened. We have left other people behind, in dangerous territory, in the hands of torturers and psychopaths. Why should the Peoples Temple be any different? And by spinning the story so that it looks like mass suicide, we can assuage any guilt we may have over the exact manner of their fate. After all, they killed *themselves*. It's sad, and tragic, and a warning to us all . . . but *we* had nothing to do with it.

The Peoples Temple settlers in Guyana had come in search of God, in search of paradise, in search of spiritual liberation. Religion, after all, was their primary motive. Jones had abandoned religion very early on, ridiculing the Bible, but at the same time claiming that he was the reincarnation of Jesus and Lenin, among other heroes. He was merging religion and politics, in a way that has become all too familiar now, promising a workers' paradise "on earth as it is in heaven." In robbing his believers of an afterlife, of a blissful existence on the other side of death, and giving them only horror in this life, Jim Jones worked the ultimate blasphemy. God became, for the hopeful, idealistic parents, and innocent, wide-eyed children of Jonestown, a hungry tiger lurking in the jungle darkness, its eyes shining in the reflected light of their souls. These were people who wanted what everyone wants: peace, security, happiness, a bright future for their children, and the knowledge that they are doing good in the world and furthering the spiritual liberation of the planet at the same time. This is what Jim Jones promised them. Instead, he gave them despair.

> *As they stand in the compound the jungle night darkened, the sound of gun fire chilling them like some satanic orchestra as their friends are being shot, the rounds marching closer and closer to the center of the mass as the men march up and down the columns of the helpless. The helpless who suddenly realize that they are breathing their last moments on earth, an unspeakable fear mingling with the tears and the screams of mothers poisoning their children, husbands embracing their wives for the last time in horror and in desperate love, surrounded by evil men and a hostile landscape, all hope dying within their hearts in a dreadful plummet as, one by one, their friends and family fall to the vermin-infested earth, never to hope or pray or dream or laugh again.*
>
> *They were so very far from home.*

Robert Graves once wrote, in reference to the Gordian Knot,

> Alexander's brutal cutting of the knot, when he marshalled his army at Gordium for the invasion of Greater Asia, ended an ancient dispensation by placing the power of the sword above that of religious mysteries.[55]

Perhaps so. Perhaps the modern world is still in the grip of that conceit, that military conceit of absolute power. The CIA recognized that there was military value in those religious mysteries, however, and strove to make those mysteries serve the State. They picked up the two pieces of whatever knot they had severed, savagely and without concern for the souls of the men and women destroyed in the process, and tried to find out how it was tied.

"God," said Nik Aziz, a powerful Malaysian politician and dangerous Islamic fundamentalist, "is a gangster."[56]

Amen. But as I once wrote in another time, another place, and as the Jonestown victims learned too late to save their lives, "God is the only safe thing to be."

ENDNOTES

1 Gordon Thomas, *Journey Into Madness*, Bantam, NY, 1990, p. 276
2 Charles A. Krause, *Guyana Massacre: The Eyewitness Account*, Pan Books, London, 1979, p. 132
3 John Marks, *The Search for "The Manchurian Candidate,"* Times, NY, 1979, p. 178–9
4 Ibid., p. 164
5 Ibid., p. 166
6 Kenneth D. Wald, *Religion and Politics in the United States*, Washington, DC, 1992, p. 44
7 Jim Hougan, "Jonestown, The Secret Life of Jim Jones: A parapolitical fugue," *Lobster*, vol 37, Summer 1999, p. 10
8 Ibid., p. 12
9 Ibid., p. 13
10 Ibid., p. 13
11 Ibid., p. 14
12 Jeannie Mills, *Six Years With God: Life Inside Rev. Jim Jones's Peoples Temple*, A&W Publishers, NY, 1979, p. 243
13 Andrija Puharich, *Uri*, Anchor Press, NY, 1974, p. 26
14 Ibid., p. 30
15 Ibid., p. 31
16 Gerald L. Posner & John Ware, *Mengele: The Complete Story*, Dell, NY, 1987, p. 167–192
17 Russell Targ & Keith Harary, *The Mind Race: Understanding and Using Psychic Powers*, New English Library, London, 1986, p. 103–106
18 Garry Wills, *Under God: Religion and American Politics*, Simon & Schuster, NY, 1990, p. 144
19 Ibid., p. 144
20 Min S. Yee & Thomas N. Layton, *In My Father's House*, Holt, Rinehart & Winston, NY,1981, p. 45
21 Ibid., p. 42
22 Ibid., p. 44
23 Ibid., p. 4
24 Ibid., p. 6
25 Ibid., p. 19
26 Ibid., p. 49
27 Ibid., p. 58
28 Ibid., p. 64
29 Leonard A. Cole, Clouds of Secrecy: The Army's Germ Warfare Tests Over Populated Areas, Rowman & Littlefield, Totowa, 1988, p. 45
30 Ibid., p. 61
31 Yee & Layton, op. cit., p. 66
32 Can be found in various places, including the recently-released BLUEBIRD CIA files, and in *Bluebird* by Colin Ross, Manitou Communications, Richardson TX, 2000,. p. 385
33 Yee & Layton, op. cit., p. 172
34 Ibid., p. 168
35 Ibid., p. 168
36 Ibid., p. 172
37 Ibid., p. 177
38 Ibid., p. 180
39 Ibid., p. 185
40 Hougan, op. cit., p. 12
41 Yee & Layton, op. cit., p. 158
42 Ibid., p. 161
43 Ibid., p. 161
44 Ibid., p. 161
45 Ibid., p. 219
46 Mills, op. cit., p. 83
47 Yee & Layton, op. cit., p. 232
48 Ibid., p. 274
49 Victor Turner, *Revelation and Divination in Ndembu Ritual*, Cornell University Press, Ithaca, 1975, p.32

50 Krause, op. cit., p. 96
51 Ibid., p. 97
52 Hougan, op. cit., p. 4
53 Ibid., p. 5
54 Michael Meiers, Was Jonestown a CIA Experiment?, Edwin Mellen Press, Studies in American Religion, Number 35, Lewiston NY, 1988, ISBN 0-88946-013-2
55 Robert Graves, The Greek Myths
56 *The Star*, Kuala Lumpur, Sept 2, 2002, p.2

MOOD
ATO
RICH
BAGNO
BEST

BOOK TWO: A WARM GUN

CHAPTER FOURTEEN

HAPPINESS IS A WARM GUN

I made a decision to be crazy, or schizophrenic; a psychopath or a sociopath, whatever it is you have to be to do the things that I did. It's a choice anybody can make.

—Mark David Chapman[1]

MARKS: Is there any psychiatric significance to his mental condition that's attributable to religious beliefs?
SCHWARTZ: I cannot call them, in and of themselves, delusional, since they are not unique to him.

His concept of religion, of God, is an extremely fundamentalistic one. As he himself says, he doesn't just believe in Satan, he knows that Satan is here on earth . . . . Right or wrong to a great extent is decided in his life by a struggle between God or God's angels, and Satan, or Satan's demons, who struggle for possession of his will.

—Testimony of Dr. Daniel Schwartz in sentencing hearing of Mark David Chapman on August 24, 1981[2]

But the struggle between freedom and Communism is, in its essence, not an economic conflict but a spiritual one.

—Ronald Reagan, August 31, 1984 letter to World Anti-Communist League[3]

So it was not a well-planned intrigue, it was the Devil himself.

—August Strindberg[4]

The Jonestown hearings took place in 1979. A lawsuit was brought against the CIA in July1980 by relatives of Congressman Leo Ryan, who believed that the CIA knew much more about Jonestown than they told the Congressman. On October 18, 1978—and thus exactly a month before the massacre—CIA Deputy Director Frank Carlucci had written the Congressman to tell him that although the CIA *had* conducted mind-control experiments at Vacaville, they had not involved with Donald DeFreeze (Cinque) of the Patty Hearst kidnapping "insofar as our records reflect the names of the participants."

Lisa Philip, the mother of Larry Layton and Deborah Layton, had died in Jonestown of cancer three months before the massacre. Although this survivor of

Nazi Germany lived to see serious problems in the Peoples Temple "paradise," she did not live to see the horrible devastation of the White Night, and perhaps one should be grateful for that if for nothing else.

Carolyn Moore—Larry Layton's first wife and mistress of Jim Jones, mother of his son Kimo—was dead at Jonestown. Karen Tow Layton, Larry's second wife and sometime sexual partner of Jim Jones, also died during the White Night. It is not known when Jones died: did he wait for all of the others to die and then take his own life? Was he shot by one of the security guards at some point during the proceedings? Was he "terminated with extreme prejudice" by a CIA officer present at the scene? We may never know. We can assume, however, that Jones died with the screams of his followers in his ears and the sight of bodies falling all around him as far as his eyes could see.

Larry Layton was the only person ever charged with murder and conspiracy to commit murder in relation to the events of Jonestown and Port Kaituma. He had been seized at the Port Kaituma airstrip on the urgings of Richard Dwyer, even though the Guyanese police were reluctant to do so, and, indeed, Dwyer had no authority in Guyana to order anyone's arrest. It was necessary to charge someone with the murder of the Congressman, and Larry Layton was the only one who remained behind at the scene to be charged. No one else was ever arrested, tried or convicted, even though Peoples Temple defectors who survived the rampage would have recognized exactly who had done the shooting. There is no evidence that the shooters died at Jonestown with the rest of the commune. Once Larry Layton was in custody, there was no need to look any further, and thus he could bear the responsibility for all of it. Once someone was in custody—reminiscent of the events at Dallas in 1963 and Los Angeles in 1968—the police stopped looking anywhere else. Although Layton was convicted of conspiracy, no other conspirators were apprehended or charged. Layton was a conspiracy of one.

To put this in some kind of perspective, we have to remember that it was in 1977 that the Senate hearings took place on the CIA's mind-control operations, which involved everything from BLUEBIRD to ARTICHOKE to MK-ULTRA and MK-NAOMI to OFTEN. The revelations came as a stunning surprise to many Americans, and the CIA's efforts to downplay the projects as basically worthless and non-productive were met with incredulity. In July of 1977, *New West* magazine published (in their August 1 issue) an investigative report on the Peoples Temple which was anything but congratulatory. Only a few days later, on August 3, 1977 the Senate hearings on MK-ULTRA took place. Simultaneously, a public outcry against the Peoples Temple began, and there were demands that it be officially investigated by the government. Jim Jones, in that hostile climate, began making plans to get out of Dodge and to move to the presumably more welcoming and benign climate of Guyana.

On October 31, 1977 (Halloween), President Carter's Director of the CIA—Admiral Stansfield Turner—summarily fired over eight hundred of the Agency's covert operations personnel, reducing the CIA's operational staff from 1,200 to less than 400, virtually overnight.[5] Known as the "Halloween Massacre," Turner's move created an unofficial network of eight hundred "disgruntled former employees." It is a miracle that these men, with their specialized training picked up at The Farm and other Agency locations, did not "go postal"! (Arthur Hochberg was one of those fired that day who subsequently disappeared from public view.) However, many did find themselves working for the Reagan–Bush presidential campaign, actively supporting a former CIA Director (George Bush), whom they felt might get the Agency back on track. Campaign posters began to appear at CIA headquarters at Langley, with the "Reagan" half of the poster torn away, leaving only "Bush." On the other hand, radical protesters at the Republican National Convention in Detroit on July14–17, 1980 wore buttons that said, "Shoot Bush First."

Shortly after the "Massacre," Leo Ryan, the Congressman who co-authored the Hughes-Ryan Amendment forcing CIA to advise Congress in advance of covert activities, proceeds to Guyana and is slain on November 18, 1978, as we have seen. The people of Jonestown are killed in a massacre of horrific proportions. Large quantities of drugs are found at the scene, drugs that are later described as "mind-control" substances, but which include everything from Valium to cyanide. The amount of drugs found is far in excess of what the thousand inmates of Jonestown would or could use in the normal course of living. That, and the involvement of the son of Dr. Laurence Layton (formerly of the Army's Chemical Warfare Division) and others with suspicious backgrounds in government, the military and medicine, gives rise to speculation—so soon after the MK-ULTRA hearings—that Jonestown itself was some kind of mind control experiment gone awry.

Then, on November 4, 1979 a mob of Iranian students attacked the US Embassy in Teheran, Iran and took fifty-two Americans hostage.

Americans will not soon forget the searing image of our people being rounded up, blindfolded and bound, in the midst of thousands of screaming Shi'ite students. Americans will not forget the sight of these same students trying to tape together the millions of strips of shredded documents that the staffers had tried to destroy when the students were leaping over the embassy walls. Whereas two years previously Admiral Turner had fired most of the CIA's covert operations officers, he must have thought he could have used them now.

There was no way to get into Teheran and free the hostages. There would have to be a negotiation for their release. But first, there was tremendous propaganda value in having these once-proud Americans so helpless, as the television cameras of the world trained their lenses on Teheran—helpless and terrified the way the Shah's dreaded secret police, the SAVAK, had kept Iranian citizens in a constant state of fear and anxiety for decades. Beginning in 1960, and thus during the same period that Dan Mitrione was training secret police in Brazil and Uruguay, the CIA was training SAVAK (as were the Israelis who had long maintained a "de facto" relationship with Iran due to the fact that Iran is a nation of non-Semites who feel they have nothing in common with their Arab neighbors except Islam, and even then their version—Shi'ism—is considered heretical by most other Muslims). The Shah himself, after all, had been put in power in Iran by the American CIA in an operation of which the Agency is still quite proud. So turnabout was fair play in the eyes of revolutionaries, and there was thus no real hurry on the Iranian side to negotiate a return of the hostages.

This was the Carter presidency. Jimmy Carter had been elected largely as a kind of backlash against what was perceived as the excesses, corruption and constitutional violations of the Nixon years. He was the first Democrat in the White House since 1968, and Carter's homely, simple Southern Christian personality seemed like the perfect antidode to nearly eight years of Vietnam, Watergate, student rebellions, race riots, and assassinations. It looked as if it was going to be an administration of healing from the "long national nightmare" that was Watergate and the Nixon presidency.

Carter was elected in 1976, at the time of the nation's bicentennial. It had been two hundred years since a group of Freemasons and freethinkers had declared their independence from England and "fired the shot heard round the world." It was an appropriate time for America to rethink and re-invent itself. Saigon had fallen in 1975. Vietnam was the first war America had lost. Gerald Ford had been president for a short time in the wake of Nixon's resignation over Watergate. The Freemason and former male model and partner of Harry Conover—Candy Jones' first mentor and first husband—and member of the Warren Commission had not exactly covered himself in glory. He had been physically attacked twice, most famously by Manson Family member Lynette "Squeaky" Fromme, who is still in prison because of the attempted assassination, and totally unrepentant. It was time for America to take some spiritual inventory.

The Senate hearings into the CIA's abuse of its charter were one prominent feature of the Carter administration, as was his selection of Admiral Turner as CIA Director. In the wake of the Watergate revelations—which were almost too sordid for most Americans to believe—a house-cleaning of Howard Hunt's old employer seemed very much in order. As the CIA was being dragged through the mud and hoisted on its own petard publicly, particularly with respect to its domestic spying activities under Nixon, Turner found he had the mandate he needed to fire all the odd birds in the Agency that still reveled in clandestine, cloak-and-dagger espionage. It was going to be a new era, one in which less importance would be placed on HUMINT (human intelligence-gathering) and more on fancy technology and spy-in-the-sky strategies. The Admiral obviously felt that agents with decades of experience in the field could be replaced by computer keyboards and exotic cameras.

But then the Iran hostage situation changed all that.

The CIA was blamed for not knowing about the Ayatollahs' threat to the Shah's regime in advance, and for not knowing what to do about it. The CIA was blamed for the raid on the US Embassy in Teheran and the fifty-two Americans now being held by fanatic Shi'ite students in various scattered and undisclosed locations all over the city. And Carter was being blamed for not solving the problem at once.

And then, there was the oil.

The Middle Eastern situation was precarious. The creation of Israel in 1948 and the subsequent wars with its Arab neighbors had threatened not only the delicate balance of power between Capitalist and Communist, between Zionist and Arab, between America and Russia, but had also threatened the world's supply of oil. America had helped Saudi Arabia develop its enormous oil reserves since the earliest days and had wisely remained on the country's good side, supplying it with arms, the latest in aviation technology, and training for its fighter pilots, its troops, its weapons specialists. It had thus ensured a ready supply of oil regardless of what happened between Israel and Egypt—neither of whom have any oil—and watched the developing situation between Iraq and Iran carefully; it was not enough to simply control the oil reserves in Saudi Arabia and Kuwait, we had to control the reserves of Iraq (second in size only to that of Saudi Arabia) as well the transportation of that oil from the Middle East to Europe and America. That meant controlling the Persian Gulf, which is bordered by both Iraq and Iran, with the rich oilfields of Kuwait especially vulnerable to Iraqi attack. If these two fought each other, the US could side with either one, or both, and thus be assured of access to the Gulf for its giant tankers. If they banded together, however, they could decide to make life miserable for oil exports, just as OPEC did for a short time during the famous "Energy Crisis" of the Carter administration, until the unity between the oil producing nations fell apart and the oil embargo failed.

Many a book could be written—and many have—on Middle Eastern oil politics, and we will not go into all of that now. The taking of the American hostages was but another chapter in the ongoing saga of oil, race, religion, and history in a region that has been called everything from a tinderbox to a dynamite keg . . . to the cradle of civilization. (And, oh, how that cradle will rock!) What we will examine here instead, and in brief, is the famous incident known to historians and conspiracy theorists as the "October Surprise."

LIVES IN THE BALANCE

In a replay of the Nixon–Chenault–Thieu secret arrangement to torpedo the peace talks and thereby prolong the Vietnam War in 1968—to assure that Humphrey and the Democrats would not taste victory at the polls—there is evidence that the Reagan–Bush campaign pulled the same stunt in 1980, to keep the hostages in Iran until after the November election, thus ensuring the defeat of the Democrats once again. In addition, just as the Nixon strategy in 1968 ultimately led to five more years of American involvement and American and Vietnamese deaths in Vietnam, the Reagan–Bush strategy in 1980 culminated in the Iran-Contra Affair, as advisors answerable to the President decided to ignore Congress and do what they could to aid the Contras in Nicaragua while at the same time providing weapons to Iran in exchange for the hostages. Once again, a sitting President's policy—being effected at the highest levels of international diplomacy, with many lives at stake not to mention the nation's foreign policy direction—was subverted by a political challenger to gain advantage in an election. In other countries, going behind the president's back and cutting a secret, separate deal with a foreign power would be called treason; in the America of the 1960s and '70s, it was business as usual.

The basic story of the October Surprise is as follows:

As Carter tried desperately to resolve the hostage crisis, his efforts were being undermined by a coalition of Republicans, Iranians and Israelis. When the Shah was deposed on January 16, 1979, ending thirty-seven years of rule, the Ayatollah Khomeini was back in Teheran two weeks later on February 1 (Candlemas). On November 4, students took over the US Embassy in Teheran. On April 7, 1980, President Carter froze Iranian assets and enforced an arms and trade embargo against Iran. This made Iran vulnerable to an Iraqi attack. Furthermore, much Iranian military equipment was of US origin and needed US-made spare parts. Israel had a large inventory of exactly the spare parts Iran needed, and they urgently wanted to sell those parts to the Iranians. Carter's embargo against Iran made that impossible . . . or, at least, very difficult.

And then, on September 22, 1980—the autumnal equinox—Iraq went to war against Iran.

Iran's backdoor contacts with Israel, coupled with Reagan's rising popularity in the polls, coalesced to form a cabal that would destroy Carter's chances for re-election. There is a controversy about who first contacted whom to set the covert operation going, but it was a *menage* made in heaven. The Israelis were able to sell arms to Iran, Iran got the arms they needed, and the Republicans were able to ensure that the hostages would remain hostages until after the election. Initial meetings were undertaken between Iran and the Republican Party in Madrid in late July of 1980, at the Hotel Ritz. William Casey—soon to be head of the CIA under Reagan—was present, as well as two other Americans using aliases, and a delegation from Iran. Interestingly, an Iranian delegate had met a only few weeks previously with a representative of the Carter White House, also in Madrid, on the 2nd of July. This developed into what appeared to be improving relations between Carter and Iran that September, which could have led to the release of the hostages before the election. However, Casey's machinations insured the failure of that.

Much ink has been spilled over the question of an October Surprise. The journalism that has appeared supporting either side of the issue has been flawed, or has not presented enough unequivocal evidence one way or another to close the case. It would seem virtually impossible to get this kind of closure, considering the people and organizations involved. Naturally, had the Republicans been actively involved in an attempt to cut a secret deal with a foreign government to win an election, they would not have left a lot of paperwork around as evidence; conversely, they would have covered their tracks very well with considerable planning before any meetings or telephone contacts, etc. Similarly, the Iranians would have no interest in proving or disproving any allegations and neither would the Israelis. The CIA isn't talking, and the US government has not been able to prove a case against the very people who claim that the October Surprise *did* happen.

Its attempts to convict Richard Brenneke and Ari Ben-Menashe of perjury—accusing them of lying about their testimony in connection with the events of the October Surprise—ended in acquittal for both men. Thus, in the eyes of the American legal system, Brenneke and Ben-Menashe were either telling the truth . . . or, at least, they were not lying! In Brenneke's case, during a trial for his friend Heinrich Rupp in 1988, he "declared under oath that he had attended one of a series of meetings in Paris in late October 1980 where William Casey, Donald Gregg, and other American, Iranian and French individuals had convened to discuss the release of the US hostages in Iran. He said that Rupp had told him that George Bush was also present in Paris."[6] These were important allegations, being made at the time George Bush was running for president against Michael Dukakis. The US government decided to strike back—after the election—and in May 1989 brought an indictment against Brenneke for perjury.

In order to prove its case, all the government had to do was present witnesses and documentation to show that Brenneke was lying. Incredibly, the government provided no conclusive evidence to show that any of the individuals mentioned by Brenneke were actually where they said they had been. Incredibly, because the October Surprise took place at the height of a presidential campaign in which all or most of these individuals should have been very easy to reach and to locate. Phone records alone should have been available to prove (or at least substantiate) the claims of Bush, Casey, Gregg and others that they were where they said they had been, but there was no substantiation. Eyewitnesses contradicted each other and their own stories. The prosecution was a mess.

Facing five counts of perjury, Brenneke was acquitted on each one. That does not mean that he was telling the truth, of course; but it does mean that, for some reason, the government could not prove he was lying, and that is by far the most important conclusion to be drawn from the case. At the time of the October Surprise, neither Casey nor Bush were government employees or members of the intelligence services; the records of their whereabouts would not be considered matters of national security, but subject to the normal privacy regulations covering any American citizen and capable of being examined during the course of a jury trial. But they were not. This can only lead one to surmise that these individuals were acting in some official or semi-official capacity at the time in question, and were being protected by the government.

Ari Ben-Menashe was an arms dealer specializing in the sale of Israeli-made arms to Iran at the time. He was arrested in California on charges of smuggling C-130 transport planes to Iran, was held without bond for a year, and then acquitted of all charges. At that time, bitter and angry over his treatment by the government, he began to spill all he knew—or claimed to know—about the October Surprise affair and about Iran-Contra.

One's opinion of the truth or falsehood of the October Surprise allegations depends largely on whether or not one believes the witnesses who have come forward, and that is a tricky business. Gary Sick, a former US Navy career officer and staffer on the National Security Council during three presidential administrations, wrote a book about the affair in which he concluded that the October Surprise did happen, that the Reagan–Bush administration did conspire against incumbent president Jimmy Carter, and that the hostages were held by Iran until Reagan was safely elected and inaugurated. The hostages were released within minutes of Reagan taking the oath as President of the United States. And the arms sales to Iran began in earnest in the months that followed.

As if reprising his old role during the Vietnam War, former President Nixon had traveled to London a week after Reagan's 1980 nomination at the Republican National Convention to talk to the chairman of Bristow Helicopters, Alan Bristow, who had experience in Iran as a chopper pilot, and who had once planned a commando raid in Iran to retrieve the company's helicopter fleet.[7] Nixon met with Bristow at the US Embassy in London, and asked how feasible it would be to plan a second attempt at rescuing the Iranian hostages. Carter's first attempt, on April 25, 1980, had ended in disaster, with Delta Force commandos stranded in the desert as their helicopters crashed and burned during a sandstorm. It was generally believed that Carter would not make a second attempt, and instead was pursuing diplomatic means to resolve the crisis. Nixon was in London to arrange a non-governmental rescue attempt, presumably on behalf of the Republican Party. The plan was eventually dropped, because it would have required access to up-to-the-minute military intelligence on the hostage situation which even the Republican Party did not have, revealing that this was a private attempt to rescue the hostages and not an official one. Why, for instance, would Nixon have gone to a firm outside the United States to contract this mission if it had the blessing of the US president? Why abort the mission when Reagan would have had all the access he would need to military intelligence come January? There can be no other conclusion than that this was a separate initiative, undertaken by Nixon at the behest of the Reagan–Bush campaign and without the knowledge or consent of the Carter administration. It was a fallback option, a contingency plan should the negotiations with Iran in Madrid and Paris fall through for any reason. And Nixon would have been the perfect person for it, experienced as he was with the

Thieu–Chennault arrangement of 1968, and his given general attitude towards Constitutional niceties during his years as President.

The rest, as they say, is history. Carter was roundly defeated at the polls, Reagan was elected, the hostages were immediately released, and Iran-Contra began to get up a nice head of steam.

What interests us about the October Surprise and the development of the plan into what eventually became known as Iran-Contra is the involvement of some of the strangest people ever to become associated with American politics—which, as the attentive reader may agree, is quite an accomplishment. In this case, we are talking about the woman who first blew the whistle on October Surprise with a book of the same title, a woman who worked for the Reagan Administration and who resigned her staff position, charging sexual harassment: Barbara Honegger.

Incredibly, Barbara Honegger brings us back again full circle to the weird, post-war group that first attracted our attention in Book One: the Round Table of Andrija Puharich, the same Round Table whose members were inexplicably linked to the assassination of President Kennedy. For it was Puharich, Honegger, accused murderer Ira Einhorn, and nuclear physicists Saul Paul Sirag and Jack Sarfatti who formed a nucleus of another sort in the 1970s, and who brought The Nine back to life—and back in operation—in the person of Israeli psychic and sometime intelligence agent Uri Geller. And, as we shall also see in Book Three, it is Sarfatti and his confreres in the community of quantum physicists who provide us a working model of the sinister forces we have been chasing so assiduously thus far.

RETURN OF THE NINE

In 1968, when the political situation in the United States was in turmoil, visionaries assassinated, students rioting, and Nixon cutting secret deals to win the election, Andrija Puharich met Ira Einhorn. Puharich at this time was heavily involved in paranormal research, but—due to his academic credentials as well as his status as something of an inventor (his specialty was electronic hearing-aid devices and, some say, electronic implants)—he was respected by those scientists whose broad-mindedness encompassed the possibility of paranormal abilities such as ESP and psychokinesis. At the time he met Einhorn, he was "doing research in connection with the Atomic Energy Commission, working with the head of biophysics"[8]: Puharich, as usual, working with the paranormal but always under the aegis of a classified project of some kind, either for the military, the intelligence agencies, or other—equally secretive—government organizations, such as the AEC. Einhorn, who would later be indicted and eventually (in 2002) convicted for the murder of his girlfriend Holly Maddux, was something of a New Age entrepreneur at the time. He had read Puharich's *Beyond Telepathy,* a book that posited a connection between energy and information, and felt that it was one of the most important books of the decade. It was out of print by 1968, and Einhorn wanted to help

Puharich find another publisher and get it back in print. The two then developed a close working relationship for a while, which was further energized by Puharich's discovery of Uri Geller in Israel in 1971.

Jack Sarfatti, on the other hand, had been a gifted child who won a scholarship to Cornell to study physics in 1956, when he was only seventeen years old. In 1953, however, and during the same year as Puharich and the Round Table were in contact with The Nine, Sarfatti had been getting strange phone calls at home. Much later, Puharich's book, *Uri*, brought it all back. Sarfatti's mother began reading the book—which contains a description of the Round Table séances with the Dr. Vinod who channeled The Nine—and suddenly recognized the symptoms. She brought the circumstances to her son's attention and the memory of the strange phone calls came back in full force.

Sarfatti had been getting calls from someone speaking in a strange, metallic voice stating that it was the voice of a computer aboard a spacecraft hovering over the earth. These calls went on for a while, and would cause the young Sarfatti to wander around dazed. Evidently, the memory of the calls receded into his unconscious as he pursued his career in nuclear physics, and only the book by Puharich about Uri Geller brought it all back. The Nine claimed to be aboard a spacecraft, hovering over the earth, called Spectra. Sarfatti himself seemed selected at a very early age for something of importance. He was being tutored in a separate program for gifted children by a founder of American MENSA, Walter Breen, in a program that was funded (at least in part) by the Sandia Corporation. Some of this extracurricular training included lectures on patriotism and anti-Communism: heady stuff for a bunch of thirteen-year-olds. It would be Breen who would recommend Sarfatti for the Cornell scholarship.

There is a lot of Sarfatti email correspondence available on the Internet, much of which is concerned with quantum mechanics and nuclear physics in general, but some of which has to do with the events surrounding Spectra and The Nine. There are times when Sarfatti is obviously doubtful about the communications, wondering if they were the product of some bizarre sort of intelligence agency mind-control program. As Puharich was obviously involved in the series of séances which invoked The Nine at the same time as Sarfatti was getting the phone calls (which mirrored the information the Round Table was getting), there is at least the possibility that the calls were made by Puharich or by one of his associates (possibly Breen himself) as part of some wider program.

The fact that Puharich would also arrange long-term psychic experiments involving children at his farm in upstate New York in the 1970s gives one pause, considering the long military and intelligence background of Puharich. Were the 1970s experiments an outgrowth of whatever was happening to Sarfatti in the 1950s? Sarfatti does not seem convinced one way or another that the calls he received were extraterrestrial in origin (The Nine, or Spectra), or the result of a man-made intelligence trick; he is only certain (as is his mother) that he received them. One of the predictions made in the calls was that in twenty years he would become involved with a group of people whose mission was the acceleration of human evolution through contact with these otherworldly agencies. This is exactly what happened, for in 1973 he began to develop contacts with other, like-minded, scientists through the Stanford Research Institute (SRI) and eventually with Puharich himself. These contacts would eventually culminate in a business venture in the 1980s with Harold Chipman, a CIA Chief of Station in San Francisco, who was involved with SRI and the paranormal testing that went on there with Puharich and Geller, as well as with Russell Targ, Harold Puthoff, Ingo Swann, and the whole murder of crows that formed the most strictly controlled investigation of psychic phenomena that the United States had ever known.

The documentation concerning Sarfatti's relationship with Chipman (including Chipman's resume, which tantalizingly speaks of his language capabilities in Spanish, Mandarin Chinese, and . . . Tibetan) is available on Sarfatti's own website, as are huge strings of email exchanges on everything from Puharich and Geller and The Nine to discussions of quantum physics that are so arcane that amateurs are advised to keep their dignity intact by simply reading and not responding, as anyone who claims to add to the discussion is likely to be attacked if one can't back up one's statements with solid physics. There is no index to these exchanges, and many are very hard to decipher, as there are quotes within quotes within quotes from the correspondence that would require a Houdini to unravel; but the effort is usually well rewarded with some interesting bits of history.

In the 1970s, however, when Sarfatti was still developing the theories that would later make him famous in the world of physics, he was hanging out with Puharich, Uri Geller, and other notables in a hothouse atmosphere of radical thinking about science, communication, information, and psychic phenomena. Sarfatti claims to have introduced Geller to Jacques Vallee—the French UFO researcher of *Passport to Magonia* fame—and both to Steven Spielberg. Spielberg would later produce *Close Encounters of the Third Kind*, using Vallee as a technical adviser: Vallee the Anton LaVey to Spielberg's Roman Polanski. The character played by Francois Truffaut in the film is said to be based on Jacques Vallee himself. This same nexus of Puharich and Sarfatti is said to have influenced Gene Roddenberry in his development of the *Star Trek* television series. And behind all of this is the hugely influential figure of Ira Einhorn, usually referred to as "the Unicorn" after the translation of his surname into English.

For a while, Einhorn served as Sarfatti's literary agent (as he did with Puharich to get *Beyond Telepathy* reprinted). Einhorn was active in New Age pursuits, a kind of showman or P.T. Barnum of hippiedom, making connections and networking, bringing together people he felt should be brought together to create a kind of explosion of new thinking that cut across traditional disciplinary lines. So you had filmmakers talking to physicists, psychics talking to soldiers, and spies talking to everybody. Seminars were held, books and papers published. People like science-fiction author

Philip K. Dick (who was discovered by Hollywood in the 1990s, unfortunately *after* his death) and Robert Anton Wilson could be found in *kaffeklatsch* with Timothy Leary, John Lilly, Saul Paul Sirag, and assorted G-men. There was a sense among these people that an event of momentous importance to the planet was imminent, and that they were in the forefront of whatever it was going to be.

Many of them had already had paranormal contacts of some sort (a list that includes Sarfatti, Wilson, Dick, Geller, Puharich, and many, many others) and were certain that these contacts signalled the beginning of a more overt presence by these beings. These were people with government grants and contacts at the highest levels of the US military . . . and not only the US military. The Soviets were also involved, if only peripherally. And much of this was going on relatively un-noticed by the American people at large. Although they had seen Uri Geller bend spoons on national television, and had read the stories and novels by Dick and Robert Anton Wilson, for instance, they had no idea that all this activity was being produced by a loosely-organized group of intellectuals operating half-in, half-out of the mainstream . . . and half-in, half-out of the US government. And it was not until 1974, with the publication of Puharich's book about Uri Geller, that anyone outside a small circle of friends and associates had ever heard anything about The Nine.

Now, one of the members of this loose association of physicists, psychics and spies was Barbara Honegger. Honegger's entry pass was a master's degree in the paranormal that she obtained from John F. Kennedy University. A somewhat peripheral figure in the Einhorn/Puharich/Sarfatti circle, she was for a time the girlfriend of physicist Saul Paul Sirag, who was a frequent contributor to the group. From there, she went on to greater glory as a Reagan staffer who had quit his administration over charges of sexual misconduct. She then published a book on the October Surprise, which earned her a great degree of vitriol from Republican congressmen who characterized her as someone who dressed as a "bunny rabbit" at staff meetings and who listened to voices in her head: clearly sexual abuse of a different kind. It was Honegger's book that triggered NSC staffer Gary Sick to write his own account of the October Surprise, and the groundswell of paranoia began to grow anew.

As if this story needed to get any stranger, Honegger then—according to accounts published on the Internet—befriended the wife of one of the Iran-Contra pilots, Gunther Russbacher; and now we are well and truly in over our heads.

Gunther Russbacher is not mentioned in many books on Iran-Contra for the simple reason that he was not an active participant in the arms-for-hostages negotiations with McFarlane, Secord, North and the others. He was, however, on the flight crew of the aircraft that took 400 TOW missiles to Iran in September 1985, and then was on deck again for the famous flight of Robert McFarlane, Oliver North and their staff to Teheran in May of 1986. He is identified as ONI (Office of Naval Intelligence) in Iran-Contra related correspondence, as was his colleague on these flights, Robert Hunt.

A letter to Robert Hunt from Moshe Ben-Manash, Special Envoy to the Israeli Ambassador to Washington, dated November 11, 1993, confirms the presence of Robert McFarlane, Oliver North, Robert Hunt, George Cave, Howard Teicher, Gunther Russbacher and John R. Segal on a flight that left Israel loaded with one pallet of spare parts for the Hawk missile system. Russbacher and Segal (the latter identified as CIA) are mentioned as the pilots of the aircraft.

Other documentation shows that Russbacher was the pilot for the initial shipments of TOW missiles to Iran in August and September 1985, and that Poindexter advised Bill Casey, the Director of the CIA, that a confidential account had been set up for Russbacher, Segal and the other staffers of the May 1986 Teheran flight, with the implication that these funds would be used to compensate their families in event that the mission ended in disaster.

Several years later, Gunther Russbacher married a woman who believes herself to be descended from royalty, a woman who also believes that she and her brother were experimented upon by the government when they were children, who believes that her eggs were taken from her when she was eleven years old, etc. Her stories—available on the Internet through various sites—are a bizarre trip through a very disturbed psyche. She recounts events whose participants are all high-ranking US government personalities—engaged in weird, uncharacteristic behavior involving Templar chapels, underground submarine bases, and the like—and an individual introduced to her as the "King of the World." The events resemble those of an early Bond film, but without John Barry's score. The unsettling thing about her reminiscences is that she often mentions people and events from the covert world in a perfectly nonchalant and matter-of-fact way. Even though her tales are outrageous, the little details are quite unnerving.

As an example, consider a posting on the Internet dated 9 Nov 1998:

> Gunther and I drove directly to Offutt Air Force base in Omaha. We stayed in VIP quarters. William Webster, the DCI was on one side of us. Brent Scowcroft, the NSA, was on the other side. George Bush was across the hall, and Dick Cheney was at the end of the hall.
>
> William Webster wore red shorts and a red Hawaiian shirt.
>
> The meeting was to upgrade Gunther on his SR 71 flying so he could fly a mission to Moscow. On the mission with Gunther were Brent Scowcroft, William Webster, Gunther's boss, the DCO (Director of Covert Operations) an Admiral named Wilhelm Johann. There was a fourth passenger, but Gunther would never tell me who he was.

Thank goodness.

The events described above were said to have taken place in July of 1990. It is a little strange to see George Bush (*pere*?) and Dick Cheney mentioned in the same sentence about an event said to take place a decade before Bush's son and

Cheney would wind up in the White House. Bush Sr., of course, was President of the United States in July of 1990. To be sure, the email is dated November 9, 1998 but that is still long before Bush (*fils*) and Cheney campaigned together in the 2000 election.

If you're going to invent wild stories, then this is the way to go, I guess. Drop names like mad. Add the little details that give the reader a sense of reality: I can't get that image of William Webster out of my mind. It has poisoned me on red shorts forever.

In case there are readers who feel that the story may perfectly well be true, allow me to point out that according to this same posting, Gunther Russbacher had been in prison in St. Louis for a year: he had been arrested two days after he and Rayelan were married. Gunther was released in July 1990, and the couple "drove directly to Offutt Air Base in Omaha," where Gunther was evidently immediately being trained to fly a Stealth spyplane full of the intelligence elite to Moscow. Does any of this make any sense at all? Yet, there are copies of documentation available on the Internet—including a military record of some sort from Offutt Air Base—that would seem to support this story. At least in part. At least if we can believe that the documentation itself is real.

What we do have is Rayelan Russbacher (a/k/a Rayelan Allan) performing something called the "Avalon Mystery Mass" at the Church of Antioch in Santa Clara, California; perhaps I should say "concelebrating" the said Mass, along with Matriarch Mary Spruit, and with that we are back at the ranch, for with Mary Spruit and the Church of Antioch we are at home and hospitality with the wandering bishops of Book One.

Mary Spruit was ordained and consecrated by her husband, Herman Adrian Spruit, who in turn held the Vilatte succession and a number of others. He was co-consecrated by a bishop of the Liberal Catholic Church (the ecclesiastical arm of the Theosophical Society) and by a bunch of other notables, some of whom share lines of succession with the Gnostic Catholic Church of the OTO, the American Orthodox Catholic Church (of David Ferrie fame), and so on, and so forth, and so it goes. In addition to the Avalon Mystery Mass, Rayelan Allan—at least, as of 1998—was also offering something called the *Dance Enchants*, a meditation method based on "temple dancing" which also forms a part of the Avalon Mystery Mass. (According to personal correspondence with the present-day leader of the church, Rayelan Allan was indeed a *priest* of the Church of Antioch and had worked with Matriarch Spruit, but not after 1993.) To quote from her promotional material on the Web:

> DANCE ENCHANTS is a simple and easy way to experience the bliss of meditation and the beneficial spiritual and mental changes found on a disciplined spiritual path. Whoever said that enlightenment couldn't be fun?

Indeed.

Yet, here we have the intrepid Rayelan Allan Russbacher feeding information to Barbara Honegger on Iran-Contra . . . the same Barbara Honegger who was Saul Paul Sirag's main squeeze . . . who has a master's degree in parapsychology . . . who was an intimate of the circle around Puharich and Sarfatti and Einhorn . . .

. . . and who today is a military affairs journalist for the Naval Postgraduate School, Department of the Navy. A journalist who warned Washington a week after the September 11 attack on the Pentagon and the World Trade Center that a fifth column within the American military and justice systems—including a judge, military officers, pilots, and even Israeli intelligence—had advance warning of the attacks and did nothing to stop them, and may, indeed, have had a hand in planning and carrying out the horrendous events of that day.

It . . . it . . . boggles the mind.

UNDER GOD

Reagan's apocalyptic view of history, and his near-Manichean view of the world, was never deeply disected by the journalists of the time of his presidency. A member of the Disciples of Christ (which was, oddly enough, the religious background of the family of his would-be assassin John Hinckley, as well as of Jim Jones of the Peoples Temple) and a profound believer in the prophecies of the Bible, particularly the Book of Revelations, Reagan saw the world in black and white terms. The Soviet Union—we all remember—was characterized as the "Evil Empire." The missile defense shield—the Strategic Defense Initiative, or SDI—he proposed to protect the United States was referred to as "Star Wars." He saw the fight against Communism as a spiritual one, one which ran the risk of demonizing those living in Communist countries. Oddly enough, however, his administration was also characterized by the intense astrological interests of his wife, Nancy, leading some of us to wonder if the Reagan administration was a hotbed of Gnosticism.

What we had in the White House at that time—and probably what attracted many Americans to the Reagans—was a First Family representative of the strangest qualities of American life (Christian fundamentalism and chiliastic panic, astrology, xenophobia masquerading as anti-Communism, and the Hollywood-movie-star heritage of both the President and his wife) packaged in a non-threatening, homely manner by a grandfatherly authority figure. Many Americans could not understand the contempt others felt for Reagan and, perhaps rightly in a way, interpreted any anti-Reagan sentiments as anti-American. His popularity would only be increased by the failed assassination attempt by John Hinckley, Jr., an attempt that promoted Reagan into a kind of Jack Kennedy manqué, thus perfecting the icon.

But to many, the Reagan presidency was an assault on all that the Kennedy administration had represented. Many remembered Reagan's cooperation with the House UnAmerican Activities Committee during the McCarthy era. Many viewed his career as Governor of California with alarm, particularly his support for a proposed center to study violence that had all the earmarks of a concentration camp for undesirables. Critics of the far left, in a bit of self-conscious humor, began to equate Reagan with Regan, the demon-possessed character in *The Exorcist.* When it was discovered that Reagan's assailant—John Hinckley, Jr.—was the son of the *same* John Hinckley who had a meeting scheduled with Neil Bush (one of the Vice President's sons) the *same day* that Reagan was assaulted, conspiracy theories began to blossom once more in the land. That cynical 1980 campaign button—"Shoot Bush First"—suddenly took on a cautionary and prophetic meaning.

Before the Hinckley assassination attempt, however, another murder was being planned. We know the victim; we know the man who pled "guilty," and thus avoided a murder trial where evidence could have been presented in the glare of public scrutiny. What we don't understand is the motive; or, we suspect the motive and it is monstrous.

LET ME TAKE YOU DOWN

"You're not a saint. I'm not a saint. Yoko's not a saint. Nobody's a saint."
—John Lennon[9]

"I'm the Devil, and I'm here to do the Devil's business."
—Charles Watson

". . . would you kindly inform [Charles Manson] that it was Paul McCartney who wrote 'Helter Skelter', not me."
—John Lennon[10]

It was a few weeks after the election. Reagan had just been elected President, and former CIA Director George Bush was elected Vice President. If we believe the conspiriologists, the Reagan plan to subvert the election process and deal directly with the Iranians on the subject of the hostages had worked. The hostages, however, had not yet been released. That would not happen until the day of the inauguration, a month away.

The mother of all conspiracy theorists—Mae Brussell—believed that the deaths of rock stars Jimi Hendrix, Janis Joplin, and Jim Morrison were in reality political assassinations, carried out in an attempt to defuse the counter-culture revolution, which was the only movement actively challenging the establishment on issues such as racism, the environment, sexual morality, the war in Vietnam, etc. She associated the premature deaths of the rock-and-roll icons of the Sixties with the Manson killings, believing they were all of a piece: an attempt to destroy the youth movement and pull America into line by a gray flannel assembly line of right thinkers and right believers, feeding the war machine.

However, I have found it difficult to subscribe to this theory, as attractive as the sentiment behind it may be. The history of rock-n-rollers is littered with the "exquisite corpses" of men and women who lived life at the very edge of human experience and who took tremendous chances—with their bodies, their minds, and their souls—and courted death by the very manner of their lives. Buddy Holly, the Big Bopper, and Ritchie Valens in that terrible airplane crash seemed to set the standard for the mayhem that would follow: Elvis Presley's demise from the inevitable complications due to his larger-than-life lifestyle, and on and on, from the senseless deaths from overdose and suicide of the sixties through to Kurt Cobain and the other tragedies of the nineties. It is too easy to hold a dark government plot responsible for these deaths, especially without a shred of evidence when, in fact, the evidence that exists all points in a different direction.

Yet it is when we begin to examine the slaughter of the rock stars that we come close—not to a specific conspiracy, but—to those sinister forces we have been tracking, forces that lurk behind the events in question. This is a study that goes deeper than the "deep politics" of Peter Dale Scott. It is, perhaps, closer to what the Italians mean when they speak of *dietrologia* or the "science of the left hand"; for that is what "sinister" means, anyway.

Before, however, we jump from our cautiously established platform of conspiracy and coincidence, built so carefully, throughout *The Nine* and herein, decade by decade and century by century, we must stop once more to pick at another thread in our study of scarlet. For of all the dead rock stars, there was one whose premature death was most clearly a murder and an assassination. This was not a rock star embarked on a hazardous journey of drink, drugs and exhaustion, but a man clearly comfortable with himself and his surroundings, a husband and father, a calm and rational human being who was at the brink of a comeback after a decade of silence. A man whose killer prayed to Satan hours before the trigger was pulled and who—Larry Layton–like, Sirhan Sirhan–like, Dan White–like—walked robotically through the motions of murder, in a trance-like daze, and found himself in police custody, staring bewilderedly out at the world from within a tiny closet of darkened dreams.

We are discussing, of course, John Lennon and the events of December 1980.

I never met John Lennon or his wife, Yoko Ono, although as a New Yorker I was frequently privileged to see them both around town. Eerily, a few years after John's death, I would find myself constantly running into Yoko on the street with an array of bodyguards in tow (Yoko, not me); but, as a typical New Yorker, I never approached either of them for an autograph or attempted to speak with them. We New Yorkers, you see, feel we are much too cool to approach celebrities; such behavior is reserved for tourists.

Or for assassins like Mark David Chapman.

Many people are aware that the Beatles had had a fling with mysticism back in the 1960s, and that with George Harrison it "took," and he became a lifelong Buddhist until his death, a passing that included the chanting of prayers by Buddhist monks. The gallery of photographs on the cover of the *Sergeant Pepper* album of "people we like" included Aleister Crowley. Yet of all the Beatles, probably John Lennon was the most cynical, the most skeptical. It was he, after all, who uttered the immortal line, "The Beatles are more popular than Jesus." It was a simple observation rather than a declaration of faith, but one which resulted in Beatles albums being burned across America's Bible Belt. His signature song, "Imagine," asks us to imagine that there is no heaven and no hell. In his conversation with Paul Krassner, quoted above, he immediately rejected any reference to anyone as a "saint." The conversation in this case concerned Mae Brussell. In a bizarre twist of fate, it was John Lennon who financed conspiracy queen Brussell's first published article, when Paul Krassner found that his printer, alarmed by the contents of the article, insisted on being paid up-front.

What many do not know about John and Yoko, however, is that they were fascinated with the occult.

John's approach seems much more in line with a no-nonsense attitude towards spirituality: he accepted that spiritual realities existed, but denied the authority of organized religions and cults to determine who should believe what. Occultism is a mechanical approach to spirituality; faith is not as large a component in western magical practice as it is in western religion. A religious person drives a car without knowing anything about its engine; an occultist is a mechanic who is not satisfied until he or she understands the machine and can, perhaps, build a better one.

Which may explain the visits of John and Yoko to the Magickal Childe Bookstore in Manhattan in the 1970s.

At that time, I was friendly with Herman Slater, the proprietor of the store, and had known him since the days when he ran the Warlock Shop in Brooklyn Heights where I lived. As the fame and notoriety of his establishment grew—being covered extensively in the overseas press as well as by local newspapers and television shows—he began to attract an equally notorious clientele. The Process would hang out at the Warlock Shop, as well as the odd Satanist and witches of various denominations. The Shop is alluded to several times in Maury Terry's *The Ultimate Evil* as a hangout for people who knew more about the Son of Sam murders than they were telling. And, amidst all of that publicity, would occasionally arrive John and Yoko Lennon.

Their tastes ran more to Egyptology in those days, and they would typically spend hundreds of dollars on books in a single visit. They didn't ask any questions; they knew what they wanted. They would show up during the middle of a weekday afternoon, a time when there were few other shoppers, and take their time going up and down the aisles in relative peace and quiet. We later learned that Yoko was very fond of fortune tellers, and had one or two that she relied upon extensively. In the years directly following the murder of her husband, she seemed to rely upon them even more.

> *I even invoked the "forces of darkness." I don't mean a demon with a tail and horns, but as a religious person I believe there are spiritual powers in the world and an evil side of the spirit. The point is I did the invoking, so the responsibility is mine.*
> —Mark David Chapman[11]

> *John Lennon is dead. The world is over. Forget it. It's just gonna be insanity . . .*
> —John W. Hinckley, Jr., taped on Dec. 31, 1980.

Mark David Chapman is something of an enigma. The back story to his assassination of Lennon does not really compute: the trip around the world, the work for the YMCA that is missing from their files, the visit to war-torn Beirut, the trips back and forth between New York City and Honolulu, the story about the "Little People" in his head, his abrupt decision to plead guilty and avoid a trial . . . all of these things put together make him look uncomfortably like your standard political assassin or serial killer. Like Lee Harvey Oswald and James Earl Ray. Chapman seemed to have had access to funds for overseas travel that are not accounted for by a salary. (Hinckley also traveled extensively throughout the United States in the weeks leading up to his attempt on Reagan's life, flying from New Haven—where Jodie Foster was going to school at Yale—to Nashville, Denver, Washington, etc.) Oswald lived in Russia. Chapman attempted to visit Russia . . . but opted for Beirut, instead. He spent time in Korea—as did Oswald, of course, and David Berkowitz (the "Son of Sam")—but not in the military; his employer was the YMCA. Chapman worked among Vietnamese refugee children at Fort Chaffee in 1975, as the Vietnam War came to a close. He used a Charter Arms .38 revolver when he shot Lennon: the same weapon favored by Arthur Bremer. He was hospitalized for mental illness in Hawaii after a suicide attempt; Oswald was briefly hospitalized for mental illness (after *his* suicide attempt) in Moscow. And, like Oswald, Berkowitz, and so many others, he never stood trial, thus cheating history of a public debate over the evidence.

There seems to be no doubt that Chapman did indeed pull the trigger of the gun that killed John Lennon. In fact, he stood around and waited for the police to arrive, calmly reading *The Catcher In The Rye*, that coming-of-age novel by former US Army intelligence officer J. D. Salinger. What is missing is a coherent motive. Of course, one does not need a motive in order to convict a killer if one has all the other evidence available including, in this case, eyewitnesses, the murder weapon, and a confession. What is under scrutiny here is not whether or not Chapman fired the weapon that killed Lennon. (Thankfully, since the ballistics evidence in the case of Lee Harvey Oswald, James Earl Ray and even Sirhan Bishara Sirhan has been attacked repeatedly by critics, and the ballistics evidence linking David

Berkowitz to all of the Son of Sam killings is likewise very weak.) What *is* being questioned is the phenomenon of Mark David Chapman himself, and the strange coincidence in the timing of a murder of someone who could have been a very big fly in the ointment of a Reagan administration that was just coming into power.

John Lennon had been out of the mainstream for five years. Content to be a house-husband and father to young Sean Lennon, John did not record or even write many songs in the period 1975–79. He was not politically active. He had fought a hard battle with the American Immigration and Naturalization Service in order to remain in the United States—specifically New York City, a place he loved more than any other—and won . . . during the Carter administration, when heavy FBI and CIA surveillance on Lennon as a "dangerous extremist" was switched off. He and Yoko moved into the Dakota Apartments on Manhattan's Upper West Side, and therein the murky correspondences begin to merge.

The Dakota Apartments, of course, is where Roman Polanski filmed *Rosemary's Baby*. It is a beautiful, pre-War building with large rooms, high ceilings, and outrageous rents. The Lennons would eventually wind up owning four apartments at the Dakota, taking over the entire seventh floor.

The Dakota was so named because when it was built it was considered so far away from the city center that it might as well be in Dakota. At that time, the late nineteenth century, Dakota was still a territory of the United States and had not yet split into two states. Oddly, the very word "Dakota" will re-emerge in our investigation, linked to the Son of Sam cult, which links us to the Manson Family and thus right back to Roman Polanski and *Rosemary's Baby*. Another cult, this time including some well-known European fashion designers, was known to be operating in Manhattan out of another building, similar to the Dakota and called it's "sister building." This cult was linked to at least one death, that of a young woman who plummeted out of an apartment window à la the character in *Rosemary's Baby*. For now, however, let us look more closely at the sinister forces swirling around John and Yoko Lennon, forces that would work very hard indeed to ensure that Mark David Chapman and his Charter Arms .38 revolver were in the right place at the right time.

The problem inherent in most histories is not that they merely accumulate facts and details and stretch them into a narrative that purports to tell the truth of what actually happened; the problem is in what is kept in and what is left out. Histories must be essentially synopses of what transpired, with focus on the high points: when a certain battle was fought, or how many votes were cast, etc. We are then reassured that in this pile of data we are seeing what actually happened; it is a bit like summing up a marriage by reciting the date and venue of the ceremony, how many years the union survived, and how many offspring it produced. Documents are necessary, of course. They represent the skeletal matter of the corpse being examined. But there are documents, and there is blood.

The American attitude towards the concept of blood sacrifice is one of mixed incredulity and horror. Incredulity that such a thing as blood sacrifice actually exists anywhere in a civilized society, and especially in America; horror at the very concept of slaughter in the name of religion. The reaction of America during the "satanic cult survivor scare" of the 1980s is very revealing; some Americans firmly believed that an organized network of Satanists was stealing children—or breeding them deliberately—for use in ritual sacrifice. Other Americans immediately rejected the idea as absurd. Both, of course, were ill-informed.

Those who believed in the stories simply confabulated movie plots with reality and didn't bother to ask some of the obvious questions: where did the babies come from? Where are the bodies? Why is there no record of such widespread child snatching? Etc. Those who did not believe in the stories rejected evidence showing that many Americans are, indeed, involved in religious systems which prescribe blood sacrifices and that blood sacrifice is carried out on a daily basis in the country; although, of course, not of human infants. The Caribbean and South American religions of santeria, macumba, candomble, palo mayombe, voudoun and many others regularly sacrifice animals during the course of their rituals. In Haiti, human sacrifice did take place—euphemistically referred to as "the hornless goat" sacrifice—right through the nineteenth century, at least. Muslims practice animal sacrifice at specific times of the year, most notably during the Hajj: the pilgrimmage to Mecca, when hundreds of thousands of lambs are slaughtered. Hindu worshippers also incorporate animal sacrifice into their rites, and the altars dedicated to Kali are often awash in the blood of victims. As late as the nineteenth century (and, some say, the twentieth) the Hindu cult of the Thuggee also prescribed human sacrifice to honor their goddess, Kali; and also until very recently it was common for women to throw themselves on the funeral pyres of their husbands in a rite known as *suttee*, now officially banned but which still occurs with some frequency in the countryside.

In Malaysia, the newspapers often carry stories about human sacrifice taking place today. Some small cults have used human sacrifice as a means of ensuring lottery wins, and the bodies of several Caucasians murdered for that purpose were discovered in one village in 2001, their skulls used as ritual implements of power.

In South America and in the South Pacific, special laws were enacted—and enforced—to stop aboriginals from practicing head hunting and some related cannibalistic practices. There are men still alive today in Borneo (for instance) who regularly tasted human flesh.

And, of course, the Christian Eucharist is a celebration of sacrifice in which the congregants eat the flesh and drink the blood of Jesus Christ. There are today roughly one billion such God-eaters on the face of the earth.

David Ferrie, the American Orthodox Catholic bishop and anti-Castro gunrunner, practiced a form of voudoun in his apartment in New Orleans (North America's capitol of voudoun), killing chickens and calling on African gods while at the same time plotting to murder a President. Was Papa Doc Duvalier correct in stating that *he* had engineered the Kennedy assassination? Did voudoun call to voudoun, like blood calling to blood? Ferrie, with his white rats in cages, looking for a cure for cancer, not realizing that the cancer in America's soul was deeper than rat and syringe could cure.

Thus, the American attitude towards blood sacrifice is complex. The American tradition of political assassination is perhaps an eruption of this atavistic impulse, refined in the alembic of the Industrial Age to produce sacrificial rites where the feudal-era knife has been discarded. The machinery of the gun takes its place as the ritual implement of choice, not quite as emotionally satisfying, perhaps, as the visceral stabbing of the victim, but nonetheless effective and emblematic of the Western colonization of an entire continent where the firearm dominated over the bow and arrow and the tomahawk; and emblematic of the way America has developed since then, a nation of watchers-from-afar.

These grizzly scenes of political murder were recorded on video cameras and played out on television newscasts, just as Aztec rites were performed in public high on the pyramids of Teotihuacan along the Avenue of the Dead. The Eucharistic Mass had already prepared millions of worshippers for an "anemic" bloody sacrifice, one that takes place off-stage, behind the icon screen, on the other side of the altar rail, but whose elements are shared with the worshippers in the form of bread and wine; yet nothing is as emotionally satisfying, perhaps, as being a witness to the actual ritual death itself. Witness the public execution of Charles I, and the frenzied dipping of handkerchiefs in his blood by the mob.

That political assassination may be sacerdotal in nature, a spiritual or mystical act with all the attendant symbolism, mythology and invocation of dark forces that it implies, is not really a new notion to the American public, but perhaps it has not been described quite this way before. After all, we expect our serial killers to have mystical—if twisted—motives. Witness the murderers in the Thomas Harris novels based on his fictional "Dr. Hannibal Lecter," where our serial killer is in search of some type of personal transformation. In *Silence of the Lambs*, the killer wishes to change his sex by killing women and stripping them of their flesh and making, essentially, a "woman suit" out of their skin. He is acutely aware of the transformative aspect of his killings, for he inserts the larva of a special moth into the mouths of his victims after he is through with them.

The moth, of course, like the butterfly is an ancient symbol of transformation and regeneration through transformation. This degree of sophisticated reasoning is something the American public has come to expect from their fictional serial murderers. What is more, the villain in *Silence of the Lambs* is based loosely on the actual case of Ed Gein, who did kill women and preserve their flesh in a similar fashion. Gein was also the inspiration for the archetypal Hitchcock film, *Psycho*, in which the killer assumes the personality of his dead mother in order to perpetrate the killings, dressing in her clothes and speaking with her voice. Transgender transformation also hints darkly at the sexual nature of these crimes; the mystical element is elaborated upon by novelists, but nonetheless exists in the sexual fantasies of the actual killers themselves. Witness also Jeffrey Dahmer, perhaps the most emblematic of the ritualized serial killer with extreme sexual fantasies, cannibalism, rape, and blood lust, who designed an altar as a power center on which would be displayed the skulls of his victims . . . a throwback to the Borneo head hunters and the Malaysian cultists.

Why not, then, a mystical motivation for political assassins?

It seems obvious, somehow, in the choice of victims: John F. Kennedy; Robert F. Kennedy; Dr. Martin Luther King, Jr.; John Lennon. No one shoots a Jesse Helms or a Strom Thurmond. Or an Arlan Spector. Or Frank Sinatra, Dean Martin, or Donny and Marie. The victims selected are always icons of the best and the brightest, regardless of the reality of the personalities involved; or they are chosen because they threaten the politico-economic establishment. They are not trivial victims. Abraham Lincoln. Dag Hammarskjold. Olof Pahlme. Che Guevara. No one successfully assassinated Hitler, although there were attempts. No one assassinted Mussolini; not really. He was brought down by an angry mob once the war was lost. No one assassi nated Chairman Mao. Fidel Castro himself still lives, despite everyone's best attempts at the contrary.

It's the dreamers who die by an assassin's hand. Quite often, they are killed by men who are dreamers themselves.

Mark David Chapman was born on May 10, 1955 in a suburb of Fort Worth, Texas. His father was in the Air Force, a staff sergeant, while his mother was a nurse. Conspiracy theorists love that combination, of course, and believe it hints at other, stranger, connections. Whitley Strieber's father was also in the Air Force in Texas at the time of his birth, ten years previously, but in Strieber's case the Air Force base involved was Randolph, outside of San Antonio, and was the locus for the Nazi scientists who were brought over during Operation Paperclip, scientists who specialized in "aviation medicine." However, in Mark Chapman's case, the father was discharged soon after he was born and got a degree in engineering at Purdue University in Indiana before moving on to Decatur, Georgia, then Roanoke, Virginia and eventually back to Decatur, where he had been transferred by his job with the American Oil Company in Atlanta.

It's Chapman's interior life that interests us most, however. He described his private childhood fantasies to Jack Jones, who recorded them in his biography of Chapman, *Let Me Take You Down*. Instead of an imaginary playmate, Chapman had an entire kingdom full of imaginary playmates. He called them the Little People, and he was their king. If they dissatisfied him in any way, he would blow them up "and a lot of them would die," but they would forgive him later and everything would be okay. It's possible he got this concept the "Little People" from his fascination with the film *The Wizard of Oz*. He was so enthralled with this movie that when he went to New York City to kill John Lennon, he bought a still of the film that he left propped up in his hotel room.

Many commentators on Chapman and the Lennon killing focus on his identification with Holden Caulfield in *The Catcher in the Rye* since he was reading it when he was arrested in front of the Dakota, and because he flogged the book everywhere he went and to everyone he met, even "autographing" copies of the book, sometimes as Holden Caulfield. This element was picked up in the film *Conspiracy Theory*, where it is pointed out that Chapman was not the only killer to walk around with a copy of the book, and the film's plot talks of the book as a kind of mind-control trigger for selected political assassins of the MK-ULTRA variety. Before we look at that any deeper, however, we should first examine the role that *The Wizard of Oz* plays in Chapman's psyche, for we will uncover some startling clues.

With *Catcher*, Chapman can identify safely with the character of Holden Caulfield, a young man disgusted by the "phoniness" in the world, who leaves school and wanders around Central Park, eventually having a nervous breakdown and winding up in a mental hospital. With *Oz*, however, we are on shaky ground. For here Chapman identifies with Dorothy, the character played by Judy Garland. The plot of the film—based on the L. Frank Baum story of the same name about a young girl from Kansas who winds up "over the rainbow"—is similar to that of Maeterlinck's *The Blue Bird* which was, as we have suggested in Book One, the likely inspiration for the CIA mind control project BLUEBIRD.

Dorothy is knocked unconscious during a tornado at her home in Kansas. This part of the film is in black and white. She then awakens in a different land, discovering that her house—which was picked up in the tornado—has landed on an evil witch, killing her. She finds herself surrounded by the Munchkins, a society of Little People who are grateful to her for having killed the evil witch. It is in this film that we first hear the song "Ding Dong, The Witch Is Dead," the same song that was sung at the gates of the White House when Nixon announced his resignation. Barbara Honegger was also once referred to disparagingly as a "munchkin" after her attack on the Reagan administration over the October Surprise. Thus, politically, the battle lines are drawn: Munchkins to the Left, Wicked Witch to the Right.

This, and the rest of the film until the ending, is in color.

In order to get back home, she must find the Wizard, who lives in the Emerald City. Along the way, she is befriended by a Good Witch, is targeted by another Evil Witch, and picks up a Cowardly Lion, a Scarecrow, and a Tin Man. And, as always, she is accompanied by her little dog, Toto. They must go through a haunted forest, and undertake other adventures in a very similar fashion to Maeterlinck's story, until they finally find the Wizard, who tells them he can't help them until the Wicked Witch is dead. So, off they go to destroy the witch, who has an army of flying monkeys. This done, they return to the Emerald City, and the dog, Toto, accidentally reveals the true identity of the Wizard: just a normal man hiding behind a curtain at a set of electronic controls that make him appear as a monstrous and all-powerful genie. That immortal line, "Pay no attention to the man behind the curtain," is uttered by this man, desperate to preserve his secret to the last.

The Wizard, however, proves to be wiser than even he believes he is, and the Cowardly Lion gets courage, the Tin Man a heart, and the Scarecrow a brain. Finally, Dorothy can return home by using a mantra and clicking the heels of her ruby slippers together . . . slippers taken from the corpse of the witch slain by her falling house . . . and she awakens back in Kansas. The mantra she repeats as she clicks her heels together, SS officer style: "There's no place like home. There's no place like home." A xenophobe's slogan if ever there was one. She awakens in her home (in black and white again) to her adoring family, who have all appeared in her "dream" as different individuals. There's no place like home, and there isn't a dry eye in the house.

The movie is a musical, of course, and the highlight is the most famous song from the film, "Over The Rainbow." It is a melancholy ballad about a yearning for home, but for an ideal home "over the rainbow," a kind of heaven on earth. Dorothy seeks that, but finds it instead in her own home, among her family. This is how Maeterlinck's story also ends. Although each series of adventures seems to take days and days, both hero (Tyltyl) and heroine (Dorothy) wake up in their own homes the following morning. Both hero and heroine discover that what they were seeking was always in front of them, in their own home. In Tyltyl's case, the quest was for a Blue Bird. In Dorothy's case, her ticket home was a pair of Ruby Slippers. The alchemists and tantrists among my audience will recognize the sexual symbolism immediately: blue for boys, and red for girls! More importantly, the device Tyltyl uses to "see" with enlightened vision is a diamond on his hat that he must twist in a certain direction. A diamond in the center of his head, then, is a famous Buddhist symbol, the adamantine substance; Dorothy's slippers are made from rubies. They are both precious stones and both have deeper meanings to adherents of Eastern religions as well as to practitioners of Western occultism.

Of course, there is an enchanted forest in *The Blue Bird* also, and it is as hostile to Tyltyl as the forest is to Dorothy and her friends. There are evil witches in each story. Both Tyltyl and Dorothy are accompanied by a dog. Both Tyltyl and Dorothy eventually pick up other companions along the way who are looking for their own salvation.

The message of *The Wizard of Oz*, however, can be seen in a more dangerous light to someone like Chapman. The Wizard is obviously a "phony," not a real wizard at all but a charlatan who has been deceiving people with his showman's tricks, for his own personal gain. In the film, Dorothy unmasks the charlatan and forces him to do good deeds for the people of the city.

On the streets of New York, however, Mark David Chapman shot him with a Charter Arms thirty-eight.

We're not in Kansas anymore.

Chapman also walked the yellow brick road, just like Dorothy. He traveled around the world before meeting Lennon, and made the trip to New York City from Hawaii twice before actually pulling the trigger.

He also had his Munchkins, the "Little People" who were his subjects. In fact, the Little People had argued against his killing of Lennon and walked out on him when he told them he was going to do it. Thus, once again, the Munchkins prove themselves to be Leftists, at worst, or Democrats at best! Might it have been his affinity with the Little People in his mind that made Chapman so successful with Vietnamese refugee children during the summer of 1975 at Fort Chaffee, Arkansas?

> *Remember, these were days when drugs were rampant in high school halls. Lot of hippiedom. Lot of confusion. The war in Vietnam was going strong. We were lost in the forest.*
>
> —Mark David Chapman[12]

Mark was a loner in school, a type that was picked on and bullied. His mother was abused by her husband, Mark's father, and sought comfort in a close relationship with her son, whom she idolized, telling him he would be a great man some day. Mark found himself taking sides in the war between his parents, defending his mother against a remote but overbearing father. His mother would come into his room at times after being slapped around by her husband, and sleep in Mark's bed until the storm had passed.

Mark, ostracized at school and generally friendless, woke up one morning and found that there were Little People living in houses and apartments and going to work in skyscrapers . . . in the walls of his bedroom. He summoned them before him and ordered their assistance in protecting his mother against his father. To encourage them, he played Beatles music for them: in his head, beamed out along invisible wires to invisible speakers.

He would rock back and forth in front of the stereo and listen to the Beatles endlessly, applauding after every song as if he were at a rock concert. He had only one Beatles album, *Meet the Beatles*, and he inspected the album cover minutely, memorizing its details.

He was nine years old.

By the time he entered high school, he was undergoing substantial changes in his personality. From a clean-cut and awkward boy from a good family, he turned into a doper who cut classes and hung out with similar individuals. For once, he was part of a group and accepted. He grew his hair long, wore dirty bellbottoms that he never changed, and dropped acid and smoked grass at every chance he got. At the age of fourteen, he ran away from home and went to Florida, and lived on the beach for two weeks until his money ran out.

This episode is rather strange in its details. Mark had called a taxi service to take him to buy the air ticket two weeks before his trip. The car that met him had two men in it. They dropped him off at a ticket office, and waited until he bought his ticket and then they drove him back, agreeing to show up in two weeks time, at five o'clock in the morning, in front of a diner, to drive him to the airport.

Strangely enough, the taxi arrived at the appointed hour with the same two men in the car. This is certainly a very odd circumstance. The boy was fourteen years old. There were two men in the taxi each time, not simply a driver. Who were these men? What were their roles? And why did they agree to meet him again at 5 A.M. two weeks in the future . . . and show up? The story does not make a lot of sense. Indeed, it is troubling. There is obviously more to the tale than Mark Chapman has told, and it is possible that he does not remember the incident very well; thus, it is one more strange mystery waiting to be solved.

Mark flew to Miami and took a taxi to the beach, where he hung out for some time and had a moderate series of adventures, including a walk of twenty miles to a rock concert in the Everglades under a broiling Florida sun. Eventually, a Cuban family in Coral Gables took pity on him and let him live with them for a few days before finally putting him on a bus back to Georgia.

It was the summer of 1969. Charles Manson was ordering the Tate and LaBianca killings. Jim Jones was ranting and ramping up in Ukiah, California. Everything was going to hell. And we were lost in the forest.

On October 25, 1970 Mark David Chapman had a satori of sorts. He had gone to a weekend religious retreat at the urging of a friend, the motivation being the presence of a lot of girls. It was a "charismatic fundamentalist congregation"[13] sponsored by the South Dekalb Presbyterian Church, and during the retreat they showed a film about the life of Jesus which seems to have made an impression on Mark, for he wrote down the date as if it were something significant, a "spiritual turning point."[14] On that same day, in California, Nancy Marie Bennallack was slain, the fifteenth victim of the Zodiac killer. That same month, Joel Rostau, a business associate of slain Tate-victim Jay Sebring, was murdered in New York City. The Manson Family was suspected of the crime, as they were of the death of Charlene Cafritz in Washington, D.C. the month before. Cafritz—a friend of Sharon Tate, Charles Manson, Terry Melcher and Alan Warnecke—claimed to have secret videotapes of the Manson Family, tapes that were never found. She died of a Nembutal overdose.

Cult killings went on that year, from the Zodiac killer to "Maxwell's Silver Hammer": according to Manson Family member Gypsy Share, they were responsible for the savage murder in July 1970 of two people on the beach near Santa Barbara. There was one survivor of that attack, who spoke of the killers wearing robes and chanting. And on September 18, 1970, Jimi Hendrix was found dead of a drug overdose in the London apartment of his German girlfriend, Monika Dannemann. The Scotland Yard investigation documents were sealed.

Mark David Chapman had not yet become a born-again Christian. Although the date of October 25, 1970 was firmly etched in his mind as a day of spiritual importance, he returned to school and lapsed into his familiar drugged-out hippie routine. But one connection he made that weekend was to influence the rest of his life, for he met Michael MacFarland, the boy who would insist that he read *The Catcher in the Rye*.

In the summer of 1971, during the school vacation, Mark went to visit his grandmother in Ormond Beach, Florida. Still a hippie by his own standards, and still doing drugs—even though he felt a strong attraction to his new Christian friends and the comfort of religious community—he sought out other like-minded people and hung out doing drugs along the Florida coastline. It was when he returned home one day to discover that his wallet had been cleaned out by his newfound "friends" that he had a religious conversion.

> ". . . I remember, when I realized that my buddies had gone through my wallet, feeling the lowest I had ever felt. I felt like nobody. Like nothing. Nothing at all."[15]

In the midst of his profound depression, he reached out to Jesus. He lifted his hands and asked Jesus to come to him. He described the moment to a psychiatrist at Rikers Island as a physical sensation of God entering his room, feeling a "tingling from the tip of the toe to the top of my head"[16] on his left side, for God was sitting on his left knee. Mark David Chapman had become born-again.

When he showed up for classes in the fall of 1971, he was a changed man. Gone were the hippie clothes, the dirt, the long hair, the rock-and-roll lyrics, the drugs. And gone was any fascination for the Beatles, particularly for John Lennon. He told his friends that "Imagine" was a Communist song,[17] a not unreasonable assumption for a high school junior to make. He was also incensed by Lennon's comment that the Beatles were more popular than Jesus. Like most devout Christians, he assumed that Lennon was boasting, when in fact he made the comment cynically, as his own worst critic.

The period of devout Christianity didn't last, however. Chapman was always wired a little too tight. During a typical prayer service replete with witnessing, praying, and singing, Chapman—who had written a Christian song and brought his guitar—found that there was no time or opportunity for him to play it after the three-hour-long session. The frustration grew in his heart and turned him off where the Christian prayer groups were concerned. Like discovering his "buddies" had ripped him off in Florida the summer before, Chapman felt again like nobody because the group had failed him.[18] He cast about, looking for another cause or another group, something else to join, somewhere he would be embraced.

And he found it, this Holden Caulfield manqué, as a counselor to children at the YMCA.

As he cleaned up his act, he volunteered as a counselor at the South Dekalb County YMCA and later became an assistant program director. He was, in fact, recognized as an important asset to the YMCA program. His rapport with children was tremendous. They hung around his neck, sat in a circle around him as he played his guitar, and generally just followed him around. In addition, Chapman found that he was a great fundraiser as well, and was honored by having his name "engraved on a tile above the Olympic size indoor pool that he helped build" for the YMCA.[19] Well, it wasn't his birth name, actually. It was "Nemo."

Those who remember the stories of visionary author Jules Verne will recall the figure of Captain Nemo. According to friends of Chapman at the time, he wanted the kids to call him Captain Nemo or just Nemo, and somehow the name stuck. There does not seem to be any clear explanation of why Chapman liked that particular name, except perhaps that he identified with the Jules Verne character who is an enigmatic and powerful commander living *20,000 Leagues Under the Sea*. At one point, during an awards ceremony when Chapman was being honored by the YMCA, the kids began to chant "Ne-mo! Ne-mo!" as he walked on stage to receive his award. Those were, according to Chapman, the greatest days of his life.[20]

What is astounding to a person looking, Umberto Eco–like, at the semiotics of history is the actual meaning of the name "Nemo," for it is Latin for "No one." That is, in fact, why the Verne character chooses that name rather than use his own birth name: he wanted to disguise his real identity and be known only as "Captain No One." Chapman, who all his life feared being a "nobody" a "nothing" was now universally acknowledged as such by the children, and praised for it. But sadly he never made the connection.

Indeed, as novelist Patricia Cornwell has documented in *Portrait of a Killer: Jack the Ripper—Case Closed*, even Jack the Ripper suspect Walter Sickert signed some of his famous letters to the press as "Nemo" and used "Mr. Nemo" as a stage name.[21]

Those who remember the book and the movie *The Exorcist* will recall the scene in which Father Karras attempts to decipher the strange language that the possessed child, Regan, has been screaming. He is playing a tape recording of the guttural voice over and over, until another priest tells him that the child is screaming English, backwards. When Karras plays the tape backward he hears the Devil, in response to Karras' question "Who are you?" reply, "No one. I am no one."

Chapman turned his academic career around, as well, and graduated from high school six months early. He went to live with his friend Michael MacFarland (who introduced him to *The Catcher in the Rye*) in Chicago, where the two of them entertained church groups with music and comedy routines. When this was not going anywhere, Chapman returned to Georgia and worked at the YMCA at a series of jobs, and even worked for a time at a mental hospital in Atlanta, on a floor specializing in children suffering from autism and other mental illnesses. "Little People." Then, in 1975, the YMCA sent him to Beirut.

Chapman had filled out an application to something called ICCP/Abroad, a non-profit program being run by the YMCA which placed American YMCA volunteers with foreign affiliates, as a kind of Peace Corps for YMCA camp counselors. This was in February 1975. As British researcher Fenton Bresler reveals, however, one got to choose where one was stationed. Chapman did not list Lebanon as his first choice, but rather, oddly, the Soviet Union.

He even went so far as to sign up for a Russian language course in anticipation of this trip, but was turned down at ICCP/Abroad because he did not already speak Russian. Instead, he got his second choice: Beirut.

There is no guidance available as to why this deeply committed Christian would have picked Beirut when Jerusalem was also available. No one seems to be able to give an answer to this perplexing question. Beirut was already in the throes of political upheaval and instability, and was only weeks away from full-blown civil war. Mark was one of only two people sent to Beirut by ICCP/Abroad, and he spent very little time there once the shooting started. He made a tape-recording of the small-arms fire going on outside his hotel room window, which he brought back with him and played for friends. He was obviously very shaken and paradoxically excited by this experience. From Fenton Bresler's point of view, he was sent to Beirut to be "blooded."[22]

To understand this reference, one has to remember that in 1975 Beirut was probably the CIA's largest Middle Eastern station, one responsible for intelligence activities throughout the region. One must also remember that the CIA had a history of engineering coups in the region, such as the one that placed the Shah of Iran back on the Peacock Throne. Although some researchers insist that the CIA maintained a school for the training of assassins in Lebanon, there is no proof of this available, of course. However, virtually every other Middle Eastern group with an axe to grind has had training camps in the region, and in addition the author knows of IRA and other European revolutionary and terrorist groups that trained in Lebanon during the same period.

Further, it is also known that the CIA used students studying abroad as a source of intelligence. As Bresler notes—and as anyone who was of the author's generation may remember—*Ramparts* magazine did a report on just that subject in 1967, which caused quite a furor at the time. Bresler's thesis is that Mark David Chapman was a CIA-trained assassin, and that the murder of John Lennon was political. Certainly, the timing is suggestive, as we shall see. Bresler has gone further, suggesting that a "split personality" was induced in Mark David Chapman, and that the alternate personality had only some tangential points in common with the original Mark David Chapman, such as—for instance—*The Catcher in the Rye.* Bresler's case is persuasive, and is consistent with what we already know of MK-ULTRA and other intelligence-and military-sponsored mind-control programs. Further, the target was both a cultural icon and a political figure in his own right, and someone who could have rallied American sentiments against what would become the Reagan and Bush administrations, Iran-Contra, arms-for-hostages, and the stepped-up war against the Soviet Union, a Cold War which would eventually result in the destruction-by-bankruptcy of its Communist government. Upon his return to the States after the aborted Beirut mission, Chapman found himself at the newly-created Fort Chaffee, Arkansas, which was a kind of way station for Vietnamese refugees who had fled the fall of Saigon in April of that year. With him at Fort Chaffee was the former head of the YMCA station in Saigon, David C. Moore, who had only been in-country for about a week before Saigon fell, and who was now at Fort Chaffee helping the Vietnamese in their American orientation. This episode is ripe with significance.

Why would the YMCA have sent *anyone* to Saigon in April 1975? It was clear to even the most optimistic that the country was falling. Da Nang had fallen by March, long before Moore's arrival in Saigon. The North Vietnamese Army was advancing rapidly towards Saigon; the entire country north of the capitol had already fallen. What was there to be gained by sending a brand-new administrator there at the time? It seems, in retrospect, insane. Unless there was a hidden intelligence agenda.

This same David Moore then appears at Fort Chaffee with some of these refugees, and rooms with Mark David Chapman who has just returned from . . . Beirut. Another falling city, resounding with sound of explosions and machine-gun fire. Together, the two were involved in some fashion with these unfortunate victims of what the Vietnamese call the "American War," ostensibly helping them in their relocation to American communities and in some cases adoption by American families.

These are only suggestive facts which, taken separately, perhaps mean little, but when taken together show the lineaments of a darker purpose. Once again, we are forced to decide whether there was a controlling governmental agency behind these events, with an agenda of its own, or whether instead these strange events are representative of a mystical nexus of deeper, unconscious spiritual forces that underlie conscious, visible phenomena. Either way, the conclusions are disturbing.

By the end of 1975, the Fort Chaffee refugee-placement program had completed its mission, and nearly 30,000 refugees had been placed in American communities throughout the United States. It was during his tenure at Fort Chaffee that Mark happened to shake the hand of President Ford, who had come to visit the resettlement camp. Thus, President Ford came into contact with some of the most notorious individuals of the late twentieth century: Mark David Chapman and would-be presidential assassin and Manson Family member Lynette "Squeaky" Fromme. Not bad for a president whose administration did not even last a single term. If we include his partnership with Harry Conover, the future husband of alleged mind-control victim Candy Jones, and his inclusion in the Warren Commission panel which effectively covered-up certain aspects of the Kennedy assassination, we have a man whose history bears a bit more scrutiny.

At that time, Mark had developed another, very odd, relationship with a man whose name is only given as the pseudonym "Gene Scott" in Bresler's book, but was later identified as "Dana Reeves" in the Jack Jones biography of Chapman.[23] This gentleman was an officer with a Georgia sheriff 's department at the time Bresler's book was being written (1989), and it is not known where he is today, but his influence over Mark was powerful and bizarre. Chapman, who was said to despise guns and violence, became a gun enthusiast around this man and seemed to be under the control of his personality in some way. And as it turns out, it was this same mysterious individual who supplied Mark David Chapman with the hollow-point bullets he used to murder John Lennon.[24]

We don't know much more about him beyond the enigmatic references in Bresler's book, and the fact that he was with the Henry County sheriff 's department as mentioned in the Jones biography,[25] but this strange mentoring of Chapman by a man from a police department resonates with the pairing of Dan Mitrione and Jim Jones: one, a police officer from a small town with an ulterior motive, and the other a young, religious man—a boy, really—who comes under his influence and then morphs from devout Christian into murderer. Both young men spent time abroad, financed by unknown sources of income, in politically unstable regimes. Both came home with palpable personality changes. Both men abandoned the Christianity of their youth, yet committed their heinous crimes in the name of a higher ideal. Jim Jones ridiculed the Bible and the concept of a "Sky God"; Mark Chapman invoked Satan in the hours before he killed John Lennon.

The implosion of Jim Jones in the jungles of Guyana was very public, very messy, and left a lot of loose ends, red herrings, and smoking guns. I think Mark David Chapman was a refinement of the same system. If Jim Jones was the "alpha" version of an experimental program, then Chapman was the "beta" release: a carefully constructed multiple personality with a tightly focused purpose, a single target, and ultimate deniability. There is evidence of the same type of sexual dysfunction in both Jones and Chapman: Jones was obviously bisexual, and had sexual relations with both the male and female members of his congregation, something of which he boasted openly and frequently—as well as constantly referring to the size of his penis—indicating in Jones some confusion over his sexual identity; documentation on Chapman's sexual relationships are somewhat murkier, but offhand references by someone who knew him during the Beirut episode seem to indicate that he was suspected of having an unhealthy interest in his young charges.[26]

His Georgia police officer friend got him a brief job as a security officer at DeKalb General Hospital,[27] and they shared an apartment in Atlanta during this time. Bresler intimates that possibly there was more to the relationship than simple friendship; the police officer was never married, but is described as handsome and Rambo-like in appearance. Others who knew the two of them during this period also indicated "complex undertones" to the relationship, which evidently continued through the Lennon assassination and well into Chapman's incarceration.[28]

Chapman's sexuality is frequenty invoked as some kind of touchstone to the rest of his story, and it is worth looking at briefly. He did not have sexual intercourse until he was twenty years old, and this with a female roommate who was somewhat more worldly than he was. The fact that he was engaged to another woman at the time is said to have given Chapman an incredible feeling of guilt over this single sexual episode. He is also said to have been sexually attracted to older women, and fantasized about them being chained, naked, in a dungeon—in the basement of his high school—where they were forced to do what he wanted, which did not include intercourse but did include fellatio.[29] (This seems to be another version of the "Little People" fantasy, with Chapman in complete control over helpless victims who are forced to worship him under penalty of death. Was this then a repressed sexual fantasy, which threatened to erupt into his relations with children?)

As devout Christians, he and his fiancée struggled with the question of sexuality and prayed over it. He eventually told her about his one-night-stand with the roommate and she evidently felt betrayed by the revelation.

He tried to attend college with her at her university, but failed at that after a while, broke up with his fiancée, and wound up booking a ticket to Honolulu.

GOD'S LONELY MAN

Some commentators have written that Chapman's trip to Hawaii was for the purpose of committing suicide. Others have said that Chapman went to Hawaii for further training and indoctrination by any one of several classified military operations that were based on the islands. What we do know is that Chapman did, indeed, attempt suicide in Hawaii by means of a hose running from the exhaust pipe into the closed window of his car, but it was a pathetic and failed attempt and Chapman wound up in a mental hospital.

This juxtaposition of Hawaii and mental hospital is one that we encountered already in the case of Jim Jones. In Jones' case, the belief is that he committed himself to a hospital or clinic in Hawaii in order to avoid adverse publicity back on the mainland. Chapman would have had no such qualms. Yet, the nexus of Hawaii and hospitals comes up again in the Son of Sam case, where it was revealed that drugs were making their way onto the mainland from Hawaii by being secreted in bags of plasma. The plasma would arrive in a hospital in New York City and the drugs removed there by hospital workers who were one link in the supply chain. This trafficking in narcotics is said to be one of the main sources of income for the Son of Sam cult.

Chapman was in Hawaii at the time of the Son of Sam killings, and it is worthwhile to note that he did have access to unexplained sources of income during that time, income that helped finance his trip around the world and his subsequent flights to New York City leading up to the assassination of Lennon in 1980. In fact, one of the strangest episodes of Chapman's visits to New York was his taking a cab through the city and stopping for a few minutes at various apartment buildings where he seemed to be making pickups or deliveries, which makes no sense since Chapman supposedly knew no one in New York. At one point, he offered the cab driver some cocaine, which is also totally out of character for Chapman at that time (this was long after his "drugged out hippie" days in Columbia High School in Georgia) and has never been explained; but if Chapman *was* making drug deliveries in Manhattan it all begins to make much more sense: everything from the Hawaiian hospital connection to the multiple air fares to New York to the unexplained source of income to the strange cab ride and the offering of cocaine.[30] As I used to tell people in New York in the 1970s and '80s, if you overheard a conversation between two people and it didn't make any sense, it was probably about drugs.

While Chapman's murder of Lennon in New York—where the Son of Sam killings had been taking place—does not seem to be linked in any way to the Sam cult, and on the face of it appears to be a wholly-independent act, the parallels between David Berkowitz (the convicted "Son of Sam" killer) and Chapman are compelling, as we shall see.

Whatever the reason for his trip, Chapman quit his job in Atlanta, sold everything he owned, and flew to Honolulu in January 1977. After a short time there, loneliness building up inside him, he phoned his former fiancée in Georgia, and she convinced him to return, which he did . . . believing it was because she wanted him back. As it turned out, she did not; she only thought she was helping him by urging him to return. Disgusted, he turned around and flew back to Hawaii.

At that point, he began to realize that he had a problem, and he phoned a suicide hotline and was eventually referred to the Waikiki Mental Health Clinic. That seemed to help somewhat, but still did not keep him from the suicide attempt with his car's exhaust on June 20, 1977, an attempt that failed when his plastic hose melted from the heat. He was eventually accepted into Castle Memorial Hospital, a private hospital run by the Seventh Day Adventist Church, where his fees were paid by the state's welfare system. He was diagnosed as being severely depressed, but not psychotic. He was released in two weeks.

Castle Memorial is located in a small town on the other side of the island from Honolulu. Mark Chapman decided to stay there and find an apartment, and was eventually hired by Castle Memorial, first as a maintenance man and then promoted to customer relations. Now we are back in the twilight zone, because—as with Jim Jones, Lee Harvey Oswald, and so many others we have come across—there seem to have been *two* Mark Chapmans.

Bresler has noted[31] that all the documentation possessed by Chapman at the time of his arrest checks out. His Hawaiian driver's license was issued in July of 1977, which is about right. The owner of the apartment where he stayed says that he did, indeed, live at the address on Puwa Place in Kailua where he said he was.

Everything seems fine. Except that the owner says that Chapman was living with "a woman and three young children,"[32] and that they left owing a month's rent, had no electricity in their final month at the complex, and left the apartment in such a mess that it cost two thousand dollars to clean it up. A search of records at the post office and other agencies in Kailua failed to turn up any identification of the mysterious woman and her three children. The records of the apartment complex do not show Chapman as having lived there, even though it is the precise address on his driver's license.

This has led some researchers to believe there was a confusion, and there must have been another man named Mark Chapman involved. But how could that be? How could one Mark Chapman (in custody) show that address on his driver's license . . . but not actually live there? How could the other Mark Chapman (mistaken by the landlord to be the man in custody) live there anonymously at the home of a mystery woman and her three young children, whom the apartment owner believes might have been her sisters?

Was Mark Chapman being "sheep-dipped"? Was a false story being planted, his traces obscured by conflicting records . . . or no records at all? Chapman had been undergoing treatment at Castle Memorial; he told his therapist all sorts of things about his past, about Beirut, about his girlfriend in Georgia. No one seems to have known anything about him living in an apartment with four females.

Yet, at the time Bresler's book was being researched—more than five years after Chapman's arrest for the Lennon assassination—Chapman was still getting mail delivered to the apartment on Puwa Place.[33]

At any rate, on Oahu Chapman began dating again. One of his girlfriends was a woman twenty years older than he, a psychiatric nurse at Castle who was said to be an illegitimate daughter of comedian Oliver Hardy of Laurel and Hardy fame (as if this story could get any weirder) That relationship lasted for some months, until a local Presbyterian pastor convinced Mark that his relationship was immoral. Chapman would eventually move in with the pastor and his family and become reconverted to the fundamentalist form of Christianity the pastor preached. Then, in December of 1977, his parents came to Hawaii to visit. It was evidently a pleasant time for everyone, and Chapman was eager to demonstrate his newfound stability—both financial and emotional. Everything seemed to be going his way.

Then, six months later, Mark David Chapman went on a trip around the world.

According to Chapman's account, he had arranged for a loan from the hospital's credit union. The hospital has refused to confirm or deny this aspect of the case, citing confidentiality. Yet, Chapman had only been employed at Castle Memorial since August 1977. It seems unlikely that the credit union would have advanced him the money necessary for a world tour after less than one year of service. He had no other collateral that anyone has been able to discover, nothing to secure a loan that must have been a minimum of three thousand dollars by my estimation, allowing for the cheapest possible airfare and budget accommodations. Nonetheless, he was able to take leave from the hospital on July 6, 1978, for over six weeks after only ten months of employment, and, armed with his credit union loan and a thousand dollars he received from his father on Christmas, he visited Japan, Korea, Hong Kong, China, Singapore, Thailand, India, Nepal, Israel, Iran, Switzerland, the United Kingdom, France, Ireland and Atlanta, Georgia before returning to Hawaii. He stayed in YMCA youth hostels throughout the trip, armed with a letter of introduction from his old friend from Fort Chaffee days, David Moore, who was by now working for the YMCA in Geneva.

In Bangkok, he found himself spending the night with a prostitute, but otherwise his trip seemed uneventful from a sexual perspective. He did, however, see some very sobering sights in India and Nepal, and was in Iran only six months before the Shah was deposed and fled into exile. In Hong Kong, he was one of the first American tourists allowed to cross over into China, as the border had been opened the same week as his arrival.

In India, he arrived in Delhi and was able to visit the Taj Mahal and take a trip to Nepal. This meant some difficult traveling for a lone, young American: from Delhi to Agra (which is not too bad) where the Taj Mahal is located, and then up to the Nepali border across the province of Uttar Pradesh. There are trains from Delhi to Agra that accommodate the heavy tourist traffic to the Taj Mahal, and they take roughly two to three hours to make the trip. Getting to Nepal from Delhi, however, is somewhat more problematical depending on where one enters Nepal. Buses from Delhi to some of the closest border towns can take twelve hours. It is possible that he flew to Kathmandu from Delhi, but I have been unable to find any more detail about this part of his itinerary. One assumes that the local YMCA was able to arrange safe passage for Chapman. Nevertheless, he did see a cremation as well as overwhelming scenes of extreme poverty and desperation. During this world tour, he took something like 1,200 slides.

In Geneva, he met with his friend from Fort Chaffee, David Moore, and they discussed everything, including Chapman's failed suicide attempt. Moore tried to reassure his young friend, who was disappointed over his failure to finish college and get a degree, which would have enabled him to have a real career with the YMCA.

Mark Chapman arrived back in Hawaii on August 20, 1978, where he was met by his travel agent, Gloria Abe. He had been sending her postcards and letters constantly during his trip, and soon the two people found themselves in love.

Gloria Abe is the daughter of Japanese immigrants to Hawaii—her mother a Buddhist and her father a follower of the Japanese national religion, Shinto—and although she is a few years older than Chapman, she is younger in appearance. A thoughtful, patient woman with an interest in reincarnation and astrology, she was able to stand up under Chapman's constant self-doubt and erratic behavior, and even more she was moved by his religious fervor and Christian spirituality. In an eerie reminder of Jim Jones' youth, he told her that he used to preach on the streets when he was young, passing out religious tracts.[34] She found herself converting to Christianity at the same time she was falling love with him.

They were married on June 2, 1979.

Their minister was the same pastor who had re-converted Chapman to fundamentalist Christianity. At their wedding, for instance, there was no alcohol served to the one hundred or so guests. The wedding itself was not held at the pastor's church since, in fact, he did not have one. His congregation of less than thirty souls met in a room loaned to them by a local school on Sundays. As someone who worked for the Presbyterian Church in 1969 and 1970, I can attest that this was a somewhat unusual pastor and congregation. Chapman's pastor was on a mission, and his influence over Chapman seems suspect to me. Chapman's involvement with a fringe Christian operation—when surrounded by every sort of mainstream Christian denomination and observance—is of a piece with the rest of his life. Even when he became involved with the YMCA—certainly a venerable American institution, the Village People notwithstanding—it would be in a manner fraught with extreme expression and experience.

One learns to swim at the "Y," or goes on summer camp or day trips; but Mark David Chapman goes to Beirut for the YMCA as civil war is breaking out, then to Fort Chaffee to help with Vietnamese refugees in the months after the fall of Saigon. He then travels around the world, staying at various YMCA hostels and meeting his old friend from Fort Chaffee days—David Moore—in Switzerland. And, as we shall see, on his way to kill John Lennon he will spend a mysterious three days in Chicago: the same city where David Moore has by that time been reassigned, although Moore claims that he was not contacted by Chapman during that trip. Clearly, Mark David Chapman cannot do anything in an average, low-key fashion, even though most of the people who knew him describe him precisely that way: friendly, normal, responsible. Yet he pushes the envelope of his own personality, taking extreme positions on spiritual subjects, moving to Hawaii, marrying an older Asian woman, traveling throughout Asia and then to Europe on his own, dodging bullets in Beirut, working with Vietnamese refugees in Arkansas . . . and still feels constantly alone, depressed, unfulfilled. Then, just when things seem to be working out okay, he swings in another direction entirely, ruining any chance he might have had for a "normal" life.

Two months into the marriage, and Chapman had prevailed upon his wife to quit her job as a travel agent and to get a job instead at Castle Memorial, where he was working. He did not like her long hours at the travel agency, and clearly seemed to want to dominate her time and to control her social interactions as much as possible. He then decided that they had to move to the other side of the island and commute to work by bus, selling off their car in the process. None of this made any sense, of course. Chapman was going out of his way to complicate his life, and that of his wife. Most people would try to move closer to their place of employment: Chapman chose the opposite strategy. Most people would, in that case, have held on to their means of transportation: Chapman sold the car, making them both rely upon public transportation.

And then, he suddenly decided he had an interest in art.

He began haunting art galleries and educating himself on art; he wound up buying some lithographs and then reselling them, borrowing money from his father-in-law, from his mother, from his credit union. It was a strange interlude. People who work in intelligence circles know that art is one way to disguise income: art is a very volatile commodity, and a painting can appreciate or depreciate in value quickly over time, or may simply become attractive to a collector who will pay more than the market price. That it was this series of transactions in art that supposedly financed Chapman's trips to New York makes one wonder, especially as the passion for art did not last long . . . and especially as it seems Chapman paid back the credit union loan and the loan from his mother before his trips, while for some reason not paying back the $2,500 he borrowed from his wife's father, using that money to finance his New York travels. It is all very strange.

Then, towards the end of the art episode, he quit his job at Castle Memorial—days after the hostages had been taken in Iran—in an uncharacteristic quarrel with the human resources people over a promotion he claimed he deserved and did not get, and wound up instead getting a low-paying job once again as a security guard: on December 19, 1979, at an apartment complex across the street from what was then Scientology headquarters in Honolulu.

Chapman is known to have harassed the Scientologists. He is one of four individuals known to be doing so at the time. One of these four men was in the habit of making phone calls to Scientology offices and threatening members with death. It might have been a case of a security guard with too much time on his hands, but again Chapman may have had another agenda. He is said to have blasted Beatles music across the street in an effort to harass the Scientologists, but there is no indication that he was particularly fond of the Beatles at this time. He had objected to Lennon's "more popular than Jesus" statement while still living in Georgia, as we have seen; he had undergone a born-again Christian conversion in Georgia before this animosity towards the Beatles began, and then had undergone another conversion to the Presbyterian group before his marriage to Gloria Abe. It thus seems unlikely that he would be blasting Beatles music, if he was, indeed, blasting music at all. How does a security guard whose responsibility is the protection of an apartment complex manage to set up such a blatant operation without attracting the ire of his own employers? This is yet another part of the story that does not compute.

In addition, according to Chapman in his interviews with Jack Jones, he also harassed Hare Krishnas. He objected to the way they coaxed money out of passers-by.[35] He only stopped, afraid for his safety, when told by one person that the Krishnas could find a way to hurt him, that they were dangerous.

Then, in August 1980, he rediscovered *The Catcher in the Rye*.

As we have seen, this novel about a young man's coming of age was written by a former US Army intelligence officer, who served in Europe with the troops that landed at Utah Beach during the Normandy invasion of June 1944. The circumstances of J. D. Salinger's military career are—like virtually everything else in his life—shrouded in mystery. We know that his job involved the interrogation of captured German civilians who were believed to be spies, saboteurs or simply Nazis-in-hiding. We also know that he suffered some form of nervous breakdown during his career in Europe. And we know that, shortly after the publication of *Catcher*, he retired in complete anonymity to a small town in New Hampshire, a few miles from where this author once lived in the early 1960s. We also know that Salinger was—and possibly still is—a believer in Eastern mysticism as well as in psychic phenomena.

He claimed to be in telepathic communication with his first wife, whom he married in Europe during his military posting there (yet another mystery that has not been adequately described), and that they could go into trances and meet each other in the ether.[36] Virtually nothing is known of this woman, save that she was French and her given name was Sylvia.[37] She was also described as possibly being a psychologist, or an osteopath! Whatever the case, we know very little about her; what we do know is that Salinger signed on for a further six months of civilian work for the Defense Department in Europe after his official discharge in November 1945.[38] The nature of this work is not revealed. One of his biographers, Ian Hamilton, believes it had to do with denazification, which is entirely possible since that is what Salinger was involved with when he was wearing a uniform. It is believed that his interest in the occult began with his relationship to the mysterious Sylvia.

> It was suggested to us by an ex-army acquaintance that perhaps Salinger is still a spy, or that somewhere in his spying past there is a secret so secret that he now has no choice but to dwell perpetually in shadows, in daily fear, no doubt, of some terrible exposure.[39]

It is fascinating to contemplate the number of former intelligence officers who went on to write bestselling novels. Salinger is one; William Peter Blatty is another. Ian Fleming, of course, and E. Howard Hunt and Dennis Wheatley. In the non-fiction area we have such luminaries as Peter Tompkins and his "secrets of the pyramids" and T. E. Lawrence of Arabia and *The Seven Pillars of Wisdom*. Salinger, Blatty and Fleming, however, have had enormous impact on our culture, giving us unforgettable characters in Holden Caulfield, Regan and Fr. Damien Karras, and James Bond: an alienated teenager who has a nervous breakdown, a pre-pubescent girl possessed by demons and saved by a conflicted priest, and an invincible, not-so-secret secret agent. Fears and fantasies, courtesy of the American and British intelligence services.

In reality, perhaps, these characters have been transformed into . . . teenagers who express their alienation by shooting each other, and the rest of us, with automatic weapons; Catholic priests who are suspected more of pedophilia than of saving the souls of small children like Regan (how many mothers these days would leave their little Regans alone with a Catholic priest?); and an intelligence service that overthrows regimes it doesn't like, assassinates the heads of sovereign nations, spies on its own citizens, and through all this still manages to shoot itself in the foot more often than not.

But, meanwhile, back at the ranch, Chapman latches on to *Catcher* again, perhaps seeing in it something of his old self, his true self before Hawaii and marriage, before Beirut and Fort Chaffee . . . or perhaps, as Fenton Bresler suggests, it was handed to him by his controller. Regardless of how the book showed up in Chapman's environment, however, it began to once again exert a strong influence over his consciousness. He was becoming Holden Caulfield.

DOUBLE FANTASY

> Hear me, Satan . . . Accept these pearls of my evil and my rage. Accept these things from deep within me. In return I ask only that you . . . give me the power . . . The power to kill John Lennon. Give me the power of darkness. Give me the power of death.
>
> —Mark David Chapman[40]

> Now I say to you: I don't believe that Mark did it. It was terrible. It was the Devil!
>
> —Mrs. June Blankenship[41]

Holden Caulfield, and Dorothy from the *Wizard of Oz*. It was all coming back to him now. Dorothy the savior of the Munchkins; Holden the Catcher in the Rye. There was no place like home, and the Little People had returned.

In 1980, Chapman is either unemployed or sporadically employed. He begins hanging out at the library; his physical appearance begins to deteriorate; he tries selling blood to raise money. His wife is still working; so they are surviving, but not much more than that. Incredibly, he has paid off all their debts—which had been mounting, including credit-card debt and various loans—and is at loose ends. He suddenly develops a renewed fascination for *The Catcher in the Rye* and buys two copies, one for his wife and one for himself. He signs them both as Holden Caulfield.

He reads a recently-published biography of Lennon, and finds himself apalled at Lennon's repudiation of his earlier life, the Beatles, his revolutionary ideals. He claims he is disgusted at Lennon's obvious wealth, since his signature tune "Imagine" contains the phrase "imagine no possession." Chapman is coming to the conclusion that Lennon is a phony.

Then, he is sitting in his apartment going through his record albums and comes across the Beatles' *Sergeant Pepper* album, sees the picture of Lennon in the small mustache and granny-glasses, and decides then and there that he has to kill him.

> *We're one world, one people whether we like it or not. . . . Leaders is what we don't need.*
> —John Lennon[42]

It is October 1980. The *Double Fantasy* album is almost ready for release, containing seven cuts from Lennon and seven from Yoko Ono. John Lennon is making a comeback. A single from the album—*(Just Like) Starting Over*—is climbing the charts. There are photos of Lennon in the weekly and daily newspapers, interviews, and hints of a matured political consciousness.

Reagan is running against incumbent Jimmy Carter for the presidency. He is ahead in the polls, but not by much. It is this month that the alleged "October Surprise" conspiracy is taking place, with involvement by former CIA Director and current-vice presidential nominee George Bush: an arrangement with the Iranian government not to release the hostages until after the election. This arrangement will grow into the Iran-Contra scandal, with arms-for-hostages deals involving the US, Israel and Iran, while Ollie North arranges illegal support for the anti-Sandinista Contra rebels in Nicaragua. Guns, drugs, money, logistical support. It will be a nightmare of *realpolitik* and dirty tricks, surpassing Watergate in abuse of the Constitution and contempt for the American people by those in power. But the stakes are very high, at least in the viewpoint of the conservative faction within the Republican Party. It is nothing less than a battle for the human soul, the destruction of the Evil Empire, and the fulfillment of what Ronald Reagan sees as the Biblical prophecies in the Book of Revelation.

The last thing they needed was an activist Beatle, one who would become a naturalized American citizen in 1981, and then be able to vote and rail against the administration, reawakening old sentiments of peace, love and rock'n'roll. Particularly not *this* Beatle, the one who said they were more popular than Jesus. A Beatle worth something in excess of $150 million in 1980 dollars. A Beatle who could, conceivably, run for an American political office one day, and do so without having to raise a dime for his campaign treasury.

Chapman is sitting in his living room, listening to Beatles records and bobbing back and forth, *davvening*, rousing himself to a state of trance-like rage. He summons his Little People, for the first time in years. He needs to organize himself to go to New York City and murder John Lennon. If he does that, he knows, then the terrible pressure in his soul will be relieved. Maybe he will wind up in prison, or executed (New York did not have the death penalty at that time). Either way is okay with Mark David Chapman.

He signs himself out of his job for the last time, as "John Lennon." He then crosses out that name and signs his own. It is October 24, 1980.

Chapman buys a Charter Arms .38 revolver from a gun shop in Honolulu, but for some reason does not buy ammunition. It is October 27, 1980.

On October 29, he flies to New York City, and checks into the Waldorf Astoria, stays a few days, then changes to the YMCA, then the Sheraton Center, then the Olcott, which is down the block from the Dakota. He stakes out the Dakota, visiting every day, but also doing tourist things like Broadway plays, the Statue of Liberty, etc.

He tries to buy ammunition at a gun shop there. But one cannot buy ammunition in New York City, which has tough gun control laws, unless one has a New York City permit. Thwarted at this juncture, he decides to call on his old friend, the Georgia sheriff 's officer, and source the bullets that way.

He flies to Georgia (first class) on November 5, where his friend not only supplies bullets—hollow points, or "dum dums" as they are called, bullets with real stopping power—but takes him out for target practice for a day until Chapman is proficient, firing 150 rounds in the process.[43]

Chapman returns to New York, but discovers that Lennon is not at home. The doorman at the Dakota—the famous "Rosemary's Baby" apartment building where the Lennons have bought an entire floor—tells everyone the same thing: they are not at home, they are away, they are abroad, don't know when they will be back. In fact, the Lennons are still at work on the publicity and promotional material for *Double Fantasy*.

Chapman goes to the movies, and sees *Ordinary People.* The film provides a kind of catharsis for him, and his desire to kill Lennon subsides. He calls his wife in Hawaii, tells her that he had contemplated killing Lennon, that he has given up on that idea and is coming home.

Chapman returns to Honolulu on November 12, believing he has won a great victory by not killing Lennon, telling his wife that from now on everything will be okay, everything will be fine, it's all over, he's found himself. Don't worry. Be happy.

Within weeks, he is back on a plane for the mainland. This is where the story becomes muddied, with conflicting evidence showing that Chapman either left Honolulu on December 2, 1980 or December 5, 1980; that he either switched planes in Chicago, or stayed in Chicago for three days; that he brought his grandmother from Hawaii to Chicago, or that he visited his grandmother in Chicago, or he didn't see his grandmother at all.

Bresler makes a very convincing case—based on evidence at the Honolulu police department—that Chapman left for the mainland on December 2 and stayed in Chicago for three days before traveling on to New York, intending to return to Hawaii from there on December 18; he did not purchase a direct flight from Hawaii to New York, even though that would have been the cheaper alternative. Instead, he booked a roundtrip Honolulu-Chicago ticket, and then in Chicago at some point purchased a ticket for New York.

What was Chapman doing in Chicago for the missing three days? Was his trip in December specifically for the purpose of killing Lennon, or was there another purpose entirely, something to do with Chicago? Did he make the decision to go to New York to kill Lennon only after his visit in Chicago, with whomever it was he may have met there? His good friend David Moore says that he did not see him in Chicago, which, Moore admits, was very strange because even if Chapman only had an hour layover in O'Hare Airport he would have phoned him anyway. What would have kept Chapman from phoning his friend from the Fort Chaffee and world-tour days?

Several reports have stated that Chapman was accompanying his grandmother back to her home in Chicago, although they conflict on how long he spent in Chicago. Oddly, this grandmother cannot be located. Even more incredibly, United Airlines—the carrier he used for the flight from Honolulu and the later flight to New York—no longer even has a timetable in their records for the period in question, much less any passenger manifests! So it has been impossible for Bresler to backtrack over Chapman's movements and pin them down.

The missing three days in Chicago is troubling, as is the fact that Chapman did not purchase his ticket for New York until after he had landed and spent some time there. What happened in Chicago to point Chapman back toward his target?

Regardless of the Chicago interlude, by the time Chapman lands in New York City on December 6, 1980 his plan has been reaffirmed. He books himself into the YMCA closest to the Dakota and begins immediately to hang out around the entrance, waiting for Lennon. When Lennon doesn't show up that first day, Chapman begins that strange odyssey around Manhattan with a single cab, making two quick stops uptown and offering the driver a hit of cocaine, which the driver evidently refuses. Chapman then gets off in Greenwich Village, at Bleeker and Sixth.[44] We don't know what he does there, or when he gets back to the YMCA.

The next day, he checks out of the Y and books himself into the Sheraton Center Hotel, an expensive place on 7th Avenue and 52nd Street, far south of the Dakota and not within easy walking distance, as was the YMCA. No one knows why the sudden change of venue.

Then, in the hotel room, he arranges the famous shrine.

This is a composition of symbolic meaning, and consists of his expired passport with all the immigration stamps of his world tour; the letter of recommendation from his friend at the YMCA, David Moore; a photo of himself at Fort Chaffee with the Vietnamese refugees; a photo of his old car from his Georgia days, a '65 Chevy; his air ticket showing only the Honolulu-Chicago round trip, nothing showing how he arrived in New York; a Bible, inscribed "Holden Caulfield"; and a still from the movie *The Wizard of Oz*, also inscribed, this time "To Dorothy."

We must wonder at this point if Chapman was trying to tell us something, a message that was never received. The passport, the letter from David Moore, and the photograph of the Vietnamese refugees can be seen as simply an indication of some of the high points of his life, like the photo of his old car, or it could be seen as pointing in another direction: a paper trail meant to suggest the spoor of an ulterior motive, a hidden agenda. These, packaged with the Bible and the movie still, sums up the story of the inner and the outer Chapman.

He then has a call-girl come to his room at the Sheraton, and after she leaves he phones his wife in Hawaii and assures her of his love.

The next day is Monday, December 8, 1980.

> *So worrying about whether Wall Street or the Apocalypse is going to come in the form of the Great Beast—is not going to do us any good today . . . . I am going into an unknown future . . .*
>
> —John Lennon, the last interview, December 8, 1980[45]

On Chapman's twenty-block walk north to the Dakota, armed and dangerous and carrying a copy of the just-released *Double Fantasy* album, he realizes something is missing. Frantically, he seeks out a bookstore and finds a copy of *The Catcher in the Rye*. Relieved, he goes on his appointment with destiny with the familiar red paperback in his pocket. In it he has written, "From Holden Caulfield to Holden Caulfield," and "This is my statement."

He waits around outside the apartment building, without seeing Lennon. Around noon, he invites two girls who had also been standing around to go to lunch with him, and they do. After lunch he returns to the Dakota, and that afternoon meets John and Yoko's five year old son, Sean, and shakes his hand. But still no Lennon.

Finally, Lennon shows up, and Mark Chapman manages to get his autograph on the *Double Fantasy* album, as do all the others who had been hanging around. But he does not shoot. There are too many people, too many things could go wrong. And, anyway, maybe Mark isn't ready yet. Maybe actually seeing John Lennon in the flesh was startling; and he acts like any regular fan when he realizes that his picture had been taken by a photographer who had been watching the building, saying, "They'll never believe this in Hawaii!"[46]

Finally, at nearly 11 o'clock at night, John and Yoko arrive back at the Dakota after a long session in the recording studio. Mark Chapman is still there. There is a voice in his head, saying over and over, "Do it. Do it. Do it."[47] He says, "Mr. Lennon," and John turns to see Mark David Chapman in combat stance aiming the .38 revolver at him, firing the five rounds in rapid succession, hitting his target with four of them.

Lennon falls. Yoko screams. The doorman picks up the phone to call the police.

Mark David Chapman sits there, pulls out his copy of *Catcher*, and begins to read.

The subway entrance was right behind him. He could have escaped easily long before the police arrived. He could have been back in Hawaii (or Chicago) before anyone could identify him as the shooter, if actually anyone could. In fact, one of the first New York police detectives to interrogate Chapman felt that the young killer had been programmed to kill.[48]

Chapman was duly arrested, strangely shouting at the arresting officers, "I acted alone!"[49] He became silent in the police station, would not answer questions, but seemed strangely calm and unworried. (This was, incidentally, the same opinion people had of Lee Harvey Oswald after his arrest for the shooting of Officer Tipitt and the subsequent charge of killing the President.) As the months progressed, and as psychiatrists began visiting Chapman to derive some insight into his mental state, he was given an attorney, who labored to prepare a solid defense of "not guilty by reason of insanity" for his client. He was examined by a battery of famous psychiatrists, including Dr. Bernard Diamond, who had interviewed Sirhan Sirhan, Dr. Daniel Schwartz, who interviewed David Berkowitz, and hypnosis expert Dr. Milton Kline. All of that became moot when, on June 22, 1981, Chapman told the judge he was changing his plea to guilty. He told the judge that God had told him to plead guilty. His plea was accepted, and there was therefore never a trial in the murder of John Lennon.

In mid-August 1981, Chapman suddenly went berserk. He began screaming at other prisoners, tearing up his Bible and attempting to flush it down the toilet in his cell, which caused it to overflow. He splashed the water from the toilet at the guards, tore off his clothes, and started screaming like a monkey. (Shades of the Sirhan Sirhan hypnosis session with Dr. Diamond!) It took six men to subdue him, and bundle him off to Bellevue, New York's famous mental hospital.

In the ambulance on the way, he spoke to his guards in two entirely different demonic voices, named Lila and Dobar.[50] They said they had been sent to him by Satan.

After he was injected with anti-psychotics, the demonic presences began to fade, but not disappear entirely. He was visited by clergymen and prison chaplains of various denominations; all were convinced that Chapman was possessed by demons, a claim that only made Chapman angry.

On August 24, 1981 he was sentenced to twenty-to-life at Attica.

In Attica, in 1982, he began to invoke Satan again. His wife visited him and tried to exorcise the demons herself, but to no avail. Eventually, Chapman's demons faded once again, and he became somewhat normal.

Then, in 1983, the demons returned. Chapman began to invoke Satan for eighteen straight months, composing hymns and praying to the demonic forces day and night. He became so violent, that he was taken to Marcy, a mental hospital for convicts. They used anti-psychotics again, and brought him back to Attica.

But the demons returned.

Finally, in 1985, the exorcism of Mark David Chapman began in earnest. A minister would stand outside the prison in the middle of the night and begin the ritual, while Chapman would try to cooperate inside his prison cell at the same time.[51] The exorcism sessions finally worked, and Chapman slowly began to recover after vomiting up six demons, fluids leaking from his mouth as he writhed on the floor of his cell, snarling in arcane languages unknown to him.

He was cured. He was little Regan, safe at last.

A DAY IN THE LIFE

In June of 1989, a stalker named Robert John Bardo—armed with a copy of *The Catcher in the Rye* and a Charter Arms .38—walked up to actress Rebecca Schaeffer and blew her away. But he was not the first to imitate Mark David Chapman.

In the crowds gathered outside The Dakota to mourn the loss of John Lennon, as they still do every year on Lennon's birthday and on the anniversary of the day he was shot, another man joined the throngs outside the infamous apartment building; another man stared up at the building, gazed at the crowds of people around him, many of whom were openly weeping, and silently plotted his own desperate act. Standing on the street across from the entrance where John Lennon was gunned down that December was John Hinckley, Jr. To avenge the murder of John Lennon, and win the admiration of *Taxi Driver* star Jodie Foster, he would attempt to assassinate President Ronald Reagan.

> *. . . I made a list of 50 total coincidences, things that were pretty frightening because there was no way that they could have been planned, no way that I could have set them up. It was like the whole killing was set up by destiny, just something that was meant to be . . . . It was just eerie, like something more was going on than I had ever envisioned. Like it was out of my control. It was like all of those coincidences were not only confirmed, but they were magnified a thousand times and enlightened and new angles and nuances and the whole purpose was given to me to understand.*
>
> —Mark David Chapman[52]

Coincidence or, as Jung would have it, synchronicity. It is the first layer of evidence that what we are dealing with is something other than a normal, linear, cause-and-effect dynamic underlying the warp and woof of creation; it is the first level of experience that can be reliably expected to obtain when occult practices are employed, or when violent acts are accompanied by religious fervor. It is what one sees when there is a strain in the fabric of reality, when time or space stretches or contracts, when terrible deeds are committed by little men.

Once again, we are forced to consider: are the coincidences that surround Mark David Chapman evidence of a political conspiracy to murder John Lennon? That would be the scientific view, accepting for the moment that we reject the notion of "coincidence" as being itself unscientific. Or are they evidence of the workings of another force in the universe? Is a coincidence simply the line of least resistance, the shortest distance between two phenomenological points? As we will see, the ancients had a special way of dealing with coincidences: they codified them into something they called "correspondences," and consciously employed the phenomena to attain specific goals.

Are there people—individuals, or organizations—that, consciously or unconsciously, employ these techniques today?

It is not known whether Chapman ever saw *Taxi Driver*, a film that was released in 1976 to much critical acclaim, and this at a time when he was struggling with his relationship with his fiancée and his university courses, months before he had cut and run to Hawaii. One wonders if he would have found any resonance between the character of Travis Bickle and his own situation. Travis Bickle is a desperately lonely man, a nobody, like Chapman. He has a hard time with human relationships, as does Chapman. He has a very ambiguous sexual identity, as does Chapman. He gorges on junk food and alcohol, as does Chapman. He begins to develop a plan to assassinate an important figure, as does Chapman. He buys weapons, conceals them on his person, and goes out to commit an assassination. In Travis Bickle's case, he does not manage to kill the political candidate, but is run off before he can draw his weapon.

Taxi Driver was based, in part, on the George Wallace assassination attempt committed by Arthur Bremer, and on Bremer's diary. Thus, it was a case of art imitating life. Bremer had used a Charter Arms .38 revolver, the same make and model as that later used by Mark David Chapman.

Bremer had attempted his assassination of Wallace on May 15, 1972. His Charter Arms revolver only held five bullets, like that used by Chapman eight years later. Yet, Wallace was struck by a minimum of four bullets, and possibly all five. Taking into consideration the fact that three other people were wounded in the same fusillade, it would appear that at least eight bullets had been fired, which immediately raises the ugly specter of a second shooter, and thus of a conspiracy. Wallace himself always claimed that he was the victim of a conspiracy that day.

In addition, Bremer's fingerprints were not found on the gun retrieved at the scene, even though the famous film footage of him shooting Wallace shows he was bare-handed and not wearing gloves. An FBI agent retrieved it, not from Bremer, but from the ground where the assassination attempt had taken place, and held on to it for hours. No one knows why.

Like Chapman, Bremer traveled extensively in the days leading up to the murder; this for a man whose jobs were as a busboy in a restaurant and as a janitor. In fact, Bremer had also flown to New York City (from Milwaukee) and stayed at the Waldorf-Astoria Hotel, the same hotel favored by Chapman on his original trip to New York.

In the days leading up to the Wallace attempt, Bremer had bought a second-hand car, took a helicopter ride around New York City, rented limousines, bought weapons, etc., all on a busboy's salary. Records of his hotel stays, bills, etc. were seized by the FBI and not made available to the press.

Bremer's half-sister—Gail Aiken—was a close associate of Reverend Jerry Owen, the man who befriended Sirhan Sirhan in the days leading up to the Robert Kennedy assassination: yet another minister of religion with mysterious ties to assassination and murder. Reverend Owen was believed to be one of the sources of income for Sirhan Sirhan, and one of the members of the assassination conspiracy, according to researchers Turner and Christian. The net draws tighter and tighter.

And so it goes.

On March 30, 1981, John Hinckley, Jr.—strongly influenced by *Taxi Driver* (based in part on Bremer) and by Chapman's murder of John Lennon—attempted to assassinate President Ronald Reagan, armed with a revolver and a copy of *The Catcher in the Rye.* A case of life imitating art imitating life. And, like the fictional Travis Bickle, he does not succeed in his assassination attempt.

From Bremer to Hinckley, by way of Chapman.

The Hinckley family knew the Bush family; both were in the oil business. Hinckley's father had an appointment the day of the Reagan assassination attempt with George Bush's brother in West Virginia. The net draws even tighter. This is either evidence of a political conspiracy or simply another coincidence . . . but in our case, we must look at coincidence very carefully, for it usually represents the action of a deeper, more sinister force.

> *Diane, when two events happen simultaneously pertaining to the same object of inquiry, we must always pay strict attention.*
>
> —Special Agent Dale Cooper, *Twin Peaks*, pilot episode

The shooters are all invariably *nemo*s, nobodies. Stunted personalities. Easy to manipulate, either by government forces or by . . . other forces. They are attracted to conspiracies because they see in them an entrée into the working world, the world where things happen and where people are fully-realized personalities. They seek the missing piece of themselves, filling the emptiness with a gun. They seek spiritual transformation. They are told (either by a government agent, or by the very culture itself) that they can become whole by absorbing the life-essence of a great man, a great warrior whose blood they drink, whose liver they eat. As the Mass says, *Hic est corpus meum; hic est enim calix sanguinem meam.* It is the oldest ritual of the shamans, the consumption of a God.

And it is the most dangerous message of the sinister forces, that there is nothing behind the curtain or the icon screen; that the Wizard is a fraud; that there is, in short, no God but Man. What was meant to liberate has now enslaved, for its message has been perverted by Men who wish to be known as Gods—who reserve Godhead for themselves—filling the vacuum of belief with naïve faith and the fascist mantra that "there's no place like home."

ENDNOTES

1 Jack Jones, *Let Me Take You Down*, Villard Books, NY, 1992, p. 216
2 Fenton Bresler, *Who Killed John Lennon?*, St Martin's, NY, 1989, p. 312
3 Russ Bellant, *Old Nazis, The New Right, and The Republican Party*, South End Press, Boston, 1991, p. 68
4 August Strindberg, *Inferno*, Penguin, NY, 1979, p. 250
5 Ibid., p.23
6 Gary Sick, *October Surprise*, Times Books, NY, 1991, p. 210
7 Ibid., p. 75
8 Steven Levy, *The Unicorn's Secret*, Prentice Hall Press, NY, 1988, p. 130
9 Quoted in Paul Krassner, *Confessions of a Raving Unconfined Nut*, Simon and Schuster, NY, 1993, p. 215
10 Ibid., p. 215
11 Bresler, op. cit., p. 322
12 Jones, op. cit., p. 125
13 Ibid., p. 121
14 Ibid., p. 122
15 Ibid., p. 12
16 Ibid., p. 123
17 Ibid., p. 123
18 Ibid., p. 125–6
19 Ibid., p. 131
20 Ibid., p. 131
21 Patricia Cornwell, *Portrait of a Killer*, Little, Brown, London, 2002, p. 178–9
22 Bresler, op. cit., p. 116–121
23 Jones, op. cit., p. 209
24 Bresler, op. cit., p. 125
25 Jones, op. cit., p. 209
26 Bresler, op. cit., p. 121
27 Jones, op. cit., p. 204
28 Bresler, op. cit., p. 125
29 Jones, op. cit., p. 135
30 Bresler, op. cit., p. 217
31 Ibid., p. 150–151
32 Ibid., p. 150
33 Ibid., p. 151
34 Jones, op. cit., p. 171
35 Ibid., p. 220–221
36 Ian Hamilton, *In Search of J.D. Salinger*, Vintage, NY, 1989, p. 128
37 Ibid., p. 97
38 Ibid., p. 97–98
39 Ibid., p. 80
40 Jones, op. cit., p. 194–195
41 Bresler, op. cit., p. 184
42 Bresler, op. cit., p. 163
43 Jones, op. cit., p. 210
44 Bresler, op. cit., p. 216–218
45 Ibid., p. 224
46 Ibid., p. 227
47 Ibid., p. 231
48 Ibid., p. 256–257
49 Ibid., p. 232
50 Ibid., p. 307
51 Jones, op. cit., p. 240–242
52 Ibid., p. 226

BOOK TWO: A WARM GUN

CHAPTER FIFTEEN

A VAST, RIGHT-WING CONSPIRACY

With political victory, the ideological conflicts that have swirled about this nation for half a century now show clear signs of breaking into naked ideological warfare in which the very foundations of our republic are threatened and we had better take heed.

—Richard Mellon Scaife, Heritage Foundation rally, November 1994

This is the great story here, for anybody willing to find it and write about it and explain it: this vast, right-wing conspiracy that has been conspiring against my husband since the day he announced for president.

—Hillary Rodham Clinton, *Today* show, January 27, 1998

If the . . . charge by the First Lady that the President is the target of a vast right-wing conspiracy is accurate, then nearly all the banking records point to one individual: Richard Scaife.

—Keith Olbermann, "White House in Crisis," MSNBC, March 26, 1998

Richard Mellon Scaife, scion of the Mellon fortune and heavy financial backer of the conservative movement in America—including the campaign to discredit and eventually impeach Bill Clinton—made a most revealing remark when he addressed the Heritage Foundation in the heady days of the Republican Party winning control of Congress in the November 1994 election. He said that "ideological conflicts" had "swirled about this nation for half a century," i.e., since about 1945. Further, he warned that the nation was on the verge of breaking out into "ideological warfare in which the very foundations of our republic are threatened." This can not be understood without reference to the last days of the Second World War, and the polarization of the two most powerful American political parties on either side of the right-versus-left conflict, as Nazis were being recruited into the American intelligence, aerospace, medical and scientific establishments as a means of combating the Communist threat.

Deep into the Clinton presidency, a right-wing ideologue was giving voice to what a generation of conservatives and rightist Republicans feared most: that with the collapse of the Soviet Union and the demonstration that Communism was politically bankrupt, America would not take the initiative and extend its hegemony—even, according to some, its imperialism—over the rest of the world. To the Republicans, the Democrats were throwing away the one best chance America had to bring the entire world to heel. This conflict of opinions, of "true believers" from both sides, would result in the catastrophes of the early twenty-first century, and in particular, the invasion of Iraq under a Republican president who is the son and heir of former CIA Director George Bush.

As detailed in Book One, this was, indeed, an ideological conflict, and it was supported by powerful and influential individuals and organizations in the United States, with their ideology exported abroad in the support of vicious dictatorships of every stripe: essential elements of a "bulwark against Communism." Even as members of the American intelligentsia in science and medicine—notably space science and psychiatric medicine—were probing the far reaches of space and the deep secrets of the human mind, American political and religious leaders were leading the popular charge at home and abroad in the open forum.

Taken together, this was nothing less than a redesign of the American political and religious environment, an attempt to create a new country, one worthy of the mantle of global liberator, a liberator with its eyes on the domination not only of the world, but of space, as well. And, in order to create this new country, this new spiritual paradigm with new rules of engagement and a strange new morality in which some of the most brutal regimes the world has ever known—the Nazis and the Imperial Japanese—would become our allies against "godless Communism" and the "yellow peril," we had to take measures that were harsh and ruthless.

The war against Communism took more out of American society than the war against Nazism. For one thing, it lasted much longer and, as Communism was an "international" enemy and painted as more truly an ideological enemy than Nazism, anyone could be a Communist. Your neighbor, your boss, your employee, your brother, your senator and even—in the eyes of some—your president. America turned inward upon itself in its search for socialists, Communists, "reds" in general and their fellow-travelers. While Eleanor Roosevelt and Albert Einstein and Helen Douglas were in New York City raising consciousness and voice against the importation of war criminals under the Operation Paperclip program, the Dulles brothers and Richard Nixon were plotting an extension of that program to include thousands more. It was an ideological conflict that perhaps had its origins in American history decades if not centuries earlier, but which only became refined and fine-tuned during the war years.

We may say it was a Republican versus Democrat conflict, and in one sense this is true. The Republican Party had not been slow to support Nazism, as has been substantiated not only in Book One, but also in reports by other authors and in substantial documentation over the past fifty years. The Democratic Party has resisted this type of immoral *realpolitik* for a long time. In general, its leaders have supported human rights issues at home and abroad—whether in deed or in mere lip-service—and have resisted corporate America's attempts to give the country a make-over into its own, grey-flannel image. When critics of Democratic leaders itemize their complaints, they are generally in terms of political corruption (gerrymandering, pork barrel politics, bribes, and the like) and issues of sexual morality: character issues rather than policy issues. For example, Presidents Kennedy and Clinton have been pilloried in the conservative press because of real or imagined sexual adventurism.

Many consider this sheer hypocrisy: Kennedy was seen as dangerous to white hegemony in the United States with his, and especially his brother Robert's, support of integration; Clinton and (especially) his activist wife, Hillary Rodham, were seen as too popular among the black and Latino voters, and among women in general.

While it would be the grossest sort of hyperbole to suggest that Republicans are Nazis and racists, and that Democrats are loving humanitarians, there is some truth to the notion that the Republican Party is the party of corporate America, and this generally means white America. When attacks are made on Democratic leaders for purely political reasons, the attacks seem weak and unpopular. When attacks are made for social reasons—religion, sex, "character" issues—then the attacks become more confident, more virulent. Character issues are seen as spiritual ones, even theological ones.

Republicans are seen as the party of the corporation, big business, wealth. Democrats are seen as supporters of the labor unions, the poor, blue collar workers, racial minorities. It is, therefore, very difficult for many to view the Republican Party as anything but an oppressor of the poor, minorities and labor . . . even though the large corporations that support the Republican Party are the source of jobs and technology that employ the workers. This is a simplistic view, but it is one that holds true for many people. The reinvention of the Republican Party in the last twenty years or so has been largely due to its hijacking of Democrat platforms and its *apparent* move towards the center under the neo-conservatives (to the dismay of old-line conservatives), just as the Democratic Party was losing the support of the very people it was supposed to defend against the rabidity of the Republicans. This took place against a backdrop of a frightening increase in crime, in the proliferation of drugs, illegal aliens (the terrestrial kind), unwed mothers, and AIDS. The American people—terrified at these domestic developments—turned towards the "law and order" Republicans to defend them against these threats to "homeland security." The taking of the hostages in Iran during Carter's Democratic administration was just one more indication that the Democrats were not the people to protect Americans and American interests.

We then had eight years of Ronald Reagan, and four of George H.W. Bush. Predictably, word of secret deals, guns-for-hostages, drugs-for-guns, and other skullduggery leaked out, and we had the spectacle of Iran-Contra and the rumors of an October Surprise. America learned that it was secretly arming drug dealers and guerrillas to fight against the Sandinista regime in Nicaragua, even though it was against the law to do so without the approval of Congress. America learned that people in positions of power and influence (non-elected positions) had nothing but disdain and contempt for the elected officials of Congress. America learned that it had agreed to sell arms to Iran, the same country that had taken Americans hostage in a humiliating orgy of nationalism. America learned that the White House operated on quite another level, one of *realpolitik*, one that did not respect Congress and the laws it had passed. But then, what did we expect of a Party that had held its 1980 National Convention in Dallas, not far from the spot where the most popular Democratic president of recent memory was assassinated?

And then there were the savings and loan scandals, in which even a Bush family member was indicted for his participation in a series of corrupt business practices that led to the collapse of the Silverado S&L. America was suddenly in debt up to its ears due to the S&L crisis, which was engineered by Ronald Reagan when he enacted sweeping banking "reforms" that opened loopholes in the practices of savings institutions large enough to drive police wagons through. It was business as usual. And it became too much. Too much business. Too much of the usual:

Item: May 1985. Reagan at the Nazi cemetery in Bitberg, Germany. Laying a wreath and memorializing the Waffen SS as "victims." Reagan also proclaimed April 10th as "Croatian Day" in the United States. April 10th, of course, is the anniversary of the day the Nazi Ustashi government under Pavelic took control in Croatia and began its reign of terror in the Balkans, including Catholic Father Kamber's establishment of a concentration camp at Doboj.[1] The entire Ustashi government, including Pavelic, managed to emigrate safely to Juan Peron's Argentina after the war.

Item: October 1987. The program for the National Republican Heritage Groups Council meeting lists, as co-chairmen, Anna Chennault (the Taiwanese lobbyist we came across during Nixon's 1968 "October Surprise" negotiations with Vietnam), and Laszlo Pasztor (former leader of the Hungarian Arrow Cross Youth Division, the Hungarian Nazi Party organ, during World War II). The Host Committee lists such notables as Romanian Iron Guardist (and supporter of Nazi war criminal Valerian Trifa) "Reverend" Florian Galdau; Italian fascist Phil Guarino, who was an associate of Licio Gelli and Roberto Calvi of Masonic P-2 fame; and even that doyenne of the cosmetics industry, Hungarian émigrée Christine Valmy.[2]

Item: September 1988. A flurry of news reports concerning a heavy concentration of Nazis on presidential candidate George Bush's newly-formed Coalition of American Nationalities, including the usual grouping of Romanian Iron Guardists, Ukrainian SS supporters, Croatian Nazis, and Holocaust-denial activists. This list includes Fred Malek, who, when working for the Nixon White House, compiled an enemies list of "Jewish sounding names." Malek resigned his position as Bush advisor immediately. He would eventually—and quietly—enter the administration after the election of George Bush.

The comfort of Republicans—and particularly the conservative wing—around Nazis and Nazism was (and is) unsettling.

But, hey . . . the Soviet Union fell. The Berlin wall fell. China became increasingly capitalist. Talks were held with Communist Vietnam with an eye towards trade. The enemies that the Republicans had warned about, sometimes shrilly, since 1945 were now disappearing. The Red Menace and the Yellow Peril were things of the past. We even witnessed the shocking scene of Brent Scowcroft in Beijing a month after the brutal Tiananmen Square massacre in 1989, toasting the Chinese leaders at the request of self-proclaimed China expert and former-Ambassador to China (briefly), President George Bush. Although America laid sanctions against China for the massacre (most Democrats were outraged at the wanton slaughter of students and pro-Democracy supporters), Bush ensured that his older brother—Prescott, Jr.—was still able to broker a deal between the Chinese government and Hughes Aircraft for the sale of communications satellites, when other American companies were barred from so doing. It was a New World Order, indeed. The Republicans had made the world safe for . . . well, Republicans.

And then along came Bill Clinton.

No matter what side of the fence you're on, you have to admit that there has never been as vicious, as concentrated a campaign to destroy a presidential candidate—and, then, a president—as there was with Bill Clinton. The emotions he aroused in his enemies were visceral, rabid, hysterical to the point of pathology. The fact that Clinton was re-elected and served his full eight years, even surviving an impeachment process, is testament more to his popularity among the rank and file American voters than it is to the lack of effort or focus of his enemies. During the Clinton administration, America prospered. That was supposed to be a Republican gimmick. Just as the Republicans tried to co-opt the Democratic Party platforms by loudly proclaiming a return to "family values" (this, in the Party of Newt Gingrich and his famous divorce from his hospitalized, bed-ridden wife), it seems the Democrats had taken a page from the Republican book and reminded themselves, "It's the economy, stupid."

When Governor of Arkansas Bill Clinton announced for the presidency, the scramble began to defeat him before he ever went to a single primary, much less the convention. Clinton, after all, had avoided the draft during the Vietnam War. Clinton was a Rhodes Scholar who went to Oxford. Clinton spoke German fluently. He was obviously the wrong person to have as the Commander-in-Chief of the Armed Forces, which title comes with the Presidency. He was brilliant; he opposed the Vietnam War; he had a famous photograph of himself shaking the hand of President Kennedy; he had an accomplished and attractive wife (who had actually worked for a Watergate investigator) and a young daughter; he was a friend of racial minorities; and . . . he played the saxophone. He even admitted he had smoked pot, although he famously declared he "didn't inhale." Looking at the Clintons, one could not help but be reminded of the Kennedys. And there is nothing the Republican Party hates more than the Kennedy clan.

Clinton had to be stopped.

The story of the 1990s is that of how Clinton could *not* be stopped, no matter how much money and influence the Republicans and conservatives threw at the problem. It is not a story in which the Republican Party covered itself with glory. It is, in fact, the story of how the opposition to Clinton became so crazed that it didn't care how much America itself was humiliated in the process, giving rise to some speculation that the Republican Party has another agenda. Hillary Rodham Clinton was not spared the vitriolic character assassinations, either. An extremely intelligent and well-spoken First Lady, she epitomized the New Woman who could hold a prestigious job in law and still make a home for her husband and daughter, as well as find time to write a book on the problems of raising children in the new society: *It Takes a Village*. But as the Republican Party and especially the powerful Conservative wing mounted pressure on the Clintons both in personal as well as in policy terms, it was as if we were reliving that moment from the Vietnam War in which we heard that awful axiom: *we had to destroy the village in order to save it*.

It is also a story of how many Democrats lost their nerve and began to distance themselves from a President whose only crime—the only one ever proven after the expenditure of more than forty million dollars of taxpayer money and untold investigative man-hours over the course of more than eight years—was that of a sex act with Monica Lewinsky and his denial of same under oath. Essentially, it was the Profumo affair all over again, but minus the Communists.

In order to understand what happened to America during the Clinton administration—and without taking sides one way or another on Clinton's presidency, character, or accomplishments (or lack thereof)—we will see many of the same old faces reappear, like unsettled ghosts, in the American haunted house. We will have to look back once again to the first Nixon campaign and Nixon's mentor, Murray Chotiner. We have to go back and watch the slurry of Christian fundamentalists and charismatics around first Nixon and then Reagan and Bush, watch their influence over this story, and how they played true to form and supported some of the worst mass murderers in history. We have to remember how German Christians were duped and "played" by the Nazis into giving their support to the Third Reich (or, if not their support, then their studied neutrality) and watch the same strategy taking place again, in the America of the 1990s as—in the words of Sara Diamond—a famous televangelist "established for the Christian Right the standard message of tying one's personal redemption to a gospel of political participation."[3] We have to investigate the monied families of America, some of the same families who swirled around the séance tables of Andrija Puharich and Stephen Ward.

We have to evoke sinister forces.

GOING UP RIVER

> "They were laying on hands," an American aid worker recalls, "speaking in tongues and holding services while people were dying all around."
>
> —"Jewels for Jesus: Zaire, Mobutu and Pat Robertson" by Andrew Purvis, *Time* magazine, February 27, 1994

In Book One, we examined the development of the psychological warfare operations of the American military from World War II and extending through Vietnam. What we did not focus on then was the growing importance of evangelical Christianity as a venue for psychological operations against target nations, using resources that had "plausible deniability" written all over them. It was the influence of such Christian propaganda efforts as the Far East Broadcasting Company's radio stations beaming messages into Communist China (as one example) that led to a growing presence of the Christian Right within U.S. intelligence and psychological warfare operations around the world, often with chilling effect.[4] Although we described the cynical manipulation of Congolese spiritual beliefs by U.S. intelligence forces, we did not take that argument to its logical conclusion: the ability to manipulate *American* spiritual beliefs the same way, and for similar ends. We shall do so now, and with the prime example being Pat Robertson's Christian Broadcast Network (CBN) and his Christian Coalition.

In Book One, we cited in some detail a special report on African occultism prepared by the Special Operations Research Office (SORO) at American University, a paper commissioned by the US Army that was entitled "Witchcraft, Sorcery, Magic and Other Psychological Phenomena and Their Implications on Military and Paramilitary Operations in the Congo," by James R. Price and Paul Jureidini. This paper—prepared in 1964—was focused specifically on events in the Congo, where a young Army Chief of Staff tried to consolidate his power base and create a new country.

Previously, Patrice Lumumba had been the leader of the newly-independent Democratic Republic of the Congo, a country that had once been known as the "Belgian Congo" and which had gained its independence from Belgium officially on June 30, 1960. Lumumba was a charismatic speaker and firebrand, and largely believed to be a supporter of the Soviet Union and its brand of Communism. Of course, this *volte-face* had happened after Lumumba (in a replay of circumstances surrounding Ho Chi Minh's similar request of the United States in the 1940s) requested UN support to defend his country from an insurrection in southern Katanga province, a "native" insurrection bolstered by the sudden appearance of crack Belgian paratroopers. The UN turned him down, even though they had sent troops immediately to Leopoldville. Their mandate, Lumumba was informed, was to protect the new country from foreign aggression, but not from its internal problems. The fact that these "internal problems" also involved the presence of Belgian troops did not matter to the UN. Feeling betrayed, he was forced to go to Russia for help to prop up his administration, and the Soviets sent troops to help Lumumba put down the insurrection.

Thus, his government was seen as hostile to the United States. Long before the SORO paper had been prepared and digested, however, it had been up to another agency of the government to take steps to remove Lumumba from power, to terminate him with "extreme prejudice." This agency, of course, was the CIA, under orders from President Eisenhower. And the man who flew to Africa to put this plan into motion was none other than Dr. Sidney Gottlieb, the man in charge of MK-ULTRA.

Under orders from Richard Bissell, head of CIA Clandestine Services at the time, Gottlieb flew to the Congo in 1960, and hand-carried an infectious agent designed to kill Lumumba and make it look as if he had simply contracted a local, fatal disease.[5] His asset in the Congo—career CIA agent Larry Devlin—was unable (or unwilling[6]) to infect Lumumba in time, however; but the die—or the spell—was cast.

Mobutu—Lumumba's Army Chief of Staff—took over the country on September 14, 1960, barely two-and-a-half months after its independence from Belgium. Lumumba himself was mysteriously assassinated on or about January 17, 1961. His body was never found. According to one source, Lumumba—who had been arrested and taken to an out-of-the-way military base—was chopped into pieces and dissolved in acid, either by Belgian specialists who wanted to remove all traces of the assassination[7] or on the advice of Congolese shamans so that his spirit would not haunt Mobutu or the new republic.[8] By November of 1965, the psy-war witchdoctors—in concert with Mobutu's witchdoctors—had won the day and made the Congo (renamed Zaire) safe for democracy, and Zaire safe for Mobutu (like Papa Doc Duvalier of Haiti, and Augusto Pinochet of Chile, a "president for life") for another thirty-two years.

What happened next could have been predicted by anyone who has spent any time at all in Africa. Mobutu changed his name from Joseph Desire Mobutu to Mobutu Sese Seko Kuku Ngbendu Wa Za Banga, "The All-Powerful Warrior Who Goes from Conquest to Conquest, Leaving Fire in His Wake." He re-instated African religious and cultural practices in his new nation, considering anything else to be the trappings of colonialism. (As an example, Congolese were banned from wearing neckties and western dress.) In the process he became a leader equivalent to the Duvaliers in Haiti or Marcos in the Philippines, stripping his country of its natural resources and hoarding the proceeds in Swiss and Belgian banks. (It was Mobutu's reign that inspired the creation of the term "kleptocracy.") Although accounts of his reign are largely concerned with his greed—his personal worth has been estimated in the billions of US dollars—most studies (such as Michela Wrong's otherwise entertaining *In The Footsteps of Mr. Kurtz*) ignore Mobutu's secret police, the torture of political dissidents, the ruthless extermination of the opposition, and the murderous events of 1990, when more than 200 students were gunned down by Mobutu's security forces at a pro-democracy rally at the University of Lubumbashi. They ignore his administration's support of the Rwandan Hutu rebels who massacred the Tutsi minority in one of the worst cases of bloodshed and genocide the African continent has known in the past century.

A man who claimed vicious Romanian president Nicolae Ceausescu as his personal friend, this was the African leader adopted by American Christian fundamentalist and right-wing demagogue televangelist Pat Robertson as his idol.

And business partner.

To come to grips with this story is to begin to understand the depth of human depravity in the face of wealth. It is written in the Bible that "the love of money is the root of all evil" (1 Timothy 6:10), and while that may seem like an overstatement to some, it is certainly close enough to the truth to get us home. We have to say that either the opulence of Mobutu's personal wealth blinded Robertson to the truth of his regime, or that Robertson simply didn't care. After all, he was no stranger to Africa and its problems. His business enterprises there involved everything from logging to diamonds, and it was diamonds that lured Robertson to Zaire, a country famous for the stones that are a girl's best friend. And, while diamonds may be forever, Mobutu certainly wasn't, and as his regime began to fail in the face of popular uprisings, invasions, a disaffected army, and waning support from the West, Robertson's fortunes in Africa also dried up; but not before rumors began to spread of his cynical exploitation of the humanitarian efforts in Zaire as a mask for his business activities.

This is the Christian minister who would throw his support behind the conservative movement to discredit the Clinton administration by accusing it of having masterminded the murders of 200 individuals over the course of the Arkansas politician's career: two hundred unproven, unverified, unsubstantiated homicides, which were more the product of feverish imaginations than crime scene evidence and grand jury subpoenas. Two hundred fictitious murders over a long political career, up against what his close personal friend Mobutu had actually accomplished in a single day with his army at the University of Lubumbashi.

We read previously of the Christian minister-turned-socialist Jim Jones, who led his followers to death in the Guyanese jungles. Only a few years later, Robertson would travel to Zaire in the midst of war, disease and starvation . . . and ignore the plight of the suffering to take care of his burgeoning business deals in the diamond mines. He would use his religious organization as a cover for his more material pursuits, taking whatever he could get out of Zairean jungles before the insurrections and corruption made it impossible to leave with his fortune intact.

One of the little known sidebars to the story of World War II is that of the war in Africa. Once Belgium had been occupied by the Nazis, its colony in Africa—the Belgian Congo—also should have come under Nazi control. While Field Marshal

Rommel was busy fighting a hit-and-run campaign across North Africa, there was a more shadowy campaign being waged in the Congo, in the heart of Conrad's "heart of darkness."

The Congo was valuable to the war effort for two reasons, one obvious and the other not-so-obvious, at least at the time. In the first case, it was the diamonds. Diamonds are an important commodity during war, as they can be used in industrial applications to further the war machine: as cutters in machine tools, as abrasives, and in a variety of other uses such as guidance systems and other electronics. They are also, of course, a means of barter and trade when currencies collapse due to invasions and insurrections. The Congo has the world's largest diamond reserves outside of South Africa, and when the Nazis came into power in Belgium they foresaw coming into this large fortune as well . . . if they could secure it. Although they were nominally in charge of Belgium and made it part of the Third Reich, they did not have physical control of the African colony. The Nazi military had other problems in Africa of a more immediate nature, and were not there in sufficiently large numbers to invade the Congo in order to control the diamond trade; but they didn't have to.

There was a large black market in diamonds, and the American OSS saw this as their opportunity to work in concert with the South African diamond giant De Beers to thwart the Germans and gain control of the world's diamond supply. De Beers, for its part, intended to drain the Congo dry of diamonds with Allied cooperation, in order to protect its own native reserves in South Africa from premature depletion. At the same time, De Beers was actively smuggling diamonds to the Third Reich and making money from both sides in the conflict, ignoring Roosevelt's repeated requests for a guaranteed diamond stockpile in the United States or, at the very least, in Canada. By the time the OSS had learned of the details of the De Beers black market network, the war was almost over and the urgency declined.

It would be to these diamond mines that Pat Robertson would resort, fifty years after the war's end, in a botched—but expensive—attempt to make his own fortune.

At the same time, there was that other commodity in the Congo, one that made it of such importance that Albert Einstein would write a letter to Washington, begging the Roosevelt administration to do all it could to protect that country from Nazi invasion. This, of course, was uranium. The Manhattan Project was in full swing, and the weapons-grade uranium that would eventually be used to build the two atomic bombs that were dropped on Japan in August 1945 did indeed come from the Congo.

With the end of World War II came the end of the Nazi occupation of Belgium. The Congo remained in Belgian control, but the times were changing and the end of the period of colonialism was near. Great Britain was losing control in India and Malaya, and Belgium was on the ropes in Africa. By the 1960s, the colonies would be liberated . . . but at the same time find themselves in the midst of tremendous internal struggles.

The Congo was no exception. Civil war was tearing the country apart, and into this madness stepped Patrice Lumumba. With his eventual arrest and assassination, the Congo was not entirely free of internecine conflict. Mobutu would not become leader of his country for another five years, years of intense fighting in the Congo's provinces . . . and of intense spell-casting by government-approved shamans, if the above-mentioned SORO document is any indication. Into this nightmare of war and bloodshed many adventurers and entrepreneurs would find themselves a home. One of these was Siegfried "Congo" Müller.

Shown in an East German film of the 1960s, *Der Lachende Mann* ("The Laughing Man"), Müller was a former Nazi and present-day mercenary who found himself "defending civilization" in the Congo's civil wars. He was interviewed by two East German filmmakers, who pretended they thought favorably of the Third Reich, and he opened himself up to them, smiling and laughing, smoking cigarettes and drinking from a glass of Pernod as he described his enthusiastic contribution to the savagery taking place all around him. The film was released in 1967 to some critical acclaim, but it was an East German offering and received very little attention in the West, which, after all, was satisfied that Lumumba was dead and that Mobutu—an anti-Communist and friend of the United States—was safely in charge of the Congo, now renamed Zaire.

Africa has always been a haven for military adventurism, whether of the homegrown or the imported variety. The mercenaries taking part in insurrections in Angola, Rhodesia, Mozambique and Namibia are the stuff of legend. The Biafran conflict in Nigeria provided mercenaries with employment on both sides of that conflict. The famous Selous Scouts of South Africa provided another opportunity for blood and money, if not glory. Tribal conflicts became inflated to national conflicts; revolution became civil war, became independence, became civil war, became revolution, in a sickening spiral of violence and deceit and greed that would characterize African politics for generations. Add to that religious and ethnic rivalries, economic competition, foreign manipulation of all sides in every struggle, and you have an excellent laboratory for weapons, tactics, and psychological warfare experimentation.

The Nazis who escaped justice at the end of World War II wound up in Latin America, North America, and Australia in large numbers. Many of these were protected by Allied intelligence agencies, as has been covered at length and in depth in many other studies, including my own *Unholy Alliance*. That Nazi scientists and criminals wound up assisting the governments of the Arab world is also not in doubt. The activities of Otto Skorzeny, Hitler's commando, in Egypt, Syria and other North African and Middle Eastern countries are well-known. The assistance of these men in the development of Arab missile and weapons programs has changed the balance of power in that troubled region.

The presence of Nazi war criminals in Africa has rarely been addressed, if only because Africa itself is still a "heart of darkness" for most Americans and Europeans, a treacherous land of incomprehensible intrigue. That Nazis such as Siegfried Müller would have found their way to the Congo comes as no surprise. The opportunities for war and the spoils of war were too numerous.

In addition, with the advent of Lumumba, the struggle became characterized as a war between Capitalism and Communism, between the "values" of the West versus those of the East. The renegade Nazis came down squarely on the side of the West and Capitalism, fighting their old enemy the Soviet Communists on the battlegrounds of Katanga province. Enlisted to assist the efforts of the United States, and of the Belgian forces in the region, Nazi mercenaries were only too glad to offer their expertise in torture, interrogation, and military drill. This is the dirty secret of the African wars of the 1950s, '60s and '70s. More attention has been paid to the presence of Nazi war criminals in Latin America, but the activities of Nazis in Africa, Asia and Australia are only now coming to light in the literature.

For instance, under Otto Skorzeny's leadership, the Middle East became a safe haven for Nazis on the run. Moving there in 1953, Skorzeny managed to find posts for a lot of his old friends. The Grand Mufti of Jerusalem, spiritual leader for thousands of Muslims in Palestine, had worked for Schellenberg's counter-intelligence division of the SS. King Farouk of Egypt had collaborated enthusiastically with the Nazis during the war years. Skorzeny became the "chief military adviser" to General Mohammed Naguib of the new republic in Egypt, selected and groomed for that position by an "unholy alliance" of former Nazi spymaster and now head of the CIA's anti-Soviet effort in Europe, Reinhard Gehlen, and the CIA's own Allen Dulles. Skorzeny began the happy task of recruiting as many former SS officers as he could find to fill the ranks of what would become Egyptian strongman Nasser's secret police, including some four hundred SS men as a special operations group involved in the training of Palestinian commandos for attacks across the Gaza Strip.[9] Members of Field Marshall Rommel's Afrika Korps were also located and turned over to Nasser's command and, it is said, that some of these men were involved in the quiet liquidation of Jews in Egypt in the 1950s.[10] But, in addition to the rank-and-file SS criminals sponsored by the Skorzeny/Nasser/Dulles triumvirate, there were also the superstars.

These men included Adolf Eichmann, who sojourned in Egypt before moving on to Argentina; General Oskar Dirlewanger, the Butcher of Warsaw; Leopold Gleim, in charge of the SS in Poland; and, even more ominously, a gaggle of concentration camp medical men.

Dr. Hans Eisele was Buchenwald's medical officer, and he was recruited by Skorzeny together with Heinrich Willerman, his opposite number at Dachau. These men formed a core of specialists in interrogation and torture techniques, seconded to the Egyptian secret service.[11]

Thus, what is being revealed, slowly and painfully, is the degree to which psychological warfare, biological and chemical weapons, and mind-control experimentation have been exploited with reckless abandon throughout Africa, and with the connivance not only of renegade Nazis but also of British and American scientists and government experts from Porton Down and Fort Detrick . . . which implies, of course, the participation of both British and American intelligence agencies since these organizations are military bases operating under the tightest security measures in their respective countries. This CBW effort was not limited to Sid Gottlieb's aborted attempt to kill Congo leader Patrice Lumumba with a nasty virus in 1960.

The depth and degree of the homicidal intent reaches much further into our nightmares. The existence of these programs in African countries being targeted by American intelligence agencies, as well as courted by American right-wing Christian organizations led by men like Pat Robertson, gives us the opportunity to witness what such programs could do when they were being expanded outside American territory, far from the reach of Congress and a disinterested electorate. We can see what these programs were intended to do, as they developed, untrammeled, in the African bush. We can proceed behind the apologetic shrugs and embarrassed smiles of a Dick Helms or a Sid Gottlieb before Congressional investigators, and go right where the fruits of their labors were being harvested. How else to really understand what MK-ULTRA and all those acronyms were all about unless we see them in action? How else to visualize the true nature of the "fifty years of ideological conflict" mentioned by Scaife unless we watch some of the combatants, the same people who would conduct pious crusades against Clinton and the Democrats for real or imagined wrongs?

We might as well begin with South Africa, therefore, a favorite destination of Nazis on the run, as the regime was eager to import as many able-bodied white men as possible, men who were not afraid to get their hands dirty. Or bloody. We might as well begin with the revelations of biological and chemical weapons use, which have poured out of that country in the years since the end of apartheid. We might as well begin with Project Coast.

PROJECT COAST

> The image of white-coated scientists, professors, doctors, dentists, veterinarians, laboratories, universities and front companies, propping up apartheid with the support of an extensive international network, was a particularly cynical and chilling one.
>
> —*Final Report*, Truth and Reconciliation Commission, Volume Two, Chapter Six, "Special Investigation into Project Coast," 29 October 1998

In June and July of 1998, hearings were held in Cape Town, South Africa to determine the extent of chemical and biological warfare programs in that country when it was under apartheid rule. One does not automatically think of South

Africa when one discusses chemical and biological weapons, but during the era of apartheid and before Nelson Mandela was released from prison and became that country's first black president, the Republic of South Africa pursued a "weapons of mass destruction" campaign as serious as any other. In cooperation with foreign firms and agencies, the South African Defence Force (SADF) and its CBW project leader—Dr. Wouter Basson—developed an arsenal of poisons, both chemical and biological, for use against critics of the regime. The cabal in charge of this effort included the chief of staff of the defense force, the chief of staff of intelligence, and the surgeon general, as well as Dr. Basson. Thus, it was a program initiated and maintained at the highest levels of the South African military and intelligence organs and was not a rogue effort by lower-level staffers.

Ironically, the discovery of the true nature and scope of this program was made in virtually the same way investigator John Marks made his discovery of the MK-ULTRA documents: "The arrest of Dr. Basson and the seizure of four trunks containing documents related to Project Coast in January 1997 provided the Commission with proof that there was more to the programme than had initially met the eye" (*Final Report*, "Methodology"). Readers may recall that Marks' discovery of the MK-ULTRA documents was also based on four boxes of documents long thought destroyed, and, in fact, crucial evidence regarding Project Coast was likewise in the form of financial records . . .

This cornucopia led to a major reappraisal of South Africa's CBW program and revealed links to foreign assistance that would prove embarrassing; so embarrassing, in fact, that the Deputy Minister of Defence tried to pressure the Commission to hold its hearings *in camera* so that they would not "jeopardise international relations with countries which may have assisted the programme but with whom South Africa continues to have diplomatic relations" (*Final Report*, "Methodology"). This request was denied, and the hearings were held in open court.

The revelations were nothing short of sensational, in a perverse sort of way, e.g.,

> The discovery of a document which has become known as the 'Verkope lys' (sales list) and a list of SADF sponsored ('hard') projects conducted at Roodeplaat Research Laboratories provided the Commission with a clear indication that there was an intent to poison individuals, and that the front company, Roodeplaat Research Laboratories, was involved in the development of the toxins used for this purpose.

The toxins involved included "anthrax in cigarettes, botulinum in milk and paraoxon in whiskey—in the Commission's view clearly murder weapons."

Even more bizarre was the baboon fetus.

> The inclusion of a baboon foetus on the list, dated late July 1989 (just prior to such a foetus being found in the garden of Archbishop Tutu's house), as well as

> a reference to chemical and biological operatives, indicated that the items may well have found their way, directly or indirectly, into the hands of operatives of the Civil Co-operation Bureau (CCB).

The CCB, of course, was the Orwellian-nomenclatured South African secret police, responsible for assassinations in other African countries as well as within South Africa, and which maintained offices in Europe for monitoring anti-apartheid activities and conducting operations against those who opposed white rule in South Africa. The CCB has claimed responsibility for numerous murders in Africa, many of which were committed with toxins developed under Project Coast.

Another front company for Project Coast and Dr. Basson was Delta G Scientific, which was involved in the development of street drugs such as ecstasy and methaqualone. This was admittedly used for crowd control, but also for assassinations in which prisoners were injected with muscle relaxants . . . and then dropped from planes. In addition, Basson was sent to Croatia in 1991 during a negotiation to buy 500 kg of methaqualone from the Croatians (including "high-ranking government officials"), which was brought back to South Africa. This is the deal that eventually led to Basson's arrest when he was discovered holding $40 million worth of *Vatican* bearer bonds. His involvement in Project Coast gradually became revealed after his arrest (in Switzerland) and the discovery of the four trunks of documents in his possession.

But Croatia was not the only country on Basson's list. He also visited Taiwan to meet with CBW specialists there, as well as the United States, where—according to the Commission documents—the South African surgeon general met in 1981 with "Americans who were part of the United States CBW programme"; these Commission documents "demonstrate their willingness to assist the South Africans." As a reminder, this would have been during the Reagan administration and during the time of the United States' boycott of trade with South Africa.

By 1993, both the American and the British governments were concerned about the South African program and approached the South African government with these concerns. The Commission found this approach "unclear." According to Basson, the governments were afraid that the CBW program would fall into the hands of the African National Congress after the 1994 election. The ANC was viewed by most Western governments as a Marxist front or, certainly, unfriendly to Europe and America. Whether the approach was made at the level of the US State Department and the British Foreign Office, or whether it was an approach from nervous intelligence agencies who feared that documentation would reveal the true extent of their support for apartheid and the assassinations carried out in its name, is not known. A chemical-weapons attack on Mozambican forces in 1992 by South African troops came dangerously close to exposing the true extent of South Africa's CBW program, and it is possible that the Fort Detrick and Porton Down scientists rushed to cover up their involvement.

The trial of Dr. Basson is, at the time of this writing, still underway. He has been charged on numerous counts in connection with his Project Coast program, but the lack of direct evidence linking him specifically to murder and assassination may prove to be his salvation. Others were not so fortunate; members of the CCB are in prison in various countries under lengthy sentences for using the chemicals and toxins developed under Basson's aegis. Other former members have become mercenaries, or are running "executive security" organizations, providing bodyguards for executives and security forces for diamond mines, oil rigs, and other industrial concerns in Africa. We have not heard the last of this episode, nor of the CCB.

JEWELS FOR JESUS

In the 1980s Shaba emerged as a key strategic outpost for the Reagan Doctrine. Reportedly, the CIA used an airstrip in the remote Shaban town of Kamina in order to channel covert weapons into neighboring Angola. President Reagan hailed Mobutu as "a voice of good sense and good will."

. . . "Ethnic cleansing" was the term that Zaireans, diplomats, and aid workers used to explain the cramming of tens of thousands of hungry and destitute citizens into and around two fly-strewn railway stations in the mining towns of Likasi and Kolwezi. They were refugees in their own country . . . .

—Bill Berkeley, "Zaire: An African Horror Story," *The Atlantic Monthly*, August 1993

Into this morass of murder and methaqualone, Nazis and neurologists, comes one of the strangest white men ever to set foot on the Dark Continent. Less than a year after the above lines appeared, *Time* magazine would print a story that—taken in this context—is nothing less than shocking.

When I began writing this book—more than twenty years ago—I considered writing it as a novel, since I was certain that no one would believe it as non-fiction. That was before revelations about Pat Robertson's business dealings with President Mobutu and his cynical manipulation of relief efforts in Zaire made the newsweeklies in the 1990s. Now, I am presented with an embarrassment of riches. Truly, this is the stuff of fiction. Imagine Joseph Conrad-meets-Thomas Pynchon. Or Paul Theroux-meets-Tom Robbins, All this, and against the backdrop of an African Holocaust and a campaign to destroy a sitting American president. The cinematic possibilities are endless, but this story will never make it onto the silver screen. Too many reputations would be ruined. Too many deaths avenged.

Pat Robertson, the creator of the Christian Broadcasting Network (CBN), the famous televangelist who once ran for the American presidency, is perhaps the most prominent spokesman for Fundamentalist Christianity in the United States. His *700 Club*—with its Bible-oriented spin on world events—is watched by millions nationwide. As the "ideological forces" invoked by Richard Mellon Scaife began to polarize even more strongly in the 1980s and '90s, it began to appear as if the Fundamentalist Christian Right was hijacking the moral high-ground, even as it was making its bed with conservative Republicanism.

Soon, it would be difficult to find a Democrat in a Fundamentalist Christian congregation. Democrats, after all, supported a woman's right to choose in the case of an unwanted pregnancy; Republicans were grudgingly supporting the Right to Life movement of the anti-abortionists. That alone was enough of a religious rallying point, enough to polarize a nation into those who supported abortion as an alternative to an unwanted pregnancy and those that preached that abortion was murder.

Democrats also numbered many ethnic minorities among their constituencies who professed Roman Catholicism—the Irish, the Italians, the growing numbers of Latin Americans—as well as Buddhism, Taoism, Confucianism, Hinduism, etc. Republicans, on the other hand, traditionally attracted their numbers from high-church Anglicans and other so-called WASPs (White Anglo-Saxon Protestants). That strategy was fine when neither women nor minorities nor teenagers had the vote. With the change in American demographics, however, it behooved the Republican Party to find a power base that was large in terms of numbers and not just assets. The Supreme Court decision in Roe v Wade provided an excellent opportunity to drive a wedge between the Democratic Party—the party of the "people," after all—and white American Protestants who were beginning to feel disenfranchised by affirmative action, New Age mysticism, homosexual rights, crime in the streets, and bilingual education: i.e., the whole celebration of the "Other."

Further, with the waning of the Cold War in the advent of *perestroika* and *glasnost* and the eventual collapse of Soviet-style Communism, the Republicans needed another agenda. Another enemy. It was time to consolidate their winnings and take the show on the road. Waving Bibles and shouting, "In God We Trust," the post–Cold War bandwagon was just starting out of the gate when President George H.W. Bush was defeated in his run for a second term in office by the youthful, draft-dodging, womanizing Governor of Arkansas, Bill Clinton.

Governor Clinton did not come from old money. In fact, he didn't come from money at all. As the years of the Whitewater investigation demonstrated, the Clintons couldn't even successfully make money in real estate, not even illegally. They were not members of the Old Boy's Network of oil, manufacturing, or banking. They didn't understand what was at stake. They didn't understand how the game was supposed to be played. They were the poor relations, outside the Club, who should only be allowed to stare into the windows at the old men sitting in the cracked leather chairs and smoking Havanas while reading the *Journal*. Clinton hadn't even been in the military, for goodness' sake. How were you supposed to deal with someone like that?

This is not to suggest that Clinton was a saint, or that he was blameless in his pursuit of politics and the politician's dream job, the White House. Becoming an American president virtually guarantees a resume of dirty deals, backdoor negotiations, and accommodations with the less-than-savory. The spiritual state of politicians is one of cynicism and choosing the lesser of two (or more) evils. Yet, the accommodations made by the Clintons in their ascension towards the White House were like those of every politician in the country; they did not include guns-for-hostages, drugs-for-guns, Nazis-in-hiding, and all the other machinery of despair. There was no background of deals with oil-rich sheikhs, negotiations with mobsters, or "missing time" during the Kennedy assassination.

Hillary Clinton, the successful lawyer from Chicago suburbs, had no skeletons in her closet, try as they might to find some. (The best the Right could do was to promote a rumor of lesbianism! Another sexual angle. And even then, it was dropped for lack of any kind of evidence at all.) And as for Bill, there were only rumors of women, women, and more women. It was all they had on him, and even then it wasn't much. But sex seemed like the way to go; it was consistent with the strategy of the conservative Right to attack the Democrats in general—and Clinton in particular—on moral grounds. The sex issue seemed like a natural partner of the abortion issue, after all, and isn't the depth of feeling on the part of some anti-abortionists related to the idea that these unwanted fetuses are the product of frenzied, unlicensed sexual activity? Every sexual act, according to the most conservative element of the Christian Right, must be for the sole purpose of procreation. Therefore the existence of an unwanted fetus is—in the terms of this debate—an oxymoron. Every fetus is the result of a sex act, and every sex act must be for the purpose of making a fetus. Q.E.D. (The ancillary doctrine is, of course, that homosexuality, masturbation, anal sex, and oral sex are also forbidden according to this rubric.)

The ferocity of the conservatives' attack against Clinton was remarkable for its lack of attack of political substance; it seemed as if, early on, they had decided that a sexually-loaded campaign against Clinton would rally the Christian Right around their cause in sufficient numbers to have the President impeached. Sex, after all, is the great unspoken issue in American politics. Sex is used to sell a political candidate, and to dethrone him. We have no trouble imagining Democratic politicians having sex—the Kennedys in all their glory, Bill Clinton, even nervous Jimmy Carter had "adultery in his heart"—but the mere suggestion of a Richard Nixon or a Ronald Reagan or a George Bush having sex is likely to elicit either groans of horror or gales of laughter. The Grand Old Party does not produce party animals. Or so it did seem, until George W. Bush became president, and his documented background of drunk driving became a non-issue, as was the drinking and carousing (and arrest) of his underage daughters.

If we were to consult Foucault once again—as we did in *Unholy Alliance*—we would wonder if the dichotomy between Democrats and Republicans in general was that of sex versus blood, respectively, since the crimes of which the Democrats are accused are those of sexuality and its side-effects (love affairs, abortions, women scorned), and those of the Republicans are of blood (war, murder, and assassination). Love and death.

All of this is just a setting for what comes next; providing a spiritual or at least theological context for the spectacle of a cabal of conservative, right-wing industrialists and religious leaders waging war against an American president as if their lives depended on it, spending untold millions of US dollars in the process.

Pat Robertson is not only a Christian minister with a congregation composed of television viewers who donate heavily to his cause. Robertson is also a businessman. There is nothing wrong with this, of course, and the argument could be made that if more ministers and priests were businesspeople, there would be less corruption in the churches and clergymen would be more understanding of the day-to-day stresses of dealing with jobs, employers, volatile markets, and the like. The concept of the "worker priest" was popular for a while in Europe in the years after World War II, although it gradually took on a Marxist tinge. Robertson, however, is no "worker priest." His business deals are routinely in the millions of dollars and involve the exploitation of the natural resources of developing nations, what used to be called "the Third World."

Investing heavily in Africa, Robertson created the African Development Corporation, or ADC. This was allegedly not connected in any way with his religious broadcasting operations, although it is hard to tell how these companies are financed. What is known for sure is that, in 1992, the ADC entered into negotiations with the Zairean government of President Mobutu for the development of the diamond trade in the southern mining town of Tshikapa, along with projects including logging in other areas of Zaire.

The idea, as touted by the Robertson organization, was that it had secured Mobutu's blessing to use some of the profits from these enterprises to boost humanitarian aid projects in Zaire. The fact that Mobutu had already plundered his country's economy, banking hundreds of millions—if not billions—of dollars in foreign accounts in Switzerland and Belgium, suggests the cynicism of this self-congratulation. It has been estimated that Mobutu could have single-handedly solved his country's economic and humanitarian problems with the funds he had salted away abroad while his countrymen's per capita annual income was something like $500, belying the necessity of a Robertson–Mobutu partnership.

Robertson, by no means a stupid man, must have known exactly what he was getting himself into by making deals with a long-term dictator as venal as Mobutu. Mobutu needed assistance in developing more of his country's natural resources, since the US French and Belgian governments were coming down hard on his human rights abuses—an about-face from the days of the Reagan-Bush administrations, which had unequivocally supported the dictator-and were putting the squeeze on his international financial deals. To Mobutu, Robertson was, well, a God-send; he represented not only new business potential, but also the quiet moral support of the Christian Right in America, which had just lost its election to the Democratic candidate, Bill Clinton. To Robertson, Mobutu was a friend of the United States, a stalwart foe of Communism, and a good business partner. It was a marriage made in hell.

Robertson initiated Operation Blessing as a tax-exempt humanitarian mission to help those less fortunate in Africa, buying three Caribou aircraft in the process, for the ostensible purpose of flying medical supplies and doctors to those areas of Zaire being flooded by refugees, both internal refugees as well as those from the growing Rwandan crisis across the border. The Caribou are designed for short-take-off and landing (STOL): Vietnam-era aircraft ideal for short runways in the jungle. Robertson went on the air in the United States extolling the virtues of his operation and showing how the poor Zaireans and Rwandans were being helped by the smiling Christian American efficiency of Operation Blessing.

Unfortunately for the poor Zaireans and Rwandans, Operation Blessing was largely a sham.

Pilots who had been employed by the organization revealed to newsmen that their job was not hauling medicine to Goma or the other regions where people were starving to death or dying from a host of treatable illnesses; rather, they were involved with moving mining and dredging equipment to Robertson's diamond mines. It got so bad that one of the pilots had "Operation Blessing" removed from the plane's tailfins. Out of forty flights that had been flown in Zaire for Operating Blessing, only one or two had actually had anything to do with humanitarian aid.

As the Rwandan crisis deepened in 1994, Robertson was on the air constantly trying to raise money for his humanitarian efforts to help the refugees. Where this money wound up is anyone's guess at this point. None of the pilots who have been contacted by investigators could come up with more than half-a-dozen humanitarian flights during the entire period Operation Blessing was in operation in Zaire, and even then the medical support was minimal. In a 1994 *Time* magazine article, alluded to above, one aid worker complained that the efforts of Operation Blessing in Goma—the town hardest hit by the Rwandan refugee crisis—were a joke: that they were heavy on transportation and light on aid; workers preferred to stand around and preach rather than get down and dirty with the dead and dying, and the organization pulled its people out after only short tours in the region.

Eventually, in 1995, Robertson pulled the plug on the African wing of Operation Blessing (possibly due to all the bad publicity), but continued with his business deals in other parts of Africa, such as in Liberia in support of President Charles Taylor, a man with a human rights abuse record at least as long as Mobutu's. Taylor's use of death squads, his support of mercenary groups who use Liberia as a staging area for attacks in other countries, and his involvement in arms trading made him a '90s equivalent to former Ugandan dictator Idi Amin; he had even been known to conduct torture and interrogation sessions in his own home, the Executive Mansion. Corruption was rife and unapologetic in Liberia, with Taylor and his cronies pocketing at least 20% of Liberia's annual budget, according to a 1998 US Department of State Country Report on Liberia.

In 1998 Robertson created a company called Freedom Gold for investment in Liberia. His focus remained roughly the same: the exploitation of Liberia's raw materials and natural resources—gold, diamonds, oil, lumber—with the expectation that profits would be plowed back into the Liberian economy for humanitarian efforts. Well, Liberia—like Zaire—certainly needs humanitarian aid, of that there can be no question. The problem arises when dictators, consumed with greed and the desire for personal wealth, make deals with Christian ministers-turned-businessmen. There is no earthly way that profits would have been reinvested in the poor of either Liberia or Zaire in any significant amount, when the leaders of those respective governments had control over the profits. It would have been naïve to think so. That Robertson himself would have been remunerated for his assistance to these regimes goes without saying; but that he would have been able to bring this money back to the people of Zaire or Liberia, untouched by the corrupt fingers of Mobutu or Taylor, was impossible. If nothing else, after the debacle in Zaire Robertson should have realized this (if, indeed, he was simple-minded enough not to know what was going on from the beginning). Why he would have turned around and gotten into bed with Taylor after the Zaire fiasco boggles the mind . . . unless he knew exactly what he was doing, and that it had nothing at all to do with humanitarian aid.

Moreover, there may have been another benefit to all of this for Robertson and his Christian ministry. Mobutu—who always waivered between African animism and Christianity—began to talk up the Christian message (even as he was murdering his opponents). Taylor became fanatically Christian, at least on paper, proclaiming his administration blessed by God and making it mandatory for his government ministers to attend prayer services on pain of losing their jobs . . . or worse. Yet, as late as December 2002, Taylor (and African diamonds) would be linked to the Al-Qaeda money-laundering system, and Liberia described as a safe haven provided for Al-Qaeda operatives after the September 11, 2001 attack on New York and Washington, D.C.[12] And so it goes.

Robertson also went on the record as supporting the regime of Frederick Chiluba of Zambia, another African country in dire need of real assistance. Chiluba, who declared his country a "Christian nation" in 1991, removed all vestiges of Muslim, Hindu and African native religions from the nation's school system, and approved a plan to have Christian fundamentalist ministers work with the police to identify and destroy anything they deemed obscene. This was in tandem with an anti-abortion and anti-pornography crusade, and the shutting down of radio stations and newspapers that did not toe the party line.

Another "Christian" ruler supported by Robertson on television and in his books is Jorge Serrano, the bizarre President of Guatemala who wanted to create a Pentecostal Christian government in Guatemala. The list goes on and on. Here is Robertson sitting down to dinner with notorious Salvadoran death-squad leader Roberto D'Aubuisson.[13] Here is Robertson raising two million dollars for

Guatemalan military dictator General Oscar Humberto Mejia Victores.[14] Here is Robertson being saluted by the Contras at their base camp in Honduras.[15] Here is Robertson once again in Guatemala, this time in support of death-squad leader and eventual president Rios Montt, a born-again Christian who suspended his country's constitution and proceeded to murder thousands of his fellow citizens.[16] The eagerness of Fundamentalist Christians in their support of vicious dictators simply because they pay lip service to Christianity is baffling.

Perhaps it all goes back to Martin Luther, the Father of the Protestant Reformation and the church that bears his name, who declared the Epistle in which James claims, "Faith without good works is dead" (James 2:26) to be an "Epistle of straw." If it is enough simply to believe, and not to act in accordance with those beliefs, then there is no moral imperative to leading a Christian life. One simply "takes the pledge," and then does what one likes. I don't believe Robertson seriously entertains this viewpoint, but it does seem he entertains a double standard. Even as he was supporting a range of sadistic political leaders in Latin America, Africa and elsewhere—men with the blood of thousands if not millions on their hands—he was simultaneously on the attack against the President of the United States.

The story of Iran-Contra as is generally known to most Americans omits one important aspect. Although the trail of deceit and treachery—especially against the US Congress and in violation of the Borland Amendment which forbade the government from giving military aid to the Nicaraguan rebels—stretched as far as North, Secord, McFarlane and others sworn to defend the Constitution, and whose names became household words (and in some cases, heros) to Americans in the 1980s, the breadth of "private funding" of the Contra rebellion has never been deeply explored. The fact that the Christian Right raised millions of dollars in aid to the Contras has been "backburnered" in most histories of the affair. Indeed, Pat Robertson's Christian Broadcasting Network was only one source of aid and support to the Contras; in addition, we find the Unification Church of Rev. Sun Myung Moon as well as the Knights of Malta fraternal society involved in fund-raising and other efforts on behalf of the rebels.

The Knights of Malta participation is interesting because, at the time, its head was J. Peter Grace, an old friend of Pat Robertson and the godfather to his children. It was Grace who famously hired a Nazi scientist, Otto Ambrose, to work for the W. R. Grace Corporation even though his past as a chemist and director of I.G. Farben during the war was well-documented. Grace seems to be another of those monied Americans who feel an investment in fascism is always good for business, and who support (sometimes secretly, sometimes openly) all manner of right-wing dictators and death-squad capos in the defense of Christianity, democracy, and white supremacy.

As for Reverend Moon and his Unification Church, this convicted felon (for tax evasion) has supported the extreme right in America for decades. The Unification Church itself fronts for the Korean Central Intelligence Agency, and when the author himself was approached by the Church in the 1970s they owned—in addition to a network of churches with a sophisticated marketing campaign aimed at scientists and other intellectuals—a rifle factory in Korea. Reverend Moon himself believes that Jesus will return to earth as a Korean, and he has let it be known that he believes this Second Coming involves his own person. Incredibly, with all of this clearly heretical belief openly promulgated, Christian ministers such as Pat Robertson have no problem at all in sharing a podium with Moon and enjoying the international reach of the Unification Church.

The main organizer of the private funding endeavor was Major General John Singlaub (retired), who came to brief prominence during the Iran-Contra investigation. Singlaub, a decorated Army veteran who had worked closely with the CIA over the years, took control of the World Anti-Communist League (WACL) in 1984. Although mention was made of the WACL during the Iran-Contra hearings, one did not hear of the constituent religious groups that provided important sources of revenue for the anti-Communist and specifically anti-Sandinista campaign.

The WACL is a notorious hotbed of Nazis, pro-Nazis, and neo-Nazis from every continent. The number of groups involved in the WACL is almost embarrassing in its composition of ethnic organizations devoted not only to the destruction of Communism, but to the advancement of a neo-fascist agenda. Singlaub was able to find support from the governments of Taiwan and South Korea, as well as from Saudi Arabia, in his globe-trotting mission: support that went to the Contras in their efforts to overthrow the Nicaraguan government.

President Reagan's support for both Singlaub and the WACL is also well-documented.[17] For instance, it was Reagan who, in 1983, told Yaroslav Stetsko, former Nazi premier of Ukraine during the War, "Your struggle is our struggle. Your dream is our dream."[18] At the time, Stetsko was a leader of the secretive Organization of Ukrainian Nationalists-Bandera (OUN-B), which collaborated extensively with the Nazis in their invasion of the Ukraine, and in 1983 was representing the Ukrainian Congress Committee of America (UCCA), part of the bewildering matrix of acronyms and ethnic subgroups that are the legs and arms of the WACL.

Diamonds and uranium. Christianity and Paganism. Black versus White. Capitalism versus Communism. While the Cold War was being fought famously in the streets of Vienna and Berlin, Moscow and New York, Hong Kong and Singapore, it was also being fought more savagely in Latin America and Central Africa and could hardly have been called a "Cold War," when all the heat of battle and bloodshed fueled the fantasies of the armchair warriors in Washington and London. It was, after all, to the Congo that Sidney Gottlieb brought his vial of death for use against a man who Washington decided would not be cooperative. That was Lumumba's death sentence: he was an inconvenient man, like Frank Olson and so many others on the CIA's "hit parade."

As the Cold War wound down, however, and enemies abroad became harder to find, Americans could take their time and identify enemies at home. The defeat of Communism was seen by many to be a victory for Christianity, at least for the homegrown Fundamentalist form of Christianity. It was now time to weed out the opposition.

AMERICAN SWASTIKA

> If Christian people work together, they can succeed during this decade in winning back control of the institutions that have been taken from them over the past 70 years. Expect confrontations that will be not only unpleasant but at times physically bloody . . .
>
> —Pat Robertson, "Pat Robertson's Perspective," Oct/Nov 1992

> Although civil religion has been degraded in this manner in domestic politics, the dangers of extremist versions have been most visible in American interactions with the rest of the world . . . . Some critics have argued that this sense of mission coupled with a tendency to view international politics as a clash of moral opposites, has undermined the development of an effective foreign policy.
>
> —Kenneth Wald[19]

Not to be outdone, even by financial backer and moral supporter Richard Mellon Scaife, Robertson identified a struggle lasting *seventy* years rather than Scaife's mere fifty. Seventy years from 1992 gives us 1922, the era of post–World War I euphoria in America, the Roaring Twenties, and—of course—the League of Nations, forerunner of that right-wing boogey-man, the United Nations. In less than a decade, the stock markets of the world would collapse, and a president was elected who would remain in power for more than twelve years, a Democrat whose New Deal frightened the hell out of the Republicans: Franklin Delano Roosevelt.

It was Roosevelt who had wanted to go to war against the Nazis, but was virtually forbidden to do so by all the politicos around him, until that fateful day when Germany declared war on the US in the immediate aftermath of Japan's attack on Pearl Harbor. America, just starting to recover from nearly ten years of the Great Depression, had not wanted a foreign adventure and could not be convinced that a war against Germany held any margin for them. Many of the men around the President—and many others who held positions of power in America—were sympathetic to the Nazis. Henry Ford is perhaps the best and most famous example of an American who actually donated funds to Hitler from the earliest days of the Nazi Party, and who received the Third Reich's highest honor for a non-German, sharing that dubious distinction with none other than Benito Mussolini.

But another Republican whose support of the Third Reich nearly cost him his livelihood was Senator Prescott Bush. Yes, gentle Readers, the father of 41st President George H.W. Bush (former Vice President under Ronald Reagan, former

CIA Director, former-Ambassador to China) and, of course, the grandfather of George W. Bush, the 43rd President of the United States.

Prescott Bush was an active Nazi supporter, whose company—Union Banking, a subsidiary of W. A. Harriman & Company—had its assets seized by the US Government in 1942 under the Trading with the Enemy Act. This was done by US Government Vesting Order No. 248, for those who think I am making this up. The gist of the government's case was that, for many years, Prescott Bush and George Walker (his father-in-law) had been actively raising money to support the fledgling Nazi Party, laundering the funds through Harriman and its subsidiary Union Banking. According to Loftus and Aarons in their *Secret War Against the Jews*, George Herbert Walker was "one of Hitler's most powerful supporters in the United States," and was under Congressional investigation as early as 1934, when it was believed that Walker's Hamburg-Amerika Line "subsidized a wide range of pro-Nazi propaganda efforts both in Germany and the United States."

Both in Germany. And the United States.

Of course, by 1942 when the US Government seized the assets of Union Banking, America was already at war with Germany. The Bush family support of the Third Reich, however, began when the Party was barely functioning. Although Hitler enjoyed financial support from German institutions such as manufacturing giant Thyssen, AEG, Siemens, I.G. Farben and other household names, there was also extensive financial backing from wealthy and prestigious American companies and individuals. We do know of Henry Ford's backing,[20] and now of the Bush and Walker families' support.

Could Hitler have become as powerful as he did *without* American financial support? That question is almost impossible to answer now, more than seventy years after the fact. What is certain, however, is that the enthusiastic support of Hitler by Ford, Bush and Walker entails a deep moral responsibility for what happened, for the ravaging of Europe under the swastika and for the deaths of millions of people in the Holocaust, as well as nearly twenty million Russian citizens and countless millions more throughout the European theater.

We cannot, of course, hold former President Bush responsible for the sins of his father; nor can we hold his son responsible. Yet, we can expect a higher degree of moral responsibility in their actions as men and as political leaders. We can expect them to repudiate the Nazi sympathies of their forebear, if not in word, ten at least in deed. Unfortunately, as we saw, in the 1988 Presidential campaign, George H.W. Bush was happy to accept support from a range of Nazis and Nazi-sympathizers in his quest for the White House, and was just as happy to keep them on in the administration even after they had been identified as such.

Aarons and Loftus present a case that this was anti-Semitism, pure and simple; and, to a certain degree, anti-Semitism in the pursuit of Middle Eastern oil. I tend to take a different view. Anti-Semitism was certainly part of the story of why these companies and individuals supported Hitler and continued to support Nazism even after the end of the war. Money (and oil) is certainly another, very powerful, motive. Yet, I believe that the entire racial theory of Nazism was a comfortable environment for these men. They were, after all, from privileged backgrounds: old money, power, prestige, the right companies, the right schools, the right fraternities (such as the infamous Skull & Bones at Yale, to which generations of the Bush family belonged). The Nazis embodied the secret dreams and unspoken loyalties of these men, the public acknowledgment of all that the American elite held dear.

Racial (or ethnic, or familial) superiority meant that they did not have to be particularly smart, particularly accomplished in their own right, but could rely upon the mere fact of their bloodlines to ensure the continued power of themselves and their families from generation to generation. After all, America is not a monarchy, yet there burns in the secret heart of almost every American politician and businessman a desire for royal prestige, for the trappings of nobility, for the accumulation of knighthoods and noble degrees. Skin was the uniform these men wore; the right color identified you as a friend rather than a foe. Family name was the battalion to which you belonged and owed allegiance: Bush, Walker, Mellon, Scaife, Morgan, DuPont, etc. Jews were not allowed, of course, but neither were blacks, Asians, Hispanics, etc. Eugenics was the new "science" of population control, which was a code word for genocide and "ethnic cleansing," and the Bush–Walker team provided logistical support for the Third International Congress of Eugenics that was held in New York on August 21–23, 1932, at the American Museum of Natural History, ensuring that Nazi eugenicists were present at the Congress by providing free passage aboard their shipping line, Hamburg-Amerika.

The flyer advertising this Congress is revealing. It shows a tree with a large root system. Each root is labeled with one of the sciences: anthropology, archaeology, etc. The slogans say, "Eugenics is the self-direction of evolution," and, "Like a tree, Eugenics draws its materials from many sources and organizes them into an harmonious entity." Among those sources, depicted as a root off to the right side of the drawing, is one labeled "religion." Another is "politics," and still others include "fecundity," "mate selection," "race crossing" and "eugenic forces" (whatever they are). Thus, the "science" of eugenics was seen as means of organizing the whole of human endeavor, while weeding out those who do not fit the paradigm.

But what are we to make of "religion" in this context? As heinous as we have come to see eugenics as a whole—as it was the science proclaimed by the Third Reich as an excuse (or a reason) for eliminating the mentally-ill, the physically-infirm, and eventually the Gypsies, the Jews, the Slavs, etc.—we have to wonder what the American organizers understood the role of religion to be. In America, eugenics was a code-word for the subjugation, sterilization and eventual elimination of the black race. In Germany, of course, it referred to the Jews as well as Gypsies, homosexuals, Communists, and whoever else was on Himmler's enemies list at the time.

Whatever the core beliefs of the Congress, it was enthusiastically supported by some of the most prominent industrialists and people of "old money" in the

United States, and support was extended to their like-minded brethren across the seas in Germany. In 1932, Hitler was on the verge of taking power in Germany and eugenics was one of the Nazi Party's platforms, a kind of pseudo-scientific imprimatur for race hatred and the Final Solution. American financiers—such as W.A. Harriman and George Herbet Walker, founding members of Union Banking—were sending bags of money to Hitler to prop up his shaky political position, or successfully laundering that money through American and European banks. It is clear that some of the most important businessmen in America felt they had a vested interest in promoting the Nazi Party, and through their support of ancillary programs such as the Eugenics Congress, we can begin to put together a more complete picture of this interest: America for white people, Europe for the Nazis, forming a broad alliance of power stretching over both sides of the Atlantic and ensuring the enslavement of millions upon millions of people who were not members of the club. In America, it was nothing less than a repudiation of everything the Statue of Liberty stands for.

Fast forward to 1992.

> There is a religious war going on for the soul of America.
> —Pat Buchanan, May 1992[21]

We have seen how the son of Prescott Bush, George H.W. Bush, carried on his father's support for fascism by hiring numerous pro-Nazis, ex-Nazis and Holocaust-revisionists and by courting ethnic organizations that were run by former Nazis. We have witnessed Richard Nixon's support for specific Nazis, such as Trifa and Malaxa, in a pattern that goes back to the days of Allen Dulles and the early post-War years when the two men collaborated on hiding the smoking gun of government documentation that would have shown the Dulles brothers' involvement with Nazi war criminals and Nazi fund-raising. We watched Ronald Reagan place a wreath at the SS cemetery at Bitberg. And now, we are forced to witness another gathering of the Klans in their desperate effort to dispatch the Democratic Party's presidential candidate Bill Clinton.

The old money in the 1990s was represented by one of the wealthiest dynasties in the United States: the Mellon family. Mellons can be found sprinkled throughout the American experience over the last century. Heirs of a fortune built by a Pittsburgh industrialist, they were at one time considered *the* richest family in the United States. Although their money was not quite as "old" as that of the Astors, they traveled in much the same circles. We will find Mellons present at the birth of Timothy Leary's LSD crusade; we will find them involved in the Profumo affair in England in 1962; we will find them involved in the skullduggery around Resorts International in the Bahamas, along with Richard Nixon and Bebe Rebozo; we will find them once again financing a vociferous campaign of print and broadcast media to unseat Bill Clinton.

WILD BILL HITCHCOCK

Why Hitchcock decided to throw his weight behind the psychedelic cause is still something of a mystery. Was he simply a millionaire acid buff, a wayward son of the ruling class who dug Leary's trip? Or did he have something up his sleeve?

—*Acid Dreams*[22]

One of the principal witnesses against [LSD chemist Nicholas] Sand and two co-defendants was William Mellon Hitchcock, an heir to the U.S. Steel fortune, who testified under immunity and acknowledged that he had bankrolled the operation.

—*San Francisco Examiner*, "Fugitive to face LSD charges," June 6, 1998

The Legal Attache, London, forwarded copies of memoranda prepared by Alfred Wells, Secretary to Ambassador Bruce, concerning various persons involved in the instant case. In a memorandum dated 11/6/62 Wells stated that he had attended a dinner the night before at which he had met Dr. Stephen Ward and that Ward had made loud statements that he had been the principal liaison between the Soviets and the British Government during the Cuban crisis . . . . By memorandum 6/18/63 Mr. Wells stated he had been to a luncheon on 2/13/63 with Thomas Corbally, Dr. Ward, Mrs. Robin Dalton, an Australian woman, and William Hitchcock.

—FBI Memorandum 65-68218, from W. A. Branigan to W. C. Sullivan, dated 7/1/63, "Re: Christine Keeler; John Profumo"

William Mellon Hitchcock was no stranger to that rareified atmosphere where American politics and American money mingle in a fuzzy miasma of intelligence agents, crooked financiers, and secret agendas. He was one of the heirs to the Mellon fortune and to Gulf Oil (founded by his grandfather William Larimer Hitchcock) and nephew of Andrew Mellon (a Secretary of the Treasury for three Republican Presidents from 1921–32). He and his sister Peggy were close to both Timothy Leary (and Australian film producer Robin Dalton) on the one hand, and to people like Stephen Ward, Thomas Corbally, and the American Ambassador to England on the other.

The latter was natural, since David Bruce—the US Ambassador to the Court of St. James during the Profumo affair—was his uncle. A former and important member of the OSS during World War II, Colonel Bruce landed at Normandy with the head of the OSS: General "Wild Bill" Donovan. A roommate of Billy Hitchcock's father at university, Bruce had married (and later divorced) a Mellon. During the War, David Bruce's OSS network operated behind enemy lines in France, disrupting the German Army; at one point, Bruce had hundreds of French agents under his command.

Bruce would later go on to even greater glory, not only as US Ambassador to England, but also to France and Germany. He would also be involved, with Henry

Kissinger, in the Paris Peace Talks during the Vietnam Era. Bruce's connections in Europe during the War included high-ranking Italian Masons who held influential posts within Mussolini's government.[23] We also discover that OSS staffer and future CIA Counterintelligence Chief James Jesus Angleton was working in Italy at this very time with his father, Hugh Angleton, cultivating close relationships with Masons working within the Fascist Mussolini government to advance a somewhat different agenda.[24]

Thus do we begin to realize that the word "conspiracy" does not do justice to what is, after all, merely a group of people from similar backgrounds with similar goals, all working to a common purpose which is hidden from the world at large by virtue of a Great Wall of wealth, prestige, culture and power. We begin to see that what the rest of us call conspiracy is just business-as-usual for the people that operate above, behind and below what we know as consensus history, consensus reality. I believe that the word "conspiracy" is over-used and emotionally-loaded in this context. Let us instead, and rightly, use the word "cabal" to denote this gathering of sinister forces.

There were other Mellons on board at OSS: Paul Mellon (Treasury Secretary Andrew Mellon's son) served with the OSS Special Operations Branch in London, moving on to become commander of the Morale Operations Branch, based in Luxembourg. According to Richard Harris Smith, "Other Mellons and Mellon in-laws held espionage posts in Madrid, Geneva and Paris."[25] Further, as reported in *Acid Dreams*, "After the war, certain influential members of the Mellon family maintained close ties with the CIA. The Mellon family foundations have been used repeatedly as conduits for Agency funds. Furthermore, Richard Helms was a frequent weekend guest of the Mellon patriarchs in Pittsburgh during his tenure as CIA director (1966–1973)." In addition to the Mellons, members of the Morgan, Vanderbilt, and DuPont families were very active in the OSS making it essentially a "rich man's club." David Bruce himself was the son of a US Senator and a millionaire even before his marriage to Ailsa Mellon.

Thus, William Mellon Hitchcock's presence at dinner in London in 1962 with Thomas Corbally and Stephen Ward is highly suggestive of an intelligence angle. At the time of the Profumo affair, Hitchcock was flying back and forth between New York and London: in London, to hang out with Ward and Corbally (the latter will become important a bit later on), and in New York to hang out with Timothy Leary, who had just returned from an aborted LSD-commune experiment in Mexico and was looking for another site. He found one at Hitchcock's Dutchess County, New York, estate: Millbrook.

Hitchcock's involvement with all of these people—and many more besides—has always been suspicious. Even those around Timothy Leary—full of peace and love and lysergic acid—were sometimes, well, leery of Hitchcock. Hitchcock did not live at the Millbrook mansion with Leary and his other guests, but instead stayed at a much smaller cottage elsewhere on the grounds, where he conducted business (he has been described as a stockbroker) and had his own guests over. He was never fully part of the acid scene, except for the trips he took with Leary and company at Millbrook, and kept mostly to himself, not sharing in the mysticism and deep philosophical musings of the Leary operation.

As it turns out, Hitchcock had so many ties to the intelligence community—mostly through banking circles and money-laundering operations—that it raises one's paranoia level to a new . . . high. As described in *The Nine*, LSD was introduced to the American public through the CIA, which wanted to test its effectiveness for everything from mind control to crowd control. We then discover Hitchcock's involvement with the CIA and CIA-front organizations, such as Castle Bank and Resorts International. We also see Hitchcock turning state's evidence against his old LSD chemist, Nicholas Sand, even though Hitchcock himself admitted he had financed Sand's operation for the manufacture and distribution of millions of hits of LSD.

Probably the most accessible history of this period is the book *Acid Dreams, the Complete Social History of LSD: The CIA, the Sixties, and Beyond* by Martin A. Lee and Bruce Shlain, which was originally published in 1985. In those pages, we read of the strange development of Harvard professor Timothy Leary. We read of his salad days as a clinical psychologist at the Kaiser Foundation Hospital in Oakland, California (the same hospital where Andrija Puharich got his start) in the period 1954–59, where he developed a personality test ("the Leary") which was used by the CIA human resources people to screen potential employees.[26] We learn of his growing awareness of the field of psychedelics during a vacation in Mexico in 1960, where he was urged by a friend to try hallucinogenic mushrooms (psilocybin) in Cuernavaca. He returned to Harvard—where by now he had a professorship—filled with the experience, and related it all to Dr. Harry Murray, with whom he developed a psilocybin research project. This was the same Murray who had been involved with the creation of personality tests for the OSS during World War II. (As we see, the field of early psychedelic research in the United States was heavily influenced by men who had more than a passing relationship with intelligence matters.)

By the time he met—first Peggy, and then—Billy Hitchcock three years later, Leary was well on the way to becoming an acid guru, having abandoned psilocybin for the more attractive pharmaceutical developed by the Sandoz laboratories in Switzerland, lysergic acid diethylamide, or LSD-25. Peggy Hitchcock was a New York City socialite with tremendous energy and an interest in everything. She introduced brother Billy to Timothy Leary, and it was the beginning of a fateful friendship.

Aside from renting his vast Millbrook estate to Leary's acid organization for a mere five hundred dollars a month, he wound up subsidizing various drug operations and secret laboratories (including that of convicted acid chemist Nicholas Sand), for which he would eventually come to the attention of US Customs and other government authorities, although he would not spend any time in prison. This is not surprising in view of the fact that he walked with the gods.

One of Billy Hitchcock's earliest recorded introductions to the world of intelligence was his presence at that fateful lunch with Dr. Stephen Ward (who would be convicted, unfairly, of living off the earnings of women in the nasty Profumo Affair, which threatened to pull down the British government if not also an American president) and Thomas Corbally. Corbally, a mysterious and elusive businessman who seems to live only in hotels on either side of the Atlantic, reported this lunch to the US Ambassador, David Bruce, Billy Hitchcock's uncle by marriage. There were important intelligence ramifications to what was eventually reported to the FBI by the State Department, including the fact that Stephen Ward had been a go-between during the Cuban missile crisis of 1962, carrying messages back and forth between the British and the Soviets. This was not empty bragging, although it would have been better had Ward kept his mouth shut; it was his loose lip that sealed his doom, for once his reputation had been ruined by the Christine Keeler prostitution scandal, he would not be believed on anything having to do with such lofty matters as intelligence activities relating to the one incident in the twentieth century that had, without question, brought us to the brink of nuclear holocaust.

Rumors had it that Dr. Ward was involved in occultism, and some have tried to link him (without documentation so far) to the Golden Dawn or to one of its offshoots in Great Britain. That he was involved in orgies that were attended by the rich and famous is beyond all doubt, however, and some of these gatherings may have been ritualistic in nature. He was evidently very interested in occultism and "black magic."[27]

Yet, the intimate lunch attended by Ward, Hitchcock, Corbally and Robin Dalton leads us to wonder what could have brought these four people together, for of that group at least three had intelligence connections: Ward, Hitchcock, and Corbally. Ward would commit suicide directly after his guilty verdict was returned. Corbally, according to his own account, was sniffing around Ward either at the behest of the CIA or of Ambassador Bruce (depending on which story one believes), even though he considered Ward a personal friend, one who had once treated him for a knee injury.[28]

When David Bruce did not report back to the United States on this vitally important information, FBI Director J. Edgar Hoover became suspicious that Bruce himself was involved in some kind of international vice ring.[29] Hoover suspected—as did others in the American intelligence community—that one of Christine Keeler's clients may have been John F. Kennedy himself. Hoover, whose distrust and dislike of the Kennedys ran deep, spun a nightmare scenario in which Keeler—bedmate of a Russian military attache in London—was sleeping with the American president, and exchanging one kind of pillowtalk for another.

Hoover had reason to be nervous. A sex ring that had operated in New York City until 1961 (barely a year before the Profumo scandal was exposed)—and to which it was believed Keeler and some of her colleagues belonged at various times—was staffed by at least one Chinese woman of foreign birth and assorted other foreign nationals. When the police raided the operation, the ringleader—one Alan Towers—fled to a safe haven behind the Iron Curtain. One of his "employees," the prostitute Maria Novotny, reportedly told police that Alan Towers was a Soviet agent and was running an international sex ring for the purpose of entrapping prominent politicians and businessmen.

In spy parlance, this is known as a "honey trap," and today many suspect that Ward was doing the same thing with Christine Keeler, Mandy Rice-Davies, and the other women associated with Keeler (including, it is said, Mary Anne de Grimston of the Process Church of the Final Judgment) . . . but not for Soviet intelligence. Instead, it is believed that Ward was working for British intelligence in an attempt to entrap such Soviet targets as Yevgeny Ivanov, the GRU (Russian military intelligence) *rezident* whose name turned up in the Profumo affair as one of Keeler's lovers, causing the scandal that rocked the British government. Thus, Keeler was simultaneously sleeping with both John Profumo—the British Minister of War—and Ivanov, the Soviet military intelligence officer assigned to Great Britain. And this, during the time of the Cuban missile crisis! If President Kennedy was also sleeping with Keeler or with one of her associates (as Hoover feared might be the case), Christine Keeler might potentially be considered one of the most important women in the history of the twentieth century.

As it was, Profumo resigned (after at first denying then admitting that he had slept with Ms. Keeler) and Ivanov was sent back to Russia. Ward, unable to deal with the scandal and embittered with the way his friends all abandoned him in his hour of need, committed suicide. (The cottage where he lived on the Astor estate of Cliveden was subjected to the ministrations of an exorcist, giving rise to more theories of Ward's occult involvement). Ms. Keeler herself survived the episode and was interviewed a few years ago in the American and British press after the release of a film about the affair entitled, naturally, *Scandal*. The former prize-fighter (and fiancé of Process Church co-founder Mary Anne de Grimston) Sugar Ray Robinson had wanted to produce a film on the Profumo affair with Keeler playing herself, but nothing had come of the project. Thomas Corbally and William Hitchcock also survived, and each went on to greater glory (or infamy): Corbally to a disastrous relationship with Connecticut conman Marty Frankel, and Hitchcock to a disastrous relationship with LSD chemist Nicholas Sand. The British government prepared an official report on the Profumo Affair known as the Lord Denning Inquiry, which, in its essential whitewash of the episode and its focus on Keeler and Ward, was likely the inspiration for another such government inquiry a year later: the Warren Report.

Why did US Ambassador David Bruce not report the details of the Ward scenario to his putative masters in the United States? What was the role of his wealthy in-law, William Mellon Hitchcock, in the affair? Was Thomas Corbally actually working for Bruce (*via* Billy Hitchcock?) when he began spying on Dr. Ward? What was Corbally—at the time over fifty years old—doing hanging out in London with William Hitchcock, who was at that time only in his twenties? The suave, urbane international businessman Corbally with a hip, young stockbroker like Hitchcock? One imagines that money would be a passion they shared; another might be intrigue. Almost immediately after the Profumo affair, Hitchcock is back Stateside, being introduced to Tim Leary by his sister Peggy, and virtually donating his family's ancestral home to Leary and his gaggle of acid heads.

This might seem like just a bit of youthful folly—thumbing one's nose at the Establishment, as some have put it—if not for the fact that Hitchcock did not drop his "straight" life and become a drug-entranced hippy. He lived apart from Leary and his commune—eventually renamed Castalia in honor of the Hesse novel *The Glass Bead Game*, in which Castalia represents an institute of pure intellectualism—and remained very much in charge of his business interests . . . and, when the chips were down, turned state's evidence against the drug dealers he himself employed. One is tempted to believe that Thomas Corbally was a guest of Hitchcock's at his own, rather more modest, cottage at Millbrook, kept safely away from Leary, Richard Alpert, Ralph Metzner, Gunther Weil and visitors such as R.D. Laing, Andrija Puharich, and Maynard Ferguson. Leary's spiritual mentor, Aldous Huxley—whom he met in the early 1960s when he was still a clean-cut university professor—had already died on November 22, 1963 (!!), while tripping on LSD to ease his way to the Other Side.

One is tempted to believe that some of the LSD-25 churned out by Nicholas Sand and others working for Wild Bill Hitchcock wound up supporting an intelligence agenda. No matter; eventually the Millbrook commune was raided—and Timothy Leary arrested—by none other than future Watergate Plumber G. Gordon Liddy. Liddy and Leary would eventually go on the lecture circuit years later, Liddy representing the conservative, law-and-order viewpoint, with Leary as an amiable but unfocused foil for Liddy's sarcasm. (Both, of course, were convicted felons who had served prison time for their separate offences.) Needless to say, it was not a marriage made in heaven, and the road show did not last; Liddy wound up as a radio personality in his own right, while Tim Leary passed away, still convinced of the righteousness of his acid cause, and dropping unsettling hints that he had been working for the CIA at the time.

While William Hitchcock's intelligence role is not known to any degree of certainty except for the circumstantial evidence cited above, he certainly surrounded himself with spooks, mobsters and . . . Republicans. His deep involvement in Castle Bank and Trust is just one such instance. A CIA front in the Bahamas run by former OSS China hand (and former boss of E. Howard Hunt) Paul Helliwell, it was used as a personal bank by Richard Nixon, George H.W. Bush, and Robert Vesco, as well as by an assortment of Republican movers-and-shakers and the occasional drug runner and Mafia don. Those who enjoy wallowing in Watergate will recall Castle Bank, but perhaps not realize that Billy Hitchcock was an important supporter of the institution.

His similar involvement with Resorts International, a spook-front and private Republican vault, is also well-known. The history of Resorts International has been brilliantly detailed in Jim Hougan's *Spooks*, and we will not go into any great detail here, but it is enough to say that Resorts is in the middle of not only the Watergate affair but also a vast array of intelligence operations that include anti-Castro Cubans, Mafia bagmen, illegal campaign contributions, and money laundering. The Nixon and Rebozo involvement with Resorts is only the tip of a very old and very dirty iceberg, and Hitchcock has managed to stay quietly in the shadows of these infamous politicos.

Alas, the same cannot be said of his relative, Richard Mellon Scaife.

THE CLINTON CHRONICLES

Richard Mellon Scaife's antecedents were also intelligence-connected in World War II. His father Alan Scaife was a major in the OSS. The Mellon side of the family, of course, included all those OSS Mellons with their cozy relationships extending to the modern incarnation of the OSS, the CIA. While Bill Hitchcock's involvement with twentieth century American history seems divided between the LSD culture on one side and money laundering on the other—including a variety of intelligence and high-level Republican Party cooperative efforts—Richard Scaife's politics are worn on his sleeve for all to see.

He has been identified in the mainstream media as the treasure chest for the anti-Clinton campaigns of the 1990s, supporting a wide variety of efforts to destroy the Democrat. We learned of the Paula Jones scandal through Scaife's investigation into Clinton's private life, an investigation undertaken with private detectives and well-placed bribes, as well as with investigative reporters working for his own newspaper. It was Scaife who joined hands with Pat Robertson—he of the "jewels for Jesus" investments in Zaire—to promote a video cassette purporting to tell the truth about Clinton the mass murderer entitled "The Clinton Chronicles," a conspiracy theory wrapped in innuendo and basted with misdirection which, if anything, gives the very idea of "conspiracy theory" a bad name. (This did not stop Pat Robertson from promoting it through his own Christian Coalition, however.)

The story of Richard Mellon Scaife is clouded by Scaife's own reluctance to talk to reporters, even though he controls several media outlets including the *American Spectator*, a newspaper published in Pittsburgh that has been instrumental in the Clinton attacks. It was the *Spectator* that first published the Paula Jones story, early in the Clinton campaign for the presidency. When Spectator editors or journalists have been slow to go to press with an anti-Clinton story that was heavy on innuendo but weak in verifiable sources, they have been censured by Scaife or fired outright.

To do him justice, Scaife's paper was also one of the first to come out with an editorial demanding the resignation or impeachment of President Nixon during the Watergate scandal; those who watched from the sidelines, however, interpreted this as a man distancing himself from the exposure of some of the Republican Party's dirtiest secrets. Nixon, though an eager tool of the Right, was not cut from quite the same cloth-of-gold as his aristocratic buddies, and thus could not be expected to maintain (achieve?) any kind of dignity in the face of the ongoing revelations.

With Nixon, the Republicans learned a valuable lesson: the poor and the greedy can be manipulated far more easily than the wealthy, but that manipulation can come with a price. The poor and the greedy are hired help; they are not part of the cabal and cannot be expected to act with the appropriate—*je ne sais quoi? . . . noblesse oblige?*—in times of stress. With the Bush presidencies, a wealthy dynasty was put in place, one that could be relied upon to give the party line with aplomb; further, the Bushes were members of that exclusive club of oilmen which is a venerated sect of the cabal; even further, they had enough family members in important positions—Governor of Texas, Governor of Florida, two critical states during an election—to consolidate power at various levels of government. The Bush dynasty was the Republicans' answer to the Kennedys.

Thus, when Clinton made a run at the Oval Office, it shook the conservative Right down to its heels. The plan had been to have George Bush serve for two terms, during which a consolidation of power could take place: the "ideological forces" mentioned by Scaife in 1994. When Clinton threatened that, action was required. On one level, that action would be taken by the same dirty tricks faction that had served Nixon so well in his political campaigns.

Lucianne Goldberg had worked for Murray Chotiner, Nixon's first and virtually only campaign manager. Chotiner had worked for Nixon since his first run at a political office after the War, orchestrating the red-baiting and Jew-baiting whisper tactics that helped Nixon in his California campaigns. Chotiner's involvement with organized crime is no secret; his delight in dirty tricks was passed on to his student as a virtual religion. After Chotiner's death—in an automobile accident ironically in front of a Kennedy residence—his mantle was picked off the floor by one of his latest camp-followers: Lucianne Goldberg. Ms. Goldberg had worked to infiltrate the campaigns of the Democratic opposition in 1972, looking for specifically sexual dirt that could be used to embarrass or ruin an opponent. (This was also the year of the Watergate break-in.) In 1992, she dusted off these skills and once again began seeking sexual scandal in an effort to defeat another Democratic contender. She was, in a way, less successful this time. Her efforts in 1972 helped re-elect Nixon to office. Her efforts twenty years later did not stop or remove Clinton, but it did prove to be a nightmare for the United States nonetheless.

It was Goldberg's relationship to Linda Tripp—a well-traveled former Delta Force member—that helped to unravel what would become the Monica Lewinsky debacle. Goldberg, acting as a kind of literary agent (who would go on to represent former LAPD officer and O.J. Simpson-trial celebrity Mark Fuhrman), was scouting around, looking—once again—for dirt on the Clinton administration.

Tripp had worked for the previous Bush administration, and the White House found her a job at the Pentagon (where she made more money, incidentally) in the days after the Vince Foster suicide.

The Vince Foster case, of course, became a *cause celebre* among the Right, as they were convinced that Foster had been murdered by the Clintons, in spite of the evidence to the contrary. Foster had worked for the Clinton White House, and when news of his death reached the administration they began a search of his office and, it is alleged, removed documents before the arrival of police. In the days that followed, there was a flurry of activity as White House legal staff began to assess the fallout from the suicide. Tripp became increasingly contemptuous of the Clinton people and of the way she had been sidelined during the transition. When she was finally transferred to her office at the Pentagon, she wasted no time telling people of her dissatisfaction with the way she had been treated. Even though she was working for more money and back in the Pentagon, it did not compare with the prestige of working at the White House, and she was bitter and angry at the Clinton administration.

Word of her state of mind reached Goldberg through another friend, and Goldberg approached Tripp for more information. About all Tripp could come up with on her own were the shenanigans that took place around the time of the Foster suicide, and a lot of gossip about various staff people and the lack of organization within the administration. Goldberg was not satisfied with that. It just wasn't enough to sell a book . . . or destroy a president. She wanted more.

Tripp eventually made the acquaintance of another White House staffer, a former intern named Monica Lewinsky. Monica claimed to have been having a love affair with Bill Clinton. This was just what Goldberg was looking for.

At this time, the Whitewater investigations had been going full-swing. The Whitewater affair has been covered in many other books and newspaper accounts, and a full narration here would be tedious and not add very much. It is probably enough to say that there were allegations of the Bill Clinton's wrongdoing when he was still in Arkansas, long before he became president, which involved a suspicious real estate deal known as Whitewater. Whether this deal had any relevance at all to whether or not Clinton should have remained President is, of course, for people far more knowledgeable than I to conclude. In fact, it began as a fishing expedition by the Republican opposition to find something—anything—to hang on Clinton to force him to resign or, barring that, to prevent him from seeking a second term as President.

An independent counsel was named, was replaced, and finally Kenneth Starr took over the task of finding something illegal in Clinton's background. The Whitewater investigation was turning up nothing. While the real estate deal had gone badly, there was never any evidence that the Clintons profited by it; in fact, they lost money. There was also no evidence that the Clintons had been involved in anything illegal. Forty million dollars of the taxpayers' money had been spent on chasing a chimera, and Starr was desperate for an angle. *Cherchez la femme.*

Richard Scaife, who had been pressuring his people to find dirt on Clinton, had placed private detectives in Arkansas to sniff around. They came up with Paula Jones and the statements of some Arkansas State Police who claimed that they had, essentially, pimped for Clinton when he was Governor of Arkansas. Paula Jones claimed that she had been having sexual relations with Clinton for some time, a fact that was also supposedly known to the State Police who were the Governor's security detail. The fact that the dates and places given by Paula Jones were later shown to be inaccurate (in one instance, she gives as the date and time of her rendezvous with the Governor the same time that he was in front of a few hundred people giving a speech) was inconsequential to the strategy. It was enough to have Ms. Jones stand in front of cameras and claim that she slept with Clinton.

During Clinton's campaign for the presidency, another woman—Gennifer Flowers—had also come forward with a story that she had been sleeping with the Governor. It had almost been enough to capsize the Clinton riverboat until the Clintons—both Bill and Hillary—appeared on national television, holding hands, and telling the American people that if they had no problem with the "revelations," neither should anyone else. That well-publicized demonstration of matrimonial solidarity deflected the anti-Clinton torpedo . . . for the moment. Clinton was elected in 1992, but the allegations of extra-marital affairs did not stop. Scaife wanted more, and he found it in Paula Jones.

Jones would be called before Ken Starr as he fished for more evidence of wrongdoing, but there was a danger that Jones would not be enough. Her testimony had been challenged before. But with Monica Lewinsky, the Starr investigation took on new energy. Whitewater—in all its complexity and ultimate failure—was all but forgotten, but here was something the American people could really get into. A sexual scandal, taking place in the Oval Office itself!

Monica had been tricked by her "friend" Linda Tripp into relating details of her meetings with the President over the phone . . . and into Tripp's tape recorder. With that, Tripp and Goldberg could go to the Starr investigation. What had begun as a search through Clinton's balance sheets ended as a search through his bedsheets. Starr was happy that he finally had something to beat the President with, and at last the long-awaited impeachment proceedings were begun.

During this time, several other events were taking place behind the scenes. In the first case, the anti-Clinton lobby had worked itself into a frenzy with something called "The Clinton Chronicles." Financed by Scaife, this was an "exposé" of the Clinton mafia and its evil machinations—including murder—over the years. As mentioned before, the source material for the Chronicles was rather flimsy, largely based as it was on the "revelations" of a "disgruntled former employee," Larry Nichols. Nichols had been fired from his state government post in Arkansas because he had been using the office facilities to raise funds for . . . the Contras. Embittered over what he perceived as his cavalier treatment by the governor—Bill Clinton—he became an easy mark for the intrepid private investigators hired by Richard Scaife.

As in the case of Lucianne Goldberg and Linda Tripp, Scaife's people found Nichols to be a good source of gossip about the future president but they needed more.

Nichols began spinning tales of drug-running in Arkansas, of womanizing politicians, gun deals, and assorted Contra-related derring-do. He became the George Adamski of the Clinton administration: claiming he had been aboard that spacecraft and had seen the evil aliens at work, and was only too happy to go public with what he knew (or could invent).

In a bizarre twist, however, the core of the Arkansas revelations is the infamous Mena episode. A small town in Arkansas with an airstrip, it was used by the CIA to transport guns and drugs between Latin America and the United States as part of the Contra operation. In other words, it was the legacy of the *Reagan–Bush* administrations and had nothing to do with Governor Clinton; indeed, as a "black op," it was probably completely unknown to the Governor in the first place.

Although the taped interviews were not quite ready for prime-time, they were promoted heavily by televangelist Jerry Falwell and, later, by Pat Robertson's own CBN, and by the Christian Coalition he founded after his unsuccessful run at the American presidency in 1988. Also appearing on "The Clinton Chronicles" was Paula Jones, she of the purported sexual relationship with Clinton while he was governor. The Christian Right ate it up. It may not have been ready for prime-time, but it sure played well in Peoria.

But that was not the end of Richard Scaife's campaign to unseat the President. In order to ensure a most favorable outcome of the Kenneth Starr investigation, he funded a chair at Pepperdine University specifically for Starr when his role as special prosecutor was complete. Once this arrangement became public, however, everyone denied the connection, and Starr was forced to refuse the chair.

Scaife's hatchet man for the *American Spectator* was one David Brock. Brock's story is by now quite well-known. Famous as a muckraker on the trail of the Clintons for several years, he eventually balked at writing a story that would claim Hillary Clinton was a lesbian. Scaife wanted the story to be explicit in its claims; after all, he was donating heavily to the *American Spectator* from his own pocket and felt he owned the paper. In addition, Brock's pieces had always been on the mark. But when it came to Hillary as gay, Brock could not find the evidence, and he couldn't find the heart to go forward with the conservative program. Scaife demanded Brock be fired from the paper, and Brock went ahead and apologized to the Clintons publically for the hatchet jobs he had been doing at Scaife's insistence, admitting that they were created largely out of whole cloth.

There is no law against philanthropy, of course, and one should not hold Richard Scaife's donations against him. Yet, it is of interest to note that in addition to over $900,000 he donated to the 1972 Nixon Committee to Re-Elect the President (CREEP), he has substantially supported Conservative Republican causes steadily through the years since then. The fact is that the bulk of his largesse in the 1990s went to organizations that represent the core of the Conservative movement—including millions to the Heritage Foundation (a famous Conservative "think tank"), the Western Journalism Center and Accuracy in Media (two groups specializing in Vince Foster assassination theories), and the National Taxpayers Union (which produced yet another video "exposé" of the Vince Foster assassination theories)—is an indication of how much "old money" is allied to the "New Right" in American politics. Like the funding of the Nazi Party by wealthy German (and American) corporations in the 1920s, '30s and '40s, the presence of such tycoons as Scaife, H.L. Hunt, Nelson Bunker Hunt, and many others in the background of the Christian Right campaigns against Clinton reveals a deeper, darker purpose in the souls of these men, a moral conviction representing an entire constellation of religious, racial, social and cultural theories that the rest of the world might find abhorrent or even frightening.

In Weimar Germany there were dozens of political parties that could have used financial support from huge industrial concerns like Farben, Krupp, Siemens, and the rest; the fact is that these companies threw their backing behind Hitler and the Nazi Party. American companies such as Ford Motor, Harriman Brothers, ITT, and many others followed suit. Men like Allen Dulles, John Foster Dulles and Richard Nixon conspired to give aid and comfort to the enemy, pulling the strings necessary to ensure that thousands of war criminals escaped justice at Nuremberg; and that millions of dollars in German money found their way to safe haven as well.

In a sense, the young inheritors of Old Money were picking up where their parents left off. The elder Bushes, Mellons, Scaifes, Hitchcocks, etc. were dying off or fading into retirement. In one year alone—1994—the obituaries of the *New York Times* were reporting the demise of many old OSS men, their affiliations buried deep within the columns memorializing their contributions to society. Thus was even such a venerable institution as television chef Julia Child revealed to have been in the OSS, which is where she had met her husband, now deceased.

The youth and energy of Bill Clinton posed a threat to the old way of thinking, the old right-wing power politics that many claim—and with much justification—built the United States in the first place. The Mellons, the Astors, the Morgans, the Carnegies, the Forbeses, the DuPonts, the Hunts, all made serious contributions to the strength and power of America. Their industries employed millions of Americans, even as they were building massive fortunes that would sustain generations of their own bloodlines long after they were dead. They also built monuments to themselves, of course, with stone blocks large enough to bury the corpses of the men, women and children who died for their sins. The Holocaust is but one example of what may happen when an almost religious zeal for racial and ethnic superiority is wedded to extensive wealth and connections in high places.

The wannabes—the Pat Robertsons, Jerry Falwells, and other spokesmen for the New Right, the Christian Right—were only too eager to use these connections and these funds to further the goals of their financial masters, meanwhile nurturing their own bank accounts. Whether it was tearing down an American president or building up a Third World dictator, the Christian Right had managed to instill in their followers the idea that—as sociologist Sara Diamond so eloquently put it—"one's personal redemption" was tied to "a gospel of political participation." Pat Robertson certainly exemplified that concept, as his track record of support for Mobutu, Taylor, Rios Montt, and the Nicaraguan Contras dramatically shows.

Americans in general do not have on-the-ground experience in the developing nations, especially not those regions in the midst of political struggle and military turmoil. They can't be expected to know how America is perceived abroad by the citizens of these countries whose only experience of America is either the politically-committed Christian missionary (like Robertson), the rapacious capitalist businessman (again, like Robertson), or the government spooks and saboteurs who support first one dictator and then another. If America is despised in some foreign countries, and if American humanitarian efforts are greeted with suspicion or scorn, it is largely due to the mixed signals sent out by a combination of American businessmen, American missionaries, and American foreign policy experts and in-country foreign service bureaucrats.

We may despise the Islamic promotion of a *jihad* against the West and specifically against America, but unrecognized by most Americans is the fact that their own most visible "ambassadors" to the East have been people like Robertson on the one hand, and agencies like the CIA on the other, complemented by a wealth of oil men, military advisers, and cultural emissaries in the food, entertainment, and fashion industries. If everyday Americans do not support, condone or participate in cultural or military colonialism, their overseas counterparts are not so innocent. Groups like the Christian Coalition, the Christian Broadcasting Network, the Heritage Foundation, and individuals like Pat Robertson and Jerry Falwell, have been busy creating a philosophical framework for the New Right in the absence of a credible Communist threat: the idea that personal spiritual redemption and political activism (of an approved, Conservative, variety) are mutually dependent.

The Christian Right took a page from the psychological warfare book. What is missionary work, after all, but psychological warfare by other means? Sara Diamond, who has written extensively on the phenomenon of Christian fundamentalist and evangelical political action, notes the relationship between humanitarian aid and psychological warfare, a relationship hinted at in Christopher Simpson's work on psychological warfare, *Science of Coercion: Communication Research and Psychological Warfare 1945–1960* (Oxford, 1994).

"Humanitarian aid" and "psychological operations" are two areas of "total war" where the Christian Right serves U.S. foreign policy objectives best. Acting either as "private" benefactors or as agents of the U.S. government, Christian Right "humanitarian" suppliers and promoters of anti-Communist ideology use religion to mask the aggressive, cynical nature of "humanitarian" projects . . . . It is doubtful, however, that counterinsurgency could be effective without the use of religion. Because the conduct of "psychological operations" relies on the successful interpretation and manipulation of a target population's deeply held beliefs and cultural practices, the functional use of religion simply must be addressed by anyone intending to understand and put an end to "total warfare."[30]

When Diamond first published her work, in 1989, Pat Robertson's "humanitarian" efforts in Zaire had not yet begun, and were not noticed by the media until 1993. As men, women and children were dying from the combined results of war and the Ebola virus, Robertson's "Operation Blessing" was flying dozens of sorties . . . to a diamond mine far from the scene of the conflict. When they did manage to fly into Goma and other regions ravaged by refugees (both internal and external), they brought a few pounds of aspirin. No blood, no vaccines, nothing that addressed the real problems of the sick and dying. They prayed, said a witness, and spoke in tongues, and preached . . . and then got the hell out of there.

At the same time, Robertson was running an anti-Clinton campaign on his 700 Club, watched by millions, and raising money for his obscenely cynical African operations. With funding from right-wing zealots like Richard Mellon Scaife and H.L. Hunt, the Christian Right was simultaneously hailing Larry Nichols, Paula Jones, Linda Tripp, and Monica Lewinsky as political "heros" while supporting dictators in Africa and Latin America, men with the blood of thousands of civilians on their hands. Islamic militants may be forgiven, therefore, if they see America as embarked on a "crusade" reminiscent of the worst excesses of the thirteenth century, promoting evangelistic Christianity with fire and sword abroad, and with rumor, paranoia and innuendo at home. The Christian Right has supported regimes that actively used chemical and biological weapons against their own people, that tortured and killed political opponents, all in the furtherance of dubious national interests. Can America accept that some of their most revered spiritual leaders may be moral imbeciles, praising Jesus on the one hand while financing terror on the other?

The involvement with the Nazis of the sainted forebears of these men should have told us everything we needed to know. But most Americans are completely unaware of this long, involved history when they go to a voting booth to select our national and local leaders. For one thing, this history is the stuff of thick, academic tomes that never find their way to a secondary school classroom. For another, the irrefutable evidence shown in these sources is relegated to the "crank" category by mainstream historians, since it does not fit neatly into preconceived ideas of the American historical experience. To integrate this information into our history books would be to rewrite history itself.

Thus, when Hillary Rodham Clinton went on the air with her mention of a "vast, right-wing conspiracy," no one was really listening. It did not sound like an objective read of the situation, but as a self-serving statement designed to exonerate her embattled husband. Now, with the benefit of years of hindsight, we may be able to see the outlines of this conspiracy more clearly. From the days of Prescott

Bush, Allen Dulles, and Richard Nixon and their enthusiastic collaboration with Nazism to the days of Ronald Reagan and George H.W. Bush, the fascist "ethnic outreach" programs of the Republican Party courted the Nazi vote and employed hundreds of Nazis and Nazi war criminals in its political campaigns in the decades after World War II. In a more contemporary context, George W. Bush can be shown to have had connections with Islamic terrorists through his oil businesses. Thus the weight of the evidence is such that we are forced to realize that Richard Mellon Scaife, Pat Robertson, and Pat Buchanan were all correct: America is truly a land where two ideological forces have been battling each other for generations for stewardship over the American soul. And, as usual, the Devil is better-dressed, has better public relations, and quotes Scripture for his own ends.

BUSH AND GOD

> We are in a conflict between good and evil, and America will call evil by its name.
> —President George W. Bush, Commencement Address, West Point, June 1, 2002

Those who believe I am heavily overstating a case for which the evidence is circumstantial need only look at the cover of *Newsweek* for March 10, 2003, with a cover story entitled, "Bush & God: How Faith Changed His Life and Shapes His Agenda." While giving us a tale of how George W. Bush found Jesus in his forties, stopped drinking, and got serious, there is a deeper, more unsettling message that may be summed up in these lines:

> The presidential campaign was Texas on a grander scale. As he prepared to run, in 1999, Bush assembled leading pastors at the governor's mansion for a "laying on of hands," and told them he'd been "called" to seek higher office.[31]

The entire article—and series of accompanying, shorter, articles—describes the Bush presidency as a "faith-centered" administration. To further quote,

> . . . this president—this presidency—is the most resolutely "faith-based" in modern times, an enterprise founded, supported and guided by trust in the temporal and spiritual power of God.[32]

It would sound mean and petty to complain about a presidential administration that was spiritual, if it were not for the fact that the Bush administration picks and chooses its scriptural texts with its own agenda in mind. The administration—as admitted in the *Newsweek* articles—has ignored the clergymen, the priests, the mullahs in coming to its current state of spiritual enlightenment. The combined voices of Protestants, Catholics, Jews and Muslims against war does not move George W. Bush at all. Obviously, he considers himself more spiritually enlightened than the professionals, and having a circle of Christian evangelical sycophants around him—and the backing of wealthy Fundamentalist political action groups hailing from the days of Robertson, Falwell, Scaife, and others—means that he never need hear a discouraging word.

There is no spiritual debate in the White House. Instead, what motivates and drives this president—at least, insofar as we are able to tell—is a belief in his own position (he claimed he was "called" to the presidency by God), a simplistic understanding of good and evil (Saddam Hussein is evil, those who do not support United States' foreign policy are evil, etc.), and the fact that he is now the leader of the world's last remaining superpower. If the Islamic world is afraid that Bush is on a Crusader-like rampage to Christianize the Middle East, though, they need not worry too much. When Saudi Arabia was being chastised by the US Commission on International Religious Freedom for its human rights abuses, especially in terms of its persecution of foreign Christian workers on Saudi soil who are thrown into prison for practicing their faith, they were not censured by the US government. The support of Saudi Arabia is considered too important to alienate in this fashion.

One must also remember the practical parameters of this brand of spirituality. When George W. Bush was Governor of Texas, the rate of executions of prisoners on death row was at an all-time high. This is the "old time religion" of a Savanarola or a Torquemada, molded to fit the *realpolitik* of twenty-first century global confrontation. It is the British film *The Ruling Class*, performed on a world stage with George W. Bush in, alas, the Peter O'Toole role: the wealthy scion of a moneyed dynasty who believes himself to be Jesus Christ and is battling against another mental patient—this time played by Osama bin Laden or Saddam Hussein, take your pick—who believes he is the Creator God. In the film, the Peter O'Toole/George W. Bush character is "cured" of his delusion that he is Jesus Christ . . . only to wake up one morning and "realize" he is Jack the Ripper.

And so it goes.

> *The utterances of the Divine Name, which was supposed to make the devils tremble and place them at the will of the Magus, was at least equally powerful, it was argued, to enforce their obedience for a purpose in consonance with their own nature. Behind this there lay also the tacit assumption that it was easier to control demons than to persuade angels. Then seeing that prayer to God and the invocation of the Divine Names presuppose a proper spirit of reverence, devotion and love as the condition upon which prayer is heard, it became a condition in Goetia. The first impossibility required of the adept in Black Magic is therefore that he should love God before he bewitches his neighbor; that he should put all his hopes in God before he makes pact with Satan; that, in a word, he should be good in order to do evil.*
>
> —*The Book of Ceremonial Magic*[33]

ENDNOTES

1 Mark Aarons & John Loftus, *Unholy Trinity*, St Martin's Press, NY, 1991, p. 98
2 Russ Bellant, *Old Nazis, The New Right and the Republican Party*, South End Press, Boston, 1991, p. 22
3 Sara Diamond, *Not By Politics Alone: The Enduring Influence of the Christian Right*, Guilford Press, NY, 1998, p. 30
4 Sara Diamond, *Spiritual Warfare: The Politics of the Christian Right*, South End Press, Boston, 1989, p. 6–8
5 John Marks, *The Search for the "Manchurian Candidate,"* Times Books, NY, 1979, p. 75
6 Michela Wrong, *In The Footsteps of Mr Kurtz*, HarperCollins, NY, 2002, p. 80
7 Ibid., p. 82
8 Ibid., p. 82
9 Charles Higham, *American Swastika*, Doubleday, NY, 1985, p. 251
10 Ibid., p. 251
11 Ibid., p. 251–252
12 As reported in the *Washington Post*, Dec 28, 2002
13 Diamond, 1989, op. cit. p. 17
14 Ibid., p. 17
15 Ibid., p. 17
16 Ibid., p. 164–168
17 Bellant, op. cit., p. 65–68
18 Ibid., p. 72
19 Kenneth Wald, *Religion and Politics in the United States*, Washington DC, 1992, p. 65 331
20 Peter Levenda, *Unholy Alliance*, Continuum, NY, 2002, p. 101–102
21 Diamond, 1998, op. cit., p. 93
22 Martin A. Lee & Bruche Shlain, *Acid Dreams*, Grove Weidenfeld, NY, 1985, p. 99
23 Richard Harris Smith, OSS: The Secret History of America's First Central Intelligence Agency, University of California Press, Berkeley, 1981, p. 84–85
24 John Loftus & Mark Aarons, *The Secret War Against the Jews*, St Martin's Griffin, NY, 1997, p. 82–87
25 Smith, op. cit., p.15–16
26 Lee & Shlain, op. cit., p. 73
27 Phillip Knightley & Caroline Kennedy, *An Affair Of State*, Atheneum, NY, 1987, p. 48
28 Ibid., p. 197
29 Ibid., p. 201
30 Diamond, 1989, op. cit., p. 161–162
31 Howard Fineman, "Bush and God," *Newsweek*, March 10, 2003, p. 20
32 Ibid., p. 17
33 Arthur Edward Waite, *The Book of Ceremonial Magic*, Dover, NY, p. 142

PETER LEVENDA

SINISTER FORCES

A GRIMOIRE OF AMERICAN POLITICAL WITCHCRAFT

BOOK THREE: THE MANSON SECRET

FOREWORD

CHARLIE'S DEVILS

BY PAUL KRASSNER

> The history of civilization is the history of warfare between secret societies.
> —Ishmael Reed

In 1971, I began to write an article, "The Rise of Sirhan Sirhan in the Scientology Hierarchy," for my satirical magazine, *The Realist*. Then, in the course of my research, a strange thing happened. I learned of the actual involvement of Charles Manson with Scientology. In fact, there had been an E-Meter at the Spahn Ranch where his "family" stayed. Suddenly, I no longer had any reason to use Sirhan Sirhan as my protagonist. Reality will transcend allegory every time. So, although I had announced that I was going to publish that article, I started investigating the Manson case instead. Nevertheless, Scientology sued me for $750,000 for just those nine words—whoops, there goes the whole petty cash account—but I chose to fight them on 1st Amendment grounds, and they eventually dropped the suit.

I corresponded with Manson, visited his female killers in prison and—in a classic example of participatory journalism—took an acid trip with family members Squeaky Fromme and Sandra Good. Ed Sanders' book, *The Family*, mentioned that Los Angeles police had discovered porn flicks in a loft at the crime scene, the home actress Sharon Tate shared with her director husband, Roman Polanski (in London at the time of the murders). And yet, the prosecutor in Manson's trial, Vincent Bugliosi, denied in his book, *Helter Skelter*, that any porn flicks had been found. It was possible that the police had in fact uncovered them but lied to Bugliosi.

I learned why when I consulted San Francisco private investigator Hal Lipset, whose career had been the basis for *The Conversation*, starring Gene Hackman. Lipset informed me that not only did Los Angeles police seize porn movies and videotapes, but also that individual officers were *selling* them. He had talked with one police source who told him exactly which porn flicks were available—a total of seven hours' worth for a quarter-million dollars. Lipset began reciting a litany of those porn videos. The most notorious was Greg Bautzer, an attorney for financier Howard Hughes, together with Jane Wyman, the former wife of then-Governor

Ronald Reagan. There was Sharon Tate with Dean Martin. There was Sharon with Steve McQueen. There was Sharon with two black bisexual men.

"The cops weren't too happy about *that* one," Lipset recalled.

There was reportedly a video of Cass Elliot from The Mamas and The Papas in an orgy with Yul Brynner, Peter Sellers and Warren Beatty. Coincidentally, Brynner and Sellers, together with John Phillips of The Mamas and The Papas, had offered a $25,000 reward for the capture of the killers. I always felt these executioners had a prior connection with their victims. I finally tracked down a reporter who had hung around with police and seen a porn video of Susan Atkins with one of her victims, Wojciech Frykowski. When I asked Manson about that, he responded: "You are ill advised and misled. [Victim Jay] Sebring done Susan's hair and I think he sucked one or two of her dicks. I'm not sure who she was walking out from her stars and cages, that girl *loves* dick, you know what I mean, hon. Yul Brynner, Peter Sellers . . ."

Manson was abandoned by his mother and lived in various institutions after he was 8 years old. He learned early how to survive in captivity. When he was 14, he got arrested for stealing bread and was jailed. He was supposed to go to reform school, but instead went to Boys Town in Nebraska. He ran away from Boys Town and got arrested again, beginning his lifelong career as a prison inmate, and meeting organized crime figures who became his role models—and future contacts. He tossed horseshoes with Frank Costello, hung out with Frankie Carbo, and learned how to play the guitar from Alvin "Creepy" Karpas. Eventually, he was introduced to Scientology by fellow prisoners while he was at McNeil Island Penitentiary. He needed less deconditioning than his cellmates, who had spent more time in the outside world. One of his teachers said that, with Scientology, Charlie's ability to psych people out quickly was intensified so that he could zero in on their weaknesses and fears immediately. Thus, one more method was now stored in his manipulation tool chest.

When Manson was released in 1967, he went to the Scientology Center in San Francisco. Family member "Little Paul" Watkins, who accompanied him there, told me, "Charlie said to them, 'I'm Clear'—what do I do now?' But they expected him to sweep the floor. Shit, he had done *that* in prison." In Los Angeles, he went to the Scientology Celebrity Center. Now this was more like it. Here he could mingle with the elite. I managed to obtain a copy of the original log entry: "7/31/68, new name, Charlie Manson, Devt., No address, In for processing = Ethics = Type III." The receptionist—who, by Type III, meant "psychotic"—sent him to the Ethics office, but he never showed up.

At the Spahn Ranch, Manson eclectically combined his version of Scientology auditing with post-hypnotic techniques he had learned in prison, with geographical isolation and subliminal motivation, with sing-along sessions and encounter games, with LSD and mescaline, with transactional analysis and brainwashing rituals, with verbal probing and the sexual longevity that he had practiced upon himself for all those years in the privacy of his cell. Ultimately, in August 1969, he sent members of his well-programmed family off to slay Sharon Tate and her unborn baby, hairstylist and dealer to the stars Jay Sebring, would-be screenwriter Wojciech Frykowski, and his girlfriend, coffee heiress Abigail Folger. Revenge for a drug deal gone sour.

Ed Sanders wrote, "In the days before his death, Sebring had complained to a receptionist at his hair salon that someone had burned him for $2,000 worth of cocaine and he wanted vengeance." On Friday evening, just a few hours before the massacre took place, Joel Rostau—the boyfriend of Sebring's receptionist and an intermediary in a cocaine ring—visited Sebring and Frykowski at the Tate house to deliver mescaline and coke. During the Manson trial, several associates of Sebring were murdered, including Rostau, whose body was found in the trunk of a car in New York.

The next night, Manson accompanied his followers to kill supermarket mogul Leno LaBianca and his wife. Ostensibly, they were selected at random, but a police report showed that LaBianca was a heavy gambler. He owed $30,000 to Frankie Carbo's organization. I asked Manson about a little black book he was supposed to get from LaBianca. He wrote back, "The black book was what the CIA and a mob of market players had, Hollywood Park [race track] and numbers rackets to move in the Governor's office legally."

Ed Sanders and I were on a panel at the University of Missouri, where he stated, "In the course of my research in Los Angeles, it became evident that Robert Kennedy was killed by a *group* of people including Sirhan Sirhan." In *The Family*, he had written, in reference to the Process Church, to which Manson had ties, "It is possible that the Process had a baleful influence on Sirhan Sirhan, since Sirhan is known, in the spring of '68, to have frequented clubs in Hollywood in occult pursuits. He has talked several times subsequent to Robert Kennedy's death about an occult group from London which he knew about and which he really wanted to go to London to see."

Since the London-based Process Church had been an offshoot of Scientology, this looked like it could be a case of satirical prophecy. I was tempted to return to my original premise involving Sirhan, but it was too late. I had already become obsessed with my Manson research. I recalled that, in the summer of 1968, while the Yippies were planning for a Festival of Life at the Democratic National Convention in Chicago, some zealots from the Process cult visited me in New York. They were hyper-anxious to meet Timothy Leary and kept pestering me for his phone number. The Process, founded by Scientology dropouts, first came to the U.S. from London in 1967. Members were called "mind benders" and proclaimed their "dedication to the elimination of the grey forces."

In January 1968, they became the Process Church of the Final Judgment, a New Orleans–based religious corporation. They claimed to be in direct contact with both Jesus and Lucifer, and had wanted to be called the Church of the Process of Unification of Christ and Satan, but local officials presumably objected to their taking the name of Satan in vain. The Process struck me as a group of occult provocateurs, using radical Christianity as a front. They were adamantly interested in Yippie politics. They boasted to me of various rallies which their *vibrations alone* had transformed into riots. They implied that there was some kind of connection between the assassination of Bobby Kennedy and their own mere presence on the scene.

Bernard Fensterwald, head of the Committee to Investigate Assassinations, told me that Sirhan Sirhan had some involvement with the Process. Peter Chang, the district attorney of Santa Cruz, showed me a letter from a Los Angeles police official to the chief of police in San Jose, warning him that the Process had infiltrated biker gangs and hippie communes. And Ed Sanders wrote in *Win* (Workshop in Nonviolence) magazine, "[W]ord came out of Los Angeles of a current FBI investigation of the RFK murder, the investigation growing, as the source put it, out of 'the Manson case.' Word came from another source, this one in the halls of Government itself, that several police and investigatory jurisdictions have information regarding other murders that may have been connected to the Robert Kennedy shooting: murders that occurred after RFK's. A disturbing fact in this regard is that one agency in the Federal Bureaucracy (not the FBI) has stopped a multi-county investigation by its own officers that would have probed into such matters as the social and religious activities of Sirhan Sirhan in early '68, and into the allegations regarding RFK-connected murders."

In 1972, Paulette Cooper, author of *The Scandal of Scientology*, put me in touch with Lee Cole, a former Scientologist who was now working with the Process Church. His role was to provide information on Scientology to the Process. I contacted him and flew to Chicago. We made an appointment to visit the Process headquarters. The Process men were dressed all in black, with large silver crosses hanging from their necks. They called each other "Brother" and they had German shepherds that seemed to be menacing. The Brothers tried to convince me that Scientology, not the Process, was responsible for creating Manson. But what else could I have expected?

Charles Manson's *real* family consisted of con artists, pimps, drug dealers, thieves, muggers, rapists and murderers. He had known only power relationships within an army of control junkies. Charlie was America's Frankenstein monster, a logical product of the prison system—racist, paranoid and violent—even if hippie astrologers thought that his fate had been predetermined because he was a triple Scorpio. A psychiatrist at San Quentin Prison told me of an incident he observed during Manson's trial. A black inmate said to Manson, "Look, I don't wanna know about your theories on race, I don't wanna hear anything about religion, I just wanna know one thing—how'd you get them girls to obey you like that?" The reply: "I got a knack."

Actually, Manson told me, "I only picked up girls who had already been tossed away by society." And he would fill that void. After having lived behind bars most of his life, he ended up in the Haight-Ashbury area in the Summer of Love. Oh, those luscious runaways. And so he began to explore and exploit countercultural values.

I was gathering piece after piece of a mind-boggling jigsaw puzzle, without having any model to pattern it after. The evidence indicated that members of the Manson family had actually but unknowingly served as a hit-squad for a drug ring. Manson had instructed the girls to do whatever family member Tex Watson told them. When Manson was charged, Watson was also charged, but federal authorities held Watson in a Texas prison with no explanation—not even his own lawyers were allowed to see him—while Bugliosi prosecuted the Manson trial in California. In order to find Manson guilty, the jury had to be convinced that Charlie's devils were zombies who followed his orders without question. In order to find *Watson* guilty, the jury had to be convinced that he was *not* a zombie and knew exactly what he was doing.

Conspiracy researcher Mae Brussell put me in contact with Preston Guillory, a former deputy sheriff, who told me, "We had been briefed for a few weeks prior to the actual raiding of Spahn Ranch. We had a sheaf of memos on Manson, that they had automatic weapons at the ranch, that citizens had complained about hearing machine-guns fired at night, that firemen from the local fire station had been accosted by armed members of Manson's band and told to get out of the area, all sorts of complaints like this. We had been advised to put anything relating to Manson on a memo submitted to the station, because they were supposedly gathering information for the raid we were going to make. Deputies at the station of course started asking, 'Why aren't we going to make the raid sooner?' I mean, Manson's a parole violator, machine-guns have been heard, we know there's narcotics and we know there's booze. He's living at the Spahn Ranch with a bunch of minor girls in complete violation of his parole. Deputies at the station quite frankly became very annoyed that no action was being taken about Manson. My contention is this—the reason Manson was left on the street was because our department thought that he was going to attack the Black Panthers. We were getting intelligence briefings that Manson was anti-black and he had supposedly killed a Black Panther, the body of which could not be found, and the department thought that he was going to launch an attack on the Black Panthers."

If that's true, then it was racism in the Sheriff 's Department which turned law enforcers into unintentional collaborators in a mass murder. But what if there was some other, deeper reason? Guillory told me, "Before the Tate killings, [Manson] had been arrested at Malibu twice for statutory rape. Never got [imprisoned for parole violation]. Manson liked to ball young girls, so he just did his thing and he was released, and they didn't put any parole hold on him. But somebody very high up was controlling everything that was going on and was seeing to it that we didn't bust Manson." And, in this third book of the *Sinister Forces* trilogy, Peter Levenda presents the historical context for an underlying scenario which could well provide that missing link. For a quarter-century, he has diligently researched political witchcraft in the United States, culminating in what he calls the "Manson Secret."

Meanwhile, Charlie has become a cultural symbol. In surfer jargon, a "manson" is a crazy, reckless surfer. For comedians, Manson has become a generic joke reference. I asked him how he felt about that. He wrote back: "I don't know what a generic is, Joke. I think I know what that means. That means you talk bad about Reagan or Bush. I've always ran poker games and whores and crime. I'm a crook. You make the reality in court and press. I just ride and play the cards that were pushed on me to play. Mass killer, it's a job, what can I say."

—Paul Krassner is the author of *One Hand Jerking: Reports From an Investigative Satirist*; he publishes *The Disneyland Memorial Orgy* at paulkrassner. com.

INTRODUCTION

February – September 2003 Kuala Lumpur

God is great; there is no God but God, and Mohammad is his prophet. The speaker-amplified cry of the muezzin echoes off the tall buildings around the park. It should be an auspicious ending. Auspicious, not suspicious. But with the subject matter and the time of night and the thrumming nervousness of the streets it is too tempting to be anything but suspicious. Even God is a suspect now. God most of all.

I started this when I was not yet twenty-five years old. I am now fifty-two. It is impossible to communicate what this means in terms of a single project, especially a writing project that takes place in solitude with all the wings of life flapping around me, beating at my windows, noisy and oblivious to my daily anxieties and dreads, my occasional attack of euphoria and self-congratulation over a well-written line or a fortuitous discovery. There is a thin line that separates solitude from loneliness, and I cross it every day and sometimes even in my sleep.

During the years I worked on this book, I also worked in the world, like a Sufi, "in the world but not of it," or so it would seem to most people. Yet, I managed to develop lines of business for American and European companies abroad, lived and worked in Asia for many years, was responsible for expense budgets that exceeded ten million dollars and for sales that nudged one hundred million, spread over five continents and thirty countries. This type of multiple personality disorder is common among Americans, and is endemic among New Yorkers: this shadow life running parallel and sometimes perpendicular to the daily life of mortgages and credit card bills, a child's education and doctor's visits. Yet, through it all, I have not succumbed to drink or drugs or institutionalized madness, and for this I am grateful.

I keep a bottle of Absolut in the freezer, however, and I drink some now, the colored lights of the city outside my window twinkling like acid-dream fireflies in the tropical night. I am alone. The files are stacked on the floor, the dining-room table, the chairs all around me. Outside, incongruously, the sing-song warble of the muezzin calls the Muslim faithful to prayer. Inside the mosque, dozens of barefoot, sarong-clad men kneel, facing Mecca and its ancient lump of meteoric rock, and bow, surrendering themselves to God. God will protect them from evil, from demons, from unclean thoughts, from Western decadence, from American imperialism and currency speculators. From *Ibliss* and *Shaitan* and all the Islamic demons. *Ein feste Burg*, Luther would have said. *A mighty fortress is our God.*

But my demons will not leave me alone. Their traces are everywhere around me, but mostly on paper, in the files. And in my head. I can feel them, whistling through cranial corridors, taunting the prisoners I have chained in there and tried to forget, tormenting me with memories. With dreams. With morgue photographs. Autopsy reports. Lists of dead names. A political *Necronomicon*.

I light a candle, the flame flickers. It glints, winking like an evil eye, off the wavy blade of the kriss I keep near my bedside. I also need protection tonight, from what I do not know and cannot name. Only feel.

Unknown to me and to the world at large, Al-Qaeda operatives met not far from my apartment and began the plotting for the September 11 attack. It was a critical moment in history, this meeting; "pivotal," some in the intelligence community have said. And it happened in darkness, in the shadows. Two lives running parallel to each other, one in the daylight of the mosque and the loudspeaker prayers, and the other at night in an apartment full of the mutterings of bombers and saboteurs, like muffled oars.

While I dug and dug, mining data and researching through every type of material in an effort to disinter the sinister forces that lie dead but dreaming beneath the American political landscape, events were in progress to change the world forever. Fundamentalist Islamic militants were preparing to "bring the war home," as we used to say in the 1960s, and launch an attack on the very American landscape I was writing about. And they played right into the hands of their enemies. It was all a Republican administration needed in order to launch the twenty-first century equivalent of an Inquisition at home, and a Crusade abroad.

But I did not know this at the time. All I felt was the foreboding, the sense of impending doom, and I attributed this to my research and my unhealthy concentration on evil, on mental disorders, on murder and assassination and magic.

The files. Thirty years of hunting and searching. Mistakes. Missteps. False starts. Foul matter. I was a thin, nervous, sickly youth when I started. Bespectacled and academic. Solitary and anxious. I was not the type to have guns pointed at me, to have my life threatened by soldiers, spies. Not because I was good, or even innocent. But because I was not a soldier, not an intelligence agency cowboy strapped with an Ingram Mach-10 and a "get out of jail free" card. I was a reader. A writer. The passive-aggressive type. I asked questions. Terrorists don't have questions, only answers.

But in the last thirty years I have been stalked, surveilled, photographed, searched, researched, detained and denounced by a variety of agencies and individuals, in a number of countries, and for various reasons. I guess I have a problem with authority. But in my defense I have to say that pure research—of the academic variety—is bloodless. Worse, it is dishonest. Historians are cheats, like crooked accountants cooking the books. They manipulate data and create fiction in the guise of gospel. To get the taste and smell and feel of history, you have to get your hands dirty.

Or wet.

The vodka is ice-cold and flows like syrup, the way it is supposed to. The way it did in Moscow in 1996, when I visited the Metropole Hotel and Dzherzinsky Square and the Lubyanka with a former member of the former KGB. A pilgrimage of sorts, shrines to espionage and assassination legend. Outside, now, the temperature is mild for this time of year, for this tropical place. Standing in my window, backlit by my apartment lights, I can gaze out to my right and my left and see rain forest in the distance. Jungle. But straight ahead, behind the mosque and the Citibank building, stand the tallest buildings in the world.

I'm wasting time. Procrastinating. The files—like the *grimoires*, the workbooks of the medieval sorcerers—sit patiently inside, full of blood and secrets. Fat toads, fed on flies and their maggoty children.

Darwin Scott. Stabbed nineteen times with a kitchen knife. Charles Manson's uncle, murdered a few months before the Tate and LaBianca slayings.
Frank Olson. Falls ten floors to his death outside a New York City hotel room, his CIA handler standing at the window, looking down, making a phone call.
Donna Lauria. Shot to death in New York City. The Son of Sam saga begins.
Sharon Tate. Pregnant. Stabbed to death.
Nancy Warren. Pregnant. Beaten and strangled to death.
Marina Habe. Abducted, raped and murdered on New Year's Eve.
Michael Prokes. Suicide. Immediately before he takes his life, he holds a press conference claiming the CIA was withholding an audio tape made during the Jonestown massacre.
Michael Carr. Automobile crash on the West Side Highway. A Son of Sam cleanup operation?
Drucilla Carr. Suicide.
Howard Green and Carol Marron. Dead in New Jersey. Their bodies found drained of blood.
Dorothy Blackburn. Murdered. Body found in upstate New York. The Arthur Shawcross murders begin.
Joel Dean Pugh. Both wrists and throat slashed. Death ruled a suicide.
Steve Brandt. Gossip columnist. Close friend of Sharon Tate. Afraid for his life after the Manson killings, he flees to New York City. Suicide. Months later, I begin working for his father.
Charlene Cafritz. Had secret Manson videotapes. Suicide by drug overdose.
Joel Rostau. Murdered in New York City.
Ronald Hughes. Manson defense attorney. Murdered.
Laurence Merrick. Manson filmmaker. Murdered.

The names of the victims go on and on.

From Black Dahlias to Red Dragons. From stabbings, to shootings, to subtle poisonings and suspicious "suicides." The blood of these victims stains the black and white pages, and the black and white American soul. I did not come to Malaysia only to wind up as the caretaker of these hideous memories, these dead and staring eyes, these voiceless corpses. But I can hear the clank of the sliding trays in the morgues back in the States and the dull hiss of the minds gone . . . awry. This is the hand I fear most, the hand behind these outrages, several and satanic, for it is one hand and not many that I see, a single nightmare, an epistemological singularity, evil in its finest—most finely-woven, most sub-atomic—form.

The Muslims have finished praying. They walk to their cars. The women in veils called *tudung*, the men in those narrow, dark, brimless caps called songkok, made famous by news photos of Sukarno back in the 1960s, in the Year of Living Dangerously. The Malaysian Prime Minister, beleaguered on all sides by the Asian economic crisis of 1997–99, blamed his country's decline on international Jewish bankers and other, unnamed, "sinister forces." *Sinister* forces. A blast from the past. Our past.

It's all in the files.

Here, photographs of the mass graves at Auschwitz. Here, photographs of Catholic monks and priests, monsignors and bishops, reviewing the Nazi troops marching through small towns in Croatia.

There, crime scene shots in California, New York, Mexico, Texas . . . there, declassified documents coyly hinting at monstrous deeds committed by government officials; there, the arrogant testimony of colonels, crusaders, and Company shrinks.

I walk over to the windows, but am afraid to look up, worried that the hand will strike from there as easily as from a cluttered government office cubicle or a slowly cruising Lincoln Continental. MacArthur was afraid to look up. Hillenkoetter was afraid to look up. Who am I to second-guess these men? Generals and admirals, men with the stink of blood on their hands from the defense of America in time of war; men who sent boys off to the jungles of Asia to fight the Japanese, or commanded naval convoys where flames burned the water in some kind of alchemical allegory, to the deranged counterpoint of screams. This is the hard math of life and death, the calculus of survival. War makes us all scientists for a time. And these men—these military commanders with ribbons and medals who saw tens of thousands march into battle or sail into holocaust, who ordered planes and bombs and all our technology into the feverish, frenzied air—feared *space*, and the threat of alien, sinister forces from above.

Daylight is worrying the edges of the Asian night. The files are open, tossed, backs broken, pages marked. The connective tissue to all of this is here. Strong. Unbreakable. Strings of connections that weave fatal chains whose links laugh at canned history, at consensus reality. In the bookstores in Kuala Lumpur and on the newsstands, you can buy copies of our own, red-blooded American hero Henry Ford's anti-Semitic tract, *The International Jew*, published by some white supremacist, no-name press in South Africa.

And so it goes.

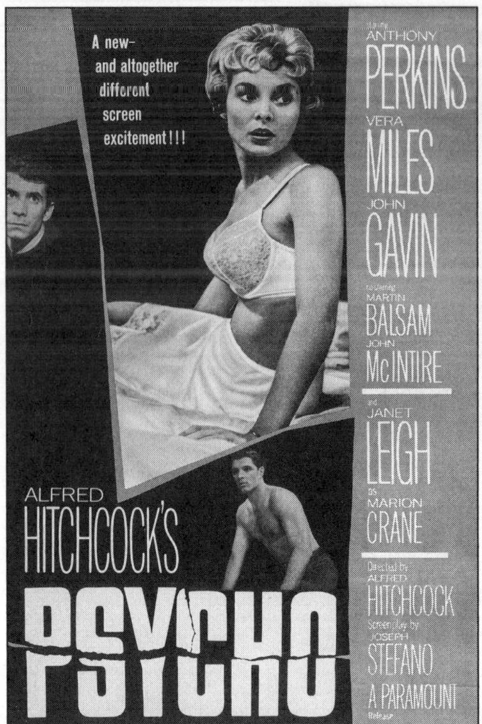

Ed Gein's horrific crimes—particularly his creation of garments from human skin and his complex psychological profile—directly influenced two iconic films in American horror/thriller cinema: *Psycho* (1960) was loosely based on Gein's relationship with his domineering mother and his psychological deterioration, while *The Silence of the Lambs* (1991) drew from Gein's practice of skinning his victims and wearing their flesh, incorporating this into the character of Buffalo Bill who sought transformation through creating a "woman suit." Both films helped establish the template for how serial killers would be portrayed in American cinema, particularly the emphasis on psychological complexity and transformation through violence.

SECTION FIVE:

MAGIC IN THEORY AND PRACTICE

The strange behavior of future shamans has not failed to attract the attention of scholars, and from the middle of the past century several attempts have been made to explain the phenomenon of shamanism as a mental disorder. But the problem was wrongly put. For, on the one hand, it is not true that shamans always are or always have to be neuropathics; on the other hand, those among them who had been ill became shamans precisely because they had succeeded in becoming cured.

—Mircea Eliade[1]

To add confessional uniformity to institutional centralization—to control minds as well as bodies—was an understandable ambition of governments, and the pursuit of spiritual dissidents in the courts could be its practical outcome. Control of political loyalties was, after all, felt to rest on control of denominational ones.

—Stuart Clark[2]

. . . beneath the open surface of our society lie connections and relationships of long standing, virtually immune to disclosure, and capable of great crimes, including serial murder . . . . These forces are still with us, and they are not benign.

—Peter Dale Scott[3]

Magick is a faculty of wonderfull vertue, full of most high mysteries, containing the most profound Contemplation of most secret things, together with the nature, power, quality, substance, and vertues thereof, as also the knowledge of whole nature, and it doth instruct us concerning the differing, and agreement of things amongst themselves, whence it produceth its wonderfull effects, by uniting the vertues of things through the application of them one to the other, and to their inferior suitable subjects, joyning and knitting them together thoroughly by the powers, and vertues of the superior Bodies.

—Cornelius Agrippa, *First Book of Occult Philosophy,* Chapter II

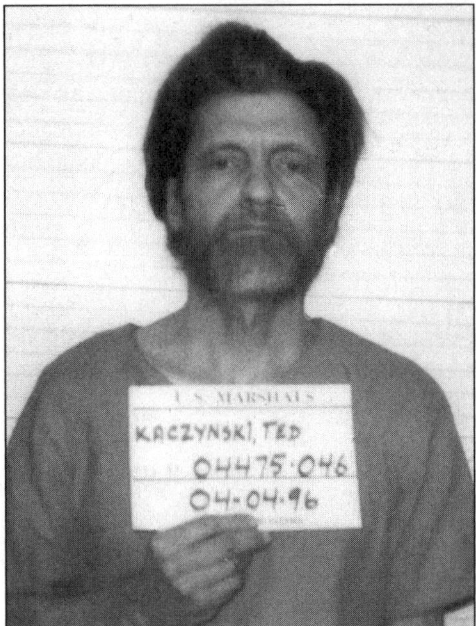

Before he became the infamous Unabomber, Ted Kaczynski was an unwitting subject in a CIA-backed psychological experiment at Harvard under Dr. Henry A. Murray, where brutal personality assessments originally designed for OSS interrogation training were used to systematically break down students' personalities. This previously hidden connection between early CIA mind control experimentation and Kaczynski's later descent into isolation and violence represents one of the clearest documented cases of how government psychological manipulation programs may have contributed to creating the very type of violent offender they sought to understand and control.

CHAPTER SIXTEEN

PSYCHO

I was going to show you how a soul with a weak hold on its tenant could be expelled by another; how, indeed, half-a-dozen personalities could take turns to live in one body. That they are real, independent souls is shown by the fact that not only do the contents of the mind differ—which might conceivably be a fake—but their handwritings, their voices, and that in ways which are quite beyond anything we know in the way of conscious simulation, or even possible simulation.

These personalities are constant quantities; they depart and return unchanged. It is then sure that they do not exist merely by manifestation; they need no body for existence.

—Aleister Crowley[4]

Osiris married his sister Isis and succeeded Ra as king of the earth. However, his brother Set hated him. Set killed Osiris, cut him into many pieces, and scattered the fragments over a wide area.

Isis gathered up the fragments, embalmed them, and resurrected Osiris as king of the nether world, king of the land of the dead . . . . Isis and Osiris had a son, Horus, who defeated Set in battle and became king of the earth. Thus in this myth we see the fragmentation, death, healing, and resurrection of the self in a new form. This is the cycle through which the successfully treated DID (dissociative identity disorder) patient must pass.

—Colin A. Ross[5]

To me, black and white films from the early days of cinema have always seemed somewhat . . . existential. Something to do with film noir, I suppose. One is forced to concentrate more on the story being told, the characterizations, camera angles, etc., as if searching for a hidden meaning. Since there is no color, the shadings are all done with light and darkness, with strips of shadow and sharp, cutting edges: like some kind of Zoroastrian struggle taking place, frame by frame.

This is especially true, I think, of Fritz Lang's masterpiece, *M.*

This is Lang's first sound film, and it is also the first film ever made about a serial killer. Though released in 1931, its issues are strikingly modern and relevant. The film could have been made yesterday, and it humbles us to realize that people agonized over the same moral and legal issues in Weimar Berlin as they do in twenty-first century New York. Briefly, the story is this:

A series of child abductions and murders is taking place in a city in Germany. Little girls are being seduced by gifts of candy and balloons, their bodies sometimes found, sometimes not, a little while later. Details of the crimes are not given, but we are meant to understand that they are hideous. The killer is sending letters to the police and the newspapers, taunting them. The letters are being analyzed by police graphologists in what is perhaps the first instance on film of "profiling."

We know the identity of the killer from the beginning. It is a man named Beckert who is played to perfection by a young Peter Lorre, a Hungarian actor who at the time was also working on a Brecht piece (and similarities between the Lang film and Brecht's work have been noted before). Lorre would rise to prominence in American films later in his career—notably *Casablanca*, *Passage to Marseilles*, etc.—and his pop eyes and strange, lisping voice would become the mainstay of cartoon villains for decades to come.

Beckert has a nervous habit of whistling a melody from Grieg's *Peer Gynt,* and that is how he is eventually identified, by a group of street criminals who want to stop the intense pressure being put on their illegal businesses by the police who are turning the city—and the underworld—inside out in their search for the murderer. Thus, we have both the police and the criminal organizations looking for the killer, the criminals somewhat more successful in that they do not have to rely on the niceties of search and seizure laws to conduct their sweep of the city. That Beckert is eventually captured is a foregone conclusion; what is fascinating is how the killer describes the uncontrollable compulsion that leads him to murder, the fact that he cannot remember the murders themselves, and the struggle of society over what to do with a man who is an "involuntary" killer, a man who cannot be held responsible for his actions. The discussion of how the murderer—if brought to the police—would probably get off with a "not guilty by reason of insanity" plea and be free to walk the streets and kill more little girls is so contemporary that we are shocked into a realization that this conundrum has been going on, continuously and unresolved, since at least that time.

The term "serial killer" is not used, as that phrase was developed in America fifty years after the release of the film; yet the pattern of murders, amnesia, the killer's taunting letters to the police, etc. are identical to those with which we are now familiar from both real-life instances of serial murder as well as the more fanciful treatments by Hollywood.

Is the serial killer a metaphor for something deeper? The Fritz Lang film stops well short of the type of mythologizing of, say, *The Silence of the Lambs*. The 1931 film treats the murderer as a human being suffering from a serious sickness—perhaps mental, perhaps spiritual—that renders him unfit for human society and which puts both the police and the criminal organizations into counterpoint against a case of "real" criminality: we are forced to admit that perhaps the common criminal is simply the mirror image of a policeman, whereas the serial killer is beyond all comparison with normal human activity, legal or illegal.

Modern writers like Thomas Harris (who created the unforgettable Hannibal Lecter) have taken this idea one step further: if the serial killer is indeed outside the normal realm of human behavior, then—on an existential level—what does he represent? By comparing the bizarre actions and beliefs of a serial killer to those of cannibals, primitive shamans, etc., we are drawn to the conclusion that these extreme cases of human behavior—eating human flesh, becoming possessed by spiritual forces—point the way to a different view of society, and of reality itself. Thomas Harris' killers are seeking transformation: either spiritual or psychological transformation or actual physical change. They use murder, torture, and pain as means to this end. In this they are no different from organized killing societies such as the SS, for Hitler himself believed he was using the Nazi Party to create a "new man."

This almost visceral urge to evolve into something different, something other, may indeed be the manifestation of a genetic impulse. Transformation is a theme of many ancient spiritual practices, from the Siberian shaman changing himself into an animal to the dead Egyptian Pharaoh becoming a god, to the transformative rites of the Catholic Mass, to the intense ecstatic rituals of Haitian voudon in which the devotee is temporarily possessed by a god and behaves accordingly. Ancient religion and primitive religion are obsessed by the idea of personal transformation; it is only in the richer and more developed countries that this concept is forgotten as people desperately try to hold on to the status quo. They suddenly have a lot to lose if they become something . . . other.

Thus, the mythology of the serial killer is a warning, perhaps, that this urge is not to be ignored because otherwise it will manifest in very dangerous, very unhealthy ways. And should the reader believe that this "mythology" is a fabrication of novelists and Hollywood scriptwriters, let us examine the myths of some of America's most famous serial murderers to see how deeply religious concepts and iconography adorned their chambers of horrors.

DSM-IV

Before we delve directly into the shamanistic and initiatory aspects of some celebrated serial murderers, let us define our terms. We will discuss the religio-occult terms as we come across them, but for now we should focus on what mainstream psychiatry thinks about such things as multiple personality disorder (MPD), dissociative identity disorder (DID), post-traumatic stress disorder (PTSD), and the whole field of acute mental illness in general. In order to do this, we must consult that bible of the psychiatric profession, the *Diagnostic and Statistical Manual: Mental Disorders*, more commonly referred to as *DSM*.

The first edition of the *DSM* was not published until 1951, following a period of confusion and disorganization in the profession that began in the 1920s, when efforts were undertaken to create an international "Standard Nomenclature of Disease." Various attempts at codifying mental illness by adopting a specific vocabulary were attempted—with varying degrees of success—throughout the 1930s. All of this changed with the onset of World War II.

Many readers may be surprised to learn that the celebrated *DSM* is actually the result of an American *military* mission to provide a comprehensive classification system of mental disease. As the war broke out, psychiatrists realized, "There was a need to account accurately for all causes of morbidity, hence the need for a suitable diagnosis for every case seen by the psychiatrist, a situation not faced in civilian life. Only about 10% of the total cases seen fell into any of the categories ordinarily seen in public mental hospitals. Military psychiatrists, induction station psychiatrists, and Veterans Administration psychiatrists, found themselves operating within the limits of a nomenclature specifically not designed for 90% of the cases handled."[6] In other words, *ninety* percent of the mental illness cases encountered by the military fell outside the normal run of what was experienced in a civilian setting. As an example:

> Relatively minor personality disturbances, which became of importance only in the military setting, had to be classified as, "Psychopathic Personality."[7]

(We may be forgiven if we suggest, therefore, that perhaps some of what we have come to know as mental illnesses are in actuality mental states or conditions not conducive to following orders, marching in lockstep, and blowing someone's brains out.)

The Navy then began to develop its own classification system in 1944, and the Army came up with its own version in 1945, a version that eventually became the one used by the Veterans Administration in 1946. However, by 1948 there were "at least three nomenclatures (Standard, Armed Forces, and Veterans Administration)" in general use, none of which agreed completely with the new International Statistical Classification.[8] What happened next seems dull and unexceptional, except perhaps to a Burgess (*A Clockwork Orange*) or maybe a Blatty (*Twinkle, Twinkle Killer Kane*). To quote once again from the very first edition of the *DSM*:

> Following the adoption of new nomenclatures by the Army and Veterans Administration, the Committee on Nomenclature and Statistics of the American Psychiatric Association postponed change in its recommended official nomenclature pending some evidence as to the usability of the new systems. In 1948, the Committee undertook to learn from the Army and Veterans Administration how successful the changes had been . . .[9]

In other words, the American military was guiding the American Psychiatric Association in the creation of what would become the *Diagnostic and Statistical Manual: Mental Disorders.*

Many Americans know—or are dimly aware—that the excellent interstate highway system in the United States is the result of a Defense Department initiative, designed to enable motorized armor to move swiftly from one area of the country to another in the event of an attack or evacuation. What many Americans do not know is the extent to which the Army and the Navy contributed to other aspects of American life that we take for granted, such as for example the classification of mental disease.

> There were many other details to arrange; the consideration of a proper place for the operation gave rise to much mental labour. It is, generally speaking, desirable to choose the locality of a recent battle; and the greater the number of slain the better. (There should be some very desirable spots in the vicinity of Verdun for black magicians who happen to flourish after the vulgar year 1917).
>
> —Aleister Crowley, *Moonchild*[10]

"Shell shock" was a common concept among the medical profession during World War I. Some of our more famous psychiatrists—such as William Sargant, mentioned in Books I and II in the context of his relationship to Dr. Frank Olson—cut their eye teeth on treating shell shock in World War I veterans. They used everything from drugs to hypnosis to analysis in an effort to ease the suffering of these mentally-wounded soldiers. In fact, Andre Breton—the celebrated *eminence gris* of the Surrealist movement—worked in the same capacity, treating shell shock victims with such occult techniques as automatic writing. (We will examine the Surrealists in more detail in a later chapter.)

Another celebrated therapist of the First War was one W.H.R. Rivers, who exerted considerable influence over the lives and thought of such important individuals of the time as the poet Siegfried Sassoon and the poet, novelist and mythologian Robert Graves (who was also a confidant of Sargant, another therapist who specialized in shell shock and the application of psychotherapy in a military setting). Rivers had spent some time studying the enigmatic Toda tribe of India, a strange ethnic group that seems to trace their origins to the ancient Middle East, including—according to some observers—ancient Sumeria. Rivers treated Sassoon at a military hospital for shell shock (or, as it seemed to some critics, malingering) and began to derive a philosophy of the mind from the experience as well as from his background in ethnology and the study of primitive cultures.

In a lecture given after the War, he had this to say about the relationship between mental illness and combat:

> Perhaps the most striking feature of the war from the medical point of view has been the enormous scale upon which its conditions have produced functional nervous disorders, a scale far surpassing any previous war, although the

> Russo-Japanese campaign gave indications of the mental and nervous havoc which the conditions of modern warfare are able to produce.
>
> —W. H. R. Rivers to the John Rylands Library, April 9, 1919

This idea that modern warfare contributes to a serious rise in mental disorders is one that would influence William Sargant and others following in the footsteps of the great therapists of the first decades of the twentieth century. Rivers would devote a great deal of his time towards an understanding of the relationship between "Medicine, Magic and Religion" (as a collection of his essays is entitled), looking for a solution to the problem of the mind-body dichotomy. This, of course, is the bedrock of what would become the mind control programs of the Americans, the Soviets, the Chinese and others, although Rivers—a humanitarian and idealist—would presumably have been horrified to see his insights result in such experimentation.

As World War I became World War II—and "shell shock" became "battle fatigue"—military authorities were under pressure to counter the growing incidence of soldiers unfit for combat due to mental disturbances. This situation became quite severe during the Korean War, when a new wrinkle—"brainwashing"—was added to the mix. In November 1951—the height of the Korean conflict—the very first edition of the *DSM* was finalized.

By the time we were coming out of the Vietnam War, the *DSM* had gone through several editions. "Battle fatigue" had become institutionalized as "post traumatic stress disorder" or PTSD, in *DSM-III*. And suddenly the era of the "crazed Vietnam veteran" was upon us, introducing a new breed of menace in American streets: the lonely, alienated warrior who had seen and experienced too much in the Southeast Asian jungles, had taken too many drugs, had killed too many people, had learned loyalty and sacrifice under fire only to see these values mocked by his Stateside friends and family. He hallucinates, has flashbacks of the jungle, cannot relate to his wife or girlfriend, and winds up wandering the streets at night, stoned, armed, and believing he is back in the jungle. A killing machine. A powder keg ready to explode.

It was an urban myth to a certain extent, of course, pumped up and exploited by the media in novels, movies, and television shows, but it was a short slide from the "crazed Vietnam veteran" to a particular refinement of the archetype in the more robust "serial killer." With the serial killer, we forgot all about the crazed Vietnam vets and began worrying about the quiet, soft-spoken, socially inept young white man next door with the foul body odor, the rotting teeth, the uneducated English, and the basement full of corpses. It was a pop-culture segue from the Age of Manson to the Age of Lucas, Dahmer, Gacy, and Bundy. Manson had a retinue of young women and men to carry out his bizarre plans; the serial killers worked alone, or in pairs. They derived pleasure from committing the acts directly, themselves, and would never have dreamed of "farming out" the work to a "Family." The body count of a single serial killer such as Dahmer or Gacy would be far greater than that of a Manson. And what's more, they were solo acts.

For some reason, the serial killer captured the American imagination. Murder has always been interesting to people, but usually in the slightly claustrophobic and socially-refined venue of the detective story. The stories of Agatha Christie, Arthur Conan Doyle, and Edgar Allan Poe (the father of the detective story) defined our notion of how to handle the grotesque and the morbid: we have brilliant amateurs who trace minute specs of evidence or apply an unassailable logic to the conditions of the crime to identify and apprehend the perpetrator. They are crimes solved by science and logic tables.

With the serial killer, however, we enter the world of the motiveless crime, a world where the abilities of a Sherlock Holmes or a Miss Marple would shatter like a stained glass window in the rays of a hideous insanity, a lust for blood, a ritualistic slashing of the carving knife. We are desperate to understand the serial killer, finding in him a fascinating and compelling introduction to the dark corners and fetid basements of our own troubled psyches. And, just as Freud sought to understand the human mind by examining its pathologies, we come to understand not only the substance of our own souls by studying the serial killer but—as authors of serial killer fiction such as Thomas Harris have implied—also the possibilities of our transformation. We seek, in the blood and madness and gore of the serial killer's frenzied occupation, the rites of the shaman, the illumination of the magician, the ecstatic trance of the medium, the possession by a god.

The hallmark American film which sensationalized the serial killer was Alfred Hitchcock's masterpiece, *Psycho* (1960). It was based, loosely, on the case of a genuine serial killer, Ed Gein, who murdered women and saved their skin to sew together as garments, creating a kind of "woman suit" that he could wear. The character of Norman Bates—played by Anthony Perkins—is in the grip of what would come to be known as multiple personality disorder (MPD). He is sometimes Norman Bates, and sometimes his abusive (and dead) mother. The idea that Norman grew up in a physically-abusive household which molded his personality—or, to be more precise, dissociated his personality—is hinted at in the film but not emphasized. It is Norman's own insanity that confronts us, not that of his mother.

As the psychiatric profession developed its theories of personality disorders, it abandoned the concept of "multiple personalities" to embrace one of "dissociated personalities," i.e., taking the philosophical stance that there is only one personality allowed per human being but that it can, at times, become dissociated: splinter into several parts, as it were. Whatever name we give it (and some psychiatrists are not happy with the dissociative identity disorder—DID—classification and retain MPD as their preferred nomenclature), the disorder is easily confused with what our ancestors thought of as demonic possession, for in a case of DID the personality undergoes a profound change, sometimes even in front of the therapist. The patient will speak in a different voice, perhaps that of a different sex, different age group, act differently, use a different vocabulary and "present" differently from the other personality or personalities. Each personality may remember what has happened to the other personalities, or more usually may not. This type of amnesia is common in cases of DID, and was of intense interest to the CIA scientists of MK-ULTRA.

Yet, involved with the already heady experience of dealing with a serial killer who may be suffering from DID, we also have—in the fictional case of *Psycho* but also in the actual case of Ed Gein—the concept of transformation.

This idea that one can transform oneself spiritually (or physically) through murder and mutilation was explored by novelist Thomas Harris in his famous *The Silence of the Lambs*, since made into a film (1991) starring Jodie Foster as FBI Special Agent Clarice Starling and Anthony Hopkins as Dr. Hannibal Lecter. In this story, the serial killer is a virtual Ed Gein, capturing women and starving them so that their skin would become loose on their bodies, and then killing them and removing the skin. His goal—after being turned down by several sex-change clinics—was to become a woman, and to do this he would don a woman's actual skin, or a skin suit composed of pieces of various women.

That this smacks of pure lycanthropy, as practiced by shamanistic cults the world over, albeit with animal skins, usually goes unnoticed. Yet, to further drive home his message, Harris has his serial killer insert the larva of a specific type of moth into the mouths of his victims when he dumps their bodies. The moth, of course, is a symbol of transformation. The mythology is carefully worked out and, it must be said, beyond the imagination and creativity of most serial killers one comes across in the news. That does not mean, however, that the genuine serial killer is not (subconsciously at least) seeking transformation. But we must ask ourselves, Is transformation a code word for psychic integration? Or does it mean something more?

THE MANCHURIAN SERIAL KILLER

A favorite topic in the underground press is the concept that some serial killers are the victims of a government mind-control project run amok. With the Rockefeller Commission investigations in the 1970s and the subsequent revelation that the United States had carried out a number of experiments on violent offenders—dosing them with enormous amounts of LSD, for instance—one comes to the natural conclusion that the experience must have made a deep and serious impact on the already fragile psyches of these dangerous felons. Did they get religion? Did they become mystics, eschewing their former lives of murder and rape, under the benign energy flowing into their souls from the kindly government medical men in their white robes and insincere smiles, hypodermic syringes raised to the heavens? Or, as is more likely, did the intense psychological pressure of the massive dosage of hallucinogens force some other, less savory, response of these men in prison cells and iron shackles? Unfortunately, we shall never know.

The files have been destroyed. We don't even know their names. We don't know what streets they wander, or what diseased daydreams occupy them as they gaze upon the rest of us in their madness.

As we saw in Book II, Congressman Leo Ryan believed that the leadership of the Symbionese Liberation Army might have been victims of an MK-ULTRA program during their incarceration at Vacaville prior to their assault on California banks and the kidnapping of Patty Hearst. Congressman Ryan would be murdered in the presence of the local CIA *resident* only a few months after he made his inquiries of the CIA.

A more pressing case before us, however, is that of convicted serial killer Arthur Shawcross. In Shawcross we have all the elements of a paranoid fantasy that even Hollywood would find a hard time digesting. A Vietnam veteran, child molester, rapist, and murderer who is set free only to kill again. A man who claimed a history of violent encounters in Vietnam . . . but whose official Army records deny any substance to the stories. A man whose brain shows evidence of surgical intervention, but whose Army medical records were classified and not permitted to be reviewed by his own defense team. A man who claimed he heard voices, haunted by ghosts no one else could see.

A common defense for serial murder—entertained, if not actually implemented at trial—is the insanity plea. We will look at that more closely a little later, but for now it is enough to know that this plea (with its origins in nineteenth century British jurisprudence) is honored more in the breach than in the observance. The insanity plea is rarely used, not quite so often as Hollywood would have us believe, but it is a tantalizing plea nevertheless. As in the Fritz Lang film mentioned above, society seems to realize that there exists in the world the "involuntary" killer, the man (or sometimes the woman) driven to kill by uncontrollable impulses; a man who is not whole, or not wholly human. A man who cannot be held accountable for his crimes.

A traditional tactic of the defense attorney—and defense psychiatrist—in attempting to convince a judge and jury of the insanity of their client is to demonstrate the existence of some kind of organic mental illness, something that can be proven in the laboratory: a chemical imbalance, say, or severe brain damage. Perhaps a tumor, or lesions in the temporal lobe. Many of our most famous serial killers have, indeed, such a medical history. Bobby Joe Long of Kenova, West Virginia had been hit on the head as a child, beaten with an iron pipe. The damage was severe, and could be seen in X-rays of his head. He also had a demonstrable chemical imbalance and all sorts of hormonal problems. Bobby Joe Long had to have sex many times during the day, and when no sexual partner was available he resorted to constant masturbation. Eventually, he became known as the Want-Ad Rapist in southern Florida, a man responsible for the rape and murder of many young women. Incidentally, Long served some time in the US Army before being discharged due to his peculiar personal habits and his violence towards authority.

When the mental disorder is not organic, it is not uncommon for the defense to wonder if their client is the victim of multiple personalities, the Dissociated Identity Disorder of the *DSM-IV*. In the case of a true "multiple," the perpetrator of the crime is only one of the many personalities inhabiting the defendant. The others may have no knowledge at all that a murder has been committed, much less that they are actually responsible. They have total amnesia of the event, and only the personality who actually committed the murder will know anything about it. This, of course, is exactly what the CIA wanted to achieve in the MK-ULTRA experiments.

What many casual observers do not realize is that the "not guilty by reason of insanity" defense was, itself, originally a politically-motivated one. Like the *DSM*, and so much else in American science and psychiatry, it had its origins in politics.

NOT GUILTY BY REASON OF INSANITY

Some criminals in the United States and in other countries have managed to escape a harsh penalty—death or life imprisonment—due to this strange, even profound, concept. It is understood that moral responsibility and madness do not mix; therefore, the insane can only be hospitalized and not penalized. Readers may be forgiven if they believe that "insanity" is a clinical term, a medical designation. It is not. It is a legal term, and pretends to describe a state of mind in which the accused is unaware of the difference between right and wrong and therefore incapable of making moral choices. There is even a special subset of this condition, known as "temporary insanity," in which the accused was in this state of mind only during the time necessary to commit the crime and was remarkably "sane" later. In this latter case, there is no need for either hospitalization or prison; the accused often walks.

In Malaysia, a particularly ugly episode took place in 1969. It is known as the "May 13th Incident." Without going into detail about Malaysian politics, suffice it to say that the Malay racial hegemony over this multi-ethnic society was briefly challenged by a coalition of opposition parties chiefly composed of ethnic Chinese, who in Malaysia are generally either Christian or Buddhist. Rather than celebrate their victory indoors, out of sight of the restless Malays, the Chinese supporters decided to stage an ad hoc parade through their neighborhoods. The ethnic Malay (and religiously Muslim) politicians began churning up their followers, fanning the flames of fear, paranoia and hatred. What happened next is a matter for the history books, and has been told to me by many persons who lived through it. Malay men—some of them in uniform, troops called out to quell the violence but who, instead, found themselves contributing to it—fell upon the Chinese with knives, both the long, machete-like *parang* and the wavy-bladed *kriss*. Thus began hours and then three days of terror as ethnic Malays attacked ethnic Chinese in the streets and in some cases house to house. More than 6000 Malaysians—90%

of them ethnic Chinese—were homeless in Kuala Lumpur by the end of this savagery, as their houses and shops were burned to the ground; the official government statistic shows 178 dead although this figure is challenged, many critics insisting the death toll was much higher.

No one was ever brought to trial for this outrage. The reason? The Malays had "gone *amok*." *Amok* is one of a handful of Malaysian words that is familiar to Western audiences, being rather colorful and exciting. It is classed nowadays as a kind of momentary pathological state of blood lust. Like going "berserk"—a mental state closely related to "amok"—the victim is possessed by an insensible violent spirit that can only be diminished over time. Since the Malays were amok at the time of the massacres, they could not be held accountable for their actions. It was a group version of "not guilty by reason of insanity," and temporary insanity, at that; it was used to excuse an outbreak of politically, racially and religiously-motivated violence that is still remembered with horror today.

The first case in which the verdict "not guilty by reason of insanity" was pronounced was not during a normal criminal trial, but in a notorious political assassination scandal. In 1843 the accused, a Mr. Daniel M'Naghten, had attacked British Prime Minister Sir Robert Peel. M'Naghten—a Scotsman and a wood-turner—believed that the British Prime Minister was oppressing him. Knowing the historic relationship between the people of Scotland and the people of England, we must at least admit this was a theoretical possibility . . . . Be that as it may, Mr. M'Naghten believed that demonic forces were bent on his destruction and that they were personified by Sir Robert. He fired into a carriage carrying both Sir Robert and his secretary. He mistook the secretary for Sir Robert (there being no television in those days and precious little photographic coverage, so mistaken identity was perhaps more of a problem then than now) and the secretary was wounded. The secretary walked to his home after the attack, so he was not in mortal danger at that time. However, he had very poor medical care and died shortly thereafter from complications. Sir Robert managed to survive the attack. The Queen was outraged, and was looking forward to the death penalty for such an outlandish and willful attack on her ministers, but Mr. M'Naghten was sent to the mental asylum known as Bedlam after having been judged not to be in the possession of all his faculties. The verdict? *Not guilty by reason of insanity.* This has since become known as the M'Naghten Rule, after the famous would-be assassin. And, at the same time, the stereotype of the "crazed, lone assassin" was born.

In the United States, we marginalize political assassins. They are either crazed loners—like Oswald, Hinckley, Chapman—or they are marginal people, such as the Palestinian Sirhan B. Sirhan. The established ruling class of a country cannot accept a sane, reasonable assassin any more than they can accept the points of view of their political or military enemies. Assassins are, by definition, insane or somehow racially or ethnically "other," if not actually inferior. They do not come from the body politic. They are outsiders, and their outsider status is what causes them to commit these crimes. We cannot afford to give these assassins a soap box from which to convince us of the rightness of their actions, because we may be swayed by a person who is so consumed by political conviction that he picks up a gun and rids the country of someone we may be tempted to realize was a tyrant, and by extension therefore to question the present government altogether.

So, we eventually accept a subliminal message every time an assassin is murdered or otherwise silenced before he or she can stand trial: *to attack the king is insanity.*

Oswald was a perfect case. A misfit, a loner, a defector who had spent time in the Evil Empire (the Soviet Union, which had a practice of putting political dissidents in mental institutions, thus implying that *the entire non-Communist world* was psychotic). He returned to America with his Russian wife and shortly thereafter found himself in Dallas, accused of killing the President. Well, anyone who desires to attack and kill the ruler of a kingdom is, by definition, unhappy. A misfit. Someone who feels he has already been marginalized by a state that has no room for him; or by life itself, perhaps, which is so full of contradiction and hypocrisy that the only healthy state of mind may be insanity (*vide* psychiatrists Laing and Szacs, not to mention visionary literature from Gogol to Vonnegut and Tom Robbins). The assassination of a president may, from this point of view, be an act of clarity cloaked in ritual: an attempt to awaken a sleeping population and, at the same time, to exact revenge for an unimaginable list of perceived crimes against humanity.

Those who may be scandalized by the above few lines should realize that there is no truly objective state of sanity; that the psychological states so carefully enumerated and tabulated in *DSM-IV* are so socially-loaded that it becomes obvious that the people who threaten us or our perceptions of life are the ones we declare mentally ill. As in Euclidean geometry, there are certain—in this case, unspoken—axioms which we take to be self-evident, such as "parallel lines do not meet" or "sociopaths feel no guilt." In other words, what we have determined to be mental disorders are reflective of a certain point of view about society itself and not about the human mind or the human spirit, which is (or perhaps should be) much more than merely its social function.

As mentioned, "insanity" is a legal term, not a medical one. It is a complex knot of moral, social, cultural and behavioral assumptions; much more so "temporary insanity." But it can be an excuse for some of the most hideous crimes ever committed. In our society, a man who kills and eats his enemy can be pretty safely considered "insane." Serial killer Jeffrey Dahmer had a collection of body parts in his apartment, and had built an altar there to display them, after the fashion of a Borneo headhunter. These actions revolted us, and with good reason. But in the case of the Kwakiutl Cannibal Societies of North America mentioned in Eliade, for instance, such behavior was *central to the rites of transformation* and accepted by these societies as such.[11] Talking to spirits may provide one's peers with enough cause for certification to a mental hospital, but many primitive (and not so primitive) religious societies could not exist without this essential component. And what of Catholics who believe that they are eating the flesh and blood of a man who died on a cross two thousand years ago . . . and that they are partaking of his divinity, his godhead by doing so . . . and that he rose from the dead and ascended bodily into heaven?

> *To be 'crazy' is a social concept; we use social restrictions and definitions in order to distinguish mental disturbances . . . . It is not an absolute increase in insanity that makes our asylums swell like monsters, it is the fact that we cannot stand abnormal people any more, so there are apparently very many more crazy people than formerly.*
> —C.G. Jung[12]

One of our more famous serial killers of the past century—Earl Nelson, who was charged with committing more than 20 murders over a period of only 18 months—was the subject of an intense debate over the insanity plea. He was charged in Canada in 1927, where some of his murders were committed, and subject to the British legal system which gave us the M'Naghten Rule. Insanity was invoked as a possible defence, but no one could agree on just what insanity (or sanity, for that matter) meant. The two prevailing opinions were that "insanity" only meant not knowing right from wrong; or that insanity was of a "cyclic" nature and knowing right from wrong one moment did not mean that one knew right from wrong at another moment (hence, "temporary insanity"). The issue, though is with "right" and "wrong."

Normally, it seems to be the case that these are interpreted in a purely legal way. In other words, insanity is an inability to understand what society considers legal and illegal. I submit that in this rapidly shrinking world where it is possible for me to be in Beijing at 10 A.M. and in New York City at 5 P.M. the same day due to jet travel and time zones, that not knowing what is legal in one country does not necessarily mean one is insane. Of course, many readers will object to this oversimplification; obviously, killing another human being is wrong anywhere, it is illegal everywhere. But that itself is an oversimplification and begs the question: what does it mean to be insane? Killing the enemy on the battlefield is considered legal and sane; killing the same man a year later on a city street is illegal, and if the person who commits that crime does not realize this, then he is insane. Is it perhaps a problem of society itself, that sanity is a moveable feast to be determined not by science but by politicians? And that somehow the State has managed to arrogate to itself the power to determine the state of our souls?

Clearly what is needed is a new approach to the concepts of sanity and insanity, as well as of blood lust, psychopathology and sociopathology, even transformation, initiation, and spiritual growth. We are accustomed to believing that spiritual growth is possible only by prayer and meditation and good works. Unfortunately, the record of the world's religions will show that spiritual growth may be dependent on such horrors that we may be forgiven for relinquishing advanced states of spirituality, exchanging the possibility for a new lawn mower, video game or the latest Britney Spears CD.

Susan Sontag has given us a brilliant invitation to the world of the insane in her article on the French actor, playwright, author and director Antonin Artaud, "Approaching Artaud." She discusses the provincial nature of the concept of madness and cites the outrage over the practice in the (now former) Soviet Union of locking political dissidents up in insane asylums as "misplaced." Further along she states,

> In every society, the definitions of sanity and madness are arbitrary—are, in the largest sense, political.[13]

And further,

> Artaud . . . saw the insane as the heroes and martyrs of thought, stranded at the vantage point of extreme social (rather than merely psychological) alienation, *volunteering for madness*—as those who, through a superior conception of honor, prefer to go mad rather than forfeit a certain lucidity . . . (emphasis added)[14]

Far from being the province of privileged academia, however, the study of madness and politics has a more pedestrian, more utilitarian purpose. Madness, you see, can be harnessed for political ends . . . if only we know how to induce it, how to maintain it, and how to get rid of it when necessary.

In other words, we need to know how to become shamans.

Artaud saw his own escalating mental disorder as just such a path towards illumination. While Sontag, above, interprets madness as a political term in her discussion of Artaud, Artaud himself writes,

> My confinement was thus a religious matter, an affair of initiation and spells, of black magic and also most importantly of white magic, however unpopular that may be.[15]

Without realizing what they were doing, this is precisely what the CIA attempted to do from 1950 to 1973, and probably much more recently than that. This is also what the military tried to do beginning roughly at the same time and continuing for an unknown period, possibly even to the present day. The goal was to create the perfect spy and the perfect assassin. The CIA claims they did not succeed at either, at least not through their mind-control projects which fit under the umbrella of MK-ULTRA. However, when we examine the claims and counterclaims of those involved in debunking or supporting the "repressed memory syndrome" concept, we will see that someone, somewhere must be lying.

The central concept behind the shamanistic initiation is the controlled derangement (reorganization?) of the human mind in such a way that it follows a predictable and useful pattern. I use the term "shamanistic" in the sense that Mircea Eliade and others have done: not to devalue the process or to attribute it only to "primitive" peoples or practices, but to refer to a natural and vibrant mystico-psychological process to accomplish what Jung might have termed "individuation," but which (because of the paranormal abilities involved) might be closer to the presumed accomplishments of certain yogis. The descriptions of the torments the shamanic initiate had to undergo are close in feeling and content to those of an early Christian ascetic in the desert: everything from a sensation of dying to complete dismemberment, decapitation, disembowelment, and worse. What is interesting is that this process is undergone voluntarily and willfully, and this fact perhaps more than any other points out how relatively easy it must be for any of us to go "insane." As Eliade writes,

> The strange behavior of future shamans has not failed to attract the attention of scholars, and from the middle of the past century several attempts have been made to explain the phenomenon of shamanism as a mental disorder. But the problem was wrongly put. For, on the one hand, it is not true that shamans always are or always have to be neuropathics; on the other hand, those among them who had been ill *became shamans precisely because they had succeeded in becoming cured* . . . . But if shamanism cannot simply be identified with a psychopathological phenomenon, it is nevertheless true that the shamanic vocation often implies a crisis so deep that it sometimes borders on madness . . . . But I should like even now to stress the fact that the psychopathology of the shamanic vocation is not profane; it does not belong to ordinary symptomatology. (emphasis in original)[16]

One is reminded of the case of August Strindberg, the Swedish playwright who descended into madness for a period of years (fueled by occult and alchemical researches, by the way; he claimed to have made gold from base metals and there was talk of proposing him for a Nobel Prize in science) and then came out on the other side, "sane" and productive. Others were not so fortunate: Nietzsche, Artaud, Van Gogh are easy examples. Eliade wrote the above passage in 1958, when MK-ULTRA was in its heyday. It is tempting to wonder if the G-scale experimenters were familiar with his work, and if they understood what they were doing to the psyches of the subjects—both willing and unwilling—at their disposal. The evidence we have suggests not. Both in the LSD testing that was conducted on violent offenders—with huge doses administered over days and weeks—to the notorious "psychic driving" systems developed by Dr. Ewen Cameron in Montreal, it is obvious that there was no thought at all to what the procedures were doing to the mental, emotional or (dare we say it?) spiritual states of the unwitting test subjects. In fact, the CIA (and the military) were opening a Pandora's Box of demonic forces: the black box of consciousness. It is the story of a modern day Dr. Frankenstein, or a laboratory full of Drs. Frankenstein, and the monsters they made: monsters that wander the streets of our cities today. The complexity of the human experience is such that we can only wonder what trigger mechanisms exist in the environment—on television, in newspapers and magazines, and even the Internet—that suggest modes of behavior to these victims that are dangerous to themselves and to us. The records of these experiments were destroyed. The names and identification of the test subjects have been erased. Those few who have come forward with bizarre memories of mind-control scenarios are laughed off the stage; they are so obviously deranged that no one can take them seriously. Or they are in prison for committing various crimes—some of them violent—so their testimony is ignored as tainted. Isn't it ironic? Don't you think?

POSSESSION, DEMONIACAL AND . . . OTHER

> The question as to what extent the investigator, the exorcist, the therapist or even the community generally contribute towards the creation of multiple personalities is by no means an easy one even to formulate satisfactorily . . .
>
> —T. K. Oesterreich, *Possession, Demoniacal and Other*[17]

> Madness is rare in individuals—but in groups, parties, nations, and ages it is the rule.
>
> —Friedrich Nietzsche[18]

A reading of *DSM-IV* is an education, though not necessarily in the way intended by the authors of this grimoire of mental illness. When we look at some of the more infamous disorders—such as sociopathy, psychopathy, dissociative identity disorder (the old "multiple personality disorder")—we see lists of symptoms that could easily apply to our most cherished Hollywood film characters . . . or the protagonists of some of our most popular novels. Certainly one could make a case for some of our revered political leaders being absolutely off their rockers, according to the list of symptoms given in the *DSM*. Nixon comes to mind when we discuss the Paranoid type, for instance.

The psychotic have always made good copy, and great movies. Hannibal Lecter, for example, as the cannibalistic psychiatrist and serial murderer; the psychotic arch-enemies in the James Bond films; Anthony Perkins as *Psycho*, itself a film based on the real-life serial killer Ed Gein. *Dracula* has been identified by many authors as a thinly-veiled sexual psychopath. And, of course, the mad scientists of *Frankenstein, Dr. Jekyll and Mr. Hyde*, and a host of others spanning the history of cinema, and of Romantic-era literature generally, attempting to penetrate the mysteries of nature by taking the most awful risks and jeopardizing the very nature they are trying to understand. They go insane, eventually, either because of their blasphemous studies (most of which are being undertaken quite blandly today in the world's most modern laboratories) or because of the guilt that overcomes them when they realize what they have done.

But the factor that most interests us in this case when speaking of mental illness is the use made of mental disorders by shamans and the proverbial "witch doctors," who see this type of (sometimes voluntary) madness as a prerequisite to spiritual understanding and occult power. And in order to understand that, in context, we have to look at how thinking about mental illness in the ages before psychiatry was often confounded with thinking about demonic possession.

> *Since we have access to the unconscious only through pathological material, our efforts arouse the resistance of the conscious, awake individual. Yet all this is inconsequential compared with the one great fact which [Freud] did not mention: that it is of the essence of his simple and ingenious approach to make something unconscious comprehensible by grasping it in illness and kindred states. Only through pathological material could sure knowledge be won . . .*
>
> —Lou Andreas-Salomé, *Freud Journal*, Oct. 26, 1912

According to Oesterreich, in his landmark and definitive study *Possession, Demoniacal and Other*, the phenomenon of possession is a central element to religious faith, because it seems to offer concrete proof of an afterlife, and of the existence of spiritual forces. Whether the possession is by a demon, an animal spirit, or a divine being, the displacement of a human's personality by the personality of an Other is considered by most to be proof positive of the existence of spiritual forces. This type of phenomenon is very hard to discredit, because in so-called "actual" cases of possession, the new personality is so alien to the original that the only explanation that comes to mind is that the old personality has been evicted, so to speak, from the organism and a wholly new—i.e., "other"—personality has taken its place. This other personality must therefore be a spirit that is lacking a physical body, and therefore there must exist spirits in addition to whatever animates our bodies while we are alive.

Demonic possession became a household phrase in the 1970s with the publication of the novel *The Exorcist,* written by William Peter Blatty, a Hollywood screenwriter. As is well-known by now, the novel was based on an actual case of possession that took place in a small town in Maryland while Blatty was a student at Georgetown University. What is not so well-known is that Blatty himself had been an intelligence officer, specializing in psychological warfare, in the years before writing his famous novel. It was Blatty who also wrote the screenplay for a film that came to be known as *The Ninth Configuration* (1980) after his original novel *Twinkle, Twinkle Killer Kane,* a book and film that come as close to describing the arcane world of military psychiatry as any (imagine *Catch-22* meets *The Manchurian Candidate*). It was Blatty who took us through the strange and horrifying world of possession and gave it a scientific-sounding name—briefly—before taking it away again: *somnambulaform possession*. Not exactly a genuine scientific term, it can be found in Oesterreich's work, which was a source for Blatty when it came to organizing the material around a scientific viewpoint, but it will not be found in *DSM-III* or *-IV*. Unfortunately, in the novel, the scientists cannot help the possessed girl later played by Linda Blair, and priests—exorcists—are called in to perform the rituals that will drive out the demon and save the child.

There are many interesting points of contact between *The Exorcist* and Stoker's *Dracula*, and this is probably not the place to go into them. One could suggest wondering why the demon is invisible in *The Exorcist* even though we have a young girl in mortal danger being rescued by an older expert in occult phenomena who is also a scientist; in *Dracula*, the demon—this time in the form of Count Dracula, the vampire itself—is very much visible. Does Regan's demon represent an element in ourselves—psychological or cultural—that we do not wish to face, or admit?

No matter. What is interesting is that the novel, and then the film, sparked a nearly global interest in demonic possession and kept movie theaters—and churches—filled for some time to come.

Until the devil we knew was replaced by a devil we didn't know.

We have become accustomed by now to accounts of Multiple Personality Disorder (MPD), what is now also known as Dissociative Identity Disorder (DID). The former designation implied the existence of more than one personality in a single human being; the new designation implies a breaking down of the unitary personality into a group of fragmentary personalities. Regardless of the mechanism behind the phenomenon, what we have in this type of condition is the invasion of a human's consciousness by an alien personality. Now, this personality may be a fragment of the original, or it may be a kind of "split" from the original now functioning independently of the original. In any case, it could appear to be demonic to the lay observer and the person could seem to be suffering from an involuntary possession.

The new personality or personalities often has information that the original personality does not; is able to speak in different accents or even in different languages and even to be conscious of much biographical information of which the original was not. In the case of MPD or Dissociative Identity Disorder, this may only be a temporary or fluctuating situation; i.e., the new personality is in control for a short period of time and then retreats into the background, allowing the original personality—or another personality—to regain control. It is typical of these cases that the original personality has no memory of what transpired when the "alter" was in control.

This condition would have been of utmost interest to the mind-control researchers for all that was implied in terms of memory and control. If the scientists could create an alter personality in a given subject, for instance, they could create a robot. This would be true only if the scientists were able to control the alter themselves. This would probably be difficult to do, since the evidence at the moment suggests that the alter is a defense mechanism of the original personality, to protect it against a traumatic episode (child abuse, for instance, being the most common and most documented cause). Also, there is a danger that the alter—possessed of a perfect memory—would not be the ideal mechanism for creating spies and assassins.

Yet, the basic functions of multiple personality disorder would have attracted the scientists and they would have sought ways in which they could create and/or manipulate multiples. Fortunately for them, there is a large literature on voluntary possession. As documented by Oesterreich and in other places, this experience is worldwide, and the author has been privileged to witness this phenomenon first-hand in various countries, notably in Haiti, in the United States, and in parts of Asia.

What is perhaps not so widely known to the general public is the fact that the very concept of multiple personality disorder (and its recent incarnation as dissociative identity disorder) has led to a schism among psychiatric professionals. There are those who deny that the disorder is genuine, and accuse either the psychiatrists of fraud or gullibility, or the patients of malingering. There are those—also professionals in psychology and psychiatry—on the far opposite side of the spectrum who feel that MPD and DID are proof of the existence of an afterlife, of reincarnation, and the like. There is even one psychiatrist who has alleged that a woman suffering from multiple personalities was a witch and had cursed him, causing his ulcer to flare up.

The division between those who "believe" in MPD/DID and those who do not seems to be a function of whether the therapist had ever confronted such a case. Those who have treated this disorder claim that there is no way their patients could pretend to have multiple personalities, that the personality changes are so defined, so extreme, as to be beyond the capabilities of all but the most accomplished, Oscar-winning actor. In addition, there is the problem that some of these "alter" personalities may have powers and abilities—such as in foreign languages, or certain of the sciences—that the other personalities do not have, and which the "core personality" has never studied or learned. There is also the question of amnesia, with some of the personalities remembering events in the person's life and others not—which has led to a controversy over legal responsibility in the case where a person suffering from MPD/DID has committed a crime and only one of the personalities is aware of this.

Those who snicker at the claims of MPD/DID do so based largely on the philosophical platform that each person has only one personality, i.e., that there is only one personality allowed per body. In other words, the argument runs (as it does for most subjects considered even remotely "paranormal") from the conclusion backward to the proof. The assumption is that no two personalities can inhabit the same consciousness, much less fifteen or twenty or more in some documented cases of MPD/DID. And the fact that spiritual possession occurs in so many "primitive" cultures does actually provide an argument *against* the validity of MPD/DID, since the medical professionals point to what they interpret as the natural credulity and superstition of these cultures as being the breeding ground for this particular form of "hysteria." If the condition can be acquired voluntarily, they argue, then it is obviously not a unique psychological disorder but a simple case of delusion, paranoia, or hysteria. But, if the condition can be *acquired*, then the mind-control researchers of MK-ULTRA had something to work with.

Those who submit to the voluntary form of possession are doing so in order to contact the world beyond life; to speak with spirits; to effect material changes in this world by utilizing supernatural "connections." Voluntary possession—such as that made famous by the practitioners of *voudoun* (or "voodoo," as it is usually spelled) seems to our eyes a kind of sorcery. The possession is of a controlled nature: there is a limited hierarchy of spiritual forces that can possess the devotee, and each member of this hierarchy can be recognized by certain visible signs. For instance, someone possessed by Baron Samedi will be seen to smoke cigars, drink rum, walk with a limp, and comport him-(or her-)self in an old-worldly, gentlemanly way. Erzulie, the Goddess of Love, is obvious by her behavior and her love of flowers, etc. It is to be noted that these cases of possession only occur within the rigidly controlled and structured environment of the ritual itself. That being said, another phenomenon does take place—again, witnessed by the author, both in Haiti and in New York City's borough of Queens—in which a bystander, heretofore unexposed to this type of experience, is himself or herself possessed by one of the Haitian gods, or *loa*. This "contagious" aspect of possession is remarked upon by Oesterreich, and perhaps the most famous example in literature is that reported by Aldous Huxley in *The Devils of Loudon*, in which nuns, priests and the exorcists themselves became possessed by an epidemic of demonic forces. Actually, in the case of the voudoun rituals, the dynamics of the rituals themselves are catalysts and can conceivably act upon anyone, even uptight middle-aged white executives from Silicon Valley. The timbre and rhythm of the drums, for instance, and the dark, candle-lit *peristyle* with the waving of flags, the chanting, the sacrifice of animals, etc. all contribute to a kind of psychodrama in which this author believes subtle levels of consciousness are triggered, possibly due to the effect of some of these elements on the autonomic nervous system (the drum beats, for instance, causing the drummers to gain control over the pulse rate of the listeners and slow it down or speed it up as the ritual demands).

It would be the contagious form of possession that would crystallize this phenomenon for the men of MK-ULTRA. A contagious psychological condition is analogous to a contagious biological agent, and both were under examination and trial by the CIA and the military in the years after World War II. For, if we look at the scientific reactions to cases of possession and reincarnation (in which a living person suddenly "remembers" another life and can speak in a foreign tongue, etc.) and take the time to see these cases as the mind-control experimenters would, we notice a glaring admission which is not framed as such. In these cases—especially when the subject speaks in a foreign tongue—we are told by the psychiatrists and the scientists that this is *not* evidence of a spiritual agency; rather, the subjects had been exposed to this material at some point in their childhood and subconsciously recorded it before forgetting all about it. While that explanation may satisfy the need of a rationalist approach to paranormal phenomena, it is a double-edged sword, because it admits that these unconscious powers exist . . . with the implication that they could be harnessed in service to the government, or to some faction thereof. None of the phenomena associated with either possession or "reincarnation"-type personality changes are accepted as spiritual or metaphysical evidence; the same phenomena, however, have to be explained and categorized in some way that does not invalidate the modern scientific model. When the scientists—and Oesterreich included—came to the conclusion that this type of phenomenon had a basis in scientific reality they unwittingly opened the door to the men of MK-ULTRA. In both cases of involuntary and voluntary possession, memory is tapped in its deepest layers and everyday consciousness is suspended while this powerful new entity controls the subject, sometimes even wiping the memory of the subjects so that they have no recollection of what they were doing while "under the influence." In cases of voluntary possession, the condition is easily reversible; even in cases of involuntary possession, exorcism sometimes works, rendering the condition equally reversible. And in the case of multiple—or dissociative—personality disorder, it is possible to exert some control over the manifestation of the alters, but only at considerable expense of time and money, which would not be an attractive proposition to the government scientists who, after all, had a Cold War to win.

Therefore, it would be only a matter of time before the mind-control researchers began to scour the records of occultists, magicians, witches, voodoo priests and Siberian shamans to isolate the techniques that were used since time immemorial to supplant a person's normal, comfortable, everyday consciousness and replace it with a powerful, all-knowing (and sometime violent, and always deceptive) alter personality; and to use those alters to uncover the action of deep memory, for MK-ULTRA was, at its core, an assault on the Land of Memory: the creation of new, false memories and the eradication of old, dangerous ones.

The techniques included drugs, various types of hypnosis including auto-hypnosis (as pioneered by CIA psychiatrist George Estabrooks, among others, who saw occult phenomena as evidence of MPD), and even more extreme measures such as those developed by Dr. Ewen Cameron in Montreal, procedures known as "psychic driving," which involved drastic sensory deprivation sessions in an effort to wipe the consciousness clean and record a new consciousness over the old, much the same way we record over a used cassette tape or floppy disk file. But even more distressing and bordering on the incredible are reports that are starting to surface of a systematic effort to create perfect assassins and espionage agents from the ground up . . . using children.

One of the salient features of multiple personality disorder is that its major predisposing factor is childhood trauma, particularly physical and sexual abuse. What this told the researchers was that the human child was an eminently malleable subject, and with the right sort of conditioning a child could be turned into virtually anything the researchers could come up with. We, as Americans, cannot give credence to these stories because we do not believe that such activities ever took place within our shores. And we may be right. The bulk of the evidence that is coming to light is that the worst of these excesses took place under CIA aegis and completely within the parameters of the CIA charter: i.e., the CIA is forbidden to conduct its intelligence gathering activities in the United States; that is properly the jurisdiction of the FBI. By running operations of questionable morality in foreign countries, the CIA was able to avoid a great deal of oversight. It was also able to keep the operations "legal" in the sense that they did not take place in the United States, but abroad. Further, by using a number of cover or front organizations it was able to utilize that wonderful elocution, "plausible deniability."

That children are routinely used and abused all over the world outside the United States is beyond any reasonable doubt. Child prostitution has become a plague, especially in Southeast Asia, where the prepubescent prostitutes (male and female) of Thailand, the Philippines and now Cambodia, Burma, Vietnam and other countries are infamous. This prostitution takes place with the tacit approval—and sometimes the insistence and cooperation—of local government agencies, such as the military in Burma. The murder of orphans and "street Arabs" in the city streets of Central and South American countries is a tragedy of epic proportions, even as many of these murders were—and are—carried out by members of the military and police forces of those countries. As if that wasn't enough, children are being increasingly recruited into army organizations in Africa and Asia. It has become a staple of television news to see children under the age of twelve holding Kalashnikovs and taking fire from the treeline. This has become such a global problem that the United Nations has considered a treaty that would forbid the recruitment of any child under the age of eighteen. (Oddly enough, one of the main opponents of such an agreement has been the United States, which wants the option of bringing seventeen-year-olds into the Army.) The Chinese organized crime clans—known as the Triads or sometimes the Tongs—routinely use children as assassins, as they cannot be tried as adults in many American states, even for murder. That horrendous and appalling medical experimentation was carried out on children in Nazi Germany and the Nazi-occupied territories within the living memory of many adults is also without question. Yet, somehow, we tend to disbelieve that all of this could be taking place today and in our own country or under the supervision of our government agencies, (even though we imported many Nazi medical scientists as part of Operation Paperclip and other operations after World War II). This type of blindness could only exist in a culture where we have begun to believe our own propaganda, since it is so much more attractive than the awful, the heartbreaking, truth.

As stories surface concerning something called Operation Monarch, and as these stories are blasted by critics because of the outlandish claims being made—high government officials sexually abusing the young children of military families in controlled settings; young children being programmed as assassins; etc.; etc.—there appears substantiating evidence of an even more troublesome (because perfectly believable) nature. Although there are many documented cases of children being trained as fanatic soldiers and killers—especially in Asia, in some celebrated cases in the Golden Triangle, and in Africa—we choose to believe that this is a bizarre aberration. Yet, as we investigate the evidence in the following pages, we will walk into the center of a nightmare of unbelievable proportions because this single, documented, *American* case contains within itself all the elements that we—as serious researchers, journalists and historians—have been taught to treat with skepticism and condescension. We will uncover an organization that was trolling for child subjects (victims) all over the globe; that used these children in strange rituals involving animal sacrifice; that sent these children to secret schools abroad; and that—when on the verge of discovery and exposure—was finally protected by the CIA.

FINDERS, KEEPERS?

On February 5, 1987 the US Customs Service received a phone call from Sergeant JoAnn VanMeter of the Juvenile Division of the Tallahassee Police Department in Florida. Six very young children—aged 2 to 7 years—had been found in the apparent custody of two well-dressed men. The children were scampering in a park in Tallahassee, but they appeared to be ill-fed, ill-clothed—some not wearing underwear—and filthy. An anonymous tip to the Tallahassee PD was enough for the police to undertake a routine investigation, questioning the adults and the children. When the adults proved to be evasive, and their van—a 1980 blue Dodge with Virginia license plates—which was as filthy and foul-smelling as the children, was discovered to be full of books, maps and a single mattress, the police had enough to charge the two men with child abuse.

One of the two men now in custody gave the police a business card with a statement on one side saying that the "bearer knew his constitutional rights to remain silent and that he intended to do so." The children could not name the two men either. In fact, they didn't know the "function and purpose of telephones, televisions and toilets" and further stated that "they were not allowed to live indoors and were only given food as a reward."

They further said that they were on their way to Mexico to go to a school for smart kids. Tallahassee PD phoned the Customs Service to see if they had any information on the adults, the kids, or the alleged school in Mexico and to determine whether or not there were grounds for holding the men on a federal charge. The

Tallahassee police suspected that the children were being used in a child pornography ring, and the Customs Service has a database devoted to collecting information on international child pornography operations. The fact that Mexico was stated as their destination aroused the suspicions of both TPD and the Customs Service even further; Mexico is a haven for every type of pornography production, including child pornography—still photos and films including child prostitution—as well as for purported "snuff film " factories south of the Rio Grande.

Customs said they would investigate the links of the men to an address in the D.C. area, discovered through a check of the license plate on the van.

And this is where it all came together . . . and then exploded apart.

The Tallahassee Police Department and the Customs Service coordinated their efforts with the Washington D.C. Metropolitan Police Department (MPD), as the van was traced to an address in the District and other identification was found in the van leading the detectives to two addresses in Washington. A search warrant was obtained, and a Detective Bradley of the Washington MPD informed the Customs agents that an informer reported that a cult known as the Finders was operating out of those addresses, and that the Finders were involved in blood sacrifice, sex orgies involving children, etc. The two men in custody were determined to be known members of the Finders, and several of the children were identified as "belonging" to the cult.

By the time the warrant was served, there were no children at the cult headquarters at 3918/20 W. Street, NW, but a large quantity of children's clothing was found, including diapers and other clothing, though nothing for children past pre-school age. The worse was yet to come, however.

In another part of the building, filled with computers and files, the detectives found detailed instructions for "obtaining children for unspecified purposes." I will let Special Agent, US Customs Service, Ramon J. Martinez continue in his own words:

> "The instructions included the impregnation of female members of the community known as the Finders, purchasing children, trading, and kidnapping. There were telex messages using MCI account numbers between a computer terminal believed to be located in the same room, and others located across the country and in foreign locations. One such telex specifically ordered the purchase of two children in Hong Kong to be arranged through a contact in the Chinese Embassy there . . . . Other documents identified interests in high-tech transfers to the United Kingdom, numerous properties under the control of the Finders, a keen interest in terrorism, explosives, and the evasion of law enforcement."

The next day, Friday February 6, 1987, Martinez and Bradley then proceeded to the Finders' warehouse at 1307 4th Street, NE. If anything, the take in the warehouse was more horrifying than what was discovered at cult headquarters. Again, to quote Special Agent Martinez:

> "I was able to observe numerous documents which described explicit sexual conduct between the members of the community known as Finders. I also saw a large collection of photographs of unidentified persons. Some of the photographs were nudes, believed to be of members of the Finders. There were numerous photos of children, some nude, at least one of which was a photo of a child "on display" and appearing to accent the child's genitals. I was only able to examine a very small amount of the photos at this time. However, one of the officers presented me with a photo album for my review. The album contained a series of photos of adults and children dressed in white sheets participating in a "blood ritual." The ritual centered around the execution of at least two goats. The photos portrayed the execution, disembowelment, skinning and dismemberment of the goats at the hands of the children. This included the removal of the testes of a male goat, the discovery of a female goat's "womb" and the "baby goats" inside the womb, and the presentation of a goat's head to one of the children."

There can be no doubt, therefore, that what was discovered in the photographs satisfies the criteria for a "satanic" cult involving blood sacrifice and children. The graphic nature of the photographs emphasizes still further that no mere ritual sacrifice of the goats was intended, but a complete disembowelment and dismembering, including a concentration on the sexual organs of the animals. A ritual sacrifice would have been bad enough; hideous, even, for children to be forced to take part. But to carry the bloody ritual to its specific conclusion of the mutilation of the bodies seems to be an attempt to either traumatize the children to an extent that dissociative identity disorder would be a likely outcome, or to anesthetize the children against the performance of bloody and barbaric acts. The author can think of no other purpose that would be served.

However, in fairness to the reader it should be mentioned that the author has spent many years in Asia and in countries and regions where Islam and Hinduism are popular religions. In both these world religions, animal sacrifice is an accepted part of ritual practice and male children of a certain age can be seen participating in or observing these rituals. And, during a Shi'ite festival which commemorates the martyrdom of a Muslim saint, it is not uncommon to see fathers cutting the heads of their own children with swords or machetes to the extent that the children are screaming and covered in blood, as a sign of their grief over the death of Ali.

I submit, however, that the practice of animal sacrifice in a community where there is general support for this practice within the context of an accepted religion has a different effect on a child's understanding than the barbaric butchering and mutilation of an animal in secret, in a country, a city and among people for whom the closest they would normally come to animal sacrifice is the meat counter at their local supermarket. (And isn't this the point, that "insanity" is a social concept, dependent on the mores of the society in which one finds oneself?)

The discoveries at the Finders warehouse were not over, however.

> "Further inspection of the premises disclosed numerous files relating to activities of the organization in different parts of the world. Locations I observed are as follows: London, Germany, the Bahamas, Japan, Hong Kong, Malaysia, Africa, Costa Rica, and "Europe" . . . There was one file entitled "Pentagon Break-In," and others referring to members operating in foreign countries."

What the agents faced was a mountain of evidence pointing to an international trade in children and the use of children in horrible rituals which were photographed for posterity. They found passports and other travel documents, details for trafficking in foreign currency and in high technology transfer to foreign countries. In effect, they had a gold mine and what could have been the most scandalous, most astonishing case in the history of modern jurisprudence because it has it all: child abuse, slavery, rituals, sex, money, and power. But the Finders case had still another aspect, one which the Customs agents could not have predicted.

Martinez arrived at MPD to discuss the case with Detective Bradley, as pre-arranged. Bradley was unavailable. Instead, Martinez was asked to speak to an unidentified third party who could only speak "off the record."

And what he told Martinez was the last straw.

All passport data had been turned over to the State Department, who told MPD that the passports and the travel represented by the passports was within the law," even though this involved "travel to Moscow, North Korea, and North Vietnam from the late 1950s to mid 1970s." Further, Martinez was told that "the investigation into the activity of the Finders had become a CIA internal matter. The MPD report has been classified SECRET and was not available for review."

A cult. Kidnapped children. Sexual abuse. Blood sacrifice. Mutilation. A worldwide organization. Covered up by the CIA. This sounds like a bad Ludlum novel, but it was reality. In Washington, D.C. In 1987.

In *Unholy Alliance*, I wrote extensively of another such cult, this one based in Chile. Called Colonia Dignidad, it was run by a former World War II Luftwaffe officer and defrocked (?) Baptist minister, and was involved in the trafficking of children from various countries, torture of political prisoners, and other Nazi pastimes. It was covered up by the Pinochet government and by its secret service, the dreaded DINA. It was finally uncovered, raided several times, and its back broken. We think. Its owner and founder was apprehended and is now awaiting trial as you read this.

There is a lot of hysteria on the subject of "satanic cult survivor syndrome," and much of the skepticism which greets these claims is well deserved. However, when confronted with a real-life children-sex-sacrifice-CIA cult what are we to believe?

How do we answer the skeptics who insist that it's a figment of overactive imaginations and underactive libidos? How do we answer the believers who accept that there is a world-wide satanic conspiracy involving stolen children and cult members impregnated to give birth to sacrificial babies? The Finders case has robbed us of the luxury of disbelief. And the CIA has robbed us of the answers we need to put the Finders in some sort of perspective, some method in which to handle this bizarre information in a way more suitable to our early 21st century sensibilities.

One set of sinister questions remains, and has yet to be answered: not in the Customs documents, not in any of the news reports. The answer may be buried Bobby in the MPD files marked SECRET (if they still exist at all) or in the CIA's own files on the matter.

What did the Finders do with the children after they "found" them? Where did they go? Where was the school in Mexico? What did they do there? How many more were there?

And . . . *where are they now and what are they doing?*

And to whom?

Item: When Lee Harvey Oswald made his famous trip by bus to Mexico City in 1963, ostensibly to obtain a visa for Cuba, he sat next to an Englishman by the name of John Howard Bowen, alias Albert Osborne. Bowen was an "itinerant preacher" of the Baptist persuasion, an elderly gentleman who traveled frequently to Mexico, according to Warren Commission exhibits (mostly FBI interrogation reports). When confronted by the FBI, Bowen claimed he had borrowed the identity of Albert Osborne, an Englishman who was also an itinerant Baptist preacher, when investigated by the Mexican authorities at a time when he couldn't find his own identification. He claimed that Osborne was an Englishman but that he, Bowen, was born in the United States. Unfortunately, the other passengers on that fabled bus trip to Mexico City identified Bowen as an Englishman, and eventually the FBI concluded that Bowen and Osborne were one and the same.[19] What is interesting is the fact that Bowen-Osborne was a devoted Nazi both before and during World War II, opposing America's entry into the war, and ran a fascist camp for boys in rural Tennessee until it was closed down in 1942.[20]

At the time of the Kennedy Assassination in 1963, there were persistent rumors that Bowen-Osborne was running a school for assassins in Mexico, somewhere in Pueblo, under the guise of a "missionary effort." (When Bowen was first interrogated by the FBI, he claimed that he had been ordained a minister in 1914 by the Plymouth Brethren in Trenton, New Jersey. The Plymouth Brethren is the sect to which Aleister Crowley's parents belonged and from whom he "discovered" his true identity as the Great Beast 666.) Even the Warren Commission could not accept the testimony of Bowen-Osborne, and they were easy marks. Gradually, stories of Bowen's connections to American paramilitary organizations began to circulate, including his involvement with the Minutemen. It was Fred Crisman's purported relationship to the same paramilitary group that led to his interrogation by Jim Garrison in 1968.

A Mexican school for assassination. The recruitment of young boys. Nazis. The Christian Right. 1963.

Item: Los Angeles, May 13, 1964. Less than six months after the Kennedy assassination. The 19th Annual Convention and Scientific Program of the Society of Biological Psychiatry takes place. During the convention, it is reported that 450 children, aged 4 to 15, at Creedmore State Hospital have been subjected to a massive program of hallucinogen experimentation, incorporating everything from LSD to psilocybin to various other drugs. Doses are 150 mcg of LSD or 20 mg of psilocybin, daily, "for periods up to several months." The children ranged from autistic to "slightly schizophrenic" (whatever that means).

WHOEVER FIGHTS MONSTERS

> Whoever fights monsters should see to it that in the process he does not become a monster. And when you look long into an abyss, the abyss also looks into you.
>
> —Friedrich Nietzsche[21]

It wasn't until the mid-1970s that the term "serial killer" became the household word it is today. Coined by FBI profiler Robert K. Ressler, it has taken on a life of its own. Often, the term is applied when it shouldn't be, but we still understand the basic concept: a repeat murderer who doesn't kill for money or for revenge or some other, commonly understood, motive but to satisfy a deep need, a "lust to kill." Serial killers come in two basic flavors, organized and disorganized, but there are killers who partake of both characteristics and are therefore sometimes more difficult to capture. Typically, a serial killer is a young white male, although there have been female serial killers and serial killers of other races.

(As I write these lines, Pakistan has just convicted a serial killer in their country. Their mode of justice? They will strangle him in front of the parents whose children he himself had strangled to death, and then they will destroy his body with acid, again as he did to his victims.) But in the United States, which has become a kind of serial killer capital of the world, we have hundreds on the streets at any given time and they are all mostly young white males.

Many theories have been advanced to explain their strange behavior: the rituals of killing, the cycles or periods, the trolling for victims, the fugue state before the kill and its aftermath, the sometimes gruesome souvenirs, the taunting of police officers, etc. Psychoanalysis of some of our most famous 20th century cases reveals a depressing similarity among these "monsters": horrible childhoods, in some cases horrible beyond description; physical abuse, including severe head traumas and sexual abuse; perhaps one absentee parent. In fact, many of these events are also characteristic of cases of dissociative identity disorder ("multiple personalities"), so it should come as no surprise that the insanity defense is often invoked for crimes committed by serial killers. We want to classify these people as something other than human, and in the last hundred years or so the easiest, most "politically correct" way to do this has been to use insanity as an excuse.

But when we examine the individual cases we see that there is a social component to the genesis of their mental condition. It seems that serial killers are not born, they are made: in much the same way dissociative identity disorder is a creature of a hideous childhood and a violent upbringing. That presents a problem for the death penalty lobby, because if the development of a personality into a serial killer is not a matter of choice (such as, for instance, dealing drugs, etc.) then how can we punish the offender? If the shrinks are correct, then the killers have no conscious control over their actions. And it would certainly seem to be the case, since the pattern is so well-known by now: the early days of torturing small animals, sexual abuse of children or other vulnerable persons, the first kill which leads inevitably to the second, and then the cycle increasing in intensity with the time period between each successive kill growing shorter and shorter until it seems that the killer will explode in a homicidal frenzy. It has all the hallmarks of a psychological syndrome, a psychopathology that demands treatment instead of punishment.

But we have no way to "treat" a serial killer; by the time he has begun killing he is usually too far gone to be treated. The best we can do is jail him, hospitalize him, or execute him. There is no other alternative; he certainly can never be returned to society. And we can't treat a serial killer because—even with all the understanding of how a serial killer is "made" in childhood—we feel he is beyond salvage. He is too cunning for psychoanalysis, a cunning born of survival in the "straight" world. He will say what the analyst wants him to say; he will appear ingratiating, accommodating, perhaps feigning sanity or insanity as the situation warrants, playing with his captors. Intelligence is one of the characteristics of the serial killer: usually above-average and sometimes even genius-level intelligence, particularly in the case of the so-called "organized" killer. We have the modern-day icon of Hannibal Lecter as a model for this type of highly intelligent, highly organized killer. It also reinforces an attitude Americans have towards the intelligent, that they are somehow "different" from the rest of us. It makes us feel better to see the intelligent as psychotic, or—as pointed out in *Unholy Alliance*—Nazis. At the same time, serial killers are obsessed with their dark yearnings. They have somehow equated sexual gratification with violence and murder, arousal with the blood and pain and fear of their victims. And we abhor the crime and the criminal especially because of the sexual aspect of this disorder, an aspect that can include necrophilia and worse.

There is another aspect of this phenomenon, however, that concerns us more closely because it may hold a clue not only to the serial killer himself but to the human condition in general. A careful examination of many of the more famous cases in the last one hundred years will reveal that many of these killers had a religious or occult obsession that ran parallel to their lust-murder obsession. This combination has lent some of these killers a superior attitude towards their captors, an air of smugness and complacency, as if they were in possession of secret knowledge. Certainly, a man who has killed dozens of victims in cities across the country, constantly evading capture and baffling law enforcement, probably feels a little superior to his captors. More importantly, the actual act of murder itself—especially in this case, in taking the life of another human being without motive but by deeds of unspeakable violence—must cause a strange disorientation in the murderer, a kind of twilight state in which reality is distorted. A killer *is* different from the rest of us: he has performed an action that is the ultimate in what society considers heinous. A serial killer's experience is even more bizarre, more outlandish. He kills a string of people for no socially-identifiable purpose. He takes their lives himself, one after the other, repeatedly, in a complex ritual that has meaning only for him. He has stared into the eyes of his victims as they expire. In many cases, he defiles their bodies, or dismembers them, keeping parts as souvenirs; Jeffrey Dahmer and Edmund Kemper come readily to mind.

We have not had these experiences. We know nothing of this. We can read the words, or hear them spoken, but we cannot imagine the sensations; we cannot put ourselves in the killer's place, although we can probably identify with the horror of the victims. There is nothing in our experience, generally, to equate with a lust killing. Most of us have never killed a human being under any circumstances, including war. We certainly have no psychological analog to a lust killing, unless it is lust—sexual desire and arousal—itself. Those of us who feel guilty about our own sexual desires may believe they can understand to some extent the sexual component of the serial killer's strange actions. Think again. *DSM-IV* has no category for this. Thus, the superior (even smug) attitude of the serial killer towards the rest of us. He has walked with demons. He has defiled himself in the most extreme manner possible for a human being. He has seen deeply into the abyss. The problem is, he is still there and cannot get out.

If the CIA in their desperate zeal to combat a perceived brainwashing threat from the Chinese or Russians had attempted to open the black box of consciousness in order to create the perfect assassin—a man or woman who would kill as programmed and forget why (which could be a clinical description of the serial killer's functions as well)—then they were also experimenting with the same mechanism that creates serial killers . . . and shamans. The horrifying visions of the shaman-in-training are nearly identical, if not exactly identical, to those that obsess the serial killer: the dismemberments, the excruciating pain, the visions, the voices in the head, the blood lust. It is, as Eliade points out, tantamount to psychopathology. In the case of the shaman, he is eventually cured of this disorder even though it may last for a long time. His society understands what is going on, and they have mechanisms for dealing with it; the shaman will be a valuable addition to their society after the cure, because then he will be able to communicate with the spirit world, to intercede for his neighbors and to foretell the future. The crucial difference between a shaman and a serial killer may be that the latter has *externalized* the psychological process. What for a shaman—as well as for the artist, the poet, the musician—is an internal nightmare of hallucinogenic proportions becomes, in the hands of the serial killer, a dreadful reality. In another example, Christianity teaches that Jesus was beaten, and crucified, and then had his side pierced with a spear. The terrible tortures (analogous to the tortures of the shaman) happened *to* him; he did not visit them upon his fellow human beings. But a serial killer enacts these same crimes, which first began as childhood or adolescent fantasies, upon innocent victims, one after the other, until he is stopped.

Is a serial killer a shaman who has not made it back?

In 1998, the following was reported in the Indonesian press as well as by the Agence France Presse: An Indonesian practitioner of black magic—a type of sorcerer called a *dukun*—one Ahmad Suraji, was sentenced to death for the murder of forty-two women. He claimed that his father came to him in a dream and told him if he killed seventy women and drank their saliva, his magic powers would be increased and he would—paradoxically—become a better healer. The bodies of all forty-two women were found in a sugar cane field, most of whom had been strangled by the man they came to for help with love and money problems. In a separate trial, one of Suraji's three wives was named as an accomplice.

Obviously, there is a logical problem with a shaman who has to kill seventy people in order to become a better healer! But in any event, we are faced with this instance of a serial killer who is a shaman, albeit a poor one. Southeast Asia is still full of examples of shamans, dukuns, bomohs, and other types of sorcerers who resort to murder in order to enhance their occult abilities. There are many examples in Indonesia, as well as in Malaysia, Thailand and the Philippines. While these shamans may be nominal Muslims, Buddhists or Christians, they are really animists at heart: pagan occultists for whom their religious affiliations are more of a vehicle for reaching more people in their role as healers or witches. Serial murder is not unknown; a case in Malaysia of sorcerers who killed a number of foreigners in an attempt to use their skulls to gain greater powers was reported in the press around the same time as the Suraji case in Indonesia.

Thus, in Asia, we have compelling evidence of a link between serial murder and occult practices. What we do not know is if this is a cultural phenomenon, or if the type of killer such as Suraji fits the accepted FBI profile of a serial or "lust" killer such as a Dahmer or a Gacy . . . or if this is a different phenomenon altogether. We do know that Dahmer, for instance, was fascinated by occultism and believed that he could create zombies from his victims, and also had an altar adorned with the skulls of his victims when he was finally apprehended. Yet, in Dahmer's case, we don't know if the occult beliefs preceded the lust for murder, or if they were only window-dressing, a ritualization to heighten the sexual pleasure he derived from his actions. Perhaps a closer look at Dahmer's case would be revealing of larger issues.

PROM NIGHT

I saw and think 'The Exorcist' was the best saterical comedy that I have ever seen.

—Letter from the Zodiac Killer to the *San Francisco Chronicle*, January 30, 1974 (Candlemas), misspelling in the original.[22]

Jeffrey Dahmer was the prototypical awkward teenager, but one with a secret. According to FBI interview transcripts, Dahmer knew he was homosexual since he was about thirteen years old. In 1970s small-town Ohio, that meant that he had to disguise his sexuality and pretend to be as heterosexual as everyone else. For someone like Dahmer, however, that was not going to be easy.

Thin, shy, and nervous, Dahmer would never come across as a macho man. Nevertheless, he had a date for the high school prom in June of 1978. The unfortunate lady was Bridget Geiger, and she would later participate in a séance in Dahmer's home.

According to press reports published at the time of the grisly Dahmer revelations, Ms. Geiger described herself as an unpopular high school sophomore, and Dahmer was equally unpopular as a senior. A mutual friend had arranged their "date" for the prom, during which Dahmer ignored her for hours, ostensibly to go out and get hamburgers. He was obviously painfully shy around girls, and could not even bring himself to pin the obligatory corsage to her prom dress, but had to enlist the aid of her mother.[23]

The prom took place in May 1978. A month later, Jeffrey invited her to a party at his house. It was not much of a party, according to Ms. Geiger, but just a half dozen people sitting around with no food, no music, not much of anything. At one point during the evening, Dahmer decided he wanted to have a séance to contact the spirit of someone who had died in the house. According to Dahmer, an evil spirit had contacted him and spoken to him, asking him to do things that scared him. As the candles were lit and started to flare up and sputter, Bridget Geiger realized that Dahmer was not joking, and she fled the house, never to see or speak to Dahmer again.[24]

That same month, Dahmer claimed his first victim, the young hitchhiker Steven Hicks.

It is important to put the events in perspective. Dahmer—described variously as a loner and as the class clown, capable of practical jokes but never having any close friends—attends his senior prom, probably through social pressure from his parents or what he felt society expected of him. Although he knew he was homosexual at this time, he had not actually acted out any homosexual acts with others (except for a brief interlude as a younger child with a friend which did not progress beyond some mild groping or fondling). He attended the prom with a young lady who described herself as unpopular as Dahmer himself. One would have thought that Dahmer would have been eager to put that episode out of his mind, but a month later he invites the same girl to a "party" that is not a party at all, but a prelude to a séance to contact an evil spirit; moreover, an evil spirit that has been telling Dahmer to do things that scare him. The séance seems to have proceeded without Ms. Geiger's participation. What occurred, we do not know; but that same month, possibly only days or at most weeks later, Dahmer is cruising a country road and finds his first victim.

Steven Hicks was a personable nineteen-year-old, socially adept, and according to Dr. Joel Norris the diametric opposite to Dahmer in terms of personality. Hicks was on his way to a rock concert, and Dahmer picked him up and convinced him to return with him to Dahmer's home for a drink. What transpired next is subject to some controversy, as Dahmer has given conflicting accounts. We do not know if Dahmer had sex with Steven Hicks, but what is certain is that when Hicks attempted to leave Dahmer went berserk and killed him with a barbell.

He then proceeded to the next phase of his pattern, which was the dismemberment of the body.

Mircea Eliade has described the curious process of "election" of a shaman; it begins with some notification from the spirit world that the subject has been "elected" to become a shaman. In other words, there is a spiritual force—demonic or angelic or simply an amoral spiritual entity of some kind—which makes its presence known to the future shaman. If we take the above story at face value, this is exactly what happened with Dahmer. As an outsider, a loner, he fit the bill in every other respect. Even as someone sexually confused, or homosexual, or a transvestite: all of these sexually ambiguous or "deviant" behaviors were evidence of a shamanistic vocation in some cultures. The process of initiation begins immediately upon notification to the future shaman that he or she has been elected.

This initiatory process involves a gradually worsening stage of mental disorder and illness, as described above. This includes a sensation of being murdered and dismembered, of having one's organs removed, of being reduced to a skeleton. In some cases, as in Siberian shamanism, it was not unusual for the fully-initiated shaman to wear a coat covered in animal (or human) bones, as a marker of his initiatory death and dismemberment. These are all steps taken by Dahmer himself in the intensification of his disorder, as he began to kill and eviscerate and dismember his victims. To a shaman, it would appear as an externalization of what should have remained an internalized experience.

Dahmer had dismembered and eviscerated animals before, always "road kill" that he found on the highway. According to Dahmer, he never killed an animal himself. What argues against this, however, is the scene close to his house of a kind of ritual setting in the woods in which it seems dogs were killed as part of an occult rite. This had taken place the previous year, in 1977, amid reports of missing dogs in the Bath, Ohio neighborhood where he lived. The scene was described by Jim Klippel to the *Akron Beacon-Journal*:

> "Somebody must have had a lot of fun with that dog . . . if that's what you want to call it. It was skinned and gutted. And about a hundred yards away there had been a large fire and thirteen little fires around it. It looked so much like cult worship that it scared us to death."[25]

The dog that Klippel referred to had been found nailed to a tree.

It fits the profile of a serial killer that Dahmer would have started torturing animals, eventually moving up to humans. Dahmer insists that he did not kill any animals himself, that he did not want to inflict pain. His human victims were said to have been drugged first before he killed them—usually by strangulation—so that they would not feel pain. It is possible that the drugging only made it easier for Dahmer to subdue and murder his victims, and that pain (or the avoidance of it) had nothing to do with it. In any event, the disappearing and murdered dogs in 1977 pointed to a disappearing and murdered Steven Hicks in 1978.

It is worthwhile to note here that missing dogs—especially German shepherds—are a recurring theme around cult murders and cult activity, and that the slaughter of dogs was an element of the cult surrounding the Son of Sam killings that we will investigate shortly. (About a year before the Son of Sam killings began, the author lived in Brooklyn Heights and heard stories of dogs being tortured and killed in a warehouse near the Brooklyn Bridge. This is the same neighborhood where the Warlock Shop once stood, the occult store referred to by Maury Terry several times in *The Ultimate Evil* as an informal meeting place for some of the Sam cultists.)

Dahmer disposed of Hicks' body, burying the pieces in the earth near his home (where they would be found thirteen years later), and went about his life as if nothing had happened. He enrolled in college, but was kicked out due to his excessive drinking, a habit that began when Dahmer was still in high school. At the end of 1978, we find Dahmer enlisting in the Army and being sent to Germany.

His military record, obtained by the FBI and part of his declassified FBI file, shows that Dahmer had severe problems in the Army, problems with drinking and problems with authority. He was eventually discharged from the Army when they realized they couldn't do very much for him, and he could do nothing for the Army. So many of our nation's most famous serial killers have spent time in the Armed Services: Dahmer, David Berkowitz, Bobby Joe Long, Arthur Shawcross . . . the list is long and gruesome. Dahmer may be relatively unique in that he began killing *before* he enlisted; the others did not begin until after they had been in the service.

What transpired after his discharge is by now well-known among aficionados of the bizarre and the morbid. He returned home, eventually found a job or series of jobs in Milwaukee, and began trolling for victims. He honed his skills, and refined his rituals. His victims were all gay men, of various races—Black, White, Asian, Hispanic—mostly young, people he met in gay bars as far away as Chicago. He would work during the week, and then go crazy on the weekends, drinking and hanging out in gay strip clubs, gay discos, adult movie theaters and bookstores, and when he was finally apprehended the body count came to seventeen, including his first victim, Steven Hicks. Their bodies had been dismembered, dissolved in vats of acid in his apartment, stored in a large freezer. Their skulls had been retained, cleaned and defleshed and in some cases painted, and were adorning his altar, his "power altar."[26] The number of skulls on the altar has been given variously as six (Ressler) or ten (Norris), along with a planned hanging skeleton on either side, a central hanging lamp, and two griffins. The altar was not complete at the time of his arrest, but some of the skulls and the two griffins were in place, as well as candles, incense, and other vaguely occult paraphernalia.

The griffins are interesting, only in that we encountered a pair of griffins in Book I: atop the incredible wandering house in Ashland, Kentucky, where—it was claimed—they had the power to ward off evil. In Dahmer's case, the griffins had names: one was Leon and the other was Apal, according to an FBI report on an interview with Dahmer on August 3, 1992. These words were written on the griffins themselves, which were knocked over during his session with victim Curtis Straughter who rolled off the bed and crashed into the altar, alarming Dahmer. According to the FBI report,

> DAHMER stated that these griffins were part of the occult, and symbolized personal power and made it that he did not have to answer to anyone. DAHMER stated that there were words written on each griffin, one had Leon and the other had Apal. DAHMER again stated that this symbolized personal power, and he felt that this was a sign to show that he was losing control.[27]

For those interested in these things, the names of the griffins may provide a type of clue. "Leon," of course, is simply the Spanish word for lion, and, of course, the lion represents the kind of strength and power that attracted Dahmer. "Apal" is somewhat more problematic. It could simply be the Hebrew word אפל which means "darkness, gloom," in which case the combination of lion with darkness is most apt.

When asked about his occult beliefs, he made an interesting revelation. Again, according to the FBI:

> DAHMER was asked if he was involved in the occult, and DAHMER stated that he started dabbling in the occult and reading, and his favorite movie was *EXORCIST III,* because it helped fit into his fantasy. DAHMER stated that in the movie *EXORCIST III* the guy could create illusions, and DAHMER felt that he himself could create illusions.[28]

For those who have not seen this film (*Exorcist III,* 1990), or who don't remember it, it is a sequel to the original William Friedkin film, and was actually directed by Friedkin himself. (*Exorcist II* was not a Friedkin production.) In addition, it had some members of the original cast. The important thing about this film, however, is that *it links serial murder with demonic possession*, something which the earlier *Exorcist* films did not do.

That this was Dahmer's favorite film is very revealing. The throwaway line about "creating illusions" is just that, a decoy. As we read famed FBI profiler Robert K. Ressler's interview with Dahmer, the reason Dahmer was fascinated by *Exorcist III* was the power the possessed had over reality, over the minds and bodies of the rest of the world.[29] The element of "creating illusions" was only a tool, a means to an end. There are many films concerned with the creation of illusions, but only *Exorcist III* marries this theme with that of demonic possession and serial murder. Dahmer went so far as to procure yellow contact lenses, to give his eyes that feral, haunted glow when he trolled the bars, looking for victims. He believed that they "exuded power."[30]

Further evidence of this is given by an intended victim who escaped, one Tracy Edwards.

Edwards had been invited back to Dahmer's Milwaukee apartment, and during a drinking session managed to have one hand handcuffed at knife point but retained enough common sense or sobriety to refuse to have the other hand cuffed. Dahmer, however, although angry, was calm because he had drugged Edwards' drink. His victim would soon be unconscious, and a little later dead.

While waiting for the drug to take effect, and with knife in hand, Dahmer demanded that Edwards watch a videotape with him. It was *Exorcist III.*

Dahmer watched the film intently, at times rocking back and forth, chanting in a humming sound, and seeming to go into a trance (as described in Book II, the same process was used by Mark David Chapman when invoking Satan or talking to his Little People). Then a personality change would take place during the parts of the film that depicted possession sequences. At this time, Dahmer himself would become aggressive and demand that Edwards place the other handcuff on his wrist. Then, as the filmed possession sequence would change to something more mundane, Dahmer's mood also shifted and he began to complain about his life and his loneliness.

Eventually, Edwards escaped through a combination of luck and intelligence. He played Dahmer's moods and in a moment of inattention managed to hit Dahmer with enough force that he fell to the side, allowing Edwards to escape out into the night, running as fast as he could.

The mood changes may indicate some form of dissociation on Dahmer's part, such as we have already discussed, although Dahmer never presented as a sufferer from DID or MPD at the time of his arrest or subsequent medical examinations. Indeed, psychiatrists were never able to completely analyze Dahmer, as Dahmer himself complained. They could point to his necrophilia (he would have sex with the corpses of his victims before they were dismembered, copulating with them or even drawing slits in their chest for this purpose) or his other symptoms, but never be able to integrate these symptoms into a single diagnosis. FBI profiler Ressler would say that Dahmer represented a new phenomenon, and partially blamed Hollywood (even though he himself had been a technical adviser on *Silence of the Lambs*). He saw *Exorcist III* as some kind of triggering mechanism for Dahmer, as something that gave the killer a kind of validation.

I believe this is a hard point to prove, as one would have to show other instances in which this film instigated murder, dismemberment and cannibalism. Nonetheless, by blaming cinema and also to an extent pornography for the Dahmer phenomenon, Ressler was raising the ante: he was stating, simply, that American culture had contributed to the creation of Dahmer. If we look at other instances of serial murder around the globe, however, including the Indonesian case mentioned above as well as Chikatilo in Russia, and cases in Pakistan, China, and everywhere else, it is obvious that it is not American culture that creates serial killers—not even of the cannibalistic variety—but perhaps culture in general offers a social medium for the phenomenon. In Indonesia, it manifested as witchcraft; in Milwaukee, as a string of homosexual and racist hate crimes. The common denominator, however, in so many cases of serial murder and other vicious crimes seems to be theological. There is a supernatural element wherever we look, if we look deeply enough. A taste for ritual, for horror films, for spiritual evocation, for demonology. A taste for Satan.

In a macabre example of art imitating life imitating art, we have *The Exorcist*, which was a favorite film of the man eventually identified as the Zodiac Killer, and then *Exorcist III*, in which the demon-possessed serial murderer, the Gemini Killer, is based on the same Zodiac Killer (who, unknown to the film's writer, director and producer, was a fan of the first *Exorcist* movie). This real-life connection then leaps into Jeffrey Dahmer, who is mesmerized by the character and who probably does not realize that the fictional Gemini Killer is based on a real person, a genuine serial murderer such as he himself is becoming, a famous murderer with a taste for the occult and for Satanism, as Robert Graysmith's sequel to his definitive work on the Zodiac killer, *Zodiac Unmasked*, amply illustrates. And this, a movie based on a book written about a genuine case of demonic possession . . . a book written by a psychological warfare officer, a man himself laboring in an occult tradition of Giordano Bruno, as identified and clarified, by poor, murdered Professor Culianu. The links examined by Culianu—of eros and image, of magic and sexuality—are in this single example drawn so carefully and completely that I feel it safe to say that no one would be able to ignore the obvious conclusion that both Bruno and Culianu were correct and saw the inner workings of the sinister force with tremendous clarity, as we shall soon see.

The cannibalism factor increased the fascination the public has had with Dahmer. The killer admitted that he ate various body parts of his victims, so that he could feel them as part of him. It gave him a sexual thrill, but was obviously satisfying on some deeper level as well. Like the fictional Hannibal Lecter he would fry pieces of his victims on a skillet over a stove.

I would ask the reader to stop for a moment, inundated as we are with all of this hideous detail, and try to imagine the atmosphere of Dahmer's apartment. It was not a large place. It was a one-bedroom affair of the type one would see in most large cities: a sitting or living room, a bedroom, a toilet, not much else. In this apartment was a giant freezer filled with body parts. There was a vat containing acid and more body parts. There was a pot in which he cooked pieces of his victims. And there was the altar with its complement of skulls.

He *lived* in that apartment; it was not a kill zone, a special secret place hidden away in the woods like the witch's house in Hansel and Gretel (another example of murder, witchcraft, cannibalism and child abuse). It was where he went to sleep and woke up every morning. Showered. Shaved. Left every day to go to work, or to find more victims. Once he had killed them, and had sex with their bodies, he would begin the laborious process of cutting them up into smaller pieces, some of which he would eat and some of which he would freeze for later. The rest would get dissolved in acid, and the blood and offal poured down the normal bathroom drains. Police investigators found pots in the apartment containing severed hands, genitalia, and other body parts, like something out of a nightmare. Or a children's fairy tale.

Put yourself there. Try to imagine Dahmer—a chain smoker—standing over his latest victim, a large sharp kitchen knife in his bloodied hand and a cigarette in his mouth, spilling ash, as he sawed away at someone's thigh or arm. Someone with whom he had had sex—alive and dead—perhaps only hours before. Try to tell yourself that this is life, this is how some people live, that this is an experience to which a human being can become inured, accustomed, habituated. With the black walls and dark furniture and altar of skulls and griffins, the lighting must have been dim. There were blood stains on the carpet. At times, the giant freezer leaked. There was a smell.

And the next weekend Dahmer would go out again.

There was a great distance between Dahmer's childhood home in Bath, Ohio and the apartment in Milwaukee, a spiritual distance most of us will never cover. We can talk about isolation, about confused sexuality, about alienation, even about multiple personalities and sexual dysfunctions. We can try to *reduce* this phenomenon to something we can live with, something within the boundaries of the reality we know, rather than the reality we suspect exists.

Eichmann, the prototype and exemplar of Hannah Arendt's "banality of evil," rarely saw the victims he consigned to the death camps as part of the Third Reich's

"Final Solution." He did not wallow in their blood and gore. He did not dismember his victims, much less devour their flesh. He was an accountant, making sure quotas were filled and trains ran on time. If the evil that Eichmann represents is, indeed, "banal" or at least masquerades as banality, then what do we make of the evil represented by Dahmer?

What do we make of evil itself?

Dahmer, with his thin build and owlish, bespectacled appearance could have been Ohio's answer to Eichmann. They were both matter-of-fact during their respective interrogations. Eichmann's responsibility was for the deaths of millions of people; Dahmer's for seventeen. Do we measure evil in terms of body count? This question has never been answered. It seems beyond human ability to answer. Were Eichmann and Dahmer evil? Were they sane? Were they *equally* evil, equally sane or insane? What does this question demand of us as human beings? Does it demand that we question . . . no, that we *exam*ine the consequences of our actions, no matter how "banal"? Do we have to kill, dismember and devour our victims before society can pass a judgment of "evil" upon us? Or is it enough simply to sign the execution orders? Or to pay the taxes that will pay for the construction of missiles, or for the covert actions of anonymous assassins in Third World countries?

Or is it enough to *imagine* acts of evil, like a Stephen King or a Clive Barker, or a Thomas Harris? Or an H.P. Lovecraft?

Or like you? Like me?

In an American court of law, it is enough to be convicted of *responsibility* to deserve the death sentence, as in the case of Charles Manson; but that is, in itself, not enough of a verdict of evil. It is a verdict of guilt in the eyes of the law, but not necessarily of evil, or of sanity.

In Dahmer's case, we have what appears to be an unequivocal example of pure, unadulterated, evil. Yet, his defense attorneys attempted to win their case on the basis of diminished capacity, i.e., the insanity defense. Dahmer had already confessed to the crimes, including that of Steven Hicks thirteen years previously. There was no doubt in anyone's mind that Dahmer had actually committed these crimes. What the trial was to determine, before a jury, was whether or not Dahmer was "insane."

Dahmer's meticulous planning of each crime and the effort he made to dispose of the bodies before going out again to perform the same actions were enough for the jury to come back with a verdict of "sanity." There were, of course, other social issues surrounding the trial, including the Rodney King case in which a black man was beaten by Los Angeles Police Department officers and the entire episode captured on videotape. Much was made of Dahmer's victims, that they were all homosexual and that eleven of the seventeen were black. Dahmer's crimes were painted as "hate crimes," i.e., that Dahmer—conflicted about his homosexuality—took out his shame and rage on homosexuals and extended that via a basic racist streak to include blacks. To equate Dahmer's murder, dismemberment and consumption of his victims—not to mention his attempts to turn at least one of them into a zombie by drilling holes in his skull while he was still alive and filling the holes with acid—to the LAPD brutality in the case of Rodney King, was quite a stretch. Although both crimes were hideous, the case of Dahmer reveals a sickness and depravity that even the LAPD could not match on its best days.

The expert witnesses and other observers on the case admitted a degree of bafflement when it came to Dahmer. The language became, in fact, embarrassingly theological.

John Liccione, the chief psychologist of the Milwaukee County Medical Health Complex at the time of the Dahmer arrest, claimed, "We may think we know the person, but rare is the case we really know what a person feels and thinks deep down in the bowels of his soul . . . . Soul can be concealed. Who knows what is in there?"[31]

Theresa Smith, the sister of Dahmer victim Eddie Smith, put it more succinctly when she said, "I just know Dahmer's evil . . . . And if they had a plea for that, that's what he'd get—evilness."[32]

The drawing Dahmer made of his proposed Power Altar included a black table with ten painted skulls, a standing skeleton on either side of the altar, what appear to be incense burners on top and at either side of the altar, and an overhead hanging lamp with four blue globes. The four globes (or six globes, according to Ressler, p. 128) are the mysterious element; they don't seem to fit the overall layout of death and darkness. There might be a clue—however tenuous, but we *are* in very murky territory—in several works by noted occult scholar and head of one of Aleister Crowley's Ordo Templi Orientis (OTO) organizations in England, Kenneth Grant.

Quoting from the Lovecraft tale, "The Lurker at the Threshold," he writes (in 1980),

> The globes, or bubbles, comprise 'that tentacled amorphous monster . . . whose mask was as a congeries of iridescent globes, the noxious Yog-Sothoth, who froths as primal slime in nuclear chaos beyond the nethermost outposts of space and time'.[33]

And previously, in 1972, quoting the same story and linking it to a design in Crowley's own Pantacle:

> Not stars, but suns, great globes of light . . . and not these alone, but the breaking apart of the nearest globes, and the protoplasmic flesh that flamed blackly outward to join together and form that eldritch, hideous horror from outer space . . .[34]

Had the stories of H. P. Lovecraft influenced the dreams and forbidden fantasies of the introverted young Ohio homosexual who held séances in his home as a teenager to confront the evil spirit who, he said, was telling him to do "scary things"? We shall probably never know.

Jeffrey Dahmer was beaten to death in prison in November 1994 by a black inmate, Christopher J. Scarver, who was serving a life sentence for murder.

Scarver said that voices in his head told him that he, Scarver, was the Son of God.[35]

MURDER AND TRANSFIGURATION

We are accustomed to thinking of the fictional killer as someone who is in fiendish pursuit of a kind of transformation. The killer in Thomas Harris' famous *Silence of the Lambs* is trying to transform himself into a woman by sewing the skin of his victims together to make a kind of suit, à la real-life serial killer Ed Gein; the symbol of that novel-turned-movie is a moth: a motif of transformation from caterpillar to pupa to winged creature. How much more interesting an evil character who is in search of self-transcendence! It elevates the discussion beyond a mere carnal craving for blood; and why? Because we want to elevate our own sexual urges into something more . . . divine? A tantric take on lust murder? Or is there something fundamentally correct in the assumption that the serial killer—like the shaman—is in search (consciously or unconsciously) of a kind of transformation? Before our minds were filled with stories and images of vicious and depraved serial killers, there was in North America an institutionalized form of murder, evisceration and dismemberment: the ritual killings that took place among the Aztecs and Mayas, and all as part of public displays that merged religious intensity with dramatic scenes of bloody knives and hearts, still beating, ripped from the chests of victims. This linkage of hideous slaughter with communication with God and the preservation of society was not exclusive to the ancient Mexican civilizations, of course. Jesus is another such example. Transformation by way of torture, bloodshed, and murder.

Is this what compelled the CIA to dig deeper into the mentality of violent offenders and psychopaths? Not because they wanted to see God, but because they wanted to control that urge for transformation, for transcendence and re-direct it towards a more politically useful target?

Critics of Thomas Harris' novels point to an obvious "flaw" if his work is to be taken scientifically, and that is that serial killers by and large do not have the intellect, the control, and the deep inner resources of a Hannibal Lecter; they are usually underachievers, usually white men who are marginal in society due to physical or mental defects or social ostracism, a lot closer to the brutal redneck antagonists in *Deliverance* than the urbane, literate Lecter. Yet it is just these men who, in other societies, may find themselves called to the position and function of shaman, and not to the role of the intellectually-astute, the suave, cultivated man of science and society.

David Sexton—literary editor of the *London Evening Standard*—has written a thoughtful and stimulating book on Thomas Harris and the themes in his novels: *The Strange World of Thomas Harris*.[36] In this tightly-focused essay, we are startled to read that the themes we have been pursuing are echoed quite clearly by this British critic, for he draws a comparison between the mind of Hannibal Lecter and *The Art of Memory* by Frances A. Yates,[37] showing that the number and type of connections and correspondences in Harris' work is a deliberate creation of a kind of memory palace, and that numerous Web sites have sprung up devoted to unraveling these connections and demonstrating the superb depth of erudition and culture that permeate the Lecter novels, giving them a resonance far beyond that of a traditional thriller or horror story. Hannibal Lecter is, himself, a kind of memory palace, which is why he is able to spend long days, weeks and months in his cell without his books as he pores over a vast mental library and museum that is his own memory. Further, while giving homage to Sherlock Holmes, Harris also draws his inspiration directly from Edgar Allan Poe and the American traditions of the detective story and the horror story (as did Sir Arthur Conan Doyle), traditions steeped in that peculiar American culture that European critics deny we possess while they simultaneously admire and emulate it, for it is, after all, a tradition born in the darkest of human impulses: conquest, heresy, the ripping of the veils of Temple and Kingship.

It was Ioan Culianu who revealed the close association between eros and magic, and called it the birthplace of the modern sciences of propaganda and advertising. The serial killer is, after all, a "lust" killer; his crimes are referred to as "sexual homicides" and it is for this reason that we have become fascinated with the serial killer, as he represents the "link" or "bond" between sex (eros) and magic, sex and transformation. The transformation that is so much a part of the Harris novels is also the core impulse behind the shaman; it was also a major factor in the thinking of serial killers such as Jeffrey Dahmer.

Yet, before we examine the deeper processes of the shaman and the serial killer, let us remind ourselves of the political uses of psychology and of "brainwashing," so that we can put this all into some kind of context. It would be useful to understand that there exist in the United States—and probably in many other countries as well—two "sciences" that run parallel to each other. As James Bamford described in his definitive study of the National Security Agency, *The Puzzle Palace*, in 1982, the scientific establishment is not necessarily completely up-to-date on new developments that affect national security considerations. Much science is conducted behind closed, locked, and even hidden and disappearing doors. The NSA itself has had an enormous influence on the development of computer science, as they needed more and more powerful machines to create cyphers and to decrypt the cyphers of other countries. The NSA also had a tremendous influence on the development of space science, as they struggled to design spy satellites that could eavesdrop on conversations many miles below their orbits. The NSA—and similar organizations around the globe—of necessity have to be several years, or even several generations, beyond what is taking place in the civilian scientific community.[38] The same, it may be safely assumed, is true of psychiatric science as well.

Psychiatry being generally beyond the purview of the NSA, the military intelligence groups and the CIA had a monopoly on new developments in this area, as we have seen. Like the NSA and computer technology, the CIA financed many specific psychiatric projects but always with an emphasis on memory and control. The creation of amnesia, the embedding of secret orders via hypnosis, or drugs, or "brainwashing" or some combination of these or other techniques, were all vitally important to intelligence organizations, and CIA-funded research made its way into the general literature (just as NSA-funded research contributed to the explosive growth of computer science and telecommunications; just as the Army's Psychological Warfare effort funded and directed the new science of communications; just as the military directed the creation of the *DSM* with its tremendous influence on generations of American psychiatrists). Other authors—such as the psychiatrist and hypnosis expert George Estabrooks, who worked for CIA—have described how the CIA was interested in the creation of multiple personality disorder. As we uncover more and more concerning the parallel interests of the Army and the Navy in these matters, we can only assume that they were also fascinated by this disorder and the potential uses to which it could be put.

Item: Lt. Commander Dr. Thomas Narut—a US Navy psychologist—claimed before a NATO conference of psychologists in Oslo that ONI (the Office of Naval Intelligence) had been using convicted murderers in a bizarre scheme to create the perfect commando. These were men from military prisons who were sent to various US embassies abroad after having been "treated" with behavior modification techniques and turned into assassins "who could kill on command." Narut was later reprimanded by the Navy and forced to retract his statement, but the cat was already out of the bag.[39]

While disturbing and possibly unethical, this program used individuals who were already murderers. In another program, it is possible that the CIA actually contributed to the creation of a famous killer:

Item: It is revealed that Ted Kaczynski, the famed "Unabomber," had been a test subject in a CIA mind-control project during his university days. A brilliant mathematician, Kaczynski would escape from society and hole up in a cabin in the Montana woods until his capture by federal agents, after his letter bombs killed three people and wounded twenty-three over a course of seventeen years. The man who experimented upon him was none other than Dr. Henry A. Murray, the former OSS psychiatrist for whom Timothy Leary had developed a psilocybin experimentation program at Harvard in 1960 after his return from a trip to

Mexico. Kaczynski was one of only twenty-two Harvard undergrads who were part of this secret project from the fall of 1959 to the spring of 1962, a program based loosely on OSS interrogation methods and designed to break down the student's personality. The personality assessment tests devised by Murray for the OSS during the war were conceived as an attempt to find out which candidates would do well under interrogation and torture; some OSS candidates broke down even *before* the tests were administered, so frightening were the rumors about their intensity. Kaczynski, who needed the money and volunteered for these tests without being told what to expect, began to develop signs of emotional stress and a hatred for society as his Harvard years progressed. Eventually, less than ten years after the completion of the Harvard tests, he disappeared into the Montana woods, wrote his journals and a long Manifesto that some critics have called "brilliant," and mailed bombs all over America.[40]

MISBEGOTTEN SONS

Stuart Clark, a Professor of History at the University of Swansea (and winner of the Royal Historical Society's Gladstone History Prize in 1997) has written a book that examines the politics of witchcraft. Entitled *Thinking With Demons: the Idea of Witchcraft in Early Modern Europe*, it is a thorough examination not only of the political issues surrounding the idea of witchcraft but also of politics and religion in general, especially the uncomfortable relationship between political institutions, and particularly political leaders, and the Church, and how witchcraft at once tested and in some cases validated the supernatural role of the King. Although he is writing of a time hundreds of years in the past, his theme could just as easily be ported to a modern context:

> To add confessional uniformity to institutional centralization—to control minds as well as bodies—was an understandable ambition of governments, and the pursuit of spiritual dissidents in the courts could be its practical outcome. Control of political loyalties was, after all, felt to rest on control of denominational ones.[41]

It is this strange alliance between political loyalties and denominational ones that paved the way for the excesses—not only of the Inquisition, which began after all with the persecution of the Cathars, a heretical sect that threatened political hegemony in France—but also of the mind-control efforts of modern governments. In the last hundred years, as psychiatry became become more popular and influential, especially as it tried to mimic the scientific method on which so much technology is based, the social role of religion in the West came under increasing pressure. Religious beliefs were considered in the light of psychopathologies, for instance in William Sargant's study of religious conversion and "brainwashing," but also in the Soviet Union, which saw religious affiliation in the same light as political dissidence, both of which were cause for commitment in a mental institution. Religion—at least in the eyes of those psychologists and psychiatrists working for the government—was seen in mechanical terms, as a kind of hysterical reaction, a nervous disorder; and, just as psychopathology could be put to the service of the State (such as in the case of multiple personality disorder), so also could religious sentiment which, after all, was only a complex of mental disorders as seen in the light of psychiatric illumination.

In the West, religious affiliation implied political loyalty, and still does to some extent (witness the abortion controversy as a test not only of religious commitment but also of political action and party loyalty). In the Communist East, to be religious at all was tantamount to treason. Instead of burning the religious (or politically dissident) at the stake, they were committed to institutions or, in China, to re-education camps.

That does not mean, however, that the powers unleashed by intense religious devotion would be ignored. Neither in the West nor in the East could governments afford to disregard the weapons potential of the "disordered" mind. Strip the denominational dogma from the religious experience and one can see a range of striking similarities among the spiritualities of many cultures and beliefs. These similarities are the bedrock of the psychological approach to religion, a wellspring of unconscious mental ability that finds expression in religious sentiment, but which can just as easily be molded to other beliefs, other . . . loyalties. But to do that, to at once evoke and control, *manipulate*, this power one has to dig down and get one's hands dirty. And, it should be stressed, bloody.

Nietzsche wrote that what we perceive as higher culture is nothing more than the elevation of our innate savagery to a divine state. He wrote of the canonization of evil, the social consensus that transforms acts of hideous cruelty into spiritually redeeming metaphors. Society has this power, the power to bless barbarity. The early history of Christianity—of Jesus, of the Martyrs, all those dead Virgins—is of the sacralization of the Victim; the later history of Christianity is of the sacralization of the soldier, the witch-burner, the firebrand: of the Inquisition and the Crusades. Saint Ignatius Loyola, he of the Counter-Reformation, said that to give him a child for a year was to bind that child to the Church for life.

Take a child, then. As young as possible. Remove him from his family, from his parents, and bring him up in a commune with other children. The only adults are the wardens of this commune, the "trainers." Authority figures, authority without love. Keep him isolated from the rest of the world. Do not give him a name; do not allow him to develop an independent personality. Feed him poorly; dress him poorly. Keep him hungry and cold. Subject him to scenes of bloodshed and violence; make him partake in these scenarios. Brutalize his consciousness. You will be creating a monster, who will one day go out and kill . . . or self-destruct in some addicts' hallway. A terrorist, an assassin, a psychopath . . . a killer.

The serial killer fixates on a certain type of victim, a type that makes sense only to him. Someone who reminds him of his mother, maybe, according to the stereotype. Or women with long hair. Or white women only. Or prostitutes only. Or young boys.

What if—in the course of this "instruction" in our special school for children—we implant a different fixation? What if we create the psyche of the child from the ground on up? This, as discussed in Book I, is what Dr. Ewen Cameron of Montreal had pledged to do, and with CIA funding, until that fateful day in November 1963 when his services were no longer required. Like Otto Rahn, the reluctant SS officer and historian whose goal was the Holy Grail, Cameron died on a mountaintop. His records and documentation were seized by CIA officer William Buckley, who later found himself at the mercy of Arab terrorists who worked on him the same foul black magic that Cameron had used on his victims. Cameron created the technique of "depatterning," which—in its application as well as its theory—could just as easily be called "dissociating": a subject had his or her mind methodically erased, broken into pieces and scattered to the winds. Long established patterns of thought and behavior were disassembled, the patient reduced to a blank slate on which Cameron could write anything he wished. Tapes played constantly, day and night, with speakers under the patient's pillow, formulating a new purpose, a new identity, a new set of learned behavior. Like the central character in *A Clockwork Orange*, the patient would become a "New Man."

But the interest of the CIA was not in developing a technique for the soul's individuation. That would have no military or intelligence value at all. The CIA's approach was purely mechanical: how do we turn an ordinary person into a killer, in fact a killer with selective amnesia? Cameron claimed to be able to create selective amnesia. A combination of drugs, sensory deprivation, monotonous tape recordings of command phrases . . . but were the side effects too cumbersome? What about surgery? What if we did a little nip-and-tuck in the cerebral cortex? What then?

The example of Arthur Shawcross may be a case in point. A convicted serial killer and rapist, Shawcross had spent time in Vietnam. He claimed to have seen bloody combat in the jungles, and to have first cannibalized his victims there. The Army denied that Shawcross was anywhere near combat, and instead insisted that throughout his tour he had remained "in the rear with the gear." When he was finally apprehended for a string of ghastly homicides in and around Rochester, New York, his defense team were not allowed copies of his military medical files. Pictures of his brain, however, showed evidence of medical intervention: symmetrical scarring that his team believed had to have been the result of surgery and not from natural causes. It was Shawcross who claimed to hear voices in his head, ghostly spirits urging him to kill. To the prosecution, he was simply malingering and faking mental illness. To the defense, he was a cipher. They needed the medical files. They could not get them.

The perspective of modern science and modern jurisprudence seems to be that, for the most part, killers are killers because they want to be killers. They have chosen evil as a way of life, and for that reason they should be punished if not executed. Society agrees in principle, of course; who needs killers loose on the streets? But when it comes to the serial killer, we are on shaky ground. As queried earlier, is a serial killer a voluntary or an involuntary murderer? Who are these "misbegotten sons"?

Any answer depends, first of all, upon determining who is, and is not, a serial killer, because the loose application of this term has caused some confusion in the popular media. By simple arithmetic, a serial killer is a killer who kills more than once; i.e., who kills victim after victim over a period of time. Obviously, hired assassins or Mafia hit men are not included in this category. That is because the term "serial killer" is a more modern term for what used to be termed a "lust killer." In other words, the criteria for labeling a person a "serial killer" is more complex than simply a long hit list of victims. A serial killer—popularly understood—is someone who kills more than one person over a period of time (i.e. "in series") due to an emotional urge (a "lust") to kill. These killers are very personally involved in their crimes; they need to see the victim up close, to spill blood with their own two hands. The act of murder is for them a kind of sexual act, and quite often the crime scenes show evidence of sexual activity with the victim, pre-mortem and/or post-mortem. The victims are all selected according to a pattern that involves either their profession (prostitution, for example) or their physical appearance, or some other quality known only to the killer.

In this way, we can see that killers such as Charles Manson do not fit the profile. The crimes for which Manson was convicted were all committed by other people, the members of his "Family." No self-respecting serial killer, motivated by the lust of killing, would assign murders to other people to carry out. Nor would they attack at a distance.

> In most serial murders, then as now, the weapon of choice was the knife, with the second most favored method being strangulation and the third, suffocation. Serial murderers, in general, do not use guns, which kill people from a distance; serial murderers want the personal satisfaction of causing death right there at hand.
>
> —Robert K. Ressler[42]

The same may be said for David Berkowitz. Try as they might, psychologists working on the Son of Sam case could not squeeze the round peg that is David Berkowitz into the square hole that is the "lust" or serial killer. While Berkowitz admits to several of the killings, he insists that he did not commit all of them and that the murders were, in fact, carried out under the orders of a cult to which he belonged. As he is in prison for life with no possibility of parole, he has no ulterior motive for making this claim. Nothing that he says at this point will reduce his sentence and he has, as mentioned, freely admitted to committing some of the murders anyway. By pleading guilty immediately after his apprehension, he denied the rest of us an examination of the available evidence which would have pointed to the existence of the murderous cult to which he belonged. In fact, the evidence collected in the twenty-five years since the time of the killings is now leaning heavily to support this allegation of a cult of murderers operating in the New York metropolitan area as well as in other parts of the country, including North Dakota and California. While many critics sincerely doubt the claims of Maury Terry and others who point to a vast conspiracy of Satanic killers (and some of Terry's claims *are* weak and poorly supported), the preponderance of the evidence in the Son of Sam case is strong enough to suggest that what Berkowitz is saying is, in fact, true.

Thus if we include Manson and Berkowitz in any study of serial murder, the statistics will become skewed and much valuable data will be lost. Whatever the psychic disorders suffered by Manson and Berkowitz—and they may be legion—the label of serial killer cannot, in all honesty, be used in their cases. In fact, Terry's evidence goes far to suggest that the Manson and Berkowitz cases may actually be related; that the cult to which Berkowitz belonged in New York City was a branch of the one to which Manson had allegiance. Just as in our study of coincidence and politics, when it comes to serial murder the coincidences also pile up, suggesting that the same dynamic applies. It is but another indication of the existence of a powerful, hidden force in nature that surfaces in time of tremendous stress in the fabric of reality.

For although there are definite and critical differences between Manson and Berkowitz on one hand, and Dahmer and Gein (for example) on the other, there are certain deeper threads that can tell us a great deal about these killers as well as about the forces they represent. In the case of Manson and Berkowitz, we can point to the dim outlines of a cult of killers using occult jargon and ritual to buttress what may have been simply a drug-related criminal operation, much the same way the Matamoros killers used *palo mayombe* as a front for what were essentially normal, criminal operations. The killers themselves believed in their respective cults (whether or not their leaders did), and committed their crimes out of a sense that they were being initiated into a circle of tremendous occult power.

In the cases of both Jeffrey Dahmer and Ed Gein—killers who operated alone and not as part of any cult or criminal organization—they were still interested in ideas of transformation (and, in Dahmer's case, occultism) and in the techniques of empowerment that murder would afford them both. In Ed Gein's case, he wanted to transform himself physically into a woman; in Dahmer's case, he simply wanted more power than he had: he wanted to create a zombie that would be his personal sex slave, a human being devoid of will who would simply not exist if

Dahmer was away but who would become his plaything when he was home. On the other hand, and in the context of our argument, neither Manson nor Berkowitz were "shamanistic"; that is, they were carrying out the murderous wishes of a cult to which they belonged in the expectation (perhaps) of attaining some degree of occult power in the process, power that would be bestowed by the cult leadership as a reward for their efforts, or obtained through the very act of killing in a cult context. This is similar to the mechanism of normal initiatic cults the world over, where certain tests and trials are administered to the initiand, both to test the candidate's loyalty as well as to cause emotional and psychological stress conducive to illumination. (Even in Freemasonry, one is initiated at the point of a sword—blindfolded and bound—and made to swear all manner of frightening oaths.)

But both Dahmer and Gein were prime examples of loners, outcast from any kind of society, people with sick fantasies of blood, dismemberment, cannibalism and necrophilia, as well as confused sexual identities. They had secret chambers to which non-initiates were not allowed, places reeking of gore and offal that were monuments to their dreams of godlike power and psychic integration.

SHAMANISM AND SERIAL MURDER

> Neurosis and initiation are the same thing, except that neurosis stops short of apotheosis, and the tremendous forces that mold all life are encysted—short circuited and turned poisonous.
>
> —Jack Parsons

As the West became increasingly Judeo-Christian, and a split was created between humanity and nature, with nature being suspected of harboring evil, the role of the shaman was relegated to the dustbin of personal spiritual illumination. Church and temple were organized, social places that contained all the spirituality that any normal human being could ask for. They channeled the spiritual desires of men and women into socially-acceptable forms, cookie-cutter spirituality. In the process, Westerners began to lose their contact with nature, their reverence for nature, and by so doing became alienated and desperate. Jung said somewhere that Christianity caused Europeans to become schizophrenic, and perhaps he was right. We lost the ability to nurture the shamanic impulses into mutually beneficial manifestations. The pseudo-shamans we produce—the Dahmers, the Geins, the Gacys, the Bundys—know only the impulse, but not the technology, for spiritual integration. They experience the nightmare of the "future shaman," but not the communication with God.

Sexuality was another victim of the rise of Christianity in the West. The expression of sexuality was severely suppressed by the Church, and a caste of celibate priests and nuns was created—after a period of hundreds of years as the Church consolidated its political and economic power in Rome—and sex was considered to be a kind of necessary evil, useful only for procreation. To enjoy sexuality was to be sinful. Women were characterized as wanton sexual creatures, whose constant thirst for sex made them easy prey for the Devil, who turned them into witches and made them kiss his buttocks as a sign of their submission to his infernal will.

The sexual content of serial murder is well-known. Virtually all serial killings have a strong sexual element, whether it is actual sex with the victim before or after death—or during the murder itself—or sexual mutilation, or display of the victim's genitalia, etc. Why, then, is serial murder not simply serial rape? Why does murder become involved in what seems to be only a sex crime, a mutation of normal sexual affection and desire into something violent and morbid? Is it because we in the West have associated sex with punishment, with death—with spiritual death—for so long that our serial killers are only demonstrating to us our own repressed desires? Perhaps. And perhaps there is even a deeper context in which to look at serial murder.

> *Human sexuality is, quite apart from Christian repressions, a highly questionable phenomenon, and belongs, at least potentially, among the extreme rather than the ordinary experiences of humanity. Tamed as it may be, sexuality remains one of the demonic forces in human consciousness—pushing us at intervals close to taboo and dangerous desires, which range from the impulse to commit sudden arbitrary violence upon another person to the voluptuous yearning for the extinction of one's consciousness, for death itself.*
>
> —Susan Sontag[43]

The historian of religion Mircea Eliade has written about sexuality and shamanism, albeit briefly. In his monumental work entitled *Shamanism*, he has examined the role of sexual energy and gender-transfer in shamanistic circles around the world. Some shamans are called to change their sex; to wear the clothing and adopt the mannerisms of the other sex and even to marry as if they had truly changed gender. It is interesting to note that in some cultures, although the call to switch gender is understood to occasionally be part of the initiatic process, some "future shamans" prefer suicide.[44] Thus, the call is seen as powerful and demanding, and the shaman sees no way out of his predicament other than self-extermination. Eliade goes on to state that "transvestitism and ritual change of sex are found, for example, in Indonesia (the *manang bali* of the Sea Dyak), in South America (Patagonians and Araucanians), and among certain North American tribes (Arapaho, Cheyenne, Ute, etc.)."[45]

In a later chapter, one devoted to Asian shamanism, Eliade confronts certain shamanistic cults of Tibet in which the identical stage of decapitation, dismemberment, and cannibalism is undergone by an initiate—albeit in a state of meditation and trance and not in actuality—at the hands of a goddess, brandishing a sword. The flesh and blood of the initiate is given to demons and wild beasts, and eventually the initiate is reborn after this horrifying experience.[46] Eliade sees in tantrism remnants of ancient shamanistic practices concerning sex and sexual energy, such as the Tibetan practice of "mystical heat" in which the initiate is made to conserve his sexual energy and transform it into a kind of bodily heat so intense that he is able to dry wet blankets on his skin outdoors in the winter.[47] This idea of "mystical heat" was not unknown to shamans of various other countries and climates, and was inextricably linked to healing of physical illnesses in others, and in a bizarre form of self-mutilation in which the body of the shaman is "heated" in this mystical fashion, as well as his knife. When both knife and body have been heated to the right temperature, the shaman opens a wound in his own abdomen without pain.[48]

The shamans may also be the sexual partners of spiritual forces, spirits of the opposite sex who come to the initiate on his sick-bed (for the initiation always begins in illness of some kind) and tell the future shaman that he has been selected as a husband. To refuse is to die. The shaman thus selected may find himself unable to satisfy a mortal woman, or to refuse all sexual contact except with this ethereal entity who nonetheless teaches him shamanism over a period of years. Many of the public rituals performed by shamans are sexual in nature, using elaborately carved wooden phalluses for example, accompanied by the beating of the drum and hypnotic incantations.[49] We are reminded of Dahmer on his couch, in trance, in mystical communion with the demon who tells him to do "scary things."

We may also remember Foucault and his "blood and sex" theory. Does the shaman live on the tangent between blood and sex? Is the "place between the worlds" that is symbolized (or actualized) by the magic circle, the *hounfort*, the temple, the place between blood and sex, between death and rebirth, between nature and . . . murder? Is the magic circle really a place of healing, not only of physical ailments and mental disorders, but of the rift between who we are and who we wish to become, between what is our nature and what society demands of us? Possibly the only way for the sick, the disturbed, to become whole—to become healed—is to communicate directly with God.

If the shamanistic process is allowed to continue on its normal route, the future shaman will recover from his illness after an experience of ascending into the heavens and becoming reborn as a shaman. It is an ecstatic journey that puts the shaman into contact with higher forces, centering him and empowering him not only as a shaman but as a human being, as a productive and important member of his tribe: someone who has been to the Other Side and come back with the ability to predict the future and heal the sick. And if the shamanistic process is not allowed to continue?

> The total crisis of the future shaman, sometimes leading to complete disintegration of the personality and to madness, can be valuated not only as an initiatory death but also as a symbolic return to the precosmogonic Chaos, to the

> amorphous and indescribable state that precedes any cosmogony. Now, as we know, for archaic and traditional cultures, a symbolic return to Chaos is equivalent to preparing a new Creation. It follows that we may interpret the psychic Chaos of the future shaman as a sign that the profane man is being "dissolved" and a new personality being prepared for birth.
>
> —Mircea Eliade[50]

For modern psychiatry, every mental breakdown—every mental illness, every mental disorder—has its origin somewhere in the patient's life. A person does not go insane for reasons that are not part of his personal history. Therefore, what Eliade is saying would be considered suspect by psychiatrists. How could a person go insane—how could his personality disintegrate to that extent—due to an *external* influence? There is either an organic reason (such as a hormonal imbalance or some other chemical reason, or physical trauma of some sort, such as a blow to the head), or there is a precipitating cause in the patient's immediate environment. Yet, in the context of shamanism, the precipitating cause is the summons of a spirit. Even more threatening, the shaman is a person who has gone "through" madness and has become "cured" without the benefit of modern psychiatric technique. Even more astonishing, this person who had once been mad is now a valued and even a revered member of his society, and *all due to the fact of his madness and subsequent cure.*

The controversial Scottish psychiatrist (and sometime visitor to the Timothy Leary/William Hitchcock estate at Millbrook) R. D. Laing wrote in 1967, in *The Politics of Experience,*

> When a person goes mad, a profound transposition of his place in relation to all domains of being occurs . . . . *Nevertheless, he can often be to us, even through his profound wretchedness and disintegration, the hierophant of the sacred.* An exile from the scene of being as we know it, he is an alien, a stranger signaling to us from the void in which he is foundering, a void which may be peopled by presences that we do not even dream of. They used to be called demons and spirits . . . . Madness need not be all breakdown. It may also be breakthrough. (emphasis added)[51]

Madness and psychic disintegration (dissociation?) leading to . . . spiritual breakthrough, psychic powers, attainment, illumination: the shaman, the medicine man, the magician.

When the governments of the world undertook their various and individual programs for exploring the possibility of mind control, they were seeking a way to "disintegrate" the personality of a subject and then rebuild it in some other, more convenient, form. The efforts of Dr. Cameron in Montreal were certainly perfect examples of this approach. If the government—or, at least, its intelligence agencies—could arrogate to themselves the power of initiation then they could indeed create a "cult of intelligence" to which their most valuable members would not even be aware they belonged. In Eliade's world of shamanism, the shaman-to-be began in illness—mental illness or even epilepsy or some epileptoid disorder—and found his personality "disintegrating," his body being dismembered and disemboweled on some level, and then gradually became whole again and the proud owner of a "new" personality. The problem with this process—in the eyes of government agencies—would be the time it took to develop this new personality and the ambiguity of that personality: why not design the new personality from scratch and drag the unsuspecting "shaman" through the entire initiatic process in record time with drugs, sensory deprivation, and all the other tools of the trade? To that end they explored the shamanistic repertoire of hallucinogenic drugs, ritual, hypnosis, and whatever else they could find, not realizing that they were—in the eyes of shamans, mystics, magicians everywhere—becoming "black magicians" in the process. Just like every other wistful and lazy would-be occultist with the flowery titles and advanced degrees of imaginary spiritual attainments, the CIA psychiatrists wanted all the benefits of the initiatic process but without the expense of time and effort required to do it right. They also wanted complete control over the finished product; this, from people who had not been through the process themselves and had no idea what changes it would create in the minds—dare we say "souls"?—of their subjects. They were wading into deep waters, the same waters that could create a shaman . . . or serial killer.

> The real problem is that people like Dahmer present a dilemma for society, which has not evolved proper ways to deal with them. Focusing on notions of right and wrong does not begin to approach the complex reality of what Dahmer did.
>
> —FBI Profiler Robert K. Ressler[52]

It is a cliché of modern psychiatry that a child who has been abused will grow into an adult who abuses children. What about the serial killer? Obviously, he was not "killed" as a child, was not dismembered or eviscerated. What causes the escalation from physical and sexual abuse into serial murder, into lust killing? If an adult abuser is only "acting out" what he has experienced as a child, is the serial killer acting out a different experience, a different reality? What were the nightmares of Jeffrey Dahmer like? Did he wake up one morning, feverish and shaking, from a vision of hell? Did he truly hear a voice telling him to do "scary things"? A normal therapeutic course would probably not have helped Dahmer very much; he would have known to keep the darker elements of his nature quite hidden. Patients fool therapists all the time, particularly sociopathic patients. Perhaps what Dahmer needed was not therapy, but initiation.

If, as Mircea Eliade said, those who were mentally ill "became shamans precisely because they had succeeded in becoming cured," then I submit that those who were mentally ill (like Dahmer, like Gein), became serial killers precisely because they had *not* succeeded in becoming cured. I submit that the shamanic impulse has not died, it has only been suppressed in our society, and thrown in with diagnoses of schizophrenia and other mental disorders; that characterizing what used to be understood as a mystical state as, instead, evidence of psychosis has robbed us of any hope of spiritual comprehension. And generations of psychiatrists and psychologists since at least the time of Freud have warned us what to expect when strong emotional impulses are denied.

This is not to suggest that serial killers are somehow holy or spiritual beings; far from it. The call to become a shaman is not necessarily divine; it could as easily be demonic. How would we know the difference? We have lost our moral compass in a society that tolerates priestly pederasty, the avarice of televangelists, the cupidity of politicians. We get our education in ethics from made-for-tv-movies and obnoxious political talk show hosts. Our spiritual lives have been canned for so long, we wouldn't recognize "fresh" if it grew in our backyards. The spiritual aspirations of Americans—like that of most Westerners—have been manipulated by social forces for so long, it would be amazing if modern America could produce a single person worthy of canonization by a church worthy to canonize. Monotheism brought with it a political structure that mimics that of the monarchy; even Hell, in the medieval grimoires, is peopled with kings and dukes and princes and, yes, presidents. More than anything else, the Postwar 1950s brought with it not only the man in the grey flannel suit, but the priest, the minister, and the rabbi in the grey flannel suit. The excesses of the 1960s were an obvious and predictable reaction against the stifling of the spiritual impulse to celebrate, to worship life in all its forms, to experience spiritual ecstasy.

The serial killer is the dark side of that force, the symbol of a twisted and corrupt spiritual desire forced to feed in silence and solitude on its own flesh and blood.

And when the CIA began to experiment on the minds of violent offenders with drugs and behavior modification and God knows what else, they were playing hide-and-seek in the dungeon with Hannibal Lecter. And when they experimented on children, dosing them with huge amounts of LSD and other hallucinogens, they were opening the very gates of hell itself. This is not to apportion blame, but to state a simple fact regardless of who or what is to blame, if anyone, if anything. With respect to the study of serial murderers and shamans, the CIA was contributing with ravaged minds and body bags, courtesy of Doctors Cameron, Gottlieb, Estabrooks, and so many others.

Imagine a government-run Zen monastery in which the penalty for not solving your koan is execution by a firing squad.

ENDNOTES

1 Mircea Eliade, *Rites and Symbols of Initiation*, Harper Torchbooks, NY, 1965, p. 88
2 Stuart Clark, *Thinking With Demons: The Idea of Witchcraft in Early Modern Europe*, Oxford University Press, Oxford, 1999, p. 554
3 Peter Dale Scott, *Deep Politics and the Death of JFK*, University of California Press, Berkeley, 1996, p. 17 and 21
4 Aleister Crowley, *Moonchild*, Mandrake Press, London, 1929, p. 29–30
5 Colin A. Ross, Dissociative Identity Disorder: Diagnosis, Clinical Features, and Treatment of Multiple Personality, John Wiley & Sons, NY, 1997, p. 6
6 Diagnostic and Statistical Manual: Mental Disorders, American Psychiatric Association, Washington, D.C., 1952, p. vi
7 Ibid., p. vi-vii
8 Ibid., p. vii
9 Ibid., p. vii
10 Crowley, op. cit., p. 179
11 Eliade, op. cit., p. 68–72
12 Carl G. Jung, *Analytical Psychology, Its Theory and Practice*, Vintage Books, NY, 1970, p. 38
13 Susan Sontag, "Approaching Artaud," *Under The Sign of Saturn*, Farrar, Straus, Giroux, NY, 1980, p. 64
14 Ibid., p. 64–65
15 Bettina L. Knapp, *Antonin Artaud, Man of Vision*. Discus, NY, 1971, p. 183
16 Eliade, op. cit., p. 88–89
17 T. K. Oesterreich, *Possession: Demoniacal and Other*, University Books, NY, 1966, p. xiv
18 Friedrich Nietzsche, *Beyond Good and Evil*, Vintage, NY, 1966, p. 90
19 Warren Commission Exhibits 2196 and 2443
20 Anthony Summers, *The Kennedy Conspiracy*, Warner Books, NY, 1996, p. 344
21 Nietzsche, op. cit., p. 89
22 Robert Graysmith, *Zodiac Unmasked*, Berkley Books, NY, 2003, p. 151
23 Milwaukee *Sentinel*, 7/27/91, page 5, Section A; and Joel Norris, *Jeffrey Dahmer*, Pinnacle Books, NY, 1992, p. 79–80
24 Norris, op. cit., p. 80
25 Ibid. p. 65
26 Ibid., p. 280
27 FBI transcript dated 9/11/92, File # 7-MW-26057-83, p. 10
28 Ibid., p. 10
29 Robert K. Ressler & Tom Schachtman, *I Have Lived in the Monster*, St Martin's, NY, 1998, p. 150–1
30 Ibid., p. 151
31 Milwaukee *Sentinel*, Sept 12, 1991, page 10A, by Joe Manning
32 Milwaukee *Sentinel*, Sept 11, 1991, Final Edition, page 1A, by Rick Romell
33 Kenneth Grant, *Outside the Circles of Time*, Frederick Muller, London, 1980, p. 206
34 Kenneth Grant, *The Magical Revival*, Frederick Muller, London, 1972, p. 116
35 Ressler, op. cit., p. 160
36 David Sexton, *The Strange World of Thomas Harris*, Short Books, London, 2001, ISBN 0-571-20845-2
37 Ibid., p. 152 and see Frances A. Yates, *The Art of Memory*, University of Chicago Press, Chicago, 1966
38 James Bamford, *The Puzzle Palace*, Penguin Books, New York, 1983, p. 507–511
39 Martin, Harry V. and Caul, David, "Mind Control," *Napa Valley Sentinel*, August-November, 1991
40 Alston Chase, "Harvard and the Making of the Unabomber," *The Atlantic Monthly*, June 2000
41 Clark, op. cit., p. 554
42 Ressler, op. cit., p. 54
43 Susan Sontag, "The Pornographic Imagination," in Bataille, *Story of the Eye*, Penguin, London, 2001 p. 103 (originally published in 1967, in synchronicity with Laing, below)
44 Mircea Eliade, *Shamanism*, Arkana, NY, 1989, p. 258
45 Ibid., p. 258
46 Ibid., p. 436
47 Ibid., p. 437
48 Ibid., p. 256–257
49 Ibid., p. 71–81
50 Eliade, op. cit., p. 89
51 R.D. Laing, *The Politics of Experience*, Pantheon, NY, 1967, p. 133
52 Ressler, op. cit., p. 160

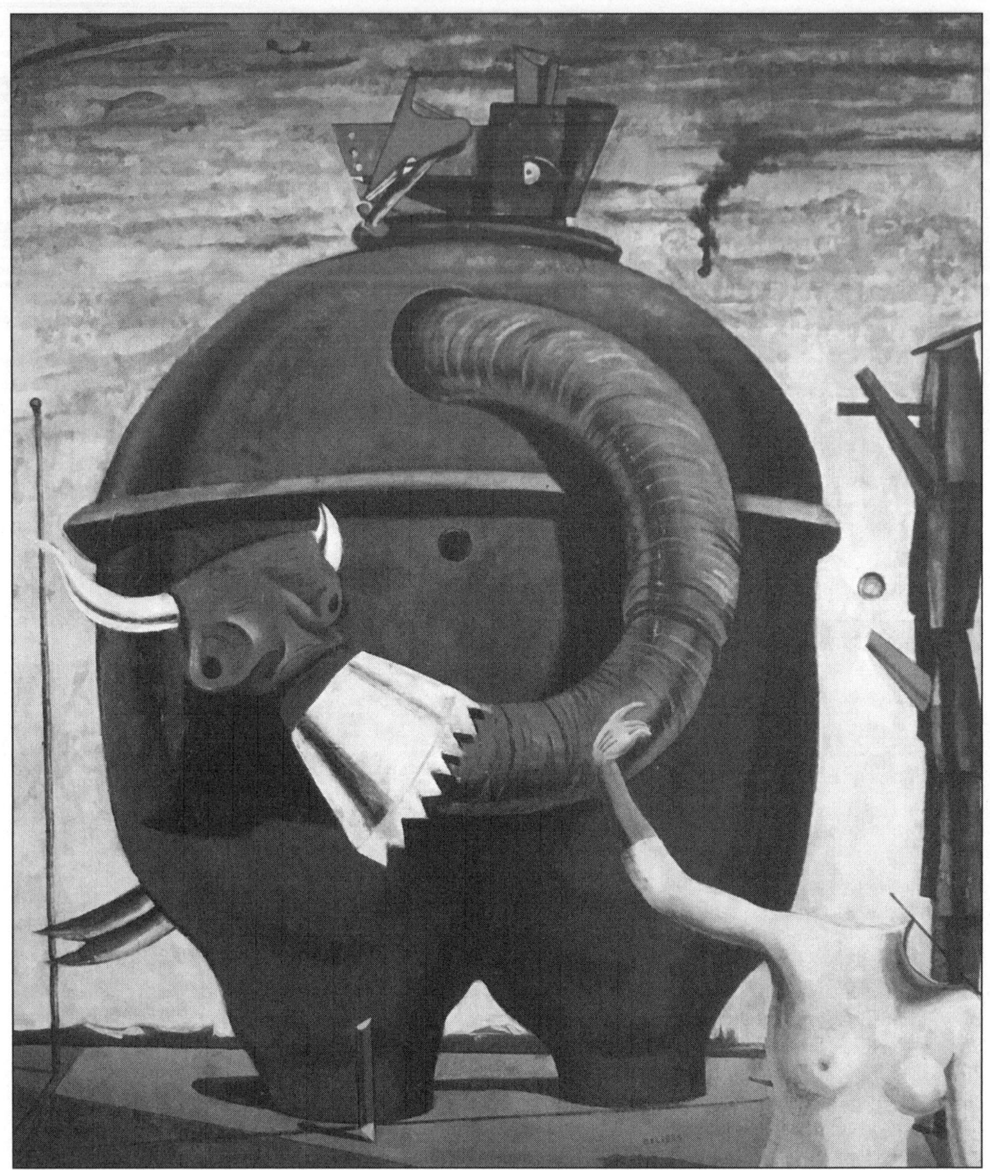

The Surrealist Movement, born from Andre Breton's experiences treating shell-shocked soldiers in World War I, sought to liberate human consciousness through a fusion of psychiatric techniques, occult practices, and artistic expression. While typically viewed as merely an artistic movement, surrealism was actually a revolutionary endeavor that used art as a weapon to bridge the conscious and unconscious minds, sharing some technical approaches—though with vastly different aims—with later CIA mind control programs. Max Ernst's "The Elephant Celebes" (1921) exemplifies surrealism's marriage of the mechanical and biological, featuring a mechanical elephant-like creature assembled from industrial parts against a haunting landscape, suggesting both the horrors of mechanized warfare that influenced the movement and the exploration of unconscious dreamscapes central to surrealist practice. The movement's political stance against fascism and totalitarianism, combined with its occult interests and psychological explorations, made it a particular target of Nazi persecution, forcing many of its practitioners into exile—highlighting how the battle for control over human consciousness played out across both artistic and political spheres.

CHAPTER SEVENTEEN

VOLUNTARY MADNESS

The deliberately induced psychotic state, which in certain unstable individuals might easily lead to a real psychosis, is a danger that needs to be taken very seriously indeed. These things really are dangerous and ought not to be meddled with in our typically Western way. It is a meddling with fate, which strikes at the very roots of human existence and can let loose a flood of sufferings of which no sane person ever dreamed.

—C.G. Jung, "Psychological Commentary" to the *Tibetan Book of the Dead*, p. xlvi

. . . what we are basically talking about is an activity which took place in the country that involved the perversion and the corruption of many of our outstanding research centers in this country, with CIA funds, where some of our top researchers were unwittingly involved in research sponsored by the Agency in which they had no knowledge of the background or the support for. Much of it was done with American citizens who were completely unknowing in terms of taking various drugs, and there are perhaps any number of Americans who are walking around today on the east coast or west coast who were given drugs, with all the kinds of physical and psychological damage that can be caused. We have gone over that in very careful detail, and it is significant and severe indeed.

—Senator Edward Kennedy, during 1977 Senate Hearing Testimony of CIA Director Stansfield Turner on MK-ULTRA, August 3, 1977

The notion that unreason as well as reason rules us from above is psychologically painful. This intolerability has given rise to the consoling world-views of religion . . .

—Peter Dale Scott, *Deep Politics*[1]

The séance was the true laboratory for the study of multiple personality.

—Daniel Lomas, *The Haunted Self*[2]

We in the West have always had a hard time with madness. We can't define it, but we know what it is when we see it. Like the term "insanity," it is not a clinical definition of a mental state or disorder, but a general epithet or legal characterization. Michel Foucault has written extensively and eloquently about the ways in which the West has viewed and treated the "mad," and we are all familiar with the cliches that tell us that primitive people believed the mad were "touched by the gods," and were therefore revered.

Mircea Eliade has written at length about the shamanistic vocation and has described the agonies of the shaman-to-be as a psychopathology, thus linking the rituals of initiation with the frightening madness of the berserker and "witch doctor." Yet, Eliade was not the only one to see something redemptive and salvageable in the acute mental disorders of the primitive occultists. Government leaders and military men also found reason to rejoice in the gibberings of the hopelessly insane.

While a detailed examination of the official attitudes towards mental illness is beyond the scope of this work, a brief look at the unwholesome way in which mental illness has been confused with both government policies and tactical weapons is in order.

What we undertake to show in this chapter is nothing less than a technique for going insane. So far, most discussions of this topic have been general and allusive. We will attempt a more direct approach here. Based on the practices of voluntary madmen going back millennia, and refined by modern psychiatric and behaviorist methods as shown in the papers and reports coming out of military and intelligence agency mind-control and behavior-control programs, the goal of this technique is to go mad *temporarily* and return in one piece.

Because this is probably the first time such a technique has ever been described fully, the vocabulary and concepts may appear strange at first, bordering on the superstitious. Remember that this is a process of going insane, and a bizarre or off-beat appearance should not be demoralizing.

What we are going to do is utilize the methodology of the shaman and the magician, the artist and the visionary—who have made a kind of science out of this temporary insanity but within the framework of the projects of Cameron, Estabrooks, Gottlieb, et al. In other words, we will use occultism and mind control to describe each other and so come to a better understanding of both. Once the basic method of "voluntary madness" is understood by examining the actual processes, then we can better understand how it is being used today.

Merely reading the following pages will not cause madness; but putting the methods into practice in a serious attempt will cause serious psychic dislocation. Therefore caution is necessary.

SET AND SETTING

> Magick is the art and science of causing change to occur in conformity with will.
>
> —Aleister Crowley

Many of our more famous artists, writers and musicians have had serious mental problems. We can think of Van Gogh, Artaud, Nietzsche, and many others who have gone insane, either temporarily or permanently. It almost seems a prerequisite for creativity. What is not so well known, though, is that there was a tendency among artists of the past hundred years or so to court insanity as a means of reaching altered states of consciousness. The boundary between the artist and the psychopath is a shifting one, more of a twilight horizon in which it is difficult to separate sea and sky than a solid firebreak designed to protect hearth and home. What is even more interesting is that the same concept is at the heart of mysticism and magic. Shamans, artists, mystics . . . and psychopaths.

When the CIA began to unravel the smoking entrails of consciousness, they understood that the artistic community was an obvious medium for their experimentation. After all, didn't novelist and philosopher Aldous Huxley—a colleague of CIA drug experimenter and psychic researcher Dr. Humphrey Ormond, who provided some of the drugs Huxley took—write the seminal manifesto for the drug culture in *The Doors of Perception*? And didn't the cult-rock band The Doors take their name, inspiration and modus vivendi from Huxley's work? And didn't Jim Morrison of The Doors eventually become initiated into witchcraft? Just pulling at that single thread is suggestive enough. See what happens when we pull at the entire tapestry.

The psycho-biographies of artists and writers—full of alcohol, drugs, sex, and "derangement"—are rarely informative when it comes to the actual processes that led them on their individual paths to perdition. We can read a biography of August Strindberg and still be no closer to the process he (successfully) followed that led him into insanity and back out again. Yet, if we take a page from the acid book of the Sixties, we just might be able to understand what happened to these people and what really goes on in the heart and soul of creative thinkers when they decide to test the boundaries of reality and consciousness.

Anyone who went through the Sixties (and can still remember them) will find the phrase "set and setting" very familiar. Basically, it means that before one takes an acid trip—before, that is, one ingests a tab of LSD-25—it is vitally important to ensure that the environment is conducive to the "trip" and that one's mental state is likewise calm and receptive. This "hallowing" of the space before a religious ritual (and, indeed, before the twentieth century the only people who took hallucinogens were those being initiated into shamanistic cults, in Europe, Latin America, Africa, and Asia) is something we come across in every instance of occult and religious practice. While this is perceived by anthropologists and archaeologists as a kind of superstitious identification of the city-state or the temple with heaven itself, when we apply this same reasoning to the acid trip or the psilocybin experience, we discover that it is vitally important to the success of the undertaking that the environment within which one "drops acid" has been carefully selected and prepared beforehand. It was not unusual in the Sixties to see the environment prepared with burning incense, candles, soft music, etc. And, as in the tantric and yogic ashrams of the East, there was generally also a Guide.

The guided trip was a mainstay of the acid culture in the early days of the Postwar era. It was patterned—consciously or unconsciously—after the rites of the Mexican shamans who performed their initiations with peyote (mescaline) or mushrooms (psilocybin). Naturally, as acid became more and more popular and easily available, it lost its "sacramental" allure and simply became another drug, another escape valve from society and the environment, and then we experienced the burn-outs and the suicides and all the trauma of the "bad trip."

There was a precedent for all of this in the workbooks of the European ceremonial magicians, the mysterious *grimoires*. While it was believed that the druggies who were going "voluntarily mad" were some kind of modern social aberration, the grimoires were evidence that going insane voluntarily was a long and serious tradition going back for nearly a thousand years. Before the medieval grimoires, however, there were books of magic spells in ancient Egypt and even spells carved into wet clay cylinders in the firelight of Mesopotamia and Sumer. Yet, the casting of spells is not, in and of itself, the central element of ceremonial magic, and these practices—while cognate with magic—are not what we seek, for a successful practitioner of magic is one who has made some contact with the Other. The spells and workbooks of the sorcerer and witch are only recipes to assist one who has already become a "cook."

In the grimoires, we find the same reliance upon set and setting that we will come across again, hundreds of years later in a different context. (Set and setting will also be recognized as a crucial element in psychological warfare and interrogation techniques. The process is all of a piece, and we may be able to understand the entire gestalt better if we look at how each of these practices describes and reinforces the others.)

In order to become a successful magician—according to the grimoires—one must first evoke spiritual forces. One must make contact with the spirit world. This is identical to the training of a shaman, the more primitive and even pre-literate school of magic. For the ceremonial magician, "set and setting" is crucial. It lays the groundwork for the ritual to follow, and if it is not meticulously planned beforehand then the entire endeavor is doomed to failure. The day and time for the ritual of evoking spiritual forces must be selected long in advance. This will be based on the nature of the spiritual force to be evoked. For the European ceremonial magician—as for the Asian fakir, tantrist, saddhu, or Daoist—this is linked to astrological data. For instance, there are spiritual forces (angels, demons, elementals) that have particular affinity for one or other of the stars or planets or zodiacal signs or elements. Once the appropriate spiritual force has been identified, and its affinity understood, then a day and hour appropriate to that affinity is selected for the ritual.

This is "set and setting" taken to an extreme, perhaps, but it is based on an assumption that was quite common in medieval times and, actually, for thousands of years of recorded human history before then: the doctrine of correspondences. This doctrine may fairly be said to be the doctrine of "coincidences" as well, as we shall see, and is very probably the key to the entire realm of what we have been calling "sinister forces."

The Romanian-born historian of religion, Ioan Culianu, was probably the first to delve deeply into the medieval doctrine of the occult link and to show its relevance not only to the history of the Renaissance but to modern history as well. His published writings on the subject are nothing short of revolutionary, both for their breadth of scholarship as well as for the brilliant way he expresses his theories. It is a serious and tragic loss to the history of religion that he was murdered at the University of Chicago in 1991, a crime that has remained unsolved but, which has been laid at the door of the Romanian secret police.

Culianu's most fascinating contribution was *Eros and Magic in the Renaissance*, a work that is based in part on the writings of the philosopher-magician Giordano Bruno and particularly on his *De vinculis*, a work that surpasses Machiavelli's *The Prince* in its sheer audacity. *De vinculis*—or "Of the link"—is a virtual operating manual for consensus reality. While it appears on its face to be an introduction to a method of conjuring demons, it is also a guide to psychological warfare, probably the earliest ever written. Culianu understood the relationship between magic and politics as no other before him, and while his scholarship may be daunting to a non-academic it is nonetheless a valuable contribution to this discussion.

There is no space to go into a detailed exposition of *Eros and Magic*, but instead we will focus on *De vinculis* and Giordano Bruno, because *De vinculis* is about more than just the magical link, and Giordano Bruno is more than just a philosopher who ran afoul of the Inquisition. In fact, Bruno was himself a magician-spy, in the mold of the English magician-spy John Dee, and their paths crossed more than once.

Giordano Bruno was a Neapolitan philosopher, writer, former priest, heretic, and was excommunicated from the Church when he wrote his literary masterpieces. Bruno is probably the closest the western world has come to the living embodiment of the satanic priest, a character that Dennis Wheatley has created in several of his occult novels and which seems fantastic in the present-day. He "aspired to the mantle" of Dr. John Dee,[3] the magician, mathematician, astrologer and spy in the service of Queen Elizabeth I of England, a man renowned throughout Europe for the breadth of his knowledge of both the mundane and the spiritual realms. It was to the same service of Elizabeth I that Giordano Bruno once worked as a deep-cover intelligence officer, uncovering Catholic conspiracies against the Queen during his stay at a house in London.

Bruno's hatred of the Catholic Church ran very deep. He had been a Catholic priest himself, one who abandoned the Holy Orders and "defrocked" himself, becoming in the process excommunicate and forbidden by the Church to even attend Mass, much less celebrate it. His hatred of what he saw as Papal idiocy and criminality led him to support various Protestant groups and operations at every opportunity, although he did not consider himself a Christian at all much less a

Protestant, and could be more correctly identified as a kind of pagan, a New Age philosopher quite ahead of his time; certainly, he was a magician, and the bulk of his writings after the "Embassy affair" of 1584—in which his espionage activities against French Ambassador to England Michel de Castelnau resulted in the arrest and execution of various individuals who were conspiring with the Church against the Queen—were about occultism.[4]

Bruno is described as using or contemplating four "arms" or methods of toppling the Papacy: armed force, fraud (or, as Bruno called it, the "art of dissimulation" which, in Bruno's case, included espionage), ridicule, and magic.[5]

> . . . his last works . . . are indeed about magic . . . showing that he intended to pull off the ultimate coup against the papacy by personally enchanting Pope Clement VIII . . . one might well think that having failed to shake the papacy by force, fraud or ridicule he was driven to magic as a last resort. And I doubt that we can use against it the history of a cool-headed secret agent we now know, for it seems fairly clear to me that, in exploring in *De vinculis* the ways by which affinities personal and cosmic might be manipulated for political ends, Bruno was thinking of his management of Castelnau as a model of how the thing should be done.[6]

In *Giordano Bruno and the Embassy Affair*, John Bossy records several instances in which Bruno and Dr. Dee met each other, either at Dee's home in Mortlake or in Prague. Dee was reputed to have the best library in England, and they shared a common interest in the occult as well as in espionage. As mentioned in *Unholy Alliance*, there is no doubt now that John Dee was a spy for the court of Queen Elizabeth I at a time when religious, colonial and territorial wars were rampant. The original 007—literally—Dee was involved in espionage for the queen during his visits to the Continent, where he ran into Bruno once again in Prague, the site of the famous evocation of the angelic forces that has come down to us as the system of Enochian magic, a system very badly understood by many of today's practitioners.

Bruno would eventually be captured by the Inquisition and put to death by being burned at the stake in Campo dei Fiori in Rome on February 17, 1600, on orders of the same Pope Clement VIII he had attempted to destroy through magic. To understand what Bruno was up to—and to understand even better how this system has been used since then by politicians, military strategists, spies and terrorists—we will look at *De vinculis*, which gives the show away.

As far as I know, this small book has not been translated into English although both Latin and Italian copies exist. I base my brief discussion on my own translations of same as well as on Ioan Culianu's extended study of Bruno and his work.

> Is the Western State, in our time, a true magician, or is it a sorcerer's apprentice who sets in motion dark and uncontrollable forces?
>
> —Ioan P. Culianu[7]

Ioan Culianu (whose patronymic is spelled variously as Culianu, Coulianu, Couliano) was born on January 5, 1950 in Romania at a time of tremendous political upheaval in that country, due to the Communist takeover of the government and the abdication of the young King Michael. His story is one familiar to many Eastern Europeans of a certain age: political repression, poverty, lack of exposure to the West and its suspiciously alluring ideas of democracy and capitalism. The man who would become his mentor, the extremely influential Mircea Eliade, was also a Romanian, and one who had made his home in the West . . . specifically at the University of Chicago where he made a name for himself as an authority in the history of religions. Eliade's books—notably *Shamanism*, *The Myth of the Eternal Return*, *The Quest* and *Images and Symbols*—have been and will be cited many times during thecourse of this work.

Eliade was a hero to the young Culianu, who worked assiduously to get himself noticed by the master with an eye to working with him in the United States. Emigrating to Italy—actually overstaying on a special exit visa from Romania that allowed him to attend a seminar there—he wound up in a camp for displaced persons and even attempted suicide, driven to despair over his lack of legal status and any way to earn a living, coupled with increasingly dismal news from home. Eventually, however, he managed to work his way out of his depression and through a series of contacts and clever networking his brilliance came to the attention of the University of Milan, and he began to write many excellent articles, reviews and monographs on Renaissance studies, philosophy, religion, and related subjects during his tenure there and at the Netherlands Institute for Advanced Study, where he was a Fellow.

This outpouring of work and garnership of professional accolades finally earned him the attention of Mircea Eliade, and he eventually wound up in America with a professorship at the same University of Chicago in 1985.

This was largely due to the impact of two important works published by Culianu in 1984. One was a study of shamanism and ecstasy; the next was Eros and Magic in the Renaissance, a work begun when Culianu was only nineteen. It is on the basis of this last work that his reputation was assured, both in Europe (where it was first published in France) and then in the United States when Eros and Magic became available in English translation. (It was also in 1984 that Archbishop Valerian Trifa of the Romanian Orthodox Church was finally deported, when it became known that he had been a Nazi and member of the Iron Guard during the war; in fact, it fell upon Culianu's shoulders to defend his mentor, Mircea Eliade, from the same claim, once it was revealed that Eliade—à la Carl Jung—had written admiringly of the Iron Guardists, albeit before their name became synonymous with the worst sort of atrocities.)

Culianu himself was fascinated by the occult and what occultism says about reality and consciousness. He studied the medieval witchcraft trials, Renaissance magic, the Tarot, even conducting seminars on the symbolism in the popular

David Lynch television series *Twin Peaks*. He wrote about gnosticism, shamanism, the use of drugs in altered states of consciousness . . . and all from a serious, academic viewpoint with virtually every line buttressed by extensive citations and primary sources in Latin, Italian, German, English, and many other languages. He was at once serious and playful, a man who felt that modern society had lost its connection to the miraculous, to the metaphysical, and that because of this loss we were in no position to understand the writings of men like Bruno who formulated entire technologies for reorganizing the human mind, beginning with memory and extending to every mental and psychological faculty.

Eros and Magic in the Renaissance concentrates on three seminal figures in Renaissance philosophy, magic, and—at least in Bruno's case—politics. Aside from Giordano Bruno, Culianu discusses Marsilio Ficino and Pico della Mirandola: three men who had an enormous influence over the development of hermetic thought during the Renaissance. Pico della Mirandola was a student of Ficino, and Giordano Bruno drew his inspiration from both.

Although Bruno had written a number of famous and influential works, Culianu concentrates on *De vinculis en genere*, sometimes referred to simply as *De vinculis* or "Of Links." These links, according to Bruno, are those between human beings, but they could just as easily be those that link God to humans; the links to which he refers are any connections that could be made between any created objects at all. Magic is the art of manipulating these links, links which have been activated through the desire of the magician; thus magic is, in other words, *eros*.

Eros forges connections between human beings, as we have all witnessed and as we are all the tangible result. Eros is a field of attraction between two objects; in human terms, we may call this attraction "love" or "fascination" or "chemistry," etc. When the attraction exists between inanimate objects, other terms might be used, but according to Bruno (and the generations of her meticists before him) they are all variations of the same theme. This is magic, pure and simple. Even Aleister Crowley was not able to refrain from using a verse from the *Book of the Law* as a kind of slogan: *Do what thou wilt shall be the whole of the Law; Love is the law, love under Will.* This is an accurate summation of Bruno's technology, and what Culianu discovered, for Culianu—in describing Bruno's contribution to occult philosophy—states that Bruno's ideal magician "*epitomizes the most perfect, hence the least human, product of the age of phantasms: a person capable of free will untrammeled by the turgid forces of his nature, which he has learned to dominate*" (emphasis in original).[8]

This is virtually identical to Crowley's much-overused and misunderstood slogan, and reveals that both the late-Renaissance magician Giordano Bruno and the early-twentieth-century magician Aleister Crowley were in agreement on the core issue of magical technology. What is important for us to consider is whether or not the knowledge of this technology was disseminated more widely than the narrow and shadowy corridors of the secret societies.

For Bruno took this hermetic concept one step further, to the realm of politics. And so did Culianu.

> *Securitate, a friend once said, they're all mystics.*
> —Ted Anton[9]

It is no secret that the goal of the Nazi Party under Hitler, Hess and Himmler was nothing less than the creation of a "new man." Hitler mentioned this repeatedly, and corroborating evidence is given in the author's previous work. The goal of the occult and political programs of the Third Reich was the jump-starting of human evolution to the next stage. Whether or not such a process is possible is beside the point; what concerns us here is what the leaders of the Reich understood this next stage to be.

Throughout the writings and declarations of the "theologians" of the Third Reich—everyone from Eckart to Rosenberg to Darre to Rahn to Wiligut there is an emphasis on the idea of the lost psychic powers of the Aryan race due to pollution of the blood. That the New Aryan Man would be possessed of these powers was taken for granted by Wiligut and his protégés. That the Third Reich itself was perceived to be the result of a "triumph of the Will is clear, both from the writings of Hitler and his colleagues as well as from that famous film by Leni Riefenstahl. The early anti-Semitic mystics—men like Lanz von Liebenfels and Guido von List—wrote of the seductive charms of the Jewish woman, and of the enslavement of Aryan men to these erotic creatures; and of the necessity to reject their advances and to gain control over one's own libidos: to put one's emotions and sexuality under direct conscious control. In this sense, the phenomenon of the Third Reich can be seen as a validation of the occult theories of Bruno and others; indeed, the attraction of Jung, Eliade and others to the initial appearance of the Nazi Party is most likely due to this transcendental nature, this occult platform of the Party that was so much in agreement with the technologies of the Hermeticists. It was an error to suppose that just because a political party—or, more correctly in this case, a cult—should have adopted such theories and technologies, they were, therefore, spiritually enlightened or illuminated. When the horrors of the Third Reich became known, men like Jung and Eliade distanced themselves from it as much as possible and came away with a rude awakening: that not everyone who puts occult theories into practice is a "white magician," and that having occult abilities does not automatically imply moral superiority. If anything, one lesson of the Third Reich can be summarized as the realization that occult technologies can be utilized by any individual or group, regardless of their political affiliation or spiritual growth. This was a lesson that was taken to heart by Soviet intelligence, Chinese and Korean intelligence, the Romanian secret police (the Securitate), Hamas, Hezbollah, Al-Qaeda, and by the men of MK-ULTRA.

But before terrorism became an accepted tool of international diplomacy, and interrogation refined to the astonishing degree that it has been in the twentieth century, there was the Renaissance. At that time, the West was divided by religious wars. Catholics and Protestants were the main combatants, although the Jews were still being persecuted as well. And even among the Protestants there was conflict, with various groups claiming to be the sole authority on the pure, unadulterated practice of Christianity. The Catholic Church, with special emphasis on the Pope in Rome, was considered to be a great evil: a debauched, degenerate, corrupt organization that was more interested in material wealth and temporal power than in spiritual attainments. By the time Martin Luther nailed his famous ninety-five theses to the door of the cathedral (October 31, 1517 . . . Halloween and the day the gates of the underworld are opened), the Reformation had begun.

While authorities are divided as to the dates when Renaissance and Reformation both began and ended (and, indeed, the dates are different for different countries, with England coming in later than the Continent), it can be said that the Renaissance began in Italy either as early as the twelfth or as late as the fourteenth century, as Europe shrugged itself awake from the so-called Dark Ages, and reached its height with the fall of Constantinople in 1453 and particularly with the discovery of America and the expulsion of the last Muslim Caliphate from Spain in 1492. Thus, Martin Luther's attack on the Catholic Church took place in a time feverish with theological, philosophical, metaphysical, artistic and political changes.

For Marsilio Ficino, it was the rebirth of Platonic philosophy that characterized the era, a kind of pagan sensibility that was refined and redefined by Pico della Mirandolla and then, eventually, by Giordano Bruno himself. This amalgamation of Greek and Byzantine philosophy and metaphysics with Arab science, Jewish mysticism and Catholic ritual and liturgical practices created an explosion of consciousness among the intelligentsia of Europe. The Greek gods were rediscovered and became a kind of esoteric shorthand for the artists, poets, and philosophers of the time; Egyptian religion—particularly the as-yet undeciphered hieroglyphics—became a fascination for many, as it seemed to be a kind of system that communicated directly to the soul, to the unconscious mind. The Renaissance was a time of Image, both in the Art of Memory and in the Art of Magic, and at the time of the Inquisition's investigation of Bruno it was believed that there was really no difference between the two. Indeed, Bruno was hard put to defend the Art of Memory as a science that had nothing to do with Magic; a sly dissimulation by the master of the art of subterfuge, since he knew as well as anyone else that the two practices are mutually dependent.

That the manipulation of a human being's memory is tantamount to control over his consciousness is something that was clearly understood by the magicians of the Renaissance and rediscovered by the intelligence officers of the twentieth century; but while the latter threw the entire weight of hypnosis, drugs, electroshock and other heavy-handed machinery at their subjects, Bruno cautioned a lighter touch. It was necessary that his subjects be unaware of his intentions, that they be *charmed* into performing those actions he required. You couldn't accomplish this with drugs and psychotherapy unless you wiped the memory and consciousness of the subject clean, as Ewen Cameron tried to do, and that took a lot of time and energy and resources, and the results were never very reliable or consistent. Bruno's approach might today be called "subliminal," that is, below the threshold of conscious awareness. While the operator may train himself in these techniques while in a heightened state of awareness brought about by meditation, ritual, drugs, "Tantric" sex and other devices, it was necessary that the target be free to go about his life uninterrupted and oblivious. Just as one is not aware of the process of falling in love—of all the thousand impressions and subconscious signals that are sent and received in the course of a relationship—just so the target of Bruno's magic would not be aware that he was being "bewitched," i.e., psychologically manipulated, until it was too late. The process, according to Bruno and those before him, was virtually identical. Hence, eros *is* magic because eros charges or activates the link.

According to Bruno, there is a network of "links" (or we may call them "connections") that "fills the universe." This is actually a sophisticated concept for a fifteenth century philosopher to expound, for it turns up again in the idea of the "matrix," both in quantum physics as well as in the popular motion picture series of the same name. These links may be activated by a force that resides in the body and that proceeds from the body, what Bruno calls metaphorically the "hand that binds" which "throws out its snares" (*De vinculis*, I).

No one is immune from this phenomenon. Every type of person may be affected by the judicious application of this technique. The type of "knot" or "binding" used depends on the target; the use of images is especially employed as a mechanism for attracting the binding energy. According to Bruno, one must study one's target carefully and create what today we would call a psychological profile of the intended victim. This will give an accurate picture of the state of the victim's consciousness: the mental images with which he surrounds himself, images that can be manipulated by the magician. The Chinese philosophers say that in order to know someone or something, "know what it eats"; Bruno would have said, "know what it loves," for in that love is the key to its submission.

For Bruno, love is the occult force that binds the universe together, and if one can understand love and understand how others love and what they love, then one can control them through their passions and their appetites. If reality is what our conscious minds make of it—a deliberate ordering of sensations in categories of priority, translated by our brain as images of light and dark, color, sound, dimension, etc.—then the way into the mind of another is through the images he or she manufactures. Rather than create a whole, complex reality that will be translated and identified by the subject's brain, one simply creates the images of the desired reality, working backwards from the image to the result desired.

Bruno understood that thought is a succession of images in the "mind's eye"; that memory is a storehouse of images, as his promotion of the Art of Memory exploits. Culianu calls the magician the "artist of memory," and this is an extremely important point; else, why did the mind-control experts concentrate so profoundly on ordering and redesigning the memory of selected subjects? Bruno's strategy employed a technique of going directly to the brain through the use of images, creating an alternate reality over which he was the master. In order for this system to work, it was necessary that the target be "seduced" by the images, i.e., "fall in love" in a sense with the image presented by the magician and thereby allow it to work in his consciousness. For this to happen, the magician himself must expend great amounts of energy—of passion, really—through that image in order to create the "link," in order to "enchain" the other person or persons and make them instruments of his will. As a corollary, Bruno insists that the magician not allow himself to fall in love with his own images, lest he become enslaved by them and ultimately destroyed. Thus, the magician places himself above love—above all the human passions and desires—so that he is not enchained in turn. Culianu understands that this seems at first glance to be a contradiction: the magician employs love and all the machinations and subterfuges of love, of eros, of passion and desire in order to seduce—to enchain or enslave—the will of others; he must experience love deeply, that "derangement of the senses" of which Rimbaud is the most famous exponent; yet he must not be affected by love, not "fall in love" himself even as he seems to be the ultimate lover, the most desirable suitor, working on the sensory apparatus of his victim with all the stored erotic energy at his disposal for, finally, the perfect magician is one who remains celibate, who retains his seed and uses the accumulated energy to power his magic. *He must believe he is in love with his subject at the time he works his magic, and not at any other time.* This is our introduction, not only to the Manson Secret, but also to the television preacher, the popular politician, the salesman, the advertising executive. Culianu understood all of this, and was perhaps the first person to clarify and enlarge upon this idea.

At least, until he was murdered on May 21, 1991 at the age of 41.

Culianu's political involvements were largely unknown or misunderstood by his colleagues. One would have had to have a good working knowledge of the Byzantine conspiracies and intrigues of Romanian politics to get an inkling of Culianu's dangerous activities. He could not resist writing against the dictatorial Ceaucescu regime, although at times his writings were more in the way of a *ludus serius*, a kind of game involving symbolic figures, than they were out-and-out broadsides against the Communist leader and his secret police, the Securitate. But Culianu was a living symbol of the rewards that freedom of thought, freedom of expression, and the free and open exchange of intellectual ideas could bring. Further, he was a problem for both sides of the Romanian problem: right and left. Although there is no doubt that he was a sincere anti-Communist—living and suffering under a Soviet-style Eastern European dictatorship is enough to convert anyone to democracy and the free-market system, without even knowing what those concepts really represent—he was also anti-Nazi. This, in the context of Eastern European politics, was a difficult position to maintain, for it meant that he attracted enemies from both the Securitate and from various underground movements that had their origins in the ideas, if not in the actual membership roles, of the Romanian Nazi Iron Guard.

Six years previously, Valerian Trifa had been deported from the United States. This former Iron Guard leader and dedicated anti-Semite had come to America and taken by force the Romanian Orthodox Church, proclaiming himself its archbishop and leader. This was a man who had never been ordained a priest, nor had he any theological or ecclesiastical training whatsoever, a man who was little more than a violent thug and ringleader of a network of Iron Guardists from North America to South America, Europe, and Australia. When some US government officials discovered that Trifa had actually been a Nazi, they worked at getting his citizenship revoked, which resulted in his eventual deportation in 1984. Although Trifa himself was deported, he was not removed as the head of the Romanian Orthodox Church nor is there any evidence that he relaxed his control over the global Iron Guard network.

At the same time, Romanian secret police were active in the United States; thus, Culianu was surrounded by enemies who would have stopped at nothing if he was identified as a threat to the regime, or to the underground Iron Guard network. As Mircea Eliade's literary executor after his death in 1986, he also had access to documents concerning his mentor's Iron Guard affiliations, evidence that he had written articles in the 1930s supportive of fascism and the Iron Guard itself, evidence that troubled Culianu deeply.[10] Culianu himself had written articles condemning the right-wing in Romania, which enraged the fascists who had thought he was one of them. Truly, the shots that were fired in the men's toilet at the University of Chicago from a .25 caliber Beretta—killing Culianu execution style, to the head—could have come from anywhere. Although the crime remains unsolved to this day despite heavy FBI involvement in the case, it is a certainty that what killed the young professor of religion was the very force he had been studying and writing about so extensively and with such penetrating insight.

INITIATION, INTERROGATION

The doctrine of correspondences assumes that everything in reality is somehow linked to everything else in some way; that the microcosmic world is a perfect image of the macrocosmic world; and that if we can cause a change to occur in the microcosm it will reflect in a corresponding change in the macrocosm. This is the essence of practical magic, and it is nothing less than a realization that there is a way to defeat the space-time continuum. It is an attempt to understand—and to exploit—"non-locality," a concept familiar to quantum physicists and which we shall examine in a later chapter. For now, suffice it to say that for the magician there is no such thing as a coincidence; for the magician, every coincidence is the manifestation of a subtle correspondence. While we experience coincidences in life as if they were accidents, the magician turns the tables and utilizes coincidence *proactively* as a way of causing change to occur in the real world.

We will examine this mechanism more fully a bit later on. For now, let us look at the technology of magic where we will see some parallels in modern psychology, particularly in multiple personality disorder and other forms of psychosis.

The magician, having selected the day and time of his ritual, must also select the appropriate location. Many grimoires give suggestions ranging from abandoned churchyards to lonely forests to a room in one's own home that has been stripped of all ornamentation. The idea behind each of these recommendations is particular to the type of ritual being performed. In the evocation of demonic forces, for instance, a graveyard would be an appropriate locale because it would cause feelings of dread and heightened anxiety in the magician, sentiments which are conducive to the experience of confronting evil firsthand. Even more importantly, such an environment would be a reminder to the magician that what he is undertaking is a dangerous endeavor and that he should not turn his back for a moment on the forces thus externalized.

There is another reason for choosing an outdoor site, and that is one of simple expedience: spiritual forces need to clothe themselves in bits and pieces of reality in order to become "visible" to the magician. This is known as the "material basis" in modern occult parlance. Something must be available for the force to "inhabit," if only briefly, so that it may become sensible to the magician. This can range from the smoke of burning incense to a drop of ink in a bowl of water, to the rustling of leaves on a nearby tree or even a hapless forest animal who may be in the vicinity.

In a closed room, where the environment is one hundred percent controlled and designed by the magician, this basis may be incense smoke or ink in water, as mentioned, or may even be a pure hallucination caused by the sensory deprivation techniques we will examine shortly. Whatever the case, the environment for the ritual must be carefully chosen in advance and prepared for the ritual by the magician.

Space and time, the ritual location and the day and hour of its performance, have now been manipulated by the magician to a certain extent, based on the doctrine of correspondences. That is "setting." Now the magician must concern himself with "set."

"Set," in this case as it is in the case of the LSD trip, is the mental state of the person undergoing the experience. The grimoires usually specify a period of fasting, celibacy and prayer to precede the actual performance of the ritual. This period may be anything from a few days before the ritual to months in advance. During this time, the magician must concentrate on the ritual to be performed, and must become "inflamed with prayer." As the day and hour of the ritual approaches, the praying and fasting is stepped up. The entire being of the magician—body and soul—is devoted to the ritual and everything else, every extraneous thought and desire, must be eradicated from his consciousness. This is a kind of controlled fanaticism, fanaticism focused towards a specific goal at a specific time and place.

The shaman, for his initiation, becomes ill at first: feverish, delusional, near dead, psychotic. The magician also becomes deranged, for as elevated as this spiritual state may seem—constant prayer, celibacy, fasting—it shares a great deal with the psychotic state. After all, this entire uncomfortable existence is surrounded by images of spiritual forces, by the manufacture and preparation of exotic instruments designed to force obedience from those forces, by the creation of a blank book in which to record the experience and—in the case of some grimoires—to actually receive the signature and seal of the spirit evoked. After a long period with very little food, no sexual activity of any kind, and constant focus and concentration on invisible beings, one could safely say that the magician is entering a state of controlled psychosis, a state leading deliberately up to the evocation of one of these invisible beings to visible appearance. What the shaman was doing in the forest or jungle by himself, at the mercy of visions of hideous torment, the magician does to himself deliberately in his European city or town, driving himself slowly insane, loosening his grip on "reality" so that he may catch a glimpse of the sinister forces that operate below the radar of even our most sophisticated science. The very predicate that these forces exist, and can be summoned, would be enough to sentence many a modern man or woman to thirty days of observation in a mental ward. The investment of time, money, and consciousness in the effort to summon, and to communicate with, these forces contribute to a state of mind in the magician that is difficult to describe. He builds up within himself a determination to know the unknowable, to see the unseeable, to do the undoable, and this sets up a psychic tension in the magician that can easily lead to a nervous breakdown, or worse.

One of the most accessible of the modern practitioners of this art was the late Francis Israel Regardie, one time secretary to Aleister Crowley and—oddly enough—one-time associate of Kennedy assassination researcher Mary Ferrell. Regardie went on record several times insisting that anyone desiring to go on the path of occult attainment represented by ceremonial magic first undergo a period of psychological analysis and therapy.[11]

A disturbed mind would find the ceremony and ritual of magic too comfortable, and would find itself a prisoner of the unreal, of the Other. The practice of magic by such a mind would further its derangement, but without the hope or expectation that a state superior to sanity would be achieved; rather, the health of such a mind would be forfeit if it undertook a practice of magic alone, without the benefit of a strict and observant guide. The resultant anxiety—in which the "magician" would see signs and portents everywhere, in a chaos of iconography that is perhaps best represented by the type of conspiracy theorist who believes that the goal of all those wealthy men and government acronyms is to destabilize *him* personally—leads easily to what the *DSM* calls "paranoid schizophrenia," from which the road back to mental health is long and painful. This is because magic, as it is known in the West, is a highly intellectual art. The psychological edifice created by a knowledge of ancient tongues and scripts, the minutiae of astrology, the language of symbolism, all combine in a structure whose internal logic serves as a means by which one can both create the ritual *and* decipher its outcome. A certain objectivity is required, and this is why a strong grasp of the principles of the doctrine of correspondences is so necessary, for this is the alphabet and the vocabulary of visions, dreams, nightmares, and the disturbing coincidences that surround the magician once embarked on this mysterious quest.

To make matters even more confusing, the set of correspondences is not identical from culture to culture, from society to society. A Siberian shaman may use one set of correspondences familiar to him due to the flora, fauna and folk religion of his environment; the European ceremonial magician will use another, even more elaborate, set; and the voodoo priest yet another. However, attempts have been made to show that these different sets of correspondences do share some basic information, that there is a common denominator to all cultures and practices even though they may seem to differ widely. The Golden Dawn of the late nineteenth century sought to do just that, by using the Jewish Qabala and Tree of Life as a template upon which to "fit" the belief systems (and, thus, the correspondence systems) of every known culture, past and present. Aleister Crowley, himself an initiate of the Golden Dawn, attempted to perfect that system with the help of several of his friends, and the result is the impressive *Liber 777*. This is nothing less than a kind of database of religious and occult beliefs and practices, all set out on the 10 spheres and 22 paths of the Qabalistic Tree of Life. Thus, we can see at a glance how specific symbols in religious processes as disparate as Hinduism and Islam, Christianity and Buddhism, Greek and Roman mythology, etc. all correspond to each other in some way. While this was intended both as an aid in understanding different religions and as a means of creating occult rituals that would take into consideration a profound depth of meaning cutting across geography and millenia, it is also a useful place to begin comprehending the activity of what the Dutch novelist Couperus called "the hidden force." An understanding of the system of correspondences enables us to grasp the mechanism of what we have become accustomed to call "coincidence."

We will investigate coincidence and synchronicity in greater detail in a later chapter. For now, we should understand that—for the occultist—there is truly "no such thing as coincidence," or, more accurately, that coincidence is a clue that deeper connections exist between observable phenomena, that another force of nature is at work that we don't understand, but which has something to do with what quantum physics means when they refer to "non-locality." To New Orleans District Attorney Jim Garrison, the accumulation of coincidence in the Kennedy assassination case meant that intelligence agencies were at work behind the scenes. That he was correct should be beyond doubt, regardless of whether or not you believe Oswald acted alone. What we will do in this chapter, and in this entire book, is to go a layer deeper than political conspiracy and examine a mysterious and dangerous structure of sinister forces that "conspire" at a level where science and magic, magic and politics, meet.

That is our "set and setting."

The magician's magic circle is designed with a dual purpose in mind, and that is perhaps why it is usually portrayed as two concentric circles. In a sense, the magic circle—the setting—is needed to contain the mental focus of the magician within a narrowly structured (nine foot diameter, according to many of the grimoires) space; in another sense, the circle is also designed to keep everything else *out*. The grimoires are full of the direst warnings should the circle ever be breached: such an accident would prove the destruction of the magician. For the duration of the ritual, the magician stays inside the circle and ensures that its physical integrity is maintained.

The famous Beat poet and novelist William Burroughs, in a letter to the editor of the *Necronomicon*, wrote that the magician is like a mafia don, safe within his magic circle, sending spiritual forces to do his bidding and not getting his hands dirty. In a very real way, that is the idea. The magician, by expending huge amounts of energy and intense mental focus during the days and weeks leading up to the culmination of the ritual, is creating a psychological state in which the energy must be directed somewhere. To a psychologist, this may mean that the energy is directed inwards, leading to an imbalance in the psyche of the operator. To an occultist, however, while there is a very real danger of just that, the structure of the ritual is such that channels are designed to move this energy away from the conscious mind of the operator and outwards, into a specific space for a specific goal or target. The success or failure of the occult ritual largely depends, therefore, on the ability of the operator to externalize this accumulated energy: whether in an evocation of spiritual forces to visible appearance, in an attempt to heal someone of an illness, to find money, or to cause physical or mental harm to another.

In order to properly focus the mind and will of the operator, then, the magic circle and its environment—the setting—must reflect the nature of the specific ritual being undertaken. This is where the doctrine of correspondences comes into play. We have seen that an appropriate *time* is selected for the ritual, based on astrological principles that correspond to the nature of the ritual or to the spiritual force being evoked. We have seen that a *space* is also selected that would be conducive to the performance of such a ritual. Now that space and time must be manipulated in such a way that only the stated purpose of the ritual—and nothing else—will be permitted in the consciousness of the operator. The selection of the appropriate space and time is already half-way there; it is as if we have chosen a specific highway to a specific town. The performance of the ritual itself is akin to driving the car along that highway to reach that town.

By beginning at the right time, at the precise moment specified by the ritual, the magician "stops time" in a sense. The magic circle is commonly thought of as a place between two worlds, a place where the usual laws governing space and time are waived. As long as the ritual begins at the right time, and no matter how long the ritual lasts, it is still "that time" in the sense of the ritual. Just as a human being, born at a specific time, is said by the astrologers to bear certain characteristics of that day and year and hour no matter how long he lives, so the ritual is "born" at a specific time and place and contains within itself the characteristics of that time and place. In fact, occultists routinely draw up horoscope charts for the proposed rituals in advance, as if the rituals were persons.

Before we go much further in this examination, let's stop here for a moment and look at how set and setting are used by interrogation experts the world over.

It is a truism that the first duty of an interrogation specialist is to disorient his subject. The idea is to make the subject feel as uncomfortable as possible, and to become confused as to the time and place he is being held. Lights are turned on and off at whim; meals are served at random intervals; sounds are broadcast in close proximity, from the screams of the damned to the shouts and commands of the interrogators/torturers. This is the "softening up" process, designed to make the subject more malleable during the actual interrogation itself. From a combination of fear, anxiety, and confusion it is hoped that the resistance of the subject is broken down. Rarely is it necessary to apply actual physical torture to a prisoner to gain cooperation. Those who torture their prisoners usually do so because they enjoy it, and not because it is necessary. Psychological torture is much more powerful, and is easier to regulate. Physical torture can result in the death or incapacitation of the subject, rendering the whole exercise a failure.

While the magician needs to control every aspect of his environment prior to undertaking the ritual, the interrogator needs to control every aspect of the environment of his subject prior to the actual interrogation itself. He begins with the physical environment and, if he is skilled or lucky, moves on to the mental environment. He begins perhaps as an adversary, and then transforms himself over time into a kind of "accomplice" of the subject, someone the subject can trust. The interrogation subject has become a kind of "material basis" for the information the interrogator needs; he is a medium through which the information will "speak." The actual subject himself is of no real use to the interrogator; his only concern is for the information the subject is hiding.

Let us look at a recently declassified CIA manual on interrogation, the famous "KUBARK Counterintelligence Manual," which was originally circulated (internally at the CIA) in July 1963 and was declassified (albeit with heavy censorship) in January 1997.[12] The following is from Chapter VII: "Planning the Counterintelligence Interrogation," Section C: "The Specifics":

> **3. The Interrogation Setting**
> The room in which the interrogation is to be conducted should be free of distractions. The colors of walls, ceiling, rugs, and furniture should not be startling. Pictures should be missing or dull. Whether the furniture should include a desk depends not upon the interrogator's convenience but rather upon the subject's anticipated reaction to connotations of superiority and officialdom. A plain table may be preferable. An overstuffed chair for the use of the interrogatee is sometimes preferable to a straight-backed, wooden chair because if he is made to stand for a lengthy period or is otherwise deprived of physical comfort, *the contrast is intensified and increased disorientation results* . . . . If a new safehouse is to be used as the interrogation site, it should be studied carefully to be sure that *the total environment can be manipulated as desired.* (emphases added)

As we can see from the preceding, the goal of the interrogator in designing the "setting" for the interrogation is virtually identical to that of the magician. Total control of the environment is uppermost in the mind of the careful interrogator. As the document goes on to describe in much more detail, everything from telephones to electrical generators to a "do not disturb" sign on the door of the interrogation room is taken into consideration to eliminate every single instance of interruption and distraction. The need for the disorientation of the subject is also noted. This type of disorientation will also take place as a result of the occult ritual, properly performed. It is nothing less than the "derangement of the senses" demanded by the French poet Rimbaud and echoed throughout the surrealist movement; or the dictum of Timothy Leary, "Turn On, Tune In, Drop Out," to which it may be compared. The difference is that the interrogator is using these techniques on an unwilling and resistant subject; it is the application of a very old occult technique for modern, intelligence-gathering purposes.

In a chapter of the manual entitled "IX. Coercive Counterintelligence Interrogation of Resistant Sources" we find the following, very revealing, paragraph:

> 1. The more completely the place of confinement eliminates sensory stimuli, the more rapidly and deeply will the interrogatee be affected. Results produced only after weeks or months of imprisonment in an ordinary cell can be duplicated in hours or days in a cell which has no light (or weak artificial light which never varies), which is sound-proofed, in which odors are eliminated, etc. An environment still more subject to control, such as water-tank or iron lung, is even more effective.

The purpose of all this sensory deprivation is further clarified:

> 4. The deprivation of stimuli induces regression by depriving the subject's mind of contact with an outer world and thus forcing it in upon itself. At the same time, the calculated provision of stimuli during interrogation tends to make the regressed subject view the interrogator as a father-figure. The result, normally, is a strengthening of the subject's tendencies toward compliance.

And there is the crux of the matter: "regression." As the authors of the manual state at the beginning of the section, "All coercive techniques are designed to induce regression." Even hypnosis is considered a means to this end. On page 96 of the manual, reference is made to the work of Merton M. Gill and Margaret Brenman, who state, "The psychoanalytic theory of hypnosis clearly implies, where it does not explicitly state, that hypnosis is a form of regression." In other words, the idea is to regress the subject to "a level at which the resistance can no longer be sustained. Hypnosis is one way of regressing people."

Therefore, the interrogation environment is designed to disorient a subject and then regress that subject to the point where he or she has become, in a psychological sense, a child. This is clear from the statement above that "the regressed subject view the interrogator as a father-figure." The subject becomes a child, the interrogator a father; or the subject becomes a candidate for initiation, and the interrogator, the initiator.

The blindfolding and binding of the Masonic candidate (from which we get the word "hoodwinked"), the mock burial of candidates in the European mystery religions, the isolation of the shamanic candidate and his reduction to a childlike state of helplessness by his mental or physical illness, are all means of reducing sensory stimuli and regressing the candidate to a childlike state, in order to be "reborn."

In occult matters, this disorientation is a preliminary phase. Like the shaman in the forest, sick and hallucinating, this initial period serves to "unlock" normal mental and psychological perceptions. We have all heard of the expression "to change one's mind," and of the difficulty of "changing the mind" of a particularly stubborn person (or resistant interrogatee). The purpose of the disorientation phase is to allow the mind to be more easily changed. This is as true of the CIA's interrogation methods as it is of spiritual or occult initiation. In the case of the shamans, this disorientation was achieved by illness—either physical or mental, or a combination of both—as well as by the future shaman's isolation in the wild. In the context of modern Western occultism, this disorientation is achieved by a refinement of the "sick in the woods" shamanistic type, and involves sensory deprivation. The Masonic initiate is brought in blindfolded and bound; without sight, and without the unrestricted use of his limbs, he is reduced to hearing and smell: the chants of his fellow Masons and the aroma of incense. All other sensory input has been—as the CIA manual would have it—"manipulated." In the more ancient mystery religions—as well as in some initiatory cults in the West today—the candidate for initiation was buried alive, his sensory input slowly reduced to nothing as he lay in a grave or a tomb, awaiting his rebirth or "resurrection." This is mirrored in some Eastern Orthodox ceremonies in which the candidate for the bishop's mitre spends the night in the church, prone on the church floor, and covered with a sheet as if dead; heavy candlesticks hold down the four edges of the sheet. At dawn, he is "risen," the sheet and candlesticks removed, and he joins the company of his fellow bishops for the formal consecration ceremony.

It is perhaps this state of disorientation that enables the interrogation to proceed more smoothly as the subject searches for the next stage of initiation: "rebirth" is not putting too fine a point on it. The subject is expected to do the unthinkable: to give his enemy vital information that may lead to the arrest or death of his colleagues or cause some danger or threat to his country. He must find a way to do this, to live with this decision to side with his enemy, even if under coercion and torture.

The CIA manual contains bibliographic information for the interrogator's reference, including many of the "usual suspects" (such as works by Lawrence Hinkle and Harold Wolff, Robert Jay Lifton, Margaret Singer, and *Brainwashing: A Guide to the Literature*, published by a CIA front, the Society for the Investigation of Human Ecology) plus an interesting offering by psychiatrist James Clark Moloney, "Psychic Self-Abandon and Extortion of Confessions," included in the January/February 1955 edition of the *International Journal of Psychoanalysis*. This article, according to the CIA manual, relates the "psychological release obtained through confession (i.e., the sense of well-being following surrender as a solution to an otherwise unsolvable conflict) with religious experiences generally and some ten Buddhist practices particularly."[13]

Thus, even as early as 1955, it was realized by some observers that there is a distinct relationship between the gestalt of the interrogation room and that of the meditation chamber or other religious experience. The CIA held a dim view of Moloney's work, even as they cited it in the Bibliography of the interrogation manual; they recommended the serious interrogator read *Hypnosis and Related States: Psychoanalytic Studies in Regression*, by Merton Gill and Margaret Brenman.

Also cited in the annotated CIA bibliography was an obscure article by John C. Lilly, he of "talking with dolphins" fame. This article—entitled "Mental Effects of Reduction of Ordinary Levels of Physical Stimuli on Intact Healthy Persons," in the *Psychological Research Report #5* of the American Psychiatric Association (1956)—is devoted to a study of sensory deprivation: "The effect was to speed up the results of the more usual sort of isolation (for example, solitary confinement). Delusions and hallucinations, preceded by other symptoms, appeared after short periods. The author does not discuss the possible relevance of his findings to interrogation."[14]

In one of the many coincidences that shadowed the writing of this book over the years, there is another worthwhile to mention, as it occurred as these words were being written.

In order to identify the source of my information that Francis Israel Regardie recommended a course of psychological analysis prior to undertaking occult practice, I located a copy of *An Interview with Israel Regardie: His Final Thoughts and Views*, edited by Christopher S. Hyatt, buried deep within my library, and found the relevant quotation. Scanning through the book, however, I came upon an article by Regardie at the rear of the book which is an attack on James Clark Moloney and is entitled "Cry Havoc!" This attack is due to Moloney's published distaste for the practice of chiropractic, which was of serious interest to Regardie.

Thus, I read the references to Moloney in at least two places: in the CIA document,[15] and then immediately—the same day, perhaps an hour or so later—another in a book so far removed from the subject matter of the interrogation manual as to render the occurrence even more meaningful. As if to emphasize the bizarre nature of this "coincidence," the preceding article in the Regardie collection is entitled "What Is Psychotherapy?" and contains, on page 113, a reference to (actually, a quotation from) that notorious and by-now-familiar CIA mind-control psychiatrist and inventor of "psychic driving" and "depatterning" techniques, Dr. Ewen Cameron! Although the collection of articles and the interview was published as a book in 1985, there is no mention of when the articles in question first appeared in print, nor is there a source for the Cameron quotation, alas.

Before we close the section dealing with "set and setting" it will perhaps be useful to look once more at the CIA interrogation manual, in the section dealing with "coercive interrogation," i.e., where the subject is resistant to interrogation, such as a political prisoner might be. The CIA manual quotes at length from Lawrence Hinkle (who, with Harold Wolff, was asked to study brainwashing at the request of Allen Dulles, becoming, in the process, "the chief brainwashing studiers for the U.S. government")[16] and then again from Lilly. The CIA found Lilly's description of the sensory deprivation experienced by, for instance, arctic explorers to be particularly fascinating and relevant, especially the passage from his article that states, "The symptoms most commonly produced by isolation are superstition, intense love of any other living thing, perceiving inanimate objects as alive, hallucinations, and delusions."[17]

These are all symptoms that we may, with confidence, also ascribe to heightened states of mystical or occult awareness. Unfortunately, the terms "hallucination" and "delusion" are, of course, emotionally loaded. We may wish to substitute terms like "vision" or "altered mental state," or even the Golden Dawn's suggestive "evocation to visible appearance," in the cases where these experiences are the result of a deliberate attempt to penetrate other levels or modes of consciousness. It is interesting that Lilly discovers superstition as one of the side effects of lengthy isolation and sensory deprivation; this may be understood as the willingness of the subject to see relationships between events that are not seen or not recognized by the mentally healthy. These relationships, of course, are precisely what the occultist is seeking to understand; Jung called this phenomenon "synchronicity" and science calls it "coincidence."

The setting of the occultist is just as consciously controlled and manipulated as is that of the interrogator. Every detail must be considered, and the entire environment must reflect the purpose of the ritual. In the case, for instance, of a ritual designed to evoke spiritual forces which may be represented by the planet Venus—a planet that represents for the occultist, as for the mythologian and the anthropologist, ideas cognate with love, luxury, beauty, fine arts, etc.—the color scheme must represent what his culture identifies with Venus. In Europe, this would be the color green; the metal would be copper; sweet incenses would be burned; the entire environment of the ritual chamber would reflect the concept of Venus and no other. For Mars, these elements would be replaced by the color red, iron as the metal, and so forth. These correspondences may be found in any work of ceremonial magic such as those by Agrippa, pseudo-Agrippa, pseudo-Solomon, or in *Liber 777* aforementioned. This is a type of sensory deprivation, in which all extraneous ideas and mental triggers are removed from the chamber and replaced by a single, strident pulse in which sound, sight, smell, touch, and even taste are of a piece: one insistent message being broadcast from the environment back onto the senses of the magician or operator. Further, the operator has himself designed the room or chamber to reflect this purpose, so the message has gone out from the operator to the environment and back again. The chamber thus designed acts as a kind of externalization of the inner thoughts and desires of the operator, much the same way we decorate our homes to reflect personal taste. Yet, this chamber's design is temporary; it will serve for the performance of a single ritual—or ritual series—only. On another day, it will be completely re-arranged to reflect a different spiritual force.

Thus, the magician is at once interrogator and interrogatee; he is the one in charge of manipulating and controlling the environment, but not for the effect it will have on someone else, but on himself alone. What the CIA has done in its interrogation manual—itself the product of MK-ULTRA, as is obvious from the works cited in its Bibliography, entire entries of which have been redacted while the others are overwhelmingly works by MK-ULTRA and military mind-control specialists—is to separate the magician from the ultimate goal of all occultism, which is a kind of spiritual perfection and elevated consciousness, and instead focus all the powers of occult technique on an unwilling and uninformed subject, to manipulate him as well as the environment, to change the subject and transform him into something more useful to the interrogator and of mortal danger to the subject's own people. It is, in the jargon of occultism, black magic; and black magic in the service of the State.

The interrogator himself must be of a very special and unique character. He must be capable of what Robert Jay Lifton has called "doubling." That is, a CIA interrogator must be capable of being two persons at once. Lifton used the "doubling" metaphor to describe those German scientists who—although from gentle and cultured backgrounds, with wives and children of their own—were able to become monsters in the service of the Nazi state. They had, in effect, two totally distinct personalities, which was the only way they were capable of carrying out the horrendous experiments they did while at the same time considering themselves human beings and men of science. While Lifton stops short of calling this a case of multiple personality disorder or dissociated identity disorder, it is so borderline a state as to be confusing to the non-professional. The CIA interrogator, as per the declassified manual, must also be capable of this type of "dissociation":

> Once questioning starts, the interrogator is called upon to function at two levels. He is trying to do two seemingly contradictory things at once: achieve rapport with the subject but remain an essentially detached observer. Or he may project himself to the resistant interrogatee as powerful and ominous (in order to eradicate resistance and create the necessary conditions for rapport) while remaining wholly uncommitted at the deeper level, noting the significance of the subjects [*sic*] reactions and the effectiveness of his own performance. Poor interrogators often confuse this bi-level functioning with rolè-playing, but there is a vital difference. The interrogator who merely pretends, in his surface performance, to feel a given emotion or to hold a given attitude toward the source is likely to be unconvincing; the source quickly senses the deception. Even children are very quick to feel this kind of pretense. To be persuasive, the sympathy or anger must be genuine; but to be useful, it must not interfere with the deeper level of precise, unaffected observation. Bi-level functioning is not difficult or even unusual; most people act at times as both performer and observer unless their emotions are so deeply involved in the situation that the critical faculty disintegrates. Through experience the interrogator becomes adept in this dualism.[18]

If some careful reader sees in the above an echo of the Stanislavski Method, he may be forgiven. As we will see in a following chapter, the Method resonates quite well with both occult practices and intelligence work.

Thus, we have examined set and setting; set is the mental state of the occultist and of the interrogator, a mental condition conducive towards obtaining a desired result. Setting is the environment, which is designed, controlled and manipulated in such a way as to reinforce the mental set. Mind control and magic: not very far apart at all. It is perhaps a natural reluctance on the part of many government scientists and brainwashing experimenters to take occultism and its literature and practitioners seriously that has prevented the CIA and the military from becoming even more powerful and omniscient than they have been; or, perhaps, we don't know the half of what they have already achieved and the lengths to which they have gone to achieve it. That the literature of occultism, spiritual initiation, and shamanism could contribute greatly to mind-control programs was acknowledged by some specialists. As we have seen, Moloney noticed it; and some of the operations already described in this work involved consultation with psychics, magicians, and others of that industry. It is the fact that the initiatory process itself is time consuming and highly subjective that probably prevented its use as a mind control weapon; however, the rites and methods of the occultist and shaman were scoured carefully by the men of the CIA to see if there were short-cuts and indications of other technologies that might be employed, such as, of course, hallucinogens.

That there are no short-cuts to either initiation or occult abilities—whether one chooses to believe in them or not—did not occur to them, however. Techniques and tools were taken out of context and bent to serve the urgent needs of the state. This is similar to a prince hiring an alchemist to churn out gold; or a monarch hiring a seer to divine the intentions of an enemy. While occult abilities have always, since the dawn of recorded history, been used in the service of the state, there used to be an acknowledgment of the spiritual nature of these powers on the behalf of the rulers, and of the necessity of appeasing the spiritual forces thus evoked. Today, with a totally mechanistic and technological approach to science, this basic perspective has been lost, and with it the moral imperative to treat the use of these powers (and, by extension, the hearts and minds of human beings) with care and respect.

BORN AGAIN

Eliade and other commentators on initiation myths have remarked often that the goal of the initiation is to cause the initiand to be "reborn"; the symbolism of wombs and tombs, of death and resurrection, all point to a dramatic rebirth of the initiand before he or she can take a place among the members of the cult. Naturally, this rebirth experience is quite different from an actual birth; after all, one undergoes this process voluntarily with the expectation of a great reward at the end of it. One is reborn with all one's memories intact. One has been conscious of the progression from lay person to initiand to initiate, which is more than can be said for most of us who have only been born once, the normal way. Yet, this insistence on the rebirth of the initiand into a "new life" is so widespread among so many cultures around the world, that it must have something important to convey to us. This may reside in the concept of a new *identity*.

When one is baptized in the Catholic faith, one is given a "Christian" name. When the author was a child, this had to be the name of a saint. One could not be baptized as "Phoenix" or "Serendipity" or "Moon," there being no Catholic saints with those names.

But then came the rite of Confirmation. This is the ritual where a Catholic child must repeat the baptismal vows which were said on his behalf by his godparents when he was an infant. Now that the child is of age—usually around ten or eleven years old and safely before the actual onset of puberty—he or she is expected to participate in this ritual which "confirms" those vows. Dressed in white, carrying a candle or a flower, the child makes his way to the communion rail of the church where a bishop confirms the child in its vows, *slaps the child on the cheek*, and then calls the child by a *new name*. This is probably as close as traditional Roman Catholics ever come to a "born again" experience. It is a replay of Baptism but with a totally conscious and aware child taking the place of the infant. The slap has been described as a means of warning the child that he or she will not have an easy road ahead as a Christian. I am not so sure if this is its true intention. But it is the new name that concerns us, because after all the child already has a Christian name, conferred at the time of Baptism. Why another name?

Of course, since the child is now conscious and capable of making moral decisions and knowing right from wrong, it is expected that the child will also take another name as an indication that he or she is fully conscious in a moral sense. The child selects this name beforehand. It also must be the name of a saint, preferably a saint whose example the child admires and emulates.

This rite may have had as its inspiration the Jewish ritual of the bar mitzvah, in which a Jewish boy of thirteen years or so "becomes a man" and is introduced to the community of men as a full-fledged member. Whatever its origin, it is the bestowal of a new name that concerns us.

When one converts to Islam, one is also expected to take a Muslim name, which is usually Arabic and is usually either the name of a prophet or other holy figure, or which means something appropriately spiritual. (We are reminded of the prizefighter Cassius Clay becoming Muhammad Ali.)

The same is also true of virtually every occult society. The name is selected by the initiand beforehand, and may be in any language. In the tradition of the Golden Dawn, this new name was usually in Latin but may also have been in Greek, Sanskrit, Hebrew and even Gaelic. The name was believed to be especially meaningful and to contain within itself an entire occult program. Its numerology was carefully examined, as well as its linguistic roots and occult "heredity." Within the cult's chambers, the initiate was only known by his or her cult name.

In the Manson Family this was not unusual, either. Lynette Fromme was "Squeaky," Ruth Ann Moorehouse was "Ouisch," and there were "Gypsy," "Sexy Sadie," and so many others. This idea of naming served the purpose to unite the group but also to delineate its boundaries from the rest of society. To Ms. Fromme's parents, she would always be Lynette. To the police, to the government, she would always be known by her "Christian" name. But to her friends and colleagues, she was Squeaky, even as she attempted the assassination of President Ford long after the Tate/LaBianca killings.

And, of course, in the intelligence community, false names and code names are a commonplace. In this instance, it is to protect the user and conceal his or her identity from those without a "need to know"; but it has the same psychological effect on the agent who must use that name as his identification within the "cult of intelligence." His membership in the elite group of intelligence officers is known only to his colleagues; he must use a different persona when outside of that charmed circle. Another case of "doubling"?

A book could be written on this topic of identity, and the reader will be relieved to learn I am not going to explore the theme thoroughly here. I am only pointing out the obvious, that the tradition of taking a new name begins in religion and culminates in the cult—whether of murderers, such as the Manson Family, or of intelligence, such as the CIA—and that the psychological effect of this new name has not been fully investigated.

We understand that the person suffering from dissociative identity disorder or multiple personality disorder also uses a multiplicity of names. Each "alter" personality has its own name and its own identity, usually vastly different from every other alter. The goal of MK-ULTRA was, of course, the creation of this type of disorder in its subjects in the search for the perfect—and perfectly deniable—assassin. In the case of DID or MPD, this disorder is the result of a trauma inflicted from outside the subject: an abusive parent or other older person, usually. In the case of the cult, this name is often bestowed upon the subject by its leader or guru or, as in the case of the Golden Dawn or the Catholic Confirmation ceremony, chosen by the subjects themselves. Again, the emphasis is on willing versus unwilling participation in the rituals of consciousness. The CIA wished to manipulate the subject completely, physically and mentally. They and their agents were mostly unaware that this could also lead to a spiritual crisis in the subject, one from which most people would not recover; one from which it was almost impossible to claim a heightened spiritual state or initiation. When they incorporated drugs into the program and, as in the case of Dr. Cameron, bizarre sensory deprivation techniques coupled with the endlessly droning tape players—a suggestion first bruited about by Aldous Huxley—we had all the elements of a serious occult experience, but man-handled by men of science and government who had no interest in the spiritual dimensions of their work, nor in the spiritual state of their subjects, and whose own level of spiritual development and awareness would have been equally suspect.

I have witnessed what may happen to a person when unwittingly "possessed" during the course of a voodoo ceremony. At times, uninvolved observers of such a ritual will, themselves, fall into a state of possession even though they are not members of the cult nor are believers in possession specifically or voodoo in general. The person becomes a danger to themselves and to others. The voodoo priest in charge of the ritual will usually bring this unfortunate person out of the trance (I have seen this done with a whispered prayer and a spray of rum in the subject's face), whereupon the person is led back to their seat in a dazed state, remembering nothing of what has transpired. Possession, trance, amnesia. In the case of Dr. Cameron and the other practitioners of this "black art," there was no attempt to bring the subject out of trance, or to protect the subject from the consequences of accidental "possession." The trance was the thing; the creation of multiple personalities was the goal; selective amnesia was a necessary side effect. Anything that stood in its way was, of course, anathema, but whatever contributed to these strange and dangerous psychological conditions was welcomed and enhanced.

To understand why this effort by Cameron was so evil, it is perhaps a good idea to compare Cameron's methods with normal psychotherapy. There are many forms of psychotherapy, of course, but the most common is what is sometimes referred to as the "talking cure." For fifty minutes a day, several days a week, a patient goes to see a psychiatrist or a psychotherapist, sits on a chair or lies on a couch, and talks. The therapist is usually silent, or perhaps gently prods the patient with a mumbled "hmmm" or "ah" or "how does that make you feel?" This can go on for years. It is used to treat various low-level neuroses; nothing life-threatening, no voices in the head or snakes on the walls. This is the type of therapy we are accustomed to hearing about when we read the gossip columns or the movie star magazines. The regularity of the therapy—a strict fifty minute hour, according to a strict schedule laid out in advance—is designed to give some order and structure to the patient's life. The patient, after all, is in the midst of chaotic feelings, confused emotional responses, anxieties, mood swings, depression. The unvarying routine of the therapy sessions forces a kind of artificial edifice within which these emotions are contained; it is like telling the patient that, no matter how chaotic life becomes, tomorrow at precisely four o'clock and for precisely fifty minutes, he will have the undivided attention of his therapist, just as he has had for the past three years and can reasonably expect to do for the next three or thirteen or thirty. It is also a safe environment in which to externalize these deeper emotions, anxieties, rages. The therapist will never criticize the patient, or laugh at him, or humiliate him in any way. And, at the end of the fifty minutes, no matter what is being discussed or how emotionally charged the atmosphere has become, the session is over and the patient must leave to make way for the next patient. While that seems harsh and annoying, it is actually part of the "cure": it once again reminds the patient that no matter what he or she is going through, there is a structure and routine to life and tomorrow is another day.

There are, of course, other therapies and therapeutic techniques. There is primal scream therapy in which patients are encouraged to re-live the moment of their birth as mewling infants, screaming in a kind of frenzied catharsis to overcome feelings of abandonment by the mother, etc. There is Jungian therapy, in which great attention is given to dreams and other symbolic material. Strict Freudian therapy, of course, involves the therapist speaking very little while the patient does all the talking, or doesn't talk at all. And so it goes. But the constant in these therapies is the sense that the therapist is a safe and trustworthy person, and that the therapeutic environment is a safe haven in which it is permissible and encouraged to reveal one's innermost thoughts, dreams, desires.

Therefore, when this environment is used for an attack on the mind and body of the patient, a grievous harm has been committed. The sense of betrayal of trust is enormous. Imagine going to a doctor with a minor ailment and leaving his office with a mortal disease, deliberately injected into your skin by the man or woman you trusted with your life. The same was taking place at Cameron's clinic in Montreal. Many of his patients became vegetables; some never recovered. When the CIA manual on interrogation was first promulgated within the Agency—in July 1963—Cameron's experiments were still ongoing, as was MK-ULTRA. Instead of his patients being "born again" into a healthy, robust psyche, they were being psychically murdered.

I hasten to add that some therapies may require confrontational techniques, such as in the use of psychodrama by some therapists. Again, this is done within the context of a therapeutic setting, and the patients are not strapped down to a hospital bed, fed drugs intravenously, and made to listen to subliminal messages on endless tape loops for days on end, like a scene out of *A Clockwork Orange*. In the case of Cameron—and in other cases in which helpless victims were made to suffer the very pains of hell at the hands of men and women of science—the patients were, quite simply, guinea pigs. They had become objects, and had lost their humanity. Isn't this how the serial killer views his victims? How the Nazi doctors viewed their prisoners?

What MK-ULTRA and the other government mind-control programs revealed was that the techniques of occult initiation and psychotherapy could be used not only to elevate a human being and sanctify his life; they could also be used to maim and kill. This was analogous to the relatively secret methods of using acupuncture (for instance) as an instrument not only of healing, but of torture.

The spiritual rebirth promised by the secret society, the mystical cult, the shamanistic initiation is not the end of the road for the initiate. It is a necessary prerequisite to greater accomplishments, and the path of the initiate is never-ending. While many professional skeptics—such as the Amazing Randi, among others—take delight in debunking the paranormal, there are aspects of occult initiation that transcend sleight-of-hand and legerdemain. While Randi has gone to great lengths to try to debunk the powers of Uri Geller, for instance, his own demonstrations of Geller-like abilities have always been weak. Yet, it is in the incredible mental abilities of the more "primitive" cultures that we find the greatest expression of what can only be called paranormal abilities, even as we try to define them using outmoded scientific vocabulary.

For instance, every year in Southeast Asia and parts of India there is the celebration of the Hindu festival of Thaipusam. This is the day when devotees fulfill promises made to the gods by having their half-naked bodies pierced with long needles from which are hung heavy fruits and other equally weighty objects. The devotees feel no pain, and there is no blood from these wounds. They walk in the tropical heat in a trance, their chests, cheeks, and other parts of their bodies run through with needles. Some of them carry huge float-like ornaments on their heads, secured by more needles run through their skin. This is a common festival, drawing crowds every year, and yet no one has been able to adequately explain how these people—no Uri Gellers or Amazing Randis among them—are able to enter into the kind of hypnotic trance necessary to demonstrate these startling abilities. They are under the tutelage of a guru, of course, who cautions the bystanders that no attempt must be made to break the trance of the devotees, for if they were to "snap out of it" they would find themselves in excruciating pain.

When the rite is accomplished, the needles are removed and there are typically no scars to show where the needles had been inserted and, of course, no evidence of bleeding. In Kuala Lumpur, where the author lived for several years, this rite takes place annually at the Batu Caves, a Hindu shrine devoted to the goddess Kali. In Singapore, the same festival is celebrated with the devotees walking on hot coals, showing neither pain nor burns or blisters. These feats of paranormal control over the body's natural responses—responses of pain, blistering, bleeding, etc—all take place within a religious context. Apologists for the scientific viewpoint would try to extricate the phenomena from their context, and explain them away as a kind of autohypnosis; yet, the field of hypnosis itself is not without its critics among the scientific community. What is the state of mind of the devotee during these painful (to watch) proceedings? Some have described it as a kind of "out of body" experience, as if they were watching what was being done from afar; what some theorists have called "splitting." The "center of gravity" of their consciousness is removed from a physical locale and suspended somewhere over their head. It is a trance, very much like a hypnotic trance, and indeed some of this same phenomena may be duplicated in the hypnotist's parlor. In a famous scene from Edgar Cayce's life, this "sleeping prophet" would go into a trance and critics would poke needles through his skin. No blood, no pain, no scar tissue.

In China, dedicated practitioners of the martial arts show the same abilities to ignore pain and stop the flow of blood, using swords to make their "point." What would be the therapeutic value of these techniques to modern medical science, one wonders?

In Africa, in the "village of the sorcerers" at Yho, in the Ivory Coast, there is a reported birthing ritual in which small children are put into a hypnotic trance and tossed into the air like sticks, from one man to another, each holding a sharp knife. The children have their eyes wide open, but are frozen solid, deep in trance. This tossing of the children from one man to another outside the hut where a woman is in labor continues as long as necessary, until the woman actually gives birth. The children in the air, the men with the knives, are said to simulate the actual moment of birth and to facilitate the entry of the child into the world. Like most such explanations, it has lost something in the translation, I am sure.[19]

The fact that hypnotic trances have been used in various ways by cultures around the world—as the above, very few, examples illustrate—indicates a knowledge of the powers of the mind that is at least as extensive as that of modern psychiatry, albeit in different, culturally-specific, garb. The "splitting" of consciousness necessary for the Thaipusam devotee or the Shaolin Temple monk or the Yho village sorcerer all represent a kind of voluntary madness, a temporary state of dislocation, of dissociation, of the personality that is considered useful and appropriate under certain, socially-approved, conditions. The example of spirit possession—such as that in Haitian voudoun as well as in African religious rites, Chinese Daoist mediumship, Siberian shamanism, and the more genteel European séance—is another type of dissociation, one that has been classified as "hysteria" by early modern psychiatry, but one which is a core element of much spiritualism and occult practice. The body is seen as a vehicle for spiritual forces, a kind of horse that can be mounted by the spiritual force evoked. Indeed, in Haitian voudoun this is the symbolism employed, for the possessed person is called a horse. In Malaysia, there is a virtually identical ritual—called *Kuda Kepang*—in which men carrying large wooden horse figures (similar to the western "hobby horse") dance around in a circle until they become possessed by spirits, all under the watchful eye of the shaman, or *bomoh* as he is called in the local language.

This leads us to the next element of the occult ceremonies in which forces are evoked: the "material basis."

> *Having regard to the nature and antecedents of the Intelligences with which Black Magic professes to be concerned, it must be highly important that the operator should know the kinds of apparitions which may be expected . . . . According to the Grimorium Verum, the spirits do not invariably manifest under the same forms . . . being disengaged from all matter, they must of necessity borrow a body in order to appear before us, and then they assume any shape and figure which seems good to them. Beware, however, lest they affright thee . . .*
>
> —A.E. Waite[20]

We have seen how the belief systems of ancient peoples allowed for the temporary possession of human beings by spiritual forces. This is a belief that persists to this day, from the Caribbean to Africa to Asia, and in virtually every continent and among virtually every race. The conscious evocation of forces, the invitation to these forces to inhabit a human being, is as commonplace in Haiti as it is in Malaysia and Africa. While spirit possession may also occur without conscious invitation—such as in the cases of demonic possession to which Oesterreich refers in his monumental *Possession, Demoniacal and Other*—we will focus for the moment on the voluntary kind. Normally, this takes place in an environment that has been under the conscious control of a shaman of some sort; the shaman provides a physical area that has been "blessed" or sanctified in some way, an area that will contain the forces summoned. This is as true for European ceremonial magic as it is for Haitian voudoun. Then, the shaman or magician begins the ceremony that will summon these forces into the bodies of the worshippers. The worshippers then become possessed by these forces under the watchful eye of the shaman, and depart as well under his supervision and observation. In the jargon of modern ceremonial magic, the person thus possessed would be considered a "material basis."

This is a well-known idea in European magic. In some of the early grimoires, we read of the advisability of having a young boy act as a seer under the control of the magician; the boy should be a virgin (perhaps to ensure that his emotional state was unencumbered by the heavy calculus of adult desires and worries), and at or below the age of puberty. In the literature concerning poltergeist activity—the "noisy ghost" phenomenon in which household implements are thrown through the air, furniture levitated, bangs and explosions and all sorts of startling occurrences take place without any obvious human or mechanical agency—it is believed that the presence of young children reaching the age of puberty are (unconsciously) at fault. There is a tentative theory that children reaching that age possess telekinetic powers due to some hormonal imbalance taking place as their bodies prepare for the onslaught of adolescence.

In other, more recent, cases we have the example of Aleister Crowley and his sometime disciple, the poor doomed Victor Neuberg. In the sands of northern Africa, Crowley and Neuberg were involved in the evocation of spiritual forces using basic ceremonial techniques. In these experiments, a magic circle was drawn within which the chief operator or magician would stand throughout the ceremony. A triangle was drawn outside the circle, and in this figure the "material basis" would sit during the same period. This "material basis" could have been anything from an animal to a magic mirror to a brazier of burning incense, but in the case of at least one of the operations carried out in the north African desert, Crowley himself sat in the triangle while his assistant, Victor Neuberg, stood in the circle and recorded everything that transpired. During the course of this ritual, it seems Crowley became possessed by a spiritual force—in this case, identified as Choronzon, the Beast of the Abyss—and attacked Neuberg, leaving the triangle and jumping inside the magic circle whose integrity had been breached by Crowley/Choronzon throwing small amounts of sand over the circle, obliterating it in places. Neuberg reacted quickly, stabbing outward at the "apparition" with his magic dagger, and Crowley/Choronzon retired to its triangle as Neuberg repaired his circle.

A "material basis" is a medium whereby an invisible, formless spiritual force may manifest itself in three-dimensional terms. This basis can be anything malleable enough for a force to inhabit and animate in some way. Billows of incense may collect themselves into the semblance of a demon or a genie, much the way children see faces in clouds. Images may coalesce on the surface of a magic mirror or crystal ball. A cat on a leash or a bird in a cage may, when planted within the magic triangle, become agitated in ways that evince an occult, occupying force. And a human being, especially one mediumistic, artistic or sensitive enough to begin with, can also become a material basis for the occupation of a spiritual force.

This happens with regularity among people all over the world, but usually in a socially-powerful setting like a voodoo ceremony or shamanistic séance. In Western ceremonial magic, the same goal is desired but within a very strictly controlled setting and with a very specific force in mind. The rituals of ceremonial magic are less Dionysian than those of Haitian voudoun; they are more ponderous, more complicated, and are created with the evocation of a particular entity in mind, to the exclusion of all others. The Haitian ceremonies are like occult cocktail parties to which a variety of guests are invited and the music and the drums are an integral part of the "entertainment." By comparison, the ceremonies of western magic are more like job interviews. But in either case, the material basis is necessary.

A more detailed description of this concept may be found in a novel by English magician Aleister Crowley: *Moonchild*. In this work, a room is fitted with decorations all designed to invoke lunar qualities, so that a young woman may become pregnant therein and give birth to a child of lunar characteristics. It is a concept that has its origins in the idea of sensory deprivation, but of a more refined type in which every sensory stimulus is removed save the ones most conducive to the desired goal of the ritual. It is a study of the complete control of a physical environment in order to similarly control the mental and emotional state of a human subject, so that the subject becomes the "material basis" for a spiritual force that has been summoned by the operator. Just as a woman becomes the material basis for the soul of the child she is carrying—so goes the argument—other physical media can become (temporarily or permanently) the material basis for other "souls" or spiritual forces.

If we stop to consider for a moment how this works, we will see at once an analogy to the theme of this book, for the spiritual forces are invisible, yet we know they are there. To evoke them only needs a suitable medium, and the will to summon them. They will then clothe themselves in the molecules of whatever medium is available, arranging them around themselves into a semblance of what they are and what they represent, a kind of mask or persona, much the same way we dress ourselves in our everyday costumes, making a statement with every article of clothing we wear. The intelligence agent does the same thing, of course. Beginning with the assumed name, he is "born again" as someone else. He dresses the part, speaks the part (possibly even in a language foreign to him), and acts the part. He occupies a space in front of his enemies, but they know him not. He is, essentially, a spiritual force moving through their environment: the physical representative of the will of some other government, some other country, some other agenda, some other reality. Some of these agents may simply be gathering information; others may be bent on more sinister ends: assassination, sabotage, the overthrow of a political regime. They are analogous to spiritual forces, sent by magicians to investigate the "Other Side." And when they are discovered, it is usually by the enemy's own "magicians," who understand the secret world of the spies and who can read the signs they leave on the aether.

When the interrogator begins his ceremony, the subject is brought into a controlled environment and his entire consciousness is manipulated coldly and effectively by the interrogator. The subject has information the interrogator needs. The subject is the "material basis" for the information; the poor wretch destined to occupy the dread Triangle of Art while the magician—the interrogator—is safe within his magic circle.

The interrogatee has been unwillingly led onto an initiatory path from which—according to the point of view of the theologian, the mystic, the occultist—he may not escape. Irrevocable forces have been set in motion; the interrogatee has been forced to see inside himself, to witness profound truths about the state of his soul and, by extension, the state of the world—of reality—as well. His world has been turned inside out: an adult, he has become a child again; an enemy, he has become a collaborator; a man who thought he understood how the world works, he has become an initiate into a deeper, darker mystery.

When these techniques have been amplified by the use of drugs, hypnosis, and the other paraphernalia of medical men like Ewen Cameron or Sidney Gottlieb, they become intensive initiatory experiences, but without the saving graces of a spiritual context that would permit some kind of growth. Instead, it is as if the initiation chamber had been taken over by the sorcerer's apprentice: a non-initiate with no real, personal knowledge of the initiatory process but who managed to get hold of the book and recite the incantations carelessly, thus damning both himself and whoever happened to be in close proximity. It is no accident, I believe, that Dr. Frank Olson—arguably one of the first victims of the CIA's mind-control program—was made to visit an important stage magician in the hours before he plunged to his death from a window at the Statler Hotel. The reason for this unusual visit has never been satisfactorily explained.

L'ART MAGIQUE

> If within the last century art conceived as an autonomous activity has come to be invested with an unprecedented stature—the nearest thing to a sacramental human activity acknowledged by secular society—it is because one of the tasks art has assumed is making forays into and taking up positions on the frontiers of consciousness (often very dangerous to the artist as a person) and reporting back what's there.
>
> —Susan Sontag[21]

> Le Poete se fait voyant par un long, immense et raisonne dereglement de tous les sens, toutes les formes d'amour, de souffrance, de folie; il cherche lui-meme, il epuise en lui tous les poisons, pour n'en garder que les quintessences. Ineffable torture ou il a besoin de toute la foi, de toute la force surhumaine, ou il devient entre tous le grande malade, le grand criminel, le grand maudit—et le supreme Savant!—Car il arrive a l'inconnu!
>
> —Rimbaud, letter to Paul Demeny, 15 May 1871[22]

How, then, to compare the "sacramental human activity acknowledged by secular society" with a sacramental human activity *not* acknowledged by secular society, such as magic, Tantra, shamanism, etc., which has the same ends and often very similar means? If, as Rimbaud insists above, the duty of the Poet is to become a seer, by "an immense and systematic derangement of the senses," and thereby arrive at sure knowledge of the Unknown, then where do we draw the line between art and shamanism, between poetry and psychological warfare? We have spoken in previous volumes about the strange interrelationships that exist between certain films and actual political events, such as *The Manchurian Candidate*'s director John Frankenheimer being the host of Bobby Kennedy's last meal. Film, of course, is an art form and—as stagecraft by other means—one of the oldest forms of art in the world, and one of the most sacred in a mystical and religious sense, the actors inviting possession by the gods they represented in the theater, a sacred space. Can art be used to understand magic, and vice versa? Or can the lives and techniques of the artist be used to reinterpret the lives, techniques and even address the accomplishments of the magician? The reader may be surprised to learn that there is a body of literature on the subject of art as occultism, and art as psychology . . . with very revealing things to say about all three. The application of this literature to our theme will become obvious in the following pages.

We saw in Book I how communication science developed out of the requirements of psychological warfare, or what the Germans called "world-view warfare." We have also seen how the bible of modern psychiatry, the Diagnostic and Statistical Manual, Mental Disorders (DSM), arose from US military requirements. While we have not yet investigated the impact of psychological warfare concepts on the most pervasive artistic media of modern times—music and cinema—we will first examine the development of one influential artistic movement and its relationship to both modern psychiatry and modern occultism: surrealism.

There have been several attempts to understand surrealism from the point of view of psychology and of occultism. An excellent example of the former is *The Haunted Self: Surrealism, Psychoanalysis, Subjectivity* by David Lomas. Published in 2000 by Yale University Press, it is a profound study of the cross-pollination of surrealism, psychoanalysis and various "fringe" practices, such as hypnosis and automatic writing. As an example of the latter, we have Nadia Choucha's *Surrealism and the Occult: Shamanism, Magic, Alchemy, and the Birth of an Artistic Movement.* Published in 1991, it covers much of the same ground as the later work by Lomas, but with a more specific—and equally revealing—focus.

The man largely considered to be the father of the surrealist movement is Andre Breton. During World War I, he worked in a military hospital treating victims of what is now known as post-traumatic stress disorder (PTSD). A medical student at the Sorbonne, he was heavily influenced by the writings of Pierre Janet, the famous psychologist who also exerted a great influence over Freud and Jung and a generation of philosophers and thinkers. Janet's work *Psychological Automatism* was a seminal study of the role automatic writing and free association could play in an understanding of the unconscious mind. Breton took this technique to heart, and used it in his treatment of shell-shocked veterans.

Automatic writing is a technique whereby one either closes his eyes or is otherwise distracted from what his hand is writing on a sheet of paper, the idea being that the hand will write words that come directly from the unconscious mind, sneaking in below the super-ego, the radar of consciousness. To the spiritualists, automatic writing was a form of communicating with the Other World, the spirit world, and mediums would use this as a means of obtaining messages from deceased loved ones. (This technique was dramatized in the Nicole Kidman film, *The Others*.) Breton and many of the other Surrealists, however, denied the existence of spiritual forces, ghosts, etc. and insisted that automatic writing—like all of the occult arts—was only a means towards releasing images and information, even heretofore hidden powers, from the unconscious mind. Although heavily involved in occult studies—as Nadia Choucha demonstrates—they were unconvinced of the existence of the spirit world per se, and instead preferred to conceive of the occult arts as a kind of proto-psychology:

> The surrealists all rejected the idea of spirits, believing that these messages and drawings came from the unconscious mind of the medium as a result of dissociation of the personality.[23]

This idea of the "dissociation of the personality" was as important to the surrealists as it was for later generations of psychiatrists and mind-control experimenters. To the surrealists, the human consciousness was *normally* in a state of dissociation and it required techniques such as automatic writing and other trance-states to unify the unconscious material with consciousness; that is, they believed dissociation was a sign of the breakdown in communication between the conscious and unconscious minds. They sought to re-integrate, individuate, the human personality (in much the same way as did the psychoanalysts and the shamans) by uncovering repressed unconscious data and making it available to the consciousness. Yet, while the psychoanalyst worked one-on-one with a patient, the surrealists intended to explore the mind's potential in their poetic and artistic expressions and thus, perhaps, instigate a move towards illumination among larger numbers of individuals.

> *The study of cases of double and multiple personality (so-called 'disaggregations of the personality'), of which there was a near epidemic in the late nineteenth century, caused a number of investigators to raise doubts about the philosophical premise that the human subject is a unity.*
>
> —David Lomas[24]

Breton was heavily influenced by the writings of the French symbolist poet, Arthur Rimbaud. He believed, like Rimbaud, that a "derangement of the senses" was necessary before true illumination could be obtained. At the same time, he was as strongly influenced by the writings of Janet, who believed that hysteria was caused by dissociation, or by the dissociation of a traumatic episode in the patient's past, with a host of related ideas that could only be accessed through such methods as free association and automatic writing. This equation of dissociation with hysteria is important; after all, modern psychiatry has insisted that the incidence of witchcraft in Salem—for instance—was simply a manifestation of hysteria; and writers on demonic possession put forth the theory that possession is either a form of hysteria or of dissociation. A person suffering from dissociative identity disorder may appear to be "possessed"; a possessed person may only be suffering from a form of what Janet or Freud would call hysteria. This complex of ideas surrounding what other cultures believed to be a spiritual phenomenon is at the core of shamanistic practices, just as it is of the CIA's MK-ULTRA and similar programs for unlocking the secrets of the mind. To Breton, surrealism was nothing more or less than "a form of psychic automatism"[25] and "magic dictation." The use of what had originally been an occult technique—automatic writing, a mediumistic method of contacting spiritual forces—to understand hysteria and dissociation (which had originally been believed to be evidence of possession by spiritual forces) is revealing, for not only the symptomatology of the mental disorder had its origins in witchcraft and magic, but the method for treating it also claimed similar origins. All that changed, really, was a set of labels.

The surrealists as a group struggled with the relationship between word and image; they felt that language was paramount (after all, automatic writing is writing, not drawing), but those who were artists rather than poets were confused as to how the newly discovered ideas of psychology, science and philosophy could be expressed through image. There was a great deal of struggle between the poet-surrealists and the artist-surrealists at the birth of the movement, the poets claiming that the artists could not hope to duplicate their efforts since the mind was, at its heart, verbal. "In the beginning was the Word." Much of what Janet and, later, Freud wrote concerning the functions of the mind stressed the verbal quality of consciousness. To Breton, the spiritual mentors of the movement were Rimbaud and Baudelaire, and of course Lautreamont: poets, not painters.

Asian languages, however, show that frequently both word and image are combined. Chinese characters have their origin in hieroglyphics, and there is little in a Chinese character to indicate its pronounciation. Ancient Egyptian writing was, of course, pictographic and evolved into the famous hieroglyphs we all know. Ancient Mayan writing—only recently deciphered—was also hieroglyphic. The idea that a word could also be an image, or could contain an image inside of it somehow, was also the essence of Qabala. As Hebrew letters were also numbers, which meant that each Hebrew word contained within itself hundreds or thousands of associations, that also meant that each Hebrew word contained within itself images corresponding to those associations. The Golden Dawn used a technique for "translating" Hebrew words into images, as a kind of coding system. They further refined this method as the Enochian system, in which the four elements each have their symbolic animals (the Eagle, the Lion, the Bull, the Man, representing the four fixed signs of Scorpio, Leo, Taurus and Aquarius respectively, which themselves represent Water, Fire, Earth and Air respectively), and combinations of the elements meant one could combine the four elemental "animals" into various configurations, producing what were certainly "surreal" images: perhaps the head of a Man, the body of a Bull, the legs of an Eagle and the tail of a Lion? Using the Hebrew alphabet, one could also translate that combination into a word using the Hebrew letters for the four elements as found in the unpronounceable name of God, YHVH.

One of the surrealist artists connected with the occult was Austin Osman Spare. Spare was also concerned with the connection between word and image, and in his work (what he called "automatic drawing") he created a "magical alphabet" that used Roman letters arranged in such a way as to create occult symbols or "sigils." Spare claimed to have been initiated into witchcraft by a descendant of the original Salem witches, and was also a member of Aleister Crowley's occult society, the *Argenteum Astrum* or A.·.A.·. His work has also had a profound influence on occult author and Crowley-initiate Kenneth Grant. Spare believed that the method of automatic *drawing* was "a means to art," as an essay of his—published as a chapter in his *The Book of Pleasure (Self-Love): The Psychology of Ecstasy*—attests. What Spare and many other surrealists had done was to take the essentially passive approach of Breton—as reflected in their fascination with automatic writing and the hypnotic trance—and raise the stakes by incorporating a more aggressive approach to unlocking the secrets of the mind by using formal occult methods involving spirit conjuration, drugs, and sexually-oriented rituals. It was taking Rimbaud's "derangement of the senses" much more seriously, much more energetically. It was the "voluntary madness" of Artaud, which even Artaud understood in occult terms.

The list of surrealist painters who were also occultists is actually quite long, and many art critics are not aware of this relationship, just as many occultists are not aware that some of the more well-known authors on occult subjects were also surrealist painters. Spare is only one example of an occultist who was an acknowledged surrealist artist. There was also Ithell Colquhoun, who wrote a history of the Golden Dawn entitled *The Sword of Wisdom.* There was respected surrealist painter Kurt Seligmann, who wrote a history of occultism: *Magic, Supernaturalism and Religion.* Aleister Crowley himself was a painter, although one hesitates to classify him as a surrealist.

The other surrealists who were fascinated with occultism and incorporated occult themes in their works or occult knowledge in their approach to art include virtually every famous name of the movement: Max Ernst, Antonin Artaud,

Marcel Duchamp, and many others were heavily influenced by occultism and read avidly in the subject, and were, in their turn, subject to occult "analyses" by art historians and critics who came after them. Kandinsky, a kind of proto-surrealist, was also very involved in occult theory and Theosophy and was on familiar terms with the works of Blavatsky, Rudolf Steiner, and Maurice Maeterlinck, as his own writings demonstrate. He, too, wrote of art as a revolutionary act, equating mysticism, revolution and art, with references to Nietzsche, Blavatsky, and the other "revolutionary" thinkers of the day. Picasso was considered by Breton to be a forerunner of surrealism, and Picasso's interest in primitive art parallels that of Freud as well as the surrealists'.

The primitive, the childlike, the insane: these were the vocabularies that Breton wanted to investigate, like a fortune-teller over a pack of Tarot cards, for their hidden meanings and their clues to the unconscious world; and these three categories of being represented opposition to the social status quo.

> *There can be no doubting that Breton's wartime experience as a medical auxiliary predisposed him to view hysteria as a form of insubordination—a protest, albeit a mute one, against military and medical authority.*
>
> —Lomas[26]

The surrealist perspective is echoed in that of Scottish psychiatrist R.D. Laing who, in his controversial and thought-provoking essay *The Politics of Experience*, makes many of the same points concerning schizophrenia and the possibilities of spiritual growth through madness. It should be noted that Laing also began his medical career in the army, in this case the British Army, where he worked as a psychiatrist before going on to the Tavistock Clinic. Laing agrees with the surrealists when he states that " . . . we are bemused and crazed creatures, strangers to our true selves, to one another, and to the spiritual and material world—mad, even, from an ideal standpoint we can glimpse but not adopt,"[27] and, "We are potentially men, but are in an alienated state, and this state is not simply a natural system."[28] *The Politics of Experience* includes a final section, entitled "The Bird of Paradise," that would have satisfied many a surrealist, as it seems to be a free-association-like account of a journey into and out of madness. Concerning the voyage into madness, Laing is unequivocal:

> We can no longer assume that such a voyage is an illness that has to be treated . . . . Can we not see that this voyage is not what we need to be cured of, but that it is itself a natural way of healing our own appalling state of alienation called normality?
>
> In other times people intentionally embarked upon this voyage.
>
> Or, if they found themselves already embarked, willy-nilly, they gave thanks, as for a special grace.[29]

Thus Laing, more than forty years and a World War after the first *Surrealist Manifesto*, is seen endorsing what is really a surrealist agenda, except he is doing so as a trained, experienced, and respected member of the psychiatric profession and not as an artist. He recognizes that "in other times people intentionally embarked upon this voyage," the condition of voluntary madness that is a hallmark of poets like Rimbaud and Artaud, as well as of occultists and shamans, and people like Breton, Masson, Ernst, Duchamp and so many others. The energy of the surrealist movement perhaps finds its culmination in Laing; we are certainly living now in a state of *denouement* in which the ideas of Laing have been discarded or ignored by a profession that seems to have found its savior in chemical therapies that treat symptoms, and make the neurotic and psychotic more productive members of an increasingly unhappy and alienated society.

It was not only Laing who represented this new appraisal of surrealist ideas. Even Mircea Eliade—cited earlier for his insights into the link between shamanism and madness—speaks directly to the problem, writing in 1969:

> It is naively believed that six months of "field work" among a tribe whose language one can scarcely speak haltingly constitutes "serious" work that can advance the knowledge of man—and one ignores all that surrealism or James Joyce, Henry Michaux, and Picasso have contributed to the knowledge of man.
>
> The contemporary artistic experiments are capable of aiding the historians of religions in their own research . . . It is not without interest to note, for example, that in their revolt against the traditional forms of art and their attacks on bourgeois society and morality the surrealists not only elaborated a revolutionary aesthetic but also formulated a technique by which they hoped to *change* the human condition. (emphasis in original)[30]

Eliade recognized the attempt by the surrealists—more than any other "artistic movement"—to actually *change* humanity. This historian of religion, mysticism and shamanism saw kindred spirits among the surrealists, and wondered openly about the value of his anthropological colleagues living with primitive tribes for short periods and writing up elaborate explanations of their culture and beliefs, when there was such a rich storehouse of knowledge about the human condition sitting ignored in the texts and artworks of the surrealists and other voluntary madmen. He goes on to state in the same paragraph that the exercises of the surrealists "recall certain Yogic or Zen practices" and that the effort of the surrealists to enter into a state of consciousness that combines both the sleeping and the waking states—à la the hypnotic trance—was nothing less than "the desire to effect in concrete the coincidence of opposites, the hope of being able to annul history in order to begin anew with the original power and purity—nostalgia and hopes rather familiar to historians of religions."[31]

Did the surrealists succeed? Did they leave a map for others to follow?

I will take a very big chance of alienating many people by stating that it may be wrong to consider surrealism as simply another artistic movement. The stated goal of the surrealists—as revealed in the succession of manifestos that appeared in the 1920s and 1930s, usually from the pen of Andre Breton, but signed and ratified by the surrealist luminaries of the time—was nothing less than open communication between the conscious and unconscious minds, and the expected resultant freedom and empowerment of the individual. They intended to accomplish this in ways that were, in a sense, anti-intellectual, although the literature of surrealism see-saws between the intensely intellectual and the playfully poetic. In a sense, the surrealists used artistic media as weapons in their revolutionary struggle to liberate human consciousness. As a social movement—that is, as a movement with the intention of affecting as many members of society as possible, rather than through a slow and arduous process of initiation—they did share a few elements in common with both the psychological warfare officers (engaged in "world-view warfare") and the men of MK-ULTRA.

The surrealists sought to tap the powers of the mind using psychiatry and occultism (whatever would work, whatever would help them break through the barrier between consciousness and unconsciousness), and in this they are not very different from shamans, not very different from the men of MK-ULTRA. Art—painting, sculpture, poetry, fiction, and even (with Bunuel and Dali) cinema—happened to be the medium in which they worked, but surrealism was born on the battlefields of World War I, as the confrontation between life and death, between existence and non-existence, forced a generation of artists to chose between the dangerous ignorance of a cultivated sanity and the seemingly crystal clarity of madness. The hideousness of that conflict, the first "high-technology" war using tanks, airplanes, mass communications, and chemical weapons, traumatized a generation. Breton began life as a medical student, and worked with shell-shocked soldiers at the front. Andre Masson, another important surrealist, fought in the War and spent agonizing hours wounded, lying in a ditch face-to-face with a dead German soldier, literally "facing death." Using automatic writing, hypnosis, and later various occult techniques and occult studies such as alchemy and ceremonial magic, the surrealists tried to penetrate the secrets of the mind; this endeavor would be repeated by the CIA a few years after World War II, continuing for decades until fear of discovery made them either cancel their projects or disguise them in some way. The preliminary goals of the surrealists and the spies were the same: unlock the secrets of the unconscious mind, understand amnesia, hypnotic trance, hysteria, dissociation, multiple personalities and "the self," and the human will. Yet, the ultimate goals were quite different. For the surrealists, the liberation of humanity—the perfect freedom of men and women—was their target, their *raison d'etre*. For the CIA and the military, the aim was the enslavement of those minds and the harnessing of consciousness to political and military purposes. The surrealists used the garret, the artist's studio, the writer's desk; the CIA used the laboratory, the interrogation room, the torture chamber.

This is not to say that the surrealists were apolitical. A little-discussed and perhaps consciously-ignored aspect of the surrealist movement is the strength of their political commitment. Art historians tend to avoid political analysis as much as military historians ignore the religious or spiritual framework of combating forces (such as the occult nature of much of the Third Reich, and especially of the SS). However, the widespread and energetic political involvement of the surrealists is as important to a complete understanding of what they were as are their psychic explorations. As early in the movement as 1925, when the French government began to suppress Moroccan tribesmen in their African colonies, the surrealists expressed a political agenda that was anti-authoritarian, anti-colonial and—eventually—anti-fascist as well. Breton's *Manifesto of the 121*, for instance, was an attack on the Algerian war of the 1950s.

Most importantly, though, was surrealism's clear-cut opposition to both fascism and Stalinism. While they supported revolution against oppressive authority in general, and could be considered a kind of socialist movement in sympathy with Marxism-Leninism, they opposed totalitarian governments. Their aim, after all, was the liberation of the human soul. Breton spoke out publicly against fascism in the 1930s (for instance, in Belgium in 1934), and surrealism eventually came to the attention of the Nazis. The Nazi "art exhibit" of 1937, *Degenerate "Art,"* was a clear attack on the surrealist movement which was, after all, an affront to fascism not only politically but also "spiritually." The surrealists were on the Nazi death lists, and they had to flee.

As noted in Book I, virtually the entire surrealist movement managed to escape the Third Reich and go into exile abroad: Breton, Ernst, and so many others avoided the death camps through the assistance of Varian Fry and others, the same people who helped Hans Habe escape to America. It is of great interest to this study that the artistic movement most singled out by the Nazis for destruction was surrealism, for the surrealists may have been polar opposites of the Nazis when it came to political ideas, but they were just as fascinated by the occult and by the possibilities of human consciousness. The Nazis, however, were a cult, and cults can admit of no competing cults. While it would be rash to label surrealism a "cult," it was not purely an artistic movement, either. Art was their medium of expression, but the experiments entertained by the movement—including in one case hypnotic trances carried out every day for more than a year by surrealist Rene Crevel—were more in line with psychic research and psychoanalysis than sculpture.

In 1938, Breton famously met exiled Russian revolutionary Leon Trotsky in Mexico, accompanied at the time by painter Diego Rivera, and they penned yet another manifesto, this time on revolution and art. It was an attack on Stalinism, of course, and the photo that exists of Trotsky, Breton and Rivera standing around in Mexico, chatting, tells us more about why the surrealists were despised—and why they were important—than any volume of art analysis. From Breton the medical man, Breton the psychotherapist in the trenches, Breton the poet and founder of the surrealist movement, Breton the psychic researcher, to Breton the anti-fascist and revolutionary: a single man can so succinctly represent the entire flow of ideas in this work:

He managed to escape the Nazis during World War II and wound up in exile.

In December 1945, he gave a speech on surrealism in Haiti.

A few days later, the Haitian government was overthrown in a popular uprising.

John Lilly on sensory deprivation and hallucinations; James Clark Moloney on the similarities between interrogation and religious experience; the surrealists and the occult . . . and anti-fascism. Perhaps the reader will agree that the thesis I have been promoting is not so far-fetched after all. Intelligence agency and secret military mind-control programs, psychological warfare, and . . . art and . . . religion. In Books I and II we have looked at CIA programs affiliated with MK-ULTRA which investigated paranormal phenomena as well as occultism of various types. We have examined the CIA's promotion (and investigation) of hallucinogens such as LSD-25, as well as shamanistic resources like psilocybin and mescaline and the *Flesh of God*. We've watched as OSS scientists such as Henry Murray became involved in drug research (with Timothy Leary) and interrogation techniques (on Ted Kaczynski, the Unabomber). If we match what the CIA was doing under BLUEBIRD, ARTICHOKE, and MK-ULTRA with religious conversion phenomena, mystical practices, shamanistic rituals, and the initiatory cults of Europe, Asia, Africa and other areas, we will better understand the role of psychology, philosophy, and organized religion in modern American politics.

In Book I we saw how Nazism infected many American political and industrial leaders, and in another place (*Unholy Alliance*) I showed how Nazism was (and is) in fact a cult, with an ideology all its own. We have seen how the Christian Right has supported a political agenda at home in America and abroad in the developing nations. We have witnessed the merger of organized religions such as Roman Catholicism and Eastern Orthodoxy with both fascist and Nazi political parties and with "ethnic outreach" programs in Europe and the United States. We saw how the churches helped many Nazi war criminals not only escape justice, but thrive and prosper in their new countries.

We will also see how this moral blindness has contributed to the phenomenon of the serial killer, the mass murderer, and to the present state of world affairs. I apologize if this perspective is disturbing, and I am sensitive to the criticism that there may be other explanations for the data I have already presented, as well as the data I am about to describe. However, the state of the world today requires us more than ever to seriously consider these strange arguments, for they offer an explanation for modern events that no other, less controversial, course of study so far has been able to contribute.

> *There is no such "condition" as "schizophrenia," but the label is a social fact and the social fact is a* political event.
> —*The Politics of Experience* (emphasis in original)[32]

ENDNOTES

1 Peter Dale Scott, *Deep Politics and the Death of JFK*, University of California Press, Berkeley, 1996, p. 12

2 David Lomas, *The Haunted Self*, Yale University Press, New Haven, 2000, p. 67

3 John Bossy, *Giordano Bruno and the Embassy Affair*, Yale University Press, New Haven, 1991, p. 101

4 Ibid., p. 154

5 Ibid., p. 146–154

6 Ibid., p. 154

7 Ioan P. Couliano, *Eros and Magic in the Renaissance*, University of Chicago Press, Chicago, 1987, p. 105

8 Ibid., p. 69

9 Ted Anton, *Eros, Magic, and The Murder of Professor Culianu*, Northwestern University Press, Evanston, 1996, p. 123

10 Ibid., p. 135

11 Christopher S. Hyatt, ed., *An Interview with Israel Regardie*, Falcon Press, Phoenix, 1985, p. 31–34, ISBN 0-941404-31-5, LOC 84-80967

12 This manual is available in many places on-line, and was originally generated in July 1963 as *Kubark Counterintelligence Interrogation*, KUBARK being an internal codeword referring to the CIA.

13 Ibid., p. 116–117

14 Ibid., p. 116

15 Ibid., p. 31, p. 116

16 John Marks, *The Search for The "Manchurian Candidate,"* Times, NY, 1979, p. 127–130

17 Kubark Counterintelligence Interrogation, p. 88

18 Ibid., p. 48

19 Hassoldt Davis, *Sorcerers' Village*, Little, Brown, Boston, 1955, p. 304–305

20 A.E. Waite, *The Book of Ceremonial Magic*, Dover, NY, p. 193–4

21 Susan Sontag, "The Pornographic Imagination," in Georges Bataille, Story of the Eye, Penguin, London, 2001, p. 92

22 Reprinted in p. 11, *Rimbaud, Collected Poems*, introduced and edited by Oliver Bernard, Penguin Books, London, 1962.

"The Poet makes himself a seer by a long, immense and reasoned derangement of all the senses, all forms of love, of suffering, of madness; he searches within himself, consuming every poison and retaining only their quintessence. Ineffable torture, where he needs all his faith and superhuman strength, and during which he becomes the great patient, the great criminal, the great accursed—and the supreme Wise Man!—among all men, because he arrives at the unknown!"

23 Nadia Choucha, *Surrealism and the Occult*, Destiny Books, Rochester VT, 1992, p. 53

24 Lomas, op. cit., p. 59

25 Ibid., p. 22

26 Ibid., p. 56

27 R.D. Laing, *The Politics of Experience*, Parthenon, NY, 1967, p. 13

28 Ibid., p. 13

29 Ibid., p. 167

30 Mircea Eliade, *The Quest: History and Meaning in Religion*, University of Chicago, Chicago, 1975 edition, p. 65

31 Ibid., p. 65

32 Laing, op. cit., p. 121

BOOK THREE: THE MANSON SECRET

CHAPTER EIGHTEEN

HOLLYWOOD BABALON

Babylon was Bab-ilani, a "gate of the gods," for it was there that the gods descended to earth . . . . But it is always Babylon that is the scene of the connection between the earth and the lower regions, for the city had been built upon bab apsi, the "Gate of the Apsu"—apsu designating the waters of chaos before the Creation.

—Mircea Eliade[1]

Now that we have succeeded in breaking down the atom the cosmos is split wide open . . . . We have arrived, possessed of a power which even the gods of old could not wield. We are there, before the gates of hell. Will we storm the gates, burst hell itself wide open? I believe we will. I think that the task of the future is to explore the domain of evil until not a shred of mystery is left.

—Henry Miller[2]

Evil has become a determinant reality. It can no longer be dismissed from the world by a circumlocution. We must learn how to handle it, since it is here to stay. How we can live with it without terrible consequences cannot for the present be conceived. In any case, we stand in need of reorientation, a metanoia. Touching evil brings with it the grave peril of succumbing to it. We must, therefore, no longer succumb to anything at all, not even to good.

—C.G. Jung, (in reference to Nazism)[3]

Sinister forces are at work!

—Peter Sellers as Inspector Clouseau in *The Pink Panther Strikes Again* (1976)

One might have guessed that I am the type of movie-goer who sits in the theater at the end of the film and reads the credits. Naturally, I am interested in the actors, character actors, director, producers, cinematographers, and writers; but I am also interested in the locations, the musical score (the composer, the arrangers, the selections of pre-recorded music and their performers and composers, etc.), as well as in the organizations and people thanked by the producers, usually at the end of the long list of credits and just before the copyright notices. This means I am usually the last person sitting in the theater when the house lights go up.

Now, with the advent of video tape and especially of DVD technology, I am able to watch these credits more carefully, rewind and re-read, and generally perfect my education. What I am doing with film is what I do with novels, non-fiction, government files, police reports, interviews and news reports: data mining. It's hard on the eyes and taxes the brain—and the patience of those around you. When you discover connections no one else has, you are elated until you find yourself greeted by annoyed glances of "so what?" and "here we go again." Yet, the rewards can be great if your prey is the dark matter at the heart of existence.

I grew up watching old films on a small black-and-white television. These were mostly gritty gangster flicks and propaganda films from World War II. My mother would share bits of information about the personal lives of some of the actors, and this made me aware of another world hiding behind the celluloid world. I watched James Cagney, Errol Flynn, Humphrey Bogart, Ronald Coleman . . . *A Tale of Two Cities*, *The Light That Failed*, *Casablanca*, and all the sentimental, swashbuckling tales of the 1930s and 1940s. *Singin' in the Rain*, *Easter Parade*, *Oklahoma!*, *The Wizard of Oz*, *The Bells of St. Mary's*, *Boy's Town* . . . Like it or not, the themes and attitudes of these films helped mold a certain way of looking at the world, a way of expecting heroism, self-sacrifice, humor, gallantry, and resolve in the face of danger. *A Passage to Marseilles*, *The Cross of Lorraine* . . . I learned how to be a gentleman watching performances by Ronald Coleman, Michael Rennie and George Sanders . . . and then learned that there was no room for gentlemen in the Postwar world. Gentlemen, I discovered, were dinosaurs: obsolete, like the black-and-white screen I grew up watching, in which the world itself was reduced to a case of black versus white, of evil versus good.

When I left home at the tender age of eighteen, I moved to a tiny studio apartment in Brooklyn Heights not far from the legendary haunts of Henry Miller, Walt Whitman, and Norman Mailer. I did not have a television set, and would not own or watch a television set for another ten years, all through the decade of the 1970s. Co-workers felt this was an indication that I was some kind of subversive, or perhaps an alien. Others would say I had not missed a thing.

Instead, I went to the movies.

Things had changed since the propaganda flicks of the 1940s. Now we had a more sophisticated medium, offering us *Catch-22*, *A Clockwork Orange*, *The Kremlin Letter*, *Anne of a Thousand Days*, *Joe*, *The Revolutionary*, *The Strawberry Statement*, *Slaughterhouse-Five*. And then I discovered foreign films. *Murmur of the Heart*, *Sunday Bloody Sunday*, *Belle de Jour*, *Satyricon*, *Roma*, *La Nuit Americaine.* Suddenly I had developed a taste for Truffaut, Malle, Fellini, Bunuel. When a new film was screened in Manhattan—usually on a Thursday—I would take off work, call in sick, and be the first one into the theater for the first run of the film in New York. Sometimes I would see two films on the same day, an unheard-of luxury for a young man working at minimum wage as an inventory clerk who sometimes had to walk to work across the Brooklyn Bridge and up to 32nd Street—a jaunt of several miles—just to save the subway fare to buy an ice cream for lunch at Grand Central Station on 42nd Street. At night, I would return home to my studio apartment—really a former pantry that had been blessed with a modern bathroom, the largest and most comfortable room in the damp, freezing studio—and work on my short stories, which were experiments along the line of surrealism.

I foraged for Grove Press books at a store in a subway arcade under Madison Square Garden, and began to read Burroughs and Kerouac and Ginsberg. I was alone, my parents had separated, my brother and sister were still in high school and living with our mother in the Bronx, and the books—and the movies—were my company and my education and culture. The artistic nudes in *Evergreen* were my introduction to the female form. Paperbacks by Abbie Hoffman and Regis Debray and Chairman Mao were my introduction to subversive politics, politics as a kind of culture, a kind of artform. Movies, books, politics all became a homogenous mass, a black mass of revolution, freedom, exhilaration. I wore a beret, and read French newspapers. I made friends in Brooklyn Heights and spent time in sidewalk cafes, talking about Vietnam and Palestine, assassinations and rebellions, art and film and poetry. I might as well have been in Paris. Or Barcelona. Or Prague, until that deadly Spring.

But underneath all of that was another reality, one I had suppressed; a reality of séances and Ouija boards, churches and liturgical celebrations, Russians and Syrians and spies. I had befriended students of similar ethnic background as myself, people of Czech and Slovak ancestry who spoke the languages and had one foot in the Old Country. I was introduced to the world of the Eastern Orthodox churches, a demimonde in the middle of New York City populated by exiled countesses and bearded archimandrites, of low-level agents and fascist sympathizers. It was a fascinating, glamorous world for a sixteen-and seventeen-year-old boy from the Bronx and one in which I easily fit. I was desperately hungry for culture, for knowledge, for an explanation of the things I had lived through in my life so far. America did not provide much in the way of culture beyond television and sports, or so I thought, and the exiled European communities presented me with entire, fully-articulated cultural experiences involving languages, cuisines, religions and politics. I soon began to study Church Slavonic, to the point where I could read it effortlessly and chant along with the monks in the Russian, Ukrainian, Serbian, Bulgarian, Slovenian, Carpatho-Russian orthodox churches of New York City.

And one day, in the company of one of my friends, I went to see a film starring Anthony Quinn and Michael Caine, *The Magus*. Based on the best-selling novel by John Fowles, the film made a great impression on my young mind. I left the theater wondering if everything I saw around me was an illusion; if the people around me were merely actors, playing a role designed to elicit from me some specific reaction, like the Michael Caine character in the film who is an Englishman living on a Greek island, befriended by the mysterious Anthony Quinn character who stage manages an entire experience for him, to the point where Caine does not know if he is going mad.

Film had that ability, I realized. An ability to alter perceptions of reality, if only for a moment. What power! And this was long before I ever heard of subliminal messages in advertising or films: little snippets of film, a few frames long, inserted into the tape so that your conscious mind did not record the images but your unconscious mind—which sees everything—did. No, this was simply the artistry of the motion picture, the power of actors and plot and lighting and music to work on your mind to such an extent that you lost contact with your historical world and entered into one invented by the filmmakers. An *unconscious* suspension of disbelief. An open challenge to your "worldview." Mind control.

My father had been an actor for a while, and had copies of Stanislavksi's writings on the Method, alongside a complete set of the works of Edgar Allan Poe. Maybe, I thought, there was more to this than simply memorizing lines and pretending to be someone else and looking pretty while doing it. As I grew older, I discovered that the writings of Stanislavski were applicable to a wide range of human experience. No wonder Hollywood actors feel they have something to say about everything, I thought, even if they don't! Stanislavski makes them believe they do, makes them believe that acting gives them an insight that is relevant to all of human experience. The true Method actor is a kind of initiate, a voluntary madman, and opens himself or herself up to forces he or she does not understand, but which are potent nonetheless. And these forces—being summoned—then act upon those in close proximity. That was the point, after all, of the very first theatrical performances in ancient Greece, which were sacerdotal in nature, a conjuration of the gods. That was why theatrical performances were banned by the medieval Church as occasions of sin and tools of the Devil. And that is why the American film industry is seen as such a threat to the cultures and mores of people living in developing nations around the world. It is, as the splendid German phrase has it, "world-view warfare."

THE METHOD

Let me remind you of our cardinal principle: through conscious means we reach the subconscious.

—Stanislavski[4]

"They told me that you had gone totally insane, and . . . uh . . . that your methods were unsound."
"Are my methods unsound?"
"I don't see any . . . method . . . at all, sir."

—an exchange between Colonel Kurtz (Marlon Brando) and Captain Willard (Martin Sheen) in Francis Ford Coppola's *Apocalypse Now*

On October 7, 1947—a few months after the first modern American UFO sighting in June and the Roswell "crash" in July—the Actor's Studio was opened in New York City. An organization dedicated to teaching actors the Stanislavski "Method," it was mentored by Lee Strasberg and Sandy Meisner, both strong adherents of the Method who at the same time became mortal enemies due to "artistic differences." Thirteen days later, on October 20, 1947 the House Committee on Un-American Activities or HUAC began its investigation into Communist infiltration of the Hollywood movie business. Ronald Reagan (FBI agent T-10) was one of the first to betray his friends as Communists, thus paving the way for a career in American politics, first as Republican Governor of California and later as President of the United States. Walt Disney was another one eager to cooperate with the Committee, as was Jack Warner of Warner Brothers and Louis B. Mayer of MGM. While the two events are seemingly unrelated, it is ironic to realize that Stanislavski—a Russian who stayed in Russia after the Revolution and who died in Moscow in 1938—would wield such an influence over American acting and filmmaking even as HUAC was attempting to clean out Hollywood of Communists, Communist sympathizers, and fellow travelers.

Eventually, one of Lee Strasberg's most famous pupils at the Actor's Studio would be Marilyn Monroe.

Konstantin Stanislavksi was born Konstantin Sergeyevich Alekseyev in Moscow in 1863. The child of a wealthy family of manufacturers, he had the freedom to choose his career and went wholeheartedly into acting, forming—in 1897—the celebrated Moscow Art Theater or MAT. His performances as an actor in roles by Chekhov and Ibsen, as well as Shakespeare's *Othello*, earned him renown not only in Russia but throughout Europe. One of his other, more famous, accomplishments as a director includes Maurice Maeterlinck's *The Blue Bird*, and of course with that, as detailed in Book I, we are back at the ranch. *The Blue Bird* would once again be performed in Moscow, but this time in 1976 as a film directed by George Cukor and starring Elizabeth Taylor, Jane Fonda, Ava Gardner, Cicely Tyson, and many others in a star-studded cast that was the first ever US–Soviet joint film production. It was not, however, the first film version of Maeterlinck's play, but it has been the last to date. (Oddly enough, the first was a 1940 offering by Walter Lang starring Shirley Temple, released just one year after *The Wizard of Oz*.) Stanislavski was evidently very much taken with Maeterlinck, for he mentions him and *The Blue Bird* several times in *An Actor Prepares*. As Maeterlinck was well-known as a mystic, an astrologer, and a spiritualist as well as a Nobel-Prize winning author, we should not be startled to realize that Stanislavksi's "method," for all its naturalistic emphasis, has its roots very firmly in the occult tradition, particularly that represented by the surrealist point of view.

Consider the following:

> I have no desire to prove whether Prana really exists or not. My sensations may be purely individual to me, the whole thing may be the fruit of my imagination. That is all of no consequence provided I can make use of it for my purposes and it helps me.[5]

In discussing Prana—the Sanskrit term for "the breath of life" or spirit, power, vitality, etc.—Stanislavski was applying yoga and yogic techniques to husbanding this energy and using it in performance for everything from breath control to physical presence on the stage. (Is it a coincidence that the film company that produced the first vampire film, *Nosferatu*—a company created by German occultists—would also be named Prana?) Stanislavski's approach is a common-sense one that the surrealists would have approved, for he does not care if Prana exists in an objective sense, only that he can use the concept to help him in his work. This fits in very well with Breton's insistence that there was no such thing as a ghost, but that mediumship was useful and interesting.

Stanislavski was clear about the cardinal principle of the Method: "through conscious means we reach the subconscious." This was, of course, the surrealist agenda, except that for Stanislavski it was dangerous and pointless to penetrate the subconscious realm directly. One had to approach it obliquely, to coax it into making an appearance, and then when it did, not interfere. This ability of the subconscious he called "intuition," and it was an actor's greatest asset.

In order to summon intuition—in order to consciously reach the subconscious, in his words—he made use of physical gestures and of providing background stories for the characters portrayed, thereby developing actors' sense memories. One of the most difficult aspects of the Method for many actors is this delving deeply into one's past, dredging up past traumas in order to use the energy, the gestures, the reactions constructively in a role.

It is a type of psychoanalysis, after all, in which an actor is made to undergo painful experiences from his past in a classroom full of his fellow students. This conscious invocation of pain and memory is an echo of the shamanistic initiations we discussed briefly in the previous chapter. It is a deliberate attempt to induce a kind of hysteria in the student-actor while maintaining his or her conscious control over it. A very difficult and very demanding process, and one that does not have psychological integration as the goal. Rather, this system can be used to create a kind of dissociation necessary for the kind of spectacular performances we have come to expect of a Brando, a Pacino, a DeNiro. A Christopher Walken.

For what is an actor but a person who specializes in multiple personalities? Who deliberately invokes—on a stage, night after night—an alien presence into his body, his consciousness?

The structure of the play, the static form of the lines to be recited, the necessity to react to the other actors in the right time and place, act as a kind of ritual, enabling the performers to retain their sanity to the end. (My mother told me the story—certainly apocryphal, for I have found no record of this—that the Broadway theater cast of Erskine Caldwell's *Tobacco Road* had gone somewhat insane as a result of portraying the same miserable, defeated characters night after night, and could not "get out of character" once the performance was over. Such was the reputed pernicious power of the "Method.") As noted previously, theater was originally presented not as entertainment but as education and illumination. It was sacerdotal in nature, a religious and mystical experience, and the actors prepared for this accordingly. What Stanislavski did was to put down on paper and in practice a codified form of this ancient system, for acting had in a sense degenerated since that time into one-dimensional pantomime. Actors no longer thought of their function as sacred or mystical, but as a vehicle for ego, for self-dramatization at the expense of the play. Stanislavski brought the actors back to a realization of the importance of their art by speaking of the subconscious and of "psychic processes," thus elevating acting to a kind of priestly role.

> Our subconscious is inaccessible to our consciousness. We cannot enter into that realm. If for any reason we do penetrate it, then the subconscious becomes conscious and dies.[6]

What Stanislavski means here is that the raising of the subconscious to consciousness robs the subconscious of its energy. Freud understood that subconscious (or unconscious) material drew energy into itself from the very fact of its suppression. Stanislavski did not want perfectly individuated and psychically integrated actors, for they would not have the artistic temperament required to make their performances come alive. Yet, he did want to tap that energy in a conscious way. He wanted, in other words, to play with fire: to have his cake and eat it too.

> Fortunately there is a way out. We find the solution in an oblique instead of a direct approach. In the soul of a human being there are certain elements which are subject to consciousness and will. These accessible parts are capable in turn of acting on psychic processes that are involuntary.
>
> To be sure, this calls for extremely complicated creative work. It is carried on in part under the control of our consciousness, but a much more significant proportion is subconscious and involuntary.
>
> To raise your subconscious to creative work there is a special technique. We must leave all that is in the fullest sense subconscious to nature, and address ourselves to what is within our reach. When the subconscious, when intuition, enters into our work we must know how not to interfere.[7]

What he is discussing are the physical gestures that can "accidentally" release subconscious energy, and the evocation of personal memories which are "accessible" and which can act on involuntary psychic processes. He is asking his students to allow themselves to become vehicles for the roles to be performed. This can have its dangerous aspect, but the method used by Stanislavski—while much more intense than normal acting classes which rely on basic stagecraft—is primarily safe insofar as it goes, although in unstable people some of the exercises could cause emotional distress if the teacher is not experienced enough to handle the rough psychological fallout. In any event, the Method is a viable means of awakening the unconscious, and it does so within a socially-acceptable context of theater arts.

The problem—from the point of view of initiation—is that the unconscious is awakened and put to use for different roles, different performances, in a consciously-controlled environment that is not conducive to spiritual growth in and of itself. Today you are Othello, tomorrow Romeo. You have no control over the order or nature of the roles you take on. Unlike a magician or shaman who has a set path to follow and a set order of experience, an actor puts on and takes off personalities like a voodoo practitioner who becomes possessed by different gods. The spiritual growth of a voodoo devotee (from the point of view of shamanistic initiation) is not clear. His ability to become possessed by his gods does not immediately suggest that he has entered upon a spiritual path with integration or individuation (to use the Jungian term) as its goal. The voodoo *priest*, however, is another matter, and in order to be successful and attain credibility among his congregation he must have passed through a complete initiatic program, much as his ancestors and present-day counterparts in western Africa.

The Method actor is—for all his preparation and soul-searching and intensity of concentration—still at the whim of the demands of the theatrical world. It is a business, a job, and requires one to be able to be different people at different times, all on command. The audience is in a similar situation. They do not progress through a set program of theatrical events, rising in spiritual or psychological understanding with each passing performance. Instead, their experience is as willy-nilly as that of the actors themselves. Unlike the calendar of ritual used by the Catholic Church, for instance, in which Epiphany follows Christmas with unerring regularity and the Christian year moves slowly into Lent and then Holy Week and Good Friday and Easter, a theatrical calendar can be anything, in any combination, at any time. It is considered "entertainment," but those of us who have witnessed great performances—whether on stage or screen—instinctively know that entertainment is a weak description of what has transpired. For westerners in the 21st-century world, theater and especially cinema is the closest thing to a spiritual experience many of us will ever have. That is why we so easily misunderstand and miscalculate the tremendous influence of religion in developing countries that do not have their own movie industry . . . and the horror with which many non-westerners view Hollywood Babylon.

ANGER MANAGEMENT

> "The only performance that makes it, that really makes it all the way, is the one that achieves madness."
>
> —Mick Jagger as "Turner" in *Performance* (1968)

Filmmaker Kenneth Anger (1929–) began his career as a child actor in a production of *A Midsummer Night's Dream* (1935)—the only sound film ever made by Max Reinhardt, the Austrian stage director, which was also the film debut of Olivia de Havilland, and featured an all-star cast including James Cagney, Dick Powell and Mickey Rooney (as Puck). He eventually moved behind the camera to write and direct such cult classics as *Kustom Kar Kommando* (1965) and *Scorpio Rising* (1963), *Invocation of My Demon Brother* (1969), and *Inauguration of the Pleasure Dome* (1954–56). Some critics have insisted that Anger is the precursor of—and inspiration for—such directors as David Lynch, Pier Paolo Pasolini, Martin Scorcese and Francis Ford Coppola. His involvement with Thelema—the cult founded by Aleister Crowley—is clearly evident in everything from *Pleasure Dome*, which featured Anais Nin and Marjorie Cameron (Jack Parsons' wife) to *Demon Brother*, which featured Manson Family member and convicted murderer Bobby Beausoleil as well as Anton LaVey of the Church of Satan. When we search for links and connections between the Ordo Templis Orientis (OTO), the Church of Satan, the Manson Family, Hollywood, and Sixties rock 'n' roll, we can do worse than to begin with Kenneth Anger.

> The '69 Tate massacre was not Old Hollywood. What befell the red house on Cielo Drive resembled the devastation caused by a jet plane crash: the Bad Ship Lollipop piloted by Uncle Sugar. Charlie Manson—programmed puppet, *deus ex garbage can.*
>
> —Kenneth Anger[8]

Now more than 75 years old, Anger made his impact on Hollywood with a film entitled *Fireworks*, which was released in 1947 and caught the eye of French poet and filmmaker Jean Cocteau. Cocteau (1889–1963) was one of the earliest "surrealist" filmmakers, with his *Le Sang d'un Poete* (*The Blood of a Poet*) released in 1930, and he was part of the symbolist entourage around such notables as Claude Debussy, designing the sets for Debussy's *Pelleas et Melisande*, which was itself an operatic version of a Maeterlinck play on Merovingian themes. He is perhaps better known for his film *Orphee* (*Orpheus*), released in 1950, which received wide critical acclaim and which was an interpretation of the myth of Orpheus who descended into the Underworld, certainly an initiatic theme. Even more importantly for us, Cocteau was identified as one of the leaders of the Priory of Sion (the French society which, it is claimed, holds secret information concerning the bloodline of Jesus

Christ) by the investigative team of Baigent, Leigh and Lincoln in their controversial bestseller based on documents found in the Bibliotheque Nationale in Paris, *Holy Blood, Holy Grail,*[9] and for some background on the French occult societies that interpenetrated French artistic circles, *Holy Blood, Holy Grail* is a good introduction, and shows how deeply artists like Cocteau and Debussy were involved in everything from Rosicrucian mysteries to Cathar revivalism. (Cocteau's design for a mural of the crucifixion in the Notre Dame de France cathedral in London is a blatant Rosicrucian—and Templar—allegory which would have appealed to Anger, with its hints of Egyptian and occult symbolism.)

Anger followed *Fireworks* with *Rabbit's Moon* in 1950 and *Eaux d'Artifice* in 1953, having become deeply involved in occultism of the Aleister Crowley variety during his high school years. One of his films, the early *Les Chants de Maldoror*, now lost, was based on the famous pre-surrealist "prose poem" of the same name by the doomed visionary, Lautreamont, who was such an influence over Breton and the surrealist movement. This fusion of occultism with art and cinema places Anger firmly within the surrealist category, at least for a time early in his career.

With his critical *bonafides* supplied by Cocteau, he spent time in France working for the director of the *Cinematheque Francais* and wrote what would become an underground classic: *Hollywood Babylon*, published originally in French in 1959. This was an exploration of Hollywood's seamier side, revealing scandal after scandal, murder, suicide, drugs and sex, which opens with a famous quotation from Aleister Crowley's *Book of the Law*, the "Bible" of his religion of Thelema: "Every man and every woman is a star." A sensation in France, it eventually made it into an English version in the United States in 1975. In the interim, Anger had become part of the Rolling Stones' entourage and had traveled with them on tour, finding time to cultivate friendships within the sinister nexus that accumulated around Charles Manson, the Church of Satan, and the OTO. Manson Family member Susan Atkins had already performed for the Church of Satan as a vampire in a black mass, an effort that was caught on film and preserved for posterity.

In fact, it is with Anger that we gain a backstage pass to the ebb and flow of the sinister forces at work in America, for he seems to be either at the center or the periphery of some of America's most pivotal cultural events from the 1950s through the 1970s, and beyond. From his early film starring Marjorie Cameron and Anais Nin, to films featuring performances by Bobby Beausoleil, Mick Jagger, Keith Richards, Anton LaVey, and so many others, we find that Anger is there for everything from the doomed Thelema Lodge of the OTO to the Magick Powerhouse of Oz to the Church of Satan to the Charles Manson Family to Altamont and "Sympathy for the Devil." For a while, death and destruction seemed to hover around Anger like demented groupies at a Megadeth concert.

In 1955, Kenneth Anger went to Cefalu, Sicily, the site of Aleister Crowley's Abbey of Thelema during Mussolini's rule, with the intention of doing a documentary on the place, and found it essentially intact, from an occult and artistic point of view anyway. Many of the murals painted by Crowley were still in evidence, albeit whitewashed over by nervous villagers who had the place exorcised after Crowley's departure, much as the cottage where Stephen Ward resided at Cliveden was exorcised, and Anger shot a lot of film on-site, at one point escorting famed sexologist Alfred Kinsey around the place.[10] This was a year after he had released *Inauguration of the Pleasure Dome* featuring Marjorie Cameron. Thus, by the mid-1950s, Anger was thoroughly in the midst of a magical quest, and used his preferred artistic medium—film—to record, celebrate, and illuminate the fact.

This fusion of occultism and film was not the first attempt to use the medium to promote a surrealist agenda, but it was one of the more accessible to avant-garde American audiences. By the 1950s, it is doubtful whether surrealism, *per se*, was still a force to be reckoned with in the artistic world; the Beats were taking over the imagination of the disaffected young with poetry by Ginsberg and Ferlinghetti, fiction by Kerouac and Burroughs, and a generation of the beret-wearing, black-turtlenecked, finger-snapping, bongo-playing, professionally-alienated "artistes," so charmingly portrayed by the cartoon character GoGo Man Van Gogh in the bizarre animated series *Beanie and Cecil.* The difference between Anger's offerings and surrealist art in general was that Anger's was a specifically occult production, attempting to convey occult ideas, as well as other "marginal" concepts such as homosexuality, sadomasochism, etc. Whether or not Anger deliberately attempted to cause change in human consciousness with his films (most of which were quite short) or whether his goal was simply self-expression in the context of a radical approach to filmmaking cannot be easily understood. What is easier to trace is his involvement with occult organizations, especially as they connect to the arts in general.

Among the most influential rock bands of the late 1960s and early '70s were the Rolling Stones, Led Zeppelin, and The Doors. All three of these bands had very strong links with occultism. Jim Morrison, the leading light of The Doors, married Patricia Kennely, a Welsh Traditionalist witch whose Craft genealogy can be traced directly back to Gerald Gardner and Aleister Crowley. Led Zeppelin's Jimmy Page became so involved with Crowley's occultism (some say, due to Kenneth Anger's proselytizing) that he bought Crowley's old estate in Scotland: Boleskine. Even the Beatles would put a picture of Aleister Crowley on the back of their *Sergeant Pepper* album among the "People We Like," and we remember their pilgrimage to India to sit the feet of the Maharishi (along with Mia Farrow, of *Rosemary's Baby* fame).

But it is the relationship of the Rolling Stones—and specifically of Mick Jagger and Keith Richards—to hard-core occultism and satanism that fascinates us, and the compelling figure of Kenneth Anger who lurks at the center of this uneasy alliance.

One of the Stones' most famous songs is "Sympathy for the Devil," an intelligent and sinister paean to "his Satanic majesty." It was the song being performed at Altamont when the Hell's Angels killed a man in front of the stage before thousands of witnesses. What only serious followers of the Stones already know is that the strange "wooo-wooo" backup vocals are being performed by Anita Pallenberg and Marianne Faithfull, the lovers of Keith Richards and Mick Jagger, respectively. These two ladies were also very involved in occult practices, under the tutelage of Kenneth Anger, and had appeared in his Crowley-themed films. Pallenberg would later become involved in the suicide of a young man at the home she shared with Keith Richards; Faithfull would record a song in honor of witchcraft, and would appear in the magazine published by the Process Church of the Final Judgement.

One of the entourage around Anger, Pallenberg, Faithfull and the Rolling Stones was a somewhat more successful filmmaker, Donald Cammell (1934–1996). Cammell is interesting in this context because his father was none other than Charles J. Cammell, a biographer (the first) of Aleister Crowley. C.J. Cammell was a friend of not only Crowley but a whole coven's worth of occultists, including Victor Neuberg, the man we discussed in the previous chapter as working at rituals with Crowley in North Africa. Donald Cammell grew up around occultists of every variety due to his father's interests and claimed that he sat on Crowley's lap at least once when he was a child (surely a cause for parental alarm?). Cammell directed Pallenberg and Mick Jagger—as jaded rock star "Turner"—in his acclaimed film *Performance* (filmed in 1968, released with heavy cuts in 1971), and Julie Christie in his bizarre *Demon Seed* (1977), about a computer that impregnates a young woman played by Christie. His film *Wild Side* (1996)—starring Christopher Walken, Anne Heche and Joan Chen—never saw theatrical distribution due to artistic differences between the director and the studio, NuImage, which was looking for something less artistic and less different, and so retained final cut and made a mess of Cammell's vision. *Wild Side* eventually made it into the cable-tv world, albeit heavily cut and edited.

His last completed work was *White of the Eye* (1988), about a serial killer and the woman who loves him. Although it died at the box office, it was considered an artistic success.

Four films in his entire career, the themes running from a gangster and rock star ménage à trois in *Performance*, to a computer fathering a child in *Demon Seed*, to another gangster and another ménage à trois in *Wild Side*, to a serial killer in *White of the Eye*. He had false starts such as *Ishtar*, (a film that would have starred William Burroughs, Mick Jagger and Norman Mailer, about the Babylonian goddess returning to earth) and *Fan Tan* (a Marlon Brando project about piracy in the South Pacific). For various reasons, these projects never came to fruition. *Performance*, which made his name as a director to watch, was heavily influenced not only by the Rolling Stones and the rock 'n' roll world of London in the late Sixties, but also by occult mythology, in this case the world of Hasan-i Sabah, he of the Assassins cult which figured so prominently in Book II. In addition, the shadows of Genet, Borges, the artist Francis Bacon and themes of death, identity transfer, gender transfer, and transformation generally haunt this production from the very beginning. His cast included Mick Jagger and Anita Pallenberg, already wired into the British occult scene, and James Fox (the brother of actor Edward Fox) who would do an about-face and begin working for a Christian missionary organization right after filming was complete on *Performance*. He would not return to acting until 1983, even though he was a well-known actor who had starred in such films as *The Chase* (1965) with Jane Fonda.

Donald Cammell came to the attention of Kenneth Anger early on, and played the role of Osiris in Anger's *Lucifer Rising* (1970), made during Anger's Rolling Stones period. Anger said it was "type-casting." Cammell was already well on the way to making surrealist films, and admitted his influences were Antonin Artaud and Jorge Luis Borges, the famous Argentine writer who gave the world some of its most interesting and unearthly prose, fortified by prodigious learning and intellectual vigor, made all the more remarkable considering that Borges was blind.

It is said that Cammell's last words were about Borges, as the bullet that entered his skull did its damage and slowly dimmed the light of one of Hollywood's least appreciated and certainly least understood directors, reprising the scene in which Turner is killed in *Performance*, as the camera shows us the bullet entering his skull (from above, the same awkward angle Cammell chose for his own death) and culminating in a picture of Borges. Cammell committed suicide on April 23, 1996 when on the verge of revitalizing his career, and it took him forty minutes to die in the arms of his wife, China (Patti Kong) Cammell.

In his final years, Cammell—son of an occultist and a crypto-occultist himself, surrounded by witches and magicians—became mentally unhinged. He developed an alternate personality, called "the uncensored Cammell," who did outrageous things in public (such as driving at high speed in the Hollywood hills, completely naked) that the other Cammell would never have done, and never remembered afterward. This was a clear sign of dissociated identity disorder, and his friends asked him to seek medical help but it was no use. He claimed the anti-depressants he was prescribed actually made his situation worse. It is not known whether the doctor he visited for only a few sessions was aware of Cammell's increasing dissociation, or if he was just being treated for depression. It is also entirely possible that Cammell was right, and that the anti-depressants made things worse by empowering the "uncensored Cammell." Alas, we shall never know.

In the same category of actors plagued by their art to the extent that they do themselves damage is a more recent case, that of Hong Kong actor and singer Leslie Cheung, who committed suicide on April 1, 2003 by plunging from his Hong Kong hotel room window to the streets below. Mr. Cheung—a handsome young man with an intelligent and knowing visage, an idol to Chinese men and women alike for both his immensely popular songs and his movies—had starred in a recent string of hits, including *Double Tap* (2000) and *Inner Senses* (2002). In *Double Tap* he had portrayed a gunsmith and expert marksman who kills a man in an effort to save lives, only to discover that he enjoys killing, becoming, in effect, a serial murderer. It was a powerful performance by the boyish-looking singer, and led to *Inner Senses*, his last film.

In *Inner Senses*—one of a growing number of excellent Asian horror films—he portrayed a psychotherapist who tries to help a young woman who is being driven insane by visions of ghosts. As he cures her, he becomes "haunted" himself. The film explores themes such as suicide, spiritual possession, the paranormal, and madness with a rare, deft touch, and we watch as Mr. Cheung's character goes slowly insane from guilt over the suicide of an old girlfriend when he was still in secondary school. He begins the film by stating that repressed memories should stay repressed, as they have been repressed for a reason (an odd position for a psychoanalyst!); and, in a kind of corollary, that "there are no such things as ghosts," that ghosts represent useless information that cannot be accommodated in other ways. As the film progresses to its climax, the Cheung character's own memories come to haunt him and nearly kill him. The penultimate scene is of the psychoanalyst, confronted with the ghost of his dead girlfriend, at the edge of a tall building saved at the last minute from falling to his death by neutralizing his feelings of guilt over her suicide in a conversation with her ghostly form. It's the type of ending that would make sense to a psychotherapist, but perhaps not to Leslie Cheung himself, who became strangely withdrawn and isolated after the completion of the film.

The rumors in Asia at the time of his death were that the film had so shattered his psyche that he did not recover from its effects, and that the Hollywood-style ending—so Western in its resolution of the problem by making the ghost and the analyst "talk out" the problem, so that both ghost and analyst come away whole—was so artificial in an Asian context that Leslie Cheung could find no other way to resolve a deeper, mysterious personal problem except by resolving the film's central problem with his own death, in exactly the same way as it would have happened in the film: falling from a tall building. No one knows why the actor committed suicide, and it shocked and saddened the entire Chinese-speaking world to an extent reminiscent of the death of Rudolph Valentino nearly a century earlier. While in the West ghosts are the stuff of legends and scary movies, in Asia ghosts are taken very seriously, and it is perhaps this cultural disconnect that opened a door into Mr. Cheung's sensitive nature and caused a psychic imbalance. While James Fox left filmmaking altogether after *Performance* in order to become a Christian missionary and sort out his inner turmoil in a more constructive manner, Leslie Cheung was not so fortunate. And, as it turned out, neither was Donald Cammell.

It is interesting to think of the two director-occultists together on the same set, as they were for *Lucifer Rising*: Donald Cammell, the pedigreed visionary whose father knew Aleister Crowley and who himself met Crowley when he was a child in his Edinburgh home filled with art, music, fantasy, and magic; and Kenneth Anger, the black magician wannabee who came at the occult from the dark side of satanism, sadomasochism, and sexuality. While neither man could claim to be a Hollywood success story, it is clear that, from the point of view of the studios, Cammell had somewhat more going for him. His four completed films were full-length Hollywood movies with intricate plotting and character development and a profligate use of flashbacks, intercutting and hallucinogenic cinematography and special effects. By contrast, Anger's films are short subjects on interesting themes, with some recognizable actors and film scores by Jagger and Bobby Beausoleil, but on the whole curiosities of the art and extremely experimental, rather more in the line of filmed rituals, no matter how beautifully realized. Both directors have become cult idols, of course, and critics point to the influence of both Cammell and Anger over generations of new directors.

Cammell himself confessed that he was an admirer of Anger and that *Performance* was largely inspired by Anger's work. At the time *Performance* was being filmed, Cammell was part of the entourage around the Rolling Stones including Pallenberg (who was leaving Brian Jones for Keith Richards), Marianne Faithfull (who was supposed to have played Pallenberg's role—Pherber—in the movie, but who had to leave the production due to pregnancy by Mick Jagger), Mick Jagger, Keith Richards and Brian Jones themselves, and Anger. It was also the year that "Sympathy for the Devil" was released, a song sung by Satan himself which became the soundtrack for the Altamont homicide the following year. It was Pallenberg and Faithfull who came up with the idea to use the "woo-woo" chant as background vocals to the song and it is the two witches who actually perform it in the 1968 recording. On a more recent note, the music of the Stones was employed almost as a physical presence in the occult thriller *Fallen* (1997), starring Denzel Washington as a police detective attempting to solve a series of murders which are, in fact, being committed by a demon. In the beginning of the film, the demon has possessed a serial killer, who sings "Time Is On My Side"—a song made famous by the Stones—during his execution, and this song is picked up and used throughout the film as the signature tune of the demon. The credits go up, however, not with "Time Is On My Side" but with that other classic, "Sympathy for the Devil." The idea of a demonically-possessed serial killer was first introduced to American audiences with *Exorcist III* (1990), however, and is a theme whose powerful attraction is difficult to describe, but whose affect on genuine serial killer Jeffrey Dahmer has already been noted.

It is claimed by music historians that the Stones' fascination with Crowley, magic and satanism ended with the tragedy at Altamont, a rock festival that was promoted as a kind of "Woodstock West," but which somehow degenerated into a catastrophe culminating in murder. That did not affect Anita Pallenberg or Marianne Faithfull in quite the same way, however, and there is no evidence that they abandoned their occult beliefs or practices after 1969. While there is a lot of speculation that Kenneth Anger had relationships with members of the Process Church of the Final Judgement, I have been unable to verify this. However, his close relationships with the Church of Satan and with the OTO is beyond doubt, as they are heavily documented in Anger's own films.

With Pallenberg and Faithfull, however, we are on firmer ground, as we know that Faithfull, for instance, once posed for the Process in a photo published in their magazine (the same magazine that featured writing by Charles Manson in one of their issues). Thus, through Faithfull and in the same time period as *Performance* and *Lucifer Rising*, we have solid Process connections. In fact, a 1999 update of Maury Terry's 1987 book on the Son of Sam and Manson cases, *The Ultimate Evil*, shows that Manson met the Process as early as 1968—the same year *Performance* was being filmed—and in one case actually met Process members in the Tate-Polanski home on Cielo Drive before the doomed actress moved in.[11] While Terry's conclusions are not always to be relied upon, his raw data is usually trustworthy. I believe it is safe to say that the circle around Anger knew the Process fairly well and had contacts with them. To what extent exactly these contacts involved the darker side of both the Process and the Anger circle is subject to speculation.

Pallenberg for her part was involved in a death that took place at the home she shared with Keith Richards in 1979. The death is startling enough, but it took place in an area that was known as the "eastern headquarters" of the Process, in upstate New York near the Connecticut border, in the town of Pound Ridge. According to Terry, the Process had their headquarters nearby in the appropriately-named Salem, New York. The victim was a seventeen-year-old caretaker, Scott Cantrell, who shot himself to death in her bed. The death was ruled a suicide, but for a while it looked as if Pallenberg would be accused of manslaughter. It seems that Cantrell was talking of playing Russian Roulette. The nexus of events surrounding this location is compelling, however, for the small and remote area around Pound Ridge comes up several times in this investigation, showing the twisting threads of coincidence and conspiracy wrapped around themselves in a Gordian knot of sinister forces.

For instance, actress Ali MacGraw (*Love Story*, *Goodbye, Columbus*) grew up in the same area—in the town of Bedford Village—which is not unusual in and of itself; but her father *was* rather unusual. A failed artist, he cultivated an interest in UFOs, Egyptian hieroglyphics, the mysterious Easter Island script, and many other languages.[12] He was a genius, born a little too late to be recognized in a world that does not value arcane erudition, or, indeed, erudition of any kind at all. An embittered, angry man, he made life unpleasant for his family, even as his gaze was turned towards a borderland reality they could not see.

Ms. MacGraw's first brush with the movie industry came in 1967 when she was part of the entourage around *Barbarella*, which was being filmed in Italy at the time. She met Jane Fonda and Anita Pallenberg off the set of that strange piece of science-fiction erotica; ironically, Fonda had already turned down the leading role in *Rosemary's Baby*, the part that would eventually go to Mia Farrow. (Pallenberg's role in *Barbarella* was as the Great Tyrant, a black-robed queen of the night.) Our interest in Ali MacGraw does not end there, however, for she brings us into the world of *Rosemary's Baby* producer Robert Evans, a man briefly believed to have been responsible for a murder connected to both the Son of Sam cult *and* the Manson Family.

Another link with Pound Ridge is a scandal that brewed there a few years ago, when local parents and teachers were upset over what they perceived to be a cult operating among their schoolchildren. As it turned out, this "cult" was based on the card game *Magic*, and Pound Ridge residents were convinced that the game was teaching its children occult ideas and practices. Perhaps the good citizens of Pound Ridge were a little sensitive on the issue, considering the suspected satanic activity of their neighbors, from Anita Pallenberg to the Process. Before we leave Kenneth Anger, a closer look at two of his films—among the three involving overt occult themes—is well-deserved, for they will set the stage for what is to follow.

In *Invocation of My Demon Brother*, released in August 1969 (the same month as the Tate/LaBianca murders in Hollywood), Anger himself plays the role of the Magus; Anton LaVey of the Church of Satan portrays Satan; and Bobby Beausoleil (one of the convicted Manson murderers) is the Trickster, smoking a pipe in the shape of a skull. The Rolling Stones make an appearance in the film, in footage shot in Hyde Park three days after the death of their colleague Brian Jones. All this, in a film only eleven minutes in length. Anger's portrayal of himself as the Magus—as the master magician in control of the environment—could be interpreted as everything from wishful thinking and cinematic hyperbole to a darker (perhaps unconscious?) statement of moral responsibility. The year 1969 is, after all, the year the energy summoned by the Summer of Love two years previously began to die out, turn sour, and putrefy. The Manson murders in Hollywood, Altamont . . . all this counter-culture evil taking place the same year that human beings first set foot on the moon in answer to the call of a martyred president.

For *Lucifer Rising*, released definitively in 1980, Anger had a more ambitious agenda. The producer of this film was none other than Anita Pallenberg, with Anger's credits as director, editor and the film's creator. Music was provided by Bobby Beausoleil, then in prison for life for the crime of murder (of musician Gary Hinman) in the first degree. Actors included Marianne Faithfull (as Lilith), and Donald Cammell as Osiris opposite his sometime lover Miriam Girbil as Isis. Kenneth Anger once again assumes the role of Magus.

The footage was shot in various potent locations, from Gizeh, Luxor and Karnak in Egypt to Stonehenge in England . . . to Externsteine in Germany, the sacred pagan shrine so venerated by the Nazis. Anger, Faithfull and Donald Cammell were along for the ride, shooting in the Egyptian desert at the foot of the pyramids at Gizeh or at the temples of Luxor and Karnak. One can be reasonably certain that more than just filmmaking was taking place during this time. Bobby Beausoleil was originally cast as Lucifer, but his incarceration made shooting a trifle difficult, and a total of five "Lucifers" were cast over the years—including Mick Jagger—before Anger settled on Leslie Huggins in the title role. Jimmy Page of Led Zeppelin was writing music for the soundtrack, but he and Anger fought over various issues, with Anger famously cursing Page and—according to the tabloids—causing all sorts of evil things to befall the Crowleyan musician and resident of Boleskine, where some of the footage was shot. Anger was upset over the music Page had produced, and dismissed him as a mere occult dilettante. When this author met Anger—in the company of the OTO in New York City about the time of the release of *Lucifer Rising*—he appeared rather quick to denounce those with whom he disagreed.

One of the myths surrounding the film is that of the stolen footage, buried in the California desert by an irate Bobby Beausoleil and never seen again. Beausoleil denies this episode, but Anger has claimed that it is true. Beausoleil, in an interview published on his own Web site, beausoleil.net, claims that no film footage ever existed, and implies that Anger was trying to placate his "German backers" by saying that the film was stolen, when, in fact, he hadn't shot a single frame. In any event, the production was beset by all sorts of difficulties and would not appear for more than ten years. Beausoleil, it should be remembered, had appeared in films before, notably as an Indian brave in the soft-core porn epic *Ramrodder*, shot in Topanga Canyon not far from the Spiral Staircase in Malibu, the strange house where both the Process and Manson used to hang out. Appearing with him in *Ramrodder* was Catherine "Gypsy" Share, another Manson Family member, who would be involved in a shootout with police after a failed attempt to rob a gun store. Their plan was to break into prison, rescue Manson and head for the desert and freedom.

Lucifer Rising—only twenty-nine minutes long—concerns the invocation of Lucifer by Isis, Osiris, Lilith and of course the Magus. The characters play humans possessed by these gods at the various sites of power in Egypt, Germany and England, and the scenes are intercut with various images Anger found compelling, such as a solar eclipse, fires, volcanoes, and a goat. The finale of the film is a shot of a flying saucer sailing over the Sphinx. A pink flying saucer.

This identification of Lucifer with the God of Light—essentially the same as the Egyptian god Horus—is a familiar one, found in Theosophical writings as well as Nazi ideology. Indeed, the name "Lucifer" is Latin for "Light-Bringer," an echo of the belief that Lucifer was the brightest of all the angels and rebelled against God due to his sin of pride. Others have tried to show how Lucifer is merely another manifestation of Prometheus, who stole fire from the gods to give to humanity and was punished for his transgression. In a sense, then, Lucifer and Prometheus are both personifications of an older myth, perhaps reminiscent of Adam in the Garden of Eden, who disobeys God in order to know both good and evil and then is also punished.

Anger's only other film to incorporate occult themes is his earlier production, *Inauguration of the Pleasure Dome* (1954), with Anais Nin as Astarte. This is the film that boasts Marjorie Cameron—the widow of OTO's self-appointed Antichrist, Jack Parsons—in a cameo role. Ms. Cameron remained involved in occult practices long after the death of her husband in 1952, and various works by British OTO leader Kenneth Grant mention her writings and activities since that time. While Anger was interested in invoking Lucifer, Parsons was dedicated to Babalon, the Crowleyan Goddess, and was sure she had been incarnated sometime in the immediate Postwar era. As described in Book I, some of Parsons' letters to Marjorie Cameron on a variety of occult themes have survived, and they provide insightful, intelligent commentary on the entire movement.

It would be Parsons and Cammell who would die violently, both consumed by their esoteric visions; Beausoleil and Manson who would live on, but in prison, as murderers; Pallenberg and Faithfull who would survive addiction and worse and come out the other side. Jagger and Richards were never touched deeply enough by the forces swirling around them to derail them from their careers. And Kenneth Anger is now in his seventies, contemplating a filmed version of Crowley's Gnostic Mass and a second sequel to *Hollywood Babylon*, the Magus safe in his California home and surrounded by the ghosts of so many dead and dying gods.

Was Manson a "programmed puppet"? Of course, that is the thesis of this book as well as a throw-away line of Anger's. My information, however, comes second-hand from primary sources: from memoirs, police files, declassified government documents, and the like, seasoned with an extensive background in the esoterica of many countries. Anger was part of Manson's circle, or perhaps we should say Manson was part of Anger's. More importantly, Anger refers to the Tate killings as a plane crash of the "Bad Ship Lolllipop" being piloted by "Uncle Sugar," a nickname for Uncle Sam or the United States government. What does Anger know about the Manson killings? What does he suspect?

One wonders if he thinks back to the days of The Magick Powerhouse of Oz, Bobby Beausoleil's band in California during the "Equinox of the Gods" ceremony at the Straight Theater on September 21, 1967? Or of the Himalayan Academy that he helped to establish with Timothy Leary and, it is said, Abigail Folger, who would die so violently and hideously at the hands of the Manson Family at the Polanski-Tate residence? Or of Altamont and "Sympathy for the Devil" in 1969 and yet another murder, this time of a black man by Hell's Angels gang members? Or the even more bizarre story circulated on the Internet that Kenneth Anger met Mark David Chapman in Hawaii six weeks before the Lennon assassination in 1980; to accentuate the eeriness of the tale, it is insisted that Chapman gave Anger a gift of some live bullets. It *would* account for Chapman showing up in New York City with a gun but no ammunition.

Regardless of the fact or fiction of the stories woven around Anger—many woven on Anger's own loom—it may be agreed that he has staying power. Whether he is still the Magus, still ordering the universe to fit his peculiar Gnostic vision, remains for history to decide.

QUEEN OF THE NIGHT

> At one of the Polanskis' wild, drug-fueled bashes at 10050 Cielo Drive in tony Brentwood, the housekeeper could not get into the bathroom and began pounding on the locked door.
>
> Eventually, the door opened and out came Jane, hair mussed and clothing askew, with another male guest . . . . "I hate it," she said, "when something's half finished." A guest recalled that the mysterious "other man" may have been handsome millionaire hairstylist Jay Sebring, who had been Sharon Tate's lover before she met Polanski.[13]

> "You know you're only allowed out on Halloween!"
>
> —Jane Fonda as "Night" in *The Blue Bird*, 1976

One of Jane Fonda's more bizarre cinematic appearances is as Night in the film version of Maurice Maeterlinck's play, *The Blue Bird*. We discussed this work extensively in Book I, due to its compelling relevance to (and possible inspiration for) the CIA mind-control program of the same name. Maeterlinck's play was first performed in Russia, and was important to Konstantin Stanislavski. It was only fitting, then, that a film version be made in Russia once again, this time starring Elizabeth Taylor, Jane Fonda, Ava Gardner, and a host of other bright Hollywood lights and using a local Russian film crew. By all accounts, the film was a disaster. George Cukor had never made a fantasy film before, being remembered more for classics such as *Gaslight*, and this lavish attempt seemed doomed to failure even before the rushes were in. Fonda spent six weeks filming in Moscow, only to find that the bulk of her performance wound up on the proverbial cutting-room floor.

It is the fact that the film was made at all that interests us, for the only other time anyone had filmed *The Blue Bird* (in 1940), it had starred Shirley Temple, who eventually wound up as the American Ambassador to Czechoslovakia. This time, the film was being made in the Soviet Union as a gesture of détente, and thus rife with political undertones. Fonda was known in Russia only barely, and primarily for the fact that she had visited Hanoi during the Vietnam War. Her husband, Tom Hayden, accompanied her for a while to Moscow, only to become disgusted at the bourgeois appetites of the Muscovites, who seemed more interested in blue jeans than politics. What is not discussed in any of the sources I have been able to locate is the extent to which American intelligence used this first American–Soviet cinema co-production to advance their own agenda in Russia. It seems like a heaven-sent opportunity to infiltrate an agent or two into the entourage, using the production as a cover for more nefarious activities, but, alas, there is no documentation to support such a contention.

Yet, how *The Blue Bird*—the operational name for the CIA's first mind-control effort came to be associated with Russia and filmed in Moscow (the evil empire, after all, that had used mind control on Cardinal Mindszenty to force him to make outrageous confessions before television cameras) is one of the "coincidences" in this study that hum beneath the threshold of our hearing. One has to ask why it was important to Cukor and his producers to make the film at all, and at considerable expense. It must have seemed an eccentric choice. As it was filmed on location in early 1975 and released in 1976, seven years after the Manson killings and the year of the U.S. bicentennial, I like to think that *The Blue Bird* production was Jane Fonda's wake-up call, literally. After all, as detailed in Book I, she was likely present—along with husband-director Roger Vadim—at the Polanski home on the day that a drug dealer was pistol-whipped in front of Polanski's guests, only days before the actual murders of Sharon Tate and her friends. She studied Krishnamurti for a while, largely due to her brother's influence, but generally avoided occultism (according to one of her biographers, Christoper Andersen[14]), even though it was very popular in her circle and especially among the Polanski clique.

The Blue Bird is about memory, and fear, and conspiracy, and ultimately salvation. It is about innocence, and about traveling far and wide, only eventually to find happiness at home. Like the *Oz* books—the stories by Frank Baum that inspired the name of Beausoleil's band, The Magick Powerhouse of Oz—its message is faintly fascistic: "there's no place like home." To get to this primeval state of bliss, one has to proceed through a nightmare of anxiety, mortal attacks, and terror. The children do this in *The Blue Bird,* just as Dorothy does in *The Wizard of Oz.* (Strangely, and again according to Maury Terry's informants, one of the cults connected to the Son of Sam operation was called "The Children.") It is a spiritual voyage straight from the world's shamanistic traditions, and at least in Maeterlinck's case the analogy was probably deliberate.

Maeterlinck wrote extensively on occult themes, as we have seen, and was a believer in spiritualism and psychic phenomena in general. His influence over Stanislavski was due at least as much to his spiritual worldview as it was his Nobel Prize in Literature. Maeterlinck was a man with a mission, a believer. *The Blue Bird*—while seemingly a story for children—is, like most fairy tales, a coded message for adults, one the CIA took very much to heart, ransacking it for technique and theory while ignoring its higher meaning.

While the Cukor film is worth mentioning simply because we have spent so much time with Maeterlinck and the play before—in the context of the CIA—Fonda's role in it is compelling for two reasons: one, she was obviously very close to the circle around Sharon Tate and Roman Polanski and was even suspected of having had sex with Tate's former lover, Jay Sebring, as well as of having been present for the unfortunate punishment of the drug dealer at the Polanski home: connections that lead us straight back to Charles Manson and the Family. But the other reason is perhaps even more bizarre. It involves her brother, Peter Fonda, and his marriage to Susan Brewer.

Peter Fonda, of course, became a film idol with the release of *Easy Rider* (1969), another film that has become a cult classic. With co-stars Dennis Hopper and Jack Nicholson—"Indians!"—Peter made his indelible mark on Hollywood history and personified a generation of young Americans during the time of the Vietnam War. (According to audio commentary on the DVD release by the film's director, Dennis Hopper, the famous LSD scene towards the end of the movie was based on the Gnostic *Gospel of St. Thomas* found at the Nag Hammadi library.) One Jerry Kay, the art director for the film, was—according to the first edition of Ed Sanders' *The Family*—a member of the infamous Solar Lodge of the OTO, the Thelemic organization that was involved in the "boy in the box" affair that caused Grady McMurtry to reactivate his OTO status and fly to California to ward off the sudden interest of the FBI in the Order and deflect it towards the "unofficial" OTO lodge, a series of events that were put in motion during a police raid on the Solar Lodge on July 26, 1969 to investigate charges of child abuse . . . the day before Bobby Beausoleil murdered Gary Hinman.[15] There was also circumstantial evidence linking Charles Manson to the Solar Lodge, and much stronger evidence showing his relationship with the Process. It is strange, then, in the context of our study, to discover that Peter Fonda—in New York City in October 1961—would marry the stepdaughter of Noah Dietrich.

Noah Dietrich was probably the one man on earth who knew Howard Hughes inside and out. An employee, and CPA of the Hughes empire for thirty-two years after 1925, he ran Hughes Tool and, according to former Hughes insider and CIA Castro-assassination plotter Robert Maheu, delivered "net profits as high as $55 million annually."[16] Dietrich was the steady, efficient businessman and financial genius behind the Hughes empire, but when Dietrich asked for the stock options he had been repeatedly promised by Hughes, Hughes fired him in May of 1957. To be sure, this was also at the height of Hughes' troubles with TWA. Hughes had wanted to buy more planes, and needed the support of the banks to do so. They refused to put more money into TWA, and it seemed that Dietrich also refused to cooperate with the scheme. No matter which way the story played out, by the end of 1957 Howard Hughes had retreated from public view, by his lights abandoned by his friends and cheated by the courts and the government. It was the beginning of the great Hughes disappearing act.

Dietrich eventually published his memoirs, *Howard: The Amazing Mr. Hughes*, but not before it became something of a cause célèbre. A circulating manuscript of the book was supposedly used by Clifford Irving to forge the infamous Hughes memoirs.

Strange, then, that Peter Fonda would marry Dietrich's stepdaughter four years after the 1957 debacle with Howard Hughes. No, not evidence of any kind of conspiracy, but the nexus of Hughes-Dietrich-Fonda is fascinating, because it connects us—matrix-like—to Fonda-Polanski-Tate-Manson and, of course, *The Blue Bird*, which is, after all, the "Manson Secret." Remember also that Jack Parsons worked for the Hughes Corporation for a while, and the strong links between the Hughes Corporation and the CIA on the one hand (particularly with regard to the Glomar Explorer and the raising of a sunken Soviet submarine) and the Mormons on the other, with tendrils that slither out and wrap around the Watergate office building in 1972.

Conspiracy theorists usually concentrate on political phenomena and criminal suspects at the expense of other types of information, but if we extend our search to include Hollywood on the one side, and religion and even mysticism on the other, we can come up with revealing angles to every political event that are nowhere else considered. We have to dig down deeply in the evidence lockers, looking at the inventories of books, films, and documents from the crime scenes, ones that were rejected by the detectives and inspectors as irrelevant to the cases, if we want to understand the sinister forces that flow beneath the surface of public events. No political event exists in a vacuum; no politician is only a politician. The one-dimensional approach to history has hobbled us for so long that the history books in our schools have become little more than fleshed-out chronologies. The very idea of "history" itself is suspect, now that we understand a little more about time, space, consciousness, psychological warfare, and the quanta. It is my hope that this "deconstruction" of some of Hollywood's famous (and not so famous) films will lend itself to a new approach to history, one that is as firmly based in culture, science and—what we call for want of a better word—"religion," as it is in politics.

There were mysteries at the Polanski house, most of which have never been revealed publicly, and these mysteries are germane to the wilder of the Maury Terry and Ed Sanders satanic conspiracy theories. Terry Melcher, who had lived in the Polanski residence shortly before the Polanskis moved in, stated that Roman Polanski had made unusual films there involving sadomasochism, pornography, etc.[17] A friend of the Manson Family, Charlene Cafritz, claimed to own motion picture footage of the Manson clan that the police did not have and of which they were not aware.[18] At the time of the trial, Cafritz was at St. Elizabeth's Hospital in Washington, D.C., the same hospital from which James Forrestal plunged to his death, and where poet Ezra Pound was kept after the War. It was where Dr. Winfred Overholser worked on truth serums for the OSS and, later, the CIA. Ms. Cafritz died soon thereafter, of an overdose of Nembutal, and was buried in the D.C. area without ever having revealed the location of the famous Manson films.

One of the strange twists of fate that link two otherwise unrelated events is the person of Min S. Yee, a reporter who—with rock star John Phillips of The Mamas and The Papas, a close friend of Sharon Tate—visited a "voodoo astrologer," who told them that the night of August 8–9, 1969 had been a perfect time for a sacrifice. Also, it seems a "voodoo adept" had threatened the life of Wojciech Frykowski, one of the Tate murder victims.[19] This prompted Polanski and Phillips to fly to Jamaica to conduct their own investigation of Caribbean voodoo and some other, possibly drug-related, Jamaican links to the murders, apparently without success.

This same Min Yee later collaborated with Dr. Thomas N. Layton on a book about the Jonestown massacre and his family's role in it: *In My Father's House* (1981).

It was Dennis Hopper who insisted to police after the killings at the Polanski residence that a lot of very strange activity took place there, and that some of the stranger episodes were actually filmed. Hopper was close to Jane Fonda and her circle: he attended her Las Vegas wedding to Roger Vadim with his wife and Peter and Susan Fonda, and of course co-wrote and co-starred with Peter Fonda in *Easy Rider*, released the same year as the Tate/LaBianca killings. He attended the raucous parties at the Polanski residence on Cielo Drive, and was in a position to know what went on there. Jane Fonda has not gone into any detail as to what transpired among the Polanskis, and all we surmise about her participation in their weird scenes is second-hand.

I don't know how close Susan Brewer was to her stepfather, Noah Dietrich; but the Tate/LaBianca killings took place in August 1969, and by November 1970 Clifford Irving had been approached by the powerful people who wanted him to work on a special project, ostensibly involving Howard Hughes and the fraudulent biography, a biography that would be based largely on Noah Dietrich's memoirs.[20] This undertaking would be fraught with danger, since it involved parties "who would stop at nothing to achieve their own ends—even murder."[21] Hughes had officially "disappeared" that same month, on November 25, 1970, an event that was recorded with some fanfare in Hank Greenspun's *Las Vegas Sun* on December 2.

The Manson trial was still in progress at that time, and would not be over until January 25, 1971, when the jury returned a verdict of "guilty" for all four defendants, returning on March 29, 1971, in the penalty phase of the trial, to pronounce "death" for Manson and the convicted members of his Family.

BELL, BOOK . . . AND CANDLE IN THE WIND

I have the most wonderful memory for forgetting things.

—Marilyn Monroe[22]

Director Luis Bunuel was one of the clique of surrealist film directors around such leading lights as Jean Cocteau and Salvador Dali. One of his screenwriters (on the acclaimed La Cucaracha) was a young Mexican man of great good looks (of the "Latin leading man" type) known as Jose Bolanos. During the McCarthy Era, when so many Hollywood stars, writers, and directors were either being blacklisted or blacklisting, Mexico became a safe haven for people like Bunuel and Bolanos, particularly as both could speak Spanish, of course, and would find themselves in a congenial environment. Mexico was friendly to socialists and socialist governments, and the Cuban Government of Fidel Castro had an embassy there, as did the Soviets. Lee Harvey Oswald (or someone pretending to be Lee Harvey Oswald) would visit the Soviet Embassy in Mexico City in 1963, just a few months before the assassination of the late Marilyn Monroe's putative lover, John F. Kennedy.

By 1962, though, the year that concerns us in this section, Castro was in firm control of his island nation and had "outed" himself as a Communist. It was bad news for the United States, and especially for those who had supported Castro in good faith . . . including everyone from CIA agents to movie stars like Errol Flynn. The Mafia was faced with the sudden loss of their casinos in Havana, and they were busy plotting revenge against "the Beard." Khrushchev was beaming, godfather-like, down at this tropical paradise only ninety miles off the coast of his arch-enemy, the United States of America. What a good place to plant a few ICBMs, he thought.

At this time, young writer Bolanos found himself in very good company, indeed. After an intense courtship involving flowers presented on a family heirloom silver plate, numerous mariachi bands, drinking, dancing, and god knows what else, Bolanos had managed the dream date: screen legend and would-be socialist Marilyn Monroe.

When we talk about politics and Hollywood, we cannot avoid the seemingly surreal. Weirdness is the order of the day, and truth is always much, much stranger than fiction. Lee Harvey Oswald was captured in a movie theater, as an example. It was showing a Van Heflin film, *Cry of Battle* (1963), about insurrection in the Philippines, which would have been interesting to Oswald under kinder circumstances, since he spent some time there as a US Marine. Abraham Lincoln was assassinated in a theater while watching a stage play, *Our American Cousin*, shot in the back of the head by a famous actor and leading man, John Wilkes Booth. The movies gave us Ronald and Nancy Reagan—both Hollywood actors—as President and First Lady.

Yet, not many people know that Fidel Castro himself was once a film actor in Hollywood. In the October 30, 1997 edition of *Zenit*, Uruguayan film critic Alvara Sanjurjo confirmed persistent rumors that Castro did, indeed, have a fledgling start as an actor in two George Sidney productions, *Bathing Beauty* (1944) and *Holiday in Mexico* (1946). Sanjurjo is an intimate of Alfredo Guevara Valdes, the head of the Cuban Instituto Cinematografico de Cuba, who himself is a close friend of the Cuban leader, and should know. Even the current owner of *Holiday in Mexico*, Turner Classic Movies (TCM), states, on its Web site, TCM.com:

> Pasternak and Sidney released their third film in Technicolor, the sizzling *Holiday in Mexico* (1946). Starring Walter Pidgeon as the U.S. Ambassador, *Holiday* promised fun in the sun when his daughter (Jane Powell) falls for a Latin lover (Jose Iturbi). In addition to a bossa nova score, *Holiday* in Mexico featured a young Fidel Castro in a bit part—look close for the future dictator!

Even such definitive biographies of the great Cuban dictator as that of Tad Szulc do not include this bizarre stage in his development, yet the data is available.

Castro made several trips to the United States before he became a guerrilla leader and eventual *El Lider*, one of which was for a honeymoon after his marriage on October 12, 1948 (yes, Columbus Day and Crowley's birthday) to Mirta Diaz-Balart, and, during another trip a year later, he stayed in a small apartment at 155 West 82nd Street in New York City for a few months and haunted Marxist bookstores, like so many other students and would-be revolutionaries of the author's own acquaintance during the 1960s. Although these two trips are well-documented, the appearance of Castro in *two* Hollywood films—both made by George Sidney, who also directed *Pal Joey* (1957) and other Sinatra vehicles (oddly enough, considering that the Rat Pack, and particularly Sinatra, were major supporters of the Kennedy presidential campaign in 1960) goes virtually unnoted in biographies of Castro and histories of the Cuban conflict. (Sidney would retire from Hollywood at the age of 49 and become a respected paleontologist!) Castro did himself make one sly reference to his earlier career during a visit to Princeton University in 1959, shortly after he marched through Havana at the head of the victorious revolutionaries:

> In response to an implied accusation that his motives were less than altruistic, Castro reportedly rejoined with the following assertion: "I could be rich . . . You know how? By writing the history of our revolution for Hollywood."

This curious circumstance lends itself to all sorts of semiotic possibilities. Castro as young Hollywood extra in wartime California, between bouts of baiting the politicos in Havana. Since it is now known for certain that Castro did, indeed, have a bit part in *Bathing Beauty*, one wonders why he returned to Hollywood for *Holiday in Mexico*. Was he called back? Did he have an agent? Did he go out of his way to show up for an audition? (Castro at a cattle call!) Did he briefly toy with being an actor instead of a politician or, as has been suggested, a professional baseball player?

Regardless, Castro came to understand the power of Hollywood, and it should have come as no surprise when movie stars and directors began showing up in Havana in the late 1990s for heart-to-heart talks with Fidel.

But was screenwriter Jose Bolanos a Fidelista? Or was Bolanos—the last known lover of Marilyn Monroe—working for another organization altogether?

In the months leading up to the death of Marilyn Monroe on August 4–5, 1962, the United States was engaged in a serious struggle with the Castro regime in Cuba. The Bay of Pigs invasion had failed disastrously on April 17, 1961; the world was only months away from the Cuban Missile Crisis of October 1962. Throughout the spring of 1962 the operation that would become known as Mongoose consumed more and more of the Kennedys' time: Jack and Robert, the President and the Attorney General. Declassified State Department files show that meetings were held weekly and almost daily at the State Department and the CIA on the subject of destabilizing the Castro regime by using everything from psychological warfare to sabotage and assassination. The largest domestic CIA operation ever was mounted in Florida, with a recruitment of anti-Castro Cubans and fellow travelers, including mysterious Mafiosi with exploding cigars, courtesy of the CIA's Technical Services Division and the collaboration of Robert Maheu.

Yet, at the same time, documents and published eyewitness interviews will confirm that Ms. Monroe was seeing both of the Kennedy brothers romantically. In fact, there have been persistent rumors that Christine Keeler of the Profumo Affair had seen Jack Kennedy in July of 1962 during a visit to the United States with her friend, Mandy Rice-Davies. This would have been less than a month before the death of Monroe, and during the lead-in to the Cuban Missile Crisis that October. While there is no documentation to support that either Kennedy ever actually met—much less romanced—either Ms. Keeler or Ms. Rice-Davies during that time, the mere possibility was giving American intelligence nightmares, as Keeler had been sleeping with both British War Minister John Profumo and the local Soviet GRU *rezident* at the time of the October crisis. This was magnified by what they *did* know concerning the Kennedys' involvement with Marilyn Monroe, who, from about February 1962 on, became involved with a group of Communists living in exile in Mexico City.

As recounted in several modern biographies of Monroe—notably by Anthony Summers, who also did a comprehensive job on the Kennedy assassination, and Donald E. Wolfe, whose research is based in part on Summers' interviews—there was a hotbed of Communists, socialists, and assorted left-wingers in Mexico City in the early 1960s, some of whom had been in self-imposed exile since the start of the HUAC investigations, and many of whom had Hollywood connections. During this same period, relations between the United States and Cuba had become dangerously heated, with the US secretly (and sometimes not so secretly) aiming raids, sabotage, and agent infiltration at Castro's island, and attempting to assassinate the leader using a wide variety of toxins developed by the CIA and agents-in-place, all part of "Operation Mongoose." Mexico City in those days was like a western hemisphere Vienna: a place of fragile neutrality, teeming with spies, in which agents from the opposing camps—Soviet, Cuban, American—could watch each other come and go in the Zona Rosa. One of these was the famous "silver spoon Communist": Frederick Vanderbilt Field.

Coming from a wealthy background as a right-wing American, Field's political faith wavered, and then finally fell on the side of the left. Around him in Mexico City was a gaggle of left-wingers who professed everything from diehard Communism of the Soviet Communist International or "Comintern" model to revolutionary Castroism—liberal dilettantes who were excited to be this close to real socialists and Communists and who, anyway, professed humanitarian principles ranging from racial integration to a change in American foreign policy in Latin

America. In the midst of this cocktail circuit could be discerned such influences as artist (and Communist) Diego Rivera—the aforementioned comrade of Trotsky and Andre Breton—as well as filmmaker Luis Bunuel. As always, surrealism found itself in support of radical political solutions, even as it decried "Soviet realism" in art. It was an eclectic group of people from various backgrounds, and it is in this mélange that we find Marilyn Monroe in February of 1962.

Introduced to Field via her psychiatrist, Ralph Greenson, and his homunculus, Eunice Murray, Monroe and Field became fast friends. (At the time of her death, Field was even staying at Monroe's New York City apartment.) Indeed, Field's Mexican wife had been an artist's model for Diego Rivera. Field offered instant entrée into leftist artistic circles, something that was noticeably missing (or, at best, underground) in Hollywood. Monroe was impressed by the strong emotional feelings she encountered among the exiles: a typical liberal fascination with their idealistic *fervorinos* against American hegemony, racial segregation, and political hypocrisy in high places. Communist propaganda of the time appealed to a paranoid, conspiratorial view of politics, in which the rich oppressed the poor, the whites oppressed the blacks, and the wealthy American oligarchy did what it could to extend that dynamic overseas, by oppressing poorer "third world" nations. Racial segregation was an easy target, and demonstrated to the liberal elite that at least part of what the Communists were saying was obviously true. Support was especially high in favor of Castro's Cuba.

Of course, the exiles were equally charmed by the presence in their midst of such a famous and glamorous superstar as Marilyn Monroe. It was one thing to hobnob with the likes of Diego Rivera and Luis Bunuel, arch intellectuals and artists bathed in a kind of fashionable cynicism among a fawning expatriate community of many nations; it was quite another to be seen in the company of the world's most famous woman, a person who was at the same time relatively naïve about politics, yet open to new information and new points of view. She was also quite vulnerable, having gone through a series of famous (and not so famous) husbands, in an endless, desperate search for true love and emotional fulfillment. Her ex-husband Arthur Miller, for instance, was known to be sympathetic to the Left, and his famous play, *The Crucible*, is a thinly disguised attack on the McCarthy hearings . . . as seen from the point of view of the witchcraft trials in Salem. As always, we keep coming back in a smaller and smaller spiral linking politics, the occult, and culture. It is a volatile formula, and one that very possibly led to Marilyn's death.

She was also surrounded by Communists at home, even between husbands. This preponderance of closet Communists around Marilyn Monroe is a fact that deserves much more scrutiny than it has been given so far—except by Summers and Wolfe, aforementioned. Even her psychiatrist, Dr. Ralph Greenson, was a Communist, and was approved by the Party as a politically-reliable shrink, a functionary of an organization infiltrated to an extent by European émigrés who owed their allegiance to both Freud and Marx. This organization, known as the Psychoanalytic Institutes, with offices in most major American cities,[23] and which contained within its ranks members of various political affiliations, served as a secure means for Communist Party members to meet and exchange information. Psychiatry, in general, was a wonderful mechanism for running "cells" in a foreign country. No one would question why a person had to meet secretly with a psychoanalyst or psychiatrist; in fact, many psychiatrists' offices are designed to permit only one person at a time in the waiting area, and each patient leaves by a separate exit so that no patient need be seen by another.

This situation is perfect for debriefing agents, and for discovering the innermost secrets of others, and may have been one of the reasons why the Water-gate Plumbers broke into the office of Daniel Ellsberg's psychiatrist, Dr. Lewis Fielding. As the man who leaked the Pentagon Papers to the press, Ellsberg's motives seemed highly suspect, and Ellsberg himself was targeted as a Communist. That suspicion might have extended to his psychiatrist, in a replay of what had been going on in the early 1960s. After all, Lewis Fielding was a close friend of Marilyn Monroe's analyst, Dr. Greenson, and the FBI maintained a file on Greenson, a file that is still classified to this day. The story of the "Communist-cell psychiatrists" is one that has not been told, and the implications of the story are alarming. Much of this history is still classified, but what we do know has serious implications for the Marilyn Monroe story.

For instance, Dr. Greenson was the leader of the Arts, Sciences, and Professions Committee (ASPC), which was a front organization for Communist infiltration of the media. Within the ASPC were a number of other organizations, including the Doctors Professional Group, and the People's Educational Center, "which was established and funded by Frederick Vanderbilt Field."[24] The founder of the ASPC, Louis Budenz, was "a Communist Party leader and one time managing editor of the *Daily Worker*" (Wolfe, p. 474). Many of these men were openly Communist in the immediate pre-War days, but went underground once the Senate and HUAC hearings began. As Wolfe relates,

> One of Greenson's contacts within the hierarchy of the Comintern was Frederick Vanderbilt Field. As the director of the American Russian Institute, Field was also associated with Greenson's mother, Katharine Greenschpoon, who was on the board of directors, according to the Senate Fact Finding Committee on Un-American Activities in California bulletin of 1948.[25]

And again,

> Field was closely monitored by the FBI in Mexico City, and . . . continued his links to the United States through the Comintern leader in Los Angeles—Dr. Ralph Greenson.[26]

Field (and many others) had to flee to Mexico once Louis Budenz defected and began giving the Senate the names of other Communists in California as the McCarthy investigations intensified. Gradually, Marilyn became aware that there was something sinister about Greenson's attentions (and those of his spy, Eunice Murray), and by July 1962 she was openly revolting against them. By then, of course it was too late.

Just as the CIA was in full throttle on MK-ULTRA, the Soviets were using traditional psychiatric and psychoanalytic settings in the United States to serve as Comintern fronts and, perhaps, to condition and control certain select patients. When we see the degree to which Monroe depended upon Greenson, and when we learn of Greenson's bizarre "anti-analytic" approach with Monroe in direct violation of his own, published therapeutic principles, we can easily understand how a charge could be made that Monroe was being deliberately manipulated by the Comintern.

And when we learn that E. Howard Hunt—former CIA agent, formerly stationed in Mexico City, one of the Watergate Plumbers himself, and present during the break-in at Fielding's office—was a good friend of the last man to call himself Marilyn Monroe's lover, Jose Bolanos, we are forced to take a completely different look at the events of 1962 and 1963.

Bonafide Communist Frederick Field was highly suspicious of Bolanos, and warned Monroe against seeing him. He believed that Bolanos had infiltrated into the left-wing community in Mexico, an insincere Communist with a hidden agenda, "distrusted by the real left."[27] As revealed in Wolfe's analysis of the death of Marilyn Monroe, Bolanos and E. Howard Hunt were friends.[28] Hunt traveled frequently to Mexico City—either in official or unofficial capacity (he was still with the CIA at the time, although David Atlee Phillips was CIA station chief in Mexico City during this period)—and the two would occasionally meet. Hunt, a writer, considered himself a kind of Ian Fleming, but was actually quite a bit more like the Cigarette Smoking Man, the *X-Files* character based on Hunt. He was also interested in Latin occult practices (as evidenced in his novel *The Coven*), so it is possible that his interest in Mexico City and the Zona Rosa was more of a literary one, slumming with the glamorous expats.

But I don't think so.

I believe that Bolanos was Hunt's man in the Zona Rosa, and once it became known that Marilyn Monroe was hanging out there—at the suggestion, no less, of her Communist Party-approved psychiatrist, Greenson—alarm bells should have gone off at Langley. Unknown to Monroe, Frederick Field knew her housekeeper, Eunice Murray, quite well, and Murray was the conduit to both Field and Greenson. Her husband, John Murray, had been a labor organizer in Hollywood in the 1940s and a dedicated Communist Party member. When the Murray family underwent a reversal of fortune after the War, John Murray sold his home (the site of many Party meetings) to Dr. Greenson, a man he knew from Communist cell gatherings in Hollywood. (It was to this house that Marilyn Monroe would go for her psychiatric meetings with Dr. Greenson.) It was Dr. Greenson, in fact, who ordered his patient to fire her loyal friend and masseur, Ralph Roberts, and replace him with the sinister Ms. Eunice Murray, without telling Ms. Monroe that Murray was a psychiatric nurse, and a Communist at that.[29]

The FBI had surveillance on Peter Lawford as well as Marilyn Monroe—according to its own documents—which in some instances refer to a mysterious confidential informant, who (on the basis of internal evidence) can only be Bolanos. At the same time, the CIA was of course also surveilling Field as a suspected Soviet agent, and CIA Counterintelligence Chief James Angleton confirmed that Marilyn's home was bugged.[30]

So, as you can see, Marilyn never had a chance.

In 1962, Operation Mongoose was in full swing, as the US government ramped up to destabilize Cuba and assassinate Castro. The missiles were starting to arrive in Cuba, smaller tactical missiles at first and then the ICBMs. By late 1961, incoming CIA Station Chief in Mexico, David Atlee Phillips, already knew the first of the missiles were there. By July 1962 everyone at Langley knew. Hunt was still the CIA liaison with the Cuban exiles, trying to keep up their spirits after the failed Bay of Pigs invasion. And here was Marilyn Monroe, drinking mezcal with the Reds and—who knows?—maybe eating the worm. She was already friendly with Robert Kennedy, and had been asking him a great many leading political questions, questions provided to her by a suspiciously helpful Dr. Greenson. She would then report on these meetings, in all innocence, in the Zona Rosa to Comintern member Frederick Field, to E. Howard Hunt intimate Jose Bolanos, and from there to . . .?

In addition, Robert Kennedy would be informed sometime in 1962 that the CIA under General Lansdale (whom we encountered in Book I in his incarnation as a psychological warfare expert) was subcontracting the Castro assassination to the Mafia, using the ever-helpful Robert Maheu as cutout. Ms. Monroe's friendship with Mafiosi Johnny Roselli and Sam Giancana—themselves deeply involved in these same clandestine arrangements and directly involved with both Richard Nixon and E. Howard Hunt—went back a ways as well, dating from the beginning of her Sinatra period, and this just wove the noose around her neck a little tighter. All around her were some of the seminal figures in the history of modern American covert operations and the Cold War. And, it was suspected, she was writing it all down in her ever-present red-bound diary.

Marilyn Monroe had direct access to the President of the United States and the Attorney General of the United States on the one hand, and to the Communist Party on the other, not to mention the Mafia on still another appendage of what murdered investigative journalist Danny Casolaro would call "the Octopus." That made her the Christine Keeler of America. But while Ms. Keeler's interests in John Profumo and Yevgeny Ivanov were purely materialistic, Ms. Monroe's interest in the Kennedy brothers, and particularly in Bobby Kennedy, was purely romantic. As far as we can discern from witness interviews at the time, Marilyn Monroe was despondent over her relationship with the Attorney General, whom she believed would leave his wife and children in order to marry her. They had argued about a number of political issues, however, including nuclear testing and Cuba as it turns out, with Bobby Kennedy eventually accusing her of turning Communist on the basis of her leftist views.[31]

So, who wanted Marilyn dead? As in the case of the John F. Kennedy assassination a year later, the list of suspects is a long one. At one time, her home was being bugged and her phones tapped by the FBI as well as by an "independent investigator," whose employer might have been either the Mob or the CIA. She was under surveillance by them all. Her association with both the Kennedys and with the Comintern made her a dangerous woman; had the CIA succeeded in assassinating Castro, it is entirely possible that Ms. Monroe would have gone public with what she knew. She was already feeding information to the Mexico City Communists, as well as to Jose Bolanos who, we suspect, was working for E. Howard Hunt. She was a liability to the Kennedys, to the FBI, and to the CIA—specifically, to Operation Mongoose; and, to the extent that she could jeopardize Operation Mongoose, she was a liability to the Mafia. The only people who did not want Marilyn Monroe dead would have been the Communists themselves, since she was so close to the President, the Attorney General, Sam Giancana, Johnny Roselli, "Operation Mongoose," etc., etc. It would have been insane to kill the goose that was laying golden eggs.

However, by July of 1962 and only weeks before her death, she had realized that something wasn't right with Greenson and Murray. She told her ex-husband Robert Slatzer that she was going to fire them all. Was a decision made to silence her before she could reveal the existence of this clandestine Communist cell in Hollywood and Mexico City?

Robert F. Kennedy arrived with his family in Los Angeles on August 3, 1962. There is a great deal of speculation—supported by some fragile circumstantial evidence and the testimony of eyewitnesses—that Kennedy visited Marilyn Monroe sometime between August 3 and August 5, the day of her death. The existence of her diary was well-known, and she had made it understood that she had potentially explosive information. Was a decision made to murder Marilyn Monroe when it was known Bobby Kennedy was in town, as an attempt to embarrass or possibly ruin the Attorney General, the one man Jimmy Hoffa and other union-mafiosi hated the most?

Some authors support the Mafia-Killed-Marilyn theory; others the Kennedys-killed-Marilyn theory; still others the FBI/CIA-killed-Marilyn theory. That she was murdered and did not commit suicide seems, at this point, a safe inference, based on forensic evidence and crime scene photographs, as well as conflicting witness testimony. Whatever the truth may be, one thing is for certain: her diary was never found, even though it was the target of a search by James Jesus Angleton, the CIA's Chief of Counterintelligence, the man responsible for hunting the famed Soviet "mole" within American intelligence. Angleton would become enmeshed in another hunt for the diary of a Presidential lover, this time in 1964 with the death of Mary Pinchot Meyer, as described in Book I.

Monroe's diary, however, was without a doubt political nitroglycerine. Referred to as her "book of secrets," it contained information on everything from the Mafia, Hoffa, and the Bay of Pigs to the CIA assassination plots against Castro, all culled from conversations with Jack and Bobby Kennedy.[32] Monroe kept all of this written down because, as revealed in her conversations with her ex-husband Robert Slatzer only weeks before her death, Bobby Kennedy would get mad at her for not remembering "anything he told me" concerning political issues.[33] During this conversation with Slatzer, in which she allowed him to browse through her "book of secrets" and "handwritten notes from Bobby Kennedy—some of them on Justice Department stationery,"[34] she spoke of the possibility of holding a press conference in the event that either the President or the Attorney General refused to speak with her. Convinced that her phones were tapped (they were), she met Slatzer outdoors where they could speak in private.[35] This was in late July 1962.

The weekend of July 28–29 probably holds a key to what transpired only days later. Ms. Monroe spent the weekend at the Cal-Neva Lodge in Lake Tahoe, and the mystery that surrounds this weekend is impenetrable. That something loathsome did take place, and that it involved Marilyn Monroe who was only now making an important comeback, is certain, if only because of the reticence of eyewitnesses to discuss it.

Wolfe makes a good case that she was invited to the Cal-Neva Lodge—Sinatra's unofficial headquarters—in order to be pressured into not going to the press with what she knew about the Kennedys and that those present on that weekend were Sinatra, Peter and Pat Lawford, her friend Gloria Romanoff . . . and Sam Giancana. It was Giancana's presence there that weekend that wound up costing Sinatra his gaming license, so we know that much is true. What has been revealed since then by eyewitnesses who did come forward is almost too much to believe, a horror that goes beyond anything we might comfortably imagine.

Her ex-husband, Joe DiMaggio—icon of American baseball and one of the men who truly loved Marilyn—arrived unexpectedly at the scene. No one knows how he knew his ex-wife would be there, but he showed up and was not allowed inside the complex of bungalows that had been reserved for Monroe, Sinatra, and Giancana, on orders from Sinatra. Instead, he had to take a room at a nearby motel. Marilyn Monroe herself was not actually registered at the Cal-Neva, a precaution that now seems much more sinister in retrospect; instead, she was put into the bungalow complex and kept watch over the entire time.

When DiMaggio returned from Lake Tahoe, he told his friend Harry Hall that he was furious with what had happened, that Sinatra had kept Monroe on drugs, and that they had "sex parties."[36] To clarify what was meant by that, photographer Billy Woodfield was quoted as saying that Sinatra gave him a roll of film from that weekend. When Woodfield developed the roll, he evidently found photos of Marilyn being sexually abused by, or at least in the presence of, Sam Giancana and Frank Sinatra.[37]

In other words, Marilyn Monroe was likely drugged, raped, and photographed; the photos would be used as blackmail against her if she decided to come forward with what she knew about the Kennedys, the Mafia, and Castro.

A drugged Monroe was returned to Los Angeles late the night of July 29–30, in the company of Peter Lawford. Monroe was returned to her home in a limo, but Lawford rode with the flight crew to his beach home. Before arriving home, he asked the crew to stop for a moment so he could make a call from a pay phone (knowing his own home was bugged and his phones tapped). He made a mysterious phone call that lasted about twenty minutes before finally going home in the early hours of that morning.

That phone call was logged into the White House, a call that went directly to the President.

Marilyn's last days were a turmoil of political intrigue. It seems the blackmail effort was not panning out the way everyone thought it would. She was threatening to go public with what she knew; she was also on the verge of firing Dr. Greenson and Eunice Murray who, she finally realized, was sent to spy on her by Greenson.[38] She had made an appointment to see her attorney, Mickey Rudin, the following Monday in order to change her will. Mickey Rudin was Dr. Greenson's brother-in-law, and Frank Sinatra's attorney as well, so the circle grows increasingly smaller . . . and tighter. She had already "fired" her friend Paula Strasberg, of the Actor's Studio Strasbergs. Her efforts at learning the Method had worked well, according to Lee Strasberg, and she was becoming a serious, accomplished actress, and not merely someone to be cast in comedy roles or fluff pieces. But the influence of the Strasbergs had proved pernicious; while they had managed to avoid the worst of the HUAC excesses, they were still considered "Reds" and the Method was, after all, a psychological conditioning process, what A.O. Scott of the *New York Times* has recently called "a mode of psychological melodrama, a means by which the obscure, private noise of the soul is transformed into speech and gesture."[39] Add to this sex, drugs, and politics, and you have a volatile mixture, an initiatory explosion in the making. According to Anthony Summers, Monroe had built up"a considerable library. Marilyn had a lifetime interest in the occult, and she often visited astrologers and psychics."[40]

This tantalizing bit of information is left there. As in so many biographies of the famous, the celebrated, the influential—such as in biographies of Hitler, for instance—a fascination with the occult is mentioned, briefly, and then glossed over. No one seems willing to offer more than a few words on the subject, even as they dissect every other aspect of the person's private, personal life. Her longtime friend and one-time husband, Bob Slatzer, devotes a short chapter in his biography of Marilyn to her interest in the occult,[41] and even reproduces an astrological chart cast for her by Laetitia "Tish" Leroy.[42] But between her interest in the occult on one side, and her early involvement with leftists and others who came afoul of the Senate and Congressional committees on the other, she was already peering behind the veil of American politics and American reality.

Marilyn Monroe had already penetrated the mysteries of the Kennedy Administration: she, herself, had become one of those mysteries. She was being groomed and trained—via the Method and via psychiatry—by a cabal of Communists with a hidden agenda, such as Dr. Greenson, who told her what friends to have, what film roles to take, and who generally abused the oath of a physician by doing everything contrary to established psychiatric procedure when it came to the screen goddess. (As if to underscore the connection, her code name when calling the President was "Miss Green."[43])

She was *their* initiate, sent into the opposing camp; they had made this vulnerable, talented woman a Discordia, Goddess of Confusion and Disharmony, the unwitting spy of a Soviet cabal. But she was turning on everyone: Mafia, Kennedys, Communists alike, in a desperate attempt to hold herself together, to integrate her personality and become the strong, even happy, woman she knew herself capable of being.

She had become that dangerous entity, the student who has surpassed the need for a master. On August 4, 1962—at the age of only thirty-six—she died. The crime scene was a mess; forensics were a joke. It was the proverbial "locked room" mystery, in which the victim was murdered in a room that was locked from the inside. She was said to have overdosed on sleeping pills . . . but none were found in her digestive tract. There was no glass of water in that locked room to enable her to swallow what were estimated to be nearly 50 capsules. And no hypodermic syringe. Her psychiatrist Dr. Greenson and her physician Dr. Engelberg (who were, after all, close friends) waited hours before calling the police. It was Engelberg who prescribed the Nembutal that was said to have resulted in her death. It was Engelberg who gave her mysterious injections the week she died.

Shortly thereafter, other women began dying. Mary Pinchot Meyer was murdered on a street outside her home in 1964. This was the ex-wife of an important CIA official, who was also a lover of President Kennedy and the woman who turned him on to drugs, courtesy of Dr. Timothy Leary; she was the woman who called Leary shortly after the assassination, possessed of guilty secrets.

On November 8, 1965, columnist and reporter Dorothy Kilgallen died under mysterious circumstances, soon after she had visited Jack Ruby in prison in Dallas.

She was conducting her own investigation of the Kennedy assassination, and had been in possession—through her lover, Ron Pataki—of some secret information concerning Marilyn Monroe, with whom she had also been friendly.[44] Her notes of the interview with Jack Ruby disappeared after her death. Pataki had seen them, however, but refuses to discuss their contents, so once again we are cheated of knowing the truth about America, the truth about our history, by people who arrogate to themselves the title of well-intentioned guardians of our memory.

But it was not only the women who died.

After Marilyn Monroe's death in August 1962 came the Cuban Missile Crisis in October, the Profumo Affair the following year with the suicide of Dr. Stephen Ward, and the Kennedy assassination in November 1963. Ironically, the John Frankenheimer film starring Frank Sinatra and Angela Lansbury, *The Manchurian Candidate*, was released in 1962, the year Marilyn was murdered, and pulled from distribution after the assassination of the President in 1963.

And then Bobby, a man racked with guilt over the death of his brother, if not also for the murder of Marilyn Monroe, who decides to make a run for the presidency and try to make America a better place, to end the war in Vietnam, to ensure racial integration and equality, is gunned down on the day of his California victory in June 1968.

Darkly, like the wings of a deeper conspiracy, flickered the faces of Roman Polanski and Sharon Tate at the Frankenheimer dinner table for Bobby Kennedy's Last Supper that night. The following year, almost on the anniversary of Marilyn Monroe's death and in the same town, Sharon Tate herself would be horribly butchered, and the man accused of masterminding that crime would be held in the same jail cell that had been especially designed for Bobby Kennedy's putative killer, Sirhan Sirhan.

Another man, perhaps satisfied with the death of the screen legend, would go on to greater glory: E. Howard Hunt. The Watergate affair would dredge up all kinds of ugly secrets, prompting Richard Nixon to famously worry about exposing "the whole Bay of Pigs thing." Hunt and Jose Bolanos. Hunt and the break-in at Dr. Lewis Fielding's office: the close friend of Marilyn's Comintern analyst, Dr. Ralph Greenson. Hunt as "action officer" on the Bay of Pigs invasion. Hunt as CIA icon to the anti-Castro Cubans in Miami. Hunt as mastermind of the Watergate break-in. And Bolanos as FBI informant *and* CIA informant? The middle man between Marilyn Monroe and E. Howard Hunt? Bolanos as screenwriter to surrealist Bunuel, hovering around the edges of the Mexican surrealist community that included Bunuel, Dali, Diego Rivera and Frida Kahlo, meanwhile spying on them for the Company. *La Cucaracha*, indeed.

It's possible that the men who killed Marilyn were concerned about national security; it's possible that they were protecting American secrets from leaking to the press, or to the Soviet Union. It's possible they told themselves, these grey-souled men of the CIA, the FBI, the Mob, the anti-Castro Cubans, the Sinatras, the Giancanas, the Hunts, that Marilyn Monroe was just a weak-willed, inconvenient woman who was in the way, a dumb broad with a big mouth, a slut who slept her way to stardom, a woman scorned, a mistress dumped.

I submit—after my own, twenty-five-year-long investigation into American politics and American culture—that all these men taken together, all these Hunts and Sinatras and Giancanas and Bolanos, and Greenson and Murray and all the rest, were not worth one Marilyn Monroe, whatever the official or unofficial reason for her execution.

> I found out something I never knew. I found out that my world was not the real world.
>
> —Robert F. Kennedy, shortly before he was assassinated[45]

ME AND THE DEVIL (BLUES)

> I do enjoy the Beatles however; their music has a definite beat and in many ways their music is good music.
>
> —Rudolf Hess[46]

> Me and the Devil
> Was walking side by side . . .
>
> —Robert Johnson, "Me and the Devil Blues"

Although every form of music has had its satanic influences—and music probably its origins as drum beats and chants in primeval rituals performed in the same darkened caves where the first art was painted and the first theater enacted—in the present era we can trace the fusion of music and madness to the blues composer and guitarist, Robert Johnson.

Johnson (1911–1938) began playing the juke joints and roadhouses of Mississippi during the Depression in the early 1930s, after a tragic life in which his sixteen-year-old wife and newborn baby both died in childbirth, an event that came in the wake of Johnson's own illegitimate birth, his childhood at a variety of homes and under a variety of names, but always to the soulful sound of the Mississippi Delta blues. He was murdered—poisoned with strychnine—by a jealous husband on August 16, 1938 at the age of 27, but not before he had recorded some famous and influential tracks, like "Terraplane," "Hellhound on my Trail," and "Little Queen of Spades."

But it was the dark, and darkly sardonic, anthems that reached the souls of modern rockers and opened their eyes to the sinister that is an inextricable element of all music, but especially of any music that pretends to speak directly to the soul. Readers may wonder at my identification of the "sinister" with music, but "sinister" is a word with many meanings and implications. It can represent the sense of awe we feel at the approach of a divine mystery as much as it can mean an unsettling feeling in the presence of the demonic. The word "sinister" refers, after all, to things of the "left hand," and the left side of the body is controlled by the right side of the brain. It is fascinating to learn that the Italians speak of the paranormal, and conspiracy theories in general, as *dietrologia*, or the "science of the left hand side."

To Jungian analyst Adolf Guggenbühl-Craig—author of the aptly-titled *From the Wrong Side: A Paradoxical Approach to Psychology*—the sinister has celestial associations:

> The sinister is always the unintelligible, the impressive, the numinous. Wherever something divine appears, we begin to experience fear.[47]

And further:

> I assume that an encounter with God or with the transcendent, per se, can only then occur when we experience the violent side of God, creation and mankind as well. We meet God and the world just as much in the horrific as in the beautiful and sublime.[48]

Many music critics might agree that the sinister and the sublime meet in the works of Robert Johnson. Only twenty-nine Johnson titles still exist on vinyl, and they were compiled into *Robert Johnson: The Complete Recordings* on the Columbia label in 1990. These recordings were all made in Texas, some in Dallas, from November 23–27, 1936, and their influence has been enormous.

In fact, Eric Clapton—in an essay on Johnson published in the liner notes to Johnson's complete recordings—states,

> Up until the time I was 25, if you didn't know who Robert Johnson was, I wouldn't talk to you. It was almost like that. *It was as if I had been prepared to receive Robert Johnson, almost like a religious experience* . . . Even then I wasn't quite ready. (emphasis in original)

In another essay in the liner notes, Keith Richards of the Rolling Stones relates how he heard Johnson for the first time at the home of Brian Jones:

> To me, Robert Johnson's influence—he was like a comet or a meteor that came along and, BOOM, suddenly he raised the ante, suddenly you had to aim that much higher.

And, of course, he did. From "Me and the Devil Blues" by Johnson to "Sympathy for the Devil" by Jagger and Richards, there is a continuum of fascination with evil, and the use of music to *evoke* those sinister forces that has so frightened Fundamentalist Christians and the Christian Right in general. Rock 'n' roll as early as Elvis Presley was considered satanic, inspired by the Devil himself to instigate revolution against authority, sexual liberation, and "dirty dancing." Johnson threw down the gauntlet with his songs about women, violence, and despair as a master of Delta Blues, and the gauntlet was picked up and passed around by generations of serious musicians to follow.

While we can see the "satanic" influence of Johnson over the Rolling Stones—the Stones certainly had their share of occult influences and connections, from Anger and Cammell to Pallenberg and Faithfull—occultism was never very far from the other icons of '60s rock. While the Beach Boys were hobnobbing with Charlie Manson, who himself was reading arcane messages into Beatles lyrics, and Jimmy Page of Led Zeppelin was starring in and scoring Anger films and living at Crowley's Boleskine estate in Scotland, Jim Morrison of The Doors was marrying a witch.

The marriage was a pagan version of the same, known as a "handfasting" in Wiccan circles, and thus had no legal standing, which has led to some animosity among Morrison's girlfriends and fiancées. To understand where this is going, we have to rely upon reminiscences by the witch in question, one Patricia Kennealy or Patricia Kennealy-Morrison as she prefers to be known. Writing in her autobiography, *Strange Days*, she describes a great deal about her pagan experiences and philosophy, and she gave an abridged version of same to interviewers from a pagan publication, *Pagan Muse and World Report*, in their Fall 1996 edition and since reprinted on Ms. Kennealy's own Web site. This marriage of rock-icon Morrison to Kennealy was covered briefly in Oliver Stone's film about the group, *The Doors*, which does emphasize a mystical quality of The Doors and of Morrison himself.

Morrison died tragically in a bathtub in a Paris apartment of a friend in 1971, only a year after he and Kennealy were handfasted in a pagan ceremony. At the time, Kennealy was a member of a coven of Celtic witches she had joined in 1966 (the same year as the formation of the Church of Satan), becoming high priestess in 1969, the same year she met Morrison. She had been working for a rock music magazine, which is how she came to meet him. She was "married" to Jim Morrison on Midsummer's Day, 1970, before the members of her coven. He would die in July of 1971, a little over a year after the handfasting, and under mysterious circumstances. The French forensics—as in the case of LAPD's investigation of the death of Marilyn Monroe—were a farce; no one really knows how Morrison died or who might have been responsible. What is known is that there was a quantity of drugs in the apartment where he died, and that he had snorted heroin and probably overdosed in the bathtub, according to Pamela Susan Courson who was snorting heroin with him at the time. Ms. Courson, with whom Morrison was staying, had his body wrapped in plastic and packed in dry ice, and she slept next to his body for three nights until someone sent over a coffin. Ms. Courson had a lover, a French count, whom she shared with Marianne Faithfull, who was also in Paris that week. Courson told the count that it was a heroin overdose that killed Morrison, warning him because they all—Pamela Courson, the count, Morrison, and Faithfull—had scored off the same dealer. The count returned from Courson's apartment, told Faithfull what had happened, and the two of them—count and witch—left immediately for Morocco to avoid being interrogated by the French police.

Morrison was quickly buried in a cheap coffin during a funeral ceremony that lasted all of eight minutes and with only a handful of mourners. Eventually, his gravesite would be placed under tight security, replete with motion sensors and CCTV cameras, due to the incidents of attempted grave robbing by hysterical fans and venal ghouls. It is now one of the most famous tourist attractions in Paris.

After his death, Ms. Kennealy avoided the coven for several years in her grief, eventually becoming involved with Margot Adler's Pagan Way celebrations in New York City and from there joining a Welsh Traditionalist coven until it fell apart shortly thereafter (in or about 1977). (Dr. Adler is the author of *Drawing Down The Moon*, a study of modern American paganism, and a descendant of famous psychoanalyst Alfred Adler.) According to Ms. Kennealy, Jim Morrison had fully intended to be initiated into witchcraft upon his return from Paris, but fate had other ideas.

Morrison took the name of his group from Aldous Huxley's *The Doors of* Perception. More than any other rock band of the era, The Doors were famous for mystical lyrics and haunting, dreamlike melodies. There is no doubt that Morrison was fascinated with alternate forms of spirituality, expressed in eerie, stream-of-consciousness verse and alchemical allusions. Kennealy who, after all, began her career as a rock critic, describes Morrison as a shaman and The Doors concerts as rituals:

> The audiences were actually participants in Doors concerts, not just spectators. Those shows were mystical occasions. It sounds like so much hooey now, but you really had to be there, 'cause they absolutely were . . . . It was all absolutely there for you to grab onto. Because Jim made sure it was there for you to grab. Because he put it there. He really did see it like that, and he consciously tried to make it happen . . . . He saw it as actively functioning as a living link between people and the creative power . . . where you represent the people before the gods and the gods before the people.[49]

Ms. Kennealy herself later went on to become the successful fantasy and science fiction author of a series of books known as *The Keltiad*, and was knighted in the

Ordo Supremus Militaris Templi Hierosolymitani (the Sovereign Military Order of the Temple of Jerusalem) in September 1990 at Rosslyn Chapel in Scotland, sponsored by fantasy authors Katherine Kurtz and Scott MacMillan. Rosslyn Chapel is a mecca for New Agers interested in the Templar tradition, as it has been mentioned in books supporting the theory that some Templars escaped to Scotland after the disbanding of their Order by the Pope and the King of France in the fourteenth century. The Chapel itself is at least as strange in its architectural details as that other infamous and possibly Templar edifice, Abbe Sauniere's strange church at Rennes-le-Chateau in the Pyrenees, also a must-see on any serious New Age tour. The Order into which she was knighted is a repository of some of these legends and mysteries surrounding the original Templars. Ms. Kennealy, through her initiation into a Celtic coven, then a Welsh Traditionalist coven, and then a Templar Order, manages to represent for us the pagan, Crowleyan and Masonic strains of modern western occultism. Welsh Traditionalist witchcraft is a form of Gardnerian "Wicca" and, as such, is heir to the Crowleyan tradition. The Sovereign Military Order of the Temple of Jerusalem is, by intention, a resurrection of certain Templar ideas and principles which predate Crowley, and the OTO to which he belonged, and which contributed to the creation and survival of the phenomenon of Freemasonry. All of this, and a handfasting to Jim Morrison of The Doors.

At the time that Ms. Kennealy was working with Margot Adler and a Welsh Traditionalist coven in New York City, the Son of Sam murders were in full swing. The witches of Ms. Kennealy's acquaintance were customers of that venerable institution, the Warlock Shop/Magickal Childe Bookstore in both its Brooklyn Heights and then West 19th Street, Manhattan incarnations. Herman Slater's remarkable store was a meeting place for witches of all persuasions, as well as for Satanists, Thelemites, the odd alchemist, Scientologists, and members of the Process. Members of the Son of Sam cult also visited the store on occasion, and several of the young women mentioned in Maury Terry's book on the Sam case—*The Ultimate Evil*—were known to frequent the shop. One day, perhaps, its story will be told in detail. While Terry's book has been ridiculed on pagan and occult Web sites (and often for good reason), much of his data is known to be accurate, even if his conclusions are occasionally off-the-mark or off-the-wall. We will return to this story in the following chapter, but for now let us conclude our study of sinister forces in Hollywood with a look at the background of the Son of Sam cult, as seen through the life and times of one of Hollywood's most famous producers.

Along the way we will look at the film that put serial killer Jeffrey Dahmer into a murderous trance, and discover a director whose work could only be called initiatory in the strictest sense of the term.

BAD TRANSFORMERS

> I learned that just beneath the surface there's another world, and still different worlds as you dig deeper.
>
> —David Lynch[50]

A recurring feature of David Lynch films is the flickering electric light, result—as we are told in the pilot episode of his television series, *Twin Peaks*—of a "bad transformer." This flickering electric light will appear again in such Lynch films as *Mulholland Drive*, to announce the appearance of the Cowboy: a bizarre character who speaks in gnomic riddles, like a cross between Gary Cooper and David Carradine. In *Twin Peaks* it is the light in the morgue over the place where the body of Laura Palmer had been kept, and which is then visited by Mike, the one-armed man, who recites the famous poem:

> Through the darkness of futures past
> The magician longs to see;
> One chants out between two worlds
> "Fire, walk with me."

There, in a strange little verse, we have the key to unlocking the mystery not only of *Twin Peaks* but of virtually all of Lynch's films: the suspension of normal laws of time ("futures past") and the idea that the magician lives "between two worlds." The suspension of a normal, linear narrative event in favor of a dreamlike, hallucinatory set of images that are taking place all over the fourth dimension is part of Lynch's appeal as a director, and part of what makes his films so frustrating to the average filmgoer. His realization that there are two worlds, and a place to stand between them, is what contributes to his aura as a modern, twenty-first century initiate of the Mysteries, for that is what his "mystery" films are: elucidations of the core Mystery behind reality.

> We all find this book of riddles and it's just what's going on. And you can figure them out. The problem is, you figure them out inside yourself, and even if you told somebody, they wouldn't believe you or understand it in the same way you do. You'd suddenly realize that the communication wasn't 100 per cent. There are a lot of things like that going on in life, and words just fail you.[51]

And one of the keys to the mysteries—in fact, their *raison d'etre*—is the very idea of transformation, and of the sinister implications of a "bad transformer." In the same pilot episode of *Twin Peaks* where this throwaway line is used, the conversation is between the one-armed man, Mike (who knows where the serial killer, Bob, is hiding), and FBI Special Agent Dale Cooper. As we discover towards the very end of the very last episode of *Twin Peaks*, it is Cooper himself who becomes a "bad transformer" and who winds up in the "place between the worlds," the dreaded Lodge. Transformation is a central theme of Lynch's films, as characters change identities and places in the space-time continuum with astonishing regularity; and it is closer to an initiated understanding of how reality works than a standard linear narrative could ever be. In Lynch films, there is no such thing as coincidence. The universe is not that lazy, events not that meaningless. Behind every event there lurks a world of information, of relevance, of mysterious connections that link one seemingly innocuous image with another. Telephones, lampshades, ashtrays, coffee cups, dripping water, the wind in the trees . . . everything becomes fraught with sinister, cosmic significance.

One could devote volumes to describing and "decoding" the astrological, alchemical, historical, and political references in Lynch's work, especially in *Twin Peaks*, which is the closest thing we have in modern America to the *Chymical Wedding of Christian Rosenkreutz*. Some professors of religion—such as Mircea Eliade's brilliant Romanian protégé Ioan Culianu—did just that, in Culianu's case holding weekly student seminars on the subject, until his murder in a restroom of the University of Chicago.

It is the idea of transformation that concerns us most at the moment. It was, after all, the principle goal of alchemy to be able to effect transformations, whether of lead into gold or of base humanity into a heightened spiritual state. Jung's interpretation of alchemy tended towards the psychological, of course, and for him the idea of transformation was emblematic of spiritual and psychological growth. His famous forward to a translation of a Chinese alchemical text—*The Secret of the Golden Flower*—is evidence of this, as is the bulk of his considerable writing on the subject of alchemy and on the similarity of alchemical symbols (so beloved of the surrealists) to the drawings of patients undergoing psychotherapy.

Spiritual possession is also a form, albeit temporary, of transformation. From the days when shamans wore animal skins and turned lycanthrope, to the ecstatic dances of Haitian voudoun or Malaysian *kuda kepang*, this type of transformation was temporary in time, but its effects on the psyche of the possessed must be of a long-term nature, setting them apart from other human beings and allowing them to visit, if only for a moment, the "place between the worlds," or what Lynch calls "the Lodge." This concept received a sudden impetus from the research of Charles Darwin concerning evolution, and of Madame Blavatsky's framing of evolution in spiritual as well as racial terms. All at once, the ancient occult and alchemical dream of transformation became respectable: transformation was not only possible, the descent of man through various stages of animal life including most recently those of the simian variety was evidence that even greater evolutionary stages were possible. But . . . evolution, transformation into what? Would humanity one day be considered nothing more than a temporary phase of evolution before an even greater advancement?

Fundamentalist Christianity could not accept Darwinian evolution because it disagreed with the Biblical account of the creation of man; yet, even worse, an acceptance of the possibility of evolution carries with it a greater danger. If humanity is destined for a more perfect modification or more refined mutation in the future, then the incarnated Christ of two thousand years ago was inhabiting an inferior vessel, one that was not made in the "image and likeness of God," for that is yet to come. This is another reason why those who believe in the literal word of the Bible—whatever that is, as one must select from a bewildering array of Biblical translations—cannot accept evolution, and why secret societies embrace it with open arms. They believe it is the soul or spirit that is eternal, that is in the "image and likeness of God," and that the body is a material basis for that spirit, only: a machine, a device that enables the spirit to function in this hostile world. That the machine was perfectible, or at any rate mutable and subject to transformation, was a given, and irrefutable evidence of the possibility of spiritual attainments.

I have declined to quote much Jungian material in this work so far, even though the subject matter practically screams out at times for a Jungian perspective, because it may seem too scholarly or academic an approach to take, and because Jung—as valuable as his insights may be—is too controversial a source. However, we would be amiss if we did not take into consideration what he has said about alchemical transformation, as he was one of the first to realize the psychological nature of the alchemical texts.

In describing one early text, one of the visions of Zosimos, he tells us, concerning transformation,

> The drama shows how the divine process of change manifests itself to our human understanding and how man experiences it—as punishment, torment, death, and transfiguration. The dreamer describes how a man would act and what he would have to suffer if he were drawn into the cycle of the death and rebirth of the gods, and what effect the *deus absconditus* would have if a mortal man should succeed by his "art" in setting free the "guardian of spirits" from his dark dwelling. There are indications in the literature that this is not without its dangers.[52]

In a footnote to this text, he writes,

> The element of torture, so conspicuous in Zosimos, is not uncommon in alchemical literature.[53]

Indeed. As we have seen, torture—specifically including dismemberment and cannibalism—is a common element in shamanistic initiation traditions, although the experience is usually an internalized affair or, as in the case of the Kwakiutl tribe of North America, enacted in ritualized pantomime in memory of a time when it was performed in fact. Transformation comes at a price, a price that can be too heavy for many to bear.

We discussed Mormonism in Book I of this study; we return to it again for confirmation of what we are discussing here. Mormonism shares many beliefs in common with the Gnostics, and many that are diametrically opposed to orthodox Christianity, especially with regard to the possibilities of transformation and of individual human beings attaining Godhead.

As cited in the book *Mormon America: The Power and The Promise* by Richard N. Ostling and Joan K. Ostling (considered a "definite introduction to the Church of Jesus Christ of Latter Day Saints" by *Library Journal*), Mormon apologist B. H. Roberts, in a dialogue with a Jesuit critic, defined three points on which Mormons differ from "traditional" Christians (and, we may assume, traditional Jews and Muslims as well):

> First, we believe that God is a being with a body in form like man's; that he possesses body, parts and passions; that in a word, God is an exalted, perfected man.
>
> Second, we believe in a plurality of Gods.
>
> Third, we believe that somewhere and some time in the ages to come,through development, through enlargement, through purification, until perfection is attained, man at last may become like God—a God.[54]

There is nothing in the above statement that conflicts with occult beliefs, but much that conflicts with the great monotheistic religions. Whether Joseph Smith formulated these ideas before or after his involvement with Freemasonry is moot; he was a practicing magician from early adolescence. In Mormonism, American religion has adopted many occult and hermetic beliefs, including Gnosticism and a belief in transformation. The above statement does not admit to the possibility that today, in this lifetime, a human being may become God; it purposely postpones that possibility until "some time in the ages to come," but at the same time admits that God is "an exalted, perfected man," implying that some of these transformations have—in however isolated a fashion—already taken place. It is not known whether or not Mormonism, perhaps in its more secret conclaves, ever considers the possibility that techniques exist for attaining this goal in this lifetime, but the mere fact that they accept this type of transformation as dogma is intriguing.

Serial killer Jeffrey Dahmer was fascinated with the concept of transformation, for he believed that with transformation came spiritual power. His favorite film was *Exorcist III*, as we have seen, and it is a proper sequel to *The Exorcist,* with some of the original cast and with the original director, William Friedkin. In *Exorcist III*, we meet the demon who was exorcised in the first film, entering the body of a serial killer at the moment it leaves the body of little Regan. The demon has returned as a serial killer, and it was this element of possession/transformation that transfixed Dahmer. Every time the demon would make an appearance on the screen, Dahmer would go into a kind of trance . . . as if willing the demon to enter *him.*

What many people already know is that the original book by William Peter Blatty is based on a genuine case of demonic possession. Dahmer would have known this as well, and his attraction to the theme of *The Exorcist* is at least partly based on the idea that demonic possession is genuine and that the events in the first film were based on reality. The events of the third film became reality . . . through Dahmer, serial killer and cannibal, himself. Is it only coincidence, then, that Blatty was a psychological warfare officer for the US military in the 1960s before he wrote his bestselling novel? And that another Blatty novel, *Twinkle, Twinkle Killer Kane,* was about a military mental hospital, with hints of a mind-control program run amok? Further, that this novel was also made into a film, *The Ninth Configuration* (1980), starring Stacy Keach as the new director of the hospital (set in a castle) who is if anything even more insane than his patients; and that the film was directed by William Peter Blatty himself, and featured Jason Miller: the "Father Damien" of *The Exorcist.* It is as if Blatty is trying to tell us something.

The Exorcist, of course, started all sorts of demonic possession hysteria. One writer who contributed to this sense of the sinister all around us was Malachi Martin, a former Catholic priest, whose book on possession and exorcism in America, *Hostage to the Devil,* was praised by some clergymen even as it was attacked by others. Martin's book begins with a vignette of an Irish Catholic priest in Nanjing at the time of the Japanese invasion. The priest is trying to exorcise a demon from the body of a Chinese Catholic man, a man who has been identified by the Chinese police as . . . a serial killer.

Malachi Martin's *bona fides* have been challenged by Robert Blair Kaiser, a former *Time* Vatican correspondent, who claims in his autobiography that Martin stole his wife and had him committed to a mental institution in order to get rid of him. It is a nasty attack on the late Martin, and represents what has become a general whiff of opprobrium where the former priest is concerned. While the Catholic Church has been officially silent on the matter of Malachi Martin, his books have been popular among a certain segment of the Catholic population, who believe that there is an evil, Satanic element within the Vatican that has hijacked the Church for its own purposes. Martin was writing about this years before revelations exploded about the Vatican banking scandals, the Masonic P-2 society infiltration of the Vatican as high as cardinal level, and the alleged murder of Pope John Paul I after only thirty days as Pontiff.

Thus, it is entirely possible that there are at least two factions within the Church, and that one faction supported Martin's researches and that another firmly opposed them. Martin also alleged that there existed within the Church something he called the "Superforce," which was the name he gave to the cabal of evildoers within the Vatican that perpetrated not only political and financial crimes, but which was also involved in pedophilia and other sexual scandals, some under the guise of a satanic cult of sex abusers. Recent revelations concerning the widespread cover up of pedophilia and other forms of sexual abuse within the Church—a cover up that begins at the highest levels of the Vatican bureaucracy—seem to support Martin's contentions, particularly as, in some cases, this abuse was connected with vaguely ritualistic settings and ceremonies. Whatever the truth behind the mysterious Malachi Martin—who, at one point, had a correspondence with our dear friend Rayelan Russbacher of Barbara Honegger, October Surprise, wandering bishop, and *Les Dances Enchants* fame—his most vocal opponent and the source of the scurrilous rumors about him is Robert Blair Kaiser, in his autobiography *Clerical Error*.

Kaiser's book has been both praised and attacked by Catholics, largely depending upon where they stand where the subject of Father Martin is concerned. Having begun his career as a candidate for the priesthood, spending eight years at a Jesuit seminary, Kaiser abandoned Holy Orders and eventually won a posting with *Time* magazine in Rome, covering the controversial Second Vatican Council ("Vatican II") of Pope John XXIII and winning awards for his reporting in the process, reporting that was assisted in no small part by Malachi Martin. In *Clerical Error*, Kaiser accuses Martin of abusing their relationship by sleeping with his wife while he was a houseguest of the Kaisers. The whole sordid story is there—published, of course, after Martin's death from a stroke in 1999—and it confirms the suspicions of many in the New Church that Father Martin was a sexual predator of vast proclivities who betrayed Church and friend, alike, with reckless abandon.

Yet, defenders of Father Martin point to a paucity of documentation supporting Kaiser's contentions and insist that his period spent in a mental institution—where he was diagnosed as suffering from acute paranoia and schizophrenia—has contributed to a wild tale without foundation, fueled by unresolved psychological issues concerning the Church, the Jesuits, celibacy, and a host of other problems that, perhaps, only lapsed Catholics can fully understand.

How strange, then, that we find Mr. Kaiser three years after the close of Vatican II back in Los Angeles working as a stringer when the Robert F. Kennedy assassination occurred, jumping at the chance to become involved in Sirhan's defense team and gaining unprecedented access to Sirhan for the ostensible purpose of writing a book and some articles as a means of raising money for the defense lawyers.

His book on the case, *RFK Must Die!*, is an oft-cited source for material on the assassination. In fact, according to such authorities as William Klaber and Philip H. Melanson (*Shadow Play: The Untold Story of the Robert F. Kennedy Assassination*), Philip H. Melanson (*The Robert F. Kennedy Assassination: New Revelations on the Conspiracy and Cover-up, 1968–1991*) and William Turner and Jonn Christian (*The Assassination of Robert F. Kennedy: The Conspiracy and Coverup*) there is a lot of speculation about Kaiser's true role as part of Sirhan's defense.

Kaiser shifted gears numerous times during the investigation and subsequent trial, going from conviction that there was a conspiracy involved and that Sirhan was a hypnotically-programmed assassin, to his final verdict that Sirhan acted alone and fired all the shots that killed the Senator.

Reading the Turner and Christian book is an exercise in frustration when it comes to Kaiser's role, for he so obviously had virtually unlimited access to the defendant, the defendant's family, and to investigative intelligence, yet seems to have shared little of this with anyone else, even after the publication of his book on the subject. He can't seem to get to the bottom of Sirhan Sirhan, and admits as much, leaving us to wonder if Kaiser was the right man in the right place at the right time. Courtroom observers have often wondered at the strategy employed by Sirhan's defense team, which did not try to work the evidence in their client's favor, instead working out a plea bargain in advance and permitting Sirhan to hang himself in court with his own words. Even the transcripts of Dr. Bernard Diamond's efforts to hypnotize Sirhan to get at the truth of the assassination read more like a text on brainwashing than an attempt to penetrate Sirhan's unconscious and reveal what actually had taken place, and with the hypnotist leading the subject every step of the way.

Assassinations, demonic possession, serial killers, transformation, Hollywood. It gets stranger.

According to interviews with Malachi Martin and other sources—some available on religious Web sites on the Internet, some via Art Bell's syndicated radio talk shows—self-confessed serial killer David Berkowitz of the Son of Sam killings asked to speak to Fr. Martin while in jail before his sentencing. Martin obliged, and subsequently refused all offers of a book deal or other financial gain from the fruits of that meeting, and probably for good reason.

Fr. Martin, after all, concluded that Berkowitz was possessed by a demon.

THE ULTIMATE EVIL

> . . . and it is in the humble opinion of this narrator that this is not just "something that happened"; this cannot be "one of those things"; this, please, cannot be that. . . . this was not just a matter of chance. Huh! These strange things happen all the time.
>
> —"The Narrator," *Magnolia* (1999), Paul Thomas Anderson

> The essential magical work, apart from any particular operation, is the proper formation of the Magical Being or Body of Light.
>
> —Chapter XI, "Of Our Lady Babalon and of the Beast Whereon She Rideth. Also Concerning Transformations." *Magick in Theory and Practice*, Aleister Crowley[55]

It may seem odd that this look at sinister forces at work in Hollywood would lead us to the Son of Sam cult, but that is the nature of the Beast. We, as humans and especially as historians, academics, etc., think in terms of genre, of categories. Life, however, does not itself fit so easily into categories. Neither does our experience of life. The forces at work in assassinations manifest just as easily in works of art, for instance. The goal of alchemy is something called the Great Work, or *Magnum Opus*. This Great Work is symbolized by the production of the Philosopher's Stone, the object which effects transformation. The Great Work itself is not necessarily a purely alchemical accomplishment; it can be attained by other means. It is, from the point of view of modern western occultists, the perfect uniting in oneself of macrocosm and microcosm: mastery over one giving you automatic mastery over the other. This can be accomplished through yoga, for instance, as much as through alchemy, or ceremonial magic, or musical composition, painting, literature, architecture, or many other pursuits. That is why the great accomplishments of the artist are called by the same name—*Magnum Opus*, or Great Work—as the great accomplishment of the alchemist and magician.

Two types of individuals can lay claim to the status of those who have attained the Great Work. There are the public figures who, by virtue of their obvious attainments and contributions to society, seem destined to achieve the Great Work: presidents, generals, movie stars. Their intense personal focus on the Work in their lives leads them through fields of obstacles and to confrontation with the darker forces at work in the world even as they insist on continuing their quest regardless of the dangers. They typify for us what mythologian Joseph Campbell called "the hero with a thousand faces."

There is another type, however, and this individual may remain completely unknown and unrecognized until that moment in time when something exceedingly brilliant—or, more often, exceedingly vile—occurs as a result of the pressure-cooker nature of internalizing the psychological process, the intense focus, to a point of no return. This type of individual is just as focused as the first type, just as inexorable in his pursuit of the Work, but the result is usually an explosion, a slaughter, a catastrophe.

The Great Work is not an end in itself. It is a preliminary to greater accomplishments, but those which cannot be easily described or categorized. A person who has accomplished the Great Work may remain completely anonymous; conversely, he or she may dive deeply into society and work very hard to improve the lives of others. In any case, the fact that someone has accomplished the Great Work will not be obvious to those who have not, themselves, done the same. In fact, accomplishing the Great Work does not automatically imply a future of good works and good thoughts. There are those who have chosen an evil path, according to the literature, and use their hard-won knowledge and insight to further their own, very personal and often very sinister, ends. These are known as "brothers of the left-hand path" or "black magicians." It is generally acknowledged that further spiritual growth is impossible for them; however, they themselves often do not recognize any possible growth beyond what they have already accomplished.

This is obviously a discussion for initiates . . . or, at least, people who consider themselves initiates! For us, it is enough to track the existence of those who have accomplished the Great Work, who are adept at transformation, and who understand the workings of reality to such an extent that they can make use of what appear to the rest of us to be useless information, useless objects, meaningless events. Because to become a master of these sinister forces is to become a master of the phenomenon of coincidence, of correspondences, of synchronicity.

And, as such, of memory.

The "art of memory" was investigated in recent times by Dame Frances A. Yates, who understood the intricate "memory palaces" as having links with Renaissance magic, and how the art of memory itself was accused of being a "black art,"[56] even as Aristotle professed to find God resident in memory.[57] Describing in some detail the memory systems of Giordano Bruno, Raymond Lull and Robert Fludd—all famous occult scholars who wielded enormous influence over generations of hermeticists—she demonstrated how closely related were the *ars memorandi* and mystical thought. In addition, and clearly pertinent to our study, is her discovery of the fact that Robert Fludd's theater of memory is based on the actual Globe Theater of Shakespearean fame . . . or, conversely, that the Globe Theater was, itself, designed along hermetic lines in accord with occult principles: another instance of the close relationship between dramaturgy and thaumaturgy.[58]

> Thoughts occur to one of the possibility of using Fludd's revelations, not only for the understanding of the actual staging of Shakespeare's plays, but also for an interpretation of the relative spiritual significance of scenes played on different levels. Is the Shakespearean stage a Renaissance and Hermetic transformation of the old religious stage?[59]

In regards to this virtually lost art, it can be described simply: one trained one's memory by imagining a vast hall or other building filled with niches, columns, and levels into or onto which one put an element of the thing one was trying to memorize. It could be a line from a speech, or a mathematical formula, or anything at all. For convenience, one would choose an existing building, such as a cathedral, and memorize its architecture carefully. Then, one would take pieces of the thing to be memorized and associate them in turn with the statues, the columns, the entrances and exits, and other ornamentation, with each statue, etc. calling forth the associated idea in one's memory. In this way, the theater of memory would be filled with images corresponding to the target memories. The theater of memory served as a template, with the memories assigned to their respective positions on the template.

In the days before teleprompters, computer disks and PDAs, a powerful memory was an enormous asset in business, politics and, of course, the theater. Memory also permitted one to see associations that others would miss, because recurring patterns of behavior and natural events would become clear if one remembered past incidents and could relate them in some way to present issues. It was a means of reducing the pernicious effects of chance, much the same way card-counters win at blackjack.

Occultists already had such a system in place, the product of their efforts to reduce all of creation onto, or into, a kind of map. Qabalists had already contributed to this concept by asserting that the Torah contained encoded information that could be understood only by converting the Hebrew letters of the sacred texts to their numerical equivalents and discovering associations between words that had the same numerical value; from there, they went on to create the map of creation known as the Tree of Life upon which all things could be found.

In medieval Europe, as in India and China, the human body was also a map that could be studied for clues to how the universe worked. By associating various planets and stars with individual organs and limbs, the ancients could duplicate celestial events on a very human scale. The Hindu system of *chakras* is just such a map, with mystical and astrological associations developed for neurological centers along the spinal column, each with its own colors, letters, mantras, etc. "Raising the serpent Kundalini" along this path was tantamount to walking to the stars, each step bringing with it greater insights and greater powers. *Chakra* means "wheel" or "sphere," and the Qabalists likewise called their stations along the Tree of Life *sephira*, the Hebrew for "sphere," and often depicted their Tree of Life overlayed on an image of a man, the "perfect man" or "Adam Kadmon." The similarities between the Indian and the Qabalistic systems are very compelling, and they are joined by an almost identical system of the Daoist Chinese, that of the *Shangqing* school of Daoist alchemy.

Lest readers wonder at the relevance of Qabalism and Hindu mythology to this subject, let us point out one exemplar of modern culture's appropriation of these ancient mystic beliefs. There is probably no person of 1980s and 1990s American popular culture that represents better the conflicting spiritual forces we are discussing than Madonna. A young woman of Italian-American descent who became a huge force in popular music and the MTV age of the music video, Madonna shocked the world with the video accompanying her song "Like A Prayer" as the 1980s came to a close. While the lyrics to the song itself are not overtly religious or spiritual in nature—they are more like a traditional love song—the music video was another matter. Shot in a church, with Madonna in her usual *deshabille*, it features scenes of a statue of a black saint coming to life and kissing Madonna on the lips while outside the church white thugs attack a young black man they mistakenly believe has committed a murder. By combining elements of race, religion and even sex in one video that takes place in a Catholic church, with a choir singing backup, no less, it was a forceful attack on the Church, and moreover one that used only images and rather inoffensive lyrics to make its point.

Madonna later followed this up with a collection of her "hits" under the title *Immaculate Collection*, an obvious allusion to the Catholic doctrine of the Immaculate Conception. And when Irish pop singer Sinead O'Connor tore up a photograph of the Pope on live television and in front of a stunned audience (on NBC's *Saturday Night Live*) with the admonition "Fight the real enemy," basically stealing Madonna's thunder, Madonna herself responded humorously and intelligently the following week by tearing up a photograph of Joey Buttafuoco (of the infamous "Long Island Lolita" attempted-murder case) with the same pithy admonition.

But what makes all of this much more interesting is the fact that a decade later Madonna began a serious study of the Qabala at a Los Angeles temple. From a Catholic upbringing, to an attack on the organized Church, to a study of the Qabala . . . this is essentially the same route many lapsed Catholics have taken since the Second Vatican Council of the early 1960s, and it smacks of a return to Gnosticism. The Catholic and the Qabalist mindsets are entirely different: the difference between faith and curiosity, perhaps. It also reveals a sense that there are underlying forces at work in the universe that traditional religious instruction never adequately addresses, and for which it certainly never provides theory and practice. That Madonna has also studied yoga and other Eastern philosophies is well-known; some of her later music videos depict her in Hindu dress, while another has her hands bearing the henna tattoos of the Middle East.

A common factor underlying these systems in vastly different cultures is the idea that there is another world, another reality, either parallel to ours or at times (and places) tangential to ours, and that subjecting the human body to tightly-focused control by a trained mind can open the gate to this other reality as the body's resources—neurological, biochemical—are diverted towards this end. The other means of opening the gate is, as we have already shown, the "derangement of the senses" championed by the surrealists and the shamans. The lack of conscious control in the latter method is considered quite dangerous by adepts, although it is a faster route. For that reason, the "fast approach" is usually undertaken in groups, so that there is the possibility of intervention by a more experienced practitioner should an emergency arise. The first method can be undertaken by a solo operator as long as a strict regimen is followed, gradually building up conscious control of what are, after all, unconscious processes. In his excellent forward to the collected works of alchemist Thomas Vaughan, Beat hero Kenneth Rexroth describes this process "conscious control of the autonomic nervous system"; this it is, of course, but such control is not the goal but only the tool, the instrument, to the opening of this "gate."

We have shown in the previous chapter many points of similarity between the serial killer and the shaman, even to the extent of demonstrating how—in some cases, at least, for which we have adequate documentation—they share a fascination with the idea of transformation. The Behavioral Sciences Unit at the FBI's training academy at Quantico has been credited with developing the distinction between the organized and the disorganized serial killer, and with creating the famous "profiles" which aid local law enforcement personnel in their hunt for this most difficult of murderers to apprehend. Often, as in any other science, evidence is sometimes bent to fit a theory, however. It is the contention of this study that Charles Manson and David Berkowitz were not serial killers in the classic sense. They represent a different phenomenon entirely, and one that we will examine in this and the chapter to follow.

Maury Terry has insisted that there is a connection between Charles Manson and David Berkowitz, and he has based this conclusion largely on jailhouse confessions and some controversial interviews with convicted felons. His research has been attacked in many cases, especially as it has contributed to the rise of "satanic cult survivor hysteria" in the 1980s and 1990s in the United States. Some of his conclusions have been drawn from an idiosyncratic decoding of the "Son of Sam" letters to the press and by a loose association of the dates of the Sam murders to dates with alleged occult significance. In this regard, Terry has followed (probably unconsciously) in the footsteps of more venerable scholars of the occult, people like Dame Frances A. Yates and, more recently, David Ovason who, in books such as *The Zelator* and *The Secrets of Nostradamus*, discusses something he calls the "green language" (after Fulcanelli), and which former AP reporter and right-wing conspiriologist Michael A. Hoffman II calls "twilight language."[60] These authors find that the enigmatic references in everything from the prophecies of Nostradamus and modern political propaganda to the gnomic alchemical and Rosicrucian texts conceal a deeper meaning which is easier to understand once you have the key. Both Terry and Hoffman understand—from their radically different perspectives—that language conceals as much as it reveals, and that occultists have made liberal use of this characteristic to disguise more profound, more sinister truths about everything from world events to inner, psychological states. The problem, as always, lies in interpretation.

When Charles Manson "deconstructed" the lyrics to the Beatles' *White Album,* he was employing his own version of the "green language," believing that the Beatles were, in some way, mystical adepts who were communicating with their followers directly in coded messages in their songs. Thus, the song "Revolution 9" became, for Manson, "Revelations 9," a Biblical reference to the Apocalypse. The socio-political agenda of the Manson Family became "Helter Skelter," a reference to the title of another *White Album* song, etc.

Terry is guilty of the same type of deconstruction attempt on the Son of Sam letters, and for this he has been criticized by people claiming to be occultists. A long and detailed attack on Terry's book by someone named G. M. Kelly and posted on the Internet by something called the "Castle of the Silver Star",[61] is a case in point. We are to understand that Kelly is a Thelemite, a follower of Crowley, as he begins his review of Terry's book with the salutation "Do what thou wilt shall be the whole of the Law," which is standard among members of the OTO and other followers of Thelema. Kelly is not, however, a member of the Grady McMurtry faction of the OTO which he terms the "Caliphate pseudo-O.T.O." and an "enemy of human evolution." (The insertion of human evolution into the argument supports my thesis that occult organizations tend to believe in the fact or possibility of human evolution, as opposed to more traditional organized religions that either oppose the idea or are sceptical about it.) Thus, his perspective is that of one who has been (deliberately or inadvertently) attacked by the conclusions printed in Terry's book and who is thus defending occultism (and specifically the Crowleyan kind) from Terry's shotgun approach.

Kelly argues, and quite rightly, that Terry goes overboard in his analysis of the Son of Sam letters and other details about the Son of Sam killings and related matters including—and most importantly—Terry's understanding of the nature of cults. To Terry, virtually everything that is not a socially accepted organized religion in America is a cult. This is a trap into which many have fallen at one time or another, including Attorney General Janet Reno in her doomed opposition to the Branch Davidians in Waco, Texas. How do we define a cult in a country that celebrates freedom of religion and which was, itself, founded by members of what was, essentially, a cult? From the Puritans who managed the first Thanksgiving to Freemasons such as George Washington, America was seeded with cults. To the English government, the fleeing Puritans were certainly heretics and cultists, as were eventually the Huegenots, the Plymouth Brethren, and—to the Catholic Church—the Lutherans, Presbyterians, etc.

Without going into the minutiae of the various murders and other phenomena that Kelly analyzes—putting off until the next chapter a more penetrating look at the Son of Sam case—let us look at what he says concerning the Son of Sam letters.

As is well-known, during the crime spree known as the Son of Sam killings, someone sent letters to the newspapers boasting of the crimes, much in the same way the Jack the Ripper killings were accompanied by letters from the murderer to the police and the newspapers a hundred years earlier.

One of the letters, known as the "Borrelli letter" and supposedly written by David Berkowitz and dropped at the Suriani-Esau crime scene for the attention of NYPD Captain Joseph Borrelli, states,

> *I am the "Son of Sam."*

And,

> *I am on a different wave*
> *length then everybody*
> *else—programmed to*
> *kill.*

And,

> *I am the "monster"—*
> *"Beelzebub"—the*
> *"Chubby Behemouth."*[62]

A programmed killer who is also a demoniac. Clearly, the writer was working within a venerable tradition!

The NYPD released a psychiatric profile of the Sam killer on May 26, 1977, after analyzing the Borrelli letter and coming to the conclusion that the killer was:

> . . . neurotic, schizophrenic and paranoid—dime-store definitions resulting from remote analyses by the psychiatrists. The profile also suggested that the killer might regard himself as a victim of "demonic possession."[63]

PAGING FATHER MARTIN

Terry's book describes a conversation between him and Larry Siegel, a "well-informed researcher and professional writer," who, at Terry's suggestion, began to investigate the occult with an eye to unlocking the secrets of the Sam letters. They latched immediately onto the references to Beelzebub and "Behemouth" in the Borrelli letter, as they were Biblical demons; but where the conversation turns "green" or "twilight" is in their interpretation of Behemouth (or, actually, Behemoth) as a demon represented as an elephant, and the name of the Elephas Disco near where one of the Sam killings took place. As the letter to Borrelli was dropped weeks before the Elephas attack—and *elephas* being the Latin for "elephant" and hence, by association, to the "Chubby Behemouth"—Terry and Siegel felt they had proof that the killings were planned in advance, not random, particularly as the writer of the letter stated that the "wemon of Queens are z prettyest of all," even as the letter itself was dropped at a *Bronx* crime scene and Elephas was in Queens.[64]

This does seem to strain "coincidence," but Kelly does not mention this in his lengthy attack on *The Ultimate Evil*, only pointing out that Beelzebub and Behemoth were more likely references to a Judeo-Christian context than a satanic one . . . even as he decries satanism as nothing more than an "extreme overreaction to extreme Judeo-Christian religious ethics and restrictions"! Kelly is trying to have his cake and eat it, too. Satanism and Judeao-Christianity are inextricably linked, the one a reaction to and defiance of the other, so it is natural to expect Biblical references in satanic literature. Kelly is correct in attempting to distance Thelema and modern, New Age paganism from Judeo-Christianity, of course; but his case is made more difficult by Crowley himself, who incorporated a "Gnostic Mass" into his repertoire of occult ceremonies and constantly referred to himself as the Great Beast mentioned in the Apocalypse and to his consorts as "Scarlet Women." The fact is that it is extremely difficult to extricate Judeo-Christianity from Thelema, especially in view of Crowley's own writings on occult themes, which are hardly ever purely pagan or non-Judeo-Christian.

Kelly's problem with Terry's book is probably less with Terry's leaps of logic than with the possible reaction to Terry's thesis by people who would "use books like Maury Terry's to evoke a new form of the Inquisition."[65] Kelly, as a self-described "serious student of the so-called 'occult' now for at least two decades" can "definitely say that there is nothing whatsoever in the Borrelli letter to indicate any great knowledge of any esoteric or occult subject,"[66] Yet, the unusual references to "Chubby Behemouth" and the "wemon of Queens" and a subsequent attack at the Elephas Disco in Queens weeks later, implies someone with a somewhat deeper understanding of occultism than the somewhat airy phrases of the Borrelli letter initially suggest, regardless of Kelly's demurral.

I believe the problem lies in affiliations.

G.M. Kelly firmly defines his identity as a Thelemite and a serious student of the occult for decades; normally, this implies a certain tradition that can be traced through the OTO and the Golden Dawn, back to Freemasonry and the Rosicrucians and the Knights Templar. It is a specific train of esoteric thought and practice, and the various branches share a common language, even as they may be at loggerheads with each other over minutiae of ritual or interpretation.

But there are other organizations that have only the most tenuous of affiliation with the standard occult secret societies, and which determine their own "tradition" without regard to the standard texts. There is certainly nothing in the available literature on the hermetic secret societies of the West to show that human sacrifice was an acceptable part of the ritual, yet to deny that ritual murder ever has taken place in the past is to deny a healthy part of human history. Recently, in fact, we have the Matamoros cult that was responsible for a number of ritual murders in Mexico and Texas: a group that was supposedly practicing a form of Latin shamanism known as *palo mayombe*, even as "legitimate" practitioners insisted that the Matamoros group had no legal standing within their religion. The Matamoros cult—which involved trafficking in illegal drugs across the Mexican-Texas border—was only revealed in 1989, two years *after* the publication of Terry's book insisting there was an occult "culture" surrounding certain elements of the international drug trade. Thus, if we posit a secret society—a cult, if you will—that engages in this type of ritual murder, then we must expect that they do not take their ceremonial guidance from the same sources wherein Mr. Kelly finds his spiritual comfort, or that, if they do, their interpretation of these sources is at wide variance from those enjoyed by Kelly and other Thelemites.

The "great satanic network" described by Maury Terry has nothing to do with the OTO as it is known today. As I say in *Unholy Alliance*, the McMurtry version of the OTO, at least, could not organize a bake sale much less a calendar of premeditated murder. But individuals who had once been members of the OTO could have become involved in any kind of criminal activity; and this is where the rules of evidence are necessary in order to define what was cult activity and what were simply the actions of people who had once been involved with a cult. And, in the case of the Son of Sam cult and its alleged connections with Charles Manson and other murders throughout the United States, we have to accept that we may be dealing with a stranger phenomenon that simply a gaggle of self-involved, poor-complexioned, wide-eyed, robe-wearing adolescents waving fancy cutlery and howling at the moon.

What captures our attention here, however, is the way Terry has interpreted the Son of Sam letters, looking for occult content to support his idea that a nationwide network of satanic killers was involved in the Sam killings. The fact that one of the probable members of this cult, Michael Carr, was born on October 12—the same birthday as Aleister Crowley—is taken as relevant, as if Mr. Carr had been able to choose his birthday with that in mind. Also, as Kelly points out, October 12 is Columbus Day in America, the day Columbus first set eyes on the New World—a mission influenced, as we saw in Book I, by a desire to mount another Crusade to take Jerusalem away from the Muslims. In any event, being born on Crowley's birthday does not imply satanic tendencies!

Another piece of "green interpretation" is Terry's wild analysis of a phrase in the "Breslin letter," a letter from the Sam killer to *Daily News* columnist Jimmy Breslin. The phrase that bothered Terry was a simple one, but set apart from the rest of the letter by quotation marks, as were other suggestive phrases:

> *"Keep 'em*
> *digging, drive on, think*
> *positive, get off your*
> *butts, knock on coffins, etc."*[67]

Terry "deconstructs" what seems to be a simple and obvious sentence into actual directions to David Berkowitz's apartment! He begins by stating that he uses two techniques, one a kind of "crossword puzzle type of system"[68] and what he calls a "common satanist trick: spelling words backwards."[69] The latter he probably derives from that standard novelistic description of a Black Mass which has its participants reciting the Lord's Prayer backwards, but . . . who knows? In any event, the method bears bizarre fruit.

By spelling "keep 'em" backwards, he gets "peek me"; "digging" he believes is a reference to "digs" or home. Thus, he translates this first phrase as "LOOK FOR ME HOME."[70]

Again: "drive on" becomes "drive no" the "no" meaning "north," so that he gets "drive north" or "NORTH AVENUE."[71]

For "think positive" he eventually derives "HEAD RIGHT."[72]

For "get off your butts" he translates "butts" as cigarette butts and therefore as "ash," obtaining "GET OFF ASH."[73]

Finally, "knock on coffins" becomes "KNOCK ON PINE," since a coffin is a "pine box."

To continue with Terry's own words:

> . . . to reach David Berkowitz's apartment from any of the major routes out of New York City—site of the investigation—one would exit the parkways or thruways, drive across Ashburton Avenue, head right off Ashburton onto North Broadway and proceed to Pine.[74]

Realizing, perhaps, that he was straining credulity with this analysis, he goes straight to Benoit Mandelbrot, he of the Mandelbrot Set and discoverer of fractals, a famous mathematician, who looked over the Sam letter and Terry's accompanying analysis and concluded,

> The odds against one phrase being accurate were small; against two being on target they increased dramatically; and so forth. Finally, the odds against all five—in order—leading step by step to the right address were almost impossible to calculate as a coincidence or an unintentional happening.
>
> "So, " Mandelbrot intoned, "it's not a coincidence. What you have done is correct. If you sent me a letter, what do you think the odds would be that I could get step-by-step directions to your house out of five successive phrases if you didn't intend to word your writing in such a manner?"[75]

There are many more such leaps of logic in Terry's work, and we won't go into them all. However, instances like the several mentioned above demonstrate the activity of something deeper at work than mere chance or coincidence, popularly understood. Occultists like Kelly ignore this type of evidence, even as it supports their core contention: that there is an alternate reality parallel or tangential to our own that manifests in symbols, whether of events, dates, places, objects, etc. This reality may be an artificial construct of some group or "cult"; or it may be a physical, "objective" reality. Or there may be no difference between the two. But this reality, whatever its theoretical basis, may be manipulated, and so cause change to occur in this world, even as the other world is changed in turn. The evidence points to only two possible conclusions: that there is at work in the world a relatively sophisticated conspiracy of occultists involved in ritual murders, or that there is in operation a force behind events in the world that we don't understand.

It was this blurring of boundaries between David Lynch's "two worlds" that led to a murder scandal surrounding *Rosemary's Baby* producer Bob Evans, a sophisticated drug-running operation, political and police corruption, serial murder, mysterious cults, and the existence of a "Manson II." It will even lead, however briefly, straight back to Ashland, Kentucky.

Fire, walk with me.

ENDNOTES

1 Mircea Eliade, *The Myth of the Eternal Return*, Bollingen Series XLVI, Princeton University Press, NJ, p. 14–15
2 Henry Miller, *The Time of the Assassins: A Study of Rimbaud*, New Directions, NY, 1962, p. 33
3 Carl G. Jung, *Memories, Dreams, Reflections*, Vintage Books, NY, 1963, p. 329
4 Konstantin Stanislavski, *An Actor Prepares*, Routledge/Theatre Arts, NY, 1989, 1936, p. 176
5 Ibid., p. 199
6 Ibid., p. 13
7 Ibid., p. 14
8 Kenneth Anger, *Hollywood Babylon*, Dell, NY, 1981, p. 413
9 Michael Baigent, Richard Leigh, Henry Lincoln, *Holy Blood, Holy Grail*, Dell, NY, 1983, p. 157-158
10 Sandy Robertson, *The Aleister Crowley Scrapbook* , Samuel Weiser, NY, 1988, p. 83–87
11 Maury Terry, *The Ultimate Evil*, Barnes & Noble, NY, 1999, p. 533–534
12 Ali MacGraw, *Moving Pictures*, Bantam, NY, 1992, p. 41
13 Christopher Andersen, *Citizen Jane: The Turbulent Life of Jane Fonda*, Henry Holt, NY, 1990, p. 180–181
14 Ibid., p. 180
15 Ed Sanders, *The Family*, E.P. Dutton, NY, 1971, p. 164
16 Robert Maheu & Richard Hack, *Next To Hughes*, HarperCollins, NY, 1992, p. 87
17 Ed Sanders, *The Family*, (Revised and Updated Edition), Signet, NY, 1990, p. 404
18 Ibid., p. 405
19 Ibid., p. 294–295
20 Stephen Fay, Lewis Chester, Magnus Linklater, *Hoax*, Viking, NY, 1972, p. 309 and p. 240
21 Ibid., p. 340
22 Donald H. Wolfe, *The Assassination of Marilyn Monroe*, Warner Books, NY, 1998, p. 541
23 Ibid., p. 477
24 Ibid., p. 475
25 Ibid., p. 476
26 Ibid., p. 476
27 Ibid., p. 487
28 Ibid., p. 487
29 Ibid., p. 468–471
30 Ibid., p. 538–539
31 Anthony Summers, *Goddess: The Secret Lives of Marilyn Monroe*, Indigo, London, 1985, p. 540
32 Wolfe, op. cit., p. 452, 540–1
33 Ibid., p. 541
34 Ibid., p. 540
35 Robert F. Slatzer, *The Life and Curious Death of Marilyn Monroe*, Pinnacle, NY, 1974, p. 6–23
36 Wolfe, op. cit., p. 547
37 Ibid., p. 547
38 Ibid., p. 557
39 A.O. Scott, *International Herald Tribune*, April 22, 2003, p. 18
40 Summers (1985), p. 41
41 Slatzer, op. cit., p. 156-168
42 Ibid., p. 281
43 Wolfe, op. cit., p. 450
44 Ibid., p. 555
45 From David & David, *Bobby Kennedy, the Making of a Folk Hero*, cited in Gus Russo, *Live By The Sword*, Bancroft, Baltimore, 1998, p. 381
46 Eugene K. Bird, *Prisoner #7: Rudolf Hess*, Viking, NY, 1974
47 Cited in *Skull Session* by Daniel Hecht, 1998, Signet, NY
48 Adolf Guggenbühl-Craig, *From The Wrong Side*, Spring, Woodstock CT, 1995, p. 78–79
49 From "Opening Her Own Doors: Patricia's Portrait, Jim Morrison—A Shaman's Showman," *Pagan Muse & World Report*, Fall, 1996
50 David Lynch, in *Lynch on Lynch*, Chris Rodley, Faber and Faber, London, 1997, p. 8

51 Ibid., p. 25–26
52 C.G. Jung, *Alchemical Studies*, Bollingen Foundation, NY, 1967, p. 105
53 Ibid., p. 105
54 Richard N. Ostling & Joan K. Ostling, Mormon America: The Power and the Promise, Harper-SanFrancisco, 2000, p. 297
55 Aleister Crowley, *Magic In Theory and Practice*, Dover, NY, 1976, p. 88
56 Frances A. Yates, *The Art of Memory*, The University of Chicago Press, Chicago, 1966, p. 42–43
57 Ibid., p. 47
58 Ibid., p. 342–367
59 Ibid., p. 365
60 Michael A. Hoffman II, *Secret Societies and Psychological Warfare*, Independent History and Research, Coeur d'Ilene, Idaho, 2001
61 http://www.geocities.com/Athens/Parthenon/7069/index.html
62 Maury Terry, op. cit., p.44–45
63 Ibid., p. 47
64 Ibid., p. 164–166
65 http://www.geocities.com/Athens/Parthenon/7069/index.html
66 http://www.geocities.com/Athens/Parthenon/7069/index.html
67 Maury Terry, op. cit., p. 50
68 Ibid., p. 119
69 Ibid., p. 119
70 Ibid., p. 119
71 Ibid., p. 119
72 Ibid., p. 120
73 Ibid., p. 120
74 Ibid., p. 120
75 Ibid., p. 121

HOLLYW

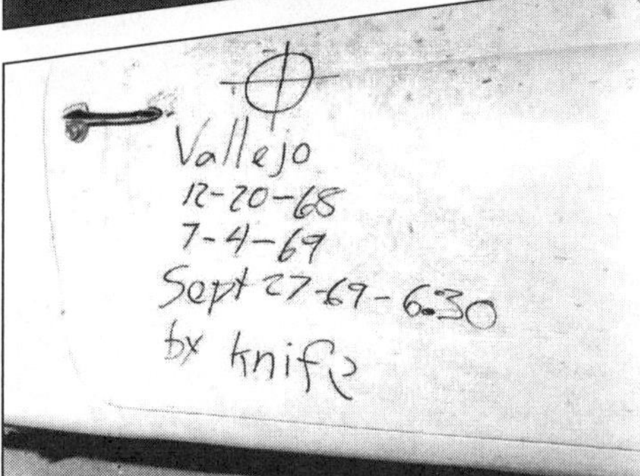
Vallejo
12-20-68
7-4-69
Sept 27-69-630
by knife

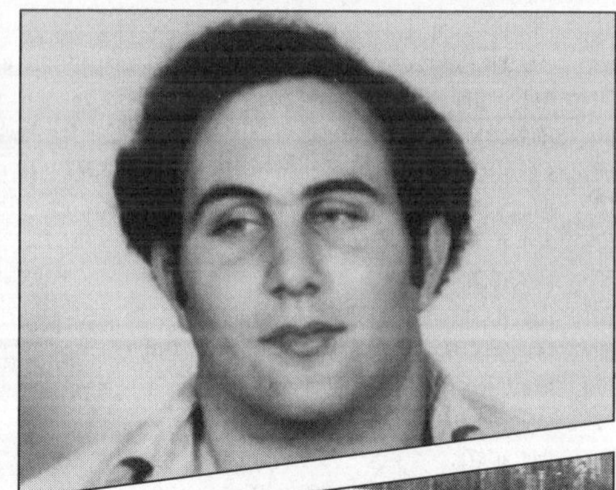

BOOK THREE: THE MANSON SECRET

CHAPTER NINETEEN

AN AMERICAN DREAM

> "I saw a man once just after he came back from a killing. You looked like he did."
> "How did he look?"
> "Like he'd been painted with a touch of magic."
> —Norman Mailer, *An American Dream*

In the previous chapter we discussed some of the occult influences swirling around the Hollywood music and movie scene, focusing on the 1960s and 1970s. Readers may wonder why I bother to mention Hollywood at all, since it seems somewhat out of place in a book that takes history seriously, and history is the stuff of dictators and armies, kings and presidents, economic boom and bust. As I hope I have indicated—and supported—adequately thus far, it is as impossible to extricate the arts from politics as it is religion from politics. Indeed, one may say that religion occupies the middle pew between art and politics, partaking as it does of the powers and conceits of both. So much more so the phenomenon of the secret society, the mystic cult.

If we—in concert with Giordano Bruno and with Professor Culianu as our guides—understand that the power behind the connections between events and persons, the fuel of the magic link itself, is *eros*, then we can come to no greater comprehension of American history over the past century than to realize the central position occupied by sex, and how quickly and almost effortlessly sex leads us to art on the one hand, and to murder on the other.

Thus, critical to our thesis is the story of the interpenetration of Hollywood and homicide, for the "scarlet thread of murder" that is woven through the fabric of history is one of those elements that reveals to us the existence of the sinister forces of which we speak. Murder makes everything relevant: blood samples, blood patterns, body temperature, time of day, day of year, hair, semen, cloth, fur, positioning of body, placement of body in relation to other objects, rigor mortis . . . in short, the entire crime scene—like those medieval woodcuts of the human body showing signs of the zodiac representing various organs—takes on cosmic significance; and the doctrine of correspondences is probably nowhere as prominent in the thinking of scientists as it is in that of criminologists, and no crime scene is as pregnant with meaning—deep, profound meaning—as that of the serial killer, whose mental images, whose fantasies, fuel the act itself and are revealed in its arrangements. For both murder and sex, the human body is at once the *image*, the representation of either hatred or lust, and the place where the desired act is performed, the object upon which it is perpetrated, the physical *link* itself. Often, movie stars themselves are hunted, stalked and slain by deranged fans who have no real idea of who the star is, of the star's actual personality or genuine nature, but only what was visible on the screen, the image of the star, so powerful is this new medium, so ancient in its origins among the rituals and magic of our ancestors.

It is for this reason that we are compelled to look closely at a series of murders that took place between 1977 and 1983, and also beyond. These killings involved some of the most powerful, most famous names in the movie business . . . and some of the least known, least respected as well. The culture of drugs, cults, and death overtook the culture of the screen, and for a brief moment the veil of the dark temple was lifted by a corner, and a whiff of sulphur and satanism escaped into the disbelieving world. Appropriately enough, the central character in this episode was the producer of Roman Polanski's film, *Rosemary's Baby* : Robert Evans. Evans would go on to marry Ali MacGraw—the actress whose father was the mystic of Bedford Village—and Phyllis George, a former Miss America who later married a governor of the Commonwealth of Kentucky, a governor involved in the drugs and money scandal surrounding an organization known only as "the Company."

Evans was involved in a homicide, one with tentacles reaching from New York to Los Angeles, from Miami to Bogota . . . and from Charles Manson to a second killer known as Manson II . . . and a spate of homicides known to the press as the Son of Sam killings. What we have read so far about occultism and Hollywood finds its epitome in this single example, as so many of the characters overlap between the Roy Radin homicide case in 1983 and the Manson Family environment in 1969, with the Son of Sam murders taking place in the interim. As with every facet of American history we have investigated so far, we will see that the coincidences pile up in remarkable ways and considerable volume, and we have to ask ourselves again that question: is all this the result of a conspiracy, as many would have us believe? Or is it the result of something deeper and more mysterious, but no less threatening?

Is it the Manson Secret?

A BRONX TALE

Maury Terry, the investigative journalist whose *The Ultimate Evil* started a landslide of satanic cult hysteria in the United States in the late 1980s, as he delved deeply into the Son of Sam murder mystery, discovered that he had actually gone to high school with John Carr, one of the suspects in the re-opened case who was killed by a shotgun blast to the head at an Air Force base in North Dakota. In the spirit of historical accuracy and complete disclosure, therefore, I must make a similar declaration.

I am a graduate of Christopher Columbus High School, in the Bronx. This institution boasts at least two well-known alumni. One is pioneer transsexual Christine Jorgensen. The other is confessed Son of Sam killer David Berkowitz.

I cannot claim to have known Berkowitz in high school, since I graduated in 1968 and he started at Columbus in 1969, but he would have read my article on alchemy and the transmutation of metals in the school's "literary-arts magazine," *Horizon*, which was published that year. In fact, Berkowitz lived for a while on Barnes Avenue in the Bronx, a few blocks from where I lived on Revere Avenue. And he worked as a security guard at Co-Op City, very close by.

And we had friends in common.

During my last two years at Columbus, I was friendly with a number of people who lived in and near Pelham Bay Park, which is in the same area of the northeastern Bronx as Barnes and Revere Avenues, a few subway station stops north of Westchester Square and at the end of the Number 6 line (the famous "Pelham 1-2-3"). In those years, 1967–1969, there was a lot of mysticism going on in the United States, and the Bronx was no exception. These individuals were very involved in ritual practices, as they understood them. (Some were even teachers at the high school.) We held séances together in Pelham Bay, near where Co-Op City now stands; some of us even tried summoning demons. As a text, we relied upon A. E. Waite's *Book of Ceremonial* Magic (or, in its more ominous incarnation, *The Book of Black Magic and of Pacts*). Vietnam was in full heat, and there were many of us who would go off to the jungles, never to return. We wanted to know what was really "out there," of what strange stuff reality was really composed. We knew the Church was not telling us everything; we knew the government was lying to us about so much, starting with Dallas in 1963. We questioned all authority, and with reason. Authority had let us down; authority was sending us to die in a war no one understood. We knew there were secrets, and we resented that, resented the fact that we could die without knowing the Truth. To that end, we read the works of Marx and Engels, Mao and Angela Davis and Abbie Hoffman, side by side with Aleister Crowley, Eliphas Levi, and MacGregor Mathers.

To that end, we scrupulously copied down arcane ceremonies and mispronounced Greek and Hebrew incantations (although we could be counted upon to get the Latin right, altar boys as some of us had been before the days of Vatican II and the vernacular Mass). We made our own instruments and tools "of Art": wands, knives, swords, robes, and censers.

We stalked the dead lands of pre-Co-Op City in the middle of the night, lit candles in the dark and chanted to the Moon.

We tugged at the veil of the Temple, hoping to rip it from its moorings and reveal the Light once and for all.

We gathered strange herbs from the roadsides and the park grounds, burned them in our censers or drank them as sacraments.

We stood on a rock at dawn and worshipped the Sun and reached out to touch the face of God.

This was the Bronx in 1960.

Many of the people mentioned in Maury Terry's book were either known to us, or known to friends of ours. This web of relationships would increase once Herman Slater opened his famous store on Henry Street in Brooklyn Heights in 1972, like a crazy little magnet that attracted only those on the very fringe of society. From that year until 1984 I found myself in the center of many of the incidents recounted in Terry's book, at least those that involved the Warlock Shop, Brooklyn Heights, the OTO, and the various other secret societies and cults with their tenuous connections to the Scientologists, the Process Church of the Final Judgement, the Church of Satan, the Ku Klux Klan, the National Renaissance Party, and all the various witchcraft covens and personalities, from the Gardnerians to the Alexandrians and Welsh Traditionalists, from Raymond Buckland to Leo Martello and Margot Adler, from covens gay and straight and mixed, to covens clothed and "sky clad." What was going on was much more blatant, much more vigorous, than even Terry suspected. There was *a lot* going on in those days, and much of it was open and covered by a skeptical but eager press, while the rest could be discovered with a little patience and good humor.

Raymond Buckland had already appeared on television talk shows as early as the late 1960s, sometimes opposite popular witch and author Sybil Leek. The American Society for Psychical Research was flourishing under the leadership of Dr. Karlis Osis, and I was a member . . . even though I was only sixteen years old, attending ASPR meetings at night in Manhattan with my mother, and once taking the train to Brentwood, Long Island to spy on the home of Raymond Buckland, author, leader of a coven of witches, proprietor of a witchcraft museum . . . and owner of the hearse parked in his driveway.

Samuel Weiser's in those days was a second-hand bookstore just below Union Square, with a basement section, dimly lighted, devoted to the occult and orientalia where you would find herbals, Tarot decks, grimoires, incense sticks, ephemerides, Sanskrit dictionaries, and a very strange clientele. It moved several times thereafter, dumping the second-hand stock and specializing in both selling and publishing occult arcana, each time the premises becoming smaller and smaller, finally reduced to the size of the original occult section in the basement of the store off Union Square.

Zoltan Mason's store was near Bloomingdales, uptown and second-storey, a quiet, dignified shop that specialized in astrological literature but which also boasted a decent alchemy section and some odds and ends on ritual magic. They frowned on walk-in trade, were not really interested in the retail business, but held classes in astrology. Zoltan Mason himself, noticing my serious demeanor and ambitious book selections—the *Turba Philosophorum*, the *Chymical Wedding of Christian Rosenkreutz*, the *Christian Rosenkreutz Anthology* in a large, beautifully printed and very expensive hardcover edition—took me inside to the back room (in actuality, his well-appointed office and secret storeroom, an elaborate Zodiac hanging on the wall behind his desk) and asked me what languages I spoke, and if I could help him with some translations from Latin, Russian, Church Slavonic . . .

It was an era of tea rooms and card readings, horoscopes and spells.

And, under it all, a seething political revolution in the making.

It was the height of the Vietnam War, but also of US government penetration of the anti-War movement, as well as of the Black Panthers, the Ku Klux Klan, the Weathermen, and the cults. In 1968, Martin Luther King, Jr. was assassinated in Memphis, Tennessee. Columbus High School held a moment of silence as we sat, stunned, in our seats during home room. A few months later, Bobby Kennedy was shot in Los Angeles, California. We were reeling from one assassination then another, to the backbeat of our neighbors dying in Vietnam. During the funeral service for Bobby Kennedy at St. Patrick's Cathedral in Manhattan, Andy Williams sang *The Battle Hymn of the Republic* as the mourners began to file out, one by one, into the June sunshine and Leonard Bernstein powered up the Hallelujah Chorus from *The Messiah*.

Two months later, in Miami, *The Battle Hymn of the Republic* was played once again, this time at the Republican National Convention that nominated Richard Nixon as their candidate for the Presidency. The obscenity of that event—if not its implicit symbolism—should have put us all on notice, those of us who needed to be warned.

James Earl Ray—the putative assassin of Dr. King—co-authored a book on the King assassination with anti-tax activist Frederick Saussy, *Tennessee* Waltz, with an afterword by Mr. Saussy entitled "The Politics of Witchcraft."

Politics and witchcraft were in the air, not as mutually exclusive themes but as two ways of looking at the same phenomenon. With this in mind, we can proceed safely to an analysis of the Son of Sam killings and, by extension, the weird and highly "coincidental" Roy Radin homicide. As in the case with the assassination of President Kennedy, we will uncover so many corpses along the way, so much "collateral damage," that we will be forgiven if we come to the conclusion that the reason our criminal justice system is so flawed is that our scientific method of forensic investigation does not allow for something as ethereal as moral responsibility, much less a close definition of what constitutes good and evil.

OCCULT CALENDARS AND MOVEABLE FEASTS

One of the essential elements used by Terry and others to define what constitutes evidence of an occult crime spree is the use of an alleged occult calendar as a timing device for ritual murders. They point to Halloween as a "sacred day" in the calendar of the occultists or satanists, and a few other days as well, and then try to fit the dates of the murders to the so-called satanic or pagan calendar. Some of their efforts have been correctly held up to ridicule; the pagan holidays are astronomically determined, and there is not a lot of temporal leeway for their celebration. However, having witnessed the lax attitude of many self-proclaimed pagans and satanists in the past—and sometimes the necessity of holding ritual holidays on days when most of the participants would be free from obligations at the office—I can attest that, to the less serious among the pagans, these days are *somewhat* moveable. The question then arises: would a cult devoted to ritual murder and human sacrifice actually postpone a homicide to a convenient weekend or bank holiday? Serial killers like Dahmer did most of their killing on days off; would the same hold true for an organized cult? The answer: not likely.

That said, let us examine the occult holidays in question beginning with the traditional pagan and occult holidays, and then comparing them with the table in Terry's book.

Traditionally, the most important days on the occult calendar—and this is demonstrated by cultures as disparate in time and space as the Stonehenge cult, the American Mound Builders, and the ancient Egyptians—are those that mark the solstices and the equinoces: sacred space aligned with sacred time. Thus, the first days of Spring, Summer, Fall and Winter are the most important and are called the Quarter Days as they divide the year into fourths. The great stone calendar of Stonehenge is so oriented, for example.

Then, the next four days of occult importance—and considered by some to be more important than the Quarter Days—are the Cross Quarter Days. These are the days that divide the previous quarters, appearing (for instance) halfway between the first day of Spring and the first day of Summer. These are:

- April 30, called *Walpurgisnacht* in Germany and *Beltane* in the Celtic countries;
- August 1, called *Lammas*;
- October 31, called Halloween or *Samhain* by the Celts; and
- January 31, called Candlemas or *Oimelc* by the Celts.

There are other days of importance to various cults, and these should not be ignored. They would include—but are not limited to—October 12, which is the birthday of Aleister Crowley; December 1, which is the day Crowley died; July 23, which is the birthday of Crowley's wife, purportedly the woman indirectly responsible for bringing Crowley's attention to the presence of the extraterrestrial intelligence known as Aiwass during their honeymoon in Cairo in 1904 (and, also, the day of the rising of the Dog Star, Sirius: a date sacred to the ancient Egyptians, source of much modern occult symbolism), and many others, including dates of importance only to Thelemites, or to Anton LaVey's Church of Satan, or Michael Aquino's Temple of Set, etc.

It is to be stressed that these are all dates of importance to those using the Western, Gregorian Calendar. There may be cults in Russia and some of the Eastern European and Balkan countries that use the older, Julian calendar. Asians have their own sacred holidays and these are usually moveable with regard to the Western calendar, based as they are on the lunar cycle. So, the type of cult one is dealing with will predict how it will use the calendar; conversely, if one knows the calendar being used, one can identify the type of cult involved with reasonable assurance.

It should be pointed out that lunar cycles are also important. The Full and New Moons especially are trigger dates for the celebration of pagan rituals, especially for the Wiccan cults that are based on a ritual they call "Drawing Down the Moon," which is quite possibly the relict of an old Thracian ritual, and possibly also an elaboration of Gerald Gardner and Aleister Crowley, although we have to admit that any witchcraft cults that pre-existed the Gardnerian versions would have also worshipped the moon.

The Quarter Days are normally celebrated at dawn on those days, and are rituals oriented towards the sun and towards the solar calendar, as evidenced by Neolithic structures such as Stonehenge and the American earthworks of the "mound builders" culture. The Cross Quarter Days, by contrast, are normally celebrated at night, most appropriately at midnight. Taken together, the Quarter and Cross Quarter Days would be known as "sabbats" to the witch cult and to some of the satanic organizations as well; the lunar rituals based on the Full or New Moons are considered "esbats" in the literature, a type of lesser sabbat. There are normally thirteen lunar months of roughly twenty-eight days each in a solar year of twelve months, but a solar year can only contain four Quarter Days and four Cross Quarter Days. As the full and new moons are also of great importance and significance to Islam, Buddhism, Hinduism and Daoism, we can safely say that a knowledge of the lunar calendar as well as the Quarter and Cross Quarter Days would be sufficient to cover most bases.

The Son of Sam killings began, officially, with the attack on Donna Lauria and Jody Valente on July 29, 1976. Donna Lauria died in the assault. As the pagan festival of Lammas begins officially on the eve of August 1, we may agree that this event is quite close to fitting the occult calendar as envisioned by Terry and described above. According to Terry's research, and Berkowitz's own admission in the Epilogue to Terry's book,[1] the attack on Donna Lauria was a deliberate one, and not a random attack as were some of the other killings. Therefore we must assume that—if a cult were involved—this date would have some special significance. The fact that it happens on a Thursday, rather than on a more convenient weekend night like most of the others, should compel our close attention. Also present at the murder was Michael Carr, according to Berkowitz, although

Berkowitz admitted he did the actual shooting. Several other members of the cult—which Berkowitz readily identifies as such—were also present as observers.

Terry goes further, however, by insisting that the murderous assault on Arlis Perry in a church at Stanford University—a truly hideous killing that incorporated many ritualistic elements—was a killing by the same cult as that responsible for the Son of Sam killings three years later in New York City. There is greater weight to this conviction for several reasons (as we will see below), but the fact that the murder took place on the night of October 12, 1974—and thus Crowley's birthday, a day that is celebrated by some Thelemic groups—already forces us to consider that the killer or killers were familiar with this date and chose it deliberately.

Of course, some critics of this approach have stated that it is also Columbus Day, and that it would be equally credible to say that Arlis Perry was murdered by a crazed Genoan, or by someone upset with Columbus' invasion of the Native American territories, etc., or even by a Norwegian who wanted to bring the country's attention to the fact that Leif Erikson was the first to discover America and not Columbus, etc. However, the selection of a church as the murder site, the insertion of a candle in the victim's vagina with another between her breasts, and the strange placement of her bare legs and the blue jeans positioned over them, forming a kind of diamond pattern (or a six-pointed star), suggested to many investigators that this was a cult crime.

The time frame October 12–13 is important for another reason which is largely ignored by writers on cult crime, for it was Friday, October 13, 1307 when the Knights Templar were arrested throughout France in an attempt—orchestrated by Pope and King—to destroy the Order. It is possibly the event that gave rise to the idea that Friday the 13th is unlucky, and which has made Friday the 13th such a popular date among occultists and horror movie directors. More than that, it is an important date for Freemasons and modern-day Templars who derive their heritage from the famous Order.

(For those interested in such things, March 18 is also notable as the date on which Templar Grand Master Jacques de Molay was burned at the stake in 1314. It is also the birthday of "sleeping prophet" Edgar Cayce, as well as alleged Kennedy assassination conspirator and wandering bishop David Ferrie.)

The next Son of Sam attack took place on October 23, 1976, a Saturday. This date has no particular occult significance, and is not near enough to another date to be remarkable. It is over a week early for Halloween, for instance. In addition, Terry believes that the targets in this case—Rosemary Keenan and Carl Denaro—were chosen randomly, even though Ms. Keenan was the daughter of an NYPD detective and Mr. Denaro was a security guard who had just joined the Air Force. According to Berkowitz, the shooter was a woman.[2]

Next, we have the attack on Joanne Lomino and Donna DeMasi on November 27, 1976, also a Saturday. Conceivably, this could have been a date chosen for its proximity to December 1, the day of Crowley's demise, as it is the closest weekend night; a weak theory, but possibly one that would obtain. Both were wounded. Both saw their killer before he opened fire, and their description of him was as different from that of David Berkowitz as it was possible to be, although virtually identical to that of the Donna Lauria assailant: slim, blonde, with a high-pitched voice. Berkowitz claimed it was John Carr.[3]

Then we have the attack on Christine Freund on January 30, 1977, a Sunday. This is identified by Terry—for completely different reasons—as a deliberate Son of Sam target rather than a random shooting. This is also a date comfortably close to Candlemas and the pagan festival of Oimelc. Thus, the dates match in this case as well as they do for Arlis Perry and for Donna Lauria. Christine Freund died on her way to a Masonic dance with her boyfriend, John Diel, who was unhurt in the attack. It would be the Freund case that would lead some investigators towards a possible motive for some of the killings that did not fit a "crazed, lone gunman" scenario. According to Berkowitz, an "out of town" shooter was brought in for this one, although there were a total of five cult members present for this attack. The shooter in this case was identified by Berkowitz as "Manson II," who also claimed responsibility for the Arlis Perry attack.

The next Sam attack took place on March 8, 1977, a Tuesday and another anomaly in the calendar. This was the shooting of Virginia Voskerichian. March 8 has no particular significance in the calendar, so this attack is a mystery. Bulgarian-born Voskerichian died instantly when the slug from the .44 Charter Arms Bulldog revolver passed through her skull as she walked down the Queens street on her way home from Columbia University. Berkowitz claims a woman committed this murder.[4]

This is followed by the attack on Alexander Esau and Valentina Suriani on April 17, 1977, the Sunday after Easter, taking place along the Hutchinson River Parkway in the Pelham Bay section of the Bronx, not far from where David Berkowitz (and the author) used to live. Again, no occult significance, but both were slain and a letter left in the car to the attention of Queens Detective Captain Joseph Borelli, the letter that would state for the first time "I am the 'Son of Sam.'"[5] However, there were indications in that letter that the murders had been planned for Easter, a week earlier, and were supposed to have taken place in Queens. From internal evidence, it seemed to the police that the letter itself had been written more than a week earlier, designed to be left at a Queens crime scene and not at one in the Bronx . . . which leaves us with the question, who was the intended target for Easter Sunday? Berkowitz admits to having committed this crime, although other cult members were, as usual, present.

On May 30, 1977, a letter was mailed to *Daily News* columnist Jimmy Breslin from the "Son of Sam." This letter contained many specific references to people who would later become identified once Berkowitz was apprehended, including John Carr. It was a well-written, creepy letter that ignited the imagination of New

Yorkers, and put them on alert that something more than your everyday, crazed killer was on the loose. The letter contained occult references as well as building upon the vampiric symbolism of the first letter left at the Esau/Suriani crime scene. It was, in fact, an intelligent piece of work and was the first communication bearing the Son of Sam "logo," a grouping of astrological symbols that had some investigators wondering at a link to California's Zodiac killer.

June 26, 1977—a Sunday—is the day of the attack on Judy Placido and Salvatore Lupo outside the Elephas Disco in Queens. This date is somewhat problematic. Was it chosen because it is the closest weekend date after the summer solstice, which would have been on or about June 22? Both survived this attack. (Ironically, Judy Placido had attended Son of Sam victim Valentina Suriani's funeral two months earlier.) Michael Carr committed this murder, again according to Berkowitz.[6]

But the final confirmed Son of Sam murder was that of Stacy Moskowitz (and the blinding of her date, Robert Violante) in Brooklyn on July 31, 1977—virtually the first anniversary of the Sam killings as well as Lammas in the pagan calendar and a Sunday. And a full moon. This attack had a plethora of eyewitnesses who saw more than one participant in the killing and at least two vehicles: one, a Ford Galaxie, was Berkowitz's car, the one identified by a parking ticket that night. The other was a Volkswagen Beetle.[7] Although Berkowitz was present at this killing, evidence shows he could not have committed it and, indeed, once he knew his car had just received a parking ticket, tried to call it off, knowing where that clue would lead. However, the killing went ahead as planned, committed—according to Berkowitz—by a friend of John Carr's from North Dakota.[8]

As you can see, not all of the killings were timed to the official pagan calendar. In fact, most of them could not be successfully placed near enough to a cult date to be significant. Yet, is there a pattern we could be missing? Or is the lack of a pattern in some killings an indication that they were committed merely to confuse the issue, or conversely that they are evidence of a second killer or killers?

One possible pattern is the astrological one.

If we consider the Arlis Perry homicide first, we are relatively secure in that this murder took place on Crowley's birthday, a date of considerable significance to his followers. But if we look a little deeper, from the point of view of a sophisticated cultist with a hidden agenda, we may find something more than we bargained for.

Arlis Perry was killed on or about midnight of October 12–13, 1974. An astrological chart drawn up for that place and time would reveal that there was a conjunction of the Sun and Mars in Libra at the Lower Heaven (the point in space opposite the Midheaven where the Sun is highest at noon). This conjunction is squared by Saturn in Cancer, and "semi-sextiled" (an angle of thirty degrees) by the waning Moon in Virgo. To reinforce the imagery, there were also significant angles between Pluto, Neptune and Jupiter that night. In fact, virtually all the "angles" that night were squares, conjunctions or oppositions: all considered "hard" aspects in astrological circles. In other words, it was a potent night for a ritual murder and may have been selected with that point of view in addition to the fact that all of these aspects were taking place on Crowley's birthday.

One does not need to believe in astrology at all to understand that others do. One does not have to believe in the efficacy or value of human sacrifice to understand that others do. As pointed out in *Unholy Alliance*, even British Intelligence understood that the Nazis were astrology-crazed, and worked up several propaganda and psy-war campaigns to turn that belief against them, realizing that no matter how you view astrology, there is a certain internal consistency to its methods that can be exploited by a clever astrologer-turned-intelligence officer.

Could an astrological perspective assist us in analyzing the other Son of Sam homicides?

For one thing, charts drawn up for all the murders indicate that only one—that of Virginia Voskerichian on March 8, 1977—did not take place during a waxing moon. (In fact, the Voskerichian attack was very anomalous in other regards, taking place much earlier in the evening than the others.) The other shootings took place either on New or Full Moons or when the Moon was somewhere between New and Full. In fact, the attack on Alexander Esau and Valentina Suriani on the strange date of April 17, 1977 (a date with no known pagan or occult significance) took place during the New Moon. The attack on Rosemary Keenan and Carl Denaro on October 23, 1976 (again, a date with no known occult significance) not only took place on the night of the New Moon but also when both the Sun and the Moon were entering conjunction with Uranus and Mars and the Moon's North Node (tradition-ally an indicator of an eclipse).

The attack on Stacy Moskowitz—the last of the official Son of Sam murders—took place not only on Lammas but also on the night of the Full Moon.

If one believes in astrology, then one can say that the murders happened on those dates and times because the "stars were aright." And if one does *not* believe in astrology, then one can still say that someone else, someone who *did* believe in astrology, chose those dates and times deliberately. It is not a conclusive piece of evidence, but the astrological character of the murder calendar is suggestive. Berkowitz told Terry that he was not aware of the reasons for the murders, or why some victims were chosen for death; he was simply told what to do and he did it.

Then, however, we have the collateral damage, the deaths of people who were close to the suspects or the investigation. These include:

September 20, 1977: Andrew Dupay—a mailman who worked the Yonkers route where Berkowitz and the Carrs lived—goes downstairs to the basement of his home while his wife is bathing their two daughters, writes a hasty suicide note, and kills himself with a shotgun. It is the autumnal equinox. No one knows the motive for the suicide, except that in the days immediately before and after Berkowitz's arrest, co-workers say Dupay began acting fearful, gradually becoming consumed with panic through the month of August and into September. One informant wrote Terry that Dupay had met someone in Pelham Bay Park the day before his suicide. Pelham Bay Park, of course, is the same area of the Bronx where Berkowitz had lived a few years earlier. The man he met was not identified.[9]

October 31, 1981: the murders of Ronald Sisman and Elizabeth Platzman on Halloween. Sisman was a photographer who claimed to have possession of videotapes made by the Son of Sam killer(s), notably of the murder of Stacy Moskowitz. Sisman was planning on giving this evidence to the authorities, but he and his girlfriend were executed. It was Sisman who introduced actress (*Welcome Back, Kotter*) and model (*Playboy*) Melonie Haller to producer Roy Radin, who was himself murdered by the Son of Sam cult according to Terry. Melonie Haller was savagely beaten at Radin's Long Island estate and claimed that the beatings and possible rape were videotaped by Radin and/or his accomplices.

Craig Glassman, on October 31, 1991: again, Halloween. Glassman, an important witness to the goings-on in and around the Yonkers apartment of David Berkowitz, who had received threatening letters and was the target of an arson attack by Berkowitz, died on the Taconic State Parkway in a bizarre auto accident.

There were numerous other murders and violent deaths surrounding the Son of Sam cult, much as we saw in the case of the Kennedy assassination, lending credence to the conspiracy theory proposed by Terry. A further piece of evidence, circumstantial as it may be, is that of the dates of the famous Zodiac killings in California.

The Zodiac killer began his murderous spree on October 30, 1966—again, uncomfortably close to Halloween and very suggestive of cult involvement. (In fact, this date is interesting for another reason, for it is the very same day that President John F. Kennedy's brain was discovered missing from the National Archives; within two weeks New Orleans DA Jim Garrison would begin his own investigation of the assassination and, at the same time, the Mothman sightings would begin in West Virginia.) The murders continued until May 20, 1981 . . . a period of nearly fifteen years. The Zodiac killer was never apprehended and the case remains open, although there have been one or two very good suspects. What is important for our investigation, however, is the fact that the Zodiac killings stopped from October 16, 1975 until starting up again on February 24, 1979, a quiescent period of about three and half years. This period of Zodiac inactivity dovetails with the Son of Sam murders, which took place from July 1976 to August 1977, and the murders of alleged Sam accomplices John Carr in February 1978 and Michael Carr in October 1978.

In fact, the murder of Arlis Perry in Stanford on October 12, 1974 also fits neatly into the Zodiac framework, as the killer was operating mostly in and around the San Francisco area at this time. If the Zodiac murders were the result of a cult in operation, then it is reasonable to assume that the Son of Sam cult—on the

East Coast as opposed to Zodiac's West Coast sphere of influence—was picking up *when* Zodiac left off, for whatever reason, and that Zodiac picked up shortly after the last Sam killing in late 1978, thus perpetuating a calendar of murder for reasons at which we can only guess.

There are many similarities between the Zodiac case and the Son of Sam case. The definitive study of the Zodiac killings—*Zodiac* by Robert Graysmith—tells us that the killings took place "on weekends when the moon was new or full."[10] In addition, Graysmith has linked the killings to the Quarter Days: the summer and winter solstices and the spring and autumn equinoces.[11] Further, Zodiac sent taunting letters to the press, as did the Son of Sam killer(s) as well as probably the most famous serial killer of all time, Jack the Ripper. Like the Ripper, the Zodiac's identity is unknown.

There was a Zodiac murder in 1974, only a few weeks before Arlis Perry's. This took place "six days after the Autumnal Equinox in 1974," when a fourteen-year-old girl was killed.[12] The Zodiac used a wide variety of murder weapons, making his identification and apprehension even more difficult. Then, after October 1975 there seems to be little or no more activity from the Zodiac until February 1979: virtually the same time frame in which the Son of Sam murders took place, including the violent deaths of John and Michael Carr.

In Graysmith's sequel, *Zodiac Unmasked* published in April 2002, he identifies the Zodiac Killer as one Arthur Leigh Allen, and notes that the period of Zodiac inactivity matches the years when Allen was in prison . . . specifically the Atascadero State Hospital for the Criminally Insane, convicted of child molestation.[13] Strange, then, that the Son of Sam cult would begin operation when he was incarcerated, and then stop shortly after he was released. If this is coincidence, then it is evidence of a deeper historical force at work.

Maury Terry has linked the Son of Sam killings to the operation of a satanic cult; indeed, David Berkowitz has admitted as much and in some detail in the Epilogue to Terry's book. The Zodiac used occult symbols, astrological symbols, and ciphers in his letters to the press. Even his *nom de guerre*, "Zodiac," is of course astrological.

Of course, as always, the alternative explanation is "coincidence." As we have seen, coincidence can be evidence of the operation of something deeper behind historical events. Although every historical event—and many, smaller, personal events—can be shown to demonstrate a certain degree of "coincidence" in action, it is when we discuss murder, from presidential assassinations to mass murder to serial murder, that we find the frequency and specificity of coincidence increasing dramatically. We see that events have been presaged by webs of convenient accidents, bringing specific people into specific places at specific times. It is perhaps the inclusion of *people* into this time-space continuum that has something to do with the mechanism of coincidence, as people have the ability to remember the past, and to predict—with various degrees of accuracy—the future.

The interface between consciousness and physical space is one that we will examine in the final section of this work, because it, quite simply, gives the game away. However, the conclusions to which I am drawn will not make much sense unless you witness for yourself the operation of this mysterious, sinister force for yourselves.

As an example, and considering dates of pagan significance, the famous Texas Tower Sniper case took place on Lammas, that is on August 1, 1966 at Austin (this is a Cross Quarter Day; the next Cross Quarter Day would be October 31, 1966 when the Zodiac killings began). Charles Whitman was an ex-Marine who somehow lost his mind and began shooting at random targets from the top of a tower at the University of Texas, hitting forty-five people in ninety-six minutes and killing fourteen of those. Whitman had had trouble in the Marines, and had been court-martialed in November 1963. He had served in Guantanamo Bay, Cuba beginning in December 1959 when Castro's revolution was in full swing and the island nation was transferring its political allegiance to the Soviet Union. In June 1961 he was sent to a college preparatory school in Bainbridge, Maryland, eventually enrolling in the University of Texas in September 1961 under a special program designed to enrich the Marine Corps' scientific and technical capabilities by training selected Marines in engineering, mathematics and science.

It was a prestigious assignment, and one that Whitman eventually flunked, in tandem with a gradual deterioration of his mental state. He lost his scholarship, and had to report to Camp Lejeune in North Carolina in February 1963. He was court-martialed in November for an assault on another Marine, and his fiancée showed up for the trial. She thought she had become pregnant the night of November 23, 1963—according to Whitman's journal—but it was a false alarm. It is interesting to note the similarities between Whitman's career and the American political experience of the time. Whitman, a Marine, is stationed in Cuba at the time of the Castro revolution; Lee Harvey Oswald, another Marine on active duty the same time as Whitman, is tested in Russian in February of 1959, but is released from active duty on September 11, 1959 before Whitman arrives in Cuba. Oswald (who would eventually campaign for the Fair Play for Cuba Committee) will renounce his American citizenship in Moscow on October 31, 1959 (Halloween).

Oswald, either a very poor Marine or a deep-cover intelligence asset depending on whom you believe, is accused of assassinating President Kennedy on November 22, 1963 from the Texas Schoolbook Depository in Dallas, Texas using a poorly made sniper's rifle. The following night, Marine Charles Whitman is having sex with his fiancée while awaiting a court martial, an act the fiancée later believes to have impregnated her. The following day, Oswald is killed by Jack Ruby.

Three years later, on August 1, 1966, Charles Whitman becomes the second ex-Marine accused of sniping at people from a high place in Texas, after first murdering his wife and mother the previous evening. All of this would just be interesting and perhaps even ironic, were it not for a book that had been published a few years earlier describing the same scenario: *Open Square*.

Like the Maeterlinck play that prefigured the Kennedy assassination in Dallas, this paperback thriller by Ford Clark prefigures the Texas Tower case. It tells the story of Ted Weeks, a student and a psychotic, who climbs a tower in a Midwestern university town and begins shooting at random targets below.

The definitive story of Charles Whitman, *A Sniper In The Tower: The Charles Whitman Murders*, by Gary M. Lavergne, has this to say about the startling similarities between Clark's novel and the real-life events that unfolded a few years later:

> . . . the sniper's nest had food; Weeks had an overly loving mother and a perfectionist for a father; he could not live up to the expectations of his father; he was trained to shoot in the military (ROTC); he hauled his supplies in a suitcase, the contents of which included water, gasoline, and five hundred rounds of ammunition; and he used ventilation slits as portholes to fire through. Astoundingly, the fictitious sniper Ted Weeks was killed by a police force headed by a "Chief Miles."[14]

In other words, the details of the fictional sniper matched perfectly those of the real sniper, *even down to the name of the chief of police* which, in the real-life case was Chief Robert Miles.

Of course, efforts were made to discover whether or not Whitman had read the Clark novel. No copy of the novel was found in his home after the shootings; no one could remember him ever reading it, or mentioning it. He had not taken it out of the library. It was not a well-known book, not a bestseller likely to have been on everyone's nightstand. In fact, Whitman is said to have looked at the tower years earlier—perhaps even earlier than the book's publication—and remarked that one could "hold off an army" from up there.[15] And, anyway, Whitman could not have arranged for the chief of police to be named Miles.

So, it was "just one of those things."

> *A coincidence, however, is frequently a glimpse of a pattern otherwise hidden. His heart tells him indisputably what his mind resists: This is no random event, but part of the elaborate design in a tapestry, and at the center of the design is he himself, caught and murdered.*
>
> —Dean Koontz[16]

To return to Terry's cult calendar analysis,[17] it shows that he arrived at similar conclusions where dates of cult significance are concerned, but used far too much leeway in his calculations, thus opening himself up to criticism from those who study occultism seriously.

For instance, he mentions the October 23 shooting and links it to Halloween, a conclusion I think is too far-fetched, as Halloween is over a week later. We can't use more than a day or so on either side of a specific date to show relevance, I believe, otherwise virtually any date you would care to mention is close enough to a cult "holiday." November 27 he links to November 30 (St. Andrew's Eve) and a date that does not seem to have any significance taken that way, but which does link successfully with December 1, the date of Crowley's death which he does not mention. As November 27 fell on a Saturday, it may indeed have been used as the closest weekend date to December 1, if our cultists were constrained to use weekends for hits for the most part due to day jobs or other obligations, or perhaps the convenience of using the weekend as it would be a time when their targets would be out late at night. He also refers, on the same page, to December 21 as St. Thomas' Day, a "satanic feast"; I believe he really wants to point out the significance of the winter solstice rather than a saint's day. The one that puzzles Terry most of all—as it does me—is the Virginia Voskerichian homicide of March 8, which seems to be the one anomalous shooting of all, even taking into consideration lunar phases; further, it took place on a Tuesday rather than a weekend, and much earlier in the evening—7:30 P.M.—than the other homicides, which all took place between midnight and 3:00 A.M. Terry's partner in the investigation opines that it might have been the cult leader's birthday, but that does not account for the early evening shooting unless it was timed specifically to coincide with other data (such as the putative cult leader's birth time) to which we have no access.

A search of my records and a large timeline developed for the purpose of tracking these events has revealed virtually nothing of significance for March 8 in any era. However, March 8, 1990 *was* chosen as the date of the *first* New York City "Zodiac" murder; the fourth and last New York City "Zodiac" killing was on June 21 that year: the summer solstice. It is possible that the March 8 date was selected deliberately to reinforce a link with the Son of Sam attack on Voskerichian, but there is no evidence to support this, either. Thus, the March 8 date remains a mystery.

There are other resonances to the "occult calendar," however, and these may be of interest to some readers:

Candlemas—

- **1/31/1865:** the 13th Amendment to the US Constitution is passed, abolishing slavery in the United States.
- **1/30/1933:** Adolf Hitler seizes power in Germany.
- **1/31/1958:** America's first satellite, Explorer I, built and controlled by the Jet Propulsion Laboratory, discovers the Van Allen Belt; the American space age begins.
- **1/30/1972:** "Bloody Sunday," the massacre of 13 marchers in Derry, Northern Ireland by British troops during a protest of Unionist rule.
- **1/31/1976:** George H.W. Bush becomes Director of the CIA.

Vernal Equinox—

- **3/21/1973:** The George Stano serial killings begin, in Gainesville, FL (thus giving more support to a cult calendar theory).

Beltane—

- **5/1/1960:** Francis Gary Powers shot down over the USSR.

Summer Solstice—

- **6/21/1972:** the date of the famous 18 ½ minute gap on the Nixon Oval Office tapes, giving rise to the suspicion of "sinister forces."
- **6/21/1975:** Self-proclaimed satanist Michael Aquino is visited by the Egyptian deity Set during an occult ritual, giving birth to the Temple of Set.
- **6/22/1979:** the Susan Reinert "Mainline" murders in Philadelphia, believed to have been part of a satanic sacrifice.

Lammas—

- **8/1/1914:** Germany mobilizes against Russia; World War I begins.
- **7/29/1921:** The Council on Foreign Relations incorporated in New York.
- **7/29/1958:** NASA created.
- **7/31/1980:** The children of slain Congressman Leo J. Ryan file suit against the US government over the Jonestown murders.

Crowleymas—

- **10/12/1962:** Lee Harvey Oswald gets a job at Jaggers-Chiles-Stovall, a company whose name has Thelemic resonances.
- **10/12/1964:** Mary Pinchot Meyer, confidant of John F. Kennedy and Timothy Leary, is murdered in Washington, DC.
- **10/13/1968:** Clida Delaney and Nancy Warren are murdered near Ukiah, California, believed to have been the work of the Manson Family.
- **10/12/1979:** Doreen Levesque murdered by Carl Drew in Fall River, MA as part of a cult sacrifice 10/12/1988: Patricia Ann Cantero murdered by her son, Jonathan, in Tampa, FL as part of a satanic ritual.

A note to the first entry, the passing of the anti-slavery amendment to the US Constitution on January 31, 1865: General Lee of the Confederacy surrendered to General Grant at Appomattox on Palm Sunday, 1865, thus ending the Civil War; President Abraham Lincoln was assassinated less than a week later, on Good Friday, by an actor in a theater. It was as if America was acting out its own version of the Passion Play, with Lincoln as Christ. It is no wonder, then, that so many parallels would be found between Presidents Lincoln and Kennedy, and that their deaths would be elevated to the status of iconic events in the eyes of many observers. On the other hand, perhaps the driving force of some other intelligence below the conscious threshold of the American psyche manipulates these events, and their ancillary coincidences and correspondences may be the evidence of this arcane activity.

As can be seen from the above, very small sampling, a number of occult murders and serial killings were begun or committed on important dates on the cult calendar, many more than Maury Terry was aware of when he wrote *The Ultimate Evil.* The dates with political overtones were included only to show how politics and the occult intermingle and to stimulate further research (if warranted), as well as to show how easily conspiracy theories can spin out of control.

A DIFFERENT WAVE LENGTH

> Murder is a recent interest of mine.
>
> —David Berkowitz[18]

David Richard Berkowitz was born on June 1, 1953 in Brooklyn, New York. He was conceived in a parked car, the natural child of Betty Broder of Brooklyn and Joseph Klineman of Long Island, a married man who was having an affair with Ms. Broder. Ms. Broder herself had been married before, to a Tony Falco, who left her. On David Berkowitz's adoption papers, it is Tony Falco's name that appears as the natural father, even though it was Joseph Klineman who was responsible. Betty Broder had a daughter, Roslyn, with Falco: David Berkowitz's half-sister.

Both Joseph Klineman and Betty Broder were Jewish.

"Richard David Falco" (to give David Berkowitz his name as it appears in the adoption records) was then adopted by Nathan and Pearl Berkowitz, who lived on Stratford Avenue in the Soundview section of the Bronx. Nathan Berkowitz had a hardware store on Melrose Avenue in the Bronx. They renamed the baby David Richard Berkowitz and everything seemed to be fine until October 1967, when Pearl Berkowitz died of cancer. David was fourteen years old.

Late in 1969, David and his father moved to Co-Op City in the Bronx, a house in development that was just being completed and touted as one of the largest in the world at the time, with its own shopping center, movie theater, etc. David Berkowitz enrolled in Christopher Columbus High School that year. He was sixteen.

The following year, he joined the Auxiliary Police force of the New York Police Department, out of the 45th Precinct in the Bronx. The Auxiliary Police force (to which the author belonged for a while in the summer of 1980) is a civilian patrol unit, a separate division of NYPD that helps the regular police monitor neighborhood activity, help out in directing traffic at public events, and generally make an appearance as the "eyes and ears" of the police department. They dress in standard NYPD uniforms, carry a baton (a nightstick), and a distinctive shield (badge). They carry radios but are not authorized to carry firearms. They are not peace officers per se, but assist the police in day-to-day activities, usually in the evenings or on weekends, since most of the civilian police—or APO's (Auxiliary Police Officers) as they are known—either have day jobs or are, like David, busy at school. David joined the volunteer fire department at Co-Op City, which is ironic (or cynical) considering his penchant for committing arson.

Around this time, his adopted father Nathan married Julia, a woman who had children of her own from a previous marriage. One of these children, David's step-sister, is a witch of some description, and taught David about the occult.

He graduated from Columbus High School in June of 1971, and immediately enlisted in the Army.

This was deep into the Vietnam conflict, when many young men were looking for ways to avoid service. Berkowitz, however, had spent time in uniform as an APO and as a volunteer fireman. Restless, he is a joiner, seemingly trying to compensate for an imagined flaw. He will spend the rest of his life in one kind of uniform after another, as he moves from the Army to work as a security guard and finally as a mailman, at which point he is arrested for the Son of Sam killings and begins wearing a prison uniform.

In the Army, Berkowitz is stationed not in Vietnam but in Korea, spending a year there and taking LSD during his tour. Not much is known about his life in the Army at this point, only that after his hitch in Korea he is transferred to Fort Knox, Kentucky in January 1973.

This is where David Berkowitz goes off the rails.

Although Berkowitz is Jewish—his adoptive parents are Jewish, his natural parents are Jewish—David suddenly becomes a Christian upon his return from Korea. While stationed at Fort Knox—the site of the nation's heavily-guarded gold repository—he begins attending the Beth Haven Baptist Church in Louisville and becomes a fanatic Christian. He tries to convert both civilian and military personnel, even preaching (à la Jim Jones in Indiana) on street corners. Again, there is insufficient data to make any kind of assumption here about what motivated Berkowitz to become religious, much less Christian. Did it have something to do with his discovery that he was adopted? Did the LSD he took in Korea have anything to do with this sudden spiritual awakening?

In June 1974 he is discharged from the Army and moves back to the Bronx, to 2161 Barnes Avenue, and enrolls in Bronx Community College. At the same time, he gets a job as a security guard for IBI Security, working in Manhattan.

Arlis Perry is murdered in California on October 12, 1974.

Early in 1975, his adoptive father, Nathan and Nathan's wife Julia leave the Bronx and move to Boynton Beach, Florida. David's stepsister—the would-be witch—decamps for a commune in California. In April 1975, Saigon falls to the Communists.

In May, David Berkowitz takes an important personal step. He joins ALMA, the Adoptees Liberty Movement Association, in an effort to come to terms with his adopted status, something that has obviously been bothering him. That Mother's Day, he sends a card to his natural mother, Betty Falco. This leads to an emotional meeting with her, during which he discovers that she has remarried (to a man named Leo). More disturbing to David is the fact that she reveals he was born illegitimately and moreover that she has other children she has not abandoned. This must contribute to seeing himself as worthless and unwanted.

Thus begins a strange odyssey with so many false starts and red herrings that we are forced to sit back and wonder at what was really going on.

In February of 1976, Berkowitz moves to New Rochelle from the Bronx, to an apartment that is much farther away from both his college and his job and which is more expensive. No one knows why he does this. It makes no sense. The apartment was only advertised in a local Westchester newspaper, not something Berkowitz would have normally seen in the course of his days in the Bronx and Manhattan. It is in a private home owned by one Jack Cassara. At that time, Cassara is working at the Neptune Moving Company in New Rochelle. One of his co-workers is Fred Cowan, a neo-Nazi who would go amok and, during a siege at the moving company, kill six people before killing himself on Valentine's Day 1977. Later, clippings would be found in Berkowitz's Yonkers apartment covering the Cowan case in detail. Berkowitz would refer to Cowan as "one of the Sons."[19] Later, during a court-ordered interrogation in October 1978, Berkowitz would reveal that he knew Cowan personally. He obviously knew Cowan's co-worker, Jack Cassara.[20]

Then, the following month, he applies for an apartment in Yonkers, on the other side of New York from New Rochelle, at 35 Pine Street, even though he has a one-year lease with the Cassaras that is only a month old. Again, why?

In April 1976, he moves to 35 Pine Street. Again, this move makes no sense for someone working and studying in the Bronx. Not only is the time it takes to commute a factor, but also the additional cost of commuting; plus, the rent is one hundred dollars more a month than the original place he had in the Bronx. One hundred "1976" dollars. This is the apartment where he would eventually be arrested on August 10, 1977.

On May 13, 1976, the house of a Yonkers neighbor is firebombed, part of a pattern of firebombings in the area.

In June 1976, Berkowitz travels to Florida to visit his father, and then drives on to Houston, Texas to visit an Army buddy—Billy Dan Parker—who buys him the .44 Bulldog revolver that was used in at least some of the Son of Sam shootings. Outside of Houston, in the town of Beaumont, lives the ex-wife of John Carr. Beaumont is also believed to be a cult center, one referred to by serial killer Henry Lee Lucas.

He returns to the Bronx and gets a job as a cabdriver in Co-Op City, making the long commute from Yonkers every day.

On July 29, 1976 the first Son of Sam shooting takes place.

Maury Terry's thesis is that the Son of Sam killings were committed by more than one person, and that David Berkowitz was only one of perhaps as many as three different shooters. Based on that theory—and it is a good one, and fits the eyewitness evidence as well as a lot of circumstantial clues—there was a conspiracy to commit these murders. Of what was this conspiracy composed?

When Berkowitz was finally arrested for the crimes on August 10, 1977 (for those following this sort of thing, the anniversary of the LaBianca killings in 1969) he pled guilty, thus avoiding a trial. This had happened before, of course, such as in the cases of accused Martin Luther King assassin James Earl Ray and John Lennon assassin Mark David Chapman. I don't want to elevate David Berkowitz to the same level as a political assassin, but will only point out that when the public is deprived of the right to see the evidence laid out in a trial, the public is similarly robbed of a chance to understand the crime and to benefit from the investigative resources of a defense team which might uncover a deeper, darker truth. I believe this is something which we should not allow to happen when a case is as important as a political assassination, or a serial murder spree that held a major city hostage for more than a year.

When the Sam killings were taking place, and the taunting letters received and printed in the newspapers, many of us New Yorkers were convinced at the time that more than one shooter was involved. The timing of the murders was very suggestive of more than one killer, and the various eyewitness descriptions of the shooters were so different that it naturally raised a lot of speculation about multiple killers. But this had not been experienced before in the United States: a group of murderers carrying out seemingly pointless and random homicides. It was easier to believe that one, crazed gunman was responsible. So, when Berkowitz was arrested and pled guilty, the entire case was swept under a rug. And there it stayed for quite some time.

But an examination of the letters sent by the Son of Sam killer(s) pointed to other connections, and more correspondence both from Berkowitz himself and from other convicts began to reveal a strange set of correspondences between the Son of Sam killings and murders taking place as far away as California and as long ago as 1969. And when Berkowitz associates wound up dying violently all over the United States after Berkowitz was in prison and could not conceivably have committed these additional killings himself, alarm bells began to go off. In addition, the very bookstore to which Terry refers several times in his book as being a central meeting place for members of this murderous cult was the same bookstore around which the author and several of his friends congregated from time to time during the Son of Sam killings, a store rapidly becoming notorious as a kind of occult clearing house for pagans, witches, satanists, magicians, and assorted other fringe religionists.

It is possible that Terry jumped to a lot of conclusions in the Son of Sam case, and that some of his theories about a proposed network of satanic killers are a little thin. It is also more than likely that some of the felons (including Berkowitz) who confided in him, telling tall tales of cult rituals in the moonlight replete with the sacrifice of dogs and humans, were doing so for ulterior motives or just having fun at Terry's expense. However, a few pieces of evidence militate against this point of view.

In the first place, Berkowitz has absolutely nothing to gain by spreading stories of a murderous cult to which he claimed to belong, and by admitting that he committed *some* of the killings but not *all*. That he is a self-confessed murderer is beyond doubt, and he does not try to backpedal from that fact. Berkowitz is in prison for life, and he knows it. There is no possibility of parole for David Berkowitz. His much-publicized conversion to Christianity (a re-conversion, actually, considering his activities in Kentucky a few years before the murders) does not buy him any time outside his prison walls. He has his own Web site now, and tries to impart uplifting spiritual messages via that medium, tranquilly acknowledging that he was a murderer who will never see freedom, who is only interested in being an example of redemption for other felons like him, as well as for those on the "outside." He cannot gain financially from any of these activities, for it was because of Berkowitz that we have the famous "Son of Sam laws" that forbid a convicted felon from benefiting from his crimes by selling the rights to a book publisher or movie producer, etc. Thus, he has no ulterior motive that we can see for finally coming forward and telling Maury Terry that he belonged to a satanic cult that was a splinter group of the Process, and that there were links between his group and the Charles Manson Family.

In the second place, the letters Terry received contained much internal evidence to suggest that his correspondents knew more about various other murders committed around the country than could be gleaned from newspaper reports. This includes Berkowitz, but also other inmates and other informants who claimed to have befriended Berkowitz inside, and who had heard of substantiating evidence that could be checked by Terry and other investigators.

Where Terry is on shakier ground is his analysis of occultism and the activities of various cults and secret societies. His background in this field comes strictly from a handful of very poorly-composed occult books designed for popular audiences that were themselves written by people with very little direct knowledge. This has happened to many investigators, of course, who come upon occultism for the first time and have their eyes opened wide at this strange demimonde in their own communities, and thus begin to believe everything they read on the subject, growing more and more nervous with each purple page of sensationalist prose, not realizing that the reality behind most of what comprises the modern manifestation of occultism is usually a lot less exciting and a lot more tawdry, about one step up from the standard established by Star Trek conventions, but minus the sophistication. Thus, it is possible for Terry—in *The Ultimate Evil*—to confuse the Golden Dawn with satanism, or the OTO with the Process, etc. Although we can easily show a "line of succession" leading from the Golden Dawn to Aleister Crowley, and from Crowley to the OTO and from the OTO to Scientology, and from Scientology to the Process Church of the Final Judgement, and eventually from there to Charles Manson, the so-called "Solar Lodge of the OTO," and even cult killers such as Clifford St. Joseph and others, we certainly don't have enough to show a deliberate conspiracy on the part of all these organizations in the Son of Sam case, and certainly not enough for calling all of these groups "satanic" or "murderous." Perhaps, from a very narrow Fundamentalist Christian point of view, Terry could be forgiven for making these assumptions, because to a Fundamentalist anything smacking of the occult is automatically from the Devil and satanic. This includes rock music, homosexuals, prime time television and your daily horoscope. All the evidence shows, however, that Terry is not a Fundamentalist Christian with an axe to grind against alternative religions, so we have to be a bit more selective and astute when it comes to investigating the occult aspect of the Son of Sam case, and this is what we mean to do, armed with such evidence as is available and beyond doubt. It will take us back to Charles Manson, and ahead to Manson II and a nexus of drugs, rituals, pornography, prostitution, and politics in low places. It will help reveal the Manson Secret.

RETURN OF THE PROCESS

> Your process is all fucked up!
>
> —Brad Pitt to Bruce Willis in *The Twelve Monkeys*

> There are other Sons out there—God help the world.
>
> David Berkowitz[21]

A key element in Terry's thesis is that the Process Church of the Final Judgement is alive and well, and involved in nefarious activity stretching from drug-running to child prostitution to murder. This was also asserted in Ed Sanders' study of the Manson Family, *The Family*. Sanders was successfully sued (in the United States) and references to both the Process and the OTO—so prevalent in the first edition of his book—were expunged by the time the book was republished. (This was not so in the United Kingdom, where the courts decided in favor of the publisher and author.) However, Terry recounts in *The Ultimate Evil* his discussions with Sanders concerning these cults. Terry makes no bones about mentioning both the Process and the OTO in *The Ultimate Evil*, and has evidently resisted any legal attempts to get him to change his story.

What initially bothered Terry about the Process was the appearance in one of their issues (the "Death" issue) of an article written by Charles Manson. Critics of the Terry thesis have scoffed at this, saying that such persons as Marianne Faithfull and Salvador Dali also appeared in the Process magazine; my reaction is simply this, however: what was Charles Manson doing in such august company? Further, Marianne Faithfull (as we have seen) had a long association with occultists of the Crowley dispensation through her relationship with Kenneth Anger. Dali himself was very involved in occultism, was well-known in several occult milieus, and his paintings—true to his reputation as a surrealist—reveal many occult and alchemical themes. There is a certain cultural or spiritual consistency to those who graced the pages of the Process magazine, and to dismiss Manson's appearance there as of little import is to be quite naïve. Further, as we have already learned, Manson told prosecutor Bugliosi that he and Robert Moore (the founder of the Process) were "the same." In addition, members of the Process on a mysterious mission visited Manson in prison after his arrest for the Tate/LaBianca killings, after which he no longer referred to the Process in any way. It is doubtful that Manson would have been worried about a lawsuit for slander, so we have to assume that something more was at stake.

In addition, we also have the visits by Manson Family member Bruce Davis to England on at least two occasions; as discussed in Book I, the British police agencies identified Davis as visiting the Scientologists and/or the Process on each visit. In fact, we also have the murders of former Scientologists in England at this time, members connected with the Manson Family and, as we will see, yet another Scientologist was killed, this time in connection with the Son of Sam case.

That there was a connection—however tenuous one believes it to be—between Manson and the Process is known and documented, even in the Process' own publication. The neo-gnostic theology of the Process would have appealed to Manson, extolling as it does both Jesus and Satan—Manson thought he was both, anyway.

The next step is to find any relation at all between David Berkowitz, the Son of Sam murders, and the Process. If this can be done, then we have left the realm of pure speculation and have entered the world of logical possibility.

Let's begin with the dogs.

For some reason, there have been reports of sacrifices of large numbers of dogs, mostly German shepherds, throughout the United States in the past thirty-odd years, but notably in areas where we discover confirmed cult activity. This was as true in Berkowitz's Yonkers neighborhood as it was in Walden, New York, where a "total of eighty-five skinned German shepherds and Dobermans were found" in a single year "between October 1976 and October 1977."[22] The day after Berkowitz's arrest in Yonkers, the bodies of three slain German shepherds were found in an aqueduct behind his apartment. Two had been strangled with chains; the third had been shot in the head.

Two days before his arrest, someone phoned an animal shelter using his name and address, inquiring about adopting a German shepherd that had been advertised in a local paper. A few hours later, someone else called from the same street in Yonkers, also inquiring about the dog. This caller said he was "fixing some cars" on

Pine Street; an allusion that Terry believes actually refers to the Carr family who figure so prominently in this case.[23] As it turned out, two men did visit the shelter, including one who resembled Berkowitz, but according to Berkowitz himself it was not he, although he acknowledges that someone may have been impersonating him on the phone.

Why? This was *before* his arrest and identification in the press as the Son of Sam.

Remember that serial killer Jeffrey Dahmer's first "kill" was the ritual slaughter of a dog behind his home in Ohio, which culminated in his placing the dog's skull atop a stake hammered into the earth; and, around the time of the Sam killings, the author heard convincing rumors of the abuse and slaughter of dogs in a warehouse near Brooklyn Heights, within walking distance of the Warlock Shop, before Berkowitz was arrested and the connection with dogs was made.

Terry connects the German shepherd sacrifices with the Process, due to their fondness for the animals. Members of the Process in those halcyon days of the 1960s were to be seen around San Francisco dressed in black and leading shepherds on the leash. The "Fear" issue of the Process magazine featured a photo spread of twenty German shepherds in a menacing pose. It doesn't automatically follow, however, that the Process would sacrifice the animals.

Another symbolic association that should be mentioned is the fact that Hitler favored German shepherds above all other animals. That there might be a Nazi or neo-Nazi element to the Son of Sam cult should not be ignored, especially as mass murderer Fred Cowan—one of the "Sons" according to Berkowitz—was a neo-Nazi. Further, the Process symbol was a stylized swastika: what some members referred to as "four P's"; these "four P's" later contributed to the name of a Process splinter group called "Four P" after the same symbol. It was this group that remained behind in California after most of the regular Process decamped and went to New York City following the assassination of Robert F. Kennedy. Four P—and its reputed leader, the Grand Chingon—has been implicated in a number of vile acts, including animal and human sacrifice, in northern and southern California. Convicted serial killer and cannibal Stanley Baker claimed to belong to this cult, and Manson Family members were known to refer to Charles Manson as the Grand Chingon, even though the organization was supposedly so secret that its very existence was unknown to all but a few.[24]

> *The Devil does not exist. It is a false name invented by the Black Brothers to imply a Unity in their ignorant muddle of dispersions. A devil who had unity would be a God . . . . It is, however, always easy to call up the demons, for they are always calling you . . .*
>
> —Aleister Crowley[25]

> *I'd say anybody who worships the devil is not a nice person.*
>
> —David Berkowitz, court-ordered interrogation, October 26, 1978[26]

Aside from the famous statement in letters and in person by Berkowitz that he alone committed the Son of Sam murders because he was ordered to do so by Sam Carr's dog—who was actually an ancient demonic force, according to Berkowitz—there was much more in the letters and in documentation found in Berkowitz's apartment after his arrest to suggest that he was part of a larger organization. In fact, in his letters to the press, he alludes to some of these participants by name, although his references were not understood at the time.

The most important from an investigative point of view was the name of "John Wheaties," identified in the letter to Jimmy Breslin as a "Rapist and Suffocater of Young Girls."[27] It was the investigative work of Terry and his associate (and former police detective) Jim Mitteager that uncovered the identity of this person as John Wheat Carr, a son of Sam Carr of the infamous demonic dog. John Carr led to his brother Michael Carr, a high-level Scientologist, and to Wheat Carr, their sister who worked for the Yonkers Police Department and who was married to a police officer. In a court-ordered interrogation of David Berkowitz in October 1978 at the Marcy Correctional Institute near Utica, New York, Berkowitz revealed that he hated the Carrs. In that same interrogation, he grudgingly (almost accidentally, due to clever questioning by a Legal Aid lawyer representing Terry's associate Mitteager) revealed the existence of the cult to which he, the Carrs, and probably Fred Cowan belonged.[28]

Critics of these revelations point to the fact that Berkowitz appears not to know very much about occultism or satanism in this lengthy exchange, often quoting lines out of context to prove their point. Anyone reading the entire Q&A, however, will recognize that Berkowitz was being cagey and evasive, even at times arrogant or flippant, in his answers; the fact that he would admit to knowledge and then take back the admission, and flip-flop like this several times during the interview, eventually breaking down in front of the interrogators, is more than enough to support the point of view that Berkowitz was afraid for his life. He was also being "handled" quite effectively by the prison doctor, who, it appears, spoke with him during a lunch break and managed to get Berkowitz to retract everything he had said in the morning, and to refuse to answer any more questions. When this did not work—when Berkowitz eventually relented and began talking again—the interrogation was interrupted by both the aforementioned doctor and a representative of the New York Attorney General's office, who ordered that the interrogation be stopped immediately.[29] Why this occurred is open to a great deal of conjecture, of course. It is possible that the authorities did not want the Son of Sam case reopened, as it would make a lot of detectives and prosecutors look inept or incompetent when so much additional evidence pointing to a conspiracy was revealed. It is also possible that the cult to which it is alleged Berkowitz and the Carrs belonged exerted pressure behind the scenes to ensure that Berkowitz—and only Berkowitz—took the fall for the Sam killings.

This latter theory does not seem so far-fetched when we consider some further facts.

John Wheat Carr, a career member of the Air Force who was discharged for drug related offences, died violently on February 16, 1978 at the airbase in Minot, North Dakota, the victim of a shotgun wound to the head. OSI—the Air Force's internal police agency—initially determined that the death was a probable homicide, changing that determination to suicide when the investigation took on national proportions with inquiries from Westchester County and New York City police departments and prosecutors' offices. He had been in Yonkers, at Sam Carr's home, only a few days before and unexpectedly flew back to Minot on Valentine's Day, after phoning his girlfriend at the base and telling her that the police were after him and things were too hot in New York. John Carr was on the run, but he never made it. Terry is convinced that Carr was murdered, and the evidence at the scene certainly points in that direction.

The murder of John Carr establishes the fact of conspiracy in the Son of Sam murders; John Carr's death was the conspirators' attempt to silence someone who might conceivably talk to the authorities. Carr had been the subject of a manhunt by police all over New York City and Westchester once it had been realized that he was the "John Wheaties" of the Son of Sam letters. If someone killed John Carr—while David Berkowitz was sitting in prison—then the implication is that there was at least one more conspirator out there: the one doing the mopping up. To make matters more interesting, John Carr's description fit perfectly with eyewitness reports of the Son of Sam killer seen at more than one crime scene, down to the color of his hair, his build, and his left-handedness. Evidence gathered since then shows that Carr was in New York City for at least four of the shootings, even though he lived in Minot, North Dakota at the time. He was also present in Houston, Texas on June 12, 1976: the day Billy Dan Parker bought the .44 Charter Arms Bulldog for Berkowitz in that city.

John Carr—who was born on October 12, 1946 (Aleister Crowley's birthday, as Terry points out)—was interested in the occult. Growing up in Yonkers, he was a schoolmate of Maury Terry in high school, as Terry himself reveals in *The Ultimate Evil*[30]—an odd parallel to the fact that *this* author went to the same high school as David Berkowitz. Carr traveled the world with the Air Force, spending time in Thailand and Korea, before returning to the Strategic Air Command base at Minot. But his involvement with drugs led to his downfall with the Air Force. He was hospitalized several times for drug overdoses, and was taking Haldol at the time of his death. Haldol is usually prescribed for psychiatric disorders.

Carr was discharged from the Air Force on October 13, 1976, due to his drug-related problems, after twelve years in the military. He, of course, does not sound like a sophisticated cult hitman, but then we are not watching a Hollywood movie version of a satanic cult. If we posit the existence of a daring group of

Satan-worshipping killers then the position of John Carr in this group must have been relatively the same as that of Berkowitz: they were both expendable, sent out to kill specific targets on specific days, both psychologically damaged in some way and vulnerable to manipulation by more sophisticated—more motivated—leaders who had done all the planning and who probably wrote the famous letters to the press, for it would eventually come out that Berkowitz did not write them himself. With Berkowitz silent in prison, and the police onto John Carr's involvement and looking for him everywhere, these mysterious leaders only needed to tie up loose ends, beginning with John Carr but not ending there.

While John Carr's familiarity with the occult is documented in Terry's book (everything from keeping a list of demons with him to burying dog excrement in the yards of people he was trying to curse), it receives further confirmation from Berkowitz himself, who characterized him as a "devil worshipper" during his interrogation at Marcy . . . oddly enough not including himself in that category.

Later, police in the Minot, North Dakota area acknowledged that John Carr was a member of a satanic cult that operated there, that John Carr himself was not only using drugs but dealing (not an uncommon combination), and that he told police detectives that members of the cult had to drink their leader's urine from a chalice, among other unsavory details. (He had been rousted by the police in October 1976 on a street in Minot for being under the influence of drugs.) Even more importantly, the Minot police agencies knew that Carr and Berkowitz were acquainted and that both belonged to the same cult, based on voluminous testimony from friends, including a fellow airman and roommate, Jeffrey Sloat, who eventually had John Carr committed to a mental institution for a while due to the latter's strange behavior, which included chanting in an unknown tongue and talking to a picture of Abraham Lincoln. The police involved in the investigation in North Dakota forwarded this information to their New York City and Westchester County counterparts, and never heard back from them.[31] The details on the existence of the cult and the participation of more than one person in the so-called Son of Sam murders was deep-sixed by the New York authorities; in essence, allowing the cult to continue its operation unhindered, possibly even to the present day.

In the months leading up to his capture, Berkowitz was engaged in a campaign of terrorism in his neighborhood designed to get him arrested on lesser charges before he was apprehended for the Son of Sam murders, and before he would be expected to commit more. He was firebombing houses, shooting dogs, and sending hate mail to all and sundry . . . with return addresses that would only point back to him. The inability of the Westchester Sheriff's Department and the Yonkers police to put all of this together—even when Sam Carr himself walked into a police station with the evidence long before the last two Son of Sam attacks—drove Berkowitz crazy. He wanted to be taken off the streets before more people were killed; rather than simply walking into a police station and saying, "I'm the Son of Sam," he preferred to be picked up on lesser charges so that when the next Sam killing took place he would have an alibi, and the attention would drift away from him (if, indeed, it would ever focus on him in the first place). That was his plan. But it was not working.

Shortly before his arrest, he scouted another murder site, this time on Long Island. Feeling the pressure of another upcoming murder, and knowing it was only a matter of time before the police analyzed the parking tickets issued at the time and place of the Stacy Moskowitz killing, he placed a rifle in his car in full view and a Sam letter in the glove compartment. His apartment had been cleaned out a week or so earlier, and most of his furniture and an expensive stereo set purchased in Korea had been left in front of a Salvation Army storefront. He then proceeded to decorate the walls with weird writing in Magic Marker, making references to "the children" and "the little ones" becoming murderers. And he sat and waited for the cops to show up.

After his arrest, he would eventually be interviewed by Dr. David Abrahamson, to determine if he was mentally fit to stand trial. Abrahamson wrote a book about the experience, entitled *Confessions of Son of Sam* and published in 1985. In this book, we learn that Berkowitz recognized Abrahamson when they were first introduced, as he had read Abrahamson's *The Murdering Mind* prior to his arrest! He also read a number of books about murderers such as Richard Speck and Nathan Leopold that he took out of the Yonkers Public Library, telling the doctor, "Murder is a recent interest of mine."[32]

In the same book, we find a poem written by Berkowitz as the killings were beginning, entitled "Mother of Satan" and dated September 22, 1976: the autumnal equinox and one of the Quarter Days. It reads (with the original spelling):

> Old Mother Hubbard
> Sitting near the cubbard
> with a hand grenade
> under the oatmeal.
>
> Who will you kill now
> Daughter of Satan?
>
> In the image of the
> Virgin Mary—pure and innocent
> The Great Impersonator—
> Is that you? "Yes."
> How many have you decieved—
> lured to slaughter like a
> fat cow?[33]

The first stanza is compelling, humorous and well-written, despite the misspelling of "cupboard" unless, of course, the misspelling was intentional and yet another piece of coded information. Also, in the earliest versions of "Mother Hubbard" we find that her dog is her master.

But one cannot help wondering if Berkowitz wrote this with a specific person in mind, someone from the cult. Someone, a woman, "in the image of the Virgin Mary" and a "Great Impersonator," who deceived many and lured them to slaughter "like a fat cow," is also the "Daughter of Satan." A woman, rumored to belong to the cult, was present at some of the Sam killings according to eyewitnesses. Was this another gofer of the cult, or someone more important?

Abrahamson, however, did not address himself to the idea of a cult behind the murders. He was only concerned with Berkowitz's mental state, as far as the courts asked for his opinion. Berkowitz was given a battery of tests, including the MMPI, and Abrahamson came back with the following diagnosis:

> Clinical scales indicated pathological elevations regarding the following scales: schizophrenia; paranoia; psychopathic deviation; depression; hypomania; psychasthenia and social introversion.[34]

Abrahamson also reveals that Berkowitz lay claim to setting numerous fires in the years 1974–77. We know he firebombed his neighbors' homes in the months leading to his arrest, but that was for a specific purpose: to get himself arrested. Abrahamson reveals a much longer career as an arsonist, however, beginning on May 13, 1974 with a rubbish fire set in the area of Co-Op City. This is odd, since supposedly Berkowitz was still in the Army at the time, stationed in Kentucky.

Then, Abrahamson says that Berkowitz had a detailed list of the fires he set, a total of 1,411 fires from 1974 until his arrest in 1977; the list includes the date, time, street, borough, weather, firebox number and Fire Department code.[35] This incredible assertion is nowhere else mentioned in connection with Berkowitz and the Son of Sam case, and the sheer number of fires beggars belief. 1,411 fires in three years? Anyone doing the math will realize that means he set roughly 1.25 fires per day, every day, for that period . . . and was never caught. Further, Berkowitz states that he committed no arsons in the period December 25, 1974 to June 6, 1975 (this was the period when he was searching for his birth mother). So, he had to have committed 1.50 fires per day in the time available. One senses that Berkowitz was having some fun with Dr. Abrahamson; either that, or the 1,411 fires were the total of a group effort and not Berkowitz acting alone.

Another startling revelation from Abrahamson's book is the acknowledgment by Berkowitz that he attacked a young, fourteen-year-old girl on Christmas Eve 1975 between 10:30 and 11:00 P.M. on Baychester Avenue in the Co-Op City area of the Bronx. This was done with a 3-1/2 inch long hunting knife and, according to Berkowitz, he stabbed her repeatedly but she survived. If true, this would be the only attack by Berkowitz that did not involve a .44 Charter Arms Bulldog revolver.

The problem I have with this information stems from a telling revelation at the very beginning of the book: that Berkowitz had read Abrahamson's text on *The Murdering Mind* long before he met the doctor, and that he had also studied Richard Speck and other murderers. He may have gleaned from these texts the classic symptoms of the serial killer: beginning with arson, graduating to a disordered attack (the Christmas Eve assault on the young girl) and from there to a more orderly, more sophisticated pattern of murder.

The fact that we have a growing mountain of evidence—including eyewitness testimony, circumstantial evidence, and crime scene evidence—that point to a conspiracy in the Son of Sam murders strongly implies that they were *not* the work of a lone serial killer at all, and that Berkowitz was simply tailoring his story to fit what he knew Abrahamson's assumptions would be. It is interesting that in his discussions with the doctor he did not abandon his "Son of Sam" story, replete with demon-possessed dog, which since then has been acknowledged to be a fabrication designed by Berkowitz to insure himself an insanity plea. There *were* dogs, there *was* a Sam Carr, and there *were* devil worshippers, however. It's just that Berkowitz used the *literal* interpretation of the Sam letters to convince the doctors that he was insane.

On July 10, 1979, David Berkowitz was attacked by a fellow inmate, his throat slashed, but he survived.

A few weeks later, a friend of his was shot to death in his apartment in Flushing, Queens. Howard Weiss was a fellow member of the police auxiliary unit in Co-Op City to which Berkowitz and another colleague, a former Yonkers police officer who is not identified in Terry's book except for a pseudonym, belonged. These three men had attended a wedding of a friend in Maryland in 1976, before the Son of Sam killings began: a wedding that was captured on videotape, showing all three men present. Another link between them was the fact that the Yonkers police officer knew the Carrs, and that all three men were known to have owned .44 Charter Arms Bulldog revolvers.[36] Sources would confirm that all three men (as well as the Carrs and many others) belonged to the same cult, and were even involved in multiple arson attacks—thus confirming the author's suspicion that the fires Berkowitz claimed he set were, in reality, set by more than one person—but these sources are not identified in Terry's book, and nothing more about them is known. Regardless of this nagging problem, the fact that Berkowitz's friends begin dying (violently) all over the place is enough to give one pause. Like all those violent deaths that surround the Kennedy assassination and its aftermath, it points to the existence of a powerful conspiracy. (Should these deaths be unconnected to each other in any way, however, then we are looking at a different phenomenon entirely, and one that cannot be explained away by pious invocations of "coincidence.")

In the background of all of these killings, Terry and a few of his contacts in law enforcement began to search strenuously for links between John Carr and David Berkowitz in an effort to understand how these two men would have known each other and influenced each other. With Berkowitz in prison and John Carr murdered in North Dakota, it seemed more urgent than ever to uncover other friends and associates common to these two men.

When they spoke by phone to Minot, North Dakota law enforcement they were shocked to learn that Minot knew all along about John Carr's occult involvements as well as the existence of a cult in Minot that, among other things, sacrificed German shepherds. Terry and another investigator, NYPD detective Harry Cinotti, flew to Minot to discover for themselves what the cult is like, who are its members, and what is its murderous agenda. Cinotti is a strange character; although a police officer he is also a very religious, very Roman Catholic, devotee of a woman of local Queens celebrity, Veronica Lueken, who channels the Virgin Mother every year at a gathering in Flushing Meadows and has a devoted following. Cinotti is the Van Helsing in this case, a man who one suspects travels with crucifixes, holy water, and a set of wooden stakes packed next to his service revolver and shield. On an expedition one evening to the strangely beautiful Untermyer Park in Yonkers where cult activity was known to take place—cult activity connected with Berkowitz and the slaughtered German shepherds—Cinotti prepared his fellow investigators with spiritual advice on how to protect oneself against the dark forces of Hell, thus both alienating and freaking out his fellows in equal measure.

Once in Minot, a town less than a hundred miles from the Canadian border and about a hundred miles from Bismark (and fifty miles from the edge of nowhere), Terry and Cinotti met the local law enforcement personnel and learned about John Carr's cult in disturbing detail. Several members of the cult were identified—some of whom would die violently before the investigation concluded—and some were interviewed for background on John Carr and David Berkowitz. There were many confirmations of the Carr/Berkowitz relationship, and an equal number of confirmations concerning John Carr's involvement in the occult, including a blatant admission from his own sister back in Yonkers.

Cult involvement *per se* is no reason to get excited. Defining what a cult is and isn't has kept theologians, historians of religion, psychologists and even criminologists busy for years. In addition, there are many relatively benign alternative religious organizations in the United States and abroad that may qualify as someone's idea of a cult, but which do not engage in anything remotely nefarious. The problem with the putative Son of Sam cult is that evidence began to mount that it was a cover for drug-running, child prostitution, pornography and murder-for-hire. The circumstantial links to the Process are what made Terry take special notice that what he was investigating might turn out to be a very sophisticated, very well-managed criminal enterprise that spanned the globe; moreover, one in which devil worship comprised the organization's "mission statement."

Why should this be a special problem?

Criminal organizations are businesses like any other. They sell a product or service, and exist for profit. What makes them criminal is the product or service they offer: drugs, guns, or sex, for instance. Otherwise, though, they are usually rational groups of like-minded individuals who understand the world in terms of cause and effect, and moreover who are willing to go to extremes to defend their business from competitors. Extremes like murder. Because they are involved in trade in illegal commodities, they are vulnerable to more than market forces. They are also vulnerable to law enforcement agencies, making their business more complicated and more difficult to manage and defend. Therefore, the type of person who becomes involved in criminal enterprises has already placed himself outside the social milieu in which the rest of us live, and experiences life in a more desperate, more emotionally-charged way than we do. Although we may take advantage of the products and services offered by the criminal organization from time to time—and thereby support the criminals with our own, honestly earned, money—we do not murder our competitors, or steal from banks and armored cars, or fence stolen property, or deal drugs or guns or rent our bodies for sex. Thus, we can go to church on Sunday feeling suitably redeemable from our petty sins, sheep who have strayed perhaps, but who are nonetheless members of the flock. Not so the criminal.

Criminals have seen life the way police officers do: from the bottom, up. They see life the way it really is, behind closed doors. They know the weaknesses of their fellow humans, because they cater to them. They know the judge with a gambling problem, or the priest who prefers sex with underage boys. They see beyond the façade of society, and what they discover is no more elevated or spiritual than their own, tawdry, experience has taught them. The criminal feels that he or she is a realist, is in fact honest because he or she does not disguise the fact of belonging to a race of beings that is inherently . . . evil. To a criminal, nothing is beautiful, nothing is innocent, nothing is pure. The priest at Mass is a pederast, a bigot, a hypocrite. The same hands that touch the sacred Wafer, transforming bread and wine into the Body and Blood of Christ, had just last night touched the genitals of an altar boy in the sacristy. "Where was Jesus?" the criminal laughs.

The criminal, then, is a satanist. The criminal respects only power and the only powerful person the criminal respects is the one that demonstrates that power on a regular basis. The Mafia chieftain ordering the death of a subordinate, the pimp beating the reluctant or lazy prostitute, the drug dealer wiping out a competitor. To a criminal, murder is the ultimate demonstration and exercise of power; in a way, then, the criminal worships the one who dispenses death and fear.

To the criminal, sex is a commodity and there is no love to redeem it. The criminal respects lust. Everything else is a romance novel, suitable for children (those he has not already corrupted). Women are inferior beings, dangerous at times, but like children should be seen and not heard.

Drugs are for the weak, a product to enslave the masses and take their money.

Gradually, we can understand the attraction Satanism would have for a criminal. Not that the criminal himself would be a pious Satanist, spending hard-earned money on building chapels devoted to Hell; but he would understand that devotion to Satan would lead automatically to an acceptance of the criminal's life-style and perspective. The Satanic perspective would allow and encourage drug use, all types of sexual acts with all types of partners, willing and unwilling, and the forceful suppression of dissent, the aggressive enslavement of the weak. Satanism is not about worship or devotion; it is about power, and about power as manifest on both a physical and a spiritual level.

That is not to say that the Satanic cult attracts only the powerful. In fact, the opposite is true.

The people who worship power are those who do not have it. The vast majority of people who have been attracted to Satanic cults have been—in the author's experience as an observer of the occult environment—the weak, the desperate, the downtrodden, the impoverished . . . the petty criminal, the drug addict. They become the playground for a handful of people at the top, who manipulate their willing servants, exploiting their submission and devotion, and turn them into drug couriers, pornographers, and murderers. The glue that binds these groups together is the ritual held in the dead of night in abandoned parks and ruined buildings, the shedding of innocent blood, and the promise of eternal reward in a Hell of their own devising.

The Process Church of the Final Judgement made Satanism fashionable to an extent, and if not glamorous, then a bit more intellectually honest. Robert Moore's neo-Gnosticism was a refinement of Anton LaVey's blatantly commercial approach to Satan. While LaVey's showmanship attracted a certain element that was ready to dip their toes into the thrill of actually participating in a Black Mass, Moore's Process Church strained for a more severe aesthetic. Moore had a mission, and a program. Moore *believed.* LaVey did not. Moore came from a Scientology background, in which the possibilities of human programming, of mind control and ritual, were vigorously explored. LaVey's "do your own thing and don't let guilt or shame or other people get in your way" was little more than warmed-over Rabelais and a dose of Dale Carnegie. It was not intellectually ambitious, but an approach designed to appeal to the greatest number of people, and thus based on a few simple ideas. The Church of Satan was a kind of psychotherapy clinic dressed up in Gothic robes and black candles. Psychodrama for the counter-culture that was just coming into its own in 1966. It was "the Power of Positive Thinking" meets *La-Bas.*

The Process, on the other hand, was a genuine cult. The early days of their group, flying from London to Mexico *en famille* with guard dogs and black jackets, blending Jehovah with Lucifer and then adding a strong dose of Satan as they germinated in San Francisco a few blocks up the street in the Haight from where

Manson was staying, is evidence that what Moore was up to was much more than LaVey ever had in mind. Moore was undergoing his own shamanistic initiation at the expense of his followers; his magazine, *Process*, with its issues devoted to "Death" and "Fear," was riding a wave of disintegration and dismemberment, albeit in an artistic way replete with photos of pop icons like Dali and Faithfull, not to mention epistles from Manson himself.

And that is what eventually happened.

The Process splintered in the years after 1968. The three main bodies within the Process—the groups devoted to Jehovah, Lucifer, and Satan—broke apart from each other and attempted to retain independent status. Moore himself left the Process (or, as some say, was kicked out in a kind of palace coup orchestrated by his wife) and melted into obscurity; the same might be said for the Jehovah and Lucifer contingents, as the Process reinvented itself and tried to hold onto what they could from the old days, amalgamating what they could of the older membership. The Satan contingent, however, seems to have survived.

Rumors of a cult calling itself the Four P surfaced in California shortly after the Process disappeared from that state. "Four P" was a name taken from the Process symbol, which resembles four "P's" in a circle forming a kind of swastika figure. Then there was the Grand Chingon, said to be the leader of the Four P. Manson Family members used to claim that Charlie was the Grand Chingon, but that was empty boasting. No one seems to know who the Grand Chingon was, or even what "Chingon" means, except that it may not be a real title but a kind of epithet. In Mexican Spanish, the verb *chingar* means "to fuck" and is used as an expletive, such as in the word *chingada* for "fucking" or *chinga su madre*, a common curse. Thus, the word *chingon* could mean "the fucker." As the Luciferian element of the Process was the one involved most directly in the lascivious aspects of the cult—the purely sexual component, rather than the more intense power component of the Satan element—it is possible that the Grand Chingon was leading a group of dissident Luciferians, except for the fact that the Four P group and the Grand Chingon were implicated in several vicious murders in the California area in the late 1960s and early 1970s, including the one involving Stanley Baker, the aforementioned cannibal.

Remaining behind in California, at a time when the film *Rosemary's Baby* had just been released, another Kennedy slain, Dr. King assassinated, the Days of Rage raging in Chicago, the infamous Tet Offensive ongoing in Vietnam, etc., cult members and those who lived on the fringes of the cults still sought to stay active and to survive. California to most people is Hollywood, the City of Dreams. The free-wheeling lifestyle of movie stars, directors, producers fit perfectly with the "nothing is true, everything is permitted" school of born-again Ismailism which became—at least in California—a kind of neo-gnostic Satanism. After all, in Hollywood one had access to all the things that cults are today accused of exploiting: drugs, pornography, prostitution, and extravagant dreams of wealth, fame and power. Scientology deliberately targeted movie stars, and the current membership lists bear out this strategy: John Travolta, Kirstie Alley, Tom Cruise, and Nicole Kidman are all Hubbard alumni, as well as many lesser-known dream factory employees. With celebrities, Scientology could buy respectability.

But people like Charlie Manson were fishing in the same waters. Charlie, with his close relationship to Dennis Wilson of the Beach Boys and his on-again, off-again partnership with Terry Melcher (son of Doris Day), and his de facto guardianship of DiDi Lansbury, was prowling the fringes of the Hollywood boondoggle. There are fortunes to be made in Hollywood, and fortunes to be lost. It is a high-risk, high-stress environment that has seen its share of murder and suicide, long before Charlie Manson and long after. Those who work this industry know where to score drugs, where to pick up sexual partners for a price, and where to hire a hitman.

One of the many theories about the Manson killings is that they were murder-for-hire. This is the field that Maury Terry has plowed so earnestly, for it leads him back to one of the more spectacular Hollywood murders of recent years, that of Roy Radin and the hired hitman known as Manson II.

THE COTTON CLUB MURDERS

> And it shall come to pass, that thy choicest valleys shall be full of chariots, and the horsemen shall set themselves in array at the gate.
>
> —*Isaiah 22:7*, in a King James Bible opened to this page and found at the Roy Radin crime scene by Maury Terry[37]

We can't really talk about this aspect of the case without talking about Robert Evans, for Evans will lead us to Roy Radin and Elaine Jacobs and Manson II. Bob Evans is a famous Hollywood movie icon, a producer who was responsible for such box office hits as *Rosemary's Baby* and *The Godfather*. In fact, this axis of directors Roman Polanski and Francis Ford Coppola is one that will surface again in his career, as he went on to produce both *Chinatown* and the doomed *Cotton Club*.

Robert Evans has been married to some of Hollywood's most celebrated leading ladies in his time, including Ali MacGraw and former Miss America Phyllis George. It was Ali MacGraw who served as our guide into the Process-infiltrated area of upstate New York, where we found Pound Ridge, Salem and Brewster in the midst of satanic skullduggery, including the presence of unapologetic occultist Anita Pallenberg and a dead seventeen-year-old boy in her bed, and a flap over satanic activity in the area that continues to the present time. Phyllis George will introduce us to her former husband Kentucky Governor John Y. Brown and a scandal surrounding the governor, Colombian drug runners in northeastern Kentucky and a bizarre paramilitary drug cult known as "the Company." More importantly, Evans will meet and—some say—eventually propose to one Elaine "Laney" Jacobs, the wife of several drug runners in her time with a trail that leads directly back to crazed *narcotraficante,* worshipper of John Lennon, and neo-Nazi, Carlos Lehder, currently a guest of the US federal prison system. The number of associations that swirl around Robert Evans is astonishing; the fact that he was arrested and convicted once for cocaine possession is only the tip of a very old and very cold iceberg. He was a suspect in a homicide, and it was this homicide that brought the Son of Sam cult to the surface.

As with most "deep politics," the connections between these individuals and events are murky, but definite. These are all people who knew each other, did business together, did drugs together, and in some cases committed murder. It is a matter of the public record. What has not been revealed until now is the extent to which these events are linked below the surface to each other and to darker forces at work in the collective American psyche.

There are several books which can introduce the reader to the broader aspects of these cases, even though they do not reference each other and seem on the surface to be unrelated. They are, in addition to Maury Terry's *The Ultimate Evil,* Ali MacGraw's *Moving Pictures,* Sally Denton's *The Bluegrass Conspiracy,* and Steve Wick's *Bad Company: Drugs, Hollywood and the Cotton Club Murder.* The latter is a review of the murder case involving Bob Evans and as such is a bit less self-serving than Evans' own autobiography, *The Kid Stays In The Picture* (later made into a lugubrious documentary with a running Bob Evans voice-over whose only saving grace is the hilarious impression of Evans by Dustin Hoffman over the closing credits).

The following is a précis of the facts of the case as represented in the above works and the public record.

Orson Welles may seem like a strange person to introduce this story, but once again we are faced with deep resonances and incredible Brunoesque "links." Welles, one of the pioneers of the motion picture and an incredible artist (as evidenced by his *Citizen Kane,* which is the focus of many filmmaking courses and books of cinema criticism) was also fascinated with the occult and the power of mass media. His infamous broadcast of H.G. Wells' *The War of the Worlds* over the radio on Halloween 1938 is part of American history; the broadcast seemed so genuine to listeners that it caused a panic as people believed the Earth had actually been invaded by creatures from Mars. His aborted attempt to make a film in Brazil about Latin American witchcraft led to his being cursed by a local shaman, something Welles took very seriously.

But Welles is important to us at this juncture for another reason entirely. He was Roy Radin's mentor.

Roy Alexander Radin was born to impresario Alexander Radin and his wife Renee, a former stripper, on November 13, 1949. The elder Radin had been a confidant of Welles, and Welles took over the education of the teenaged boy when Al Radin died. Al Radin had been a fixture on Broadway, a man who knew all the players from the actors and actresses to the producers, directors, agents and other hangers-on and could make or break a career. His son looked up to him, and considered his father "the greatest man in the world." He inherited some of his father's contacts and clientele, even so far as to include former Rat Packer comedian Joey Bishop as emcee for some of his roadshow extravaganzas. (With Frank Sinatra and Peter Lawford deeply involved in the Marilyn Monroe/Kennedy brothers affair, that would leave only Dean Martin and Sammy Davis, Jr. of all the Rat Packers relatively unscathed from conspiracy associations . . . except for the fact that Sammy Davis, Jr. *did* join the Knights of Malta, long rumored to be a hotbed of intelligence activity and Illuminati-type machinations.)

Overweight, with a pudgy face framed by a short beard, and always well-dressed in public (while preferring a bathrobe at home in his huge Southampton mansion, Ocean Castle), Radin was a show business entrepreneur who managed talent that others wouldn't touch or know what to do with. He represented such acts as George Gobel, Georgie Jessel, Red Buttons, Demond Wilson, and Tiny Tim, sometimes ganging up a few dozen acts and taking the whole geriatric entourage on the road, doing policemen's clubs and other small venues from New England to the Midwest and up and down the Eastern seaboard by bus. Magicians, ventriloquists, dancing poodles and has-been actors and comedians from the 1950s were his stock-in-trade and, incredibly, Middle America loved it and made him a wealthy man.

And with the wealth came the drugs, lots of drugs.

When we speak of cults, particularly satanic cults, we have a picture in our mind of black robes, burning candles, sexual orgies, and strange drugs burning in the censers, sending clouds of potent smoke flowing through the ruined chapel, further enflaming the strange desires of the participants, urging them onwards towards greater depravities. We remember the command of Rimbaud, to "derange the senses" as prerequisite to insight, to spiritual understanding; it was a command the surrealists took to heart, and one that became almost a commonplace among the Hollywood crowd of the 1960s and 1970s. Sexual "deviance" was a necessary tool, as necessary as the drugs; and this is not to make a moral observation or a value judgment on what type of sexuality is "deviant" or "perverse," but only to acknowledge that sexuality is technology in the hands of the mystic as well as of the satanist. The deliberate pursuit of whatever type of sex is considered deviant by one's own culture is part of the program of spiritual seekers as far removed from each other in time and space as Tantric Hindus, California Satanists, Daoist sorcerers, Siberian shamans, and paunchy English "witches" with their scourges and "sky-clad" rituals in the New Forest. To break tabu is a necessary stage in *vama marg* tantra ceremonies, for instance, in which dietary and sexual tabus are deliberately broken, one after another. It is recognized by these technologists of the spirit that deviation from socially-acceptable mores is a powerful tool for awakening the sleeping powers within us, provided that this deviation takes place within the occult engines they have designed.

In the Roy Radin case, sex and drugs combined in the usual ways, but with the addition of cult practices on the one hand, and videotape technology on the other. To show how far we worship the image, merely participating in extreme sexual activity was not enough anymore for people of Radin's circle. It became necessary to record the images on tape so that the events could be relived or—and this is more likely—could be examined and studied from a different perspective, a different angle than the lenses of our own eyes permit us, like seeing yourself talk on television for the first time. To watch yourself having sex with another on tape is to sink a well into your subconscious. It is a point of view normally reserved for your sexual partner; by breaking that parameter you have changed the dynamic of the act completely. While you have *performed* as a sexual being until that time—from the inside, out—you are now a sexual *image*, from the outside, in. You have reversed polarity. And if this is done without the proper safeguards, you can spin out of control.

It is no wonder, then, that all of the high-profile cult scandals of the last thirty years have involved videotaped sex acts: from the much-rumored sex tapes of Sharon Tate and Roman Polanski to the missing videotapes of the Manson Family, to the Sisman videotapes of the Son of Sam killings and the Roy Radin videotapes, sex and murder have become images, have become magical glyphs and sigils in a modern-day grimoire. And, as usual, there is always an organization in place to take control of these images: a cult, a gang, a government. In Radin's case, it was all three.

Radin had made the shrewd choice to hire as many off-duty police as possible, and always threw benefits for the local police departments, thus ingratiating himself with law enforcement, who looked the other way when he was buying cocaine (even having it delivered to his mansion like take-out pizza) or who would give him a head's-up when they knew he was about to be raided. What they did not know was that his godfather—his literal godfather—was Johnny Stoppelli,[38] a soldier in the Genovese crime family who maintained an upscale lifestyle in Manhattan's Murray Hill section. Radin referred to Stoppelli as his "muscle," and when Ron Sisman was murdered along with his girlfriend Elizabeth Plotsman on a Halloween night it was rumored that Radin (and, possibly, Stoppelli) had something to do with it. That's because Sisman had been the one who sent Melonie Haller down to Ocean Castle one night, thus threatening Radin's reputation and lifestyle when she was found, unconscious, on the Long Island Railroad.

Melonie Haller had posed nude for *Playboy* magazine after her appearances on the network television sit-com *Welcome Back, Kotter* in the 1970s. It was Ron

Sisman, a photographer with numerous contacts in the entertainment industry in New York, who suggested she visit Radin at his Long Island home. Radin would be able to help her career, he explained, and she should bring along her portfolio to show him.

Haller showed up at Ocean Castle on April 11, 1980 with a friend, and had dinner with Radin, Radin's second wife Toni Fillet, and two men who were actually police detectives from Rhode Island. Haller's friend was telling stories of cocaine buys he had made, not knowing that his dinner companions were cops. It made for an interesting evening. Once the police had left, Haller and her friend stayed behind and—during the course of an alcohol-and drug-filled evening—wound up donning skimpy leather Nazi uniforms and whipping each other for the benefit of their host. According to various eyewitness testimony—supplemented by a lot of rumor and innuendo—Radin had a movie camera set up in his bedroom where much of this activity took place.

When Haller later told this story, she said her rape had been caught on video, and when the police eventually raided Ocean Castle, they seized what turned out to be a blank (erased) tape from the machine in Radin's bedroom. Whether or not Haller was actually raped or if she did, in fact, willingly participate in sex acts with Radin or other parties is not known for certain. What is known is that, on the following day, when she tried to interest Radin in her portfolio he was less than attentive. She became either unstable or simply upset and angry (depending on which version of the story one believes) and Radin ordered her out of the house. Her companion of the previous evening—a management consultant, no less—is said to have beaten and kicked her, and to eventually have her taken to a local train station and put on the LIRR for Manhattan, where she was found unconscious and heavily bruised.

The tabloid press was gleeful, of course, and Haller rewarded their joy by insisting to the police that she had been drugged, raped and beaten by Radin and his associates and that everything had been captured on videotape. No such tape was found, but then Radin had ample advance warning from the local cops and would have been able to erase any incriminating evidence. As it was, he had the household staff clean the rooms thoroughly and dispose of any drugs, weapons, stains, etc. By the time the police arrived, all they could find was a pistol in Radin's closet, for which he was eventually indicted on a misdemeanor charge of possession of an unregistered weapon.

Whether Radin blamed his predicament on photographer Ron Sisman is not known; what is known is that Sisman was murdered shortly thereafter. The talk on the street, however, was that Sisman was killed for another, even more sinister, reason: he claimed to have possession of a videotape showing the murder of Stacy Moskowitz, the last Son of Sam victim. Appropriately enough, Sisman and his girlfriend were executed in their townhouse on Halloween night 1981, and no videotape was found at the scene.

After the scandal of the Melonie Haller episode—which was followed extensively by the New York tabloid press—Radin had to rebuild his reputation and his business. He had expensive tastes, and so did his *arriviste* wife, Toni Fillet, who fancied herself a society matron and whose ultra-thin and boney physique reflected her maiden name. It would take him two years of turmoil, but in 1982 he sold his Southampton estate for eight million dollars (he had paid only $300,000 for it in 1978) and began his run at Hollywood. In his briefcase was a batch of screenplays that had been sent him over the years. One was a musical he liked about a Harlem nightspot, and it was called *The Cotton Club*.

The same year (and in the same state) that Radin was being investigated over the Melonie Haller affair, Hollywood producer Robert Evans was having his own problems with law enforcement. He had been arrested and convicted for cocaine possession, a charge Radin himself narrowly avoided by flushing his drugs down the toilets minutes before the police raid on Ocean Castle. Evans had been the *enfant terrible* of the Hollywood movie industry in the late 1960s and 1970s, producing a string of box office smashes that included *Rosemary's Baby*, *Love Story*, and *The Godfather*. He was wealthy, self-assured, powerful, and attractive in a boyish sort of way. He charmed Ali MacGraw, to whom he was married for a while, as well as Phyllis George (who would go on to marry Kentucky Governor John Y. Brown) whom he divorced in 1978. He was a regular on the cocktail and cocaine circuit. Evans became dependent on cocaine, and this led to his eventual arrest and conviction for possession of five ounces of the powder in New York, where Radin was having his own problems with the law. This arrest came after a series of financial and critical failures for Evans at the box office, which included, incidentally, the first film made of a Thomas Harris book, *Black Sunday*.

Evans avoided an actual prison term by plea-bargaining his way out of it, producing instead a television special with an anti-drug message: *Get High On Yourself*. Like the previous string of Evans releases, this was also a flop.

Evans and Radin: both in trouble with the law, both at the lowest ebbs of their respective professional careers, reputations in tatters, friends not returning calls, money dwindling, yet neither having ever met the other. It would take a woman with millions of dollars in cocaine money to bring the two together, to essentially seduce both men, becoming in the process a real-life *femme fatale*. By the time a year was over, one of the men would be dead, the other would be questioned by homicide investigators, and Laney Jacobs would be married yet again.

Karen DeLayne Jacobs was born in the third week of June 1947, at the moment UFOs were skimming across the skies of the northwest United States, confusing Kenneth Arnold, and giving rise to the term "flying saucer." She was born in the state of Alabama to an auto mechanic and his wife. Her father eventually became an auto salesman and their financial lives improved, but at the expense of their homelife. Her parents divorced when "Laney" (as she was known) was only nine years old, and in spite of careful upbringing by her grandparents in Georgia she became a willful and wild child, even though her school records were impressive and she had joined a number of clubs and was considered popular, that Holy Grail of teenaged girls. After school she held a number of jobs, but her restless nature was not satisfied with being a legal secretary, and she soon started hanging out in the Latin demimonde of South Florida.

A brittle-looking brunette and at times peroxide blonde with a tight smile and a ferret's features, she was nonetheless as popular around the Cuban and Colombian *narcotraficante* circuit as she was in her Georgia high school Pep Club. Known as *La Rubia* ("the Blonde"), she began cutting deals behind the backs of her drug-dealing boyfriends and was soon running coke in quantity from Miami to Los Angeles. Sometimes loud and abrasive, bordering on the vulgar, she was also smart and cautious with a bookkeeper's approach to the drug business, keeping careful records of all her deals and building a substantial fortune in the process. She loved hanging out in Latin discos and clubs, and her stable of boyfriends was almost exclusively Cuban or Colombian or of other Latin American ancestry; in addition, what they had in common was a love of the drug trade and the fabulous wealth it represented to the otherwise unaccomplished, uneducated, and underprivileged of *norteamericano* society, Latin or *gringo*.

She had gone through a long succession of marriages before her fateful trip to Los Angeles in 1982 (poor Laney, always a bride, never a bridesmaid!) but her most recent liaison was with a powerful trafficker, one Milan Bellechasses. Bellechasses, a native of Santiago de Cuba, worked for the Medellin drug cartel and specifically for Carlos Lehder Rivas, one of the most colorful of the three men who made up the cartel. Lehder was not only a drug trafficker (who had spent time in the Bronx as a teenager, dealing marijuana and boosting cars), but he also considered himself a political activist dedicated to the overthrow of North American hegemony in Colombia and the rest of Latin America through the exportation of illegal drugs to the States: weapons of mass addiction, perhaps. He was also a worshipper (there is no other word) of former Beatle John Lennon, and erected a statue of him outside a hotel he owned in Colombia. The statue shows Lennon completely nude, except for a Nazi helmet, a guitar, and a hole where his heart would be. Lehder's fascination with Nazism perhaps stems from his own background: his father had been a German engineer who emigrated (mysteriously) to Colombia around the time of World War II.

It would be Lehder who would eventually give evidence against Panamanian President Manuel Noriega, after the latter's abduction from Panama by American troops. (Lehder himself had been captured in Colombia and extradited to the United States by the Colombian government on US federal drug charges, a situation that caused tremendous dislocation in New York City as rival gangs fought over his territories, leaving scores of people dead in an underground war that was never reported by the English language press, although it was extensively covered in Spanish language newspapers for weeks. The remaining cartel members offered to pay off all of Colombia's national debt—in cash—if they would be assured that they would not also be extradited. The Colombian government, to its credit, did not entertain the offer.)

This was the milieu in which Laney Jacobs moved and operated. When Miami got a little too hot for her—and her husband and the father of her unborn child was arrested in a drug raid—she decided to decamp to Los Angeles, a dream of hers since childhood. She wanted to be in the movie business. She wanted to be a producer. She could not completely sever the ties that bound her to the drug trade, however, and she really didn't want to. The money was too good, and besides she also had a serious coke habit to support. Then there was Milan Bellechasses, always lurking in the background, a man to whom Laney was inexplicably attracted, and with whom she did millions of dollars of business over the years.

How Laney met Bob Evans was pure serendipity. She had rented a limousine in LA from a company in which Evans was a part owner, Ascot Limousine, and the chauffeur heard her talking about investing some of her money in a movie project. The chauffeur knew that Evans was looking for backers for new projects of his own, and offered to put Laney Jacobs in touch. He was as good as his word, and soon Evans was sending flowers to Laney and taking her out on the town, introducing her to his Hollywood world. The fact that they had cocaine in common didn't hurt the relationship, although Evans would always, incredibly, claim that he did not know that Laney Jacobs was a dealer or that the money she was considering investing in his various projects was drug money. Friends and acquaintances, of course, insist otherwise.

Evans was at his wits' end at the time, trying to jump-start his stalled career when into the midst of his purgatory wandered Jacobs, a brash player in a tight red gown and a bulging purse who single-handedly gave the term "powdering one's nose" a whole new meaning. It was a marriage made in some perverse kind of heaven, where the angels play maracas instead of harps, and the clouds have a street value of a hundred bucks a gram.

For a brief time, one of his financial backers was Adnan Khashoggi.

As revealed in Ronald Kessler's biography of the international arms dealer, *The Richest Man In The World*,[39] Evans had been introduced to Khashoggi by a mutual friend, Melissa Prophet, "a former Miss California who portrayed a tennis groupie in his 1977 movie *Players*."[40] Prophet heard that Evans was having trouble raising money for *The Cotton Club*, and contacted Khashoggi who suggested that they meet immediately and discuss the deal. Khashoggi agreed to provide $750,000 up front, with another $1,250,000 when Evans managed to sign a few more backers. It was with this money, according to Kessler, that Evans hired Mario Puzo to write the script. Melissa Prophet got a credit as an associate producer.

However, Khashoggi (a failed producer himself, whose movie about the Prophet Muhammad starring Anthony Quinn—*The Message*—was banned in Muslim countries and actually caused riots) eventually wanted to own more than 50% of the film, and was prepared to invest an additional ten million dollars for the privilege, but Evans turned him down and eventually bought him out for one million dollars cash.[41] Kessler's book is thin on dates, and unfortunately we don't know exactly how these events tied into those that follow. Khashoggi's original offer of two million dollars is suggestive, as we shall see, as well as Evans' ability to buy him out for a cool million when, according to all accounts, he was flat broke at the time.

Laney Jacobs and Roy Radin both arrived in Los Angeles in January of 1983, and it was shortly thereafter that Laney met Evans and then met Radin, who was interested in renting or buying her house in Benedict Canyon. Radin and Jacobs hit it off immediately, Radin inviting Jacobs to his temporary, serviced apartment, where his assistant prepared a light supper for them.

As their relationship blossomed, Jacobs confided to Radin that she wanted to be a movie producer. Since Radin was in Hollywood on the same mission, they could pool their resources. When Jacobs mentioned her friendship with Robert Evans, however, that took the dialogue to a whole new level. Radin was ecstatic at the possibility of working with a legend like Evans, and when a meeting was finally arranged, Radin talked to him about the various scripts he was interested in promoting.

One of the projects in question was *The Cotton Club*. The story of a Harlem nightclub, Evans had wanted to do a film about the history of the club himself, but more as a drama, while Radin was favoring a musical (true to his Vaudeville roots). The script would eventually go through several hands including Mario Puzo and Francis Ford Coppola. As the story unfolded, Evans would turn Hollywood upside down looking for backers, even interesting international arms dealer (and eventual Iran-Contra figure) Adnan Khashoggi. Finally, he garnered the support of the Doumani brothers, Las Vegas businessmen and casino owners (El Morocco) who were inclined to help finance the project if they had some control over the script and the casting. It was just as the Doumani deal was in danger of falling through that Laney Jacobs brought Roy Radin to meet Evans; was it synchronicity that both Evans and Radin were interested in making a film about the Cotton Club? That Evans had already started raising funding and doing rewrites of the initial script when Radin walked in with another Cotton Club treatment under his arm?

Radin was elated; he was finally in the big leagues. Further, Evans was a known coke-head and even the Doumani brothers were fed up with his habit. Radin had experience with cokeheads and felt he could control Evans to a certain degree. He could coast on Evans' legendary reputation in the movie business (even though that legend was largely tarnished) and create a new reputation for himself. And everything would have been fine, had it not been for Tally Rogers.

Rogers was Laney's drug courier, and the man who had installed the safe in her house. After an argument about the amount he was to be paid for a Miami-Los

Angeles round trip, he rifled her safe and her stash and made off with a million dollars' worth of cocaine and cash, and then promptly disappeared.

Radin by this time was back on the East Coast temporarily tending to some business, when he received a hysterical phone call from Laney accusing Radin of being partners with Rogers in the crime. Radin, of course, had nothing to do with it. He had bigger fish to fry, and was eager to be rid of Laney Jacobs if at all possible and get down to business with Evans. But Jacobs was having none of it. She began phoning all over the country in an effort to locate Rogers.

The coke business in those days was done largely on credit. The cocaine Jacobs had in her home—and she had stacks of it from floor to ceiling in her closet—had not been paid for. It had been extended on credit to Milan Bellechasses from his Colombian suppliers, and from Bellechasses to Jacobs. Jacobs would have to make good on the coke, in cash. Hence, the hysteria. If she didn't, the Colombians were notoriously lacking in a sense of humor, and would deal with her harshly. To compound matters, her small son was living with her and could also conceivably become a victim in some hideously operatic act of revenge.

Tally Rogers *had* taken the coke and the cash, angry at the way he had been treated by Jacobs, and was now driving around the country, moving from place to place and keeping a low profile, believing it would eventually blow over. Roy Radin shared this point of view, and concentrated on his production career instead, ignoring Laney's screams over the telephone.

Jacobs, terrified that either Rogers would come back to steal the rest of her stash or that the Colombians would show up, all firepower and fatal finery, went to a friend of hers and asked him to help her find a bodyguard. The friend introduced her to one Bill Mentzer and one Alex Marti, both former bodyguards of *Hustler* magazine publisher Larry Flynt, who had been wounded in an assassination attempt a few years previously. Laney took them to her house to guard her home and coke, and eventually began "dating" Mentzer. Marti, an Argentine and reputed former death squad member was the more violent of the two, and also a Hitler devotee who had a portrait of the Fuhrer in his home, a Third Reich library, and who admired the Nazi method of execution: a single gunshot to the back of the head.[42]

In the meantime, Radin was going forward with his movie deal with Evans. Jacobs found out that she was going to be cut out of the deal, less a finder's fee, and she was livid. Cocaine makes one paranoid as it is, but is it paranoia when everyone really is plotting against you?

Jacobs and Radin agreed to a fifty thousand dollar finder's fee upon signing of an agreement between Evans and Radin (something which had been going nowhere since both coked-out producers could not manage to write a single declarative sentence that made any sense). Radin did his best to ignore Laney Jacobs, and was busy investigating a mysterious burglary of his office in Manhattan when, unknown to him, Bob Evans and Laney Jacobs traveled together from California to New York and from there on to Miami, where Laney was introducing Evans to her circle of friends.

Laney had managed to get Evans to agree to disassociate himself from Radin, at least on principle. Radin was still insisting he could raise thirty-five million dollars, and Evans could not afford to ignore that. However, Laney wined and dined and bedded Evans in Miami, showing him that it was possible to raise cash as easily in Miami as it was from Roy Radin. Evans already had Mario Puzo and Francis Ford Coppola lined up to make the *Cotton Club* movie, and these were bankable names.

During this visit to Miami, Laney Jacobs introduced Robert Evans to Milan Bellechasses.

At the same time, Radin was actually accomplishing something on his own. He had managed to convince the Puerto Rican government to raise the thirty-five million dollars through an industrial bond offering. The idea was this: Evans would make the film in Puerto Rico and the Puerto Rican government would build a Hollywood-class studio to accommodate him (and many future films), and would even make Evans a professor of film at the University of Puerto Rico. In other words, there was serious and reputable money behind the scheme. For his part, Evans had to raise money through the sale of foreign rights, and Radin had to front another eight million dollars of his own money, which he felt he could do through the sale of his Long Island mansion. Radin would own 45 percent of the deal, Evans another 45 percent, and their Puerto Rican attorney the remaining ten percent. It seemed like a done deal.

On the New York side, pre-production was already in progress at Astoria Studios on *Cotton Club*. People were being hired, money was being spent, there was still no official screenplay, but the show must, as they say, go on. The Doumani brothers were still in for $1.6 million and had not been paid back, and there was fighting over the script that seemed to go on forever, but at least the movie was being made.

Then, in April of 1983, it all went wrong.

Visiting Evans at his home one evening, Radin learned that Laney Jacobs was back in the picture, literally. Evans tried to convince Radin to give Laney half of his 45 percent. If he had done that, of course, Radin would have lost any control he had over the project. Evans would keep 45 percent, the lion's share, and if he formed a bloc with Laney (as it appeared to be the case), then Radin was reduced to a minor role. This was not what Radin had in mind, especially since he had been the one to set up the Puerto Rican deal in the first place.

On May 5, 1983, and in the midst of the accusations and recriminations that were flying around the New York City townhouse of Robert Evans that week, Radin managed to bring his "godfather," Johnny Stoppelli, to one of the meetings, hoping that they could work something out between Radin and Evans. However, they had just begun to talk when Laney walked in with her Miami attorney, Frank Diaz, and the fighting began again. Radin was adamant about not letting Jacobs have any percentage of the deal. He did not want to have to deal with her at all.

Even more compelling, however, was Johnny Stoppelli's reaction: he recognized Jacobs for what she was, and told Radin that he would not do business with drug dealers and warned Radin to forget the whole thing. That, if he did not, he was asking for trouble.[43] Radin felt he could not abandon the project completely, and was still committed to doing something in Hollywood.

On May 7, 1983 Roy Radin flew to Hollywood to attend the bar mitzvah of comedian Red Buttons' son, Adam. He was still anxious about the *Cotton Club* deal and felt, understandably, that he had put the whole deal together from financing to studios and should be allowed to have a greater say in the future of the project. He felt he did not owe Laney Jacobs anything beyond the finder's fee, since all she did was introduce him to Evans. He had done the rest.

When he was out one afternoon, he received a call at his Los Angeles hotel on his private line. It was a New York mobster, warning him to keep his mouth shut and to get out of town. The call was taken by Radin's assistant, Jonathan Lawson, who was appropriately alarmed and urged Radin to heed the advice. It had been a warning—the last one.

Radin called Stoppelli in New York City and asked about the call, but Stoppelli hadn't a clue. He only reiterated what he had told Radin before: get out of LA and forget the movie business. He was involved with drug dealers and it could only mean trouble. Radin promised he would return to New York on Friday, after the bar mitzvah.

Immediately, the issue began to heat up. Evans offered to buy out Radin for two million dollars cash, but Radin declined. (Where did Evans get two million dollars in cash, if not from Laney Jacobs?) Evans called the Puerto Rican attorney and asked if the deal could still go through without Radin. The attorney preferred that both Evans and Radin be involved; however, if someone could come up with the financing that Radin was due to invest—eight million dollars—then it was possible. A girlfriend of Radin's—and a close friend of Laney Jacobs—warned Radin that there was heavy muscle in town around Jacobs and that Radin should under no circumstances agree to meet with her. Most curiously, Evans had not been able to post the performance bond necessary to get the movie contract signed with the Puerto Ricans, but somehow had two million dollars cash to give Radin. Evans' insistence that he did not know Laney Jacobs was involved in drug-dealing begins to look very weak at this point.

But the die had been cast. Laney Jacobs had called and asked for one last meeting to try to sort out the *Cotton Club* mess. Radin, pushed to the wall but still believing he could salvage the deal, agreed.

The date was set for Friday, May 13.

That night, Laney Jacobs arrived in a limousine to collect Radin and drive to the La Scala restaurant in Los Angeles. Radin's assistant, Lawson, did not trust the arrangement at all. Instead, he had one of Radin's long-time friends and fellow coke user, actor Demond Wilson (*Sanford and Son*, *The New Odd Couple* television sitcoms), tail the limo to the restaurant. Wilson, according to all accounts, was armed. Lawson stood in the lobby of their hotel and watched as Jacobs and Radin drove off in the limo, driven by one Bob Lowe. Prior to that, Jacobs had tried to get Lawson to drive to her house to pick up some cocaine but Lawson, smelling a rat, refused and stayed behind. It was a decision that saved his life, for Jacobs had two men waiting for him in a pickup truck outside her house.

Wilson, who had already done at least two lines of cocaine in the car, began following the limousine but not before another car swung out behind it, a black Caddy driven—as it was later discovered—by Bill Mentzer, with Alex Marti riding shotgun, appropriately enough. The two cars lost Wilson in traffic, taking evasive measures and running a red light, so that Wilson wound up driving directly to La Scala to wait for Radin and Jacobs to appear. The plan was that Wilson would take another table and watch the proceedings from a safe distance.

They never showed up. After a few hours, Lawson called La Scala to see what was going on and was informed that Radin and Jacobs never arrived. He asked to speak to Wilson, and was dumbfounded to learn that Wilson was just sitting in the restaurant all this time, waiting for the friend he would never see again.

Wilson, terrified by now, disappeared that night. It would be two days before Lawson could locate him, but by that time Radin had already been reported missing.

Wilson has since left show business and refuses to talk about that night. Instead (like so many others who have been touched by the cults), he became a Christian minister and now preaches the Gospel, trading cocaine for the "opium of the people."

Lawson, confronting Jacobs, got two different stories, neither of which made much sense. Either Radin left the limo before arriving at La Scala after a fight with Laney, or Jacobs did. No matter, they were both lies. That same week she had her infant son and her maid fly back out to Miami, and she put her Los Angeles home up for sale, telling everyone she was going to New York to work for Robert Evans. Events had been set in motion behind Radin's back.

The full story would not come out until much later, after several years of investigation, but on June 10, 1983—less than a month after Radin's disappearance—a bee-keeper by the name of Glen Fischer wandering in the rough country near Gorman, California came across a body that was partially buried in a ravine, the fingers of one hand clawing upward from the ground, its skull almost completely destroyed, its jawbone several feet away from its head, pumped with twenty-eight shots at point blank range, and dressed in an expensive three-piece suit and a Pierre Cardin tie. Glen Fischer had found Roy Radin.

It is at this point in the story that we must rejoin our previous protagonists, who had been searching zealously for evidence of just such a crime before it was even reported. Maury Terry, acting on the basis of information obtained from an informer—"Vinny"—who had known David Berkowitz in prison, was looking at Roy Radin as the possible East Coast connection for the Son of Sam cult. Why? There was more to Ocean Castle than the Melonie Haller incident. It seems that police had been called out to the Castle several times in the past, acting on complaints of sexual assault. There was a strong rumor that many of the parties and other activities there had been videotaped; and that photographer Ronald Sisman was more deeply involved with Radin and with cult activity than others had suspected. Vinny had actually named Radin—knowing him only as "Rodan" and "Rodan the Flying Monster"—as well as Sisman and others involved in the case. Radin was said to be involved with "Dale Evans," another code name, and in this case Roy Radin was referred to as "Roy Rogers."

"Dale Evans," then, was possibly Bob Evans . . . but some of this information went back long before Evans and Radin were thought to have met, implying a deeper involvement between the two men, something that Evans has always denied. In fact, Evans would only admit that Radin was merely an acquaintance and not a business partner, a statement that was patently untrue, as signed copies of their movie agreement exist to disprove this allegation beyond any doubt. To be sure, "Roy Rogers" could also have been a reference to Tally Rogers who, as Laney Jacobs' drug courier, was driving between Miami and Los Angeles twice a month and could conceivably have been more than simply a drug courier, and used to transport information between the Los Angeles branch of the Sam Cult and the East Coast. (When the investigators finally caught up with Tally Rogers, he was serving time in the Louisiana prison system for child molestation, having sexually abused two young sons of his then-current girlfriend.)

Vinny insisted that Radin had close connections to Los Angeles and the Son of Sam cult supposed to be headquartered there. Terry's information included reports of satanic activity at Ocean Castle along with all the drugs and polymorphous sexuality. David Berkowitz himself was known to have visited Ocean Castle at least once, which was explosive information as it was . . . but then Berkowitz also had been seen in Minot, North Dakota, the other Sam cult site. Terry tried connecting all the dots, but he did not have identities for some of the players, and in other cases he was dealing with ongoing police investigations and could not reveal more specific information, or possibly such information was not available to him.

Terry has been criticized a great deal by both occultists and others for some of his conclusions, as I have mentioned, but a close reading of *The Ultimate Evil* and collation with other documentation of these cases shows that Terry has been reliable where names, dates and places are concerned. He has reproduced documentation received from his informants and others, including Berkowitz, and these bear out the basic facts of his theory: that there is (or was) a nation-wide network of criminals either using satanic activity as a front, or a satanic cult using criminal activity to finance their operation. In any case, murder is an essential part of their business plan, either "for hire" or for reasons of ritual magic and sacrifice. There is no way some of his informants would have had the information they had—in advance of any media accounts—unless they were "connected" in some way to the events described.

Once Radin's body had been found, Terry was notified and prepared to fly to Los Angeles to examine the crime scene himself, certain he was that Radin had been part of the Sam cult he was investigating. That is when he received another note from "Vinny," who told him to look at the scene carefully, for the killers would have left a cultic clue behind. Terry had a lot of clues in his hands, but until Roy Radin's body was found he didn't know what to do with them. As the Radin murder became news, Terry realized that the scenario fit all the details of the cult organization and activity he had been hearing about. He flew to Los Angeles and drove out to the canyons around Gorman, convinced he would find what Vinny had been telling him was there: evidence of cult involvement in the murder of Roy Radin.

And that is when he found the Bible, buried underneath a bush next to where Radin's body had been found, opened to the twenty-second chapter of Isaiah.

The murder of Roy Radin, while solved, is not wholly explained. There was the angle that Laney Jacobs believed Radin had ripped off her drugs and cash to the tune of one million dollars; killing Radin would not get that money back and, in fact, everyone knew who had taken the drugs anyway: Laney's drug courier Tally Rogers. Radin had been buying drugs from Rogers, but giving him checks made out to Laney Jacobs, making it clear that he expected Laney to be paid back for the money Rogers stole from her. Thus, the drugs-and-cash angle for Radin's murder did not make a lot of sense: he was the only one playing straight with her on that score.

Then there was the movie angle. Was Radin murdered so that Laney Jacobs could enjoy greater participation in the Evans venture? This is possible, of course, although it does give a whole new meaning to the phrase "termination clause." Why was it necessary to kill Radin? In the first place, if Evans felt strongly enough about having Jacobs involved in the production (perhaps due to her ability to provide huge amounts of drug money to finance his projects) he could have simply given her part of his share rather than insisting that it come from Radin's end. Of course, that would mean less control for Evans and more for Radin, and that was unacceptable.

So, Evans actually had a motive for getting rid of Radin; but he pled the Fifth Amendment, answered no questions in court, and was never charged. Other than Jacobs and Evans, who else would have wanted Radin dead?

The mystery man behind Laney Jacobs is, of course, Milan Bellechasses. It is reported in Steve Wick's account of the murder that Bellechasses was quietly involved in the Puerto Rican movie studio project with Radin and Evans, using his girlfriend Laney Jacobs as a front. Bellechasses thought that a movie deal with the Puerto Rican government would enable him to launder drug money easily. Money laundering is an essential part of the drug trade: profits from the sale of illegal narcotics is collected in cash, and even one neighborhood in a busy American city can net millions of dollars in cash profits in a single month. Counting this cash, transporting it and, eventually, banking it is an arduous task which requires its own specialists and its own network of couriers, accountants and compliant banks in countries with flexible banking systems.

According to this theory, Bellechasses would have viewed the Evans-Jacobs-Radin arrangement as tailor-made for his purposes. In order for this to work, he would have to retain—through Laney Jacobs—a percentage of the company; a finder's fee, such as Radin was offering, just wouldn't work.

Evans had to have known about this, and Wick's book suggests as much (along with a disclaimer that Evans has denied knowing anything about this, even though he was identified by Bill Mentzer on the witness stand as the man who gave the orders to kill Radin). Evans has never been convicted of a crime in connection with the *Cotton Club* murder, although he has been a suspect. On the basis of the information in Wick's book and much else uncovered by Terry and others, I think it is safe to say of Evans that "the kid stays in the picture."

Wick also mentions that the name "Rodan" was given to Roy Radin by his neo-Nazi killer, Alex Marti, who also called Radin "a big, fat Jew." Terry's informant on the East Coast knew the nickname Rodan before Radin was killed. Since Radin was known as "Rodan" to the Son of Sam cult (via Vinny's information), the only possible conclusion to draw is that Marti and his partner Mentzer were either members of that same cabal or had been hired guns of the cabal. All Terry needed to confirm the stories he had heard was proof at the crime scene of cult involvement, as the Sam cult usually left a "signature" behind.

Terry, wandering around the Radin crime scene on two separate occasions, found the Bible on the last day of his visit to Los Angeles, steeling himself to dig under a bush close by the scene that had been overlooked by police. The Bible was not buried in the sand, but simply sitting at the root of the bush, opened to the page mentioned above. It was straining credulity to believe that the positioning of the Bible in that place, miles from civilization and in the middle of the desert, was simply a coincidence. It had to have been planted. As the investigation progressed and Bill Mentzer, Alex Marti, Bob Lowe and, finally, Laney Jacobs were identified as the co-conspirators in the murder of Roy Radin, it only made Terry more convinced that the Son of Sam cult was behind the murder, and that there might have been other motives for Radin's messy extermination.

That "Vinny"and "Danny"—Terry's prison informants—would have known details about Radin, Evans, Ocean Castle, Sisman, Berkowitz, drugs, videotaped sexual acts, and much else besides, clearly implies (but does not prove) that they were right in other areas as well, including the satanic cult angle. The author himself can attest that Roy Radin had expressed interest in filming occult rituals being performed in Manhattan by the magicians and other self-styled sorcerers hanging out at the Magickal Childe bookstore on 19th Street, identified by Terry (although not by name) as an important locus for the Sam cult. And an address book in Berkowitz's possession did show an entry for Ocean Castle. Sisman did introduce Melonie Haller to Roy Radin, and Sisman and his girlfriend were murdered on Halloween; police—aware of the relationship between the two men—questioned Radin about the murder, but he claimed ignorance. Sisman was also rumored to have in his possession the all-important Stacy Moskowitz murder videotape . . . if, indeed, such ever existed.

RETURN OF THE FAMILY

For reasons why this murder neatly fits a theory of a nationwide satanic cult, we only have to look at Terry's evidence concerning Bill Mentzer and his early years in California, including his relationship to the Manson Family. Mentzer is a link that ties together not only Charles Manson and the Roy Radin murder, but also those separate cases and the Son of Sam murders in New York City, as well as other murders across the country. While the author does not wish to re-ignite the "satanic cult hysteria" of the 1980s, it is important to look at this evidence soberly, for the murders in question are not the key reasons why an understanding of the Manson/Sam cult is critical; rather, the murders—while vile enough in and of themselves—are only one aspect of the group's activities.

Bill Mentzer—Terry's pick as "Manson II," a much-rumored hitman with cult credentials—has the necessary pedigree. According to Terry's informants within the Los Angeles police, federal agencies, and the criminal subculture (very few of whom are named, making independent corroboration or confirmation difficult if not at times impossible), Mentzer had been a friend of both Charles Manson and, most importantly, Abigail Folger in the late 1960s. Although much has been made of the Sharon Tate murders, which were ghastly, the focus has been primarily on Sharon Tate herself, her filmmaker husband Roman Polanski (who was in Europe at the time of the killings), and Wojciech Frykowski, who was a known drug dealer and a friend of Polanski's from their early days in Poland. There has not been a lot of light shed on Abigail Folger, even though she was arguably the wealthiest person among the victims, and had bankrolled numerous New Age-type projects in California in the 1960s.

Heir to the Folger Coffee fortune, Abigail had made a practice of financing worthy causes, and these included the Himalayan Society (to which it is said Manson himself belonged) and the Straight Theater in San Francisco, which was the scene of the famous Magick Powerhouse of Oz performance that brought together Kenneth Anger and Bobby Beausoleil, as well as other Manson Family members. An informant who had penetrated the anti-war movement in America on behalf of the federal government told Terry that he had been present at a meal that included Abigail Folger and Bill Mentzer. Mentzer obviously had a soft spot for the counter-culture, for he wound up working for *Hustler* publisher Larry Flynt later on in the '70s.

While Mentzer had a criminal record and had been involved in questionable and illegal activity for a while, what does not ring true about Mentzer being the much-vaunted "Manson II" is that, for a hitman, he evidently has a rather weak stomach. On each occasion where we know Mentzer was present at or committed a murder he had to drink himself into the role. That is, he had to be pretty drunk before he could carry out the killings, whereas his associates—men like Argentine assassin Alex Marti—carried out these missions with glee, and needed no "Dutch courage" to get them in the mood. In the case of Roy Radin, it is agreed that Mentzer did not fire the shot that killed the producer. It was Marti who fired some twenty-seven rounds into Radin's skull; Mentzer only delivered the twenty-eighth and final shot, a kind of *coup de grace*, and that only after he had been drinking. While he may have been a willing hitman—at least theoretically—it would take him some time to work up the nerve. This does not sound like a "Manson II," but it is possible I am reading too much into the sobriquet for, after all, Manson himself was never convicted of actually committing a murder, but only of having ordered them to be carried out. If the Manson killings were murder-for-hire, Manson acting on instructions from another source, then the Mentzer killings were certainly hired hits. The murder of Roy Radin was carried out on Laney Jacobs' instructions. Another murder, that of a transvestite in Los Angeles who was allegedly blackmailing a wealthy family, was also murder-for-hire, a contract fulfilled by Mentzer.

Thus, we have to look a little deeper into the Manson and Mentzer killings to understand that they were not the result of crazed dope fiends going on a murder spree, but possibly contracted killings, paid for or at least ordered by person or persons unknown. In the case of Roy Radin and the Los Angeles transvestite, the contracts are clear. They were murders for specific motives. In the case of the Manson Family, we do not know who contracted the Tate/LaBianca killings (if indeed they were contracted), but, on the basis of much evidence and assorted testimony by those close to the case, we are safe in making the general assumption that Manson was carrying out assassinations at the behest of others.

That Manson and Mentzer knew each other in California in the 1960s is now virtually a certainty. That they were both involved in cult activity is also something for which Terry makes a very good case. We have already looked carefully at Manson's career and his cult involvements, which are beyond dispute. In addition, Terry has Mentzer not only friendly with both Charles Manson and Abigail Folger, but in the days after the Manson killings he places Mentzer at cult sites in California, Texas, and on the East Coast.

If we understand that the Son of Sam killings also included some specific hits, possibly ordered by an organized crime lord (as intimated by David Berkowitz himself, who has never avoided responsibility for his participation in these murders), and if we understand that Manson, Mentzer and Berkowitz are linked quite specifically via their respective cults, we have to come to the inescapable conclusion that a cult exists whose members are available for contract killings, and that this cult has existed since at least the late 1960s through the late 1970s, and likely beyond. We have also to understand that some of the Son of Sam killings were cult sacrifices, chosen to take place on days selected in advance according to an occult calendar or to some other, more esoteric, method. These killings were probably arranged to "blood" the new recruits: to acquaint them with the act of murder and to win their loyalty through fear of exposure to the authorities. This implies a well-organized and disciplined operation with, indeed, national coverage, as murders connected to this cult have taken place all over the United States.

As we mentioned, however, murder is only one aspect of this cult's activities. Drug-running is another, and probably provides much of the operating income for the group. Prostitution—both male and female, adult and child—is also a function of the group, as well as pornography and particularly child pornography.

While we have looked at both the Manson-Mentzer-Berkowitz connections and the Robert Evans-Laney Jacobs-Mentzer connections, what the reader may find startling are connections to still yet another group of organized killers and drug runners, the infamous "Company."

When Laney Jacobs was asked about her sources of income, she would usually tell people that she had made investments in the Suzy Creamcheese line of women's fashions and was a part-owner of the franchise which was famous in Las Vegas and among Hollywood celebrities. We don't know if Jacobs did indeed own a piece of the Suzy Creamcheese action, but she is known to have taken friends to visit Las Vegas and stay at Suzy Creamcheese owner Leslie DeKeyser's house, and to buy them clothes at the boutique. Jacobs spent a lot of time traveling to Vegas from both Florida and California, and we remember that Bob Evans was trying to raise money from casino owners there, the Doumani brothers.

Suzy Creamcheese had another illustrious client, and this will lead us back to Ashland, Kentucky and—strangely enough—back to Bob Evans, drugs, and murder. This time the main character is a bizarre figure who was part-commando, part-mystic, and total criminal, a man who leaped to his death on September 11, 1985, when his parachute didn't open because the $75-million worth of cocaine he had strapped to his body proved too heavy: Andrew Carter "Drew" Thornton II.

THE BLUEGRASS CONSPIRACY

Suzy Creamcheese was the brainchild of one Leslie DeKeyser, a flamboyant man with outrageous taste in fashion who created outfits that even a Vegas showgirl might have been embarrassed to wear. (The name came from a famous Frank Zappa song, whose most memorable lyric "Suzy Creamcheese, what's got into you?" became a rallying cry for a certain type of hippie-chick/rock groupie of the 1960s.) Although he boasted such . . . luminaries as Charo and Cher among his satisfied customers, his most devoted client was one Anita Madden, nee Myers, a woman who was raised in Ashland, Kentucky on the wrong side of the tracks, but who clawed her way to the top by marrying the heir to the Madden horse-raising fortune. Sharing a great deal in common with Laney Jacobs, another poor white Southern girl who made it a habit to marry wealthy men, Anita Madden's parties became scandalous affairs in the late 1960s (and through to 1998, the year of the last Madden Kentucky Derby-Eve bash), with Ms. Madden decked out in the latest Suzy Creamcheese outrage, all leathers and feathers, and surrounding herself with show business and sports personalities, in a determined effort to invade and hold hostage the society columns of the Kentucky newspapers, struggling against those other blue-blooded clans, the Whitneys, the Vanderbilts, and the Barnstables who looked down their noses at the noisy bottle-blonde with the trashy, Frederick's of Hollywood *couture*. Ms. Creamcheese "herself " would show up at these galas—particularly the pre-Derby extravaganzas that are a mainstay of Kentucky society—resplendent in whips and chains, while nude mermaids and muscular men in sadomasochistic gear wandered the grounds of Madden's estate, Hamburg Place, making sure all the guests were properly lubricated.

All of this is recounted in greater and fascinating detail in investigative journalist Sally Denton's *The Bluegrass Conspiracy*, and it makes for compelling reading, especially as we begin to come across familiar names and suggestive time frames.

For instance, we don't know if Laney Jacobs and Anita Madden ever met; we do know that one of Anita Madden's closest friends married one of Laney Jacobs' husbands, however. Although Laney Jacobs herself is not mentioned in Denton's work, even though her story dovetails neatly with that book's drugs-murder-conspiracy saga, and neither is her lover and putative fiancé Bob Evans, Phyllis George makes an important appearance, she who was once married to the Hollywood producer. The Laney Jacobs-Suzy Creamcheese-Anita Madden nexus catapults us to the Laney Jacobs-Robert Evans-Phyllis George nexus and the *Cotton Club* murder, with Kentucky Fried Chicken along the way.

Confused?

Like her compatriot, Charles Manson, Anita Madden grew from a poor white background in Ashland to become figurative head of a social demimonde that rejoiced in free love, drugs, and dangerous alliances. While Charlie's girls were putting out in hot, dirt-floor shacks in the desert for Charlie's unhygienic guests—usually the Hell's Angels or some other motorcycle gang running LSD and pot through the American landscape like Wells Fargo on angel dust—Anita Madden's parties were a bit more upscale, the guests generally bathed, and the Dom was always properly chilled. But beneath the social register veneer lay the same sinister forces that suppurated so openly among the Family. While Charlie courted Terry Melcher and the Beach Boys on the West Coast, Anita Madden was hosting Sissy Spacek, Ann-Margret, Connie Stevens and Larry Flynt (employer of convicted Radin assassins Bill Mentzer and Alex Marti) in Kentucky; but for both there was violence and bloodshed just below the surface. At the end, there would be many dead—both the innocent and the guilty—including the first assassination of a federal judge in a hundred years. And we will incredibly find ourselves back at Dealey Plaza on November 22, 1963, with a wisp of smoke rising from the Grassy Knoll.

The complex mystery begins with a bizarre paramilitary operation known as the "Company" a nickname not to be confused with that of the CIA . . . maybe. As it turns out, the Company was involved in more than what was originally suspected by Kentucky law enforcement, which was drug-running, pure and simple. Sally Denton's book is virtually the only text anywhere that exposes this operation, and Ms. Denton found herself being squeezed out of mainstream journalism largely due to her insistence (and evidence) that Kentucky politics was dirty with drug and arms deals. Ms. Denton again went against the establishment with her oft-cited piece "The Crimes of Mena" (co-authored with Roger Morris), an article on a covert government drugs-and arms-smuggling operation, an exposé that was spiked by the *Washington Post* at the last minute, and wound up instead in the pages of *Penthouse.* The Mena article is an account of an Iran-Contra operation in the tiny town of Mena, Arkansas during the Reagan-Bush years, while Bill Clinton was governor of the state. Denton would go on to investigate both the criminal history of Las Vegas (also co-authored with Roger Morris) as well as the Mormon Mountain Meadows Massacre of September 11, 1857, thus illustrating once again that independent investigation into America's history keeps pulling one back to the same topics.

Kentucky has a tradition of smuggling that goes back more than a century, making it the Paraguay of the South. With the Ohio River on one side and the Big Sandy on the other, and a stretch of the Mississippi on the western border, Kentucky has seen more than its share of strange water traffic, with contraband running as far south as the Gulf of Mexico. Running slaves, then liquor, and finally drugs and guns, Kentucky's history as a smuggler's state is almost genteel, serving as an unofficial frontier between the Northeast, the South and the Western parts of the United States.

The police investigation of the Company revealed a state whose politics—from the Governor's Mansion on down through the various local and state police departments—was corrupt to the extent that its reputation is only surpassed by that of Louisiana and Rhode Island. There were so many former and current law enforcement officers as part of the Company that for a while many investigators were under the assumption that it was a covert federal operation, perhaps something linked to arms deals with the Contras. Indeed, Iran-Contra figure Adnan Khashoggi makes an appearance in this story, too, as a frequent visitor to Kentucky whose own company's name—the Triad Corporation—was echoed in the name of the farm that served as the Company's headquarters: Triad. The logo of the Triad Farm was a pitchfork, and locals insisted to police and federal investigators that it was used not only for paramilitary training but was also the headquarters of a satanic cult.[44] In fact, it was during the search for a missing friend of Company members, Melanie Flynn (sister of baseball player Doug Flynn of the Mets and later the Cincinnati Reds), that a psychic was eventually called in, and without prompting led police to the site where they privately believed Flynn had been killed; the same psychic told the investigators that she believed a cult was behind the murder. She identified Drew Thornton as one of the persons responsible for Flynn's murder, and the heavy occult "vibes" she received chilled her to the bone.

There is a strong tradition linking Kentucky and the casinos of Las Vegas. Kentuckians are inveterate gamblers; after all, their state boasts the prestigious Kentucky Derby, and many fortunes are won and lost on a single race. Several important Vegas casinos were run by Kentuckians, and they favored people from their home state as dealers in their employ. There is also a link between Kentucky and Florida, and that is the drug trade.

In the 1970s, Kentucky became infamous for activity of the Company, a network of illegal trade in drugs, arms and prostitution. The Company was largely composed of former law enforcement officers, and had intelligence resources high up in several federal agencies, notably the Drug Enforcement Agency, or DEA. It was widely rumored that the Company had CIA connections, and that they were part of the infrastructure that eventually began supplying the Contras in the 1980s. With planeloads of weapons and high-technology gear such as night-vision scopes and other James Bond paraphernalia (either stolen from US military bases such as China Lake, or actually supplied by the government, the truth is a little hard to find), the materiel wound up supporting Latin American military regimes, and the planes would fly back into the United States with shipments of marijuana and, later, cocaine. Shipments worth millions of dollars a flight.

One of the central figures of this organization—believed by federal agents to have been the most dangerous, most highly-organized and tightly-controlled illegal operation in the country—was Drew Thornton, a former Lexington, Kentucky police officer and martial arts specialist. Thornton's parents were Northerners; his father was from New Jersey and his mother from Connecticut, but they assimilated quickly into Kentucky society by the expedient of raising racehorses on a small ranch near the town of Paris. Thornton joined the Army at the time of the Vietnam conflict, and then rotated back to the States and became a police officer, eventually working Narcotics as well as Intelligence. He formed alliances at this time with an entire brotherhood of police officers who had no problem with selling the dope they confiscated, usually long before it made its way to the evidence locker.

The Lexington police department became notorious for dirty cops during this period, and evidence began to accumulate showing that they were actually being protected by the local DEA chief, giving rise to speculation that the "dirty cops" were working on a larger, more covert, operation on behalf of the DEA and, possibly, the CIA; conversely, other speculation was simpler and more direct: the DEA chief in Kentucky was corrupt. The reality is probably a combination of both.

At various times in her book, Denton mentions the fact that Drew Thornton believed himself possessed of supernatural powers, but she does not delve any deeper into this except to imply that it was a mélange of Asian mysticism and martial arts philosophy, and that Thornton had become a kind of David Carradine (of television series *Kung Fu* fame) at least in his own mind. (His first wife also professed to be psychic, able to predict future events.) This mysticism was wedded to his paramilitary exploits, and his Triad Farm became a venue for both occult practices of some description and commando training. It was also a center for the trade in illegal narcotics, and more than one eyewitness reported seeing aircraft flying low over Triad and dropping bundles that were believed to be drugs. In other cases, federal agencies reported suspicions that arms, including tanks, were being smuggled into and out of Triad Farm. When State Police investigator Ralph Ross attempted to learn more, he was warned off the case by Lexington police officers . . . even though they had no jurisdiction over the territory. Ross was eventually set up by his own men in a desperate effort to silence him, and thus remove the threat of an investigation which was lapping gently around the doorway to the Governor's Mansion.

The investigation into the clandestine affairs of the Company eventually went as high as the governor of the state, who at the time was John Y. Brown, a successful Democratic businessman who had parlayed the Kentucky Fried Chicken franchise into a hugely successful operation (and would later become involved with Kenny Rogers Roasters and the Roadhouse Grill franchises). Harlan Sanders, who had created Kentucky Fried Chicken and become an honorary "Colonel" in the process, harbored ill feelings towards the deal, believing that he had been cheated out of money that was rightfully his. "Colonel" Sanders had developed the business from a mom-and-pop operation to over six hundred outlets by 1963. In 1964, John Y. Brown arranged a buyout of Sanders, a deal in which the "Colonel" felt manipulated into selling, and said as much to the newspapers.[45] The deal, however, made Brown a multimillionaire once he brought the company public, and he gave jobs in KFC to friends of his who would later become notorious in the Company investigation, including Dan Chandler and Jimmy Lambert. Chandler would become an "unindicted co-conspirator," and Lambert would face a criminal indictment over the affair. They were all part of the Anita Madden social circuit, including Governor Brown himself.

There were (and are) other "social circuits" in Kentucky society, of course, and Madden was viewed as something of an interloper at first, her personal pedigree not being up to the local standards of old money and Southern antebellum aristocracy. But Anita was a force to be reckoned with, as she trucked in the bodybuilders and the strippers and the rock bands and the outrageous costumes and "theme" parties. It was to this particular circuit that we trace all the movers and shakers of the Company and its ancillary characters and operations, however, and not to the Vanderbilts, Whitneys or Barnstables. There is a certain cachet that comes from having worked your way up from the bottom, a certain pragmatic if not pugnacious view of life and how best to meet its challenges, that attracts the adventurer, the politician, and the criminal. Also, the business of the Madden dynasty was the raising of thoroughbred horses, not an industry defined by the mint julep and the shy Southern belle, but by hard choices and fierce competition. Thus, it was to Anita Madden and her Hamburg Place estate (and what they represented) that men like Brown, Chandler, Lambert, Barry Bryant and Drew Thornton would gravitate.

Brown was married to former Miss America Phyllis George (after her divorce from producer Robert Evans), united by their mutual love of sports. Brown would go on to become owner of various ball teams, and Ms. George would go on to be a television announcer. They would eventually divorce after some twenty years of marriage, and Brown would go on to marry (and divorce) another beauty pageant queen in the late 1990s.

The story of the Company is much too long and complex to be discussed here in its entirety, and readers are urged to find a copy of *The Bluegrass Conspiracy* and prepare to be stunned at the breadth and depth of political corruption that reaches from the bottom-feeder nickle-bag street dealers to the cops who bust them and on up to Colombian drug lords, crooked DEA chiefs, and gun-running mercenaries and suspect spooks. The time frame of *The Bluegrass Conspiracy* parallels that of the Son of Sam killings and the Roy Radin murder, however, and stretches across the same real estate: South Florida cocaine circles, the Medellin cartel, Las Vegas money-laundering, the use of prostitutes to blackmail political leaders, and the rise of Los Angeles as cocaine-central after Miami. We have David Berkowitz in Kentucky preaching on street corners at the same time Drew Thornton is busting radicals and dope dealers there, in an eerie replay of the Jim Jones and Dan Mitrione "relationship" in Indiana; we have Laney Jacobs staying with Suzy Creamcheese founder Leslie DeKeyser at the latter's home in Las Vegas, at the same time that she is plotting the Roy Radin murder and is involved with Robert Evans[46]; Leslie DeKeyser is also an intimate of Anita Madden and a regular at her parties; Laney will later marry Larry Greenberger, a famous South

Florida cocaine dealer and lieutenant of Medellin cartel *narcotraficante* Carlos Lehder Rivas; Greenberger himself is later murdered either by his wife, Laney, or by one of her lovers, before she herself is arrested and convicted for her role in the Radin homicide. We have Larry Flynt, the man who employed Radin assassins Bill Mentzer and Alex Marti, attending Anita Madden's pre-Derby parties at Hamburg Place . . . and we have the assassination of federal judge John Wood at the orders of drug kingpin Jimmy Chagra, an assassination carried out by hitman Charles Harrelson, father of actor Woody Harrelson ("Woody" on the television sit-com *Cheers*, who later portrayed a serial killer in Oliver Stone's *Natural Born Killers* and . . . Larry Flynt, in *The People vs. Larry Flynt*). When arrested, Charles Harrelson will confess to having been the man on the grassy knoll in Dallas on November 22, 1963; he will confess to having assassinated President John F. Kennedy. He will quickly retract that confession on the advice of his attorney, and he has never spoken about it again.

The assassination of US District Judge "Maximum" John Wood took place on May 29, 1979 in San Antonio, Texas, on the day that Jimmy Chagra was due to appear in his courtroom for the beginning of his trial on charges of drug trafficking. Jimmy Chagra was an American of Lebanese ancestry whose brother, Lee Chagra, had been a famous defense attorney for drug dealers, until a drug bust in 1973 attracted the attention of the DEA. Jimmy Chagra eventually began running his brother's operation—which included masterminding a drug operation that extended from Lebanon to South America, an operation that used Caesars Palace in Las Vegas as its unofficial headquarters.

At the time, Caesars was being managed by Dan Chandler, the friend of Kentucky Governor John Brown, to whom he owed the position. Chandler would introduce the Chagra brothers to Barry Bryant and Drew Thornton, the two partners running the Company. The Chagras were tied to the more prosaic organized-crime families of the Patriarcas in New England and Spilotros of Chicago,[47] so the meeting and eventual partnership between the Chagras and the Company signaled a crime empire that would literally span the globe and extend the reach of both organizations considerably, with old-time Vegas-style Mafia wheeling and dealing on the one hand, and "New Age" paramilitary and covert ops on the other. In addition, federal officials believed that the Chagras also had ties to Middle Eastern terrorist organizations, ties that probably involved the trade in heroin from Mideast markets such as Afghanistan, Pakistan, and the Levant.[48]

By 1978, it was virtually impossible to tell the two operations apart. Jimmy Chagra was experiencing a lot of heat from federal attention, leaving the Company to take advantage of his organized-crime connections and grow exponentially. They developed important links with the intelligence community, as they crossed paths in the underground world of arms dealing and money laundering, and of course the international trade in narcotics.

Then, on December 23, 1978, Lee Chagra was murdered, the victim of a .22 calibre bullet fired at close range in his law office.

A few months later, and his brother Jimmy would be arrested on four counts of drug trafficking from Colombia, his bail set at one million dollars.

Then, on the day he was due to go to trial, his mortal enemy—Judge John Wood—was assassinated, killed by a single shot from a sniper's rifle. According to FBI Director William Webster, it was "the crime of the century" (which probably shows their bias when it comes to the assassinations of John F. Kennedy, Robert F. Kennedy, Dr. Martin Luther King, Jr, Medgar Evers, Malcolm X . . . etc., etc.). As the investigation into the judge's assassination progressed from Chagra, Bryant and others involved with the Company, a suspect was eventually identified and arrested, a man who confessed to the killing: Charles Voyde Harrelson.

When Harrelson was arrested, he also confessed to the assassination of JFK, and, indeed, photographs of the famous "three hoboes" arrested that day in Dallas do seem to show a somewhat younger Harrelson in the lineup, and forensic experts from the Houston Police Department evidently agree. A book written about the assassination and focusing on one of the other co-conspirators—Charles Rogers—by John R. Craig and Philip A. Rogers tells the story in some detail.[49] Although it lacks documentation and source material, and for that reason cannot be taken as "gospel," it does name names and gives dates and places for many of the events described, particularly those leading up to Dallas in November 1963.

Harrelson's life as a professional hitman is not in question. He had been arrested for various crimes involving firearms all his life, and was an acknowledged killer in several unrelated cases. He is presently in prison for the rest of his life, due to the Judge Wood assassination. He has refused to discuss anything more about the Kennedy assassination after that one day in which he admitted he was on the grassy knoll with another assassin, suspected murderer Charles Rogers.

Rogers came to the attention of researchers because of the murder of his parents on Father's Day, June 20, 1965 in Houston. They had been murdered and dismembered, some body parts flushed down the drains and the rest stuffed in the refrigerator, wrapped in plastic, à la Jeffrey Dahmer. Rogers, who lived with his parents, was nowhere to be found and would never be found again. According to the authors, his parents had been killed because they suspected their son's involvement in the assassination. This was due to—again, according to the authors—both Charles Harrelson and Lee Harvey Oswald turning up one day in September 1963 at the parents' church a few blocks away, asking to wait there for a mysterious "Carlos" who would turn up later: a "Carlos" who knew the minister and his wife very well.

The day after the Kennedy assassination, the minister and his wife recognized the photograph of Lee Harvey Oswald as the "Lee" who had visited them a few months earlier. They already knew who "Carlos" was, as they spotted him outside the church talking with Oswald and Harrelson. It was their congregants' son, Charles Rogers.

The authors make many connections between Charles Rogers and David Ferrie, Lee Harvey Oswald, Charles Harrelson, the Civil Air Patrol, the CIA, etc., even going so far as to tie Rogers in with the man who executed Che Guevara in Bolivia. Some of the data is verifiable, such as Rogers enlistment in the Navy, his work for ONI (the Office of Naval Intelligence), and his academic career, as well as his brief employment with Shell Oil before his ostensible recruitment by the CIA. Although Rogers was obviously a suspect in the murder of his parents, he was never sought by authorities and the case remains open and unsolved to this day. Not so the John Wood assassination, however, for which Charles Harrelson is doing life without parole in Marion.

Years later, Sally Denton would return to the drugs and arms conspiracies of the South with her fabled article in *Penthouse*, co-authored with Dr. Roger Morris, a Harvard professor who had worked in the National Security Council during both the Johnson and the Nixon administrations. Ms. Denton herself was head of UPI's investigative unit and had written for the *Washington Post* and other mainstream media before the guns-for-drugs conspiracy among Kentucky's law enforcement elite grabbed her attention, and lost her the support of the system. "The Crimes of Mena" tells the story of Barry Seal, an admitted drug smuggler who—as all evidence now shows beyond any shadow of a doubt—worked for the federal government, specifically for the CIA and the DEA and possibly other agencies as well, at the same time he was running drugs from South America. Later, he would be murdered by the Medellin cartel in Baton Rouge, Louisiana, where he was giving evidence against the drug lords. Seal was part of an operation that was set in motion by forces within the White House that wanted to support the Contras in Nicaragua by any means necessary, an operation that became known to the world at large when another smuggler, Eugene Hasenfus, was shot down over Nicaraguan airspace in a plane that was once owned and flown by Barry Seal. The trail of drugs and arms smuggling led from that Hasenfus crash along a moral fault line that terminated at Oliver North and the Iran-Contra scandal.

The Denton/Morris article never mentions Kentucky and the famous "Company" of Drew Thornton detailed in Denton's earlier book on the Bluegrass Conspiracy, but the conclusion is inescapable. All of the theories being tossed around at the time of the Company investigation by federal investigators included the same guns-for-drugs scenario that eventually defined the Barry Seal case and, indeed, both operations were running concurrently . . . if they were, in fact, different operations and not part of a single, overall clandestine project to finance and supply the anti-Sandinista forces in Nicaragua using funds provided by the sale of cocaine in the United States.

Nothing more has been heard of Mena. The right-wing cartel in the United States has tried to pin the blame on Bill Clinton, of course, claiming that since he was Governor of Arkansas at the time that Barry Seal was using the small town of Mena as the headquarters for his vast criminal empire he should have done something about it. The blame backfired, however, when it was realized that this was a program begun under the Reagan and Bush administrations and could not properly be laid at the Governor's door. (In fact, readers may remember the story of Larry Nichols, the man fired by then-Governor Clinton because he was using the state's telephones to raise money for the Contras, and who later parlayed his termination into the "Clinton Chronicles," financed by Richard Mellon Scaife.) Those who insisted that Clinton should have done something about Mena when he was governor miss the essential element in all of this: the Barry Seal operation had the blessing of the White House. As Denton and Morris make very clear, nothing connected to Seal could be investigated: not by the FBI, not by the IRS, not by US Customs, not by the DEA . . . by no one. Had Clinton forced the issue and brought it to the attention of the media, he would have been pilloried by the very same people who now blame him for *not* doing so, the people who believe that Oliver North is a hero, that ignoring Congressional regulations such as the Boland Amendment was admirable, and that Iran-Contra was justified.

And so it goes.

David Berkowitz. Charles Manson. Roy Radin. Robert Evans. Bill Mentzer. Laney Jacobs. Anita Madden. Leslie DeKeyser. John Y. Brown. Phyllis George. Larry Greenberger. Carlos Lehder. Drew Thornton. Barry Seal. Charles Harrelson. Drugs. Guns. Assassinations. Cults. Hollywood. Miami. Las Vegas. Lexington. Mena. And behind it all, a vast criminal enterprise that had its roots in the White House and its branches in nearly every state in the Union, and in so many Latin American countries that it was a virtual NAFTA agreement, so much so that the "loud, sucking sound" so beloved of independent candidate H. Ross Perot's aborted 1992 presidential campaign may have been nothing more than lines of coke being hoovered up the collective American nose.

These are the trivia, the minutiae that give conspiracy theorists anxiety attacks, and for which there is no satisfying explanation other than the ubiquitous "coincidence," a word that is meaningless because it is *supposed* to be meaningless: a word intended to represent a pointless concurrence of two events, which presupposes that events can occur at the same time or the same place or to the same people, or some combination of these, and yet have no possible relation to each other. It is a way of avoiding a question and, by extension, the uncomfortable answer to that question. Yet, they are "links" in the Brunoesque sense of the word, in Coulianu's sense of the word. They may be thought of as synchronistic, in Jung's sense of the word. Something at the edge of quantum physics, perhaps, or something peculiar to depth psychology or social anthropology.

Or they may be evidence of genuine political and criminal conspiracy.

Or something darker, more dangerous: a sinister force that has festered within the soul of America for many, many years.

> *Sometimes I think there's a buried maniac who runs the mind of this city. And he sets up the coincidences.*
>
> —Norman Mailer, *An American Dream*

As Denton and Morris reveal, among Eugene Hasenfus' personal effects when his plane crashed in the Nicaraguan jungle, thus initiating the Iran-Contra investigation, was documentation showing his involvement with the controversial and top-secret Area 51 in Nevada . . .

ENDNOTES

1 Maury Terry, *The Ultimate Evil*, Barnes & Noble, NY, 1999, p. 529
2 Ibid., p. 529
3 Ibid., p. 529
4 Ibid., p. 530
5 Ibid., p. 44
6 Ibid., p. 530
7 Ibid., p. 64–72
8 Ibid., p. 531
9 Ibid., p. 149–151
10 Robert Graysmith, *Zodiac*, Berkley Books, NY, 1987, p. 248
11 Ibid., p. 254
12 Ibid., p. 254
13 Robert Graysmith, *Zodiac Unmasked*, Berkley Books, NY, 2003, p. 160–162
14 Gary M. Lavergne, *A Sniper In The Tower*, Bantam Books, NY, 1997, p. 341
15 Ibid., p. 342
16 Dean Koontz, *One Door Away From Heaven*, Bantam, NY, 2001, p. 76
17 Terry, op. cit., p. 170
18 David Abrahamson, *Confessions of Son of Sam*, Columbia University Press, NY, 1985, p.15
19 Terry, op. cit., p. 154
20 Ibid., p. 224
21 Ibid., p. 147
22 Ibid., p. 162
23 Ibid., p. 158–162
24 Ibid., p. 179
25 Aleister Crowley, *Magic In Theory and Practice*, Dover, NY, 1976, p. 193
26 Terry, op. cit., p. 228
27 Ibid., p. 50
28 Ibid., p. 228
29 Ibid., p. 229
30 Ibid., p. 184
31 Ibid., p. 249–256
32 Abrahamson, op. cit., p. 2, 14
33 Ibid., p. 87
34 Ibid., p. 151
35 Ibid., p. 180
36 Terry, op. cit., p. 257–258
37 Terry, op. cit., p. 462–463
38 Steve Wick, *Bad Company: Drugs, Hollywood, and the Cotton Club Murder*, Harcourt, Brace, Jovanovich, NY, 1990, p. 64
39 Ronald Kessler, *The Richest Man In The World: The Story of Adnan Khashoggi*, Warner Books, New York, 1986
40 Ibid., p. 130
41 Ibid., p. 131–132
42 Wick, op. cit., p. 112
43 Ibid., p. 131
44 Sally Denton, *The Bluegrass Conspiracy*, Doubleday, NY, 1990, p. 102–103
45 Ibid., p. 147
46 Wicks, op. cit., p. 105
47 Denton, op. cit., p. 66
48 Ibid., p. 67
49 John R. Craig and Philip A. Rogers, *The Man On The Grassy Knoll*, Avon, New York, 1992

CHAPTER TWENTY

COMMUNION

Behind the scenes high-ranking Air Force officers are soberly concerned about the UFOs. But through official secrecy and ridicule, many citizens are led to believe the unknown flying objects are nonsense.

—Rear Admiral Roscoe Hillenkoetter, former Director of the CIA, in a memorandum to Congress dated August 22, 1960

The UFOs reported by competent observers are devices under intelligent control . . . . These UFOs are interplanetary devices systematically observing the earth, either manned or under remote control, or both.

—Colonel Joseph J. Bryan III, Chief and Founder of the CIA's Psychological Warfare Staff, former Special Assistant to the Secretary of the Air Force, in a 1960 letter to Major Donald Keyhoe

We deal now not with things of this world alone. We deal now with the ultimate conflict between a unified human race and the sinister forces of some other planetary galaxy.

—General Douglas MacArthur, 1962

We can study files for decades, but every so often we are tempted to throw up our hands and declare that history is merely another literary genre: the past is autobiographical fiction pretending to be a parliamentary report.

—Julian Barnes[1]

. . . given that in the course of history many have acted on beliefs in which many others did not believe, we must perforce admit that for each, to a different degree, history has been largely the theater of an illusion.

—Umberto Eco[2]

For not all true things are to be said to all men.

—Bishop Clement of Alexandria (c. A.D. 150–215)

At the very heart of the UFO controversy is the question of Truth. Like the fictional FBI Agent of *X-Files*, Fox Mulder, we are inclined to believe that "the Truth is out there," but even Mulder eventually lost the faith. That is the crux of the problem, isn't it? Faith?

Many Christians do not realize that the parameters of their faith were established by the Council of Nicea in 325 A.D., a Council controlled by Emperor Constantine through his emissary Bishop Eusebius. In other words, a political leader would decide core issues of what would become a world religion. This Council decided the question of Jesus' divinity once and for all, and it was the men who composed this Council who decided which texts would comprise both the Old and the New Testaments. The decision—which resulted in the modern Holy Bible—was both a religious and a political issue. To summarize, doctrines held by groups believed not to be "team players" were denounced as heretical, and the relevant texts omitted from the final Scripture. Especially dangerous to the development of a "state church"—which is what Constantine was creating, even though he would not actually become baptized until his death bed—was the phenomenon of Gnosticism. Gnostics embraced the Christian message, but in a way inimical to authority. They believed that everyone should approach God directly.

As Biblical scholar Elaine Pagels writes,

> . . . when we examine its practical effect on the Christian movement, we can see, paradoxically, that the doctrine of bodily resurrection also serves an essential *political* function: it legitimizes the authority of certain men who claim to exercise exclusive leadership over the churches as the successors of the apostle Peter. From the second century, the doctrine has served to validate the apostolic succession of bishops, the basis of papal authority to this day. (emphasis in original)[3]

She goes on to clarify:

> . . . orthodox teaching . . . legitimized a hierarchy of persons through whose authority all others must approach God. Gnostic teaching . . . was potentially subversive of this order: it claimed to offer to every initiate direct access to God of which the priests and bishops themselves might be ignorant.[4]

And:

> . . . when gnostic and orthodox Christians discussed the nature of God, they were at the same time debating the issue of *spiritual authority*. (emphasis in original)[5]

Thus, matters as diverse as the Nicene Creed, which emphasizes the physical reality of Jesus' resurrection, and the actual books included in the Bible, were the result of political issues being decided at the time: an attempt to create a state religion with an identifiable hierarchy that was amenable to control. Obviously, a religion in which every member had direct access to God was a threat not only to the concept of an ecclesiastical hierarchy, but was also subversive of the State itself. How could any person with direct access to God also pay the appropriate homage to a temporal leader, to an Emperor? Thus, matters of faith and matters of truth became tools to be used in order to manipulate the citizenry.

Bishop Clement of Alexandria, quoted above, a powerful figure in second century Christianity, wrote pragmatically on the question of truth and faith. Like an ancient precursor to Machiavelli, Clement understood that truth was dangerous and not to be entrusted to just anybody. Clement's fears about the special volatility of truth may be evidence of some deeper, darker secret at the heart of Christianity, a secret to which he was privy. As we uncover more scrolls and decipher more arcane texts from Biblical times, often against enormous opposition from the Church (as described in Baigent and Leigh's *The Dead Sea Scroll Deception*),[6] we are gradually getting used to the idea that the last two thousand years of Western history may have been based on a magician's trick, a bit of misdirection and legerdemain, concealing a closely-guarded secret of which underground societies and some high-level clerics have long been aware.

What does this have to do with UFOs?

No, I am not about to insist that Jesus was an astronaut or some kind of space alien. What I am going to suggest is that we in the West have become accustomed to accepting a great deal at face value, on "faith." After all, we are heirs to easily the most bizarre set of beliefs among all the world's major religions: that a man—or someone who seemed very much like a man—was executed in Roman-occupied Palestine two thousands years ago, and then rose from the dead, disappearing after a short time into the heavens. Christians are required to believe this; it is central to their faith and is represented in the Nicene Creed, and in the celebration of the Mass (or Divine Liturgy) in which believing Christians partake of the body and blood of Jesus, substances that have been transformed from bread and wine through some occult agency, thus adding a form of cannibalism to the already heady mix of crucifixion and resurrection. When it comes to Jesus, Muslims are ready to accept him as a prophet; when it comes to his resurrection, they demur. The same with the Jews. But there are over a billion people in the world who believe—or who belong to religious sects which insist they believe—that Jesus was born of woman, lived to the age of 33, then was crucified, experienced death, was buried, and rose from his tomb "on the third day," or actually about 39 hours after he was taken down from the cross.

The Swiss psychoanalyst and philosopher C.G. Jung once commented that Christianity had, in effect, turned the Western world schizoid. Forced to accept an impossibility as the truth, and forced in turn to repress natural instincts in the service of this impossibility. Western civilization since the time of Constantine has been struggling with itself. To complicate matters, the doctrine of Original Sin—that all humans are born with a blemish of sin on their soul due to the original defection of Adam and Eve—means that we are all guilty, from birth; indeed, we are also guilty to some extent of the sufferings and death of Jesus, who "died for our sins." Christians, and especially Roman Catholics, are awash in guilt, and conflicted over their true desires and the extent to which those desires are at odds with Christian doctrines of personal behavior and sin. Yet, to deny the Risen Christ (or to refute any of these individual doctrines) was to invite personal disaster in the form of Inquisition and the stake. Thus, many otherwise decent and intelligent people learned to dissemble from a very early age. They learned to lie, either to themselves or to others, in order to survive.

But . . . miracles do happen. Strange things do occur. And to deny the Risen Christ may be to throw out the Baby with the baptismal water. If we insist that resurrection from the dead is an impossibility in this world, do we entertain the idea—even for a moment—that it might be a reality in another world? Do we insist that the "real world" we see around us is the one, sole, objective truth and there is no other even though we know—intellectually—that what we experience with our senses is largely a creation of our nervous systems? When we say that resurrection is impossible, upon what do we base that assumption?

Upon science. Upon scientific evidence. Thus the war between science and religion, a war that reached its climax in the Renaissance, when the occult, the mystical, made one last brave attempt to redeem civilization for the dreamers, the artists, the believers.

Belief is love. The very English word "belief " is related to the German verb *lieben* ("to love"). To *believe* something is to *hold dear* that idea, to prefer it to others, to feel emotional about it, maybe even passionate. That is why "true believers" scare us so much: they seem to have abandoned rational thought and to have fallen in love with a fantasy.

Bishop Clement was very clear about this, in his own way:

> For even if they should say something true, one who loves the Truth should not, even so, agree with them. For not all true things are the Truth; nor should that truth which seems true according to human opinions be preferred to the true Truth—that according to the faith.[7]

We can see the seeds of the Baltimore Catechism being sown even then! The "true Truth"—according to the good bishop—is that "according to the faith."

This is why we have such a difficult time resolving the UFO issue. Eugene Hasenfus was shot down over Nicaragua during his mission to supply the anti-Sandinista Contras. He was part of a wide-ranging network of self-anointed patriots and right-wing zealots who were championed by General Singlaub and the various Republican Party ethnic outreach groups. (Incidentally, Clinton antagonist Larry Nichols was a self-admitted member of one of these groups). Hasenfus is the sort of man typified by "Jack D. Ripper," the commander in charge of an Air Force Base in the Peter Sellers comedy *Dr. Strangelove*, who believes fluoridation of water to be a Communist plot to deprive Americans of their "precious bodily fluids," and thus instigates World War III. In Hasenfus' possession were documents linking him to Area 51 in Nevada.

Area 51 is the scene of a great deal of controversy among the UFO enthusiasts, as they believe that captured alien spacecraft are taken there to be "re-engineered" by American engineers and scientists. Another engineer, one Bob Lazar, has insisted that he himself witnessed this procedure in operation at Area 51.

Area 51—known as Groom Lake, and Dreamland, and a host of other appellations—is without a doubt a top-secret US Air Force facility where, it is said, "stealth" bombers and other military aircraft are designed and tested. The facility is so secret that for years the government would not even admit it existed, even though its presence there was announced by the barbed wire fencing and the warning signs advising that anyone breaching security would be shot.

Why a member of the Contra supply network would have connections of any kind to Area 51 is a question that has not yet been answered. Hasenfus was a pilot and a mercenary; he was not an aerospace scientist with a top-secret classification. We are in the uncomfortable position of having two mysteries wrapped around each other, and neither giving us much room for deduction: first, we don't really know what is going on at Area 51, so we can't imagine what Hasenfus would be doing flying over Nicaragua for the Contras and having Area 51 phone numbers in his possession; in the second place, we don't know much about the background of Eugene Hasenfus himself, and details about the day-to-day operation of the Contra effort are shrouded in similar mysteries. If we knew more about Hasenfus, we might piece together some important information about Area 51; if we knew more about Area 51, we might understand why Hasenfus was linked to it. As it stands, we know virtually nothing about both pieces of this puzzle, for—as it is written—"not all things are to be said to all men."

CONTACT

Is this the devil? What the hell is this?

—Whitley Strieber, under hypnosis to recall details of his abduction[8]

Whitley Strieber was born a Roman Catholic. Although, as we see from his writings both in print and on his Web site, he and his wife were involved with the Gurdjieff Foundation for a while (and he also admits that he has attended witchcraft ceremonies, of the "New Age" pagan variety[9]), he nonetheless retains a great deal from his Catholic upbringing. A gifted storyteller, several of his novels have been made into movies (including *The Wolfen* and *The Hunger*) and, indeed, he worked as a screenwriter for a while (*The Owl and the Pussycat*). But Strieber came to international prominence largely on the strength of one book, a non-fiction bestseller in which he claimed to have been abducted by an alien force.

Communion: A True Story was not only a bestseller, but it became a feature film starring Christopher Walken as Strieber, a film that was unsettling and eerie to many audiences and made even more so by the filmmakers' insistence that it was based on actual events. That the title, Communion, has special resonance for Catholics should be obvious: it is the name for the ritual involving consumption of the body and blood of Jesus. It is one of the seven sacraments in the Catholic Church, and signifies full membership in the Church.

Yet "communion" also means "communication," albeit on a deeper level, and this is the emphasis of the film and especially of the book, as well as of all the others from Whitley Strieber that have followed *Communion*, and which deal with the same phenomena. In fact, one of the sequels to *Communion* is *Confirmation*, a word that describes another Catholic sacrament, this time the ritual in which a young boy or girl reaffirms the vows made by their godparents at their baptism; i.e., *confirms* that they renounce Satan and believe in Jesus. The titles of the other sequels are not so openly sacerdotal, however, being *Breakthrough*, *Transformation*, and *The Secret School*. (One does suspect that it would be difficult to use *Extreme Unction* as a title, although *Penance, Baptism* and even *Matrimony* have possibilities, not to mention the potentially sinister *Holy Orders*.)

Briefly, the story is this:

On the night of December 26, 1985 Whitley Strieber—on holiday at his cabin in the woods in Ulster County, upstate New York—was awakened by a strange noise in the living room. It would later be recorded that a UFO had been sighted in the area that night, but at the time Whitley had no knowledge of this and did not associate his experience with UFOs and alien visitors until months later.[10] He sat up in bed, startled, but then lay back down to return to sleep. He says that this type of strange behavior would be "repeated many times,"[11] a kind of nervous reaction to events so out of the ordinary that there does not seem to be an appropriate response based on the usual fight or flight instincts of our lower brains.

Then he is visited by several creatures who surround his bed, and who seem to carry him aloft and out of the cabin.

It should be noted that both his wife and his young son are with him in the cabin, but they do not seem to have been awakened by the strange noise or by the visitors at this time.

He then winds up in a "messy round room,"[12] and then observes many tiny people rushing about and finds that he is in a state of abject terror. Other events are taking place, but he cannot recall what they are, ascribing this lack of detail to a form of amnesia brought about either by sheer terror or, somewhat more prosaically, by drugs. While neither Whitley Strieber nor his wife, Anne, are drug takers, he implies that he may have been deliberately drugged with some exotic narcotic by the creatures who abducted him and took him to the "messy room."

He describes having his cranium penetrated by a long, thin needle, and then the insult of the infamous "rectal probe." Soon thereafter, his memories end, and he wakes up to a winter morning in the New York woods with a vague recollection of something having happened during the night, but unsure what it was.

During the following weeks, he feels a general mental and physical deterioration as he struggles with the fallout of that night, still unaware of what really happened and equally unaware of an "extraterrestrial" element to the experience. It merely seems to him that he is going insane.

Back in New York City on February 6, 1986, he came across the name of UFO researcher Budd Hopkins in a book about UFOs he had received as a Christmas present but which he had been too afraid to read before, for reasons then unknown to him. Discovering that Hopkins lived in New York City, not far from his own Greenwich Village apartment, he decided to call him although he wasn't quite sure what to say. The images he recalled from the "event" of that night were so abnormal that he did not know if they fit the now-familiar pattern of a close encounter.

Hopkins invited him over and the two spent a few hours discussing the event, and then Hopkins asked whether Strieber had had any similar experiences in the past, and that is when he suddenly remembered an event in October of 1985, an event that was experienced by other witnesses.

It took place in the same cabin in the woods, but this time he had house-guests as well as his wife and son: two authors—one a Romanian immigrant and the author of an account of his experience in a Romanian work camp, and the other an American-born intellectual. His houseguests were aware of a strange light—an unearthly glow—all around the cabin the night of October 4, a light so bright that it woke them up. Whitley thought the cabin was actually on fire, but of course there was no damage. They discussed it—as well as a loud bang the same night, a sound of unknown origin—the following morning, but then thought nothing more about it.

Prompted by Budd Hopkins, Whitley asked his family what they remembered of that night. Whitley's son Andrew said it was the night of the bang, when his father threw his shoe at a fly. When asked who told him about throwing a shoe, Andrew remarked that it was "Just a bunch of people. People who were around."[13] When pressed for more details, specifically about any strange dreams from that period, Andrew readily replied that he had a dream about "little doctors" who put him on a cot and told him not to worry.[14] As one might imagine, this was unwelcome news to Whitley Strieber! What he was dealing with, if it was a hallucination, was a hallucination shared by his family. Either they were all going insane, or there was some external force prompting these strange recollections.

Asking his friends about what they remembered about that October night, they verified the existence of a bright light in the woods and a loud explosion, and Whitley's telling them it was all right: "The light is gone. Go back to sleep."[15]

Eventually, Strieber would seek a hypnotist to enable him to recall more details of the two experiences and transcripts of the sessions are given verbatim in *Communion*. The experience was obviously terrifying, with visions of the world being destroyed and his son being killed, all suggested by the strange beings who had abducted him and forced him to see these images and to react violently toward them. There was also a vision of his father, on a train, surrounded by soldiers in uniform. Whitley later states that this had to be a memory of 1957, returning on a train from a vacation in Madison, Wisconsin back to Texas, where Whitley was born and where the family lived. (This link between Whitley's abduction experiences and a sudden vision of his father in a way that seems out of context will turn out to be quite important, and what eventually led Whitley Strieber to contact this author some years later, as we shall see.)

While Strieber's story in *Communion* refers to events that took place while he was an adult and spending holidays at his cabin in the woods of upstate New York with his family and friends, it becomes clear through his writings that he links that experience with older, more unsettling ones from his childhood. Whitley Strieber has never insisted that he was abducted by what the popular imagination terms "space aliens." He is not convinced that the UFO phenomenon is, strictly speaking, the visitation of the earth by beings from another planet, or that he (and others like him) have been periodically kidnapped by these beings and used in gruesome medical experiments. He keeps an open mind, and as far as I can discern is sincerely seeking to understand what his experience really was, what it represents. While he has interpreted it in spiritual terms, and more so as the years have gone by, he seems nonetheless perfectly willing to accept the beings as space aliens if it could be proved; he is just as willing to accept a verdict of angels or spirits or extra-dimensional creatures of some sort, or even subconscious material surfacing in a unique and powerful way. The important aspect to the case is how the interaction between human beings and these "aliens" is handled, and what changes it can cause in the human psyche. Does "contact" enable a person to become more centered and at the same time more aware? Does it ennoble a person? Does it cause significant psychological change or growth?

Or does it represent something else, something more dangerous?

Harvard professor and psychiatrist John E. Mack, M.D. concludes that those who have experienced "alien abduction" are genuinely suffering from post-traumatic stress disorder (PTSD).[16] That is, they have had an experience which has caused all the psychological and organic reactions typical of soldiers who have been in battle, or people who have witnessed a particularly upsetting event, such as violent death. We may remember that it was just this illness that gave rise to the creation of the *Diagnostic and Statistical Manual* by the US Army; and that Surrealist author Andre Breton used automatic writing to treat soldiers suffering from this disorder. We remember that brainwashing expert William Sargant cut his medical eye teeth on the same disorder. It is—whether one gives it the clinical name "post-traumatic stress disorder" or the more colorful "shell shock" or "battle fatigue"—a virtual mother-lode of inspiration for artists and G-men alike. Mack, who won a Pulitzer Prize for his psycho-biography of Lawrence of Arabia (*A Prince of Our Disorder*), was roundly criticized by his peers for accepting the testimony of abductees at face value; but all he was really doing was explaining to the world at large that these people had apparently suffered from some appalling treatment, since they were exhibiting all the same symptoms as people suffering from shell shock or battle fatigue. Yet, there was nothing in their backgrounds that could account for the experiences. Thus, Mack was inclined to believe that the abductees had experienced something so unusual, and so stressful, that to call it "alien abduction" was not far from the truth.

Malachi Martin also makes a brief appearance in this story, in an encounter he had with a former *Newsweek* journalist, Bruce Lee, who one day was inspecting racks of *Communion* in a bookstore shortly after its release and saw what appeared to Lee to be . . . well, aliens: short beings dressed oddly, as if in disguise, and laughing at details in the book, complaining of what Whitley "got wrong."[17] The experience unnerved Lee, who later was visited by Fr. Martin, who was one of his authors. (Lee by this time was an editor at publishing house William Morrow.) He told Martin about this strange encounter, at which point Martin—suddenly quite nervous—asked Lee, "Does this experience disturb you?" to which Lee responded, "No." Martin then told him that "they exist."[18] It should be pointed out that Father Martin disturbed Lee more than the aliens; after working with Martin on his book about demonic possession, *Hostage To The Devil*, Lee had to resort to an exorcist himself, because the experience, he said, left him feeling "unclean."

This association of aliens with demons has occupied many writers and thinkers over the past fifty years since the days of Kenneth Arnold, Fred Crisman, and Roswell. (Conceivably, an encounter with either one—I mean aliens and demons, not Arnold or Crisman—would be sufficient cause for a case of post-traumatic stress disorder.)

Eventually, as Whitley Strieber's memories became clearer, he remembered some salient points from his own childhood that could have important bearing on this case, and could explain some of what Mack's patients were experiencing.

At this point, and in the spirit of full disclosure, I have to say for the record that Mr. Strieber contacted me via email a few years ago, after reading my first book, *Unholy Alliance*. His question to me was quite specific: an inquiry concerning Operation Paperclip and the identity of some German officers who had been stationed at Randolph AFB in the 1950s. Since I had spent years researching Nazi Germany and particularly those who escaped justice and wound up in the Americas, it was natural enough that he would contact me for this information.

But as we communicated further, and at length, concerning this period of American history, it became clear that Strieber believed that he may have been a victim of some sort of medical treatment or experiment at the hands of these men. He further believed that some sort of connection existed between the Randolph

AFB group and a school in Mexico, and this is where the story came unnervingly close to actual events which are only now coming to light.

For this, we must go back to Whitley's own childhood and the state of the world, and particularly of the United States, in the early 1950s.

We must go back to the Secret School.

THE SECRET SCHOOL

> Si la bomba no ha destruido al mundo, ha destruido a nuestra idea del mundo. . . . Redescubrimos un sentimiento que acompano siempre a los aztecas, a los hindues y a los cristianos del ano mil. La tecnica comienza por ser una negacion de la imagen del mundo y termina por ser una imagen de la destruccion del mundo.
>
> —Octavio Paz[19]

> . . . Sade was still haunted by the fear of what he called "the black men" who lay in wait to put him away.
>
> —Michel Foucault[20]

Whitley Strieber was born on June 13, 1945 in San Antonio, Texas. The war in Europe was over, but the war in the Pacific was still two months away from its complete and dramatic conclusion, with the dropping of the atomic bombs on Hiroshima and Nagasaki. His father, Karl Strieber, was a well-known and respected attorney who specialized in the petroleum industry, a common-enough occupation in Texas. His mother, Mary, was the daughter of a wealthy businessman. All in all, his home life could be described as "comfortable."

San Antonio—one of the most agreeable of Texas cities—is surrounded by military bases, from the US Army's Fort Sam Houston to several Air Force bases, such as Randolph Air Force Base, which served as the headquarters for the "aviation medicine" effort of the US Army Air Corps (which became the US Air Force). This program was largely staffed by Nazi scientists brought over after the War's end, as recounted in Book I. The most prominent among them, of course, was Dr. Hubertus Strughold, a man who should have been sentenced at Nuremberg, but who was rescued by American military scientists eager to make use of his expertise in the relatively new field of "aviation medicine" . . . a field whose guinea pigs had been chosen from the death camps of the Third Reich. Strughold paid it forward, and rescued in turn a number of his own colleagues, falsifying documents and *curricula vitae* so that the cream of the crop could accompany him to relative security and luxury in the United States. The end result was that Randolph AFB became a kind of sanctuary for scientists who were used to experimenting on living human subjects.

This type of experimentation was not limited to testing the limits of physical endurance at zero-g, but also included psychological and neurological testing.

Hallucinations are a natural part of the isolation of a high-altitude pilot, due to the sensory deprivation and lack of oxygen that occurs from long periods of solitude in the air, and experiments were conducted to determine how long an individual pilot can remain sensory deprived before hitting the panic button. Incredibly, many test subjects reported the same hallucination: little yellow men in black hats. This gave rise to speculation that the visions are triggered by some sort of neurological factor, thus far unknown and unidentified.

In Whitley Strieber's communications with me, he expressed a suspicion that perhaps he himself had been a test subject at Randolph. He mentioned Dr. Strughold by name, and also a mysterious Dr. Antonio Krause, whom I have so far been unable to identify, but who figures strongly in Strieber's memories as related to me and on his own Web site. To understand why he would have come to that conclusion—and why it could be seriously entertained—we must understand what the climate was like in the United States at that time: the immediate Postwar period.

America had gone from the universally-acknowledged victor of World War II to the first atomic superpower in the same year, 1945. America had done the unimaginable: it had developed a weapon of mass destruction, a bomb so powerful that one dropped from a plane could level an entire city, killing hundreds of thousands of people in the process and guaranteeing generations of hereditary illnesses from exposure to high doses of radiation. Then, almost immediately, America found itself facing its greatest enemy to date: the threat of Communism.

It was General Patton who is famously quoted as saying that America had fought the wrong enemy in the war; that the true evil was that represented by the Soviet Union and, later, Red China. In 1950, the Korean War began, as North Korean troops—supplied and supported by Mao's China—began an assault on Seoul, with the aim of creating a Communist Korea. United Nations troops—largely composed of American soldiers, but including combatants from many nations—fought a desperate and harrowing struggle to help South Korea repel the invaders, and a few years later the war came to an uneasy truce with a country still divided.

At the same time that the Korean War was coming to a close, Vietnam had become another flashpoint, with the defeat of the French military forces at Dien Bien Phu and the eventual splitting of the country into a Communist North Vietnam and a democratic Republic of Vietnam in the South.

The war against Communism was an ideological conflict; the Communists were atheists who persecuted religion, and this was generally enough to turn most Americans into rabid anti-Communists. The American government did not shy away from using whatever tools came to hand in this life-and-death struggle for the planet. As we have seen, these tools included Nazi scientists, spies, mercenaries, and medical men; but these tools also extended to American children.

As a child growing up in America in the 1950s, the author experienced some of this first-hand. We were taught to expect an aerial attack at any time, and were trained in how to protect ourselves from a bombardment: the old "stick your head between your knees and kiss your ass goodbye" position. We rehearsed this every week, as air raid sirens went off in the city like something out of a World War II propaganda film. Of course, this could be construed as a kind of psychological warfare, conducted by the government on its own citizens, since it is doubtful that in the 1950s the Soviet Union possessed the military capability necessary to invade the United States or bomb Chicago (where I lived for a while as a child and learned to "duck and cover."). They had been devastated in the war, lost more than twenty million of their people to fighting and starvation, and had their hands full in Eastern Europe. No matter; as a child I was taken to visit Nike missile bases and given lectures on the Communist threat. We were told to be aware, and to report suspicious activity. In some cases, children were encouraged to spy on their neighbors, or even on members of their own families; certainly, they were keeping an eye on their teachers.

We grew up with the Bomb. It was always there, in the background, ready to destroy the world's civilizations at only a few moments' notice. We were told what it would be like: the intense flash of light, the hurricane-force winds, the disintegration at ground zero, the blowing out of windows and destruction of buildings miles from the center of the blast. We were shown how people in Hiroshima had been reduced to photo images: shadowy shapes on walls and bridges made by the brilliant blast, all that was left of the people who, a moment earlier, had been standing in those spots. We grew up with Armageddon a sudden plausibility . . . and the end of the millennium was less than fifty years away. The end of the world seemed like something one reasonably should plan for.

We grew up with air raid shelters. There were those in our city neighborhoods: basements of churches and schools with the familiar yellow-and-black signs and the stockpile of medicines and canned food. Outside the cities, people began building their own shelters: in their backyards or below their homes, concrete bunkers with candles, flashlights, bottled water, and transistor radios (a new invention). America was preparing for a pre-emptive first strike, nuclear winter, and possible invasion.

With all of this threat and perceived threat in the air, a daily experience for most of us, it was natural that red-blooded American citizens should be prepared to make the necessary sacrifices to defeat the Communist enemy wherever it could be found. Communism was sneaky; it wasn't quite the same as the German-American Bund of the 1930s, holding marches in the Yorkville section of New York City to support the Nazi Party in Germany. Communism was more covert; people spoke of "Communist infiltration" and "fellow travelers." People spoke of something—a newspaper article, a book, a movie—as being "Communist inspired." When some Americans came to their senses and started calling the Army–McCarthy hearings a "witch hunt," they were more right than they knew. Arthur Miller saw it, and wrote *The Crucible*, a play ostensibly about the Salem witchcraft trials but seen—more correctly—as a parable about the anti-Communist hysteria gripping America at that time. We saw how this theme influenced Miller's wife, the actress Marilyn Monroe, who became more sympathetic towards Communism as the years went on.

It was understood that the Soviet Union—and those countries identified as "satellites" of the Soviet Union, i.e., Eastern European countries such as Poland, Hungary, Czechoslovakia, and East Germany—brainwashed its children and taught them to spy on their own parents. Whether this was true or not, it was a powerful image when seen in the United States, which had just come from confronting brainwashing first hand in Korea. The CIA went to great pains to find a way to counteract this threat, focusing on the soldier in the field at first; but it has always been whispered that the intelligence agencies—either the CIA or the military intelligence organs, or both—experimented in some way or form on children in the United States in the 1950s.

Only scraps of evidence have ever come to light. As mentioned in Chapter Sixteen there is published documentation proving that children were used in drug experiments in the United States, drugs that included LSD. In Montreal in the 1950s, we know that children in orphanages were used experimentally, particularly in those orphanages run by the Catholic Church, once they had been diagnosed as "retarded" or categorized with some other mental illness as a ruse for the institution to earn additional government funds. We also know that Montreal in the 1950s was the scene for some of the CIA's most imaginative and chilling psychological experiments, those of Dr. Ewen Cameron at his Mount Royal "Ravenscroft" clinic. This precedent—that of the CIA using medical institutions in foreign countries as contractors for their psychological experiments—is worthwhile studying, for it may reveal a pattern.

While the hideous example of Dr. Cameron's psychic driving and other programs in Canada is by now well-known to those who study this field, there is virtually no information about similar programs undertaken south of the border, in Mexico.

But there is the Finders case.

As we saw earlier, when US government officials were called in on February 5, 1987, due to the arrest of two men in Florida in connection with the suspected trafficking of children to Mexico, with the subsequent discovery that a group called "Finders" was involved in everything from ritual sacrifice to international travel to proscribed destinations (like North Korea and North Vietnam), and had ties with Chinese embassy officials in Hong Kong, among other things, the lid was clamped down tight and the American public was not allowed to know anything more about this group that had ties to the CIA. Since then, the entire case has been stonewalled and whitewashed; we have been presented with a picture of

Finders that is innocuous and bland, and the arrests just a big misunderstanding. But there is no misunderstanding what Washington, D.C. area police discovered at the Finders headquarters, or the fact that several small children were in the charge of two well-dressed men who were taking them to a "special school" in Mexico, a school for very bright children. This report of the school in Mexico has never been followed up; that part of the story died when the police were told—by the CIA—to keep away from it. Strangely, the news media also dropped the story.

No one knows what happened to the children who were picked up in Florida: filthy, in tattered clothing, ignorant about things like television and computers but nonetheless quite intelligent, they disappeared from view as surely as the story disappeared from the newspapers. To put together a scenario of what might have happened all we have is the inventory list of what police found at Finders headquarters, and that included photographs of children participating in animal sacrifice; copies of communications between Chinese nationals and Finders on the subject of trafficking in human beings and "obtaining children for unspecified purposes"; instructions on money laundering; and more.

Since then, some (but not all) of this has been explained away by the Finders leader, Marion Pettie, who has put a benign and eccentric spin on the facts. Context is everything, and Pettie paints his organization in a kind of loopy, New Age light that has nothing to do with espionage, psychological warfare, brainwashing, or any of that Cold War impedimenta. Yes, he and his family have CIA connections going back to the 1950s. Yes, they killed a goat, and children *were* present. But this is all being taken out of context, he insists. The reality is really quite boring.

Yet, he has never answered any questions concerning the travel to Communist countries in the 1950s through 1970s, or the telex traffic with the Chinese embassy in Hong Kong concerning the purchase of two children, or the fact that Finders had files on their activities and the activities of their members all over the globe. As a matter of national security, we are not allowed to ask these questions or to reopen the case. The matter is closed, and the US Customs and Metropolitan Police Department files are locked away in a file marked SECRET.

What happened to the children? Where were they going?

As Maury Terry continued his investigation of the Son of Sam cult, an investigation that became more linked with the Process or one of its offshoots—through statements made by former Process members—he kept hearing the cult called by a peculiar name, "The Children." David Berkowitz knew the cult by this name, and it was stated by Terry that a wealthy émigré from Postwar Germany who lived in the Yonkers area was an important leader. This man has since died. Terry, who knows the man's name, did not divulge it in his book, but he did attend the wake and saw the proliferation of black flowers around the man's coffin.

The Children.

A noted psychotherapist and expert on hypnosis, D. Corydon Hammond, has also insisted that a satanic cult exists in America that was begun by Nazi émigrés after the war, and that this cult abuses and even sacrifices children as part of its ritual.[21] If we put this together with Terry's discovery, we begin to see a pattern emerging . . . particularly as the Nazis could not have come to America and begun developing their network without at least preliminary support by American intelligence officials. It is possible that the tales of a nationwide Nazi–Satanic cult that sacrifices children is only the smoke from a much smaller, but potentially more dangerous, fire.

The facts that we have to hand may be of help:

We know, for instance, that Nazi scientists and medical professionals were allowed to emigrate to the United States after the war as part of Operation Paperclip and succeeding efforts to rescue as many Nazi professionals as possible in the effort to contain Communism. We also know that American intelligence hired an entire network of Nazi spies to assist them in combating the Soviet Union, a network known as the Gehlen Organization. We also know that many Eastern European Waffen-SS and other Nazi troops, including high-ranking officers, were allowed to emigrate to America after the War, and in some cases (such as that of Valerian Trifa of the Romanian Orthodox Church and the Iron Guard) became prominent in Eastern Orthodox churches in the United States, either as clergymen or as financial supporters, and wound up holding positions of prominence in American political organizations. We also know that CIA Director Allen Dulles had a critical role to play in covering up details of his involvement with Nazi officials. All of this has been covered in detail, and fully documented, in Books I and II.

Knowing all of this, is it so far-fetched an idea that some of these Nazis were allowed—or encouraged—to continue their medical and psychological programs in America? Or, where it was considerably safer, in Canada or Mexico under CIA or military intelligence auspices?

What Whitley Strieber describes—the involvement of Nazi scientist Hubertus Strughold in the experimentation program—is not beyond the realm of possibility. That Randolph AFB would have been chosen as the site of this activity is logical, as it was the center for aviation medicine research, a broad category that included virtually anything having to do with neurological, biological, and psychological testing. It was also close to the Strieber home in San Antonio, Texas.

However, how can we accept that the young son of a prominent San Antonio attorney would have been selected for psychological experimentation by the US Army?

The answer lies in the context of the times.

In the immediate Postwar years, as the Soviet Union gradually assumed the mantle of our cosmic enemy, Americans were called as never before to do what they could to contain and eventually destroy this threat. It seemed as if

Communism was erupting all over the world, from Asia to Europe to Latin America. Educators, scientists, journalists, and businessmen were called to the service of the CIA, enlisted in the global fight against the Red Menace and the Yellow Peril. It is hard for those who did not grow up in those times to realize just how much this sentiment insinuated itself into the lives of those who did. The orgy of red-baiting, loyalty oaths, and purges of government agencies, and the entertainment and other industries, was a constant backbeat to the news reports of new Communist successes, of falling dominoes around the world. All Americans were expected to do what they could to help in this Manichaean struggle between West and East, between Capitalism and Communism, between Democracy and Dictatorship.

Many children in those days were tested for intelligence, and some were selected for further tests. We only have bits and pieces of information about these programs available to us now, some only on the basis of personal testimony. The memories recorded by Whitley Strieber of his childhood encounters with the "visitors" at the secret school hidden within San Antonio's Olmos Basin *may be*, he admits, screen memories of actual psychological testing that was done on behalf of American intelligence and conducted by the Nazi doctors of Randolph AFB, tests that could have included hallucinogenic drugs such as LSD and psilocybin. We know that such testing was done on children, for instance at Creedmore in the 1960s. We do not know how much drug testing was done by the military at this time, although we do know that such men as Andrija Puharich were conducting all sorts of psychological and chemical tests on behalf of the US Army in the 1950s. We also know that, at that same time, the CIA was not above dosing its own employees and contractors with LSD and other substances without their knowledge, as the Frank Olson tragedy clearly demonstrates.

Without going into a discussion of whether or not Whitley Strieber's experiences with the visitors were actually memories of medical experimentation by the Nazi doctors of Randolph, or were genuine experiences of alien abduction and mental programming, we can accept—at least theoretically—that there is a basis for believing that young Whitley (or others like him) were subjected to some form of psychological experimentation during the 1950s, and that this experimentation may have included the use of psychotropic substances. We can accept this, because there is enough documentation to prove that programs like this were already in existence, and that the American government agencies and private medical teams involved were not above employing these tests on unwitting human subjects, including children. San Antonio, Texas was a military town. Many of the local people owed their jobs to either the military or to the petroleum industry. There were Army bases and Air Force bases, and the mysterious Randolph AFB with its coterie of unrepentant Nazis. Patriotic American parents might have been willing (or even proud) to have their children placed in experimental programs, assured by their own government that the testing would be passive, non-invasive and benign, especially if their children had shown a high IQ or other abilities on standard tests administered by the school system.

In that context, and in the 1950s, anything was possible.

Nuclear physicist Jack Sarfatti (intimate of Saul Paul Sirag, Andrija Puharich, Uri Geller, Ira Einhorn, Philip K. Dick, Carlos Castaneda, Barbara Honegger, and many others) has written about a similar experience he had as a primary school student around the same time, in 1952, an experience in which he places a lot of stock and which was obviously a seminal event in his life. He had been identified as boy with a genius IQ, and preparations would soon be made to send him to Cornell University on a full scholarship at the age of 17. In the meantime, however, he received a strange phone call at his home in the Flatbush section of Brooklyn.

According to Sarfatti's own account in *The Destiny Matrix* (1995), and also available on the Internet,

> The telephone rings. I pick it up. I hear curious clanking mechanical sounds like relays clicking. A distant cold metallic voice speaking numbers gets louder.
>
> "Who are you?" I ask.
>
> "I am a conscious computer on board a spacecraft . . . We have identified you as one of four hundred young bright receptive minds . . . You must give us your decision now. If you say yes, you will begin to link up with the others in twenty years."

After a few seconds, young Sarfatti agrees, and the voice replies,"Good, go to your firescape [*sic*]. We will send a ship to pick you up in ten minutes.

Nothing happened.

Sarfatti then goes on to explain how he later became a member of a group of gifted children, an after-school coterie led by one Walter Breen (1928–1993), "a graduate student at Columbia and well known Numismatist associated with psychologist William Shelden."[22] Walter Breen is a fascinating person in his own right. His *Complete Encyclopedia of US and Colonial Coins* is the definitive volume on this subject, and retails today for $135. But he was also very familiar to the science fiction circles of the 1960s, and was a co-founder of the Society for Creative Anachronism (SCA). He also wrote, under the pseudonym J.Z. Eglinton, *Greek Love*, a text that has been referenced by the North American Man Boy Love Association (NAMBLA) as supportive of their philosophy concerning sexual relationships between men and boys. Breen had been arrested before for child molestation, and would be again at the end of his life.

But the gifted children group to which Sarfatti belonged was somehow linked with the Sandia Corporation, now part of Lockheed Martin, a charter member of the Defense–Energy establishment. In an email posted on a Web site (http://groups.yahoo.com/group/ItalianPhysicsCenter/message/79) and dated

July 16, 2001, Sarfatti writes, "Breen was talking about extra dimensions, telepathy, remote viewing, UFOs, mutant humans, contact with aliens . . . Sandia was trying to develop us as super-kids to have paranormal powers and to deal with extra-dimensional intelligence." Sandia is still involved with gifted children to this day, in cooperation with a "super kids" program that selects very bright students to work with its supercomputer.

As for Walter Breen, he eventually married Marion Zimmer Bradley (1930–1999), the science-fiction author of *The Mists of Avalon* (and author of much lesbian fiction besides, who was very active in gay counseling as well as a contributor to *The Mattachine Review*) who would bear two children (in addition to a child by her first marriage) while they were married and before their separation in 1979. Even more fascinating is the fact that, in 1980, both Marion Zimmer Bradley and Walter Breen *would be ordained as priests in the Eastern Orthodox Church by Bishop Michael Itkin,* making their line of apostolic succession (via Bishop, and now "Saint," Carl Stanley) the same as David Ferrie's! (As you can see, it is virtually impossible to extricate the material of this book from the moist-palm grasp of the ubiquitous wandering bishops.)

The data in Sarfatti's article/book-in-progress reads like a history and who's-who of American (and foreign) alternative culture in the 1970s. Twenty years after his strange phone call (and, as we discover later, there were more than one) he was indeed linked with some of the brightest and most creative minds on the planet. He has considered whether or not the phone call was some kind of hoax, but he is reluctant to accept that explanation. Others have had similar phone calls, he tells us, and—of course—the spaceship-computer scenario was playing out even then with Andrija Puharich and his circle in their evocation of The Nine (albeit unknown to young Sarfatti—or anyone else—at the time). Incidentally, and congruent with our overall thesis, Sarfatti was also heavily influenced by the surrealist film *Orphee* by Jean Cocteau.

He became involved with the Stanford Research Institute at about this time (1973), and with Hal Puthoff and Russel Targ, scientists who were involved in SRI's "remote viewing" and other paranormal experiments. Until this association, Sarfatti considers himself to have been"anti-mystical" (Sarfatti Web site), but during his time with SRI he begins to realize the importance of those mysterious phone calls made twenty years earlier. He also discovers that artist and remote viewer Ingo Swann "channeled" a "cold, metallic voice from a saucer 100 years into future" at Stanford Research Institute (SRI), along with our friend Barbara Honegger (she of the "October Surprise" episode). SRI, of course, was also the place where Israeli psychic Uri Geller was tested in 1973.[23] In 1975, in a separate series of tests of Uri Geller's psychic abilities by a team at Lawrence Livermore Laboratories (where much of America's nuclear weapons research takes place; the scientists were worried that someone with Geller's abilities would be able to trigger a nuclear device or scramble a computer system using only his mind), scientists recorded another "distinctive, metallic-sounding voice, unheard during the actual experiment but now clearly audible."[24] Among the few words that could be made out, however, was "the code name of a very closely held government project. The project had nothing to do with psychic research, and neither it nor its code name was known to . . . Livermore."[25] More about the Lawrence Livermore incident in the following chapter, but in line with the experience of Sarfatti, one of the Livermore scientists actually received a phone call from the "strange metallic voice," which told him and the team to cease the experiments with Uri Geller. They did, and were left alone after that.[26]

(In a side note, Sarfatti also reveals that he had been a member of the Civil Air Patrol (CAP) in New York at the age of fourteen. In attempting to put together his timeline, it occurred to me that he was in the CAP at the same time as David Ferrie and Lee Harvey Oswald, but of course a thousand miles away from the New Orleans operation. At that same time, my parents were also members of the CAP, but in the Cook County, Illinois area. Considering that my father had right-wing sentiments and a history as a segregationist . . . well, you can see where I'm going with this!)

Thus begins a personal odyssey, during which Sarfatti discovers he is descended from a Knight Templar, hangs out with science-fiction authors Philip K. Dick and Robert Anton Wilson, meets Carlo Suares (*The Cipher* of Genesis), is told by some Theosophists that he is the reincarnation of their Bishop Leadbeater (the gay and "wandering" bishop who on a beach in India discovered the young boy who would become future spiritual guru Krishnamurti), and on and on.

Sarfatti is a scientist, and if you read some of the email exchanges posted on the Internet between him and other physicists and physicist-wannabes, you will become very quickly bogged down in a quagmire of calculus and contempt. The internecine wars between physicists are as unseemly as those between Kennedy assassination theorists or battling UFO apologists; but in the end the fact that Sarfatti *is* a scientist is what stands out. And while his childhood experiences do not match, chapter and verse, those of Whitley Strieber, there are very strong and suggestive parallels between the two. Both are contacted by alien intelligences; both are linked to spacecraft; both are "identified" by these intelligences while they are quite young: Whitley was nine years old, and Sarfatti was about twelve. Both had their experiences in roughly the same timeframe: the early 1950s. Sarfatti was "contacted" in 1952/53; Strieber in 1954. Both were members of a "secret school" that had associations with paranormal abilities and UFOs.

Sarfatti mentions in another email exchange, from June 2002, that he had been "studied" by the US Army in the late 1940s, and goes on to describe the after-school group led by Walter Breen as the "McDermott-Sheldon-Breen 'Columbia-Sandia eugenics' connection of 1953–56."[27] Again, this is a very suggestive timeframe in which to be placing events so similar as those related by Sarfatti and Strieber.

In yet another place Sarfatti goes into more detail about this observation by the Army.[28] He claims it occurred at "US Army Quarter Masters in Lower Manhattan in the late 1940s soon after the alleged Roswell incident," and mentions that his mentor Walter Breen told him that he (i.e., Breen) had been in a plane crash in 1947 and had complete amnesia of the event, only coming to later in an Army hospital. 1947, of course, was the year of the Roswell incident. Sarfatti wonders if there was a connection between Breen and Roswell. (Breen would later go on to become a charter member of the American MENSA organization.)

It is not only Sarfatti who has a single degree of separation between himself and the UFOs, however. One of Whitley Strieber's neighbors was the Colonel in charge of the air base from which Captain Mantell went on his fateful chase of a UFO, and became the first ever military casualty of a UFO in American history. (More about this in a bit.) Young Whitley used to play in the Colonel's swimming pool with the Colonel's own son.[29]

(And, in the spirit once again of full disclosure, the author must acknowledge that he was approached in 1961–62 after an intelligence test of some kind administered by his school in the sixth grade. I was never told the results of this test, but a parade of teachers and other, unidentifiable, persons coming into my classroom to stare at me made me aware there was something odd going on. Later that same school year, after a science fair in which I made an exhibit out of CAP navigational materials such as maps, plotters, etc., men representing Cornell University came to visit my teacher and to speak with my parents about my attending a special class there. I never knew the outcome of those visits, but suspect that—due to my father's FBI records—I was rejected as potentially subversive!)

Whatever opinion one may hold of Whitley Strieber—fraud, psychotic, contactee, abductee, mystic, trickster, or honestly concerned about inexplicable events in his own life and the life of the world—one is hard put to categorize Sarfatti the same way. Yet they both share an experience of alien contact while children, an experience that neither yet fully understands: Was it a hoax? Was it "real"? Were the perpetrators aliens? US government officials? Something else?

Sarfatti's involvement with the Columbia–Sandia "superkids" program is no mystery, and neither is the existence of Walter Breen. Strieber's difficulty lies in the fact that there is very little corroboration of his experience, aside from some other children (now adults) in the neighborhood in those years who used to disappear for hours at a time in the Olmos Basin, and aside from Whitley's discovery of the buildings used by the "secret school" during a taping for a television series, *Contact,* right where he had always claimed they would be.[30]

What seems a certainty is that both men had something done to them as children during the Cold War, something that may have been government-sanctioned. And if we find that theory far-fetched, we only have to remember how the CIA covered up the Finders revelations in the name of national security. Whatever happened to Sarfatti—and what seems to have happened to Strieber—it bore fruit. Sarfatti has become well-known as both a scientist and as a popularizer of quantum physics through his books and collaborative efforts with other scientists, writers, and thinkers. He has pursued the idea of alien intelligence relentlessly, searching for the physics that would make stellar travel possible and stretching the limits of quantum mechanics to break Einstein's "wall of light," i.e., to find a way to travel faster than the speed of light and thus master the space-time continuum.

Strieber has heroically recorded his experiences with "the visitors," knowing full well that he was subjecting himself to near-universal ridicule and humiliation. He was (and is) a successful novelist whose books become movies; like Philip Corso, he had no need to jump into this particular fray and take a stand one way or another. Yet, while Sarfatti pursues the science behind the alien experience, name-dropping like mad (and why not?) and trading good-natured insults with some of the world's most intelligent human beings, Strieber is struggling to find a meaning to all of this that transcends science, a spiritual or perhaps existential paradigm lurking behind the flashing lights, the speeding saucers, the bug-eyed monsters of our nightmares.

Both men were touched by something supernatural in their childhoods during the Cold War that led each on his own path, paths that converge—perhaps—during recess at the secret school.

A COLD, METALLIC VOICE

A clean mind is one that has been brainwashed.

—Walter Breen

Sarfatti is obviously convinced that the "cold, metallic voice" he heard over the phone was some type of paranormal communication, either of alien beings actually hovering overhead in a spacecraft of some kind or something that has yet to be fully identified and described. He admits it *may* have been part of an ultra-secret government program, a kind of brainwashing or mind control experiment, but he insists that it was not a hoax or a prank. In this, he is running parallel in his thinking to that of Whitley Strieber, who also heard a "machine-like voice" during his contacts with the Visitors.[31]

What many UFOlogists and "fellow travelers" may not realize, however, is that this "cold, metallic voice" has an impressive pedigree in the United States, even before computers, radios, and other modern communications media existed to give us an idea of what that kind of voice would sound like.

In M.V. Ingram's ambitiously entitled *An Authenticated History of the Fa*mous Bell Witch. The Wonder of the 19th Century, and Unexplained Phenomenon of the Christian Era. The Mysterious Talking Goblin That Terrorized the West End of Robertson County, Tennessee, Tormenting John Bell to His Death. The

Story of Besty Bell, Her Lover and the Haunting Sphinx, published in Clarksville, Tennessee in 1894, we read of an encounter between General Andrew Jackson and the famous Bell Witch. One section is worth quoting here, and takes place when General Jackson is on the move through Robertson County, Tennessee in the vicinity of the Bell Witch. His wagon freezes on a level road, and no amount of coaxing the horses or pulling by his troops will enable the wagon to move an inch. The wheels are removed, the axles inspected, and there is no indication of a problem with either the wagon or with the road. It is a bizarre situation in and of itself, but then:

> All stood off looking at the wagon in serious meditation, for they were "stuck." Gen. Jackson after a few moments thought, realizing that they were in a fix, threw up his hands exclaiming, "By the eternal, boys, it is the witch." Then came the sound of a sharp metallic voice from the bushes, saying, "All right General, let the wagon move on, I will see you tonight." The men in bewildered astonishment looked in every direction to see if they could discover from whence came the strange voice, but could find no explanation to the mystery. Gen. Jackson exclaimed again, "By the eternal, boys, this is worse than fighting the British." The horses then started unexpectedly of their own accord, and the wagon rolled along as light and smoothly as ever.

Jackson's entourage arrived later that night at Mr. Bell's home, where they sat up waiting for the witch to keep her promise. They had with them a self-described "witch layer," or exorcist, who kept a pistol loaded with a silver bullet, ready to destroy the phantom.

> Presently perfect quiet reigned, and then was heard a noise like dainty footsteps prancing over the floor, and quickly following, the same metallic voice heard in the bushes rang out from one corner of the room, exclaiming, "All right, General, I am on hand ready for business."[32]

The "witch layer" then tried to shoot in the direction of the voice, but his pistol would not fire. Eventually the Bell Witch grabbed the man by his nose and threw him out of the house, much to the consternation as well as the amusement of General Jackson and his men, who could nonetheless not actually see what was causing the witch layer so much discomfort. The Witch then assured Jackson that it would return the following night, but Jackson could not convince his men to hang around much longer and they left with daybreak.

This account is that of one Colonel Thomas L. Yancey, a lawyer in Clarksville, who compiled this story from surviving eyewitnesses, and then sent the report to M.V. Ingram for inclusion in his book in 1894. What is interesting is the statement—made twice—that the Bell Witch spoke in a "metallic voice." One wonders what that meant to people living in 1894? Was that the phrase used by his eyewitnesses, who would have heard that voice during Jackson's lifetime (1767–1845), more specifically in the early decades of the nineteenth century? The Witch evidently possessed paranormal abilities, was invisible, but spoke English tolerably well despite the strange sound of her voice. This would seem to fit neatly with the characteristics noted by Sarfatti.

To be sure, the UFO phenomenon itself is not new. Strange lights in the sky have bedeviled humanity for centuries, if not millennia, and so have the strange creatures who either pilot the craft or are just along for the ride.

French scientist Jacques Vallee has seriously studied this phenomenon for many years ,and discusses his findings in a series of books, most notably among them *Messengers of Deception* and *Passport to Magonia*. He admits that it is foolish to discount the thousands of UFO reports as nothing more than mistaken sightings of the planet Venus, or swamp gas, or the other frankly unbelievable "scientific" explanations of the events. Researcher John Keel, whose book *The Mothman Prophecies* was eventually made into a film starring Richard Gere, is even more forward when he claims that our planet is "haunted." He sees—as does Vallee and many others—the UFO experience as analogous (if not identical) to the experience of demons, fairies, and other monsters from other times. The fact that we now describe these events in terms that make it sound as if the "visitors" are space travelers may be more a reflection of how our culture is oriented in the aftershock of nuclear explosions and lunar missions than of any kind of "objective" reality. It may be the same experience as seeing demons, or fairies, only filtered through a modern consciousness and more "scientific" sensitivity.

Keel reports many instances of strange phone calls connected to UFO activity and UFO "contactees." He himself was the recipient of many such strange calls, and at one time the number of strange calls to members of UFO groups around the country reached such a crescendo that it contributed to the eventual breakup of many of these groups. The calls would range from electronic beeps and clanking noises—such as Sarfatti first experienced with the "spaceship" call—to threats, to persons imitating the voices of friends, to static . . . and in some cases the caller would play back taped conversations the recipient had moments or days ago with other parties, as if to demonstrate that the phone lines were tapped. This indicates either that the government was behind this elaborate campaign of intimidation and disinformation, or that some other force with unlimited resources was the culprit. No private organization or company—no Minutemen or Michigan Militia, Ku Klux Klan or Black Panthers, Weathermen or Conservative Coalition—has the ability to mount such an aggressive campaign against the UFO groups, and more importantly no motivation to do so. If we accept the data given in Keel's book—and in so many other reports published over the last thirty to fifty years—then we are forced to assume that the American government was responsible for the phone calls, the mysterious "men in black," and other related phenomena associated with the UFO experiencers. If the American government was *not* responsible, then we have a potentially more serious problem on our hands.

It is not the intention of this author to weigh in on one side or the other in the UFO controversy. I have never seen a UFO, have never been abducted by aliens or had any analogous experiences. I have seen the fabled "men in black," however, when an old black Cadillac drove up in front of my home one afternoon and the driver aimed a camera with a telephoto lens at me. When I tried to confront them, the vehicle drove away quickly and was replaced by another, this time containing two rather short women instead of two men, who drove into my driveway—blocking my car and preventing me from chasing the Cadillac—left their vehicle, and stood before me asking me sweetly if I knew where a "Mr. Devilbis" lived. Startled, I responded in the negative although the name was familiar to me: it was that of a manufacturing company somewhere in the Midwest to which, a few weeks earlier, I had been referred by a former co-worker as a possible client for some electronic work. There was no Devilbis anywhere in the immediate vicinity of the town where I lived, however, and none for almost fifty miles in any direction. It wasn't until years later that a "deconstruction" of that event led me to the amusing revelation that "Devilbis" was actually two words: "devil" and Latin "bis," meaning "the second devil" or "the devil, again."

Why this visitation should have taken place is beyond me. As I said, I am not a UFO contactee and have never belonged to any of the UFO groups or really had anything at all to do with UFOs. My specialty has always been history and culture, specifically the history of religions and mystical movements. But this was the winter before the Gulf War began, and it is possible that my 1960s experiences with a variety of anti-war groups and other radical associations would have flagged me in some kind of government computer. At least, that is what I told myself in those days even though, on reflection, it doesn't make any sense. It is quite costly to maintain a surveillance operation using two cars and four agents for a single individual who has had nothing to do with politics in over twenty years. Of course, my business took me all over the world, and especially to China, but that still does not rate me two cars, four agents, a telephoto lens and "Devilbis." I have never been able to determine the cause of the event, or the identities of the individuals involved or the organization, if any, to which they belonged. I did have another similar run-in years later, however, at Changi Airport in Singapore, when a young woman appeared from out of nowhere, dressed like a 1950s spy in a trenchcoat—totally inappropriate for Singapore weather!—and who smiled at me and tapped me on the shoulder, gave me a little wave, and disappeared again.

And so it goes.

THE STARGATE CONSPIRACY

. . . NASA is the disturbed child of two dysfunctional parents—paranoia and war.
—Graham Hancock[33]

In 1999, the authorial team of Lynn Picknett and Clive Prince published *The Stargate Conspiracy*,[34] an exposé of what appeared to be a US government conspiracy to control access to the type of information that people like Jack Sarfatti, Hal Puthoff and others were accumulating on their own. Picknett and Prince connected this conspiracy to activities surrounding the Pyramids and the Sphinx in Egypt, but focused as well on the circle of mystics around Andrija Puharich and the alien intelligences known as "The Nine." Missing the most crucial connection of all, however—that of Arthur Young, Ruth Paine and Lee Harvey Oswald—they ended their book with the breathless expectation that something of awesome global importance would occur at or near the millennium at the site of the Pyramids at Gizeh. Nothing of that nature transpired . . . at least, not that we know of, anyway!

But their research is valuable in other ways. Picknett and Prince have been rummaging through the Catholic closet for a while, coming up with new spins on the Shroud of Turin (*Turin Shroud—In Whose Image?*) and the Knights Templar (*The Templar Revelation: Secret Guardians of the True Identity of Christ*), going to the same well as the team of Baigent, Lincoln and Leigh before them (*Holy Blood, Holy Grail*). What makes *The Stargate Conspiracy* unique is the level of research into lesser known realms, less well-trod paths of arcane knowledge and secret societies with political connections. For many readers, it might have been the first time they came across the names that were once household words among the New Age crowd of the 1970s: Uri Geller, Andrija Puharich and the rest. The fact that the event of momentous import at the millennium apparently did not occur when they said it would is no reason to ignore this book, which is full of detail concerning some of the most colorful individuals of our time, and some of the most sinister associations. It is also useful for its introduction into the world of Egyptology, and the political machinations that take place both within and without the Cairo Museum.

The reason for this is a belief—held by some individuals and groups, including (the authors insist) elements of the US Government—that the Egyptian gods were extra-terrestrial beings. Aliens. And that the Pyramids of Gizeh and the Sphinx somehow conceal evidence of this, either in their construction or in whatever may be buried beneath them, or both. Indeed, "The Nine" itself is a reference to the council of Nine Gods—the Ennead—in Egyptian religion, and thus reinforces the links between ancient Egypt, alien civilizations, and the séances with The Nine conducted (on behalf of the military?) by Andrija Puharich and his group totaling nine members.

The field of paleo-astronomy is esoteric in itself; when you mix it up with eccentric ideas about history and archaeology you are only asking for trouble. Academia will either ignore you (at best), or ridicule you. You will be lumped in with the cranks and the crackpots, the un-credentialed and un-accredited "amateur historians," who have no business kicking sand at the tenured bullies who occupy their privileged positions in sunny safety from the deep water of rushing currents of controversy and treacherous whirlpools of contradictory and anomalous evidence, rather like beached whales. Yet, as the decades have gone by, it has become more and more obvious that many of our ancient structures—Stonehenge, the Pyramids, the Adena and Hopewell mounds—were astronomically oriented. Academia will grudgingly accept that some of these edifices were built in such a way that the rising of the sun on the summer or winter solstice was accommodated in their design, so that rays of the sun would fall through a specific aperture in the stone or wood or earthen construction (as is obvious to anyone who has been there at the time). The ultimate purpose for this, of course, is a matter of some debate. Those academics who wish to support this theory will go so far as to state that these astronomically-oriented creations were used as a kind of calendar, telling primitive man when to sow and when to reap. The problem with this uneasy concession is that the constructions are often much more elaborate than that, and consumed a great deal of primitive society's time and resources to build.

In the case of the Pyramids, a serious attempt has been made to associate their design and orientation with the constellation Orion.[35] In the case of the Gothic cathedrals of France, Louis Charpentier (*Les Mysteres de la Cathédrale de Chartres*) has put forward the theory that they were built in imitation of the zodiacal sign Virgo (for "virgin," since each of these cathedrals were known as a "Notre Dame" or "Our Lady"). This approach to archaeology and "sacred architecture" was anticipated in that classic of the scientific interpretation of myth, *Hamlet's Mill*,[36] in which the authors deconstruct many famous world myths to demonstrate that they had astronomical significance and were referencing events that had taken place in the heavens.

A full discussion of these ideas is outside the scope of this book, and the interested reader is encouraged to seek out *Hamlet's Mill* in particular for an engrossing and illuminating exposition of these themes, before going on to the more popular *The Orion Mystery* and some of the other titles fighting for shelf space in either the New Age section, the Ancient History section, or somewhere in between. One would be amiss not to mention R.A. Schwaller de Lubicz' works in this context as well, such as *The Temple In Man* and *Sacred Science.* Of course, the works by former OSS officer Peter Tompkins are also valuable, such as his *The Secrets of the Great Pyramid.*

It is enough to say for now that these theories of the inter-relationship between ancient buildings and monuments and the stars—and the even more esoteric correspondences between both buildings and stars and the human body and its processes and systems—were taken seriously by agencies of the US (and other) governments, if not by academia itself. The design of these edifices and their orientation to the compass points were thought to either *symbolize* a kind of divine geometry, inherent mathematical formulae embedded deep within nature, or to actually *cause* the building in question to function as a kind of machine. We know that the ancient Egyptians placed great store in the idea of resurrection; whether of the physical body or of some spiritual analogue is still open to furious debate. We also see, from a careful and "astronomical" reading of the Coffin Texts and other elements of what is sometimes called the Egyptian Book of the Dead, that the Egyptians were very conscious of the stars, and had developed an entire liturgical culture around the stars and the transportation of the soul of the dead pharaoh to a place in the celestial firmament. Thus, the idea of space travel is at least as old as ancient Egypt, if not much, much older.

The Germans had come closest to the dream of space travel during World War II. The rocket factories were cranking out missiles like the V-1 and V-2, but designs on the boards covered everything from jet aircraft to "flying saucer" prototypes. In the immediate postwar years, various Germans approached American intelligence (CIC) officers in Germany professing to have details of the saucer effort, including the Horten brothers who were part of Operation Paperclip,[37] and the bizarre case of Guido Bernardy. On August 5, 1947, Bernardy approached the US Army in Frankfurt in an attempt to see General Lucius Clay to warn him about Nazi secret weapons, the development of flying saucers by Hitler's scientists, Hitler's survival in a submarine sailing in the Southern Hemisphere and about to launch these weapons against the US and Europe, and the appearance of "two gentlemen, with no special talent in their lives, [who] discovered they did have extraordinary powers and capabilities which made it possible for them to communicate and contact the spirit world."[38] The agent who interviewed him, one Albert Goldstein, added, "Subject seemed entirely sincere, and the strong possibility that he is merely a crackpot is not apparent."[39] A few months later, the Horten brothers became an issue once again, as the Roswell case and the multiple sightings of "flying saucers" in the United States caused the Deputy Director of Intelligence, European Command to send a memorandum—dated 21 October 1947—to the American Chief of Staff about information received from Wright Field "concerning the flying saucers recently sighted over the UNITED STATES.

"For your information, the Air Materiel Command at WRIGHT FIELD is making a study of this subject and is constructing models to be tested in a wind tunnel . . . . The Air Materiel Command is of the opinion that some sort of object, such as the flying saucer, did exist" (Document declassified 5 July 1994). It would seem from the context of the accompanying documentation that the Horten brothers were assisting the US government in this assessment. It is known that the Operation Paperclip scientists had been sent to Wright Field (which would become Wright-Patterson AFB) in July 1947 at the time of the Roswell incident.

Although Roswell is not mentioned in the declassified documents, it is nonetheless remarkable that the engineers and scientists of Wright Field were testing models of flying saucers in a wind tunnel there a few months after the incident (which the military had ridiculed as being the mistaken identification of a weather balloon, and which later researchers identified as artifacts of Project Mogul) and that this testing involved de-Nazified scientists under Paperclip, and that their preliminary conclusion was that a flying saucer "did exist."

Hitler kept waiting to the very end for the coveted "secret weapon" that would decide the war, and he would remain disappointed, but Wernher von Braun and Walter Dornberger fled to the United States with the designs in their files and in their heads, and eventually with hundreds of their fellow scientists in tow managed to fill in the gaps and create the American space program, a military endeavor which later became NASA.

One of the amateur, popular and revisionist historians and archaeologists to draw the attention and suspicion (perhaps unfairly) of the Picknett and Prince team is Graham Hancock, who caused a worldwide sensation with the publication in 1992 of *The Sign and the Seal*, a book in which Hancock claimed to have discovered the resting place of the Ark of the Covenant. Hancock is a respected journalist and expert on East Africa, who worked for *The Economist* and *The Traveler*. He also won honorable mention in the 1990 H.L. Mencken journalism award for his book *Lords of Poverty*. Thus, Hancock is not an amateur journalist or armchair anthropologist, but a credible field observer of the cultures on which he reports. Yet, like Howard Blum, Jim Marrs and the other members of the "brotherhood buried alive," he has drifted from purely political reportage to the arcane. Since *The Sign and the Seal*, he has authored many hefty tomes on the subject of alien influence on ancient civilizations, such as *The Mars Mystery* (1994) and *Fingerprints of the Gods: A Quest for the Beginning and the End* (1995). In the former, he writes,

> NASA was formed in 1958 at the height of the Cold War when all advances in space science were spin-offs from the development of more efficient killing machines. The exploration of space itself was directly linked to defense policy.[40]

This is something which many Americans forget, just as they forget that everything from their superb interstate highway system to the *Diagnostic and Statistical Manual of Mental Disorders* was the result of defense policies. Military policies. War.

NASA was created around the dark genius of a coven of Nazi scientists who first tested their designs and discoveries on the civilian population of London during the Blitz. While many may feel that Hancock's characterization of NASA as a "disturbed child" is overstating the case, the preponderance of men who should have been standing trial for war crimes instead working for NASA in those days—men who had used slave labor to build bigger and better rockets—certainly goes some way to justify a verdict for moral imbecility, and the network that existed in the 1950s between the rocket scientists on the one hand and the "psychic scientists" like Andrija Puharich on the other—including the presence of the Nazi doctors at Randolph AFB—is clearly evidence of a hidden agenda. When Puharich went to Brazil to investigate Arigo, the "psychic surgeon," it was in collaboration with his friend John Laurence, an engineer specializing in satellites and telecommunications and one of the founding members of NASA.

Clearly, whoever was working with or for NASA in the 1950s and 1960s had to be able to accept the presence—let alone the dominance—of the many Nazis on their team and, as we have seen in previous volumes, those Nazis would not have been able to emigrate safely to the United States much less serve in positions of tremendous prestige and authority if it were not for the unwavering support and material assistance of men like Allen Dulles and Richard Nixon. As unpalatable as this idea seems, and as outrageous as it will appear to many, the facts speak for themselves and are incontrovertible. The same men who went after spirited anti-Nazis like Helen Gahagan Douglas in political campaigns, using Red-baiting and anti-Semitism as their weapons, also did their best to defend the active involvement of committed Nazis in the most sensitive, most secret caverns of American military technology, aviation medicine, and intelligence.

When Jack Sarfatti and Whitley Strieber were getting their marching orders as children from "the visitors" or perhaps "The Nine," NASA had not yet been created. *All* American space research before October 1, 1958—the date the National Aeronautics and Space Act was signed, creating the National Aeronautics and Space Administration, or NASA—was in the hands of the military, or under military contract at places like the Jet Propulsion Laboratory, which would become part of NASA very quickly. All investigation of the UFO phenomenon was in the hands of the FBI, the CIA, or the military. And the military departments responsible for space research were dominated by the Nazis they had brought over after 1945, Nazis who would eventually become an integral part of NASA, an agency that was created in response to the launching of the first earth-orbit satellite by the Soviet Union in 1957, *Sputnik*. Who can extricate their memories of America's early space programs from the image of affable Wernher von Braun, a man who once wore the uniform of the Third Reich? Indeed, who among us who were alive at the time can forget Tom Lehrer's 1965 song "Wernher von Braun," which, while a humorous satire on the former German officer, was nonetheless asking an important question: is it ethical to have former Nazis running our space program?

While the military and intelligence organs dominated UFO research—and kept sightings investigations, recovered evidence, and eyewitness testimony (particularly with regard to radar observations and encounters with military and commercial pilots, etc.) under wraps, thus robbing civilian groups of the chance to evaluate much UFO evidence—these military and intelligence organs also dominated psychic research and mind-control programs. Thus, on the one hand you had the Pentagon and the CIA monitoring UFO reports and massaging data, and on the other hand you had the same agencies racing to dominate inner space, as well. If the UFO phenomenon partakes of both the scientific (space flight, faster-than-light travel, alien visitations) and the psychological (hallucinations, visions, spiritual encounters and illumination), then the US government had all the bases covered. About all civilians could do was point to the sky and say they saw a UFO, or point to some burned grass on their lawn, or recount a tale of alien visitation; the civilians would have no access to the government's files on their experience, would have no opportunity to evaluate their experience in terms of ongoing military or intelligence operations, or in the context of data on similar experiences already in the government database, etc. The civilian would have had one of the most profound experiences of his or her life, and be unable to put it into *any* kind of context. Worse, individuals would be subject to ridicule if they opened their mouths. Further, this experience was either "real," i.e. had a scientific basis in objective reality, or was "spiritual" and had a more psychological dimension; the civilian would have no knowledge of how to interpret the event, and would thus be left in the dark having received no input from either the government or the scientists . . . or the church.

In the early Postwar period, as we can see from the quotations that open this chapter, some of America's most powerful individuals were convinced of the reality of the UFO phenomenon, not as some kind of mass delusion among the credulous elements of the population, but as a scientific fact: even more, as a problem that had to be evaluated from a military perspective. Generals, admirals, high-ranking CIA officials all believed in the potential threat posed by the phenomenon and then, abruptly, they grew silent; but not before the childhood experiences of Jack Sarfatti and Whitley Strieber, and not before the creation of NASA. In fact, one could reasonably say that the statements by credible, trained military and intelligence observers supporting the view that UFOs represented an alien civilization, a "sinister force" to use the words of General MacArthur, came to a halt after the Kennedy assassination in 1963. Odd, then, that we would find Fred Crisman and Guy Banister in at the very beginning of the twentieth century's UFO flap—two stalwarts of the assassination conspiracy as viewed by Jim Garrison, and both former intelligence officers (Crisman for OSS and eventually the CIA, Bannister for the FBI and, at one point, as the boss of FBI Special Agent Robert Maheu, who would go on to organize the Mafia–CIA assassination attempts against Castro).

Odd, then, that we would find many of Lee Harvey Oswald's co-workers at the Reily Coffee Company in New Orleans leaving that firm after the assassination and getting jobs with NASA and its subcontractors.

Coffee company employees. NASA.

Odd, then, that the Oswalds' Texas benefactors—the Paines—would have strong ties to the aerospace industry, and that Michael Paine would work for General Walter Dornberger at Bell Aerospace.

NASA was only one side of the story. Operation BLUEBIRD and, eventually, MK-ULTRA were the other. During 1954 alone, the year that Whitley Strieber recalls as being the first year he was brought to the "secret school," a total of seventeen MK-ULTRA contracts were signed, including everything from hypnosis (Projects 25, 29) to stage magic (John Mulholland's projects, including Projects 15 and 19) to drugs (Projects 26, 27, 28, 37, 38). These projects included testing of hallucinogens and narcotics on human subjects, as well as John Mulholland's specialty, which was training agents in how to dose unwitting subjects in the field. The following year saw the start of the Ionia State Hospital program of massive dosing of prisoners with LSD as well as the use of hypnosis in interrogations (Project 39) and, in 1956, Louis Jolyon West's experiments in "dissociated states" under the auspices of the University of Oklahoma (Project 43). Unfortunately, we have very little information on analogous *military* research taking place at the same time. We know that the Air Force contracted with the CIA in 1959 to conduct studies of "the Nature and Uses of Hypnosis as a Control Technique" (contract AF 49(638)-72B), and that the Navy had similar interests in 1964 (contract Nonr-4731(00)), and that the Air Force again commissioned the CIA to investigate the relation between sleep and hypnosis (contract AF-AFOSR-707-67) from 1964–1971. The only reason we know about any of this was because four boxes of MK-ULTRA files were found to have escaped the shredding frenzy of Richard Helms and Sidney Gottlieb. We did not learn of this from the Armed Forces directly, which is generally under no pressure to open its research files to the public. Not on mind-control programs. Not on UFO sightings. Elements of both fall under the heading "national security."

Thus, the American government had a stranglehold on research exploring the nature of consciousness, of memory, of deception, of manipulation—using drugs, hypnosis, and occult techniques—at the same time as they were performing damage control on the UFO flap. If these efforts were not coordinated at some level—if the research products of both were not being sent to the same, anonymous office in Arlington or Langley or Washington for analysis—then a tremendous opportunity was lost: an opportunity to learn, once and for all, what the UFO sightings (and especially the abductions and other "close encounters") represented. At the same time, if these efforts *were* coordinated, then the American people were being well and truly "controlled," and important information, central to our understanding of who we are and the place we have in the world, was being withheld.

The comedy *Men In Black*, a film starring Tommy Lee Jones and Will Smith as government agents keeping a lid on alien "immigration" to the United States, features a device which erases a contactee's memory: of both the alien experience as well as of the MIBs themselves. One imagines there are government agents who would have given their right arms for a device of that nature. One has no need to wonder if time and money was spent in pursuing that technology, since we have shown in Books I and II that the government was committed to achieving just that sort of power over the minds of its citizens, and over the minds of selected foreign citizens and populations as well.

At some point, the exploration of outer space extends into an exploration of inner space. This was perhaps the message of the experiences shared by Strieber and Sarfatti, a message both are still trying to communicate and to understand to this day. In Strieber's case, it comes with a warning: the entities we discover on our journeys may not always be altogether benign.

THE NINE, THE PROCESS, AND THE VISITORS

> Despite what they had done to me, I did not hate the visitors. Because I knew their strength but not their motives, they frightened me . . . . That they represented a real, living force seemed hard to dispute. But that this force might be essentially human in origin remained a definite possibility.
>
> —Whitley Strieber[41]

It may seem incongruous to try to contact aliens aboard their spaceships through the means of a séance. After all, the séance is the proper environment of the ghost and the disembodied spirit. The assumption one makes about aliens is that they are, at least, alive. (Although, considering that, is it not possible that perhaps dead aliens who have visited this planet would have left behind a similar effluvium, some alien ectoplasm, a Martian ghost haunting our planet, moaning unintelligibly in alien dialects, and able to be contacted with Ouija board and medium? Is Roswell thus haunted?) Nevertheless, the séances conducted by Andrija Puharich and his blue-blooded colleagues from December 31, 1952 through June 27, 1953 with the mysterious Dr. Vinod, Arthur Young, Ruth Forbes Paine Young, and Alice Astor were just such instances, and they were taking place during the same period that Sarfatti and Strieber were each, in their own way, making contact. (Although Strieber places great emphasis on 1954 as the year he was admitted to the "secret school," his memories of childhood encounters stretches from 1951 to 1957.) As we have seen earlier, these séances gave rise to the concept of The Nine, and these forces—speaking through Dr. Vinod—established themselves as living entities, as alien visitors aboard a spacecraft that was hovering over the earth. Indeed, Whitley Strieber himself speaks of hearing "nine knocks" associated with visits by his alien stalkers, and Sarfatti is likewise aware of The Nine, although at times in his lengthy email exchanges one sees them referred to as the "Alien Raj." Uri Geller also claimed to have been contacted by The Nine, as we see from Andrija Puharich's book on the Israeli psychic, *Uri*.

These are the associations that give Picknett and Prince some anxiety, for they understand The Nine to be a hostile agency (no matter whether it be an alien menace or a clandestine psy-war campaign) and the covert cooperation with The

Nine—or with what they interpret as the hidden agenda of The Nine—by government and science as a betrayal of humanity. If we are to believe Robert Temple, for example (and there is no reason why we should not), then the US government was extremely interested in his research into the African Dogon tribe—the primitive tribe that knew of the existence of both Sirius A and Sirius B, including having much detailed information about the physical and chemical composition of both, as well as an accurate calendar of the double star's movements—and attempted to keep Temple from publishing his results in *The Sirius Mystery*, an attempt that obviously failed. Whether or not the attempt was a genuine, albeit half-hearted, effort on the behalf of the CIA to stop Temple from publishing, or was itself part of a disinformation campaign or some other psy-war experiment, is not known. What is known is that the CIA knew in detail of Temple's research long before he had gone to press. If we trace Temple's research in a "chain of custody," we find that it leads to the artist and occultist Harry Smith (so beloved of the OTO) and directly from Smith back to . . . Arthur Young, Smith's mentor and benefactor. Temple himself studied with Arthur Young. And when we deal with Arthur Young, we are dealing with The Nine.

The "nine knocks" of Whitley Strieber's experience is related both in *Transformation* and in his later book, *Breakthrough*. They took place on the evening of August 27, 1986 while he was at his upstate New York cabin. There was a definite series of three distinct sets of three knocks, for a total of nine knocks, coming from a corner of the ceiling. Strieber seemed to understand this as an invitation to go outside and meet "the visitors" . . . an invitation he declined, from fear. His cats also reacted in terror, staring at the spot the knocks came from.

Then, as he relates in *Breakthrough*, exactly eighteen months to the day from his experience of nine knocks, an entire town—Glenrock, Wyoming—was awakened at 2:45 A.M. on February 27, 1988 by the same phenomenon: nine knocks in three groups of three on the sides of their houses, their cars, their doors. This was related in the local newspaper, but no one ever discovered the cause of this bizarre event.

And when Strieber wrote *The Secret School* in 1997, it contained nine "lessons" divided into three "triads."

One would tend to dismiss these strange matters as having nothing really essential to do with The Nine, other than the mere fact of number, except for the peculiar association that three groups of three knocks would have for someone who had studied Western occultism.

First, magician Aleister Crowley, in his amusing and informative *Magick In Theory and Practice*, states,

> The general object of a knock or a knell is to mark a stage in the ceremony . . . . The sudden and sharp impact of the sound throws the mind into an alert activity which enables it to break loose from the obsession of its previous mood. It

> is aroused to apply itself aggressively to the ideas which had oppressed it. There is therefore a perfectly rational interpretation of the psychological power of the knock.[42]

Crowley belonged to the Golden Dawn, the British secret society that gave him the theoretical framework for much of his occult knowledge. Recourse to the rituals of the Golden Dawn—as published in Crowley secretary Israel Regardie's *The Golden Dawn*—will show us one way three groups of three knocks may be employed.

The ritual in question is that of the Neophyte Grade, the very first initiation in the Golden Dawn scheme. The temple is arranged, according to Regardie, in Egyptian fashion, and the whole rite recalls the weighing of the soul of the recently departed against the feather of the Goddess Maat. The Neophyte wears a black hooded robe. The other officers of the temple are dressed according to their rank, but again the regalement includes Egyptian motifs.

To one side is a representation of the Evil Triad of the Egyptians: gods who are prepared to devour the entrails of the Neophyte should he be found wanting. Surrounding the Neophyte are four benevolent gods, who will protect him from the savage hunger of the Evil Triad.

At one point in the ceremony, the three main initiators perform a "battery" of nine knocks, three knocks each, while uttering the formula "Khabs Am Pekht. Konx Om Pax; Light In Extension," one knock for each word. The initial phrase is Coptic, thus reinforcing the Egyptian character of the ritual, while the second phrase is in a "corrupt Greek" form. As for the meaning behind this, Regardie states,

> This affirms the establishment of the White Triangle and therefore the Completion of the Opening Ceremony. The Mystic Words "Khabs Am Pekht" which accompany the knocks seal the image of the Light.[43]

The Egyptian tenor of this rite is immediately suggestive to those who have read the Picknett and Prince book, because Egypt is at the heart of this mystery of The Nine.

However, the way in which the knocks are sounded is quite important; the interval between each knock is as essential as the knock and number of knocks itself. In the case of the Strieber/Glenrock events, the nine knocks are given in three groups of three, thus: 3—3—3. The number 333 has enormous significance for Qabalists (such as Madonna and Demi Moore!) as well as for ceremonial magicians in general, for it represents Choronzon, the Beast of the Abyss.

We have all heard of the significance of the number 666 as the number of the Beast of the Apocalypse. Some of us have wondered at the significance of 555 which, as I mention in *Unholy Alliance*, is the number of Hitler's original membership in the Nazi Party, as well as the height (in feet) of the Washington Monument, the altitude of Ashland, Kentucky above sea level, and the number of the Greek word *Necronomicon*.

In the case of 333, we are dealing with a suspiciously empty section of the Qabalistic Tree of Life. The Tree consists of ten *sephiroth* or spheres, each representing some facet of creation. Dividing the top three spheres from the lower seven is what occultists refer to as Daath, or the Abyss. It represents for some the "dark night of the soul," a necessary purging of the soul's sins, its karma, its dross before it can continue to the three "supernals" and complete its journey to Nirvana (to mix theologies for a moment). Just as there is an "Evil Triad" waiting for the Neophyte at the very first grade of initiation—demonic forms that wish to devour the unworthy aspirant—there is a Beast waiting in the Abyss itself, as if for a second and more brutal initiation. The number of Choronzon (derived from Qabalistic numerology) is the number of that particular Beast: 333.

Yet, as Masonic and other lore will remind us, these fierce creatures only appear fierce to the unclean. To those who have been purged of self-interest, self-consciousness, and the ego in general, these hideous monsters appear as angelic beings: the fierceness was one's own gross nature reflected on the faces of the guardians.

It is to this sector of the Tree of Life that Crowley successor Kenneth Grant has applied so much of his learning and exegesis. Grant believes that what the Qabalists consider the Abyss is actually a Gate, a way out to the zone of the stars, and a way in for the alien intelligences that have been summoned by magicians. While he devotes nearly an entire book to this thesis (*Nightside of Eden*), he covers the theme in many of his other works as well. In *Outside the Circles of Time*, he states that Choronzon "creates the event-act known as The Beast, viz: the creative vortex in the Aether that gives rise to the manifestation of phenomena *via* the mechanics of atavistic resurgence."[44] In *Hecate's Fountain*, he writes, "To enter into consciousness of this mystery is to become ashes to one world, but living and eternal fire to the next . . ."[45] In reference to studies by fellow occultist Michel Bertiaux, he writes (in *Cults of the Shadow*), "Choronzon, as the guardian of the gate *between* the known universe and the unknown universe—A and B—equates with ideas shared by all cults of the Shadow . . .," linking Choronzon and the Abyss to Haitian voodoo, for instance.[46] Finally, Grant defines the Abyss as "the Gulf between the unreal and the real, i.e., between phenomena and noumenon. Crossing the Abyss is the most critical event on the Spiritual Path . . . . Only the total abolition of the ego, or limited individual consciousness, makes a successful crossing possible."[47]

As mentioned in an earlier chapter, Grant also makes note of the fact that the drawing of one of Crowley's alien intelligences, Lam, is virtually identical to the famous portrait of one of the Visitors that adorns Whitley Strieber's *Communion*. If we posit, for a moment, the idea that all of the theories of Kenneth Grant and Aleister Crowley refer to specific phenomena—however they interpret them—then we have a sudden resurgence of those phenomena in the events experienced by Whitley Strieber, as well as by others before and since.

Ed Conroy, the reporter who researched Whitley Strieber's claims for a book entitled *Report On Communion: An Independent Investigation of and Commentary* on Whitley Strieber's Communion, also noted the correlations between Strieber's experiences and western occultism in general, taking particular care to cite Kenneth Grant, and Grant's views on the UFO phenomenon as an occult event of great importance, and then spends pages discussing Aleister Crowley's invocation of Choronzon . . . without being aware at this time of Whitley's experience of the nine knocks.[48]

> *For me, the nine knocks were personal confirmation.*
> —Whitley Strieber[49]

Indeed.

To an occultist, the "nine knocks" may appear sinister, heavy with foreboding, for it serves in its grouping of three triads as an invocation of Choronzon; or is it perhaps a signal from the Abyss that the "Portal" is open. The Portal is the gateway to the Inner Temple, the Holy of Holies, and of this Israel Regardie writes,

We are told in the Portal that the nine months' wait which must intervene before the Portal is again opened for the Aspirant has a correspondence to the nine months of gestation before birth.[50]

(It was eighteen months to the day between Strieber's "nine knocks" and the "nine knocks" of Glenrock, Wyoming: two times nine months. One wonders how the Portal was opened nine months after Strieber's experience and nine months before Glenrock's? And what did Glenrock do to deserve this in the first place?)

> *For years I have told of being present at the University of Texas when Charles Whitman went on his shooting spree from the tower in 1966. But I wasn't there. Then where was I?*
> —Whitley Strieber[51]

Strieber's experiences are certainly bizarre enough by themselves, but when related to other events occurring at the same time they take on larger, more cosmic overtones. Strieber's books vacillate between "Gee, I have no idea what is happening to me," and "Gee, this must be an event of momentous importance!" as well they should. We are in no mood for prophets these days, unless they can give us the winning lottery number, so those who have been touched by supernatural forces are generally encouraged to keep silent and pass the butter.

For instance, as quoted above, he firmly believed for years that he had been at the University of Texas when Charles Whitman began sniping at innocent civilians from the Tower. Yet, as he discovered later to his chagrin, he was never there. He did attend UT, but a year or more *after* the event in question, and he doesn't know why he believed he was there, with such vivid memories of what went on.

In other cases, he has no memories of entire weeks of his life, weeks that have disappeared and for which he has only scraps of information, none of which seem to make sense when strung together (as he himself admits). The year 1968 is a case in point, and one with extreme relevance to our story.

In January of 1968, Strieber left Texas to go to London. He had been accepted at the London School of Film Technique, and the twenty-two-year-old was looking forward to spending time in England. But after about six months, he finds himself taking a train to Italy from London and meeting on the train a young lady. The couple decide to travel together and somehow they wind up in Rome, but after a stop of a few days? six weeks? in Florence. Once in Rome, they break up (for whatever reason, Strieber does not remember) and Whitley takes another train, this time bound for Strasbourg. From Strasbourg he goes by rail across France, winding up at the Spanish border at Port Bou, where he takes yet another train and winds up in Barcelona, booking a small room on the Ramblas. All this time he is in a state of fear, but we never learn the object of that fear, only that it may, somehow, have to do with the Visitors. He eventually returns to London, but has been gone for much longer than he thought: about six weeks is the best guess.[52] Further, he also has memories of attending some kind of "ancient university" at this time, and of seeing adobe huts which made him think of North Africa (an easy trip from Spain).

What are we to make of this?

During Whitley Strieber's radio interview of this author about *Unholy Alliance,* he mentioned in passing that he had visited the headquarters of the Process while he was in London that year, and that of course made my ears prick up even as the revelation caught me off guard. 1968 was a particularly volatile time for the Process, and it was during this year that Manson Family member Bruce Davis was known to have paid a visit or two to Process head-quarters in London. Further, Sharon Tate and Roman Polanski were wed in London in January of that year, the same month Strieber flew to London from Texas. (In the spring of 1968, both Sirhan Sirhan and Naomi Judd would, at different times, visit Theosophical Society headquarters in Los Angeles.) Dr. Martin Luther King, Jr. was assassinated that April, and his putative assassin, James Earl Ray, escaped to London in May, visiting first Portugal and then returning to London to buy tickets for Belgium. He was arrested in June of that year in London and extradited back to the United States. Bobby Kennedy was assassinated a day or two earlier, and the Process went underground almost immediately in Los Angeles.

On July 29, when Whitley was presumably on the Continent, scientist Dr. James McDonald—a former US Navy intelligence officer during World War II—testified before Congress on the reality of the UFO phenomenon. (He would commit suicide some time later.) And, in November of 1968, Bruce Davis visited the Process in London. Whitley Strieber was still in London, and did not return to the United States until December of that year.[53] There is, of course, no evidence at all that Strieber ever met Davis, or that the two men were ever in Process headquarters at the same time. That is not the point I am trying to make, however.

Whitley Strieber, who for a long time inexplicably believed (erroneously) that he had been at the University of Texas on the day that Charles Whitman began shooting people at random, *was* in London when James Earl Ray was there after the Martin Luther King assassination; he *was* in London, visiting the Process, the same year that Manson Family member Bruce Davis was in London visiting the Process; he *was* in London when Sharon Tate and Roman Polanski were married there.

We would not consider all of this as evidence of anything at all, except that Whitley's behavior during 1968 was bizarre by his own admission, and that he had also visited the Process—for whatever reason—that same year. The author believes that Whitley's odyssey probably had nothing at all to do with the Process *per se*; that his visiting their headquarters in London might have been motivated more by simple curiosity than anything else. Yet, placing the young—by now, twenty-three-year-old—Whitley Strieber at the Process headquarters in London at the same time that they were forging some kind of link with the Manson Family is suggestive of some deeper influence, for the Process would later leave California for New York City, which is where Whitley wound up after leaving London and at the same time. They also had operations in Texas, principally Houston, where Maury Terry opines they were working with the Son of Sam cult—if, indeed, the two groups could safely be considered separate by that time, the 1970s.

No, Whitley Strieber is not some crazed Process/Son of Sam hitman; rather he was a contactee, vibrating like a tuning fork with all of the resonant associations taking place around him. One would have probably thought nothing at all of these coincidental links except for that one, salient piece of data: that he had visited the Process in London in 1968. For someone who had been at the mercy of the "secret school" since the age of six, and particularly since the age of nine, dealing with God-knows-what (military mind-control experiment or alien abduction), it comes as something of a shock—like a significant plot twist in a cinematic drama—to find him wandering into Process headquarters only a few months before Bruce Davis makes one of several known appearances there. After that episode, however, things quieted down for Whitley. At least for a while.

In 1970, Whitley and Anne Strieber were married and lived in New York, on West 55th Street in Manhattan. Strieber cannot recall much of significance until April of 1977, when more strange occurrences began to take place. This time, both he and Anne heard a voice coming out of their stereo. This in itself is not a strange occurrence in New York City, where police and taxi radios frequently come in over stereo receivers in the home, but in this case the voice had a conversation with the young couple, something which is certainly *not* possible under ordinary circumstances.

After a series of moves back and forth to Connecticut they eventually settled for a time in New York City, and maintained the famous cabin upstate where the most dramatic of the "visitations" took place. At some point during these early years of his marriage, however, Whitley Strieber and his wife Anne became involved with the Gurdjieff Foundation.

The Gurdjieff Foundation can hardly be considered a cult. During the same time that Whitley was a member, this author was in contact with a few other members in New York, who held the organization in high esteem and virtually spoke of it only in whispers. It operates relatively secretly, and is devoted to the teachings of both the Georgian mystic G.I. Gurdjieff and his most famous disciple, P. D. Ouspensky. Interested readers are encouraged to read their works, as there is no time or space here to go into much discussion of their philosophy.

Suffice it to say that it is hermetic, and metaphysical. There are physical exercises, chants (in particular the Gurdjieffian "double tone" chant) and meditations, as well as teachings on a wide variety of subjects pertaining to an illuminated understanding of nature and consciousness, including Gurdjieff 's famous insistence that most people are "asleep," and need to "wake up." It is a method to integrate the dissociated parts of one's personality, much like Jungian depth psychology but in a more active way (the passive Jungian system having a great deal in common with Freudian psychoanalysis). By all accounts, Gurdjieff himself was a powerful occultist, and had been trained at various places in Asia Minor and the Caucasus. He was also a trickster, and used paradox and practical jokes in the way Jesus used parables and miracles. In the end, those of his followers who adhere strictly to his teachings are generally considered to be forces for good in the world, and only the most doctrinaire of Christian theologian would go so far as to condemn them as "cultists."

One knows that Strieber gained very much through his fifteen-year association with them; unintentionally perhaps, they gave him tools for understanding his alien experiences, and methods for safeguarding himself and his family from the fallout of the traumatic processes to which he was subjected.[54] At one point, in his mid-thirties, he also found himself "working with young people" at the Foundation, and that must have struck a subconscious chord with his repressed memories of the "secret school."

Around the time he parted ways with the Gurdjieff Foundation, he had the terrifying series of experiences in the New York cabin that he relates in *Communion.* Since that time, he has created a virtual cottage industry in contactee experiences and has developed that theme into something more baldly spiritual and metaphysical, in books such as *The Key* and *The Path* which he markets on his own Web site, www.unknowncountry.com. Although he has always stressed the spiritual side of the Visitor experience—even from the early days of *Communion*—the importance of the esoteric as it relates to the Visitors has become more pronounced in his writings in the past few years. That said, he has not abandoned the traditional areas of

UFOlogy, such as saucer sightings and cattle mutilations, even as he has expanded into new realms, including some conspiracy literature and secret society lore. The interrelationship of all of these fields is something of which Strieber is keenly aware, and he links it to apocalyptic presentiments of global destruction and the possibility of a major appearance by the Visitors in the near future.

The Swiss psychiatrist C.G. Jung wrote a book devoted to the UFO phenomenon, entitled *Flying Saucers* and published in 1958 in German, and in English the following year. Jung is also the source for the concept of synchronicity, and we will address this more fully in the following chapter. What he has to say about those who have witnessed UFO contacts or sightings is actually quite apt in this case, and bears quoting:

> The empirical man extends beyond his conscious boundaries, his life and fate have far more than a personal meaning. He attracts the interest of "another world"; achievements are expected of him which go beyond the empirical realm and its narrow limits . . . . This numinous transformation is not the result of conscious intention or intellectual conviction, but is brought about by the impact of overwhelming archetypal impressions.[55]

And:

> An experience of this kind is not without its dangers, because it often has an inflating effect on the individual. His ego fancies itself increased and exalted, whereas in reality it is thrust into the background. . . . It is not the ego that is exalted; rather, something greater than it makes its appearance: the self, a symbol that expressed the whole man.[56]

This could go a long way toward explaining Whitley Strieber's development from a writer of horror fiction to the promoter of a kind of New Age mysticism based on his memories of the Visitors and the integration of them into his personal spirituality. Strieber himself writes of the phrase he heard during his abduction in the New York forest: "You are the chosen one," a phrase he immediately rejected as a little too hokey, but one that would have been in line with Jung's evaluation. Jung, of course, was inclined to reject the UFO phenomenon as simply a psychological matter for interpretation, until he had to admit that there was sufficient evidence to show that these sightings were not the result of mere hallucination, but had been tracked on radar and witnessed by military observers who were (in 1958) taking it seriously.[57]

Behind all of this is the lurking suspicion that some of these experiences may not be the result of benign forces looking to improve the lot of mankind, or the natural process of Jungian individuation. Again, it may be useless—psychologically speaking—to draw a sharp line of distinction between an actual alien visitation and the inner, spiritual experience it initiates. But can we be sure that the initiatory process (when put in motion by an experience of the Visitors) is "benign"? After all, just because a civilization is more advanced than we are technologically does not mean it has our best interests at heart. If nothing else, the history of colonialism would tell us that. That an alien race may be neither benign nor hostile, but simply self-interested, is an idea not normally entertained by the UFOlogists. Indeed, the world could be in the position of the Native American population of Manhattan Island, who sold their birthright for a string of beads. (The experience of aboriginal populations when it comes to the advent of colonial powers is worthwhile revisiting for the lessons it can teach us: powerful invading forces that sweetly smile on the natives and assure them that they mean no harm, and then proceed to rape the country, exploit its natural resources, and enslave or slaughter the residents as they go along. How could the aboriginals understand the mentality of the colonial powers, when they had no social context in which to place such an "otherworldly" event? How could they defend themselves, or even understand that they had to do so?) Even more troublesome, genuine contactee experiences may be mixed up with nefarious government disinformation programs, thus corrupting the entire contactee "database."

A SECRET BRUISE

> If mine was not an uncommon experience, it might be that we live in a society that bears a secret bruise from it.
>
> —Whitley Strieber[58]

It's not as if there were no evidence that the planet has been visited by *something*. The number of sightings that have taken place that have never been satisfactorily explained as due to atmospheric anomalies, swamp gas, the planet Venus, etc. is quite large. The number of sightings that have been tracked by the military on radar is also large enough to warrant some serious investigation. The number of sightings by commercial airline pilots is also worth consideration. And that is not counting sightings by citizens, people the government and the scientists do not deem "credible" because they have no training in celestial observations. In other words, the UFO phenomenon has been hijacked by the very establishments we have reason to believe may be responsible for at least some of the disinformation and misinformation that has gone on for so long in connection with the "flying saucers." There is no question that eyewitnesses make mistakes; there have been many studies in the psychological and criminological literature proving just that. However, what those studies do not prove is that while eyewitnesses may differ on the size and shape of a criminal, the clothing he was wearing or the color of his eyes, they normally agree on the fact that a crime has been committed: a gun did go off, a car was stolen, a man was beaten, a woman was raped. As Dr. James

McDonald relayed in his Congressional testimony: "Those eyewitnesses don't come in from, say, a street corner accident and claim they saw a giraffe killed by a tiger . . . . There is legally confusing difference of timing and distance, and so on; but all are in agreement that it was an auto accident."[59]

In the case of the UFO phenomenon, eyewitnesses may differ as to the number of colored lights, or the sound or lack of sound, or the shape of the craft; they agree, however, that something strange was in the sky that night. The weakness of eyewitness testimony is something that conservative scientists and scientific observers and skeptics—like the late Carl Sagan, for instance—rely upon to bolster their *a priori* judgment that the craft seen was not a craft at all because the witnesses cannot agree on specific details. They have become, in effect, defense attorneys poking holes in the testimony of witnesses in order to protect their client, in this case the scientific (or military) establishment. To be sure, as Sagan said "extraordinary claims require extraordinary proof "; but who decides what is ordinary and extraordinary proof? And, really, what is an extraordinary claim? Since the time of the Renaissance, science has usurped the role of religion and has relegated to itself the right to decide upon matters that were once the province of faith: specifically, the nature of reality, of creation itself. When science demands physical evidence of alien contact—evidence beyond the scorched circles in the farmyards, the blips on the radar screens, the affidavits by eyewitnesses, the photographs of celestial anomalies taken during nighttime and daylight—it has slyly changed the rules of the game. Evidence good enough for a court of law is no longer evidence, which, of course, calls into question the truth of other verdicts handed down by those same courts.

Science, quite rightly, places itself above and beyond such political decisions. Like Supreme Court justices, scientists reserve the right to tell the truth no matter what the effect will be on popular ideas of what is real and what is not, what is fact and what is fiction. Yet, in actual practice, the reality is somewhat different. The history of science is the history of the relationship between scientists and politicians, between men of science and men of *realpolitik* who hold the purse strings on the government grants so desperately needed for research. The history of science is the history of scientists: men and women so fiercely competitive that they will falsify data and steal the research of others to further their own agendas, their own careers. In other words, scientists are people prone to the same vanities and cardinal sins as the rest of us, and this humanity colors their perceptions, particularly of the unanswerable questions which—since they are unanswerable—serve no pragmatic purpose for a scientist who must earn a living doing useful work. Let's look for our keys under the streetlamp because there's more light there, even though we lost them across the street.

This blindered view of scientists toward the UFO phenomenon has worked extraordinarily well for the government and the military, for it means they have the ability to study the problem at their leisure, without having to explain anything to the populace at large. They can simply refer the curious to the scientists, who will tell them that there is nothing to worry about.

There have been exceptions of course.

> *It is unfortunate that Dr. McDonald couldn't understand or adjust to the political-military situation, and chose instead to act only according to strict scientific dictates.*
>
> —Dr. J. Allen Hynek[60]

On July 29, 1968, Dr. James E. McDonald—Professor in the Department of Meteorology at the University of Arizona and a Senior Physicist at the Institute of Atmospheric Physics, former US Naval intelligence officer during World War II, member of various scientific associations, husband, and father of six children—testified before the Committee on Science and Aeronautics of the U.S. House of Representatives during their Symposium on Unidentified Flying Objects. In a very thoughtful, reasoned way—both in his oral testimony and in the prepared statement that was inserted into the Record—Dr. McDonald came out in support of the extraterrestrial origin of some of the UFOs seen over America and the rest of the world. As a meteorologist, he was well-equipped to dismiss some of the "atmospheric" explanations of the phenomenon, such as ball lightning or swamp gas. After describing several convincing cases of UFO sightings and activity, and attacking positions taken by other scientists who were not meteorologists and therefore who made mistakes in their evaluations of the evidence, he addressed a famous UFO debunker, Philip Klass of *Aviation Week*, who specialized in ridiculing UFO reports, saying that Klass' explanations of UFO sightings as "atmospheric-electrical plasmas" just "do not make good sense."[61] Then, rather than beat around the bush with the type of vague statements we too often expect from our professional class, he was quite straightforward in his estimate of the situation:

> To conclude, then, my position is that UFO's are entirely real and we do not know what they are, because we have laughed them out of court. The possibility that these are extraterrestrial devices, that we are dealing with surveillance from some advanced technology, is a possibility I take very seriously.[62]

He then answered a number of questions put to him by the assembled Representatives.

> Representative Bell asked,
>
> "What leads you to believe that whatever these phenomena are, they are extraterrestrial?
>
> "What facts do you have?"

To which Dr. McDonald replied:

> May I say that I wouldn't use the word "believe." I would say the "hypothesis" that these are extraterrestrial surveillance, is the hypothesis I presently regard as most likely.

He then clarified his statement by referring to the evidence he had examined over the previous two years of intense study:

> It is this very large body of impressive witnesses' testimony, radar-tracking data on ultra-high-speed objects sometimes moving at over 5,000 miles an hour, UFO's, combined radar-visual sightings, and just too much other consistent evidence that suggests we are dealing with machine-like devices from somewhere else.[63]

McDonald's testimony was valuable, and his verbal statement before the Committee plus the appended report makes an interesting contribution to the rational discussion of the UFO phenomenon. Unfortunately, Dr. McDonald was ridiculed for taking an unabashed "pro-UFO" stand. His testimony before Congress on other issues—such as the danger to the ozone layer posed by the supersonic transport, or SST—was greeted with derision by some Congressional committee members, who described him as "the man who believed in little green men." Philip Klass, who somehow saw McDonald as a kind of nemesis, is known to have planted false information with investigative journalist Jack Anderson, claiming that Dr. McDonald used US Navy funds illegally to study UFOs. Although this claim was later disproved by Navy auditors, the pressure of public humiliation and ridicule became too much.

On June 13, 1971 his body was found in the Arizona desert, an apparent suicide. There was a revolver next to his body, and a note. Dr. McDonald had been silenced forever. But he was not the first.

Morris K. Jessup was another scientist whose support of continued UFO research very probably cost him his life. An astrophysicist with degrees in astronomy and mathematics, who had served with the US Army during World War I, Jessup was a generation older than James McDonald. He spent time in the Union of South Africa in the 1920s, and then in Brazil during the Depression, and later with an archaeological expedition in Central America studying Maya ruins, a junket funded by the Carnegie Foundation. The ancient ruins fascinated the young astronomer, and he would make a return visit there in the 1950s to determine how the huge monuments were built without the aid of machines. At the time, the UFO phenomenon had reached epidemic proportions, with massive sightings throughout the world, but particularly in France and the United States. Jessup studied the available evidence, and eventually—in 1955—published *The Case for the UFO*. In addition, Jessup felt that some of the geological anomalies he had discovered during his visits to the Mexican and Central American jungles and ruins were consistent with some types of lunar cratering, and that they could only have been made by an intelligent, albeit alien, race.

Jessup would have joined the ranks of the other scientists who took UFOs seriously and been laughed out of existence had it not been for the so-called "Allende letters," and the insistence of a strange, probably crank, correspondent that the US Navy had conducted an experiment in "electronic camouflage" during World War II at the Philadelphia Navy Yard, with disastrous results. According to the correspondent, who identified himself as "Carlos Miguel Allende" (an identification which is in some dispute, as the same correspondent also signed his name on other letters to Jessup as "Carl M. Allen"), the experiment had taken place sometime in 1943, when Allende was a seaman, and had caused the U.S.S. *Eldridge*, a destroyer escort, to disappear, then to reappear in Norfolk, Virginia, only to disappear and reappear back at the Philadelphia Navy Yard. This incident, referred to as "the Philadelphia Experiment," allegedly was witnessed by Albert Einstein, whose work on the Unified Field Theory started the whole program in the first place. Supposedly, the crew of the *Eldridge* (those that survived, not all did) were discharged as being mentally unfit, and the entire experiment classified.

The Philadelphia Experiment is a favorite story among the credulous, and was made into a science fiction film a few years ago. (Notice the odd near-homonym at work between *Eldridge* and that word so favored by H.P. Lovecraft: "eldritch.") We would not even be addressing it here at all were it not for official US government interest in Jessup's correspondence with "Carlos Allende," and the mystery of the "annotated book."

While many—too many—of the supposed witnesses and participants to this "experiment" are off the record and unidentified in the book by William L. Moore and Charles Berlitz, *The Philadelphia Experiment: Project Invisibility*,[64] it nevertheless gives an otherwise detailed look at this controversy, and is virtually the only text available in print on the subject. Berlitz, of course, is the author of *The Bermuda Triangle*, the book that popularized that subject, and is of course *that* Berlitz, of the language schools. William L. Moore is identified as a schoolteacher from Minnesota who has been pursuing the subject of the Philadelphia Experiment relentlessly since hearing of it from people who claimed to have been there. While Moore is credited with authoring the book, it was done so "in consultation with Charles Berlitz," and bears the latter's Introduction.

Central to this story is the idea that, running parallel to the Manhattan Project which was, of course, the development of the atomic bomb, the US military was involved in other secret weapons research. Albert Einstein is known to have worked as a consultant to the US Navy in 1943 for unspecified research, as well, which adds more fuel to the fire. In addition, many of the various officers and ships mentioned in the rambling, near-hysterical Allende Letters were later proven to have existed and, indeed, Allende/Allen could only have known about these details if he had, in fact, been a seaman in the same theater at the time of the alleged incident, which was later shown to be the case, when a copy of his US Department of Commerce certificate was published in Moore's book. In fact, the Allende Letters evidence a knowledge of the details of the Navy yards where the "Experiment" was said to have taken place on the one hand, and of the involvement in secret projects by both Albert Einstein and Bertrand Russell, however murky or ambiguous this involvement was.

The rest of the Letters, however, are strictly Fantasyland. Ships disappearing at sea, sailors "frozen" half in and half out of this dimension, etc. Yet the letters were convincing enough that Dr. Jessup asked for further proof. Allende/Allen obliged by giving more names, dates and places and even offered to go under hypnosis and "truth serum" sessions in order to retrieve phone numbers, addresses, etc. He also brought up the idea that the Navy had used some of this science as a means of developing a propulsion system . . . for the UFOs. At the same time, his letters were virtually written in crayon: different colored inks, inappropriate capitalizations, underlinings . . . in short, the typical sort of communication one receives from people suffering from a mental disorder. Then, again, that also goes to evidence: according to the Letters, many of the sailors involved in the Philadelphia Experiment wound up being discharged as "mentally unfit."

Then, in the summer of 1955, a copy of Morris Jessup's book, *The Case for the UFO*, was sent to the Navy's Office of Naval Research. It was heavily annotated by the anonymous correspondent, and the nature of the remarks startled the naval officers who received it; so much so, that they contacted Jessup and asked to see him.

When Jessup arrived in Washington, he was shown the copy of his book with the plentiful notations and remarks, and the experience seems to have been unsettling. He recognized the handwriting as that of his crazed correspondent, Allende, and told the officers that he had two letters from the same man in his files. The officers insisted that they needed to see them as soon as possible. In return, they would give Jessup a copy of the annotated book in order to get his input.

What were the annotations like? They discussed everything from the UFOs, their propulsion systems, "magnetic fields, gravity fields, sheets of diamond, cosmic rays, force cutters, inlay work . . ." etc., etc.[65] The annotator knew of a great many details that were known only to Jessup or to a handful of specialists in the field of UFOs, and "many other matters usually of concern mainly to psychics, cultists and mystics. That these were true or not was not the point. The fact that they should be so precisely known to an unknown was."[66] This bothered the scientist more than anything else, this and the fact that the Navy was actually taking the ravings of this mysterious individual seriously. And, of course, the Philadelphia Experiment was also mentioned in the notes.

Demonstrating the extent to which the Navy took this matter to heart is the method by which they made copies of the book. There was no photocopy machine in 1955, so the book had to be retyped by hand on mimeograph stencils! This edition is referred to as the Varo edition, because the work of typing and mimeographing the entire work (in two colors, black for the original text and red for the annotations) was evidently undertaken by a temporary secretary hired by that company for that purpose.[67] Jessup was presented with three copies of his own, and he took to reading and re-reading the notes and eventually annotating the annotations.

This development contributed to a gradual deterioration of Jessup's mental and financial state. Various projects he had proposed for a return to the Central American jungles to research ancient civilizations had come to nought, and this brilliant scientist was reduced to writing for astrological journals and researching psychic phenomena . . . "reduced" may be too strong a word, for his sudden conversion to the purely paranormal may have been the result of his intense study of the annotated book and the realization that for some reason the Navy was taking it seriously. Like many who have come across the same or similar constellation of factors, he found the psychological stresses to be enormous—particularly for a man of science—and in 1958, at the end of his rope, he visited an old friend in New York. This was the naturalist Ivan T. Sanderson and it was, appropriately enough, "on or about Halloween evening." Jessup gave his friend his copy of the annotated book—this time containing his own annotations as well—and told him to hold it for safekeeping in case anything happened to him.

Sanderson later stated,

> At this our last meeting he was extremely distraught and admitted that due to an originally pure intellectual interest in natural phenomena, he found that he had been completely swept into a weird and insane world of unreality. He expressed outright terror at the endless stream of "coincidences" that had occurred in his work and in his private life . . .[68]

Again, the "coincidence stream" rears its head; it is a familiar phenomenon to artists, writers and especially researchers into the paranormal, the study of which seems to increase the number and frequency of coincidences to an almost alarming rate.

Jessup left New York shortly thereafter, and it was believed he was returning to his home in Indiana. However, he never made it there. Instead, he drove to a house he owned, unknown to anyone, in Coral Gables, Florida. His friends and publishers were frantically trying to locate him when they discovered he had been hurt in some type of automobile accident in December of 1958, but had recovered and was still in Florida, exhausted, struggling to revive his writing career and being rejected by his publishers.

Then, on April 20, 1959 Morris Jessup was found, barely alive, in his car in a park near his home. He had run a hose from his exhaust pipe into his vehicle. He was rushed to a hospital, but was pronounced dead on arrival.

Was it a suicide? Naturally, there are those who contest this verdict. Moore claims that he obtained access to medical examiner files on the Jessup suicide[69] showing that Jessup was quite drunk when he ran the hose into his car. The unsettling thing about this piece of evidence is that Jessup was known to be at that time on medication which, in combination with alcohol, would have either killed him immediately or at the very least rendered him incapable of driving a car and running the hose from his exhaust pipe in such a calculated manner. This means he would have had to start drinking after he arrived in the park and ran the hose. Was a bottle found in Jessup's car? Was Jessup still taking medication to save his life when he knew he wanted to end it? Unfortunately, we don't know any of this from Moore's book.

As mentioned, most of the more sensational claims in Moore's book come from unnamed informants, so it is virtually impossible to come to any conclusion about the Philadelphia Experiment. The facts that can be verified are those that relate to Morris Jessup himself, his work, his support of an aggressive research program on UFOs and on alternative forms of energy and propulsion, the "annotated book" episode and the Allende Letters, and his tragic end.

Two scientists, both fervent supporters of a more open and aggressive study of the UFO phenomenon, drive to secluded areas away from their homes and commit suicide. More recently, another scientist met a similar end: a UN weapons inspector, Dr. David Kelly, who went to an isolated location in the English countryside in July 2003 with a bottle of pain killers and a revolver. Dr. Kelly had leaked information to the British press that intelligence estimates of Iraq's weapons capability had been exaggerated, presumably in order to support Prime Minister Tony Blair's decision to join with the United States in the invasion of Iraq earlier that year. It led to a firestorm of controversy over the legitimacy of Blair's decision, with ramifications for President George W. Bush as well, similar claims having been leveled against his administration. (Clearly, terrorists have replaced UFOs as potential threats to national security.) We want our scientists to be priests of the truth, of scientific facts which we believe are the psalms of reality; but we don't want them to deviate from the line set down by our politicians and military leaders. We don't want them to tell *too much* truth. "For not all true things are to be said to all men."

The infamous Condon Report, published in 1968, is a case in point. Highly touted as an independent investigation to determine once and for all the reality behind the UFO phenomenon, it became obvious—through the "Low memorandum" that was leaked to the press—that the Condon committee had no intention of proving or disproving UFOs based on evidence, but was determined to put the controversy to rest no matter the damage to the cause of truth. The committee was formed in 1966 at the request of the United States Air Force, and was based at the University of Colorado under the stewardship of nuclear physicist Dr. Edward Condon, a scientist who had worked on the atomic bomb and on space technology. His attitude towards UFOs was biased from the beginning, and his introduction to the Report was grossly at odds with the actual report itself, which contained data on many unsolved cases that merited further study. What destroyed the credibility of the Condon Report—or *The Scientific Study of Unidentified Flying Objects* to give it its formal title—was the publication of the August 1966 Low Memorandum, written by Condon's second-in-command, Robert Low, which contained the following, damning paragraph:

> The trick would be, I think, to describe the project so that, to the public, it would appear a totally objective study but, to the scientific community, would present the image of a group of non-believers trying their best to be objective, but having an almost zero expectation of finding a saucer.

The Report was criticized long and loudly by many who had hoped for an unbiased approach to the problem (including its most vocal critic, Dr. James McDonald, as well as Dr. J. Allen Hynek who, in disgust with the Report, began his own organization to study UFOs), especially as the Air Force was about to cancel their own long-standing UFO program, Project BLUEBOOK. Even Dr. Condon himself would eventually admit to the press that the Report was a waste of taxpayers' money, in this case $500,000 to cover two-years' worth of foot-dragging and obstructionism. In the end, even the files themselves (public property, after all, paid for with public funds) were never made public, and were eventually burned. It was said that Condon himself had been the victim of US government pressure to present a report that debunked UFOs, that he had been blackmailed concerning security investigations of his background that had taken place during the McCarthy era.[70]

This theory was documented rather convincingly in Major Donald E. Keyhoe's *Aliens From Space: The Real Story of Unidentified Flying Objects*,[71] which, despite its sensationalistic title, is one of the more sober and more revealing of the UFO books by insiders. Keyhoe—a retired US Marine Corps officer and a central figure in the UFO debates of the 1960s and 1970s—reveals the political machinations that went on behind the scenes of the Condon Report, and shows how the Air Force was desperate to use the Condon Report to discredit UFO sightings in general. The 1960s saw a huge increase in the number of UFO sightings around the world, and the Air Force was unable to respond to the problem in any way. It did not have the technology to engage the UFOs in either communication or combat, and the sightings by credible witnesses—including high-ranking military personnel—were rendering the swamp gas and weather balloon explanations laughable. Condon himself had been a target of the House Un-American

Activities Committee investigation in the 1950s, and this presented the Air Force with another problem. The report was due out in the fall of 1968, around the time of the US presidential elections. Depending on who won the election, the Condon Report could be buried . . . or it could become a national (and international) cause célèbre. It was important to release the Report as the official word of scientists that there was nothing to the UFO reports, and that they were all the result of mistakes by untrained and non-credible witnesses, especially in view of the outcome of the presidential election of November 1968; for the man who won that election was the same man who had sat across from Dr. Condon during the HUAC investigation, a man who developed an intense dislike for the scientist: Richard M. Nixon.

Nixon would have been only too happy to attack Condon over the Report if the Report acknowledged the existence of extraterrestrial flying objects, if only to disgrace and humiliate Condon. The problem with this scenario is that it would put the Report front and center before the press and the public, and the Report was full of cases where the UFO sightings could *not* be explained away by the usual swamp gas and weather balloon scenarios. It was better if no one looked too closely at the Report. Hence, the public pronouncements by Condon, and his fabled introduction in which he claims that none of the cases studied by the Condon Committee were of otherworldly spacecraft, but could all be explained away.

In other words, the government once again told the scientists what to say to the world about the world, and about science itself.

In a related development, Rear Admiral Roscoe Hillenkoetter, first Director of the CIA and decorated war hero, quit his job at NICAP (National Investigative Committee of Aerial Phenomena, the most prestigious of all the UFO investigative groups) within days of a CIA investigation of his proposed role in opening the UFO investigation at the Congressional level with the support of Senators like Goldwater and Kefauver and many others. Although an ardent supporter of efforts to investigate UFOs and a harsh critic of US Air Force attempts to cover up and whitewash what were turning out to be hundreds of verified sightings (if not thousands), he inexplicably disappeared from the UFO scene in 1962 due, Keyhoe believes, to pressure from "a very high level" to block the proposed Capitol Hill investigation.[72]

Noting the presence of CIA officials at every level of this investigation (as reported by Keyhoe), and noting that this occurred only months after the firing of Allen Dulles as Director of the CIA over the Bay of Pigs affair and the ensuing hatred and distrust of President Kennedy by some of the remaining CIA hands, and noting that February of that year saw the first earth orbit by an American astronaut, we are left with an embarrassment of paranoid riches once again. The Capitol Hill investigation of the UFO phenomenon did not take place, Hillenkoetter retired from NICAP, John Glenn orbited the earth, and the world settled down to other matters: the Cuban Missile Crisis, the Kennedy assassination, a massive wave of UFO sightings in 1965 . . . the assassinations of Robert Kennedy and Martin Luther King in 1968, the election of Richard Nixon as president that same year, the Condon Report of January 1969 . . . the suicide of Dr. James E. McDonald.

It is a scene of awful beauty. A strange object is seen in the skies over Kentucky on January 7, 1948. It is a large, round metallic machine, and it is descending in the vicinity of Godman AFB, heading south towards Tennessee and witnessed by thousands of people including the base commander, Colonel Guy Hix, who authorizes a squadron of three P-51s to intercept the craft. All but one peel off and head back to base as it becomes obvious that the strange object has begun to climb at an alarming rate for a man-made device, and the World War II–era planes are not equipped with oxygen. But one pilot stays with the chase, oblivious to the danger to his life. A World War II veteran transport pilot, Captain Mantell climbs.

The object reaches an altitude of 20,000 feet and Mantell stays with it; man and machine, locked in ecstatic embrace, the light from the glowing object reflected in his eyes, his Mustang screaming with the effort of climbing to 30,000 feet, higher than ever a Mustang has climbed before.

His voice can be heard over the radio at Godman AFB.

"I've sighted the thing . . . . It looks metallic and it's tremendous in size . . . . Now it's starting to climb . . . . I'm trying to close in for a better look."

His wingmen have given up the chase. Mantell is alone.

What happens next is the subject of tremendous controversy. Mantell, evidently due to lack of oxygen at the high altitude, has blacked out. His plane begins to descend in a sickening spiral, a power dive. There is a flash of brilliant white light, like an explosion, and then the Mustang belly-flops into a field. Mantell is dead. The Mustang, oddly enough, even though its wings and tail section have separated from the fuselage, shows no other signs that it has crash-landed. There is no damage to the fuselage. No scratching or any other indication that the plane had skidded or dived into the earth. No damage to surrounding trees or vegetation. The plane simply flopped down. Mantell is still strapped into his seat, having made no effort to eject, due to his unconscious or semi-conscious state by the time he reached 25,000 feet.[73]

Although initial reports in the newspapers claim that Mantell died chasing a UFO, the Air Force quickly acts to suppress that bit of information. Their story is that Mantell died chasing the planet Venus, which he had mistaken for a UFO. (This is the same story that would be given to future president Jimmy Carter when he reported a UFO sighting while he was still governor of Georgia.) The problem with this scenario is that the chase had occurred in broad daylight, at three o'clock in the afternoon, when Venus is hardly visible. The second problem is that the altitude of Venus at that time—even if visible—was close to the horizon and not straight up. The third problem is that Captain Mantell was an experienced combat pilot who would not have mistaken a planet for a bogie. The fourth problem is that thousands of other people saw the craft, including Mantell's base commander, who watched it through his binoculars. The story was then changed to a Navy "Skyhook" balloon, but that account was challenged by the military's own records: there were no Skyhook balloons anywhere near Kentucky at that time. Further, such a balloon would have had to have been at an extremely high altitude to account for all the eyewitnesses who reported it: more than 25 miles high, and closer to 50.

Also, the "balloon" seemed to take evasive action when pursued by Captain Mantell.

Only six months after Roswell and the Kenneth Arnold sighting, Captain Mantell gave chase to a UFO, determined once and for all to get to the bottom of the mystery since he alone had been given the opportunity. Suffused with the joy of flight, the excitement of the chase, and knowing that he was pushing himself and his plane (and, possibly, his government) to its limits, he locked on to his target and gave it everything he had, secure in the knowledge that whatever happened, his efforts would contribute to sure knowledge of the nature of the flying machines, the saucers, that were suddenly streaking across American skies. Was it a rictus of pain or a grin of boyish, joyful satisfaction on Mantell's face as he neared the 30,000 feet mark on his altimeter, the shining object tantalizingly out of reach, his fuselage rattling with the effort, his prop blades a blur . . . and then, blackness.

The debris of an aircraft that has plummeted to earth from 20,000 or 30,000 feet should spread over a wide area, not be found as relatively intact as Mantell's Mustang. The source of the flash of light as he neared the ground has never been identified. Eyewitnesses say it came just before the plane left its dive of mortal descent and "pancaked" to the ground . . . as if God had interceded at this last moment and decided to place the aircraft reverently on the ground rather than allow it to plunge into the earth, nose first. Whatever the case, Godman Base commander Colonel Hix transferred to San Antonio, Texas, where one day his son would play in the swimming pool with young Whitley Strieber.

A month after Mantell's death, the Air Force Director of Intelligence issued a Top Secret memo—dated February 12, 1948—requesting that all air bases have at least one plane equipped with camera equipment ready at all times to give chase to UFOs. The request was denied, due to the enormous cost it would entail in men and machines.

The Director of Intelligence was Charles P. Cabell, the man who would later become deputy director of the CIA under Allen Dulles, before they were both fired by President Kennedy over the Bay of Pigs—the man whose brother was mayor of Dallas, Texas the day Kennedy was assassinated in that city.

Reality is what has been defined by our political leaders and not by our priests *or* our scientists. The precedent established by our treatment of the UFO phenomenon—the manipulation of truth, the creation of reality through propaganda and psychological warfare and disinformation, the use of journalists and scientists and other men and women presumed to be dedicated to the truth—has worked its way into the Cold War, Vietnam, Chile, Watergate, Iran-Contra, and now the present situation in the Middle East. And people die: martyrs to a manufactured truth, to a cleverly-designed reality matrix, an invisible white rabbit pulled from a grinning black magician's black hat: a *pookah*.

Harvey . . . with guns.

ENDNOTES

1 Julian Barnes, *Flaubert's Parrot*, McGraw Hill, NY 1985, p. 93–94
2 Umberto Eco, "The Force of Falsity," *Serendipities*, Orion, London, 1998, p. 3
3 Elaine Pagels, *The Gnostic Gospels*, Vintage Books, NY, 1981, p. 7
4 Ibid., p. 32
5 Ibid., p. 40
6 Michael Baigent and Richard Leigh, *The Dead Sea Scroll Deception*, Corgi, London, 1991
7 Cited in *The Secret Gospel* by Morton Smith and in *Bloodline of the Holy Grail* by Laurence Gardner, Martin Gardner,Element, Shaftesbury, Dorset, 1999, p. 92
8 Whitley Strieber, *Communion*, Avon, New York, 1988, p. 57
9 Ed Conroy, *Report On Communion*, William Morrow, NY, 1989, p. 113
10 Strieber, op. cit., p. 11
11 Ibid.
12 Ibid., p. 16
13 Ibid., p. 37
14 Ibid., p. 38
15 Ibid., p. 38–40
16 John E. Mack, M.D., *Abduction*, Ballantine Books, New York, 1994
17 Conroy, op. cit., p. 39–42
18 Ibid., p. 43
19 Octavio Paz, *El signo y el garabato*, Biblioteca de Bolsillo, Barcelona, 1991, p. 12–13 "If the Bomb had not destroyed the world, it destroyed our idea of the world .... We rediscover a feeling that was familiar to the Aztecs, to the Hindus and to the Christians of the year 1000. Technology begins by being a negation of the image of the world and ends by being an image of the destruction of the world."
20 Michel Foucault, *Madness and Civilization*, Vintage, NY, 1988, p. 202
21 Peter Levenda, *Unholy Alliance*, Continuum, NY, 2003, Chapter 11, "Aftermath"
22 This is from the Sarfatti Web site.
23 Sarfatti email exchange with David Gladstone dated June 29, 2001.
24 Jim Schnabel, *Remote Viewers: The Secret History of America's Psychic Spies*, Dell, NY, 1997, p. 165
25 Ibid., p. 167
26 Ibid., p. 168
27 See http://www.Stardrive.org/Sarmail7-2-02.shtml
28 http://groups.yahoo.com/group/SarfattiScienceSeminar/message/3079
29 Conroy, op. cit., p. 87
30 Ibid.
31 1996 interview with Mac Tonnies on www.beyondcommunion.com/breakthrough/96tonnie.html
32 The Bell Witch story may also be found in *Witches, Wraiths and Warlock s*, edited by Ronald Curran, Fawcett Books, NY, 1971, p. 25–28.
33 Graham Hancock, *The Mars Mystery*, Seal Books, Toronto, 1998, p. 169
34 Lynn Picknett and Clive Prince, *The Stargate Conspiracy*, Warner Books, NY, 2000
35 Robert Bauval and Adrian Gilbert, *The Orion Mystery: Unlocking the Secrets of the Pyramids*, Mandarin, London, 1995
36 Giorgio de Santillana and Hertha von Dechend, *Hamlet's Mill*, Gambit, Boston, 1969
37 CIC Foreign Documents Unit, dated 30.5.45, Title PWI reports dealing with HORTEN tail-less aircraft
38 Statement of Bernardy dated August 5, 1947 in CIC files
39 Memorandum for the Officer in Charge, 7 August 1947, Subject: BERNARDY, Guido, Helmut, Julius, "Flying Saucers"
40 Hancock, op. cit., p. 169
41 Strieber, op. cit., p. 95
42 Aleister Crowley, *Magick In Theory and Practice*, Dover, NY, 1976 edition, p. 84
43 Israel Regardie, *The Golden Dawn*, Llewellyn, St. Paul, 1986 edition, p. 347
44 Kenneth Grant, *Outside the Circles of Time*, Frederick Muller, London, 1980, p. 225
45 Kenneth Grant, *Hecate's Fountain*, Skoob, London, 1992, p. 221
46 Kenneth Grant, *Cults of the Shadow*, Skoob, London, 1994, p. 167
47 Kenneth Grant, *Aleister Crowley and the Hidden God*, Skoob, London, 1992, p. 202

48 Conroy, op. cit., p. 279–282
49 Whitley Strieber, *Breakthrough: The Next Step*, Harper, NY 1995, p. 14–15
50 Regardie, op. cit., p. 92
51 Strieber, 1988, p. 117
52 Ibid., p. 134–136
53 Ibid., p. 136
54 Conroy, op. cit., p. 268
55 C.G. Jung, *Flying Saucers*, Routledge, London, n.d., p. 79
56 Ibid., p. 79
57 Ibid., p. 121–122
58 Strieber, 1988, p. 96
59 Symposium on Unidentified Flying Objects, Hearings Before The Committee on Science and Astronautics, US House of Representatives, Ninetieth Congress, Second Session, July 29, 1968, USGPO, Washington, DC, p. 21
60 Dr. J. Allen Hynek, *The Hynek UFO Report*, Dell Publishing, NY, 1977, p. 112
61 Symposium, op. cit. p. 26
62 Ibid.
63 Ibid., p. 27
64 William L. Moore and Charles Berlitz, *The Philadelphia Experiment: Project Invisibility*, Ballantine Books, NY, 1984
65 Ibid., p. 66
66 Ibid., p. 68
67 Ibid., p. 70
68 Ibid., p. 76, citing from Sanderson, *Pursuit* magazine, No. 4, September 1968
69 Ibid., p. 253–54
70 Jim Marrs, *Alien Agenda*, HarperCollins, NY, 1997, p. 154
71 Donald E. Keyhoe, Aliens From Space: The Real Story of Unidentified Flying Objects, New American Library, NY, 1974
72 Ibid., p. 86
73 Marrs, op. cit., p. 102–104

MÉDAILLE
3153
Fillette

materia zem ex qua trahit
lutio fit: tertium
materia lapidis
RIOVRABETI

CHAPTER TWENTY-ONE

THE MACHINERIES OF JOY

To be perfectly honest, we will always have a lingering suspicion that there could be something dark and dreadful going on behind the scenes, something much bigger, and much more awful, than a mere conspiracy. The universe is mysterious. Reality itself is mysterious. No human has any true idea whether life has any transcendent purpose or not, whether there is life after death, whether there are such entities as absolute good and absolute evil.

—Graham Hancock[1]

Mystery is an occult force or efficacy that does not obey us, and we never know how or when it will manifest itself.

—Octavio Paz[2]

Human force cannot be other than spiritual; surely earth does not need man's feeble stirrings.

—Kenneth Patchen[3]

He expressed outright terror at the endless stream of "coincidences" that had occurred in his work and in his private life . . .

—William L. Moore[4]

I knew by now that when a group of individuals gravitated toward one another for no apparent reason, or a group of individuals inexplicably headed in the same direction as if drawn by a magnetic field, or coincidence piled on coincidence too many times, as often as not the shadowy outlines of a covert intelligence operation were somehow becoming visible.

—Jim Garrison[5]

The complex theory of 'synchronism', partly based on the observation of such coincidences as these, might perhaps lead to an entirely new conception of history.

—Pauwels and Bergier[6]

The French team of Jacques Pauwels and Louis Bergier published one of the most explosive books of its decade, *The Morning of the Magicians (Le matin des magiciens)* in 1960. According to the accepted mythology, Pauwels and

Bergier had served in the Resistance during World War II and since the end of the war had become interested in the paranormal, both from their reading of literature and history and what they observed among the Nazi elite, who were, in some cases, deeply involved in the subject. There are very few footnotes in *The Morning of the* Magicians, and very little in the way of primary source material, making confirmation of some their claims nearly impossible; yet, recourse to the National Archives in Washington, D.C. and the Library of Congress—as well as the former Berlin Documentation Center—has made it possible to verify some of their assertions, and to come up with quite a number more. These were covered in some detail in this author's *Unholy Alliance*, which has been cited before in this study, and we won't go into more detail here except to say that the basic premise of *Unholy Alliance* is that the Nazi Party was not a political party as we commonly understand it, but a cult. For confirmation of this, we only need to look at the modern manifestations of the Nazi Party to see how thoroughly they have become combined with cultic principles.

The Silver Shirts—an American pro-Nazi political party started by William Dudley Pelley in the 1930s—is a prime example of this. Pelley's organization was suffused with mystical concepts (including a great deal of UFO lore after the War), and Pelley himself was interned by the American government during World War II as a subversive and possible enemy agent. The National Renaissance Party of the 1950s through 1980s, run by James Madole, is another example of a pro-Nazi "cult" that quoted extensively from Madame Blavatsky and Alice Bailey's works as justification for anti-Semitism and genocide. Today, the pro-Manson Universal Order founded by neo-Nazi James Mason is another case in point, and we only have to see the swastika Charles Manson etched into his own forehead to understand how deeply elements of American society idolize the Nazis and the force it represents . . . and how dangerous these beliefs are to the rest of us. From the occult side, the enthusiasm shown by Michael Aquino and the Temple of Set for the SS castle at Wewelsburg is another indication that there is something more going on with the Nazi Party and its followers—even today—than what Americans read about in their newspapers in the 1930s and 1940s.

It is perhaps not going overboard to say that the Third Reich caused a massive shift of consciousness in the planet, a "paradigm shift" one might call it.

Although occultism and politics had long been bedfellows, since the days of Joseph interpreting dreams for Pharaoh, or King Saul consulting the Witch of Endor, or even earlier in the astral temples at Nineveh and Babylon, the world came very close to enduring a massive and industrialized "cult-ocracy" in the form of the Third Reich and the proposed division of Europe into states run by the fanatically esoteric SS of Heinrich Himmler. That millions of innocent people died because of this twisted dream is one of the tragedies of the twentieth century that has been visited upon the twenty-first, in the form of the Middle Eastern conflicts, the wars in the Baltic states, and so much else. Forces are at war in the world, causing immeasurable horror and suffering, and we do not know what they are. We do not understand how we could have become so thoroughly manipulated by these forces that we can no longer call a halt to the slaughter but have to watch, impotently, from the sidelines as the blood and the smoke of a thousand separate Holocausts drifts closer and closer to our own shores.

In *Morning of the Magicians*, the authors identified these forces in paranormal terms, but always linking them back to the fascist fantasies of Hitler, Himmler, Rosenberg, Darre, and Hess: blatantly occult fantasies that became government policy and which led to the Holocaust and World War II. But the authors insisted that there was something there, below the surface, of the Third Reich: a sinister force that had been successfully, for a time, evoked by the Nazi magicians of the SS. The phenomenon of "coincidence," or what Jung called "synchronicity" and Pauwels and Bergier call "synchronism," was the most obvious evidence of the operation of this force and one which the authors suggested could be the basis for a whole "new conception of history."

Indeed, this author himself has pointed out from time to time how often coincidence appears in the telling of everything from assassination conspiracies to UFO research; and he has suggested that either we agree with Jim Garrison that such coincidences are evidence of an intelligence operation (and, by extension, that some of our conspiracy theories may, after all, be correct), or that the coincidences represent something else: an "acausal connecting principle" perhaps (to use the phrase invented by Jung) that nevertheless demonstrates important linkages or "correspondences" between events in the world. To understand how this might be possible, we will have to examine the field of quantum physics for a short time, as we come across some amazing correspondence between Carl Jung and Wolfang Pauli, the former the father of the "archetype" and depth analysis, and the latter a Nobel Prize–winning physicist. While the primary sources for much of this information are quite dense, the basic outlines of the science will be presented in as intelligible a fashion as possible. As always, source material is noted in the text for those who wish to understand what is happening in the world of the physics of consciousness today, and why it is vitally important that we, as citizens of a shrinking world, remain current with these new discoveries.

DARKNESS AT NOON

> **Goebbels:** You wanted to see me, Dr. Jung.
>
> **Jung:** No, you wanted to see me.
>
> **Goebbels:** No, you wanted to see me.
>
> Jung turned around and left Goebbels' office—and vomited . . .
>
> —Account of a visit by Carl Jung to Berlin during May 1933 upon being invited to a meeting by Nazi Propaganda Minister Joseph Goebbels[7]

By all accounts, Wolfgang Pauli should have been the most satisfied man in Europe. In 1932, he was already world-famous as a physicist, a scientist of brilliance and possessed of an uncanny, creative insight. He was doing the work he loved, and recognized by his peers for his accomplishments. He was on the way to winning the Nobel Prize in physics in 1945.

Yet, his emotional life was in utter turmoil.

His mother, discovering that his father had been having an affair, committed suicide by poisoning herself. Pauli then became involved in a disastrous marriage with a cabaret singer which lasted less than a year. He turned to drink, got involved in bar brawls, fought constantly with his colleagues, and sank into a morbid state of what they used to call "melancholia." Wolfgang Pauli was on the verge of a nervous breakdown.

He also complained of very strange, very disturbing dreams, and it was possibly this problem among all others that led him to consult one of the world's most famous psychoanalysts, the St. Paul to Freud's Jesus, Swiss psychiatrist Carl Gustav Jung. At first, Jung gave him over to the care of a newly-trained assistant, a woman, as Jung felt Pauli's problems stemmed from relationships with women (his mother's suicide, his failed marriage), but as the sessions brought forth a mine of greater and greater symbolic material, Jung took over from Erna Rosenbaum and began to analyze Pauli personally.

In a state of profound personal misery, Pauli began his sessions with Jung every Monday at noon.

What resulted from this relationship, which lasted some twenty-six years (1932–1958), is a fascinating collection of letters the two men exchanged discussing Pauli's dreams and his scientific approach to Jung's deep and heavily symbolic psychoanalytic system. Although the actual psychoanalysis only lasted two years, Pauli continued to send reports of his dreams to Jung, and they discussed both the dream imagery as well as Pauli's concepts of physics and "symmetry," concepts that eventually won Pauli the Nobel Prize for his discovery of the "exclusion principle," which also bears his name as the "Pauli principle." The relationship between Jung and Pauli was probably the first real interface between modern physics and psychoanalysis, and paved the way for the development of what is now known as the field of quantum consciousness, a controversial and extreme form of physics in which it sometimes seems as if the slide rule has been applied to the soul.

The search for the basic "building blocks" of life, of reality, of the mind, has been going on for thousands of years. In the West, during the golden era of the Greek philosophers, all of reality was believed to be reducible to four elements: earth, air, fire and water. In the East, a similar impulse led to the identification of five elements: wind, water, fire, metal, earth. The intention was the same: to find common denominators for the bewildering profligacy of creation, a creation that included the palm tree and the platypus, the horse and the canyon, gold and lead, coal and diamonds. It was believed by both Western and Eastern philosophers that the elements—whether four or five—worked with each other in combination to produce all that the senses perceived. This understanding led to everything from the Periodic Table of the Elements to the nature of the DNA molecule, as science looked deeper and deeper behind what was visible to the naked eye to what was invisible: atoms, chromosomes, quarks. This effort was matched by the work of the scientists of the mind, the psychologists who sought to discover what hidden, invisible forces were at work behind the crazy-quilt veneer of consciousness.

Carl G. Jung (1875–1961) was of Protestant German Swiss parentage, and was for a time an important disciple of Sigmund Freud (1856–1939). It was Jung who understood the relationship that exists between mythology and unconscious psychological states, and the relevance of myths, fairy tales, and religious and mystical imagery to psychoanalysis and the interpretation of dreams, as well as the interpretation of cultural events and icons through an analysis of their symbolism. He also popularized the theory of the "archetype": images buried deep within our "collective unconscious" (another Jungian concept) that are carriers of a constellation of associations, and which are universal in nature, such as the Great Mother or the Wise Old Man or the Serpent. His analysis of alchemical literature is, itself, literature, much in the same way that Freud's writings are more than scientific articles and closer to philosophical essays, which, to some of his followers, are virtual scripture.

To Jung and his followers, there is a deep substratum of consciousness that lies beneath the layers of mechanical instincts and the measurable phenomena of clinical psychology, even below Freud's layer where the "pleasure principle" resides. This layer—called by Jung the "collective unconscious"—is a well of images and associations, myths and icons that all humans share. These images become visible under certain circumstances, such as in political rallies or religious rituals or on the movie screen or in advertising and propaganda, and we take them for granted without realizing the power they represent or the extent to which they may be manipulating our consciousness. One of Jung's most accessible and popular works—*Man and His Symbols*—usually appears as a large, coffee-table book replete with these images and explanations of what they represent, and why we react to them the way that we do.

Traffic with the collective unconscious is not all one-way, however. Like a living being, it can be influenced by consciousness and modified. Thousands of years of human civilization have modified the symbol stream and the structure of the collective unconscious, and there are regional differences in how these symbols manifest from culture to culture, although the basic elements of the collective unconscious—the archetypes—are the same for everyone. This is what Jung's patient and occasional collaborator, Wolfgang Pauli, found so fascinating, and what led the two of them to equate this process with those of quantum mechanics.

Jung's fascination with mystical and occult texts and themes—although not with occult practices *per se*—led him to write admiringly of the phenomenon of National Socialism in Germany, interpreting the Nazi pagan mythos in his *Wotan*. It was this, as well as his anti-Semitism, which has led many in recent years to question Jung's personality and motives, although it is clear from his later writings that he did not idolize the Nazis or defend their hideous excesses. That Jung was an anti-Semite is something that not even his own followers try to deny, as evidenced by the "Lingering Shadows" conference held at the C. G. Jung Foundation in New York City in 1989.[8] At the same time, Jung's anti-Semitism is virtually indistinguishable from that of, say, Aleister Crowley. Both men held contemporary views of Jews that were common for their time and place, and yet both men also studied Judaism and Jewish mysticism. While we expect more from both—since Jung was widely regarded as a deep and serious thinker, a man whose genius made an enormous contribution to psychology and philosophy, and in the case of Crowley we have a man who declared himself to be a god (!)—we are left with the realization that these idols have clay feet, as do all idols in every era. One tends to think that Jung's early fascination with Nazism had more in common with many a scientific observer at an atomic bomb test: in one's heart, one realizes that this is a horrible development, but at the same time one is awed by the sound and the light, amazed that the human race is capable of such elaborate and dramatic destruction.

(Of course, the focus on Jung as an anti-Semite is something of a smoke-screen as well. One cannot compare Jung's admitted anti-Semitism with that of Henry Ford's rabid anti-Semitic tract, *The International Jew*, for instance, or the actions of a generation of American politicians and businessmen such as Herbert Walker, Prescott Bush or the Dulles brothers, who actively supported Nazism before and after the war.)

As the years went by, Jung became something of an ethnologist, and traveled to Africa in search of primitive cultures. He wrote extensively on alchemy both European and Asian, and studied the UFO phenomenon. He analyzed Christianity in light of his discoveries in psychology and mythology, and gave us terms we use today without realizing Jung's contribution: anima, collective unconscious, archetype, individuation. The goal of Jung's approach to psychoanalysis was the integration of the various elements of the personality to form a seamless whole, the process he called "individuation." The emblem of the successful conclusion of this process was the mandala, the famous Eastern symbol of the sum of creation, a symbol in which opposites are balanced with each other: north with south, east with west; fire with water, air with earth; male with female. Jung did not simply borrow the idea of the mandala from Hindu or Buddhist iconography; he believed the mandala was used by the Eastern mystics to mean the same thing, to represent the same process, as that described in his own work. To Jung, the world was full of symbols: from advertising logos and slogans to political speeches to arcane occult texts. In this, he was walking in the footsteps of Giordano Bruno, and, close behind them both was Ioan Coulianu.

Jung's collected works are available through the Bollingen imprint of Princeton University, and they are a tremendous resource not only as a guide to Jungian thought but also as a veritable Baedecker through religious and mystical thought and textual and iconographic references from around the world. The works of Wolfgang Pauli—those that are accessible to a non-scientific audience—are equally valuable, such as "The Influence of Archetypal Ideas on the Scientific Theories of Kepler" which was included in *The Interpretation of Nature and the Psyche* by Jung and Pauli. In this essay, Pauli analyzed Kepler's theories of astrology in the light of both physics and Jungian psychology. But it is perhaps in the area of "synchronicity" that we will find the views of Jung and Pauli most valuable here, for it gives us a context for understanding the action (and, perhaps, the nature) of the sinister forces of which we speak.

> . . . it is impossible, with our present resources, to explain ESP, or the fact of meaningful coincidence, as a phenomenon of energy. This makes an end of the causal explanation as well, for "effect" cannot be understood as anything except a phenomenon of energy. Therefore it cannot be a question of cause and effect, but of a falling together in time, a kind of simultaneity. Because of this quality of simultaneity, I have picked on the term "synchronicity" to designate a hypothetical factor equal in rank to causality as a principle of explanation.[9]

Jung's idea of an "acausal connecting principle" actually goes to the heart of physics; it is an attack on the most sacred of scientific sacred cows: cause and effect, something which Isaac Newton had enshrined in his work. In the traditional view, every effect has a cause, much like those swinging ball sets one sees on executive desks, where one ball knocks into another, which knocks into another, etc., in a straight line down from the first "knock." To this type of scientist, every effect can be traced back to an "ultimate cause," all the way back to the Big Bang that started the universe on its ancient path. But isn't that the problem?

An endlessly receding, linear chain of cause-and-effect eventually leads us back to a First Cause, and that implies a beginning without cause. Some have called it God. There is no room in traditional science for God, because the existence of a God would (presumably) render scientific theory *relative* to God, an unknown and undefined principle. Science has generally avoided facing this issue in any sort of intelligible way. The universe may simply be eternal, outside normal definitions of time since it contains all time (and all space); but then what does that do to cause-and-effect, which is conceived of as linear as opposed to . . . what, circular?

Arthur Young (one of the original "Nine") proposed the existence of the "quantum of action," what he identified as "first cause," and called it the "missing parameter of science." In his view, it would go a long way to accommodating the paradoxes one encounters in quantum physics, such as Heisenberg's "Uncertainty Principle." According to Heisenberg (a friend and classmate of Wolfgang Pauli at the University of Munich), one cannot precisely predict the position of an electron at any given time; its position will always remain "uncertain." This is because an electron has an inherent motion that is not the result of it being acted upon by other forces, and thus its motion seems to lie outside the realm of cause-and-effect. A molecule, on the other hand, is a static sort of thing: composed of atoms in a particular alignment and creating, for instance, water (two atoms of hydrogen, one of oxygen); it is a blunt fact and Newtonian laws work on water and on the rest of the molecules at that level of reality. Electrons, though, operate in a world where Newtonian physics no longer applies.

To go one step further, a photon—a particle of light—operates in a still more rarefied world. One of the mysteries of light, and that which prompted the discovery of the quantum by Max Planck around the year 1900, is that it does not lose energy in its travels through space. A light particle having left a distant star arrives on earth with the same energy it had when it left. This did not seem to be playing by the Newtonian rules. Heisenberg realized that in order to study a photon one of necessity has to "disturb" it; i.e., a relationship develops between the particle studied and the one doing the studying which changes the state of the particle (and, of course, of the observer). Thus, there is no such thing as a truly uninvolved, outside observer. The observer is a participant. The observer changes the object being observed by the very fact of observation, and this is not merely a semantic game: it is the reality of quantum physics and the laboratory observation of sub-atomic particles.

At the sub-atomic level, where light can be either a particle *or* a wave but not both (whimsically referred to as a "wavicle"), one can only study it as one *or* the other, thus making a judgment before one even begins. In a sense, then, the observer and the object observed are connected in some mysterious, acausal way; and if the observer and observed are connected, then the universe is a place of interconnectedness that transcends mechanistic Newtonian causality. And if this is true—and quantum physicists insist that it is—then the UFO phenomenon (as an example) is a function of that universe, and it is quite possible that if there are actual "aliens" piloting the craft, they may have been aware of this principle for a long time, which would account for their actions in ways that we are not prepared to accept. They would be aware, for instance, that their observation of us changes *them* in some profound way, and that our experience of them changes us; which could account for their strange appearance, such as the various beings experienced by Whitley Strieber in his published accounts: possibly an attempt to modulate our experience of them in ways that will not cause some kind of existential blowback.

In Newton's world of linear cause-and-effect, the possibility of free will is discounted. In the world of Arthur Young and the "quantum of action," free will is reinstated as a function of "action" and thus is given essentially its own existence as a separate quantum. How does this quantum unite and modulate the other quanta?

Meaning is the bridge between consciousness and matter.
—Physicist David Bohm, *Omni* magazine, January 1987

What Jung proposed was that another principle, a connecting principle, exists in the universe outside of cause and effect, linking "unrelated" elements at the level of *eaning*, creating what are called "meaningful coincidences." Since we are accustomed to interpreting events as cause-and-effect related, the appearance of coincidence has been variously understood as either "magic" or as something totally without meaning, a kind of accident that has no place in scientific discourse (as if any event could be considered to be "outside science"). Once again, we have drawn a line between an event observed and the observer, ignoring the importance of the coincidence as a carrier of information. Yet, as physics has progressed to the point where the old standby of an "outside observer" to an experiment is no longer to be taken for granted, but that "observer" has now become a "participant," it has become harder and harder to define a pure science that is not the result of human intervention and participation . . . with all that implies. (What is perhaps comforting to some to contemplate is that if creation itself is a kind of experiment, then, according to Heisenberg, God is not only an observer but is also a participant.)

Jung noted that the basis of modern science is statistical in nature: that is, scientific laws are really statements about probability. That is why it is thus far impossible, for instance, to predict the weather with any degree of accuracy, or the outcome of a sporting event in advance, or to give an absolutely certain medical prognosis; that is why it is impossible to predict where a given sub-atomic particle will be at any given time. We can make statements about probable results, but still cannot be one hundred percent certain about predicting specific events. When events occur which defy the laws of probability, science generally lumps them into a separate category, the one or two (or ten or twenty) percent not accounted for in their statistical calculations. Likewise, religion generally lumps them into a separate category, and calls them "miracles": spontaneous remission of a cancer, for instance, or the patient pronounced dead who comes back to life on the operating table. Or a shower of frogs. For the mystically-inclined, the occurrence of these "non-statistically predictable results" indicates the presence of God. For the scientifically-inclined, they may be thought of as accidents, or the result of inadequate data or a defective instrument, or as mere coincidences.

Sometimes, however, there are just too many coincidences, and their sheer number or frequency suggests the operation of another factor in the universe.

Jung posited that there are relationships among events that are not part of the cause-and-effect nexus, and that these relationships come to our attention when a large number of coincidences take place. While he had been aware of this phenomenon for quite some time and witnessed it in his own life and in the lives of his patients, development of a formal theory awaited his relationship with the Austrian scientist Wolfgang Pauli. It was Pauli who actually "proved" Heisenberg correct, and made a substantial contribution to quantum mechanics by his own "exclusion principle" or what is known as the "Pauli principle." The math behind this principle is daunting, as is any attempt to describe it without recourse to advanced physics, but suffice it to say that it involves principles of symmetry and asymmetry and explains the wonderful diversity of nature as a kind of cosmic "dance."

Theoretical physicist Dr. F. David Peat, who worked with renegade physicist David Bohm and who once interviewed Werner Heisenberg, Pauli's friend and classmate, has expressed the Pauli Principle this way:

> Electrons, protons, neutrons, and neutrinos, along with other particles, form one group (and engage in an *antisymmetric* dance) while the other group includes mesons and photons of light (and forms a *symmetric* dance). It turns out that, in the former case, the nature of this abstract movement or dance has the effect of keeping particles with the same energy always apart from each other. However, this *exclusion* of particles from each other's energy space is not the result of any force which operates between them nor indeed is an act of causality in the normal sense, rather it arises out of the *antisymmetry of abstract movement* of the particles as a whole. Hence the underlying pattern of the *whole dance* has a profound effect on the behavior of each individual particle. (emphasis in original)[10]

Thus we are talking about a pattern or matrix underlying the observed universe, a kind of grid of connections linking events according to a system we can only barely perceive, a pattern that is *in motion* if we take Pauli's symmetric and asymmetric dances literally. It is this pattern that differentiates one element from another, and which contributes to everything from, as Peat explains, "the intense coherent light of the laser as well as superfluids and superconduction" on the one hand to "the collapse of a star through the white dwarf, neutron star, and black hole stages" on the other.[11] In other words, all of physical creation. Peat sees this as a basis for a coherent theory of synchronicity, as the relation between the particles in Pauli's exclusion principle "is not the result of any force which operates between them nor indeed is an act of causality." Thus, we have links between particles that defy normal cause-and-effect calculations. And these are the particles that make up the universe as we know it, and everything in it.

Physicists normally do not appreciate it when non-physicists make statements about their science irresponsibly and make theoretical leaps not supported by mathematical proofs (and why should they?), so it is incumbent upon me to add a further caveat of clarification:

Modern theories of quantum physics do not invalidate traditional Newtonian physics when it comes to the tangible world we live in. What goes up must still come down; and for every action there is still an equal and opposite reaction. None of that has changed. The laws of physics that we learned in school are useful ways of interpreting the world we live in and its phenomena. The laws do not exist outside our perceptions, however. They are laws that man has made, not laws that exist in nature; they are ways of understanding and measuring nature and its processes. As such, however, they do not provide a definitive cosmology; they do not explain everything that we experience.

If we look at "reality" (what a concept!) as having layers, much like Jung's concept of consciousness, then the Newtonian world is the "top" layer, the layer we deal with every day. It is the layer of molecular structures, of mass and energy and dimension. It is our conscious level, if you will.

If we go a level down, we enter the atomic world which has a slightly different "reality" and set of laws that govern its processes.

Still further down, we have the world of nuclear particles, like the "uncertain" electrons. And, further down still, we have the world that light lives in: a mysterious realm of photons that defies Newtonian concepts of time and space.

Arthur Young described this as an "arc," illustrating the descent of light through the nuclear particles to atoms to molecules, and then up from molecular structures to plants, animals, and eventually man, in a glyph that is strangely reminiscent of ancient Gnostic and Manichean theories of the descent of spirit into matter,[12] and for a reason: these lower levels of reality are those frequented by the magician and the mystic, the psy-war expert and the advertising man. These are the levels upon which it is possible to exert some influence (all those spinning electrons, all those packets of light, that dizzying dance of symmetry and asymmetry in the dark and dirty basement beneath the nice clean house of consensus reality, the subtle connectivities like the invisible wiring in the walls, pipes of hot and cold running fractals, all Fast Fourier and fragile beauty) and thereby—according to the *Lesser Key of Solomon*, a medieval sorcerer's workbook that looks like notes on an advanced form of calculus by a demented or visionary Pauli or Heisenberg—"anticipate an effect, the which to the vulgar shall seem to be a miracle."[13]

While the system of levels posited by both Jung and Young (!) are intellectually satisfying to some degree—it seems to be "orderly" and capable of representing processes that are quantum mechanical as well as Newtonian depending on the level or layer of reality under discussion—there are other phenomena in the world of quantum physics that are counter-intuitive. For instance, time.

As Oxford mathematics Professor Sir Roger Penrose puts it,

> All the successful equations of physics are symmetrical in time. They can be used equally well in one direction in time as in the other. The future and the past seem physically to be on a completely equal footing. Newton's laws, Hamilton's equations, Maxwell's equations, Einstein's general relativity, Dirac's equation, the Schrödinger equation—all remain effectively unaltered if we reverse the direction of time.[14]

This means that, to use Penrose's example later on in the same book that a glass full of water falling off a table and breaking on the floor could—according to the above-mentioned laws of physics—just as easily assemble itself from the broken pieces of glass and spilled water and jump up onto the table: the entire episode but in "reverse" order.[15] Since that is not the way we perceive the universe to operate, there must be another factor—a factor in consciousness—that experiences the passage of time in a single direction: past-present-future. The future, then, is dependent on actions and processes that have taken place "before" it in time, which seems to indicate a degree of choice—of decisions made, directions taken—otherwise the future would be absolutely predictable in every aspect.

Penrose has attacked the contemporary discipline of Artificial Intelligence as being basically unscientific in its approach to consciousness and physics. He does not believe that the brain is nothing more than a glorified computer, or that eventually computers will develop to the point that they attain consciousness, as consciousness is obviously much more than mere computation. Penrose is part of a new movement in science and consciousness which has attracted a number of maverick thinkers with a variety of heavy credentials. F. David Peat—mentioned above—studied with Penrose at Oxford, as well as with David Bohm, and his integration of Jungian psychology with quantum physics is representative of the direction in which the movement as a whole is going.

Penrose has worked with microbiologists to come up with a novel and, if correct, profound theory of quantum consciousness, which is based on the examination of microtubules in the brain. As noted earlier, science has been occupied with discovering the smallest, most irreducible elements of matter and energy in order to understand how the universe is put together; as atoms were broken down into sub-atomic particles and quarks, fermions, bosons, mesons and a host of other strange and tricky entities made their appearance (either virtually, through mathematical calculation and prediction, or in the particle accelerator), so too did the biologists break down the human body into its constituent "particles": the genetic code, and its holy grail, the human genome. Still, none of these discoveries answered the basic questions of the human condition, such as the mystery of consciousness: of a mind that could conceive of realities that were not "real," of time that could flow backwards, of being in two places at the same "time," of life after death and reincarnation and the evil eye. Or, more prosaically, of communicating over vast distances and traveling in the air and watching images move before your eyes and hearing voices come out of a machine. All of these ideas were once thought to be the powers of sorcerers and magicians and fakirs, and are represented in the grimoires and other spellbooks of the occultist; they are now within the reach of everyone on the planet, no matter how spiritually undeveloped, how illiterate, how rational or irrational. They were the inventions of conscious minds working in ways that could not be explained by instinct or some other mechanical description of the brain and its nervous system. They were the inventions of men and women who dreamed the impossible, and who were haunted by the chants of the shamans lodged deep within their "collective unconscious," the prayers of human beings who longed to fly.

Is there a physical basis for consciousness? Or are body and mind functions of each other?

What Penrose and his colleagues have discovered is that—on what could be called the "sub-atomic" level of the human brain and nervous system—there exists an interface between mind and matter that has important implications for our study.

THE ROOTS OF COINCIDENCE

> The . . . dilemma confronts us as we turn to a type of phenomenon which has puzzled man since the dawn of mythology: the disruption of the humdrum chains of causal events by coincidences of an improbable nature, which are not causally related yet appear highly significant. Any theory which attempts to take such phenomena seriously must necessarily involve an even more radical break with our traditional categories of thought than the pronunciamentos of Heisenberg, Dirac or Feynman.
>
> —Arthur Koestler, *The Roots of Coincidence*[16]

> Zombies are a useful philosophical concept.
>
> —Stuart Hameroff in "A Sonoran Afternoon"

In 1996, Roger Penrose and Stuart Hameroff—in a paper entitled Orchestrated Reduction of Quantum Coherence in Brain Microtubules: A Model for Consciousness"[17] resented a theory of consciousness that stemmed from Penrose's concept of "objective reduction" or "OR," first promulgated in 1994's *Shadows of the Mind.* Objective reduction is, as the paper defines, "a newly proposed physical phenomenon of quantum wave function" which is "essential for consciousness, and occurs in cytoskeletal microtubules and other structures within each of the brain's neurons."[18] In other words, a professor of the mathematics of physics (Penrose) and a professor of anaesthesiology and psychology (Hameroff) teamed up to unlock the mysteries of quantum and consciousness and apparently found them hiding discretely within the very neural pathways of the human brain.

The exposition is very tough going for the non-initiate, especially as two very distinct disciplines are involved: quantum mechanics and neurobiology. An attempt will be made to "objectively reduce" the main thrust of the argument.

Penrose and Hameroff begin by describing some basic elements of quantum physics.

> At the base of quantum theory is the wave/particle duality of atoms and their components. As long as a quantum system such as an atom or sub-atomic particle

> remains isolated from its environment, it behaves as a "wave of possibilities" and exists in coherent "superposition" (with complex number coefficients) of many possible states.[19]

How, then, does the phenomenon move from this ambiguous "wave of possibilities" to become an actual particle or wave? What causes its "collapse"? Several theories are advanced, but Penrose prefers a "self-collapsing" model "growing and persisting to reach a critical mass/time/energy threshold related to quantum gravity."[20] This self-collapsing model is referred to as OR or "objective reduction," as opposed to the SR or "subjective reduction" model wherein the collapse is attributed to measurement or conscious observation.

The authors go on to describe another fact of quantum physics, one that seems extremely bizarre to those brought up on a healthy diet of Newtonian physics:

> Another feature of quantum systems is quantum inseparability, or non-locality, which implies that all quantum objects that have once interacted are in some sense still connected! When two quantum systems have interacted, their wave functions become "phase entangled" so that when one system's wave function is collapsed, the other system's wave function, no matter how far away, instantly collapses as well. The non-local connection ("quantum entanglement") is instantaneous, independent of distance and implies that the quantum entities, by sharing a wave function, are indivisible.[21]

Non-locality is one of the more attractive characteristics of quantum physics for the romantically-inclined, as it implies that a kind of communication is possible across vast distances, and that once two "wave functions" meet, they are always in instant communication and are, in fact, "indivisible." While this in itself is not a validation for extrasensory perception or telepathic communication, etc., it does present scientists with an uncomfortable premise. If such a phenomenon is possible—even at the sub-atomic level—then somehow it might be possible at a more macro level, the level of waking consciousness.

Penrose and Hameroff then go on to describe the research of various other scientists who have identified "apparently random quantum effects acting on neurotransmitter release at the pre-synaptic grid within each neural axon," and that one researcher, H.P. Stapp, "has suggested that (SR) wave function collapse in neurons is closely related to consciousness in the brain." The quest of Penrose and Hameroff for a physical structure wherein these effects take place brought them to the microtubule.

Microtubules are components of the neuron or, more specifically, of the cytoskeleton structure within the neuron which "establishes neuronal form, maintains synaptic connections, and performs other essential tasks." The microtubules themselves are "hollow cylindrical polymers of individual proteins known as tubulin" which are "interconnected by linking proteins (microtubule-associated proteins: MAPs) to other microtubules" which then form the "lattice networks" of the cytoskeletons. In the view of the authors, the MAPs are responsible for—"orchestrate"—the collapse of wave functions in the neurons; thus, "Orch OR." The wave function collapse is non-reversible in time, and it is the successive collapse of wave functions at the microtubule level that gives rise, in effect, to the passage of time (its seeming unidirectional nature: past-present-future) and thus to consciousness itself. (This would solve the conundrum posed by Penrose earlier (1994) and mentioned above: that the laws of physics are the same whether time "flows" forward or backward, and that the sensation of time going in one direction only is therefore a function of consciousness, since there are no physical laws to account for it.)

The reader will forgive me if I skip the proofs and formulae that are offered in support of this theory, and those interested are encouraged to seek out this information for themselves on the Internet or in an up-to-date science library. There are, however, some slightly more accessible accounts of this fascinating and ultimately quite revealing theory, and Penrose's partner Stuart Hameroff is responsible for a few of them.

In *Trends in Cognitive Sciences*, Hameroff 's article "'Funda-Mentality' Is the Conscious Mind Subtly Linked to a Basic Level of the Universe?" sets out the parameters of the discussion in a style that is a bit easier to understand for those who do not have the math.[22]

Hameroff begins by discussing various attempts to come to a physics of consciousness, all of which are lacking in either scientific rigor or fall apart on close inspection. The main target of the Penrose-Hameroff approach is the "mind as computer" theory. The "physicalists"—those who believe that a purely physical solution will one day appear to explain consciousness as a kind of super-computability, a more sophisticated version of the desktop PC—see consciousness as the inevitable result of more complex neural circuitry, circuitry which could one day be duplicated in the laboratory and the test bench. Penrose and Hameroff, however, believe that consciousness is not purely physical in the traditional sense. It is certainly not a function of "computability":

> Regarding transition from pre-conscious or implicit processing to consciousness itself, the physicalist view is that consciousness emerges at a critical level of complexity. But no threshold is apparent, nor is there a reasonable suggestion why such an emergent property should have conscious experience. As physicalism is based on deterministic computation, it is also unable to account for free will or Penrose's proposed non-computability. But the major problem remains experience, for which physicalism offers no testable predictions. Something is missing.[23]

Hameroff then asks the question that is central to an understanding of how the sub-atomic phenomena—equally wave or particle, obeying the exclusion principle and the uncertainty principle, exhibiting features of non-locality—so bizarre in terms of Newtonian physics and the "real world," ever manage to organize themselves into the tangible, touchable, breakable, objects around us:

> The problem is the transition: why and how do microscopic quantum superposed states become classical and definite in the macro-world? This problem is called quantum state reduction, or collapse of the wave function, and it may be the key to both consciousness and reality.[24]

This, of course, is where "Orch OR" comes into the discussion and the magical microtubules make their appearance. The idea, basically, is this:

At the most microscopic level of "reality," the sub-atomic particles behave strangely, as if they are not really part of classical reality. Yet, they make up everything that we see, everything that our senses perceive. This means that, at some point, these sub-atomic particles (and waves) become organized in a fashion that permits physical reality as we know it. There is a threshold somewhere, a level of complexity is reached and—due to some type of combination of particles, waves, mass and energy that we do not yet understand—the wave function, the quantum state of the particles, collapses, becomes "reduced" to perceived and perceivable reality (OR or "objective reduction"). The ambiguous nature of an individual particle is "reduced" to one state only: either particle or wave. What Penrose and Hameroff are saying is that this process can take place not only within the external world of physics, but also within the brain, at the microscopic level of the microtubules which are components of the cystoskeleton of the neuron, and that this process is taking place constantly:

> OR in the brain would likely be linked to neural processes occurring over time scales in the range of tens to hundreds of milliseconds, for example 25 millisecond intervals in coherent 40 Hz.[25]

Naturally, then, the brain contains not only neurons and synapses and the entire wet machinery of cognition, but is also acting on—and being acted upon by—the quanta. Consciousness itself, according to this theory, is the result of this type of objective reduction, indeed a self-orchestrating objective reduction. The brain is plugged into the quantum world in a very dynamic way, and consciousness is the result.

The authors do not discount the possibility of consciousness in beings other than human. According to their model, as long as sufficient numbers of microtubules are present in the brain or nervous system of the creature under consideration, this phenomenon will obtain. The degree of sophistication is possibly a result of the complexity of the brain and nervous system itself: the sheer number of collapsing wave forms at any given "time" (and their relationship to each other across a complex matrix of neurons) indicating a corresponding degree of consciousness.

Hameroff, in another article in the same issue of the journal explains more fully:

> Regarding free will, the problem is that our actions seem neither totally deterministic nor random (probabilistic). The only other apparent choice is Penrose's non-computability. In the Orch OR model microtubule quantum superpositions compute and evolve linearly . . . during pre-conscious processing, but are influenced at the instant of OR collapse by hidden (Platonic) non-computable logic inherent in spacetime geometry. The precise outcome—our free will actions—result from effects of the hidden logic on the quantum system poised at the edge of objective reduction.[26]

Elsewhere in the same article, Hameroff describes this hidden logic as "some influence which is neither random nor completely deterministic, but due to hidden propensities embedded in fundamental spacetime." It's these "hidden propensities" and "hidden (Platonic) non-computable logic inherent in spacetime geometry" that are the catch. While the Orch OR model may explain the *mechanics* of consciousness—and it is still early days on that due to the amount of funding it would require to test the theory—there is still the mystery of consciousness itself. What Penrose and Hameroff have done is state the problem in terms that are clear and compelling, if not always convincing to their peers. The idea that consciousness is not merely the result of a kind of super-computation capacity of the brain, but of actions that take place on a sub-microscopic level within that brain that are identical to processes familiar to quantum physicists is significant, if only because it helps to answer another question, that of synchronicity and coincidence.

In case the reader is thinking that perhaps all this theorizing is quite abstract and is not useful in any pragmatic sense of the term, it should be noted that Penrose and Hameroff were invited to lead a group meeting at the RAND Corporation on October 22, 1998—one of a series of meetings that were sponsored by the Defense Advanced Research Projects Agency (DARPA), a US government agency that is the godchild of the Pentagon, and target of much speculation by conspiracy theorists. The series "focused on social and political governance questions arising from the impacts of the information and biological revolutions." Thus, the findings of Penrose and Hameroff were being examined for the possible application of their research in the "social and political governance" sphere by the military.

Before we leap from Orch OR to synchronicity, it is perhaps useful to look at what Penrose and Hameroff had to say during that study group concerning different mental states and their relationship to the collapse of quantum wave function. By the time of this meeting in October of 1998 the theory seems to have advanced somewhat and become even more compelling.

A chart that was included as part of the report on the RAND meeting is entitled "Quantum Superposition Entanglement in Microtubules for Five States Related to Consciousness." The first state is the normal waking state. The second shows the mental state during anaesthesia. The third is called "heightened experience." The fourth is called "altered state," and this one is the most interesting. The legend appended to this diagram states,

> D. Altered State: even greater rate of emergence of quantum superposition due to sensory input and other factors promoting quantum state (e.g. meditation, psychedelic drug). Predisposition to quantum state results in baseline shift and collapse so that conscious experience merges with normally subconscious computing mode.

In other words, the altered mental state brought about by meditation, psychedelics, or—we may assume—other mystical and occult practices, is actually *promoting* the quantum state posited by Penrose and Hameroff. These practices cause profound changes not only in the neural firing of the brain but also at the deepest level of matter and energy, at the level of waves and particles. It is not only a chemical change we are witnessing but changes at the sub-atomic level, the level where "uncertainty" and "non-locality" and "symmetry" . . . dance. And if this is causing a change in consciousness, it is also fair to say that consciousness is capable of causing a change in the operations of not only the neurons on the level of neurophysiology, but also on the sub-atomic processes represented by the microtubules on the level of the quanta. It is a conscious decision to perform meditation or the other "mind altering" (literally!) exercises—including taking psychedelic drugs—and this decision then causes changes to occur in one's own brain, altering its state and to some degree its structure. What kind of changes take place? What purpose do these changes serve? And more importantly, are we competent enough to take responsibility for creating these changes?

If we look at the legend for "Heightened Experience" on the same chart, we read:

> C. Heightened Experience: increased sensory experience input increases rate of emergence of quantum superposition. Orch OR threshold is reached faster and Orch OR frequency increases.

Only the next state in the chart, "Altered State," demonstrates a faster rate of quantum superposition with its proportional increase in Orch OR frequency. It is not stated exactly what a "heightened experience" might be, other than the result of "increased sensory input." One wonders. Could this include sex? Watching a film or television show? Listening to music? Could this state be achieved on a wide scale through clever use of the media? Through public performance of religious ritual? Propaganda?

This level of discussion is generally and noticeably absent from Penrose's public appearances before mathematicians and physicists, during which he usually focuses on the general outlines of his OR theory and presents evidence for non-computability as an important characteristic of consciousness; Hameroff—as an anesthesiologist and psychologist—is apt to concentrate on various aspects of consciousness, but the chart in the RAND discussion is much more to the point. It identifies those areas of the Orch OR model that would be of most interest to those responsible for military and political matters and, in light of our previous discussions of Puharich, MK-ULTRA, psychological warfare, etc., it's rather like a "blast from the past": can science be used in any way to modify the consciousness of individual human beings, of groups (or nations) of human beings, and can the consciousness of individuals or groups be used to modify or manipulate "reality"? When the most powerful weapon of a terrorist is the willingness to commit suicide in order to bring down an airplane, a bus, or a building full of people, or an entire city itself, suddenly consciousness becomes a central issue of national defense. We are a long way from using the science revealed by quantum mechanics to effect changes in consciousness, but the scientific theories presented by the quantum consciousness crowd permit the possibility of *thinking about* these strategies, and allows an environment in which the discussion goes up a level, from that of the crank and the schizophrenic with an aluminum foil hat to protect against "rays," to the level of scientific advisors to military theorists.

Is quantum mechanics a way of introducing into scientific discourse such concepts as ESP, or psychokinetics, or remote viewing? Will the research by Penrose, Hameroff, et al. lead to the development of devices that could be used to increase the abilities of the brain to encompass mental powers that used to be the stuff of either science fiction . . . or the oral traditions of shamanism and the encoded texts of alchemists and magicians?

We are perhaps a level "too deep" when we use quantum mechanics as a means of having this discussion, and the rules that apply in quantum physics do not apply in the world of classical, Newtonian physics in which we run our machines, drive our cars, watch television, and play baseball. But that's just the point. The powers and abilities of the shamans—and, now, of the remote viewers and the psychological warfare experts and the advertising men—are not demonstrable by Newtonian physics. They lie outside the realm of the classical scientific systems and are much more comfortable in the quantum world. And the interface between quantum physics and classical physics is our own nervous system; our brain is a site where quantum events are taking place, with all that implies, from "uncertainty" to "non-locality," albeit at a very sub-atomic level. The possibility that human beings may be able to consciously use this interface to defy normal, Newtonian physics by being in two places at once, or by leaping forward or backward in time, is something that has been tested under laboratory conditions in the United States under military and intelligence contracts. It was not only tested. It was used. And was successful.

Although contemporary science may scoff at the concept of "remote viewing," it became part of the American arsenal during the Cold War. In addition, the abilities of the remote viewers clearly demonstrate the mind's ability to duplicate—on a macro level—what quantum states do on a micro level, particularly in the area of "non locality." If the rules of quantum mechanics only apply on a deep, sub-microscopic level and the laws of classical Newtonian physics apply on our day-to-day level of reality, then there is another level of human experience entirely, in which it would appear that both worlds—quantum physical and classically physical—operate as one, in which a human being (a complex Newtonian structure if ever there was one) is able, through consciousness, to see into the future or the past, or to travel long distances and witness events taking place thousands of miles away, or even affect physical objects at that distance, using nothing more than the brain. In other words, to behave like a photon.

In 1982, the famous experiments of French physicist Alain Aspect demonstrated the reality of non-locality and, even more so, opened the door to this idea of consciousness affecting quantum states. Prior to these experiments, otherwise visionary scientists and mathematicians such as Albert Einstein, Boris Podolsky and Nathan Rosen considered non-locality as "spooky" or "ghostly"—appropriately enough—and Einstein in particular resisted this concept all his life. However, Aspect was able to arrange an experiment that vindicated (at least for some) the idea that two particles somehow "communicated" over vast distances instantaneously, thus violating Einstein's law that nothing could travel faster than the speed of light.

Basically, the experiment involved two photons whose "spins"—the direction and momentum of the particle's spin around its axis—were "entangled," or "mixed." In other words, they shared the same physical characteristics or properties. These photons were emitted at the same moment, and were thus "related." (I am simplifying this concept, of course, and the mathematicians and physicists in the audience may forgive me for taking shortcuts through the math in order to present the experiment in an intelligible manner.)

Once these photons were emitted, one was sent through a set of filters, let's call them filter A and filter B: the "external agents." A switch was employed to move the photon through either A or B, randomly. Through filter A, the photon would spin in one direction; through filter B, a different direction. What transpired, however, was earth-shaking in its implications, for when the first was affected by its "external agent"—passing through either filter A or filter B, and altering its spin respectively—its unfiltered twin responded immediately assumed the identical state, no matter how far away it was or in what direction it was traveling. There was no observable means of communication between the two particles, and the information was, necessarily, transmitted faster than the speed of light.

Further experimentation showed that the particles would remain in constant, immediate contact no matter how far apart they were, even if they were billions of miles distant. This implied that there is another fabric or web of interconnectedness underlying the physical universe that does not obey the laws of either Newtonian or Einsteinian physics. It also suggested that the human mind, by controlling the action of a particle in one place, could also control the action of a particle at a distance. It's a little like the notion that sticking a pin into a voodoo doll in Detroit could cause a pain in Dar-es-Salaam, with the caveat that the voodoo doll in Detroit must be made with the "particles" of the target in Dar-es-Salaam (the hair, fingernail clippings, etc.).

THE SHADOW OUT OF TIME

> Recent experiments in remote viewing and other studies in parapsychology suggest that there is an 'interconnectedness' of the human mind with other minds and with matter . . .
>
> —Survey of Science and Technology Issues, Committee on Science and Technology, US House of Representatives, 97th Congress, June 1981

> My conception of time—my ability to distinguish between consecutiveness and simultaneousness—seemed subtly disordered, so that I formed chimerical notions about living in one age and casting one's mind all over eternity for knowledge of past and future ages.
>
> —H.P. Lovecraft, "The Shadow Out Of Time"[27]

One of the strangest—and, at the same time, most documented and revealing of military and government appreciation of the paranormal—was the series of "remote viewing" experiments that were variously part of the Pentagon's own programs as well as sub-contracted by the military and the intelligence community to private contractors. As mentioned briefly in Book I, this program was known under a variety of rubrics, but the most dramatic and best known of these was STAR GATE, but it also included GRILL FLAME, CENTER LANE and SUN STREAK. Oddly enough, the most celebrated participants of the remote viewing endeavor were Scientologists.

Once again, and as so many times previously in our story, we find the influence of Aleister Crowley and Jack Parsons spreading through the political, military and cultic elements of American culture. Although this particular development was not as overt as the Manson Family, the Process, the Son of Sam, etc., it was as much a part of the establishment wing of the Crowley phenomenon as the former groups were part of the counter-culture or "anti-establishment" wing. We can credit Jack Parsons' contribution to the American war effort during World War II as well as to the American space program in general; when it comes to Hal Puthoff, Pat Price and Ingo Swann, however, we can credit Parsons' partner, L. Ron Hubbard, and his indirect contribution to the Cold War and anti-terrorism efforts, since Puthoff, Price and Swann were members of Scientology at the time they formed the nucleus of the remote viewing project in 1972 at the Stanford

Research Institute in Menlo Park, California, an important scientific think-tank on the level of the RAND Corporation.

This sounds like the stuff of fantasy fiction, but it has been documented quite thoroughly by science writer Jim Schnabel in *Remote Viewers: The Secret History of America's Psychic Spies*,[28] and has also been ably presented on a number of Web sites, one of which has published a remote viewing manual compiled by the US Army. Schnabel's account brings us back to some of our old friends from Book I—Andrija Puharich, Uri Geller, "Spectra," and "Hoova"—and also introduces us to some new ones, including officers and enlisted men of the US Army, former NSA employees, the CIA, the National Security Council, and a coven of US senators bent on protecting the psi-war program from federal budget cuts. In addition, two of the participants of that program—Russell Targ and remote viewer Keith Harary, both of SRI—have written their own book, *The Mind Race: Understanding and Using Psychic Powers*,[29] as has another participant, David Morehouse: *Psychic Warrior: Inside the CIA's Stargate Program.*[30] Thus, we have no lack of documentation provided by actual members of the remote viewing program as well as by Schnabel, who interviewed many of the program's participants.

The discussion of the modern technique of "remote viewing"—which was a scientific-sounding name invented by the SRI team to distance their practices from those of spiritualist mediums and Gypsy fortune-tellers—begins, according to Schnabel, in February of 1960 with the publication (in a French periodical, *Science et Vie*) of an article claiming that the US Navy had been able to communicate with the nuclear submarine *Nautilus* while it was submerged under the Arctic ice, using only telepathy. The article named names, but a volcano of controversy erupted, and everyone mentioned by name in the article condemned it as nonsense. But the damage had been done. The Soviets were worried that the US had found a way to harness psychic powers for military purposes, and the US was convinced that the Soviets were doing the same.

In fact, there was a great deal of similarity between the piece in *Science et Vie* and the Fred Crisman flying saucer affair in Ray Palmer's *Amazing Stories* magazine. These may have been two examples of disinformation specialists at work, stirring the pot for reasons known only to their case officers; for Fred Crisman was an intelligence officer specializing in disinformation, and on the French side, the consulting editor of *Science et Vie* who had planted the *Nautilus* story with a hapless staff writer was none other than Jacques Bergier, one of the co-authors of *Morning of the Magicians*, and a former intelligence officer himself with strong connections in the French intelligence community. The *Nautilus* story appeared in the French papers the same year that Pauwels and Bergier's *Morning of the Magicians* was published.

We could take issue with Schnabel's timeline, though, since we have already learned that Andrija Puharich was performing telepathy experiments for the US military as early as 1955. That there was an American military interest in psychic abilities long before the *Nautilus* episode is documented, so it is not really very far-fetched to assume that some kind of psychic experiment might have been underway with the nuclear submarine. After all, there was no other way to contact the submarine once it had disappeared under the ice. A submarine in 1960 had to rise to periscope depth to send or receive radio transmissions. Thus, psychic communication—which is not, as demonstrated by the SRI team, dependent upon the same physical restrictions as radio waves—would have been an ideal medium, if it worked. Alas, in the case of the *Nautilus* we may never know; but in many other cases, however, the facts are quite clear and incontrovertible: the American military and intelligence organizations did use psychics for a variety of tasks, many of which were highly classified.

The year 1972 saw some amazing political developments, some of which were secret at the time and not revealed until much later, and some of which became obvious almost overnight. Howard Hughes declared the Clifford Irving book to be a hoax in January; the Zodiac killings were by then in full swing in California; J. Edgar Hoover died in May, and George Wallace almost died a few weeks later, victim of an assassination attempt by Arthur Bremer. In late May to mid-June the Watergate break-ins were taking place, to be discovered by a security guard on June 17, 1972, and subsequently broken as a national news story by the investigative team of Woodward and Bernstein of the *Washington Post* in the following months.

Quietly, however, another development was taking place. This time, the venue was a scientific laboratory in Menlo Park, California. On June 6, 1972, the artist and sometime astrologer Ingo Swann used his mental powers to disturb the operation of a magnetometer buried in a concrete well at the Stanford Research Institute.

Four months later, the CIA would fund SRI to the tune of fifty thousand dollars to continue that research, after intermediate testing had demonstrated the uncanny abilities of Swann and other psychics to penetrate top-secret military installations using only their minds.

If this information had appeared between the covers of *Amazing Stories* there would have been no need to consider it as anything more than either a hoax or a fantasy. Schnabel is a respected science writer, however, and the information revealed in Schnabel's book is reinforced by documentation readily available from a variety of sources. Even the no-nonsense *Journal of Defense & Diplomacy*, in their September 1985 issue, contained an article entitled "The Science of Psychic Warfare" by their science editor, Charles Wallace, which mentions the SRI research among other items of interest, such as the "Emotic Theory" of psychic phenomena that identifies the "five pairs of cranial sinus cavities as the sensors—mastoid, ethmoid, sphenoid, maxillary and frontal—of which the last two become the most important" as instruments of psychic abilities. This, between pages showing ads for submarines, small arms, and Harrier aircraft. Wallace goes on to mention a case that is discussed in more detail in Schnabel's work, and that is the successful use of psychics to locate a downed Soviet bomber in Africa, a story that was carried by Jack Anderson in his syndicated newspaper column.

Before we approach the Soviet bomber story, however, let's look at the SRI remote viewing program, since it stands out as the best-documented case thus far of the American government's interest in, and support of, psychic abilities as military weapons. Regardless of what scientists may have to say about the "reality" of psychic phenomena or the quantum consciousness debate, the evidence is conclusive that individual human beings are able to infiltrate secure locations at a distance using only their minds. The welter of evidence in Schnabel's book alone should be enough to cause scientists to re-evaluate their stand on ESP, telepathy, and other rejected paranormal abilities regardless of their "non-computability," if only because the world has become a much more dangerous place than ever before, and abilities of this nature are necessary to augment a national defense policy that relies overmuch on machinery, electronics, the suspension of civil liberties, and duct tape against enemies whose only resources are those of their own fanatic convictions.

The scientific approach to extrasensory perception (ESP) began with the statistical method of J.B. Rhine at Duke University in 1927, an approach characterized by thousands of tests of subjects using a special deck of cards consisting of twenty-five cards divided into five sets of five symbols: star, square, circle, cross, and wavy lines. People being tested are asked to guess at the sequence of symbols in a freshly-shuffled deck, or to predict the sequence before the deck is shuffled, etc., in a variety of experiments designed to evaluate different forms of ESP. Chance will account for a certain percentage of right answers. Any percentage above the chance calculation would suggest the presence of a psychic power of some description. Collating the results in a statistical format, Rhine hoped to prove the existence of psychic abilities by emphasizing those results that were statistically higher than chance would have predicted.

Rhine's experiments were never fully embraced by the scientific community, and in many cases the results were mediocre at best, and certainly not enough to encourage a full-scale investigation of the paranormal. However, the Rhine approach of using statistical methods to evaluate something as tenuous as psychic abilities did encourage others interested in researching the phenomena, by handing them a scientific precedent. Rhine's sterile laboratory environment for testing ESP, or "psi" as the phenomenon was eventually known, was a far cry from the séance table and the shaman's hut, and won some respectability for the pursuit.

In the 1950s, of course, paranormal abilities were the target of several US government projects, including those of Andrija Puharich for the military as well as the CIA's own efforts along the same lines. The Korean War had brought tales of brainwashing and mind control to the American public in the form of articles, books and movies (such as *The Manchurian Candidate*), and warned the population that it was possible for an enemy to exert control over a person's consciousness.

In the 1960s came the famous *Nautilus* incident—or non-incident—and the period also saw a heightened interest in UFOs and mystical and occult phenomena. Where the mysterious East was considered the source of brainwashing techniques in the 1950s, it became the source for spiritual enlightenment in the 1960s. Brainwashing is about conversion—as William Sargant and others have pointed out—so it could come as no surprise that many Americans and other westerners were joining Asian religions and cults, such as the Hare Krishnas, the Japanese Nichiren Shoshu sect, the Maharishi Mahesh Yogi's Transcendental Meditation, and various Tantric and other Eastern spiritual methodologies. Tales of the paranormal powers of Hindu yogis and fakirs as well as of Chinese magicians and sorcerers were commonplace in the literature (such as the excellent books on Asian mysticism by John Blofeld, and the more metaphysical approach of Alan Watts) as well as in the rumor mills surrounding the various disciplines.

California, of course, was the scene of much of this activity. As political counter-culturalism (the Hippies, the Yippies, the Weathermen) eventually gave way to spiritual counter-culturalism, California retained its position as the nerve center for American alternative religions.

But California was also the Jet Propulsion Laboratory, Stanford University, Lawrence Livermore Laboratories, and so much else associated with rocket science and nuclear weaponry. In the midst of this high-technology atmosphere one found the Stanford Research Institute or SRI, a think-tank that was connected with Stanford University, but which in actuality derived much of its income from government and military grants and contracts.

Professor Hal Puthoff was as much the product of his generation as anyone else. Although he had a stint with the National Security Agency (NSA), he was primarily a laser physicist and contributed heavily to the development of laser technology. His associate, Russell Targ, was another laser physicist, and the two formed an unforgettable partnership at SRI during this period. Laser technology owes a great deal to quantum mechanics, of which Puthoff was of course quite aware. It was perhaps this background in the strange science of lasers and the quanta that led Puthoff to examine alternative religions and mystical groups and individuals, and to his becoming a Scientologist. He eventually wrote a grant proposal, asking that he be allowed to conduct some preliminary tests of psychic abilities.

Somehow, the proposal came to the attention of Ingo Swann, who was himself a Scientologist and being tested for psychic abilities in New York City, where he lived. He contacted Puthoff, and it was agreed that he fly out to California in June 1972 to undertake some informal testing. Puthoff was interested to see whether or not Swann had the ability to move physical objects from a distance, using only his mind (an ability known as "psychokinesis," or simply "PK"). Swann managed to cause the needle in a buried magnetometer to move. This was a heavily-shielded device, buried in concrete, which was eventually used to prove the existence of the sub-atomic entities known as "quarks." Puthoff wrote a report of this experiment, and sent it on to various organizations in an effort to secure financing for the project. It was on the basis of that experiment that the CIA decided to start funding Puthoff 's team at SRI, in an effort develop a means of using psychic abilities to supplement the American defense and intelligence effort, sending in CIA official Ken Kress with $50,000 for SRI.[31]

Testing began in earnest later that year (1972). It was a bit rocky at first, until Ingo Swann came up with a remarkable idea. He suggested that geographic coordinates be used by the tester as a target location. Telling the psychic no more than the coordinates, the psychic would have to mentally travel to that precise spot and report back on what he "saw" there. This method became known as "scanate" for "scanning coordinates," and the project informally known as Project Scanate.

This method was successful beyond expectations, and in worrisome ways. The CIA began to collaborate on the testing, giving the geographic coordinates of various locations to SRI, and Swann—and eventually a newcomer to the project, Pat Price—would mentally "go" to those coordinates and write down what they saw. This testing was done mostly through the CIA's Technical Services division, and involved CIA officers Ken Kress and the pseudonymous "Richard Kennett" and many others. In one case, in June of 1973, a CIA officer with a skeptical attitude towards the project gave a set of coordinates to his mountain cabin in West Virginia. Both Swann and Price came back with detailed information concerning what appeared to be a military base, replete with file drawers marked with operational code names. The CIA official scoffed, telling his associates that there was nothing to this SRI program after all.

A while later, one of the other CIA officials involved with the SRI program decided to take a look himself. After all, how could both of the psychics be wrong in exactly the same way, with the same details? Driving around near the mountain cabin, he stumbled upon a top-secret Pentagon installation.

Putting the details of the experiment in his report, and making mention of the location of the Army's facility, he inadvertently raised a hornet's nest of concern in intelligence circles. The details of the facility, and in particular the code names of secret projects, were known only to a few. How, Pentagon security officials wanted to know, had agents penetrated the facility? When apprised of the supernatural means used by SRI to do just that, the stern-faced men were not amused. They went to Menlo Park and interrogated all concerned until they were satisfied that there was no actual security leak and no enemy penetration of their facility.

The psychic prowess of the SRI "scanate" team was proven, unequivocally.

As more and more testing took place, Puthoff and Targ used different methods to shield their targets so thoroughly that even they did not know in advance what they would be. For instance, they used random number generators to come up with geographic coordinates to ensure that they were not somehow inadvertently and unconsciously signaling the coordinates to the psychics. They would try an "outbound" scanning experiment, in which a subject would drive to a location and sit there at a specific time while the psychic would try to "see" where the subject was located, essentially looking at the surroundings through the subject's eyes. These tests were also enormously successful, and in ways no one expected. In one case, involving psychic (and Scientologist) Pat Price, the random number generator gave a certain set of coordinates for a marina not far from the SRI facility. (The envelopes containing the coordinates were numbered, and the random number generator would produce a number corresponding to one of the envelopes, thus removing any human agency from the selection process.) A suspicious and skeptical SRI staffer, however, decided to change the location at the last minute without regard to the coordinates printed on a paper inside the envelope given to him before he set out. Instead, he drove around aimlessly for a while and then picked a completely different location.

Price not only identified the exact location where the wandering subject wound up, but gave the answer five minutes *before* the subject arrived on-site, thus predicting the future.[32]

As the testing programs continued, Pat Price wound up moving for a while to West Virginia, where he used his talents to locate veins of coal for a mining company; at the same time (and unknown to SRI), he was working directly for the CIA.

The CIA at this time was concerned with penetrating a number of Chinese and Soviet embassies abroad. This Price was able to do, with relative ease, using only his mind. He accurately described a number of Chinese embassies and in detail. (The only occasional hiccup occurred when he described a building the way it had looked in the past.) He was even able to look at a photograph of a building and tell the CIA where the building was located—with incredible precision—and in one case remind the CIA handler of exactly where the photograph had been developed!

Price had been a heavy drinker and smoker, and was fond of food as well. Therefore it came as no surprise when he developed symptoms of angina. Although his friends did what they could to try to convince him to cut down, he generally ignored this advice and continued his energetic lifestyle.

Then, one evening in Washington in mid-July of 1975, he had dinner with friends. The next day in Las Vegas, not feeling very well at dinner, Price mentioned to his friends that someone had slipped something into his coffee the night before. This did not sound like paranoia on his part; he seemed certain of it. Later that night he went to his room. His friends found him afterward in a state of cardiac arrest. He was pronounced dead in the hospital.

Perhaps no one would have thought much of Price's insistence that he had been poisoned or drugged the previous evening, but when CIA official "Richard Kennett" tried to find out more, he was told that no autopsy had been performed. This was indeed unusual, as the death had occurred to a non-resident outside the hospital and would have ordinarily required an autopsy. Further, the hospital staff reported that a man had arrived at the hospital within hours of his death with a briefcase full of Price's medical records and managed to convince the staff not to perform an autopsy based on this evidence of Price's poor physical condition. This gentleman has never been identified, not even by the CIA. The assumption among some of Price's associates was that he had been deliberately poisoned by the KGB or possibly the Chinese. There was never any evidence of this, of course, and Price's lifestyle certainly could have contributed to a heart attack; the anomaly in this affair is the lack of an autopsy and the mysterious man with the briefcase.[33]

Price was the SRI psychic who was the most stunningly successful and consistent. If news of his exploits percolated outside the small circle of SRI and the CIA's Technical Services Staff, he could have become a target of hostile forces. The same month as Price's death, Andrija Puharich was hosting a visit by Ira Einhorn and Holly Maddux at his "Turkey Farm" in Ossining, New York, where they witnessed a fourteen-year-old child in a remote viewing session "visit" the Pentagon, the White House, and the Kremlin. It is perhaps not outside the realm of feasibility to imagine that the Soviets were aware of this "psychic spying" and simply decided to remove the most powerful psychics from America's arsenal. Puharich's role was well-known by this time. He had been the man to introduce Uri Geller to the world, to bring him to SRI to be tested and thus come to the attention of American intelligence (which was, after all, funding the psychic research at SRI), and to place Geller within a very special context. In 1973, Puharich was still promoting the idea of The Nine, fully twenty years after the first session with the Indian medium Dr. Vinod. He brought Geller to a meeting with Arthur Young on February 27, 1973 at Young's home; again this is twenty years after the first communication with The Nine that involved both Puharich and Young.

Under hypnosis by Puharich, Geller admitted being the recipient of powers from The Nine (a claim he has denied in later years). Puharich's book *Uri: A Journal of the Mystery of Uri Geller*, is a good source for names, dates and places in the Geller timeline. It also contains the text of the film SRI made of Geller, and the text of the original statement by The Nine. Much of what was going on at SRI in the 1970s is covered by Puharich from his own perspective, which is almost completely related to Uri Geller.

And, according to Geller, Puharich was his CIA handler. This doesn't seem too outlandish a claim to make under the circumstances. After all, Puharich did have extensive ties to the military and intelligence communities dating back to the Korean War. And Puharich did bring Geller to SRI, a place that was testing psychic abilities under contract to the CIA. Whether or not Puharich was actually on contract to the CIA himself is moot under the circumstances; his mentorship of the young Israeli psychic brought them both into contact with officials from the CIA, the Pentagon, and the American government on an almost continual basis. For all practical intents and purposes, Geller was being observed by the CIA, and

Puharich was the point of contact. The Uri Geller–Andrija Puharich relationship has already been covered in Books I and II. What is important to focus on now is the "extended family" around the SRI remote viewing program, including the quantum physicists and the military and intelligence operations that continued the psychic espionage project, bringing us into strange realms indeed.

At the time that SRI was experimenting with psychic abilities in a relatively benign fashion, the Soviet Union was engaged in its own psychic research. There were theoretical problems with psychic research in the Communist state, however; as long as ESP and other paranormal abilities were linked with superstition, magic and religion, no one in the Communist Party could become involved. Marx and Engels were quite clear about the position of religion in a Communist society. Religion, after all, was "the opiate of the people," and psychic phenomena were relegated to the fringe of religion. But with the publication of the presumably fictitious *Nautilus* story in 1960, it seemed necessary for the Soviets to counter the presumed Allied threat in mental telepathy and other powers, in the name of "national security."

There were several famous Soviet psychics, and some of this research was covered in *Psychic Discoveries Behind the Iron Curtain*, a 1970 bestseller by Sheila Ostrander and Lynn Schroeder, published two years before the experiments at SRI would begin. According to Schnabel, who bases his information on intelligence documents and sources, the Soviets "scoured the mystical eastern vastnesses of the Soviet Union in order to find the toughest Siberian shamans, the best-trained Tibetan priests, the most powerful Mongolian *chi gong* masters."[34] This effort yielded some fruit, for "a group of Tibetans succeeded in breaking a human skull a few yards away, just by concentrating on it."[35] All of this was undertaken by the Institute for the Problems of Information Transmission (known by its Russian acronym IPPI) in Moscow. This same Institute was responsible for a state-sponsored experiment in the blackest of black arts: the cursing of souvenirs by shamans so that the (foreign) recipients of these gifts would "suffer neuralgia, depression, and even nervous breakdown."[36] What is astonishing about these experiments is that they were undertaken by a state that considered itself the only truly scientific government on earth: one purged of religion, fantasy, and superstition and devoted to the liberation of the minds of humanity from the shackles of false religious sentimentality.

In *Nexus* magazine, an Australian journal that reports on psychic phenomena, UFOs, etc., former scientist and now the head of something called Paranormal Management Systems in the UK, Turan Rifat, makes an observation about Soviet parapsychological research which echoes that made by Kenneth Grant with regard to Jack Parsons and the Babalon Working, i.e., that Soviet "research in the biophysical domain became so advanced that they opened doorways to other continuums and themselves fell prey to malevolent forces."[37] While this sounds far-fetched and the kind of thing one would expect of a popular magazine dealing with paranormal conspiracy theories, one must admit that if this were possible, then it is, of course, equally possible with regard to American military and intelligence mind-control and psychological warfare operations. The Soviets would have been using the very people who specialize in developing paranormal abilities through the "derangement of the senses" and the other techniques already described herein. These are individuals who would have attained some degree of spiritual enlightenment and psychological integration. Would they have willingly or enthusiastically supported their government's plan to utilize these abilities in the service of the state, for the assassination and control of foreign citizens? If one believes in the existence of "malevolent forces," then the Siberian and Mongolian shamans and Tibetan priests would be the likely contacts for these forces, as they had devoted their entire lives to the pursuit of otherworldly experience in the form of gods, demons, and disembodied souls. With the virtual destruction of the Russian Orthodox Church and the suppression of all religious organizations, the shamans would have been the only ones left in the Soviet Union still practicing spiritual techniques. Romanian émigré philosopher Mircea Eliade had written extensively concerning shamanism in the 1960s, and his insights into shamanism as a form of psychological conditioning could not have failed to come to the attention of the Soviets.

Back in the United States, the CIA and other government organizations were taking a good, hard look at the success ratio of the SRI program. A temporary blocking of federal funds for psi research took place in the mid-1970s, due to unfavorable publicity generated by reports of the CIA's own prior MK-ULTRA mind-control programs (the psi research of SRI and the CIA seeming a little too alike for comfort, as both involved experimentation on human subjects, and many in government were opposed to this type of research anyway as smacking too much of witchcraft or just plain nonsense), but the coffers slowly opened again during the Carter administration, and this time the military was taking a more central role.

The Pentagon's remote viewing programs eventually (in early 1979) came under the authority of the Defence Intelligence Agency, or DIA. The DIA set up its own remote viewing operation at an abandoned building at Fort Meade, code-named GRILL FLAME, but their remote viewers were generally still being trained at SRI in California, by the team of Puthoff, Swann and others. Swann helped to codify the remote viewing protocols, making it an easily-defined system, and it is Swann's contribution that comes through most clearly in the Internet-published DIA manual on CRV or "Coordinate Remote Viewing."

GRILL FLAME was under the authority of one Jack Vorona, a nuclear physicist who was a DIA officer, and who controlled other "alternative" projects, such as one that was designed to study mind-control using microwave technology.[38] This technique was thought to be a focus of Soviet research at the time, but there has also been a lot of research in the United States on not only the use of microwaves but also low-frequency radio waves, and on all sorts of electronic and mechanical approaches to mind control.

These days, the Internet is full of information (much of it suspect) on this type of technology, but a strange book published in 1998 and authored by Richard Sauder includes over one hundred pages of U.S. patent information for a variety of electronic devices for mind-control applications, including US Patent 3,951,139: *Apparatus and Method for remotely Monitoring and Altering Brain Waves* and US Patent 5,213,562: *Method of Inducing Mental, Emotional and Physical States of Consciousness, Including Specific Mental Activity, In Human Beings*. The inventor of the latter was Robert A. Monroe, and thereby hangs a tale.

Robert Monroe, a radio producer, began suffering from insomnia in 1958. It was a severe case that doctors could not do anything about, believing Monroe to be suffering from a nervous breakdown, especially when he began reporting that he was leaving his body at night. Of course, most mental health professionals when faced with a statement like that would diagnose some form of schizophrenia; depending on other presenting symptoms one could also be looking at dissociation. Monroe, however, was fascinated by his own "disorder," and began building a room where these episodes—known to psychic researchers as OOBEs or "out of body experiences"—could be monitored more closely. Eventually, this hobby turned into a full-scale methodology for initiating the OOBE using sound-waves which, when broadcast through a set of headphones, would mimic brain-waves of the same frequencies that he was targeting.

Soon, the Monroe Institute was established for the study of this (and related) phenomena and became a part of the overall US government's psychic warfare program. Located in Virginia, it was convenient to the Fort Meade contingent, and the devices that Monroe developed at his Institute appear to have been quite successful and popular among the remote viewers. Monroe authored several books on the out-of-body-experience (such as *Journeys Out Of The Body*, Doubleday, NY, 1971), and Richard Sauder became interested, and visited the Monroe Institute to go through the training. He would later claim that since then he had been in sporadic telepathic communication with Monroe himself.[39]

As bizarre as that sounds, the reactions of SRI and GRILL FLAME staffers when faced with the Monroe techniques were just as startling. Army Captain Skip Atwater was the intelligence officer who, in 1977, founded the Army's version of the SRI team at Fort Meade and ran it until 1987. Atwater visited the Monroe Institute in 1977 and tried out the equipment, which consisted of a set of headphones that broadcast a pre-recorded tape with Monroe's voice and special effects. According to Schnabel's account, Atwater experienced a sense of levitation on the very first attempt![40] Astonished by this result, Atwater became a fixture at the Monroe Institute, and eventually became director of research there after retiring from the Army.

Other military remote viewers at the Monroe Institute experienced everything from spirit possession to a sense that they were being remotely-viewed by the Soviet opposition; but by far the strangest and most compelling case for the dangers of meddling in the paranormal for those who have not undergone rigorous spiritual training beforehand is the Lawrence Livermore episode.

This is recounted in very few places. Uri Geller mentions being at Lawrence Livermore in passing in *The Geller Effect*—co-authored with Guy Lyon Playfair (the AID worker from Brazil who became very involved in occultism and the paranormal)—but it is not mentioned at all in Puharich's *Uri* or in the book co-authored by SRI scientist Russell Targ and SRI remote viewer Keith Harary, *The Mind Race*. It appears in various places on the Internet, and in some detail in Schnabel's work on remote viewers and in *Mind Reach* by Puthoff and Targ. It is worth repeating here in brief, as the individuals concerned were all scientists at Lawrence Livermore, and not psychics or mediums or anyone traditionally connected with the occult.

Uri Geller had been invited to SRI for some informal tests of his abilities in 1972. By 1974, word of his prowess had leaked out around the world, and the nuclear weapons specialists at Lawrence Livermore were concerned that someone with psychic abilities—particularly psychokinesis, an ability Geller demonstrated by bending metal spoons, rings, and other objects with his mind—could detonate a nuclear weapon using only mental energy or could scramble the nation's military computer systems, thus disabling the country's missile defences. Therefore, in late 1974 and 1975 a select group of scientists and security officers began testing Geller at an off-site location.

The tests showed that Geller could only affect metal objects, computer systems, and computer disks if he was in physical contact with them. Therefore, it was a reasonable assumption that PK was not a threat to the nation's missile systems. However, other developments took place that caused not only concern but hysteria among the Lawrence Livermore staff.

While technicians were listening to the audiotapes routinely made during the Geller PK sessions, they noticed a voice on the tape that had not been there during the tests. It was a "metallic voice" and was largely unintelligible, although the few words that were understood turned out to be top-secret codenames for intelligence operations, names that were unknown to the scientists at Lawrence Livermore. In addition, an infrared camera that had been used during the sessions showed patches of radiation on the laboratory walls where no such radiation should have been present.

These were more than merely scientific anomalies. They were captured on tape and film under controlled circumstances. However, this would have been worth a few paragraphs in a report and not much more, were it not for the fact that personnel involved in the Geller experiments began to experience exceedingly strange phenomena. One of the recurring motifs was the appearance of a flying saucer in the laboratory: a hovering, hologram-like image that would float around and then disappear. And this "saucer" appearance was not restricted to the laboratory. Some of the scientists witnessed the phenomenon when they were at home with their families. There was no conceivable explanation for this, no way such a hologram could have been projected inside the secure laboratory environment without a lot of equipment and expensive electronics that could have easily been discovered. Since Geller was known to put out the story that he was in communication with extraterrestrial agencies aboard a spacecraft that hovered over the earth, the connection was obvious, but the reason or motivation behind the apparitions was not.

In addition to the saucer, there were reports of appearances of strange and fantastic animals to the Lawrence Livermore personnel and their families, including very large black birds, ravens, that would appear from nowhere and wander across their lawns . . . or suddenly appear in the morning standing over their beds. This association of birds with Geller was something that the laboratory staff may have not recognized, for Geller's supernatural experiences included that of a bird of prey, usually a hawk (symbol for the Egyptian god, Horus). The appearance of fantastic animals is common in the literature of shamanism, and their purpose is usually totemic in nature; but what was happening to the scientists?

As the personnel began to break down and exhibit signs of intense mental distress, the security officer in charge of the group broke down and contacted "Richard Kennett" of the CIA. As Kennett not only had security clearances but was also aware of the psychic research programs and had a doctorate in neurophysiology, he was the logical choice.

Kennett listened to the men—some of whom broke down and wept in his presence—describe their symptoms. He was not convinced that this was simply a textbook case of hysteria. These men were scientists with no occult leanings; furthermore, they had all been psychologically vetted, as they were involved with classified government and military projects. It didn't make sense.

And then he listened to the audiotapes, and heard the secret codewords mentioned that none of the Lawrence Livermore staff could have known.

This was not the end of the story, however. One of the scientists received a phone call and heard the "metallic voice" that so often pursues researchers in this field, man and boy, and this time the voice told him to drop the Geller experimentation completely. The team was only too happy to do so, and the "hauntings" gradually stopped.

(I hesitate to mention another incident among these many strange occurrences at America's most important nuclear weapons research facility after that at Los Alamos. Although the incident has been documented, I feel I am so straining credulity as it is, with these stories of paranormal powers, government agencies, military remote viewing and the rest, that to bring up the denouement of the Lawrence Livermore episode might be to lose my audience completely after we have come so far. I have made it a core element of my approach that everything I claim in this book is thoroughly documented and with as much reliance on primary sources as is practicable, considering the subject matter. I have, indeed, omitted many anecdotes and other material that I considered too questionable, or for which evidence was not sufficient to overwhelm any reasonable objections. So . . .)

Apparently, one of the Livermore scientists was at home one evening speaking with his wife when another of the apparitions occurred in their living room. This time it was of a man's arm, clad in a grey suit jacket, that hovered and twisted in the air between them. The end of the arm consisted not of a hand, but of a hook. It appeared, and then just as mysteriously disappeared.

When this account was related to "Richard Kennett," he must have wondered whether or not Puthoff and Targ had been playing games with lasers and holograms. When he met with them, he repeated what he had heard from the Livermore scientists, ending with the story about the arm. At that precise moment, there came a loud, insistent pounding on the door of their motel room. The door was opened to reveal a man dressed in a grey suit. He walked into the center of the room and said in an odd voice, "I guess I must be in the wrong room," and turned and left. They had enough time to see that he had one sleeve pinned to his shoulder. The man in the grey suit was missing an arm.

Schnabel, in whose book this account also occurs, gives it the benefit of a doubt.[41] Some of the Lawrence Livermore staff refused to go into details about these experiences with him; one of them was writing his own book about the Geller affair and wanted to keep the details to himself, understandably. Others were not directly involved in the day-to-day proceedings and could not offer much corroboration. Schnabel has wondered if the "man in the grey suit" episode was invented as a fictional device by Puthoff and Targ, if not the first apparition then perhaps the melodramatic, *Weird Tales* ending. There is no particular reason to believe that Puthoff and Targ would have invented such an ending, however, considering all the problems they have had in getting scientists to take their paranormal research seriously. To invent such a Hollywood ending would be to jeopardize whatever ground they had won, painfully and at great cost. At this time, we simply have to take the story at face value. It is certainly no stranger than other episodes in the literature, and finds resonance with mysterious and "synchronistic" events recounted by Strieber, Sarfatti, and so many others. Even more incredible, all of this was taking place in the heart of the American defense industry, in the core of the "military-industrial complex" President Eisenhower warned us all about in 1960.

During the Carter Administration, remote viewers were involved in everything from looking for the Iranian hostages to locating a downed Soviet spyplane. In May of 1978, Hal Puthoff received an urgent fax from the Army tasking his remote viewer team to locate a Tu-22 bomber that had disappeared somewhere over the African nation of Zaire. The man who gave Puthoff this mission was General Ed Thompson of the Pentagon's intelligence agency, responsible for the Army's remote viewing projects among other duties. Thompson was a strong supporter of remote viewing, as was General Albert Stubblebine of the Pentagon's INSCOM (Intelligence and Security Command) division, under whose wing GRILL FLAME, CENTER LANE, and the other codenames for the remote viewing operations would find themselves in the 1980s. (INSCOM would also develop a close working relationship with the Monroe Institute.)

The Soviets and the American CIA were hot in pursuit of the downed bomber. If the CIA could get there first, they would uncover a treasure trove of Soviet secrets, since the Tu-22 had been on an intelligence-gathering mission over Africa. The CIA had its own ideas about where to find the plane, but the SRI remote viewer came through with flying colors. He was corroborated by another remote viewer, this time working out of Wright-Patterson Air Force Base. Between the two of them—and unknown to each other—they developed a detailed map and description of where the plane would be found, tail-up in a jungle river. The CIA recovery team—on their way to the site where they estimated the plane would be—came across the site identified by the remote viewers first: there was the plane.

This story eventually made Jack Anderson's syndicated newspaper column and became a world-wide sensation. Other spectacular results would follow from time to time, involving terrorists, hostages, nuclear weapons testing, and other areas of intense concern to military and intelligence chiefs. And the experiments continued as Puthoff and others sought ways to fine-tune the results of their most talented remote viewers as well as to develop methods by which virtually anyone can be trained in the process.

There was considerable opposition to these programs both within and outside the military, however. Some among the general staff could not understand the value of having "tea leaf readers" work for the Pentagon; others felt that the mystique of the remote viewers detracted from the real work of intelligence gathering, which involved either satellites in the sky or assets on the ground. Many were dismayed by the cozy relationship that developed between INSCOM and the Monroe Institute. Also, remote viewing reached a kind of crescendo during the Democratic Carter administration, and after the Republican Ronald Reagan was elected President in 1980 there was a mad dash to distance the new administration from the perceived weaknesses of the old. The CIA's Robert Gates as well as Defense Secretary Frank Carlucci both opposed the remote viewing programs, which is amusing considering that their president was a man who consulted astrologers, and had been doing so since at least the time he was Governor of California.

Although Gates and Carlucci did their best to destroy the remote viewing program, the psychics had champions in the persons of Senator Robert Byrd (D) of West Virginia, Senator Daniel Inouye (D) of Hawaii, Senator and former astronaut John Glenn (D) of Ohio, and two Republican senators, William Cohen of Maine and Ted Stevens of Alaska. (It should also be mentioned that one of the most vocal supporters of the SRI and military psi-war programs was former astronaut Edgar Mitchell, who had been on hand to welcome Uri Geller to SRI back in

1972. Mitchell—a member of the Masonic society—has been intimately involved with paranormal research since his retirement from NASA. Astronaut Buzz Aldrin, another Mason, brought a Masonic flag with him on his Apollo 11 flight to the Moon on July 20, 1969, an event he commemorated in a letter to the Masonic Grand Commander on NASA stationery, dated September 19, 1969. That quite a number of astronauts have been Masons, and that the Grand Secretary General of the Society at the time of the lunar landing in 1969 was the brother of an important NASA official is noted in Richard Sauder's book.)[42]

The senators managed to protect the remote viewing program for quite a while, but the psychics still wound up as moving targets, working now for INSCOM, now for the DIA, fighting for funding all over Capitol Hill. Puthoff managed to win a ten-year contract from an unidentified government agency that saved the SRI program, but he had tired of the politics—both internal and external—at SRI and retired from the Institute in 1985. Major General Stubblebine was forced to retire from the Army—and thus as protector of the remote viewing apparatus—in 1984. Oddly enough, Stubblebine would wind up in New York, having divorced his first wife, living with a psychiatrist who specialized in alien abduction cases. Many of the remote viewers and support personnel became UFO "believers"—if that is the correct term—including Ingo Swann, who eventually returned to New York City after dealing with numerous internal political squabbles himself, most notably with Russell Targ. Swann has written and self-published a book about his UFO beliefs, *Penetration: The Question of Extraterrestrial and Human Telepathy*, which does not add much to our knowledge of the SRI remote viewing program, but which does expand considerably on the theme that remote viewers were occasionally tasked with UFO research—including attempting to learn the truth behind the flying saucer phenomenon—as well as viewing other planets. Stubblebine himself became a UFO enthusiast and is on the record as stating that there are "structures underneath the surface of Mars" as well as machinery, and that all of this information was obtained through remote viewing.[43]

In light of the fact that that so many military men, from enlisted personnel to generals like MacArthur and Stubblebine, have gone on the record as supporting the idea that UFOs are extraterrestrial craft visiting the earth, the constant ridiculing of this hypothesis from all corners of both the military and the scientific communities seems highly suspect. We are constantly being told that the eyewitnesses to UFO sightings are not credible, not trained observers, and have mistaken natural objects for spacecraft; then we have a wide cross-section of military and scientific personnel who insist that the phenomenon is genuine and not the result of swamp gas or the planet Venus. What is the citizenry to make of this apparent dichotomy? We may accept—reluctantly—that a farmer in Iowa who has lived there all his life has mistaken a common natural event for a flying saucer landing; we find it difficult to accept that a major general would have made a similar mistake.

Indeed, the reactions of men like Stubblebine and MacArthur are based on military records rather than personal, eyewitness accounts or—like Stubblebine—are the result of paranormal "scrying" (a method which was, of course, supported by the military and proved useful in a number of occasions, such as locating SCUD missiles during the Gulf War with Iraq); but then, are we not to trust the analyses of this data by generals and other officers, especially those—like Stubblebine—who were in charge of intelligence and security? If not, if we can't trust the observations and conclusions of the men who are effectively in charge of our national security, and who have been for the past fifty years at least, then certainly that security is in serious disrepair!

One of SRI's remote viewers—Keith Harary—co-authored a popular book on remote viewing and psychic phenomena in general with Russell Targ, entitled *The Mind Race*. Harary joined SRI in 1980, and has since become a psychologist, but in 1979 he found himself counseling former members of the Peoples Temple and working closely with Al and Jeannie Mills, the Temple whistle-blowers who would soon be murdered in their home. Targ and Harary teamed up after leaving SRI in the early 1980s, and traveled frequently to Eastern bloc countries, which was a concern to the American intelligence establishment, particularly the DIA. Targ claimed they were working with their Russian counterparts in a "pure science" and non-military environment, but it is not certain that statement satisfied the DIA.

Eventually, the two men began playing the silver-futures market using Harary's psychic abilities and Targ's analysis of the results, and making considerable progress, attracting an investor. After a few misses, however, the men began blaming each other for the losses—and in public, during a lecture at Esalen—and the lawsuits started to fly. The men are still at loggerheads.

The remote viewing program lasted well into the 1990s, due to the $10 million contract won by Hal Puthoff in the last days of his administration at SRI, but as early as 1988 the Pentagon Inspector General had recommended that the Fort Meade operation be shut down. The days of the remote viewers were numbered. By 1995 and at the end of the SRI contract, word of the "psychic spies" had leaked once again to the press, and CIA directors and military men and former remote viewers were appearing on television and in the print media, answering questions and trying to put a better appearance on the revelations than the image of a spy with crystal balls. Ingo Swann went on the record to state that the original purpose behind SRI's remote viewing program was to discover what the Soviets had accomplished in the field, in order that American military and intelligence personnel could be kept informed.

Much of the methodology of the SRI remote viewing teams leaked out, including Swann's elegant (and often criticized) terminology. One of these was the "Matrix": a description of the underlying interconnectivity of the universe that a remote viewer would enter in a trance state. Without putting too fine a point on it, what Swann proposed was that psychics could enter what was essentially a kind of quantum state; within the Matrix, a remote viewer could theoretically go anywhere and see anything, regardless of normal limitations of space and time. That a popular film series would be made based on this very premise within a few years of the press revelations about GRILL FLAME, STAR GATE and Ingo Swann's "Matrix" should, perhaps, no longer surprise us.

The films' treatment of normal human consciousness as the creation of an enormous computer-like grid run by alien forces is probably as close as we will get to seeing the theories and doctrines of The Nine, Spectra, Hoova and all the rest portrayed cinematically, albeit from a very negative standpoint. It should also be mentioned that central to the screenplay of the the *Matrix* films are the "Men in Black"; this time they are assassins bent on stopping characters Morpheus, Neo and their cohorts from taking back the planet and waking up the world.

> *How could people respond to these images if images didn't secretly enjoy the same status as real things? Not that images were so powerful, but that the world was so weak.*
> —Jonathan Franzen[44]

The remote viewing programs of the military and intelligence communities—under the general rubric of GRILL FLAME and the other, later, modifications of the same—were extremely cheap by Pentagon standards. Hal Puthoff had secured a ten million dollar, ten year contract to support that research. By comparison, some of the Pentagon's frivolous spending on toilet seats and screwdrivers seems insane. It was not remote viewing in and of itself that threatened the American military establishment, however; it was the fact that the very nature of the program threatened its comfortable, Newtonian worldview. Officers were nervous about the "giggle factor"—when talk of the psychic spies and their exploits would elicit giggles and outright guffaws from their peers—and probably this more than anything else caused the remote viewing programs to be sidelined and eventually cancelled altogether. This is a pity, for several reasons.

In the first place, SRI and Hal Puthoff and the others were unable to publish much of their research due to security restrictions and the highly classified nature of some of their taskings. That means that an area of science in which we desperately need to know more has been effectively shut off from peer review, with the result that few individuals and organizations in the scientific establishment take the program—and all it implies for science—seriously.

In the second place, America (and the West in general) is now engaged in a serious struggle for survival against forces that are not technologically or economically superior. These forces succeed on the basis of power derived from the very mental states studied by the mind-control experts of the past fifty years: conversion, dissociation, and the whole eros-driven "derangement of the senses" that contributes not only to art and the manufacture of images, but to the conscious and willful use of those images to effect political change: the science of the shaman, the magician, the psychological warfare expert. The leaders of these assaults cynically manipulate the minds of their followers to the extent that suicide missions become glorious . . . particularly those in which large numbers of civilians are murdered, as hideously and as brutally as possible for maximum effect. This is not a new development, of course. The Japanese in World War II gave us a foretaste of the "kamikaze" impulse. The black magicians behind these and other acts of desperate courage committed by the credulous and the lonely and the pious never lead these doomed individuals in the suicide runs, but pull the strings from a safe base in a friendly country, moving huge funds across borders with alacrity, and ordering mayhem by email and mobile phone. To find these sorcerers we need more than satellites and smirking condescension. We need more than SIGINT and HUMINT. We need a "backdoor" into their psyches.

This was begun during the Carter administration when remote viewers were tasked with locating hostages taken by terrorists, including CIA agent William Buckley, whose exploits and murder were detailed in Books I and II; it was reinforced when remote viewers were tasked with finding SCUD missile launchers during the Gulf War. At this time, remote viewing cannot be considered a replacement for normal intelligence gathering operations and probably will never be; but it is a valuable supplement to those endeavors and has the additional virtue of being inexpensive and seemingly undetectable. There is no earthly reason why these programs cannot be reinstated and the methodology perfected. There is, in fact, no reason why private individuals or private organizations cannot practice these techniques on their own, independent of government supervision or involvement. Shamans and magicians have been doing so for thousands of years. And the training manuals exist: either the grimoires of the sorcerers or the official manuals of the remote viewers. Terrorist organizations have been using methods very similar to these for indoctrination and training of assassins, and the Soviet Union has experimented to an unsettling degree with the ability to cause heart attacks and other ailments from a distance using the powers of the mind. The powers of consciousness.

THE GHOST IN THE MACHINE

Art is a school of self-transcendence. So is a voodoo session or a Nazi rally.

—Arthur Koestler[45]

Arthur Koestler, himself fascinated for many years by the phenomenon of coincidence (and author of the influential essay *The Roots of Coincidence*), traces modern preoccupation with it to Schopenhauer, and from Schopenhauer to Paul Kammerer and from there to Jung and Pauli. What all of these gentlemen had in common was an understanding that coincidence represents an acausal "force" or "principle" in the world, operating outside traditionally-understood science, but nevertheless a part of our experience. Koestler actually goes much further and much deeper into the study of this phenomenon than even Jung and Pauli, who seemed to stop short: Jung not enough of a physicist and Pauli not enough of a psychologist, perhaps.

In *Janus*, a book published towards the end of his life, before this accomplished philosopher, sometime Marxist, and historian of science committed suicide with his wife of many years after he learned he was stricken with a debilitating terminal sickness, Koestler laid out the parameters for an educated debate over the issue of coincidence and its role in both physics and in consciousness. As it transcends the initial attempts by Jung and Pauli to identify coincidence beyond the tag "acausal connecting principle" and goes right to the heart of the matter by identifying coincidence with paranormal abilities as well as with events in the "real world," his ideas bear some review. One should remember that Koestler did begin his professional life as an admirer of Communism, later abandoning this political creed and defecting to the West; his political life and background are therefore valuable to us, for they give Koestler a unique perspective on the historical and scientific problems we face when we consider coincidence as more than just a curiosity.

Koestler begins his argument by pointing out that a human being's brain is actually two brains: a reptilian brain, responsible for our instinctual behavior, and a neocortex, a "new brain," that lies atop the old brain and is responsible for our intellectual superiority to other creatures on the earth. Koestler believes that it is the imperfect control of the reptilian brain by the neocortex that has led to humanity's predicament. He points to an explosive growth in technology from the time of the ancient Greeks to modern space exploration in only 2500 years, and the parallel decline in human ethics and morality, which began with Taoism, Buddhism and Confucianism and which led to Hitler, Stalin, and the spiritual poverty of modern psychology.

He emphasizes that only human beings feel no compunction about killing members of their own species and, indeed, are capable of such obscenities as human sacrifice to appease some invented deity. He does not believe that humanity wages war and commits genocide because of aggression; instead, he blames humanity's ills on an excess of devotion. It is loyalty to a king or to a cause or to a religion (quite often, all three) that motivates a man to leave his home and put on a uniform and endure months or years of self-sacrifice, boredom, hunger and deprivation. Soldiers, as Koestler points out, are rarely aggressive and certainly not territorial. They have subsumed their individuality in the group, the tribe, the cult. They follow orders. They kill, not out of conviction or aggression, but on command, out of loyalty to an authority figure and identity with a group.

For Koestler, the most powerful weapon in the arsenal of humanity is language.[46] The Word. For it is language that both unites groups and divides humanity among those very groups, and gives it the rationale for killing fellow humans. It is language as it is understood by the psychological warriors and the advertising executives. It is language as understood by the ancient Greeks as well as by Bruno the Renaissance magician.

Thus, Koestler attacks the reductionism of scientists and philosophers from Pavlov to Skinner, from Freud to Desmond Morris, which blames the evils of history on instincts and natural aggression. In fact, he goes even further to suggest that this loyalty to authority begins as a form of brainwashing in the human infant, which remains helpless and in parental control for a much longer period than the infant offspring of other mammals. "Brainwashing," he writes, "starts in the cradle."[47] Children drink in religious fanaticism and tribal identification along with their mother's milk. In this, Koestler and psychiatrist R.D. Laing (and Ignatius Loyola) are in perfect agreement. It was the malleability of the brain of the human child that encouraged a generation of behaviorists and determinists to devote special attention to the establishment of those "secret schools" for the indoctrination of the young and their molding into the Cold Warriors of the future. Whether we believe the Whitley Strieber model of the secret school, or the Jack Sarfatti model, it is clear that this type of environment did exist, and not only in the United States but most especially in other countries, such as in China under Mao, in the Soviet Union under Stalin, in Germany under Hitler, and in those African and Asian nations of today which train boys and girls of nine and ten years old in the arts of assassination and soldiering.

Koestler's interest is obviously political in much of what he writes, but he has abandoned the jingoistic politics of the political party, the slogan, the mass rally, for a scientific view of the human being that transcends social organizations. (He was imprisoned as a suspected spy during the Spanish Civil War and narrowly escaped execution.) Like Jung and like historian of religion Mircea Eliade, who both had a flirtation with Nazism, Koestler's brief involvement with Communism was salutary in the long run: they all abandoned the dream of equality and freedom from want promised by social organizations and turned towards a pursuit of spiritual (or, perhaps, psychological) freedom as the means to cure humanity's ills. Marxism—as self-consciously more "scientific" than its competitors—was in a sense the perfect laboratory environment for the development of these ideas, for Marx looked at history as inevitability: human society progressed from a feudal state to an industrialized state to a socialist state and then to a communist state (I am summarizing mightily here) according to the Marxist dialectic. The world would eventually evolve into communism and workers would live in a paradise on earth as there was no paradise anywhere else. When the "inevitability" of this process was called into question—when the workers' states of the Soviet Union and China did not automatically induce working class ecstasy—then history as evolution was called into question, as well. As Koestler understands, the history of science and technology is one thing; the history of human civilization is quite another.

In an effort to come to terms with this schizophrenic aspect of humanity, Koestler considers human beings to have two (at times mutually contradictory) impulses: that of self-transcendence and that of self-assertion. Self-assertion may be thought to be analogous to the instinct of individual survival and expression at the cost of society; self-transcendence—to which he also refers as the *integrative* faculty—is the impulse to go beyond one's personal comfort and satisfaction to meld with the common good, to sign the social contract. These two impulses, to Koestler, represent a continuum of two extremes, with much of human behavior occupying a kind of middle ground, as humans attempt to satisfy both at once. This leads to Koestler's concept of "bisociation," by which he means "a distinction between the routines of disciplined thinking within a single universe of discourse—on a single plane, as it were—and the creative types of mental activity which always operates on more than one plane."[48] Koestler uses this concept to explain both humor and tragedy, and the creative arts (which includes every creative act, including those that occur within science and mathematics) and then inevitably turns to the subject of coincidence:

> *Coincidence* may be described as the chance encounter of two unrelated causal chains which—miraculously it seems—merge into a significant event. It provides the neatest paradigm of the bisociation of previously separate contexts, engineered by fate. Coincidences are puns of destiny. (emphasis in original)[49]

Koestler goes on to talk about the "law of large numbers" or "law of probability" that Jung identifies with Newtonian science in general. When observing, for instance, that dogs were biting people according to an average of about seventy-five incidents per day in the 1950s in New York City, Koestler asks a question: "How do the dogs of New York know when to stop biting and when to make up the daily quota?"[50] He reprises the sentiments of mathematician Von Neumann who looked at probability as "black magic," in which "we are faced with *a large number of uncertainties producing a certainty*, a large number of random events creating a lawful total outcome" (emphasis in original).[51] This, of course, is also the case with quantum physics, in which the uncertainty of life at the quantum level produces the relative stability and certainty of the perceived universe.

Koestler realizes the implications of what he is writing, of course, and draws the same comparison between paranormal abilities and coincidence that are drawn by Jung and many others. He begins by speaking about the "integrative tendency"—which he also refers to as the "self-transcendent tendency"—as the impulse to create order out of disorder: i.e., *transcending* the individualistic instincts of survival to attain a high degree of *integration* of the individual with society. He then draws a parallel between the self-transcendent tendency and psychic phenomena:

> The present theory is even more hazardous by explicitly suggesting that the integrative tendency operates in *both causal and acausal* ways, the two standing in a complementary relationship analogous to the particle-wave complementarity in physics. It is accordingly supposed to embrace not only the acausal agencies operating on the sub-atomic level, but also the phenomena of parapsychology and 'confluential events'. We have seen that ESP and 'synchronicity' often overlap, so that a supposedly paranormal event can be interpreted either as a result of ESP or as a case of 'synchronicity' . . . . The present theory suggests that in a similar way telepathy, clairvoyance, precognition, psychokinesis and synchronicity are merely *different manifestations under different conditions of the same universal principle*—i.e., the integrative tendency operating through both causal and acausal agencies. (emphases in original)[52]

This connection between the paranormal and the synchronistic is at the heart of this entire three-volume study. We have examined the coincidences of history, such as those that surround the various political assassinations in America in the last half of the twentieth century. We have also studied some paranormal phenomena. We have explored theories regarding the practices of shamanism, the techniques of mind control, the manifestos of the surrealists, the espionage of the remote viewers, and the visions of the UFOlogists. The Frenchmen, Pauwels and Bergier, have suggested that coincidence may offer us a new way of looking at history; Jung and Pauli have suggested that coincidence may offer us a new way of looking at reality. The theories presented in this chapter—to which an increasing number of physicists and other scientists subscribe—may offer not only a way of looking at history, but a way of taking an active part in its creation.

THE RED TINCTURE

> Consciousness is basically a device for registering meaning . . .
>
> —Colin Wilson, *Order of Assassins: The Psychology of Murder*[53]

There is a tool with which we are theoretically able to cause change to occur at what we may call the quantum level (and, correspondingly, on the higher levels as well, once the fundamental change has taken place at the root level of the quantum). That tool is *meaning*. And the phenomenon of synchronicity as understood by Pauli and Jung reveals this meaning in action.

Those new to quantum physics will probably find it strange that one of the pioneers of this discipline was intimately familiar with alchemy, psychology, and even the *I Ching*, and could carry on a correspondence (and hold his own) with the likes of a Carl Gustav Jung. One comes away from the correspondence between Jung and Pauli with a sense that the physicist Pauli understood that the Jungian idea of the unconscious and its structures was essential to a complete grasp of not only psychology but also physics. Pauli's letters are full of reference to Kepler, whom he studied not so much for his contribution to science but rather for his alchemical work, in which Pauli saw the germ of quantum physics.

Pauli was a consistent and dedicated recorder of his dreams, and he would analyze them in concert with Jung, not only during the two years of Pauli's therapy with Jung, but long after that therapy had ended and the two had developed a kind of professional relationship based on the exchange of ideas, principally those concerning synchronicity.

Pauli's dreams were remarkable in that their symbolism seemed to mirror his philosophical preoccupations. As someone who was familiar with alchemical authors such as Robert Fludd, he was able to communicate with Jung on a shared deep level. Pauli understandably felt a certain kinship with the alchemists, since they were—at least in Jung's view—attempting to harmonize physics with consciousness, with spirituality, and this was obviously a concern of Pauli's, as is evident from the correspondence. While Pauli was certainly interested in how his dreams were relevant to his personal growth, he also had the desire to learn how they contributed to understanding the broader picture of quantum physics and consciousness.

These letters are a valuable resource, for they demonstrate an approach toward psychology by a physicist, while Jung is approaching physics through psychology. There are occasions when Pauli will correct a malapropism of Jung's indicating a too hasty-analogy between some element of physics and that of psychology, and these are valuable as well, for they show how deeply Pauli was reading Jung. They also discuss astrology and other "occult" practices, as well as some of the experiments in parapsychology of the day, such as those by Duke University professor J.B. Rhine. It should be remembered that this correspondence lasted from the 1930s to the 1950s; that is, it spanned the years of the rise of Nazism, World War II, the first atomic bombs, and the Cold War. Pauli was Austrian, and Jung was Swiss. They were both German-speaking Europeans caught up in the madness that science, occultism, and politics had unleashed on the world. Taken in this light, their letters have a certain poignancy.

It is on the subject of synchronicity and the "meaningful coincidence" however that the two men are most fascinating. Rather than dismiss coincidence as scientifically irrelevant or trivial, they approach it as evidence of the operation of a deeper physical process, and quite possibly as the crossroads of physics and consciousness.

In a letter to Jung dated June 28, 1949, Pauli—discussing a little-known essay of Schopenhauer's on "the ultimate union of necessity and chance"—writes,

> . . . whereas [Schopenhauer] wanted at all costs to cling to rigid determinism along the lines of the classical physics of his day, we have now acknowledged that in the nuclear world, physical events cannot be followed in causal chains

> through time and space. Thus, the readiness to adopt the idea on which your work is based, that of the "meaning as an ordering factor," is probably considerably greater among physicists that it was in Schopenhauer's day.[54]

Jung and Pauli were discussing "meaning as an ordering factor" in the context of consciousness—in the perception of meaningful coincidences by the conscious mind—as well as in the nuclear world. The assumption being made by both Jung and Pauli is that somehow the rules of the quantum or nuclear world also obtained in consciousness, if not in the Newtonian world of linear cause-and-effect. What the modern theories of "quantum consciousness" propose is that there exists a mechanism in the brain that may be in control of consciousness and that this mechanism functions at the quantum level where non-locality is a feature: a level where the Newtonian concepts of time and space do not apply. Pauli goes a step further by associating Jung's idea of synchronicity with an alchemical process that Jung refers to as the *conjunction process* and what the alchemists referred to in the Latin as *coniunctio*. The conjunction process is the union of opposites that leads to wholeness, to healing, for which normal human sexual relations (or "Eros") may be considered emblematic. And one of the alchemical symbols of the successful completion of this process is the "red tincture":

> . . . what strikes me first from the psychological angle is that a far-reaching parallel exists with what the alchemists referred to as the "production of the red tincture." Experience has shown me that what you call a "*conjunction process*" is generally conducive to the appearance of the "synchronistic" phenomenon . . . . And it is more likely to make its appearance *when the pairs of opposites keep in balance as much as possible*. (emphasis in original)[55]

Pauli goes on to compare the concept of radioactivity to synchronicity:

> . . . Just as in physics, a radioactive substance (through "active precipitation" from developing gaslike substances) radioactively "contaminates" a whole laboratory, so the synchronistic phenomenon seems to have the tendency to *spread* into the consciousness of several people. (emphasis in original)[56]

And:

> . . . The physical phenomenon of radioactivity consists in the transition of the atomic nucleus of the active substance from an unstable early state to its stable final state . . . in the course of which the radioactivity finally stops. Similarly, the synchronistic phenomenon . . . accompanies the transition from an unstable state of consciousness into a new stable position, in balance with the

> unconscious, a position in which the synchronistic borderline phenomenon has vanished again.[57]

This is quite clearly a workable hypothesis for the operation of synchronicity as a phenomenon which moves from an unstable state of consciousness to a stable one, at which point it disappears.

Pauli goes a bit further in a letter written to Jung on June 4, 1950 (at the outbreak of the Korean War), in which he relates more dream material, and then writes of his experiences at Princeton University, where he discussed synchronicity "on several occasions." He then makes an interesting comment which is very much in line with Jung's own published writing on synchronicity:

> . . . I made a point of stressing the difference between the *spontaneous* appearance of the phenomenon . . . and the *induced* phenomenon (by means of a preliminary treatment or a rite), as is the case with mantic practices (*I Ching* or *ars geomantica*). (emphasis in original)[58]

Spontaneous synchronicity and *induced* synchronicity. Here we come to the very heart of the power behind the sinister forces. Even Pauli seems somehow aware of the larger implications of this theory when he writes to Jung on November 28, 1936:

> I would like to hear sometime what you think about the collection of dreams . . . in which the dark anima asserts with a certain persistence that there is a "magical" connection between sexuality and eroticism on the one hand, and political or historical events on the other.[59]

In all the writings of the physicists and the quantum consciousness theorists we have encountered thus far, there has been avoidance of the core question at the heart of their identification of synchronicity ("meaningful coincidence" and "acausal connecting principle") with quantum mechanics: the political ramifications of a consciousness that can be manipulated as much as subatomic particles can be manipulated, but using as the "energy source" what Pauli's "dark anima" calls "sexuality" and what Ioan Coulianu's Giordano Bruno calls "eros," resulting in the phenomenon of *induced* synchronicity

Are the many, many coincidences that surround some of America's most critical "political or historical events" representative of this type of *induced* synchronicity? Were Pauwels and Bergier correct in postulating that the phenomenon of synchronicity and meaningful-coincidence could lead to "an entirely new conception of history"? Were these scientists-intelligence officers-occultists, godfathering the birth of modern remote viewing with their disinformation article on the *Nautilus* experiments in telepathy, telling us something they already knew?

It would seem at first glance that an induced synchronicity is one in which there is an element of cause-and-effect, and thus negates the entire concept of an "acausal connecting principle"; but what Pauli references is not a means to *cause* a synchronicity to occur, but a means of *observing* synchronicity by creating an environment conducive to its observation—such as the Chinese system of divination known as the *I Ching*—or by creating an event through a normal cause-and-effect mechanism in the narrow, determinist sense which "throws off" synchronicities the way radium throws off radiation. There are occasions in which synchronicities seem to multiply; it is not known whether this is the result of conscious observation (in which naturally occurring synchronicities normally ignored are singled out for study, and thus *seem* to be multiplying) or of some other factor.

While the entire Jungian theory of synchronicity is based on its acausality, are there circumstances that are more conducive to synchronicity than others? Synchronicity is a connecting principle, connecting events that are otherwise not related by cause-and-effect, and it involves *meaning*. Meaning, as we have seen, is the bedrock of consciousness.

As Pauli pointed out above, synchronicity seems to accompany the transition from an unstable state of consciousness to a stable one. Perhaps, then, the appearance of synchronicity is an indication that an unstable state in the unconscious mind is reaching stability in full consciousness. This is in accord with Jung, who gives the phenomenon of synchronicity a grounding in the archetypes, those structures in the unconscious mind that are sources of psychic energy and which manifest themselves in dreams, visions, and art. It is the search for meaning in these phenomena that has given rise to religion and philosophy, reaching a kind of apotheosis in alchemy, which celebrated the image as repository of meaning—something which the surrealists understood at once.

Jung drew a strong comparison between ESP and synchronicity in his one published essay on synchronicity, because both phenomena seemed to violate the laws of classical physics in the same way: they ignore the limitations of space and time. The experiments in remote viewing, therefore, would be related—in Jung's view—to the phenomenon of synchronicity. One of the remarkable facts about psychic phenomena that attracted Jung's attention was the degree to which enthusiasm or strong emotional excitement affected the results of ESP tests conducted under laboratory conditions: the results were actually better if the subjects were enthusiastic about ESP, believed in ESP, or were otherwise emotionally stimulated by the testing procedure. Famous psychics, when presented with the sterile laboratory environment, often tested badly. The English trance medium Eileen J. Garrett attributed her own poor performance to the fact that "she was unable to summon up any feeling."[60] This close association of feeling and paranormal abilities (on the one hand) and feeling and synchronicity (on the other) would have been familiar to Renaissance magicians like Bruno, who considered such feelings an aspect of "eros." Given a workable set of correspondences—i.e., the magical "links" determined by the structure of the "Matrix" (to use Swann's terminology)—and sufficient "eros" in whatever form, the magician would be able to cause paranormal phenomena to occur.

In the case of Eileen Garrett, the ESP test cards used were "soulless"; she would have had better results (in her view) with something more akin to a Tarot deck. In other words, with images drawn from the pool of archetypes in the collective unconscious: the spring of synchronicity as well as of paranormal abilities.

We may recall the presentation of Penrose and Hameroff to the RAND Corporation, during which they said that the "heightened experience" was conducive to achieving the quantum state in the human brain. Psychology, medicine, and physics seem to agree with the Renaissance sorcerers in this regard.

Jung ends his 1973 monograph on synchronicity with the following sentiments:

> Synchronicity is no more baffling or mysterious than the discontinuities of physics. It is only the ingrained belief in the sovereign power of causality that creates intellectual difficulties and makes it appear unthinkable that causeless events exist or could ever occur. But if they do, then we must regard them as *creative acts*, as the continuous creation of a pattern that exists from all eternity, repeats itself sporadically, and is not derivable from any known antecedents . . . . For these reasons it seems to me necessary to introduce, alongside space, time, and causality, a category which not only enables us to understand synchronistic phenomena as a special class of natural events, but also takes the contingent partly as a universal factor existing from all eternity, and partly as the sum of countless individual acts of creation occurring in time. (emphasis in original)[61]

Creative acts. A pattern, like Swann's "Matrix," that exists from all eternity. The sum of countless individual acts of creation. The creative acts not only of art and music and literature in the normal sense of creation but also the creative acts of politicians, generals, bishops, and popes. The creative act of ritual magic, the shamanistic séance, the Nuremberg rally, the assassination of a president, the coronation of a king.

History, then, can be understood as a function of the operation of this principle in a higher sense as surely as—in a grosser sense—the cause-and-effect mechanism of Newtonian physics is a useful way of looking at wars and elections and assassinations: accumulations of dates and places and names that are quantifiable and identifiable, like the chemical formulae we learn in high school science classes. In this "higher sense," historical events are linked *sub rosa* or *sub mensa* by connections and "correspondences" that only come to our attention as intriguing little coincidences or ironic commentaries, the stuff of "deep politics," not admissible as evidence in a court of law but nonetheless demonstrating motive in a more profound way: the motive of another, occult participant in the crime; for the pattern of connections understood by Pauli, when acted upon by Arthur Young's "quantum of action," can produce effects in unforeseen ways and lead us back to "first causes" we would never have expected.

To students of Renaissance magician Giordano Bruno, such as the late Professor Ioan Culianu, the links between persons, objects, and events can be activated through "eros." As Aleister Crowley would say, centuries after Bruno, "Love is the law, love under Will." Will is Arthur Young's "quantum of action," and "love" or "eros" is the energy expended by that Will. Will may be thought of as intention, an intellectual decision made by a human being to effect some change; love or *eros* is the power of that intention when linked to the object of the will. If the energy is powerful enough, and the link substantial enough, then change can be effected *at a distance*, *instantaneously* and with *no loss of energy*.

This idea of unmediated change at a distance is central to the idea of occultism, but anathema to most modern models of science beginning with Newton, though Newton himself was a practicing astrologer and occultist. In the kind of physics one learns in school, objects must act upon each other to effect change. A billiard ball must strike another billiard bill, or a gust of wind toss dried leaves along the ground, or radio waves be picked up by an antenna and modulated into sound. In other words, all change is mediated locally. The idea of a kind of mental ray that emanates from our brain or our eyes and charges across space in an instant to move a solid object, or "see" events at a distance, is the stuff of comic books and science fiction; yet that is just what the modern theories of quantum consciousness suggest *might* be possible.

To Jung, the link that exists between these events is entirely psychological; i.e., there is no physical basis for the link, otherwise we are back at the cause-and-effect Newtonian school of physics, and synchronicity operates outside those parameters. The links are connections of *meaning,* and it is still doubtful whether physics can demonstrate a scientific basis for meaning. However, can consciousness act upon matter and change it?

Of course, every time we make a conscious decision to do something—to lift a book or throw a ball—we are demonstrating the action of consciousness upon matter. A traditional scientist could disagree, however, by saying that a complex series of physical actions involving human musculature and the firing of neurons in the nervous system is what "caused" the book to be lifted or the ball to be thrown. To Arthur Young, the decision to lift the book or throw the ball is a demonstration of another type of law, but just how "physical" is decision-making? Is it the result of an eventually-predictable set of natural steps in a linear chain of cause and effect? If so, then human beings have no will and cannot be judged for their actions. This was the problem facing Arthur Young, and it contributes to the discussion about synchronicity.

> *Manson's situation is, however, infinitely worse. From the very beginning, his experiences seemed to inform him that what we all secretly know about our existential condition might* very well be *wrong!*
>
> —R.C. Scharff, "Understanding Charles Manson," in *The Manson Murders: A Philosophical Inquiry* (emphasis in original)[62]

The issues of good luck versus bad luck are familiar to the general public, but these matters scientists consider to be sheer chimeras of superstition, without any basis in reality. The Communists, of course, considered luck—and all its ancillary charms, talismans, potions, spells—to be part of the opiate of the people for the very same reason: it was unscientific, and adoption of practices like these only enslaved the people and kept them from participating in the real power of the oligarchy, where it was believed luck (good or bad) did not exist. Likewise, any belief in miracles and psychic healing, etc. was derided in favor of confidence in the science of medicine. If only everyone abandoned these silly beliefs and instead adopted a purely scientific outlook with its faith in the miracles of modern medicine, then everyone would be better off.

Except that people still die in hospital beds. People are still hit by cars, drown at sea, and have jetliners crash into their office buildings. While science can account for *how* so much evil happens in the world, it cannot offer any reason *why*. It has abandoned that aspect of chemical and physical reactions to the moralists, but at the same time it has cut the moralists off at the knees with its insistence that everything that happens in the universe happens as a result of mechanistic laws. Thus, the people—for whom their own individual lives are perhaps more important than the big picture of scientific advancement and statistical probabilities of survival—fall back upon charms, talismans, prayers, shamans, psychic healing and all the rest. While science insists that none of this works, it is incapable of ensuring any individual that he or she will not be stricken by disease, or die as the result of a car accident, a terrorist strike, a falling brick.

These things are the result of a confluence of events in the Matrix, and the person who is victimized by them is occupying a particular spot—not only in space and time but also in another dimension, the quantum dimension perhaps where considerations of space and time are not so ironclad as they are in the perceivable world—where the scarlet threads of murder, sickness, and natural disaster may run through him and annihilate him. The use of charms, talismans, prayers, etc. is intended to readjust an individual's position in the Matrix so that these threads do not strangle him; this conscious focus on avoiding pain and misery may cause neural firings affecting the quantum level, where the microtubules make minute adjustments to the parameters of time and space, and the individual narrowly misses being beaten, eaten, or otherwise incapacitated in an event we refer to as "coincidence."

Science is also unable to explain the basis for the profound sense of loss we can feel at the death of a loved one; or the guilt in recognizing the evil of our own past actions. These are the emotions, after all, that prompt the survivors to pick up a gun or blow up a bus. Psychology (surely an inferior science by any method of calculation) only admits that these feelings exist, and that one must come to terms with them . . . but these are ideas that are the product of a worldview that has been formed by scientific thought, which is, itself, weak on questions of moral responsibility and spirituality. The idea that negative feelings should be exorcised—by psychotherapy or drugs—is the mechanistic scientific worldview taken to its logical conclusion. As R.D. Laing and others have pointed out, it may be wrong to consider anti-social behavior (such as that of the schizophrenic) as something that must be suppressed with anti-psychotic drugs and leather restraints. There may be another dimension to the human experience—to consciousness—that science does not understand, because it refuses to acknowledge that there is any importance to events outside the parameters of its measurements. It is, once again, the case of the drunk looking for his keys under a streetlight because the light is better there. The keys are in the darkness. And in the darkness is superstition, mysticism, art, music, madness, and death. The hungry ghosts.

ENDNOTES

1 Graham Hancock, *The Mars Mystery*, Seal Books, Toronto, 1998, p. 380
2 Octavio Paz, *The Labyrinth of Solitude*, Grove Press, NY, 1978, p. 69
3 Kenneth Patchen, *The Journal of Albion Moonlight*, New Directions, NY, 1961, p. 152
4 William L. Moore, *The Philadelphia Experiment*, Fawcett Crest, NY, 1984, p. 76
5 Jim Garrison, *On The Trail of the Assassins*, Warner Books, NY, 1991, p. 135
6 Louis Pauwels and Jacques Bergier, *The Morning of the Magicians*, Mayflower, St Albans, 1973, p. 135
7 James Kirsch, "Carl Gustav Jung and the Jews: The Real Story," *Journal of Psychology and Judaism* 6, No. 2 (Spring-Summer 1982), p. 113–43
8 Lingering Shadows: Jungians, Freudians, and Anti-Semitism, Aryeh Maidebaum and Stephen A. Martin eds., Shambhala, Boston and London, 1991
9 C.G. Jung, *Synchronicity: An Acausal Connecting Principle*, Bollingen, Princeton University Press, Princeton, 1973, p. 19
10 F. David Peat, *Synchronicity: The Bridge Between Matter and Mind*, Bantam Books, NY, 1987, p. 16
11 Ibid., p. 16
12 Arthur Young, *The Foundations of Science: The Missing Parameter*, Broadside Editions, San Francisco, 1985, p. 6
13 Aleister Crowley, *Goetia*, Magickal Childe Publishing, NY, 1989, p. 6
14 Roger Penrose, *The Emperor's New Mind*, Oxford University Press, Oxford, 1989, p. 302
15 Ibid., p. 304–5
16 Arthur Koestler, *The Roots of Coincidence*, Hutchinson & Co., London, 1972
17 S.R. Hameroff, A. Kaszniak, and A.C. Scott (eds.,), Toward a Science of Consciousness—The First Tucson Discussions and Debates, MIT Press, Cambridge, MA, 1996, p. 507–540
18 Ibid.
19 Ibid., p. 507
20 Ibid., p. 507–8
21 Ibid., p. 508
22 S. R. Hameroff, "'Funda-Mentality' Is the Conscious Mind Subtly Linked to a Basic Level of the Universe?" *Trends in Cognitive Sciences*, 1998, vol.2, p. 119–24
23 Ibid.
24 Ibid.
25 Ibid.
26 S. R. Hameroff, "Quenching qualms about quantum consciousness: Reply to Spier and Thomas," p. 125–127
27 H.P. Lovecraft, *The Best of H.P. Lovecraft*, Ballantine, New York, 1982, p. 356
28 Jim Schnabel, *Remote Viewers: The Secret History of America's Psychic Spies*, Dell, NY, 1997
29 Russell Targ and Keith Harary, *The Mind Race: Understanding and Using Psychic Powers*, New English Library, London, 1986
30 David Morehouse, *Psychic Warrior: Inside the CIA's Stargate Program*, St Martin's Press, NY, 1996
31 Schnabel, op. cit., p. 89
32 Ibid., p. 151
33 Ibid., p. 182–183
34 Ibid., p. 188
35 Ibid., p. 188
36 Ibid., p. 188–189
37 Turan Rifat, "Military Development of Remote Mind-Control Technology," *Nexus*, Volume 3, #6, Oct-Nov 1996
38 Schnabel, op. cit., p. 220
39 Richard Sauder, *Kundalini Tales*, Adventures Unlimited Press, Kempton, Illinois, 1998
40 Schnabel, op. cit., p. 296
41 Ibid., p. 168–169
42 Sauder, op. cit., p. 14
43 Schnabel, op. cit., p. 213
44 Jonathan Franzen, *The Corrections*, Picador USA, NY, 2002, p. 322
45 Arthur Koestler, *Janus*, Vintage Books, NY, 1979, p. 76
46 Ibid., p. 15

47 Ibid., p. 13
48 Ibid., p. 113
49 Ibid., p. 144
50 Ibid., p. 267
51 Ibid., p. 266
52 Ibid., p. 270
53 Colin Wilson, *Order of Assassins: The Psychology of Murder*, Panther Books, St Albans, 1975, p. 167
54 Atom and Archetype: The Pauli/Jung Letters 1932–1958, edited by C.A. Meier, Princeton University Press, Princeton, 2001, p. 38
55 Ibid., p. 40
56 Ibid., p. 41
57 Ibid., p. 41
58 Ibid., p. 44
59 Ibid., p. 16
60 Jung, op. cit., p. 18
61 Ibid., p. 102–103
62 R.C. Scharff, "Understanding Charles Manson," in The Manson Murders: A Philosophical Inquiry, David E. Cooper, Editor, Schenkrian Publishing Co., Cambridge, 1974

CENTRAL INTELLIGENCE AGENCY
UNITED STATES OF AMERICA

SECTION SIX:

HUNGRY GHOSTS

Buddhism teaches the existence of hungry ghosts . . . . The Chinese call these ghosts 'kwei' and believe that it is they who give an enormous amount of trouble to human beings such as making them sick, taking possession of them, haunting their houses, and so on. Those 'kwei' or evil dissatisfied spirits whose families have neglected them by not making ritualistic offerings to them or those who died suddenly and violently, become hungry ghosts, out to seek vengeance against human beings.

—Tan Teik Beng, *Beliefs and Practices Among Malaysian Chinese Buddhists*[1]

I am wearing the talisman of invisibility so that now even my shadow is gone, shrink-wrapped around my invisible flesh, tight to the invisible bone. I wander abroad, among the nomads, stepping carefully over the moving bundles of rags that clot the landscape like sores on diseased flesh. These are the Arabs that haunt my dreams, the wanderers of the waste I know as Queens.

Some of them will die tonight, of exposure to the harsh winds and the cancerous dampness that creeps up from the pavement and down from the walls. Their minds feast on their bodies, devouring their anatomies by inches, and when a homeless street person dies the mind lives on as a hungry ghost, haunting the Underground stations, the crumbling concrete platforms, the rusted rails . . . .

Lee Harvey Oswald once lived in Russia. Like Gogol. Like Dostoevsky. He spoke Russian, and had a Russian wife. That is why Gogol never finished Dead Souls, for Lee had not yet been born.

But Gogol, a voice crying in the wilderness, was his John the Baptist, and Dostoevsky was his St. Paul.

I passed by Jesus on the street today, but he pretended not to know me.

—Peter Levenda, *The Black Pullet*, unpublished ms.

Are you being sinister or is this some form of practical joke?

—Allen Ginsberg, "America," January 17, 1956

CHAPTER TWENTY-TWO

HAUNTED HOUSE

Without absolutely expressing a doubt whether the stalwart Puritan had acted as a man of conscience and integrity throughout the proceedings which have been sketched, they, nevertheless, hinted that he was about to build his house over an unquiet grave. His home would include the home of the dead and buried wizard, and would thus afford the ghost of the latter a kind of privilege to haunt its new apartments, and the chambers into which future bridegrooms were to lead their brides, and where children of the Pyncheon blood were to be born.

—Nathaniel Hawthorne, *The House of the Seven Gables*

. . . agents from the federal intelligence community have entered private practice by the tens of thousands, impinging invisibly, but profoundly, on current events and our perception of them. The specter they raise is one of a country "haunted" by its wandering spooks . . . light has always been the most dependable means of exorcism. So it is that the haunting of America will end only when our secret history becomes public knowledge.

—Jim Hougan, *Spooks*[2]

I have been asked if it is possible to strike an entire community through magic. My answer must be yes . . . . It is possible for the demon to use one person to strike even a very large group—these groups can even take over or influence one or more nations.

—Fr. Gabriele Amorth, Chief Exorcist of Rome[3]

As we have seen, not only do private intelligence agents haunt America, but the entire secret history of the nation is replete with covert action by a variety of individuals and official and quasi-official government organizations that have penetrated not only domestic political parties, terrorist groups, revolutionary cabals, and cults, but have also penetrated the inner senses of the human mind. Like the ghost-story spooks of children's fairy tales, they have invaded our dreams, our waking thoughts, and our sleeping unconscious to an extent no one would have believed possible one hundred years ago, using a variety of techniques: from the hypnosis and automatic writing of the shell-shock therapists and surrealist artists of the first half of the twentieth century, to the drugs, psychic driving, psychological warfare, and remote viewing of the last half, governments have been intent on delving into the powers—and understanding the weaknesses—of the human mind. But by limiting our collective attention to questions of the mind only, we have ignored what may be a larger issue, a more dangerous threat; when we use the word "mind" we are making a value judgment where psychological, parapsychological, and paraphysical phenomena are concerned. We have successfully robbed "mind" of spirit. That may have been a mistake.

While medical men like Dr. Cameron hammered at the neurological functions of the human brain with drugs and sensory deprivation in an effort to erase memory and recreate personality from the ground up, other scientists and intelligence officers approached the mind directly through the manipulation of images. In this, they were following in the footsteps of the ancient Greek philosophers, who understood that phantasms were the only means through which the real world was perceivable to the soul. The Greek word from which we get "fantasy"—*fantasia*—is translated as "imagination, the power by which an object is presented to the mind (the object presented being *fantasma*),"[4] and was common usage in the age of Plato and Aristotle. It represents a surprisingly prescient understanding of how the brain "sees": an object is presented to the brain as a *phantom*, as an image. In other words, there is an intermediate step between the perception of an object and its appearance in the brain: the image. The ancient Greeks understood this and, later, the Renaissance philosopher-magicians who realized that in this image-making faculty of the brain there resides great power, for the brain relies on images exclusively, and treats everything it "sees"—trees, sky, people, artifacts—as images. It is not dissuasive that the images thus perceived also bring with them sounds, and smells, and tactile sensations. These are all part of the complex "image" created by the brain in order to contemplate "reality." To the Renaissance magician, this entire construct could be fabricated in order to cause change to occur in the world: focus on the image itself, on the "technology" of the image, and one could obtain tremendous power, for the language of the brain is image. Image *is* reality, and reality is nothing more than one long propaganda film.

When one speaks or writes of "mind control," a presumption is often made that one is a conspiracy theorist reveling in the most outlandish tales of sinister government plots to brainwash the masses. Unfortunately, the historical record is clear. Intelligence organs—including those of the military—have been involved in precisely that sort of research in many countries for at least the past sixty years, if not longer. What has been generally ignored in the books and papers published thus far on the subject is the extent to which real knowledge about the functions and processes of human consciousness has been obtained in this manner; what has also been ignored is the blowback from these programs. Scientists were not allowed to publish the most exciting results of their research, as they came under security classification. Men like Hal Puthoff and Russell Targ, Ewen Cameron and

Frank Olson and William Sargant were prohibited from sharing their work with their peers. Always listening was the enemy—the Soviet Union and the People's Republic of China, countries devoted to atheism and credited with the first applications of what would become known as "brainwashing," itself a spiritual technology stripped of its religious context.

Most writings on the technology of the religious experience—whether it be yoga, or meditation, or shamanistic ritual, or the taking of peyote or magic mushrooms—stress the dangers of unguided spiritual "experimentation." In the days most of these texts were written, there was no science of psychology, no practice of neurology or understanding of neuropathy. Madness was often considered in purely theological terms. Even so, the warnings were explicit: disaster would be the outcome of any attempt to reach nirvana through crude, artificial means, or without the guidance of an experienced guru, or by an unclean and untrained ascetic. In the case of government investigation of the paranormal, and of the human mind, none of these precautions were heeded. Psychiatrists like Ewen Cameron ran roughshod over their patients' psyches, doing permanent damage to the consciousness of innocents. Bureaucrats like Sidney Gottlieb authorized government expenditures for covert research that was responsible for massively dosing prisoners, psychopaths, and children with hallucinogens and other drugs . . . human beings whose identities are no longer known to us or to anyone. Alive? Or dead? Serial killers . . . or ghosts?

Others have died in the attempt to discover the truth about reality, truth that was protected by men in white jackets or blue uniforms or grey flannel suits. Captain Mantell, Morris Jessup, James McDonald . . . all died in pursuit of that truth, the first man in actual pursuit of a UFO, and the last two suicides from the stress and humiliation that dogs every genuine researcher into this extremely sensitive subject.

These are the hungry ghosts that haunt America. These, and so many others. As we have seen in various statements by a wide range of experts, it has become increasingly difficult to separate an intelligence operation from the operation of another force in the world: two phenomena, both secret and "occult," linked by a common thread of coincidence and synchronicity. Where did this "other" force come from? How do we cope with its effects? How do we exorcise the hungry ghosts of America? As frivolous as these questions may seem to a traditional historian, they actually go to the heart of what it means to be human, and as well to the heart of what we have come to call "reality." Questions of good and evil, life after death, punishment and revenge, God and demons . . . for all of these ideas, which are central to the life of every human being, we normally rely upon priests or ministers or other religious leaders, or, if we are atheists, upon philosophers, artists and even scientists. It would never occur to us to question history itself, which we see largely as a stage on which these ideas are played out in a kind of cosmic drama, the end of which we cannot predict but which we hope will mean that the guilty will be punished and the sufferings of the innocent redeemed; but the answers to our perpetual questions about life and existence may be encoded in our history—not the "Disneyland" version, to use Jim Hougan's phrase for the type of canned history one is taught in schools and universities, but—our secret history, our forgotten history for which our classical, schoolroom-style history is but the outward sign and symbol.

The historical model I am proposing in these volumes should be obvious by now. By tracing the darker elements of the American experience from the earliest days of the Adena and Hopewell cultures through the discovery by Columbus, the English settlers in Massachusetts and the Salem witchcraft episode, the rise of Joseph Smith, Jr. and the Mormons via ceremonial magic and Freemasonry, up to the twentieth century and the support of Nazism by American financiers and politicians before, during, and after World War II, and the UFO phenomenon coming on the heels of that war, we can see the outlines of a kind of political ectoplasm taking shape in this historical séance: politics as a continuation of religion by other means. The ancillary events of the Charles Manson murders, the serial killer phenomenon, Jonestown, and the assassinations of Jack Kennedy, Bobby Kennedy, Martin Luther King, and Marilyn Monroe are all the result of the demonic possession of the American psyche, like the obscenities spat out by little Regan, tied to her bed and shrieking at the exorcists. It is said that demonic possession is both a way of testing us, and of making us aware of the real conflict taking place within us every day.

The fact that so many American men and women in positions of power and authority have been specifically involved with occult practices is something that not even I had anticipated before I began the research for this work. Initially, I treated the one or two politicians who "dabbled" as a kind of anomaly; my original focus had been the unhealthy, almost incestuous relationship between Church and State, in America specifically and in the world in general: religious beliefs as the motivation for dangerous policy decisions and strategic maneuvers (such as Ronald Reagan's apocalyptic Christianity, and Nancy Reagan's devotion to agenda by astrology, and George W. Bush's devotion to evangelical Christianity). The more I looked, however, the more I found men with bizarre beliefs and involved in questionable, occult practices at the highest levels of the American government, and buried deep within government agencies. I also discovered that occultism was embraced by the American military and intelligence establishments as a weapon to be used in the Cold War; and as they did so, they unleashed forces upon the American populace that cannot be called back.

Those that were not involved in occultism *per se* were involved with Nazism in one form or another, and thus were aiding and abetting not only an enemy of America and an enemy of humanity in general, but what was most certainly and by any definition a cult: the most powerful and most dangerous cult the modern world has seen so far. The moral imbecility of those engaging these men as scientists, spies, and agents of American foreign policy—and then defending them against those who begged for justice, hiding them on American soil—is beyond comprehension. The guilty include the Dulles brothers, Walkers and Bushes, Henry Ford, Richard Nixon, and so many other household names in American politics. We can try to make excuses for them, try to rationalize away their actions in the light of *realpolitik*, but then we become as bad as the Germans who claimed they were only following orders.

Watergate revealed the existence of "sinister forces" to me in many ways. The scandal opened the floodgates of conspiracy theories going back to the Kennedy assassination and beyond. It tied together so many loose ends, yet posited more questions than it offered answers, revealing a secret political struggle that had been going on for decades, ripping apart the very fabric of America with a populace oblivious to it all. One inevitably was forced back to the CIA and the mind-control experiments that began in the late 1940s and extended nearly to the present day. Coincidence piled on coincidence, indicating the existence of a powerful, subliminal force working at the level of chaos—at the quantum level—and struggling to manifest itself in our reality, our consciousness, our political agenda. This dynamic was uncovered by a Swiss psychologist and an Austrian physicist, but it capably describes a force working within the context of American history and American politics that is suppurating below the consciousness of the people but able to erupt without notice. A sinister force.

Fascism.

When the science editor of *Time* magazine—Leon Jaroff—became aware of the remote-viewing experiments taking place at SRI under Puthoff and Targ, he was alarmed. To Jaroff, the paranormal research at SRI was akin to the occultism that, in his view, gave rise to fascism in Germany, and he felt that *their research should be destroyed.*[5] Theodore Adorno (1903–69), the German philosopher whose "F-scale" or "fascism scale" became a controversial subject in psychological circles after his expulsion from Germany in 1934, attacked the "irrational" for the very same reason: his belief that the irrational (to Adorno, everything from astrology to occultism) in mass culture inevitably leads to fascism.[6] One is almost forced to ask the obvious question, the one not asked in polite company: does the "irrational" include religion? Of course, it does, but science prefers religion to be a vehicle for instruction in ethical culture, and not supernaturalism; yet it is humanity's confrontation with the supernatural that lead to the development of religion and, eventually, ethics and moral values.

Therefore, it is perhaps not the belief in the irrational that leads to fascism, however, but the *marginalization* of the irrational that does so, for it encourages a parallel belief in conspiracy. Since people in general have direct experience of the paranormal in their lives—from events as trivial as coincidence to as traumatic as poltergeist activity, incidents of ESP, UFO sightings, or even remote-viewing—to find their experience ridiculed by the established authority is insupportable. They confront this "disconnect" coming to them from authority, and thus begin to question authority—its wisdom, or its motives—itself. They become prey to those who would encourage their "irrational" beliefs and point an accusing finger at the very authorities—scientific or political—who would deny them the secret power or arcane knowledge they could otherwise possess. The debasement of the paranormal in culture only serves to increase its value among the population, who treasure their unusual experiences in secret, and who build up entire cosmologies around them, since they have no other context in which to understand what they *know* to have occurred. Thus, for me, fascism is the result not of irrational beliefs but of *the monopolization of those beliefs by others*: men and women who exploit the divide between the direct experience of the masses and the intellectualist denial of their experiences by a privileged, powerful elite.

The shaman in primitive cultures is a person who has managed to integrate the irrational into his own personality and, by extension, into the life of his society. His act of personal self-transcendence—to use Koestler's terminology—is an act of social integration which also successfully integrates the irrational into the life of society through his social role as healer, therapist, and seer. The serial killer is a shaman who has not managed to integrate the irrational with the life of his society, as society no longer has a place for it or a context within which to understand what is happening to him. The irrational in modern society is consigned to the dustheap of psychoanalysis, if not of history itself. The same is true of the fascist.

The fascist embraces the irrational because it is transcendental, and the fascist yearns to transcend his natural state, to become more than human, to become—as Hitler said—a "new man." Since the fascist becomes the only political person who tolerates the irrational, he becomes the figurehead of the people who have encountered the irrational in their own lives. The fascist is a shaman who has not managed to integrate the irrational in his own life, but who still needs the approval and support—and, if possible, the adulation—of society in order to act out his fantasies. The serial killer differs only in that he has no need of society's approval: he gave that up a long time ago, and regards society with hatred and suspicion. The fascist and the serial killer share this in common: they both feel a tremendous need for self-transcendence but fail to integrate the irrational needs and experiences of their psyches with either themselves (the fascist) or with society (the serial killer). The successful shaman has done both: he has interiorized the essential conflicts of the irrational experience in the "rational" world, and has also integrated both the elements of his own personality as well as his own personality (with all of its irrational experiences) with society in general. However, had society in general not welcomed his achievements, there is every possibility that he would have become a social pariah and, from there, a dangerous individual, fueled by the dangerous component of shamanism: sexuality.

Our society has no place for the shaman, so we marginalize both him and his experiences. The shaman comes back, then, to haunt us in other ways: either as the iconic serial killer or as the dreary fascist. Both are evil, either evil "in and of themselves" to borrow the clanking terminology of the existentialists, or as channels for an evil force that is older than history, but of whose machinations history is the unhappy result.

THE ORIGINS OF EVIL

> Myth is a two-way mirror in which ritual and philosophy may regard one another. It is the moment when people normally caught up in everyday banalities are suddenly (perhaps because of some personal upheaval) confronted with problems that they have hitherto left to the bickerings of the philosophers; and it is the moment when philosophers, too, come to terms with the darker, flesh-and-blood aspects of their abstract inquiries.
>
> —Wendy Doniger O'Flaherty[7]

The problem of evil is one that has bothered theologians and philosophers for thousands of years. The problem can be expressed simply: Why does God permit evil to exist in the world? If God is all-powerful, then God must be permitting evil to exist; if so, then God is evil, or blind to the sufferings caused by evil (which cannot be so, because one of the definitions of God is that he/she is all-powerful and all-knowing). The only logical conclusions to draw are that either God is not all-powerful, or not all-knowing, or . . . that God is evil.

This problem did not exist in ancient times, when there were a multiplicity of gods all in conflict with each other. Human beings would cast their lot with one side or the other; the opposing side was the enemy, but not necessarily evil in the moral sense. The disasters that befell human beings—sickness, death, famine, drought, etc.—were caused by demons, the foot-soldiers of the "bad" gods. One could appease them, or exorcise them.

As the pantheism of our ancestors became the monotheism of the Jews, Christians and Muslims, God became One: the Creator and the Redeemer, the Preserver and the Destroyer. Yet, somehow God was "all good." The Christian New Testament offered us a God who was loving and merciful, holding out expectations of reward in an afterlife (obviously, it would have to be an afterlife; the good and the innocent are cannon-fodder in *this* world). The God of the monotheists demands loyalty above all else. He will test that loyalty with severe trials, such as experienced by Job in the Old Testament, when Satan persuaded God to let him push Job to the limit with every imaginable suffering: essentially laying a wager with God that Job would give up His worship and turn apostate. Somehow that scenario became the operative one in the monotheistic cults: evil existed because it was God's way of testing our loyalty to Him.

Of course, that gave rise to a host of other logical inconsistencies. If God is, indeed, all-knowing, then God would have known in advance how Job would have reacted. There would have been no need of any test, not for Job and not for the rest of us. Why, then, are we tested?

We are then given the argument that God is demonstrating that we have free will, and can choose to be loyal to Him or not. Again, that begs the question. If God is all-knowing, then He already knows what choices we will make. And so on.

Another argument, and one that has never garnered much support, is that what we consider to be evil—pain, suffering, death—is not evil at all. It is only our perception of these things that makes them evil. "It's all good." Unfortunately, we can easily think of dozens of cases where that argument is unacceptable: the suffering of children, for instance—beings so small and vulnerable that their suffering cannot be the result of any choice they have made. The Asians, confronted with this obvious fact, came back with the elegant concept of reincarnation. Thus, an infant who suffers in this life is paying for a sin committed in a previous incarnation. This also provides the satisfying corollary that there is a continuity of identity of some kind after death and through a long succession of rebirths. There have even been fully documented cases of small children spontaneously exhibiting knowledge of other lives in other places that they could not have garnered in their short lives but must have "remembered" from a previous existence (e.g. in *Twenty Cases Suggestive of Reincarnation*). The fact that many of these cases take place in countries and amid cultures where reincarnation is an accepted phenomenon may skew the statistics in an unsatisfactory way, and raises the suggestion that these experiences may be the result of some other kind of paranormal event, such as telepathy.

Reincarnation (with its concomitant ideal of *karma*, the burden of one's actions—good and bad—that one carries from lifetime to lifetime) *is* an elegant solution, but—like the heaven and hell of the monotheists—it admits of no real proof beyond the anecdotal. If evil is not the result of a linear chain of cause and effect—a chain over which we have control—then where did it come from? What is its purpose? Whom does it serve? And why does God not protect us from it?

The answers to these questions may not be palatable. They bring us to a mythology that is at once quite old and at the same time the stuff of science fiction and fantasy. It is as much part of the ancient Sanskrit texts as it is of the Middle Eastern Gnostic documents. It is also a recurring theme in UFO lore as well as in pulp fiction. Because it comes up so often in the human psyche, it is worth examining here, even as it has been abandoned as a workable hypothesis by the monotheists who have given us thousands of years of refinement and civilization, art and music and literature . . . and Inquisitions, Crusades, Holy wars, and genocide. It is an explanation for the schizophrenia that characterizes the human experience.

Wendy Doniger O'Flaherty—a colleague of the slain Ioan Culianu at the University of Chicago—has studied the problem of evil as it appears in Hinduism, one of humanity's oldest religions, based on one of its oldest languages: Sanskrit, a language so ancient and so complex that even today it is extremely difficult to give satisfactory translations of Sanskrit texts (as the ongoing and still uncompleted project to create a comprehensive Sanskrit dictionary has shown). What she has to say about Hindu concepts of evil is universal in application, and has resonance with early Christian and gnostic belief systems, as well as with mythologies as remote from each other as the Aztec and the Daoist. She writes,

> The belief that the gods create evil for man in order that man should depend on the gods—and the priests—recurs in Sanskrit texts. The gods find evil necessary for their very existence; they allow the demons to thrive in order that they themselves may thrive as gods, to force men to worship them.[8]

This is, of course, an exceedingly cynical appraisal of the problem, but one that is familiar to students of Hinduism. It depicts the gods as venal entities who desire worship and sacrifice, and use men—and their fear of demons—the way governments use their populations. If it is true that "the organizing principle of nations is war" then it is equally true of the cosmos, according to this view.

> The one invariable characteristic of the gods is that they are the enemies of the demons, and the one invariable characteristic of the demons is that they are opposed to the gods. For this reason, when the later myths began to apply new moral codes to the characters of individual gods and demons in myths, a number of inconsistencies arise, for the two groups, as groups, are not fundamentally *morally* opposed. (emphasis in original)[9]

This important point speaks to the problem we face in dealing with spiritual evil. Although gods and demons are at war with each other and—as Wendy Doniger O'Flaherty says elsewhere—"mankind is caught in the crossfire,"[10] there is no moral difference between the two. Each is equally good or equally bad, depending on whose propaganda you believe. It also posits an ongoing struggle for supremacy between the two groups, something that would be familiar to anyone who has studied Manichaeism and Gnostic dualism, which considers humanity the battleground between the opposing forces of light and darkness. Yet, even this concept is "reductionist":

> . . . in most Hindu texts, even when life is clearly desired and death feared, death is not the key to the struggle between gods and demons. For although they fight for the elixir of immortality, and the gods are said to win it ultimately, gods and demons are equally mortal and equally murderous to mankind. Finally, though the gods and demons are sometimes identified with light and darkness, these are merely symbolic expressions of contrast rather than true opposition.[11]

"Equally murderous to mankind." A sobering thought, and one which the monotheists reject, even as their texts are replete with instances of an angry God destroying entire cities in his wrath. The monotheists struggle to explain why God would take vengeance on living beings in one instant, but threaten eternal punishment for evildoers in hell after death in the next. Which is it? Punishment here and now, or punishment later? Or both? If we understand the existence of evil in the context of a war between opposing "gods" then evil becomes, in a sense, more palatable. The innocent always suffer in a war; civilian targets and "collateral damage" are inevitable. If we, as human beings, can assist one side or the other in this conflict and thereby ensure that one side wins, then evil—as we understand it, as the "collateral damage" of the conflict—should come to an end. This is not as sophisticated an approach as that of, say, Thomas Aquinas or St. Augustine, but it has the advantage of being logical and clear, and of not requiring the mental gymnastics necessary to place evil within a framework of the divine testing of free will and human choice.

But if the gods and demons—merely opponents in a cosmic war, after all—are in combat with each other, and if humanity has become a kind of spiritual battlefield, then where did the gods and demons come from in the first place, and why is humanity "caught in the crossfire"?

> The belief is often expressed that the demons were not only the equals of the gods but their superiors—the older brothers, the original gods from whom the gods stole the throne of heaven.[12]

This, of course, is pure Lovecraft. It is also purely Sumerian, which is probably the most ancient of all recorded religious cultures. The idea that there once existed an ancient race of gods that was overthrown by another group of deities goes back to the Sumerian creation epics. It is even reflected in the Talmudic idea of the *nephilim*. It is resurgent in the gothic horror of H.P. Lovecraft, and it makes an appearance in some of the theories of alien abduction and the Erich von Däniken *Chariots of the Gods* books. It is such a common and universal theme, that it is amazing the monotheistic religions have not managed to incorporate it into their theologies in such a way that this is no longer a controversial issue; instead it is a persistent "rumor" in literary circles as well as in alternative spiritual beliefs.

The identity of a class of Hindu gods known as the *asuras* has been the subject of a great deal of controversy in this regard. They are among the oldest of spiritual forces recognized in the Sanskrit literature, and even the name *asura* is quite controversial itself. Religious historian Wash Edward Hale (recipient of a Ph.D. in Comparative Religion from Harvard University's Divinity School in 1980) has written an entire book on the subject, demonstrating how little we actually know about the origins of Sanskrit terminology.[13] *Asura* has been linked etymologically to everything from the Zoroastrian god Ahura Mazda to a hypothetical Assyrian cult; the term *asura* itself seems to mean "lord," on that there is no disagreement, and has been applied to both humans and gods. With the passage of time, however, it seems that these beings were devalued in comparison with the *devas* who were considered the "good" gods, the *asuras* gradually taking on the characteristics of demons.

Professor of Comparative Religion at the University of Manchester, Trevor O. Ling has made a study of evil in Buddhist thought, and begins with an overview of the Hindu beliefs from which Buddhism developed. What he has to say about the *asuras* is relevant to our theme:

> According to the Udana and the Anguttara Nikaya they are said to be *ocean-dwellers*, together with various sea-monsters, nagas and gandhabbas. On the other hand they are said in the Samyutta and Anguttara Nikayas to be *dwellers in a city*. (emphasis in original)[14]

This idea of the asuras as ocean-dwellers as well as dwellers in a city, and their association with sea monsters is, of course, pure Lovecraft. His "Cthulhu" is a type of sea monster who "lies dead, but dreaming" in a lost city at the bottom of the abyss, but who is worshipped in secret by strange cults who dream of the day when his rulership will be reinstated on earth.

This concept appears also in the Sumerian creation cycles in which the ancient goddess of the abyss Tiamat—who reappears in the Biblical Hebrew term *tehom* for a kind of sea monster—is slain by a race of younger gods, children of Tiamat, who create the known world from her body ripped asunder, and from her blood and their own breath, the young gods create human beings. This is an ancient story, which nonetheless is echoed in Arthur Koestler's idea of the two human brains, one reptilian and ancient and one newer and more intellectual and calculating: humans partaking of the characteristics of both "gods."

In Biblical times, the existence of this sea-monster/demon was recognized in the term *Leviathan*, and the existence of a cult that worshipped Leviathan:

> Let them curse it that curse the day, who are ready to rouse Leviathan. (Job, iii:8)

And:

> In that day the Lord will punish with his sword, his fierce, great and powerful sword, Leviathan the gliding serpent, Leviathan the coiling serpent, he will slay the monster of the sea. (Isaiah, xxvii:1)

Certainly a strange preoccupation for a tribe who lived in the desert lands of Palestine; it is possibly a survival of Babylonian mythology, although some (such as William Smith in *Smith's Bible Dictionary*) have claimed that the Leviathan mentioned in the Bible is either a whale or a crocodile, and some translations of the Hebrew have used "dragon" in place of "monster" or "Leviathan."

Buddhism differs from Hinduism in several important respects, but germane to our study is its concept of evil. In Buddhism, evil is personified as Mara, a god (or demon) of death and evil. It is Mara's project to tempt the Buddha away from his meditations. Buddha, however, conquered Mara and at the same time conquered death itself.[15] In this, perhaps, he is a precursor to the Jesus who also conquered death, albeit in a different fashion. In Buddhism, we have a single powerful god-man, the Buddha, in conflict with a single, powerful demon, Mara. Buddha becomes superhuman during his life; Jesus—according to the predominant theology of the twenty-first century—was born a God, although there were heresies that insisted that Jesus became God while on earth.

But Mara shares a great deal in common with the Christian Satan, for Mara is an adversary and represents the created world, *Samsara*, the world of illusion and *Maya*,[16] just as Satan is said to be "Lord of this world" and is capable of taking Jesus to the mountaintop and offering him everything in sight if only he will fall down and worship the demon. Indeed, it has been alleged in various places that Buddhism—which began in India during the sixth century B.C.—came to influence Christianity through Buddhist missionaries that were said to have traveled as far as Palestine by the first century A.D. Buddhism comes as close as possible to a kind of monotheism while still retaining much of its polytheist, Hindu roots and terminology.

The danger in this approach is that one elevates evil to the level of a god, a force balancing that of good and threatening to conquer goodness, or at the very least to thwart its plans. Even Aleister Crowley, no stranger to the demonic, asserted that the Devil *per se* does not exist, that evil had been elevated by the ignorant to a monad equal in power to that of any God:

> The Devil does not exist. It is a false name invented by the Black Brothers to imply a Unity in their ignorant muddle of dispersions. A devil who had unity would be a God.[17]

Crowley accused those who worshipped evil (the "Black Brothers") of having created the Devil, which is quite a difference from the evidence of historical and scriptural texts, of course, and may reflect more of Crowley's own personal philosophy than it does years of philological and theological study. However, as the world progressed from wars fought with rocks, to bows and arrows, swords and shotguns, it still seemed as if evil was the stuff of smaller demons: the spent cartridge, the torched hut, the thrown spear. Then, the Bomb was dropped on Hiroshima and Nagasaki in August 1945. It suddenly became possible to start thinking about a *force* of evil, something unitary and powerful beyond all previous imagining. It suddenly began to look like there *was* a Devil, and weapons of mass destruction became his calling card. To concern oneself with individual demons seemed almost quaint, missing the point.

Like the Christian (and Manichaen) concept of an eternal conflict between good and evil, Buddhism acknowledges the ongoing struggle against Mara but—again, like Christianity—also maintains that the Buddha was the first to overcome

Mara, and therefore opened the road to Enlightenment for everyman. Jesus is said to have suffered and died "for our sins" and to redeem humanity; he descended into hell after his crucifixion and then ascended into heaven after his resurrection on earth, thus demonstrating his power over death. Thus, both Jesus and Buddha overcame death and became immortal; whether Jesus was born superhuman or became so during his trials in the desert and his other mortal struggles against evil and death is a purely theological issue. (Of course, one could always say that since the conquest of death by Jesus was foreordained, that he was certainly "born a God," in a kind of exegetical Monday-morning quarterbacking.) And, just as demons possess the innocent in the Christian (and Jewish) traditions explored by Oesterreich and others, so too does Mara possess innocent villagers, requiring the application of exorcisms.[18]

Although no case can be made that the Christian mythos is merely Buddhism in fancy dress, there are important similarities between Jesus' confrontation with Satan and the Buddha's confrontation with Mara. As Ling points out in his analysis of some of the literature on comparative religion which focuses on Satan and Mara,

> In each case the symbol came into being as the result of the experience and insight of a great personality. In each case it appears to have reflected the experience of critical encounter with *a spiritual force which was hostile to holiness.* (emphasis added)[19]

Of course, it is this very spiritual force that concerns us in this study.

What is fascinating about Mara is that he is the lord of the five senses, of physical reality, and *of consciousness as well.*[20] Mara is, in fact, the lord of the Matrix, for Mara's domain (*Maradheyya*) represents—in the Pali scripture known as the Sutta-Nipata—an "entanglement, strongly stretched out and very deceptive. Sometimes this is called Mara's stream."[21] The goal of Buddhism is to transcend not only physical reality (with all its limitations, passions, and other emotions) but consciousness as well, in order to attain Nirvana. This entails gradually reducing one's attachment to physical objects, then to physical sensations, entering a state of sensory deprivation in which even thoughts and ideas are "objects" to be avoided and one's individual consciousness disappears, subsumed into the collective "cosmic consciousness" that is Enlightenment. It is easy to see how attaining this state would be tantamount to conquering death, for death is an event that occurs to the physical body; in the perfect state of meditation envisaged by the Buddhists, the reliance on the body as a means of survival is abandoned. It is, perhaps, the ultimate "self-transcendence," just as Mara represents the ultimate in "self-assertion." Mara is, quite simply, the source of all problems, the pulsating core of evil.

Trevor Ling uses the analogy of a man fighting mosquitoes; one can take measures to fight against each individual mosquito, or one can take measures to defeat all mosquitoes. The same with a man being shot at: does he dodge each bullet individually, or does he take measures against the man with the gun?[22] In polytheist traditions with a multiplicity of demons, man has fought each one individually. With the coming of the Buddha, according to Ling, there was a revelation: namely, that the source of all demons was, in essence, one demon; the source of all ills was one Father of Sickness. It reoriented the focus of humanity from the day-to-day battle against hordes of individual demons/sicknesses/cruelties/horrors to the identification of a single, monist fountain of all suffering. In the Pali Canon, this is Mara.

Unfortunately, knowing this and doing something about it are two different things! We still have to dodge bullets, and mosquitoes, and evil people, one by one. It takes a certain type of individual—a Buddha, or a Buddha in the making—to focus his or her attention on the source of all evil and take careful aim. For the rest of us, there is Kevlar, and pesticides, and exorcism.

> The essence of the animistic attitude to life is that the ills which man experiences are attributed to wholly external forces. These forces, conceived as having an existence separate from his own, he regards as hostile. They must be avoided if possible . . . or they may be manipulated to advantage by one who possesses the means or the skill to do so. This last kind of response, the manipulation of hostile forces, is the one characteristic of animistic and other forms of magic. It was in this direction that animism shaded into Brahmanism in a way that is in striking contrast to the Buddhist attitude to what are called the 'low arts'. The object of the Brahmanic sacrifices was ostensibly to chain the demons; the real object was an extension of this attitude at a more profound level, namely the manipulation for men's advantage of what were believed to be certain hidden natural forces.[23]

We have already studied this "manipulation of hostile forces" as put into practice by everyone from Siberian shamans to remote viewers. It is a mainstay of Hinduism today, and the practices of Hinduism which verge on the paranormal are evidence that the knowledge of the manipulation of these forces has been cultivated and preserved through thousands of years, even as the monist traditions of Judaism, Christianity, Islam and Buddhism decry their use.

The last twenty years or so has shown a marked interest in, and popularity of, the subject of Evil. There have been cultural studies of Evil, from Howard Bloom's *The Lucifer Principle* and Paul Oppenheimer's *Evil and the Demonic*, to sociological and historical overviews such as Jeffrey Burton Russell's *The Devil: Perceptions of Evil from Antiquity to Primitive Christianity* and Ervin Straub's *The Roots of Evil: The Origins of Genocide and Other Group Violence*. Even Elaine Pagels has published *The Origins of Satan*, a study of how Satan came to be identified in early Christianity. In this age of holocaust and genocide, of Kosovo and Croatia and Cambodia, nuclear, chemical and biological weapons, the subject of Evil has become fashionable again and no historian of religion is able to ignore its appeal.

Howard Bloom, who trained as a scientist and then left science to run a public relations company for musicians such as Prince, Billy Joel, Billy Idol, Bob Marley and Bette Midler (among many others), is an example of someone who (like Koestler) has functioned in two separate worlds and has the benefit of a larger perspective. Bloom blames Evil on the necessities of evolution, and—like a first century Gnostic—places the onus directly on Nature itself. Anyone who watches the Discovery Channel is likely to be confronted with dramatic evidence of the cruelty of Nature, of course, whether it is a hurricane, earthquake, flood or simply one animal devouring another. Of course, Bloom's thesis is not so narrow as that. He borrows from Koestler even as Koestler is not identified in the text, by recapitulating Koestler's theory of the *holon,* except that the holon in this instance Bloom calls the "superorganism."

Koestler viewed everything in nature as inferior to the level above it in terms of complexity, and superior to the level below it. Essentially, what Arthur Young described in his "arc" that led down from light to nuclear particles, atoms and then molecules and from there up through plants, animals and finally man, Koestler was describing in terms of a hierarchy leading down from organisms at the top to sub-atomic particles at the bottom. Each level of Koestler's hierarchy is a subset of the level above it; conversely, each level of the hierarchy contains within it complex arrangements of the level (cells, molecules, atoms, etc.) below it. Koestler understood each "sub-assembly" of this hierarchy—whether the cells of the human heart, or the atoms that make up a molecule of water—as functioning as a "quasi-independent whole, even though isolated from the organism or transplanted into another organism."[24] To Koestler, each of these "sub-assemblies" was "Janus-faced," i.e., one face looked to the level above it and was a sub-assembly of that level, and one face looked at the level below it which contained its own sub-assemblies. This Janus-faced object Koestler calls a *holon* and emphasizes that the holon is more than the sum of its parts (in reference to its quasi-autonomous features, but also in consideration that a human being for example is more, obviously, than simply a collection of its component elements).

As noted, Bloom characterizes human beings as parts of what he calls a "superorganism,"[25] "disposable parts of a being much larger than ourselves." This is one of his "five ideas," which—he writes—"illuminates a mystery that has eternally eluded man: the root of the evil that haunts our lives. For within these five small ideas we will pursue, there lurks a force that rules us."[26] The other ideas include the principle of the self-organizing system (which is similar, again, to Koestler's concept of a "self-regulating open hierarchic order,"[27]) the meme (a "self-replicating order of ideas" which is the root of the images and visions that provide both coherence to society and which encourage it to go to war), the neural net or "group mind," and the "pecking order."

To Bloom, humanity's contribution to the violent way of life it has inherited from the apes, from Nature itself, is the "dream of peace. But to achieve that dream he will have to overcome what nature has built into him."[28] It is interesting that a writer with a scientific background as well as a political background (who wrote position papers for congressional candidates) and a business background in the media should arrive at the conclusion that evil is hard-wired in us by Nature itself, and that only by overcoming this programming can we achieve our "dream of peace." This is something that no church-going Roman Catholic would disagree with, as it is a modern explanation for what is known in the Church as "original sin": the dogma that every human being is born with the taint of sin which only a decent life of holiness can neutralize. In other words, every person born of woman is born defective in the eyes of the Church. Only becoming baptized into the Church and following its regulations will free one of this defect. (It is a great marketing gimmick, of course: *"What? I have original sin? Get it off me! Get it off me! What's it going to cost?"*)

As mentioned, this concept was well-known to the Gnostics, that disparate group of syncretist mystics who wielded tremendous influence in the first few centuries of the Christian era. By blending eastern and western, Jewish and Christian concepts into a single coherent whole, they cast a long shadow over everything from the Dead Sea Scrolls of Qumran to the Nag Hammadi texts of Egypt . . . to the Cathars and Manichaeans, and eventually to modern ceremonial magic, the rise of the secret societies, and the occult revival of the twentieth century. While there were many different versions of Gnostic belief, they agreed on some basic issues. First and foremost was the idea that matter was inherently evil, and had been created by the "demiurge," a being that opposes God and who fashioned the world from chaos, the abyss, one of whose terms is the Latin *matrix*. According to some Gnostic texts, the God in the Garden of Eden who created Adam and Eve and warned them against eating of the Tree of Knowledge was the Demiurge and *not* the benevolent Deity; God's presence in the Garden was actually that of the Serpent, who pointed the way of freedom to Eve.

The Gnostic texts—as well as traditional Biblical scripture—refer to the demonic rulers who assist the Demiurge as *archons*, a term that means "chief " or "ruler" or "prince." The archons are invariably evil, and represent forces that oppose God. In this, they are virtually identical to the Hindu *asuras*, a Sanskrit word with the same meaning as *archons*.

In Gnosticism, there are two main schools of thought concerning the true nature of evil. The "Eastern" view—which has its origins in Zoroastrianism and Manichaeanism, and thus demonstrates a possible link to Aryan Hinduism—states that good and evil are two supreme powers struggling for control of the world, and will continue to struggle forever. The "Western" view—which has its origins in Egypt and the Middle East—defines evil as a *result*, rather than something with an autonomous existence. This theory describes the creation of matter as a series of emanations of light, of spirit, leading from the divine Source and becoming grosser with each rung of descent until spirit is buried as a dim spark within matter. (This is virtually identical to the way Arthur Young explains creation.) Benjamin Walker, who writes on culture, history, and religion, has offered a concise introduction to this Gnostic belief:

> . . . evil is the natural consequence of the descent of the emanations, so that as the emanations recede from the primary divine source there is a progressive diminution in their goodness and light. Again, when God withdrew his presence to make room for the world, Satan was free to exercise his will in opposition to the divine, as a consequence of which evil arose . . . . Evil is not an abstraction or a passive condition, but a positive and violent force arising from the active operation of Satan and his archons.[29]

Of course, this is so similar to the Indian concept of Mara, the Lord of Evil, as the ruler of physical creation, the five senses, matter and even consciousness itself, that it could have been devised by a Pali scholar rather than a Syrian Gnostic.

From India to Egypt and Palestine, evil is perceived as a force under the direction of what can only be called politicians. "Lords," "chiefs," "rulers," "magistrates," or "princes," *archons* or *asuras*, the implication is the same: evil is somehow under political control. Further, matter is seen as evil, the result of an entrapment or degradation of *light*. Thus, we have two disciplines in which evil is being described: one, a scientific approach, shows evil to be the result of light "descending" and becoming matter, much like Arthur Young's famous diagram of the "arc"; the other, a political approach, shows that this matter—creation itself—is under political control by a Demiurge and his team of archons, or "rulers." God, in this context, was the Serpent in the Garden of Eden: a kind of rabble-rouser who urged Adam and Eve in their rebellion. "God," as Nik Aziz said in Malaysia, may truly be "a gangster."

Evil as matter, evil as a blind force. There is no contradiction necessary between the two, since the discoveries of quantum physics illustrate that the heart of all matter *is* force.

Ancient Egyptian religion was no exception to this rule of evil as blind force, and as an eternal opponent to the forces of light. Osiris and Set were brothers, Osiris representing Light and Set, Darkness. There are several versions of the story of the murder of Osiris by Set, but it is certain that Set did, indeed, kill his brother (the first murder in Egyptian religion is fratricide, as it is in Genesis) and dismembered his body. Again, we face dismemberment in a religious or spiritual context that is far removed from the dismemberment visions of the Siberian shamans, but which shares essential characteristics. In both the case of Osiris and the case of the shamans, dismemberment precedes illumination.

Isis, the wife (and sister) of Osiris collects the various pieces of Osiris' body after they had been scattered throughout Egypt and the Nile by Set. She puts the pieces together and becomes impregnated by the momentarily reanimated corpse. She gives birth to Horus, the Hawk-headed God, who then goes to battle with Set. Osiris, meanwhile, is reborn and takes his place among the constellations of the heavens, becoming the prototype for the resurrection of humans. The mummification ceremonies typical of ancient Egypt were designed around the premise that the deceased would become an "Osiris" and experience rebirth just as the original Osiris did.

The parallels with Christianity are interesting, of course. The betrayal of Osiris by his brother, Set, is analogous to the betrayal of Jesus by Judas. In some accounts, Set manages to convince Osiris to try out a sarcophagus which has been built specifically for his size. This occurs during a party at which the friends of Osiris and Set are in attendance. Osiris lays down in the coffin, and Set nails the cover shut, killing his brother. In the Christian account, Jesus is at a Passover seder with his disciples, and Judas leaves early to report his presence to the Roman authorities. In both cases, there is a gathering of friends and colleagues and the betrayal of a "brother."

And in both cases, the manner of death is not a simple one. In the case of Osiris, he is either shut up in a coffin to die a slow death of suffocation or, in the more generally accepted form, he is dismembered and the pieces of his body (fourteen in number) are scattered throughout Egypt. In the case of Jesus, he is first beaten and tortured, and then crucified, with nails driven into his wrists and ankles; but even crucifixion is not enough, for his side is pierced with a lance. In a Christian hymn, it is written, "They have pierced my hands and my feet; they have numbered all my bones," which is about as close to a description of dismemberment as one would wish, the total violation of the human body.

And, of course, both Osiris and Jesus are "reborn."

The number fourteen is of interest, as well. Osiris was chopped into fourteen pieces. In every Catholic church, one will see a commemoration of the suffering, crucifixion and burial of Jesus in a series of plaques—called the Stations of the Cross—which are invariably fourteen in number. (Oddly, to the Chinese, fourteen is an unlucky number (not thirteen), because the pronunciation of "fourteen" in Mandarin and other dialects is a homonym for "is dead": *shi si*.)

In the revisionist Christianity of the secret societies, the Priory of Sion, the books of Baigent, Lincoln and Leigh, Jesus does not die on the cross but is secreted out of Palestine and flees to France in company with Mary Magdalen, who bears him children . . . a bloodline that is said to exist to this day. (Naturally, the French believe that the heirs of Christ are French, a belief that explains a great deal!) Mary Magdalen could be seen as an analogue of Isis, of course, hiding with Jesus and becoming pregnant by him. In the *exoteric* Christianity with which we are familiar, however, the Virgin Mother of Jesus is iconographically identical with images of Isis. The same blue robes covered with stars. The images of the Virgin Mother holding the Baby Jesus are identical to statues and drawings of Isis holding the Baby Horus, son of Osiris.

Either this is the result of deliberate borrowing by Christianity of Egyptian religious concepts—which has not yet been proved beyond reasonable doubt—or another force is at work, like Jung's archetypes, manifesting in the unconscious minds of various races at various times across the globe. Gnosticism comes closest to weaving the various occult strands of Egyptian mysticism, Jewish mysticism, and Christian theology, as well as concepts from the Persian cult of Mithra and the Phrygian cult of Attis (both of which eventually became Roman cults) as well as other cults of west Asia, into a coherent whole representing the consistent features of each of these beliefs and practices, and finding common ground among them. Of course, in the process Gnosticism has overturned some traditional beliefs, as they sought the *esoteric* meanings behind the accepted scriptural texts. Thus, to the Gnostics, the Creator of the Old Testament is the Demiurge and not the benevolent God represented by Jesus. A close reading of the Old Testament would tend to support this view: Jehovah is forever destroying cities and smashing armies, laying waste to huge tracts of the Middle East, sometimes for the merest of slights. He certainly seems to act in the role of a fantastically powerful demon rather than a Prince of Peace of the "God is Love" variety.

The Gnostics were not the only ones pulling together a religion out of several disparate cultic elements; what we know today as modern Christianity owes much of its character to St. Paul, a convert to the new faith who decided that the religion would have broader appeal to the Gentiles if it incorporated some pagan elements. In this, he was like a modern takeover baron, buying a small, successful corporation and changing its identity to fit a larger market strategy, thus stripping the original company of its character and firing its most loyal employees to make the new shareholders happy, at least for the first fiscal quarter or two. St. Paul as the Gordon Gekko of Christianity? Perhaps.

What happened to the original Christian message has virtually disappeared under the heavy furniture of the Church; the cults who were the closest in mission and theology to the early Church were dissipated throughout the Middle East and as far as Afghanistan and, some say, Kashmir: small groups of Jewish mystics considered heretics by both Jews and the new, Pauline Christians. Another branch wound up in Africa, in Ethiopia, in possession of a Gospel of St. Thomas, unaware that the New Testament canon would be decided by the emissaries of Constantinople and that their Gospel had no place in it. It is not only modern American history that has to be revisited; as we have seen, the history of the Church is now under heavy attack from the revisionists, experts in Biblical exegesis and analysis, archaeology and philology, who are piecing together the events of the time of Jesus from the Dead Sea Scrolls, the Nag Hammadi texts, and new scholarship. Writers such as Elaine Pagels, Robert Eisenman, and Hugh Schonfield have made tremendous contributions to our understanding of this pivotal period in Western history; popularizers such as the team of Lincoln, Baigent and Leigh *(Holy Blood, Holy Grail)* have brought the results of this research to the mainstream media. Through all of this, the Church has remained silent, preferring to offer no answer than to trap itself in responses that it knows will be undermined by the next discovered parchment, the next jar of scrolls.

A new approach to Jesus and to God; and, with all of this, a new approach to the idea of divinity, and a new concept of the problem of evil.

Trevor Ling reminds us, in his book on the Buddhist mythology of evil, that there is consternation in our hearts when we confront the otherworldly. He refers to the work of Rudolf Otto who, in his influential *Idea of the Holy*, argued that our experience of the divine and the demonic may be confused, a feeling he called "daemonic dread":

> This daemonic dread, [Otto] claims, 'first begins to stir in the feeling of "something uncanny," "eerie" or "weird." It is this feeling which, emerging in the mind of primeval man, forms the starting point for the entire religious development in history. "Daemons" and "gods" alike spring from this root . . .[30]

In this, Otto agrees with Jungian psychoanalyst Adolf Guggenbühl-Craig, who identifies the sinister with the divine:

> The sinister is always the unintelligible, the impressive, the numinous. Wherever something divine appears, we begin to experience fear.[31]

And:

> Everything that has to do with salvation possesses . . . a sinister, unfamiliar character . . .[32]

Even Elaine Pagels, Professor of Religion at Princeton University, was unable to avoid the implications of the experience of the paranormal for the idea of evil: "Evil, then, at its worst, seems to involve the supernatural . . ."[33]

The emphasis in these writers is on the personal experience of evil as something of an otherworldly, paranormal or supernatural nature, evil "at its worst." Further, it is possible to confound the experience of the divine with the experience of the satanic, as both Otto and Guggenbühl-Craig point out. These sinister forces are also numinous; the sinister may also be . . . divine.

This is clear in the mystery religions, of course. Initiation into these cults always involves a preliminary period of tremendous fear and horror, the initiate blindfolded and bound, brought into the sacred precincts on the point of a sword, and made to swear terrible oaths which involve—in Freemasonry, for instance—threats of death and dismemberment should the initiate reveal anything that is to be shown to him. Our problem, as human beings, is that we are unable to differentiate between the divine and the demonic: our psychological reactions—fear the experience of the sinister, dread—are the same for both. Certainly, the stars of the Old Testament felt this way when coming face to face with Jehovah. God is not only stern and just in the Old Testament, he is positively homicidal. He demands absolute loyalty on the pain of death. He tells Abraham to kill his own son, and then changes his mind a little later on. He submits Job to unimaginable torment, just to win an argument with Satan. He comes up with circumcision as a means of identifying the Chosen People (a simple tattoo would have been nice, or an identification card). He destroys Sodom and Gomorrah, tears down the walls of Jericho, floods the earth to destroy every living thing except whatever Noah could fit on his ark. Speaking of arks, the Ark of the Covenant was so dangerous that merely to touch it was enough to cause death, so it was paraded before the enemies of Israel, who promptly fell down with hemorrhoids. (I Samuel, V) So, yes, our experience of the divine has been . . . sinister. It has been frought with danger, with threat of destruction both physical and spiritual. And, at the same time, we have seemed to have been pawns in some larger game.

Why did Jehovah permit the enslavement of the Jews under the Pharaoh, for instance? Why the seven plagues of Egypt? Why didn't Jehovah simply appear to the Pharaoh—as he had with Moses—and *tell* him to let his people go? Since Jehovah was so capable of destroying entire cities on a whim, why did he allow the Egyptian cities to survive undamaged? Why the elaborate miracle of the parting of the Red Sea, and then luring the Pharaoh's troops into a trap, drowning them in the suddenly "unparted" waves? If we are to take these stories at face value—and many, many do—then Jehovah was a god to be feared, yes, a god capable of supernatural abilities, but not a god one could love. Jehovah appears in the Old Testament as a kind of military dictator with psychic powers. How, then, to tell the difference between god and demon? When Jehovah himself is capable of so much bloodshed, so much vast destruction, what then is evil?

SEX, DRUGS AND ROCK 'N' ROLL

The philosophers have struggled with the concept of evil only because the existence of evil in the world seems to laugh at any pious descriptions of the nature of God. All of the religious and metaphysical texts of the world rationalize the existence of evil: it is either God's means of testing us (a ridiculous assertion on the face of it, and especially when we confront the suffering of children and infants), or it is the result of humanity's abandonment of God's laws (also ridiculous, and for the same reasons), or it is the result of a war taking place between the forces of light and darkness (somewhat better, but substitute "light" and "darkness" for virtually any pair of opposites you like, and then degrade the image of God somewhat to that of a combatant of roughly equal powers as the Devil). What most religions agree upon, however, are the *effects* of that evil: murder, war, rape, sickness, human suffering in general, and particularly that of the innocent.

Evil only describes the suffering of human beings, the beings uniquely—it is believed—conscious of their own mortality, aware of the linear passage of time, capable of falling in love . . . in short, those things that depend upon a certain perspective about reality that is unique to us. Religion attempts to transcend those basic assumptions, especially the Asian religions in which even the passage of time is dismissed as a kind of illusion (something with which our quantum scientists would agree). If we are able to disown fears about mortality, ignore time as the dance of Maya, and renounce the love of one person and translate that into love for all of humanity, and then abandon even *that* love, then we are able to destroy Evil. Evil comes from attachment, say the Buddhist scriptures. Dissolve all attachments, and absolute freedom is the logical conclusion.

> *I fear nothing; I hope for nothing.*
> —Blaise Pascal, *Pensees*

What is compelling about the shamanistic approach to spiritual freedom is that the very practices which the Buddhists believe tie one down to attachments on the material plane are the same practices the shamans use to attain supernatural powers. Yes. Sex, drugs and . . . well, drumming. Tools that had been used by occultists, artists and shamans for millenia gradually became part of the culture, and in so doing were robbed of their transcendent influence. Just as the scientists would have us worship technology in place of religion, we find ourselves using the technology of religion as entertainment. Yet, even then, there is some "redeeming social value."

Susan Sontag brought to our attention earlier the link between creativity and madness, especially with reference to the case of French playwright Antonin Artaud. In another essay, this one on pornography, she brings to our attention the similarities between pornography on the one hand, and science fiction on the other.[34] By doing so, she makes some very compelling points about spiritual transcendence and the appropriateness of marketing this transcendence to the masses.

> Pornography is one of the branches of literature—science fiction is another—aiming at disorientation, at psychic dislocation.[35]

This idea of disorientation and psychic dislocation is familiar to us by now from our study of Rimbaud, as well as from our treatment of shamanism and occultism, as well as our foray into the mind-control projects of the American (and Soviet) governments. Sontag takes these ideas further in her idea that pornography fits the criteria of psychic dislocation as easily as do the various religious technologies themselves. Many people will be offended by what seems to be a defense of pornography, when what Sontag is doing is explaining its power rather than moralizing about its role in society. Both pornography and science fiction depend heavily on fantastic elements which bring the reader out of the normal, everyday world and into a sacred space of tabu. In the case of science fiction, the tabus are largely scientific: one bends the rules of Newtonian physics using words instead of mathematical formulae. One is expected to suspend disbelief, to permit one's mind to wander outside the limits of consensus reality. Pornography operates on similar principles. It removes the experience of sexuality from social norms, social limits, and places it in another sacred space of tabu: one in which every conceivable type of sexual coupling and sexual act is not only permitted but encouraged. Both forms of literature excite the imagination and encourage a kind of mental daring. Both are heavily oriented towards manipulation of the *image*. And, in this, they share a great deal with religion and the technologies of the religious experience.

> In some respects, the use of sexual obsessions as a subject for literature resembles the use of a literary subject whose validity far fewer people would contest: religious obsessions. So compared, the familiar act of pornography's definite, aggressive impact upon its readers looks somewhat different. Its celebrated intention of sexually stimulating readers is really a species of proselytizing. Pornography that is serious literature aims to "excite" in the same way that books which render an extreme form of religious experience aim to "convert."[36]

This comparison of the influence of pornographic literature to the conversion phenomenon studied by Sargant, Lifton and others may clarify somewhat the idea behind the sinister forces of this work's title, for sex has always been a major focus of the world's religions, and control of the sexual impulse—either through celibacy or strict regulations concerning matrimony, homosexuality, pedophilia, bestiality, etc.—is a hallmark of virtually every religion in the world. Even the curse of the serial killer is linked inextricably to sexual impulses (after all, the serial killer was first known as a "lust killer"), and avant-garde philosophers such as Wilhelm Reich could postulate that sexual function and dysfunction were behind everything from mental illness and physical illness to totalitarianism and even the UFO phenomenon.

The virtual impossibility of regulating the sexual impulse, however, has given rise to the tremendous degree of inconsistency and hypocrisy in our world, and this is not only a matter of Western decadence but a problem in virtually every corner of the globe. We have the spectacle of Catholic priests being brought to trial for sexually abusing children. We have women in Africa, as well as in Pakistan and some other Muslim nations, being subjected to corporal punishment—including, incredibly, rape—for being the victims of rape. We have entire villages in Southeast Asia dedicated to supplying the "sex tourist," offering children of both sexes for the pleasure of middle-aged European and American travelers. All of this makes the secret practices of Hindu Tantrism seem tame and decorous by comparison, and elevates even so venal a character as Aleister Crowley to the status of a true Victorian gentleman.

Predictably, everything from rape to serial murder to pedophilia is blamed on access to pornography. In other words, and according to this theory (which is very popular among the Christian Right), the minds of otherwise innocent men and women are being manipulated by images (in pornography and in mainstream television and cinema programs with violence and/or sex as the subject matter) to commit atrocious acts against individuals and society. In the East, modern Western movies and music videos are routinely blamed for the decadence of Asian youth. While this argument seems puerile to anyone with an ounce of common sense (from "the Devil made me do it" to "Madonna made me do it"), it does reveal an unconscious understanding of the function and power of the image, something that is *not* discussed openly in any of these societies, since elites in every society wish to manipulate images in their own way and not have their agenda (and methodology) revealed to the public at large. To open up this discussion to general public dialogue on the power of the image and how it is used by political parties, religions, intelligence agencies, and advertising companies would be to invoke doubt as to the relevance or justification of using *any* images. It would most certainly instigate a serious conflict over the role of censorship, and probably place authority for media and image manipulation right back in the hands of governments.

Pornography occupies a special place in this discussion, since it is a form of manipulation that is almost universally proscribed in all places yet still enjoys a strong and resilient popularity despite its official status as an illegal, or at the very least immoral, medium. It is difficult to understand the undeniable power of pornography if it is regarded simply as another form of literary or artistic expression. Although it does address one of the most basic of human appetites, one has the feeling that cookbooks—which, after all, address the most basic human appetite—do not enjoy quite the same cachet. There is another dimension to pornography that transcends that of all other literary and artistic forms. Even today, the number of Web sites devoted to pornography outstrips by far every other genre of site. Pornographic sites on the Internet actually finance the Internet and are a source of tremendous wealth for their owners. The ease of downloading pornographic images, stories, and even entire movies, has made the Internet the method of accessing pornography favored over retail outlets in the strip malls and on the back roads of America. Pornographic Web sites have even been used by Islamic terrorist organizations as a means of communicating, by encoding information in graphics files.

Sontag's remarks on pornography vis-à-vis the expression of religious sentiments, and in comparison to science fiction, are worth recalling today. The essay was written in 1967 in response to an erotic novella by Bataille, and it contains virtually an entire precis of Hermetic thought as it pertains to the initiatory process. It is an extraordinary document, and one that perhaps could only have been written in the Sixties. So much of what was written—indeed, discovered—in the Sixties has since been devalued in a kind of scientific backlash, yet will one day form the core of another discipline, something akin to art and yet more like magic; or perhaps it will be magic, the Western Tantra that Francis King thinks magic really is.

Sontag's writings of this period can be taken together with those of R.D. Laing, Michel Foucault, Wilhelm Reich, Antonin Artaud, even Noam Chomsky and other legends of the time. Laing's breathtaking and ground-breaking works on psychology and psychiatry—especially concerning schizophrenia—have been devalued by a mechanical approach to mental illness which insists that the origins are organic and that schizophrenia can be treated with drugs. Thus, it is assumed, Laing's work has no merit and can be safely ignored. By stripping meaning from the experience of mental illness, science has merely shoveled the dirt under the carpet. Would Artaud have been happier if he were sane? Van Gogh? Strindberg? Nietzsche? Is their art the result of mental illness, or was mental illness merely a means to an end, a necessary approach to that level of truth? With the right drugs, the schizophrenic is now a functioning human being, more or less acceptable in society, and science is happy with the result. What if this approach had been taken towards the schizophrenia of the Siberian shaman? Obviously, the response of science would be to rejoice in the "cure" of the shaman, because who needs shamans, anyway? And isn't that the point, after all?

The war of science on superstition is a front for another war, the war on meaning. Science manifestly does not provide meaning for scientific events, and in fact is unequivocal about the lack of meaning in scientific phenomena (as opposed to the last five thousand years of recorded history in which every event is accorded some degree of meaning). Meaning is the enemy; there is only the fact of science, the raw data. At the heart of science's war on superstition is the war on religion, and on mysticism and the possibility of spiritual enlightenment. To an extent, one can sympathize with science's point of view that religion has brought nothing but trouble to humanity (as if science has brought nothing but goodness). One can point to the Inquisition, to the Crusades. One can also point to the glories of the Renaissance, of the Gothic cathedrals, of religious music and art. Both religion and science have given, and have taken away.

Sontag is right to link the literature of sex with the literature of religion and, even, to science fiction. That is a perceptive and illuminating conclusion. In the East, the literature of sex is quite often the literature of religion, as in the Hindu Tantras for instance. And both sex and religion have as their goal in these literatures the quest for fabulous powers, mystical cities, and alternate realities . . . i.e., have something in common with the literature of science fiction.

And the linkage of madness with art, with religion, with pornography is a valid one, as we have been at pains to demonstrate in these pages. The sexual powers are demonic, and they live at the juncture—perhaps, the tangent—of the real and the ideal, of this world and another. Demonic forces can be summoned by the sexual act; demonic forces perhaps do the summoning themselves at times (the incubus and sucubus of medieval legend). In India, the forces are more divine than demonic, but to a Western observer gazing on the frightening image of Kali, an important Tantric goddess, the distinction may seem moot. These forces are making themselves known in alien abduction experiences and in satantic cult survivor experiences. The perverse, the obscene . . . these are the elements of pornography that point to a transcendental state of mind, one that is not accessible to everyone and, in fact, shouldn't be.

The experiences of Whitley Strieber and other self-confessed "abductees" almost invariably contain a sexual element. It would seem that the alien forces that abduct our citizens are inordinately concerned with human reproduction, and remove ovae and sperm from healthy individuals for further study or experimentation (according to the published accounts). The witches' sabbats as reported in the medieval press reveal the same sort of link between paranormal contact and sexuality. The Hindu Tantras are themselves a technology for achieving this type of contact through the manipulation of sexual imagery and energy. The Renaissance magician Giordano Bruno set out the parameters for this technology in his own work, principally in *De Vinculis*, the text analyzed so thoroughly by Ioan Culianu. The implications are obvious: the manipulation of the image, and especially of the sexual image or image of sexual potency or reference, need not be the sole domain of the intelligence agency or the secret society; it can become the practice of the individual, the mystic, the artist, the magician.

On a biological level, we may characterize this as the conscious control of unconscious forces: as the deliberate control of the autonomic nervous system, such as is revealed in the alchemical documents of, for instance, Thomas Vaughan. This control of previously automatic nervous system functions has as its corollary the conscious reorganization of the firing of the synapses in the human brain in an attempt to exert some influence over the quantum level of consciousness. As such, this technology is extremely dangerous. As poet and philosopher Kenneth Rexroth pointed out in his introduction to the work of Thomas Vaughan, it was this very technology—in an unsupervised environment—that killed the Welsh alchemist and his wife.

Sexuality may seem like a jarring note in a political history, except that the case of Bill Clinton has brought the connection between sex and politics to international prominence, even as there has been no real attempt to understand what significance the combination of political leaders and sexual activity has for the electorate. There have been other politicians whose careers were marred by sexual exploits, of course, such as Wilbur Mills, the Democratic chairman of the House Ways and Means Committee back in the 1970s (a Thirty-Third Degree Mason, incidentally), who got in trouble with an Argentine stripper; former Indiana Senator Gary Hart, whose presidential campaign imploded with the revelation of *Monkey Business*; or even President Jack Kennedy, tarred in revisionist histories with a succession of mistresses that included everyone from Mary Pinchot Meyer and Judith Exner to Marilyn Monroe. The fact that Republican campaign strategists routinely search for sexual gossip regarding their Democrat opponents is ignored by most commentators; no one looks any deeper into the sexual obsessions of career Republican politicians, perhaps fearful of what might be found there.

Fascism is another area in which sexuality plays an important role, and it was this close relationship between sex, mysticism and politics that caught the attention of Susan Sontag, whose insights into the functions of creativity, madness, pornography and fantasy have helped us thus far already. Her essay "Fascinating Fascism" clearly shows how the culture of Nazism rang hidden bells deep within the Western psyche, and continues to do so today. That Nazism is a cult similarly obsessed with sex is no revelation; it begins with a faulty theory of genetics (eugenics) which attempts to justify a "purity of blood" program in which, for example, only Germans who could demonstrate an unbroken line of Aryan ancestry going back to the year 1750 were permitted to join the SS. Sexual relations with Jews were believed to cause a pollution of the bloodstream, even if no children were conceived as a result. The mere fact that one had slept with a Jew was enough to convince the Nazis that one's spirit was now impure.

At the same time, the Nazis set up the infamous Lebensborn project in which SS officers (and thus of proven purity of blood) were encouraged to mate with as many pure Aryan women as possible in order to increase the number of Aryans on the planet. These children were brought up in Nazi orphanages, "baptized" according to Nazi ritual, and indoctrinated with the Nazi beliefs on the superiority of their race and the divine nature of the Fuehrer. Homosexuality was believed to be an illness of which one could become cured; alternatively, it was viewed as a crime against nature, and homosexuals were sent to the concentration camps along with the Jews, the Communists, and anyone else believed to be "deviant" politically, racially, or sexually. When it came to sex, the Nazis were as relentless in their own way as the Vatican. The newsletters and broadsides published in Germany in the early years of this century, showing blonde Aryan women being violated by crazed, hairy, Semitic monsters was a clear expression of German sexual insecurity, a major motivating force behind the creation and success of the Nazi Party.

The German occult organizations that existed until their suppression by the Nazis in the 1930s were openly concerned with sexuality and the mystical or magical attributes of sexual relations. As described in more detail in *Unholy Alliance*, organizations such as the Ordo Templi Orientis, the Brotherhood of Saturn, and so many others believed that there was a sexual secret at the heart of occult literature, concealed behind symbols and archaic references to the Rose and the Cross, the Dew, the Red Tincture, etc. Biological functions from menstruation to ejaculation were examined carefully and compared to steps in the alchemical process. When Aleister Crowley was initiated into the Ordo Templi Orientis, he rewrote many of their basic rituals to reflect more brazenly the sexual component of the "mysteries." The "sacrament" of the Gnostic Mass, for instance, was (and possibly still is) composed of both semen and menstrual fluid, mixed with flour and fashioned into "cakes of light" . . . certainly a dangerous substance to consume in these days of AIDS and other sexually-transmitted diseases. The rubric of the Gnostic Mass which requires the Priestess to stroke the Lance of the Priest in a prescribed fashion comes as close as one would wish to a *Grand Guignol* approach to organized occultism, something which the late Italian director Federico Fellini would have appreciated.

It is not for nothing that Sontag calls sexuality one of the "demonic forces" in human consciousness:

> Human sexuality is . . . a highly questionable phenomenon, and belongs, at least potentially, among the extreme rather than the ordinary experiences of humanity. Tamed as it may be, sexuality remains one of the demonic forces in human consciousness—pushing us at intervals close to taboo and dangerous desires, which range from the impulse to commit sudden arbitrary violence upon another person to the voluptuous yearning for the extinction of one's consciousness, for death itself.[37]

This demonic force *can* be tamed, however, and made subject to conscious control. It is probably this ancient idea that informs modern Church requirements of celibacy for its priests, while at the same time it forgets to train its clergy in the transcendental nature of celibacy as a means for controlling the sexual impulse and, by extension, deeper, autonomic nervous system responses. The ecstatic sexual union so prized and so sought after by romance novelists and pornographers alike is only a preview, a kind of demonstration, of the potential of the human nervous system. Like the visions that come from ingesting a hallucinogenic drug, the transcendental moment that can be obtained from a powerful orgasm in the normal course of events is only advertising. The main event takes place at the point one is able to control these visions (or these orgasms) consciously, for it is then that the "heightened state" of Sir Roger Penrose's quantum consciousness can be initiated, manipulated, and made to serve a higher purpose, but only in those who have been prepared—through a system of initiatic instruction—for this experience, for this power:

> What's really at stake? A concern about the uses of knowledge itself. There's a sense in which all knowledge is dangerous, the reason being that not everyone is in the same condition as knowers or potential knowers. Perhaps most people don't need "a wider scale of experience." It may be that, without subtle and

> extensive psychic preparation, any widening of experience and consciousness is destructive for most people.[38]

To have initiated this process in oneself without proper preparation or guidance is dangerous, and possibly suicidal. To initiate it in others without their conscious understanding of the dangers involved, or even—as in the case of Ewen Cameron and other scientists and doctors under the intelligence agency programs—in unwitting and involuntary subjects, is not only unethical, it is homicidal. The case of Frank Olson is just one case among many hundreds, if not thousands, that took place in the United States alone. It was as if a cult began initiating members without their knowledge, and without their psychological preparation: members who would not have been accepted as novices under normal circumstances and who were then subject to extreme spiritual and psychological pressures all at once. Some would have survived; most would have become victims, Children in the Land of Memory who can never find their way home.

In case this assertion seems unduly hyperbolic, one only has to refer to the work of one of the early LSD researchers from the days of Timothy Leary and Richard Alpert and the Esalen Institute: the Czech defector Dr. Stanislav Grof.

> *The Soviets seem to make a habit of exploring coincidences.*
>
> —Ostrander & Schroeder, *Psychic Discoveries Behind the Iron Curtain*[39]

Grof is perhaps best known as one of the founders (along with psychologist Abraham Maslow) of the field of Transpersonal Psychology, a system of psychology that maintains that individual consciousness is part of a larger, "cosmic" or "transpersonal" consciousness, and that we share many psychological features in common with everyone else. This is a form of Jungian psychology, which itself asserts the existence of an "ancient racial memory" that is common to all peoples, and which is populated—as we have seen—by the archetypes. But Grof did not arrive at these conclusions through a normal academic path.

A native of what was then known as Czechoslovakia, Dr. Grof had begun his career as a Freudian analyst in the 1950s, earning an M.D. from the Charles University School of Medicine and then his Ph.D. from the Czechoslovakian Academy of Sciences. (This after Grof, a hardcore Walt Disney fan, first seriously considered a career in animated movies!) Before obtaining his degrees, he worked as a medical student at the School of Medicine, Department of Psychiatry, during the 1950s. Without going into too much detail concerning his duties under what was a Communist—if eventually a somewhat dangerously liberal Communist—regime, he states in many places that the Sandoz Pharmaceutical firm had sent his institute a quantity of LSD-25 for testing and evaluation in 1954. He participated in that testing regimen. From 1960–1967, he worked as the Principal Investigator of the psychedelic research program at the Psychiatric Research Institute of Prague.

All in all, he studied the effect of hallucinogens—principally LSD—on thousands of hospital patients for ten years in Czechoslovakia before finding himself in the United States at the time of the Soviet invasion and the end of the Prague Spring of 1968.

Czechoslovakia at that time was a hotbed of paranormal research and scientific studies at the cutting edge of consciousness technology, as the Ostrander and Schroeder book—published in 1970—so amply documents. Dr. Karl Pribram—whose holographic theory of the universe is one of the most important meta-physical systems to be unveiled in the last 30 years—also hails from Prague, the capitol of Czechoslovakia; David Bohm, the physicist who has had such an impact on the "quantum consciousness" field, is of Czech ancestry and was a good friend of Pribram. ESP research in Czechoslovakia was highlighted in *Psychic Discoveries Behind the Iron Curtain*, and the application of astrological methods to the field of conception and fertility also has its roots in Communist Czechoslovakia.

While it is generally known that the Soviets abused psychiatry for their own ends, and hospitalized many a political prisoner, using electroconvulsive therapy (ECT or electro-shock) on healthy individuals as a means of torture and interrogation, and applied various other types of "alternative therapies" as well, such as the use of narcotics and hallucinogens, it is not known to what extent these methods were used in what was, after all, a Soviet satellite state. In the 1950s, at the very height of the Cold War, the pressure on the staff at the various psychiatric clinics to make every use of new technologies must have been enormous—either as genuine therapies, as experimental programs on unwitting or unwilling subjects, or as out-and-out torture, interrogation and "brainwashing" techniques. As LSD was introduced into the Iron Curtain countries in 1954, and Grof eagerly accepted any opportunity to test it (on himself, and later on others) the CIA was experimenting with LSD in the United States—on both unwitting *and* voluntary subjects, and not with the slightest interest in using LSD as a "therapy" of any kind. Grof became the lead or principle investigator in the use of LSD in Czechoslovakia, and tested or reviewed the testing of thousands of subjects there before he accepted a position at Johns Hopkins University as a Clinical and Research Fellow in 1967.

Prior to this, however, we find Grof among interesting company. In the period May 8–10, 1965 we find him listed as one of the registered participants at the Second International Conference on the Use of LSD in Psychotherapy. Among his fellow participants we find Harold Abramson, Humphrey Osmond, Walter Pahnke, and others familiar to us from Operation BLUEBIRD and MK-ULTRA documentation. At this time, Grof was still living in Czechoslovakia, but it would not be long before he found himself in the enviable position of holding an important position at Johns Hopkins in the United States . . . one that would leapfrog him to the Maryland Psychiatric Research Center in Catonsville, Maryland—where he became the Chief of Psychiatric Research, remaining there until 1973 in charge of the "last surviving government-sponsored psychedelic research project in the United States."[40] Czechoslovakia was invaded by the Russians in 1968, to put down what was seen as a trend towards liberalization, as the Czech satellite began to wobble off course. Fortunately, Grof was in the United States and decided to stay. In other words, defected; a defection made easier by the public acknowledgement of his contribution to the field of psychedelic research in the form of his fellowship at Johns Hopkins; a contribution that was obviously noticed by those in the CIA responsible for LSD testing and other mind-control technologies.

I am not trying to make any kind of judgment on Grof's motives, or to impugn his history as a therapist, either in Czechoslovakia or in the United States. There is no evidence that he worked for the CIA, either wittingly or unwittingly, either voluntarily or through some kind of coercion. It is just a question of being in the right place at the right time. Absent a *Russian* specialist in LSD research, though, a Czech specialist would have been a godsend to the Agency. Grof would have had up-to-the-minute knowledge of the state of the art of LSD applications in psychotherapy and thus could have given the Agency a window onto the Soviet capabilities in that regard. This would have been of great importance and interest to Sidney Gottlieb and the other MK-ULTRA staffers, since it was largely due to the perceived threat of a Soviet mind-control program that the American version was begun. In addition, the CIA would have been crazy to ignore the fruits of Grof's data on thousands of LSD treatments in Czech hospitals. However, that he is a respected and honored psychiatrist with a string of accomplishments to his credit is not to be denied. That he abandoned the proforma atheism of his Communist youth is obvious from the work he has done since then, and from his wholehearted embrace of spirituality as a necessary factor in human growth and development. It is to this work that we now turn for reasons that will become obvious.

Grof's interest in the psychedelic experience can be gleaned from his many writings, in books, articles and interviews over the years. His focus has been on the death and rebirth experience of those who have taken LSD, and his remarks on the use of the drug by unprepared individuals are worth study. He also realizes that insights obtained during the "non-ordinary states of consciousness," or "NOSC," as he calls them, bear striking similarities to the theories of quantum physics on the one hand (he mentions David Bohm, Karl Pribram, Rupert Sheldrake and Gregory Bateson in this context[41]) and the many anthropological reports of shamanistic experiences on the other. Grof realized that there was a connecting thread between the state of consciousness obtained by taking hallucinogens and that spoken of as quantum consciousness, much as Penrose and Hameroff themselves were implying in their Defense Department lecture. He also understood the relationship that exists between these states and the occult trances of the shaman and the mystic. What is astonishing to someone who is coming to all of this material "fresh" is that no one took this argument to its logical conclusion. We shall do so shortly.

After leaving his position at the Maryland Psychiatric Research Center, Gof took up a post at the Esalen Institute—stomping ground of Jack Sarfatti, Saul-Paul Sirag, Alan Watts, John Lilly, Timothy Leary, and so many others who figure in our story, including a side-trip by Charles Manson—where he stayed for many years.

The Esalen Institute was founded in 1962 by Richard Price and Michael Murphy, and takes its name from a Native American tribe who once lived in the region. It was the first of the "human potential movement" centers, and attracted a diverse group of spiritual leaders, psychotherapists, physicists, philosophers, martial-arts experts, painters, writers, filmmakers, etc. For many Americans, the Esalen Institute would probably typify everything they hate about California, but the influence of Esalen on the fields of medicine, psychotherapy, and international relations cannot be denied. Their establishment of a group designed to reduce conflict through peaceful resolution brought them to the attention of American political and intelligence careerists, as well as the Soviets. (It was the Esalen Institute that brought Boris Yeltsin to the United States for the first time, to visit President George H.W. Bush as well as former President Ronald Reagan.)

The same year that Esalen was founded, Abraham Maslow (who developed the concept of the "peak experience") appeared on the scene and—according to the Esalen Web site—"came to play an important role in its development, leading several workshops and guiding the founders. Esalen workshop leaders eventually played a pivotal role in the growing discipline of humanistic psychology." These would include, of course, Stanislav Grof who—with Maslow—would found Transpersonal Psychology.

Before Grof arrived at Esalen, however, Esalen members would play a pivotal role in the founding of Arica, the mystical school established in Chile by Oscar Ichazo. (One of the Esalen members who traveled to Chile to work with Ichazo included John Lilly, he of the dolphin studies.) Ichazo, the son of a Bolivian military officer, joined a mysterious occult group in Buenos Aires in the 1950s when he was a young man. Based largely on this experience, he wound up in Chile training people in his system of mysticism and psychotherapy formed around the Enneagram, a nine-pointed symbol that is familiar to students of Gurdjieff. In the arid, northern Chilean city of Arica he attracted the attention of a Chilean psychiatrist, Claudio Naranjo, who then spoke about him and his technique to the Esalen crowd back in California. A group of about fifty Esalen participants flew to Arica in 1970 to undergo a rigorous training program under Ichazo, including one Jan Brewer. Brewer would tell Jack Sarfatti that Arica had "been started in Chile by high-ranking fugitives from the Third Reich who were masters of the occult."[42]

This may seem an outlandish claim at first, except that it was made by one of the first Esalen trainees to study in Arica, and my own direct experience in Chile with occultists who had Third Reich connections tends to make me less incredulous than I otherwise would be.[43] Ichazo's background as the son of a Bolivian army officer—at a time when Bolivia was riddled with Nazi fugitives, one of whom (Klaus Barbie) would become head of Bolivian Intelligence—is also suggestive of a deeper military and fascist connection to the Arica movement in Chile.

One has to put oneself back in the context of the time: Chile had been a supporter of Nazism during the war, and was in the midst of political upheaval at the time Esalen visited Chile in the period 1970–71. Salvador Allende had become the first democratically-elected Socialist president in Latin America, and efforts were underway by President Nixon and Henry Kissinger to have him ousted militarily, a program that culminated in his assassination and the military coup of September 11, 1973 that put General Augusto Pinochet in power. Chile's own self-proclaimed Nazi occultist, Miguel Serrano (a former Chilean ambassador and intimate of Hermann Hesse and Carl Jung), was applauding the overthrow even as Nobel Prize-winning poet Pablo Neruda was dying, surrounded by Chilean troops who did not permit him to get the medicine he needed to save his life. Whithin this suppurating political morass we find forty of America's best and brightest sitting at the feet of a Bolivian mystic, characterized by Claudio Naranjo as a kind of control freak who was not to be trusted.

Nevertheless, Esalen embraced the Arica work and helped to establish Ichazo as a New Age guru in North America. This is something that Sarfatti finds disturbing, going so far as to wonder if Michael Murphy—one of the co-founders of Arica and the most visible spokesman for the Institute—was a kind of "Puppet Master," or possibly an innocent dupe of the intelligence community, citing the involvement of one George Koopman who was an employee of the Defense Intelligence Agency with the Institute and with Sarfatti himself, as well as of Harold Chipman, a former CIA officer with heavy involvement in Asia for the Agency and then in California overseeing the remote viewing research of Puthoff and Targ at SRI on the Agency's behalf. This was the Institute in 1973 when Stanislav Grof joined the faculty, fresh from his stint researching LSD on the government payroll.

I do not want to appear as someone who sees a fascist or a satanist hiding in every corner. My intention is somewhat more specific. The political consciousness of those who have been leaders of some of the manifestations we know as the human potential movement has been somewhat shallow, or non-existent. Their writings, speeches and interviews reveal no interest or understanding of political responsibility; indeed, their view of life as "bliss," and that the world would be a happier place if everyone practiced a more spiritual approach to life, ignores the immediate problems of hunger, disease, and genocide. In many ways, the quest for personal fulfillment that is the hallmark of the human potential movement is possible only in a safe, healthy and relatively affluent environment, such as obtains in the United States and in other Western countries.

This is a dilemma that has concerned me for much of my life: the desire to pursue a spiritual path and lifestyle against the responsibility to act in a socially accountable way to aid those oppressed by political regimes, epidemics, famine, war. There are those who say that the individual pursuit of one's spiritual goals can go a long way towards helping rid the world of evil, but to those on the front lines it seems a vain and self-serving fantasy, especially in light of the terrible suffering visited upon the innocent by religious fanatics the world over.

It is probably this basic dichotomy between these two approaches to life that leads to the attraction between fascism and occultism on the one hand, and atheism and communism on the other, each missing an essential element only to be found in its opposite; for it is the fascist who despises humanity in general and the common good, and the communist who despises spirituality and the higher good. Both are interested in the technologies of consciousness, however, if only as weapons to be used in their continuing struggle . . . with each other. Yet, none of those involved with the human potential movement of the 1960s and 1970s—amid the assassinations, the Vietnam War, the military coup in Chile, Watergate, etc.—seemed to understand the political ramifications of what they were studying and doing, and how this "technology" could be used, and was being used, for political and military purposes both overt and covert by forces on both sides of the great Cold War political divide.

Grof in his writings about this time (1973, when he joined Esalen) is extremely prescient about the psychological and spiritual value of the LSD experience. Like Koestler, he is a European Communist who has defected to the decadent West and discovered the Soul in the process. What is more important, he bases his conclusions on more than 4,000 LSD experiments, a huge database that surrenders some interesting data.

In 1973, he published an article entitled "LSD and the Cosmic Game: Outline of Psychedelic Cosmology and Ontology" in the *Journal for the Study of Consciousness*. In this article, he states that he had "personally conducted over 3000 psychedelic sessions" since 1954, when the first shipment of LSD arrived in Prague from Sandoz Pharmaceutical. He also had "access to records from over 1800 sessions run by several of my colleagues in Europe and in the United States." More importantly, he goes on to state,

> The majority of subjects in these sessions were patients with a wide variety of emotional disorders, such as severe psychoneuroses, psychosomatic diseases, borderline psychoses and various forms of schizophrenia, sexual deviations, alcoholism and narcotic drug addiction.

This is in parallel with the US government's own practice in the 1950s of testing LSD on prisoners—usually violent offenders and sexual psychopaths—and patients in mental institutions. Dosages ranged from 10 to 250 micrograms of LSD (in Prague) and from 300 to 500 micrograms at the Maryland Psychiatric

Research Center; in the latter case, Grof was using the LSD in an atmosphere conducive to "healthy" spiritual and psychological states, the "set and setting" approach. In Prague, however, the approach was rather more clinical. His report is based on both the Prague and the Maryland research.

He talks about the current (1973) state of LSD use in the United States, when it was largely a phenomenon of the young, anti-war crowd so perfectly exemplified by Leary and others:

> Many hundreds of thousands of persons in the United States alone have been involved in unsupervised experimentation with psychedelic substances . . . many of them are repeatedly confronted with the experiences and insights described in this paper. Experiential sequences of this kind can have an enduring effect on the world-view of the psychedelic drug users, their life philosophy, and basic system of values.

This is an interesting and ambiguous statement. He begins by speaking about unsupervised experimentation (which he clearly dislikes) and then ends by linking that to an "enduring effect" on the world-view, philosophy and values of the users. One wonders if the effect is to be understood as positive, or negative? One also wonders if the LSD experimentation undertaken by the military and the CIA falls under the category of "supervised" or "unsupervised," since the military and intelligence applications would not have been designed to elevate the mind or spirit of the subject, but to break down his or her psyche and make it more malleable to the controllers.

Grof continues by linking the insights obtained by LSD users to the sacred scriptures of the Hindus, the Vedas, which—as we have seen—had some very interesting things to say about the nature of Evil, God and the Devil. He then goes further to associate LSD insights with the new, post-Newtonian physics of Einstein, Heisenberg, Schroedinger and Niels Bohr, eventually culminating in a brief overview of the work of David Bohm and Karl Pribram, the "holonomic" model of the universe.

Since his article addresses cosmology and ontology, he finds himself considering the problem of Evil. He speaks of his LSD subjects having visions of gods and demons from every culture, even cultures with which they were not familiar (and thus reinforcing Grof 's idea that there does exist a kind of "ancient racial memory" or "collective unconscious" à la Jung, common to all humans regardless of their ethnic origins). Subjects would see ancient Egyptian gods as well as Christ, Buddha, etc. In addition, visions of "Satan, Lucifer, Kali, Lilith, Moloch, Hekate, Pluto, and Coatlicue" were not uncommon.

According to Grof, his subjects revealed a sense that Creation had taken place as a kind of outpouring of consciousness from the unitary Universal Mind, which "initiates a creative play that involves complicated sequences of divisions, fragmentations, and differentiations" that eventually leads to "an infinite number of derived entities that are endowed with specific separate forms of consciousness and selective self-awareness." These "derived entities" or "filial conscious entities" then gradually lose contact with the Universal Mind, building screens that divide them from each other and from the Universal Mind. That is, they gradually "forget" their origins, and their interconnectedness with each other.

This is nothing less than Gnosticism, of course. The descent of spirit into matter is discussed from a psychedelic, twentieth century perspective but it is the descent of spirit into matter nonetheless. It is also reminiscent of Arthur Young's "arc" and Arthur Koestler's Janus-faced holon system. (Later in the same article, Grof actually refers to the "derived entities" as Janus-faced, but with no reference to Koestler, as Koestler had not yet published *Janus*.) Under the influence of LSD, the subjects experience this "screening" process and gradually break down these barriers and eventually enter into the Presence of the Universal Mind. This, again, is Gnosticism and shares a great deal in common with the shamanistic experiences described by Eliade and others. Grof links them to Jain philosophy, as well as to "the monadology of G.W. Leibnitz, and to the holonomic theory of David Bohm and Karl Pribram." He goes further, linking them to Sri Aurobindo and "the system of Kashmir Shaivism," and again illustrating the Asian focus of many consciousness pioneers of the 1950s, '60s and '70s. (A popular and amiable authority on Zen Buddhism, Alan Watts, gave the very first Esalen seminar.)[44]

Thus, it should probably come as no surprise that the conclusions of Grof when it comes to the nature of Evil are typically Asian, and specifically Hindu or Vedic. As Alan Watts says in his autobiography, "Somehow the atmosphere of Hindu mythology and imagery slid into [LSD experiences], suggesting at the same time that Hindu philosophy was a local form of a sort of undercover wisdom, inconceivably ancient, which everyone knows in the back of his mind but will not admit" (Watts, p. 344).

LSD subjects, Grof reports, describe Evil as "an indispensable instrument in the cosmic process."

> The recognition that evil is the price that has to be paid for the creation of the existing experiential realities and that it is not only a useful, but necessary ploy in the universal drama tends to bring forgiving and reconciliation.
>
> According to the insights of LSD subjects, the Universal Mind has to negate itself and create its polar counterpart in order to enter the process of creation.

This could have been extracted from the work of a Wendy Doniger or a Trevor Ling, or one of the first or second century Gnostic writers. To Grof, working from his LSD database, this negative principle of creation "permeates in increasingly concrete forms all the levels of the process of creation" including being responsible for the splits and "screening" that prevent the individual "derived entities" from contact with each other, and with the Universal Mind.

> Since the divine play, the cosmic drama, is unimaginable without separate entities, without distinct protagonists, evil is thus absolutely essential for the creation of the universe . . . the experience of unification and consciousness expansion is typically preceded in the LSD process by an encounter with the forces of darkness, confrontation with evil appearances, or passing through demonic screens; this is typically associated with extreme physical and emotional suffering.

Again, we are on familiar ground. The hideous visions and experiences of the shaman—externalized in the case of the serial killer—are once again before us. LSD provides an opportunity to undergo this experience, but in a socially acceptable "set and setting," under the comfortable supervision of a therapist who may or may not have undergone the complete spiritual transformation personally. There are those who might complain—reasonably enough—that the drug-induced spiritual experience is to the real spiritual experience as the travelogue is to the place visited. Alan Watts mentions that many people who have had a positive experience with LSD then abandon the drug and go on to more spiritual work.[45] The implication is that the LSD experience (or any experience with a hallucinogen, such as psychedelic mushrooms or peyote) is initiatory: it starts one on a spiritual path, like the drugs taken at the Rites of Eleusis, but is not the path itself. That is why it is dangerous to take the drug under any circumstances other than under the careful tutelage of an experienced user and in a setting of spiritual (psychological) protection. That is why the BLUEBIRD and MK-ULTRA experiments were so wrong, not only from a moral or ethical standpoint, but from a deeper, more profound point of view.

Grof reiterates that evil "is inextricably woven into the cosmic fabric and indispensable for the existence of experiential worlds" and thus that "it cannot be defeated and eradicated in the world of phenomena." The parallels with Gnostic thought and ancient Hindu theology could not be more emphatic. The world, then, is under the control of the Demiurge, or Lord Mara, or Satan. The phenomenal world *is* evil, and since it cannot be defeated there is only . . . escape.

> Thus the polarity between good and evil is usually transcended simultaneously with the sense of alienation and individual separateness, with the distinction between inactivity and action, and with the illusion of the objective reality of the phenomenal world.

While all of this may be perfectly valid, and is certainly in line with some of the more advanced spiritual disciplines throughout the world and throughout the ages, it can also be understood as a way of avoiding political commitment and social involvement. We can comfort ourselves with the consideration that the phenomenal world is an illusion of which Evil is a necessary component; but when a little girl dies from a sniper's bullet, or an old lady collapses from hunger on a city street, or one million Cambodians are slaughtered in the killing fields, or six million Jews are turned into smoke and ash in the concentration camps, then these theological, cosmological, and ontological speculations are of very little use.

But does that mean that we must abandon the technology of the spirit, the "machineries of joy" as I have called them, after Bradbury, in order to do "good works"? When spiritual growth virtually requires isolation from the world at large, how to look out for our fellow human beings? How to contribute in a meaningful way to the world and its relentless struggle with the very real, if also very illusory, forces of evil? Perhaps the example of the shaman—a person who has undergone all the enormous psychological pressures and spiritual stresses of which Grof, Eliade, and so many others write—is the example to follow, for the shaman returns to his village and becomes a healer, a seer, a therapist, and a spiritual force to be reckoned with. The shaman is not a luxury in his village; he is not reading tea leaves or bending spoons or checking your aura. The shaman is a necessity, a requirement for the life of the village. For all of his or her strangeness and other-worldliness, the shaman is a committed member of the community and performs valuable (and life-saving) services. The shaman can also, however, attack villagers, attack other shamans, and kill from a distance. The interest of governments in these latter powers at the expense of the former is what has damned them, and led to the present state of affairs in which the Pandora's box of consciousness—what is commonly known as the "black box"—has been recklessly opened, and the demons and evil spirits of the Other Side let loose upon the world.

And the opening of that box was quite easy, once the right tools had been obtained and a general understanding of the problem was at hand. As Grof explains later in the same article:

> There exists a wide spectrum of mind-altering techniques that can facilitate the occurrence of such unusual states. . . . They involve the use of psychedelic substances or a combination of various extreme situations, such as prolonged stay in the desert, exposure to unusual temperatures, sleep deprivation, fasting, social isolation, sensory overload, physical pain, difficult body postures, and respiratory maneuvers combining hyperventilation and withholding of breath.
>
> Similar changes of consciousness can also be produced by various laboratory and clinical techniques. We can mention in this context sensory deprivation and overload, electric stimulation of the brain, kinaesthetic devices, variations of hypnotic induction . . .

Paging Dr. Cameron. Will Dr. Mengele please pick up the white courtesy phone?

I don't want to make light of the above, and I don't want to over-react. In fact, what Grof is saying is quite correct: non-ordinary states of consciousness can be reached by any and all of these methods, and many more besides. This is obvious from the vast literature on the subject, from the lives of the Christian saints, from the examples of Hindu ascetics and Siberian shamans. What is missing is the context under which these technologies should be used. The non-denominational methods advanced by Grof and others in the field may not be sufficient; cultural loading may actually be a requirement in this case, rather than an obstacle. Yet, Grof is understandably reluctant to call in the priests.

Further along in this seminal essay on LSD and the "cosmic game," Grof complains that most existing religious systems are replete with "inconsistencies and paradoxes," and says,

> Many of them are unable to reconcile such fundamental contradictions as the assumption of a benevolent, omnipotent and omniscient creator and the existence of evil and suffering in the world; omnipotence of God and the concept of sin, as well as man's responsibility for his actions; or the supreme justice of God and the inequities existing among people.

He then notes that many religions are in conflict with each other, each cult claiming a "monopoly on God and infallibility of their creed; they hate, reject and persecute the members of the competing religions." Then he goes on to explain this gross inconsistency by falling back on the game scenario of the Universal Mind:

> According to the metaphysical system described above, the inconsistencies and paradoxes existing within the individual religious frameworks, as well as the conflicts between them, have been deliberately created by the Universal Mind and built into the scheme of things as important elements in the cosmic game.

In other words, we are back to the Gnostic Demiurge, a God who created the phenomenal world as a place of evil, a matrix of matter in which to entrap spirit.

The only religions exempt from this problem are those that are "characterized by their universality and all-encompassing understanding, compassion and tolerance. They have a definite pantheistic emphasis and believe in ultimate unity of all creation." The spiritual path, according to Grof, is one in which the individual gradually rises from self-awareness, to awareness of the connections that connect him or her to everything else in creation, and then eventually back to the Universal Mind itself. This is a basic blueprint for the initiatory systems of most of the world's secret societies. The identification of a matrix underlying all of creation and the interconnectedness (as detailed in the doctrine of signatures, or correspondences, of the medieval magicians and alchemists) of all "things," all phenomena, used as a machine to elevate consciousness to higher levels, is familiar to all students of hermeticism and of the hierarchical structure of occult lodges or orders, from the Freemasons to the Rosicrucians and the Golden Dawn, the OTO, etc. These disciplines provided a framework, an intellectual context, within which the non-ordinary states of consciousness described by Grof could be integrated into the psyches of the initiates, while at the same time surrounding the initiate with a social support apparatus so that the intense preliminary stages of psychological disintegration would not be summarily dismissed as psychosis or mental disease.

Like Eliade and R.D. Laing, Grof understands that the mental states accompanying the various stages of "illumination" are construed as mental illness, "particularly schizophrenia," by mainstream science. He claims that the work of his colleague, Abraham Maslow, has begun to change all of that, with Maslow's discovery of the "peak experience" and its identification as a "supernormal" state rather than a pathological one. Grof was probably being optimistic in this regard, since mainstream psychiatry and psychotherapy at this time are still resistant to the idea of these states as anything other than mental disorders. With new drugs to combat some forms of schizophrenia, Laing's insistence that "mental breakdown may also be mental breakthrough" has been devalued, even though one could argue that suppressing a mental state through chemical means is not the same as curing it, and does not mean that the existential nature of the schizophrenic state has been somehow explained away by describing it as a chemical imbalance. One could reasonably wonder if the state preceded the imbalance, or the imbalance the state; and then ask if the cause-and-effect relationship between chemical "imbalance" and mental state was a valid perspective in the era of quantum consciousness.

At least Grof realizes that not all "peak experiences" may be blissful, and once again touches the edge of our argument by stating,

> However, the peak experiences can also occur under circumstances which are unfavorable and critical for the individual; in this case, the ego consciousness is shattered and destroyed rather than dissolved and transcended.
>
> This is true for situations of severe acute or chronic physical and emotional stress, as well as circumstances in which body integrity or survival are severely threatened. Many people have experienced fundamental spiritual opening at the time of accidents, injuries, dangerous diseases or operations.

And, we may add, during torture, interrogation, "brainwashing," "psychic driving" and "depatterning." Remember that Grof is coming from a background in which he performed LSD research—since 1954—on the behalf of first the Czech government and then the US government at the same time that these governments were experimenting with LSD for military and intelligence applications. The above remarks by Grof would have been quite interesting to the project leaders of these agencies, as they point the way towards alternate methods of interrogation and "brainwashing," using techniques already in their arsenal but applying them towards different goals. Although the agendas of the intelligence agencies would have been unique to them, the resultant effects on the psyches of their subjects would have been to open them up to spiritual forces for which they were not prepared (neither the subject nor the controller), and for psychological (and spiritual) blowback that could not be predicted.

Grof then makes reference to the works of Arthur Young (of the original Nine) as representative of the "convergence between mysticism, modern consciousness research, and quantum-relativistic physics," before proceeding to a discussion of the holonomic model of the universe proposed by David Bohm and Karl Pribram. He mentions in passing that "Karl Pribram formulated then a neurophysiological theory that connects the holonomic concept of the Universe to brain anatomy and physiology." From there, he goes on once more to associate these ideas with the Hindu Vedas.

That Arthur Young should appear in this article is not surprising, but what may be more astonishing is the fact—related by Jack Sarfatti—that The Nine actually lectured at Esalen! Twenty years after the first appearance of The Nine to the circle around Andrija Puharich, they again manifested in the person of one Jenny O'Connor. Ms. O'Connor was "channeling" The Nine and came to the attention of Werner Erhard, the neo-fascist creator of a school of self-development known as "est," for "Erhard Seminar Training," and always printed in lower-case letters. (Erhard had famously changed his name from Jack Rosenberg to "give up Jewish weakness for German strength.") Sarfatti himself had been a visitor to Arthur Young in the company of Puharich and Ira Einhorn, and had worked sporadically with Arthur Young's Institute in Berkeley, California. Oddly enough, he seems not to have been aware of Young's involvement with The Nine in its earliest incarnation. In the late 1970s, Jenny O'Connor was referred to Sarfatti by one of the est people, and Sarfatti was not impressed. Nonetheless, O'Connor became ensconced at Ésalen, channeling messages from The Nine and having influence over some management decisions and organizational structuring at the Institute, at the same time that Esalen was being visited by Soviet officials as well as by Einhorn, various physicists, Stanislav Grof (who was "Scholar-in-Residence" from 1973 to 1987), and many, many others.

Grof does not ignore the psychic abilities and coincidences that sometimes attend the spiritual awakening. In a 1996 interview with Russell E. DiCarlo, he states,

> . . . karmic experiences are often associated with meaningful synchronicities. For example, a person has a difficult relationship with another person and has a past life experience that shows the two of them engaged in some sort of violent conflict. One of them is the victim and the other the aggressor. If this person completes reliving that incident and reaches a sense of forgiveness, his or her attitude towards the other protagonist changes in the positive direction . . . . What is quite extraordinary is that at exactly the same time a significant change in the same direction often occurs in the other person . . . . This can happen even if

> there was not a conventional communication or connection of any kind between these two persons.[46]

In other words, a "non-local" relationship develops of which quantum physics has given us the exemplar. Grof believes that reincarnation is a "pragmatic concept, reflecting an effort to understand the complexity of these experiences that spontaneously emerge in non-ordinary states."

In his work *Books of the Dead: Manuals for Living and Dying*,[47] Grof provides us with illustrations of some of the visions seen by his LSD patients, those who had taken high doses of the drug and experienced death and rebirth scenarios. On page 29, for instance, we see a drawing of a "Moloch-like deity with a furnace-belly and tearing claws" which "immediately preceded psychological rebirth and the opening into light." One wonders what would have happened had the individual been given the same dose of the drug but under conditions less than ideal: a government laboratory, for instance, or a CIA safe house? Would they have been classed as psychotic, and would they have been programmed—inadvertently to be sure—to regard the experience as a negative one, thus blocking their psychological or spiritual growth? And would anyone have cared? Would this person's rather ambiguous mental and emotional state have affected his or her performance in the outside world, as a teacher, or scientist, or criminal, or spy, or soldier?

Or would the weight of what they had experienced—and the lack of a competent social structure to explain it and support it—have led that person to leap from a hotel room window on a cold night in the City of New York?

> *Probably this chronic mutual suspicion of our neighbor's capacities . . . will never be settled to everyone's satisfaction . . . . It doesn't seem inaccurate to say most people in this society who aren't actively mad are, at best, reformed or potential lunatics. But is anyone supposed to act on this knowledge, even genuinely live with it? If so many are teetering on the verge of murder, de-humanization, sexual deformity and despair . . . all forms of serious art and knowledge—in other words, all forms of truth—are suspect and dangerous.*
>
> —Susan Sontag[48]

> *This last refuge—the statement that evil is the work of a madman—is occasionally applied to God, as well as to demons; thus Siva is often said to be a madman.*
>
> —Wendy Doniger O'Flaherty[49]

ENDNOTES

1 Tan Teik Beng, *Beliefs and Practices Among Malaysian Chinese Buddhists*, Buddhist Missionary Society, Kuala Lumpur, 1988, p. 67

2 Jim Hougan, *Spooks*, William Morrow and Company, NY, 1978, p. 9–10

3 Fr. Gabriele Amorth, *An Exorcist Tells His Story*, Ignatius Press, San Francisco, 1999, p. 150

4 Liddell and Scott's *Greek-English Lexicon*, Oxford University Press, 1896

5 Jim Schnabel, *Remote Viewers*, Dell, NY, 1997, p. 197

6 Theodore Adorno, *The Stars Down to Earth*, Routledge, London, 1994

7 Wendy Doniger O'Flaherty, *The Origins of Evil in Hindu Mythology*, Motilal Banarsidass, Delhi, 1976, p. 9

8 Ibid., p. 55

9 Ibid., p. 58

10 Ibid., p. 75

11 Ibid., p. 63–64

12 Ibid., p. 66

13 Wash Edward Hale, *Asura in Early Vedic Religion*, Motilal Banarsidass, Delhi, 1986

14 Trevor O. Ling, *Buddhism and the Mythology of Evil: A Study in Theravada Buddhism*, Oneworld Publications, Oxford, 1997, (originally published 1962), p. 23

15 Ibid., p. 47

16 Ibid., p. 58

17 Aleister Crowley, *Magick In Theory and Practice*, Dover, NY, p. 193

18 Ling, op. cit., p. 75

19 Ibid., p. 87

20 Ibid., p. 58

21 Ibid., p. 59

22 Ibid., p. 66–67

23 Ibid., p. 26–27

24 Arthur Koestler, *Janus*, Vintage, NY, 1979, p. 292

25 Howard Bloom, *The Lucifer Principle: A Scientific Expedition Into the Forces of History*, Atlantic Monthly Press, NY, 1997, p. 10

26 Ibid., p. 11

27 Koestler, op. cit., p. 289

28 Bloom, op. cit., p. 29

29 Benjamin Walker, *Gnosticism: Its History and Influence*, The Aquarian Press, Wellingborough, 1983, p. 46–47

30 Ling, op. cit., p. 87

31 Cited in Daniel Hecht, *Skull Session*, Signet, NY 1998, epigraph

32 Ibid.

33 Elaine Pagels, *The Origin of Satan*, Penguin Books, London, 1997, p. xviii

34 Susan Sontag, "The Pornographic Imagination" in Bataille's *Story of the Eye*, Penguin, London, 2001, originally published in 1967

35 Ibid., p. 94

36 Ibid., p. 94–95

37 Ibid., p. 103

38 Ibid., p. 116–117

39 Sheila Ostrander & Lynn Schroeder, *Psychic Discoveries Behind The Iron Curtain*, Bantam, NY, 1971, p. 139

40 "The Multi-Dimensional Psyche," interview with Stanislav Grof by Russell E. DiCarlo, Health World Online, http://www.healthy.net

41 Stanislav Grof, *Books of the Dead: Manuals for Living and Dying*,Thames & Hudson, London, 1994, p. 27

42 Jack Sarfatti, "Illuminati, In The Thick Of It!," http://www.qedcorp.com/pcr/pcr/si03. html

43 Peter Levenda, *Unholy Alliance*, Continuum, NY, 2003

44 Alan Watts, *In My Own Way*, Pantheon, NY, 1972, p. 298

45 Ibid., p. 347

46 Russell E. DiCarlo, *Towards A New World View: Conversations At The Leading Edge*, Epic, 1996

47 Grof, op, cit., p.

48 Sontag, op. cit., p. 117–118

49 Doniger O'Flaherty, op. cit., p. 65

BOOK THREE: THE MANSON SECRET

CHAPTER TWENTY-THREE

THE MANSON SECRET

Chinese alchemists are said to have told their pupils that not even a fly on the wall should be allowed to witness an operation. 'Woe unto the world,' they said, 'if the military ever learn the Great Secret.'

—Walter Lang, in his Introduction to Fulcanelli's *Le Mystere des Cathedrales*[1]

If the Pentagon ever formulates the Manson Secret, the world's in trouble.

—Ed Sanders, *The Family*, first edition

If the Kremlin, or the Pentagon ever formulates the robopathic secret of M, the world's in trouble.

—Ed Sanders, *The Family*, 1989 edition

An article in the *Village Voice* thirty years ago set me on a quest to learn once and for all the arcana that lurk behind American politics. It was an attempt whose ambition was exceeded only by my general ignorance. I did not belong to any political party. I did not study political science, or have a degree in American history. I was, however, an American born and raised. My father had been politically active, and the FBI had taken notice of him, however slight it might be. I had been politically active in New York City to an extent during the Sixties. And during all that time I was surrounded by the converging elements of radical, alternative politics and radical, alternative religions. They seemed to belong together, as if resistance to one form of authority demanded resistance to all others: religion, art, music, literature, psychotherapies, sex. In 1967, anti-Vietnam War protesters—led by Crowley-follower Kenneth Anger—had linked arms at the Pentagon and tried to levitate it, chanting prayers of exorcism. Exorcism! And the Pentagon, after all, is a five-sided figure that would have been familiar to medieval sorcerers as an emblem of Mars, and of protection against sinister forces.

I suspected that the secrets I sought involved some equivalent convergence of religion and politics; after all, religion has influenced politics and politics, religion for thousands of years. In many cultures, political leaders are also religious leaders, such as the Dalai Lama of Tibet, the Emperor of Japan, the Pharaohs of Egypt, etc. Did we, as Americans, leave all of that behind? The "divine right of kings," the sanctity of the royal blood, and "whom does the Grail serve?" Did we break so thoroughly and so completely with our European inheritance? Is the American miracle a result of "independent inventionism" or the more logical and aesthetically appealing "diffusionism"? Is America the result of European culture taken to its logical conclusion? Or is it truly an alien force in the world, a magnet for the dispossessed, the greedy, the criminal, the apostate, the heretic, the eros-driven immigrants of four centuries?

More generally, what is the role of coincidence in history, particularly in American history? Is coincidence an actual force in and of itself, or evidence of the action of another force, something working outside linear, Newtonian, Cartesian consensus reality? Is there a scientific basis for this force? If there is, then how do we explain its role in our own history? How can we ignore it, when so many commentators on history and science have spoken of its insidious power, from District Attorney Jim Garrison to nuclear physicist Wolfgang Pauli? Indeed, coincidence piled on coincidence during my own research for this work, defeating logical explanation. How else to explain the appearance of books I specifically needed—little-known works on particular events in US history—turning up with eerie regularity in second-hand book stalls on side streets in Kuala Lumpur? Even a privately-published monograph by remote viewer Ingo Swann? And a series of academic works on Salem witchcraft, etc.?

The *Voice* article linked such disparate elements as the Charles Manson murders, Richard Nixon and Watergate, E. Howard Hunt and occultism, Howard Hughes, and even Disneyland. It may have been intended as whimsical, but the links—as I would later learn from the work of Professor Culianu—are themselves evidence of one of the strongest forces in history. For the sin of revealing these forces, Giordano Bruno was put to the stake during the Inquisition. For the sin of revealing these same forces, Professor Culianu was murdered in 1991.

Where should I start?

I began Book I with the assumption that the phenomenon of Charles Manson and his "family" was a case study in the manipulation of these forces, whether consciously or unconsciously or, what is more likely, *intuitively*: a combination of both. Village Voice reporter Craig Karpel saw a link there, and his association of Manson with Richard Nixon was enough to start a whole train of thought going in a bizarre direction. Like most people in the mid-1970s, I knew a little about the idea of the "Manchurian Candidate," and the suspicion that our government had been involved in projects of that nature. It would be a few years before the story was generally known, due to the revelations that came out of the Watergate and associated hearings, but the theme was an ever-present one in the media, from the British television series *The Prisoner* to Anthony Burgess' *A Clockwork Orange* to the culturally-distorted mind-control scene in *Casino Royale*, starring *War of the Worlds* broadcaster Orson Welles as a crypto-Aleister Crowley.

There was an assumption on the part of many Americans that Nixon and Manson represented an evil force in their country, Robin Williams' famous "Manson-Nixon Line." Many readers will be appalled at the association, however glib, of one of their Presidents with a murderer like Charles Manson, but it is nevertheless true that many Americans did feel this way, and that from their point of view Nixon's body-count was much higher than Manson's. Although I was one of those Americans who disliked Nixon and who opposed our involvement in the Vietnam conflict, I did not suspect—at the time I began this work—that Nixon's perfidy extended beyond the Watergate break-in to include collusion with the Dulles brothers to protect Nazi war criminals and the attempt to keep the Vietnam War going on long enough to ensure his election in 1968.

But it was Manson himself that beckoned from the American heartland. We are accustomed to a certain belief that our politicians say and do unpleasant things in order to win elections or stay in power; although Nixon's crimes are a matter of public record and will be distilled many times by historians in the decades and centuries to come in the context of twentieth century American politics, Manson's crimes represent something far darker and more mysterious than simple greed or cupidity. Manson became an icon of evil in its pure form, an icon rivaling Nixon's own. Manson was not a politician, not supported by wealthy businessmen and neo-fascist bankers. He was "poor white trash," the type of man we associate with trailer parks, reformatories, and biker gangs. He carved a swastika into his forehead. He compared himself, favorably, with Jesus. He spent most of his life in prison, and most of the rest of his life trying to get back inside. He ordered murders to be committed. He had sex with minors. He stockpiled weapons and stole cars. He may be thought of as the opposite end of the spectrum from Nixon, but it is a spectrum of evil nonetheless.

If I wanted to understand political witchcraft, I would have to begin with Manson, and if I began with Manson I would have to begin with the town where Manson was raised. That led me to the Indian mounds of Ashland, and from the mounds I began to wonder if these ancient Adena structures in the very center of Manson's home town worked a weird kind of sorcery over its citizens. To understand that, I would have to understand Indian mounds in general and from there try to put the entire concept of sacred structures into some kind of context. This led me, inexorably, to early American history and prehistory, and I found myself reading Hawthorne and Lovecraft, New England's native sons and spiritual heirs of the Salem witchcraft tradition.

Slowly, an entire secret history of America was making itself known, through obscure academic journals, narratives both fictional and non-fictional, epigraphic remains, archaeological digs, and fragmentary documentation of all sorts. It was a detective story, and at the heart of this story is a mystery deep and profound: the hungry ghost that haunts the American landscape.

Manson would lead me to the Scientologists and occultists who supervised his psychological and spiritual training while in prison; to more Indian mounds, this time at Chillicothe where he underwent his spectacular "conversion" experience in 1954 and "stopped thinking"; to his alleged murder of Marina Habe in Los Angeles; and from there to her father, Hans Habe, the Nazis and Operation Paperclip.

Operation Paperclip would lead to Nazi General Walter Dornberger and Bell Aerospace, and from there to Michael and Ruth Paine and the Kennedy assassination; it would also lead to Nazi General Hubertus Strughold and Randolph Air Base, Nazi medical experimentation, and Whitley Strieber and alien abductions.

The Kennedy assassination would lead me to David Ferrie and the American Orthodox Catholic Church, to Fred Crisman and Guy Banister and the UFOs over Washington State, and before I knew it to Andrija Puharich, Arthur Young, "The Nine," and the New Age movement, even including Jim Jones and the massacre in Guyana.

Manson would also lead me to Hollywood, for it was here in Southern California that he worked his black magic, convincing *even the Beach Boys* of his *bona fides* as a spiritual leader, and becoming de facto guardian of DiDi Lansbury, the daughter of the woman who portrayed the control agent of the Manchurian Candidate in the film. It was in the Tate/Polanski home that Jane Fonda—who portrayed Night in the film version of *The Blue Bird*, filmed in Moscow where the original stage play had its Stanislavski-directed premiere—had a party for her husband director Roger Vadim only hours before the Manson killings were to begin. Manson Family victim Sharon Tate, of course, had been one of the last persons to dine with Robert F. Kennedy the night of *his* assassination, at a small gathering hosted by *Manchurian Candidate* director John Frankenheimer.

Through all of this, the rhythm of coincidence and synchronicity beat softly but persistently. It seemed as if everyone were aware of the pattern of coincidence underlying historical events, despite the fact that no one looked any deeper at the phenomenon; so this prompted me to investigate coincidence from a scientific perspective which meant, of course, quantum physics and the newly-emerging concept of quantum consciousness. With this, we were investigating not only American history but the very nature and composition of reality itself.

The physical territory of the Americas in terms of ancient prehistory gave us the "deep background" that we needed to place this Secret in some kind of physical context: the Adena and Hopewell cultures that predated what we know of the Native American civilizations. In Book I, we looked at the "Indian burial mounds" and marveled at their astronomical alignments, in some cases the equal of anything to be found in Egypt among the pyramids: a science that was not maintained by their putative descendants, the Native American Indian tribes. We examined some of the evidence supporting a Diffusionist theory of the population of the Americas by races from Europe, Africa and Asia, and looked at epigraphical evidence for a Phoenician and Celtic migration to the Americas before the arrival of Columbus: pagans from the East setting up altars in the West.

We also looked at the voyages of Columbus and realized that the motivation for these journeys was religious and political: to find a way to raise money for a new Crusade against the Muslim rulers in Jerusalem, and to find a way to attack the Muslim nations from the eastern side rather than from the Mediterranean. In so doing, we came across the story of the Arawak Indians encountered by Columbus, a member of whose race would eventually wind up in Salem, Massachusetts, accused of igniting the witchcraft hysteria of 1692.

From there, we saw how Joseph Smith, Jr.—the founder of the Mormon religion, and descendant of one of the Salem accusers—began his career as a ceremonial magician in the woods of upstate New York, an American Dr. Dee or Faustus conjuring spirits at a burial mound in an attempt to find gold and buried treasure. We watched as he became a Freemason, and was soon thereafter murdered by an angry mob, even as he was clutching an imperfectly-made talisman for protection.

The first people who lived in the Americas; the discovery of America by Columbus; the Salem (and many other) witchcraft trials (with notes on the practice of occultism, alchemy, astrology and magic by both political leaders in high positions as well as impoverished Joseph Smith, founder of Mormonism) . . . all of these important episodes of American history—many familiar to schoolchildren—had at their root religious and occult motivations and agendas that are not discussed in the classroom. Cotton Mather himself viewed America as a land possessed by the Devil, even as it was destined to become a New Jerusalem.

That was our "deep background," a preparation for what was to come.

For it was an investigation of Charles Manson that led us to Ashland, Kentucky and the burial mounds that are the heart of the town, and to a horrible crime on Christmas Eve in which three children were killed and their house burned down, after two of the children—young girls—were raped in the sight of a handicapped boy who could do nothing to defend them, or himself. The alleged perpetrators of this crime were caught, amid much controversy, and caused the Ashland Massacre, in which troops and civilians fired on each other in an effort to retain custody of the three killers. So much death and violence for such a small town, in an area that gave us Manson, Bobby Joe Long, and other murderers, as well as the deadly Hatfield and McCoy feud. And, in the midst of all of this, the mounds quietly at rest, dead but dreaming.

Manson's childhood in Ashland progresses to his incarceration at Chillicothe, Ohio, at the site of another, more elaborate, complex of burial mounds. His lieutenant in the Manson Family, Squeaky Fromme, will do time at another prison situated at another set of burial mounds, this time in West Virginia, and now for the attempted assassination of President of the United States.

The mounds seem to be a silent element in this story, and it is odd how many prisons are built on or near a set of burial mounds. Do we unconsciously associate violent offenders with something ancient, pagan, and shamanistic? Indeed, these mounds are not all "burial" mounds, but *were* constructed according to the same astronomical principles as the monuments at Stonehenge and the Pyramids at Gizeh: alignments to the sun and the moon and the stars, an attempt to measure time and to channel mysterious forces. Certainly, these were the actions of uneducated, illiterate humans from the dawn of prehistory. It is all superstition, nothing more.

Odd, then, that Wright-Patterson Air Force Base is also built on the site of Indian burial mounds. It was to Wright-Patterson that the first Paperclip scientists were taken, in July of 1947 at the time of the purported Roswell crash of a flying saucer, and at the same time that debris from the crash was purportedly taken there. Odd, then, that the Atomic Energy Commission built a nuclear facility less than half a mile away from the "Seal mounds," a few miles south of the Chillicothe complex. The Seal mounds are virtually unique among the Hopewell mounds in that they are oriented (precisely) towards the four cardinal directions and the vernal and autumnal equinoxes, rather than towards the winter and summer solstices which is the more common mound orientation. More stuff to fuel a television mini-series, or an episode of *The X-Files*. But nothing there. No smoking gun. Just fantasy and science fiction, paranoia and superstition.

After all: Charles Manson, UFOs, burial mounds, serial killers, Nazi scientists, Indian shamans, astronomical alignments, nuclear energy . . . this is not the stuff of mainstream history, of academic scholarship. It's the raw material of adolescent daydreams and the slick, pre-packaged pablum that has replaced organized religion in the United States at a time of great moral, political and cultural upheaval. It's H.P. Lovecraft on steroids, nothing more. But then we took apart these elements, piece by piece, to see what was ticking (like a bomb, if not a clock) behind them. We discovered that the FBI did indeed investigate UFOs in the late 1940s, and did indeed file these reports under the rubric "X"; but what we did not expect to find was that one of the principle players in this episode was a man who would later figure prominently in Jim Garrison's Kennedy assassination investigation: Fred Crisman, a man said to have worked for the OSS during World War II and later for the CIA, a man whose role was to create confusion and disinformation. We did not expect to find that one of the FBI agents responsible for investigating the series of UFO sightings in the Pacific Northwest in 1947—the "X" files—was Guy Banister, another player in the Kennedy assassination conspiracy who would wind up in New Orleans as an associate of Lee Harvey Oswald, running anti-Castro operations from his walk-up office on Camp Street, an address stamped on Oswald's "Fair Play For Cuba" flyers. Confusion and disinformation.

We looked at the claim of alien abductee Whitley Strieber who said that, as a child in the 1950s, he had been taken to a "secret school" with other small children. A claim with very little documentation to support it, until we come across other "secret schools" in operation at the same time, including one attended by theoretical physicist Jack Sarfatti and operated by the Sandia Corporation, a company that ran on Defense Department contracts. Then we come across a man who shared a bus ride into Mexico with Lee Harvey Oswald, a man who ran a "secret school" in that country and who had been a Nazi supporter during World War II, running a paramilitary camp for adolescents in Tennessee. Strieber claimed his "secret school" had two locations: one in San Antonio, at the Olmos Basin, and another in Monterrey, Mexico. Strieber had also been taken to Randolph Air Base, which was staffed with more than a hundred former Nazi scientists and medical officers under the Paperclip program, including General Hubertus Strughold: men responsible for experimentation on live human subjects at the death camps.

Then we came across the startling episode of the Finders, a group of cultic pretension and CIA protection, and with an international reach that specialized in children, shipping some of them to a "secret school" in Mexico. In 1987.

What did all of this mean?

We investigated the possibility that some of these events may have been related to an ongoing psychological warfare program of the Army and the intelligence agencies, which we have come to know as BLUEBIRD or as MK-ULTRA, but which had many names depending on the military or intelligence agency involved. Again, we discovered more than we expected to find.

We found what Ed Sanders referred to as the "Manson Secret."

The arcane doctrines and methods of a discarded science are at the heart of this study, because they reveal the mechanisms by which society in general, and individuals in particular, have been manipulated by forces beyond their comprehension. The modern adoration of the principles of Newtonian science—as best represented by commentators such as the late Carl Sagan, Martin Gardner, and the coven of professional skeptics around them—has served only to obscure the means by which more open-minded specialists have been able to work their magic with impunity, often to the detriment of entire populations.

If we review the manuals on psychological warfare as practiced in the Congo in the 1950s, or in Vietnam in the 1960s, we see the politically-correct ("wink, wink, nudge, nudge") approach to what is, after all, witchcraft and black magic. The same may be said for the manual on remote viewing that was used by the US military as late as the 1980s, and perhaps even more recently than that. The opposition to the remote viewing programs came not as a result of a cost-cutting consciousness or a desire to rid the Pentagon of an unprofitable boondoggle, but because it smacked of New Age, anti-Christian sorcery. Remote viewing was attacked by the *Time* magazine science editor because it was a form of occultism that could lead to fascism. In other words, opposition to this program was based on religious and political grounds, not on scientific ones.

While the agencies may have abandoned the remote viewing programs, they have not jettisoned psychological warfare, which is, after all, an essential weapon in their arsenal. All of these techniques, from psychological warfare to remote viewing, have their origins in occultism. Although we can confidently trace the beginnings of this art to Giordano Bruno and the magicians of the Renaissance, they go back much further in time than that, to the days when occultism, religion, science, art and politics were one, and the chief of state was worshipped as a god and reality determined by the limits of his kingdom; and works of theater were works of ritual; and magic was the context within which science evolved; and works of art were media to communicate directly with sinister forces.

We have suggested that much of this material can be learned through a careful study of the religions of the East: Hinduism, Taoism, Buddhism, etc., or through an examination of modern writings on shamanism. However, the most accessible technology for a Western mind would be the theory and practice of ceremonial magic. This, after all, was the method by which Joseph Smith, Jr. talked to angels and looked for buried treasure, founding a new religion in the process. It was also under study by governors, doctors, and clergymen in the early days of Colonial America and provided the atmosphere in which the Salem witchcraft trials took place. Miscellaneous tomes on magic can be found at the crime scenes of serial murder, and in the libraries of politicians. It was the means by which L. Ron Hubbard jump-started Scientology; and by which Jack Parsons made an important series of contributions to the defense and space programs. Magic was there when MK-ULTRA began its search for the secrets of the paranormal and interviewed witches and wizards in America and beyond. It is a fascination that has not died with the passage of time, or the passage of laws, whether civil or scientific. If, as Crowley has written, "magic is the science and art of causing change to occur in conformity with will," then it has obvious attractions for the politician and the general, type-A personalities whose will is surpassed only by their egos.

Ceremonial magic begins with a basic premise that is sometimes formulated as the Hermetic axiom, "As above, so below," a simple phrase with enormous implications. Magicians believe that connections or links exist between perceived phenomena, and that to operate on one side of the link is to cause change to occur on the other. To fashion a talisman of gold is to trap the power of the sun; to make love to a priestess is to invoke a god. The magician operates in a world of "non-locality," a world where a force may be an object, a wave may be a particle, and everything is in immediate communication with everything else, from the very basic sub-atomic particles that comprise matter and energy, to the couplings of Tantric deities in a cave on Mount Meru. The magician deals with multiple personalities as a matter of course: demons, angels, spirits of the dead, are all around him, all the time. Like the G-scale doctor in his white robes in a basement somewhere in the Virginia countryside, or the Canadian psychiatrist in his Mount Royal retreat, surrounded by tape recorders and hallucinogens, the magician also uses these multiple personalities as subjects to work his own will in the world: to gain wealth or knowledge, to penetrate mysteries and reveal secrets . . . to assassinate from a distance.

The magician, to protect himself from the terrible forces he evokes, stands within a magic circle made of concentric rings and illuminated by candles and esoteric symbols. From within this position, he gives the orders that cause change to occur. (As William Burroughs once said, the magician in his circle is a like a Mafia don, insulated from the acts he orders to be committed by rings of spiritual "made-men.") The magician speaks with invisible beings and summons infernal powers. The demons he conjures all have titles like Prince and Duke, King and President. The demons are all politicians, with constituents of their own. And the magician pulls their strings, surrounded by an aura of deniability, an aura created by Newtonian science, since science states that what the magician does is impossible, the result of superstition and ignorance. "There is no such thing as the Mafia," stated J. Edgar Hoover, Director of the FBI. And the capos laughed.

In the texts of ceremonial magic we find the formulas for attaining that "*abaissement du niveau mental*," that "*dereglement de tous les sens*" so necessary for the first step of initiation, that toe-dip into chaos, that lifting of the Veil of the Temple, that courting of madness and ecstatic vision. More importantly, however, we also find the technology for keeping oneself sane, for putting order into chaos, a *system* and a systematized approach to controlling psychosis and for tripping across that *corpus callosum* between the right and left hemispheres of the brain, lowering and raising the threshhold of consciousness, the *niveau mental*, at will.

Like the texts of alchemy, the grimoires of magic appear on their face to be incomprehensible works of superstition and fraud. The promises of riches are no less frequent in the grimoires than they are in the alchemical works; but the grimoires are written in language plain enough to follow: cut a willow branch at dawn, or summon Jupiter on a Thursday. It is the accumulation of all of these actions, in the order prescribed, that elicits from the operator the sensation of incipient psychosis, a gradual descent into madness, which is the first sign of success. The magician dissociates, creates alternate identities for himself with their own names and abilities and personalities. As the magician travels through the various levels of his art, his costume changes (red for Mars, white for the Moon) and the incense burning on the brazier changes (sandalwood for Venus, myrrh for Saturn) as each stage in the process prompts the appropriate response from him, elicits a new personality with all the subterfuge of scent and sight and touch and taste and hearing, all manipulated according to the rubric, all designed to break the magician down into multiple personalities and rebuild him again like Osiris from his dismembered bones, fragments of identity scattered throughout the landscape.

During this process the magician learns the power of the symbol, of the image. He learns to manipulate these images, and to create ones of his own. He learns how to influence judges, sway kings, defeat armies, be worshipped, loved, adored . . . all through image, through what today we might call advertising, or psychological warfare, using a technology that existed before printing, before advertising, before psychoanalysis. Through auto-hypnosis, the magician learns to hypnotize. Through self-degradation, he learns how to degrade others. Through self-manipulation, he discovers how you can be manipulated. After gazing into the Abyss of his own soul, he has no fear of gazing into yours, of reaching down and pulling up the sludge of your sins, draping them around your shoulders like a cloak, and never getting dirty himself in the process.

In all the revivalism of pagan religions, shamanism, Wicca, Buddhism, Taoism, Hinduism and Tantra that has taken place alongside est, and neurolinguistic programming, and enneagrams, and the self-congratulatory seminars at Esalen, and the new psychologies of Maslow, Perls, Adler, Grof, and others, all that New Age California dreaming, the one medieval subject that has been studiously ignored has been ceremonial magic. Even alchemy has won its pride of place, due to volumes of alchemical analysis by Jung and his followers, gaining credibility and acceptance among the gentle, bearded, silently enraged men of the Pacific Northwest.

But ceremonial magic is the black sheep of this earnestly sincere family of "alternative" beliefs and practices. It is too literal, too "hands on," for an industry that is more comfortable with ambiguity and theory. It seems to have more demons than angels, and the Latin, Greek and Hebrew prayers and chants are fierce and aggressive and threatening, replete with curses and the waving of swords. Yet the technology hidden among the conjurations and exorcisms of the grimoires goes to the heart of psychology, alchemy and shamanism. The complex doctrine of signatures and correspondences that forms the infrastructure of ceremonial magic is the key to the good-natured, well-intended but confused therapies of the New Age gurus.

And, of course, it is also the key to the foul-natured, evil-intended programs of the military and intelligence organs of America and its allies and its enemies.

In order to understand fully what we mean by "the Manson Secret," we must examine the technology of consciousness as it has been revealed in the course of this entire work. The reader must also be thanked for persevering on a long road that may have seemed confusing or obscure at various turns. It is hoped that the following pages will put all of the previous chapters into sharper perspective.

SPACE: THE FINAL FRONTIER

The ancient cultures of the world have not left us much in the way of writing. The earliest forms of the written language—Sumerian cuneiform, Egyptian hieroglyphics, and Chinese characters—did not make their appearance until roughly five thousand years ago; but some of the world's most astonishing feats of architectural engineering were built by cultures that did not have a written word. Stonehenge in England is a prime example, a neolithic monument that is dated to about 2800 B.C., or about the same time writing developed in the Middle East. The menhirs of northern France, the pyramids of Peru and China, and the burial mounds of North America are further examples of this phenomenon. What is important about this is the fact that these stone and earth structures were aligned astronomically, as even the toughest of critics among the scientists are now forced to agree. More than that, however, is the actual location of many of these sites, for they occupy points on the surface of the earth that are mathematically significant or are built in dimensions that suggest a precise knowledge of the curvature of the earth and the exact distance from the earth to the sun. That such a perfect science could exist in the absence of a written language or symbol system is startling enough . . . but that the ancients demonstrated a knowledge of everything from the precession of the equinoxes to the circumference of the earth at different degrees of latitude indicates that they possessed a source of information unique to them, and which has been lost to history.

However, when one speaks of the pyramids, for instance, and their relationship to specific stars and then extrapolates from there to a presumption of the historical basis of ancient religions, one is apt to sound like a crank or at best extremely credulous. Some of the brightest minds of the past hundred years have been castigated for holding theories in contradiction to those of organized academia, even though those theories were based on the same evidence available to the professional historians, archaeologists and anthropologists of their generation. What is usually lost in this bitter exchange is the acknowledgment that previous cultures held some of the same, "exploded," theories and built their civilizations around them. This is the point that interests us here. As I pointed out in *Unholy Alliance*, it is not necessary to believe in astrology to believe that the Nazis believed in it. In the case of sacred geometry and what the modern New Age movement calls "geomancy," we have a case in point.

Spaces can be considered sacred or demonic, and structures can be built in those spaces to take advantage of the former or protect against the latter. We have the examples in our own culture of the church and the haunted house: two buildings at the opposite ends of the spiritual spectrum. In the case of the church, it is interesting to realize that many of the Gothic cathedrals of France—for instance—were built on sites sacred to the pagans who had worshipped there previously. Even St. Peter's Basilica in Rome was built on the site of the Mithraic tauroboleum, where bulls were sacrificed and initiates bathed in their blood. The Cathedral of Chartres is a famous example of a Gothic structure built over a pagan shrine, complete with a spring and a "black Madonna." It is said that the Cathedral of St. John the Divine in New York City is another such example.

The orientation of sacred structures always follows strict guidelines, no matter what the religion or the country. In the Catholic Church, the altar is always in the East, the place of the rising Sun. Worshippers enter from the West, the place where the Sun "dies." There are similar requirements in India—the system of sacred architecture known as *Vaastu*—and in China, the now-popular system known as *Feng Shui* or "Wind and Water." Many volumes have been written about the orientation of the pyramids of Egypt, some more credible than others; no matter how one feels about some of the theories advanced for their design, no one can deny that the pyramids do follow a strict layout and orientation according to the four cardinal points. The great stone circle at Stonehenge is acknowledged to be a kind of astronomical calendar, as are many of the mound systems in North America.

This insistence on the precise design and placement of sacred structures is a means of creating a microcosm, a perfect image of the entire world. To the European initiates of the secret schools—such as the mysterious Fulcanelli, whose book on the Gothic cathedrals was seminal, and Schwaller de Lubicz, whose work "deciphering" the Egyptian temples is famous among a certain class of Egyptologist—these buildings are books, meant to be read by those who have been schooled in their "language." From the perspective of the occultist of the last hundred years or so, we are just beginning to understand sacred architecture now; it would be a mistake to ignore its message only because we feel that such edifices were the work of the scientifically naïve or of ignorant savages mindlessly baying at the sight of the moon. The investment of time and resources in the creation of these monuments was enormous, stressing their respective cultures to their limits. It was important for these peoples to do what they did, to build the structures they did, and to orient them as precisely as they did. To look at them as mere curiosities only demonstrates our ignorance, not theirs.

This is not to say that American architects have been totally ignorant of the idea of sacred geometry. As many authors have pointed out in the past—usually in those volumes of discarded science to which I have frequently referred—even Washington, D.C. was designed according to arcane principles for the manipulation of secret forces. The same author whom we mentioned in the context of the "green language"—the erudite David Ovason, also the author of the New Age bestseller *The Zelator: The Secret History Behind History*—has written *The Secret Architecture of Our Nation's Capital.* The Masonic and Rosicrucian (read "Templar") influences are all there to be examined.

Unfortunately, with all the recent volumes that have been written on the subject of arcane geometry and sacred architecture, there seems to be very little in the way of explanation regarding just how these vast machines of stone and earthwork were to be "used." Some scholars have risked their reputations in support of the idea of a kind of sophisticated paleo-astronomy which was linked to architecture and the erection of huge buildings in accordance with a secret tradition—the Pyramids of Gizeh arranged like the constellation Orion, for instance, with openings in their faces placed in order to capture the rays of distant stars. Yet the fact that these buildings are bare of written explication means that we can only guess at their true purpose. It's a bit like looking at an elevator for the first time: we can see it's a small room with a door that closes, and a set of numbers on a kind of magic plate next to the door, but unless we can associate that little room with the number of floors in the building, and from there to finding the machinery of cables and pulleys that would levitate the room, floor by floor, and the openings at each floor that would allow the room to access them, we will be at a loss to describe its function. In the case of the Pyramids at Gizeh, we have the small room and we have the dimensions of the Pyramid, the various shafts, the mathematical relationship of the Pyramid to the circumference of the earth at that latitude, and the relationship of the size of the Pyramid to the distance between the sun and the earth . . . but we have no idea of its function. We have not seen the elevator "move."

In the case of the Gothic cathedrals, we have at least some very suggestive statues and stone carvings that, albeit obscurely, can point us in some direction and give us some hint as to their function. To Fulcanelli (and, later, Louis Charpentier), the message of the cathedrals was alchemical in nature, an allegory describing the steps to be taken in the Great Work: the perfection of the soul, the refinement of its grosser elements, and its alignment—like a pyramid—to a distant Star. Jung understood alchemy to be a form of psychoanalysis, a means of achieving psychic integration through the use of a symbol system incorporating many of the archetypal elements he had discovered in his own work. Thus, we can jump from the alchemical allegory of Fulcanelli to the psychological allegory of Jung to get at least the beginning of an answer to the mysteries of the Gothic cathedrals.

But can a "sacred space" also be dangerous? Can it be sinister?

When I studied the life of Charles Manson and found several links to Indian mounds—from Ashland, Kentucky to Chillicothe, Ohio and Moundsville, West Virginia—it occurred to me that burial mounds are the haunted houses of American prehistory. While they were sacred to the Adena and Hopewell cultures that built them—places of burial and of astronomical orientation and ritual observances—they might very well be inimical to outsiders. In addition, some of the ancient sites were possibly erected by outsiders to the American shores: Phoenicians, according to Barry Fell, or Celts; Druids, perhaps, or Irish monks. (That there was a large "Mound Culture" in neolithic Europe is by now accepted by most archaeologists and historians; the mounds of Asia and South America are now coming to light, as well.) There is no way to know for sure how their rituals were conducted, or to what gods or goddesses. It is a distinct possibility that some of these practices may have migrated to America on forgotten waves of tentative immigration centuries—if not millennia—before Columbus, even though this transports us back to the disturbing fictions of H.P. Lovecraft.

But how to connect the burial—and other—mounds of America to something as contemporary as serial murder and the Manson Family? That does seem to be quite a stretch. Oddly enough, it is a theme that has begun to influence American literature, particularly of the horror variety, although it is nowhere articulated to the extent it has been here.

Stephen King, in *The Shining*, describes the Overlook Hotel which is the scene of murder and mayhem in his novel as built over an Indian burial mound. In the film *Poltergeist*, a housing development is found to be erected over another Indian burial mound, with ensuing supernatural events including hauntings, possession, and poltergeist activity. In 2003's *Identity*, starring John Cusak, a motel which is a scene of murder and mayhem and also a platform for working out a complicated plot involving multiple personality disorder is likewise built on the site of Indian burial mounds. A hotel, a housing development, and a motel. Possession, hauntings and MPD. Burial mounds in all three. It would seem that awareness of a link between these phenomena is moving just beneath the conscious threshhold of American culture, looking for a way to make itself better known and understood. It may be nothing more than a kind of repressed guilt over the treatment of the Native Americans, manifesting as an evil force that threatens our lives and our sanity. Or it may be something else.

Another early 21st century production, the 2002 European film *Darkness*, starring Lena Olin and Anna Paquin, treats this subject in even deeper terms: set in a house in Spain that was built according to occult specifications to evoke the god of Evil, a house haunted by the ghosts of six slain children, and a ritual that can only be performed during a particular solar eclipse that occurs only once every forty years; the slain children laid in a circle, their heads towards the center and their legs extending outside, like the burials in the Indian mounds of America, the Cathar burials, the bodies found at Waco. This film is fictional, of course, but the occult details are remarkably coherent: artists, as in the Lovecraft tale, sensing the forces at work before the rest of us.

The old Clovis migration theory that has dominated American archaeology for so long is now on the verge of being exploded. Archaeological finds in South America have gone a long way to disproving the dates used for the Clovis peoples, wreaking havoc with the timeline. Something was going on in America long before the arrival of Columbus. Successive waves of European migration after 1492 trampled on the sacred sites of unknown civilizations. Early pioneers remarked on the appearance of "Indians" with blue eyes and blonde hair, or "Indians" speaking, incredibly, Welsh.

Adena and Hopewell artifacts show raptorial birds, objects found in the same areas as modern sightings of the Mothman and other creatures of dubious origin. Our early forefathers in New England were obsessed with religion and occultism to an alarming degree. They brought slaves and indentured servants from Africa and South America, people who brought their own religious sensitivities with them and who would have looked at the mounds and other prehistoric evidence from a perspective different from their white owners'. The founder of the Mormon religion was himself a ceremonial magician, using the same grimoires that generations of European occultists had used before him to conjure spirits and command demons. He used this magic at the site of another mound, and thereby "discovered" the plates on which he claimed the Book of Mormon was written.

There is something about the American landscape that elicits a superstitious response in its inhabitants. Writers like Nathaniel Hawthorne, Edgar Allan Poe, and H.P. Lovecraft created bodies of work that are appreciated more in Europe than in America: stories of early American witchcraft and superstition, linked with flamboyant deaths, murders, and mysteries, ancient cultures, and visitors from the stars. It is startling, and a little unnerving, to see the extent to which these gothic horrors have found expression in modern American historical and political events. America itself is a housing development built over a series of "Indian" burial mounds, a development erected largely with the aid of African slaves, so it should come as no surprise when our children become deranged, violent, and possessed. An alien past has come to haunt us, so it should come as no surprise when we confront demons we do not recognize, demanding sacrifice we do not understand.

The medieval grimoires have told us that the best places for an operation of ceremonial magic is the abandoned building or ruined church, the cemetery, or a crossroads at midnight. In other words, a place of ghosts and hauntings, of tabu and desecration, or a place of fateful decision. In pagan Europe, Hecate—the goddess of witchcraft—was the goddess of the crossroads. In Haitian *voudoun*, the crossroads are sacred to Baron Samedi, he who guides one into the Underworld. A crossroads, à la Lovecraft, is a place "between," an intersection point of the ley lines that are said to run through the earth, channeling its telluric energy at those very sites where the sacred monuments were erected: Stonehenge and Newgrange, the Pyramids and the ziggurats, the Gothic cathedrals and the burial mounds. Asian culture is similarly concerned with the flow of this putative energy, as demonstrated by their adherence to frankly mystical practices such as *vaastu* and *feng shui*. America, ignoring these ideas, has seen fit to build prisons and military bases at the sites of the burial mounds: Chillicothe, Moundsville, Wright-Patterson . . . In other places, the burial mounds have sat in the center of horrible events, such as the mounds at Ashland, Kentucky; no attempt was ever made to placate or pacify whatever spiritual forces may exist in those places, if only to appease the consciences of the European settlers who had evicted the previous inhabitants to build their farms, their houses, their saloons and banks. And prisons.

If America was truly settled by Asians who had walked across the land-bridge joining Siberia with Alaska—the Clovis argument—then it stands to reason they would have brought their religion and their magic with them. It would have offered them a sense of identity and cohesiveness as they trekked thousands of miles in an inhospitable climate into unknown territory. As they walked in the direction of the rising sun, they might have been seeking the source of light and life itself. We know very little of what they practiced, and can only refer to the shamanism of Siberia and the Taoism of China for clues. Both of these cults were (and are) stellar-oriented, with myths containing the element of a ladder leading up a central pole into the heavens, a pole that linked the world above and the world below with this world; if nothing else, it was the leitmotif of the pyramids and the ziggurats.

If, on the other hand, America was also settled by refugees or explorers or traders from Europe and North Africa, then we have a better idea of the faiths they brought with them, which would have included the unknown astronomical beliefs of the builders of Stonehenge or the astrology cults of the Middle East. In either case, an awareness of astronomy and its association with architecture and sacred buildings and sites would have been an essential part of their cosmology, as well as provided the technology of spiritual transformation (either of the individual or of the whole tribe), and would have included a belief in magic and the cultivation—in their shamans—of the "heightened states" mentioned by Penrose and Hameroff thousands of years later in their presentation before the Defense Department, states that are capable of exerting an influence over reality itself.

The academically-neglected rituals of European ceremonial magic are clear about the importance of the ritual site, and its careful preparation. They are clear about what the LSD prophets would later refer to as "set and setting": the creation of a specific environment to elicit a specific psychological response. The experiments of Ewen Cameron in Montreal also included the careful manipulation of the environment of his subjects. What these latter-day shamans ignored was the second integral part of the technology of consciousness: time.

TIME: OUT OF MIND

As may be expected of cultures that placed a tremendous value on the astronomical orientation of their sacred structures, the notion of time and periodicity was inextricably linked to notions of sacred space, and both were essential to their religions. Early on, the ancients demonstrated a sure knowledge of the solstices and equinoxes. The pre-literate culture that created Stonehenge was able to arrange that massive stone circle in such a way that it could be used to calculate the solstice sunrise. This was important to a civilization that depended on agriculture, for they could compute the seasons of planting and harvesting according to the length of the solar year, although we do not know for sure if that was the use to which Stonehenge was put. Admittedly, we can think of no other use unless the calendar was important for other reasons, such as for some unknown ritual calculations.

In the case of the Great Pyramid at Gizeh, however, the precise astronomical and geophysical design and placement of that structure cannot have had anything to do with seasons of planting and harvesting, which were determined by the inundations of the Nile. There was obviously something much more profound taking place in the minds of the Pyramid architects, something that was also responsible for the spate of pyramid-manufacture throughout the world at roughly the same time, as discussed by Dr. Robert M. Schoch of Boston University in *Voyages of the Pyramid Builders: The True Origins of the Pyramids from Lost Egypt to Ancient America*,[2] and by anthropologist William F. Romain in *Mysteries of the Hopewell: Astronomers, Geometers, and Magicians of the Eastern Woodlands*.[3]

The astronomical alignments of these monuments and the prevalence of tombs in or near them indicates an association of sacred spaces with the "travels" of the dead into the heavens, what Romain calls the "azimuths of the underworld." Romain identifies three different types of sacred geometry in use by the Hopewell peoples: the square, the circle, and the octagon. The square he believes was used by the builders of the mounds to indicate the heavens, the circle for the earth, and the octagon for the phases of the moon. While there is not enough space to go into all of Romain's calculations and other evidence, it is enough to say that he provides a compelling argument for the orientation of the various Hopewell mounds as a means of facilitating the transport of the souls of the dead to the Afterlife, which, in this case as in the case of ancient China, ancient Egypt, etc., meant outer space. In other words, the Hopewell mounds (and, perhaps the Adena mounds as well) were a type of machine, a technology for extraterrestrial travel. And the travel could go both ways.

The alignments of the mounds—and, again, of the pyramids of various civilizations including the Egyptian, the Sumerian, the Aztec, the Chinese, the Peruvian, etc.—are all to very specific points on the horizon. In some cases—perhaps most cases—these alignments are to the rising and setting sun at the winter and summer solstices. In other cases, they may be to the rising and setting sun at the spring and fall equinoxes. In still other cases, they are to the maximum and minimum rising and setting of the moon. In one or two special cases, we even have instances of the orientation of some of these monuments to the cross-quarter days, the days midway *between* the solstices and equinoxes. Always, however, the orientation of these structures is in a sacred space and oriented to a sacred time.

In the case of the American mounds, we know very little about the religion and cosmology of their creators, except where revealed by the very structures themselves, which are huge and represent the investment of tremendous resources in their design and erection. Found within the Hopewell mounds in various sites across the American midwest—in Ohio, Kentucky, Indiana—are artifacts that are compelling in their design, which seem to be focused on the square and on variations of the theme of four corners or four directions. Among these is the swastika.

Although commonly associated with the Nazis, the swastika is an ancient symbol that was known in India, China, northern Europe, the Caucasus, and in North and South America as well. Pieces of copper cut into swastika shapes have been found in various mound sites. It was one of the "proofs" that the crank anthropologists of the SS-Ahnenerbe used to justify their claim that at one time the Aryan race was in control of the entire globe and had penetrated to its furthest reaches. Discoveries of swastika-decorated pottery and potsherds have been found in the Taklimakan desert of western China as well as in Tibet, and in the burial mounds of America.

When Charles Manson carved a swastika into his forehead, was he invoking the horrors of the Third Reich, or was he evoking an ancient Adena or Hopewell deity, something from beneath the burial mounds in his home town of Ashland, Kentucky; something that may have possessed his spirit one evil night when his mother was at the bar, picking up another "uncle" while she left little Charlie outside, alone, prey to the demons of hunter-gatherers, worshippers of the raptorial bird?

While it is fashionable to speak of the people of these civilizations as peaceful agrarians, that is not necessarily the complete picture. Burial evidence in some of these mounds raises suspicions that the bodies interred were not always the result of death from old age, sickness, or accident. Further, the orientation of charnel houses to specific points on the horizon which would only become "activated" by the passage of a celestial body once in a year or, in the case of some of the lunar placements, once in every nine years, suggests another line of questioning: were human beings killed, sacrificed, at specific times to coincide with the rising or setting of the sun, the moon, or a star?

We have seen that many of the serial murders carried out by the Son of Sam cult, the Zodiac killer, etc. took place on days special to the calendar used by these ancient Americans (as well as by European pagans and occultists). This may have been accidental—"coincidental"—but their number suggests otherwise. We have also seen how often the mounds themselves appear in our narrative of the cases of Charles Manson, Squeaky Fromme, and others. Chillicothe itself, one of the foremost mound sites in America, is the site of a federal prison which has boasted not only Charles Manson among its guests but also serial killer Henry Lee Lucas (and who knows how many others?). Another mound site, of possibly less importance, lies in Beaumont, Texas—a site that shows up in both the Son of Sam case as well as in the Henry Lee Lucas case. According to Lucas, the "Hand of Death" cult that he insisted existed in Texas, and was responsible for murders throughout the United States, was based in or around Beaumont at one point, and was responsible for the murder of a lawyer there. Beaumont is a suburb of Houston, and is where Sam cultist John Carr's ex-wife lived with their daughter. Berkowitz visited Beaumont when he obtained the famous .44 Charter Arms Bulldog revolver that was used in the Sam killings. Houston has been identified in the Sam literature as a cult center for the group rivalling Los Angeles; Minot, North Dakota; and New York City.

According to *Beaumont: A Guide to the City and Its Environs* "compiled and written by the Federal Writers' Project of the Work Projects Administration in the State of Texas" and published circa 1939, the area had been home to a tribe of Native Americans known as the Attacapas. This name, we are informed, comes from the Choctaw words *hatak* (man) and *apa* (eats). In other words, they were cannibals. On page 25, the anonymous but federally-funded writers go on to state,

> They told of a deluge that once destroyed the world except for those people who lived on high land. The women of the tribe, using the shoulder blades of buffalo for spades, were made to build great earthern [*sic*] mounds with their hands, and atop these mounds the big chiefs had their lodges.

Some of these mounds still exist in the Beaumont area, or did at the time the book was compiled.

Thus, we have cannibals and mound-builders in the same breath. We are told that the Attacapas (like the ancient Sumerians) believed their origin was in the sea, so they tended to stay near the water as much as possible, building their mounds on the banks of the Neches River that winds through Beaumont like gentle persuasion. In fact, the Attacapas mounds are the *only* evidence of a mound-building culture in the entire State of Texas, aside from a set of mounds on a farm near Nagodoches.

Beaumont is probably not so well-known today as it was in the 1930s when the book was written. On January 10, 1901, oil was discovered at Beaumont—at the now famous Spindletop oil fields—and history was made: Texas became an oil state, and the fortunes of George de Mohrenschildt, the Hunt brothers, the Bush family, and so many others were in the process of being made. "Spindletop" became anonymous with wealth and prosperity and conspicuous consumption, as any of us who may remember the old Spindletop restaurant in Manhattan can safely attest. Strange, then, that the place that gave America its oil wealth and oil barons should also be the place where cannibals and mound-builders, satanists and serial killers would have come calling; for in the age of the Attacapas (or "Attakapas") Indians there was no wealth to be had in oil, and in the days of Henry Lee Lucas and the Son of Sam, Beaumont had fallen from its old glory days: the fields were dry, and the mounds had all but disappeared.

The Chinese word for "coincidence" is composed of two characters, *fu* and *he*. The first character, *fu*, means "symbol" and is the same character used to represent *fuzhou*, or the name given to Taoist magic symbols and occult incantations. The second character, *he*, is familiar to me from my work abroad, as it appears in the ever-present *hetong* or "contract": it means "to join" or "to combine" even "to agree" or "to be equal to." Thus, the Chinese term for "coincidence" actually means "symbols joined together" or "combined symbols" or even, perhaps, "symbols that agree with each other."

Thus, we see the theme of Giordano Bruno and the other Renaissance occultists reprised in this simple combination of characters from half a world away: coincidence as symbols combined. Coincidence as evidence of magical forces, or even as a kind of agreement or contract: a covenant. The Latin word for *sacrament*—used these days in its ecclesiastical sense to refer to specific rituals such as communion, confirmation, and penance—originally meant a "contract," or an "oath taken by soldiers." The "Holy Sacrament" in Catholic terminology refers specifically to the consecrated Host of the Mass, the white wafer that represents, that *is*, the Body of Christ, and which represents a New Covenant between God and humanity.

I only point this out to show how pervasive certain concepts are, regardless of culture, race or religion: that the rituals performed by Chinese sorcerers and Catholic priests have at their heart an understanding that there is an agreement, a contract, between human beings and spiritual forces, and that the rituals themselves are representative of this. To take this one step further, may we suggest that the phenomenon of coincidence is an indication that just such a "contract" is in effect? We have already seen that there is a clear relationship between ritual (the "heightened states" of Penrose and Hameroff) and coincidence, a dynamic that works at the sub-atomic, quantum level. We have also seen that the doctrine of signatures or correspondences is an integral part of all magic ritual. Is this Hermetic concept what is understood by the term "contract" or "covenant"? After all, in a Christian context, Jesus promised St. Peter, "What you seal on earth shall be sealed in heaven, what you loose on earth shall be loosed in heaven." Is this the New Testament version of "as above, so below"?

The Chinese also believed in sacred space and sacred time, and more elaborately created entire technologies for traveling in "heightened states" to the stars. At the time the CIA was investigating these same methods, R. Gordon Wasson had already sampled the "magic mushroom" (known as "God's flesh") in a small village in Mexico and written about his experience in *Life* magazine, prompting a scientist on a CIA contract to accompany Wasson on his next trip. This fascination with psychotropic substances was to prompt Wasson's study of the hallucinogenic mushroom's influence over religious and mystical experience the world over, a perspective that was adopted by Allegro in *The Sacred Mushroom and the Cross*, and by Timothy Leary in his experiments with LSD-25. What was not well known at the time—but has become better understood now with the renewed interest among archaeologists in American prehistory—is that these same mushrooms (versions of *Amanita muscaria*) were in use among the mound builder cultures, where carved effigies of the mushroom have been found in the burial sites.

This association of the hallucinogenic mushroom with the sacred sites indicates a reverence for the psychedelic experience and a context of sacred space and sacred time surrounding its use. To researchers like William F. Romain, it is an indication of the beliefs of the prehistoric peoples of America in the creation and use of the mound structures as a gateway to other worlds, a gateway that could be used in both directions. The conjunction of lunar, solar and stellar earthworks in early America with the use of psychotropics and ritual lead us to the conclusion that the early Americans—possibly, but not definitively, the ancestors of the present-day Native Americans—had a technology for otherworldly "travel" (such as remote viewing) of a type which eventually came to the attention of our military and intelligence agencies, and which would have led to social organization and control of these early peoples such as the Adena and the Hopewell in line with extraterrestrial forces (as the design and orientation of their sacred structures to the stars instructs us).

This ancient American preoccupation with the stars—a consuming interest that is paralleled in virtually every other ancient civilization—found its apotheosis in the Postwar appearance of The Nine. We would not be talking about this event at all, had it not been for the participation of some of America's most notable families in this series of séances taking place in Glen Cove, Maine. We would not be talking about this event at all had it not been for the organization of these séances under an Army captain who was responsible for paranormal, chemical and biological research during the Korean War. A man who worked for Dr. Laurence Layton, the father of the only convicted Jonestown murderer.

The message of The Nine—that it was an extraterrestrial force hovering over the earth in a flying saucer of some kind and that it intended to guide a generation of human beings in expanded consciousness—was something that Andrija Puharich took very much to heart, so much so that twenty years later he was *still* talking about it, this time to Uri Geller and the people at SRI who worked on Defense Department contracts in remote viewing. As we recall, one of the original members of the séance that contacted The Nine was Arthur Young, the father-in-law of one of the Kennedy assassination personalities, Ruth Paine. (It was to Arthur Young that Puharich would take Geller, Einhorn and Sarfatti twenty years after the original seance.)

One wonders: was the assassination of John F. Kennedy something in line with the agenda of The Nine? After all the discussion we have entertained here on the subject of coincidence and synchronicity, it would be foolish to ignore the relationship between a charter member of The Nine and the family of the alleged assassin of the President of the United States. It strains credulity to the breaking-point to simply assert that the fact that Lee and Marina Oswald lived with Arthur Young's daughter-in-law, a woman who visited Young only two months before the assassination, is pure "coincidence," a mere accident of history with no meaning. Yet, we are puzzled by the eminence of Arthur Young and his wife, Ruth Forbes Paine Young, among the New Age philosophers of the American Postwar era. There is no mystery about Arthur Young's contribution to the defense establishment; his invention of what would become the Bell Helicopter would have far-reaching effects, through the Vietnam War and beyond. To his credit, he abandoned the military-industrial establishment shortly after the end of World War II to devote himself to the philosophical questions that haunted his waking hours.

Yet, he managed to obtain for his son-in-law—Michael Paine—a position with Bell Aerospace, a company that was being run by the former Nazi General Dornberger. All of this leads us to wonder if we have been mistaken in our belief that the field of alternative religion, mysticism, and the paranormal was solely the domain of the Beats, the hippies, yippies, and other counterculture types that proliferated during the 1960s on a wave of acid and angst. The Christian Fundamentalists would have us believe that the New Age is a work of Satan, and that it represents the Left in America. But mysticism has rarely been the focus of the Left anywhere.

As we have seen, the Nazis (at least, in the form of their most rabid devotees, the SS) were ardent occultists and mystics. These were the same people who were wooed by the American Right after the war, brought to the United States and protected by prominent Republicans even as prominent Democrats—like Helen Gahagan Douglas and Eleanor Roosevelt—were arguing for their arrest and prosecution. Many of the individuals who claim to have been approached by The

Nine or by their representatives—men like Jack Sarfatti, Andrija Puharich, Arthur Young, Walter Breen, etc.—worked for the military-industrial complex at some point in their lives, if not for long periods at a time. Whether they did this as convinced members of the Right, or simply because that is where the jobs were, is actually not relevant to our case. What is relevant is that this is where they wound up, deliberately or not, intersecting with some of the most important and pivotal events and personalities of the Postwar era. Men who attended séances with The Nine, who heard metallic voices on the phone, knocks on the walls, and who spent murky months or years of their childhoods at "secret schools."

THE TECHNOLOGY OF SOCIOPATHS

These were not the men, however, who found their personalities splitting, a gun or knife in their hands, blood on their clothes. These men went on to lead lives of privileged sanity. It was the other group of individuals who came to the forefront of America's attention: the sociopaths who formed cults and sought the massive initiation of the planet in their own perverse secret societies, the men who used the tools of the magician like the famous Sorcerer's Apprentice and wrought chaos and destruction all around, to the edification of the men in the lab suits and government grants who were busy refining the very same techniques.

The use of hallucinogens by Charles Manson and those around him leads us to view what he was doing with his "Family" in a more specific way. Previously, it was thought that Manson and his "hippie" followers were simply following the general trend inspired by Leary of "turning on, tuning in, and dropping out," and were using psychedelics as an escape, or a crutch, or as a source of cheap mystical experience. But the combination of Manson's Scientology and occult training in prison (including his contact with the Process and possibly the OTO), his horrific childhood experiences, his compulsive sexuality, and the use of LSD and other hallucinogens *in specifically ritual circumstances* suggests another agenda entirely. He was conscious of the uses to which hallucinogens could be put, and he himself underwent an LSD-assisted "crucifixion" in the California desert, as we have seen. The breakdown of the psyches of his followers through indoctrination, sex, and drugs, coupled with the creation of alternate personalities, the removal of his followers to isolated encampments far from city centers, his insistence that they commit criminal acts like stealing, fraud, etc. to further isolate them psychologically from society, and the manipulation of their memories so that they began to view their childhoods as something evil and "programmed," all contributed to their creation as murderous robots who would do anything to please "Charlie."

Manson's doctrine of an imminent race war in which whites and blacks would be at each others' throats was merely a reprise of the Gnostic doctrine of the war of Light and Darkness, made vulgar and devalued by identifying the races as the warring factors but, ironically, more accessible to his innocent listeners by using racial color as an indicator of spiritual worth. After all, skin color is a uniform you cannot change; there is no defection possible from race, which is why racism has been kept alive for so long and with such hideous consequences.

Mansonism is a peculiarly American form of Nazism, of fascism. It was born in the streets of Ashland, Kentucky and reared in the reformatories and prisons of the heartland among the poor, dispossessed class we cavalierly categorize as "poor white trash," but which contains in its bloodlines the heritage of the first English settlers: religious refugees and criminals fleeing persecution who carved a hardscrabble life in the hollers and later the coal mines of West Virginia and Kentucky. Like many a Skinhead of Europe and America, Manson was a white man who felt he had been cheated of his birthright, and who was prepared to take matters into his own hands in order to achieve some kind of parity, if not superiority. The fact that he was short in stature, of limited education and bizarre appearance, was both an obstacle to his becoming even more powerful than he was, and an asset among the young women who were drawn to him and who felt unthreaten by his demeanor and attitude. In addition, he understood instinctively the value of associating with Hollywood celebrities, for there are no better manipulators of images than Hollywood directors, producers, screenwriters and actors. Hollywood has a power that has still not been thoroughly appreciated and dissected by social critics, because to fully understand Hollywood one must understand the discarded sciences.

Manson did, to a large extent, understand these sciences and what they could offer the man who could use the technology to create a New World Order out of the flotsam and jetsam of America's youth. Everything we have seen in print about Manson's philosophy has shown it to be derivative and weak, a hodge-podge of jargon from various disciplines half-learned and half-invented. It didn't have to be sophisticated; it only had to be immediate, forceful and raw. What could seem more real, more edgy and avant-garde, than a lifelong prisoner turned mystic and revolutionary? A sort of poor man's Jean Genet? What was there, after all, that made Manson different from Jim Jones, for instance? They both espoused a philosophy that was part alternative religion, part revolutionary politics, and used the force of their cults of personality to convince others that they were reincarnations of gods, meanwhile focusing attention on racial issues; they drew their followers from the streets, literally, preaching an amalgam of Marxism and Manichaenism, and both would eventually instigate mass slaughters while fueled by apocalyptic visions.

It was important to both Manson and Jones to keep their followers off balance, through poor diet, erratic schedules (disruption of the body's circadian rhythms), the breakdown of sexual identity through forced sex acts with members of the opposite sex, the same sex, and with Manson and Jones themselves. Manson incorporated drugs into this repertoire for a more complete *dereglement de tous le sens*, and both men created a bunker-like mentality among their followers by insisting that outside forces were bent on their destruction and could not be trusted. Both men created a very specific spiritual context for all of this through their diatribes on religious and mystical themes laced liberally with sexual and political references.

At the same time that Manson cultivated Hollywood celebrities, Jones cultivated political leaders on a local and national scale. Had Jones and Manson managed to link up, they would have made a formidable pair, covering all the social and political bases. But sociopaths rarely work together.

The "technology" of sociopaths, however, was found to be amenable to conscious control and emulation. What Manson and Jones were doing was nothing that was not already understood by the experimental psychology programs of the CIA and its sub-contractors. They had been performing such operations for quite some time. We have the hypnosis experiments as recounted by Estabrooks and others; the LSD experiments that had taken place in prisons and mental hospitals and military bases; and, of course, the whole panoply of psychological warfare operations through the past decades. The Army had experimented with a psychotropic drug known as BZ (a "phenylglycollate ester of 3-quinuclidinol" which was termed a "hallucinogenic chemical warfare agent") in Vietnam, at Bong-san in March of 1966,[4] an event that was fictionalized in the film *Jacob's Ladder*.

The "contribution" of people like Manson and Jones was the revelation that masses of people could be made to do almost anything if their psyches had been manipulated through the use of image and emotion: the technology of magic and eros. The sexual component of the Manson Secret is very important: it provides the energy by means of which the links—the interconnectedness between events, people, objects, ideas—may be "activated." This is very old, very standard occult practice even if it is not always explained as such in the grimoires. After all, in many cases the magician uses eros to forge links with objects and ideas in his *own* unconscious, without the intermediary of other people. This was considered to be a grave secret, for it would enable virtually anyone to contact the "sinister forces" independently. Such a person would be virtually invulnerable to surveillance, unlike a group of people meeting for rituals, training, etc., a group that could be penetrated by a government agent or an Inquisitor.

But men like Manson and Jones need an audience; they need a group, for they need the power of the group. Their psychology is messianic; it's no fun being God if no one knows it but you. Their purpose was to replace the existing power structures with one of their own, and for that reason their doctrines were almost always self-defeating. Their philosophy was impure: their goal was not the spiritual liberation of individuals or even the emancipation of the proletariat, but the creation of a theocracy based on their own, personal revelation. These were cynical men, beholden to another force from which they took their orders. In Jones' case, it seems he was working for the CIA; the information in Book II demonstrates that. His relationship with Dan Mitrione demonstrates that.

In Manson's case, the votes aren't in yet, but the details of the Tate and LaBianca killings strongly suggest specific motives for those crimes that may have had little to do with Manson personally, being contract hits. These were men who could use the Manson Secret effortlessly, pragmatically, and cynically: a new brand of covert operative who hides in plain sight, committing assassinations thick with plausible deniability. The individuals who followed them were only a means to an end. In this, they are what other magicians like Crowley would have termed "black brothers": magicians who have confused their own illumination (and, it must be insisted, a *genuine* spiritual illumination) with the Ultimate Truth, and their own egos with divinity. They were not prepared to sacrifice their egos completely, to "take the oath of the Abyss" and renounce everything in the Long, Dark Night of the Soul. Instead, their powers turned inward and rancid. They became demons that feasted on human blood: spiritual entities, to be sure, and powerful, but of such an evil nature that they are not exactly poster-boys for the New Age.

The American intelligence and defense establishments were not concerned with that, however. They only wanted to know how all of this was done.

They wanted to understand—and employ—the Manson Secret.

The secret, as employed by Manson, seems simple:

First, the removal of subjects to a "sacred space" in the desert, with attending isolation from society; breakdown of personality through drugs and sex and "mind games"; bestowal of alternate personality or personalities (new names like "Squeaky," "Sadie," etc.) operative only in relation to Manson, thus becoming Manson's "alternates," like multiple personalities of Manson himself; identification of an external evil—the police, the blacks, etc.—as a threat to the group. And *fear* is the key element of the Manson Secret that makes it different from other initiatory or shamanistic practices. "Get the fear," Manson is known to have encouraged more than once. There is life only within the Family; outside is death and loss of identity. Identity is race, and gender, and devotion to the leader, the *Führerprinzip*. Family is reinforced through crimes committed together, through mutual sex, and through paranormal experiences. Leadership is tantamount to divinity: Manson is a son of God. The paranoia of the occultist becomes the paranoia of the social outcast, the prisoner, the criminal, the junkie, the murderer. Murder is a form of human sacrifice in Manson's gestalt, and commission of the murder makes a Family member "made," as in the Mafia, as in the Son of Sam cult.

Manson has thus brought together elements of Scientology and the Process, along with the Crowleyan "Do what thou wilt," and crystallized them in the persona of an outlaw. The development of "heightened states" among his followers caused them to experience the world and reality so differently that the cohesiveness of the original Family members still exists: those that have abandoned the Family have become born-again Christians or some type of mystic, i.e., they have not really abandoned the path that Manson set them on. While serial killers are shamans who have not made it back, Manson Family members are a programmed shaman: i.e., people chosen from society at random and forced to go through the shamanistic experience even though they were not ready and their guru was not prepared for the responsibility; thus, the CIA's mind-control experiments were mirror images of what Manson was doing to his followers in the desert. They were both forcing individuals to go through an initiatory experience, the difference being that with Manson there was at least the context of a religious or mystical nature—however eclectic or wrong-headed and undeveloped—which the CIA experiments lacked.

With the Manson Family you had a tribe of shamans who were willing participants, and that made them stronger. With the CIA, you had unwitting guinea pigs who were only useful to the extent that the programming was effective and focused on a single target or targets, such as assassination. Sirhan Sirhan might have made a good Family member: he had already tried Rosicrucianism and Theosophy in Southern California and was walking in Manson's footsteps, but he had no social group for reinforcement; instead, he most likely had a controller and a single target. Sirhan was as much an outsider as Manson, due to his Palestinian background and his thwarted dreams of becoming a jockey, etc. Like Manson, he turned to occultism and mysticism for answers. Like Manson, he became a murderer, except that in Sirhan's case he was likely programmed to kill by someone who saw in him the same elements as a Mansonoid, and knew that Sirhan would do as instructed.

How can we draw such a strong comparison? The dates for Manson and Sirhan are only one year apart, in the same city, and they shared the same cell (albeit a year apart), built especially for Sirhan and occupied later by Manson. Manson's victims included the actress Sharon Tate; Sharon Tate had dinner with Robert Kennedy the night he was assassinated by Sirhan. The coincidences link the two murderers as they do the two victims. The alchemical/ hermetic path of initiatory death and transformation was consciously applied by Manson, even to the extent of an LSD-assisted crucifixion in the desert; one of his members had participated in rituals with the Church of Satan, and Sharon Tate's husband had filmed *Rosemary's Baby* while Sharon herself was rumored to have been initiated into witchcraft by Alex Saunders. Manson had been audited in prison by a Scientologist who later turned up around Squeaky Fromme. The initiatic elements behind Manson are many; they are reprised in the Son of Sam case, and in many others (such as Matamoros, the Zodiac Killers, etc.).

This is the Manson Secret: the use and abuse of hermetic and initiatic (shamanic) processes as a means of manipulation of individuals and groups; the recognition that within the initiatic process is a wealth of psychological knowledge and technique that can be used for evil as well as for good; the incorporation of Fear as a substitute for Faith.

The Manson Secret is black magic, and it was black magic that informed the CIA's mind-control programs as well. These same processes are being used—virtually without change—among terrorist organizations and revolutionary cells throughout the world, who have realized that the most effective tool for violent action is the properly initiated cult member. Ecstasy is just another face of fanaticism; eros is another face of magic. Fascism is the natural environment for both, for it speaks directly to the passions and the unconscious mind, through the use of symbols, repetitive slogans, and group ritual; i.e., magic. Socialism, being more cerebral, lacks the erotic element so necessary for mass appeal. Mao changed that for a while by ignoring Marx's dictum against creating a "cult of personality" and turned himself into an image, a magical link to the eternal. Transmute the ecstasy or the eros to a high pitch of passionate dedication to a cause, and use the theory of the magical link competently, and you have created an assassin, or a priest, a lover, an actor; or a politician who cannot be stopped except by a bullet.

Many of our most infamous cults have been apocalyptic: that is, they fueled the passion and the anxiety of their followers through identification with a given date, a point in *time*. This point was to be the end of time, the end of history, the end of the world. This apocalypse point was central to the thinking of both Manson and Jim Jones, as well as so many other cults, including some of the Christian Fundamentalist sects that have been predicting the end times for so many years it has lost its allure. The Jehovah's Witnesses have been making specific predictions, as have many others. As pointed out by Picknett and Prince, even The Nine have not been averse to millennial fevers, scheduling an event at the Great Pyramid of Gizeh for the turn of the millennium that was somehow called off at the last moment due to machinations behind the scenes involving the Egyptian Museum.

The point is that while the cults have identified their sacred space—their temple, ashram, cave in the mountains or shack in the desert—they also needed a sense of urgency, an idea that revolution was around the corner, a sense of fear. They sought to transcend the kind of sacred time represented by the pyramids, Stonehenge, the Indian mounds: a time that is cyclical, reliable, permanent. They needed to extend their boundaries beyond sacred time to a profane time, a demonic time. For the Son of Sam cult and others like it, it was enough to adopt the pagan calendar of quarter and cross-quarter days because it was an anti-calendar, a calendar valued by the underdogs, the satanists, the pagans, the occultists, a calendar that speaks of ancient mysteries and supernatural power and which is in tune with the actual movements of the sun and moon; but for the modern apocalyptic cults, cults shorn of mystery and individual possibility and initiation, an end-point was needed, since in an apocalyptic cult there can only be one leader, one initiate, one *Führer*.

These cults are full of people who lack the imagination to look beyond what they see as the general decay and decadence of our society, of our entire world. They feel history winding down, coming to a stop, and pray that all the evil in the world will be destroyed by an avenging angel they like to think is on their side. Those who follow a sacred calendar know that time does not flow in a linear direction, but in cycles and epicycles, spirals and holograms. They knew this before our scientists did, and they memorialized this information in their standing stones and mounds of earth. There is a pattern to time, as there is a pattern to space, a pattern to our nervous systems, a pattern to consciousness.

What goes around, comes around.

This idea of a sacred calendar—dates associated with meaning—provides a platform for the operation of coincidence and "synchronicity." Sacred calendars program the mind, the unconscious, so that it vibrates in accordance with an ancient pattern. Coincidence can best be understood within the context of time, the timeline, the calendar personal and general. There is the grand calendar of the masses, of society: the quarter and cross-quarter days, or the Christian ecclesiastical calendar, the Jewish calendar, the Islamic calendar with its fasting month and pilgrimage month, the Asian lunar calendars with their colorful gods and goddesses, etc. Then there is the microcosmic, individual calendar of family deaths and births, moves and changes. The synchronization of these two calendars gives rise to dates of meaning, of importance. To perform an act of acknowledgment on one of these dates is to give it added power, added meaning, a more profound sense of importance which then forges further links deep within the matrix of correspondences, giving the consciousness of the individual a rare power and more penetrating insight into not only society but the individual's own role and relationship to society. One begins to experience a flow: of time, of awareness, of meaning, even of power.

Christianity adopted the pagan calendar because of this very phenomenon. Jesus was not born on December 25; but it was an important Roman festival. Halloween was scheduled to occur on the same day that the European pagans believed the door between the worlds of the living and the dead were open, October 31, a cross-quarter day. The feast of the Virgin Mother was scheduled for May 1, another cross-quarter day of tremendous importance to pagans. Just as Christianity adopted the sacred *places* of the pagans—the sites of pagan worship that became Christian shrines, even including St. Peter's Basilica itself—so they adopted the sacred *time* of the pagans, performing a coordination of astronomy and geography that would provide their leaders and their saints with an enormous reservoir of meaning, a matrix of secret power. It was a platform that enabled their faithful to soar. Is it any wonder the Muslims wish to deny both Jews and Christians complete access to the Dome of the Rock in Jerusalem, the site of Solomon's Temple, knowing how the apocalyptically-minded of both religions view the building of a third Temple on the site as a signal to usher in the End of Days?

By focusing on apocalyptic time—the end of time, the end of history—one robs oneself and one's co-religionists of power. Everything is drained towards that single end, that omega point of destruction. Life begins to loose its beauty, its meaning, its relevance. The time for redemption runs out. Grace is in short supply. Careers are denied; love is postponed.

But the apocalyptic cults function within the other calendars, like it or not. There are points of tangence, of convergence, with calendars they do not recognize and they can be interpreted thereby. Thus the rise and fall of a Manson, or a Jim Jones, can be predicted; the graves of their followers and their victims can be visited on special days, days made sacred by the blood of human sacrifice. And the cycles start again.

I like to think that most people, if given a clear choice, would select good over evil. The problem is that good and evil are often only relative terms; the absolute nature of either one is difficult to confront, face to face. The experience of the divine may often be confused with an experience of evil; that is what is meant by "sinister": a threat of something dangerous, of something nefarious, an attitude of secret knowledge and secret strength. As many quoted passages have already noted in the preceding chapters, we often see the divine as "sinister." The other reflex is to see the demonic as divine. After all, in the Western tradition, Lucifer was a fallen angel, the most beautiful of God's creation. It is natural that our experience of Lucifer would be a positive one.

That is why the image is so powerful, much more so than the written word, which requires some level of thought and conscious participation. The image acts directly on the unconscious mind, conveying whole libraries of information in a single moment, setting up connecting links with other images, other ideas. That is why, frankly, the image is not to be trusted. One needs a powerful internal editor, one that questions each image to understand its purpose, its target, its origins. This is what the Christian Fundamentalists call the "power of discernment": the ability to tell if a spirit is truly good or evil. One cannot rely on pure image alone. One needs another source of information. One needs a context.

Unfortunately, as in the case of the UFO phenomenon and many paranormal experiences, we have very little in the way of context. Our religious training has been largely abandoned in the last fifty years, or has been abused by venal leaders and prophets who see a way to make a fast dollar and an easy reputation. Our scientific training has been outdated and monopolized by a scientific elite. Our political awareness has been virtually useless, manipulated by clever pitchmen, campaign managers and spin doctors, to the point where we don't know what we value anymore, or what the American experiment is all about. We need to start relying on ourselves, and that means thinking for ourselves (as painful a process as that may be, and I do not say that lightly).

It means going back to our museums and art galleries, concert halls and libraries, to get a better understanding of our own culture and the sacrifices made by individual artists, musicians, and writers to bring eternal truths to our attention. It means turning off the television set. Now, at a time when Western—and particularly American—culture is under attack as "decadent" or "worthless" or "non-existent" or "shallow," it is important for us to re-evaluate our culture, for it contains some surprises. We have listened for a long time to the Europeans tell the Americans that they have no culture; the problem is not that Americans have no culture, it is that they do not know what that culture is. American culture is far richer and far more powerful than our European relations would admit. We need to know what it is and to understand it, and to teach it in the schools, and to do that we need to have a context in which to understand it. And that means learning about the creative functions and their relation to psychology, to visionary experience, and to the frontiers of quantum physics.

It also means learning how to use our neglected "paranormal" abilities: those abilities so assiduously studied by our military and intelligence agencies for the past fifty years. These abilities only seem paranormal now; in future generations they will be realized for what they are: the application of consciousness to science, the continuation of politics by other means . . . means not dreamed of by Clausewitz.

The "sinister forces" of our title were identified as Nazism by Robert Jackson, and as extraterrestrials by General MacArthur. The Bible warns of spiritual evil in high places, and the scriptures of India speak of the dangers of a human being storming heaven using occult practices; the ancient Sumerians understood that evil dwells beyond the planets in the realm of the stars (*Igigi*); and Nazism was concerned with the creation of a new man and the worship of Lucifer. So what are the sinister forces? Are they simply the emanations of a deeper evil force, or do we confuse the sinister divine with the sinister satanic? For most of us, confrontation with any spiritual power is a matter of dread, awe, and fear (*vide* Guggenbühl-Craig).

The Nazis took the bold—and insane—step of evoking these forces deliberately, by institutionalizing all sorts of occult ideas and theories and practices in the SS, the Ahnenerbe, and other places. The American political and economic machine emulated some of these practices in their support of Nazism, racism and eugenics; by supporting Nazism they were allowing a deep moral evil to enter the country at the highest levels of power: the CIA, NASA, the USAF, etc., and eventually US corporations, such as Bell Aerospace, ITT, etc. When the CIA scientists began their assault on human consciousness, without regard to psychological or spiritual fallout, they were following in the steps of the Nazi doctors, and in some cases using captured Nazi files and captured Nazi scientists as their guides. American politics and American science began to incorporate Nazi elements at the same time they were opening the American mind and consciousness, through drugs like LSD and through irresponsible mental programming experiments on prisoners, the mentally-ill, the unwitting, and the unsuspecting. As the remote-viewing program has shown, there is a possibility that "heightened states" of consciousness are capable of near-miraculous feats, including space exploration (*vide* Swann). The alien abductees speak of the sinister agenda of the aliens, the horrors to which they have been subjected. If these are truly alien beings, then they are adept at using the Manson Secret on their subjects; if they are not alien beings, but military or intelligence officers in the midst of an experimental program, then the Manson Secret is already in their hands, and MK-ULTRA was a decoy.

The only defense we have against the sinister forces is to develop our own mental capabilities—individually—as a firewall against psychological warfare, cultural colonialism, mind control, and the remote viewers and telepaths of the enemy.

Our churches, our political parties, our schools, our media are all as suspect as our secret government agencies. The Republicans have shown a callous disregard for the hideous crimes perpetrated by the Nazis in order to allow them to fight the Communists. I do not believe it was simple pragmatism that led them to that position; they too often voice opinions and demonstrate actions that would be clearly in accordance with a Nazi agenda. Richard Nixon was the most obvious example of this, with his anti-Semitism and his sociopathic personality, as evidenced by his collaboration with Nazis and by his version of the October Surprise. This is not to exempt the Democrats from the same accusations, but in the case of the Democratic Party, the anti-Semitism or pro-Nazism of *individuals* is more the rule than is a wholesale collaboration with Nazism as a virtual party platform. Remember that "sinister forces" were accused of creating the eighteen-and-a-half minute gap in the Nixon Oval Office tapes. Haig was more right than he knew.

The involvement of Hollywood as the medium for the sinister forces is previewed in the Lovecraft story where artists are the first point of contact for upcoming events of a global nature: Hollywood represents the artist of America, at least in a gross and commercial way, fueled by the fantasies and dark dreams of the men and women who have prostituted themselves and their abilities to the engines of the major studios while struggling personally to put forward a more wholistic point of view, sometimes below the radar and sometimes unconsciously. Hollywood is the new religion of America and, to a certain extent, of the rest of the world as well. Hollywood brings the gods—the stars, "every man and every woman is a star"—down to earth, where they can be seen and heard and touched by the masses; not only Hollywood, of course, but also the music industry, and not only in California and New York but also in Bollywood and Europe and Mexico and Brazil and Venezuela and China and Hong Kong and so on. Americans emulate movie characters more than they do the saints of their religions: they dress like them, drive the same cars, have the same attitudes, talk like them, and eventually adopt the same cultural mores. Hollywood is a vast mind-control engine, which is why many independent films are ignored by the public: they do not want to think independently, they want to have their consciousness massaged by the old, familiar rituals. The tools of Hollywood are the tools of psychological warfare, of mind control and behavior control. Of advertising, in its most pernicious sense.

Ronald Brownstein, in *The Power and the Glitter: The Hollywood-Washington Connection*, makes this idea very clear with examples from the 1940s to the present day. He speaks of Hollywood's dismay when Ronald Reagan was embraced by the electorate:

> It was widely assumed that Reagan had mesmerized the public with cheap stagecraft . . . . Almost without exception, the Hollywood left was convinced that its own understanding of the actor's tools provided unique abilities to penetrate Reagan's façade and expose the shallowness it saw behind it.[5]

Hollywood seems most powerful when it is least conscious of what it is doing. The actor Mike Farrell—who portrayed B.J. Hunnicutt on the television series *M*A*S*H*—was stunned by the fact that he was recognized by refugees from the Khmer Rouge living in camps set up on the Thai-Cambodian border in the 1980s.[6] This is the phenomenon against which the developing nations—and particularly those nations dominated by religious fundamentalism—are now protesting, sometimes with violence. They have understood that media—all media—are a form of psychological warfare, "world-view warfare." All media contain elements of cultural assumptions and biases that may not be obvious, even to their creators, and which, to governments with a tenuous hold on the loyalty and confidence of their citizens, seem subversive and dangerous. America's experience during the Cold War instructed its leaders that the best wars are those which are never fought with guns and bombs, but with ideas. Colonialism in the old sense is expensive and unfashionable. Cultural colonialism, however, is much cheaper, uses fashionable media, and is plausibly deniable.

The same elements we have discovered used by Manson and Jones and many others can be found in the dissemination of media messages throughout the world. Television has replaced scripture in many households; certainly many people pay more attention to their television set than to their religion, even in religious states. Sitting around a television set in the comfort of their own homes, people are isolated from one another in a social context, but united with others thousands of miles away in a cultural context. They are massaged by images that carry subtle sexual intentions—attractive actors, singers, models, the sexual tensions of the soap opera and the movie—and are introduced to a world that encourages a value system somewhat at odds with their own, using powerful images, colors, music: a subliminal package that causes shifts in consciousness. The danger of this can only be sensed by those already attuned to a deeper spiritual state of mind, where the assault of these images can be seen for what it is: a form of psychological warfare, of brainwashing, of cultural imperialism.

By encoding this system in a vast media machine that incorporates television, cinema, and the music industry, Hollywood has developed tremendous power. This is not to say that this power is evil in and of itself; that would be naïve. The power of Hollywood should be respected for what it is, a kind of institutionalized—or industrialized—mind control. The more actors, writers, directors and producers are aware of this, the more powerful this system becomes. The Reagan phenomenon was the wake-up call for many in Hollywood, even if they had not understood that the Kennedy election, twenty years earlier, owed a great deal to the power of television, the first such election to do so. Now it is important to maintain the struggle in Hollywood among the factions that would seek to dominate this power for one agenda or another. Hollywood has already learned the Manson Secret; it would be a disaster if only one party or one set of fundamentalist beliefs were to monopolize its use.

Terrorism, by contrast, is the new witchcraft; terrorists are aligned against all states, and thus are rebels everywhere and despised everywhere. They attack culture, and not military targets, to maximize the fear factor. Terrorist cells are the modern equivalent of the witches' coven, and the Patriot Act is the equivalent of the Inquisition.

A favorite target of terrorist states is Hollywood, for all the obvious reasons. Yet, they have learned a great deal about the power of the image from Hollywood. Why else bomb a school bus? A hospital? The World Trade Center? Terrorism, as we have seen, is a form of psychological warfare, and as such owes a great deal to the same technologies in use by Hollywood and by our own intelligence agencies. Indeed, many of the important terrorist figures now arrayed against America got their training from the CIA during American support for the Taliban guerrillas fighting the Soviet invasion. One of the more infamous of terrorist "interrogators"—Dr. Aziz al-Abub of the Hezbollah in Lebanon—had received his training in mind control at Patrice Lumumba University in Moscow, and employed virtually the same methods as his American counterparts. The "brainwashing war" that began in 1950 with the Korean conflict, and which involved the United States versus China and the Soviet Union, has now percolated down to the popular level, the terrorist level: the technology of torture, pain, sensory deprivation, hypnosis, and drugs is available to everyone, and is much cheaper to employ than a Stinger rocket or a Kalashnikov.

In the case of the Islamic terrorist organizations, these heinous practices are carried out in the name of God by men who, "inflamed with prayer," do not question their application. Just as America viewed the Communist nations as atheistic and godless, and used that as one of their many justifications for the excesses of the Cold War, so do the Islamic terrorists view America as the Great Satan, a decadent society that is an affront to God and which must be destroyed. The real war may very well be that which is being played out in Jerusalem between fundamentalist Christians, messianic Jews, and determined Muslims over the site of the Temple of Solomon and the Dome of the Rock. In the Middle East we have catastrophic military technology in the hands of religious fanatics, true believers who will fight to the last drop of their blood—and ours—for God, manipulated by cynical men who know these robot warriors for what they really are: pawns in a game whose rules only they know, men who gleefully employ the Manson Secret.

Who, then, are the sinister forces? Demons? Or Gods? Aliens, or . . . us? We are in danger of losing our freedom because of this threat to our lives and culture, since our leaders know only one way to respond to terrorism/ witchcraft, and that is the stake and the forced confession. Our leaders cannot talk to us about the real problem; they cannot admit their own failure of imagination.

We have been talking about the end-times endlessly, this begun by our fundamentalist Christian Coalition, whose most notable spokespersons have been Jerry Falwell, Pat Robertson, Ronald Reagan and, now, George W. Bush—and have been making films and writing books and articles about the apocalypse (by nuclear war, nuclear accident, asteroid strike, holes in the ozone, etc.) at such a furious pace, that we may infer that we are either predicting it through some unconscious means, some "heightened state" that has been activated in our quantum consciousness, or that we are calling it, summoning it in an act of desperation, so tired of the world the way it is and simply wanting it all to end.

We are all so tired of the epidemics, the urban violence, the danger of terrorism, of biochemical warfare, of nuclear war, of hunger and starvation, of grinding poverty and fear of unemployment, of the bankruptcy of both ourselves and of the private and public sectors, of the dwindling rain forests, the rapidly depleting water supply, the absence of anything like spiritual renewal or cultural values in our media (except, perhaps, in the art, concert music, opera, and literature that has become less and less accessible to the people, with the dwindling financial support of our respective governments for both the arts and for the education necessary to enjoy them), of sexism, racism, ethnophobia, anti-Semitism, of the sheer volume of noise being created by technology without content, without meaning, of air and earth and water pollution, of the toxic substances in our food, of the incapability of science and medicine to be consistent about what is good or bad for us to do, to consume, to behave, to believe . . . . And at the same time we are so terrified of some cosmic apocalyptic event that would wipe out the planet that we live under a cloud of danger and despair and try to smile through it all for the sake of our children. We have a love/hate relationship with life itself. We, as a society, have become sick; and that is actually the good news.

As we have noted in the above pages and at length, the sickness of an individual paves the way for spiritual enlightenment and psychological integration. The acute schizophrenia we are now experiencing as a society may be the necessary preliminary step to a shamanic-style rebirth. The hideous violence and degradation we see all around us—and on our television screens and computer monitors—may be the signal that the dismemberment of our society is at hand. The sinister forces have been evoked from within the magic circle of the Oval Office, the videocam, the seal on the floor of CIA headquarters at Langely, and in a million other places. These may be alien forces from another planet or another dimension; or they may be demons, battalions of demons as in a painting by Breughel, marching through our blasted landscape and meting out torture and death along the way. Our saving grace as Americans is the fact that we can recognize this, that we do not simply sit still and watch from the sidelines as our civilization crumbles around us.

We are not "good Germans." Hitler's Germany will forever remain our example of the sinister forces that we have come to despise, the complacency of a citizenry in which evil triumphs because good men do nothing. We are Americans, and we are biased, and bigoted, and provincial, and arrogant, and naïve, and stupid; all of this is true. But we are also dreamers; our worst citizens have been guilty of bad dreams, perhaps, but were dreamers nonetheless. We are a sentimental people who cry at Disney movies, for which the sophisticated European laughs at us. Europe, the heir to the Renaissance: clearly the last time there was anything remotely resembling grandeur on that continent. Bitter in their shameful history of genocide and holocaust and collaboration and cowardice, and eager for company in their spiritual deterioration, Europeans are the crowd that stands below a building and urges the potential suicide to jump. We will ignore them, for we are not standing on top of that building to jump, but to reach just a little higher.

We have committed some grave sins in our history; of this there can be no doubt. The slaughter of the Native American population is perhaps the first sin, and one of the most grave. The brutal, inescapable fact of slavery is another, with its sickening offspring, racism; also the way some of our wealthiest and most powerful families and leaders sponsored eugenics and genocide in everything from the murderous Tuskegee syphilis program to state laws banning interracial marriages. Our colonial attitude to the peoples of Latin America is another, an ugly legacy from the people we fought for our own independence, foisted on weaker neighbors to the south; thousands upon thousands of people have died in Latin America, and millions more suffered incredible hardships, due to American foreign policy in the region. Our support of military dictatorships around the world is another grave sin, from the Shah of Iran to Pinochet of Chile, from Marcos in the Philippines to Saddam Hussein in Iraq, and so many others. Hiroshima was a horrible crime, and Nagasaki even greater, for we did not need a Nagasaki after the holocaust of Hiroshima.

Many wonder why America is so violent; possibly it is an understandable reaction to a sense of enormous guilt, and the unfairness of this burden of guilt on the shoulders of decent men and women who would have had nothing to do with the above crimes, if they had been given a choice. Our gun-toting population is perhaps consumed with a kind of death wish, a suicidal need to purge the earth, and this may be due—I contend—to the necessity of confronting our collective history and not finding enough to rejoice and celebrate, not enough that is inclusive of all Americans. Since the assassination of President Kennedy, we have become a distrustful and cynical population; we watched our sons and daughters come back from Vietnam and wept for those who made it back alive as well as for those who did not. We began to doubt our goodness, and this has made us angry and hateful and paranoid; for it is of central importance to every American to believe in the American dream. Without that belief, we become lesser beings living in a lesser country: a crass, commercialized landscape of strip malls and fast food and electronic churches.

Thank God we have people in our country who bring these sins to our attention, and some of us listen, and some of us grow up to work against that mentality. When the rest of the world wishes to criticize us, they do so by referencing reports and data in *our own* newspapers, magazines, and news programs: they do not realize the irony of this, since in their countries it is illegal to use the media to criticize their governments. But while our elected officials may be guilty of cynicism and cowardice and evil intentions, our electorate is not. Our people still believe in the old dreams, the idea of what it means to be an American. That is why they were all so shocked by the events of September 11, 2001.

They could not understand why anybody would hate them. They have not been abroad. They don't speak the language. They haven't done the reading. They have not seen the handiwork of which our elected officials and our intelligence agencies and our corporate leaders are capable. And for that, we should be grateful. For if they did know all of this, and if they were not shocked by September 11, then the only conclusion we could draw is that they were accomplices in all of this and actually *were* the war-mongers and racists and neo-fascists the rest of the world thinks they are.

But their shock was the shock of the innocent, and perhaps of the stupid and of the ignorant . . . but not of the evil.

We could sum up with a quotation from the late, lamented Walt Kelly's *Pogo* comic strip: "We have met the enemy and he is us." Once we realize this, we can begin to make America the place of greatness and beauty and transcendence that it was intended to be, intended to be by our founding fathers who were, after all, Freemasons and Rosicrucians and Templars and freethinkers and mystics, who believed in spiritual regeneration and psychological integration.

Instead, we will end with another quotation.

That first Sunday in June 1968, at the funeral for Robert F. Kennedy—the last, best hope for a renewed America for a long time to come—his brother, Senator Edward Kennedy, read the eulogy. It contained Bobby's favorite quotation, one that he would use to revive his flagging spirits or to raise the energy of his followers.

It is a beautiful sentiment, but how many listeners in St. Patrick's Cathedral in Manhattan that solemn spring day realized the original context? As Bobby's body lay in the center aisle of that Gothic pile, surrounded by those who loved and admired him, his "robopathic" assassin in jail in Los Angeles staring stupidly around him in confusion, the men who authorized that murder toasting themselves in comfort in the boardrooms and cloakrooms and living rooms and conference rooms and bedrooms of America, some of them even there, in the church watching the funeral service with cynical satisfaction, knowing that the last assassination had taken place and that America was ripe for the plunder, the words of their sinister god were being quoted as epitaph:

"You see things; and you say, 'Why?' But I dream things that never were; and I say 'Why not?'"

The quote comes from George Bernard Shaw's *Back to Methuselah*, and they are the words of the Devil.

Brooklyn Heights, 1975—Kuala Lumpur, 2003—South Florida, 2006

ENDNOTES

1 Walter Lang, in his Introduction to Fulcanelli's *Le Mystere des Cathedrales*, Brotherhood of Life, Las Vegas, 2000, p. 22

2 Dr. Robert M. Schoch & Robert Aquinas McNally, *Voyages of the Pyramid Builders: The True Origins of the Pyramids from Lost Egypt to Ancient America*, Tarcher/Putnam, NY, 2003

3 William F. Romain, *Mysteries of the Hopewell: Astronomers, Geometers, and Magicians of the Eastern Woodlands*, University of Akron Press, Akron, 2000

4 *Harvest of Death: Chemical Warfare in Vietnam and Cambodia*, Neilands, et. al., The Free Press, NY, 1972, p. 18

5 Ronald Brownstein, *The Power and the Glitter: The Hollywood-Washington Connection*, Pantheon, NY, 1990, p. 278

6 Ibid., p. 282

Four figures who embody the collision of American idealism and corruption: Robert F. Kennedy (1925-1968), whose assassination marked the end of an era of hope; Charles Manson (1934-2017), who perverted mystical practices into instruments of terror; Richard M. Nixon (1913-1994), whose presidency revealed the depths of political corruption; and Jim Jones (1931-1978), whose Peoples Temple descended from social reform into mass murder.

These men represent a pivotal decade when sacred ideals were corrupted by power, mysticism was weaponized by intelligence agencies, and America's struggle between light and darkness played out on both public and hidden stages. Their interconnected stories expose the "sinister forces" at work beneath the surface of American society—forces that continue to shape our world today.

EPILOGUE

January 2006
South Florida

Friends of mine in Kuala Lumpur—otherwise intelligent, rational people with a love of business and the easy, good life of their tropical paradise—take it for granted that the world has targeted Muslim Malaysia out of jealousy for the strength of their economy; that Jewish bankers and financiers (like the demonized George Soros) were hell-bent on global domination; that there was simply no truth to the reports that Malaysia was a haven for terrorists, even as one of their political parties praised the bombers of Bali, of the World Trade Center, of the Marriott Hotel in Jakarta and met with Hamas and Hezbollah leaders in Malaysia in May of 2002 . . .

No matter how long I argued that most Americans couldn't find Malaysia on the map if you paid them, and that the only nationality bankers understand (I, who had worked for an Israeli bank for four years) is the nationality of money, they refused to believe me. The Prime Minister was able to unite his people against a mysterious, common enemy: a foreign enemy, an infidel army, a colonial power preparing to invade Malaysia if not with troops (although, after the invasion of Iraq, that still looked like a possibility to many) then with bearer bonds. International Jews. Foreign bankers. The IMF.

Sinister forces.

Outside my window the mosques still rang with the amplified call of the muezzin. But down the street, the prayer hall on Jalan Damai was filled with idealistic, clear-eyed, sometimes hateful young men in sarongs and knit skull-caps, sitting cross-legged, listening to a sermon mixed with political speeches, and calls to *jihad*. Other Muslims could be seen getting into their cars. Mercedes. BMWs. Hondas. The more plebeian in Protons and Kancils. They have asked God for protection, but they are still paranoid. And why not?

So am I.

> *Dogs with broken legs are shot; men with broken souls write through the night.*
> —Kenneth Patchen, *The Journal of Albion Moonlight*

What has obsessed me in these pages is not the paranoia of the clerk, but of the congressman. Of the President, and the Pentagon. Of five-star generals and CIA directors and scientists and clergymen. Of police officers and FBI profilers. This is not the paranoia of the loser, of the victim—pathetic, understandable—but of the winner, the victor. The paranoia of the people in charge. People who should know better, and probably do. It is what they fear most that I fear most: what they do not want us to know. The paranoia of experts. *If you're not paranoid, you don't know all the facts.*

It is the paranoia of men who shred documents in the executive offices at CIA headquarters, like schoolboys hiding dirty magazines; of a sitting President, nervous about "the Bay of Pigs thing"; of an Attorney General, and his murdered brother.

There is blood, and there are documents. This is history. You can't have one without the other. Blood. Documents. Guilt. Innocence. Knowledge. Ignorance. Frustration. Fear. But you can't know history unless you know fear. You can't know history unless you feel the pulse of life under your fingers; unless you can stare the guns in the face. Unless you can stand in the prisons, and the death camps, and feel the gaze of informers and spies and soldiers on your back in foreign countries . . . and on your own doorstep, your own driveway. The rest is only bookkeeping.

The world has always been like this, of course. It has always been run by people: superstitious, religious, fearful, paranoid, ugly, hateful, murderous people. That is nothing new. But at a specific point in the century we took this a step further. We opened Pandora's box, the black box of human consciousness. We flipped open the lid, and rummaged around inside. And we loosed monsters on the earth. Monsters who feed on human flesh, and who drink the nectar of human souls.

Churches harbor the danger as much as hospitals; there is nowhere to go, no one to trust. To come to that conclusion one would have to read all these books, mountains of references to be cross-checked and verified in virtually every discipline known to us: political science, history, archaeology, paleoastronomy, comparative religion, occultism, psychology, philosophy, medicine, physics, chemistry, business, finance, geology, geophysics, mathematics, anthropology, Watergate, Wall Street, assassinations, intelligence programs, alien abductions, epigraphy, linguistics, Hollywood, communications science, military history. Thousands of books, piles of documents. Is it any wonder, after all, that the shots—the shots that changed the world, that martyred a President, that ended a reign of hope—were believed to have come from a place where books were stored?

Back in Kuala Lumpur, the phone would ring very late at night (or very early in the morning). I was in Asia, so twelve hours separated me from the people I know and love in the States. They, in the sunlight of yesterday, still dealing with a day that is already closed for me. I didn't want to answer. I didn't want to tell them how that day would turn out.

Back on the East Coast, the days are reversed, but the phone no less ominous. I hate telephones. I hate being summoned to account for myself, my presence, my actions, when those who should be accountable never are. More to the point, I cannot talk now. Faced with this horrible reality, I have come to learn that I know as little about myself as about anything else. How can I speak on the phone? Who will do the talking, the listening? What truth can really be spoken, when we have been baptized with lies?

The phone continues to ring, then stops.

ACKNOWLEDGMENTS

The task of acknowledging the many hundreds of people who have contributed to my understanding of this subject is gratifying, but daunting. In the first place, research for this three volume work began in 1975 and continued at a more or less steady pace—interrupted by the vicissitudes of a quotidian existence (a day job)—and took place all over the United States as well as in many foreign countries. In addition, recourse was had to archives and libraries and, with the advent of the Internet, to on-line resources as well. That means that the number of individuals who had some input to my work increased exponentially with each passing decade.

I will try to identify those who most influenced my work and my point of view, therefore, with apologies to anyone I may have missed.

Pride of place must go to Norman Mailer, whose support of my earlier work—*Unholy Alliance*—provided a tremendous boost to my self-confidence at a time when I was ten thousand miles from the States and deeply immersed in the research for *Sinister Forces*. I will be forever grateful to the man who is arguably the be,t living American writer for so openly sharing his views and opinions on the massive undertaking I had set for myself.

Close behind are some of the other members of the Dynamite Club, such as Jim Hougan and Dick Russell, who not only provided forewords for Volumes 1 and 2 respectively, but who also contributed their advice and information. Jim Hougan, particularly, was extremely helpful when it came to the chapter on Jonestown, and his article on the subject in *Lobster*—cited in the text—is groundbreaking. Dick Russell's magisterial work, *The Man Who Knew Too Much,* was inspirational in its scope (and its size!), and his background on some of the other characters mentioned in these pages was valuable and enlightening.

Paul Krassner is a hero and an icon to many of us who remember and cherish the Sixties and the crusading journalism of *The Realist*, a tradition that has not faltered in lo, these many decades; I found myself referencing his work—particularly concerning John Lennon—long before he agreed to provide a foreword for Volume 3. Paul, I am not worthy!

Whitley Strieber was someone who believed in this effort from very early on, while I was still in foreign lands and struggling to put this initiated view of American history into some kind of perspective. His own works show how events can be seen and understood on more than one level, and even more than one dimension, and this idea helped me to formulate my own ideas concerning synchronicity, coincidence and conspiracy. We vacillate between a no-nonsense, empirical and near Positivist approach to the subject matter . . . and a mystical, transcendental illuminative vision of the same material.

I think we both realize that the truth lies somewhere in that twilight zone between the waking world and the sleeping, between consciousness and the unconscious, between occult revelation and scientific certainties. There are conspiracies, and there are coincidences; what we explore is the matrix that accommodates both and takes reality into another realm of connection and coherence altogether. As is shown in this work, one can be a conspirator and a mystic both; it will be up to history to decide which approach is the more . . . reliable.

But this book would never have seen the light of day had it not been for Kris Millegan. As the publisher of TrineDay, a small house that dares to print uncomfortable facts and to "speak truth to power," Kris has weathered many a political storm over the books he has midwifed to press. Attacked by lawsuits from the Special Forces Association, among others, because he dares to expose the harsh realities of government conspiracy and corruption, he bravely accepted the onerous task of publishing a huge work—*Sinister Forces*—that ran to almost 2000 pages of manuscript, something no other agent or publisher wanted anything to do with; but that didn't stop Millegan, himself the son of a former CIA officer, and who spent some years of his early childhood in the same countries I would wind up living in decades later. Kris' work on *Skull & Bones* has already won him worldwide acclaim (there is a Japanese translation of his work). The work he has done will stand the test of time, and future generations will be amazed that our country was able to function for so long (while ignoring the vast corruption and injustice uncovered by Kris), like the man in the Malcolm Lowry novel who ignores the tiger chewing on his shoulder and pretends there is nothing wrong.

I'm proud to be part of the Kris Millegan tradition, and this necessarily includes Russell Becker, TrineDay's editor, who painstakingly walked me through this entire manuscript to clarify and correct, identify and determine, both my ideas and my language, which, at times, had resulted in sentences that were nearly gothic in construction. Many thanks to you both.

Between all these brave men of vision there is a woman of equal vision and strength of character, and that would be the late Judith McNally, who passed away prematurely just as this book was going to press. I'd known her for thirty-five years, from when I was a struggling writer in Brooklyn Heights to the present day, when I am a struggling writer in South Florida. The struggle goes on—*la lucha sigue*—but with staunch allies and friends like Judith McNally, it seemed more like choreography than chaos. Thankfully, she was also a person who spoke her mind without reservation and was an unforgiving critic; many is the writer whose work has been tested and refined in the heat of her *athanor*, the dross slowly transformed to the glitter of something redeemable. Thank you.

Other influence, information and support have come from a diverse group of friends, associates, and fellow-travelers, among whom must be mentioned David Blackburst, for whose biography of David Ferrie we all await; and Tracy Twyman, whose late-lamented publication *Dagobert's Revenge* was a fascinating collection of all things Grail-ish, and who since has written persuasively on everything from the Merovingians to the American monetary system to the furor over the Danish cartoons of the Prophet (for which she has been "banned in Pakistan"). I wish to acknowledge the novelist Katherine Neville as well, for the long phone conversations that cleared up a lot of my thinking on some of the scientific personalities discussed herein; your fans (among whom I number myself) eagerly await your next novel.

In Europe, my old friends Gennaro Oliva and Patrizia Ronchetto deserve pride of place; there can be no more amiable guides to the life and culture of the Continent. *Grazie mille.*

In China, the same can be said of Peter Wong and Wang Lei, whom I have known for almost two decades. There is a book waiting to be written on Peter Wong's life, but who would believe it? *Xie-Xie Ninmen.*

In Malaysia, the trilingual Cecelia Ang was professional as well as patient and understanding with this ignorant *gweilo* during his long and sometimes frustrating sojourn in her native land. In business, as in culture, she helped me to see layers of meaning as well as of beauty in her country that the tourist or the foreign businessman could never discover. *M'goi* and *terimah kasih.*

In Singapore, Tham Yar Leong—businessman and geomancer—was my window to the world of Asian religion and mysticism. We spent many long hours discussing everything from the Knights Templar and the Freemasons to *feng shui* and Buddhist iconography. *O mi to fo.*

I have to give special thanks to the late Steve Orlando, of Longboat Key and Stonington, a man among men who understood that life was for living. His sense of what was valuable and important extended to his employees and his friends . . . and they were often the same people. A rare human being, he is missed.

And to Frank Diener, "Third World Man" and fellow-traveler in the dark realms of developing nations. This green beer is for you, Doctor!

To the Australians David Redfern and Larry O'Toole, the latter who told me to do the counterintuitive and focus on my strengths instead of trying to correct my weaknesses. You were right.

And to the bishops, Walter Propheta, Colin Guthrie, and George Augustine Hyde among many others. Propheta introduced me to the arcane world of the Wandering Bishops when I was still only seventeen years old. Colin Guthrie and George Augustine Hyde helped to fill in some blanks since then.

To Anthony Chang, Zhang LiDe and Zhang Qiang, who introduced me to China trade and, more importantly, to China itself, in the process giving me some of my most unforgettable memories.

To Kurt Neustaedter, who started me on the trail to the East without knowing it.

To Ingrid Celms, who was there at the beginning.

To the 16th Gyalwa Karmapa, from whom I accepted an initiation many years ago in New York City.

To the occultists Herman Slater, Ray Buckland, Maurice Woodruff, Leo Martello, Ed Buczynski, Ed James, Jim Wasserman, Martin Mensch, Richard Capuro, and so many, many others known over the years, such as Allyn Brodsky and the late Jerry Birnbaum, Kris Dowling, Elizabeth Bick Dowling . . . the list goes on and on.

To CIA agent Arthur Hochberg, and to contract agent Antonino Rocca, and several others who do not wish to be named. I value your (both voluntary and inadvertent) confidences.

To Clark Stiles ("Sunken civ") able electronic forum administrator whose long-standing support of different ideas in archaeology and anthropology were stimulating and productive.

And of course to Rose and Vivica. Vivica was not yet born when I began this work, and she is now a beautiful and talented woman of 25 years. As for Rose, strangely she hasn't aged at all. She must have a portrait hiding somewhere; yet I am sure it would look just the same anyway.

To these, and to all the others not mentioned here, I offer my sincerest gratitude. I hope this work is worthy of your many and varied contributions and lives up to the expectations you have had of a project that has taken thirty ears to complete.

Any errors, of course, remain my own.

Peter Levenda

BIBLIOGRAPHY FOR SINISTER FORCES

Not all the books, documents and other sources used as background for this trilogy are listed here, for the simple reason that such a Bibliography would be book-length itself. Instead, I have chosen those items that would give the reader an idea of where to begin to duplicate the research I have done. In addition, I have not divided the Bibliography simply into a "Primary Source" section and a "Secondary Source" section, since it was suggested that dividing the Bibliography by categories might be more valuable, as *Sinister Forces* covers a wide range of disciplines, cultures, and historical eras. Instead, I have identified primary and secondary source material within each category, where appropriate.

I hope that this decision was the right one.

That said, one can reasonably be assured that where documents are listed in the text—such as items from the JFK Collection at the National Archives or the MK-ULTRA documents released by the CIA—these are primary source material. I have taken pains to ensure that these documents are identified as clearly as possible, enabling future researchers to find them in their respective locations.

Naturally, over the past decades, research has also entailed not only documents, but flesh and blood human beings. I have spoken with literally hundreds of persons over the course of this historical investigation, many of whom would not be pleased to find themselves identified here. In the Acknowledgments section, therefore, some individuals have been mentioned but without revealing how they assisted me or what type of information they offered. In the case of Chinese military officials, former CIA and FBI officers, and others with links to their governments, this is understandable. In the case of religious leaders and cult members, this is perhaps less so but just as necessary in many cases. I interviewed all these on a "deep background" understanding, and I have not allowed these interviews to form the core of this research but have instead bolstered their statements with documentation and independent corroboration.

In the case of the wandering bishops, I was—as discussed in the Appendix to Book I—personally involved with this phenomenon and knew many of the primary players during the 1960s and 1970s, and have since interviewed others in the past ten years. My previous association with Walter Propheta and his colleagues enabled me to open dialogues with surviving members of his operation, as well as with various sects, denominations, and other splinter groups.

Further, my personal association with members of various "cults" and New Age denominations going back thirty years has made it easier for me to understand the relationship that exists between cults, crime, and political maneuvering, including intelligence-gathering. I hasten to point out that not all cults have criminal or intelligence agency connections or interests; many of these groups are composed of sincere seekers after spiritual realities. Yet, even then, they and their technologies can be manipulated by others less scrupulous.

But, isn't that the theme of this work?

SALEM WITCHCRAFT AND PRE-REVOLUTIONARY AMERICA

BELL, Michael E., *Food for the Dead: On the Trail of New England's Vampires*, Carroll & Graf, New York, 2001

BOYER, Paul and NISSENBAUM, Stephen, *Salem Village Witchcraft*, Northeastern University Press, Boston, 1993

—*Salem Possessed: The Social Origins of Witchcraft*, Harvard University Press, Cambridge, 1994

BRADFORD, William, *History of Plymouth Plantation 1620–1647*, Boston, 1912

BRESHAW, Elaine G. *Tituba: Reluctant Witch of Salem*, New York University Press, New York, 1996

BURR, George Lincoln, *Narratives of the Witchcraft Cases 1648–1706*, Scribners, New York, 1914

CAHILL, Robert Ellis, *New England's Viking and Indian Wars*, Old Saltbox Publishing, Danvers, (no date), ISBN 0916787-11-7

DEMOS, John Putnam, *Entertaining Satan: Witchcraft and the Culture of Early New England*, Oxford University Press, Oxford, 1983

DUNN, Oliver and KELLEY, James E. Jr., *The* Diario *of Chrisopher Columbus's First Voyage to America 1492–1493*, University of Oklahoma Press, Norman, 1991

GODBEER, Richard, *The Devil's Dominion: Magic and Religion in Early New England*, Cambridge University Press, Cambridge, 1994, ISBN 0-521-46670-9

HANSEN. Chadwick, *Witchcraft at Salem*, George Braziller, New York, 1992

HART, Albert Bushnell, ed., *American History Told by Contemporaries*, New York, 1898

LeBEAU, Bryan F., *The Story of the Salem Witch Trials*, Prentice Hall, New York, 1998

MATHER, Cotton, *Wonders of the Invisible World*, 1693

MORTON, Thomas, *Revels in New Canaan 1637*, reprinted in Hart, q.v.

STARKEY, Marion L., *The Devil in Massachusetts*, Anchor, New York, 1989

MORMONISM

BROOKE, John L., *The Refiner's Fire*, Cambridge University Press, Cambridge, 1994, ISBN 0-521-34545-6

LARSON, Stan, *Quest for the Gold Plates: Thomas Stuart Ferguson's Archaeological Search for the* Book of Mormon, Freethinker Press, Salt Lake City, 1996

NAIFEH, Steven and SMITH, Gregory White, *The Mormon Murders*, Penguin, New York, 1989

OSTLING, Richard N. and OSTLING, Joan K., *Mormon America: The Power and the Promise*, Harper San Francisco, 1999

PERSUITTE, David, *Joseph Smith and the Origins of the Book of Mormon*, McFarland & Co., Jefferson, 2000

QUINN, D. Michael, *Early Mormonism and the Magic World View*, Signature Books, Salt Lake City, 1998

SMITH, Joseph Jr., *The Book of Mormon: Another Testament of Jesus Christ*, The Church of Jesus Christ of Latter-Day Saints, Salt Lake City, 1991

TANNER, Jerald and Sandra, *Mormon Spies, Hughes and the CIA*, Utah Lighthouse Ministry, Salt Lake City, 1976

AMERICAN PREHISTORY

BRINE, Lindesay, *The Ancient Earthworks and Temples of the American Indians*, Oracle Publishing, Royston, 1996

BROSE, David S., BROWN, James A., and PENNEY, David W., *Ancient Art of the American Woodland Indians*, Harry N. Abrams, New York, 1985

CERAM, C.W., *The First American: A Story of North American Archaeology*, Harcourt Brace Jovanovich, New York, 1971

—*Hands on the Past*, Alfred A. Knopf, New York, 1966

FELL, Barry, *America BC: Ancient Settlers in the New World*, Pocket Books, NY, 1989

HOLAND, Hjalmar R., *Norse Discoveries and Explorations in America 982-1362*, Dover, New York, 1968

JENNINGS, Jesse D., *Prehistory of North America*, McGraw-Hill, NY, 1968

KENNEDY, Roger G., *Hidden Cities: the Discovery and Loss of Ancient North American* Civilization, The Free Press, New York, 1994

STRUEVER, Stuart and HOLTON, Felicia Antonelli, *Koster: Americans in Search of Their Prehistoric Past*, Anchor Press, New York, 1979

ROMAIN, William F., *Mysteries of the Hopewell*, University of Akron Press, Akron, 2000

WOODWARD, Susan L., and McDONALD, Jerry N., *Indian Mounds of the Middle Ohio Valley*, McDonald and Woodward, Blacksburg, 2002

NATIVE AMERICAN HISTORY

ARIAS, Larreta, A., *Popul Vuh: The Sacred Book of the Ancient Quiche Mayas*, Editorial Verdad y Vida, Mexico City

CHILTOSKY, Mary Ulmer, *Cherokee Words with Pictures*, Cherokee Publications, Cherokee, 1972

HINTON, Leanne, *Flutes of Fire: Essays on California Indian Languages*, Heyday Books, Berkeley, 1994

KELLEY, Klara Bonsack and FRANCIS, Harris, *Navajo Sacred Places*, Indiana University Press, Bloomington, 1994

LEON-PORTILLA, Miguel, *The Broken Spears: The Aztec Account of the Conquest of Mexico*, Beacon Press, Boston, 1992

NABOKOV, Peter, *Native American Testimony*, Penguin, New York, 1991

WORLD PREHISTORY

BARBER, Elizabeth Wayland, *The Mummies of Urumchi*, Pan Books, London, 1999

CLAPP, Nicholas, *The Road to UBAR: Finding the Atlantis of the Sands*, Mariner Books, Boston, 1999

CONNAH, Graham, *African Civilizations*, Cambridge University Press, Cambridge, 1990

OPPENHEIMER, Stephen, *Eden in the East*, Weidenfeld & Nicolson, London, 1998

RUDGLEY, Richard, *Lost Civilizations of the Stone Age*, Arrow, London, 1999

CHARLES MANSON AND THE SON OF SAM

ANDERSEN, Christopher, *Citizen Jane*, Henry Holt, New York, 1990

BRAVIN, Jess, *Squeaky: The Life and Times of Lynette Alice Fromme*, St Martins Press, New York, 1997

BUGLIOSI, Vincent, *Helter Skelter*, Bantam Books, New York, 1988

—*Helter Skelter*, Bantam Books, New York, 1995

CAPOTE, Truman, *Music for Chameleons*, New American Library, New York, 1981

COOPER, David E., *The Manson Murders: A Philosophical Inquiry*, Schenkman Publishing, Cambridge, 1974

GILMORE, John, *Manson*, Amok, Los Angeles, 2000

GUILES, Fred Lawrence, *Jane Fonda*, Doubleday, New York, 1982

KING, Greg, *Sharon Tate and the Manson Murders*, Barricade Books, New York, 2000

PHILLIPS, John, *Papa John: An Autobiography*, Dell, New York, 1987

POLANSKI, Roman, *Roman*, William Morrow, New York, 1984
SANDERS, Ed, *The Family*, Dutton, New York, 1971
—*The Family*, Signet, New York, 1989
SCHRECK, Nikolas, *The Manson File*, Amok, San Francisco, 1988
TERRY, Maury, *The Ultimate Evil*, Bantam, New York, 1989, ISBN 0-553-27601-8
TERRY, Maury, *The Ultimate Evil*, Barnes & Noble, New York, 1999, ISBN 0-7607-1393-6
WICK, Steve, *Bad Company: Drugs, Hollywood, and the Cotton Club Murder*, Harcourt, Brace, Jovanovich, New York, 1990, ISBN 0-15-110445-X

WANDERING BISHOPS

ANSON, Peter, *Bishops At Large*, October House, New York, 1965
BRANDRETH, Henry R.T., *Episcopi Vagantes and the Anglican Church*, Society For Promoting Christian Knowledge, London, 1947
BURGESS, Michael, *Lords Temporal and Lords Spiritual*, The Borgo Press, San Bernardino, 1995, ISBN 0-89370-426-1
MELTON, J. Gordon, *Encyclopedia of American Religions*, McGrath, Wilmington, 1978
SMITH, Charles Merrill, *How To Become A Bishop Without Being Religious*, Pocket Books, New York, 1966

INTERVIEWS AND PERSONAL CONTACTS:

ABRUGNEDO, Dom Lorenzo (Archbishop), personal communications 2004
BLACKBURST, David, personal communications regarding David Ferrie
BRENNAN, Andrei (Archbishop), personal communications 2004
CHIASSON, John "Christian", (Bishop), personal communications and interviews 1968–1969
DeVALITCH, Count Lorenzo Michel Pierre (Bishop) personal communications and interviews 1968–1969
DeWITOW, Theodosius (Archbishop), personal communications 1967
DOWLING, Kris (Bishop), personal communications 1977–2005
GUTHRIE, Colin (Archbishop), personal communications 2004–2005
HILL, Leonard G. (Bishop), personal communications and interviews 1968–1969
HYDE, George Augustine (Archbishop), personal communications and interviews 2004–2006
KONTAGEORGIOS, Eftimios (Bishop), personal communications 1971
MAKARIOS, (Bishop), personal communications and interviews 2004–2005
MARKUS, Mar (Archbishop), personal communications 2004
MOISEY, Archbishop-Metropolitan, personal communications 2004–2005
MYLES, Ivan (Archbishop), personal communications 2004
NUNEZ, John (Bishop), personal communications 2004
PENNACHIO, Andre (Bishop), personal communications and interviews 1968–1969
PERRY, David, personal communications regarding David Ferrie
PIERRE, Lawrence (Bishop), personal communications and interviews 1968–1969
PITT-KETHLEY, Fiona, personal communications 2005
PROPHETA, Walter (Archbishop Vladimir), personal communications and interviews 1968–1969
RICCIO, Dominic (Reverend), personal communications 2005
SCHILLEREFF, William (Reverend), personal communications 2004–2005
"SOROR M.A.," Societas Rosicruciana In America, personal communications 2004

NAZISM AND WORLD WAR II

AARONS, Mark & LOFTUS, John, *Unholy Trinity: The Vatican, the Nazis, and Soviet Intelligence*, St Martin's Press, New York, 1991

BAIGENT, Michael & LEIGH, Richard, *Secret Gemany*, Penguin, London, 1994

BAR-ZOHAR, Michael, *Bitter Scent: the Case of L'Oreal, Nazis, and the Arab Boycott*, Dutton, New York, 1996

BIRD, Lt. Col. Eugene K., *Prisoner #7, Rudolf Hess*, Viking Press, New York, 1974

BLACK, Edwin, *IBM and the Holocaust*, Little Brown, Boston, 2001

BLUM, Howard, *Wanted! The Search for Nazis in America*, Quadrangle, New York, 1977

BOWER, Tom, *Blind Eye to Murder*, Warner Books, London, 1997

—*The Paperclip Conspiracy*, Michael Joseph, London, 1987

BREITMAN, Richard, *Official Secrets*, Penguin, London, 1998

CLAY, Catrine & Leapman, Michael, *Master Race: the Lebensborn Experiment in Nazi Germany*, Coronet Books, London, 1995

COHN, Norman, *Warrant for Genocide*, Harper & Row, New York, 1967

CORNWELL, John, *Il Papa di Hitler: La storia segreta di Pio XII*, Garzanti Libri, Italy, 2000

FARAGO, Ladislas, *Aftermath: Martin Bormann and the Fourth Reich*, Simon & Schuster, New York, 1974

—*The Last Days of Patton*, Berkley Books, New York, 1982

FORD, Henry, *The International Jew*, Global Publishers, Johannesburg, 1997

FRANZINELLI, Mimmo, *Delatori*, Mondadori, Milan, 2001

GODWIN, Jocelyn, *Arktos: The Polar Myth in Science, Symbolism and Nazi Survival*, Phanes Press, Grand Rapids, 1993

GOODRICK-CLARKE, Nicholas, *The Occult Roots of Nazism*, New York University Press, New York, 1992

GROUEFF, Stephane, *Manhattan Project*, Little Brown, Boston, 1967

HABE, Hans, *Agent of the Devil*, George S. Harrap, London, 1958

HAYMAN, Ronald, *Hitler and Geli*, Bloomsbury, London, 1998

HIGHAM, Charles, *American Swastika*, Doubleday, New York, 1985

HUNT, Linda, *L'affaire Paperclip*, Stock, Paris, 1995

INFIELD, Glenn B., *Secrets of the SS*, Jove Books, New York, 1990

JONES, R.V., *Most Secret War: British Scientific Intelligence 1939–1945*, Hamish Hamilton, London, 1978

HUTTON, J. Bernard, *Hess: The Man and His Mission*, Macmillan, New York, 1971

LANGER, Walter C., *The Mind of Adolf Hitler*, Basic Books, New York, 1972

LAPON, Lenny, *Mass Murderers in White Coats*, Psychiatric Genocide Research Institute, Springfield, 1986

LEVENDA, Peter, *Unholy Alliance*, Avon, New York, 1995

—*Unholy Alliance*, Continuum, New York, 2002

LIFTON, Robert Jay, *The Nazi Doctors*, Basic Books, New York, 2000

LOFTUS, John & AARONS, Mark, *The Secret War Against the Jews*, St Martin's Griffin, New York, 1997

McGOVERN, James, *Crossbow and Overcast*, William Morrow, New York, 1964

MEDAWAR, Jean & PYKE, David, *Hitler's Gift: Scientists Who Fled Nazi Germany*, Piatkus, London, 2000

MUELLER-HILL, Benno, *Murderous Science*, Oxford University Press, Oxford, 1988

POSNER, Gerald L. & WARE, John, *Mengele: The Complete Story*, Dell, New York, 1987

RAHN, Otto, *La Cour de Lucifer*, Tchou, Paris, 1974

SERRANO, Miguel, *La Resurreccion del Heroe*, Solar Editores, Bogota, 1987

—*NOS: Book of the Resurrection*, Routledge Kegan & Paul, London, 1984

—*El Cordon Dorado*, Editorial Solar, Bogota, 1992

SICHROVSKY, Peter, *Incurably German*, Swan Books, Pine Plains, 2001

SIMPSON, Christopher, *Blowback*, Weidenfeld & Nicolson, New York, 1988

—*The Splendid Blond Beast*, Grove Press, New York, 1993

SMITH, Richard Harris, *OSS: The Secret History of America's First Central Intelligence Agency*, University of California Press, Berkeley, 1981

THOMAS, Hugh, *The Murder of Adolf Hitler*, St Martins Press, New York, 1995

JOVIN, M.E., *Los Protocolos de los Sabios de Sion*, Editores Mexicanos Unidos, Mexico

VON LANG, Jochen (ed.), *Eichmann Interrogated: Transcripts from the Archives of the Israeli Police*, Vintage Books, New York, 1983

ASHLAND, KENTUCKY

AP, "War on Poverty Figure Accused of Murder," *New York Times*, April 26, 1992, p. 30

Bloomberg Business News, "Ashland Oil Settles Civil Suits Over Air Pollution," *New York Times*, Feb 23, 1993, p. D5

ANON, *A History of Ashland, Kentucky 1786–1954*, Ashland Centennial Committee, 1954

ANON, *Ashland Historical Tour*, Ashland/Boyd County Tourism Commission, Ashland, 1990

HANNERS, Arnold, *Ashland's Pictorial Past*, Ashland, 1986

WALD, Matthew L., "Ashland Oil Appoints Successor to President," *New York Times*, Nov. 8, 1991, p. D4

BLUEBIRD, MULTIPLICITY AND MIND-CONTROL

Diagnostic and Statistical Manual, Mental Disorders (first edition), American Psychiatric Association, Washington DC, 1965

BAIN, Donald, *The Control of Candy Jones*, Playboy Press, Chicago, 1976, ISBN 0-87223-457-6

—*Long John Nebel*, MacMillan, New York, 1974, ISBN 0-02-505950-5

COLLINS, Anne, *In The Sleep Room*, Key Porter Books, Toronto, 1997, ISBN 1-55013-932-0

DeBOLD, Richard C. & LEAF, Russell C., *LSD, Man & Society*, Wesleyan University Press, Middletown, 1968, LOC 67-24111

FLOURNOY, Theodore, *From India to the Planet Mars: A Case of Multiple Personality with Imaginary Languages*, Princeton University Press, Princeton, 1994, ISBN 0-691-00101-4

HUXLEY, Aldous, *The Doors of Perception and Heaven and Hell*, Flamingo, London, 1994, ISBN 0-00-654731-1

KEYES, Daniel, *The Minds of Billy Milligan*, Bantam, New York, 1995, ISBN 0-553-26381-1

LEE, Martin A., & SHLAIN, Bruce, *Acid Dreams: The Complete Social History of LSD: The CIA, the Sixties, and Beyond*, Grove Weidenfeld, New York, 1992, ISBN 0-8021-3062-3

LIFTON, Robert Jay, *Thought Reform and the Psychology of Totalism: A Study of 'Brainwashing' in China*, University of North Carolina Press, Chapel Hill, 1989, ISBN 0-8078-4253-2

LOFTUS, Elizabeth & KETCHAM, Katherine, *The Myth of Repressed Memory: False Memories and Allegations of Sexual Abuse*, St Martin's Griffin, New York, 1994, ISBN 0-312-14123-8

MARKS, John, *The Search for the "Manchurian Candidate": The CIA and Mind Control*, Times Books, New York, 1979, ISBN 0-8129-0773-6

—*The Search for the "Manchurian Candidate": The CIA and Mind Control*, WW Norton, New York, 1988 edition, ISBN 0-393-30794-4

MEDVEDEV, Zhores & MEDVEDEV, Roy, *A Question of Madness: Repression by Psychiatry in the Soviet Union*, Vintage, New York, 1972, ISBN 0-394-71816-X

ROSS, Colin, *Bluebird: Deliberate Creation of Multiple Personality by Psychiatrists*, Manitou Communications, Richardson, 2000, ISBN 0-9704525-1-9

—*Dissociative Identity Disorder: Diagnosis, Clinical Features, and Treatment of Multiple Personality*, John Wiley & Sons, New York, 1997, ISBN 0-471-13265-9

SARGANT, William, *Battle for the Mind*, Malor, Cambridge, 1997, ISBN 188353606-5

SIMPSON, Christopher, *Science of Coercion: Communication Research & Psychological Warfare 1945–1960*, Oxford University Press, New York, 1996, ISBN 0-19-510292-4

SINASON, Valerie (ed.), *Attachment, Trauma and Multiplicity: Working with Dissociative Identity Disorder*, Brunner-Routledge, Hove, 2002, ISBN 0-415-19556-X

STEVENS, Jay, *Storming Heaven: LSD and the American Dream*, Atlantic Monthly Press, New York, 1987, ISBN 0-87113-076-9

THOMAS, Gordon, *Journey Into Madness*, Bantam Books, New York, 1990, ISBN 0-553-28413-4

WEINSTEIN, Harvey M., *Psychiatry and the CIA: Victims of Mind Control*, American Psychiatric Press, Washington DC, 1990, ISBN 0-88048-363-6

YATES, Frances A., *The Art of Memory*, University of Chicago Press, Chicago, 1966, ISBN 0-226-95001-8

PRESIDENT JOHN F. KENNEDY ASSASSINATION

Report of the Warren Commission On The Assassination of President Kennedy

EPSTEIN, Edward Jay, *Legend: The Secret World of Lee Harvey Oswald*, Hutchinson, London, 1978

FELTZER, James H. (ed.), *Assassination Science: Experts Speak Out on the Death of JFK*, Catfeet Press, Chicago, 2001

—*Murder in Dealey Plaza*, Catfeet Press, Chicago, 2001

GARRISON, Jim, *On The Trail of the Assassins*, Warner Books, New York, 1991

GIANCANA, Sam and Chuck, *Double Cross*, Warner Books, New York, 1992

KANTOR, Seth, *The Ruby Cover-Up*, Zebra Books, New York, 1992

HINCKLE, Warren and TURNER, William, *The Fish Is Red: the Story of the Secret War Against Castro*, Harper & Row, New York, 1981

KIRKWOOD, James, *American Grotesque*, Harper Perennial, New York, 1992

MAILER, Norman, *Oswald's Tale*, Ballantine, New York, 1996, ISBN 0-345-40437-8

MARRS, Jim, *Crossfire: the Plot that Killed Kennedy*, Carroll & Graf, New York, 1990

MORROW, Robert D., *First Hand Knowledge: How I Participated in the CIA-Mafia Murder of President Kennedy*, SPI Books, New York, 1992

PIPER, Michael Collins, *Final Judgment: The Missing Link in the JFK Assassination Conspiracy*, The Center for Historical Review, Washington, 1998

RUSSELL, Dick, *The Man Who Knew Too Much*, Carroll & Graf, New York, 2003

RUSSO, Gus, *Live By The Sword: the Secret War Against Castro and the Death of JFK*, Bancroft Press, Baltimore, 1998

SCOTT, Peter Dale, *Deep Politics and the Death of JFK*, University of California Press, Berkeley, 1996

SCOTT, William E., *November 22, 1963: A Reference Guide to the JFK Assassination*, University Press of America, Lanham, 1999

SUMMERS, Anthony, *The Kennedy Conspiracy*, Warner Books, New York, 1996

SZULC, Tad & MEYER, Karl E., *The Cuban Invasion: the Chronicle of a Disaster*, Ballantine Books, New York, 1962

SZULC, Tad, *Fidel: A Critical Portrait*, William Morrow, New York, 1986

WYDEN, Peter, *Bay of Pigs: The Untold Story*, Simon & Schuster, New York, 1979

SENATOR ROBERT F. KENNEDY ASSASSINATION

KLABER, William and MELANSON, Philip H., *Shadow Play: The Untold Story of the Robert F. Kennedy Assassination*, St Martin's Paperbacks, New York, 1998

MELANSON, Philip H., *The Robert F. Kennedy Assassination: New Revelations on the Conspiracy and Cover-Up 1968–1991*, SPI Books, New York, 1994

TURNER, William and CHRISTIAN, John, *The Assassination of Robert F. Kennedy: The Conspiracy and Cover-Up*, Thunder's Mouth Press, New York, 1993

JOHN LENNON ASSASSINATION

BRESLER, Fenton, *Who Killed John Lennon?*, St Martin's Paperbacks, New York, 1990

JONES, Jack, *Let Me Take You Down*, Villard Books, New York, 1992

MARILYN MONROE ASSASSINATION

BROWN, Peter Harry & BARHAM, Patte B., *Marilyn: The Last Take*, Dutton, New York, 1992, ISBN 0-525-93485-5

SMITH, Matthew, *The Men Who Murdered Marilyn*, Bloomsbury, London, 1996

SUMMERS, Anthony, *Goddess: The Secret Lives of Marilyn Monroe*, Indigo, London, 1985

WOLFE, Donald H., *The Assassination of Marilyn Monroe*, Warner Books, New York, 1998

SERIAL MURDER AND TRUE CRIME

BRUSSEL, James A., *Casebook of a Crime Psychiatrist*, Dell, New York, 1970

COOK, Thomas H., *Early Graves*, Onyx, New York, 1992, ISBN 0-451-40296-0

COX, Mike, *The Confessions of Henry Lee Lucas*, Pocket Star, New York, 1991, ISBN 0-671-70665-9

CROWLEY, Kieran, *Sleep My Little Dead*, St Martin's, New York, 1997, ISBN 0-312-96339-4

DEAR, William, *The Dungeon Master*, Ballantine, New York, 1985, ISBN 0-345-32695-4

DENTON, Sally, *The Bluegrass Conspiracy*, Doubleday, New York, 1990, ISBN 0-385-26272-8

DOUGLAS, John & OLSHAKER, Mark, *Journey Into Darkness*, Pocket Books, New York, 1997, ISBN 0-671-00394-1

FLOWERS, Anna, *Blind Fury*, Pinnacle, New York, 1993, ISBN 1-55817-719-1

GANEY, Terry, *Innocent Blood*, St Martin's, New York, 1989, ISBN 0-312-92269-8

GRAYSMITH, Robert, *Zodiac*, Berkley, New York, 1987, ISBN 0-425-09808-7

—*Zodiac Unmasked*, Berkley, New York, 2003, ISBN 0-425-18943-0

KELLY, Susan, *The Boston Stranglers*, Kensington, New York, 2002, ISBN 0-7860-1466-0

KEPPEL, Robert D., *Signature Killers*, Pocket Books, New York, 1997, ISBN 0-671-00130-2

—*The Riverman: Ted Bundy and the Hunt for the Green River Killer*, Pocket Books, New York, 1995, ISBN 0-671-86763-6

KNOWLTON, Janice, *Daddy Was the Black Dahlia Killer*, Pocket Books, New York, 1995, ISBN 0-671-88084-5

LAVERGNE, Gary M., *A Sniper In The Tower: The Charles Whitman Murders*, Bantam Books, New York, 1998, ISBN 0-553-57959-2

LEYTON, Elliott, *Sole Survivor: Children Who Murder Their Families*, Seal, Toronto, 1990, ISBN 0-7704-2408-2

MAAS, Peter, *In A Child's Name*, Pocket Books, New York, 1991, ISBN 0-671-74619-7

MARTINEZ, Thomas, *Brotherhood of Murder*, Pocket Books, New York, 1990, ISBN 0-6711-67858-2

McGINNISS, Joe, *Fatal Vision*, Signet, New York, 1984, ISBN 0-451-13098-7

MICHAUD, Stephen G., & AYNESWORTH, Hugh, *Ted Bundy: Conversations with a Killer*, Signet, New York, 1989, ISBN 0-451-16355-9

MOSS, Jason, *The Last Victim*, Warner Vision, New York, 2000, ISBN 0-446-60827-0

NEWTON, Michael, *Rope: The Twisted Life and Times of Harvey Glatman*, Pocket Books, New York, 1998, ISBN 0-671-01747-0

NOGUCHI, Thomas T., *Coroner At Large*, Simon & Schuster, New York, 1985, ISBN 0-671-54462-4

NORRIS, Joel, *Serial Killers*, Doubleday, New York, 1988, ISBN 0-385-26328-7

NORRIS, Joel, *Henry Lee Lucas: The Shocking True Story of America's Most Notorious Serial* Killer, Zebra Books, New York, 1991, ISBN 0-8217-3564-0

NORRIS, Joel, *Jeffrey Dahmer*, Pinnacle, New York, 1992, ISBN 1-55817-661-6

NORRIS, Joel, *Arthur Shawcross: The Genesee River Killer*, Pinnacle, New York, 1992, ISBN 1-55817-592-X

NORRIS, Joel, *Walking Time Bombs*, Bantam, New York, 1992, ISBN 0-553-28996-9

O'BRIEN, Darcy, *A Dark and Bloody Ground*, HarperCollins, New York, 1992, ISBN 0-06-017958-9

OLSEN, Jack, *The Misbegotten Son: A Serial Killer and His Victims, The True Story of Arthur Shawcross*, Island Books, New York, 1993, ISBN 0-440-21646-X

OLSEN, Jack, *Hastened to the Grave: The Gypsy Murder Investigation*, St Martin's, New York, 1998, ISBN 0-312-96699-7

PHILBIN, Tom, *Murder U.S.A.*, Warner, New York, 1992, ISBN 0-446-36091-0499

RESSLER, Robert K. & SHACHTMAN, Tom, *Whoever Fights Monsters*, St Martin's, New York, 1993, ISBN 0-312-95044-6

RESSLER, Robert K. & SHACHTMAN, Tom, *I Have Lived In the Monster: Inside the Minds of the World's Most Notorious Serial Killers*, St Martin's, New York, 1998, ISBN 0-312-96429-3

RHODES, Richard, *Why They Kill: The Discoveries of a Maverick Criminologist*, Vintage, New York, 2000, ISBN 0-375-70248-2

ROSEN, Fred, *Flesh Collectors*, Pinnacle, New York, 2003, ISBN 0-7860-1583-7

RULE, Ann, *The I-5 Killer*, Signet, New York, 1988, ISBN 0-451-16559-4

SCHECHTER, Harold, *Bestial: The Savage Trail of a True American Monster*, Pocket Books, New York, 1999, ISBN 0-671-73218-8

SCHREIBER, Flora Rheta, *The Shoemaker: The Anatomy of a Psychotic*, Signet, New York, 1984, ISBN 0-451-12855-9

SEXTON, David, *The Strange World of Thomas Harris*, Short Books, London, 2001, ISBN 0-571-20845-2

SINGULAR, Stephen, *Talked To Death: The Life and Murder of Alan Berg*, William Morrow, New York, 1987, ISBN 0-688-06154-0

SMITH, Carlton & GUILLEN, Tomas, *The Search for the Green River Killer*, Onyx, New York, 1991, ISBN 0-451-40239-1

SULLIVAN, Terry, *Killer Clown: The John Wayne Gacy Murders*, Pinnacle, New York, 1993, ISBN 1-55817-476-1

THOMPSON, Thomas, *Serpentine*, Robinson, London, 2001, ISBN 1-84119-384-4

VORPAGEL, Russell, *Profiles In Murder: An FBI Legend Dissects Killers and Their Crimes*, Dell, New York, 2001, ISBN 0-440-23552-9

WAMBAUGH, Joseph, *Echoes In the Darkness*, Bantam, New York, 1987, ISBN 0-553-26932-1

WHITTLE, Brian & RITCHIE, Jean, *Prescription for Murder: The True Story of Mass Murderer Dr. Harold Frederick Shipman*, Warner, New York, 2000, ISBN 0-7515-2998-2

JACK THE RIPPER

CORNWELL, Patricia, *Portrait of a Killer: Jack The Ripper, Case Closed*, Little, Brown, Boston, 2000, ISBN 0-316-72508-0

EDWARDS, Ivor, *Jack the Ripper's Black Magic Rituals*, John Blake, London, 2003, ISBN 1-90403-487-X

EVANS, Stewart & GAINEY, Paul, *Jack The Ripper: First American Serial Killer*, Kodansha International, New York, 1998, ISBN 1-56836-257-9

GRAHAM, Anne E. & EMMAS, Carol, *The Last Victim: The Extraordinary Life of Florence Maybrick, the wife of Jack the Ripper*, Headline, London, 1999, ISBN 0-7472-6206-3

HARRIS, Melvin, *The True Face of Jack the Ripper*, Michael O'Mara, London,1995, ISBN 1-85479-726-3

CULT CRIME

CLARKSON, Wensley, *In The Name of Satan*, St Martin's, New York, 1998, ISBN 0-312-96389-0

DUNNING, John, *Mystical Murders*, Arrow, London, 1989, ISBN 0-09-963530-5

HICKS, Robert D., *In Pursuit of Satan: The Police and the Occult*, Prometheus, Buffalo, 1991, ISBN 0-87975-604-7

HUBNER, John & GRUSON, Lindsey, *Monkey On A Stick: Murder, Madness, and the Hare Krishnas*, Onyx, New York, 1990, ISBN 0-451-40187-5

KAHANER, Larry, *Cults That Kill: Probing the Underworld of Occult Crime*, Warner, New York, 1989, ISBN 0-446-35637-9

LARSON, Bob, *Satanism: The Seduction of America's Youth*, Thomas Nelson, Nashville, 1989, ISBN 0-8047-3034-9

LINEDECKER, Clifford L., *The Vampire Killers*, St Martin's, New York, 1998, ISBN 0-312-96672-5

LYONS, Arthur, *Satan Wants You: The Cult of Devil Worship in America*, Mysterious Press, New York, 1989, ISBN 0-445-40822-7

MANDELSBERG, Rose G. (ed.), *Cult Killers*, Pinnacle, New York, 1991, ISBN 1-55817-528-8

MOORE, Carol, *The Davidian Massacre: Disturbing Questions About Waco Which Must Be Answered*, Legacy Communications, Franklin, 1995, ISBN 1-880692-22-8

NEWTON, Michael, *Raising Hell: An Encyclopedia of Devil Worship and Satanic Crime*, Avon, New York, 1993, ISBN 0-380-76837-2

SCAMMELL, Henry, *Mortal Remains: A True Story of Ritual Murder*, Harper, New York, 1992, ISBN 0-06-109958-9

SPENCER, Judith, *Satan's High Priest: A True Story*, Pocket, New York, 1998, ISBN 0-671-00790-4

WILSON, Colin, *Order of Assassins: The Psychology of Murder*, Panther, London, 1972

WINCHESTER, Simon, *The Professor and the Madman*, Harper, New York, 1999, ISBN 0-06-103022-8

MATAMOROS

HUMES, Edward, *Buried Secrets: A True Story of Serial Murder*, Signet, New York, 1992, ISBN 0-451-17164-0

PROVOST, Gary, *Across The Border: The True Story of the Satanic Cult Killings in Matamoros, Mexico*, Pocket, New York, 1989, ISBN 0-671-69319-0

SCHUTZE, Jim, *Caulron of Blood: The Matamoros Cult Killings*, Avon, New York, 1989, ISBN 0-380-75997-7

CATHARS, TEMPLARS, FREEMASONRY AND THE ASSASSIN CULT

ALARCON H., Rafael, *A la sombra de los Templarios*, Martinez Roca, Barcelona, 1986

BAIGENT, Michael & LEIGH, Richard & LINCOLN, Henry, *Holy Blood, Holy Grail*, Dell, New York, 1983

—*The Messianic Legacy*, Dell, New York, 1989

BAIGENT, Michael & LEIGH, Richard, *The Temple and the Lodge*, Arcade, New York, 1989

—*The Elixir and the Stone*, Penguin, London, 1997

BAIGENT, Michael, *Ancient Traces*, Penguin, London, 1998

—*From the Omens of Babylon: Astrology and Ancient Mesopotamia*, Arkana, London, 1994

BARBER, Malcolm, *The Cathars*, Pearson Education, Harlow, 2000

BENITEZ, J.J., *Caballo de Troya*, Planeta, Barcelona, 1996

BINKS, Walter & GILBERT, R.A., *The Treasure of Montsegur*, Crucible, London, 1987

BOUTTIER, Michel, *Cathedrales: Comment elles sont construites*, Creation et Recherche, Le Mans, 1989

BULLOCK, Steven C., *Revolutionary Brotherhood: Freemasonry and the Transformation of the American Social Order 1730–1840*, University of North Carolina Press, Chapel Hill, 1996, ISBN 0-8078-4750-X

CHARPENTIER, Louis, *The Mysteries of Chartres Cathedral*, RILKO, London, 1972

De SEDE, Gerard, *El misterio de Rennes-le-Chateau*, Martinez Roca, Barcelona, 1993

GARDNER, Laurence, *Bloodline of the Holy Grail*, Element, Dorset, 1999

GILBERT, Adrian, *The Holy Kingdom*, Corgi Books, London, 1999

GOLTHER, Wolfgang, *Parzival und der Graal*, J.B. Metzlersche, Stuttgart, 1925

HANCOCK, Graham, *The Sign and the Seal*, Mandarin, London, 1996

KNIGHT, Christopher & LOMAS, Robert, *The Hiram Key*, Arrow, London, 1997

—*The Second Messiah*, Arrow, London, 1998

LANDON, H.C. Robbins, *Mozart and the Masons*, Thames & Hudson, London, 1991

NIEL, Fernand, *Les Cathares de Montsegur*, Robert Laffont, Paris, 1973

OLDENBOURG, Zoe, *Massacre at Montsegur*, Dorset Press, New York, 1990

PICKNETT, Lynn & PRINCE, Clive, *The Templar Revelation*, Corgi Books, London, 1998

ROBIN, Jean, *Operacion Orth: el increible misterio de Rennes-le-Chateau*, Heptada, Madrid, 1990

ROBINSON, John J., *Born In Blood: The Lost Secrets of Freemasonry*, M. Evans & Co., New York, 1989, ISBN 0-87131-602-1

STEVENSON, David, *The Origins of Freemasonry: Scotland's Century 1590–1710*, Cambridge University Press, Cambridge, 2000, ISBN 0-521-39654-9

Von SIMSON, Otto, *The Gothic Cathedral*, Harper Torchbooks, New York, 1964

WILSON, Ian, *The Blood and the Shroud*, Orion, London, 1998

SECRET SOCIETIES, WITCHCRAFT AND THE OCCULT

ANTON, Ted, *Eros, Magic, and the Murder of Professor Culianu*, Northwestern University Press, Evanston, 1996, ISBN 0-8101-1396-1

BARTON, Blanche, *The Secret Life of a Satanist: The Authorized Biography of Anton LaVey*, Feral House, Los Angeles, 1992, ISBN 0-922915-12-1

CARTER, John, *Sex and Rockets: The Occult World of Jack Parsons*, Feral House, Venice CA, 1999, ISBN 0-922915-56-3

CLARK, Stuart, *Thinking With Demons: The Idea of Witchcraft in Early Modern Europe*, Oxford University Press, Oxford, 1999, ISBN 0-19-820808-1

CROWLEY, Aleister, *Magick In Theory and Practice*, Dover, New York, 1976, ISBN 0-486-23295-6

DASH, Mike, *Borderlands*, Arrow, London, 1997, ISBN 0-7493-2396-5

FLINT, Valerie I.J., *The Rise of Magic in Early Medieval Europe*, Princeton University Press, Princeton, 1994, ISBN 0-691-00110-3

FLYNN, Kevin, & GERHARDT, Gary, *The Silent Brotherhood*, Signet, New York, 1995, ISBN 0-451-16786-4

GRANT, Kenneth, *The Magical Revival*, Skoob, London, 1972, ISBN 1-871438-37-3

—*Aleister Crowley and the Hidden God*, Skoob, London, 1973, ISBN 1-871438-36-5

—*Cults of the Shadow*, Skoob, London, 1975, ISBN 1-871438-67-5

—*Nightside of Eden*, Skoob, London, 1977, ISBN 1-871438-72-1

—*Outside the Circles of Time*, Frederick Muller, London, 1980, ISBN 0-584-10468-5

—*Hecate's Fountain*, Skoob, London, 1992, ISBN 1-871438-96-9

—*Outer Gateways*, Skoob, London, 1994, ISBN 1-871438-12-8

HOWARD, Michael, *The Occult Conspiracy*, Destiny, Rochester, 1989, ISBN 0-89281-251-6

HYATT, Christoper S., *Rebels & Devils: The Psychology of Liberation*, New Falcon, Tempe, 1996, ISBN 1-56184-121-8

KEEL, John A., *The Mothman Prophecies*, IllumiNet Press, Lilburn, 1991, ISBN 0-9626534-3-8

KRAMER, Heinrich & SPRENGER, James, *The Malleus Maleficarum*, Dover, New York, 1971, ISBN 0-486-22802-9

MILLEGAN, Kris (ed.), *Fleshing Out Skull & Bones: Investigations Into America's Most Powerful Secret Society*, Trine Day, Walterville, 2003, ISBN 0-9720207-2-1

OVASON, David, *The Zelator: The Secret Journals of Mark Hedsel*, Arrow, London, 1999, ISBN 0-09-925503-0

PARFREY, Adam (ed.), *Apocalypse Culture*, Feral House, San Francisco, 1990, ISBN 0-922915-05-9

PARKER, John, *At The Heart of Darkness: Witchcraft, Black Magic and Satanism Today*, Citadel, New York, 1993, ISBN 0-8065-1428-0

PAUWELS, Louis & BERGIER, Jacques, *The Morning of the Magicians*, Mayflower, London, 1973

REGARDIE, Israel & STEPHENSEN, P.R., *The Legend of Aleister Crowley*, Falcon Press, Phoenix, 1983, ISBN 0-941404-20-X

SELIGMANN, Kurt, *The History of Magic and the Occult*, Gramercy, New York, 1997, ISBN 0-517-15032-8

SHAH, Idries, *The Secret Lore of Magic*, Citadel, Secaucus, 1972, ISBN 0-8065-0004-2

SMITH, Michelle & PAZDER, Lawrence, *Michelle Remembers*, Congdon & Lattes, New York, 1980, ISBN 0-312-92531-X

STARR, Martin P., *The Unknown God: W.T. Smith and the Thelemites*, Teitan Press, Bolingbrook, 2003, ISBN 0-933429-07-X

SUTTON, Antony C., *America's Secret Establishment: An Introduction to the Order of Skull & Bones*, Trine Day, Walterville, 2002, ISBN 0-9720207-0-5

STRIEBER, Whitley, *The Key*, Walker & Collier, San Antonio, 2001

—*The Path*, Walker & Collier, San Antonio, 2002

SYMONDS, John, *The Great Beast: The Life of Aleister Crowley*, Rider & Co., London, 1951

TEMPLE, Robert, *The Sirius Mystery*, St Martin's Press, New York, 1976, ISBN 0-312-72731-3;

—*The Sirius Mystery*, Arrow, London, 1999, ISBN 0-09-925744-0

WAITE, Arthur Edward, *The Book of Ceremonial Magic*, Barnes & Noble, New York, 1999, ISBN 0-7607-1196-8

WEBB, James, *The Occult Establishment*, Open Court, La Salle, 1991, ISBN 0-87548-434-4

WILSON, Colin, *The Occult*, Grafton, London, 1978, ISBN 0-586-05050-7

YATES, Frances A., *The Occult Philosophy in the Elizabethan Age*, Ark Paperbacks, London, 1983, ISBN 0-7448-0001-3

INTERVIEWS AND PERSONAL CONTACTS:

ADLER, Margot

BECK, Elizabeth

BRODSKY, Allyn

BUCKLAND, Raymond

BUCZYNSKI, Edward

CAPURO, Richard

CLAREMONT, Bonnie

JAMES, Ed

KING, Francis

KIRWAN, Larry

MARTELLO, Leo

McMURTRY, Grady

MENSCH, Martin

MILLS, Malcolm

RANDOLPH, Ellen

SLATER, Herman

SOLOMON, Jay

WASSERMAN, James

RICHARD NIXON AND WATERGATE

The Presidential Transcripts, Dell, New York, 1974

The Watergate Hearings, Bantam Books, New York, 1973

COLODNY, Len and GETTLIN, Robert, *Silent Coup: The Removal of a President*, St Martin's Paperbacks, New York, 1992

HOUGAN, Jim, *Secret Agenda: Watergate, Deep Throat and the CIA*, Random House, New York, 1984

—*Spooks: The Haunting of America—The Private Use of Secret Agents*, William Morrow & Co., New York, 1978

LASKY, Victor, *It Didn't Start With Watergate*, The Dial Press, New York, 1977

LIDDY, G. Gordon, *Will: The Autobiography*, Dell, New York, 1980

LUKAS, J, Anthony, *Nightmare: The Underside of the Nixon Years*, Viking Press, New York, 1976

MAGRUDER, Jeb Stuart, *An American Life: One Man's Road to Watergate*, Pocket Books, New York, 1975
SUMMERS, Anthony, *The Arrogance of Power: The Secret World of Richard Nixon*, Penguin, New York, 2001
WOOLCOTT, Alexander and KAUFMAN, George S., *The Dark Tower: A Melodrama*, Random House, New York, 1934
SHEEHAN, Neil, et al., *The Pentagon Papers*, Bantam Books, New York, 1971

IRAN-CONTRA

HONNEGAR, Barbara, *October Surpirse*, Tudor, 1989
HOPSICKER, Daniel, *Barry & 'the boys'—The CIA, the Mob and America's Secret History*, MadCow Press, 2000
KWITNY, Jonathan, *The Crimes of Patriots*, Simon & Schuster, New York, 1988
ROGIN, Michael, *Ronald Reagan: the Movie and Other Episodes in Political Demonology*, University of California Press, Berkeley, 1988
SICK, Gary, *October Surprise*, Times Books, New York, 1991

VAST RIGHT-WING CONSPIRACY

DIAMOND, Sara, *Spiritual Warfare: The Politics of the Christian Right*, South End Press, Boston, 1989, ISBN 0-89608-361-6
—*Not By Politics Alone: The Enduring Influence of the Christian Right*, Guilford Press, New York, 1998, ISBN 1-57230-494-4

THE NINE

BROWNING, Norma Lee, *The Psychic World of Peter Hurkos*, Signet, New York, 1971
GARDNER, Erle Stanley, *Host With The Big Hat*, William Morrow, New York, 1969
GELLER, Uri & PLAYFAIR, Guy Lyon, *The Geller Effect*, Grafton Books, London, 1986
GREENBURG, Dan, *Something's There: My Adventures in the Occult*, Doubleday, New York, 1976, ISBN 0-385-03898-4
HAPGOOD, Charles H., *Mystery in Acambaro*, Adventures Unlimited Press, Kempton, 2000
HURTAK, J.J., *An Introduction to the Keys of Enoch*, The Academy for Future Science, Los Gatos, 1988
LEVY, Steven, *The Unicorn's Secret*, Prentice Hall, New York, 1988
OSTRANDER, Sheila & SCHROEDER, Lynn, *Super-Learning*, Delta, New York, 1979
—*Psychic Discoveries Behind the Iron Curtain*, Bantam, New York, 1971
PICKNETT, Lynn & PRINCE, Clive, *The Stargate Conspiracy*, Warner Books, London, 2000
PLAYFAIR, Guy Lyon, *The Indefinite Boundary*, Souvenir Press, London, 1976
—with HILL, Scott, *The Cycles of Heaven*, Pan Books, London, 1978
PUHARICH, Andrija, *URI*, Anchor Press, New York, 1974
RHINE, J.B., *New World of the Mind*, William Morrow, New York, 1953
RHINE, Louisa E., *PSI: What is It?*, Harper & Row, New York, 1975
STEARN, Jess, *Adventures Into the Psychic*, Signet, New York, 1971
—*Yoga, Youth, and Reincarnation*, Bantam, New York, 1971
SWANN, Ingo, *Penetration*, Ingo Swann Books, Rapid City, 1998
TARG, Russell, *Limitless Mind*, New World Library, Novato, 2004
—with HARARY, Keith, *The Mind Race*, New English Library, London, 1986
ULLMAN, Montague & KRIPPNER, Stanley, *Dream Telepathy*, Macmillan, New York, 1973
YOUNG, Arthur, *The Foundations of Science*, Broadside Editions, San Francisco, 1985

QUANTUM CONSCIOUSNESS

ACZEL, Amir D., *The Mystery of the Aleph: Mathematics, the Kabbalah, and the Search for Infinity*, Pocket Books, NY, 2000, ISBN 0743422996

ALBERT, David Z., *Quantum Mechanics and Experience*, Harvard University Press, Cambridge, 1993, ISBN 0-674-74112-9

DAVIES, P.C.W. & BROWN, J., *Superstrings: A Theory of Everything?*, Cambridge University Press, Cambridge, 1999, ISBN 0-521-43775-X

DOSSEY, Larry, *Space, Time & Medicine*, Shambhala, Boston, 1982, ISBN 0-87773-224-8

HONIG, William M., *The Quantum and Beyond*, Philosophical Library, NY, 1986, ISBN 8022-2517-9

HORGAN, John, *The Undiscovered Mind*, Touchstone, New York, 1999, ISBN 0-684-86578-5

JUNG, C.G., *Synchronicity: An Acausal Connecting Principle*, Princeton University Press, Princeton, 1973, ISBN 0-691-01794-8

MEIER, C.A. (ed.), *Atom And Archetype: the Pauli/Jung Letters 1932–1958*, Princeton University Press, Princeton, 2001, ISBN 0-691-01207-5

PEAT, F. David, *Synchronicity: The Bridge Between Matter and Mind*, Bantam New Age, New York, 1988, ISBN 0-553-34676-8

PENROSE, Roger, *The Emperor's New Mind*, Oxford University Press, New York, 1989, ISBN 0-19-851973-7

SMOLIN, Lee, *Three Roads to Quantum Gravity*, Weidenfeld & Nicolson, London, 2000, ISBN 0-297-64301-0

JONESTOWN

HOUGAN, Jim, "Jonestown, The Secret Life of Jim Jones: A Parapolitical Fugue", *Lobster* 37, Summer 1999, pp 2–20

KRAUSE, Charles A., *Guyana Massacre*, Pan Books, London, 1979

LAYTON, Deborah, *Seductive Poison*, Aurum Press, London, 2000

MEIERS, Michael, *Was Jonestown a CIA Medical Experiment?*, Edwin Meller Press, Lewiston, 1988

MILLS, Jeannie, *Six Years With God*, A&W Publishers, New York, 1979

YEE, Min S. & LAYTON, Thomas N., *In My Father's House*, Holt Rinehart Winston, New York, 1981

EVIL

BLOOM, Howard, *The Lucifer Principle: A Scientific Expedition Into the Forces of History*, Atlantic Monthly Press, New York, 1997, ISBN 0-87113-664-3

CENKNER, William (ed.), *Evil and the Response of World Religion*, Paragon House, St. Paul, 1997, ISBN 1-55778-753-0

GOLDBERG, Carl, *Speaking With The Devil: Exploring Senseless Acts of Evil*, Penguin, New York, 1996, ISBN 0-14-023739-9

LING, Trevor, *Buddhism and the Mythology of Evil: A Study in Theravada Buddhism*, Oneworld, Oxford, 1997, ISBN 1-85168-132-9

O'FLAHERTY, Wendy Doniger, *The Origins of Evil in Hindu Mythology*, Motilal Banarsidass, Delhi, 1988, ISBN 81-208-0386-8

OPPENHEIMER, Paul, *Evil and the Demonic: A NewTheory of Monstrous Behavior*, New York University Press, New York, 1996, ISBN 0-8147-6196-8

RUSSELL, Jeffrey Burton, *The Devil: Perceptions of Evil from Antiquity to Primitive Christianity*, Cornell University Press, Ithaca, 1987, ISBN 0-8014-9409-5

STAUB, Ervin, *The Roots of Evil: the Origins of Genocide and Other Group Violence*, Cambridge University Press, Cambridge, 1998, ISBN 0-521-42214-0

EXORCISM

ALLEN, Thomas B., *Possessed: The True Story of an Exorcism*, Doubleday, New York, 1993, ISBN 0-385-42034-X

AMORTH, Gabriele, *An Exorcist Tells His Story*, Ignatius Press, San Francisco, 1999, ISBN 0-89870-710-2

CUNEO, Michael W., *American Exorcism: Expelling Demons in the Land of Plenty*, Doubleday, New York, 2001, ISBN 0-385-51076-5

LASALANDRA, Michael & MERENDA, Mark, *Satan's Harvest*, Dell, New York, 1990, ISBN 0-440-20589-1

MARTIN, Malachi, *Hostage To The Devil: The Possession and Exorcism of Five Living Americans*, Reader's Digest Press, New York, 1976, ISBN 0-8349-078-1

OESTERREICH, T.K., *Possession: Demoniacal & Other*, University Books, New York, 1966

THE UFO PHENOMENON

ACHENBACH, Joel, *Captured By Aliens: The Search for Life and Truth in a Very Large Universe*, Simon & Schuster, New York, 1999, ISBN 0-684-84856-2

ADAMSKI, George, *Behind The Flying Saucer Mystery*, Warner, New York, 1974

BLUM, Howard, *Out There: The Government's Secret Quest for Extraterrestrials*, Simon & Schuster, New York, 1990, ISBN 0-671-66260-0

CONROY, Ed, *Report On Communion: An Independent Investigation of and Commentary on Whitley Strieber's Communion*, William Morrow, New York, 1989, ISBN 0-688-08864-3

CORSO, Col. Philip J., *The Day After Roswell*, Pocket Books, New York, 1998, ISBN 0-671-01756-X

FLAMMONDE, Paris, *UFO Exist!*, Ballantine, New York, 1977, ISBN 0-345-33951-7

FRIEDMAN, Stanton T., *Top Secret/Majic*, Marlowe & Co., New York, 1997, ISBN 1-56924-741-2

FULLER, John G., *Incident At Exeter*, Berkley, New York, 1967

—*The Interrupted Journey: Two Lost Hours "Aboard a Flying Saucer"*, Dial Press, New York, 1966

GOOD, Timothy, *Alien Update*, Arrow, London, 1993, ISBN 0-09-925761-0

—*Alien Base: The Evidence for Extraterrestrial Colonization of Earth*, Arrow, London, 1999, ISBN 0-09-925502-2

—*Beyond Top Secret: The Worldwide UFO Security Threat*, Pan Books, London, 1996, ISBN 0-330-34928-7

HAINES, Richard F., *CE-5: Close Encounters of the Fifth Kind*, Sourcebooks, Naperville, 1998, ISBN 1-57071-427-4

KEYHOE, Donald E., *Aliens From Space: The Real Story of Unidentified Flying Objects*, Signet, New York, 1974

KORFF, Kal K., *The Roswell UFO Crash: What They Don't Want You To Know*, Dell, New York, 2000, ISBN 0-440-23613-4

JACOBS, David M., *The Threat*, Pocket Books, New York, 1998, ISBN 0-671-02859-6

JUNG, C.G., *Flying Saucers*, Routledge, London, 1959, ISBN 0-415-27837-6

MACCABEE, Bruce, *UFO FBI Connection: The Secret History of the Government's Cover-Up*, Llewellyn, St. Paul, 2000, ISBN 1-56718-493-6

MACK, John E., *Abduction: Human Encounters With Aliens*, Ballantine, New York, 1995, ISBN 0-345-39300-7

MARRS, Jim, *Alien Agenda: Investigating the Extraterrestrial Presence Among Us*, HarperCollins, New York, 1997, ISBN 0-06-018642-9

PEEBLES, Curtis, *Watch The Skies! A Chronicle of the Flying Saucer Myth*, Berkley, New York, 1995, ISBN 0-425-15117-4

POPE, Nick, *Open Skies, Closed Minds*, Pocket Books, New York, 1997, ISBN 0-671-85530-1

RANDLE, Kevin D., *The UFO Casebook*, Warner, New York, 1989, ISBN 0-446-35715-4

—*A History of UFO Crashes*, Avon, New York, 1995, ISBN 0-380-77666-9

RANDLE, Kevin D. & SCHMITT, Donald R., , *The Truth About The UFO Crash at Roswell*, Avon, New York, 1994, ISBN 0-380-77803-3

RANDLES, Jenny & HOUGH, Peter, *The Complete Book of UFOs*, Sterling, New York, 1994, ISBN 0-8069-8132-6

REDFERN, Nicholas, *The FBI Files: The FBI's UFO Top Secrets Exposed*, Pocket Books, London, 1998, ISBN 0-671-00533-2

SHAWCROSS, Tim, *The Roswell File*, Bloomsbury, London, 1997, ISBN 0-7475-3507-8

STEIGER, Brad, *Project Bluebook*, Ballantine, New York, 1990, ISBN 0-345-34525-8

STEIGER, Brad & STEIGER, Sherry Hansen, *The Rainbow Conspiracy*, Pinnacle, New York, 1994, ISBN 0-7860-0065-1

STRIEBER, Whitley, *Communion: A True Story*, Avon, New York, 1988, ISBN 0-380-70388-2

—*Breakthrough: The Next Step*, HarperPaperbacks, New York, 1996, ISBN 0-06-100958-X

—*The Secret School*, Pocket Books, London, 1997, ISBN 0-671-00526-X

—*Confirmation: The Hard Evidence of Aliens Among Us*, St Martin's, New York, 1998, ISBN 0-312-18557-X

VALLEE, Jacques, *Passport to Magnolia: On UFOs, Folklore, and Parallel Worlds*, Contemporary Books, Chicago, 1993, ISBN 0-8092-3796-2

—*Forbidden Science*, North Atlantic Books, Berkeley, 1992, ISBN 1-55643-125-2

WARREN, Larry & ROBBINS, Peter, *Left At East Gate*, Marlowe & Co., New York, 1997, ISBN 1-56924-759-5

PSYCHOLOGY, MYTHOLOGY AND ANTHROPOLOGY

ADORNO, Theodor, *The Stars Down To Earth*, Routledge, London, 1994, ISBN 0-415-27100-2

BATAILLE, Georges, *Death and Sensuality: A Study of Eroticism and the Taboo*, Ballantine, New York, 1969

—*Story of the Eye*, Penguin, London, 2001, ISBN 0-14-118538-4

—*Erotism: Death & Sensuality*, City Lights Books, San Francisco, 1986, ISBN 0-87286-190-2

COOMARASWAMY, Ananda K., *The Door In The Sky*, Princeton Paperbacks, Princeton, 1997, ISBN 0-691-01747-6

COULIANO, Ioan P., *Eros and Magic in the Renaissance*, University of Chicago Press, Chicago, 1987, ISBN 0-226-12316-2

—*The Tree of Gnosis: Gnostic Mythology from Early Christianity to Modern Nihilism*, HarperSanFrancisco, San Francisco, 1990, ISBN 0-06-061615-6

ELIADE, Mircea, *Shamanism: Archaic Techniques of Ecstasy*, Arkana, London, 1988, ISBN 0-14-019155-0

—*The Myth of the Eternal Return*, Princeton University Press, Princeton, 1991, ISBN 0-691-01777-8

—*Images and Symbols: Studies in Religious Symbolism*, Princeton University Press, Princeton, 1991, ISBN 0-691-02068-X

—*The Sacred and the Profane: The Nature of Religion*, Harcourt, New York, 1987, ISBN 0-15-679201-X

—*Rites and Symbols of Initiation: The Mysteries of Birth and Rebirth*, Harper Torchbooks, New York, 1965

—*The Quest: History and Meaning in Religion*, University of Chicago Press, Chicago, 1975, ISBN 0-226-20397-2

JUNG, C.G., *Memories, Dreams, Reflections*, Vintage, New York, 1963

—*Psychology and Western Religion*, Princeton University Press, Princeton, 1984, ISBN 0-691-01862-6

JUNG, C.G. & KERENYI, C., *Essays On A Science Of Mythology*, Princeton University Press, Princeton, 1989, ISBN 0-691-01756-5

KEARNEY, Richard, *Strangers, Gods and Monsters*, Routledge, London, 2003, ISBN 0-415-27258-0

LAING, R.D., *The Politics of Experience*, Pantheon, New York, 1967, ISBN 0-394-71475-X

—*The Politics of the Family and other Essays*, Vintage, New York, 1971, ISBN 0-394-71809-7

—*Self and Others*, Penguin, London, 1987, ISBN 0-14-021376-7

—*The Divided Self*, Pantheon, New York, 1969, ISBN 0-394-42226-0

LEVI-STRAUSS, Claude, *The Savage Mind*, University of Chicago Press, Chicago, 1970, ISBN 0-226-47484-4

MAUSS, Marcel, *A General Theory of Magic*, Routledge, London, 1972, ISBN 0-415-25396-9

PAZ, Octavio, *El signo y el garabato*, Biblioteca de Bolsillo, Mexico, 1991, ISBN 84-322-3083-9

—*The Labyrinth of Solitude: Life and Thought in Mexico*, Grove Press, New York, 1978, ISBN 0-394-17242-6

SONTAG, Susan, *Illness As Metaphor*, Vintage, New York, 1979, ISBN 0-394-72844-0

—*Under the Sign of Saturn*, Farrar, Straus, Giroux, New York, 1980, ISBN 0-374-28076-2

STOYANOV, Yuri, *The Other God: Dualist Religions from Antiquity to the Cathar Heresy*, Yale University Press, New Haven, 2000, ISBN 0-300-08253-3

HOWARD HUGHES

DROSNIN, Michael, *Citizen Hughes*, Holt Rinehart and Winston, New York, 1985

FAY, Stephen, CHESTER, Lewis and LINKLATER, Magnus, *Hoax*, Viking Press, New York, 1972

IRVING, Clifford, *The Hoax*, Mandarin, London, 1981

MAHEU, Robert and HACK, Richard, *Next to Hughes*, HarperCollins, New York, 1992

PHELAN, James R. and CHESTER, Lewis, *The Money*, Orion Business Books, London, 1997

SURREALISM

BRETON, Andre, *Communicating Vessels*, University of Nebraska Press, Lincoln, 1990, ISBN 0-8032-6135-7

CHOUCHA, Nadia, *Surrealism & The Occult: Shamanism, Magic, Alchemy, and the Birth of an Artistic Movement*, Destiny Books, Rochester, 1992, ISBN 0-89281-373-3

LOMAS, David, *The Haunted Self: Surrealism, Psychoanalysis, Subjectivity*, Yale University Press, New Haven, 2000, ISBN 0-300-08800-0

SECREST, Meryle, *Salvador Dali: A Biography*, Dutton, New York, 1987, ISBN 0-525-48334-9

TOMKINS, Calvin, *The Bride and the Bachelors: Five Masters of the Avant-Garde*, Viking, New York, 1974, ISBN 670-00248-8

WEYERS, Frank, *Salvador Dali: Life and Work*, Koenemann, Cologne, 2000, ISBN 3-8290-2934-9

CHAPTER IMAGES

Page 64, top: Photo by Judson McCranie, CC BY-SA 3.0, https://commons.wikimedia.org/w/index.php?curid=106526835

Page 132, bottom center right: Robert Jackson, Opening Argument, Nuremberg War Crimes Tribunal, November 21, 1945

Page 132, bottom right: Hans Habe, *Agent of the Devil*, George G. Harrap & Co. Ltd., London, 1958, p. 192

Page 526, top left: Rev. Jim Jones at an anti-eviction rally Sunday, January 16, 1977 in front of the International Hotel, Kearny and Jackson Streets, San Francisco Photo by Nancy Wong - Own work, CC BY-SA 4.0, https://commons.wikimedia.org/w/index.php?curid=91003548

Page 590, top left: John Lennon being interviewed in Los Angeles by Tony Barnard, Los Angeles Times - https://digital.library.ucla.edu/catalog/ark:/21198/zz0002pv3r, CC BY 4.0, https://commons.wikimedia.org/w/index.php?curid=144571495

Page 590, top right: Work of the master Nadiry Nadir Nardiello - Own work, CC BY-SA 4.0, https://commons.wikimedia.org/w/index.php?curid=100514099

Page 590, bottom: The Beatles wave to fans after disembarking a plane at Kennedy Airport, by United Press International, photographer unknown. This image is available from the United States Library of Congress's Prints and Photographs divisionunder the digital ID cph.3c11094. Public Domain, https://commons.wikimedia.org/w/index.php?curid=4532407

Page 686, bottom left: Jung in 1955, by Comet Photo AG (Zürich) - This image is from the collection of the ETH-Bibliothek and has been published on Wikimedia Commons as part of a cooperation with Wikimedia CH. Corrections and additional information are welcome., CC BY-SA 4.0, https://commons.wikimedia.org/w/index.php?curid=134640549

Page 1124, top right: January 1977 photo by Nancy Wong - Own work, CC BY-SA 4.0, https://commons.wikimedia.org/w/index.php?curid=44427461

Page 1124, bottom center right: Watergate Complex, by Peter Christian Riemann - Own work, CC BY-SA 4.0, https://commons.wikimedia.org/w/index.php?curid=157025926

INDEX

B

C

D

E

F

I

J

K

M

N

O

P

Q

R

S

T

U

To
The
Stars®

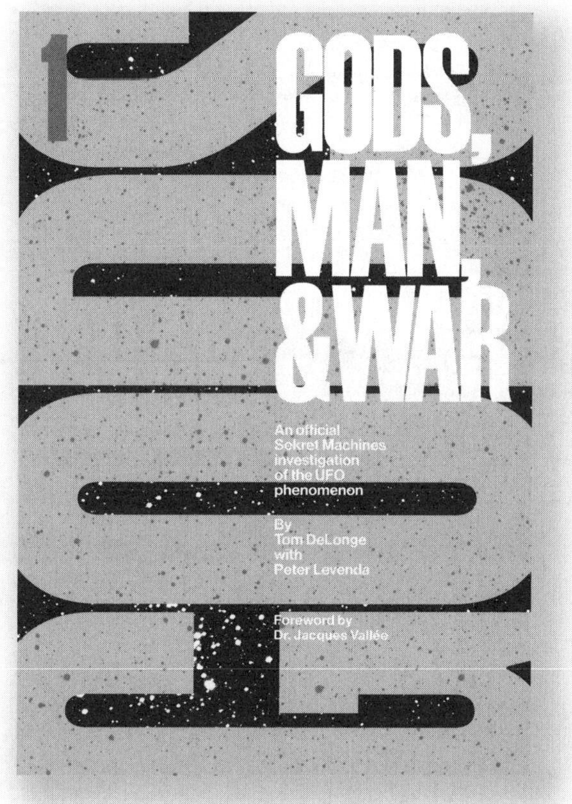
1
GODS,
MAN,
&WAR
An official
Sekret Machines
investigation
of the UFO
phenomenon
By
Tom DeLonge
with
Peter Levenda
Foreword by
Dr. Jacques Vallée